Evaluation Guide for *Biology:Living Systems*

Biology:Living Systems gives teachers an up-to-date presentation of biology. Concepts and principles are developed in a logical yet flexible order to make the students' study of biology both interesting and challenging. To strengthen the presentation and increase students' interest in and understanding of biology, many features have been included.

To examine the features of *Biology:Living Systems*, please turn to the following pages.

TEACHER'S ANNOTATED EDITION
BIOLOGY

Living Systems

Raymond F. Oram
The Peddie School
Hightstown, NJ

CONSULTANTS
Paul J. Hummer, Jr.
Gov. Thomas Johnson High School
Frederick, MD

Robert C. Smoot
McDonogh School
McDonogh, MD

Fourth Edition

Charles E. Merrill Publishing Company
A Bell & Howell Company
Columbus, Ohio

Toronto, London, Sydney

PREFACE

The Teacher's Annotated Edition for *Biology: Living Systems* provides in one book answers to all questions in the text, suggestions for effective demonstrations and activities, additional background information related to text material, and relevant references for further information. Experienced and inexperienced teachers alike will find that the Teacher's Annotated Edition provides a useful guide for the organization and teaching of a modern course in biology. It is not necessary for teachers to carry supplementary books; the material included eliminates searches for additional information.

The Teacher's Annotated Edition is composed of two parts—annotations and a teacher's guide.
Annotations: Annotations are concise statements overprinted in red on the student text. The annotations are directly applicable to the section near which they are printed. Annotations include teaching techniques, demonstrations, activities, related background material, and answers to questions within the text paragraphs. Answers to Reviewing Your Ideas section-end questions also are given in annotated form.

Teacher's Guide: The teacher's guide bound at the front of the Teacher's Annotated Edition includes complete answers to all chapter-end questions and problems, in order as they appear in the text, as well as additional material not covered in annotations. The introductory part of the teacher's guide provides insight into both the philosophy and teaching features of the text. A complete planning guide and alternate approaches are provided. A special addition to the teacher's guide is a reading feature that gives suggestions for fusing reading and science instruction. Teaching aids listed in the teacher's guide include audiovisuals, audiovisual and biological suppliers, additional sources for information, and literature references. A discussion of performance objectives and how to use them is provided, and goals and performance objectives are included for each text chapter.

Project Editor: Mary Joan Arnett
Project Artist: Dennis L. Smith
Artist: Katie White

ISBN 0-675-07022-8

Published by
Charles E. Merrill Publishing Company
A Bell & Howell Company
Columbus, Ohio 43216

TABLE OF CONTENTS

Introductory Material

Chapter-by-Chapter Material

PHILOSOPHY AND THEMES

Biology is the study of all living things. Therefore, understanding life and life processes depends on mastering the unifying principles and concepts applicable to all life forms. The approach of this text emphasizes the fundamental unity in the diversity of life forms.

Biology: Living Systems focuses on major life processes. In so doing, each process is discussed using a variety of examples from the five kingdoms of organisms. Students become aware that all organisms carry out the same life functions and thus, the ways that organisms are adapted to carry out those functions can be better appreciated.

Life processes of organisms from different kingdoms are discussed in separate units of the text. Thus, students can readily compare a variety of similar organisms. Those processes in separate units, however, are presented in the same order. Therefore, students can easily compare more diverse organisms (unit to unit) and can maintain an understanding of classification of living things.

Throughout the text are examples of the methods of science. Several classic experiments leading to the development of major principles are discussed and analyzed historically. In this way, students learn to appreciate how scientists gather and organize information about the world.

The text material contains the following unifying themes:

1. Energy is required to maintain organization of living things.

2. Traits of organisms are determined by heredity and environment.

3. Organisms evolve and relationships exist among living things.

4. The characteristics of the major phyla of organisms is the basis of taxonomy.

5. The proper functioning of a living thing requires homeostasis.

6. Functions of living things are integrated.

7. Organisms interact with each other and with their environments.

8. Advances continually are made in both biological science and biological technology.

In *Biology: Living Systems* topics are presented from the simplest to the most complex levels of biological organization. Unit I presents an introduction to the methods of science, beginning chemistry needed for an understanding of biology, and principles of cellular biology. Unit II presents traditional and modern genetics including sample problems with complete solutions. The third unit discusses evolutionary change, adaptation, and classification. Unit IV presents an overview of living organisms utilizing a five-kingdom system of classification. Life processes of organisms in the five kingdoms are discussed in the following three units. The final unit of the text presents biology of organisms in their environments.

Many features and aids have been incorporated into *Biology: Living Systems* to make your biology course easier to teach and to make the material easier for students to understand. Sample pages showing text design features and teaching and learning aids follow.

BIOLOGY: LIVING SYSTEMS . . .
A COMPREHENSIVE INTRODUCTORY BIOLOGY TEXT

Unit organization to meet planning and teaching needs—

Unit openings conveniently divide text material in a logical, yet flexible way. Each opening is a 2-page photograph with interesting paragraphs relating ideas to be covered in the unit and interesting students in the world in which they live.

Units cover the following **main areas of biology:**
1. Introduction, chemistry, cell biology
2. Genetics
3. Evolution and classification
4. Survey of organisms
5. Simple organisms
6. Plants
7. Animals
8. Environment

HEREDITY

When living things reproduce. what ensures that their offspring will resemble them? What determines that dandelions will produce only dandelions and that praying mantises will produce only praying mantises? How are the features of these and other living things determined? The results of reproduction are determined by genetic messages that are copied and passed on to the offspring. The study of genetic messages and the traits that result from them is called genetics or heredity.

In this unit, you will learn about cell reproduction and the "vehicles" which carry genetic messages to new cells. Knowledge of how genetic information is passed on will enable you to predict some of the traits new organisms will have. You also will investigate the chemical basis of heredity. You will study the materials of which genetic messages are composed and learn how those messages are decoded to produce an organism's features.

Praying Mantises
on Dandelion

94

4T

Attractive, workable format to expand student interest and learning—

Each **chapter opening** includes a large color photograph and introductory paragraph that interest students and give reasons to study the chapter.

Red **teacher's annotations** appear overprinted on the pupil's text in the TAE giving teaching suggestions and answers conveniently located with the text material.

A **goal statement** related to chapter performance objectives in the teacher's guide begins each chapter.

Each chapter is divided into two to four **major sections** which in turn are divided into several numbered subsections.

A **one column format** leaves margins open for student and teacher notes.

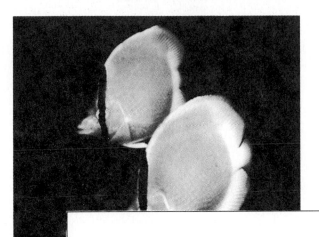

298

95

Introduction: You may wish to encourage a variety of related projects such as setting up and maintaining aquaria or terraria or collection of insects. (See Extending Your Ideas, numbers 2 and 3, in the Teacher's Guide.) Some students will be interested in observing a variety of animals in the lab; e.g., hermit crabs, salamanders, turtles, snakes, and small mammals. Care *must* be taken to treat these animals properly with arrangements made for times when school is not in session. If at all possible, also coordinate the teaching of this chapter with a trip to a zoo or museum. Consider the use of selected films or other media which bring the chapter to life. (See *Suggested Audio-Visuals* in the Teacher's Guide.)

Chapter
16

ANIMALS: ARTHROPODS THROUGH VERTEBRATES

Chapter 16 presents the characteristics of the major groups of complex animals.

Study of the characteristics of simple invertebrates (Chapter 15) reveals a variety of animal adaptations. Each phylum of organisms has particular features which make it unique. Yet, the animals have much in common as they carry out the same basic life functions. Their adaptations enable them to survive and reproduce in a variety of habitats. In this chapter, you will study three other phyla of animals—arthropods, echinoderms, and chordates. They, too, have a variety of adaptations and particular features which make each group unique. The arthropods and vertebrates have complex adaptations which make them the most successful of the animal phyla.

GOAL: You will gain an understanding of the basic features of the major groups of complex organisms in the animal kingdom.

Arthropods and vertebrates are the most successful animal phyla.

ARTHROPODS AND ECHINODERMS

Arthropods (AR thruh pahdz) are the most advanced invertebrates. This phylum has more living members than all other phyla combined. In this sense, these animals are the most successful. They are found almost everywhere. The many species illustrate the diversity of adaptations which have come about in living systems.

Echinoderms (ih KI nuh durmz) are less complex and diverse than arthropods. They are slow-moving organisms with a body plan different from other animals. However, they seem to be more closely related to the chordates than any other animal phylum.

Arthropods are the most abundant of all animals.

299

5T

BIOLOGY: LIVING SYSTEMS . . .

Teaching and learning aids to enhance readability and understanding—

Blue **student margin notes** highlight important ideas in the text. The notes can be used for preview, review, and study.

New terms are boldfaced where they are defined. Many are accompanied by phonetic spellings.

Over 1000 relevant illustrations—including photographs, photomicrographs, and artwork—give examples and details to show or explain concepts on the page.

Tables are used to summarize and consolidate information and appear in proper reading position.

FIGURE 13-3. The flagellated bacterium, *Proteus vulgaris*, shows many of the bacterial cell parts. This cell is shown magnified 21 000 times.

American Society for Microbiology

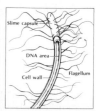

The bacterial cell wall is important in maintaining an osmotic balance between the cell and the environment.

Besides the main chromosome, bacteria have small segments of DNA called plasmids.

Most bacterial cells are enclosed by a cell wall. This wall protects the cell and helps maintain an osmotic balance (Section 5:5) between the bacterium and its environment. Penicillin is effective against many bacteria because it hinders the production of murein needed to make new cell walls. Thus, the bacteria cannot reproduce. Often the cell wall is surrounded by an outer slime capsule which may protect the cell. Some bacteria have flagella and can move by "wiggling."

Each bacterium has one main chromosome. In addition, bacteria contain smaller, circular segments of DNA called **plasmids**. Replication of plasmids is independent of the main chromosome. Sometimes part of a plasmid may become part of the chromosome. Then it replicates along with the chromosome. Other plasmids never join with the chromosome. Many of these plasmids carry genes which make the bacterium resistant to antibiotics. When the cell in which they are located comes into contact with an antibiotic, these plasmids may replicate many times. This replication aids the survival of the bacterium.

Despite their small size and simple structure, bacteria can survive in a wide variety of environments. One reason for their success in many places is that they vary in their metabolic
...rry on aerobic
...on, and so, they
...he presence of

...many places is
...ny bacteria are

...s parasites or
...rganisms often
...organisms are
...ld not survive

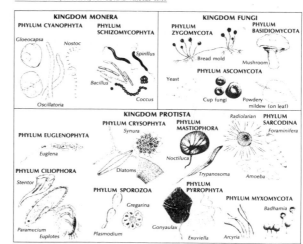

TABLE 13-2. SUMMARY OF MAJOR CHARACTERISTICS OF MONERANS, PROTISTS, AND FUNGI

Kingdom	Phylum	Common Name	Structure	Nutrition	Examples
Monera	Cyanophyta	Blue-Green Algae	Prokaryotic; Mostly Unicellular	Autotrophic	Nostoc
	Schizomycophyta	Bacteria	Prokaryotic; Unicellular	Mostly Heterotrophic	Diplococcus
Protista	Euglenophyta	Euglenoids	Unicellular	Autotrophic	Euglena
	Chrysophyta	Golden Algae	Mostly Unicellular	Autotrophic	diatoms
	Pyrrophyta	Dinoflagellates	Unicellular	Autotrophic	Gonyaulax
	Sarcodina	Sarcodines	Unicellular	Heterotrophic	Amoeba
	Ciliophora	Ciliates	Unicellular	Heterotrophic	Paramecium
	Mastigophora	Flagellates	Unicellular	Heterotrophic	Trypanasoma
	Sporozoa	Sporozoans	Unicellular	Heterotrophic	Plasmodium
	Myxomycota	Slime Molds	Unicellular and Multicellular stages	Heterotrophic	Physarum
Fungi	Zygomycota	Sporangium Fungi	Multicellular	Heterotrophic	Rhizopus
	Basidiomycota	Club Fungi	Multicellular	Heterotrophic	mushroom
	Ascomycota	Sac Fungi	Multicellular	Heterotrophic	cup fungus

Fortunately, many people realize the results of pollution, poor conservation methods, and overpopulation. Scientists and nonscientists alike are aware of and concerned about these problems. Humans should continue to use their reason and intelligence to ensure their survival and that of all that is living.

REVIEWING YOUR IDEAS

11. What are resources? How are resources classified?
12. How can food become a nonrenewable resource?
13. What is soil depletion? How does soil depletion occur?
14. What is erosion? Explain what humans can do to prevent erosion.
15. How are fuels used today? Are fuels a renewable resource? Explain.
16. Distinguish between nuclear fusion and nuclear fission.
17. What has caused the extinction or near extinction of many animals?
18. Why has much of the original forest land of the United States been cleared?

ADVANCES IN BIOLOGY

35:14 Alternative Solutions in Pest Control

Although the use of pesticides continues, it is not the only answer to pest control. Biological control methods are also being developed. **Biological control** is the use of organisms to check pest populations. Such methods retain a more natural, balanced ecosystem and avoid the disadvantages of chemicals.

One biological method used to control pests is to preserve their natural enemies—insects, spiders, frogs, and birds. Predators of pests may also be introduced into a new area. This method was first used in introduced in that was dest industry.

Wasps (Fi other insects species of para in controlling causes damag million acres caterpillars. W the host cater

FIGURE 35-20. **This wasp is laying eggs in a gypsy moth pupa. When the eggs hatch, the wasp larvae will feed on and kill the pupa. Introduction of the parasitic wasps into the area thus can control the moths.**

Thomas Zimmerman/Alpha   *Thomas Zimmerman/Alpha*

FIGURE 4-1. (a) A bobsled team at the top of the run has high potential energy and low kinetic energy. (b) While on the run, the potential energy is converted to kinetic energy.

Potential energy can be converted to kinetic energy.

Energy is conserved as it changes form.

In cells, potential chemical energy is converted to kinetic energy used for work.

Both the rock at the top of the hill and the wood have high potential energy. **Potential energy** is energy of position or stored energy. As the rock rolls down the hill or as the wood is burned, the potential energy is converted to kinetic energy. **Kinetic energy** is energy of motion. The rock at the bottom of the hill and the products formed from burning the wood have low potential energy. The difference between the high and low potential energies equals the energy released.

Energy, either potential or kinetic, can be in many forms and can change from one form to another. The potential energy in the wood molecules is called **chemical energy.** That energy is "stored" in the bonds of the molecules in wood cells. (Where did that energy come from originally?) When wood is burned, old bonds are broken and new bonds are formed. The potential chemical energy is changed to heat and light (radiant energy).

Any time energy changes form, it is conserved so that the total amount of energy in a system is constant. For example, in the burning of wood, some energy is released and can be used for work. Some of the original energy exists in the bonds of the new compounds formed, carbon dioxide and water. The total amount of this energy is equal to the amount of energy in the wood and the oxygen with which it reacted. The **law of conservation of energy** is: *energy is neither created nor destroyed, but it can be changed from one form to another.*

Changes of energy are important to living things. *Cells depend upon potential chemical energy in the bonds of energy-rich molecules. When the bonds are broken, the potential energy is converted to kinetic energy which can be used by cells for biological work.*

Review questions appear throughout the chapter material. **Reviewing Your Ideas** sections check for immediate understanding. All review questions are answered in the TAE on the pages with the questions.

Short, **numbered sections** facilitate planning lessons and assigning readings.

Informative captions tie illustrations to the text material.

Principles or **major concepts** are highlighted in **italic type.**

BIOLOGY: LIVING SYSTEMS . . .

Special features to motivate, to enrich, to inform—

People in Biology are biographies that highlight the lives and work of scientists who have made significant contributions to biology and who serve as good role models for students.

Advances in Biology features give up-to-date information about biology, biotechnology, and current areas of biological research.

PEOPLE IN BIOLOGY

Medicine was a family tradition in Jane Wright's family—both her father and grandfather were doctors—so it surprised no one when she decided to go to medical school after graduating from Smith College. She received her M.D. in 1945 from the New York Medical College and began to specialize in cancer research, especially chemotherapy. Chemotherapy is the use of chemicals, often injected into the bloodstream, to treat disease. She succeeded her father as head of the Harlem Hospital Cancer Research Foundation in 1949. In 1955 she joined the New York University Medical School as an instructor in research surgery, and later became director of cancer chemotherapy there. In 1967 Dr. Wright was appointed dean and

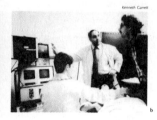

(1919 -   )

Gerard Photography

Kenneth Garrett

FIGURE 8-24. (a) This echogram shows the head and shoulders of an unborn baby. (b) Sound waves

A technique called **ultrasonography** (ul truh suh NAHG ruh fee) can be used to determine the position and anatomy of a fetus. An

ADVANCES IN BIOLOGY

8:12 Detecting Human Genetic Disease

More than 200 000 babies each year in the United States are born with genetic disorders or birth defects. Although many of them are minor, others cause severe health problems. Some cause death. Several techniques allow physicians to detect dangerous problems in the fetus (unborn child).

Amniocentesis (am nee oh sen TEE sus) is a process in which a sample of fluid surrounding the fetus is withdrawn through a long, thin needle. The fluid can be analyzed for the presence or absence of certain chemicals which indicate genetic disease. Examples of diseases detected are hemophilia, some forms of muscular dystrophy, Tay-Sachs disease, and sickle-cell anemia.

Some diseases are detected by studying fetal cells found in the fluid that is withdrawn in amniocentesis. The chromosomes in these fetal cells can be studied. Recall that the chromosomes, when photographed and paired, are called a karyotype. Karyotypes of cells can reveal if the fetus has certain diseases, such as Down Syndrome. Other examples of diseases that show in karyotypes are Turner and Kleinfelter Syndromes. (Sex of the fetus may also be determined this way.)

Amniocentesis can be used to determine if a fetus has certain genetic diseases.

FIGURE 8-23. In amniocentesis, fluid from the amnion is withdrawn. The fluid contains some of the unborn baby's cells. The cells are grown and their chromosomes are analyzed. Certain diseases can be determined from this procedure.

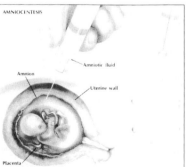

AMNIOCENTESIS

Amniotic fluid

Amnion

Uterine wall

Placenta

Kenneth Garrett

CHAPTER REVIEW

SUMMARY

1. When light strikes an object, certain wavelengths may be absorbed and the energy form changed.
2. Chlorophyll reflects mostly the green portion of the spectrum. The other wavelengths are absorbed and the light is changed to chemical energy. Carotenes aid in the absorption of light energy.
3. During photosynthesis, radiant energy is trapped and converted to chemical energy.
4. During the light reactions of photosynthesis, light energy is converted to chemical energy of ATP. Water is split into hydrogen and oxygen. The oxygen is released.
5. In the dark reactions of photosynthesis, the ATP and hydrogen from the light reactions are used in the synthesis of glucose.
6. Glucose made in photosynthesis may be used in respiration or converted to fats, amino acids, starch, or cellulose.
7. Photosynthesis and respiration are interdependent reactions. During photosynthesis, energy is used to produce glucose from carbon dioxide and water. During respiration, energy is released as glucose is converted to carbon dioxide and water.
8. In photosynthesis, light energy is changed to the chemical energy of glucose. During respiration, energy from glucose is changed to the chemical energy of ATP. ATP energy is used for work.
9. Most plant
   as they co
   vorous pla
   other nutr
   tion of ins
10. In additio
    plants req
    nitrogen,
    phosphor
11. Experimen
    fuels from

LANGUAGE OF BIOLOGY

absorption spectrum
carotene
chlorophyll
dark reactions
fossil fuels
guard cell
insectivorous plant
light reactions
palisade cells

phloem
photosynthesis
spongy layer
stomata
synfuels
visible spectrum
wavelength
xylem

CHECKING YOUR IDEAS

On a separate paper, indicate whether each of the following statements is true or false. Do not write in this book.

1. Chlorophyll absorbs mostly wavelengths of light in the green part of the spectrum.
2. Overall, the reactions of photosynthesis are endergonic.
3. Synthesis of glucose occurs in the dark reactions.
4. The products of respiration are the reactants of photosynthesis.
5. Hydrogen in a glucose molecule comes from water.
6. Light energy is changed to chemical energy of glucose during the light reactions.
7. Carbon dioxide and water are the only essential nutrients of plants.
8. Digestion is extracellular in most plants.

CHAPTER REVIEW

3. What does an absorption spectrum reveal about chlorophyll? What is the significance of the absorption spectrum of chlorophyll?
4. What are carotenes? When are they visible in leaves?
5. What are the reactants and products of photosynthesis?
6. Describe the major events of the light reactions.
7. Explain how the light reactions and dark reactions are related.
8. Once glucose is produced in photosynthesis, what are some ways in which it is used by the plant?
9. How is photosynthesis the opposite of respiration?
10. How is the chemical energy produced during photosynthesis used? What happens to some of the chemical energy?
11. Write an essay about the interdependence of photosynthesis and respiration. Your essay should include a discussion of both materials and energy.
12. How does a Venus's-flytrap trap and digest insects?
13. Explain how magnesium, nitrogen, and sulfur are used by plants.
14. Explain several ways in which photosynthesis might be used to provide new fuels.

APPLYING YOUR IDEAS

1. Relate the events of photosynthesis to the structure of the leaf.
2. What would the absorption spectrum of carotenes be like? Explain.
3. Why are fertilizers often used in growing plants?
4. Explain how photosynthesis and respiration result in the recycling of materials.
5. From where does the oxygen necessary for aerobic respiration come?

6. Trace the "flow of energy" from light to energy used for work. Is energy recycled? Explain.
7. Nitrogen is important to plants. From where does it come? How is it made available to plants?
8. What is phosphorus used for in plants?

EXTENDING YOUR IDEAS

1. Using reference materials, prepare a brief report on the contributions of van Helmont, Priestley, and Ingen-Housz to our understanding of photosynthesis.
2. Will a developing plant grown in the dark produce chlorophyll? Conduct a controlled experiment to determine the answer. As a follow up, test other developing plants using different colored lights. Does any particular color seem to favor chlorophyll production?
3. Conduct an experiment to determine the effect of different wavelengths of light on the rate of photosynthesis.
4. Find out how Spanish moss, which grows on the branches of trees, obtains its nutrients.
5. Grow two groups of insectivorous plants during the school year. Keep all conditions for both groups the same except that group A is fed insects and group B is not. Compare the growth and appearance of the two groups.

SUGGESTED READINGS

Bold, Harold C., and Hundell, C. L., *The Plant Kingdom*, 4th ed. Englewood Cliffs, NJ, Prentice-Hall Inc., 1977.
Slack, Adrian, *Carnivorous Plants*. Cambridge, MA, M.I.T. Press, 1980.
Whittingham, L. P., *Photosynthesis*, 2nd ed. Carolina Biology Reader. Burlington, NC, Carolina Biological Supply Co., 1977.

Complete chapter end material for reinforcement and further study—

The **Summary** is a numbered listing of the major concepts and principles presented in the chapter.

Language of Biology lists science terms of importance presented and discussed in the chapter.

Checking Your Ideas and **Evaluating Your Ideas** include questions to check recall of material in the chapter. Answers are given in the Teacher's Guide.

Applying Your Ideas contains application questions not directly answered in the text material. Some questions tie chapter information to material studied in earlier chapters. Answers are given in the Teacher's Guide.

Extending Your Ideas takes students beyond chapter material. Experiments, reports, projects, and debate topics are included. Suggestions and additional information are given in the Teacher's Guide.

Suggested Readings give student references for more in-depth study.

BIOLOGY: LIVING SYSTEMS . . .

Relevant appendices to expand text material—

Appendix A lists traits and examples of the major phyla and certain subgroups of the five kingdoms of organisms.

Appendix B details biochemistry of respiration and photosynthesis presented in the text.

Appendix C gives career information including addresses to write for additional information.

Appendix D lists chemical elements and some compounds with their chemical symbols.

Appendix E details SI prefixes and conversion from one SI measurement to another.

APPENDIX C

Biology-Related Careers

Careers in biology-related fields are many and varied. Some jobs in these fields may require only on-the-job training. Others may require up to eight years of formal college training plus on-the-job training. Below is a list of a few of the biology-related careers with brief descriptions and training requirements. The training requirements may vary from place to place. You will want to check with local companies, schools, and professional groups for details.

Training and education are indicated below using the following abbreviations: On-the-job training—JOB, High school diploma—HS, Vocational or technical school training—VT, Junior college (2 yr)—JC, Bachelor of Science degree—BS, Master of Science degree—MS, Internship—IN.

APPENDIX B

Respiration and Photosynthesis
Cellular Respiration

How is the energy of glucose changed to that of ATP in aerobic cell respiration? Aerobic respiration can be written generally as:

$$2ATP + 38ADP + 38 \text{—}\textcircled{P} + C_6H_{12}O_6 + 6O_2$$
$$\rightarrow 6CO_2 + 6H_2O + 38ATP + 2ADP + 2 \text{—}\textcircled{P}$$

Attempt to relate the details of aerobic respiration, which occurs in four major stages (Figure B-1), to the general purpose of ATP production. Also, compare the specific details to the general equation.

APPENDIX A

A Classification Of Living Systems

The following is a classification showing five kingdoms. Major phyla of these kingdoms are included. Several minor phyla have been omitted. Classification includes the classes for several phyla and important orders of insects and mammals. For more complete descriptions of most groups, refer to Chapter 13 (Monerans, Protists, and Fungi), Chapter 14 (Plants), and Chapters 15 and 16 (Animals).

KINGDOM MONERA
(All are prokaryotes.)

Phylum Schizomycophyta: Bacteria. Very small cells; usually unicellular; some chains or clusters; mostly heterotrophic.

Phylum Cyanophyta: Blue-green algae. Usually unicellular; some chains or filaments; chlorophyll throughout cells (chloroplasts absent).

KINGDOM FUNGI
(All are eukaryotes.)

Phylum Zygomycota: Sporangium fungi. Multicellular; heterotrophic; spores produced in sporangia.

Phylum Basidiomycota: Club fungi. Multicellular; heterotrophic; spores produced in basidia.

Phylum Ascomycota: Sac fungi. Mostly multicellular; heterotrophic; spores produced in asci.

KINGDOM PROTISTA
(All are eukaryotes.)

Phylum Euglenophyta: Euglenoids. Unicellular algae; mostly autotrophic; usually one flagellum for locomotion; mainly freshwater forms; some animal parasites.

Phylum Chrysophyta: Golden algae. Yellow-brown color; mostly unicellular; marine.

Phylum Pyrrophyta: Dinoflagellates. Unicellular; two flagella for locomotion; marine and freshwater forms.

Phylum Sarcodina: Sarcodines. Unicellular; pseudopods (false feet) for locomotion and obtaining food; heterotrophic.

Phylum Ciliophora: Ciliates. Unicellular; many cilia for both locomotion and obtaining food; heterotrophic.

Phylum Mastigophora: Flagellates. Unicellular; have flagella; heterotrophic.

Phylum Sporozoa: Sporozoans. Unicellular; reproduce by spores; no locomotion adaptations; parasitic.

Phylum Myxomycota: Slime molds. Mostly colonial; some cells amoebalike; spores; multinucleate.

Full glossary and index for quick reference—

The **Glossary** gives concise definitions of the terms presented in the text along with phonetic pronunciations. A key to the pronunciations appears on the first page of the glossary.

The **Index** references not only topics discussed in the text but also lists pages of illustrations and tables.

INDEX

GLOSSARY

Pronunciation Key

a . . . back (BAK)	i (i + con + e) . . . idea, life (i DEE uh, LIFE)	sh . . . shelf (SHELF)
er . . . care, fair (KER, FER)	oh . . . go (GOH)	ch . . . nature (NAY chur)
ay . . . day (DAY)	aw . . . soft (SAWFT)	g . . . gift (GIHFT)
ah . . . father (FAHTH ur)	or . . . orbit (OR but)	j . . . gem, edge (JEM, EJ)
ar . . . car (KAR)	oy . . . coin (KOYN)	ing . . . sing (SING)
ow . . . flower, loud (FLOW ur, LOWD)	oo . . . foot (FOOT)	zh . . . vision (VIHZH un)
e . . . less (LES)	yoo . . . pure (PYOOR)	k . . . cake (KAYK)
ee . . . leaf (LEEF)	ew . . . food (FEWD)	s . . . seed, cent (SEED, SENT)
ih . . . trip (TRIHP)	yew . . . few (FYEW)	z . . . zone, raise (ZOHN, RAYZ)
	uh (u + con) . . . comma, mother (KAHM uh, MUTH ur)	

abdomen: posterior body region of an arthropod; region in vertebrates housing many internal organs

abiotic (ay bi AHT ihk) **factors:** physical (nonliving) aspects which interact with the organisms of an ecosystem

abscission (ab SIHZH un): the falling of leaves from trees

abscission layer: group of cells which forms between the stem and the petiole of a leaf

absorption spectra (ub SORP shun • SPEC truh): spectra which have some wavelengths of light either reduced or absent

abyssal (uh BIHS ul) **zone:** deepest part of the ocean where light is absent

acceleration center: area in the medulla oblongata from which the accelerator nerves originate

accelerator nerves: nerves which increase the heart-beat by stimulating the S-A node

acetylcholine (uh seet ul KOH leen): neurotransmitter which is produced by the vagus nerves and inhibits the rate of contraction of heart muscle in humans

acid: substance which in solution has a greater concentration of hydrogen ions than hydroxide ions

acid rain: rain with a low pH

acquired characteristic: change in an organism caused by use or disuse of certain body parts

actin (AK tun): protein which makes up part of the filaments in striated muscle

action potential: reversal of polarity and flow of ions in a neuron caused by a stimulus

activation energy: energy necessary to start some chemical reactions

active immunity (ihm YEW nut ee): immunity or disease resistance resulting from production of antibodies by the host

active site: particular portion of an enzyme molecule which fits a substrate

active transport: energy-requiring process in which a membrane has an active role in the passage of materials across it

adaptation: inherited characteristic which promotes survival and reproduction in a natural environment

adaptive advantage: possessing a trait which makes a species better suited to its environment and makes its chances of reproducing better

adaptive radiation: the evolution of many new species from a common ancestor in a new environment

adenine (AD un een): one of the bases in nucleic acids

adenosine diphosphate (uh DEN uh seen • di FAHS fayt) **(ADP):** complex molecule containing adenine, ribose, and two phosphates

adenosine triphosphate (uh DEN uh seen • tri FAHS fayt) **(ATP):** complex molecule containing adenine, ribose, and three phosphates; used as an energy source in all organisms

adhesion (ad HEE zhun): attraction between unlike molecules

adrenal (uh DREEN ul) **cortex:** outer portion of the adrenal gland

adrenal gland: endocrine gland on top of each kidney

adrenal medulla (muh DUL uh): inner portion of the adrenal gland

adrenaline (uh DREN ul un): hormone secreted by the adrenal medulla; helps the body respond to emergencies; also called epinephrine

adrenocorticotrophic hormone (ACTH): hormone secreted by the anterior pituitary; stimulates the adrenal cortex to secrete its hormones

---

11T

USING BIOLOGY: LIVING SYSTEMS

Organization and Sequence

The *Teacher's Annotated Edition* of *Biology: Living Systems* is divided into two sections—the Teacher's Guide, which has pages with grey edges and is bound at the front, and the pupil's text overprinted with red annotations and answers.

The *Pupil's Edition* is divided into eight units which break up the text material in a logical manner. The units are divided into 35 chapters. Each chapter is further divided into major sections and numbered sections. The numbering and headings of the sections aid students in locating specific topics and assist you in arranging class and homework assignments.

Biology: Living Systems follows a development of biological principles from simple levels of biological organization to complex levels. The text begins with introductory information about the scientific method and measurement, the tools of the biological scientist. An introduction to basic chemistry is included in the first unit. The text then deals with cell biology, genetics, organisms, populations, communities, and ecosystems. It also includes descriptive material about diseases, nutrition, and the environment.

Teacher's Guide

The Teacher's Guide of *Biology: Living Systems* is designed to make the features of the text more useful to you as you teach the course, to give information that aids in adapting your course to your teaching style, and to provide you with additional references and resources you may want to use in your presentations, discussions, or other classroom teaching. The first forty pages of the teacher's guide include this introductory material.

Beginning on page 41T is chapter-by-chapter information. This information includes Teaching Techniques, Performance Objectives, Answers to Chapter Review, and Additional Readings.

Teaching Techniques. The chapter-by-chapter material starts with ideas and suggestions for what and how to emphasize certain principles. Teaching suggestions additional to those that appear within the chapter in the form of annotations also are given.

Performance Objectives. The major Goal of the chapter is followed by a list of specific suggested performance objectives. Thus, you are aware of what to emphasize to ensure that your students achieve these objectives. When designing your chapter tests or course of study for beginning biology, these objectives will be useful as a framework. The *Evaluation Program for Biology: Living Systems* is written based on these objectives. A thorough explanation of what performance objectives are and how to use them is found on pages 39T-40T.

Answers to Chapter Review. All answers to chapter-end questions are provided in this section. Diagrams are included where necessary and added suggestions are given for some of the extension questions.

Additional Readings. Additional student and teacher readings are provided to accompany each chapter. No readings with copyright dates earlier than 1975 are included. Therefore, locating these optional readings is facilitated.

Teacher's Annotations

The red Teacher Annotations consist of science background, points of emphasis, suggested demonstrations, teaching strategies, and answers to all Reviewing Your Ideas questions. These annotations are located conveniently with the appropriate text material.

Pupil's Text

Readability

Readability plays a major role in determining the success of a textbook in the classroom. Biology which can be comprehended by the majority of students stimulates their interest and involvement in the subject area. Readability promotes teachability and helps facilitate classroom management.

In controlling reading level, careful attention has been given to vocabulary, sentence construction, paragraph structure, unit and chapter organization, illustrations, and text format.

The vocabulary in the text is consistent with the developmental level of average high school students. Words with a large number of syllables have been avoided whenever possible. In addition, important science terms are printed in boldface type the first time they appear and are often accompanied by phonetic spellings. Italic type is used for emphasis. Defined terms are used repeatedly to reinforce meanings.

The one-column format leaves margins open for student margin notes which highlight important ideas in the text. Teacher annotations and captions are also in the margins. Thus, the flow of ideas in the main body of the text is not disrupted. Spacing around graphics and text type gives an open appearance. Tables and summary statements also enhance readability.

Because reading has become in various degrees a learning obstacle for many students, a reading feature has been included in this Teacher's Guide (pp. 22T-29T). The aim of the feature is to aid you in assisting students who have difficulties with reading in the content area. Additional reading references are listed in General References for Teachers on page 30T.

Photographs and Illustrations

A sound visual presentation stimulates student interest and adds to the level of understanding. The use of material which provides students with visual links between biological principles and real-world happenings is vital to the learning process. Each unit and chapter begins with a color photograph and thought-provoking paragraph to introduce what will be presented and to stimulate student interest. In addition, over 1100 graphics — photographs, artwork, graphs—are used to reinforce, clarify, and give relevant examples of biological concepts in adjacent paragraphs. Use these graphics as part of your presentation as much as possible to increase comprehension and to have students learn to think of them as an active part of the text.

Student Notes and Review Questions

Student margin notes printed in blue aid students in review. Using the section titles as a framework, these notes can provide students with a ready outline of the concepts discussed within the chapter. They are also an excellent reading aid in providing students with a concise statement of a paragraph or concept.

Review questions within the chapters, called Reviewing Your Ideas, aid students in determining immediately their understanding of text material. If they cannot answer the review questions, students should reread the sections just before the questions. These questions, which are answered in the teacher's edition in red on the pages they appear, are a valuable reading aid.

Advances in Biology

Features called Advances in Biology present supplemental discussions of chapter concepts and insights into current areas of biological and biotechnological research. These pages should be used to motivate students to seek additional information concerning timely issues such as recombinant DNA, fuel from plants, aging, and pest control. All of these features are related to the material of the chapters in which they appear.

People in Biology

Biographies called People in Biology highlight the lives and careers of scientists who have made valuable contributions to the field of biology. The biographies are designed to bring out the human aspects of scientists in general and to relate their work to the relevant problems of their times. Those scientists included serve as good role models for students. The features are located in the chapters where the scientists' contributions most closely coincide with the text material.

Chapter-End Material

The chapter-end material begins with a Summary which concisely reviews the major concepts and principles in the chapter in statement form. You can begin the chapter using the Summary to determine how much your students know about a topic from previous science courses. The Summary is an excellent reading aid in that it helps students discern the major points from the information in the chapter. It also gives you insight as to what the author feels you should emphasize in presenting the material.

Language of Biology is a list of important biological terms used in the chapter. Students should have an understanding of these terms to have a good understanding of the material in the chapter. This list can be used before a chapter is covered in class to determine what students may have learned from previous science courses and to determine some misunderstandings or misconceptions students may have.

Chapter-end questions fall under three headings—Checking Your Ideas, Evaluating Your Ideas, and Applying Your Ideas. Checking Your Ideas includes short answer (fill-ins, matching, true-false), recall questions. Evaluating Your Ideas is composed of explanation, recall questions as well as processing questions. To aid students in drawing material together and developing communicative skills, many questions require the organization of a short essay. Applying Your Ideas provides application questions. Students must use the chapter material to answer these questions which are not answered directly in the text. Occasionally questions are included in this section that tie ideas in the chapter with information covered in previous chapters. When these questions appear, they are marked in the teacher's edition with a chapter reference.

Extending Your Ideas presents a series of questions and activities which lead the student beyond the text and the classroom. Suggested topics can provide a variety of open-ended activities including experiments, written reports, projects, and classroom debates. Because these items include a wide range of activities from simple library reports to more complex experiments, they can be assigned to students at all ability levels. Use these items to develop positive attitudes toward science and to extend text material for capable students.

Suggested Readings provides the able and interested students with references for further study. Some references expand on topics presented in the chapter. Others treat new but related areas of interest. Also, encourage students to read articles concerning science in the local newspaper and in popular news magazines. Establish the idea that the study of science need not occur only in the laboratory or classroom.

Appendices

Appendix A contains a listing of the major phyla of the five kingdoms of biological classification with brief descriptions of traits and some examples. The appendix also includes the classes of several phyla and important orders of insects and mammals.

Appendix B details the processes of respiration and photosynthesis that are briefly discussed within the text material. This appendix is very useful if your approach to biology is biochemical or molecular and/or if your students easily handle the text material on these topics.

Appendix C provides information on biology-related careers focusing on life science, environmental conservation, and health care careers. An address list of additional information sources is also provided.

Appendix D gives tables listing chemical symbols and formulas to expand student appreciation for chemical shorthand and to be a quick reference if students forget the meanings of some of the simple symbols and formulas used in the text.

Appendix E provides an extended version of Table 2-1 in the text. Information about converting from one SI unit to another is given also.

Glossary and Index

A glossary of major terms and their phonetic spellings is provided along with a pronunciation key. The glossary and the complete index give students a quick reference to key terms and topics in the text.

PLANNING YOUR BIOLOGY COURSE

Biology: Living Systems is organized to present the study of biology from simple levels of organization to complex levels. Basic chemistry, cell biology, and genetics precede information about organisms, populations, communities, and ecosystems. This logical organization also is flexible to meet your planning requirements. You are in the best position to design a biology course that satisfies your students' needs. The planning guide shown is provided to assist you with both long range and daily planning and with designing the best possible biology program.

The guide is organized to present a suggested number of class sessions for each chapter. The entire course is based on 180 class sessions in the school year, which is equivalent to 160 hours of combined class and laboratory time.

The sections of each chapter are classified as being of primary importance or secondary importance. A basic biology program should include those sections designated as of primary importance. The sections listed in this category provide a minimum program. After presenting the essential sections in each chapter, you may have the time to select from additional text topics and laboratory exercises.

Below are listings of suggested chapters to cover if you are on six or nine week reporting periods. These listings are approximate. Exactly how you divide the time among the chapters will depend on your teaching style, your main concerns for emphasis, and the ability levels of your students.

Six Week Periods		Nine Week Periods	
Period	**Chapters**	**Period**	**Chapters**
1	1-6	1	1-9
2	7-12	2	10-18
3	13-18	3	19-27
4	19-24	4	28-35
5	25-30		
6	31-35		

Once you have determined your goals for the year, use the planning guide to aid you in scheduling. The number of class sessions suggested includes time for laboratory work and testing. You may find that some classes will take longer to cover a chapter than what is projected in the planning guide. Use the planning guide as a framework rather than as a rigid schedule.

PLANNING GUIDE FOR BIOLOGY: LIVING SYSTEMS

			Emphasis Level		
Unit	Chapter	Class Sessions	Of Primary Importance	Of Secondary Importance	Suggested Laboratory Topics
I	1	5	All sections		Appreciation of environment What is life?
	2	4	All sections		Microscope use Problem solving Measurement
	3	5	3:1-3:7, 3:9-3:16	3:8, 3:17	Chemistry of fats, proteins, carbohydrates
	4	5	4:1-4:5, 4:7-4:9	4:6	Respiration Fermentation Enzymes
	5	6	5:1-5:12, 5:14-5:15	5:13, 5:16	Diffusion Cell examination Osmosis
II	6	6	All sections		Mitosis Meiosis
	7	6	All sections		Probability Pedigrees Genetics

PLANNING GUIDE FOR BIOLOGY: LIVING SYSTEMS

Unit	Chapter	Class Sessions	Emphasis Level Of Primary Importance	Of Secondary Importance	Suggested Laboratory Topics
II continued	8	4	8:1-8:4, 8:8-8:12	8:5-8:7	Genetics
	9	7	9:1-9:10	9:11-9:13	DNA RNA Protein building
III	10	5	All sections		Adaptations Fossils Variations
	11	5	11:1-11:6, 11:9-11:12	11:7-11:8	Adaptations Anatomy Skull Studies
	12	3	All sections		Classification
IV	13	6	13:1-13:5, 13:8-13:15, 13:17-13:19	13:6-13:7, 13:16	Monerans, Fungi, and Protists: Growth and identification Survey
	14	5	14:1, 14:4-14:6, 14:8-14:10, 14:12	14:2-14:3, 14:7, 14:11, 14:13-14:14	Plants: Anatomy Survey
	15	6	15:1-15:4, 15:6-15:8	15:5	Animals: Anatomy Survey
	16	5	All sections		Animals: Anatomy Survey
V	17	4	17:1-17:7	17:8-17:9	Fungal, moneran and protistan reproduction
	18	4	All sections		Locomotion and responses in protozoa
	19	5	19:1-19:5, 19:7-19:13, 19:15	19:6, 19:14	Effect of antibiotics on bacterial cultures
VI	20	5	20:1, 20:3-20:5, 20:7-20:11, 20:13	20:2, 20:6, 20:12, 20:14	Plant life cycles Seeds and fruits Germination
	21	5	All sections		Photosynthesis Chromatography Leaf anatomy
	22	5	22:1-22:4, 22:6, 22:8-22:10	22:5, 22:7, 22:11-22:12	Root and stem anatomy Tropisms
VII	23	6	23:1-23:6	23:7	Regeneration in planaria Budding in Hydra
	24	4	24:1-24:7, 24:13	24:8-24:12	Chick embryology Tadpole metamorphosis
	25	6	25:1-25:4, 25:6-25:12	25:5	Digestion: Anatomy and physiology
	26	5	26:1-26:5, 26:7, 26:9-26:11, 26:13	26:6, 26:8, 26:12, 26:14-26:15	Transport: Anatomy and physiology Blood typing

PLANNING GUIDE FOR BIOLOGY: LIVING SYSTEMS

Unit	Chapter	Class Sessions	Emphasis Level Of Primary Importance	Of Secondary Importance	Suggested Laboratory Topics
VII continued	27	5	27:1-27:4, 27:6-27:8, 27:10	27:5, 27:9, 27:11-27:12	Respiration and excretion: Anatomy and physiology
	28	5	28:1-28:3, 28:5-28:9	28:4, 28:10-28:11	Skeletons and muscles: Anatomy and physiology
	29	5	29:1-29:5, 29:7, 29:9-29:10	29:6, 29:8	Effect of thyroxine on tadpole metamorphosis
	30	6	30:1, 30:4-30:11	30:2-30:3, 30:12-30:14	Nervous system: Anatomy and physiology Senses
VIII	31	5	31:1-31:3, 31:6-31:7, 31:9-31:12	31:4-31:5, 31:8 31:13-31:14	Behavior learning
	32	6	32:1-32:6, 32:9-32:12	32:7-32:8	Populations Relationships between populations
	33	6	33:1-33:2, 33:4, 33:6-33:11	33:3, 33:5, 33:12	Soil Weather Ecosystems
	34	5	All sections		Microcommunities Succession
	35	5	All sections		Pollution Energy Populations

ALTERNATE APPROACHES

You may choose to teach the chapters in an order other than as presented in the preceding planning guide. An effort has been made to allow for this flexibility by concisely repeating relevant ideas presented in previous chapters and by providing section-number references for topics treated elsewhere. In this way, if necessary, students can read a related section of another chapter to gain information they may not have already studied. The chapters studied out of sequence, therefore, have more meaning.

The following guides show how chapters can be rearranged if you choose to teach the course with an ecological, microbiological, biochemical, physiological, or phylogenetic approach. Each of these guides shows use of all chapters in the text; however, if you are interested in teaching a minicourse or one-term course, only the chapters marked with asterisks are needed. Each guide also shows what should be the main emphasis of the topics presented in each of the alternate approaches. These guides just as the original planning guide should be used as frameworks for your planning and not as rigid plans.

ECOLOGICAL APPROACH

Chapters	Emphasis
1-2*	Introduction to science Organism-environment interaction and interdependence
13-16*	Survey of organisms
31-35*	Responses to environment Main concepts of ecology Protection of environment Conservation of resources
17-30	How organisms function
3-12	Continuity in the biosphere Energy relationships Cell responses Heredity and environment Changes in organisms

* Include these chapters in one-term ecology course.

MICROBIOLOGICAL APPROACH

Chapters	Emphasis
1-5*	Introduction to science Introductory chemistry Cell structures and functions
13*	Survey of microorganisms
17-19*	Life processes of microorganisms Microorganisms and disease
31-35*	Roles of microorganisms in environment, e.g., parasitism, decomposition, etc.
6-9 10-12	Genetics, adaptation, etc., as related to all organisms, including microbes
14-16, 20- 22, 23-30	Plant and animal functions to round out course

* Include needed portions of these chapters in one-term microbiology course.

BIOCHEMICAL APPROACH

Chapters	Emphasis
1-5* Appendix B*	Introduction to science Introductory chemistry Energy transformations Cell structures and functions
6-9*	Replication, transcription, and translation of genetic material

17-19*	Biochemical aspects of life processes in simple
	   organisms, e.g., macromolecule digestion,
	   formation of nitrogenous wastes, etc.

20-22*
Appendix B*
	Biochemical aspects of life processes in plants,
	   e.g., photosynthesis, chlorophyll function,
	   gibberellin function, etc.

23-30*	Biochemical aspects of life processes in
	   animals, e.g., molecular aspects of aging,
	   function of hemoglobin, antigen-antibody
	   interactions, energetics of muscle
	   contraction, hormone functions,
	   neurotransmitter functions, etc.

10-12	Molecular aspects of evolution
13-16	Survey of organisms

31-35	Effect of chemical aspects of environment, e.g.,
	   pheromones, pesticides, radioactive wastes,
	   etc., on organisms

* Include needed portions of these chapters in one-term biochemistry course.

PHYSIOLOGICAL APPROACH

Chapters	Emphasis
1-5*	Introduction to science Chemistry as a basis of physiology Cell physiology
13-16	Survey of organisms
17-30*	Physiology of life processes
6-12 31-35	Genetics, Evolution, and Environment to round out course

* Include needed portions of these chapters in one-term physiology course.

In *Biology: Living Systems*, descriptions of the major characteristics of the main phyla of organisms are included in Unit IV. Units V, VI, and VII give greater detail about the anatomy and physiology of organisms within those phyla. In each chapter of these units, the organisms are discussed in phylogenetic order — from simple organisms to complex organisms. You, however, may prefer to use representative examples of organisms to show traits of the different phyla as you teach the course. For your convenience, the following tables are provided to show you how this material may be sequenced to follow a more strict phylogenetic approach if preferred. Those organisms highlighted in the second table are representative organisms most commonly used by biology teachers. The text section numbers are provided for your quick reference and to facilitate your planning. Many examples of organisms other than those in this chart are included throughout the text. You may choose to use them as supplementary examples as you teach.

PHYLOGENETIC APPROACH

Chapters	Emphasis
1-2*	Introduction to science
12*	Classification of organisms
13, 17-19*	Traits of phyla of simple organisms (Organisms and chapter sections to use are listed in table that follows.)
14, 20-22*	Traits of phyla of plants (Organisms and chapter sections to use are listed in table that follows.)
15-16, 23-30*	Traits of phyla of animals (Organisms and chapter sections to use are listed in table that follows.)
3-9	Introductory chemistry, cell structure and function, basic genetics
10-11	Evolution, adaptation and speciation
31-35	How organisms interact with the environment

* Include needed portions from these chapters in one-term phylogenetic course.

REPRESENTATIVE ORGANISMS

Organisms	Sections
Simple organisms	
Bacteria	13:1, 13:3-13:4, 17:1, 17:5, 18:1, 19:1-19:4
Amoeba, Paramecium	13:8, 13:9, 17:2, 18:1, 18:3, 18:5-18:10, 19:8
Fungi	13:13-13:16, 17:4, 17:6, 18:1, 18:4, 19:7
Plants	
Nonvascular plants	14:1-14:5, 20:1-20:4, 22:3
Ferns, Conifers	14:6, 14:8-14:9, 20:5-20:6
Flowering plants	14:6, 14:10-14:14, 20:7-20:14, 21:1-21:9, 22:1-22:2, 22:4-22:12
Animals	
Hydra	15:2, 23:1, 25:2, 28:6, 30:7
Planaria	15:4, 25:3, 27:Intro, 27:8, 30:7
Earthworm	15:7, 23:2, 25:4, 26:1, 27:1, 27:9, 28:6
Grasshopper	16:1, 16:4, 23:3, 23:5, 24:3, 25:5, 26:2, 27:3, 27:9, 28:1, 28:8
Fish	16:7-16:10, 26:3, 27:2, 27:12, 28:8
Frog	16:7, 16:11, 23:3-23:4, 24:1-24:2, 24:8-24:12, 26:4, 27:4, 28:8, 29:9
Bird	16:7, 16:13, 24:4, 24:8-24:10, 26:5, 28:8
Human	16:7, 16:14, 23:6-23:7, 24:6-24:10, 24:13, 25:6-25:12, 26:5-26:15, 27:4-27:7; 27:10-27:11, 28:2-28:5, 28:8-28:11, 29:1-29:8, 30:1-30:6, 30:8-30:14

ANCILLARY MATERIALS

Laboratory Biology: Investigating Living Systems

A practical, workable laboratory program, *Laboratory Biology: Investigating Living Systems* combines basic biological processes and concepts with successful laboratory experiences. With over 80 laboratory investigations (two or three per text chapter) from which to choose, you can select those which best meet your classroom needs.

Laboratory Biology: Investigating Living Systems is a completely self-contained laboratory manual. All observations, data, and answers are recorded in the spaces provided in the manual. No extra laboratory notebook is required.

Among the features which make this laboratory program a useful teaching and learning tool are the following.

1. The investigations are readable. Procedural steps are short and simple.

2. The self-pacing format facilitates individualized learning. Questions are placed throughout the steps to evaluate understanding while the investigation is being done.

3. Many illustrations are used, accurately showing procedural steps.

4. Many investigations use models and simulations. Thus, topics which otherwise might pose some difficulties in laboratory preparation, cost, or safety become no problem to present.

5. Behavioral objectives are included in each investigation. Therefore, students know what they are expected to do.

6. Three aspects of scientific literacy are developed. Students learn to use scientific vocabulary, scientific method, and graphs and charts.

Most of the investigations require simple, inexpensive equipment. Only about one-third require living or preserved specimens. All paper models needed for investigations are included in the teacher's edition for reproduction in proper class quantities.

Almost every investigation can be completed within one class period. If time or supplies are more limited, you also may choose to do some as class demonstrations.

Probing Levels of Life: A Laboratory Manual

Levels of life from molecules to biomes are presented in teacher-directed, student-involved investigations in *Probing Levels of Life: A Laboratory Manual.* You can select from over 80 investigations (2 or 3 per text chapter) to best meet your classroom needs.

Using *Probing Levels of Life: A Laboratory Manual*, students learn firsthand the value of making accurate observations and of recording data in arriving at valid conclusions. All laboratory records—observations, data graphs, diagrams, answers, conclusions—are to be kept in a separate, student-supplied notebook. With some assistance and supervision, students can become actively involved in understanding biological principles and concepts.

Among the teaching and learning features of this laboratory manual are the following.

1. Clear and concise step-by-step directions are in paragraph form.

2. Collection of both individual and class data is stressed.

3. Illustrations are used extensively, showing procedural steps and specimens.

4. Some investigations use models and simulations. Living organisms are used extensively.

5. Behavioral objectives are included in each investigation.

6. Students learn to use scientific vocabulary, to organize data in tables, charts, and graphs, and to use the scientific method.

The time needed to complete most all the investigations is one laboratory period. Some investigations, however, involve daily or weekly observations. Also, some investigations have been designed to take students outside the school to investigate organisms in their environments.

Evaluation Program for Biology: Living Systems

Available in both spirit master and black line master forms, the *Evaluation Program for Biology: Living Systems* is a complete testing program designed to be a teaching as well as an evaluating tool in the classroom. The program is composed of one 4-page test to go with each chapter of *Biology: Living Systems.* The questions and problems are of varying difficulty to focus on different levels of learning.

Each test has three main parts. **Part A—Reviewing Concepts** can be used as a review or testing component. Each is one page long and focuses on recall of specific facts or definitions from the chapter. **Part B—Testing Concepts,** a 2-page section, is a complete test that requires students to interpret basic concepts as well as to recall specifics. **Part C—Applying Concepts** is a one-page enrichment section allowing students to show their ability to apply their knowledge.

THE BIOLOGICAL CLASSROOM

Care of Living Material

Teaching biology offers an opportunity to develop a respect for life by applying humane principles in the educational use of living organisms. Students need to understand the importance of providing good care for pets, animals used in class, and animals used in science projects. Students should not conduct activities which will cause pain, hardship, or death to animals. All activities involving living organisms should be conducted with care, discretion, and respect for those organisms.

Many times, students wish to bring live animals to class. The teacher should discourage this practice unless there are adequate facilities and designated people to care for the animals. If adequate facilities are available, having animals in the classroom can be a learning experience for students. Students can learn the importance and responsibilities of providing food, space, fresh water, and adequate light and ventilation for animals.

Weekends and vacation periods can create problems if there has been no formal planning concerning the care of animals in the class. It is recommended that some type of provisions with school custodians or responsible students be pursued for those days when school is not in session. Some custodians may volunteer to care for the animals during a weekend or small vacation period. However, it may become necessary to take the animals home for long vacation periods. In these cases, responsible students should be available to take the animals home and care for them.

Having live animals in the classroom is not a small responsibility. However, with careful teacher planning, students can learn the responsibility and cooperation required when caring for living things.

Safety in the Classroom

The biology classroom is a safe place to conduct demonstrations and activities if you and your students are careful. The success of demonstrations and activities depends on their being conducted safely. Your students must assume responsibility for their safety and the safety of others.

Review safety rules with your students at regular intervals. Make sure students are aware of emergency and first aid procedures. Post fire drill regulations and a chart of emergency procedures in a prominent place in the classroom. Encourage the development of serious attitudes about safety. Always supervise your students when they are working. Some safety and first aid guidelines are provided in the laboratory manuals that accompany this text.

Setting Up Classroom Aquaria and Terraria

Aquaria. An empty aquarium should be washed with soapy water and rinsed thoroughly. Place it on a flat surface where it will not have to be moved again. Do not place the aquarium near heat sources.

Conditioned tap water can be used to fill the aquarium. Allow tap water to set out for two days before its use to "condition" it. A dechlorinating chemical can be purchased in pet stores to add to tap water if you want to add living things to the water sooner.

Aquarium gravel for the bottom should be washed with hot running water until the water runs clear. If an undergravel filter is going to be used in the aquarium, the filter should be put in the aquarium before the gravel is added. The bottom of the aquarium should be covered with about 4 cm of gravel. If other larger rocks are being added, avoid use of soluble rocks such as limestone.

A variety of aquatic plants may then be added to the aquarium. They are obtainable from the aquarium section in pet stores. Rooted plants should be placed in the back of the aquarium. Too few plants are better than too many. Overstocking may cause all of them to die.

Make sure the fish you select are good for a community tank. Someone in your pet store can give you advice on what fish get along well with each other. Adding one 3-cm fish per gallon of water works well. Fish should be introduced to the tank slowly so that they can adjust to the temperature, other fish, and so on, more easily. Add some of the aquarium water to the fish first. Gradually add more, and finally add the fish to the aquarium.

For best results, an aquarium filter and aerator should be used. The charcoal for the filter should be rinsed thoroughly before use. Directions for setting up a filter are included with the filter.

Terraria. Any glass container with a glass plate cover can be used as a terrarium. The container should be at least four liters in size. If animals are to be kept in the terrarium, it should be 60 to 80 liter capacity. An old aquarium makes an excellent terrarium.

Wash and rinse the container thoroughly. Place 2 to 3 cm of washed gravel on the bottom of the container. Add 2 cm clean sand. Then add about 6 cm of moist soil. On top of the soil, place a layer of healthy, green moss. Then add small ferns, liverworts, and horsetails. Lichens also can be added. Cover the terrarium and place it in filtered light. The gravel layer allows for drainage. If water accumulates in the pebble layer, remove the cover of the terrarium for a time.

SUGGESTIONS FOR FUSING READING AND SCIENCE INSTRUCTION

The Basic Relationship Between Reading and Science Content

As you review your biology textbook and the course syllabus you regard yourself correctly as a science teacher of biology. You see the many understandings and concepts which you want your students to know and be able to use. In fact, you can regard your assigned responsibility as one to help students become knowledgeable about this small segment of human knowledge. This is a major charge you have.

However, instruction merely in understandings and concepts are *not* enough. Your realistic responsibility must be a two-fold one. You will need to guide, instruct and develop with your students the techniques needed to read and understand the language of biology as well. In other words, you are a *language teacher!* As one reads biology, or any specific subject, one realizes quickly that the understandings and ideas are *understood* only as the reader comprehends the language used. Therefore, you become a teacher of language; but, in your case, the language as it is used to express biology. This dual responsibility, teaching content and developing reading techniques, is mutually supportive. One enhances the other.

The basic premise for your classroom procedure is to emphasize *process* rather than merely content. Reading is a process; it is a way of gaining information from the printed language. Consequently, reading does not contain any factual content, whereas biology does. In teaching the process of reading biology, the content is learned at the same time. The techniques and skills of reading cannot be taught in a vacuum but must be given meaning through content. This, then, is where you see how you can implement your responsibility which is to teach the reading process through biological content. The fusion of these two responsibilities into one classroom procedure make it possible for the students to learn the course content as they apply the needed reading techniques. The ultimate goal is to lead your students toward the greatest degree of independence possible.

Reading Requirements Needed in Biology

The style of writing in your biology text, *Biology: Living Systems*, is likely to be different from the material used to teach your students the techniques of reading in earlier grades. There, they were probably taught to read through narrative and fictional materials. Here, they have factual prose filled with pertinent details which must be under-

stood, classified and interrelated. In addition, there is a formidable vocabulary load used to express the biological ideas and which the students must master in order to use the language of biology as a means of acquiring the subject content.

The students who are using this textbook are not likely to be the ones in your school who are known to have difficulties in reading competently. These students have acquired the basic general techniques of reading competently. However, do not be misled. Your students may be ill-prepared to read scientific language, to organize precisely, to be definitive in their word meanings, or to use appropriate reading-study techniques. They probably have had little instruction in how to read factual prose containing many details as is characterized by scientific writing.

Here, you must help them to adapt their general techniques to the specifics required for reading a biology textbook. In developing this idea with your students, you can have an interesting discussion about the differences, as they perceive them, between reading their biology textbook and a selection of English literature. This would serve to alert them to the different techniques needed to read various types of material.

Essentially, the skills needed for your students in reading this text are

1. to know why one is reading—a purpose—what one wishes to find out.

2. to use the various parts of the textbook effectively.

3. to understand the vocabulary which includes technical terms and general words used technically, *i.e.*, cell.

4. to gain accurate information from the graphic aids: pictures, tables, diagrams, charts and graphs.

5. to read for exact meaning and to see the organization of the information: to note main ideas and to relate the appropriate details to each.

6. to read directions accurately.

7. to evaluate science materials in noting evidence, drawing conclusions, making judgments, and seeing implications.

8. to apply data from reading to practical problems and to student experience.

A valid time to begin to alert your students about the fusion of their competence in reading technique and their mastery of content is when you introduce the textbook to them. Direct them to the "To the Student," and discuss the ideas with them. Questions asked in the first paragraph will stimulate much interesting discussion, widen their perceptions of biology and, indeed, set overall purposes for the study of biology—and for reading about it. Then, note that each chapter begins with a photograph and an introductory paragraph. Conjecture with the students what an introductory paragraph might include. Check to see if clues are given in "To the Student," such as the theme of the chapter, goal statement and objective. Look, then, at such a paragraph for the first chapter. What do they see? What do they think will be explained? How can such information help them in the study of their textbook? Review with the students how new words are highlighted, topical headings can be used, and how the study aids such as "Reviewing Your Ideas" questions, which are scattered throughout each chapter, can be helpful. Emphasize with the students that such features are aids to their study of the textbook. Finally turn to the end of a chapter and discuss how the study aids there can be profitably used by them. For example, what does the *summary* include and what is meant by the *language* of biology (an excellent place to develop the idea that reading as a process is using language). Then check such words as *checking, evaluating, applying, extending;* all found in study aids at the end of each chapter. Brainstorm with the students and evolve with them ways they can use such aids. What you are concerned with here is student independent competence in using his or her textbook as a source of information and as a reference. The immediate application and constant reinforcement will enable your students to acquire competence in how to use factual prose materials successfully.

A Note on Basic Procedure

A vital part of all effective classroom procedure is preparing the student for the reading assignment. Indeed, how an assignment is made can determine greatly the student's competence in acquiring and understanding the information from the textbook. Adequate preparation for a reading assignment helps the student to relate the new information to that *already* known. Four aspects of preparation are needed and they are most often accomplished together.

1. Investigate what the students know and do not know about the topic(s) to be studied. Search with them and help to bring back to consciousness whatever background they may have. Begin immediately to help them to apply the information to their personal experiences.

2. Preview the reading assignment. In this, note the new vocabulary, the topical headings that indicate the organization, and discuss the various graphic aids and the ideas they show. You may read together the introductory goal statement. Also, you will note the summary ideas, the vocabulary and the specific questions at the end of the chapter—all as a means of helping the student to begin to understand the scope

and emphasis of the chapter. This procedure is indicated in the "To the Student."

3. Introduce and begin to develop the basic vocabulary (new concepts). Keep these to those fundamental concepts in which students must have some understanding—if the material is to make sense. (For instance, Chapter Two is titled, *"Biology as a Science."* There are two basic concepts which should be developed before the students read. They are, "what is biology" and "what is science." And then, "how is biology classified as a science." Obviously, after the material is read, their understanding of these terms should be enriched.

4. Establish questions for the students to keep in mind as they read. These will guide their reading and assist their concentration. Keep the questions few in number, usually one or two. You often can evolve these questions while you preview the assignment with the students. A purpose question for reading the first section of Chapter One might be, what relationship is there between community and living organism? For Chapter Two, the purpose question might be, how does biology qualify as a field of science?

Pertinent Classroom Activities to Foster the Skills

1. Having a reason—purpose—for reading
  a. Always be sure that the students know specifically what they are to find out.
  b. Check to be sure that your students can change the topical headings into questions. Use *who, what, when, where, why* and *how* as possible starters for the questions.

2. Using parts of the book
  a. Instead of telling students to look on a specific page or at a particular section and its page, tell them only the topic and have them locate the page by either the Table of Contents or the Index.
  b. Guide students to see how the proper use of the parts of a book can help their study techniques, particularly such features as introductions, summaries and so on.

3. Using vocabulary
  a. Use an open discussion—brainstorm—with your students about the meaning of a scientific term. Evolve a meaning from the discussion; then check the meaning with a dictionary or glossary meaning. Use as many experiences of the students as possible.
  b. In your discussion of word meanings
    1. help students to use context, particularly noting the meaning of a new word which may appear in boldfaced type.

2. alert the students to the etymology of words through the roots used.

c. Develop throughout the year a listing of Latin and Greek roots used in the scientific terms. For example in Chapter 2 there are two such words in the title: *Biology as a Science*

Biology: bios—life
           logy—science of, study of
Science: sci—knowledge

d. Classify the vocabulary listed at the end of a chapter. For instance, on page 34 the words introduced in Chapter 2 are listed alphabetically thusly:

Celsius	observation
controlled experiment	resolving power
data	scanning electron
experimentation	microscope (SEM)
hypothesis	second
International System	technology
of Measurement	theory
kilogram	transmission electron
liter	microscope (TEM)
mass	variable factor
meter	weight

Determine with students which words refer to (1) quantity—measurement, (2) scientific processes, (3) scientific equipment. Further establish the relationship of such terms as *theory, hypothesis, controlled experiment, data,* and *variable factor.*

4. Gaining accurate information from graphic aids

a. Actively and continuously use the graphic aids with the students to increase their ease and accuracy of use.

b. Guide students to have a guide question—purpose—when using a graphic aid so that the student is looking for something specific.

c. Use the photo at the beginning of each chapter for discussion. Conjecture what the main point is before the students read. After the reading for a chapter is done, go back to the photo and note if there are any new ideas or changes. This suggestion is made in "To the Students," however the students will not likely do this unless you structure the procedure and discuss their ideas with them.

5. Reading for exact meaning

a. Have students note the main topic of a section by the heading.

b. Have students note the author's outline by means of the chapter sections and topical headings.

c. Note the structure of paragraphs as shown in the excerpt on pages 16 and 17.

6. Reading directions accurately

a. Have students read a set of directions, then have them restate them.

b. Check specific action words to be sure students know exactly what is required. For example, what precisely do students do when they see such words or terms as *compute, classify, place next to, record your findings,* and so on.

c. Be sure students can identify the equipment needed for various experiments.

7. Evaluating science information and applying scientific data.

a. Use the exercise at the end of each chapter, *Applying Your Ideas.* Discuss what each means and implies.

b. Conjecture what changes there would be if such a fact or principle did not exist.

c. Have students relate experiences they have had that would show the application of the fact or principle.

Dr. David L. Shepherd
Professor, Reading/Education
Hofstra University

More detailed information for teaching reading in content areas is found in *Comprehensive High School Reading* by David L. Shepherd, published by Charles E. Merrill Publishing Co.

6   THE WORLD OF LIVING THINGS 1:1

At first you see plant life such as grasses, weeds, shrubs, and other plants. As you enter the forest, you are aware of the most striking forms of life, the trees.

You then see much more. There are other types of plants such as ferns and mosses growing on the forest floor. Leaves and fallen branches litter the earth. You look under them and find many kinds of animal life. Insects are plentiful. Ants scurry about, each doing its special job. You see spiders, worms, and many-legged creatures. Other animal life is also plentiful. Birds sing their songs and a rabbit bounds quickly out of sight. Perhaps you see a deer nibbling leaves or a snake sliding off into the undergrowth. You look more closely at the trees and find many other living things. Bees swarm around their hive. A small butterfly, almost the same color as the bark, clings to the trunk of a tree. You also see a caterpillar moving silently across a leaf, eating as it goes.

A community is a naturally occurring group of different kinds of organisms.

Your trip has been an eventful one. Yet you saw only a fraction of the living things in such a community. A community is a naturally occurring group of organisms living in a certain area. You missed the countless microscopic (mi kruh SKAHP ihk) organisms that live in the soil, in puddles of water, and inside other plants and animals. If you had taken a sample of soil or water, you would have found that it contains a vast amount of life. With a microscope, you would see many bacteria, very small living things. You might also have seen many other tiny creatures, larger than bacteria and more complex. These creatures include mites and insects and very small worms.

bacteria (singular, bacterium)

FIGURE 1-1.   A forest community may include organisms such as (a) red fox and (b) orange Indian pipe.

Gene Frazier

┌ Did students note this definition of community?

┌ Check to see if students know how to use the pronunciation key, the phonetic spelling, and why a syllable is capitalized.

Chapter

I

THE WORLD OF LIVING THINGS

┌ **Introduction:** Discuss as indicated on the left. Three basic concepts: biology, life processes, life.

Develop the etymology of biology: bios—life, logy—study of ─────

Check to see if students note the meaning of *organisms.*

Conjecture with students on the meaning of *life processes.* What clue to the meaning is given? ─────

Brainstorm with students: Is this the basic concept (idea) they are to study in biology? Get their views. Check them by previewing the textbook or by investigating the Table of Contents to see what is covered.

In previewing this chapter, determine with students why the heading THE COMMUNITY is used. What point is suggested here about living organisms? Have students read Section 1:1 to check.

You are about to begin a course in **biology,** the study of life. Naturally, you want to know what you will be learning. Your study will involve different kinds of **organisms** (living things). Part of the course will examine the major groups of organisms which exist today. You will learn about the physical characteristics which set one type of organism apart from others.

Biology is more than just a study which describes the many differences among living things. There are nearly two million known kinds of living organisms. You could not possibly learn about all or even most of them. Therefore, your study of life will focus on the similarities among organisms. These similarities most often involve the **life processes** of organisms—their activities and functions. By studying these processes, you will see that there are certain features common to all living things. By the time you complete the course, you will have a good understanding of what is meant by the word "life."

GOAL: You will gain an understanding of the basic features of life common to all organisms.

Biology is the study of life.

A living thing is called an organism.

Organisms are similar in their activities and functions.

THE COMMUNITY

1:1 Organisms

Have you ever had the chance to spend a day exploring the natural surroundings where you live? Perhaps you live in an area near a forest. Imagine that you are about to walk through the forest. As you near the edge of the forest, you see many things.

5

Main idea

Definition/main idea

Paragraph pattern: Main idea followed by illustrations.

Paragraph pattern: Question followed by illustrative answers. (See photos below.)

Paragraph pattern: Definition. Determine with students what is being defined and discuss with them the implications of the definition. Use examples.

Paragraph pattern: Definition. Ask students what is being defined.

ORGANISM AND ENVIRONMENT

1:9 Adaptation

When you think about a community, you naturally think about the organisms living in it. A lake is inhabited by fish, snails, and algae. Cactus plants, scorpions, and lizards live in a desert. Crabs, jellyfish, and whales are found in the ocean. Deer, birds, and maple trees live in a forest.

Has it occurred to you that organisms are suited to particular kinds of environments? A fish has gills that obtain oxygen from the water. A deer has teeth that grind plant material. Birds have wings. A cactus stores water. Maple trees have broad leaves which trap sunlight in photosynthesis.

These special parts and activities of organisms are examples of adaptations. An **adaptation** is a feature of a living thing which enables it to survive in its environment. Adaptations are another common feature of living things. You will learn more about adaptations in Chapter 11.

1:10 Relationships Within the Environment

Each living thing is a complex organization of interacting parts. Without the proper working of all of its parts, the organism would be in trouble. So, too, the success of a community depends on the organisms in it. Living things do not exist alone; they live together and depend on each other. The study of the relationship between organisms and their environment is **ecology.** An ecologist wants to know how organisms live with each other and how they interact with the things around them.

Organisms are suited to particular environments.

Adaptations promote survival.

Ecology is the study of the relationship between organisms and their environment.

FIGURE 1-11. (a) Water lilies and (b) a hermit crab have special adaptations which aid their survival. What are some of their adaptations?

Richard Brom... / Sharon Kurgis

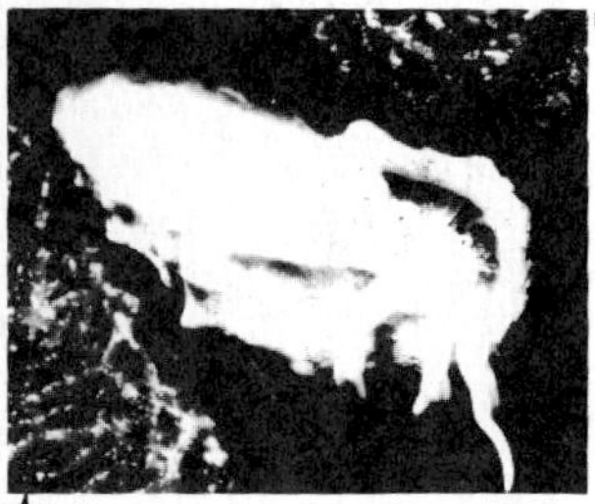

How do these photos contribute to the main idea of paragraph #2 of Section 1:9?

Definition/main idea. Ask students the main idea of the paragraph.

Main idea

Main idea

Gene Frazier   Don Nieman

a   b

A study of a community reveals many ways in which plants and animals interact. Many birds build nests in trees and other plants. Bees transfer pollen from flower to flower. Seeds of some plants are transported in the fur of mammals. Molds may grow on rotting wood, and some insects live under the bark of trees. Many organisms require mates in order to reproduce, and many young organisms must be cared for by their parents. The predator and prey relationship (Section 1:4) is another way organisms depend on each other.

Physical factors of the environment are also important to a community. Without water, carbon dioxide, and oxygen, most organisms could not live. The type of soil and amount of water determine the kinds of plants which can live and grow in a certain place. The amount of shade the plants provide affects temperature which in turn affects the kinds of plants and animals that can live there.

Can you see that a community, like an organism, is a well-organized system? Also, in nature the community is a feature of life because no organism, regardless of its adaptations and complexity, can exist by itself. In many ways humans depend on their environment. They also affect their environment in many ways. Explain. What do you think is the responsibility of humans concerning the environment?

FIGURE 1-12. Physical factors of the environment determine the kinds of organisms that can live in different places. (a) Trees cannot grow above a certain altitude mainly due to colder temperatures. (b) Due to the amount of water, hippos can live in areas where certain other organisms cannot.

Organisms depend on one another in many ways.

Physical factors of the environment determine the kinds of organisms living in a given community.

REVIEWING YOUR IDEAS

12. What is an adaptation? List three animal adaptations.
13. What does an ecologist want to find out about a community?
14. List several ways in which organisms depend on one another.

Paragraph pattern: Main idea followed by examples as details.

Paragraph pattern: Main idea followed by three details.

Paragraph pattern: One of purpose through questioning to guide thinking during further study.

No specifically stated main idea

Discuss quickly with the students how these questions, and others such as these throughout the text, are and will be useful to them. Note with the students the specific chapter sections where these questions are answered.

Brainstorm with the students the implications of these two ideas. Refer to them throughout the year.

Discuss with the students how these two pages (pages 18 and 19) can be used as a review.

Check on factual content—a good review.

18

CHAPTER REVIEW

SUMMARY

Review with students what a summary is and what its purpose is.

1. The nearly two million kinds of known living things share certain common features.
2. Organisms live together in communities.
3. All organisms need food. Producers make their own food while consumers depend on other living things for food.
4. The energy in food comes from sunlight through photosynthesis. "Burning" of food transfers energy.
5. Materials in a community are recycled. Because energy is not recycled, a community must have a constant supply of energy.

Can the students find the section where each item of the summary is explained and discussed?

6. Energy from the "burning" of food is used for growth and development, maintenance and repair, reproduction, and organization.
7. Scientists have defined several levels of organization to describe living things—cell, tissue, organ, system, organism, and community. Higher levels also exist.
8. Organisms are adapted for life in particular environments. Organisms also interact in and with their environments.

CHECKING YOUR IDEAS

①

On a separate paper, match each phrase from the left column with the proper term from the right column. Do not write in this book.

1. necessary for decay process
2. balance of internal processes
3. released during photosynthesis
4. characteristic promoting survival
5. interaction of organisms and environment
6. increase in living material
7. obtains food from host
8. necessary for work
9. substance "burned" by all organisms
10. Like produces like.
11. tissues working together
12. makes own food

a. adaptation
b. decomposer
c. ecology
d. producer
e. energy
f. growth
g. homeostasis
h. organ
i. oxygen
j. parasite
k. reproduction
l. sugar

EVALUATING YOUR IDEAS

②

1. Why is it difficult to define "life"? What is important to an understanding of "life"?
2. What are some similarities between an automobile engine and a living thing? What are some differences?
3. Distinguish between parasites and saprophytes. Are they producers or consumers?
4. What is energy? What is the source of energy in every community? How is it transferred to all members of a community? Is energy recyclable? Explain.
5. How are decomposers important to a community? What would happen to a community in which there were no decomposers? Why?

LANGUAGE OF BIOLOGY

Can the students categorize the terms? For example, which other words would relate to these words also in the list?
organism
predator
photosynthesis
community
ecology
(You may note others.) Discuss such categorizations with the class to note the interrelationships of the ideas represented.

adaptation
biology
cellular respiration
chlorophyll
community
consumer
decomposer
development
ecology
energy
food chain
growth
heredity

homeostasis
host
organ
organism
organization
parasite
photosynthesis
predator
producer
reproduction
saprophyte
system
tissue

Interpretation of the factual information leading toward practical conclusions.

Note: Items numbered 1 through 4
follow the steps of organizing and
using information:
  1. understanding
  2. interpretation
  3. application
  4. enlarging ideas

19

CHAPTER REVIEW

6. How are photosynthesis and cellular respiration important to each other?

7. What is homeostasis? Why is it important to living things?

8. What is meant by the phrase "like produces like"? Why does it occur?

9. Why is it possible to say that the process of life is continuous?

10. What is meant by "organization" of living things?

11. What is a tissue? What is an organ? What is a system? List some examples of each.

12. What is an adaptation?

13. What are some physical factors of the environment?

8. List three adaptations of a tree. List three adaptations of a human. How do the adaptations you listed help the organism survive in its environment?

9. Why are there few producers at the bottom of a deep lake or ocean?

EXTENDING YOUR IDEAS

1. Search the area near your home for different kinds of organisms. Classify each one as either producer or consumer. Identify any parasites or saprophytes you find. Determine how each organism fits into food chains of the community. List several adaptations of each organism.

2. Create your own miniature community by setting up a freshwater aquarium or a terrarium.

3. Make a list of five specific ways in which your body uses energy.

③ — Try to get these for your school library.

APPLYING YOUR IDEAS

1. List several types of communities. What do they have in common? How do they differ?

2. Indian pipe is classified as a green plant, but it lacks chlorophyll. Why is it able to survive on a forest floor better than green plants with chlorophyll?

3. Classify each of the following as a parasite or saprophyte.
  (a) tick on a dog
  (b) termites in dead wood
  (c) tapeworm in a cow

4. Give an example of a possible food chain in a lake and in a desert.

5. What would be the simplest possible food chain in a community? Explain.

6. A piece of potato immersed in water absorbs some of the water and swells. Has the potato grown? Explain.

7. How are availability of water, temperature, light, and type of soil important to a community?

SUGGESTED READINGS

Bauer, Erwin A., "How to Get Close to Wildlife." *National Wildlife*, October-November, 1981.

Deyrup, Mark, "Deadwood Decomposers." *Natural History*, March, 1981.

Feininger, Andreas, *Nature through the Seasons*. New York, Dover Publications, Inc., 1979.

Milne, Lorus J. and Margery, "The Social Behavior of Burying Beetles." *Scientific American*, August, 1976.

Smith, R. L., *Ecology and Field Biology*. New York, Harper and Row, 1980.

Way Things Work Book of Nature. New York, Simon and Schuster, Inc., 1980.

④ — Enrichment and reinforcement activities.

Using the ideas in a practical sense—how the information can be used which shows understanding and accomplishes the purpose of the content.

These are excellent for class discussion in which the ideas are considered, analyzed and, when necessary, researched.

GENERAL REFERENCES FOR TEACHERS

Allen, Dorothea, *The Biology Teacher's Desk Book*. Englewood Cliffs, NJ, Parker Publishing Co., 1979.

Behringer, Marjorie P., *Techniques and Materials in Biology*. Huntington, NY, Krieger Publishing Co., 1981.

Hickman, Faith, and Kahle, June B., eds., *New Directions in Teaching Biology*. Reston, VA, National Association of Biology Teachers, 1981.

Duke, D., *Classroom Management*. Chicago, Univ. of Chicago Press, 1979.

Estes, Thomas H. and Joseph Vaughan, *Reading and Learning in the Content Classroom*. Boston, Allyn and Bacon, 1978.

Falk, Doris, *Biology Teaching Methods*. Melbourne, FL, Krieger Publishing Co., 1980.

Shepherd, David L., *Comprehensive High School Reading Methods*. Columbus, OH, Charles E. Merrill Publishing Co., 1982.

Smith, Carl B., Sharon Smith, and Larry Mikulecky, *Teaching Reading in Secondary School Content Subjects: A Bookthinking Process*. New York, Holt, Rinehart and Winston, 1978.

West, Gail B., *Teaching Reading Skills in Content Areas: A Practical Guide to the Construction of Student Exercises*. Orlando, FL, Sandpiper Press, Inc., 1975.

Science Books and Films
American Ass'n. for the Advancement of Science
1515 Massachusetts Avenue, NW
Washington DC 20005

A Reference List of Audiovisual Materials Produced by the United States Government, #052-003
Superintendent of Documents
US Government Printing Office
Washington DC 20005

GENERAL REFERENCES FOR STUDENTS

The following magazines and journals should be available as references for students. They should be accessible in the classroom or school library.

BioScience
American Institute of Biological Sciences
1401 Wilson Blvd.
Arlington, VA 22209

Discover
Time-Life Building
541 N. Fairbanks Court
Chicago, IL 60672

FDA Consumer
Superintendent of Documents
Government Printing Office
Washington, DC 20402

International Wildlife
National Wildlife Federation
8925 Leesburg Pike
Vienna VA 22180

National Geographic Society
1155 Sixteenth St., NW
Washington, DC 20036

National Wildlife
National Wildlife Federation
1412 16th Street NW
Washington, DC 20036

Oceans
A Publication of the Oceanic Society
PO Box 10167
Des Moines, IA 50340

Omni
Omni Publications International Ltd.
909 Third Ave.
New York, NY 10022

Science
American Association for the Advancement of Science
1515 Massachusetts Ave., NW
Washington, DC 20005

Science Digest
P.O. Box 10076
Des Moines, IA 50350

Science News
Science Service, Inc.
231 W. Center St.
Marion, OH 43302

Science 8__
Subscription Department
Xerox Publications
Columbus, OH 43216

Scientific American
Scientific American Inc.
415 Madison Ave.
New York, NY 10017

SciQuest
Circulation Manager
American Chemical Society
P.O. Box 2895
Washington, DC 20013

Scientific American offprints (W. H. Freeman Co.) and *Carolina Biology Readers* (Carolina Biological Supply Co.) can be ordered in quantity for classroom use.

AUDIOVISUAL SUPPLIERS

Catalogs of audiovisual aids for purchase or rent may be obtained from the listed suppliers. Some suppliers have branch offices in various regions of the country. In obtaining supplies, try to locate the nearest branch office. Audiovisual aids should be ordered at least three months before their intended use in class.

Carolina Biological Supply Company
Burlington, NC 27215

Carolina Biological Supply Company
Powell Laboratories Division
Gladstone, OR 97027

Current Affairs
P.O. Box 246
346 Ethan Allen Highway (Rte. 7)
Ridgefield, CT 06877

Educational Audio Visual, Inc.
Pleasantville, NY 10570

Educational Development Center
39 Chapel Street
Newton, MA 02160

Educational Materials and Equipment Co.
P.O. Box 17
Pelham, NY 10803

Guidance Associates
Communications Park
Box 300
White Plains, NY 10602

Holt, Rinehart and Winston, Inc.
383 Madison Ave.
New York, NY 10017

Indiana University
Audio-Visual Center
Bloomington, IN 47401

Inquiry Audio-Visuals
1754 West Farragut Ave.
Chicago, IL 60640

Kent State University
Audio Visual Services
Kent, OH 44242

Modern Film Rentals
West: 1145 N. McCadden Place
     Los Angeles, CA 90038
Midwest: 1087 Elmhurst Road
     Elk Grove Village, IL 60007
South: 4705-F Bakers Ferry Road
     Atlanta, GA 30336
Northeast: 315 Springfield Ave.
     Summit, NJ 07901
Canada: 1875 Leslie Street
     Don Mills, Ontario M3B 2M6

National Geographic Society
12th and M Streets, NW
Washington, DC 20036

Nova Scientific Corp.
111 Tucker St.
P.O. Box 500
Burlington, NC 27215

Prentice Hall Media
Servcode HC2
150 White Plains Road
Tarrytown, NY 10591

Primary Communications
P.O. Box 480
Southern Pines, NC 28387

Science and Mankind, Inc.
Communications Park
Box 200
White Plains, NY 10602

Science Software Systems, Inc.
11899 West Pico Blvd.
West Los Angeles, CA 90064

Time-Life Films
43 W. 16th Street
New York, NY 10011

Ward's Natural Science Establishment, Inc.
P.O. Box 1712   P.O. Box 1749
Rochester, NY 14603   or   Monterey, CA 93940

University of Illinois Film Center
1325 S. Oak St.
Champaign, IL 61820

AUDIOVISUAL AIDS

The audiovisual aids listed are useful in presenting various concepts to the class. You may find that some are best understood when shown more than once. The first showing in class will allow students to get an overview of the content; the second will reinforce concepts presented. To increase attention and retention, you may want to give students a short list of questions to try to answer as you show the material. Whatever your techniques, always preview the materials before you show them in class. Those materials listed vary in complexity and some overlap in content, so you will want to be sure that what you show is appropriate for your class.

UNIT I   CHARACTERISTICS OF LIFE

Chapter 1 The World of Living Things
Biological Communities, Inquiry Audio-Visuals, filmstrip, #67022
Ecology: the Temperate Deciduous Forest, U. of Illinois, 16mm, #60327
Food Chains: Producers and Consumers, Inquiry Audio-Visuals, slide set, #69155
The Forest Floor Environment, Prentice Hall Media, Super-8, #SCT650
What Is Ecology?, Prentice Hall Media, filmstrip and cassette, #SCC457, or filmstrip and record, #SCR457.

Chapter 2 Biology as a Science
Biology Career Challenges, Prentice Hall Media, 2 filmstrips with 2 cassettes, #SCC687
Electron Microscopy, Ward's Natural Science Establishment, 16mm, #195X6005
Scientific Method in Action, U. of Illinois, 16mm, #50893
SI Metrics in Science. Prentice Hall Media, Super-8, #SCT650

Chapter 3 Materials of Life
Basic Chemistry for the Biologist, Prentice Hall Media, 2 filmstrips and 2 cassettes, #SCC816, or 2 filmstrips and 2 records, #SCR816
Chemistry for Biology, Inquiry Audio-Visuals, overhead transparency set, #44402
Macromolecules in Biology. Inquiry Audio-Visuals, filmstrip, #67073

Chapter 4 Energy for Life
Biochemistry of Enzyme Action. Inquiry Audio-Visuals, filmstrip, #67765
Enzyme Action: Catalase, Prentice Hall Media, Super-8, #SCT600

Enzyme Action: Effect of Temperature, Prentice Hall Media, Super-8, #SCT603
Respiration: Aerobic Respiration, Prentice Hall Media, Super-8, #SCT611
Respiration: Fermentation, Prentice Hall Media, Super-8, #SCT610

Chapter 5 Cell Structure and Function
Inside the Cell: Microstructure, Mechanisms, and Molecules, Science and Mankind, sound-slide program, #1043-2070
Microtubules in Echinosphaerium Nucleofilum, Ward's Natural Science Establishment, 16mm, #194X8000
Osmosis: Dialysis, Prentice Hall Media, Super-8, #SCT616
The Modern Cell, Inquiry Audio-Visuals, overhead transparency set, #68725

UNIT II   HEREDITY

Chapter 6 The Cellular Basis of Heredity
DNA and Cell Reproduction: Fertilization, Prentice Hall Media, Super-8, #SCT620
Mitosis: In Endosperm of Haemanthys katherinae, Holt, Rinehart and Winston, Super-8, #81-5340/1
Meiosis, Holt, Rinehart, and Winston, Super-8, #81-7833/1

Chapter 7 Principles of Heredity
Genetics, #4: Inheritance in Man, U. of Illinois, 16mm, #80586
Genetics: Mendel's Laws, U. of Illinois, 16mm, #60238
Mendelian Genetics, Inquiry Audio-Visuals, slide set, #69191
Mendel's Experiments, Indiana U., 16mm (bw), #NS-544

Chapter 8 Genes and Chromosomes
Experimenting with Drosophila, Holt, Rinehart, and Winston, Super-8, #81-0762/1
Giant Chromosomes of Drosophila, Prentice Hall Media, Super-8, #SCT618
Handling Drosophila, Holt, Rinehart, and Winston, Super-8, #81-0754/1
Sara Has Down's Syndrome, Educational Development Center, 16mm
Sickle Cell Anemia, Educational Development Center, 16mm
Squash Techniques, Holt, Rinehart, and Winston, Super-8, #81-0770/1

Chapter 9 The Genetic Code

Bacterial Sensitivity to Radiation, Prentice Hall Media, Super-8, #SCT050

DNA and Cell Chemistry, Ward's Natural Science Establishment, set of filmstrips, #70W3300

DNA—Composition, Prentice Hall Media, Super-8, #SCT617-2

DNA Structure: Backbones and Bases, Holt, Rinehart, and Winston, Super-8, #81-7403/1

DNA Transformation Experiment, Holt, Rinehart, and Winston, Super-8, #81-6058/1

Identifying the Genetic Material: Transformation, Holt, Rinehart, and Winston, Super-8, #81-7387/1

UNIT III   CHANGES

Chapter 10 Change with Time

Darwin and the Theory of Natural Selection, Modern Film Rentals, 16mm, #130-4025

Darwin's Theory of Evolution, Inquiry Audio-Visuals, slide set, #69182

Evolution and the Gene Pool, Inquiry Audio-Visuals, slide set, #69195

Great Scientists Speak Again: Charles Darwin, U. of Illinois, 16mm, #54613

Records in the Rocks, Time-Life Films, 16mm (bw)

The Beginnings, U. of Illinois, 16mm, #82064

The Galapagos: Darwin's Finches, Holt, Rinehart, and Winston, Super-8, #81-7528/1

Voyage to the Enchanted Isles, U. of Illinois, 16mm, #81956

Chapter 11 Adaptation and Speciation

Adaptation: Life Form and Landform, Current Affairs, sound filmstrip, #752

Animal Camouflage, Holt, Rinehart, and Winston, Super-8, #81-3360/1

Camouflage, Prentice Hall Media, Super-8, #SCT667

Hominid Evolution, Inquiry Audio-Visuals, slide set, #69201

How Life Survives: Adaptation and Evolution, Science and Mankind, sound-slide program, #1007-2070

Mimicry and Camouflage in Nature, Inquiry Audio-Visuals, filmstrip, #67021

Monkeys, Apes, and Man, U. of Illinois, 16mm, #82370

The Evolution of Man, Ward's Natural Science Establishment, set of filmstrips, #70W3500

Warning Coloration and Behavior: Insects, Holt, Rinehart, and Winston, Super-8, #81-3378/1

Chapter 12 Classification

Classifying Plants and Animals, U. of Illinois, 16mm, #01158

Taxonomy: How Living Organisms Differ, Science and Mankind, sound-slide program, #1031-2070

The Diversity of Living Things, Time-Life Films, 16mm (bw)

UNIT IV   DIVERSITY

Chapter 13 Monerans, Protists, Fungi, and Viruses

Algae, U. of Illinois, 16mm, #51332

A New Look at Leeuwenhoek's "Wee Beasties," Ward's Natural Science Establishment, 16mm, #194X2000

Fungi, Ward's Natural Science Establishment, 16mm, #194X2070

Fungi (Diversity and Ecology), Ward's Natural Science Establishment, filmstrip and cassette, #70W6320

Simple Organisms: Algae and Fungi, U. of Illinois, 16mm, #50393

The Amoebas, Prentice Hall Media, Super-8, #SCT175

The Flagellates Part 2—Termite Symbionts, Prentice Hall Media, Super-8, #SCT177

Viruses and Thallophytes, Ward's Natural Science Establishment, overhead transparency set, #75W0410

Chapter 14 Plants

Botany: Plants, Inquiry Audio-Visuals, overhead transparency set, #68733

Higher Plants, Ward's Natural Science Establishment, overhead transparency set, #75W0430

Roll Call of the Plants, Inquiry Audio-Visuals, filmstrip, #67002

Chapter 15 Animals: Sponges through Mollusks

Clam, Prentice Hall Media, Super-8, #SCT509

Earthworm, Prentice Hall Media, Super-8, #SCT515

Lower Invertebrates, Ward's Natural Science Establishment, filmstrip and cassette, #70W6410

Nematoda, Prentice Hall Media, Super-8, #SCT513

Obelia, Prentice Hall Media, Super-8, #SCT577

Octopus, Prentice Hall Media, Super-8, #SCT511

Parasitic Worms That Invade the Body, Inquiry Audio-Visuals, filmstrip, #66871

Roll Call of the Animals, Inquiry Audio-Visuals, filmstrip, #67001

The Coelenterates, Holt, Rinehart and Winston, Super-8, #81-6744/1

Zoology: Animals, Inquiry Audio-Visuals, overhead transparency set, #68734

Chapter 16 Animals: Arthropods through Vertebrates

Black Widow Spider, Prentice Hall Media, Super-8, #SCT526

Chordates, Ward's Natural Science Establishment, overhead transparency set, #75W0350

Crayfish, Prentice Hall Media, Super-8, #SCT541

Insects, National Geographic Society, 16mm, #05044, or videocassette, #05046

Sea Cucumber, Prentice Hall Media, Super-8, #SCT523

Spiders; Aggression and Mating, National Geographic Society, 16mm, #05892, or videocassette, #05898

Starfishes, Prentice Hall Media, Super-8, #SCT518

Vertebrate Classification, Inquiry Audio-Visuals, slide set, #69184

Unit V SIMPLE ORGANISMS

Chapter 17 Simple Organisms: Reproduction

Budding of Yeast Cells, Holt, Rinehart and Winston, Super-8, #81-4285/1

Growth of Molds, Ward's Natural Science Establishment, Super-8, #73W0505(T)

Mushroom Development, Ward's Natural Science Establishment, Super-8, #73W0525(T)

Mushroom Growth and Development, Holt, Rinehart and Winston, Super-8, #81-4509/1

Paramecium—Part 3, Reproduction, Prentice Hall Media, Super-8, #SCT559

Protist Reproduction, Ward's Natural Science Establishment, 16mm, #194X2020

Chapter 18 Simple Organisms: Other Life Functions

Diatoms in a Food Web, Ward's Natural Science Establishment, Super-8, #168W5131(T)

Euglena gracilis, Holt, Rinehart and Winston, Super-8, #81-5050/1

Euglena—Part 2, Behavior, Prentice Hall Media, Super-8, #SCT543

Paramecium—Part 2, Physiology, Prentice Hall Media, Super-8, #SCT558

Paramecium—Part 4, Behavior, Prentice Hall Media, Super-8, #SCT560

Protist Behavior, Ward's Natural Science Establishment, 16mm, #194X2015

Protist Physiology, Ward's Natural Science Establishment, 16mm, #194X2010

Rhizopus, Holt, Rinehart and Winston, Super-8, #81-4459/1

Chapter 19 Simple Organisms and Disease

Antibiotics—Disease Fighting Champions, Inquiry Audio-Visuals, #66874

Penicillium, Holt, Rinehart and Winston, Super-8, #81-4475/1

Viruses, Ward's Natural Science Establishment, 16mm, #194W2055

UNIT VI PLANTS

Chapter 20 Plant Reproduction and Development

Algal Syngamy: Isogamy in Chlamydomonas, Holt, Rinehart and Winston, Super-8, #81-5159/1

Bean Sprouts, Holt, Rinehart and Winston, Super-8, #81-4244/1

Early Development of the Root System, Holt, Rinehart and Winston, Super-8, #81-5563/1

Life and Death of a Tree, National Geographic Society, 16mm, #05086, or videocassette, #05088

Plant Growth Regions, Prentice-Hall Media, Super-8, #SCT635

Plant Propagation: from Seed to Tissue Culture, U. of Illinois, 16mm, #84019

Plants through the Seasons: Structure, Growth, and Change, Current Affairs, sound filmstrip, #764

Pollination and Fertilization in Flowering Plants, Ward's Natural Science Establishment, 16mm, #194W8190

Seed Dispersal, Holt, Rinehart and Winston, Super-8, #81-9946/1

Seed Distribution and Germination, Ward's Natural Science Establishment, Super-8, #73W0585(T)

Seeds Sprouting, Holt, Rinehart and Winston, Super-8, #81-9920/1

Sexual Reproduction in Ferns, Ward's Natural Science Establishment, 16mm, #194X8180

The Life Cycle of a Flowering Plant, Prentice Hall Media, 16mm, #SC178

Chapter 21 Plant Nutrition

Carnivorous Plants, National Geographic Society, 16mm, #05893, or videocassette, #05899

Insectivorous Plants, Ward's Natural Science Establishment, filmstrip and cassettes, #70W6355

Photosynthesis: Absorption of Light by Chlorophyll, Prentice Hall Media, Super-8, #SCT607

Photosynthesis: Effect of Wavelength, Prentice Hall Media, Super-8, #SCT606

Photosynthesis: End Products, Prentice Hall Media, Super-8, #SCT604

Chapter 22 Plants: Other Life Functions

Apical Dominance, Holt, Rinehart and Winston, Super-8, #81-5712/1

How Hormones Regulate Plant Growth, Inquiry Audio-Visuals, filmstrip, #67038

Phototropic Response in Coleoptiles, Holt, Rinehart and Winston, Super-8, #81-5746/1

Plant Tropisms and Other Movements, Modern Film Rentals, 16mm, #130-4091

The Flowering Stimulus: Location of the Photoreceptor, Ward's Natural Science Establishment, Super-8, #168W5128(T)

Water Movement in Stems, Prentice Hall Media, Super-8, #SCT640

UNIT VII ANIMALS

Chapter 23 Animal Reproduction

Courtship Behavior of the Stickleback, Holt, Rinehart, and Winston, Super-8, #81-5985/1

Menstruation and Sexual Development, Carolina Biological, 16mm, #93-0450-FR

Pregnancy, A Teenage Epidemic? Nova Scientific, filmstrip, #530-8415

Sex Education, Nova Scientific, transparencies with overlays, #525-1250

The Biology of Human Sexuality: Reproduction, Birth Control, and Development, Science and Mankind, filmstrip, #2-4011-2850

Chapter 24 Animal Development

Chick Embryology, National Geographic Society, 16mm, #05889, or videocassette, #05895

Development and Metamorphosis of the Leopard Frog: Rana pipiens, Ward's Natural Science Establishment, 16mm, #194X8070

Mosquito Life Cycle, Prentice-Hall Media, Super-8, #SCT590

Nuclear Transplantation, U. of Illinois, 16mm, #56306

Chapter 25 Food Getting and Digestion

Biochemistry of Vitamin Action, Inquiry Audio-Visuals, filmstrip, #67074

Digestive Systems: Annelids to Mammals, Inquiry Audio-Visuals, slide set, #69172

Digestion: Enzymatic Hydrolysis, Prentice Hall Media, Super-8, #SCT612

Human Body: Digestive System, Modern Film Rentals, 16mm, #130-4048

Nutrition: Energy, Growth and Repair, Inquiry Audio-Visuals, filmstrip, #66865

Chapter 26 Transport

Circulatory Systems: Annelids to Mammals, Inquiry Audio-Visuals, slide set, #69174

Frog: Circulatory System, Prentice Hall Media, Super-8, #SCT906

Hearts and Circulatory Systems, Modern Film Rentals, 16mm, #130-4041

Human Blood Typing, Prentice Hall Media, Super-8, #SCT639

The Work of the Blood, Inquiry Audio-Visuals, filmstrip, #66840

Chapter 27 Respiration and Excretion

Human Respiratory System, Carolina Biological Supply Co., overhead transparencies, #50-6915 and #50-6917

Respiratory Movement, Ward's Natural Science Establishment, Super-8, #73W7477(T)

Respiratory Systems: Roundworms to Mammals, Inquiry Audio-Visuals, slide set, #69178

Your Kidneys—Living Filters, Inquiry Audio-Visuals, filmstrip, #66847

Chapter 28 Support and Locomotion

Flexors and Extensors, Ward's Natural Science Establishment, Super-8, #73W7475(T)

Frog Heart Muscle Response, Holt, Rinehart, and Winston, Super-8, #81-5621/1

Frog Skeletal Muscle Response, Prentice Hall Media, Super-8, #SCT015

Locomotion in Invertebrates, Prentice Hall Media, Super-8, #SCT661

Chapter 29 Chemical Control

Tadpoles and Frogs, National Geographic Society, 16mm, #05228, or videocassette, #05230

Multicellular Animals No. 7—Hormones, U. of Illinois, 16mm, #80565

Chapter 30 Nervous Control

Man: the Incredible Machine, National Geographic Society, 16mm, #05981, or videocassette, #05982

Our Pill Society, Nova Scientific, 2 filmstrips with cassettes, #530-8430

Unit VIII ENVIRONMENT

Chapter 31 Behavior

Aggressive Display in the Siamese Fighting Fish, Prentice Hall Media, Super-8, #SCT649

Biological Clocks, Inquiry Audio-Visuals, filmstrip, #67060

Biological Societies, Inquiry Audio-Visuals, filmstrip, #67025

Miss Goodall and the Wild Chimpanzees, U. of Illinois, 16mm, #70483

Psychobiology: the Brain and Behavior, Science and Mankind, sound-slide program, #1-1013-2850

Reflex and Conditioning, Inquiry Audio-Visuals, filmstrip, #66858

Territoriality in Reef Animals, Prentice Hall Media, Super-8, #SCT664

Chapter 32 Population Biology

Man, Technology, and Pollution, Ward's Natural Science Establishment, Super-8, #73W7443(T)

Nutritional Relationships, Inquiry Audio-Visuals, slide set, #69156

Pond Life Food Web, National Geographic Society, 16mm (#06003) or videocassette (#06004)

Populations: Limiting Factors, Inquiry Audio-Visuals, slide set, #69153

Chapter 33 The Ecosystem

Bacteria and the Ecology of Planet Earth, Ward's Natural Science Establishment, 16mm, #194X2065

Cycles of the Biosphere: Matter and Energy Pathways, Current Affairs, sound filmstrip, #761

Ecosystem Processes, Ward's Natural Science Establishment, Super-8, #73W7453(T)

Food Chains and Pyramids, Inquiry Audio-Visuals, slide set, #69159

Life in the Soil, Inquiry Audio-Visuals, filmstrip, #67027

Root Nodule Formation, Ward's Natural Science Establishment, Super-8, #168W5138(T)

Chapter 34 Origin and Distribution of Communities

Ecological Successions, Inquiry Audio-Visuals, slide set, #69161

Freshwater: the Aquatic Environments, Nova Scientific, filmstrip and cassette, #530-4015

The Biomes, Ward's Natural Science Establishment, Super-8, #73W7455(T)

The Coral Reef Environment, Prentice Hall Media, Super-8, #SCT652

The Deciduous Forest, Prentice Hall Media, 2 filmstrips and 2 cassettes, #SCC462, or 2 filmstrips and 2 records, #SCR462

The Oceans, Prentice Hall Media, 2 filmstrips and 2 cassettes, #SCC473, or 2 filmstrips and 2 records, #SCR473

Chapter 35 Humans and the Environment

Acid Rain, Nova Scientific, overhead transparency set, #525-4005

Air Pollution, Inquiry Audio-Visuals, filmstrip, #67071

A Freshwater Algal Bloom, Ward's Natural Science Establishment, Super-8, #168W5132(T)

Conservation, Nova Scientific, overhead transparency set, #525-4050

Killing Weeds with 2,4 D, Ward's Natural Science Establishment, Super-8, #168W5129(T)

Man's Impact on the Environment, Ward's Natural Science Establishment, 16mm, #192X3030

Water Pollution, Prentice Hall Media, 2 filmstrips and 2 cassettes, #SCC453, or 2 filmstrips and 2 records, #SCR453

RESOURCE MATERIAL

Many pamphlets, posters, and teaching packets can be obtained from government agencies, voluntary agencies, professional associations, and business and commercial organizations. Teachers should be aware of local school system criteria used in the selection of all resource materials.

Government Agencies

Centers for Disease Control
1600 Clifton Road NE
Atlanta, GA 30333

Department of Health and Human Services
Washington, DC 20025

National Coordinating Council on Drug Abuse
P.O. Box 19400
Washington, DC 20036

National Institute on Mental Health
Barlow Building
Chevy Chase, MD 20015

National Interagency Council on Smoking & Health
P.O. Box 3654, Central Station
Arlington, VA 22203

Superintendent of Documents
U.S. Government Printing Office
Washington, DC 20025

U.S. Environmental Protection Agency
Office of Public Affairs
Washington, DC 20460

U.S. Public Health Service
Department of Health and Human Services
Washington, DC 20201

Voluntary Agencies

Voluntary agencies, supported by donations, provide valuable resources for teachers. Before contacting them, check your phone directory for a local, district, or state office.

Alcoholics Anonymous
General Service Board
P.O. Box 459, Grand Central Station
New York, NY 10017

Allergy Foundation of America
801 Second Avenue
New York, NY 10017

American Cancer Society, Inc.
219 East 42nd Street
New York, NY 10017

American Dental Association
Bureau of Dental Health Education

211 East Chicago Avenue
Chicago, IL 60611

American Diabetes Association, Inc.
600 Fifth Avenue
New York, NY 10020

American Dietetic Association
620 North Michigan Avenue
Chicago, IL 60611

American Foundation for the Blind
15 West 16th Street
New York, NY 10011

American Hearing Society
919 18th Street, N.W.
Washington, DC 20006

American Heart Association
The National Center
7230 Greenville Avenue
Dallas, TX 75231

American Home Economics Association
1600 20th Street, N.W.
Washington, DC 20009

American Hospital Association
840 North Lake Shore Drive
Chicago, IL 60611

American Lung Association
1740 Broadway
New York, NY 10019

American Medical Association
Department of Health Education
535 North Dearborn Street
Chicago, IL 60610

American National Red Cross
17th and D Streets, N.W.
Washington, DC 20006

American Nurses' Association
2420 Pershing Road
Kansas City, MO 64108

American Pharmaceutical Association
2215 Constitution Avenue, N.W.
Washington, DC 20037

American Physical Therapy Association
1740 Broadway
New York, NY 10019

American Public Health Association, Inc.
1015 18th Street, N.W.
Washington, DC 20036

Arthritis Foundation
3400 Peachtree Road, N.E.
Atlanta, GA 30326

Association for the Aid of Crippled Children
345 East 46th Street
New York, NY 10017

Epilepsy Foundation of America
Suite 1116
733 15th Street, N.W.
Washington, DC 20005

Leukemia Society of America, Inc.
211 East 43rd Street
New York, NY 10016

Muscular Dystrophy Association
of America, Inc.
1790 Broadway
New York, NY 10019

Narcotics Anonymous
Box 2000
Lexington, KY 40501

National Association for Mental Health, Inc.
1800 N. Kent Street
Arlington, VA 22209

National Dairy Council (Nutrition)
6300 North River Road
Rosemont, IL 60018

National Foundation for
Jewish Genetic Diseases, Inc.
608 Fifth Avenue, Room 702
New York, NY 10020

The National Foundation—March of Dimes
1275 Marmaroneck Avenue
White Plains, NY 10601

National Cystic Fibrosis Research Foundation
3379 Peachtree Rd., N.E.
Atlanta, GA 30326

National Health Council
1740 Broadway
New York, NY 10019

National Kidney Foundation
116 East 27th Street
New York, NY 10016

National Multiple Sclerosis Society
257 Park Avenue South
New York, NY 10010

National Safety Council
425 North Michigan Avenue
Chicago, IL 60611

National Sickle Cell Disease Program
Building 31, Room 4A-27 NIH
Bethesda, MD 20041

National Society for Crippled Children and
Adults
2023 West Ogden Avenue
Chicago, IL 60603

National Society To Prevent Blindness
79 Madison Avenue
New York, NY 10016

National Tay-Sachs & Allied Diseases Assn.
122 East 42nd Street
New York, NY 10168

United Cerebral Palsy Association, Inc.
66 East 34th Street
New York, NY 10016

Professional Associations

The following professional associations make resources for instruction available.

American Association for the Advancement
of Science
1515 Massachusetts Avenue, N.W.
Washington, DC 20036

Society for Nutrition Education
2140 Shattuck Avenue, Suite 1110
Berkeley, CA 94704

Society for Public Health Education
655 Sutter Street
San Francisco, CA 94102

Business and Commercial Organizations

Many business and commercial organizations have educational departments that supply resources for classroom instruction. Be careful to check your school policy on distribution of commercially advertised educational material.

Abbott Laboratories
145th and Sheridan Road
North Chicago, IL 60064

American Meat Institute
59 East Van Buren Street
Chicago, IL 60605

Armour and Company
Public Relations Department
401 North Wabash Street
Chicago, IL 60690

The Borden Company
Consumer's Service
180 East Broad Street
Columbus, OH 43215

Carnation Company
Medical Marketing
5045 Wilshire Boulevard
Los Angeles, CA 90036

Cereal Institute, Inc.
Educational Director
135 South LaSalle Street
Chicago, IL 60603

Colgate-Palmolive Company
300 Park Avenue
New York, NY 10022

Connecticut Mutual Life Insurance Co.
140 Garden Street
Hartford, CT 06105

Cream of Wheat Corporation
Box M
Minneapolis, MN 55413

Eli Lilly Company
740 South Alabama Street
Indianapolis, IN 46206

General Mills, Inc.
Nutrition Service
P.O. Box 1113
Minneapolis, MN 55401

Good Housekeeping Institute
8th Avenue and 57th Street
New York, NY 10019

H.J. Heinz and Company
P.O. Box 57
Pittsburgh, PA 15230

Kraft Cheese Company
500 Peshtigo Court
Chicago, IL 60690

Lederle Laboratories
Division, American Cyanamid Company
Pearl River
New York, NY 10965

Mead Johnson & Company
Public Relations Department
2404 Pennsylvania Avenue
Evansville, IN 47721

Merck Sharpe & Dohme
Division of Merck & Co., Inc.
West Point, PA 19486

Metropolitan Life Insurance Company
Health and Welfare Division
1 Madison Avenue
New York, NY 10010

E.R. Squibb & Sons
Division of Olin Mathieson Chemical
  Company
909 Third Avenue
New York, NY 10022

United Fresh Fruit and Vegetable Association
777 14th Street, N.W.
Washington, DC 20025

Upjohn Company
7000 Portage Road
Kalamazoo, MI 49002

WHAT IS A PERFORMANCE OBJECTIVE?

Statements of what science education intends to accomplish are no doubt valid and justifiable. But, how do you know if *you* are accomplishing the goals of science education in your teaching? Herein, lies the value of performance objectives—the behaviors which you, the teacher, can observe and which indicate that students are achieving the goals of science education.

As an example, here are some behaviors you might observe if you wanted to know if students were thinking critically. Students may ask questions related to the topic being discussed. They may gather and share evidence that supports their answers. They may question theories that are posed by others, and so on. An unlimited number of behaviors could be cited which would indicate if students were thinking critically.

Other behaviors will indicate if students are learning other things. These behaviors can be written as performance objectives to aid you in accessing student accomplishment. A good performance objective can usually be written in three parts—1) the condition, 2) the performance or criterion, and 3) the criterion measure.

The condition tells what causes, stimulates, or motivates the student to perform the behaviors, or under what circumstances those behaviors will be performed. For example, "Working in groups of four students, when presented with a microscope and four microscope slides, and without the aid of labeled diagrams" might be the conditions you set up for a certain behavior.

The performance or criterion tells exactly what behavior you are looking for. For example, for the condition above the performance might be "students will recall the names of the parts of a microscope and label each on a blank diagram. They also will place slides on the microscope and correctly focus the instrument and evaluate each other's proficiency at this task." The performance should avoid terms like "know about" or "appreciate" and should, rather, describe exactly what it is students *do* if they "know about" and "appreciate" science. What the students do should be expressed as some observable action such as identifying, listing, matching, or measuring.

The criterion measure tells how many of the students have achieved the objective or to what degree of accuracy or level of performance the behavior should be performed in order that you will know the students have really achieved the objective. For example, would you be satisfied if 50% of your class could perform the behavior? 80%? 100%? If measuring is involved in the behavior, how accurately do you want measurements to be made? Also, how many times do you want students to perform the behavior to show they have learned it? The answers to these questions will vary with the students' abilities. For some students you may be pleased if they measure something to the nearest centimeter once. For others, you may require measurements to the nearest millimeter, expecting perfect measurements on four out of five trials.

Why Use Performance Objectives?

A performance objective cannot and should not tell you how to teach. A performance objective, however, can be used in several different ways. It can aid you in planning instruction. It can help you provide evidence that your students are learning if you keep records of student progress. A performance objective can help you diagnose a student's abilities and better individualize student instruction. Also, a performance objective can help students tune in to what you are trying to achieve. Many teachers have found that when they share with students what objectives are sought, much of the teaching job is accomplished.

Where Do Performance Objectives Come From?

The task of selecting, composing, and evaluating performance objectives is up to you. Whereas books are available which contain objectives for science and there is even an Instructional Objectives Exchange to which you can subscribe,* only you can decide what objectives are appropriate for you, your students, your school, your situation, and your materials and resources. You should draw on the performance objectives in this guide and on other sources. Students are good sources of performance objectives as they express their interests, goals, and questions.

Any performance objective for teaching science should be based on one or more of the goals of science education. Your working to accomplish an objective should be because it is one part of a long range goal. For example, if your goal is to develop methods of problem solving, then the purpose of one lesson might be to recognize what an experiment is.

Performance Objectives for
Biology: Living Systems

The performance objectives in this guide are not meant to be all-inclusive. You will need to modify and supplement them as you see fit. Following a goal statement listed for each chapter, the specific objectives for each section are listed and are numbered to correspond to that section of each chapter. Each objective is also designated by a letter **A, P, K,** or **S.** These letters indicate to which broad goal of science education each objective is related. The four broad goals are the development of Attitudes, Processes, Knowledge, and Skills.

1. Attitudes—Performance objectives that show that students have attitudes of curiosity, of wonderment, and of appreciation of science are attitude objectives. In general, these behaviors are not prompted by the teacher. They are voluntary behaviors which indicate a preference for science. For example, do students volunteer to conduct additional experiments, or do they request the use of science equipment during free periods? Attitude goals are especially important at the completion of each chapter when students may have an opportunity to go beyond the information presented in the text.

2. Processes—Performance objectives that show that students have intellectual processes of inquiry are process objectives. These behaviors you might observe as students contrast, compare, hypothesize, theorize, classify, and observe. For example, can students predict what will happen if a member of a food chain is removed? Can students form hypotheses given sets of data?

3. Knowledge—Performance objectives that show that students know facts, terms, concepts, generalizations, and principles are knowledge objectives. Generally, a knowledge objective calls on students to recall or explain information learned in the past. For example, can students correctly define photosynthesis? Can students correctly describe the effects of insufficient sunlight on plants?

4. Skills—Performance objectives that show that students have an ability to handle materials and equipment in a productive and safe manner and to measure, organize and communicate scientific information are skill objectives. For example, can students use a pipette to accurately measure and transfer a solution from one container to another? Can students accurately record the data they gather?

How Do You Know You've
Achieved Your Objectives?

When you try to find out if students have learned anything, you probably give some form of written test—true-false, completion, matching, or essay type of examination. All of these forms of evaluation are important in determining whether or not students have achieved some of the objectives. Questions are located within chapters and at chapter ends in the text. Also, evaluation materials are available to accompany the Merrill Science Programs.

*Information and a catalog of objective collections can be obtained from: Instructional Objectives Exchange, Center for the Study of Evaluation, Graduate School of Education, University of California, Los Angeles, CA 90024.

CHAPTER 1   THE WORLD OF LIVING THINGS

Teaching Techniques

This chapter not only serves as an introduction to the course but is also ecologically oriented and, therefore, of immediate interest to students. Many students will be somewhat familiar with some of the ideas and concepts presented and you will be able to stimulate class participation at the outset. For example, choose a community other than the forest described in the chapter and invite your students to identify the kinds of organisms and physical factors to be found there. Lead them to see that the same generalities apply to all communities. Ask students what kinds of materials are not naturally recycled and why.

General features of life discussed in this chapter should be referred to throughout the course. Remind students continually that growth and development, maintenance and repair, reproduction, and organization are the broad characteristics which tie the world of living things together in a meaningful way for the study of biology. Emphasize that life exhibits unity within diversity.

Performance Objectives

Goal: Students will gain an understanding of the basic features of life common to all organisms.

Objectives: Upon completion of the reading and activities and when asked to respond orally or on a written test, students will:

Section
Number

1:0	K	define biology as the study of life.
1:1	P	identify the types of organisms found in a community and suggest reasons they must live together.
1:2	P	differentiate between food producers and consumers.
1:2	K	identify photosynthesis as the process by which producers use sunlight to make their food.
1:2	P/K	distinguish between and give examples of parasites and saprophytes.
1:3	K	explain that organisms require energy for their biological work.
1:4	K	identify the raw materials and products of photosynthesis and explain the role of sunlight and chlorophyll in the process.
1:4	K	explain how the sun can be the source of energy for producers, consumers, predators, and decomposers.
1:4	K	identify the raw materials and products of cellular respiration.
1:4	P	give an example of a food chain and explain what happens to the materials and the energy used by a community.
1:4	K	explain that a community depends on a constant supply of energy for its survival.
1:5	P	differentiate between growth and development of an organism.
1:6	K	define homeostasis and explain how this balance of life processes allows an organism to survive in a wide range of environmental conditions.
1:7	K	explain the functions of the egg and sperm in the reproduction process.
1:7	P	explain why life is a continuous process.
1:8	K	list and give examples of the levels of biological organization.
1:8	K	indicate that organization is the major result of energy used by an organism.
1:9	K	explain how adaptations enable living things to survive in their environments.
1:10	K	define ecology as the study of the relationship between organisms and their environments.
1:10	P	list several ways in which organisms interact in a community.

The following performance objectives apply to all chapters.

S/A		When conducting activities or experiments, students will use laboratory materials and equipment in the prescribed manner.
		Upon completion of the reading and activities, students will exhibit an interest in biology by:
A		citing the need for an understanding of biological concepts as basic to ecological awareness.
A/S		voluntarily discussing or conducting one or more of the activities listed at the end of the chapter.
A		reading unassigned literature related to ideas presented in the chapter.

Answers to Chapter 1 Review

Page 18. Checking Your Ideas

1.	b	5.	c	9.	l
2.	g	6.	f	10.	k
3.	i	7.	j	11.	h
4.	a	8.	e	12.	d

Page 18. Evaluating Your Ideas

1. "Life" is a difficult word to define because of the great variety of organisms which inhabit the earth. It is important to study the broad similarities found among living things in order to better understand the process of "life."

2. Both an automobile engine and a living thing require an energy source. In both, energy is used for work. They differ in that an engine is not characterized by the major features of living systems: growth and development, maintenance and repair, highly complex organization, and reproduction. Also, an organism requires a continual input of fuel and constant operation, whereas an engine can be deprived of fuel for a long while and then operate again when fuel is supplied.

3. A parasite obtains necessary materials from another living thing, the host. A saprophyte obtains its necessary materials from dead organisms and waste products. Both are consumers.

4. Energy is a property which describes a material's ability to do work. The sun is the source of energy to every community. Part of the solar energy used in making sugar becomes stored in the sugar. By means of food chains, this energy is transferred through the community. Stored energy is not recyclable because as it is used for work, it changes to heat.

5. In feeding on waste materials and dead organisms, decomposers make available materials necessary for photosynthesis and the production of essential substances. A community lacking decomposers would cease to exist because waste materials would accumulate and not be recycled.

6. During photosynthesis, oxygen necessary for cellular respiration is produced. During cellular respiration, carbon dioxide and water necessary for photosynthesis are produced.

7. Homeostasis is the balance of internal operation of an organism despite external changes. This balance is important to maintain regulation in a broad range of environments.

8. Living things produce similar living things. It occurs because during reproduction parents pass on a set of instructions which guide the development of the offspring.

9. Although individual organisms die, the "code" for life continues to be passed along to future generations.

10. Organization is the orderly functioning of an organism, involving the coordination and interaction of all processes. Organization exists on a structural level, too. Living things may have one or more levels of organization.

11. A tissue is composed of groups of cells with similar origin, structure, and function. Examples of tissues are muscle and nerve (animals) and bark and conductive tissue (plants). An organ is composed of groups of tissues. The heart and liver (animals) and leaf and flower (plants) are examples of organs. A system is composed of several organs working together. Animal systems include digestive, circulatory, and excretory systems. Transport and reproductive systems are examples of plant systems.

12. An adaptation is a characteristic which promotes the survival of an organism.

13. Physical factors of the environment include temperature, availability of light, amount of oxygen, and type of soil.

Page 19. Applying Your Ideas

1. Student answers will vary. Examples include forests, plains, deserts, oceans, rivers, lakes, marshes, and estuaries. All communities are characterized by the presence of producers and consumers which depend on them. Communities differ in the types of organisms which inhabit them and in the physical characteristics that they have.

2. Green plants with chlorophyll do not survive on the forest floor because there is insufficient sunlight for photosynthesis. Indian pipe is a saprophyte, living on dead materials for food.

3. (a) parasite; (b) saprophyte; (c) parasite.

4. Student answers will vary. Algae → snail → fish is a possible lake food chain. A desert food chain might be cactus → rodent → snake.

5. The simplest food chain would consist of producers and decomposers. Producers would be capable of trapping energy and manufacturing food. Decomposers could then obtain energy from this food by "burning" the materials of dead producers. As a result of "burning," necessary materials would be recycled.

6. The potato is larger and heavier but it has not grown because there has been no increase in the amount of living material.

7. Student answers will vary. Water supply influences the growth of producers and, hence, the food supply of consumers. Water supply is also important to animal survival. Temperature affects the activities of animals, the rate of evaporation, and germination of seeds. Light influences the rate of photosynthesis and the ability of animals to see. Type of soil influences the kinds of plants which can grow and therefore indirectly determines the variety of animal life as well.

8. Examples of adaptation in trees include broad leaves which absorb sunlight, roots which absorb water, and a stem or trunk which supports the leaves. Examples of human adaptation include the ability to reason, upright posture, and hands which grasp. All of these adaptations promote survival of the organism by making it better suited to its environment.

9. Producers are not found at the bottom of deep lakes or oceans because light does not penetrate to those depths. Without light, producers are unable to produce food by photosynthesis.

Page 19. Extending Your Ideas

1. You might wish to have a student prepare an oral report on findings. The report could include collected samples and a map of the area. Several reports about different types of communities, e.g. forest, pond, and field, might lead to a discussion of general unifying principles of community life.

2. Sophisticated equipment is not required. A simple, open glass container can serve as an aquarium. Encourage the

student to consider the factors important in maintaining a balanced "ecosystem" in the aquarium; e.g., water content, temperature, light, ratio of plants to animals, and size of organisms. Terrarium specimens can be collected easily. The terrarium should be covered with glass to prevent evaporation. If you are considering a year-long class project, more complex equipment could be constructed or purchased. Also, various types of systems could be set up.

3. Student answers will vary. Energy is used for locomotion, conducting nerve impulses, beating of the heart, breathing, growth, and synthesis of necessary substances.

Additional Student Readings

Brown, Vinson, *The Amateur Naturalist's Handbook.* Englewood Cliffs, NJ, Prentice-Hall, Inc., 1980.

Chinery, Michael, *Enjoying Nature With Your Family.* New York, Crown Publishers, Inc., 1977.

Lawrence, Gale, *The Beginning Naturalist.* Shelburne, VT, New England Press, Inc., 1979.

Suggested Teacher Readings

De Filippo, Shirley, "Aquarium Problems: How to Solve Them." *The Science Teacher*, May, 1975.

Hurd, Paul D., "Back-to-Basics: a Critical Juncture in Biology Education." *The American Biology Teacher*, March, 1979.

Kahle, Jane B., Hurd, Paul D., and Harms, Norris, "High School Biology Education in Transition." *The American Biology Teacher*, April, 1979.

"NABT Guidelines for the Use of Live Animals at the Pre-University Level." *The American Biology Teacher*, October, 1980.

CHAPTER 2   BIOLOGY AS A SCIENCE

Teaching Techniques

Emphasis in this chapter is placed on the uniqueness of scientific methods, especially controlled experimentation. After discussing Fleming's discovery of penicillin as an example of scientific investigation, guide students to apply what they have learned to other scientific questions. Spend some time suggesting the relationship of what they have learned in this chapter to their own experiences in the laboratory.

Use of material concerning the International System of Measurement will depend on your evaluation of your students' competence and confidence in this area. You may wish to omit it, cover it thoroughly, or refer to it at the appropriate times when measurement is an integral part of a laboratory exercise.

Performance Objectives

Goal: Students will gain an understanding of how a scientist conducts an investigation and how to use the International System of Measurement.

Objectives: Upon completion of the reading and activities and when asked to respond orally or on a written test, students will:

Section Number		
2:0	P	compare the quality and quantity of the earliest scientific knowledge with the scientific knowledge gathered since the late 1800's.
2:1	P	compare science and technology.
2:1	K	list the four principle processes of scientific investigation which distinguish it from other areas of study: observation, interpretation, hypothesis formation, and experimentation.
2:2	K	explain what a scientist does when involved in the observation phase of an investigation.
2:3	A	describe the importance of using reason and logic when interpreting facts.
2:4	K	define the term "hypothesis," explain how hypotheses are formed, and describe the function of a hypothesis.
2:4	P	explain why the hypothesis is not the conclusion of a problem.
2:5	K	indicate that the factor being tested in a controlled experiment is the variable factor.
2:5	K	differentiate between a control group and an experimental group.
2:5	P	describe an example of how scientific knowledge advances by making use of previous findings.
2:4,6	K	differentiate between a hypothesis and a theory.
2:7	K	explain why scientists use the International System of Measurement.
2:8	K	identify the meter as the basic unit of length in the International System.
2:8	K	list the prefixes used to indicate fractions or multiples of tens in the International System.

2:9	P	explain how solid, liquid, and gas volumes are expressed in SI.
2:10	P/K	differentiate between weight and mass and list the kilogram as the basic unit of mass.
2:11	K	identify the freezing point and boiling point of water on the Celsius temperature scale.
2:11	K	list the second as the basic SI unit of time.
2:12	P	distinguish between resolving power and magnification.
2:12	P	compare a light microscope and an electron microscope, and distinguish between TEM and SEM.

(See page 41T for performance objectives that apply to all chapters.)

Answers to Chapter 2 Review

Page 34. Checking Your Ideas

1. hypothesis
2. ten
3. variable
4. meter
5. technology
6. 1000
7. mass
8. theory
9. data
10. scanning
11. resolving power
12. Celsius

Page 34. Evaluating Your Ideas

1. Unconfirmed conclusions prevailed because later scientists did not examine them in a scientific manner.

2. Major biological discoveries include the discovery that all organisms are composed of cells, that microbes cause disease, the fact that life comes from life, the discovery of the laws of heredity, knowledge of the genetic code, and advances in medicine.

3. A good hypothesis predicts new facts and is testable. No, experimentation may show that a hypothesis is partially or totally incorrect.

4. Fleming hypothesized that *Penicillium* produced a chemical which was responsible for the death of *Staphylococcus* bacteria. He tested the hypothesis by growing *Penicillium* in nutrient broth solutions. When the broth containing the chemical produced by *Penicillium* was added to the bacteria, they died. Fleming verified that the chemical was responsible by adding broth alone to the bacteria; the precaution was testing the broth alone.

5. As a result of Fleming's discovery, a variety of antibiotic drugs have been developed. This result illustrates that practical benefits often arise from research which scientists carry on as a result of curiosity. It also shows that scientific knowledge builds upon the foundations of previous findings.

6. Scientists avoid the word "proof" because there is always a possibility that a hypothesis or theory will be revised in light of newly discovered information.

7. The milliliter directly measures liquid volume. The cubic centimeter measures liquid or solid volume and is derived from the meter.

8. Weight is a measure of gravitational attraction between two objects. Mass is a measure of the amount of matter in an object.

9. (a) $50 \text{ cm} \times 1 \text{ m}/100 \text{ cm} = 0.5 \text{ m}$
(b) $50 \text{ cm} \times 10 \text{ mm}/1 \text{ cm} = 500 \text{ mm}$

10. (a) $1.5 \text{ kg} \times 1000 \text{ g}/1 \text{ kg} = 1500 \text{ g}$
(b) $1.5 \text{ kg} \times 1000 \text{ g}/1 \text{ kg} \times 1000 \text{ mg}/1 \text{ g} = 1\,500\,000 \text{ mg}$
(c) $1.5 \text{ kg} \times 1000 \text{ g}/1 \text{ kg} \times 1\,000\,000 \,\mu\text{g}/1 \text{ g} = 1.5 \times 10^9 \,\mu\text{g}$

11. (a) $8 \text{ mL} \times 1 \text{ L}/1000 \text{ mL} = 0.008 \text{ L}$
(b) $800 \text{ L} \times 1000 \text{ mL}/1 \text{ L} = 800\,000 \text{ mL}$

12. (a)

$$
\begin{array}{ll}
1.2 \text{ km} = & 1200.000 \text{ m} \\
844 \text{ mm} = & 0.844 \text{ m} \\
125 \text{ cm} = & \underline{1.250 \text{ m}} \\
& 1202.094 \text{ m}
\end{array}
$$

(b)

$$
\begin{array}{ll}
1.2 \text{ km} = & 120\,000.0 \text{ cm} \\
844 \text{ mm} = & 84.4 \text{ cm} \\
125 \text{ cm} = & \underline{125.0 \text{ cm}} \\
& 120\,209.4 \text{ cm}
\end{array}
$$

or $1202.094 \text{ m} \times 100 \text{ cm}/1 \text{ m} = 12\,029.4 \text{ cm}$

(c)

$$
\begin{array}{ll}
1.2 \text{ km} = & 1\,200\,000.0 \text{ mm} \\
844 \text{ mm} = & 844.0 \text{ mm} \\
125 \text{ cm} = & \underline{1\,250.0 \text{ mm}} \\
& 1\,202\,094.0 \text{ mm}
\end{array}
$$

or $1202.094 \text{ m} \times 1000 \text{ mm}/1 \text{ m} = 1\,202\,094.0 \text{ mm}$

(d)

$$
\begin{array}{ll}
1.2 \text{ km} = & 1.200\,000 \text{ km} \\
844 \text{ mm} = & 0.000\,844 \text{ km} \\
125 \text{ cm} = & \underline{0.001\,250 \text{ km}} \\
& 1.202\,094 \text{ km}
\end{array}
$$

or $1202.094 \text{ m} \times 1 \text{ km}/1000 \text{ m} = 1.202\,094 \text{ km}$

13. (a)

$$
\begin{array}{ll}
2.2 \text{ L} = & 2.200\,000 \text{ L} \\
176 \text{ mL} = & 0.176\,000 \text{ L} \\
250 \,\mu\text{L} = & \underline{0.000\,250 \text{ L}} \\
& 2.376\,250 \text{ L}
\end{array}
$$

(b)

$$
\begin{array}{ll}
2.2 \text{ L} = & 2200.000 \text{ mL} \\
176 \text{ mL} = & 176.000 \text{ mL} \\
250 \,\mu\text{L} = & \underline{0.250 \text{ mL}} \\
& 2376.250 \text{ mL}
\end{array}
$$

or $2.376\,250 \text{ L} \times 1000 \text{ mL}/1 \text{ L} = 2376.25 \text{ mL}$

(c)

$$
\begin{array}{ll}
2.2 \text{ L} = & 2\,200\,000.0 \,\mu\text{L} \\
176 \text{ mL} = & 176\,000.0 \,\mu\text{L} \\
250 \,\mu\text{L} = & \underline{250.0 \,\mu\text{L}} \\
& 2\,376\,250.0 \,\mu\text{L}
\end{array}
$$

or $2.376\,250 \text{ L} \times 1\,000\,000 \,\mu\text{L}/1 \text{ L} = 2\,376\,250 \,\mu\text{L}$

14. In light microscopes, light passes through the object and is focused by glass lenses. Light microscopes have a maximum magnification of 2000 times and a resolving power of about 500 nm. In an electron microscope, a beam of electrons passes through or bounces off the object and is focused by magnets. Electron microscopes magnify hundreds of thousands of times and have a resolving power of about 0.5 nm.

15. The TEM is used for studying internal structures, such as those within cells. Thin sections are prepared for examination with the TEM. The SEM is used for study of whole structures, such as whole cells. Surface properties can be examined because the specimen is not sectioned for examination with the SEM and the image produced is three-dimensional.

Page 35. Applying Your Ideas

1. Rate of photosynthesis must be tested indirectly. A standard method is to determine the amount of oxygen

given off per unit time. This experiment is best accomplished with submerged aquatic plants and should include two (or more) groups of plants—a control group and experimental group(s). The variable factor would be the amount of light each group receives. Light intensity could be varied by using bulbs of different wattage or bulbs located at varying distances from the plants. Each group would be exposed to light for the same period of time. Amounts of oxygen given off by each plant could then be compared. Counting bubbles of oxygen given off is a suitable indicator.
2. Student answers will vary, but their plans should center around the idea of controlled experimentation with one variable factor. Evaluate each on how well variables are controlled.
3. Weight varies; mass does not. If you climbed a mountain, your weight would decrease slightly but your mass would remain constant. A dieter tries to lose mass.
4. The micrometer and nanometer are important in the study of cells and subcellular structures.

Page 35. Extending Your Ideas

1. A standard microbiology text will be helpful in gathering information for this topic. An interview with a nurse or physician would also be useful. Important antibiotics include streptomycin, erythromycin, chloramphenicol, and tetracycline.
2. Soil samples (10 g each) can be collected 10-15 cm below the soil surface. Shake each sample in a tube containing 10 mL sterile distilled water. Using sterile techniques streak the soil liquid onto nutrient agar plates. After mold colonies form, isolate the different kinds, each in its own liquid broth tube. Sterile disks soaked in the mold liquid tubes can then be placed on agar plates that were streaked with bacteria. (*Sarcina lutea* works well as a test bacteria because of its yellow color.) Examine the plates after incubation for zones of inhibition.

Additional Student Readings

Asimov, Isaac, "Science Stands Alone." *Science Digest*, November, 1978.
"Computerized Discovery." *SciQuest*, December, 1980.
Hopkins, R. A., "Metrics Ahead—How You Can Cope." *Science Digest*, February, 1977.
Hunter, J. S., "National System of Scientific Measurement." *Science*, November 21, 1980.

Suggested Teacher Readings

Baumel, Howard B., "Lysozyme, Penicillin, and Chance Discovery." *American Biology Teacher*, January, 1976.
Birnie, Howard H., "The Revolution in Science Teaching: Where Do You Stand?" *The Science Teacher*, October, 1975.
Goldstein, Martin, and Goldstein, Inge F. *How We Know: An Exploration of the Scientific Process.* New York, Plenum Press, 1978.
Kadar, Agnes, and Shupe, Barbara, "Science: A History of Woman's Work." *The Science Teacher*, April, 1977.
Lunetta, Vincent N., Hofstein, Avi, and Giddings, Geoffrey, "Evaluating Science Laboratory Skills." *The Science Teacher*, January, 1981.

CHAPTER 3   MATERIALS OF LIFE

Teaching Techniques

The intent of this chapter is to provide an adequate basis for the many contemporary topics in physiology. Emphasis should be placed on the *understanding* of bonding, formulas, equations, and conservation of matter and energy. Thus, when students are confronted with biochemical topics later on, they will have an idea of what formulas, ions, potential energy, and other terms mean. With the exception, perhaps, of honors or advanced groups, you should not make application of these topics a primary goal. It is not important for students to learn to balance equations or predict formulas. Rather, they must understand what balanced equations or chemical formulas represent. Students should learn to *recognize* structural formulas of the organic compounds discussed, but they should not be asked to draw them from memory. Stress the major uses of these compounds within living things.

For the simple molecules discussed in this chapter, the idea of "filling" outer energy levels with electrons during bonding will suffice. More accurately, an energy level is stabilized, rather than filled.

Atoms whose outer energy levels can hold more than eight electrons may still be stabilized with eight electrons because of the order in which energy levels are filled. However, for simplification such atoms are not considered in this chapter.

Performance Objectives

Goal: Students will gain some understanding of chemistry and its relationship to the study of living things.

Objectives: Upon completion of the reading and activities and when asked to respond orally or on a written test, students will:

Section Number		
3:0	K	explain that a knowledge of matter and its properties is needed to understand physiological processes.
3:1	K	define matter as anything which has mass and occupies space.

3:1	K	diagram an atom indicating the location and electrical charge of the protons, neutrons, and electrons.
3:2	K	indicate that it is the number of protons, neutrons, and electrons in an atom of one element which distinguishes it from an atom of another element.
3:2	K	explain the differences among isotopes of an element.
3:3	P/K	explain the octet rule and duet rule and use these rules to predict the number of electrons that will be shared or transferred by atoms when they combine.
3:3	K	explain the formation of a covalent bond.
3:3,4	P	differentiate between a molecule and a compound.
3:5	K	explain the formation of an ionic bond.
3:5	K	predict the formula of an ionic compound given the charges of the combining ions.
3:6	K	explain that a chemical formula shows the number and kind of each atom in a compound.
3:7	P	differentiate between solutes and solvents in a solution.
3:7	P	compare and contrast the manner in which covalent compounds and ionic compounds dissolve in water.
3:8	P	compare and contrast neutral, basic, and acidic solutions.
3:8	K	describe the pH scale and its use.
3:9	P	compare and contrast physical changes and chemical changes.
3:10	K	state the law of conservation of mass.
3:10	K	indicate the relationship between a chemical reaction and a chemical equation.
3:11	K	identify organic compounds as carbon compounds and explain why they can be so complex.
3:12	P	differentiate between structural and simple formulas and explain why structural formulas are used to represent various isomers.
3:13-15	P	compare and contrast the building blocks and biological uses of carbohydrates, lipids, and proteins.
3:13-15	K	list the functions of carbohydrates, lipids, and proteins.
3:16	K	describe a major biological function of nucleic acids.
3:17	P	compare, contrast, and give examples of the processes of dehydration synthesis and hydrolysis.

(See page 41T for performance objectives that apply to all chapters.)

Answers to Chapter 3 Review

Page 56. Checking Your Ideas

1. electrons
2. transfer
3. proteins
4. structural
5. solution
6. physical
7. molecule
8. 12
9. carbohydrates, lipids
10. hydrolysis
11. two
12. DNA, RNA
13. chemical
14. electron
15. neutrons

Page 56. Evaluating Your Ideas

1. It is necessary for a better understanding of physiological processes.

2. carbon (C), hydrogen (H), nitrogen (N), and oxygen (O)

3. Their outer energy levels obtain an outer octet (or duet) of electrons.

4. This ratio is determined by the octet and duet rules. Because an atom of oxygen requires two electrons to obtain an octet and an atom of hydrogen can provide only one of these electrons, two atoms of hydrogen are required for each atom of oxygen. By sharing electrons, each hydrogen obtains an outer duet of electrons.

5. An ion is a charged atom. In a chlorine atom, the number of protons and electrons is equal. In a chloride ion, the number of electrons is one greater than the number of protons.

6. Molecules of molecular compounds are distinct units. Ionic compounds consist of a continuous network of positive and negative ions.

7. H_2O represents one molecule of water, $3 H_2O$ represents three molecules of water. Nine atoms are contained in $3 H_2O$.

8. In water, sugar molecules separate from one another and are dispersed. The atoms of the sugar molecules do not separate. Salt dissociates in water to form sodium ions and chloride ions.

9. Hydrogen chloride dissociates in water to form chloride ions and hydrogen ions. The solution then contains an excess of hydrogen ions and is acidic. Sodium hydroxide dissociates in water to form sodium ions and hydroxide ions. The solution then contains an excess of hydroxide ions and is basic.

10. A pH of 2 is more acidic than a pH of 6 because the solution with pH of 2 has a greater concentration of hydrogen ions.

11. Carbon can form bonds with other carbon atoms to create long chains resulting in complex molecules. A carbon atom has 4 electrons in the outer energy level and forms bonds by sharing electrons.

12. A double bond is the sharing of two pairs of electrons. A triple bond is the sharing of three pairs of electrons.

Hydrogen has only one electron to share; therefore, it cannot form double or triple bonds.
13. The carboxyl group, —COOH, is common to both fatty acids and amino acids.
14. Nitrogen is found in proteins but is in neither carbohydrates nor lipids.
15. Proteins differ in the kind, number, sequence and arrangement of amino acids.
16. Nucleic acids play an important role in heredity.
17. (a) hydrolysis
    (b) dehydration synthesis
    (c) dehydration synthesis
    (d) hydrolysis
    (e) hydrolysis

Page 57. Applying Your Ideas

1. The atom has 8 electrons.

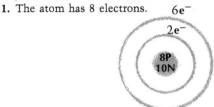

2. One positive ion combines with three negative ions.
3. Because the outer energy levels of these atoms are filled, they do not tend to share, acquire, or lose electrons. Therefore, they are usually chemically inactive.
4. The water, after CO_2 is added, will be yellow-green. As the plant undergoes photosynthesis, the CO_2 will be removed from solution and the yellow-green color will change to blue.
5. (a) physical
    (b) physical
    (c) chemical
6.

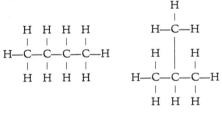

7. The pH of acid rain would be less than seven. Acid rain might disrupt the environment by altering the pH of soil and water, thus changing the forms of life able to survive. It might also directly harm or kill organisms.

Page 57. Extending Your Ideas

1. Common chemical changes include (among others):
  (1) rusting of iron
  (2) burning of gas, coal, or oil
  (3) spoiling of food
  (4) digestion
  (5) burning of leaves
  (6) photosynthesis
  (7) "burning" of sugar by organisms
  (8) corrosion of metals
  (9) production of ozone from oxygen
 (10) synthesis of protein
2. Use a magnet to attract the iron filings to separate sand and iron filings. Add water to separate sand and salt. The salt will dissolve and the sand can be removed from the salt water.
3. A general physiology text would be a good source for students. HPO_4^{-2} and $H_2PO_4^-$ are important blood buffers. Excess H^+ combines with HPO_4^{-2} to form $H_2PO_4^-$ thereby reducing the concentration of H^+ ions. Acidosis and alkalosis can result from improper regulation of blood pH. Both may lead to death if not quickly treated.
4. Cholesterol is a steroid found in animal fats, oils, egg yolk, bile, and blood. It serves as a precursor for the synthesis of many important steroids. Cholesterol is implicated in a variety of human illnesses and dysfunctions including gallstones, high blood pressure, and hardening of the arteries. Cholesterol production may be increased by a high intake of saturated fatty acids.
5. Encourage students to use indicators such as bromthymol blue, phenolphthalein, litmus paper, or pH paper. A pH meter might be available. Have students use weak solutions of HCl and NaOH.

Additional Student Readings

Asimov, Isaac, *How Did We Find Out About Atoms?* New York, Walker and Company, 1976.
Garmon, Linda, "Chemistry by Computer." *Science News*, February 28, 1981.
Thomsen, Dietrick E., "A Matter of Energy Levels." *Science News*, March 13, 1982.

Suggested Teacher Readings

Phillips, D.C., and North, A.C.T., *Protein Structure*, 2nd ed. Carolina Biological Reader. Burlington, NC, Carolina Biological Supply Co., 1978.
Smoot, Robert C., Price, Jack, and Smith, Richard G., *Chemistry: A Modern Course.* Columbus, OH, Charles E. Merrill Publishing Co., 1983.

CHAPTER 4   ENERGY FOR LIFE

Teaching Techniques

The topics in this chapter, as in other chapters of Unit One, are those applicable to all living things. Because photosynthesis is a process unique to autotrophs, it is not discussed in detail here (see Chapter 21). However, you may wish to remind students of the ultimate importance of photosynthesis as the process which incorporates energy for all life.

Make certain that students see that the details presented in this chapter elaborate general ideas presented in Chapter 1. Students should also understand that the ideas of energy flow apply to both the cellular and community levels of organization (as well as higher levels). Draw on the ideas of dehydration synthesis and hydrolysis (Chapter 3) as typical cellular reactions involving energy.

For honors or advanced groups, you should consider teaching the biochemistry of cellular respiration, covered in greater detail in Appendix B.

Performance Objectives

Goal: Students will gain an understanding of how energy is made available to cells and how that energy is used in the biological work of organisms.

Objectives: Upon completion of the reading and activities and when asked to respond orally or on a written test, students will:

Section Number		
4:0	K	define energy as the ability to do work or cause motion and explain several uses of energy in living systems.
4:1	P	compare and contrast potential energy and kinetic energy.
4:1	K	state the law of conservation of energy.
4:1	K	explain that organisms obtain usable energy from high energy molecules.
4:2	K	explain that activation energy is needed to begin reactions.
4:3	P	explain the relationship between activation energy and enzymes.
4:4	K	explain that enzymes are specific and reusable and that they are proteins.
4:5	K/S	explain the lock and key hypothesis and diagram the series of steps which occur during an enzymatic reaction.
4:5	K	give evidence which supports the lock and key hypothesis.
4:6	K	explain the roles of coenzymes.
4:7	P	distinguish between exergonic and endergonic reactions.
4:7	K	describe the function of adenosine triphosphate (ATP) in endergonic reactions.
4:8	K	identify cellular respiration as the process by which a cell releases the energy of glucose.
4:8	K/S	diagram the ATP-ADP cycle and explain what happens during the cycle.
4:8,9	P	compare and contrast aerobic respiration and anaerobic respiration.
4:9	K	list two practical uses of yeast fermentation.

(See page 41T for performance objectives that apply to all chapters.)

Answers to Chapter 4 Review

Page 70. Checking Your Ideas

1.	false	6.	false
2.	true	7.	false
3.	false	8.	true
4.	true	9.	true
5.	true	10.	true

Page 70. Evaluating Your Ideas

1. Forms of energy include electric, mechanical, chemical, radiant, and nuclear. An example of transformation of energy is the conversion of electric energy to radiant energy in a light bulb. Students may give other answers.

2. Student answers may vary. Some may answer chemical energy because it is used for biological work. Others may answer radiant energy because it is the ultimate source of energy for living things.

3. Energy is neither created nor destroyed, but it can be transformed to other kinds of energy. When gasoline is burned in an automobile, energy is transformed from chemical to mechanical energy and heat. The amount of heat and mechanical energy produced is equal to the amount of chemical energy which was present in the gasoline molecules. Thus, energy is conserved. Students may give other examples.

4. Heat would activate many reactions simultaneously. Also, cells could not survive the amount of heat necessary to activate some reactions.

5. According to the lock and key hypothesis, the active site of an enzyme is like a key which fits a lock (the substrate). When enzyme and substrate are joined, bonds can break or new bonds can form. The lock and key hypothesis explains why enzymes are specific and are not consumed during a reaction.

6. (a)

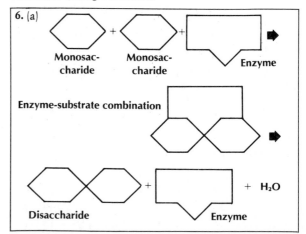

Monosaccharide + Monosaccharide + Enzyme

Enzyme-substrate combination

Disaccharide + Enzyme + H_2O

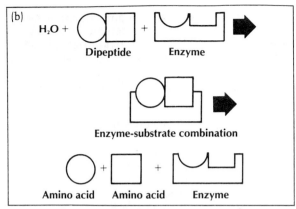

(b)

H₂O + ◯▢ + ⌒⌣ ➡

Dipeptide   **Enzyme**

◯▢ ➡

Enzyme-substrate combination

◯ + ▢ + ⌒⌣

Amino acid   **Amino acid**   **Enzyme**

7. An endergonic reaction requires an input of energy. An exergonic reaction liberates energy.

8. Breaking the phosphate groups from an ATP molecule releases energy. This energy can be used to start many endergonic reactions.

9. After a molecule of ATP has been used, a molecule of ADP and a low-energy phosphate remain. These two molecules combine to form ATP provided an energy source is supplied.

10. The reactants of cellular respiration are glucose and oxygen. The products are carbon dioxide and water.

11. Energy released from glucose is not directly used by cells. Chemical energy of glucose is stored in cells in the form of ATP. Without ATP, energy conversions within cells would be less efficient.

12. ATP is hydrolyzed and releases energy which is used for cellular work. The hydrolysis produces ADP and —Ⓟ. These can be recombined by use of the energy from cellular respiration. They are recombined to form ATP.

13. Before respiration begins, glucose, like a rock at the top of a hill, has high potential energy. Both need a source of activation energy. During the respiration process, the potential energy of glucose is converted into kinetic energy just as the potential energy of the rock is changed to kinetic energy as the rock rolls down the hill. After respiration, carbon dioxide and water, like the rock at the bottom of the hill, have low potential energy. The two processes differ in the forms of energy involved, the source of activation energy, and the use of the kinetic energy produced.

14. Anaerobic respiration is less "profitable" than aerobic respiration because fewer ATP molecules are produced. This result occurs because glucose is not broken down as much in anaerobic respiration. Therefore, less energy is released.

15. Fermentation of yeasts produces valuable industrial by-products. Ethyl alcohol is used in the production of certain alcoholic beverages. Yeasts are used in the baking industry because their fermentation produces carbon dioxide.

Page 71. Applying Your Ideas

1. The rate will increase because there will be a greater chance of an enzyme's colliding with a substrate. At the point when all of the enzyme is combined with the substrate, a further increase in substrate amount will not increase the reaction rate.

2. Glucose would be paper currency which can be changed into the "coins" of ATP. Glucose, in the analogy, should be another form of money because it is another form of chemical energy in the cell.

3. Yeasts undergoing aerobic respiration produce more energy for growth and reproduction.

4. A diver on a high board has the most potential energy. As the dive occurs, potential energy is converted to kinetic..

5. The glucose is used as an energy source. Through cellular respiration, its energy is used to make ATP just as in consumers.

6. In photosynthesis, radiant energy (light) is converted to chemical energy.

Page 72. Extending Your Ideas

1. Invertase (sucrase) can be prepared by making an extract of yeast cells. A cake of yeast is placed in 100 mL of water and broken apart in a blender. The yeast cell fragments can be separated from the extract by centrifugation. The extract contains invertase which will hydrolyze sucrose (table sugar) into glucose and fructose. Benedict's solution will give a positive test with glucose and, therefore, serve as an indicator of how the enzyme is operating. To test the effect of temperature have the student prepare several test tubes each containing the same amount of a 1% sucrose solution and extract. Place each test tube in a different temperature environment for five minutes. Then add Benedict's solution to each tube and immerse the tubes in a boiling water bath. Have the student record the time necessary for evidence of a chemical change to first appear. To test pH add various buffers to the solutions of sucrose and extract keeping the temperature constant.

2. Students should investigate scurvy, rickets, beriberi, xeropthalmia, pellagra, and pernicious anemia.

3. "Cold" light is produced as a result of the interaction of the enzyme luciferase on the substrate luciferin. Bioluminescence helps some organisms to attract food and mates. Kits demonstrating bioluminescence are available from biological supply houses.

4. Pasteur showed that the souring or acidifying of alcoholic beverages was due to the action of bacteria.

5. Prepare a solution of powdered or cake yeast in water. Add a small amount of glucose (or other sugar). Place the sugar-yeast solution in a fermentation tube stoppered with cotton. Tilt the tube so that the solution occupies part of the bowl of the tube and all of the arm. As fermentation proceeds, CO_2 will displace the liquid in the arm. Have students vary the type of sugar used to determine which sugars are more easily metabolized. To quantify the experiment, use a grease pencil to mark lines a centimeter apart on the arm of the tube so that the amount of CO_2 produced per unit time can be measured.

Additional Student Readings

Hoagland, Mahlon B., *The Roots of Life*. Boston, Houghton Mifflin Co., 1978.

Ray, Karen L., "Flexible Proteins." *SciQuest*, July/August, 1979.

Suggested Teacher Readings

Chappell, J. B., "ATP," *Carolina Biology Reader*. Burlington, NC, Carolina Biological Supply Co., 1977.

Nicholls, P., "Cytochromes and Biological Oxidation." *Oxford Biology Reader*. London, Oxford U. Press, 1975.

CHAPTER 5   CELL STRUCTURE AND FUNCTION

Teaching Techniques

Refer to the idea of organization discussed in Chapter 1 and review the role of energy (Chapter 4) in maintaining this organization. Point out that other general characteristics of life are evident at the cellular level too—reproduction (the nucleus), maintenance and repair (in discussion of phagocytosis), and growth and development (after cell division).

Make certain that students learn the major organelles and cell parts and their functions. They will be referred to and expanded on in later chapters. A fundamental understanding of passive and active transport is also important for later work.

Performance Objectives

Goal: Students will gain an understanding of the structure and functions of the cell.

Objectives: Upon completion of the reading and activities and when asked to respond orally or on a written test, students will:

Section Number		
5:0,1	K	list contributions made by Hooke, Schleidin, Schwann, and Virchow in the development of the cell theory.
5:1	K	state and explain the two components of the cell theory.
5:2	P	distinguish between unicellular and multicellular organisms.
5:2	K	list the various functions carried out by cells.
5:3	K	describe the fluid mosaic model of cell membrane structure.
5:4	P	explain why it is important that the cell membrane is semipermeable.
5:4	P	describe the process of diffusion through a semipermeable membrane and indicate the direction a substance will move relative to its concentration.
5:5	P	describe the process of osmosis.
5:6	K	explain the movement of particles across a cell membrane by facilitated diffusion.
5:6,7	P	compare and contrast passive transport and active transport.
5:8	K	list the factors which determine whether or not a particle will permeate the cell membrane.
5:9	P	compare and contrast endocytosis, phagocytosis, pinocytosis, and exocytosis.
5:10	K	describe protoplasm and differentiate between nucleoplasm and cytoplasm.
5:10	K	explain and give examples of reactions involved in metabolism.
5:11	P	explain how organelles contribute to division of labor in a cell.
5:12	K	distinguish between eukaryotes and prokaryotes.
5:12	K/S	diagram, label, and describe the functions of mitochondria, endoplasmic reticulum, ribosomes, Golgi bodies, vacuoles, lysosomes, microfilaments, and microtubules.
5:13	P	explain the formation of lysosomes and their contents and relate lysosome function to phagocytosis.
5:13	K	describe the production and secretion of certain cellular chemicals.
5:14	K	state the functions of chloroplasts, cell wall, centrioles, cilia, and flagella and identify the types of cells in which they are found.
5:15	K	list the structures and functions of the parts of the nucleus.
5:16	K	describe cell fractionation as a separation of cell parts, which makes use of properties of cell parts.
5:16	K	distinguish a step density gradient from a linear density gradient.

(See page 41T for performance objectives that apply to all chapters.)

Answers to Chapter 5 Review

Page 92. Checking Your Ideas

1. d		**5.** b		**8.** f	
2. e		**6.** j		**9.** g	
3. h		**7.** i		**10.** c	
4. a					

Page 93. Evaluating Your Ideas

1. The cell theory applies to all living things.

2. Cells in both unicellular and multicellular organisms carry out similar functions: obtaining food and other needed materials, gas exchange, excretion, synthesis of living material, regulation of water balance, response to stimuli, and reproduction.

3. Materials must be exchanged between cells and their environment. As the outer boundary of a cell, the cell membrane regulates the passage of materials into and out of the cell. If the membrane were permeable to all molecules, important molecules or particles in the cell might escape or potentially dangerous molecules or particles might enter.

4. Osmosis, the diffusion of water through a semipermeable membrane, is important to cells because organisms are composed of so much water and water is involved in many cellular reactions.

5. Carbon dioxide is in greater concentration inside a cell (as a result of cellular respiration) than in the blood. It moves by diffusion from cell to blood.

6. This alga can accumulate ions by active transport.

7. In passive transport, particles pass from a region of greater concentration to a region of lesser concentration. In active transport, often particles pass from a region of lesser concentration to one of higher concentration. Active transport requires energy. By active transport, particles can move to regions of lower concentration, in other words, in the direction they would normally move by diffusion but at a faster rate than by diffusion alone. This process requires energy.

8. Smaller particles permeate a cell membrane more easily than large ones, maybe because of the size of pores or spaces between lipid and protein molecules in the membrane. The fat content of the membrane causes fat-soluble particles to permeate more easily than those which do not dissolve in fat.

9. Cells differ in permeability due to differences in the space between proteins and lipids and because of the presence or absence of carriers in the membrane.

10. In phagocytosis, the cell membrane engulfs a food organism or large chunk of food. In pinocytosis, liquid droplets or small particles enter the cell through channels. In both cases, the food becomes surrounded by a part of the cell membrane. The food is digested inside the cell.

11. (a) protection and support—plants; algae; fungi
(b) cell reproduction—animals, some algae and fungi
(c) photosynthesis—plants; algae
(d) locomotion—all kinds of organisms
(e) intracellular transport—all kinds of organisms
(f) storage and secretion—all kinds of organisms
(g) intracellular digestion—all kinds of organisms
(h) movement—all kinds of organisms
(i) support and movement—all kinds of organisms
(j) cellular respiration—all kinds of organisms
(k) production of ribosomes—all kinds of organisms
(l) control and heredity—all kinds of organisms
(m) protein synthesis—all kinds of organisms
(n) storage—all kinds of organisms
Note: the above answers apply only to *eukaryotes*.

12. The chemicals, if free in the cytoplasm, would digest many molecules and possibly cell parts.

13. Rough ER has ribosomes on its surface. Smooth ER does not.

14. The protein to be secreted is manufactured on the ribosomes and then may pass into the endoplasmic reticulum. It may travel, via a temporary connection, to a Golgi body where carbohydrate molecules may be added to it. The chemical can be pinched off the Golgi body in a small packet which fuses with the cell membrane, pouring the secretions from the cell.

15. Cell fractionation techniques are used to isolate cell parts. After cells are ground up and suspended in liquid, they are subjected to centrifugation at varying speeds. Particles of different sizes can be separated by the spinning. Parts can also be separated by density using density gradients. The function of each part is determined by measuring chemicals within and by studying reactions of the cell part.

Page 93. Applying Your Ideas

1. *Paramecium* constantly gains water by osmosis. *Paramecium* rids itself of excess water by means of a contractile vacuole. If the concentration of salt were small, the *Paramecium* might reach an osmotic balance in which case the contractile vacuole would cease to function. If the concentration of salt were greater, the *Paramecium* might lose excess water by osmosis and die.

2. Because the oxygen that enters a cell is used in cellular respiration, its concentration inside the cell is always less than in the blood.

3. Protoplasm is not a fixed material with a definite composition. It constantly changes as chemical reactions occur within it.

4. Muscle cells require a large amount of energy for contraction. Because mitochondria are the organelles in which energy is released, mitochondria would be plentiful in muscle cells.

5. Golgi bodies would be abundant because they are the cell parts in which secretions are packaged. (If the hormone were a protein, ribosomes would also be plentiful.)

Page 93. Extending Your Ideas

1. You may wish to have students report on the following kinds of cells: xylem, phloem, red blood cells, white blood cells, muscle cells, nerve cells, bone cells, and unicellular organisms. Have students investigate how a particular cell is similar and dissimilar to the generalized cell discussed in this chapter.

2. A basal metabolism test measures rate of metabolism. It is conducted under resting and fasting conditions. During the test the amount of oxygen consumed is measured. This step indicates how quickly the body is burning food and, in turn, provides information about the thyroid gland.

3. The membrane of the model should be a transparent material given shape by a supporting structure of wire or wood. Polystyrene plastic is a workable material for modeling the organelles within the cell. There is really no typical cell because the structure of a cell is suited to its particular function. However, most cells have most of the organelles and parts mentioned in this chapter.

Additional Student Readings

Burger, M. M. and Meyer, D. I., "Puzzling Role of Cell Surfaces." *Chemistry*, January, 1977.

Miller, Julie Ann, "Puzzling Out the Cell's Power Plant." *Science News*, September 15, 1979.

Suggested Teacher Readings

de Robertis, E. D. P., and de Robertis, E. M. F., *Cell and Molecular Biology*, 7th ed. Philadelphia, W. B. Saunders, Co., 1980.

Jordan, E. G., "The Nucleolus," *Carolina Biology Reader*, 2nd ed. Burlington, NC, Carolina Biological Supply Co., 1978.

Lazarides, Elias, and Revel, Jean Paul, "The Molecular Basis of Cell Movement." *Scientific American*, May, 1979.

Lodish, Harvey F., and Rothman, James E., "The Assembly of Cell Membranes," *Scientific American*, January, 1979.

Lucy, J. A., "The Plasma Membrane," 2nd ed. *Carolina Biology Reader*. Burlington, NC, Carolina Biological Supply Co., 1978.

Speer, Henry L., "Using Lettuce Seeds to Demonstrate Osmosis." *American Biology Teacher*, March, 1976.

Swanson, Carl P., and Webster, Peter L., *The Cell*, 4th ed. Englewood Cliffs, NJ, Prentice-Hall, Inc., 1977.

Tucker, Jonathan B., "The Ground Substance of the Living Cell." *Scientific American*, March, 1981.

CHAPTER 6   THE CELLULAR BASIS OF HEREDITY

Teaching Techniques

Cytogenetic, hereditary, and biochemical aspects of reproduction are covered in this and the next three chapters. This material provides a foundation for study of reproduction at the organism level, covered in later chapters.

In teaching the downfall of spontaneous generation, lead students to be critical in their analysis of scientific experiments by reminding them of the methods of science (Chapter 2). Also, point out the history of science and the length of time often necessary to solve a problem.

Understanding of mitosis and meiosis are critical for later work in heredity and genetics. Stress the *result* of each process before proceeding with the details so that students can easily see how each stage leads to the result. It will be helpful to draw out each process on the board and to have students practice drawing them, too.

In teaching Section 6:12, drawings will also be helpful. Understanding of how meiosis and fertilization lead to variation is important for understanding of genetics problems.

Performance Objectives

Goal: Students will gain an understanding of the development of the theory of biogenesis and the cellular basis of heredity.

Objectives: Upon completion of the reading and activities and when asked to respond orally or on a written test, students will:

Section
Number

6:1	K	explain what is meant by the term spontaneous generation.
6:1	P	describe and evaluate the experiment Francesco Redi conducted to test his hypothesis that maggots come from other living things.
6:2	P	describe the experiment conducted by Louis Pasteur which discredited the belief in spontaneous generation.
6:2	K	state the theory of biogenesis.
6:3	P	distinguish between chromatin and chromosomes.
6:3	K	define mitosis as the process in which chromosomes are replicated and distributed to new nuclei.
6:4	K	describe the part of a cell's life cycle known as interphase.
6:4,5	S/P	diagram interphase and the four phases of mitosis, identify the various structures, and explain what happens in each phase.
6:6	P	explain how mitosis usually results in genetic continuity.
6:7	P	differentiate between the diploid number and the monoploid number of chromosomes in a cell.
6:7	K	define homologous and homolog.
6:8	P	compare and contrast zygote, sperm, and egg.
6:8	K	define meiosis as the process which produces sex cells having the monoploid number of chromosomes.
6:9	K/S	diagram the phases of meiosis in a male, identify the various structures, and exlain what happens in each phase.
6:9,10	P	compare and contrast meiosis in a male and a female.
6:5,9,10	P	compare and contrast the process of meiosis and the process of mitosis.
6:11,12	P	explain how the process of meiosis provides for variation among offspring.
6:12	P	explain how meiosis promotes a better chance for survival in the event changes occur in the environment and predict what could happen to an organism if meiosis did not occur.

(See page 41T for performance objectives that apply to all chapters.)

Answers to Chapter 6 Review

Page 114. Checking Your Ideas

1. diploid (2n)
2. biogenesis
3. gametes
4. interphase
5. centromeres
6. cell plate
7. variability
8. monoploid (n)
9. spontaneous generation
10. homologs

Page 114. Evaluating Your Ideas

1. Aristotle believed that some organisms could be produced from nonliving materials; *e.g.*, eels from slime.

2. Redi did not disprove the theory of spontaneous generation. He showed only that maggots are not spontaneously generated. Redi was the first to use experimental procedures to examine spontaneous generation.

3. The essay should focus on Pasteur's realization that microorganisms developed from spores in the air. The neck of the flask was drawn into an S-shape to trap these spores. At the same time air could enter; thus, that objection of the advocates of spontaneous generation was overcome. No spontaneous generation occurred.

4. The theory of biogenesis applies to all living things.

5. The theory of biogenesis states that all living things are reproduced from other living things. Because cells are the basic units of life, cells must be reproduced from other cells.

6. (a) Each chromosome replicates. Cells receive and make needed substances.

(b) The nucleus and nuclear membrane gradually disappear. Chromosomes become distinct as double-stranded structures. In animal cells, the centrioles move apart and the spindle forms between them. (No centrioles are present in plant cells.)

(c) Each centromere attaches to a spindle fiber along the cell's "equator."

(d) The replicated centromeres split. One chromatid of each chromosome is pulled to each pole of the cell. In animal cells, the membrane begins to pinch in. In plant cells, the cell plate begins to form.

(e) The nuclear membrane and nucleolus begin to reform. The chromosomes become indistinct. In animal cells, the membrane continues to pinch in. In plant cells, the cell plate is completed. In both plants and animals, two daughter cells are finally formed.

7. Plant cells have no centrioles or asters. The animal cell divides when the cell membrane pinches together at the cell's center. The plant cell divides by forming a new structure, the cell plate, midway across the original cell.

8. Genetic continuity results in the reproduction of offspring having the same set of characteristics as the parent. Mitosis contributes to genetic continuity by providing each daughter cell with the same kind and number of chromosomes present in the parent cell.

9. Homologous chromosomes are similar pairs of chromosomes. They are similar in size and shape and in the genetic information they carry. They differ slightly in the specific genetic information they contain. For example, one homolog may carry information for brown eyes and the other for blue eyes.

10. The gamete will contain 6 chromosomes, the monoploid number. Each gamete contains the monoploid number; thus, after fertilization the zygote will contain the diploid number.

11. One member of each homologous pair is from the male parent and one is from the female parent.

12. If each gamete did not contain the monoploid number, the zygote would not have 23 pairs of homologs and genetic continuity would be disrupted.

13. (a) Chromosomes appear single-stranded although they may have replicated during interphase. The homologous chromosomes then move close together in synapsis. Pairs of double-stranded chromosomes, tetrads, are clearly visible. The nuclear membrane and nucleolus disappear and the spindle is formed.

(b) Each pair of homologs attaches to a spindle fiber.

(c) One double-stranded homolog of each pair is pulled to each pole.

(d) The original cell is divided into two secondary spermatocyte cells. These cells are monoploid.

14. Meiosis II is normal mitosis except that prophase may be reduced. The cell undergoing meiosis II is monoploid so the products are monoploid. (If the cell undergoing mitosis is diploid the products are diploid.)

15. Meiosis I begins in females before birth and proceeds through the primary oocyte stage. There meiosis ceases until the onset of puberty. Then, each month, several primary oocytes continue meiosis I. In humans and other organisms, prophase I is a very important stage of making and storing needed materials. Unequal division of the oocyte cytoplasm results in most of these materials ending up in the egg. The primary oocyte divides unevenly to produce a smaller cell, the first polar body, and a larger cell, the secondary oocyte. Each cell enters meiosis II. The first polar body may divide again but the products do not survive. The secondary oocyte divides unequally again producing the second polar body and the larger ootid. The polar body disintegrates and the ootid develops into a mature ovum. Eggs can be fertilized before they are mature; sperm must be in their final form before they are functional. An oocyte undergoing meiosis yields one ovum; a spermatocyte yields four sperm.

16. Meiosis reduces the number of chromosomes in gametes to the monoploid number, one of each homologous pair. At fertilization, the diploid number of chromosomes is restored. Mitosis of the zygote results in the production of many cells, each possessing the diploid number. Thus, the new organism has the same genetic information as its parents and develops in the same way.

17. The arrangement of homologs in metaphase I determines the combination of chromosomes in each gamete. Fusion of gametes leads to different combinations of homologs in the zygote.

18. Asexual reproduction results in identical number and kind of chromosomes in each daughter cell. There is no means for genetic recombination. However, mutation can cause changes in chromosomes and chromosomes can separate improperly in mitosis causing variations.

Page 115. Applying Your Ideas

1. By claiming that air was necessary for spontaneous generation, these scientists were perhaps making use of their knowing that they required air to live. In scientific testing it is good to eliminate all but one variable. However, in this case the scientists did not have firm scientific reason to assume air was needed for spontaneous generation.

2. Redi's experiments were controlled with only one variable factor. His work was marked by careful observation and logical thinking.

3. By tipping some flasks so that the infusion comes into contact with the S-shaped neck, it could be shown that microorganisms would then develop in the infusion.

4. Art should follow Figure 6-12 but use 6 rather than 4 chromosomes.

5. Art should follow Figure 6-18 but use 6 chromosomes rather than 4.

6. The sperm cell is equipped with a flagellum which enables it to swim to the egg. Also, it is small, consisting mainly of DNA and very little protoplasm. Thus, it is more motile. The egg is large and contains many nutrients for early development.

7. Student answers will vary. Organisms show variations in size, color, physical structures, behavior, and physiology. Variation in color, for example, could be important if the environment changes. Suppose the environment of a population of dark colored rodents changes so that the color of the ground becomes lighter. Rodents which had the variation of light fur coloration would be less likely to be preyed on. Thus, they would be more likely to survive and reproduce.

8. Each daughter cell would contain four chromosomes of each type because mitosis produces cells with the same number of chromosomes as the parent cell.

Page 115. Extending Your Ideas

1. To prepare temporary mounts of onion root tips, first fix the tips to harden the tissue. Rinse in distilled water one minute and soak in 6N HCl for 3 min. Rinse again in distilled water one minute; then stain with Feulgen reagent for 20 min. Rinse the tips in 45% acetic acid. With a razor blade tease off thin sections on a clean glass slide. Add a coverslip, cover with filter paper and apply pressure to spread out the root tissue. Examine under low, then high power.

2. To examine the giant chromosomes, remove the salivary glands from third instar *Drosophila* larvae under a dissecting microscope by pulling the anterior and posterior ends of the larvae apart with dissecting needles. Put the salivary glands in a drop of aceto-carmine (or aceto-orcein) stain on a clean glass slide. Add coverslip. Put filter paper or a cork stopper on top of the coverslip and gently apply pressure to squash the salivary glands and spread out the chromosomes. Do not smash them. You may want to set these slides up under light microscopes (low and high power) as a demonstration.

3. A yeast solution to be used as an "infusion" for these experiments can be made using powdered yeast or yeast cakes. Other nutrient media can be prepared using clear broths made from bouillon cubes, etc. Some students might use a cork or rubber stopper to prevent air from entering, while others might cover flasks with foil or plastic wrap. To "duplicate" Pasteur's experiment, one end of a piece of glass tubing could be shaped into an "S." The other end could be inserted into a one hole rubber stopper.

Additional Student Readings

John, B. and Lewis, K. R., *Somatic Cell Division*. Carolina Biology Reader, Burlington, NC, Carolina Biological Supply Co., 1980.

Little, M., *et. al.*, eds., *Mitosis: Facts and Questions.* New York, Springer Verlag, Inc., 1977.

Prescott, D. M., *Reproduction of Eukaryotic Cells*. Carolina Biology Reader, Burlington, NC, Carolina Biological Supply Co., 1978.

Suggested Teacher Readings

Epel, David, "The Program of Fertilization." *Scientific American*, November, 1977.

Hawk, J. A., and Crowder, L. V., "Demonstrating Mitosis and Meiosis." *American Biology Teacher*, February, 1976.

Prescott, David M. *The Reproduction of Eukaryotic Cells.* Carolina Biology Reader. Burlington, NC, Carolina Biological Supply Co., 1978.

Sundberg, Marshall D., "Making the Most of Onion Root Tip Mitosis." *The American Biology Teacher*, October, 1981.

CHAPTER 7   PRINCIPLES OF HEREDITY

Teaching Techniques

In going over Mendel's experiments, stress the insight and logic which he used in making his assumptions. His discoveries were extremely amazing considering that he developed his ideas without any knowledge of the cellular basis of heredity. Tie in the facts of meiosis (Chapter 6) while pointing out that Mendel knew nothing of that process. Emphasize that his hypothesis offered a prediction which could be tested by further experimentation.

Spend a good deal of time going over sample and other genetics problems in class, making certain that students become familiar with the sequence of steps necessary. Punnett square solutions may be more advisable with students of lesser mathematical ability. Point out to students that in solving problems where parental genotypes must be determined on the basis of the offspring's characteristics, the recessive genotypes offer the best clue because one of each allele in the offspring must come from each parent. Have them first write out each allele they know for certain and then reason out the other allele.

Performance Objectives

Goal: Students will gain an understanding of genetics and probability and will learn to solve genetics problems.

Objectives: Upon completion of the reading and activities and when asked to respond orally or on a written test, students will:

Section Number		
7:0	K	define genetics as the study of heredity.
7:1	K	describe Mendel's observations of the pea plants.
7:2	K	differentiate between the F_1 generation and the F_2 generation.

7:2	K	state the law of dominance, explain how Mendel arrived at this conclusion, and distinguish dominant and recessive traits.
7:3	K	explain the reasoning by which Mendel assumed that genes segregate during gamete formation.
7:3	S/P	describe a Punnett square and demonstrate its use in determining the possible combinations of characters among offspring.
7:4	K	explain how Mendel tested his hypothesis about segregation and state the law of segregation.
7:5	P	compare and contrast genotype and phenotype.
7:5	K	differentiate between homozygous and heterozygous.
7:6	P	compare and contrast the Punnett square method and the product rule method of solving genetics problems and use one of these methods to solve genetics problems.
7:7	P	compare the genotypic and phenotypic ratios in the solution of a genetics problem.
7:8	P	explain what is meant by incomplete dominance and use either the Punnett square method or product rule method to solve genetics problems involving this concept.
7:9	K/P	state the law of independent assortment and give an example.
7:9	P	use either the Punnett square method or product rule method to solve genetics problems involving two traits.
7:10	P	describe an example in which a trait is governed by more than two alleles.
7:10	P	use either the Punnett square method or product rule method to solve genetics problems involving multiple alleles.

(See page 41T for performance objectives that apply to all chapters.)

Answers to Chapter 7 Review

Page 130. Checking Your Ideas

1.	true	5.	false	9.	false	13.	false
2.	false	6.	false	10.	false	14.	true
3.	true	7.	true	11.	false	15.	false
4.	true	8.	false	12.	true		

Page 130. Evaluating Your Ideas

1. Only one trait of each pair of traits appeared among the offspring. Mendel assumed that one form of each trait dominates the other.

2. The F_2 plants had a ratio of three plants with the dominant trait to one plant with the recessive trait.
3. Mendel reasoned that the sperm and the egg each contained one character for each trait. Thus, at fertilization the offspring would contain two characters for each trait.
4. Mendel tested the law of segregation by predicting the results of a cross which he had not yet performed, $Rr \times rr$. He predicted that the offspring would show a ratio of ½ round and ½ wrinkled. His results confirmed his prediction.
5. Law of dominance: one form of a hereditary trait, the dominant trait, dominates or prevents the expression of the recessive trait. Law of segregation: during gamete formation the pair of genes responsible for each trait separate so that each gamete contains only one gene for each trait. Law of independent assortment: alleles segregate independently during gamete formation.

Page 131. Applying Your Ideas

1. (a) $BB \times bb$
   black $= BB \rightarrow$ all B
   white $= bb \rightarrow$ all b
    all B
   $\underline{\times \text{ all } b}$
    all Bb (genotype)   all black (phenotype)

   (b) $Bb \times Bb$
   black $= Bb \rightarrow$ ½ B + ½ b
    ½ B + ½ b
   $\underline{\times \text{ ½ } B + \text{ ½ } b}$
    ¼ BB + ¼ Bb
   $\underline{ + \text{ ¼ } Bb + \text{ ¼ } bb}$
    ¼ BB + ½ Bb + ¼ bb (genotypic ratio)
    ¾ black : ¼ white (phenotypic ratio)

   (c) $Bb \times bb$
   black $= Bb \rightarrow$ ½ B + ½ b
   white $= bb \rightarrow$ all b
    ½ B + ½ b
   $\underline{ \times \text{ all } b}$
    ½ Bb + ½ bb (genotypic ratio)
    ½ black : ½ white (phenotypic ratio)

2. Genotype of the parents must be Pp. Phenotypes of the parents must be purple-eyed. Purple-eyed offspring could be either PP or Pp. Yellow-eyed offspring must be pp.
3. The ratio among the offspring is 3 dominant (long wing) to 1 recessive (short wing). Therefore, each parent must have been heterozygous *(Ll)*. Three fourths of the offspring would be long wing *(LL or Ll)*. Of these, two thirds would be heterozygous.
4. Brown-eyed man can be either BB or Bb. Blue-eyed woman must be bb. All children must be Bb.
5. (a) $BB \times Bb$
   black $= BB \rightarrow$ all B
   blue $= Bb \rightarrow$ ½ B + ½ b
    ½ B + ½ b
   $\underline{ \times \text{ all } B}$
    ½ BB + ½ Bb (genotypic ratio)
   ½ black: ½ blue (phenotypic ratio)

   (b) $Bb \times Bb$
   blue $= Bb \rightarrow$ ½ B + ½ b
    ½ B + ½ b
   $\underline{\times \text{ ½ } B + \text{ ½ } b}$
    ¼ BB + ¼ Bb
   $\underline{ + \text{ ¼ } Bb + \text{ ¼ } bb}$
    ¼ BB + ½ Bb + ¼ bb (genotypic ratio)
   ¼ black: ½ blue: ¼ white (phenotypic ratio)

(c) $Bb \times bb$

blue $= Bb \rightarrow \frac{1}{2} B + \frac{1}{2} b$

white $= bb \rightarrow$ all b

$\quad\quad \frac{1}{2} B + \frac{1}{2} b$

$\quad\quad \times$ all b

$\quad\quad \overline{\frac{1}{2} Bb + \frac{1}{2} bb}$ (genotypic ratio)

$\quad\quad \frac{1}{2}$ blue: $\frac{1}{2}$ white (phenotypic ratio)

6. The farmer can breed the male to recessive females. If the male is homozygous, no white offspring will be produced. If he is heterozygous, half his offspring should be white.

7. Black smooth parent was $BBrr$. White rough parent was $bbRr$.

8. $I^A I^O \times I^A I^B$

$I^A I^O \rightarrow \frac{1}{2} I^A + \frac{1}{2} I^O$

$I^A I^B \rightarrow \frac{1}{2} I^A + \frac{1}{2} I^B$

$\quad\quad \frac{1}{2} I^A + \frac{1}{2} I^O$

$\quad\quad \times \frac{1}{2} I^A + \frac{1}{2} I^B$

$\overline{\frac{1}{4} I^A I^A + \frac{1}{4} I^A I^O + \frac{1}{4} I^A I^B + \frac{1}{4} I^B I^O}$

(genotypic ratio)

9. (a) Type A is $I^A I^A$. Type B is $I^B I^B$.

(b) Type A is $I^A I^O$. Type B is $I^B I^B$.

(c) Type A is $I^A I^A$. Type B is $I^B I^O$.

(d) Type A is $I^A I^O$. Type B is $I^B I^O$.

10. Mother is $I^B I^O$. Child is $I^O I^O$. Father could not be $I^A I^A$, $I^B I^B$, or $I^A I^B$.

Page 131. Extending Your Ideas

1. Consider each trait separately. For the A's the probability of aa is $\frac{1}{4}$. For the B's, the probability of Bb is $\frac{1}{2}$. For the C's, the probability of Cc is $\frac{1}{2}$. For the D's, the probability of Dd is $\frac{1}{2}$. Therefore, the expected frequency of $aaBbCcDd$ is $\frac{1}{4} \times \frac{1}{2} \times \frac{1}{2} \times \frac{1}{2} = 1/32$.

2. The parental cross will result in offspring all of which have the genotype $AaBb$. A plant of this genotype can then be crossed with a recessive parent. Among the offspring will be plants having the genotypes $AaBb$ and $Aabb$ which can be recognized phenotypically. These plants can then be crossed. Among the offspring will be plants with the genotypes $AAbb$ and $Aabb$. To determine which plant has the desired genotype, cross each plant with a plant $AaBb$ (from the first cross). The plant with the desired genotype, when crossed with $AaBb$, will produce offspring half of which show the dominant A trait and the recessive b trait. The other plant ($Aabb$) when crossed with $AaBb$ will produce some offspring showing the recessive A trait.

3. The ratios of the offspring produced by the various crosses suggest incomplete dominance where oval is the heterozygous condition. Long and round must both be homozygous.

Additional Genetics Problems

1. The parents of a blue-eyed man were both brown-eyed. He marries a brown-eyed woman whose father was brown-eyed and whose mother was blue-eyed. They have one child who is blue-eyed. What are the most probable genotypes of the individuals mentioned?

Answer: Blue-eyed man must be bb. His mother and father must both be Bb. Brown-eyed woman must be Bb. Her father could be either BB or Bb; her mother must be bb. The blue-eyed child must be bb.

2. A man and his wife are both heterozygous for brown eyes. They have six children all of whom have blue eyes. How is this explained? What are the chances that their next child will have brown eyes? What are the chances that their next child will have blue eyes?

Answer: By probability, their children should show a phenotypic ratio of $\frac{3}{4}$ brown eyes: $\frac{1}{4}$ blue eyes. In this case, the probable results simply did not occur. The chances that their next child will have blue eyes are 1 out of 4.

3. In guinea pigs, black coat color, B, is dominant to albino, b. Rough coat, R, is dominant to smooth coat, r. Two animals are selected for breeding. Their genotypes are $BBRR$ and $bbrr$. Specify the expected genotypic and phenotypic ratios (a) in the F_1 generation, (b) in the F_2 generation, and (c) among the offspring produced from crossing one of the F_1 pigs with a pig having the genotype $BBRr$.

Answer:

(a) $BBRR \times bbrr$

black $= BB \rightarrow$ all B

albino $= bb \rightarrow$ all b

$\quad\quad$ all B

$\quad\quad \times$ all b

$\quad\quad \overline{\text{all } Bb}$

rough $= RR \rightarrow$ all R

smooth $= rr \rightarrow$ all r

$\quad\quad$ all R

$\quad\quad \times$ all r

$\quad\quad \overline{\text{all } Rr}$

$\quad\quad$ all Bb

$\quad\quad \times$ all Rr

$\quad\quad \overline{\text{all } BbRr}$ (F_1 genotype)

all black and rough (F_1 phenotype)

(b) $BbRr \times BbRr$

black $= Bb \rightarrow \frac{1}{2} B + \frac{1}{2} b$

$\quad\quad \frac{1}{2} B + \frac{1}{2} b$

$\quad\quad \times \frac{1}{2} B + \frac{1}{2} b$

$\quad\quad \overline{\frac{1}{4} BB + \frac{1}{4} Bb}$

$\quad\quad\quad + \frac{1}{4} Bb + \frac{1}{4} bb$

$\quad\quad \overline{\frac{1}{4} BB + \frac{1}{2} Bb + \frac{1}{4} bb}$

rough $= Rr \rightarrow \frac{1}{2} R + \frac{1}{2} r$

$\quad\quad \frac{1}{2} R + \frac{1}{2} r$

$\quad\quad \times \frac{1}{2} R + \frac{1}{2} r$

$\quad\quad \overline{\frac{1}{4} RR + \frac{1}{4} Rr}$

$\quad\quad\quad + \frac{1}{4} Rr + \frac{1}{4} rr$

$\quad\quad \overline{\frac{1}{4} RR + \frac{1}{2} Rr + \frac{1}{4} rr}$

$\quad\quad \frac{1}{4} BB + \frac{1}{2} Bb + \frac{1}{4} bb$

$\quad\quad \times \frac{1}{4} RR + \frac{1}{2} Rr + \frac{1}{4} rr$

$\overline{1/16\ BBRR + 1/8\ BbRR +}$

$1/16\ bbRR + 1/8\ BBRr +$

$1/4\ BbRr + 1/8\ bbRr +$

$1/16\ BBRR + 1/8\ Bbrr +$

$1/16\ bbrr$ (F_2 genotypic ratio)

9/16 black, rough: 3/16 albino, rough: 3/16 black, smooth: 1/16 albino, smooth (F_2 phenotypic ratio)

(c) $BbRr \times BBRr$

black $= Bb \rightarrow \frac{1}{2} B + \frac{1}{2} b$

black $= BB \rightarrow$ all B

$\quad\quad \frac{1}{2} B + \frac{1}{2} b$

$\quad\quad \times$ all B

$\quad\quad \overline{\frac{1}{2} BB + \frac{1}{2} Bb}$

rough $= Rr \rightarrow \frac{1}{2} R + \frac{1}{2} r$

$$
\begin{array}{l}
\frac{1}{2}\ R\ +\ \frac{1}{2}\ r \\
\times\ \frac{1}{2}\ R\ +\ \frac{1}{2}\ r \\
\hline
\frac{1}{4}\ RR +\ \frac{1}{4}\ Rr \\
\ \ \ \ \ \ +\ \frac{1}{4}\ Rr\ +\ \frac{1}{4}\ rr \\
\hline
\frac{1}{4}\ RR +\ \frac{1}{2}\ Rr\ +\ \frac{1}{4}\ rr \\
\frac{1}{2}\ BB +\ \frac{1}{2}\ Bb \\
\times\ \frac{1}{4}\ RR +\ \frac{1}{2}\ Rr\ +\ \frac{1}{4}\ rr \\
\hline
\frac{1}{8}\ BBRR\ +\ \frac{1}{8}\ BbRR + \\
\frac{1}{4}\ BBRr\ +\ \frac{1}{4}\ BbRr + \\
\frac{1}{8}\ BBrr\ +\ \frac{1}{8}\ Bbrr\ \text{(genotypic ratio)}
\end{array}
$$

$\frac{3}{4}$ black and rough: $\frac{1}{4}$ black and smooth (phenotypic ratio)

4. In fruit flies, red eye, *R*, is dominant to magenta-eyes, *r*. Long wing, *L*, is dominant to short wing, *l*. A heterozygous red-eyed, short-winged male is bred to a magenta-eyed, heterozygous long-winged female. What percentage of their offspring should have magenta eyes and short wings?

Answer: *Rrll* × *rrLl*. Consider each trait separately. Probability of magenta-eyed offspring is $\frac{1}{2}$. Probability of short-winged offspring is $\frac{1}{2}$. Therefore, by the product rule, the probability of a magenta-eyed, short-winged offspring is $\frac{1}{2} \times \frac{1}{2} = \frac{1}{4}$. The problem can also be solved by working out all the possibilities and looking for the genotype, *rrll*.

5. In cattle, black coat, *R*, is dominant to red coat, *r*. Hornlessness, or polled, *H*, is dominant to horned, *h*. A certain bull was mated to four cows. Cow 1, black and hornless, gave birth to a hornless red calf. Cow 2, hornless red, gave birth to a horned black calf. Cow 3, horned black, gave birth to a horned red calf. Cow 4, horned red, gave birth to a hornless black calf. What is the genotype of the bull? What are the possible genotypes of each of the cows and their calves?

Answer: Bull is *RrHh*. Cow 1 could be either *RrHH* or *RrHh*. Calf 1 could be *rrHH* or *rrHh*. Cow 2 is *rrHh*. Calf 2 is *Rrhh*. Cow 3 is *Rrhh*. Calf 3 is *rrhh*. Cow 4 is *rrhh*. Calf 4 is *RrHh*.

6. In a certain kind of flowering plant, tall, *T*, is dominant to short, *t*. Axial flowers, *A*, are dominant to terminal flowers, *a*. Green pods, *G*, are dominant to yellow pods, *g*. Organisms with the genotype *TtAagg* and *TTAaGg* are crossed. Without working out the entire cross, calculate the expected frequency of offspring which will be tall with terminal flowers and green pods.

Answer: The probability for tall is $\frac{1}{1}$. The probability for terminal flowers is $\frac{1}{4}$. The probability for green pods is $\frac{1}{2}$. Therefore, the expected frequency of offspring which will be tall with terminal flowers and green pods is $\frac{1}{1} \times \frac{1}{4} \times \frac{1}{2} = \frac{1}{8}$.

Additional Student Readings

Fincham, J. R., *A Study of Genetic Recombination*, rev. ed. Carolina Biology Reader, Burlington, NC, Carolina Biological Supply Co., 1982.

Vietmeyer, N. D., "Wild Relative May Give Corn Perennial Genes." *Smithsonian*, December, 1979.

Suggested Teacher Readings

Crow, James F., "Genes That Violate Mendel's Rules." *Scientific American*, February, 1979.

Herskowitz, Irwin H., *The Elements of Genetics.* New York, Macmillan Publishing Co., 1979.

Jinks, J. L., "Cytoplasmic Inheritance," 2nd ed. *Carolina Biology Reader.* Burlington, NC, Carolina Biological Supply Co., 1978.

CHAPTER 8   GENES AND CHROMOSOMES

Teaching Techniques

In sections 8:1–8:4, emphasize the accumulation of knowledge which led from Mendel's postulating of hereditary factors to the development of the chromosome theory of heredity. Point out that discoveries made early in this century tied together two branches of biology—genetics and cytology—to produce the field of cytogenetics.

Show students how the work of Mendel, Morgan, and Bridges gradually resulted in the formation of the chromosome theory of heredity. Morgan's and Bridges' discoveries, like those of Fleming (Chapter 2), were unexpected and proved to be extremely valuable.

Review again the concept of meiosis when teaching genetics problems involving sex-linked characteristics and in presenting the concept of nondisjunction. Sections 8:5–8:7 are optional and should be used with students who have clearly demonstrated a mastery of previous genetics problems. (You might wish to consider teaching these topics by assigning them as independent work for able students.)

Sections 8:8–8:10 are relevant and should serve to stimulate class discussion. You might wish to have students present short oral reports about specific human genetic diseases and genetic counseling.

Performance Objectives

Goal: Students will gain an understanding of the chromosomal basis of heredity and the development of genetics since Mendel's time.

Objectives: Upon completion of the reading and activities and when asked to respond orally or on a written test, students will:

Section
Number

8:0   K   describe the reasoning used in developing the hypothesis that one allele for a particular trait is carried on one homolog and that the other allele is carried on the other homolog.

8:1	P	differentiate between the X and Y chromosomes and their role in sex determination.
8:2	K	describe Morgan's experiments with white-eyed fruit flies and explain how the results led to the discovery of sex-linked characteristics.
8:2	K	explain Morgan's hypothesis about the inheritance of sex-linked characteristics and describe the experiment he used to test that hypothesis.
8:3	P	apply the rules of probability or use the Punnett square method to solve a problem involving a sex-linked characteristic.
8:4	K	describe an example of nondisjunction during meiosis.
8:4	P	state and explain the chromosome theory of heredity.
8:5	P	explain how linked genes reduce the chances of genetic recombination and variety among offspring.
8:6	K	explain how crossing-over tends to increase variety among offspring by separating linked genes.
8:6	K	explain how scientists use the results of crossing-over to develop genetic maps.
8:7	K/P	explain continuous variation and describe an example of several pairs of genes controlling one characteristic.
8:8	P	describe examples which indicate that environment may affect the expression of genes.
8:9	K	list several examples of human genetic disease caused by recessive alleles.
8:10	K	explain the causes and symptoms of hemophilia and color-blindness
8:11	K	list and explain the causes of human diseases caused by chromosome defects.
8:12	K	describe several ways genetic diseases may be detected in humans.

(See page 41T for performance objectives that apply to all chapters.)

Answers to Chapter 8 Review

Page 152. Checking Your Ideas

1. environment
2. genes
3. nondisjunction
4. one half
5. oxygen
6. one half
7. linked
8. recessive
9. male
10. crossing-over

Page 152. Evaluating Your Ideas

1. Observation of meiosis did not verify that genes are carried on chromosomes. Similarities between the activities of chromosomes during meiosis and fertilization and Mendel's law of segregation only *suggested* that genes are carried on chromosomes.

2. A human cell contains twenty-two pairs of autosomes.

3. The chances are 50:50.

4. Morgan tested his hypothesis by predicting the results of a cross which he had not yet performed. He predicted that white-eyed females would appear among the offspring produced from crossing a heterozygous female $(X^R X^r)$ with a white-eyed-male $(X^r Y)$. His results confirmed his prediction.

5. Morgan's results did not absolutely verify that genes are carried on chromosomes. He lacked direct evidence. However, his results supported the hypothesis.

6. Nondisjunction occurs when homologous chromosomes fail to segregate properly during meiosis. Gametes missing a chromosome or with an extra chromosome may be produced as a result of nondisjunction.

7. Genes are located on chromosomes.

8. If no crossing-over occurs, gametes would contain A and b or a and B. If crossing-over occurs, gametes would contain A and b, a and B, A and B, or a and b.

9. The plant heights are governed by multiple factors.

10. Nondisjunction could result in the production of abnormal eggs (XX) or abnormal sperm (XY). If either of these joined with a normal gamete, the result would be XXY. The person would be male.

11. Identical twins have the same genotypes. Therefore, differences in their development are at least partially caused by the environment.

12. (a) $X^R X^r \times X^R Y$ (parental genotypes)
$X^R X^r \rightarrow \frac{1}{2} X^R + \frac{1}{2} X^r$
$X^R Y \rightarrow \frac{1}{2} X^R + \frac{1}{2} Y$

$\frac{1}{2} X^R + \frac{1}{2} X^r$
$\times \frac{1}{2} X^R + \frac{1}{2} Y$
$\overline{\frac{1}{4} X^R X^R + \frac{1}{4} X^R X^r + \frac{1}{4} X^R Y + \frac{1}{4} X^r Y}$
(genotypic ratio)
$\frac{1}{2}$ red-eyed females: $\frac{1}{4}$ red-eyed males: $\frac{1}{4}$ white-eyed males (phenotypic ratio)

(b) $X^R X^r \times X^r Y$ (parental genotypes)
$X^R X^r \rightarrow \frac{1}{2} X^R + \frac{1}{2} X^r$
$X^r Y \rightarrow \frac{1}{2} X^r + \frac{1}{2} Y$

$\frac{1}{2} X^R + \frac{1}{2} X^r$
$\times \frac{1}{2} X^r + \frac{1}{2} Y$
$\overline{\frac{1}{4} X^R X^r + \frac{1}{4} X^r X^r + \frac{1}{4} X^R Y + \frac{1}{4} X^r Y}$
(genotypic ratio)
$\frac{1}{4}$ red-eyed females: $\frac{1}{4}$ white-eyed females: $\frac{1}{4}$ red-eyed males: $\frac{1}{4}$ white-eyed males (phenotypic ratio)

(c) $X^R X^R \times X^R Y$ (parental genotypes)
$X^R X^R \rightarrow$ all X^R
$X^R Y \rightarrow \frac{1}{2} X^R + \frac{1}{2} Y$

$\frac{1}{2} X^R + \frac{1}{2} Y$
$\times$ all X^R
$\overline{\frac{1}{2} X^R X^R + \frac{1}{2} X^R Y}$ (genotypic ratio)
$\frac{1}{2}$ red-eyed females: $\frac{1}{2}$ red-eyed males (phenotypic ratio)

(d) $X^R X^R \times X^r Y$ (parental genotypes)

$X^R X^R \rightarrow$ all X^R

$X^r Y \rightarrow \frac{1}{2} X^r + \frac{1}{2} Y$

$$\frac{\frac{1}{2} X^r + \frac{1}{2} Y \times \text{all } X^R}{\frac{1}{2} X^R X^r + \frac{1}{2} X^R Y}$$
(genotypic ratio)

$\frac{1}{2}$ red-eyed females: $\frac{1}{2}$ red-eyed males (phenotypic ratio)

13. Mother is $X^H X^h$. Father is $X^H Y$. Normal son is $X^H Y$. Hemophiliac son is $X^h Y$. Two normal daughters could be either $X^H X^H$ or $X^H X^h$.

14. $X^C X^c bb \times X^c Y Bb$ (parental genotypes)

$X^C X^c \rightarrow \frac{1}{2} X^C + \frac{1}{2} X^c$

$X^c Y \rightarrow \frac{1}{2} X^c + \frac{1}{2} Y$

$$\frac{\frac{1}{2} X^C + \frac{1}{2} X^c \times \frac{1}{2} X^c + \frac{1}{2} Y}{\frac{1}{4} X^C X^c + \frac{1}{4} X^c X^c + \frac{1}{4} X^C Y + \frac{1}{4} X^c Y}$$

$bb \rightarrow$ all b

$Bb \rightarrow \frac{1}{2} B + \frac{1}{2} b$

$$\frac{\frac{1}{2} B + \frac{1}{2} b \times \text{all } b}{\frac{1}{2} Bb + \frac{1}{2} bb}$$

$\frac{1}{4} X^C X^c + \frac{1}{4} X^c X^c + \frac{1}{4} X^C Y + \frac{1}{4} X^c Y$

$\times \frac{1}{2} Bb + \frac{1}{2} bb$

$\frac{1}{8} X^C X^c Bb + \frac{1}{8} X^c X^c Bb + \frac{1}{8} X^C Y Bb + \frac{1}{8} X^c Y Bb + \frac{1}{8} X^C X^c bb + \frac{1}{8} X^c X^c bb + \frac{1}{8} X^C Y bb + \frac{1}{8} X^c Y bb$ (genotypic ratio)

$\frac{1}{8}$ brown-eyed females with normal vision: $\frac{1}{8}$ blue-eyed females with normal vision: $\frac{1}{8}$ brown-eyed, color blind females: $\frac{1}{8}$ blue-eyed, color blind females: $\frac{1}{8}$ brown-eyed males with normal vision: $\frac{1}{8}$ blue-eyed males with normal vision: $\frac{1}{8}$ brown-eyed, color blind males: $\frac{1}{8}$ blue-eyed, color blind males (phenotypic ratio)

15. The alleles governing these traits are probably linked.

16. Human genetic diseases may be a result of abnormal autosomal alleles (sickle-cell anemia, Tay-Sachs, PKU), sex-linked alleles (hemophilia and color-blindness), or chromosomal defects (Down, Turner, and Klinefelter syndromes).

17. Some genetic diseases can be detected by amniocentesis. In amniocentesis, some of the fluid surrounding the fetus is withdrawn and analyzed for the presence or absence of certain chemicals. Fetal cells found in this fluid can also be studied for chromosomal abnormalities. Ultrasound gives an image produced by sound waves that "echo" back from the fetus. Fetoscopy allows direct observation of a fetus through use of an endoscope. These procedures may reveal abnormalities, also.

Page 153. Applying Your Ideas

1. Alleles A and B are 10 linear units apart. Alleles A and C are 20 linear units apart. Alleles B and C are 10 linear units apart. Since B is 10 units from A and C is 20 units from A and 10 units from B, the sequence must be $A—B—C$.

2. The alleles must be linked; therefore, they do not segregate independently. If the genes were not linked the phenotypic ratio would be $\frac{1}{4}$ tall and red: $\frac{1}{4}$ short and red: $\frac{1}{4}$ tall and white: $\frac{1}{4}$ short and white.

3. There would be no phenotypic change because chromatids of the same chromosome contain exactly the same genes; they are replicas.

Page 153. Extending Your Ideas

1. If the sample is large enough, the graph should be bell-shaped. This result indicates continuous variation and multiple genes.

2. Special stocks of *Drosophila* having two linked, recessive alleles can be obtained from biological supply houses. Cross these with wild type flies. Then, backcross virgin F_1 females to the recessive male parents. Since the genes are linked, the expected phenotypic results are one-half both wild traits and one-half both recessive traits. Small numbers of flies having other combinations (one wild and one recessive trait) indicate crossing over.

3. A kit for this experiment may be obtained from Carolina Biological Supply Co. Seeds are F_2 and show incomplete dominance. A phenotypic ratio of 1 green: 2 yellow-green: 1 yellow results under normal lighting conditions. However, varying lighting conditions will alter the ratio. This experiment illustrates heredity-environment interaction.

Additional Student Readings

Randal, Judith, "Breeding the Perfect Cow." *Science 81*, November, 1981.

Rensberger, Boyce, "Tinkering With Life." *Science 81*, November, 1981.

Rosenfeld, Albert, "The Heartbreak Gene." *Science 81*, December, 1981.

"Seeing Inside a Living Fetus." *Science Digest*, August, 1981.

Suggested Teacher Readings

Chedd, Graham, "Who Shall Be Born?", "Wrongful Life." *Science 81*, January-February, 1981.

Fuchs, Fritz, "Genetic Amniocentesis." *Scientific American*, June, 1980.

Herskowitz, Irwin H., *The Elements of Genetics*. New York, Macmillan Publishing Co., 1979.

Rosenfeld, Albert, "The Patient in the Womb." *Science 82*, January, 1982.

CHAPTER 9   THE GENETIC CODE

Teaching Techniques

This chapter deals with some of the most exciting and contemporary aspects of genetics. Moreover, it expands topics covered in Chapters 6–8. Students should understand that knowledge about nucleic acid control explains more fully and complements knowledge about mitosis, meiosis, and genetics. Refer back to these concepts as you teach the replication and functions of DNA and tie them all together.

Visual aids are valuable in teaching this chapter. You may wish to have students "build" some kinds of models to demonstrate the structure, replication, and functions of DNA and RNA. Sections 9:12 and 9:13 are optional and geared for more able students.

Performance Objectives

Goal: Students will gain an understanding of the chemical basis for the transmission of traits and of the features of genes and their chemical structure.

Objectives: Upon completion of the reading and activities and when asked to respond orally or on a written test, students will:

Section Number		
9:1	K	describe Griffith's experiment in which DNA caused transformation to occur in *Pneumococcus* bacteria.
9:2	K	indicate how DNA nucleotides join and sketch a segment of a DNA molecule.
9:3	P	describe the structure and replication of DNA and relate this to the process of mitosis and meiosis.
9:4	K	explain how differences in enzymes and other proteins can cause differences among cells.
9:5	K	indicate that genes are responsible for the synthesis of proteins.
9:6	K	explain why at least three bases in a row are needed to represent one amino acid.
9:6	P	compare and contrast the structure of RNA and DNA.
9:7	K	describe the production of messenger RNA.
9:8	K	explain the structure and function of transfer RNA.
9:7, 8	P	compare and contrast transcription and translation.
9:9	P	distinguish gene mutations and chromosome mutations.
9:9	P	describe an example in which a mutation affecting the sex cells might spread throughout an entire population.
9:10	K	describe functions of DNA outside the cell nucleus.
9:11	K	explain how a given genotype results in a particular phenotype.
9:12	P	compare and contrast structural, regulator, and operator genes.
9:12	K	explain the process of enzyme induction in a prokaryote.
9:13	K	identify several factors which influence genetic control in eukaryotes.

(See page 41T for performance objectives that apply to all chapters.)

Answers to Chapter 9 Review.

Page 174. Checking Your Ideas

1.	h	6.	c
2.	j	7.	e
3.	d	8.	b
4.	g	9.	f
5.	a	10.	i

Page 174. Evaluating Your Ideas

1. He assumed that they were originally rough *Pneumococcus* which had been transformed by the dead, smooth cells. He assumed that a chemical was responsible.

2. Griffith's experiment was tested by adding an extract from smooth *Pneumococcus* to a culture medium on which rough cells were growing. Some of the rough cells were transformed into smooth cells. These smooth cells reproduced to form other smooth cells. The controls, rough cell cultures to which no extract was added, produced no smooth cells.

3. A model is a description that helps one visualize or picture something. By constructing a model of DNA, Watson and Crick hoped to explain the properties of DNA, especially its ability to replicate. They succeeded in explaining certain properties of DNA with their model.

4. Student sketches will vary depending on the sequence of bases they choose. It is important that they show proper base pairing in their drawings. The drawings should be similar to (although they may be simpler than) Figure 9-6.

5. During interphase, DNA is replicated. Replication is necessary so that after mitosis each daughter cell has a set of DNA identical to that of the parent cell. If replication did not occur during interphase, daughter cells would not get DNA identical to the parent cell in mitosis.

6. Genes direct the synthesis of proteins (or polypeptides).

7. To provide enough code "words," a sequence of at least three bases in a row must make up a codon. Each codon represents a particular amino acid.

8. Student sketches should show an mRNA segment that is complementary to one strand of the DNA they drew in question 4. (See Figure 9-10.) The mRNA contains information about the kind and sequence of amino acids needed to synthesize a particular protein.

9. There are as many different kinds of tRNA molecules as there are codons, at least one for each kind of amino acid.

10. Student sketches will vary. (See Figure 9-12). It is crucial that student drawings show proper base pairing.

11. The gene would be at leat 4500 bases long. (It could be longer if it contained introns.)

12. Mutations may be caused spontaneously or by outside agents such as radiation, extreme heat, or chemicals. The mutation can be passed to future generations if it occurs in the DNA of sex cells and if the DNA is replicated as if it were normal.

13. Parts of chromosomes may be dropped off or improperly rearranged during crossing-over.

14. Mutations occurring in body cells are not passed on to future generations. However, mutations in sex organs can lead to the production of abnormal gametes. Therefore, they may affect future generations. Some may be lethal in

homozygous form. Other mutations contribute to variety among the population.

15. Some DNA outside the nucleus is found in certain organelles, such as mitochondria and chloroplasts. Organelle DNA codes for tRNA's, RNA of ribosomes, and other proteins involved in respiration and photosynthesis.

16. Manufacture of sucrase is an example of enzyme induction. Sucrose is an inducer. It combines with repressor molecules produced by a regulator gene. The repressors can no longer block the operator gene. Thus, sucrase can be synthesized. This process is adaptive because the cell makes these enzymes only when necessary.

17. Addition of proteins, methylation, RNA processing, splicing, unmasking of messages, transport, and addition of other chemicals are all thought to be involved in eukaryotic gene control. Students may detail any of these processes in their answers.

Page 175. Applying Your Ideas

1. The enzyme would be closer to normal if the mutation occurred near the end of the gene because most codons would be translated correctly. Thus, the enzyme might still have the proper active site. If the mutation occurred at the beginning of the gene, the entire sequence of codons would be shifted and an entirely different enzyme would be produced.

2. The supposed free-living ancestors of mitochondria and chloroplasts would have had their own genetic machinery. Some of this machinery may have remained after they became organelles if in fact this is the way they arose. Evidence indicates that chloroplasts may have arisen this way but that mitochondria probably did not. (See Section 10:13.)

3. (a) The R alleles produce an enzyme which is used to make red pigment.

(b) The r alleles produce an enzyme which is used to make blue pigment.

(c) The R allele and the r allele are both active. The enzymes produced result in purple pigment.

4. Because both alleles are present in each red cell, part of the hemoglobin will be normal and part abnormal. The cells might be expected to have some sickled cells and some normal cells.

Page 175. Extending Your Ideas

1. Styrene plastic, balsa wood, or clay could be used. Toothpicks or pieces of wire could be used to hold parts together.

2. X-ray diffraction involves passing a beam of X rays through a crystallized material. The beam is diffracted (scattered) as it hits the individual atoms of the crystal. A special X-ray sensitive film positioned behind the crystal records a pattern which indicates the molecular structure of the material. Although the molecule itself is not visible, a good idea of its structure is possible. When the technique was used to analyze DNA, the pattern showed that the molecule is a spiral with the bases stacked atop one another in a linear arrangement.

3. Meselson and Stahl labelled the DNA of *E. coli* with isotopes of ^{15}N. The *E. coli* were then transferred to media containing ^{14}N. After one division, the DNA was found, by means of centrifugation, to contain 50% ^{14}N and 50% ^{15}N. After two generations, the DNA was found to contain 75%

^{14}N and 25% ^{15}N. These data are expected if each strand of the DNA molecule serves as a template for the synthesis of another strand. Each new strand would contain only the ^{14}N isotope.

Taylor, Woods, and Hughes used a technique called radioautography in which a sensitive film records radioactive emissions. Cells of a bean plant were made radioactive by exposure to tritium (^3H) atoms. Cells were then grown in a medium containing nonradioactive hydrogen. After one division, the film showed that only one strand of each chromosome contained tritium. Again, this result is expected if the chromosomes are composed of double-stranded DNA in which one strand serves as a template for the synthesis of another.

4. You will be able to find several good references from journals such as *Science* by a quick check of the *Reader's Guide to Periodic Literature.*

5. "Killer" paramecia produce a poison. It has been found that this trait is not governed by nuclear DNA, but by kappa particles, small bodies in the cytoplasm. Biochemical analysis reveals that kappa particles contain DNA. Kappa particles are capable of replication. However, a certain nuclear gene is necessary for this replication.

Additional Student Readings

Chedd, Graham, "Genetic Gibberish in the Code of Life." *Science 81*, November, 1981.

"How Are Proteins Made?" *Science Digest*, March, 1982.

Keller, Evelyn Fox, "McClintock's Maize." *Science 81*, October, 1981.

Suggested Teacher Readings

Baumel, Howard B., "Archibald Garrod: Forgotten Link to Modern Genetics." *The Science Teacher*, September, 1975.

Chambon, Pierre, "Split Genes." *Scientific American*, May, 1981.

Chedd, Graham, "Genetic Gibberish in the Code of Life." *Science 81*, November, 1981.

Fiddes, John C., "The Nucleotide Sequence of a Viral DNA." *Scientific American*, December, 1977.

Gorman, James, "The Case of the Selfish DNA." *Science 81*, June, 1981.

Herskowitz, Irwin H., *The Elements of Genetics.* New York, Macmillan Publishing Co., 1979.

Howard-Flanders, Paul, "Inducible Repair of DNA." *Scientific American*, November, 1981.

Jackson, Richard J., *Protein Biosynthesis.* Carolina Biology Reader. Burlington, NC, Carolina Biological Supply Co., 1978.

Maniatis, Tom, and Ptashne, Mark, "A DNA Operator-Repressor System." *Scientific American*, January, 1976.

Schimke, Robert T., "Gene Amplification and Drug Resistance." *Scientific American*, November, 1980.

Stein, Gary S., Stein, Janet Swinehart, and Kleinsmith, Lewis J., "Chromosomal Proteins and Gene Regulation." *Scientific American*, February, 1975.

Vigue, Charles L., "A Short History of the Discovery of Gene Function." *American Biology Teacher*, December, 1976.

Watson, James D., *Molecular Biology of the Gene*, 3rd ed. Menlo Park, CA, W. A. Benjamin, Inc., 1976.

CHAPTER 10 CHANGE WITH TIME

Teaching Techniques

Discuss with students at the outset that evolution is the way that most biologists explain the answers to the questions posed in the Unit Introduction. Sections 10:1–10:6 show students that there is a great deal of evidence that evolution occurs. The evidence becomes even more meaningful considering that there are so many different lines of it and that the lines tend to support one another.

Teaching of Lamarckism is valuable for three reasons. It (1) shows the history of the development of a major biological principle, (2) is the way many laypersons conceive of evolutionary change, and (3) shows the weakness of an early "scientific explanation."

In teaching Darwin's theory of evolution by natural selection, emphasize the differences between his explanation and that of Lamarck. Have students explain hypothetical evolutionary changes in Lamarckian and Darwinian terms and lead them to see the inadequacies of the former and the strengths of the latter. Point out that all the subsequent discoveries in genetics support and strengthen Darwin's concept of evolution.

Performance Objectives

Goal: Students will gain an understanding of evolution, the causes of changes in population gene pools, and how a biologist studies relationships among organisms and their ancestors as evidence supporting the theory of evolution.

Objectives: Upon completion of the reading and activities and when asked to respond orally or on a written test, students will:

Section
Number

10:1	K	define and cite examples of fossils and describe how they are formed.
10:1	K	describe how scientists use radioactive isotopes to determine the age of fossils.
10:2	K	describe how fossil records are used to support the ideas that organisms evolve and that organisms living today are descendants of organisms which lived previously.
10:3	K	list ways in which comparative anatomy supports the concept of evolution and cite examples of homologous organs or parts.
10:4	P	explain how comparative embryology and biochemistry support the concept of evolution.
10:5	P	indicate the relationship between genetic recombination resulting from mutations and evolution.
10:6	K	explain how bacterial resistance to penicillin provides direct evidence of evolution.
10:7	K	state Lamarck's law of use and disuse and law of inheritance of acquired characteristics.
10:7	P	explain why it is not possible for organisms to inherit acquired characteristics.
10:8	K	give lines of evidence which led Darwin to conclude that organisms evolve.
10:9	K	explain what is meant by Darwin's theory of natural selection and use it to explain an example of evolutionary change.
10:10	P	compare and contrast explanations of change given by Lamarck and Darwin.
10:11	K	describe the experiments conducted by Miller to test Oparin's hypothesis concerning the origin of life.
10:12	K	explain the steps which might have led to the evolution of the first cells.
10:13	P	compare and contrast the two theories of the origin of eukaryotic cells.

(See page 41T for performance objectives that apply to all chapters.)

About Evolution and Creation

In addition to the answers furnished by biologists, there are, of course, the answers furnished by theologians and other religious people. Some of their answers agree with those of the biologists; some do not. Many biologists, as well as theologians, believe in God as the Creator of the world. But they also believe that God gave living creatures the ability to adapt to changing environments—and that, because of this ability, living creatures have evolved and developed into today's species. Some of these species closely resemble one another and some are quite different. In other words, there need not be a conflict between those who believe that God created all living things and those who believe that living things have evolved over time. One can believe in evolution (or not believe in it) regardless of one's *religious* beliefs.

There is nothing in the theory of evolution that is contrary to the religious beliefs of many people; and there is nothing in their religious beliefs that is *necessarily* contrary to the theory of evolution. Religious and biological explanations need not be mutually exclusive.

Some may say that the theory of evolution is in conflict with the biblical account of the creation of humans. Strictly speaking, this is not so. If one takes every statement in the Bible as being *literally* true, there will indeed be conflict. But one can accept the *spirit* of the biblical account, recognizing God as the Creator of humans, and still regard them as the product of eons of evolutionary development. In this view, the evolutionary development which ended in humans was set in motion by God.

Answers to Chapter 10 Review

Page 198. Checking Your Ideas

1. true	**6.** false
2. false	**7.** true
3. true	**8.** false
4. true	**9.** true
5. true	**10.** false

Page 198. Evaluating Your Ideas

1. Most fossils form when something prevents the decay of a dead organism or any of its parts. If an organism or any of its parts is quickly surrounded and compressed by clay or sand after its death, decomposition is prevented. As the sediments turn to rock, the organism or part is preserved.

2. The fossil record reveals that many organisms are extinct. Also, older fossils are generally less complex than more recent ones. These observations have led scientists to conclude that simple forms of life existed first and that they were gradually replaced by more complex organisms. In general, it seems that life has changed.

3. It can be determined if the structures are homologous. Homologous structures indicate organisms had a common ancestor.

4. Homologous structures indicate a common ancestry and, therefore, a close relationship.

5. Closely related organisms share a common pattern of development. Organisms with similar chemicals, especially proteins, share a common heritage. Because proteins are synthesized according to DNA instructions, comparison of proteins is an indirect way of comparing genes. Modern genetics explains the origins of genetic change—mutation and recombination.

6. Several bacterial cells, when exposed to drugs, may survive while most cells die. Those that survive produce offspring which are also resistant to the drugs. The population of bacteria evolves in that, over a period of time, all bacteria become drug resistant.

7. (a) Lamarck's law of use and disuse is poor because it implies a degree of awareness on the part of each individual. Plants and other organisms are not capable of this effort.

(b) Inheritance of acquired characteristics requires a mechanism whereby changes in body cells are transmitted to sex cells. This mechanism doesn't exist. More significantly, no experiment has ever verified Lamarck's assumptions.

8. Darwin thought that if conditions on Earth had changed then organisms must also have changed because they must be suited to their environments. His study of the fossil record suggested that one form of life evolved into another. Analysis of unique life forms on the Galapagos Islands revealed their relationship to organisms in other geographic areas.

9. From reading Malthus' essay, Darwin reasoned that there must be a struggle for existence because many more organisms are produced than survive. In thinking about selective breeding, he realized that variations can be inherited. From these things he envisioned a process in nature which resembled the process of artificial selection. He called this process natural selection.

10. In nature there is a tendency toward overproduction. Some organisms fail to survive in the struggle for existence. Variations exist in any population. Variations are inherited. Those organisms having variations suitable to their environment tend to survive and pass on their variations to future generations. Unsuitable variations are gradually eliminated and the population as a whole becomes better suited to its environment.

11. Miller's experiment shows that if the presumed conditions on primitive Earth were as believed, it is possible that organic compounds could have been spontaneously produced. However, because no one knows exactly what these primitive conditions were, the question is not definitely answerable.

12. Simple, organic molecules might have reacted to form larger compounds such as fats, proteins, and nucleotides. In the oceans, groups of these molecules might have come together and a membrane could have formed around them. Organic molecules in the ocean (sugars) might have served as an energy source, with some proteins used as enzymes in anaerobic respiration. Eventually, nucleic acids took control of cellular activities and reproduction, which could have led to a simple, prokaryotic cell.

13. Autotrophs provided a source of food to heterotrophs. In addition, they produced free oxygen which could be used in aerobic respiration. Thus, food could be oxidized more efficiently.

14. Photosynthesis is a more complex process than fermentation. It seems more likely that the simpler process would evolve first.

Page 199. Applying Your Ideas

1. The half-life of carbon 14 is approximately 5730 years. After that period, half of the original carbon would remain. After another 5730 years, only one quarter of the original carbon would remain. Therefore, the fossil is about 11 460 years old.

2. Answers c and d are example of homologous pairs of structures.

3. Organisms which produce many of the same enzymes would have similar genes. Thus, the organisms would be related.

4. Lamarck would have said that the insects evolved their color by "use," i.e. conscious effort. Each generation would pass this acquired characteristic on to its offspring and eventually the entire population had the protective color. Darwin would have said that originally the population contained some insects with a nonprotective color and some with a protective color. Those with the protective color would have a better chance to survive and reproduce. Therefore, the variation for protective color would be inherited by the next generation. Insects having the variation for the nonprotective color would be less likely to survive and reproduce. Therefore, that variation would be gradually eliminated from the population.

5. Bacteria might become resistant to the drugs. Then, when needed, the antibiotic would give no protection from (would not kill) the bacteria.

6. (a) Mendel showed that genetic characteristics were inherited in a predictable way. This finding supports the idea that variations exist and can be inherited.

(b) Mitosis explains the mechanism by which variations (on chromosomes) are replicated. Meiosis and fertilization explain how different combinations of variations arise among offspring.

(c) Mutation and crossing-over explain the sources of variations.

(d) The role of DNA explains how variations arise on a biochemical level.

Page 199. Extending Your Ideas

1. *Archaeopteryx*, a primitive bird, retained many reptilian characteristics. Among these were teeth, forelimbs modified as wings but with three claws, large hind limbs, and a long tail composed of numerous small bones.

2. Students might investigate methods of breeding in plants such as corn and wheat and fruits such as apples. Among animals, cattle, horses, and poultry are interesting examples.

3. Darwin also analyzed causes of positive phototropism (Section 22:9), investigated communication in animals, and studied methods of fertilization in plants.

4. Students will be interested in the forms of life found only on the Galapagos Islands. Land birds were rare but one group, commonly called Darwin's finches (Section 11:6), greatly influenced Darwin's thinking about evolution.

5. The Gingko tree, *Ginkgo biloba*, is the only surviving member of a class of primitive gymnosperms which once were abundant. Unlike today's gymnosperms, they have motile, flagellated sperms which develop from pollen. Fertilization occurs within the female reproductive structure (separate sexes of trees exist). The unprotected seed develops into a structure which resembles a fruit. Students should be able to find other "living fossils" on which to report, too.

6. A paleontologist studies fossils. Study of fossils may reveal not only the physical details of extinct organisms, but also their behavior. Paleontology may also provide clues about the physical environment and evolutionary relationships.

Additional Student Readings

Garmon, Linda, "A New Recipe for Primordial Soup." *Science News*, January 31, 1981.

"New Carbon Calendar." *Science Digest*, June, 1982.

Olshevsky, George, "Dinosaur Renaissance." *Science Digest*, August, 1981.

Suggested Teacher Readings

Baumel, Howard B., "Alfred Wallace: Man in a Shadow." *The Science Teacher*, April, 1976.

Dickerson, Richard E., "Chemical Evolution and the Origin of Life." *Scientific American*, September, 1978.

Grant, V., *Organic Evolution*. San Francisco, W. H. Freeman, 1977.

Henig, Robin M., "The Evolution Revolution." *Sciquest*, January, 1982.

Hinds, David S., and Amundson, John C., "Demonstrating Natural Selection." *The American Biology Teacher*, January, 1975.

Mayr, Ernst, "Evolution." *Scientific American*, September, 1978.

Schopf, J. W., "The Evolution of the Earliest Cells." *Scientific American*, September, 1978.

Rosenthal, Dorothy B., "Using Species of *Drosophila* to Teach Evolution." *American Biology Teacher*, December, 1979.

Russell, Dale A., "The Mass Extinctions of the Late Mesozoic." *Scientific American*, January, 1982.

CHAPTER 11   ADAPTATION AND SPECIATION

Teaching Techniques

A primary criticism of the idea of evolution is that complex adaptations could not possibly have arisen as a result of "mistakes" (mutations). Section 11:2 discusses the idea that evolution is a slow and gradual process characterized by descent with modification. There is no goal or final form to evolution (the philosophy of teleology); rather, natural selection works with characteristics already present. If a variation occurs which in any way is a selective advantage, then it is likely to spread through a population. Emphasize the gradualness of evolution throughout the chapter.

In discussing speciation, make certain that students distinguish between geographic isolation and reproductive isolation. The former *initiates* whereas the latter marks completion of speciation. Confusion may arise because students will (correctly) think that, when geographically isolated, organisms also are reproductively isolated. This phenomenon is known as extrinsic reproductive isolation. It is due only to the fact that the groups cannot get together to mate. After speciation is complete, the two groups could not mate even if the barrier were removed. This phenomenon is intrinsic reproductive isolation, the type referred to in the text.

Performance Objectives

Goal: Students will gain an understanding of the evolution of adaptations and of new groups of organisms.

Objectives: Upon completion of the reading and activities and when asked to respond orally or on a written test, students will:

Section Number		
11:1	P	explain the relationship between adaptation and ability for survival and reproduction.
11:2	P	cite an example of a series of adaptations which would support the idea that evolution is a series of minor changes.
11:3	P	describe industrial melanism and how it illustrates interaction of organism and environment.
11:3	P	explain how neutral mutations may later become important to a population.
11:4	P	compare and contrast morphological adaptations, physiological adaptations, and behavioral adaptations and give examples.
11:5	P	compare and contrast adaptations involving camouflage, warning coloration, and mimicry.
11:6	K	define the term species.
11:6	K	explain events which may lead to subspecies and then species.
11:6	K	explain what is meant by reproductive isolation.
11:7	K	list conditions necessary for adaptive radiation to occur.
11:7	K/P	define ecological niche and give an example.
11:8	P	explain convergence and give an example.
11:9	K	list several adaptations that make humans unique.
11:8, 9	K	describe the theory of divergent evolution in explaining how humans and apes may have had a common ancestor.
11:10	K/P	list the characteristics of *Australopithecus* and compare them with those of humans.
11:11	P	compare and contrast the characteristics and age of *Homo habilis* and *Homo erectus*.
11:12	P	compare and contrast the characteristics and age of Neanderthals and Cro-Magnons.

(See page 41T for performance objectives that apply to all chapters.)

Answers to Chapter 11 Review

Page 220. Checking Your Ideas

1. convergence
2. geographic
3. hominid
4. behavioral
5. ecological niche
6. reproductive isolation
7. adaptive radiation
8. *Homo*
9. model
10. cryptic coloration

Page 220. Evaluating Your Ideas

1. If a population is "successful" in terms of surviving but the organisms cannot reproduce, the population will not survive through time.

2. In mid-nineteenth century England, most peppered moths were light in color. This light color enabled the moths to blend in with the light color of tree trunks. Black moths were rare. Industrialization created soot which covered the tree trunks. At this point, black moths had an advantage because they blended in with the tree trunks. Light moths were more often eaten by birds. Therefore, the genes for dark color were passed on more often than those for light color. Thus, the gene pool has changed, the organisms have changed over time, and thus, evolution has occurred.

3. Student answers will vary. Examples of morphological adaptations include the muscular walls of the heart for pumping blood, claws of a carnivore for tearing flesh, and wood of a tree for support. Examples of physiological adaptations include conduction of a nerve impulse, influence of hormones on metabolism, and photosynthetic reactions. Behavioral adaptations include the blinking response, the snapping shut of a Venus'-flytrap's leaves, and the pouncing of a cat on a mouse. Of course, the distinctions among the different types is not always clear-cut, as physiological adaptations have morphological aspects, behavioral adaptations have physiological aspects, etc.

4. The eye might have evolved as a result of many discrete steps, each of which resulted in modification of previously existing structures. The sequence of events might have been perception of light → blurred images → clear images.

5. Geographic isolation separates the gene pool of an original population into two gene pools. Thus, the two groups cannot interbreed.

6. In isolated gene pools, different mutations and patterns of genetic recombination occur. The environments also are different. Thus, each group evolves adaptations to the environment in which it is living.

7. One species becomes two new species when those two groups can no longer interbreed to produce fertile offspring.

8. (a) Organisms must be able to reach a new environment, Darwin's finches flew to the Galapagos Islands.
   (b) The ancestors must have basic adaptations for survival in the new environment. The finches survived because the environment of the islands was not very different from that of the mainland.

(c) The new environment must be free from competition with similar, better adapted species. Very few bird species inhabited the islands, and those that did occupied different ecological niches.

9. Humans are not well adapted for a predatory way of life. Tools took the place of their "missing" physical adaptations and enabled them to become more efficient predators as well as permitting them to defend themselves from would-be predators.

10. Early humans, in order to survive, probably had to outsmart animals better adapted for life on the ground. Natural selection favored those early humans who had larger brains. Thus, larger brains evolved and with that greater intelligence. Had human ancestors remained in the trees, a much larger brain might not have evolved because there might not have been the competition that resulted in selection that favored larger brains.

11. *Australopithecus* had upright posture. Its teeth more closely resembled those of humans than apes, but its skull was more apelike. It lived in Africa where there were probably several different species. They may have lived from less than 2 million to 3 to 4 million years ago.

12. *Homo habilis* lived in Africa about 2.0 million years ago. It had a larger brain capacity than *Australopithecus* (700-800 cm³) and was a toolmaker.

13. *Homo erectus* may have lived as long as 1.5 million years ago in Africa. It is possible that this prehuman might have led to the extinction of *Homo habilis* and *Australopithecus*.

14. Neanderthals were more advanced than Java and Peking people, the former having a brain capacity of modern dimensions (1450 cm³) compared to the average of 1000 cm³ of the latter. Their facial features were more like those of modern humans than the features of Java and Peking people.

15. The first modern humans were Neanderthals. They were excellent toolmakers and good hunters. They sometimes buried their dead with sacrifices.

Page 221. Applying Your Ideas

1. It would be better to say that the basis for learning is an adaptation. Some learning is not really adaptive because it does not promote survival and reproduction and is not an inherited characteristic.

2. Many traits may have little adaptive value or their adaptive value may not be apparent. Certainly it seems that eye color and blood type are not essential to survival and reproduction. Such traits, however, may be examples of pleiotropy; i.e., a single pair of genes may have many effects. Perhaps blood type is a phenotype resulting from genes whose other, perhaps adaptive, effects are not understood.

3. The frequency of light-colored moths seems to be increasing slowly.

4. One form is probably the mimic of the other. The butterfly mimicked is probably distasteful or in some other way unattractive to predators. Birds (predators) could be fed both kinds of butterflies. The distasteful form would be rejected while the mimic would be eaten. In another test, the birds could be given free access to the butterflies. The birds, if this is a case of mimicry, should be confused and would avoid eating either of the butterflies.

5. The tiger's stripes tend to hide it as a predator whereas a zebra's stripes protect it as a possible prey organism.

6. The basic structure of the finch was developed over millions of years. In the relatively short time since then, various features of the finch have changed slightly by natural selection, but the finch remains a bird.

7. The two species would have had to evolve in geographic isolation. Later, once they had become distinct species, they might have come to inhabit the same lake.

8. Tooth structure and type of teeth are indicative of eating habits of the organism.

Page 221. Extending Your Ideas

1. The Irish elk evolved an elaborate and large set of antlers. It is hypothesized that at some time these antlers became too much of a burden in terms of both weight and the problem of growing new antlers each year. When they arose, the antlers were probably adaptive; however, it is assumed that environmental changes later caused them to become a hindrance and, in fact, caused the extinction of the organism.

2. These structures were derived from the gill arches of the mammal's fish ancestors.

3. To help students with internal anatomy, provide them with a source of information. If a student is unfamiliar with the functions of the organs discovered, use of reference sources to learn about them is needed. However, encourage the students to think independently in analyzing how each structure is adapted to carry out its functions.

4. Student answers will vary. Present biological evolution of humans is probably more physiological than morphological, especially in less civilized societies. Most human change today is the product of cultural, rather than biological, changes (see Chapter 32).

Additional Student Readings

Hiam, Alexander W., "Airborne Models and Flying Mimics." *Natural History*, April, 1982.

Jastrow, Robert, "Evolution: Selection for Perfection." *Science Digest*, December, 1981.

Suggested Teacher Readings

Day, M. H., *The Fossil History of Man.*, 2nd ed. Carolina Biology Reader. Burlington, NC, Carolina Biological Supply Co., 1977.

DeBeer, Gavin, *Adaptation*, 2nd ed. Carolina Biology Reader. Burlington, NC, Carolina Biological Supply Co., 1978.

Johanson, Donald C., and Edey, Maitland A., *Lucy: the Beginnings of Humankind*. New York, Simon and Schuster, 1981.

Lane, Patricia A., "The Evolutionary Strategy of Mimicry." *The American Biology Teacher*, April, 1977.

Lewontin, Richard C., "Adaptation." *Scientific American*, September, 1978.

Oxnard, Charles E., "Human Fossils: New Views of Old Bones." *American Biology Teacher*, May, 1979.

Sisson, Robert F., "Deception: Formula for Survival." *National Geographic*, March, 1980.

Walker, Alan, and Leakey, Richard E. F., "The Hominids of East Turkana." *Scientific American*, August, 1978.

CHAPTER 12   CLASSIFICATION

Teaching Techniques

Additional examples will be useful in teaching this short but essential chapter. For example, have students suggest ways to classify types of automobiles, schools, or sports.

Explain that classification of organisms varies among biologists and that the modern science of taxonomy is based on the understanding of relationships among organisms. As knowledge of relationships among organisms has improved, biologists have changed from a two-kingdom classification scheme to a five-kingdom system. Modern systems of taxonomy are not only more accurate, but also overcome the inconsistencies inherent in older systems.

Performance Objectives

Goal: Students will gain an understanding of the development and use of the universal system of classification.

Objectives: Upon completion of the reading and activities and when asked to respond orally or on a written test, students will:

Section Number		
12:0	K	identify taxonomy as the science of classifying organisms.
12:1	P	explain why it is necessary that all scientists use a common system of naming and classifying organisms.
12:2	P	describe Aristotle's system for classification.
12:2	P	compare and contrast the classification system used by Aristotle and the system used by Linnaeus.
12:2	K	describe the system of binomial nomenclature.
12:3	K	list factors which are used in classifying organisms: homologous structures, biochemical similarities, and genetics.
12:4	K	list the classification categories in order from general to specific.
12:5	P	explain that more closely related organisms have more similar classifications.
12:6	K	distinguish autotrophs and heterotrophs.
12:6	P	explain why many scientists use a five-kingdom system of classification.
12:6	K	list major traits of organisms in each of the five kingdoms.

(See page 41T for performance objectives that apply to all chapters.)

Answers to Chapter 12 Review

Page 232. Checking Your Ideas

1. c	**5.** i	**8.** f
2. g	**6.** a	**9.** b
3. e	**7.** j	**10.** h
4. d		

Page 232. Evaluating Your Ideas

1. Classification provides a logical means for organizing knowledge about the many forms of life. Living things also are classified so that biologists the world over have a common system for naming organisms. In this way, scientists can communicate without confusion about which organism they are discussing.

2. Aristotle classified animals on the basis of temporary "habitat." Because these habitats could vary, i.e., birds on land, etc., the system was not as useful as one using traits that were more permanent and involved less interpretation, such as the system he used for plants.

3. Linnaeus' classifications were based entirely on structure. His system was better than Aristotle's because it was applied in the same way to all organisms. The theory of evolution would have been helpful to Linnaeus.

4. The *species* level of classification is the most *specific*; it applies to one particular kind of organism.

5. Classification today is based on evolutionary relationships. Therefore, by examining factors such as comparative anatomy, comparative embryology, and the fossil record, taxonomists gain a better insight into the proper classification of organisms.

6. Student answers will vary. The three organisms have hair, mammary glands, placental development, internal skeleton of bone, etc. Humans are different in that they have upright posture, grasping hands, stereoscopic vision, etc.

7. A two-kingdom system of classification is inadequate because there are problems classifying unicellular organisms and organisms which have both plantlike and animal-like characteristics.

8. Plants are mostly multicellular, autotrophic organisms with complex structure. Animals are multicellular, usually mobile organisms. Animals are heterotrophic, ingest their food, and (except for sponges) have nerve cells.

9. Monerans are prokaryotes. Protists are mostly unicellular eukaryotes including both autotrophic and heterotrophic forms. Fungi are mostly multicellular heterotrophs which absorb food.

Page 233. Applying Your Ideas

1. Student answers will vary. Common characteristics include a backbone, a tail, hair, mammary glands, similar internal anatomy, four limbs, and sharp teeth. Cats and dogs differ in shape of skull, arrangement of muscles and bones, climbing abilities, retractility of claws, relative length of tail, and shape of ears.

2. Student answers will vary depending on their familiarity with the animals listed. Encourage students to think of structural similarities and differences. The proper taxonomic groupings are as follows: coelenterates—jellyfish; flatworms—planaria; segmented worms—earthworm; mollusks—clam; arthropods—fruit fly and mosquito (insects) and lobster (crustacean); vertebrates—frog (amphibian), turtle (reptile), ostrich and robin (birds), and baboon, bear, cheetah, horse, human and panther (mammals).

3. The two species are probably products of divergent evolution (speciation).

4. The two groups would be classified as separate species because they are reproductively isolated. The two groups would not interbreed because of the differences in breeding seasons.

5. rat, zebra, elephant, gorilla, ponderosa pine, camel

Page 233. Extending Your Ideas

1. All domesticated dogs are subspecies of the same species. Common examples are the collie, beagle, boxer, terrier, dachshund, and cocker spaniel.

2. In addition to or instead of using a prepared key, you might interest students in constructing a key of their own. Also, students will find differences in the use of a key depending on the season.

3. Classification of protists is more difficult because it involves microscopic examination and many forms are fast-moving. A drop of methyl cellulose solution added to each slide may prove helpful. Refer students to Chapter 13 and Appendix A for classifications.

4. In the two-kingdom system, organisms are grouped as either plants or animals. This system is weak in that many organisms do not fit neatly into either category. The three-kingdom system lumps together simple organisms as protists. Thus, true plants and animals are easily identified. A weakness in the system is that simple organisms have such a variety of features there is no clear basis for grouping them together. Rather, their being classified together is a matter of convenience. The four-kingdom system attempts to solve this problem by splitting off the monerans as a

fourth kingdom. They are placed in a separate kingdom because of their prokaryotic structure. More recently, a five-kingdom system has been accepted. According to this scheme, the fungi are a separate kingdom. Placing the fungi in a separate kingdom provides a separate category for multicellular, heterotrophic, plantlike organisms. The five kingdoms are animals, plants, fungi, protists, and monerans.

5. *Euglena* cultured in the presence of light at room temperature will remain green. Culturing in the dark, at elevated temperature, or in the presence of streptomycin will cause *Euglena* to lose their chloroplasts. This experiment illustrates well a problem of taxonomy. Essentially, a strain of heterotrophic *Euglena* can be produced from autotrophic *Euglena*.

Additional Student Readings

Durant, Mary, *Who Named the Daisy? Who Named the Rose?* New York, Dodd, Mead and Co., 1976.

Gutrick, Martin J., *Science of Classification: Finding Order Among Living and Nonliving Objects.* New York, Watts, Franklin, Inc., 1980.

Rose, Kenneth Jon, *Classification of the Animal Kingdom*, New York, David McKay Co., Inc., 1980.

Suggested Teacher Readings

Gavenas, Emil, "Scavenger Hunt: A Teaching Tool to Reinforce the Basics." *American Biology Teacher*, May, 1981.

Jackson, Donald W., "Tree Bark for Winter Identification." *The Conservationist*, January-February, 1982.

Margulis, Lynn, "How Many Kingdoms? Current Views of Biological Classification." *American Biology Teacher*, December, 1981.

Mayer, E., "Biological Classification: Toward a Synthesis of Opposing Methodologies." *Science*, October 30, 1981.

Morton, George, and Bradley, James, "A More Realistic Approach to Teaching Taxonomy." *American Biology Teacher*, April, 1979.

CHAPTER 13   MONERANS, PROTISTS, FUNGI, AND VIRUSES

Teaching Techniques

This chapter surveys the major phyla of monerans, protists, and fungi, and also includes viruses. In addition to providing phylum names and major characteristics of various representative organisms, it also stresses relevant, practical material which will be of interest to your students.

You may wish to have students learn the phylum names, but that is a matter of choice. However, it is suggested that you have your students learn the major structural characteristics of each phylum as well as some examples. Refer them to Appendix A, *A Classification of Living Systems*, as a self-check on their learning of phylum characteristics. This ap-

pendix can also be used in conjunction with such assignments as you may wish to devise.

Because the simple organisms are less familiar to students than are plants and animals, it will be especially useful to use a variety of supplementary materials such as living and preserved specimens, prepared slides, and projection slides.

Performance Objectives

Goal: Students will gain an understanding of what the moneran, protist, and fungi kingdoms include and learn the basic features of the major groups of organisms in these kingdoms. They will also learn about viruses.

Objectives: Upon completion of the reading and activities and when asked to respond orally or on a written test, students will:

Section Number		
13:1	P	compare and contrast the features of prokaryotes and eukaryotes.
13:2	K	list the characteristics which identify blue-green algae.
13:3	K	list the characteristics which identify the bacteria.
13:4	K	explain how bacteria are important in nature and industry.
13:5, 6 7	P	compare and contrast the algal protists.
13:8	K	list the characteristics of the sarcodines.
13:9	K	list the characteristics of the ciliates.
13:10 11	P	compare and contrast the flagellates and sporozoans.
13:12	K	list the characteristics of the slime molds.
13:13I	K	list the characteristics and classification of fungi.
13:13	K	describe the structures of *Rhizopus* and state their functions.
13:14	K	identify and give the functions of the various parts of a mushroom.
13:15	K	describe several ways in which sac fungi are important.
13:16	K	describe the condition of mutualism in a lichen.
13:17	K	describe the characteristics which identify viruses.
13:18	K	explain why there is a debate as to whether viruses are living.
13:18	K	explain why it is thought that viruses are products of degenerative evolution.
13:19	P	explain how a bacterium can produce a product such as human insulin.

(See page 41T for performance objectives that apply to all chapters).

Answers to Chapter 13 Review

Page 258. Checking Your Ideas

1. prokaryotes
2. mutualism
3. hyphae
4. locomotion
5. fungi
6. Protista
7. nucleic acid
8. bacillus
9. Fungi
10. endospores
11. respiration
12. blue-green
13. ciliates
14. slime mold
15. dinoflagellates

Page 258. Evaluating Your Ideas

1. (a) Eukaryotes have a definite nucleus and nuclear membrane; prokaryotes do not.

(b) The cell wall in eukaryotes, if present, does not contain murein; the cell wall of prokaryotes contains murein.

(c) Eukaryotes have mitochondria, ER, Golgi bodies, and lysosomes; prokaryotes do not have membrane-bound organelles.

(d) Eukaryotic flagella have microtubules; prokaryotic flagella do not.

(e) Chlorophyll in eukaryotes, if present, is located in chloroplasts; if present in prokaryotes, chlorophyll is not located in chloroplasts.

(f) Eukaryotes have several linear chromosomes of DNA and protein; prokaryotes (bacteria) have a single, circular chromosome of DNA and plasmids.

2. Photosynthesis occurs on membrane fragments. There are no chloroplasts.

3. Plasmids are small, circular segments of DNA in bacteria. Some plasmids carry genes which make bacteria resistant to certain antibiotics.

4. Most bacteria are heterotrophic and lead either a parasitic or saprophytic existence. Some species are photosynthetic or chemosynthetic, the latter deriving energy by oxidizing inorganic compounds and using the energy to synthesize carbohydrates.

5. Bacteria are important in nature as they decompose organic materials and aid in the recycling of needed elements. Bacteria are used in the making of many dairy products, vinegar, certain fibers, leather, and antibiotics. They are also important in producing substances by recombinant DNA techniques.

6. Protists include mostly unicellular organisms and some multicellular forms with simple structure and little division of labor. Both autotrophic and heterotrophic forms are found, and some protists employ both types of nutrition. Groups include simple algae, protozoa, and slime molds.

7. Algal protists are mostly aquatic, unicellular producers. They are eukaryotes and have chlorophyll in chloroplasts.

8. Diatoms are a source of silica in the form of diatomaceous earth. Diatoms are also important in the ocean food chain.

9. Protozoa are unicellular, animal-like organisms, most of which are motile. Some are predators, whereas others are parasites. Protozoa undergo both sexual and asexual reproduction.

10. In an amoeba, food-getting and locomotion involve pseudopodia. Paramecia move and obtain food by means of cilia.

11. *Paramecium* is a very complex cell showing much division of labor. Some scientists feel that two nuclei are necessary to control this degree of complexity.

12. The slime mold cycle begins with the yellowish, slimy mass, the plasmodium, composed of many nuclei but no cell walls. The plasmodium moves like an amoeba and eventually develops into many fruiting bodies. The fruiting bodies produce spores by mitosis and release them. Spores develop into swarm cells. In favorable conditions, the flagellated swarm cells congregate to form a new plasmodium. The swarm cells are attracted by a chemical which they secrete. In some species, sexual reproduction occurs from a fusion of two spores. Fused spores may then produce a new plasmodium.

13. Fungi are mostly multicellular heterotrophs which absorb their food from a host or the environment.
14. Thickened walls or hyphae reduce evaporation of water from fungi. Spores are resistant and provide protection until suitable growth conditions occur.
15. Fungi reproduce by forming spores.
16. Zygomycota (sporangium fungi)—*Rhizopus*; Basidiomycota (club fungi)—mushroom; Ascomycota (sac fungi)—yeast.
17. In a lichen, the alga manufactures food by photosynthesis. The food is used by both the alga and fungus. The fungus may protect the alga and hold moisture necessary for the alga's photosynthesis. It may also provide inorganic materials.
18. Degenerative evolution is the loss of certain parts or structures with time. Viruses may be products of such evolution. They may be descendants of more complex living systems which had the characteristics usually associated with life.
19. A gene for a particular product is isolated and inserted into a bacterial plasmid. Both the plasmid and bacterium are reproduced resulting in many copies. The gene product is then made and purified.
20. If the source gene is inserted into a plasmid that contains a drug resistance gene, only bacteria with those plasmids will grow in the presence of the drug.

Page 259. Applying Your Ideas

1. An endospore is a dormant form of bacterial cell which may later become active again. It is a protective adaptation and is not considered reproductive because it does not lead to an increase in the number of organisms.
2. Heterotrophic euglenoids have no stigma. Detection of light does not seem to be adaptive in these organisms.
3. Protozoa were classified as animals because they are heterotrophic and motile. Fungi were classified as plants, mainly because they do not move.
4. The plasmodium stage and swarm cells are animal-like because of their movement, whereas the fruiting body and spore stages are plantlike.
5. A virus resembles a eukaryotic chromosome in that it is a nucleic acid wrapped in protein.
6. Because today's viruses require a host cell to reproduce, it is unlikely that they could have been the first kind of living thing.

Page 259. Extending Your Ideas

1. Students can investigate the manufacturing details of some products such as yogurt, buttermilk, cheese, and butter.

2. Both wheat rust (Section 19:7) and corn smut have complex life cycles. Corn smut is a club fungus which attacks young corn plants. Spores are carried by the wind to other corn plants which they infect.
3. Bacteria can be cultured on sterile agar plates in the laboratory or cultures can be ordered from supply houses. Using sterile procedures, add a drop of disinfectant, mouthwash, etc., to each culture. If the "germ killer" is effective, a clear zone should form around the spot where it was added. Have students try a variety of household products. By marking the bottom of each culture plate in such a way to divide it into sections and then numbering each section, several substances can be tested on a single plate.
4. The fungi develop from spores in the air. Have students observe the fungi with a stereoscopic microscope or hand lens.
5. Some factors thought responsible for changes in form of slime molds include changes in temperature and moisture, diminished food supply, and an excess of violet and blue light. Chemical factors which may be involved include the presence of niacin or the amino acid tryptophan.

Additional Student Readings

Ahmadjian, Vernon, "The Nature of Lichens." *Natural History*, March, 1982.
Keher, Daniel M., "Genes for Profit." *Science Digest*, May, 1982.
"The Littlest Creature." *Science Digest*, December, 1981.

Suggested Teacher Readings

Alexopoulos, C. J., and Mims, C. W., *Introductory Mycology*, 3rd ed. New York, John Wiley, 1979.
Baumel, Howard B., "Genetic Engineering Gains Momentum." *The Science Teacher*, April, 1980.
Gilbert, Walter, and Villa-Komaroff, Lydia, "Useful Protein from Recombinant Bacteria." *Scientific American*, April, 1980.
Lee, Douglas, "Slime Mold—the Fungus That Walks." *National Geographic*, July, 1981.
Raham, R. Gary, "Exploiting the Lichen Liaison." *American Biology Teacher*, November, 1978.
Rensberger, Boyce, "Tinkering with Life." *Science 81*, November, 1981.
Sanders, F. Kingsley, *Viruses*, 2nd ed. Carolina Biology Reader. Burlington, NC, Carolina Biological Supply Co., 1981.

CHAPTER 14   PLANTS

Teaching Techniques

This chapter begins with a discussion of the major groups of complex algae. Section 14:4 identifies the adaptations which allow land plants to survive in a terrestrial environment. This section serves as a focus for class discussion and as a bridge between algae and higher plants. Have students identify how each of the functions is carried out by the algae. Students will be able to see that an aquatic environment is "less demanding" than a dry one and will come to understand reasons for the complexity of the land plants.

Subsequent sections identify the major characteristics of nonvascular (mosses and liverworts) and vascular (club mosses, horsetails, ferns, gymnosperms, and angiosperms) plants. Taxonomy is kept to a minimum. Emphasize how each group is adapted for life on land and the relative limitations and advances from group to group.

Because angiosperms are the most abundant and most familiar plants, their structure is examined in more detail (Sections 14:12, 13, and 14). Basic material about roots, stems, and leaves is presented. More detailed information about angiosperm anatomy is presented in Chapter 22, where plant functions are considered.

Performance Objectives

Goal: Students will gain an understanding of the Plant Kingdom and learn the basic features of the major groups of plants.

Objectives: Upon completion of the reading and activities and when asked to respond orally or on a written test, students will:

Section Number		
14:1I	K	list the characteristics of the algal plants.
14:1	K/P	list the characteristics of green algae and compare and contrast the features of *Chlamydomonas*, *Ulothrix*, and *Volvox*.
14:2, 3	K	list the characteristics of brown algae and red algae.
14:4	K	list plant adaptations for living in a dry environment.
14:4	K	differentiate between vascular plants and nonvascular plants.
14:5	K	list characteristics of bryophytes and why they are limited in size and habitat.
14:5	P	explain how a liverwort is adapted for life on land.
14:6	K	list the characteristics of the plants classified in the phylum Tracheophyta.
14:7	K	describe the features of club mosses and horsetails.
14:8	K	describe the structures of ferns, their means of reproduction, and their adaptations for land life.
14:8	P	explain why ferns are restricted to a moist habitat.
14:9, 10	K	differentiate between gymnosperms and angiosperms.
14:9	K	list the major characteristics of the conifers and describe their means of reproduction.
14:9	P	explain how conifers are better adapted for land life than ferns.
14:10	P	explain the adaptations for reproduction which make angiosperms even more successful than gymnosperms.
14:11	P	compare and contrast the characteristics of monocots and dicots.
14:12	K	identify the major functions of roots.
14:12	K	differentiate between a fibrous root and a taproot system.
14:13	K	identify the major functions of stems and differentiate between herbaceous and woody stems.
14:13	K/P	compare and contrast the functions of terminal and lateral buds and identify the various kinds of scars visible on a stem.
14:14	P	compare and contrast the patterns of palmate and pinnate venation and the patterns of palmately and pinnately compound leaves.

(See page 41T for performance objectives that apply to all chapters.)

Answers to Chapter 14 Review

Page 278. Checking Your Ideas

1. false		**6.** false
2. true		**7.** false
3. true		**8.** false
4. false		**9.** true
5. true		**10.** true

Page 279. Evaluating Your Ideas

1. Algal plants are mostly multicellular. They usually lack tissues, but have some division of labor. The algal body is in the form of a thallus, usually flattened. Development occurs in the water, and there is no protection of the developing plant by the parent plant.

2. *Volvox* is colonial—neither unicellular nor truly multicellular. Cells appear similar but there is some specialization. Some cells are light sensitive. Other cells function in reproduction.

3. Some brown algae have a branched thallus and specialized tissues and organs. They have much greater division of labor than other algae.

4. Red algae contain a type of chlorophyll which can absorb light deeper in the ocean.

5. Land plants are adapted for obtaining and transporting water and dissolved minerals, distributing food, retaining water, obtaining carbon dioxide, support, fertilization on land, and protection of the embryo.

6. Bryophytes have rhizoids which absorb water and minerals from the soil. These materials are transported by diffusion. Food is distributed by diffusion to nonphotosynthetic cells. An outer layer of cutin and the relatively small size of bryophytes decrease water loss by evaporation. Carbon dioxide enters through pores and dissolves in a thin film of water. Bryophytes lack any specialized support system and grow close to the ground. Eggs are enclosed by and fertilized in the tissue of the female plant. Thus, they are protected. Development of the embryo within the female protects the new generation.

7. Bryophytes are limited by their need for water to a moist environment. Lack of transport tissue within bryophytes limits their size. Water also is needed to provide a medium through which sperm can move.

8. Club mosses are small plants with true roots, stems, and leaves. They produce spores in conelike structures. Horsetails are small and have a slender stem upon which wedgeshaped leaves are arranged at several points. Some stems have spore-producing structures.

9. Ferns have vascular tissue for rapid transport of materials. Because ferns do not distribute materials entirely by diffusion, they can attain a greater size. They also have specialized cells for support and control of pore size. Ferns are limited in habitat because they require water for reproduction.

10. Conifers have wood for support. They have male and female cones, each of which produces spores by meiosis. Pollen grains are carried to the female cones by wind. After fertilization, a protective coating (the seed) forms around the embryo. Unlike bryophytes and ferns, conifers do not need water for fertilization. There is also no multicellular monoploid plant like ferns have.

11. Student answers will vary. In angiosperms, reproduction occurs within flowers and seeds are formed within fruits. Pollen grains may be carried from flower to flower by wind or animals. Fruits aid in the dispersal of seeds to regions suitable for growth and development. Make sure students are aware that, in some areas, the conifer's method of reproduction is more successful than the angiosperm's illustrating how terms such as "better" can be misleading sometimes.

12. A pollen grain contains the male gametes. A seed contains the embryo. Seeds are enclosed in fruit which aids in their dispersal.

13. A fibrous root system is composed of many secondary roots and root hairs. A taproot system has one large primary root with a few secondary roots. Both systems absorb water and anchor the plant.

14. Buds are protected, dormant tissues which may develop into stems, flowers, or leaves.

15. Leaves, flowers, fruits, and bud scales may leave scars on stems.

16. In pinnate venation, veins branch from a central midrib whereas in palmate venation, many large veins branch out from the point of attachment of the blade and petiole. Leaflets of compound leaves can be arranged in a similar pattern; i.e., leaflets are all attached to the petiole at a central point in palmately compound leaves and branch out all along the petiole in pinnately compound leaves.

Page 279. Applying Your Ideas

1. Algal plants and protistan algae are eukaryotes whereas blue-green (moneran) algae are prokaryotes. Compared to both moneran and protistan algae, algal plants are generally larger, multicellular organisms with greater division of labor.

2. Plants, unlike fungi, are autotrophic, and most plants have a more complex structure.

3. Embryos of land plants would dry out if not protected in some way. Algal plant embryos are not in danger of dessication outside the parent.

4. This example is convergence. The two kinds of plants are descended from different kinds of ancestors.

5. Indian pipe is thought to have descended from autotrophic plants. Perhaps through degenerative evolution, Indian pipe developed a saprophytic existence and lost its ability to synthesize chlorophyll.

6. A taproot generally extends down farther and can absorb water from deeper layers of soil than can a fibrous root. Fibrous roots spread out farther in the soil and absorb water from a larger area.

7. This pattern of branch growth allows for maximum exposure to sunlight by all leaves.

8. Venation and leaf patterns could be an aid in classifying or identifying plants.

Page 279. Extending Your Ideas

1. In collecting plants, students should include specimens with fruits or flowers where applicable. In some areas collecting leaves is destructive or illegal. Under these circumstances, students could sketch the leaves they observe rather than collect specimens. You may choose to collect leaves and photocopy them so students can compare various leaf traits without making their own collections.

2. Spanish moss is not a moss; it is an angiosperm, a relative of the pineapple. Spanish moss lives as an epiphyte in trees such as oak. It is common in the southern United States.

Additional Student Readings

Milne, Lorus Johnson, *Living Plants of the World*. New York, Random House, 1975.

Schaeffer, Elizabeth R., *Dandelion, Pokeweed, and Goosefoot*. Reading, MA, Addison Wesley Publishing Co., Inc., 1979.

Suggested Teacher Readings

Bidwell, R. G. S., *Plant Physiology*, 2nd ed. New York, Macmillan Publishing Co., 1979.

Galston, A., Davies, P., and Satter, R., *The Life of the Plant*, 3rd ed. Englewood Cliffs, NJ, Prentice-Hall, Inc., 1980.

Muller, Walter H., *Botany: A Functional Approach*, 4th ed. New York, Macmillan Publishing Co., 1979.

CHAPTER 15   ANIMALS: SPONGES THROUGH MOLLUSKS

Teaching Techniques

Chapter 15 surveys the major phyla of simpler invertebrates—sponges through mollusks. (Arthropods, echinoderms, and chordates are presented in Chapter 16.) Phyla are identified and distinguishing characteristics are presented by studying representative members. In teaching the material, stress the fact that animal complexity is understandable in terms of the heterotrophic way of life.

As you proceed from phylum to phylum, make certain that students see the new adaptations and characteristics which appear in each group, such as number of cell layers, number of body openings, and presence of special systems. Point out that although the animals of each phylum are adapted for life in certain environments, some phyla are more successful and widespread than others. Relate that success to their variety of adaptations.

The structures and characteristics discussed for each phylum are not intended to be extensive or all-inclusive. They provide a basis for distinguishing the phyla and later, for study of animal physiology. Equally important in this chapter is the material dealing with various animals' roles in nature, especially those affecting humans.

Performance Objectives

Goal: Students will gain an understanding of the basic features of some of the major groups of organisms in the animal kingdom.

Objectives: Upon completion of the reading and activities and when asked to respond orally or on a written test, students will:

Section Number		
15:0	K	differentiate between invertebrates and vertebrates.
15:1	K	list the characteristics of sponges and describe their reproduction.
15:2	K	list the characteristics of coelenterates.
15:2	P	distinguish between the polyp and medusa forms.
15:3	K	compare and contrast animals which have bilateral symmetry and those which have radial symmetry.
15:4	K	list the characteristics of flatworms.
15:5	K	describe the life cycle of the beef tapeworm.
15:6	P	list the characteristics of roundworms and compare roundworms with less complex animals.
15:6	K	identify several nematodes which are parasites of humans and discuss their effects.
15:7	P	list the characteristics of segmented worms and compare them with less complex worms.
15:7	P	explain how earthworms are important in soil ecology.
15:8	K	list the characteristics of the phylum Mollusca and indicate features not found in less complex animals.

(See page 41T for performance objectives that apply to all chapters.)

Answers to Chapter 15 Review

Page 296. Checking Your Ideas

1. h	4. e	8. a
2. c	5. j	9. f
3. d	6. g	10. i
	7. b	

Page 296. Evaluating Your Ideas

1. Answers will vary. Some examples follow. Animals move to capture food. A muscular and/or skeletal system permits locomotion. Animals often have a specialized support system. Nerves coordinate an animal's activities. Sense organs aid in detecting prey and avoiding predators. Digestive systems are necessary to break down the food which animals trap. Excretory systems permit the removal of harmful metabolic by-products.

2. Sponges are multicellular and heterotrophic.

3. Sponges are essentially at the cellular level of organization. They have no true tissues.

4. Sponges can reproduce sexually by producing sperm and eggs. Asexual reproduction includes budding, fragmentation, and production of gemmules.

5. Coelenterates have mesoglea, nerve cells, a tissue level of organization, and, in some forms, motility.

6. Tentacles, stinging cells, and motility are factors in coelenterates' trapping of food.

7. The polyp form of *Aurelia* reproduces asexually. The top sections of the polyp break off, forming medusae. The medusae reproduce sexually, the embryos developing into new polyps.

8. Flatworms have three cell layers and bilateral symmetry. Flatworms have the organ level of organization. Flatworms have organs such as a primitive brain and specialized structures for maintaining water balance.

9. Gas exchange and waste removal (except excess water) occur by diffusion.

10. A cow may ingest tapeworm embryos while grazing. In the cow's intestine the embryos develop into larvae, dig through the intestinal wall, and travel, via the blood, to the muscles. Improperly cooked beef may contain larvae which, in the human, attach by hooks to the intestinal wall. The tapeworm develops a series of sections, each of which contains sex organs. Fertilized eggs develop into embryos which pass out of the intestine along with undigested wastes. These wastes can contaminate grasses and the embryos can enter another cow completing the cycle.

11. A roundworm has two body openings, mouth and anus.

12. In flatworms, reproduction is sexual by mating of hermaphrodites. In roundworms separate sexes exist.

13. Diseases caused by roundworms include hookworm infestations, elephantiasis, and trichinosis.

14. Segmented worms have digestive, excretory, circulatory, and reproductive systems. They have no gas exchange or skeletal systems.

15. Earthworms burrow through and eat soil. The spaces permit oxygen to enter and improve soil drainage. Castings, mostly undigested soil which passes through the earthworms, are deposited on the surface. Thus, the soil is turned

over, exposing it to air. Wastes excreted by earthworms enrich the soil.

16. An earthworm is limited to the moist environment of the soil. Earthworms lack a respiratory system. Gases are exchanged across the moist, outer cuticle of the worm. Because earthworms live only in moist environments, some people think of them as "aquatic" animals.

17. Aquatic annelids undergo external fertilization and the fertilized eggs go through a larval stage of development. Earthworms are hermaphrodites with internal fertilization. Fertilized eggs are enclosed within a capsule and develop in the soil with no larval stage. Internal fertilization is adaptive on land because the gametes probably could not survive externally.

18. Mollusks have soft bodies enclosed by hard outer shells of calcium carbonate. Most have a folded tissue, the mantle, which covers the internal organs.

19. Mollusks are classified on the basis of their number of shells. Bivalves have two shells, univalves have one shell, and cephalopods have a very small shell or no shell.

20. Snails and slugs obtain food by scraping plant material with their radulas. Bivalves filter food from the water. Some head-foot mollusks are active predators.

Page 297. Applying Your Ideas

1. Animals and protozoa are similar in that they are heterotrophic and most forms can move. Animals are multicellular whereas protozoa are unicellular, and animals have a more complex structure, often including systems for carrying out life processes.

2. In many ways sponges are more like colonies than multicellular animals. They have no tissue differentiation and lack both motility and nervous control, two features usually associated with animals. Cells of a sponge can be separated and they will reaggregate to form a new sponge.

3. A sessile animal must depend on its food coming to it. Radial symmetry is adaptive because it enables the animal to take in food from all directions.

4. Tapeworms must be able to resist the digestive enzymes produced by the intestine.

5. Often only one tapeworm is present in the host.

6. It was thought that "bleeding" (removal of blood) would rid the person of the agents of disease.

7. The bivalves and univalves move very slowly because of their being totally or partially enclosed by their shell. In certain head-foot mollusks such as squids and octopi, the shell is absent or greatly reduced and locomotion is quite rapid.

8. Both bivalve mollusks and sponges are filter feeders. They extract food from water passing through them.

9. Fungi absorb food after it is digested. Animals ingest food which is later digested.

10. An ecological means of eliminating tapeworms is modern sewage treatment.

Page 297. Extending Your Ideas

1. Not only mollusks and annelids, but bryozoans and brachiopods, have trocophore larvae. These larvae have certain traits in common. Externally, all have a band or ring of cilia. Mouth and anus are evident and internally there is a distinct alimentary canal. The patterns of development are very similar. Comparison of these larvae suggests that mollusks and annelids have common ancestry.

2. For a clear presentation of many parasitic life cycles, refer students to Buchsbaum, *Animals Without Backbones* (see *Suggested Readings*).

3. Flukes are flatworms (class Trematoda), leeches are annelids (class Hirudinea). Both are parasitic.

4. Comb jellies belong to the phylum Ctenophora and resemble coelenterates. They have no stinging cells and, in some cases, no tentacles. They are characterized by eight bands of cilia which run from top to bottom of their walnut-shaped body. Brachiopods look somewhat like mollusks, but belong to phylum Brachiopoda. They have a shape like an old oil lamp and are therefore sometimes called lamp shells.

Additional Student Readings

Lincoln, R. J. and Sheals, J. G., *Collecting Invertebrate Animals.* New York, Cambridge University Press, 1980.

Shostak, Stanley, *The Hydra.* New York, McCann and Geoghegan, Inc., 1977.

Suggested Teacher Readings

Hummer, Paul J., Jr., "Fresh Water Bryozoa in the Laboratory," *The American Biology Teacher*, September, 1977.

Laverack, M. S., and Dando, J., *Essential Invertebrate Zoology.* Somerset, NJ, Halsted Press/John Wiley and Sons, Inc., 1979.

Orlans, F. Barbara, *Animal Care From Small Protozoa to Small Mammals.* Reading, MA, Addison-Wesley Publishing Co., 1977.

Russell-Hunter, W. D., *A Life of Invertebrates.* New York, Macmillan Publishing Co., 1979.

Storer, Tracy L., et.al., *General Zoology*, 6th ed. New York, McGraw-Hill Book Co., 1979.

CHAPTER 16 ANIMALS: ARTHROPODS THROUGH VERTEBRATES

Teaching Techniques

This chapter continues the survey of animal phyla begun in Chapter 15, concentrating on echinoderms, arthropods, and chordates. As an introduction to this chapter, remind students of the major features associated with animal life and review animal characteristics such as number of cell layers and body openings, types of symmetry, and diversity of systems. Introduce the more complex animals by pointing out that they share the general features of animals already studied, but have even more complex adaptations.

Major *classes* of arthropods and vertebrate chordates have been named. Most students will not find this burdensome because they are already familiar with some of the common term names, such as insect and reptile.

Performance Objectives

Goal: Students will gain an understanding of the basic features of the major groups of complex animals.

Objectives: Upon completion of the reading and activities and when asked to respond orally or on a written test, students will:

Section Number		
16:1	K	list the traits of arthropods and indicate features not found in less complex animals.
16:2	P	compare and contrast centipedes and millipedes.
16:3-5	K	list the traits of crustaceans, insects, and arachnids, and give examples of each.
16:3	K	describe the functions of a lobster's chelipeds and swimmerets.
16:4	K	give examples of how some insects are harmful and others are beneficial.
16:2-5	P	compare and contrast traits of the classes of arthropods.
16:6	K	list the characteristics of echinoderms and give examples.
16:7	K	list the characteristics of chordates and then of both nonvertebrate and vertebrate chordates.
16:8-14	K	list traits of each of the classes of vertebrates and give examples of members of each class.
16:8-14	P	compare and contrast vertebrates in terms of integument, body temperature, limb structure, means of gas exchange, and fertilization.
16:12	P	compare and contrast reproduction and development in reptiles with these processes in fish and amphibians.
16:13	K	explain the adaptations for flight in birds.
16:14	K	give several unique human traits.

(See page 41T for performance objectives that apply to all chapters.)

Answers to Chapter 16 Review

Page 322. Checking Your Ideas

1. true
2. false
3. true
4. false
5. false
6. true (of the phyla presented in detail in the chapter)
7. false
8. false
9. true
10. false

Page 322. Evaluating Your Ideas

1. Arthropods are successful in the sense that there are more living members of this phylum than in all other phyla combined. They exhibit a great diversity of adaptations. The exoskeleton permits greater mobility, support, and protection. The muscular system, along with jointed appendages and the skeleton, provides better motion and locomotion. Elaborate sensory organs enable arthropods to detect environmental stimuli.

2. In annelids, each segment is separate and contains about the same structures. In arthropods, segments are fused into distinct body regions.

3. Chilopoda: head and segments; mandibles; one pair of legs on most segments; tracheae. Diplopoda: head and segments; mandibles; two pairs of legs on most segments; tracheae. Crustacea: cephalothorax and abdomen; mandibles; five pairs of legs; gills. Insecta: head, thorax, and abdomen; mandibles; three pairs of legs; tracheae. Arachnida: cephalothorax and abdomen; chelicerae; four pairs of legs; tracheae and/or book lungs.

4. Chelipeds function in trapping and crushing food and in defense. Swimmerets function in swimming and as a site of attachment for fertilized eggs.

5. Insects damage food crops, destroy forests, parasitize animals and cause disease. They aid in pollination, prey upon other harmful insects, and produce some substances used by humans.

6. Chordates, at some stage of their lives, have a stiff rod of cartilage called the notochord. They also have gill pouches, a dorsal nerve cord, and a ventral heart.

7. Tunicates and lancelets are nonvertebrate chordates. They are marine and filter food from the water.

8. Invertebrates have dorsal hearts and ventral nerve cords. Vertebrates have ventral hearts and dorsal nerve cords.

9. Integumentary systems are the outer coverings of vertebrates; e.g., scales, hair, and feathers.

10. Agnathans are jawless, have no scales, and lack paired fins.

11. Lampreys eat other fish, attaching to them and cutting holes in them. Hagfish may eat fish caught in nets, boring into their bodies. Many of these prey fish are those commercially sought.

12. Cartilage fish have a skeleton of cartilage and their gill openings are not covered. Bony fish have a skeleton of bone, and their gill openings are covered.

13. Most amphibians must reproduce in an aquatic environment.

14. As larvae, amphibians exchange gases through gills. In most forms, gills are replaced by lungs in the adult stage. Gas exchange also occurs through the thin, moist skin.

15. Reptiles have dry, scaly skin which prevents water loss. Internal fertilization and development in a shelled egg permit reproduction on land.

16. Some snake venoms act on the nerves, and thus, affect breathing and heartbeat. Others destroy red blood cells and walls of blood vessels.

17. Beak structure of birds is related to diet. For example, pelicans have bills adapted for catching fish and cardinals have beaks adapted for crushing seeds.

18. Molting in reptiles involves shedding the outer skin whereas in birds it involves loss of feathers.

19. Monotremes develop in shelled eggs. In marsupials, development begins within the female and is completed in the female's pouch. Placental mammals have complete internal development. The platypus is a monotreme, the opposum is a marsupial, and humans are placentals.

Page 323. Applying Your Ideas

1. A barnacle has a hard outer shell and is sessile. In these ways, it resembles mollusks such as oysters.

2. Because barnacles are attached, reproduction involving two parents might be less adaptive.

3. Birds have high energy demands.

4. Migration and hibernation are adaptations which allow ectotherms to avoid temperature extremes.

5. Arthropods and vertebrates have complex sensory equipment and behavior, well developed means of locomotion, and they have the ability to trap and utilize a variety of food sources. Their specific adaptations differ, but both groups have adaptations for occupying many ecological niches.

6. The placentals and marsupials are products of convergence.

Page 323. Extending Your Ideas

1. These organisms will avoid both light and touch. Exposure to light will cause movement away from the light. When touched, a sowbug will curl up into a ball. Sowbugs can be kept in a closed (with air vents) container with moist soil or leaf litter.

2. Some students may wish to observe a tarantula, available in some pet stores and from biological supply houses. Be sure that guidelines for animal care are followed for any animals brought into the classroom.

3. An excellent source of insect life is an abandoned field. The net can be swept along at various levels (depths) in the vegetation. A twisting motion will help trap the insects in the bottom of the net. A killing jar can be prepared by covering the inside bottom of the jar with a thin layer of plaster. When dry, chloroform can be poured into the plaster and the jar sealed. Nail polish remover can be used in place of chloroform. Have students study insect traits and then identify the insects and classify them by order. An insect pin can be inserted through the thorax of the insect. The insect can then be pushed so it is near the pinhead. A small triangle of paper labeled with the insect's order can be placed on the other end of the pin before the pin is pushed into the cardboard. Fragile insects can be pinned through a wing or glued to the paper triangle.

4. Icthyology is the study of fish, entomology the study of insects, and herpetology the study of reptiles.

Additional Student Readings

Dunkle, Terry, "A Perfect Serpent." *Science 81*, October, 1981.

McCosker, John E., "Great White Shark." *Science 81*, July/August, 1981.

Suggested Teacher Readings

Bone, Q., *The Origin of Chordates*, 2nd ed. Carolina Biology Reader. Burlington, NC, Carolina Biological Supply Co., 1979.

Baumann, Richard W., "Water Insects and Their Relatives." *American Biology Teacher*, May, 1977.

Gibbons, Michael F., Jr., "Marsupials—Their Place in the Natural History of Mammals." *Biology Digest*, October, 1981.

Hunt, John D., "A Microhabitat for an Amphibian." *The Science Teacher*, May, 1975.

Napier, J. R., *Primates and Their Adaptations*, 2nd ed. Carolina Biology Reader, Burlington, NC, Carolina Biological Supply Co., 1977.

Orlans, F. Barbara, *Animal Care from Small Protozoa to Small Mammals*. Reading, MA, Addison-Wesley Publishing Co., 1977.

Storer, Tracy L., *et. al.*, *General Zoology*, 6th ed. New York, McGraw-Hill Book Co., 1979.

CHAPTER 17 SIMPLE ORGANISMS: REPRODUCTION

Teaching Techniques

In teaching reproduction of simple organisms, stress that although organisms differ in terms of particular physical features, the same modes of reproduction are seen in many life forms—conjugation, fission, budding, and spore formation. Emphasize that although details may vary, in general, these processes are similar from organism to organism.

As you introduce the general ideas of asexual and sexual reproduction, it may be useful to review the major events and consequences of mitosis and meiosis (Chapter 6).

Performance Objectives

Goal: Students will gain an understanding of reproduction in monerans, protists, fungi, and viruses.

Objectives: Upon completion of the reading and activities and when asked to respond orally or on a written test, students will:

Section
Number

17:0   K   define asexual reproduction and indicate that it results in the production of offspring which are genetically identical to the parent.

17:1, 2	P	compare and contrast fission in prokaryotes and eukaryotes.
17:2	K	describe fission in *Paramecium*.
17:3	K/P	compare and contrast budding and fragmentation and give an example of each.
17:4	K	describe the process of asexual reproduction through spore formation.
17:5I	P	compare and contrast fission (asexual reproduction) and fusion (sexual reproduction).
17:5	P	compare and contrast the processes of conjugation and transformation in bacteria.
17:6	K	describe the conjugationlike process in bread mold.
17:7	P	compare and contrast the lytic cycle and lysogenic cycles of viruses.
17:7	K	explain how proviruses may be responsible for disease.
17:8	K	describe the process of transduction and explain how it contributes to variety among bacteria.
17:9	K	describe the structure of RNA tumor viruses.
17:9	K	explain the life cycle of an RNA tumor virus.

(See page 41T for performance objectives that apply to all chapters.)

Answers to Chapter 17 Review

Page 338. Checking Your Ideas

1. DNA
2. conjugation
3. asexual
4. transformation (or conjugation)
5. sexual
6. fertility factor
7. budding
8. mitosis
9. bacteriophage
10. lytic

Page 338. Evaluating Your Ideas

1. The circular chromosome attaches to the inside of the cell membrane, a copy is made, and the new chromosome attaches to the membrane at a point near the original chromosome. New cell membrane and cell wall form and the cell elongates. New membrane and cell wall pinch inward from the center of the cell, separating the two chromosomes and two distinct cells are formed.

2. Fission in eukaryotes involves mitosis. In *Paramecium*, the micronucleus divides by mitosis. The chromosomes are pulled to each pole of the cell. The macronucleus divides by a nonmitotic process. The cell membrane pinches in to produce two daughter cells.

3. In yeast, asexual reproduction occurs by budding. A part of the cell wall grows out to form a bud. During mitosis, one set of chromosomes remains in the parent cell and one set moves to the bud. The new cell may give rise to a chain of buds or may be pinched off.

4. *Rhizopus* produces spores from sporangia. *Penicillium* produces spores (conidia) at the tips of conidiophore hyphae.

5. The outer wall of spores can resist harsh conditions and evaporation.

6. Sexual reproduction contributes to variety among offspring. Variety is important to survival if environments change.

7. A cytoplasm bridge forms between F+ and F− bacteria. The genetic material of the F+ type moves through the bridge into the F− cell. Both the fertility factor and other genes on plasmids are transferred.

8. Transformation and transduction may lead to genetic recombination in bacteria. In transformation, DNA from a bacterium that has broken open enters another bacterium. In transduction, genes from one bacterium may be introduced into another bacterium by a phage.

9. Different types of hyphae, + and −, grow branches which meet. The tip of each branch becomes a separate cell and acts as a "gamete". Fusion of the cells produces a zygospore. After a dormant period, the zygospore undergoes meiosis, and new hyphae develop from the spores produced.

10. Both yeast and other fungi reproduce by conjugation or conjugationlike processes. In yeast, two cells fuse to form a zygote. The zygote undergoes meiosis to produce four spores. The zygote is modified into an ascus from which the spores are freed. In mushrooms, different types of underground hyphae fuse and give rise to the rest of the mycelium. Cells of the basidia contain two nuclei which fuse to form zygotes. A zygote undergoes meiosis to produce four spores, each of which may develop into a new underground mycelium.

11. The tail-like portion of the phage attaches to a receptor in the wall of the bacterium. Part of the tail pierces the cell wall, and the phage's DNA is injected into the host cell. The phage DNA uses the bacterium's materials, enzymes, ATP, and cell parts to reproduce. Shortly thereafter, the bacterium lyses, releasing new phage particles.

12. No, in the lysogenic cycle, the viral DNA becomes part of the host's DNA and replicates along with it. Such a virus is called a provirus. Later, changes may occur which cause the provirus to become active and destroy the host cell by lysis.

13. Answers may vary. Examples are given. RNA tumor viruses have RNA rather than DNA as their genetic material. RNA tumor viruses do not lyse host cells when they exit.

14. Reverse transcriptase is an enzyme which directs the synthesis of a DNA strand from the viral RNA.

Page 339. Applying Your Ideas

1. In *Rhizopus*, the zygote is diploid. In yeast, the diploid zygote can bud producing other diploid cells. Those cells can also bud and all the cells produced in this way are diploid. The other cells of the life cycle of these organisms are monoploid.

2. Conjugation occurred between some mutants. This process resulted in genetic recombination. Some offspring obtained the genes necessary for synthesis of all four substances.

3. The mutants could not produce the substances because of missing or altered genes.

4. The original F− bacterium becomes F+ because it receives the fertility factor.

5. Asexual reproduction increases the number of organisms by dividing parent organisms.
6. During the lytic cycle, viruses destroy host cells. During the lysogenic cycle, proviruses may interfere with the host cell's metabolism.
7. Because the host cell is not destroyed, it can continue making new viral particles.

Page 339. Extending Your Ideas

1. Use 10% sugar or molasses solutions. Add the same amount of yeast to each solution tested. Plug each solution and incubate at 30° C for 24 hours. (This temperature will hasten the budding process.) Prepare wet mounts of the solutions for observation. Stains such as methylene blue or neutral red may be drawn under the cover slip to facilitate observation.
2. Hfr cells are ones in which the fertility factor becomes part of the bacterial chromosome. Hfr stands for high frequency; Hfr cells have a high frequency of recombination for characters other than F$^+$. During conjugation, the chromosome moves from the Hfr (male) cell through the conjugation bridge and into the F$^-$ cell. Hfr strains do not usually "donate" the F$^+$ capacity to F$^-$ cells as F$^+$ strains do.
3. Have students "grow" their own molds by keeping pieces of moist bread or fruit in containers kept in the dark. Use wet paper towels or blotting paper to keep the food in the containers moist. Growth may be accelerated by adding dust to the bread or fruit. Cheese, soil, or softened seeds are other possible substances for growth of mold.
4. *Paramecium* may reproduce sexually by conjugation. Two cells of different strains fuse, and a bridge of cytoplasm forms between them. The macronucleus disintegrates. The diploid micronucleus of each cell undergoes meiosis to produce four monoploid nuclei, three of which die. The surviving nucleus next undergoes mitosis to produce two monoploid nuclei. One of these nuclei from each cell moves through the bridge to the other cell. There it fuses with the remaining monoploid nucleus to form a diploid nucleus. The cells separate and the diploid nucleus in each cell divides three times (or more in some species which have several micronuclei per cell) to form eight diploid nuclei. Each cell divides twice giving a total of eight cells. Two diploid nuclei enter each cell. One becomes the micronucleus; the other becomes the macronucleus.

Additional Student Readings

Miller, Julie Ann, "Max Delbrück Remembered." *Science News*, April 25, 1981.
Patent, Dorothy H., *Bacteria*. New York, Holiday House, 1975.

Suggested Teacher Readings

Holloway, M. R., *The Mechanism of Enzyme Action*. Oxford Biology Reader. London, Oxford University Press, 1976.
Luria, S. E., *et. al.*, *General Virology*, 3rd ed. New York, John Wiley, 1978.
Nester, Eugene W., *et. al.*, *Microbiology*, 2nd ed. New York, Holt, Rinehart and Winston, 1978.

CHAPTER 18   SIMPLE ORGANISMS: OTHER LIFE FUNCTIONS

Teaching Techniques

In teaching material about life functions of simple organisms, make certain students understand the role of each life function. Basic concepts about nutrition and digestion, transport, gas exchange, excretion, locomotion, and responses introduced in this chapter are important in later chapters dealing with plant and animal physiology.

Each function is treated separately, with examples drawn from the three kingdoms of organisms. Make certain that students understand the universality of each process and that each involves a relationship between organisms and their environment. Stress the fundamental similarities among the ways that organisms carry out each function.

Performance Objectives

Goal: Students will gain an understanding of the life functions of monerans, protists, and fungi.

Objectives: Upon completion of the reading and activities and when asked to respond orally or on a written test, students will:

Section Number		
18:0	K	identify nutrients as materials required by cells and name several types of nutrients.
18:1	P	compare and contrast the nutrients required by autotrophs and heterotrophs.
18:1	K	define digestion as the process by which organisms break large molecules into smaller ones.
18:2	K	describe the process of intracellular digestion in simple autotrophs.
18:3	P	compare and contrast food-getting, digestion, and egestion in *Amoeba* and *Paramecium*.
18:4	K	describe the process of extracellular digestion by *Rhizopus*.
18:4	P	compare and contrast food-getting and digestion in parasitic and "predator" fungi.
18:5	K	list examples of substances which are transported within organisms.

18:5	K	explain ways in which transport occurs within simple organisms.
18:6	K	define gas exchange as the movement of oxygen and carbon dioxide between organisms and their environment.
18:6	K	explain that gases must be dissolved in a liquid to pass across a cell membrane.
18:6	K	identify diffusion as the means by which gas exchange occurs in simple organisms.
18:7	K	define excretion as the process by which harmful by-products (waste materials) are removed.
18:7	K	explain how ammonia is excreted by protozoa.
18:7	P/K	compare and contrast water balance in simple marine and freshwater organisms and explain how *Paramecium* maintains osmotic balance.
18:8, 9	P	compare and contrast amoeboid motion to ciliary and flagellar motion.
18:10	K	cite examples of responses to environment by simple organisms.

(See page 41T for performance objectives that apply to all chapters.)

Answers to Chapter 18 Review

Page 350. Checking Your Ideas

1. c
2. f
3. a
4. i
5. e
6. j
7. d
8. b
9. h
10. g

Page 350. Evaluating Your Ideas

1. Autotrophs take in simple molecules like carbon dioxide, water, and mineral ions. Heterotrophs take in water and mineral ions, vitamins, and complex organic molecules. Autotrophs make complex organic molecules from simple nutrients. Heterotrophs cannot.

2. Digestion is necessary to break large molecules into smaller molecules that can permeate cell membranes.

3. Digestion in autotrophs is different from that of heterotrophs in that in autotrophs there is breakdown of large molecules that the autotrophs have made. Heterotrophs take in complex molecules that are broken down.

4. Molecules are digested by hydrolysis.

5. *Amoeba* ingests food by phagocytosis, digests it within food vacuoles, and egests undigestible material by exocytosis. *Paramecium* ingests food by the action of cilia in the oral groove, and digests it within a food vacuole. When the food vacuole fuses with the anal pore, egestion occurs. Both protozoans digest food intracellularly within food vacuoles, but their methods of ingestion and egestion are different.

6. Many fungi obtain food as saprophytes. They secrete enzymes from their rhizoids into the food source, extracellular digestion occurs, food molecules are absorbed by the rhizoids, and food moves by diffusion to the rest of the fungus. Some fungi are parasites. Those that live entirely within cells of their host may absorb food already digested by the host. A few fungi have special hyphae which can trap nematode worms. Other hyphae secrete enzymes and digestion occurs as in most fungi.

7. Materials are moved by diffusion and cytoplasmic streaming.

8. Gases must be dissolved in a liquid to permeate cell membranes. Simple organisms exchange gases by diffusion.

9. Nitrogenous wastes of protozoa are removed by diffusion. Excess water is removed by contractile vacuoles.

10. Seawater and the cytoplasm of marine protists contains about the same concentration of dissolved particles. Water enters and leaves the cells by osmosis in equal amounts.

11. *Paramecium* has contractile vacuoles. Water entering the cell collects in canals around the vacuoles and then passes into the vacuoles. When the vacuole is full, it contracts, forcing the water out.

12. Amoeboid motion depends on changes between the sol and gel states of cytoplasm. As sol state cytoplasm flows toward the membrane, that part of the membrane begins to bulge outward to form a pseudopodium. The sol cytoplasm then moves back in the other direction and changes to a gel state. The gel changes back to sol and again flows toward the forming pseudopodium. Flow of cytoplasm is controlled by contraction of microfilaments.

13. It is thought that some of the microtubules in cilia or flagella contract and slide over the others causing the cilium or flagellum to bend forward in a power stroke. The power stroke is followed by a recovery stroke in which some microtubules relax and others contract. Alternation of power and recovery strokes results in locomotion.

14. Discharge of the trichocysts is a protective response of *Paramecium*. *Paramecium* reacts to objects in its path by reversing the beating of its cilia, backing away from the object, and turning about 30°. These responses are repeated until the *Paramecium* avoids the object.

Page 351. Applying Your Ideas

1. Extracellular digestion provides a means by which fungi can absorb their food in the form of small molecules. Fungi lack adaptations for ingesting large chunks of food.

2. Digestion by fungi contributes to decomposition and helps in the recycling of materials.

3. The endoplasmic reticulum functions in intracellular transport in eukaryotes.

4. Protozoa are more complex than other simple organisms in that they have cell parts for a variety of functions such as trapping food, digestion, egestion, locomotion, and excretion, although other simple organisms have special adaptations for some of these functions. One reason why protozoa are so adapted may be that they do not make their own food. Many of the adaptations that make them more complex are related to heterotrophic nutrition.

5. Those substances made by the bacteria do not have to be obtained from the environment.

6. *Euglena* swims through water changing from cigar shaped to round. It swims by flagellum movement. *Euglena* has a stigma which responds to light and the *Euglena*

responds to light by moving toward it, a behavior that is adaptive because *Euglena* is autotrophic. *Paramecium* moves by cilia, discharges trichocysts when disturbed, and has special behavior for moving around objects in its path. The behaviors are adaptive to its heterotrophic nutrition.

Page 351. Extending Your Ideas

1. The iodine or vinegar should be added to the edge of the coverslip. If iodine-potassium iodide solution is used, it will stain the cells so that the threads can be easily observed.
2. The *Paramecium* will exhibit the responses described in Section 18:10. Addition of a drop of methyl cellulose to the slide will slow the *Paramecium* down if necessary.
3. Students should observe amoeboid motion as described in Section 18:8 and cytoplasmic streaming as described in Section 18:5.

Additional Student Readings

Burchard, R. P., "Gliding Motility of Bacteria." *Bioscience*, March, 1980.
Ford, Brian J., *Microbe Power*. New York, Stein and Day, 1976.
Scholtyseck, E., *Fine Structures of Parasitic Protozoa*. New York, Springer-Verlag, Inc., 1979.

Suggested Teacher Readings

Bold, H. C., and Wynne, M. J., *Introduction to the Algae.* Englewood Cliffs, NJ, Prentice-Hall, Inc., 1978.
Lechevalier, H. A. and Pramer, D., *The Microbes*. Philadelphia, J. B. Lippincott, 1977.
Stanier, R. Y., Adelberg, E. A., and Ingraham, J. L., *The Microbial World*, 4th ed. Englewood Cliffs, NJ, Prentice-Hall, Inc., 1976.

CHAPTER 19   SIMPLE ORGANISMS AND DISEASE

Teaching Techniques

This chapter focuses on agents of infectious disease, adaptations for preventing and combating disease, and modern methods of treating disease. Before beginning the chapter you may wish to have your students list various infectious diseases of humans and other organisms and identify the types of organisms which cause the diseases. This identification of diseases and disease organisms can lead to subsequent discussion of treatment and prevention of diseases. Students are usually not reticent about this subject because disease is so relevant in their lives. A lively class discussion can generate an outline of the material to be studied in the chapter.

Many students may be interested in finding out how knowledge of infectious disease accumulated. You may wish to assign written or oral reports on pioneers such as Jenner, Pasteur, Lister, Walter Reed, Salk, and Sabin (see *Extending Your Ideas*, number 3).

Performance Objectives

Goal: Students will gain an understanding of how pathogens cause disease and the means by which humans prevent and treat diseases.
Objectives: Upon completion of the reading and activities and when asked to respond orally or on a written test, students will:

Section Number		
19:0	K	define pathogens as organisms which cause infectious disease.
19:1	K	outline Koch's postulates for the detection of pathogens.
19:2	K	name several diseases caused by bacteria.
19:2	K	explain the various ways in which infectious disease may spread.
19:3	P	compare and contrast the production of exotoxins and endotoxins.
19:4	K	give the cause of botulism and its effects.
19:4	P	compare and contrast pasteurization and freezing as methods of preventing food spoilage.
19:5	K	name several diseases caused by viruses.
19:6	P	compare and contrast the structure of rickettsia and viroids.
19:7	K	list several human diseases caused by fungi.
19:7	K	describe the life cycle of wheat rust.
19:8	K	describe the life cycle of *Plasmodium* and its effect on humans.
19:9	K	identify several adaptations which prevent pathogens from entering the body.
19:10	K	identify antigens as any foreign chemical.
19:10	P	distinguish among the various structures of the immune system: lymphocytes, lymph nodes, spleen, thymus gland, and macrophages.
19:11	K	explain the means by which the immune system recognizes and destroys antigens.
19:12	P	compare and contrast active immunity and passive immunity.

19:12	P	distinguish between vaccines and antisera.
19:12	K	identify antibiotics as drugs which destroy bacteria.
19:13	K	explain how interferon protects cells against viruses.
19:14	K	identify cancer as a disease in which there is uncontrolled production of certain cells.
19:15	K	explain the method by which synthetic vaccines are made and give advantages of making vaccines in this way.
19:15	K	discuss the production of monoclonal antibodies and explain how these antibodies may be used.

(See page 41T for performance objectives that apply to all chapters.)

Answers to Chapter 19 Review

Page 370. Checking Your Ideas.

1. true	**6.** false
2. true	**7.** true
3. false	**8.** true
4. false	**9.** true
5. true	**10.** false

Page 371. Evaluating Your Ideas

1. The germ theory of disease states that bacteria can cause disease.

2. Koch's postulates, which explain this procedure, are as follows:

(1) The organism suspected of causing the disease must be present in the diseased host and isolated from it.

(2) The organism then must be grown in pure culture.

(3) Organisms taken from that pure culture and injected into a healthy host must cause the disease in the host.

(4) The organism must be isolated from the newly diseased host, grown in pure culture, and compared to the original culture.

3. Infectious disease may be spread by air or water, by direct contact, or by organisms such as arthropods.

4. Answers may vary, but examples are syphillis, gonorrhea, and genital herpes. Sexually transmitted diseases are spread by sexual intercourse.

5. Exotoxins are produced by living bacteria, travel in the bloodstream, and affect particular tissues. Tetanus and diphtheria are caused by exotoxins. Endotoxins are not released until bacteria die and break open. Cholera, tuberculosis, and bubonic plague are caused by endotoxins.

6. Botulism results from a potent exotoxin released by *Clostridium sp.* The bacteria may be present in improperly canned food. The toxin affects the nervous system, causing problems in vision, paralysis, and sometimes death.

7. Pasteurization involves heating of milk or other foods followed by a rapid cooling. The heating kills most of the bacteria and the cooling retards the growth of remaining bacteria. The process is necessary to kill harmful bacteria.

8. Viroids are small segments of RNA. They may cause disease by regulating the host's genes abnormally.

9. Wheat rust attacks stem and leaf cells of young wheat plants. It produces spores which spread to and attack other wheat plants. Later, a different type of spore is produced which invades the barberry bush. In the bush, the original type of spore is produced and it attacks young wheat plants.

10. *Plasmodium* from an infected human's blood cells are taken in by the female *Anopheles* mosquito when it bites the human. Growth and development of *Plasmodium* occurs in the mosquito's stomach and pass from there to the salivary glands. When the mosquito bites a healthy person, some of the parasites enter the human's blood. The parasites travel to the liver where they develop for about eight days, after which they invade red blood cells. Spores form in the red cells. The red cells burst, liberating spores which invade other red cells. Each time the red cells burst, the parasites' wastes are released into the human's blood stream. Symptoms associated with this release are chills, headache, fever, and sweating. Between bursting of red cells the person feels well, but weak.

11. Pathogens enter their hosts through the skin and body openings.

12. The outer layer of skin is composed of dead cells which microbes cannot penetrate. Hairs in the nose filter many microbes from the air. The action of cilia moves microbe-trapping mucus upwards in the windpipe. Acids and enzymes produced by the body destroy some pathogens.

13. Antigens are recognized by lymphocytes which have matching antibodies on their surface.

14. After recognition of an antigen, the lymphocyte forms a clone of plasma cells. The plasma cells produce and release antibodies which combine with the antigens. Antibodies, once attached to antigens, may make bacteria and viruses more vulnerable to macrophages or cause the microbes to clump together, making them inactive. Complement in the blood breaks open foreign cells.

15. Lymph nodes contain white cells which destroy microbes.

16. Active immunity is disease resistance resulting from production of antibodies by the host. It may develop as a result of having an infectious disease or as a response to a vaccination.

17. Passive immunity is disease resistance resulting from antibodies made by another organism. It results from an injection of antiserum of those antibodies. Antisera are used in situations in which the host cannot make antibodies quickly enough to fight off the infection.

18. Active immunity lasts longer than passive immunity.

19. Antibiotics are used to treat bacterial diseases, but there are no drugs which destroy viruses in host cells.

20. Interferon travels from an infected cell to a healthy cell. In the healthy cell, it causes the synthesis of a protein which protects the healthy cell against viral attack. Interferon might be useful as a drug against viral infections.

21. Synthetic vaccines are made from a part of a specific antigen molecule—the part that elicits antibody production by a host. Synthetic vaccines can be made inexpensively, and are pure. It may be possible to produce a synthetic vaccine that would provide immunity against several diseases.

22. Monoclonal antibodies are pure antibodies made by a process in which mice are injected with a microbe or chemical. Lymphocytes in the mouse's spleen respond by making antibodies against the antigens. Lymphocytes are removed from the spleen and fused with certain cancer cells to form hybridomas. Hybridomas are cultured and form clones, each of which makes a particular antibody. Pure antibodies can be obtained from each clone. Monoclonal antibodies might provide new vaccines. They might also be used to diagnose pregnancy and certain diseases. In research, they may provide information about cell surface proteins, transplant rejections, and different aspects of the process of development.

Page 371. Applying Your Ideas

1. Pathogens are heterotrophs which lead a parasitic type of existence. They cause disease as they obtain needed materials from their hosts. Autotrophs make their own needed materials.

2. Wheat rust can be eliminated by removing its barberry bush host from areas near wheat crops.

3. Booster shots are necessary to activate the immune system to produce more "memory" cells.

4. Transplanted organs are usually rejected because they contain foreign proteins. (This topic is discussed in Chapter 26, but students should have some ideas about its answer after studying immunity presented here.)

5. Swollen lymph nodes may be a sign of infection in the body.

6. Some diseases are genetic in origin. Others may result from parasitic infestation.

7. The treatment relieves symptoms, but does not destroy the viruses which cause a cold or flu.

Page 371. Extending Your Ideas

1. Located on either side of the throat, the tonsils are lymphoid tissue thought to produce lymphocytes. As such, they are considered part of the immune system. However, they are prone to infection as a result of their constant exposure to incoming air and foods. Tonsillitis, infection of the tonsils, is not, in itself, usually dangerous. In extreme cases, though, the tonsils may become so swollen as to block the opening of the pharynx. If untreated, the infection can spread and lead to acute nephritis or rheumatic fever. Because of this tendency toward infection and the fact that lymphocytes are produced elsewhere, many physicians long felt that tonsils should be surgically removed in early childhood. However, this viewpoint has changed and tonsillectomies now are performed less frequently.

2. Poliomyelitis is caused by three different strains of virus. Many cases are mild but the disease may result in paralysis. Although persons of all ages may contact poliomyelitis, it is prevalent among children. The virus is transmitted through the air or by hands contaminated with feces containing the viruses.

The Salk vaccine was developed by Dr. Jonas Salk. The three strains of virus are first cultured in monkey kidney immersed in nutrient media. The kidney cells are killed as the viruses reproduce and the dead tissue is separated and removed from the fluid portion. Then formaldehyde is added to the fluid to destroy the viruses. After one week the vaccine is tested for inactivity of the viruses. The formaldehyde is then removed and the vaccine is usable. Usually a series of four injections is necessary to ensure lasting active immunity.

3. Jenner demonstrated the concept of vaccination when he showed that a vaccine could be used to prevent cowpox. Lister was a pioneer in the idea of antiseptic procedures, especially during surgery.

4. A disease not mentioned in the chapter but one with which some students may be familiar is legionnaire's disease. See Fraser, David W., and McDade, Joseph E., "Legionellosis." *Scientific American*, October, 1979.

5. Public health officers may conduct inspection of food stores, kitchens, and restaurants, provide health information and clinics for the community, investigate and report certain diseases, and test the quality of air and water.

Additional Student Readings

"Camouflaged Cancer Cells." *Science Digest*, September, 1981.

Epps, Garrett, "Synthetic Vaccines." *Science 81*, April, 1981.

Rodgers, Joann Ellison, "Dr. Thymosin's Remedy." *Science 81*, March, 1981.

Shodell, Michael, "Enlisting Cancer." *Science 80*, September/October, 1980.

Simpson, Lance L., "Deadly Botulism." *Natural History*, January, 1980.

Suggested Teacher Readings

Easton, Thomas A., "Viruses and Human Disease." *Biology Digest*, January, 1980.

Gowans, J. L., *Cellular Immunology*. Carolina Biology Reader. Burlington, NC, Carolina Biological Supply Co., 1977.

Hart, Gavin, *Sexually Transmitted Diseases*. Carolina Biology Reader. Burlington, NC, Carolina Biological Supply Co., 1976.

Henle, Werner, Henle, Gertrude, and Lennette, Evelyne, "The Epstein-Barr Virus." *Scientific American*, July, 1979.

Hyde, Richard M., and Patnode, Robert A., *Immunology*. Reston, VA., Reston Publishing Co., Inc., 1978.

Julien. Robert M., *A Primer of Drug Action*, 3rd ed. San Francisco, W. H. Freeman and Co., 1981.

McKean, Kevin, "Closing in on the Herpes Virus." *Discover*, October, 1981.

Porter, R. R., *Chemical Aspects of Immunology*. Carolina Biology Reader. Burlington, NC, Carolina Biological Supply Co., 1976.

Trager, William, "The Biochemistry of the Resistance of Malaria." *Scientific American*, March, 1981.

Wheeler, B. E. J., *The Control of Plant Disease*. Oxford Biology Reader. London, Oxford University Press, 1975.

CHAPTER 20   PLANT REPRODUCTION AND DEVELOPMENT

Teaching Techniques

Before discussing reproduction in specific plants, spend some time analyzing plant life cycles in general. Make certain that students master the idea that gametes are produced by mitosis from monoploid plants and that spores are produced by meiosis from diploid plants. Because they have previously learned that diploid animals produce monoploid gametes by meiosis, students may at first be confused. Stress, however, that the processes of mitosis and meiosis are essentially the same in all organisms. Mitosis always results in daughter nuclei which have the same number of chromosomes as the parent nucleus, and meiosis always produces daughter nuclei with half the number of chromosomes as the parent nucleus.

In teaching the life cycles of land plants, relate each cycle to the generalized plant life cycle. When you get to the seed plants, point out that the general cycle is still followed, but the multicellular gametophyte has been eliminated. Spores are produced, as in other plants, but they are modified to become gametes without the intervening multicellular monoploid stage present in less complex plants.

Performance Objectives

Goal: Students will gain an understanding of patterns of reproduction and development found among plants.

Objectives: Upon completion of the reading and activities and when asked to respond orally or on a written test, students will:

Section
Number

20:0	K	explain that in a plant life cycle the monoploid and diploid generations follow one another in an alternation of generations.
20:1	K	describe the stages in the life cycle of *Spirogyra*.
20:2	K	discuss the means of asexual and sexual reproduction in *Ulothrix*.
20:3	K	describe the life cycle of *Ulva*.
20:3	P	compare and contrast the sporophyte and gametophyte generations.
20:4	K	describe the life cycle of mosses.
20:4,5	P	describe the life cycle of ferns and compare it to that of the mosses.
20:6	P	compare and contrast gamete production in male and female cones.
20:6	K	describe fertilization and seed formation in a conifer.
20:6	K	list several adaptations of conifers which are not present in mosses and ferns.
20:7	K/S	diagram a flower, identify the parts, and describe the function of each part.
20:8	K	describe the formation of a pollen grain in a flowering plant.
20:8	K	describe the formation of the polar nuclei and true egg in a flowering plant.
20:9	K	describe fertilization and seed formation in a flowering plant.
20:10	K	describe the formation of fruits in flowering plants and explain how fruits play a role in seed dispersal.
20:11	P	compare and contrast self-pollination and cross-pollination.
20:11	K	list some adaptations which have helped seed plants to be successful in many environments.
20:12	K	explain and cite examples of vegetative propagation in plants.
20:13	K	identify the parts of flowering plant seeds, the functions of the parts, and describe early seed development.
20:14	K	identify and state the functions of the regions in a developing tree root.
20:14	K	explain the means by which a tree root increases in diameter.

(See page 41T for performance objectives that apply to all chapters.)

Answers to Chapter 20 Review

Page 390. Checking Your Ideas

1. mitosis	6. self
2. diploid (or 2n)	7. seeds
3. radicle	8. vegetative propagation
4. fruit	9. monoploid (or n)
5. seed plants	10. gametophyte

Page 390. Evaluating Your Ideas

1. Sexual reproduction in *Spirogyra* occurs by conjugation. Cell contents of adjacent filaments fuse to form zygotes. In *Ulothrix*, certain cells along the filament produce flagellated gametes. The motile gametes fuse to form a zygote.

2. *Ulva* has a multicellular diploid stage not present in *Spirogyra* and *Ulothrix.*

3. Plants undergo a life cycle in which a monoploid gametophyte generation alternates with a diploid sporophyte generation. By meiosis, spores are produced from sporophytes. The monoploid spores are the beginning of the gametophyte generation. The gametophyte plants produce gametes by mitosis. Gametes fuse to form the diploid zygote, the beginning of the sporophyte generation. Both gametophytes and sporophytes may be capable of vegetative propagation.

4. In mosses, the gametophyte is predominant. Each gametophyte, male and female, produces gametes by mitosis. Sperm are produced in the antheridium. They swim to the eggs which are produced by and retained in the archegonium. Fertilization occurs in the archegonium. The zygote produced develops into a mature sporophyte. Each spore of the sporophyte may grow into a small protonema which then develops into a mature gametophyte.

5. The egg is retained within the archegonium and is protected from environmental hazards. Chances for fertilization there are better and the zygote is protected during its development.

6. Mosses require a moist environment. They need a liquid medium through which sperm can travel to the eggs.

7. The sporophyte is predominant in ferns. The sporophyte produces spores by meiosis. The monoploid spores may develop into small gametophytes called prothallia. Each prothallium contains both archegonia and antheridia in which eggs and sperm are produced by mitosis. The sperm swim to and fertilize the eggs which are retained in the archegonium. The young sporophyte begins development there but soon becomes an independent plant. Ferns are limited by their need for water and the delicacy of their small gametophyte.

8. The sporophyte is predominant in conifers. In male cones, certain diploid cells undergo meiosis to form monoploid spores which become pollen grains. Certain diploid cells in female cones produce spores which are later modified to form eggs. After pollination (by wind), a monoploid sperm cell is formed within the pollen grain. The sperm fertilizes the egg in the female cone to produce a diploid zygote, the beginning of a new sporophyte generation. The zygote develops into an embryo within a seed. Seeds are dispersed by wind and develop into multicellular diploid plants. Conifers do not require water for fertilization as sperm cells in pollen grains are carried to eggs by wind. Pollen grains also prevent sperm from drying out. The embryo is protected by the outer seed coat and by the cone in which seeds are formed.

9. Pollen sacs within the anthers contain diploid cells which undergo meiosis to produce four monoploid microspores. Each microspore nucleus divides by mitosis to form two monoploid nuclei, the tube nucleus and the generative nucleus. The outer wall of the microspore then hardens and the entire structure is called a pollen grain.

10. Certain cells of the ovule divide meiotically to form four monoploid cells, one of which survives. The survivor is called a megaspore. The megaspore nucleus undergoes mitosis to form two monoploid nuclei. The nuclei divide twice more to produce a total of eight monoploid nuclei, five of which die. The remaining nuclei form the two polar nuclei and the true egg.

11. After reaching the pistil, a pollen grain sprouts a pollen tube which tunnels through the style to the micropyle of the ovule. The generative nucleus divides by mitosis to form two sperm nuclei both of which travel via the pollen tube to the micropyle. Once inside the ovule one sperm nucleus joins with the polar nuclei to form a triploid structure, the endosperm nucleus. The other sperm nucleus fertilizes the true egg to form a zygote, the beginning of a new sporophyte generation. After this the endosperm nucleus divides repeatedly to form endosperm tissue which will act as a food source for the developing plant. The outer wall of the ovule hardens into the seed coat and the ovule is now a seed. Meanwhile the ovary enlarges rapidly to become the fruit.

12. The fruit acts as a dispersal agent. Many fruits are eaten by animals which deposit the seeds after digestion. Other fruits are dispersed by sticking to animals, or by water or air. Dispersal is necessary for moving seeds to a suitable environment.

13. Seed plants do not require water for fertilization. Therefore, they are not limited to a moist environment. Embryos are protected within seeds which, in turn, are partly or completely protected. The sporophyte is predominant, thus decreasing the chances for expression of harmful genes. Flowering plants have even greater success in that their pollen is often carried by animals as well as by the wind. Also, fruits aid in dispersal of seeds.

14. The structures are the radicle, hypocotyl, and epicotyl. The radicle develops into the primary root of the plant; the hypocotyl gives rise to part of the root system and the lower part of the stem; the epicotyl forms the first leaves of the plant and the rest of the stem.

15. Cotyledons contain food which serves as an energy source until the young plant is capable of photosynthesis. The first leaves take over the function of the cotyledons.

16. New root cap cells are produced on the tip of the growing root by the meristem region. New cells also are produced further from the root tip on the other side of the meristem. These cells grow in length and form the elongation region. They add to the length of the root, pushing it deeper into the soil. Above the elongation region is the maturation region where cells grow larger and differentiate into various tissues. The tissues include those for conduction of water and food, for storage, for uptake of water and minerals, and for cell division (vascular cambium).

17. A root becomes thicker as the vascular cambium undergoes mitosis producing new conductive tissue. Cells on the inside of the cambium differentiate into tissue which transports water; cells on the outside differentiate into tissue which transports food.

18. Favorable genotypes (and phenotypes) can be preserved through artificial vegetative propagation.

Page 391. Applying Your Ideas

1. Such a tree might be "produced" by grafting. Different types of fruits are produced according to the genetic instructions of each plant type.

2. Mosses require moisture for fertilization. An open field might be too dry.

3. All but the pine and redwood are flowering plants.

4. A plant produced by vegetative propagation is genetically identical to the parent plant, making it a clone.

5. Many of the internal structures of a stem and root are the same. However, the stem also develops structures such as leaves and cones or flowers.

6. Plants have meristematic tissue which produces cells continually.

7. A tomato root develops similarly to a woody root but has no vascular cambium. It lives for only one growing season.

Page 391. Extending Your Ideas

1. Students should investigate vegetative propagation by cuttings, grafting, and budding.

2. These algae reveal a shift from predominance of gametophyte generation (*Chlamydomonas* and *Oedogonium*) to predominance of sporophyte (*Fucus*). This same trend is seen in land plants.

3. A sweet potato will develop root, shoot, and leaf systems by vegetative means.

4. Sweet corn seeds can be used in this experiment. Seeds can be planted in soil or vermiculite. Graph **a** is called a growth curve. Graph **b** is a growth increment curve. Graph **c** is a percentage growth curve. Make certain that students realize what each graph reflects.

5. Data will vary depending on the variable factor. Amount of light or water should affect the pattern of growth.

Additional Student Readings

Martin, Willard K., "Protean Beauty." *Natural History*, December, 1981.

Walker, Donald M., "Jewelweed's Sexual Skills." *Natural History*, May, 1982.

Suggested Teacher Readings

Blair, John G., "Test-Tube Gardens." *Science 82*, January, 1982.

Brookbank, John W., *Developmental Biology, Embryos, Plants, and Regeneration*. New York, Harper and Row, Publishers, Inc., 1978.

Leopold, A.C., and Kriedemann, P.E., *Plant Growth and Development*, 2nd ed. New York, McGraw-Hill, 1975.

Northcote, D. H., *Differentiation in Higher Plants*, 2nd ed. Carolina Biology Reader. Burlington, NC, Carolina Biological Supply Co., 1980.

CHAPTER 21   PLANT NUTRITION

Teaching Techniques

As you begin this chapter, you may wish to take some time to review with students some of the basic ideas about energy studied in previous chapters. Remind students that energy is needed for biological work and that ATP is the source of energy used for that work. Energy needed to make ATP comes from glucose (and other high-energy compounds) and is released during cellular respiration. Continue this review as necessary, leading to the idea that the energy of glucose comes originally from the sun and is incorporated during the process of photosynthesis. Emphasize that organisms, both autotrophic and heterotrophic, carry out respiration, but that only autotrophs are capable of photosynthesis.

Section 21:6 is an important review which relates respiration and photosynthesis in terms of both energy and materials. Before leaving this section, make certain that students see that details presented here augment general ideas presented in Chapter 1. For honors or advanced groups, you should consider teaching the mechanism of photosynthesis as presented in Appendix B.

Performance Objectives

Goal: Students will gain an understanding of photosynthesis and plant nutrition.

Objectives: Upon completion of the reading and activities and when asked to respond orally or on a written test, students will:

Section Number		
21:1	S/K	diagram a cross section of a leaf, identify the various structures, and indicate the function of each structure.
21:2	K	list the colors of visible spectrum.
21:2	K	explain that when light energy is absorbed, it is changed to another form of energy.
21:3	K	describe the absorption spectrum of chlorophyll and explain that the wavelengths absorbed are changed to chemical energy.
21:3	P	compare and contrast the location of chlorophyll in eukaryotes, blue-green algae, and autotrophic bacteria.
21:3	K	identify carotenes as plant pigments which also are involved in the trapping of light energy.
21:4	K	identify photosynthesis as the process by which light energy is absorbed and converted to chemical energy of glucose.
21:4	K	explain the events of the light reactions of photosynthesis.
21:4,5	P	relate the events of the light reactions to the events of the dark reactions.
21:6	P	compare, contrast, and relate respiration and photosynthesis.

21:7	P	compare and contrast digestion in the insectivorous and noninsectivorous plants.
21:8	K	list several plant nutrients and explain how they are used.
21:9	K	explain several ways in which plants may be used to produce fuels.

(See page 41T for performance objectives that apply to all chapters.)

Answers to Chapter 21 Review

Page 404. Checking Your Ideas

1. false
2. true
3. true
4. true
5. true
6. false
7. false
8. false
9. false
10. false

Page 404. Evaluating Your Ideas

1. (a) upper epidermis—protection
   (b) palisade cells—photosynthesis
   (c) spongy layer—photosynthesis
   (d) xylem—transport of water and minerals
   (e) lower epidermis—protection, intake of CO_2
   (f) cutin—protection against water loss
   (g) phloem—transport of food
2. Photosynthesis is the means by which light energy is converted to chemical energy, the energy form usable in living things. Humans depend on photosynthesis for food—the plants (fruits, vegetables, nuts) and indirectly the animals—they consume.
3. An absorption spectrum shows that chlorophyll absorbs most of the violet, blue, red, and orange light and reflects green and yellow. The absorbed light energy is transformed into chemical energy.
4. Carotenes are a class of pigments which reflect yellow, orange, and red. They are visible in leaves when chlorophyll production ceases.
5. The reactants of photosynthesis are carbon dioxide and water. The products are glucose and oxygen.
6. During the light reactions, light is absorbed by chlorophyll and carotene molecules. Then, in a series of steps, the light energy is converted to chemical energy in the form of ATP molecules. Water is split into hydrogen, used later in photosynthesis, and oxygen, given off as a by-product.
7. During the dark reactions, the hydrogen ions produced during the light reactions are added to carbon dioxide to form glucose. This process is endergonic utilizing the energy of ATP produced during the light reactions.
8. Glucose can be used as an energy source or converted to other organic molecules such as fats and amino acids. Some glucose is stored as starch and some is converted to cellulose.
9. The overall reaction in photosynthesis is the reverse of the respiration reaction. Also, photosynthesis is endergonic whereas respiration is exergonic.

10. The chemical energy produced during photosynthesis is used to rearrange the atoms of carbon dioxide and water to produce glucose. Some of the chemical energy is stored in glucose.
11. The essay should include the following points:
(a) Photosynthesis converts the carbon dioxide and water produced during respiration to glucose.
(b) Photosynthesis produces, as a by-product, the oxygen necessary for respiration.
(c) The flow of energy is: radiant (sunlight) → chemical (glucose) → chemical (ATP) → energy used for work of the cell → heat.
(d) The changes of potential energy are: low potential energy (carbon dioxide and water) $\xrightarrow{photosynthesis}$ high potential energy (glucose) $\xrightarrow{respiration}$ low potential energy (carbon dioxide and water).
12. Leaves of the Venus's-flytrap are modified for trapping insects. Spines border the upper edge of the leaves which are hinged along the midrib. Sensory hairs are located on the upper surface of each lobe of the leaf. Stimulation of these hairs by the touch of an insect causes the leaf to snap shut, trapping the insect inside. Digestive enzymes are secreted into the hollow and extracellular digestion takes place. The digested molecules are then absorbed and transported.
13. Magnesium is present in chlorophyll; sulfur is present in some amino acids. Nitrogen is present in amino acids and nitrogen bases.
14. Sugars produced by plants such as sugarcane and corn can be fermented by bacteria to produce alcohol. This alcohol mixed with gasoline forms gasohol. Plants such as certain Euphorbias produce hydrocarbons that can be used directly as fuels or converted to a variety of petroleum substitutes.

Page 405. Applying Your Ideas

1. The leaf's structure is related to its chief function—photosynthesis. The leaf is flattened giving a large surface area for trapping light energy. The palisade cells, containing chlorophyll, are numerous, and are close to the upper surface where light is available. Stomata are openings through which carbon dioxide can enter. Xylem brings water and nutrients to the leaf and phloem distributes glucose to nonphotosynthetic parts of the plant.
2. An absorption spectrum of carotenes would show that they absorb blue, green, and violet wavelengths. They reflect yellow, orange, and red. Pigments reflect the colors that they are.
3. Fertilizers contain nutrients required by plants. They supplement nutrients found in the soil.
4. The products of respiration, carbon dioxide and water, are the reactants of photosynthesis. As photosynthesis occurs, glucose is produced and oxygen is released. The glucose and oxygen are used during respiration.
5. It is given off during the light reactions of photosynthesis.
6. Light energy is trapped by the chlorophyll of autotrophs and converted to chemical energy of ATP in the light reactions of photosynthesis. The ATP is used in the dark reactions and energy becomes stored in glucose. During respiration, energy of glucose is released and converted to ATP. Energy of ATP is used for endergonic reactions. Once it is converted to heat, it cannot be reused. Thus, energy cannot be recycled.

7. Decomposers break down amino acids, proteins, and nucleic acids in dead organisms and wastes and return the nitrogen to the soil from which it is absorbed by plants.
8. Phosphorus is part of ATP and nucleic acids.

Page 405. Extending Your Ideas

1. Van Helmont concluded that the increase in mass of a willow tree plant was due to water. Priestley showed that oxygen is liberated by plants as a by-product of photosynthesis. Ingen-Housz found that light is necessary for photosynthesis.
2. Plants which germinate in darkness will not produce chlorophyll. The seedling is abnormally long and slender and leaves do not expand fully. This phenomenon is known as etiolation. To test the effectiveness of different wavelengths, expose germinating seedlings to white light and a variety of colors of light. (Transparent filters of different colors can be used.) Seeds developing in red light will have normal development except for color. Seeds developing in white light will exhibit normal development and coloration. Other colors will produce a variety of patterns. Keep plants in cardboard containers as they develop. The containers should be closed except for an area through which light passes.
3. This experiment should be done with submerged aquatic plants. White light and filtered light can be shined upon different plants, e.g., *Elodea* sprigs. Counting bubbles of oxygen escaping from each sprig is a means of determining relative photosynthetic rate. Blue light should produce the greatest rate; green light, the slowest.

4. Spanish moss obtains its nutrients through its leaves from the air and from water in the air.
5. Sundews, pitcher plants, or Venus's-flytraps may be ordered from biological supply houses and set up in two terraria. Fruit flies should be introduced into one terrarium, but not the other. Caution students that differences which may appear between the two groups may not be due solely to the availability of insects as a food source.

Additional Student Readings

Ognibene, Peter, "Growing Fuel." *Science Digest*, August, 1981.
"Photosynthetic Electricity." *Science Digest*, September, 1981.

Suggested Teacher Readings

Bidwell, R.G.S., *Plant Physiology*, 2nd ed. New York, Macmillan Publishing Co., 1979.
Goldsworthy, A., *Photorespiration*. Carolina Biology Reader. Burlington, NC. Carolina Biological Supply Co., 1976.
Heath, O.V.S., *Stomata*, 2nd ed. Carolina Biology Reader. Burlington, NC, Carolina Biological Supply Co., 1981.
Miller, Kenneth R., "The Photosynthetic Membrane." *Scientific American*, October, 1979.
Noggle, G. Ray, and Fritz, George J., *Introductory Plant Physiology*. Englewood Cliffs, NJ, Prentice-Hall, Inc., 1976.

CHAPTER 22 PLANTS: OTHER LIFE FUNCTIONS

Teaching Techniques

Sections 22:1 and 22:2 present the basic anatomy of angiosperm roots and stems for both monocots and dicots. These two sections provide a basis for understanding the plant physiology presented in subsequent sections of the chapter. As you teach this material, emphasize the concept of structure and function complementing each other. You can begin the emphasis using the chapter opening photo in a discussion. Stress also how the various tissues of roots and stems interact in carrying out activities such as protection, transport, and storage. Point out that although monocots and dicots differ in details of their anatomy, their general plans are fundamentally similar. If time permits, have students examine prepared slides of roots and stems, or as an alternative, use overhead transparencies.

Students may wonder why excretion is not covered. Excretion in plants is a minor activity. Protein metabolism is limited and the by-products of such metabolism can be utilized in other biochemical pathways. In any event, plants have no excretory organs. Some wastes are deposited in dead wood cells of the stem or in vacuoles.

Performance Objectives

Goal: Students will gain an understanding of plant anatomy and physiology.

Objectives: Upon completion of the reading and activities and when asked to respond orally or on a written test, students will:

Section Number		
22:1	P	compare and contrast the internal structures of monocot and dicot roots.
22:2	P	compare and contrast the internal structure of herbaceous monocot and herbaceous dicot stems.
22:2	S/K	diagram the cross section view of a woody stem, identify the various structures, and indicate the function of each structure.
22:3	K	explain the means of transport and gas exchange in algae, liverworts, and mosses.
22:4	K	describe the process whereby water travels from root hairs to xylem by successive osmosis.

22:5	K	describe the transpiration-cohesion theory and explain how this phenomenon is beneficial to complex plants.
22:6	K	explain how guard cells regulate the size of stomata and why this regulation is adaptive.
22:7	K	describe the process of translocation and indicate the structures involved in this process.
22:8	K	explain the various ways gases are exchanged in plants.
22:9	P	compare, contrast, and give examples of positive and negative tropisms.
22:9	K	describe the role of the auxin indoleacetic acid in positive phototropism.
22:10	K	list and describe other effects of auxins.
22:11	K	explain the functions of gibberellins.
22:12	P	distinguish among short-day, long-day, and day-neutral plants.
22:12	K	explain the means by which flowering is thought to occur in some plants.

(See page 41T for performance objectives that apply to all chapters.)

Answers to Chapter 22 Review

Page 424. Checking Your Ideas

1. hormones
2. lenticels
3. photoperiodism
4. pressure-flow hypothesis
5. stele
6. positive
7. abscission
8. transpiration-cohesion
9. successive osmosis
10. translocation

Page 424. Evaluating Your Ideas

1. Epidermis—protection; cortex—food storage; pericycle—formation of branch roots; xylem—water and mineral transport; phloem—food transport. In a dicot root, xylem is arranged in a star-shaped pattern with phloem vessels between the arms of the star. In a monocot root, the stele is larger, and xylem vessels are arranged in a circle with phloem vessels between them.

2. The major difference between herbaceous monocot and dicot stems is the arrangement of the vascular bundles which are scattered in the former and close to the edge in the latter. Also, vascular bundles of dicots have vascular cambium which produces cells which later develop into xylem (water and mineral transport) and phloem (food transport). Other stem structures include pith (food storage) and, in dicots, cortex (food storage or, in some plants, food production). A woody plant is a dicot. It has vascular cambium and its vascular bundles are arranged in a circle near the edge of the stem.

3. The outer bark of a woody stem consists of cork and cork cambium. The cork cambium produces new cork cells which protect the stem and reduce water loss. The inner bark consists of phloem and cortex. Phloem conducts food materials throughout the plant. Cortex stores excess food.

4. Spring wood consists mostly of large xylem vessels whereas summer wood is composed of vessels of smaller diameter.

5. In algae and mosses, materials are transported by diffusion, osmosis, or cytoplasmic streaming. Gas exchange in algae occurs between each cell and the environment. In mosses, gases are exchanged through pores.

6. In complex plants, individual cells cannot exchange materials directly with the environment because they are too far removed from it. Instead, materials enter and leave the organism only at specific points and are carried to and away from these points by a transport system. The transport system exchanges the materials with the cells.

7. Water enters a plant through its roots. Root hairs, projections of outer epidermis cells of the secondary roots, greatly increase the surface area for absorption. Water moves from the spaces between soil particles into root hairs by osmosis.

8. From root hairs, water passes by osmosis across the cell layers of the root into the vascular bundle where it enters xylem vessels. These xylem vessels are continuous with xylem of the stems and leaves. Water is conducted up the plant through this xylem "pipeline."

9. In narrow xylem vessels, water exhibits cohesion and adhesion. In combination these properties cause water in xylem vessels to be very dense. As water molecules escape from the stomata of the leaves, other water molecules from the xylem vessels of the leaf replace them. This movement creates tension, or pull, on the rest of the water column extending even to the roots. As water in the root xylem is pulled up, more water moves into the xylem from the surrounding root cells. The source of this water is the soil.

10. Guard cells swell as they use carbon dioxide during the day. When they swell, the size of a space between them, the stoma, increases. Thus, more carbon dioxide can enter the leaf. No carbon dioxide is necessary at night. At night, the guard cells collapse and the size of the stoma is reduced. Therefore, water is conserved.

11. In plants, food is transported by phloem cells in the vascular bundles. Food synthesized in a leaf dissolves in water and enters the phloem cells of the veins. From here, food may be transported (translocated) anywhere within the plant. Food probably enters the cytoplasm of phloem and moves along with it. Translocation may result from pressure differences between sieve cells. As sugar enters sieve cells of leaves, water moves in from neighboring cells by osmosis and the pressure inside the sieve cell is increased. The pressure is thought to force sugar into the next sieve cell where pressure is lower. This pressure difference exists from leaves to roots. Pressure remains lower in the roots because sugar and water leave the sieve cells there.

12. Gas exchange occurs by diffusion and plants are adapted with large surface areas for exchange and some with pores. The gas exchange that occurs is adequate to supply the needs of the plant without an elaborate gas exchange system.

13. Root cells require oxygen for cell respiration, the process that produces energy in usable form. The energy is used for the life processes in the root cells. For example, root cells actively transport minerals in. Oxygen is obtained from the air dissolved in the moisture of the soil. It diffuses into the root hairs from the soil spaces and is transported to other cells of the root.

14. Lenticels are tiny openings on stems and some large roots. Oxygen and carbon dioxide are exchanged through lenticels.

15. Gases are exchanged in leaves through the stomata. Carbon dioxide necessary for photosynthesis enters the leaf via stomata from the air. Some oxygen leaves the plant through the stomata. The rest is used in cellular respiration. Some of the carbon dioxide given off during respiration may be used in photosynthesis.

16. While investigating positive phototropism in plants, biologists learned that auxin secreted by the tip of a coleoptile is responsible for the bending of a plant toward a light source.

17. Auxin migrates away from the lighted side of the plant. This migration results in a greater concentration of auxin in the shaded side. The cells in the shaded side elongate more quickly than those on the lighted side. These unequal growth rates cause the stem or shoot to bend toward the light.

18. In roots, excess auxin causes a decrease in growth rate. Auxins accumulate in the lower side of a root. Thus, the upper side grows more rapidly and the root bends downward.

19. Knowledge that abscission is controlled by auxins has resulted in means for delaying the fall of fruits until they are ready for eating.

20. Gibberellins stimulate the growth of some plants. They are used to produce large fruits and vegetables, to stimulate germination of seeds, and to stimulate development of buds.

21. The leaves of some plants are thought to contain phytochrome, a pigment which is sensitive to light. Somehow, the proper length of uninterrupted darkness for the particular plant is detected. Evidence suggests that the leaves then release a hormone, florigen, which travels via the phloem to the flower buds and causes them to flower. Florigen has not been isolated.

Page 425. Applying Your Ideas

1. The shape caused by apical dominance affords the leaves maximum exposure to sunlight.

2. Because a critical amount of continued darkness is needed for flowering, a plant subjected to a flash of light during its required dark period would not flower.

3. A short-day plant might flower in July if it were grown in conditions where it was subjected to an artificial, lengthy period of continual darkness.

4. Most animal responses are caused by nerves. Plant responses are controlled by hormones.

5. Transport and gas exchange in all these organisms occur by diffusion. Transport also occurs in some by cytoplasmic streaming.

6. Increase in light would increase rate of photosynthesis in the guard cells and lead to an increase in size of stomata. Decrease in amount of carbon dioxide would decrease rate of photosynthesis and decrease the size of stomata.

7. The leaf would not be able to exchange gases because the jelly would seal the stomata. The leaf would die.

8. The stomata of water lily leaves (lily pads) are located on the upper surface, the side exposed to air. This structure is adaptive, allowing gas exchange through the top side of the leaf.

Page 425. Extending Your Ideas

1. Petioles to which auxin has been applied will fall off less quickly than the controls. A solution of IAA dissolved in petroleum jelly can be used for the experiment. Students could also determine the effect of different concentrations of auxin.

2. Remove the apical bud from two plants. Leave one plant untreated. Apply a solution of IAA paste to the point from which the apical bud was removed from the second plant. The plant to which the IAA has been added should continue to show apical dominance. Lateral bud formation will increase in the untreated plant.

3. Cytokinins are important in stimulating cell division. They may also induce lateral growth of cells. Ethylene plays a role in the ripening of fruit and abscission of leaves. It has been called a hormone of senescence.

Additional Student Readings

Ehleringer, J. and Forseth, I., "Solar Tracking by Plants." *Science*, December 5, 1980.

Gwyne, P. and Carey, J., "Hormones for Profit." *Newsweek*, October 27, 1980.

"Plants Ups and Downs." *Science Digest*, February, 1982.

Suggested Teacher Readings

Bidwell, R.G.S., *Plant Physiology*, 2nd ed. New York, Macmillan Publishing Co., 1979.

Hendricks, Sterling B., *Phytochrome and Plant Growth*. Carolina Biology Reader. Burlington, NC, Carolina Biological Supply Co., 1980.

Salisbury, F., and Ross, C., *Plant Physiology*, 2nd ed. Belmont, CA, Wadsworth, 1978.

Thimann, K.V., *Hormone Action in the Whole Life of Plants*. Amherst, MA, University of Massachusetts Press, 1977.

CHAPTER 23 ANIMAL REPRODUCTION

Teaching Techniques

When comparing animal reproduction to that of plants, stress that the life cycles in both types of organisms involve meiosis and fertilization, and thus, variation among offspring is ensured. However, point out that animal life cycles in general do not involve a multicellular monoploid phase. Animal life cycles also in general do not have asexual and sexual phases that must follow each other in turns. In teaching the conditions for fertilization among animals (Sections 23:3-23:5), point out that plants must meet these same conditions. See also *Applying Your Ideas*, question 5 in this Teacher's Guide.

A logical consequence of the discussion of human reproduction is the topic of birth control. For a description of various family planning methods, see Chapter 32 of this Teacher's Guide.

Performance Objectives

Goal: Students will gain an understanding of some of the patterns of reproduction of animals.

Objectives: Upon completion of the reading and activities and when asked to respond orally or on a written test, students will:

Section
Number

23:1	P	compare and contrast budding and fragmentation in animals and give an example of each.
23:1	K	explain asexual reproduction by parthenogenesis.
23:2	P	compare and contrast animal and plant life cycles.
23:3	K	list four conditions necessary for fertilization in animals.
23:4	K	describe external reproduction in frogs and explain how the conditions necessary for fertilization are met.
23:5	K	describe internal reproduction in grasshoppers and explain how the conditions necessary for fertilization are met.
23:5	K	explain how estrous cycles and courtship patterns are adaptive.
23:6	K	list the major structures of the human female and male reproductive systems and state the function of each structure.
23:6	K	describe the fertilization process as it occurs in humans.
23:7	K	describe the human menstrual cycle and explain how hormones control this cycle.

(See page 41T for performance objectives that apply to all chapters.)

Answers to Chapter 23 Review

Page 440. Checking Your Ideas

1. i	5. n	9. k	13. a
2. g	6. o	10. e	14. b
3. c	7. f	11. h	15. l
4. m	8. d	12. j	

Page 440. Evaluating Your Ideas

1. *Planaria* reproduce asexually by fragmentation. A planarian may break into two or more parts. Each part regenerates forming new individuals.

2. Animal life cycles in general do not include a multicellular monoploid phase, and animal gametes are produced from diploid cells by meiosis. Most animal life cycles do not have sexual and asexual stages that must follow each other in turns.

3. Earthworms are hermaphrodites. During mating, worms lie parallel to one another and sperm are passed from each worm to its mating partner. The sperm are stored in receptacles and later fertilize eggs. The fertilized eggs are deposited in soil where they will develop.

4. Conditions of fertilization are proper timing of release of gametes, protection of gametes, a pathway for sperm to reach eggs, and a liquid medium in which sperm may swim to the eggs.

5. Female: ovaries—egg production; oviducts—transfer eggs to abdomen; ovisac—storage of eggs; cloaca—exit point for eggs. Male: testes—sperm production; sperm ducts—transfer sperm to cloaca; cloaca—exit point for sperm.

6. Proper timing is met by amplexus. Production of large numbers of gametes provides "safety in numbers" and helps ensure fertilization will occur without a specific pathway for the sperm. The jellylike coating of the eggs also provides protection. Fertilization in water meets the need for a liquid environment.

7. Courtship patterns result in synchronized release of gametes by both sexes. This simultaneous release is important because gametes have short life spans.

8. In a female grasshopper, eggs are produced in ovaries and enter oviducts. In the male, sperm are produced in testes and travel to sperm ducts where fluids are added. As the eggs pass through the vagina in the female, sperm injected into the female enter the eggs through small pores in the shells. Fertilized eggs are expelled from the vagina and deposited in the soil where they develop.

9. The internal organs of the male and female reproductive systems protect the gametes and afford a pathway for sperm to reach eggs. A liquid medium accompanies the sperm. Proper timing is met by storage of sperm in the sperm receptacle until the eggs are ready for fertilization.

10. Female: ovaries—egg production; oviducts—egg transport to uterus; uterus—organ for growth of fetus; vagina—organ for sperm entry. Male: testes—sperm production; sperm ducts—transport of sperm to penis; penis—organ for sperm release from male.

11. During the follicle stage, the egg grows and matures within the follicle and the uterine tissue becomes thicker and more richly supplied with blood. The next stage, ovulation, marks the point at which the mature egg leaves the ovary. Next is the corpus luteum stage during which the ruptured follicle is changed to the corpus luteum. The uterine tissue is maintained during this time. (a) If no pregnancy has occurred, the corpus luteum, and then the uterine tissue, break down. This breakdown results in menstruation, the passage of blood, some uterine tissue, and the unfertilized egg from the vagina. (b) If pregnancy occurs, the uterine lining is maintained because progesterone level remains high.

12. The menstrual cycle is controlled by hormones. FSH is secreted from the pituitary during the follicle stage. It stimulates egg maturation and also causes the ovary to secrete estrogen necessary for the uterine build-up. As the level of estrogen increases, FSH decreases and LH is secreted. Ovulation and the formation of the corpus luteum occur. LH causes the corpus luteum to secrete progesterone which keeps the uterine tissue enriched. Breakdown of the corpus luteum and reduction of progesterone result in uterine breakdown and menstruation.

Page 441. Applying Your Ideas

1. Sexual reproduction ensures variety among offspring. (This question reviews Chapters 7 and 8.)

2. The production of so many sperm is adaptive because it helps ensure that fertilization will occur. Many sperm die or do not reach the egg.

3. Hermaphroditism is adaptive because it can ensure sexual reproduction of the parasite even if only one is present in the host.

4. Exchange of sperm is adaptive, providing a greater degree of genetic recombination and variety among offspring.

5. (1) pathway—moss: plants grow in a dense pattern and sperm are likely to encounter eggs; flowering plant: animals, especially insects, transfer pollen in flowers.

(2) protection—moss: egg is retained within archegonium, many sperm are released; flowering plant: pollen grains protect sperm, ovule and ovary protect eggs, and fertilization is entirely internal.

(3) liquid medium—moss: fertilization occurs in moist areas; flowering plant: no need for liquid to transport sperm because of pollen grains; fertilization occurs in moist flower parts.

(4) timing—in both groups of plants, gametes are produced at about the same time.

6. Only some algal plants have external fertilization. In mosses and liverworts, ferns, and seed plants, the egg is retained and fertilized in the female reproductive structure. However, in mosses and ferns, sperm must swim from the male to the female plant.

7. Semen is stored at a cold temperature to preserve viability of the sperm. Bulls would be selected on the basis of those hereditary traits desirable in the particular breeding.

8. Regeneration occurs in repair of tissues, such as a starfish's ray and a lizard's tail.

Page 441. Extending Your Ideas

1. *Planaria* can be cut in half using a sharp single-edged razor blade. Transfer planaria with a cotton swab to the flat surface of a moistened rubber stopper. As the blade gently presses against the planaria, the worm will extend. Then push through the body until the halves are separated. Place each half of the planaria in a covered petri dish (or other container which allows some air to enter) containing pond or aquarium water. Label each dish "head" or "tail." Each half can be observed daily using a binocular microscope or hand lens. Change water at least once weekly to prevent contamination. Do *not* feed planaria while they are regenerating.

2. Ring doves, the great crested grebe, pheasants, peacocks, the South American stone grouse, hummingbirds, bowerbirds, and jackdaws are only a few of the birds with elaborate courtship patterns.

3. See the reference by Grobstein in *Suggested Readings*, page 441 and by Edwards at the end of the material for this chapter of the Teacher's Guide.

4. Oral contraceptives contain a combination of estrogens and progesterone at a level normally present during the corpus luteum stage of the menstrual cycle. Thus, they prevent ovulation.

Additional Student Readings

Batten, Mary, "Mating Strategies." *Science Digest*, January/February, 1981.

Frisch, Rose E., "Fatness, Puberty, and Fertility." *Natural History*, October, 1980.

Lenard, Lane, "High-Tech Babies." *Science Digest*, August, 1981.

Suggested Teacher Readings

Ebon, Martin, ed., *The Cloning of Man*. New York, Signet Books, 1978.

Edwards, R.G., *Test-Tube Babies*. Carolina Biology Reader. Burlington, NC, Carolina Biological Supply Co., 1981.

Randal, Judith, "Breeding the Perfect Cow." *Science 81*, November, 1981.

CHAPTER 24   ANIMAL DEVELOPMENT

Teaching Techniques

As you discuss the various patterns of development found among animals, you may wish to take the opportunity to review the means by which the developing animals were produced. Students will be better able to see the life functions of reproduction and development as one continuous process.

Emphasize that all embryos require protection, both when fertilization occurs and later in development. Stress the kinds of adaptations for protection of developing young that can be seen in different animals. Sections 24:8-24:12 may be omitted except for more able students.

Performance Objectives

Goal: Students will gain some understanding of embryology and the changes by which an organism attains a final form.

Objectives: Upon completion of the reading and activities and when asked to respond orally or on a written test, students will:

Section
Number

24:0   K   define embryology as the study of development of organisms and list life functions of an embryo.

24:1	K	list different ways by which embryos that develop externally are protected.
24:2	K	describe frog metamorphosis and relate this pattern of development to the basic functions carried out by all embryos.
24:3	P	compare and contrast complete and incomplete metamorphosis.
24:4	K	list the four membranes which develop from the embryo within the shelled egg and describe the function of each.
24:4	K	describe development in monotremes.
24:5	K	describe the development of marsupials and explain why this development is only partially internal.
24:6	K	describe the formation of the placenta and the umbilical cord in placental mammals.
24:6	K	explain the exchange of materials between embryo and mother in placental mammals.
24:7	K	describe the birth process in humans.
24:7	P	compare and contrast parental care of mammals with that of other animals.
24:8	P	compare and contrast cleavage in a frog and a chick.
24:8	K	identify the blastula as a ball of cells with a blastocoel.
24:8	P	compare and contrast the development and characteristics of fraternal twins and identical twins.
24:9	K	describe the series of events by which a blastula develops into a gastrula.
24:9	K	define morphogenesis.
24:10	K	explain that differentiation is that part of development leading to the formation of specialized body parts.
24:10	K	describe the formation of the neural tube.
24:11	K	discuss the experiments which led to stating the principle of embryonic induction.
24:12	K	explain the hypothesis which describes how cells of a developing embryo become different from one another.
24:13	K	discuss several ways in which aging may occur in humans.

(See page 41T for performance objectives that apply to all chapters.)

Answers to Chapter 24 Review

Page 466. Checking Your Ideas

1. embryo
2. allantois
3. metamorphosis
4. cleavage
5. umbilical cord
6. amnion
7. marsupials
8. uterus
9. yolk sac
10. embryonic induction

Page 467. Evaluating Your Ideas

1. Fertilized frog eggs are protected by a jellylike layer and possibly by protective coloration.

2. Eggs hatch into larvae (tadpoles). The inactive tadpole becomes active as it develops a tail. The tail is needed for locomotion. Gills, necessary for exchange of oxygen and carbon dioxide in the water, also develop. Further development includes formation of hind and front legs and lungs. Legs are used for locomotion on land and lungs are used for breathing air. The length of the different stages varies in different species.

3. The larva can live independent of the parents and obtain food and oxygen necessary for its further development.

4. Internal development provides greater protection for the embryo.

5. The chorion functions in gas exchange. The yolk sac encloses the yolk. The allantois is a site for depositing metabolic wastes. The amnion cushions the embryo and keeps it moist.

6. Development of marsupials begins in the uterus of the mother. After a short time, the tiny embryos are expelled from the uterus and crawl into a pouch on the mother's abdomen. The pouch contains mammary glands by which the embryos are nourished. Partial internal development occurs because there is limited means for feeding the young within the uterus.

7. The egg is fertilized in the oviduct and develops into a ball of cells, the blastocyst, as it travels toward the uterus. The outer layer of cells (trophoblast) produces enzymes which digest some uterine cells and the embryo embeds in the uterine wall. This process of attachment and embedding is called implantation. The amnion forms and soon the trophoblast and embryo are connected to the uterine wall by the body stalk. Four membranes develop. Many branches form from the chorion and become embedded in the uterine wall. In these branches, capillaries develop from the allantois and become part of the placenta. The rest of the placenta is composed of spongy, blood-enriched uterine tissue. The umbilical cord develops from the body stalk and contains blood vessels derived from the allantois.

8. The placenta exchanges food, oxygen, and waste materials between mother and embryo.

9. Labor, a series of uterine muscle contractions, is initiated by hormones. The amniotic sac bursts as the cervix and vaginal openings enlarge. Further, more intense contractions force the child out of the mother's body through the vagina, usually headfirst. A final series of contractions causes the placenta to be expelled. In humans, the umbilical cord attached to the baby is tied and cut and falls off after several days.

10. In mammals, usually a small number of offspring is born at a time because it is adaptive, the advantage being that the parents can better care for and train them.

11. A blastula and a zygote are about equal in volume. No growth occurs during cleavage; the volume of the zygote is divided among many cells.

12. Cleavage results in a new mass of cells from which a multicellular animal can develop and a shape which allows for further rearrangement of cells.

13. Fraternal twins are produced as a result of two different eggs being fertilized by two different sperm. They have different genotypes and phenotypes. Identical twins are produced when cells of a dividing zygote separate during early cleavage. The cells develop into organisms having identical genotypes and phenotypes. (The phenotype could be altered, however, by environmental influences.)

14. During gastrulation, cells migrate inward through the blastopore to form an internal cavity, the archenteron. The archenteron later develops into digestive organs.

15. Differentiation is the series of changes resulting in the formation of the body parts. Embryonic induction is a phenomenon in which one part of an embryo influences the development of another part.

16. All cells must have the same genotypes because they are produced by mitosis from the zygote. However, each kind of cell has unique characteristics. Therefore, it is assumed that only a portion of the total genotype is active in each kind of cell. The remaining genes must be "switched off." Thus, each kind of cell produces a certain combination of enzymes which direct that cell's development.

17. Experiments with frogs show that the nucleus of the specialized intestinal cell still has the full DNA code needed to construct a new frog. However, some of it must not be operating. When the nucleus is placed in an undifferentiated cell, the DNA must be "switched on" again. Cloning experiments also support the hypothesis. They show that certain mature cells have all the DNA necessary to construct new organisms.

18. Through random mistakes in protein synthesis, defective proteins accumulate in cells. The number of defective proteins increases with age. At some point, there will be so many that needed cellular functions are affected and the cell dies.

19. Free radicals cause DNA mutations which result in the synthesis of faulty proteins. They also can inactivate proteins directly.

Page 467. Applying Your Ideas

1. Yolk and shells are added to insect eggs prior to fertilization, but they are added to bird and reptile eggs after fertilization.

2. Two eggs become enclosed by the same shell while traveling down the oviduct.

3. Possible pregnancy is prevented, enabling the mother to better care for the infant.

4. The mother's immune system must adjust to the presence of the embryo.

5. A mammal grows and attains sexual maturity. Learning may be considered a type of development, too.

6. Both plants and animals, while developing, require food and must exchange gases. Their development involves cell division, growth, morphogenesis, and differentiation. A major difference is that many complex plants produce new tissues and organs such as xylem, phloem, cones, flowers, and fruits each growing season. These tissues and organs develop from cells produced by meristems.

7. Development in water prevents drying out of the embryo.

8. Certain plants, such as trees, have a longer life span than many animals. Older plants are usually larger than younger plants, but continue to produce new (young) parts each year. Unicellular organisms age in the sense that they have a breakdown of cell functions when they die.

Page 467. Extending Your Ideas

1. Student answers will vary with the drugs or diseases they choose to investigate. Ethyl alcohol and German measles are just two of the factors students may want to examine. Ethyl alcohol is a drug which causes fetal alcohol syndrome in the baby when consumed by the mother during pregnancy. German measles is a viral disease dangerous to the developing fetus if contracted by the mother in the first three months of pregnancy. It causes severe malformations of the baby.

2. Cloning in mammals is being studied using three techniques. In one method, a type of parthenogenesis is effected. A sperm fertilizes an egg, but is removed from the egg before the nuclei fuse. The penetration of the egg triggers development through early stages. In a similar procedure, the sperm is removed before fusion of the nuclei, and a chemical which induces replication of the egg nucleus is added. The two egg nuclei fuse, and development occurs after the eggs are implanted in a recipient female. A third method involves transplantation of nuclei from embryonic donor cells into fertilized eggs whose own nuclei have been removed. These eggs are grown in culture and then implanted in a female recipient for the rest of the gestation period. All three approaches differ from plant cloning techniques in which an isolated cell from a parent plant develops in culture media or when means of vegetative propagation are employed. Plant cloning does not involve transplantation of genetic information or techniques which mimic fertilization.

Additional Student Readings

Conniff, Richard, "Supergene." *Science Digest*, March, 1982.

Gwyne, Peter, "DNA: New Clues to the Ultimate Secret." *Science Digest*, September, 1981.

Patrusky, Ben, "How Do Cells Know What to Become?" *Science 81*, May, 1981.

Restak, Richard M., "Newborn Knowledge." *Science 82*, January/February, 1982.

Rodgers, Joann, "Me, Myself, and Us: Twins." *Science Digest*, November/December, 1980.

Suggested Teacher Readings

Beaconsfield, Peter, Birdwood, George, and Beaconsfield, Rebecca, "The Placenta." *Scientific American*, August, 1980.

Bonner, John T., *On Development: The Biology of Form*. Lawrence, MA, Harvard University Press, 1977.

deRobertis, E.M., and Gurdon, J.B., "Gene Transplantation and the Analysis of Development." *Scientific American*, December, 1979.

Edwards, R.G., *The Beginnings of Human Life*. Carolina Biology Reader. Burlington, NC, Carolina Biological Supply Co., 1981.

Gurdon, J.B., *Gene Expression during Cell Differentiation*, 2nd ed. Carolina Biology Reader. Burlington, NC, Carolina Biological Supply Co., 1978.

Holden, David J., "Cloning: Learning to Replay the Genetic Tape." *The Science Teacher*, November, 1979.

Hopper, A.F., and Hart, N.H., *Foundations of Animal Development*. New York, Oxford University Press, 1980.

Oppenheimer, Steven B., *Introduction to Embryonic Development*. Boston, Allyn and Bacon, Inc., 1980.

CHAPTER 25   FOOD GETTING AND DIGESTION

Teaching Techniques

In this text, a variety of patterns of digestion are presented to illustrate the diversity of ways in which the function is carried out. Point out that while specific adaptations differ, each type of system meets the requirements of obtaining, processing, and distributing food. Stress the difference between the *absorptive* nutrition of fungi (Chapter 18) and the *ingestion* of nutrients by animals.

In comparing the digestive equipment of different types of animals, relate structure to function and stress both the physical and chemical events of digestion. It is not necessary to have students memorize each of the human digestive enzymes and the specific reactions they catalyze. Rather, emphasize the gradual breakdown of complex molecules to smaller forms which can enter and be utilized by body cells.

Performance Objectives

Goal: Students will gain an understanding of digestion as it occurs in simple and complex animals.

Objectives: Upon completion of the reading and activities and when asked to respond orally or on a written test, students will:

Section
Number

25:1-4	K	describe the processes of filter-feeding, chunk feeding, and digestion in sponges, hydra, planaria, and earthworms.
25:2-4	P	compare and contrast "two way traffic" and "one way traffic" digestive systems.
25:5	P	compare and contrast food getting and digestion in an arthropod and a starfish.
25:6	K	list the six types of nutrients required by humans.
25:6	K	discuss several ways in which water is important in the body.
25:7	K	identify the four basic food groups.
25:7	K	discuss various health problems which may arise from obesity.
25:7	K	explain how an excess of salt or sugar in the diet may lead to health problems.
25:8	K	describe the functions of the mouth, pharynx, and esophagus in the human digestive system.
25:9	K	list and describe the digestive processes which occur in the stomach of a human.
25:10	K	indicate the role of the liver, gall bladder, and pancreas in the digestive process.
25:10	K	list the enzymes which function in the small intestine and indicate the types of food the enzymes affect and the products of the reactions.
25:11	K	describe the absorption process and the various structures and systems involved as it occurs in the small intestine.
25:12	K	describe the structure and function of the large intestine.

(See page 41T for performance objectives that apply to all chapters.)

Answers to Chapter 25 Review

Page 484. Checking Your Ideas

1. false		6. false	
2. false		7. true	
3. false		8. true	
4. false		9. false	
5. false		10. true	

Page 484. Evaluating Your Ideas

1. Sponges are filter-feeders. Flagella of collar cells draw water into the sponge and microscopic food particles stick to the collar. Digestion occurs within vacuoles of the collar cells or within amoebocytes.

2. Both have a single body opening and "two-way traffic." Both undergo a combination of extracellular and intracellular digestion. In *Hydra*, extracellular digestion occurs in the gastrovascular cavity and intracellular digestion is completed in cells of the endoderm. In *Planaria*, extracellular digestion occurs in the intestine. Digestion is completed intracellularly in cells of the intestinal lining. In both organisms, undigestible materials leave through the single opening.

3. There is no real specialization of individual digestive organs. Rather there is a "two-way traffic" of food and wastes and one cavity for digestion. Further specialization did not develop because this system is adaptive for these animals.

4. A digestive system with two openings permits "one-way traffic" and specialization of digestive organs. Thus, food is more efficiently digested.

5. Digestion in an earthworm is one-way and involves a number of specialized regions for physical and chemical digestion. Food enters through the mouth and is passed, in order, from esophagus, to crop, to gizzard, to intestine. Wastes are egested from the anus. In a planarian, there is only one body opening. All digestion occurs in one region, the intestine. Wastes must be egested through the mouth.

6. In earthworms and most other animals, diffusion alone would not be able to transport digested food quickly enough because there are too many cells and most are distant from the intestine.

7. A starfish forces open the shells of mollusks by use of its water pressure system. Its stomach protrudes from its mouth and secretes enzymes which digest the food extracellularly. Food then passes to digestive glands in each ray where digestion is completed. Undigestible wastes are egested from the anus.

8. Nutrients are used as energy sources and as materials for growth and maintenance.

9. Water is a solvent for and an ingredient in many cellular reactions. It is part of protoplasm and blood. Water is lost through evaporation, exhalation, and urination. Some is replaced through cellular respiration and dehydration synthesis reactions. Most is replaced as water in food or beverages.

10. Minerals are parts of molecules such as hemoglobin, ATP, and DNA. Vitamins are needed to make coenzymes.

11. Obesity may lead to high blood pressure, heart disease, stroke, and diabetes. Obesity can be avoided by lowering Calorie intake and by daily exercise.

12. Excess sugar contributes to obesity, tooth decay and hyperactivity in children. Excess salt causes the body to retain water and contributes to high blood pressure and heart disease.

13. Chewing breaks food into small chunks that can be swallowed. It also creates a greater surface area of food on which enzymes can operate. Mucin in saliva moistens food so it can be swallowed more easily. If these processes did not occur, transfer of food along the alimentary canal would be impeded and the rate of digestion would be decreased.

14. The esophagus transfers food from the mouth to the stomach by means of peristalsis. No chemical digestion occurs within this organ.

15. Gastrin is a hormone which stimulates the release of gastric juice from the gastric glands of the stomach.

16. Hydrochloric acid converts pepsinogen to the active enzyme pepsin. Pepsin, in turn, hydrolyzes proteins to polypeptides.

17. Bile is not an enzyme. It causes a physical rather than chemical change. Bile is necessary for the breaking down of fats to small globules. Once fats are converted to globules, they can be hydrolyzed by lipase.

18. Carbohydrates, fats, and proteins are complex molecules. They must be converted to simple molecules which can be absorbed by the bloodstream and then permeate cell membranes. Carbohydrates are converted to simple sugars (glucose, etc.), fats are converted to fatty acids and glycerol, and proteins are converted to amino acids.

19. Enzymes necessary for human digestion are secreted by the salivary glands, stomach, pancreas, and small intestine. Food passes through all but the salivary glands and pancreas. Salivary gland secretions enter the mouth. Pancreatic enzymes are transported to the small intestine where they perform their functions.

20. Most chemical digestion occurs in the mouth, stomach, and small intestine.

21. Villi are tiny projections lining the interior of the intestine. Small polypeptides and disaccharides seem to be actively transported into the villi. Villi provide a large surface area for absorption of these molecules. In cells of the villi, enzymes convert these larger molecules to amino acids and monosaccharides respectively.

22. Monosaccharides, amino acids, vitamins, and minerals absorbed into the capillaries of the villi are first transported to the liver by the hepatic portal vein. In the liver, excess glucose is extracted and converted to animal starch (glycogen). The blood then leaves the liver and is circulated around the body. Monosaccharides and amino acids reach the body cells via the capillaries. Fatty acids and glycerol enter the lacteals of the villi and are transported to tissue cells by the lymphatic system.

23. The large intestine absorbs water from undigestible food materials. When water is not absorbed, diarrhea and dehydration can result.

24. Some bacteria in the large intestine synthesize vitamin B_{12} which is necessary for proper red blood cell and hemoglobin production.

Page 484. Applying Your Ideas

1. Digestion in *Paramecium* is similar to that in complex animals in that it occurs within a special cavity which can be considered analogous to a digestive organ. In that sense, it is like extracellular digestion. Both *Paramecium* and animals ingest complex, organic molecules.

2. A planarian can distribute digested food by diffusion because the intestine is branched. Thus, no cell is very far from the source of digested food. The fact that the flatworm is flat contributes to this method. If the planarian were bulkier, diffusion would be inefficient regardless of the branching intestine.

3. The gizzard is an organ of physical digestion which is adaptive because birds have no teeth.

4. Regurgitation is a reflex which serves to rid the stomach of spoiled or excess food. It may also be a response to infection due to viruses or bacteria.

5. Fat would be restricted because, without a gall bladder, the secretion of bile would be reduced and fat digestion would be difficult.

6. Acid indigestion may result from hypersecretion of gastric juice containing hydrochloric acid. Sodium bicarbonate serves to neutralize the acid.

7. The coiling provides greater surface area for digestion and absorption of food.

8. Plants have no digestive systems. They take in simple, inorganic materials rather than large, complex ones. Digestion is intracellular only. Insectivorous plants are similar to animals in that they trap and digest prey organisms and then absorb the small molecules.

9. Both animals are flatworms. However, the tapeworm, a parasite, has no digestive system. It absorbs small nutrient molecules produced as a result of digestion by its host. A planarian is free-living. It has a simple digestive system to process ingested food.

10. Large amounts of energy for activity and growth are needed by young people. Hence, more nutrients are needed to meet these requirements.

11. A person eating a balanced diet usually does not need additional nutrients. The nutrients are provided by the food.

12. The salivary amylase would not be effective in the acidic environment of the stomach.

13. Rhizoids of fungi secrete large molecules (enzymes) into the food source. Small molecules are then absorbed and distributed. Animals ingest complex molecules and digest them inside the body.

14. Fad diets may exclude certain important nutrients. Many persons who lose weight on such a diet quickly gain it back as they return to their previous eating habits. Proper weight loss can only be sustained by reducing Calorie intake while eating a balanced diet.

Page 485. Extending Your Ideas

1. This survey could lead to a composite report which might be presented to the entire class. Students conducting the survey should provide a questionnaire or record chart which those participating in the survey can fill in over a set period of time.

2. The cow has a series of four chambers or stomachs for digestion, the first of which is the rumen. Food is continually regurgitated and chewed after being partially digested in these chambers. Chewing the cud (regurgitated food) is necessary to physically break down the cellulose-rich grasses upon which cows feed. This alternation of chemical and physical digestion allows more thorough digestion to take place.

3. Research on Alexis St. Martin was carried out by William Beaumont, an army physician. When the wound healed, the edges of the stomach opening became attached to the edges of the muscle and skin opening. This resulted in a permanent hole in the body wall. Beaumont discovered and isolated gastric juice whose effects he then tested. He also learned about physical aspects of digestion within the stomach.

4. Student answers will vary depending on the food additives they choose to study. The *FDA Consumer* ran a three part series on food additives in 1979 giving information students might find interesting about the uses, side effects, and overuse of food additives. The reference is

Lehmann, Phyllis, "More Than You Ever Thought You Would Know About Food Additives. . .Part I (Part II and Part III)", *FDA Consumer*, April (May and June), 1979.

5. Nutritionists are scientists who specialize in the study of nutrition, some of whom carry out research about diet, the nutrient requirements of the body, and the utilization of nutrients. Dieticians plan nutritious meals and supervise food service workers. They are often hired by schools and nursing homes because proper diet is vital to both younger and older people.

6. Some other names for "sugar" are glucose, dextrose, galactose, sucrose, lactose, and maltose. Salt may be listed as sodium chloride or other sodium compounds.

Additional Student Readings

Bennet, William and Gurin, Joel, "Do Diets Really Work?" *Science 82*, March, 1982.

Dubos, René, "Nutritional Ambiguities." *Natural History*, July, 1980.

Suggested Teacher Readings

Kirschmann, John D., *Nutrition Almanac.* New York, McGraw-Hill Book Co., 1979.

Moog, Florence, "The Lining of the Small Intestine." *Scientific American*, November, 1981.

"Salt: A New Villain." *Time*, March 15, 1982.

Scrimshaw, Nevin S., and Young, Vernon R., "The Requirements of Human Nutrition." *Scientific American*, September, 1976.

Sherlock, Sheila, *The Human Liver.* Carolina Biology Reader. Burlington, NC, Carolina Biological Supply Co., 1978.

CHAPTER 26   TRANSPORT

Teaching Techniques

In teaching circulation, stress the concept of blood and other fluids as the internal environment of body cells. It is important that students understand that simple animals can exchange materials directly with their environment because of the proximity of their cells to the water in which they live. Complex animals, however, have most cells far removed from the external environment. Moreover, that external environment is often not a moist one. Therefore, the circulatory system links the external environment to the body cells and serves as a liquid medium necessary for dissolution of gases and other particles.

Emphasize the crucial role played by a circulatory system in the proper functioning of other systems. Remind students that the distribution of digested food depends on the blood and lymphatic system (Chapter 25). The circulatory system's roles in respiratory, excretory, and endocrine functions are discussed in the following chapters.

Performance Objectives

Goal: Students will gain an understanding of what transport is and how it occurs in animals.

Objectives: Upon completion of the reading and activities and when asked to respond orally or on a written test, students will:

Section Number		
26:0	K	describe the transport system as a link between the cells of an animal and its environment.
26:1, 2	K/P	describe the circulatory system in earthworms and compare and contrast it with that of arthropods.
26:1-3	P	describe the circulatory system in fish and indicate how it is different from those in earthworms and arthropods.
26:4	P	compare and contrast the heart structures and circulatory systems in amphibians and reptiles.
26:5	K	describe the heart structure and circulatory system in a human.
26:3-5	P	compare the circulatory systems of fish, amphibians, reptiles, and humans in terms of pressure of blood going to the tissues and amount of oxygen in that blood.
26:6	P	explain the functions of the S-A and A-V nodes in the human heart.
26:6	K	explain the functions of the accelerator and vagus nerves in controlling the heartbeat.
26:7	P	distinguish between systolic and diastolic pressure.
26:7	K	explain the various health problems associated with hypertension.
26:8	K	describe the lymphatic system and its functions and indicate the origin of lymph.
26:9	K	explain the function of hemoglobin.
26:10	K	explain the role of platelets in blood clotting.
26:10	K	identify leukocytes as blood cells which play a role in the body's immune system.
26:11	P	list the four blood types, indicate how they can be cross matched, and explain why some combinations agglutinate.
26:12	K	explain what is meant by the Rh factor.
26:13	K	explain the series of events which may lead to a heart attack.
26:13	K	discuss several ways in which some forms of heart disease may be prevented.
26:14	K	explain the problem of rejection in the transplanting of organs such as the heart.
26:15	K	explain the operation of an artificial heart and discuss the limitations of such a device.

(See page 41T for performance objectives that apply to all chapters.)

Answers to Chapter 26 Review

Page 510. Checking Your Ideas

1. a	**5.** c	**8.** f
2. h	**6.** b	**9.** e
3. i	**7.** j	**10.** g
4. d		

Page 510. Evaluating Your Ideas

1. In complex animals, individual cells cannot exchange materials directly with the environment because they are too far removed from it. Instead, materials enter and leave the organism only at specific points and are carried to and away from these points by a transport system. The transport system exchanges the materials with cells.

2. The "internal environment" of an organism is the fluid which links the cells of an organism to its external environment.

3. The earthworm has a closed circulatory system. Blood remains in blood vessels as it circulates around the body. The grasshopper has an open circulatory system. Most of the circulation in a grasshopper occurs outside blood vessels. Blood travels through sinuses in the hemocoel and bathes cells directly. The blood, moved by muscular contractions, eventually empties into the heart and is then recirculated.

4. Oxygen and carbon dioxide are conveyed directly to and away from a grasshopper's cells by special tubes.

5. A fish has a two-chambered heart composed of an atrium and a ventricle. Blood reaches and leaves the heart in a deoxygenated state. It is then transported to the gills where oxygenation occurs. From the gills, oxygenated blood is circulated around the body. However, blood pressure is greatly reduced as a result of the blood's first passing through the gill capillaries and circulation is slow. A frog has a three-chambered heart consisting of two atria and a ventricle. Blood from the right atrium is deoxygenated whereas that from the left atrium is oxygenated. Thus, a mixture of blood enters the single ventricle. Most of the oxygen-rich blood is deflected to the brain. The rest of the blood is distributed to other parts of the body. Unlike the blood of the fish, oxygenated frog blood is also pumped through the heart. Therefore, there is less loss of blood pressure and circulation is not as slow.

6. See answer 5. Circulation is slow because blood must pass through gill capillaries after being pumped through the heart.

7. See answer 5. Oxygenated blood is pumped back through the heart.

8. Most reptiles, like amphibians, have a three-chambered heart. However, in reptiles, the ventricle is partially divided by a muscular wall, the septum. The septum keeps oxygenated and deoxygenated blood almost completely separated. Therefore, most of the deoxygenated blood is sent only to the lungs while most of the oxygenated blood is sent to all other tissues.

9. The path is as follows: inferior and superior vena cavae, right atrium, tricuspid valve, right ventricle, semilunar valve, pulmonary artery, lung capillaries, pulmonary veins, left atrium, bicuspid valve, left ventricle, semilunar valve, aorta, arteries, arterioles, capillaries, venules, veins, vena cavae.

10. The valves maintain proper direction of blood flow. Without valves, contractions and relaxations of the heart chambers would result in simultaneous transport of blood forward and backward.

11. Mammals have a complete separation of oxygenated and deoxygenated blood in the heart. Thus, blood going to the lungs is deoxygenated and blood going to the body cells is oxygenated before it leaves the heart. With this arrangement, cells of mammals receive enough oxygen for life activities.

12. The source of the human heartbeat is the S-A node in the right atrium. A flow of current sweeps out from the S-A node and across the atria causing them to contract. The current then reaches the A-V node and sweeps across the ventricles causing them to contract. The heartbeat is felt on the left side of the chest because ventricles, whose contractions are detectable, are pointed toward the left.

13. Heartbeat rate must vary so that necessary materials such as food and oxygen reach the cells in sufficient amounts under varying conditions. The heartbeat rate is controlled by accelerator nerves and vagus nerves. The former cause an increase and the latter a decrease in the rate. The control center for heartbeat is located in the medulla oblongata of the brain. Stimulation of the acceleration center in the medulla results in an increase. Stimulation of the inhibition center decreases the rate.

14. Hypertension is prolonged high blood pressure. It can lead to enlargement of and damage to the heart, shortness of breath, kidney failure, heart failure, and death. These effects can be avoided by early detection of the disease and treatment with certain drugs.

15. Tissue fluid is derived from blood and directly bathes the body cells with which it exchanges needed and waste materials. Some returns directly to capillaries while the rest enters the lymphatic vessels where it is known as lymph. Eventually the lymph fluid enters the blood, thus keeping the water level of the blood constant. Thus, the tissue fluid and lymph are integral parts of the internal environment.

16. In the lungs, oxygen combines with hemoglobin to form oxyhemoglobin. Oxyhemoglobin is transported from the lungs to the heart and then to the body cells. In the capillaries, oxyhemoglobin breaks down into hemoglobin and oxygen. Oxygen diffuses from red cells to body cells. Carbon dioxide diffuses from the body cells to the blood. Some of it dissolves and ionizes in the plasma. Some combines with hemoglobin to form carboxyhemoglobin. The remainder combines with the liquid in the red cells. Eventually, the carbon dioxide reaches the capillaries in the lungs where it diffuses into the lungs and is exhaled.

17. Blood clots result from a chain of chemical reactions. When injury occurs, platelets release chemicals which react with other chemicals in the blood to form thromboplastin.

Thromboplastin plus calcium ions cause prothrombin in the blood to be changed to thrombin. Thrombin, an enzyme, catalyzes the conversion of fibrinogen to fibrin. Fibrin is insoluble and settles out as long strands which form a tangled network. The network traps other blood parts and forms a blood clot. The blood clot covers the wound.

18. Blood cells of the Rh positive embryo may pass across the placenta and into the mother's bloodstream. The mother makes antibodies against these cells which may pass back across the placenta into the embryo's bloodstream, causing anemia or death to the embryo.

19. Prolonged hypertension damages the lining of coronary arteries and can cause heart muscle to become thickened and overworked. The strain on the heart may lead to abnormal pumping action which interferes with normal blood flow. A blood clot blocking a coronary vessel may lead to the death of a portion of the heart muscle and result in a heart attack. Certain heart conditions can be prevented by a proper diet avoiding large amounts of fats such as those in animal and dairy products. Weight control, not smoking cigarettes, and regular exercise are also important in maintaining a healthy heart.

20. The primary danger in organ transplantation is rejection of the foreign donor tissue. Chances of rejection can be diminished by using donor tissues which closely match the recipient's. Also, certain drugs which combat the body's natural tendency to reject foreign tissue can be administered.

21. The artificial heart is composed of two chambers which are grafted to the patient's atria and the pulmonary artery and aorta. The chambers replace the damaged ventricles. An external air compressor forces air into a portion of the chambers of the artificial heart, pushing blood up and out into the arteries. Between compressions, blood enters from the atria. Some see artificial hearts as temporary measures to be used until a donor heart becomes available for transplantation. Others feel that an artificial heart may be a permanent solution for those with serious heart problems. Artificial hearts are limited in that the patient is not able to move around freely, the rate of pumping is limited, and the potential for infection exists.

Page 511. Applying Your Ideas

1. Enlargement of blood vessels near the skin permits greater blood flow and, thus, greater heat loss by radiation. Constriction of these same vessels has an opposite effect.

2. After eating, capillary beds near the digestive organs are open whereas some of the beds in the skeletal muscles are closed. Therefore, heavy exercise can lead to muscle fatigue and cramps due to insufficiency of oxygen to those tissues. If an injury resulting in internal bleeding occurred, the capillaries of the brain would open, an adaptation supplying blood where it is most needed.

3. Such an opening would lead to a mixing of oxygenated and deoxygenated blood.

4. High blood pressure indicates that the heart has been "working hard" and has increased the output of blood. (This condition is dangerous if it continues for too long.) Lowered carbon dioxide content indicates that the cells are not metabolizing rapidly and therefore do not require as great a blood supply.

5. A blood clot within a vessel would restrict blood flow and could lead to damage or death of the tissue fed by the vessel.

6. The anti-A agglutinins in the type B blood would agglutinate with the A antigens in the type A blood.

7. Transfusion of type A blood into a type AB person would be successful, because type AB blood has no agglutinins to agglutinate with the A antigens in the type A blood.

8. The resting heart rate of an athlete would be lower, in general, than that of an unathletic person. The athlete's heart, because it is in good condition from exercise beats more slowly and pumps more blood with each beat.

9. In general, animal transport involves circulation of a single fluid which carries a variety of materials. The fluid is circulated by a heart. In plants, fluids do not circulate, there is no heart, and different materials are transported by different vascular tissues.

Page 511. Extending Your Ideas

1. It may be possible to obtain both heart and lungs intact. If so, the specimen could be studied again after Chapter 27. Preserved specimens can also be ordered from biological supply houses.

2. Before Harvey (1628), it was believed that the blood ebbed and flowed in the body. By studying the structure of the heart and by tying off arteries and veins, Harvey reasoned that blood must travel in a one-way cycle involving the heart to arteries to veins and back to the heart.

However, Harvey was unable to discover the link between arteries and veins. When microscopy became available as an investigative tool, the missing connections, capillaries, were discovered by Marcello Malphigi in 1660. Malphigi's discovery came three years after Harvey's death.

Additional Student Readings

Franklin, Deborah, "Putting the Squeeze on Hypertension." *Science News*, April 10, 1982.

Garmon, Linda, "Globin's Role in Oxygen Binding." *Science News*, December 13, 1980.

"Lasers to Unclog Arteries." *Science Digest*, June, 1982.

Suggested Teacher Readings

Backos, Ronald A., "Dracula Experiment." *The Science Teacher*, November, 1976.

"Culture Network." *Sciquest*, March, 1981.

Doolittle, Russell F., "Fibrinogen and Fibrin." *Scientific American*, December, 1981.

Perutz, M.F., "Hemoglobin Structure and Respiratory Transport." *Scientific American*, December, 1978.

Zucker, Marjorie B., "The Functioning of Blood Platelets." *Scientific American*, June, 1980.

CHAPTER 27 RESPIRATION AND EXCRETION

Teaching Techniques

In teaching about gas exchange in animals, analyze with students the adaptations of the various animals studied in terms of how their systems meet two major needs, the need for a moist surface for exchange and the need for a large surface area over which the exchange can occur. Each respiratory system also can be related to the animal's habitat. Point out that the physical location of the gas exchange areas on the animals also is related to the animal's habitat. Aquatic animals often have external respiratory organs whereas land animals have internal respiratory organs protected from drying out by their internal location.

In teaching excretion, emphasize that excretory organs generally act as filtration units for the separation of needed and harmful materials. Also, whereas in simpler animals excretion and water balance are carried out independently, in more complex animals the excretory organs perform both functions. Complex animals have circulatory fluids containing both water and wastes. Stress the importance of the excretory organs in maintaining homeostasis of the body fluids.

Study of both respiratory and excretory systems in complex animals may necessitate a review of those animals' circulatory systems (Chapter 26). After completing this chapter, you may wish to tie together the systems covered in Chapters 25-27. Emphasize the importance of the circulatory system to the proper functioning of other systems.

Performance Objectives

Goal: Students will gain an understanding of the processes of respiration and excretion as they occur in various animals.

Objectives: Upon completion of the reading and activities and when asked to respond orally or on a written test, students will:

Section Number		
27:0	K	define respiration, differentiate between internal and external respiration, and explain that a moist area with a large surface is necessary for gas exchange.
27:1	P	compare and contrast respiration in *Nereis* and an earthworm.
27:2	K	describe the respiratory system in complex aquatic animals and explain the function of the gills.
27:3	K	describe the respiratory system of insects.
27:4	K	describe the various means of respiration in adult amphibians.

27:4	K	identify and indicate the function of each of the structures of the human respiratory system.
27:0, 5	K/P	differentiate between respiration and breathing.
27:5	P	compare and contrast inspiration and expiration.
27:5	K	indicate how the breathing rate in humans is controlled.
27:6	K	give examples of respiratory diseases.
27:7	K	explain several ways that smoking contributes to health problems.
27:8I	K	define excretion and explain why organisms must rid themselves of nitrogenous wastes.
27:8	K	describe how planarians maintain water balance and remove wastes.
27:9	P	compare and contrast excretion in the earthworm and grasshopper.
27:10	K/S	diagram the human kidney nephron, identify its various structures, and describe the function of each structure.
27:11	K	describe the function of vasopressin in water balance.
27:12	P	compare and contrast the function of the kidney in freshwater fish, marine fish, amphibians, birds, reptiles, and desert mammals.

(See page 41T for performance objectives that apply to all chapters.)

Answers to Chapter 27 Review

Page 530. Checking Your Ideas

1. external
2. kidneys
3. diaphragm
4. tracheal
5. surface area
6. skin
7. gills
8. urea
9. flame
10. nephrons

Page 531. Evaluating Your Ideas

1. An earthworm has no specialized respiratory system. A thin film of moisture surrounds the animal as it moves through the soil. Oxygen can dissolve in the moisture on the skin, move inward, and enter the blood where it combines with hemoglobin and is transported around the body. Carbon dioxide leaves the body by the same route but in the opposite direction. In *Nereis*, gases are exchanged at the parapods. Each parapod contains blood vessels into which oxygen passes and from which carbon dioxide escapes. Both *Nereis* and the earthworm have respiratory systems adapted to moist environments. The respiratory surfaces, parapods and skin, are in direct contact with moisture.

2. Water containing oxygen enters the mouth, passes to the pharynx, and then to the gill chamber. As water enters the mouth, the operculum closes. As the pharynx contracts, water is forced over the gills, the operculum opens, and water is expelled. Each gill is composed of a cartilaginous gill arch from which gill filaments protrude. The filaments contain capillaries. Deoxygenated blood from the heart passes to the gill capillaries where oxygen enters from the water. Oxygenated blood passes out of the gills and is distributed throughout the body.

3. Gases are exchanged between cells and the environment by means of a network of tubes. The respiratory system of grasshoppers is not interrelated with the circulatory system. Neither carbon dioxide nor oxygen enters or is carried by the blood.

4. Air enters through the nose or mouth and passes to the trachea which subdivides to form smaller channels, the bronchi, bronchial tubes, and bronchioles. Each bronchiole leads to a cluster of moist alveoli surrounded by capillaries. Oxygen in the alveoli diffuses to the blood and is carried to the body cells. Carbon dioxide diffuses from the blood to the alveoli and is exhaled.

5. During inspiration, the diaphragm moves down and the ribs move up and out, thus increasing the size of the chest cavity and decreasing pressure. As a result, air from the atmosphere rushes into the lungs. During expiration, an opposite set of movements occurs and air is forced out of the lungs as the pressure in the chest cavity increases.

6. Breathing rate is controlled by the breathing center in the medulla oblongata. The level of carbon dioxide in the blood is an index of how rapid or slow the breathing rate should be. As carbon dioxide level increases, nerves carry impulses from the breathing center to the muscles of the ribs and diaphragm. As these muscles are stimulated, breathing rate increases. As the carbon dioxide level falls, the breathing center is inhibited. The rate of impulses to the muscles of the ribs and diaphragm declines and breathing rate decreases.

7. Cigarette smoke damages the cilia so that they cannot move properly. Thus, mucus cannot be swept toward the mouth. Coughing may occur and the respiratory system becomes more vulnerable to infection.

8. In emphysema, the bronchioles become inflamed and the alveoli become scarred and may break. When alveoli break, air escapes from the lungs and less oxygen is delivered to the bloodstream. Labored breathing and a heavy cough may develop and the heart becomes strained as it beats more quickly to force more blood to the lungs. In lung cancer, cancer cells crowd out and destroy healthy tissue. Death may occur as a result of damage to the lungs and other tissues to which the cancer may spread.

9. Simple marine organisms have cell contents similar to the salt water in which they live. Therefore, water enters and leaves by osmosis at about the same rate.

10. Planarians collect excess water by osmosis. Water is drawn into the flame cells of excretory canals from tissues. The water moves along the excretory canals and leaves the organism through the excretory ducts which open as pores on the planarian's surface, a process that requires energy.

11. Ammonia requires a great amount of water for its safe removal.

12. Lymph fluid circulating in the coelom of the earthworm contains both useful materials and harmful nitrogenous wastes. Lymph enters the funnel-shaped nephrostome of a nephridium and is passed along the tubule by ciliary and muscular action. Useful lymph materials are absorbed by certain cells of the tubule and passed into surrounding

capillaries. They can then be recirculated. Harmful wastes remain in the tubule and pass to the bladder. Wastes leave the bladder and are discharged into the environment through the nephridiopore.

13. Nitrogenous wastes and water pass from the blood of the hemocoel into the free ends of the Malphigian tubules. In the tubules, water is reabsorbed but the nitrogenous wastes (uric acid) are passed to the intestine. The wastes are eventually excreted through the anus as solid material. Uric acid is excreted because it forms insoluble crystals which require little water for their excretion. Thus, water is conserved during the excretory process in these animals.

14. Kidneys in humans are a pair of fist-sized, bean-shaped organs which lie near the dorsal abdominal wall. The outer part is called the cortex; the inner part is the medulla. There is a central, hollow cavity called the pelvis. Each kidney contains about one million excretory units, the nephrons. Each nephron consists of a Bowman's capsule which tapers into a long, coiled tubule. The Bowman's capsule surrounds a mass of capillaries, the glomerulus. Capillaries emerging from the glomerulus surround the tubule. A glomerulus originates from arterioles which branch from the renal arteries. Capillaries surrounding the tubule return blood to the renal vein.

15. Blood containing urea, excess salts and ions, water, food molecules, and hormones enters the renal arteries and is channeled to the glomeruli. Blood pressure forces most of the liquid portion of the blood into the Bowman's capsules and along the tubules. In the tubules, energy is used to actively transport necessary materials such as food molecules, hormones, and ions back to the capillaries. Most of the water is also reabsorbed by osmosis. This purified blood is then recirculated.

Urea, excess salts, and a small amount of water remain in the tubules. This combination of materials (urine) passes from the tubules to the collecting ducts in the medulla and then to the kidney pelvis. Urine then enters a long tube, the ureter, and is transported to the urinary bladder for storage before removal from the body. Urine is excreted through the urethra.

16. The amount of water excreted by the kidney is controlled by a hormone called vasopressin secreted by the pituitary gland. The hypothalamus region of the brain detects the amount of water in the blood. If the level is too low, the hypothalamus stimulates the pituitary to release vasopressin. When vasopressin reaches the kidneys, it causes the tubules and collecting ducts to reabsorb more water. Hence, less water is excreted and the urine becomes more concentrated. When too much water is present in the blood, vasopressin output is reduced. Thus, more water is excreted and the urine becomes more dilute.

17. The kidneys of freshwater fish reabsorb very little water. Instead they reabsorb mostly salts. The result is a very dilute urine. Also, a large volume of urine is excreted and these fish drink very little water. These adaptations allow freshwater fish to counteract the constant input of water by osmosis from the surrounding environment.

18. Marine fish must conserve water because they tend to lose it by osmosis. Therefore, they drink a large amount of water. Because the salt in the water must be removed, it is actively transported from the surface of the gills to the surrounding water. Also, little urine is excreted because only a small amount of water enters the kidneys.

19. A kangaroo rat conserves water by producing an extremely concentrated urine containing almost no water.

These mammals are able to derive necessary water from the food they eat and from the by-products of their metabolism.

Page 531. Applying Your Ideas

1. Most annelids live in water because they lack respiratory systems which would enable them to exchange gases with the dry, terrestrial atmosphere. They are adapted for respiration in the water environment.

2. In both, gases travel through a series of tubes which link the cells of the body with the external environment. Both tracheal systems consist of moistened sacs in which gases dissolve. However, in grasshoppers these sacs (tracheoles) are located all around the body and gases are exchanged directly between the sacs and body cells. In humans the sacs (alveoli) are concentrated in two organs, the lungs. Gases are exchanged between the sacs and the blood. The blood transports the gases to and from the body cells.

3. Elevated carbon dioxide level in the blood indicates that the cells' rate of metabolism is increasing. In order to maintain homeostasis, more oxygen must be brought to the cells. Moving oxygenated blood more quickly requires more rapid breathing and an increase in heartbeat rate.

4. Because uric acid is insoluble, it can be safely deposited in the egg without poisoning the embryo.

5. Urine would be more concentrated, an adaptation for conservation of water.

6. Ocean water is salt water. The human kidney cannot extract all of the excess salt which would enter the blood if a person drank seawater. Therefore, the blood would have more salt (less water) than the tissues. Water would pass from the tissues to the blood and the person would become dehydrated.

Page 531. Extending Your Ideas

1. In a crustacean like the lobster pairs of gills are located beneath the carapace (exoskeleton of the thorax). One gill of each pair occupies each side of the body. The gills are attached to the walking legs. Leg movement helps to bring water under the carapace. The water passes over the gills and then out. Some of the blood from the sinuses enters the gills. At this point oxygen diffuses into the blood from the water and carbon dioxide diffuses into the water. The oxygenated blood then is circulated throughout the rest of the open circulatory system. (Note: In aquatic crustaceans, unlike terrestrial insects, respiration and circulation are linked.) See *Evaluating Your Ideas*, answer 2 for a description of fish gill operation.

2. Breathing rate can be taken in a normal or resting situation as a control. Students can speed up breathing rate by walking, running in place, or running up stairs. After each trial, the students must rest until the rate is restored to normal. As an additional exercise, the pulse rate can be determined under each of the conditions suggested. If a gauge is available, data also may be collected on blood pressure.

3. The skin is an organ of excretion in the sense that water, urea, and salts may pour out of the sweat glands. These materials enter the glands from the blood. The skin is not a major organ of excretion. Loss of water from the skin serves a more important function—the regulation of body temperature by evaporation and cooling.

4. The bends is a disorder resulting from the large amount of dissolved blood nitrogen at high external pressure coming out of solution quickly when the external pressure is lowered. The nitrogen accumulates as bubbles in the blood, a condition which is painful and can cause death. The bends occur when deep-sea divers surface too quickly. The condition can be avoided by a slow ascent during which nitrogen will come out of the blood slowly. If bends occur, the patient can be treated in a pressure-controlled chamber in which the pressure is slowly decreased so nitrogen will come out of the blood slowly.

Additional Student Readings

Clark, M. and Gosnell, M., "Clues to the Cause of Emphysema." *Newsweek*, April 14, 1980.

Clark, M. and Shapiro, D., "Secondhand Smoke and Lung Cancer." *Newsweek*, January 26, 1981.

Speads, Carola H., *Breathing: The ABC's*. New York, Harper and Row, Publishers, Inc., 1978.

Suggested Teacher Readings

Crouch, James E., and McClintic, Robert J., *Human Anatomy and Physiology*, 2nd ed. New York, John Wiley and Sons, Inc., 1976.

Schmidt-Nielson, K., *Animal Physiology: Adaptation and Environment*, 2nd ed. London, Cambridge University Press, 1979.

CHAPTER 28   SUPPORT AND LOCOMOTION

Teaching Techniques

In comparing the skeletons of arthropods and vertebrates, you may want to point out that these two systems are evolutionary alternatives. Both plans contribute to the protection, support, and movement of the animals and both groups of animals are successful. Although the exoskeletons of arthropods limit their size, they certainly do not limit the numbers of arthropods!

Grocery store items are useful in showing skeletons, muscles, and interactions of skeletal parts with muscles in a variety of animals. Obtain a selection of whole animals such as clams and fish or parts of animals such as ox tails, chicken wings, and chicken necks for examination. Many can be obtained inexpensively and can serve as good examples for muscle attachment, ligaments, and so on, as well as for study of skeletal parts. Cook the meat on the skeletons before examination to make muscle tissue firmer, to reduce odor in the classroom, and to avoid possible blood poisoning from handling raw meat. If students touch the raw meats, be sure they wash their hands immediately with soap and water. Although cooked, none of the materials should be eaten. You may want to obtain whole fish, cook them, and have students carefully remove the tissue to leave the entire skeletons intact for observation. If you have a collection of mounted skeletons, have students analyze the similarities and differences among them. Discussion of the functions of the skeleton follows students' seeing some of the ways the skeletons are adapted.

Performance Objectives

Goal: Students will gain an understanding of the structure and function of skeletal and muscular systems and their relationships to protection, support, and locomotion.

Objectives: Upon completion of the reading and activities and when asked to respond orally or on a written test, students will:

Section Number		
28:0	P	compare and contrast support in aquatic and land animals.
28:1I	P	compare and contrast the activities of animals lacking skeletal systems with those having skeletal systems.
28:1	P	compare and contrast the advantages and disadvantages of an exoskeleton.
28:1, 2	P	compare and contrast the structures and functions of an exoskeleton and an endoskeleton.
28:3	K	describe the composition of bone and explain the importance of ossification in bone formation.
28:4	K	identify and state the function of the parts of a bone.
28:5	K	list and describe the kinds of joints and explain how the bones are held together.
28:6	K	describe locomotion in coelenterates, the earthworm, and *Nereis*.
28:7	P	compare and contrast locomotion in clams and starfish.
28:8	P	compare and contrast the point of origin and point of insertion of a muscle.
28:8	P	describe the interaction of flexor and extensor muscles.
28:8	P	explain why muscle tone is important for support of the body.
28:9	P	compare and contrast the structures and functions of the three kinds of muscle found in verte-

brates—striated, smooth, and cardiac.

28:9   P   compare and contrast voluntary and involuntary muscles.

28:10   K   explain the sliding filament hypothesis of skeletal muscle contraction.

28:10   P   explain how it is possible to exert varying degrees of force with a set of muscles.

28:11   K   discuss the various ways in which energy needed for muscle contraction is made available.

28:11   K   define oxygen debt and explain how this debt is "paid."

(See page 41T for performance objectives that apply to all chapters.)

Answers to Chapter 28 Review

Page 548. Checking Your Ideas

1. true
2. true
3. false
4. false
5. false
6. false
7. true
8. true
9. true
10. false

Page 548. Evaluating Your Ideas

1. Aquatic organisms usually are at least partially supported by the water.

2. The exoskeleton provides support, protection, and locomotion and is, therefore, adaptive. However, the exoskeleton limits the size of the organism. The weight of an exoskeleton needed to support a large animal would be great and movement, especially on land, would be difficult. Flying would be impossible. The exoskeleton also limits growth because the exoskeleton must be shed as the organism grows. While the new exoskeleton is hardening, the organism is vulnerable to attack, has limited movement, and tends to lose water.

3. Joints permit flexibility so that individual body parts can be moved.

4. Each bone has a structure complementary to its particular function. Also, the interaction of specialized bones permits a wider variety of movements.

5. Size is not as critical in animals with an endoskeleton because the bones which support the body are thick and strong. Growth is not a "problem" because bones grow at each end. There is also no loss of protection or mobility during growth.

6. In a young embryo, the skeleton is mostly cartilage. During development of the embryo and continuing into childhood, osteocytes (bone cells) replace cartilage cells. Ossification, the hardening of cartilage into bone, occurs by the addition of minerals (calcium salts).

7. Bone consists of living and nonliving substances. The outer layer of long bones is the periosteum. Muscles are attached to the periosteum. Beneath the periosteum is the bony layer composed of mineral deposits. Haversian canals penetrate the bony layer. The canals contain blood vessels which nourish the osteocytes. Some bones contain a central cavity filled with blood vessels and nerves. This tissue, called marrow, either produces red and white blood cells or stores excess fat.

8. A ball and socket joint allows rotation as well as movement from side to side or front to back. Hinge joints allow motion in only one direction. In gliding joints, the bones move easily over one another. A pivot joint provides a rotational and up and down movement. Fixed joints allow no movement. The skull is composed of several bones allowing for growth of the brain. The joints are not fixed during the growth period. They become fixed afterward.

9. Jellyfish may be either free-floating or move by jet-propulsion. The latter results from contraction of the muscles in the bell. As water is expelled from the bell, the animal moves in the opposite direction. Movement in the starfish is effected by the tube feet of its water-vascular system. Expansion and contraction of the tube feet enable the starfish to creep along the ocean bottom. An earthworm's locomotion results from interaction of its longitudinal and circular muscles. Setae provide leverage in the soil. A clam moves by extending a muscular foot into the mud. As the muscles in the foot contract, the clam is pulled forward. Compared to insects and vertebrates, locomotion in these animals in general is slower.

10. Muscles are attached to bones by tendons. During contraction, the end of the muscle (and what it is attached to) that does not move is called the point of origin. The muscle end (and what it is attached to) that does move is called the point of insertion.

11. The biceps muscle is anchored to the humerus and also attached to the radius bone of the lower arm. The biceps is a flexor. When it contracts, the arm bends because a force is exerted across the hinge joint of the elbow. As the biceps contracts, the triceps relaxes. The triceps links the back of the humerus with the ulna of the lower arm. It is called an extensor because when it contracts, it pulls the ulna down and extends the arm. As the triceps contracts, the biceps relaxes.

12. Muscle tone is the constant partial contraction of skeletal muscles. Muscle tone contributes to body support and keeps the muscles ready for more powerful contractions. Without muscle tone, the body might collapse.

13. Striated muscle is attached to bones. It has a striped appearance, functions in skeletal movement, and is voluntary. Separate striated cells are difficult to distinguish and nuclei are scattered throughout the muscle fibers. Smooth muscle is found in internal organs and blood vessels. It is involuntary and composed of distinct, spindle-shaped cells with a nucleus. Cardiac muscle is located in the heart and is involuntary. It is similar to striated muscle but has branched fibers.

14. Striated muscle is composed of fibers which, in turn, are composed of fibrils. Fibrils consist of filaments made of myosin and actin, proteins. Actin is attached to crossbands called Z-lines. Myosin and actin molecules are linked by bridges attached to the myosin molecules. After a fiber receives a nerve impulse, ATP binds with myosin and the bridges bond with and move the actin. The bridges break, re-form at other places on the actin, and cause further movement. A series of such small moves cause the filaments to slide over one another.

15. The all or none response means that once an impulse reaches a muscle fiber, the fiber contracts fully or not at all. Degree of muscle contraction depends on the number of muscle fibers contracting at one time.

16. Creatine phosphate is formed when ATP donates a phosphate group to a molecule of creatine. As muscles become active, the phosphate can be transferred to ADP forming ATP. The ATP can be used as an energy source for muscle contraction.

17. During prolonged or heavy exercise, ATP is generated by anaerobic respiration. This process occurs after stored ATP and CP have been consumed and when oxygen cannot be brought to the muscles quickly enough for aerobic respiration to occur.

18. An oxygen debt is the amount of oxygen needed to convert the lactic acid accumulated during anaerobic respiration to carbon dioxide and water by means of aerobic respiration.

Page 549. Applying Your Ideas

1. The amount of living material in a small animal will not cause the animal to collapse of its own weight. A larger animal, composed of much more tissue, would collapse without some skeletal support.

2. Arthropods have adapted to almost all conditions of moisture, temperature, and food. This adaptability has resulted in great variety among arthropods.

3. The forelimbs are modified as wings. Some bones are hollow with bone extensions that serve as braces. The breastbone is enlarged. These adaptations aid in flight.

4. The thickness of the femur supports the weight of the body whereas the thin foot bones provide flexibility necessary for balance and locomotion.

5. The knee is a hinge joint and is not well adapted for the sudden turns and lateral movements of football players.

6. Slow contraction of smooth muscle allows for a more constant and less forceful reaction which is adaptive for internal processes.

7. More ATP is generated in aerobic respiration than in anaerobic respiration.

8. Protozoans move by amoeboid, ciliary, or flagellar motion. They have neither muscle nor skeletal tissues.

9. Skeletal muscles work in pairs. When one member of a pair is contracted, the other is relaxed.

Page 549. Extending Your Ideas

1. If it is impractical for a student to prepare and mount a skeleton, you may wish to purchase premounted skeletons or skeletal models.

2. Eventually, the student will find it difficult to keep up the pace, the rate of tapping will decrease, and finally the student will stop.

3. Three basic processes are involved in bone repair. (1) Blood clots form at the break area to close off the broken blood vessels. (2) A cartilage type material forms in the break area. (3) The cartilage is replaced by bone tissue.

4. Myoglobin is similar in structure to hemoglobin. It forms a loose combination with excess oxygen in muscle tissue, thus storing oxygen. As oxygen supplies are depleted during exercise, myoglobin releases oxygen which can then be used in aerobic respiration.

Additional Student Readings

Arehart-Treichel, Ann, "Marrow Transplants." *Science News*, February 14, 1981.

Garmon, Linda, "Building Better Bones." *Science News*, May 16, 1981.

"How Muscles Work." *Science Digest*, August, 1981.

Miller, Julie Ann, "Connective Tissue Disease." *Science News*, February 20, 1982.

Suggested Teacher Reading

Grand, Theodore I., "The Anatomical Basis of Locomotion." *American Biology Teacher*, March, 1976.

CHAPTER 29   CHEMICAL CONTROL

Teaching Techniques

As the discussion of human hormones proceeds, stress the many lines of evidence which show a close relationship between the endocrine system and the nervous system. If students clearly understand that both systems are concerned with the same general function, response to stimuli, they will more easily make sense of the overlapping features of these systems.

In teaching this material, point out that hormones interact in effecting homeostasis. For example, both insulin and cortisol contribute to glucose metabolism. Availability of glucose is related to metabolic rate, controlled by thyroxine. Anterior pituitary hormones such as TSH, FSH, LH, and ACTH control, in turn, the output of hormones secreted by other glands of the body.

In presenting human endocrinology, only several hormones are discussed, namely those about which students have heard. Table 29-1 presents information about these and other hormones. You may want to consider assigning students to report on still other human hormones, such as calcitonin and angiotensin.

Performance Objectives

Goal: Students will gain an understanding of how many of the functions of an animal are directed by chemical control systems.

Objectives: Upon completion of the reading and activities and when asked to respond orally or on a written test, students will:

Section
Number

29:0   P   explain that homeostasis is maintained by chemical and nervous control systems.

29:1I	K	describe hormones involved in chemical control mechanisms as being steroids, proteins, polypeptides, or amino acids.
29:1	P	describe the functions of insulin.
29:1	P	compare and contrast the causes of the two forms of diabetes mellitus.
29:2	K	describe the function of the hormone thyroxine and indicate the conditions caused by an excess or deficiency of this hormone.
29:3-5	K	list the hormones secreted by the adrenal glands, the gonads, and the anterior pituitary gland and indicate the function of each.
29:6	K	explain the interrelationship among the hypothalamus, anterior pituitary, and other endocrine glands in hormonal control.
29:7	K	list the hormones secreted by the posterior pituitary gland and indicate the function of each.
29:7	P	explain how the production of posterior pituitary hormones by the hypothalamus shows a close relationship between the endocrine and nervous systems.
29:8	K	explain the second messenger hypothesis and identify cyclic AMP as a second messenger.
29:8	K	explain the means by which steroid hormones are thought to exert their effects.
29:8	K	list several functions of prostaglandins.
29:9	K	describe the involvement of hormones in metamorphosis of insects and frogs.
29:10	K	explain how insulin pumps work and how they may solve the problems associated with taking insulin by injection.

(See page 41T for performance objectives that apply to all chapters.)

Answers to Chapter 29 Review

Page 566. Checking Your Ideas

1. c	5. i	8. h
2. e	6. a	9. j
3. g	7. f	10. d
4. b		

Page 566. Evaluating Your Ideas

1. One form of diabetes usually develops in people less than twenty years old. Beta cells become destroyed and not enough insulin is produced. Excess glucose cannot be converted to glycogen or fats, and glucose cannot be effectively transported out of the blood. People with this form of diabetes take regular injections of insulin. In another form of diabetes, which usually occurs in overweight people over forty years old, sufficient insulin is produced by the beta cells, but glucose does not easily permeate cells of the muscles and liver. Glucose accumulates, therefore, in the blood. Persons suffering from this form of diabetes can be helped by diet, exercise, and certain drugs. When the disease is not treated, persons with diabetes may be very thirsty and urinate frequently. Diabetes can lead to problems such as blindness.

2. Insulin regulates the level of sugar in the blood. The amount of sugar in blood must be kept within certain limits. Insulin causes the conversion of excess glucose into glycogen within the liver and muscles and also causes the conversion of some glucose to fats. In addition, insulin increases the permeability of cell membranes to glucose. All of these activities reduce the level of glucose in the blood. Insulin must be taken by injection because, as a protein, it would be digested if taken orally.

3. Thyroxine controls the rate of metabolism in body cells. Too little thyroxine produced may result in obesity. A severe deficiency of thyroxine in infancy causes cretinism. Too much thyroxine produced can cause loss of weight, irritability, and nervousness.

4. Iodine is an important ingredient of thyroxine. In one kind of goiter, the thyroid gland enlarges due to the lack of iodine.

5. Secretion of adrenaline increases during stress. This increase causes the heartbeat to speed and blood pressure to rise. Adrenaline also increases the level of sugar in the blood and speeds up the rate of metabolism. More blood is routed to the brain, skeletal muscles, lungs, and heart.

6. The cells of the adrenal medulla are more like nerve cells than gland cells. Also, the reactions caused by adrenaline can also be caused by the nervous system.

7. Aldosterone controls salt level by causing the kidneys to absorb sodium and chloride ions. Cortisol causes fats and proteins to be converted to glucose, thus maintaining a proper blood sugar level. It also prevents inflammation. Cortisone also prevents inflammation. All three hormones function in stress situations. Androgens and estrogens (male and female sex hormones) are also secreted in small amounts by the adrenal cortex.

8. Estrogens are responsible for secondary sexual characteristics in females and initiate the buildup of uterine tissue during the menstrual cycle. Progesterone, secreted by the corpus luteum, maintains the uterus. During pregnancy the placenta secretes hormones which also maintain the uterus. Testosterone, an androgen, is responsible for secondary sexual characteristics in males.

9. In females, FSH stimulates development of eggs within the follicle of the ovary. In males, FSH stimulates production of sperm cells. In females, LH causes ovulation and the conversion of the follicle to the corpus luteum. In males, LH causes the release of androgens from the testes. These facts suggest that the target organ plays an important role in determining the response.

10. Excess HGH in childhood may cause giantism. Deficiency in childhood results in dwarfism.

11. Thyroxine production is controlled by a feedback mechanism. In the brain, the hypothalamus detects the

level of thyroxine circulating in the blood. If the level is too low, the hypothalamus secretes a releasing factor which stimulates the anterior pituitary to secrete TSH. This hormone, when it reaches the thyroid gland via the blood, causes the thyroid to secrete thyroxine. If the level of thyroxine in the blood becomes too high, the hypothalamus causes the anterior pituitary to decrease production of TSH and thyroxine level is subsequently decreased.

12. Oxytocin stimulates the contraction of uterine muscles prior to the birth of a child. Vasopressin controls water balance by regulating the amount of water resorbed by the kidneys. Both oxytocin and vasopressin are produced by the hypothalamus.

13. Cells of the posterior pituitary more closely resemble nerve cells than gland cells. The hypothalamus is composed of nerve cells. The fact that both these structures are concerned with the production of hormones indicates a close link between the endocrine and nervous systems.

14. According to the second messenger hypothesis, hormones are thought to recognize their target organs by combining with specific receptor molecules located in the cell membrane. Each target organ has a different set of receptors. After the hormone combines with the receptor, a compound, called the second messenger, is produced within the cells of the target organ. This second messenger (often cyclic AMP) initiates a metabolic change by altering a specific chemical reaction within the cells. In this way, the hormonal change is effected.

15. Steroid hormones enter a cell where they combine with a receptor. The combined hormone-receptor complex enters the nucleus where it is thought to activate a gene. The protein produced affects the cell's chemistry, thereby indirectly carrying out the function of the hormone.

16. Some prostaglandins seem to play a role in the production of cAMP in target cells. Thus, they may help regulate a target organ's response to a hormone. Other prostaglandins control smooth muscle contraction, regulate pulse rate and blood pressure, cause swelling, and contribute to an awareness of pain.

17. An insect's brain secretes a hormone which causes the secretion of a second hormone, ecdyson, in the thorax. Ecdyson causes molting. The final transition to adult form occurs as a result of reduced production of a third hormone, juvenile hormone. When no more juvenile hormone is secreted, molting stops. Pupa formation and metamorphosis begin and the adult is formed. The same effects occur in the molting of nymphs and their change to adulthood.

18. Taking insulin by injection involves release of sudden high level of insulin rather than a "steady" output of small amounts. Also, the level of insulin in the blood fluctuates a greater amount in a person taking injections of insulin.

19. In one kind of battery powered, external insulin pump, constant, small amounts of insulin are released into the blood through needles implanted under the skin. By pushing a button, the patient can increase the amount of insulin released at times such as before eating. Another pump operates on the same principle, but is implanted under the skin. To be most effective, an insulin pump should be able to monitor blood sugar level and automatically adjust the amount of insulin released.

Page 567. Applying Your Ideas

1. If taken orally, insulin would be digested. (There are oral hypoglycemic agents that sometimes are effective in adult onset diabetes. Their action is to stimulate the production of insulin by the pancreas. However, insulin is not taken orally.)

2. The slight difference in structure of these two hormones can be detected by different receptors located on different target organs.

3. Removal of the corpora allata during an early molt would result in a very small adult because there would be no juvenile hormone. If juvenile hormone were added to a larva prior to its final molt, it would result in another growth period and produce an unusually large adult.

4. This activation step may be a "safety valve" which prevents an excess of insulin being formed and released.

5. Insulin produced by recombinant DNA methods can be produced in large amounts less expensively. Also, insulin produced by recombinant DNA techniques is human insulin (because the human gene is inserted into the bacterium) rather than insulin from another animal and therefore, would not cause any adverse reaction. The human insulin made by this technique is identical to that made in the human body.

6. Glucagon controls blood sugar level by increasing the level of sugar in the blood.

7. If cAMP were not changed to a different compound, the target organ would continue to respond to it long after the desired response were needed.

8. Chemical control in both plants and animals results in rather slow responses. In both kinds of organisms hormones travel from their sites of production to their target organs, and the target organs determine the responses. Most animal hormones are secreted from endocrine glands. There are no such structures in plants.

Page 567. Extending Your Ideas

1. Histamine is released by certain leukocytes and damaged tissues. It relaxes smooth muscle in the walls of blood vessels and increases the permeability of the vessels. It is thought that this increased permeability permits a greater flow of white cells and antibodies to the damaged area. Histamines also constrict the bronchioles. Histamines are released in allergies such as hay fever in which the mucus membrane of the nose becomes irritated. A large amount of fluid is then released from the blood vessels. Antihistamines, drugs used to counter the effects of histamines, are administered to patients experiencing allergic responses.

2. The hypothalamus secretes releasing factors which control the output of FSH and LH.

3. Hypoglycemia is a disease which results from the production of too much insulin. Thus, the blood sugar level is too low. It is treated by means of a special diet.

Additional Student Readings

Block, Irvin, "Body Barometers." *Science Digest*, January/February, 1981.

Solomon, Stephen, "Organ Capsules." *Science Digest*, July, 1982.

Suggested Teacher Readings

O'Malley, Bert W., and Schrader, William T., "The Receptors of Steroid Hormones." *Scientific American*, February, 1976.

Turner, C. D., and Bagnara, J. T., *General Endocrinology*, 6th ed. Philadelphia, W. B. Saunders, 1976.

CHAPTER 30   NERVOUS CONTROL

Teaching Techniques

In beginning this chapter, briefly review the evidence of the close relationship between chemical control and nervous systems (Chapter 29) and alert students to look for more of such evidence. They will see that secretion of neurotransmitters at synapses provides an especially strong line of evidence for the idea that the two systems may simply be two ways of carrying out essentially the same functions.

Teaching of the sodium-potassium pump and the nerve impulse will be aided by step by step drawings on the chalkboard. Stress that the sudden influx of ions sets up a current which stimulates polarity reversals in adjacent areas. Make certain, also, that students understand that all nerve impulses are essentially identical and that the intensity depends on the frequency of impulses and the number of neurons stimulated. Similarly, interpretation of stimuli depends on the part of the central nervous system reached by the impulse. The target idea can be reemphasized as you discuss the effect of neurotransmitters on postsynaptic membranes. Students should realize that a more complete understanding of nervous control remains a major frontier of biology.

Performance Objectives

Goal: Students will gain an understanding of nervous system structures and their functions in animals of varying complexity.

Objectives: Upon completion of the reading and activities and when asked to respond orally or on a written test, students will:

Section Number		
30:0	P	compare and contrast the functions of receptors, conductors, and effectors.
30:1	P	compare and contrast the functions of sensory neurons, motor neurons, and association neurons.
30:1	K	differentiate between axons and dendrites and indicate their functions.
30:2	K	explain the factors which produce a resting potential in a neuron.
30:3	K	describe an action potential and the passage of a nerve impulse along an axon and give an example of action potential in muscles.
30:3	K	describe the refractory period involved in nerve impulses.
30:4	K	describe the all or none response.
30:4	P	explain how a person detects different strengths of stimuli and interprets those stimuli.
30:5	K	describe a synapse and explain how an action potential can cross a synapse.
30:5	P	explain why some neurotransmitters prevent and some activate action potentials in postsynaptic fibers.
30:5	P	compare and contrast the effects of acetylcholine and noradrenaline on heart muscle.
30:5	K	explain why it is necessary that neurotransmitters be inactivated.
30:6	P	compare and contrast the effects of depressants and stimulants and give examples of each.
30:7	P	compare and contrast the nervous systems in coelenterates and planarians.
30:7	K	explain how the nervous sytem of planarians is similar to those of more complex animals.
30:8	K	list the major structures of the vertebrate nervous system.
30:9	K	explain how the human central nervous system is protected.
30:9	K	describe the structure of the human cerebrum and list its major functions.
30:10	P	explain the functions of the human midbrain and hindbrain.
30:11	K	describe the structures and functions of a reflex arc.
30:12	P	compare and contrast the sensory-somatic system and the autonomic system.
30:12	K	differentiate between the sympathetic and parasympathetic systems.
30:13	K	identify the five major human senses and explain hearing in detail.
30:14	K	define neuropeptide and give functions of endorphins and enkephalins.

(See page 41T for performance objectives that apply to all chapters.)

Answers to Chapter 30 Review

Page 588. Checking Your Ideas

1. autonomic
2. neurotransmitters
3. cerebrum
4. nerve net
5. sodium
6. motor
7. stimulants
8. central
9. receptors
10. cerebellum

Page 588. Evaluating Your Ideas

1. Both the endocrine and nervous systems are involved in responses to stimuli. The nervous system causes responses to occur more quickly. However, both systems involve production of chemicals which ultimately lead to responses.

2. Receptors detect stimuli. Conductors transmit stimuli as impulses. Effectors are responding organs. These three functional parts are necessary for a nervous system response.

3. The motor neuron resembles a fine, wire-like fiber. This long, thin shape is ideal for transmitting impulses quickly from one part of the organism to another.

4. Impulses travel from the dendrite to the cell body to the axon and then on to the dendrite of another neuron or to an effector.

5. The myelin sheath and nodes of Ranvier speed impulse transmission.

6. Stimulation of a neuron causes a change in permeability of its membrane and sodium ions rush in. Permeability quickly changes and potassium ions rush out. Movement of these ions results in reversal of polarity and causes a current. The initial reversal of polarity causes similar changes in adjacent areas of the neuron and the action potential sweeps along the neuron—a nerve impulse.

7. The refractory period is the period when the sodium-potassium pump restores the membrane to its original resting potential, during which time the neuron cannot carry an impulse. Once completed, another impulse can be transmitted.

8. An electric current in a wire travels close to the speed of light and involves the flow of electrons along the wire. A nerve impulse is caused by the flow of ions across the cell membrane and is an electrochemical reaction. It is analogous to the sputtering fuse of a firecracker.

9. To cause an impulse, a stimulus must have a minimum intensity, the threshold. When the threshold is reached, reversal of polarity occurs. Stimuli greater than the threshold level cause the same impulse as stimuli just at the threshold level. Thus, the impulse is either transmitted or it is not. There is no in-between state.

10. Strength of a stimulus depends on the frequency with which impulses are transmitted and the number of neurons carrying the impulses.

11. An impulse moving along an axon of a presynaptic fiber causes the release of certain chemicals, neurotransmitters, from the ends of the axons. The neurotransmitter diffuses toward a postsynaptic fiber where it alters the permeability of its membrane.

12. No, some neurotransmitters inhibit the postsynaptic fiber by decreasing the permeability of its membrane. An example is the vagus nerves leading to the heart. The neurotransmitter which these nerves secrete inhibits muscle cells and, therefore, decreases the heartbeat rate.

13. The effect of neurotransmitters, like hormones, depends on the target. Also, the chemical structure of neurotransmitters is very similar to that of certain hormones.

14. A neurotransmitter may be inactivated by an enzyme or may be reabsorbed by the postsynaptic fiber from which it was secreted.

15. Tranquilizers have chemical structures similar to brain neurotransmitters. Some decrease transmission at synapses. Others block receptors for neurotransmitters. Marijuana contains drugs which alter the amounts of neurotransmitters in the brain. LSD is similar to a brain neurotransmitter and interferes with normal forwarding of impulses. Curare combines with receptors for acetylcholine on muscle cells, thus preventing contraction and causing paralysis.

16. A hydra has a nerve net composed of randomly scattered neurons. The neurons are short and many synapses must be crossed. Conduction is slow. Also, only strong stimuli produce impulses which are carried very far. Usually, only individual body parts respond to stimuli.

17. The human brain is protected by a thick cranium and three membranes called the meninges. Cerebrospinal fluid which circulates between the inner two meninges cushions the brain against shock and acts as an exchange agent with the blood in the walls of the ventricles.

18. The human cerebrum receives and interprets sensory stimuli and sends out impulses for motor responses. It is also the center of speech, intelligence, emotions, memory, and personality.

19. The human midbrain is essentially a relay center between the forebrain and hindbrain. It also plays a role in vision, hearing, and orientation.

20. The cerebellum coordinates impulses leaving the cerebrum. By analyzing incoming sensory impulses then comparing them to the outgoing cerebral impulses which it receives, the cerebellum can determine whether a particular response is appropriate. If it is not, the cerebellum sends messages to alter the cerebral impulses. The cerebellum also controls posture and balance and maintains muscle tone. The medulla oblongata controls the involuntary responses of internal organs.

21. The spinal cord is protected by the vertebrae through which it passes and by meninges and cerebrospinal fluid.

22. Reflexes are simple responses which involve no conscious control. They are adaptive in that they occur quickly and may protect the animal from harm.

23. The sensory-somatic system is composed of nerves which result in responses of the skeletal muscles. Spinal nerves, cranial nerves, the brain, and spinal cord are parts of this system.

24. The autonomic nervous system controls involuntary responses. The system is subdivided into the sympathetic and parasympathetic systems. The former initiates responses which prepare the body for emergencies. The latter balances the former after the emergency has passed.

25. Touch includes pressure, pain, heat, and cold.

26. Sound waves cause the tympanum to begin vibrating. The vibrations are transmitted to and amplified by the bones of the middle ear. The oval window picks up the vibrations, causing the cochlear fluid to move. Movement of this fluid bends sensitive hairs of the organ of Corti.

Bending of the hairs initiates action potentials in auditory nerve fibers. Impulses are sent via the auditory nerve to the temporal lobe of the cerebrum where they are interpreted as sound.

27. Neuropeptides are chains of amino acids made in the hypothalamus and pituitary gland.

28. Endorphins and enkephalins are involved in the body's response to pain. These substances (or substances like them) might be used in pain relief.

Page 589. Applying Your Ideas

1. Carrying of impulses in one direction provides greater organization in that impulses follow certain routes to the central nervous system.

2. In an animal, neurons are usually stimulated at the dendrite end.

3. This requirement ensures that only meaningful stimuli will ever reach the central nervous system. If all incidental stimuli with which an animal is bombarded reached the central nervous system, it would be impossible for the central nervous system to function normally.

4. Receptors in the buttocks are stimulated. They pass the impulse along to sensory neurons which lead to the spinal cord. In the spinal cord, an association neuron is stimulated and in turn, stimulates motor neurons. The motor neurons carry the impulses to the legs and thighs whose muscles contract causing the person to jump up.

5. In muscles, each fiber, when stimulated by a nerve impulse, contracts fully. In nerves, a stimulus at or above threshold level causes an action potential. Muscle contractions and action potentials are essentially the same.

6. The nerves secrete different neurotransmitters.

7. Sponges lack nervous systems.

8. Plants are sessile organisms and need not capture food. They can survive with the slow responses dictated by hormones.

Page 589. Extending Your Ideas

1. This reflex act is the classical kneejerk reaction. Some people are capable of preventing the response.

2. Examples of stimuli are bright light, electric shock, change in salinity or pH of the environment, noise, and direct touch.

Additional Student Readings

Cherry, Lawrence, "The Power of the Empty Pill." *Science Digest*, September, 1981.

Epps, Garrett, "The Brain Biologist and the Mud Leech." *Science 82*, January/February, 1982.

"The Mind's Eye." *Science Digest*, September, 1981.

Oldendorf, William, "See Inside Your Eye." *Science Digest*, January/February, 1981.

Suggested Teacher Readings

Adrian, R. H., *The Nerve Impulse*, 2nd ed. Carolina Biology Reader. Carolina Biological Supply Co., 1981.

Bloom, Floyd E., "Neuropeptides." *Scientific American*, October, 1981.

Epps, Garrett, "The Brain Biologist and the Mud Leech." *Science 82*, January, 1982.

Gray, E. G., *The Synapse*, 2nd ed. Carolina Biology Reader. Burlington, NC, Carolina Biological Supply Co., 1977.

Keynes, Richard D., "Ion Channels in the Nerve-Cell Membrane." *Scientific American*. March, 1979.

MacLean, Paul D., M.D., "A Mind of Three Minds: Evolution of the Human Brain." *The Science Teacher*, April, 1978.

Routtenberg, Arych, "The Reward System of the Brain." *Scientific American*, November, 1978.

Silberstein, Evan P., "Constructing a Model of Nerve Cell Transmission." *The Science Teacher*, January, 1981.

CHAPTER 31   BEHAVIOR

Teaching Techniques

It is important that students understand that behavior has a biological basis and that they analyze an organism's behavior in terms of its biological "equipment." In that sense this chapter indirectly provides a good review of the systems previously studied. The principles of muscular and skeletal structure, chemical control, and nervous control can be readily applied. Make certain that students realize that there is usually an interplay between innate and learned behavior, even in the most complex animals.

Encourage students to cite examples of behavior in organisms with which they are familiar and to analyze how various behavioral actions are adaptive in those organisms. They will, of course, be most interested in human behavior and you might wish to pursue the relative importance of learned and innate behavior during the various phases of life from early infancy through adulthood.

Analysis of behavior of organisms which you may already have in the classroom can be a focus for lively discussion. Activities of mice or other small mammals, reactions of sensitive or insectivorous plants, or feeding behavior in fish are a few of the many examples.

Performance Objectives

Goal: Students will gain an understanding of the patterns of responses made by organisms to stimuli of their environments.

Objectives: Upon completion of the reading and activities and when asked to respond orally or on a written test, students will:

Section
Number
31:0   K   define behavior as the pattern of activities of an organism in reacting to stimuli.

31:0	P	explain the relationship between the complexity of an organism and the complexity of its behavior.
31:1I	K	define innate behavior as behavior which is inherited.
31:1	P	compare and contrast plant tropisms and rapid responses due to changes in turgidity.
31:2	P	explain why a reflex is considered to be innate behavior.
31:2,3	K	distinguish between a reflex and instinct.
31:3	K	list factors which may be involved in the migration of birds.
31:4	K	explain the adaptive advantages of courtship behavior and give an example of such behavior.
31:5	K	describe examples of behavior controlled by a biological clock.
31:1I 6I	P	compare and contrast learned behavior and innate behavior.
31:6	K	describe the use of motivation, reward, and punishment in the experiment involving the T-maze and earthworm.
31:7	P	distinguish between the two types of conditioning.
31:8	K	describe the learning pattern called imprinting.
31:6,9	P	compare and contrast trial and error learning and insight.
31:10	K	describe the manner of communication among bees as observed by Karl von Frisch.
31:11	K	define pheromones and give several examples of their functions.
31:12	P	explain how language has allowed humans to expand their concept formation and reasoning abilities.
31:12	P	compare and contrast human language and language in chimps.
31:13I	K	define a society as a group of animals living together in an organized way.
31:13	P	explain ways in which social hierarchy is beneficial to a society.
31:14	K	list several adaptive advantages of territoriality.

(See page 41T for performance objectives that apply to all chapters.)

Answers to Chapter 31 Review

Page 612. Checking Your Ideas

1. true	5. false	8. true
2. true	6. true	9. true
3. false	7. false	10. false
4. true		

Page 612. Evaluating Your Ideas

1. An organism's behavior is limited by its biological "equipment." In general, organisms with the most complex biological systems exhibit the most complex behavior.

2. Innate behaviors are adaptations because they aid survival and reproduction of a species. Innate responses are predictable because there is no choice involved in such a response. Each organism of a species reacts to a given stimulus in the same way.

3. When touched, leaflets of *Mimosa* plants quickly fold. Specialized areas at the bases of the petioles and leaflets contain sensitive cells which, when touched, lose water. As turgidity in the leaf decreases, the leaflets fold.

4. Reflexes serve a protective function in humans. Examples of human reflexes include the blinking response, the rapid removal of a foot from a sharp surface, and the knee-jerk.

5. Bird migration involves a set of complicated, innate responses to a stimulus or stimuli.

6. Navigation may involve the recognition of angles between the sun or stars and the horizon. Some species follow geographic features such as coastlines and rivers. Some birds may navigate by magnetic cues. Birds probably learn the features of their own nesting sites.

7. Migration enables an animal to move from a seasonally harsh climate to a milder area where food is plentiful. Courtship prepares the male and female for release of gametes and mating. These behaviors are adaptive, aiding in survival and reproduction of the species.

8. Activities probably controlled by a biological clock include flowering of plants at certain times of day, "telling time" by bees, and physiological activities within organisms. Students may give other answers.

9. The complexity of the nervous system may be an important factor in learning. The more complex the nervous system, the wider the range of possible learned behaviors.

10. The earthworm is motivated to reach the moist, dark chamber containing food. However, it makes errors and often reaches the electric shock chamber. Eventually, the worm learns that turning in the proper direction will bring the reward of the dark chamber.

11. Pavlov rang a bell at the same time he presented the dog with its dinner. The dog salivated as food was presented. After a while, the ringing of the bell alone caused salivation. The dog had been conditioned (had learned) to respond to the bell by salivating.

12. Young ducks and geese exhibit a following response to whatever they see at a critical time after they hatch. The "object" they follow may be the mother, but if she is substituted with something else the young animals will follow whatever it is they see at that critical time. This following behavior is adaptive because usually what the young see in the critical time is the mother; the mother will protect and care for the young.

13. Insight involves reasoning and allows the animal to "plan" ahead. Trial and error learning is the random approach of learning by correcting errors.

14. The bee does the round dance on the inside wall of the hive. The dance consists of circling first in one direction and then the other. This dance is interpreted to mean "There is food somewhere within a radius of one hundred meters."

15. In the waggle dance, a bee does a series of "figure eights" while it wags its abdomen. Distance of the food source is indicated by the frequency of complete dance cycles per

fifteen-second interval. The farther the food source from the hive, the smaller the frequency. Direction of the food source is indicated by the angle (in comparison with an imaginary vertical line on the wall of the hive) at which each figure eight is danced. The angle from the vertical indicates the angle of the food source from the sun.

16. In some insect species, the female releases a pheromone which can be detected by a male who follows the scent to the female and mates with her. In mice, males secrete a pheromone which triggers the onset of the female's estrous cycle. Some female mammals secrete pheromones which inform males that they are in heat. In ant societies, ants returning to the nest from a food source deposit a pheromone which ants in the nest can follow back to the food source.

17. Communication in humans increases the chances for survival and reproduction. A record of all previous human experience is available to each generation. Thus, a great deal of trial and error learning is avoided and humans can benefit immediately from what others have learned.

18. Chimps have learned to use symbols to represent ideas. Whales make a variety of sounds which may be a form of communication. Whether either of these animals has a true language has yet to be determined.

19. In a flock of chickens, social hierarchy is established as a result of chickens' pecking at each other. As one chicken gives way to another, a dominance relationship will result. As contacts occur throughout a flock, a total hierarchy emerges. A social hierarchy is one in which the strong dominate the weak, the old dominate the young, and strangers usually are dominated by those within the group. The overall result is increased order. Aggression is reduced as animals "learn their places." There is less fighting over food and mates. Therefore, under adverse conditions, the dominant organisms survive and pass on the "best" genes.

20. Territoriality strengthens a species in the sense that only the "strongest" males mate. It spreads the members of a group over a large area, thus ensuring a better food supply for all members. A large area in which to live reduces conflict.

Page 613. Applying Your Ideas

1. Student answers will vary. Most trial and error learning is common in young children, such as learning to avoid a hot stove or to ride a bicycle.

2. Student answers will vary. An argument can be made that both the dog and the person are conditioned because each does a specific behavior to get a desired effect (reward).

3. Some feel that a human infant imprints on its mother. However, further research is necessary to confirm this idea.

4. Student answers will vary. In terms of basic needs, agriculture provides a variety of readily available foods. Technology provides shelters, fuels for heating and cooking, clothes, everyday products, medicines, and means of transportation and communication.

5. Pheromones could be used to lure insects into traps where they can be destroyed. They might also be used to confuse insects about food sources, thus leading to their death. Confusion about location of mates would also cause a decrease in population size.

6. Limiting defense of territory to gestures, bluffs, and loud noises is adaptive because it maintains an animal's territory but does not result in severe injury or death. These results must be avoided if the species as a whole is to benefit

from territoriality. Many deaths or injuries would jeopardize the species' chances for survival.

7. The queen bee normally passes to worker bees a pheromone which inhibits both ovarian development and the behavior needed to make a queen cell. In the absence of the pheromone, a new queen cell will be constructed.

8. The reflex response is dictated by a specific nervous pathway, the reflex arc.

9. The effectiveness of medicines seems to be related to differences in metabolism at different times of the day, which may follow a biological clock.

10. The *Paramecium's* behavior is innate. It reverses the beating of its cilia, moves backwards, turns thirty degrees, and approaches the object again. This behavior is repeated until the object is avoided.

11. Plants have no nervous systems.

Page 613. Extending Your Ideas

1. *Stentor* responds in a variety of ways. It may bend away from the flow of ink particles. It may reverse the beating of its cilia setting up a current which will deflect the particles. It may withdraw into the tube it builds or leave the tube and swim away.

2. Pill bugs move toward the light source. This kind of behavior is called a taxis and in this case, a positive phototaxis. A taxis involves the movement of a whole organism whereas a tropism involves the movement of a part of an organism. Therefore, this behavior is not considered a tropism. The reaction of the pill bug is innate behavior.

3. Mazes can be made in boxes with cardboard or wooden dividers. Be sure students make the mazes deep enough so that the test animals cannot "hop" over the tops of the dividers.

4. Baboon societies involve much learning unlike insect societies which involve innate behavior. Baboons form social hierarchies in which older males dominate younger males and females. Grooming of young and each other is an important social activity. A baboon troop may move from place to place, defending its territories as it goes if necessary. A baboon society lacks the diversity of roles and level of complexity found in a human society.

5. When two sets of mice are placed together in another cage, conflict will occur. It would be interesting to mark each mouse for later identification so that the hierarchy can be noted. The mice can be marked on the tails with a cotton swab dipped in a weak iodine solution. Have students determine whether there are differences if one set of mice is placed in the other's original cage or if both sets are placed in a new cage. Do *not* allow mice to fight until they are injured. Only allow students to observe their behavior for a short time and then separate the mice again.

6. Temperature varies during the day. For example, it is lower during sleep and upon awakening.

Additional Student Readings

Bohannan, Paul, "Rhythm and Language: That Sync'ing Feeling." *Science 81*, October, 1981.
Garmon, Linda, "The Voice of the Deaf." *Science News*, August 8, 1981.
"Sociobiology: A New View of Human Behavior." Special Section, *Science Digest*, July, 1982.

Suggested Teacher Readings

Burton, Maurice, *Just Like an Animal*. New York, Charles Scribner's Sons, 1978.

Goodenough, Judith, Williams, Gregory F., and Palmer, John D., "The Biological Clock: Regulating the Pulse of Life." *The Science Teacher*, May, 1977.

Hinde, R. A., and Hinde, J. S., *Instinct and Intelligence*, 2nd ed. Carolina Biology Reader. Burlington, NC, Carolina Biological Supply Co., 1980.

Menzel, Randolf and Erber, Jochen, "Learning and Memory in Bees." *Scientific American*, July, 1978.

Reynolds, Vernon, *The Biology of Human Action*. San Francisco, W. H. Freeman and Co., 1976.

Smith, John M., "The Evolution of Behavior." *Scientific American*, September, 1978.

CHAPTER 32 POPULATION BIOLOGY

Teaching Techniques

In presenting the concepts of biotic potential, population growth, and population growth rate, it will be helpful to reproduce the data on the board and then draw the appropriate graphs based on those data. You may wish to have students carry out population growth studies using organisms such as yeasts, protozoans, or *Drosophila* (see *Extending Your Ideas*, number 1). Also, consider having students make estimates of populations in nature, both plant and animal. Such a study can be related to the idea of population density, such as the number of dandelions per square meter or number of diatoms per cubic centimeter. Does the population density for dandelions vary in different microclimates? Have students suggest reasons for any patterns they may discover.

In discussing the growth of the human population, stress that the graph of human population growth in many ways resembles an ideal situation in which there are no limiting factors. For the most part, the rapid growth of the human population can be explained in terms of humans' cultural evolution. Humans have, in many ways, escaped the forces of natural selection and, therefore, have avoided factors which limit the sizes of other populations. Agricultural and technological advances are primarily responsible for the large human population size.

Performance Objectives

Goal: Students will gain an understanding of the factors which affect the growth of populations.

Objectives: Upon completion of the reading and activities and when asked to respond orally or on a written test, students will:

Section Number		
32:0	K	identify population size as the number of organisms in a population.
32:1	K	identify biotic potential as the highest rate of reproduction of a population under ideal conditions.
32:1	K	identify a limiting factor as one which prevents an increase in population size at any given time.
32:2	P	compare and contrast population growth, population growth curve, and population growth rate curve.
32:2	K	differentiate between birthrate and death rate, and relate these rates to the carrying capacity of an environment.
32:2	K	explain the relationship between carrying capacity and environmental resistance.
32:3I	K	differentiate between density-dependent and density-independent limiting factors.
32:3	K	explain how space and food can act as limiting factors.
32:4	P	describe the predator-prey interaction cycle and its effect on the population size of each group.
32:5	K	explain how parasitism as a limiting factor is related to population density.
32:6	P	explain why malaria is a space-related disease and suggest a means of controlling it.
32:6	P	explain why the introduction of a lethal virus into the Australian rabbit population did not kill all of the rabbits.
32:7	K/P	explain what is meant by the competitive exclusion principle and describe an experiment which supports the principle.
32:7,8	P	compare and contrast interspecific and intraspecific competition and describe an example of each.
32:8	P	explain how hierarchies and territoriality reduce conflict.
32:8	K	describe the results of experiments involving the overcrowding of rats and explain the relationship be-

32:9	P	explain how temperature and amount of oxygen can act as density-independent limiting factors.
32:10	K	explain how the development of agriculture has been responsible for variety in human diet and increases in human population size.
32:11	K	explain how advances in technology have contributed to the growth of the human population.
32:12	K	list the factors which have been responsible for the human population explosion.
32:12	K	identify zero population growth as a condition in which the birthrate equals the death rate and the rate of population growth equals zero.

tween internal activities caused by external forces and how they affect population size.

(See page 41T for performance objectives that apply to all chapters.)

Page 628. Family Planning Methods

You may wish to include an extended section on family planning methods with the discussion of the population explosion. In presenting this material to your class, emphasize that family planning is one method for lowering the birthrate. If practiced by enough people over a long period of time, family planning could reduce the rate of population increase.

In addition to its relevance to population problems, information about family planning methods is important to young men and women as they near maturity. Stress that the type of family planning best suited for a particular couple depends on their physical and emotional conditions, moral views, and religious beliefs.

Oral contraceptives

The use of oral contraceptives (birth control pills) is the most effective method of family planning, resulting in about 99% efficiency when properly used. Birth control pills contain a combination of hormones which prevents ovulation. If there is no egg release from the ovary, there can be no pregnancy.

Use of most pills requires that a woman take a pill each day for a given number of days each month and then discontinue for several days. The prescription and schedule for taking pills is determined by a physician. The physician is also important in determining the nature of any side effects which may be brought on by taking oral contraceptives. Side effects sometimes occur. They prevent some individuals from using this method of birth control.

Intrauterine devices

This method of family planning is based on physically preventing either fertilization or implantation. Intrauterine devices (IUD's) are small, flexible, plastic or metal devices of varying sizes and shapes. They are prescribed and inserted by a physician through the opening of a woman's cervix. The IUD rests in the uterus where it either causes a rejection reaction which prevents fertilization of the egg or prevents implantation of a fertilized egg in the uterine tissue. IUD's can be removed by a physician if a pregnancy is desired.

An IUD does not interfere with sexual intercourse or normal physiological functions. Some women, however, find the IUD at least temporarily uncomfortable.

IUD's are effective over 90% of the time. The chief hazard to family planning is that the device may slip out of place without the wearer's being aware of it. Thus, an unplanned pregnancy can occur.

Diaphragm

The diaphragm physically prevents fertilization. It is a thin, flexible rubber cap which covers the cervix. The woman herself inserts the diaphragm before she has intercourse. The inside and outer edge of the diaphragm are coated with a spermicidal jelly prior to the insertion of the diaphragm. The device should not be removed for at least six hours following intercourse.

Diaphragms are prescribed by a physician who decides the size and shape best suited to the woman. The size may have to be changed with time or after a pregnancy.

Effectiveness of diaphragms as a contraceptive device is limited, largely as a result of improper use. Proper positioning of the diaphragm and spermicidal jelly prevent fertilization by not allowing the sperm to reach the egg. A physician or nurse must teach the woman how to insert the diaphragm. If properly inserted and used at all times, the diaphragm is effective. However, improper insertion of or failure to use the diaphragm regularly make this method of family planning only about 85% effective.

Spermicidal foams, creams, and jellies

This method of family planning is based on killing sperm cells and thus preventing fertilization. These substances are available without prescription from drugstores. The woman applies them inside the vagina just prior to intercourse. Many spermicides are not intended for use without a diaphragm. Those that are intended for use without a diaphragm are only about 85% effective.

Condom

The condom (prophylactic or "rubber") is a thin rubber sheath which prevents fertilization physically. The condom is placed over the erect penis just prior to intercourse and sperm are prevented from entering the female reproductive tract. Effectiveness is reduced when there are invisible perforations in the rubber, when the condom tears during intercourse, or if it slips off when the penis is withdrawn. Sometimes the woman uses spermicides simultaneously. Condoms are available in drugstores without prescription and are about 90% effective.

Sterilization

This is a surgical procedure which may be undertaken by both men and women. It is usually an irreversible procedure because it involves the cutting or tying off of tubes which convey the sperm or eggs. For this reason, this method of family planning should be undertaken only by mature couples who are certain they want no more children.

In males, a *vasectomy* is performed. The vas deferens, a coiled set of tubes, is severed. Thus, sperm do not enter the female's reproductive tract. The operation can be quickly performed in a physician's office and is followed by a brief recovery period.

In females, a *tubectomy* or *tubal ligation* is performed. The oviducts are cut and tied. Thus, eggs cannot pass into the region of the reproductive tract where fertilization occurs. This operation is more complex than a vasectomy. Neither operation impairs sexual desire, performance, masculinity, or femininity.

Rhythm method

This is a natural, rather than an artificial, method of family planning. It is based on abstinence from intercourse during the time of ovulation. A woman may keep a record of her menstrual cycle. Such a record may indicate the times before and after ovulation when no egg will be present. Body temperature drops just before ovulation then rises slightly during the last fourteen days of the cycle. A woman can take her temperature each morning. When the temperature has been elevated about one degree and remains at that level for several days, it can be presumed that ovulation has occurred. By this method of recording temperatures, the "safe" days for intercourse may be determined.

The difficulty in the rhythm method lies in that menstrual cycles are not completely regular and, in some women, are very irregular. Because of irregularities in the cycle, much of the method depends on guesswork and "safe" days cannot be accurately determined. Therefore, this method of family planning is one of the least reliable being only about 80% effective.

Answers to Chapter 32 Review

Page 630. Checking Your Ideas

1. carrying capacity
2. population growth
3. interspecific
4. dependent
5. population size
6. population density
7. intraspecific
8. zero population growth
9. biotic potential
10. environmental resistance

Page 630. Evaluating Your Ideas

1. If no limits existed, the size of the yeast population would continue to increase indefinitely. However, when a limiting factor is present, the size of the yeast population levels off and shows a characteristic S-shaped curve.

2. The population growth rate decreases because of environmental resistance.

3. The size of a population is determined by the birthrate and the death rate.

4. Biotic potential is the highest rate of reproduction of a population under ideal conditions. Carrying capacity is the number of individuals which a certain environment can support.

5. Plants cannot move and must, therefore, occupy a given area. Their roots extend downward to obtain water and minerals and their leaves are exposed to sunlight. Only a certain number of plants can occupy a fixed space and, therefore, the size of a plant population may be limited by space. Animal populations are not as often limited by space because population members can move. However, sometimes usable space can limit an animal population and also, increased population density can cause other factors to limit an animal population.

6. Availability of food depends on population density. A small population of animals may have a food supply that will last all through the year. However, doubling the population may lead to quick exhaustion of the food supply and the whole population might starve.

7. Predator and prey populations determine each other's size. An abundance of prey leads to an increase in the predator population. As predators eat the prey, the prey population begins to decline. The number of predators also decreases because they have a reduced food supply. As the number of predators decreases, the prey population begins to increase. A cycle is created in which the change of one population's size follows that of the other.

8. Parasites usually do not cause the death of their host. Infestation with a very large number of parasites, though, can cause death. This infestation with many parasites usually occurs only in a region of high population density. In such a population, parasites are more likely to be transmitted from organism to organism. As the rate of transmission increases, the number of parasites living at the expense of each individual host also increases. The host may then die.

9. The introduction of the lethal virus did not completely eliminate the Australian rabbit population because the population became less dense as rabbits died. Thus, there was a decrease in the rate of transmission of the virus from rabbit to rabbit. Some rabbits survived. Another rise in the rabbit population could be controlled as before. The virus could be reintroduced and would pass rapidly from rabbit to rabbit until the population density again decreased.

10. Each population occupies a particular ecological niche, or place in nature. Therefore, if two populations compete for the same limiting factor, the competition itself may become limiting.

11. When *Paramecium caudatum* and *Paramecium aurelia* were placed in the same culture medium, only *P. aurelia* survived as a result of interspecific competition. The two species were competing for the same limiting factor, the bacteria (food source).

12. Some degree of intraspecific competition contributes to natural selection of the "more fit" for survival. Too much of this type of competition could lead to severe injury or death. Therefore, the species as a whole would suffer.

13. Life cycles often tend to avoid intraspecific competition. Adult frogs do not compete with larval tadpoles for the same habitat and food. In some animal species, adults die shortly after young are born. This reduces competition between young and old. Dispersal of spores and seeds increases distance between young and old plants and thus reduces competition for necessary materials. Many complex animals care for their young and do not compete with them.

14. Once a social hierarchy is established, conflict is reduced. Competition for food, mates, and space is reduced and nonproductive activity is minimized. Establishment of a territory enables a male to attract a female. After the territory is established, mating occurs and aggression is later avoided. Thus, the young can be better reared with adequate space.

15. Overcrowding in rats leads to stress which becomes evident in both physiological and behavioral changes. Aggressive behavior becomes more frequent, resulting in a greater number of deaths. Nests may be poorly built or not built at all. Litter size may be reduced or the litter may be completely eliminated. Adults may eat young or abandon offspring.

16. Student answers may vary. Two examples of density-independent factors are given. 1) Insect populations grow rapidly during the summer months. Then, after the first frost and into late autumn, the population size decreases sharply. A graph of this would show an S-shaped curve then a sharp drop off. 2) Thermal pollution results in less oxygen being dissolved in the water. Therefore, there may not be sufficient oxygen to support all the organisms in the community. Dumping of raw sewage into an aquatic community leads to a decrease in dissolved oxygen because much oxygen is consumed by the bacteria metabolizing the organic material.

17. Agricultural advances have led to an increased food supply and greater variety in the diet. Technological advances have resulted in better sanitation, medicine, and surgery. The consequences of these improvements have been a decrease in the death rate and the lengthening of the life span. For these reasons, the growth of the human population has been rapid.

Page 631. Applying Your Ideas

1. High biotic potential ensures that some offspring will be able to survive and that the species will therefore survive.
2. Hypothetically, in 30 years a human female could produce 40 children. If half of them were females, they could produce a total of 800 offspring during their reproductive life span. This calculation shows that the biotic potential of humans, like all other organisms, is high.

3. Humans could be limited by space because the earth has a limited amount of available space. Also certain areas of the available space have higher population density (locally) so locally humans can be limited by space. Although sometimes humans can move away from more crowded areas, moving is not always possible and would not be beneficial if the other areas become crowded, too.

4. These activities are adaptive because as the birthrate decreases and the death rate increases, the population size is reduced to a number the environment can support.

5. Technological advances often completely eliminate natural biomes. Some United States biomes have been replaced by cities, factories, highways, railroad yards, and airports. Concrete and steel have replaced trees and grasses and little, if any, of the natural biome remains. Pollution of air and water are results of some technological advances. Other answers may be given by students.

6. Increase in height is due more to cultural, rather than biological changes. It is most probably a result of better diets and availability of food as well as medical care. It may not be adaptive because it may not aid survival and reproduction.

7. A low population density could be harmful to continued reproduction (finding a mate) and interaction of individuals living in a society. A population with few individuals might easily become extinct if the environment changed.

Page 631. Extending Your Ideas

1. Techniques for breeding and handling *Drosophila* are readily accessible from a variety of sources. *Drosophila* must be anesthetized for counting. They can then be placed in a "morgue," a jar of alcohol. Have students continue counting until the rate of increase decreases. Have them suggest what limiting factor influences the growth of the population. (Eventually, food supply will run out. To test the hypothesis that food is a limiting factor, a second vial can be used. Add new food material to the vial periodically. Compare the growth of the two populations.)

2. Review the limiting factors which are known to check the size of other populations. Have students predict some possible consequences if the human population continues to grow at a rapid rate.

3. In analyzing the deleterious effects of technology, consider its impact on the environment.

4. Students could prepare color-keyed maps or charts comparing various countries. They might also wish to make projections on population size at various future dates, both for individual countries and for the world. These projections could be graphed. Results of this project would make an excellent report or display for the entire class.

5. Evaluate stories on how well students use present facts and data to project future conditions. You may want to have students share their stories with the class.

6. A given area for study would be chosen, appropriate to the size and range of the animal. A certain number of animals would be captured, "tagged," and then released over a period of time. Later, a sample of the population is taken in the same area. The total size of the population can then be estimated according to the formula $N = \frac{nT}{t}$ where N = the estimated size; n = the total animals trapped; T = the number of animals marked; and t = the number of marked animals recaptured. For further discussion of this and other methods see Smith, Robert L., *Ecology and Field Biology*, 3rd. ed. New York, Harper and Row, 1979.

Additional Student Readings

Arehart-Triechel, Joan, "Life Expectancy: The Great 20th Century Leap." *Science News*, March 13, 1982.

Haber, Gordon C., "The Balancing Act of Moose and Wolves." *Natural History*, October, 1980.

Miller, Julie Ann, "Prairie Dog Problems." *Science News*, January 10, 1981.

Suggested Teacher Readings

Cherfus, Jeremy, "The Population Bomb Revisited." *Science 80*, November, 1980.

Odell, Rice, "Living Space: Land Use or Misuse." *American Biology Teacher*, February, 1978.

Zipko, Stephen J., "A Model for the Study of Population Dynamics." *American Biology Teacher*, May, 1979.

CHAPTER 33   THE ECOSYSTEM

Teaching Techniques

Throughout the chapter, emphasize the *interaction* of organisms and the environment. Each has an effect on the other. Organisms modify their environment while the environment determines the diversity of organisms.

Outdoor activities should play a major role in your students' learning about ecology. Study of school-area or other, perhaps more natural, communities can involve a variety of topics. For example, have some students identify various relationships in the food web of the site. Others can attempt to find evidence of pyramids of numbers or biomass. Still others may be able to find evidence of symbiotic relationships. An aquatic ecosystem such as a pond, lake, or stream makes an excellent focus of study and students can analzye such a community in terms of both biotic and abiotic factors. Teams of students can synthesize their results and endeavor to relate physical aspects of the ecosystem to the life forms inhabiting it. (See *Extending Your Ideas*, number 2.)

Study of natural chemical cycles will probably lead to a lively discussion of the effects of human intervention in ecosystems. Many students will be aware of materials which are not recyclable. This topic is discussed fully in Chapter 35.

Performance Objectives

Goal: Students will gain an understanding of biotic and abiotic factors which affect an ecosystem.

Objectives: Upon completion of the reading and activities and when asked to respond orally or on a written test, students will:

Section
Number

33:0	K	define ecological system or ecosystem.
33:1I	K	define biotic factors as the living elements of an ecosystem.
33:1	K	explain how the sun acts as a constant source of energy for an ecosystem.
33:1	K/P	compare and contrast herbivores, carnivores, and omnivores as well as first-, second-, and third-order consumers.
33:1	P	compare and contrast food chains and food webs.
33:2	P	explain the factors which result in a pyramid of energy in an ecosystem.
33:2,3	P	compare and contrast the pyramids of numbers and biomass and relate them to the pyramid of energy.
33:4	P	compare and contrast decomposers and scavengers.
33:5	K	describe the nitrogen cycle and explain its major pathways.
33:6	P	compare and contrast commensalism, mutualism, and parasitism and list examples.
33:7I	K	indicate how abiotic factors influence ecosystems.
33:7	K	explain that organisms live in air or water and list the ways these media influence life.
33:8	P	explain several ways in which water affects organisms.
33:9	K	describe the process by which soil is formed.
33:9	P	explain the importance of soil and the nature of the soil as factors which affect the structure of a community.
33:10	P	explain several ways in which light affects organisms.
33:11	K	differentiate between latitudinal and altitudinal succession.
33:11	K	explain why water is a more stable environment than land.
33:11	K	list examples of how temperature triggers some biological processes.
33:12	P	compare and contrast ectotherms and endotherms.

(See page 41T for performance objectives that apply to all chapters.)

Answers to Chapter 33 Review

Page 652. Checking Your Ideas

1. herbivore
2. carnivores
3. commensalism
4. omnivore
5. food web
6. bacteria
7. body temperature
8. latitudinal succession
9. mutualism
10. humus

Page 652. Evaluating Your Ideas

1. An ecosystem, like other levels of biological organization, is highly organized. Energy is necessary to maintain organization. Energy also is necessary for the life processes of an ecosystem. The source of energy for an ecosystem is the sun.

2. Producers are the first link in a food chain. They are eaten by first-order consumers (herbivores). First-order consumers are eaten by second-order consumers (carnivores). Third-order consumers, also carnivores, eat second-order consumers.

3. Although specific food chains may be traced, any ecosystem has a variety of possible feeding patterns. Many species are found at each feeding level and one species does not always eat the same species. All the possible feeding relationships in an ecosystem make up a food web.

4. Energy, in the form of food, is transferred along a food chain. Much usable energy is lost between each link of a food chain. Some of it escapes as a result of metabolism (cellular respiration) and some is used as life functions are carried out. Much of the potential energy at each level is never transferred to the next level. Therefore, each successive link in a food chain has less potential energy available to it than the previous link.

5. A large animal requires more energy than a smaller animal. It gets more energy from eating other large animals than from eating small animals. By trapping one large animal, less energy is expended than is gained.

6. A pyramid of numbers is related to a pyramid of energy. Because energy is lost between each feeding level, each higher feeding level has fewer organisms than the previous level.

7. A pyramid of biomass is due to the loss of energy between feeding levels. There is less energy available to maintain living material at each level. Therefore, the total mass of a group of organisms at one level is less than that of the group at the previous level.

8. Plants need nitrogen for the synthesis of amino acids, proteins, nucleotides, and nucleic acids. The nitrogen cycle is the set of events which results in the ecosystem's being able to use nitrogen over and over again. Without the nitrogen cycle, nitrogen would accumulate in the form of dead organisms and waste materials. Eventually so much nitrogen would be removed from a community that the community could not survive. In one pathway, bacteria in the soil convert proteins and other nitrogen compounds to ammonia. The ammonia reacts with water to form ammonium ions which are converted to nitrite ions and then nitrate ions by other bacteria. Nitrate ions are absorbed by plants and used in the synthesis of proteins and other organic nitrogen compounds. Nitrogen-fixing bacteria in the root nodules of legumes convert atmospheric nitrogen to ammonia. Some ammonia enters the soil and is converted by bacteria there to nitrates. Most of the ammonia is converted by the nitrogen-fixing bacteria to amino acids which enter the plant cells. There, they can be converted to other organic nitrogen compounds.

9. In commensalism, the commensal benefits from the host. The host is neither harmed nor helped. An epiphyte is an example of a commensal. It obtains solar energy by living in the canopy of its host tree. The tree is unaffected. In mutualism, two organisms depend on each other. In a lichen, for example, the alga provides food while the fungus provides moisture and protection. Each benefits the other.

10. In parasitism, one organism, the host, is harmed in some way by the other organism, the parasite.

11. (a) The density of water is much greater than that of air. Therefore, aquatic organisms are better supported than land organisms and many aquatic organisms survive without skeletal systems.

(b) Water is more dense and offers more resistance to movement than air does. Therefore, movement in water and air varies. In water, some animals move by propulsion or by "rowing." In air (on land), many crawl or run.

(c) In water, some animals can exist as filter feeders by removing food from the water as it passes through them. Land forms must go to the food. The medium does not bring the food to the predator.

12. All plants require water for photosynthesis. Some plants such as mosses and ferns must have water for reproduction. The amount of rainfall determines what kinds of plants will be dominant in a given region.

13. The formation of soil is a long process involving both living and nonliving factors. Weathering causes the breakdown of rock into smaller particles. Small organisms release carbon dioxide which dissolves in water to form carbonic acid. The action of carbonic acid and leaching continue the breakdown of rock until fine particles are formed. Gradually more organisms inhabit the area. Dead organisms and wastes enrich the soil as humus is formed.

14. The nature of the soil determines what kinds of plants will live there, which in turn, determines the variety of animals which will inhabit an area.

15. In a forest, trees are dominant because they are able to capture most of the sunlight. Other forest plants must be able to grow in the dim light of the forest floor. Some grow before leaves appear on the trees. Others are epiphytic, obtaining sunlight in the tops of trees.

16. Light is converted to heat energy as it is absorbed by the atmosphere, land, and seas. Heat energy maintains a temperature range beneficial for life. Heat is also necessary for the transpiration of water from plants and the evaporation of water from oceans and rivers. These activities contribute to the water cycle.

17. Distribution of life forms varies with climate. Climates vary altitudinally and latitudinally. Communities vary from the equator to the poles (latitudinal succession) and with changes in altitude (altitudinal succession). The two types parallel one another.

18. Water is a more stable environment because there is relatively little temperature fluctuation in water. On land, temperature may vary as much as forty Celsius degrees between day and night. In the same time period, the top ten meters of ocean water may change only four Celsius degrees. Below ten meters there is no noticeable change in temperature.

19. Some spores and seeds can survive temperature extremes which would kill a mature plant. Thus, a species can survive extreme temperatures.

20. Metabolic rate of animals varies with environmental temperature. Up to about 45°C metabolic rate increases two or three times for every ten degrees the temperature is raised. Near 50°C, the rate slows then falls sharply to zero because enzymes are destroyed by high temperatures.

21. Ectotherms have adaptations which prevent dangerous changes in body temperature and metabolism. Many of these are behavioral, e.g., hibernation and periods of inactivity. Some endotherms also avoid cold temperatures by hibernating.

22. The constant body temperatures of endotherms are adaptive in allowing proper enzyme function, metabolic reactions, and so on. Therefore, sufficient energy is made available for body functions.

Page 653. Applying Your Ideas

1. Humans are omnivores and fit into food chains at all levels. When eating fruits, nuts, and vegetables, humans act as first-order consumers. When eating meat, they are second or third-order consumers. Humans are not usually preyed on by carnivores because either they do not live in proximity to such animals or they are capable of escaping them.

2. Student answers will vary. A possible aquatic food chain is algae → crustacean → small fish → large fish. A possible desert food chain is desert plant → mouse → snake.

3. In general, and considering only animals, each successive feeding level is composed of larger animals. Larger animals tend to prey on smaller ones. However, there are many exceptions to this trend.

4. Shorter extremities in cold climates decrease heat loss from radiation. Therefore, the feature is adaptive.

5. Cactus root patterns vary. Some cactus roots grow close to the soil because water, when available, does not penetrate to great depths. Others have deep roots to get the water from much deeper in the substrate.

6. Introduction of nitrogenase enzymes into plants would enable them to fix atmospheric nitrogen, thus augmenting the supply of nitrogen absorbed from the soil. These enzymes could reduce the need for fertilizers in growing agricultural crops.

7. Wood, cell walls of dead xylem, is composed of molecules that contain much potential energy.

8. Too much energy would be lost through food chains composed of many links. By eliminating foods such as poultry, beef, and pork, energy could be conserved and more people could be fed.

9. A dog remains inactive and pants in hot weather.

10. Clearing land for agriculture disrupts existing food webs and may interfere with other biotic relationships and the recycling of materials.

Page 653. Extending Your Ideas

1. The students' plans should consider the following broad areas: constant energy input and food supply; mechanism for recycling materials; control of temperature range, rainfall, and climate; and the nature and effect of abiotic factors such as those discussed in this chapter.

2. Accurate quantitative determinations of dissolved materials and other abiotic factors can be made by using kits especially designed for high school students. As a class project, different groups of students can be assigned one or more tests. Other students can survey and/or collect specimens. Taxonomic keys can be used to identify life forms. As a whole, the class can then synthesize their information, correlate data about biotic and abiotic factors, and come to conclusions about the "health" of the ecosystem.

3. In terms of human needs, the report should focus upon food, materials necessary in a technological society, and energy for that technology. Effects of humans on the ecosystem include pollution, wildlife conservation, and overpopulation. See Chapters 32 and 35.

4. Direct students to any good ecology text. Phosphorus is usually in short supply, and its main reserves are in rock and natural phosphate deposits. Phosphorus is released into the ecosystem by weathering, leaching, erosion, and mining. It is then reduced by bacteria to inorganic phosphates which are utilized by plants and microorganisms. Upon decomposition of these organisms, phosphorus usually is washed to the sea.

Additional Student Readings

Batten, Mary, "Earth's Odd Couples." *Science Digest*, November/December, 1980.

Pringle, Lawrence, *Chains, Webs, and Pyramids: The Flow of Energy in Nature.* New York, Harper and Row Publishers, Inc., 1975.

Suggested Teacher Readings

Brill, Winston J., "Biological Nitrogen Fixation." *Scientific American*, March, 1977.

Crenshaw, Neil, "Food Webs in the Classroom." *American Biology Teacher*, February, 1981.

Freeman, Peter, "An Ecology Field Trip Focusing on Inquiry: A Northern Perspective." *American Biology Teacher*, October, 1980.

Heller, H. Craig, Crawshaw, Larry I., and Hammel, Harold T., "The Thermostat of Vertebrate Animals." *Scientific American*, August, 1978.

Sharp, John D., Jr., "Symbiosis: Creatures Living Together in Nature." *American Biology Teacher*, May, 1980.

Smith, Robert L., *Ecology and Field Biology*, 3rd ed. New York, Harper and Row, Publishers, 1979.

Zampella, Robert A., "A Simulated Stream Ecology Study." *American Biology Teacher*, May, 1979.

CHAPTER 34 ORIGIN AND DISTRIBUTION OF COMMUNITIES

Teaching Techniques

Students are frequently surprised to learn that communities, like populations of organisms, change with time. Their understanding of this phenomenon will be enhanced if they can observe an area actually in the midst of succession. If your school is near an abandoned field or a large lake surrounded by a natural community, it will be worthwhile to plan a trip there. In teaching succession, emphasize that each stage leads the way to its own ultimate destruction by modifications of the environment.

Your class probably will include students who are familiar with biomes other than the type in which you live. Encourage them to share their knowledge with the class. Stress the idea that although biomes vary greatly in terms of physical and biotic factors, all of them share basic, fundamental features.

Performance Objectives

Goal: Students will gain an understanding of ecological succession and the features and distribution of the world's major biomes.

Objectives: Upon completion of the reading and activities and when asked to respond orally or on a written test, students will:

Section
Number

34:1*I* K define ecological succession as the series of changes in a community during its development.

34:1,2 P compare and contrast the pioneering stage with the climax community and describe the intermediate stages.

34:3 P compare and contrast primary and secondary succession.

34:3 K describe how climax communities form in a given geographic area.

34:4 K describe the ecological succession of a lake ecosystem to a climax community.

34:5I K list factors that determine the type of biome an area will be.

34:5,6 P compare and contrast a tundra biome and a taiga biome.

34:7-9 K list the characteristics of the temperate deciduous forest, tropical rain forest, and grassland biomes and describe organisms of each.

34:7 K describe what is meant by vertical stratification in a temperate deciduous forest.

34:8,9 K describe the way humans have changed tropical rain forests and grasslands.

34:9,10 P compare and contrast desert and grassland biomes.

34:10 K explain several ways in which plants and animals are adapted for life in a desert.

34:11 P explain the influence of light as a limiting factor for life in the oceans.

34:11 P compare and contrast plankton, nekton, and benthos.

34:12,13 P compare and contrast the littoral, neritic, and abyssal zones.

34:13 K describe how decomposed materials are recycled in the oceans.

34:14 K describe the life forms found in abyssal communities centered around vents in the ocean floor.

34:14 K explain how energy is available to the organisms in newly-discovered abyssal communities.

(See page 41T for performance objectives that apply to all chapters.)

Answers to Chapter 34 Review

Page 674. Checking Your Ideas

1.	false	**6.**	false
2.	false	**7.**	true
3.	true	**8.**	true
4.	false	**9.**	true
5.	true	**10.**	true

Page 674. Evaluating Your Ideas

1. Primary succession begins as lichens grow on bare rock. The lichens then produce acids which begin to break rock into small particles. Decomposers break down the lichens producing organic material which enriches the forming soil. Plants begin to grow in the soil. More complex plants such as weeds and shrubs grow. Their decay also enriches the soil as does the decay of animals such as worms and insects. Then trees such as pines or oaks grow. These are finally replaced by beeches and maples as the dominant species. In secondary succession, an abandoned field is first inhabited by hardy grasses and weeds. Shrubs later appear and then junipers, poplars, and white pine. Eventually beeches and maples become predominant. The processes are much the same except that primary succession begins from bare rock whereas secondary succession occurs after vegetation of an area has been disrupted (such as from farming).

2. A lake is not a climax community. As a lake ages, soil and humus collect at its bottom and near the shoreline. Simple plants such as *Sphagnum* moss, insectivorous plants, and shrubs take root in the marshy soil. As this occurs, soil and humus continue to collect toward the center of the lake. Simple plants continue to colonize the newly formed soil. The areas first colonized undergo further succession as shrubs are replaced by trees, eventually beech and maple. This pattern continues until the lake is replaced by forest.

3. Permafrost is a permanent layer of frozen ground. It prevents the rooting of large plants, thus limiting plant life to forms such as lichens, mosses, and some small shrubs and bushes.

4. Animal life in the tundra includes examples such as mosquitoes, mice, moles, lemmings, snowshoe hares, polar bears, caribou, and fox. Birds migrate to the tundra in summer, but few are permanent residents.

5. Taiga is an area of relatively low precipitation. The rate of evaporation is very low and so the soil is wet. Temperature is warmer than that in the tundra and the soil is acidic. Because there is no permafrost, trees are able to root in taiga soil. Conifers like spruce and firs are common.

6. Microenvironments are small areas in an ecosystem which differ in conditions from the rest of the ecosystem. Microenvironments modify an area and permit certain organisms which ordinarily would not be able to inhabit that community to live there.

7. Moose, caribou, weasels, mink, and ermine are examples of animals that inhabit the taiga. Birds such as crossbills are common.

8. Temperate deciduous forest biomes receive a relatively even distribution of rain totaling about 100 cm per year. These biomes have definite seasons.

9. Vertical stratification is the organization of a forest into a series of strata or layers from top to bottom. In a temperate deciduous forest the top layer is the canopy of trees. Animals such as insects, squirrels, and birds inhabit the canopy. Most of the food is produced in this layer. Shrubs and other small plants occupy the shrub layer. On the forest floor, light is scarce and only plants which can thrive in the shade are present. Insects, other arthropods, and snakes are common on the forest floor. Rotting logs may contain microcommunities of life. Another level exists beneath the ground. Small arthropods, worms, and decomposers live in this layer.

10. A tropical rain forest receives heavy rainfall and has an almost constant temperature of 25°C. This hot, humid climate causes luxuriant growth of plants.

11. In a tropical rain forest, the canopy is the major level. Lianas are rooted in the ground but their leaves are in the canopy where sunlight is plentiful. Epiphytes are common in the canopy and support their own animal life. Arthropods and vertebrates abound in the canopy. The forest floor is very dark and plant life is scarce there. A few shrubs may survive, but usually the forest floor is barren.

12. Grasslands receive between 25 and 75 cm of rain per year. The rainfall is unevenly distributed throughout the year.

13. In the United States' grasslands, natural grasses have been replaced by cereal grains such as wheat and corn. Cattle have replaced bison. Although these changes have been beneficial in terms of human needs, people have been careless with this valuable land. Poor farming methods have led to the removal of much rich topsoil by wind and water erosion. The dust bowl of the 1930's, a result of misuse of grassland, caused many farms to be abandoned.

14. Scattering is an adaptation to a lack of water. Although plants are few in number, each has water available to it.

15. Many desert animals are adapted for water conservation. The kangaroo rat, for example, excretes very little water in its urine and is able to derive water from its food and metabolism. Burrowing rodents are adapted to temperature extremes. By remaining in their burrows, they can avoid the heat of the day and the cold of the night. Some of these animals estivate. Ectotherms such as snakes and lizards have behavioral adaptations which protect them from temperature extremes.

16. Light intensity quickly diminishes with depth because light is reflected and absorbed by the water. Light generally does not penetrate a depth greater than 200 m. Because light does not penetrate very far, the zone in which autotrophs live (in which photosynthesis occurs) is small.

17. Life in the ocean is classified as plankton, nekton, and benthos. Plankton are organisms which float in the water. Nekton are animals which can move freely through the water by their own means. Benthos are animals which live attached to or crawl on the bottom of the ocean. Plankton are most numerous; they include the producers of the ocean biome.

18. The littoral zone is the area close to the shore. It is a transitional area between land and sea. The neritic zone is the area above the continental shelf and is more stable than the littoral zone because there is no exposure to air. Plankton and nekton are plentiful in the neritic zone. The abyssal zone is the deepest part of the ocean. Light is absent; there are no producers. Nekton and benthos are common. Decomposition occurs here.

19. Decomposition occurs on the ocean bottom. Return of materials to the ocean surface is influenced by temperature and wind. In cold climates the surface water becomes colder than the water below. The heavier cold water sinks and the lighter warm water rises. Wind causes currents which move the surface water. Water below the surface rises to replace the water displaced by wind. The combination of these processes results in the recycling of decomposed materials.

20. Geothermal-heated water that escapes from ocean vents reacts with rocks forming hydrogen sulfide. Chemosynthetic bacteria use hydrogen sulfide in the synthesis of carbohydrates. These bacteria serve as food for animals like mussels and clams which, in turn, are eaten by larger animals.

Page 675. Applying Your Ideas

1. If the dominant species were damaged by parasites, the entire community would be affected. Not only may food chains be disrupted, but also many abiotic and biotic factors such as nesting sites, availability of light, humidity, and microenvironments will be altered.

2. Life in the canopy layer affects the shrubs, floor, and soil levels in terms of both abiotic and biotic factors. For example, the amount of light, temperature, and humidity are determined by the leaf distribution in the community. Leaves are a potential energy source to animals in all levels, and dead leaves and twigs are a source of materials which can be recycled by soil organisms.

3. If a forest were cleared, animal life including birds, immature and adult insects, and mammals would be affected. If these animals could not migrate to another, similar forest, they would die.

4. The algae and other plankton are the most numerous forms of ocean life.

5. Vertical stratification exists in oceans as well as forests. Surface waters are inhabited by plankton. Deeper areas contain nekton. At the ocean bottom are benthos. Light is present only in the surface waters, and photosynthesis occurs there. Deeper regions are dark and contain different organisms.

6. Student answers will vary, but should include an accurate description of the biome. Examples of how humans have changed the biome might include buildings, electric and phone wires, and removal of natural vegetation.

7. Abyssal communities centered around ocean vents are temporary in that only if geothermal rifts are present can the community continue to exist.

Page 675. Extending Your Ideas

1. If an abandoned field is accessible, you might wish to consider an entire class trip to the area. Look for succession in the field and surrounding natural biome. If there is no surrounding natural biome, have students suggest what plant forms would later replace those forms now living in the area.

2. Encourage students to think about factors such as light or shade, temperature, and humidity as well as the insides of rotten logs, and so on.

3. Estuaries are ecosystems located where fresh water and salt water meet. Salinity varies with depth and width, and is influenced by tides. Shifts in salinity may occur between high and low tides. Organisms must be adapted to changes in salinity and the action of tides. Animals adjust to changing salinity conditions by a variety of physiological mechanisms. Oysters, sponges, barnacles, and crabs are common forms of estuarine life.

Additional Student Readings

Clark, Eugenie, "Secrets of the Red Sea." *Science Digest,* April, 1982.

High, Colin, "New England Returns to Wood." *Natural History,* February, 1980.

MacMahon, James A., "Mount St. Helens Revisited." *Natural History,* May, 1982.

Raloff, Janet and Silberner, Joanne, "Saving the Amazon." *Science News,* October 4, 1980.

Suggested Teacher Readings

Cushing, D. H., *The Productivity of the Sea.* Oxford Biology Reader. London, Oxford University Press, 1975.

Engleke, Dianne, "Life in the Desert." *Biology Digest,* January, 1981.

Smail, James R., "What's in the Ocean?" *American Biology Teacher,* September, 1981.

Sumich, James L., *An Introduction to the Biology of Marine Life,* 2nd ed. Dubuque, IA, William C. Brown, Co., 1980.

CHAPTER 35   HUMANS AND THE ENVIRONMENT

Teaching Techniques

Because this chapter focuses on the environment, it should produce some spirited and vital class discussion. In directing such discussions, emphasize that humans have caused many problems for themselves and other organisms. Accentuate the positive; namely, that awareness of and concern for the problems of our environment are sound starting points for rectifying past mistakes. Instill in your students the idea that contributions by *all* individuals add up to major improvements.

Have students report on or directly investigate cases of pollution. A lake or stream can be analyzed for evidence of pollution by standard chemical and biological tests and often sources of pollution can be determined. Tests to determine air quality are also available.

Performance Objectives

Goal: Students will gain an understanding of the place of humans in the biosphere and how human influence on the environment can affect the future of humans and other organisms.

Objectives: Upon completion of the reading and activities and when asked to respond orally or on a written test, students will:

Section Number		
35:1I	K	explain what is meant by pollution.
35:1	K	list several ways in which organisms are pests to humans.
35:2	K	give two examples of unforeseen effects of DDT.
35:3	P	explain how DDT as a nonbiodegradable substance is accumulated in tissues.
35:3	P	compare and contrast the ecological effects of pesticides like parathion and malathion with the effects of pesticides like DDT.
35:4	P	explain how the use of pesticides is related to the economy.
35:5	K/P	list several common air pollutants and explain how they affect the environment.
35:5	K	discuss two possible ways in which burning of fossil fuels may have a long-range effect on average global temperatures.
35:6	K	explain how acid rain is formed and describe its ecological effects.
35:7	K	explain the sequence of events leading to an algal bloom and the results of this process.

35:7	K	explain the cause and effects of thermal pollution of water.
35:8	K	list examples of pollution other than chemical pollution of air and water.
35:8	P	identify sources of pollution in the local community and suggest changes which could decrease pollution.
35:9I	K	distinguish between renewable and nonrenewable resources.
35:9	K	explain how food for humans may become a nonrenewable resource.
35:9	K	discuss ways in which protein shortage problems may be solved.
35:10	K	explain what is meant by crop rotation and how this process prevents soil depletion.
35:10	K	list ways of reducing wind and water erosion on agricultural land.
35:11	P	compare and contrast the generation of nuclear energy by nuclear fission and nuclear fusion.
35:12,13P		suggest several ways in which humans can help to improve the environment.
35:14	K	discuss various means of biological control of pests.

(See page 41T for performance objectives that apply to all chapters.)

Answers to Chapter 35 Review

Page 698. Checking Your Ideas

1. pollutant
2. eutrophication
3. nonbiodegradable
4. nonrenewable
5. algal bloom
6. pheromones
7. biological magnification
8. erosion
9. lead
10. crop rotation

Page 698. Evaluating Your Ideas

1. Student answers will vary. Some examples are listed. Termites destroy wood; moths destroy woolen products; Japanese beetles attack plants and shrubs; weeds crowd out cultivated plants; medflies destroy fruit; fungi damage wheat.

2. Many pests were purposely or accidentally brought to this country. Humans have also altered natural ecosystems and planted large areas with single food crops. In so doing, they have destroyed natural predators and created a high population density suitable for the transmission of parasites.

3. The predator insects may be entirely eliminated by the pesticide. The pest population size may be initially reduced, but in the absence of their natural predators, the pest population will eventually grow larger than its original size, and therefore, cause greater damage.

4. Pesticides can become ineffective if some of the insects originally exposed were genetically resistant to the pesticide. These insects survive, passing on the resistance to future generations. Eventually, an entirely resistant population may result.

5. DDT causes eggshells to become thin and they are easily broken. DDT may also interfere with breeding behavior of large birds.

6. Pesticides such as malathion are biodegradable, but they affect organisms other than insects before they break down. When spread over a large area, they may kill many predators of pests. Vertebrates, including humans, may be affected.

7. Hydrocarbons may cause cancer. Carbon monoxide deprives the body of oxygen. Oxides of nitrogen may damage plants and harm animals. PAN, a combination of hydrocarbons and nitrogen oxides, damages the eyes and lungs. Lead is a poison. Sulfur dioxide causes damage to plant leaves and the respiratory tracts of animals. Sulfur dioxide and nitrogen oxide result in acid rain.

8. Phosphates and nitrates accumulate in high concentrations in rivers and lakes where they contribute to rapid growth of algal populations. As the population size increases, most of the other available nutrients necessary for life are consumed. Then, most of the algae die. A great deal of oxygen is used in the decomposition of the algae. As a result, less oxygen is available for other aquatic organisms and other plants and animals die off. Their death results in further decomposition and oxygen depletion and eutrophication of the river or lake.

9. Radioactive isotopes may accumulate in tissues and cause mutations in those tissues. They could also become concentrated in cow's milk making the milk unsuitable for human consumption.

10. Better crops have been produced by selective breeding. Plants with large heads of grain and good fertilizer response have been produced. Protein-rich crops are also being developed, and scientists are interbreeding nutritious species of plants.

11. Crop rotation is an alternation of crops on a timely (such as yearly) basis. A soil enriching plant such as a legume is alternated with a principal crop such as corn or wheat. The legumes contain nitrogen-fixing bacteria which return nitrogen to the soil. Rotation counteracts the depletion of valuable materials from the soil.

12. Humans can prevent erosion by carefully planned farming methods. Contour plowing reduces water runoff. Terracing creates banks of land on a slope, thus slowing the flow of water. Both of these methods, by reducing water flow, result in the removal of less topsoil. Planting trees to break the wind and plowing at right angles to the wind reduce wind erosion.

13. Fossil fuel formation requires millions of years. However, humans have almost totally exhausted the fossil fuel supply in only a few hundred years. Possible new alternatives include nuclear energy, solar energy, wind energy, and geothermal energy.

14. Use of nuclear energy conserves fossil fuels, although the radioactive isotopes used are nonrenewable. More importantly, radioactive wastes are produced by nuclear reactors and must be disposed of safely. Also, water used in cooling the reactors is heated and can result in thermal pollution.

15. Solar energy is being used to heat and cool homes and other buildings. Among other uses, solar energy is used to power satellites and to fuel a plant that makes fresh water out of salt water.

16. Wildlife can be conserved by the thoughtfulness of humans. Wild game preserves protect some species. Strict hunting and fishing limits help to prevent a species from declining to extinction.

17. Forests can be conserved by planting trees every few years so that some trees will be ready for cutting at regular intervals. Also, entire forests should not be cut at once. Instead, blocks of trees must be left to reseed the areas from which trees have been removed. In selective cutting, only mature trees are cut. In improvement cutting, old, crooked, or diseased trees are removed permitting more space for the growth of healthy, young trees. Recycling would help forest conservation because fewer trees would have to be cut. Recycling paper, for example, would reduce the demand for wood pulp.

18. Microorganisms are specific, affecting only certain insects. A problem is that they often work slowly; therefore, a great deal of damage may be done before the insect pests die.

19. Hormones are used to alter the insect pest's metamorphosis. Some speed up the time needed to reach maturity, and are effective against larval pests. Others retard development and are used in cases where adults cause damage or where reproduction must be controlled. Pheromones can be placed in traps to attract insects or be spread over a large area, "confusing" insects in search of mates.

Page 699. Applying Your Ideas

1. Insects have become resistant to many pesticides through the process of natural selection.

2. Increase in water temperature decreases the amount of dissolved oxygen. With less oxygen available, many organisms might die.

3. Offshore drilling procedures must guard against the hazard of possible oil leaks or spills which can kill a variety of marine animal life.

4. Student answers will vary. Home heating, transportation, production of goods, and modern agriculture would all be affected.

5. Industrial areas are most heavily polluted, but other areas become affected as pollutants are carried by wind and rain.

Page 699. Extending Your Ideas

1. Answers to these questions will vary. Perhaps these questions will serve as an impetus for the formation of an environmental group or club in your school. The club could consider ways to inform the school and community about the problems of pollution and their roles in helping to solve them.

2. In addition to demonstrating contour plowing and terracing, some students might wish to devise models to illustrate wind erosion. A small electric fan can be used as a wind source and models showing plowing at right angles to the wind and trees planted to obstruct the wind can be constructed.

3. This question might serve as the nucleus of a debate involving many class members.

4. Many communities are currently involved in recycling wastes. Perhaps a committee of students could be assigned to visit local recycling centers and gather information for a report to the class.

5. Encourage students to think about factors such as insulation, thermostat settings, number and sizes of windows and doors, and electrical demands and usage.

Additional Student Readings

Brown, Lester R., "The Coming of the Solar Age." *Natural History*, February, 1982.

Carothers, Steven W. and Dolan, Robert, "Dam Changes on the Colorado River." *Natural History*, January, 1982.

Jordan, William H. Jr., "Invasion of the Medfly." *Natural History*, May, 1982.

Metcalf, R. L. and Kelman, A., "Integrated Pest Management in China." *Environment*, May, 1981.

Suggested Teacher Readings

Ambroggi, Robert P., "Water." *Scientific American*, September, 1980.

Bonner, James, *The World's People and the World's Food Supply.* Carolina Biology Reader. Burlington, NC, Carolina Biological Supply Co., 1980.

Brill, Winston J., "Agricultural Microbiology." *Scientific American*, September, 1981.

Drummond, A. H., Jr., "Acid Rain: Precipitating a Crisis for Wildlife?" *The Science Teacher*, January, 1979.

Iker, Sam, "The Promise and Peril of Pesticides." *International Wildlife*, July-August, 1982.

Kidder, Tracy, "Taming a Star." *Science 82*, March, 1982.

Morgan, Michael D., and Moran, Joseph M., "The Human Organism and Environmental Issues: Putting It All Together." *American Biology Teacher*, September, 1981.

Sassin, Wolfgang, "Energy." *Scientific American*, September, 1980.

Scrimshaw, Nevin S., and Taylor, Lance, "Food." *Scientific American*, September, 1980.

Teacher Questionnaire

Perhaps one of the best ways to ensure that effective educational materials are produced is to let authors and publishers know how you feel concerning the ones you are using. Please help us in our planning of revisions and new programs by completing and returning the form found on the next page. After removing the questionnaire from the book, fold and staple it so that the address label shows. We would certainly appreciate hearing from you.

1 2 3 4 5 6 7 8 9 10 11 12 13 14 15 — 89 88 87 86 85 84 83 82

BIOLOGY: LIVING SYSTEMS

Circle the number which corresponds most nearly to your opinion of each of the following items of the BIOLOGY: LIVING SYSTEMS program. Please also star (*) three factors which most influence your evaluation or choice of a text.

Student Text

	Excellent	Very Good	Satisfactory	Fair	Poor	Comments
1. Format	1	2	3	4	5	_____
2. Readability	1	2	3	4	5	_____
3. Concept development	1	2	3	4	5	_____
4. Approach	1	2	3	4	5	_____
5. Organization	1	2	3	4	5	_____
6. Thoroughness & accuracy	1	2	3	4	5	_____
7. Margin notes	1	2	3	4	5	_____
8. Treatment of new terms	1	2	3	4	5	_____
9. Illustrations	1	2	3	4	5	_____
10. Chapter-end materials	1	2	3	4	5	_____
11. Appendices	1	2	3	4	5	_____
12. Glossary	1	2	3	4	5	_____
13. Index	1	2	3	4	5	_____
14. Advances in Biology	1	2	3	4	5	_____
15. Biographies	1	2	3	4	5	_____

Teacher's Annotated Edition

	Excellent	Very Good	Satisfactory	Fair	Poor	Comments
1. Teachability	1	2	3	4	5	_____
2. Text design and use pages	1	2	3	4	5	_____
3. Planning guide	1	2	3	4	5	_____
4. Reading and science feature	1	2	3	4	5	_____
5. Performance objectives	1	2	3	4	5	_____
6. Reference information	1	2	3	4	5	_____
7. Chapter material	1	2	3	4	5	_____
8. Annotations and answers	1	2	3	4	5	_____

Supplements

	Excellent	Very Good	Satisfactory	Fair	Poor	Comments
1. Evaluation Program	1	2	3	4	5	_____
2. Probing Levels of Life	1	2	3	4	5	_____
3. Probing Levels of Life, TAE	1	2	3	4	5	_____
4. Investigating Living Systems	1	2	3	4	5	_____
5. Investigating Living Systems, TAE	1	2	3	4	5	_____

School Information

1. Grade level of students	7	8	9	10	11	12
2. Enrollment of that grade	1-50	51-100		101-200		200+
3. Average class size	25 or less	26-30	31-35	36-40		41 or more
4. Total school enrollment	1-200	201-500		501-1000		1000+
5. Locale of school	rural	small town		suburban		large city
6. Ability level of class	below average		average			above average
7. Appropriateness of text for class	easy		about right			difficult
8. Number of years text used	1	2	3	4		5
9. May we quote you?	yes	no				

Name _____ Date _____

School _____ City _____ State _____ Zip _____

- -

Fold

- -

Fold

NO POSTAGE
NECESSARY
IF MAILED
IN THE
UNITED STATES

BUSINESS REPLY MAIL
FIRST CLASS   PERMIT NO. 284   COLUMBUS, OHIO
POSTAGE WILL BE PAID BY ADDRESSEE
Managing Editor, Elhi Science
CHARLES E. MERRILL PUBLISHING CO.
A BELL & HOWELL COMPANY
1300 ALUM CREEK DRIVE
COLUMBUS, OHIO 43216

TEACHER'S ANNOTATED EDITION

BIOLOGY

Living Systems

Raymond F. Oram
The Peddie School
Hightstown, NJ

CONSULTANTS
Paul J. Hummer, Jr.
Gov. Thomas Johnson High School
Frederick, MD

Robert C. Smoot
McDonogh School
McDonogh, MD

Fourth Edition

Charles E. Merrill Publishing Company
A Bell & Howell Company
Columbus, Ohio

Toronto, London, Sydney

A MERRILL SCIENCE PROGRAM

Biology: Living Systems, Pupil's Edition & Teacher's Annotated Edition
Probing Levels of Life: A Laboratory Manual, Pupil's Edition & Teacher's Annotated Edition
Laboratory Biology: Investigating Living Systems, Pupil's Edition & Teacher's Annotated Edition
Biology: Living Systems, Evaluation Program (Spirit Duplicating Masters)

About the Author:

Raymond F. Oram is a teacher/administrator at The Peddie School, Hightstown, NJ, with twenty years of teaching experience. As well as being a teacher, his positions have included Science Department Head and Assistant Headmaster. He received his A.B. degree from Princeton University and his M.S.T. from Union College, Schenectady, NY. In 1976, Mr. Oram was recognized with the Princeton Prize for Distinguished Secondary School Teaching in the State of New Jersey.

Consultants:

Paul J. Hummer is a science teacher in the Frederick, MD, schools with twenty-four years teaching experience. He received his B.S.Ed. from Lock Haven State Teacher's College in Lock Haven, PA, and his M.A.S.T. from Union College, Schenectady, NY. Mr. Hummer is also a co-author of Merrill's *Biology: An Everyday Experience*.

Robert C. Smoot is a chemistry teacher and Chairman of the Science Department at the McDonogh School, McDonogh, MD. He earned his B.S. in Chemical Engineering from Pennsylvania State University and his M.A.T. from Johns Hopkins University. Mr. Smoot is author of Merrill's *Chemistry: A Modern Course* and co-author of *Physics: Principles and Problems*.

Reviewers:

Ms. Barbara Anderson, *Science Dept. Chairperson, Foothill High School, San Jose, CA*
Mr. Thomas Atkins, *Science Dept. Chairperson, Mount View High School, Mesa, AZ*
Mr. John Boege, *Science Dept. Chairperson, Anoka Senior High School, Anoka, MN*
Mr. Carmen Ciarrocca, *Science Supervisor, Cumberland Valley High School, Mechanicsburg, PA*
Ms. Linda Dixon, *Science Teacher, Foothill Senior High School, Sacramento, CA*
Mrs. Betty Greer, *Biology Teacher, Robert E. Lee High School, Baton Rouge, LA*
Dr. Paul Hovsepian, *Director/Math and Science Education, Detroit Public Schools, Detroit, MI*
Mr. Robert Miller, *Science Dept. Chairperson, Oak Forest High School, Oak Forest, IL*
Mr. Edward Schroth, *Science Coordinator, Quaker Valley Senior High School, Leetsdale, PA*
Dr. Donald W. Urbancic, *Science Dept. Chairperson, Loyola High School, Towson, MD*
Mr. Robert Wyble, *Science Dept. Chairperson, Penn Manor High School, Millersville, PA*

Project Editor: Mary Joan Arnett; *Editors:* Mary Baker, Joyce L. Timmons; *Book Designer:* Larry P. Koons;
Project Artist: Dennis L. Smith; *Artists:* Kip Frankenberry, David L. Gossell, Shirley Beltz, Barbara White,
Lynn Norton; *Illustrators:* Juan Carlos Barberis, Lewis H. Bolen, David Dennis, Peg Dougherty, Nancy A. Heim,
Jean Helmer, Pat and Paul Karch, Bill Robison, Don Robison, Jim Robison, Jim Shough; *Photo Editor:*
Russell T. Lappa; *Production Editors:* Kimberly Munsie, Annette Hoffman; *Cover Photo:* Gene Frazier

ISBN 0-675-07021-X

Published by
Charles E. Merrill Publishing Company
A Bell & Howell Company
Columbus, Ohio 43216

Printed in the United States of America

PREFACE

BIOLOGY: Living Systems, Fourth Edition, maintains the high standards of the previous editions while adding new and current material of prime importance to high school students. Input from hundreds of teachers has played a role in updating, rewriting, and reorganizing this edition. Emphasis is placed on broad concepts applicable to all living systems. Details concerning the diversity of processes, structures, and organisms are related to the unifying principles and features of all life. Basic concepts are repeated at different points and at varying degrees of depth. Thus, the student builds upon the foundation of previously mastered ideas.

Living systems are characterized by organization. Maintenance of this organization depends on the interrelationship of matter and energy. *BIOLOGY: Living Systems*, Fourth Edition, begins by introducing these important concepts. The relationship is then emphasized and repeated throughout the text as it applies to different levels of biological organization.

Uniqueness of science is then discussed. Whenever possible, important principles and concepts are presented and developed on the basis of the experimental evidence supporting them. Thus, the student gains an insight into, and an appreciation for, the way scientific knowledge is produced. The text stresses the interrelationships and differences among facts, observations, interpretations, and experimentation. It also stresses that scientific theories are always subject to revision in the light of new evidence. Evolution, for example, is treated as a theory rather than as fact.

Chemical aspects of living systems are a basic part of today's biology. Only those principles of chemistry needed for an understanding of biochemical processes are presented. When these processes are presented with other concepts, the significance of the processes is emphasized. Chemical details are minimized. A chapter on energy ties the chemical aspects of living systems to the following chapter which explores cell structure and function.

Following the introductory unit, reproduction is analyzed in terms of the cell, genetics, and biochemistry. The text then proceeds to a discussion of the evidence regarding change in living things. Adaptations, speciation, and human origins are considered. Succeeding chapters deal with principles of taxonomy and a survey of the five kingdoms.

The next three units are devoted to the anatomy and physiology of simple organisms, plants, and animals respectively. Because these three groups of organisms are adapted to very different ways of life, it is more practical to present these organisms separately. Therefore, a major change in *BIOLOGY: Living Systems*, Fourth Edition, is the separation of anatomy and physiology of simple organisms, plants, and animals into different units. However, the organization of all three units is similar so that if preferred, systems of all may be presented concurrently.

The book concludes with a unit on environment. Chapters in this unit include an examination of behavior, population biology, and ecology. An analysis of the role of humans in causing, coping with, and solving contemporary problems of pollution, conservation, and overpopulation is incorporated.

The content is presented in a logical manner—from the simplest to the most complex level of biological organization. However, the presentation is flexible enough so that chapters may be studied in a variety of sequences.

Many aids to student learning are incorporated into the text. Each unit begins with a discussion and a photograph that provide a preview of the material to be covered. A chapter-opening photograph and an introductory paragraph are used to convey the theme of each chapter to the student. A goal statement identifies the major objectives of each chapter. Margin notes, section-end and chapter-end questions, vocabulary lists, and chapter summaries provide guides for self-assessment, review, and study. Reading lists, project ideas, appendices (including information on biology related careers), a complete glossary, and an extensive index complete the many learning aids. Together, these features provide a guide by which students may efficiently approach their study of biology.

Biology, as a study of life, is a relevant and vital discipline. *BIOLOGY: Living Systems,* Fourth Edition, presents basic biological principles by using examples which best illustrate these principles. Concepts and theories are augmented by practical, applied, and familiar examples and illustrations. Thus, the text appeals to non-science students as well as to those who will continue their study of science.

TO THE STUDENT

What common bond do you share with the more than two million other known kinds of organisms on Earth? You and the other organisms are *living* things. What makes you and other life forms "alive"? What needs do you share? What activities do you all carry out? How are you all different? In what ways do you interact? How do you and your fellow living things affect the environment, and how does the environment affect you? How do you play a role in the lives of other living things?

You are about to begin a course in biology which will enable you to answer some of these questions. You may or may not consider yourself a young "scientist." You may or may not ever take another course in biology. However, what you learn in this course will be valuable to you always. Knowledge of biology will be useful and important to you now as you learn about what makes you and other living things "tick." It will also be important later in helping you make responsible decisions as an adult.

BIOLOGY: Living Systems, Fourth Edition, contains much interesting and up-to-date information. Understanding how to use your text will help make your study of biology easier. Each unit begins with a photograph and a discussion that preview the material in the unit to follow. Each chapter begins with a photograph and introductory paragraph which convey the theme of the chapter to you as a living system. A goal statement explains the objectives for your study of the chapter. Throughout the chapter, margin notes emphasize the major

ideas. Use these notes as a self-check to evaluate your understanding of facts and major ideas. Major terms are highlighted in boldface type.

Review questions and/or problems have been placed throughout the chapter. These, too, provide a means for you to check your understanding. At the end of each chapter, a *Summary* provides a list of the major points and ideas presented. (Some of you will find it useful to read this both *before and after* reading the chapter.) A word list, *Language of Biology,* reminds you of the most important terms.

Also at the end of each chapter are sets of questions and problems. *Checking Your Ideas* is a set of questions stressing your understanding of major facts and terms. *Evaluating Your Ideas* contains questions and problems that are useful as a review of the chapter's concepts. *Applying Your Ideas* includes questions and problems which require you to apply what you have learned to new but related ideas. In addition, a set of project ideas is presented in *Extending Your Ideas.* Included among the five Appendices are *A Classification of Living Systems* and *Biology-Related Careers.* The glossary contains complete definitions of the major terms in the text. The complete index will be valuable to you in locating particular topics.

With these thoughts in mind, it is time to begin. Our hope is that your study will result in an increased awareness and understanding of yourself and your relationship with other living things. Also, we hope you will come to share with us the excitement such understanding can bring. Good luck.

TABLE OF CONTENTS

CHARACTERISTICS OF LIFE

Biology, the study of life, is a vital and challenging field. Each year that field grows as old questions are answered and new questions are raised. What determines how a living thing grows? Why do some life forms better resist disease than others? These and other questions and their answers affect you, for you are a part of the world of life.

When you think of living things, you no doubt think of many different kinds. Think about the characteristics of this hummingbird and the plant from which it is feeding. Think about other living things. Each life form has a special set of features; there is a great diversity in life forms. What is not so obvious is that within that diversity of life, there is unity. There are certain characteristics of life shared by all living things.

Unit I focuses on common characteristics of life. For example, all living things require energy. All interact with other living things and with the environment. The hummingbird interacts with plants for food, an energy source. You will learn about the characteristics common to life forms. You also will learn some of the methods by which living things are studied and you will be introduced to some ideas of chemistry needed for today's study of biology.

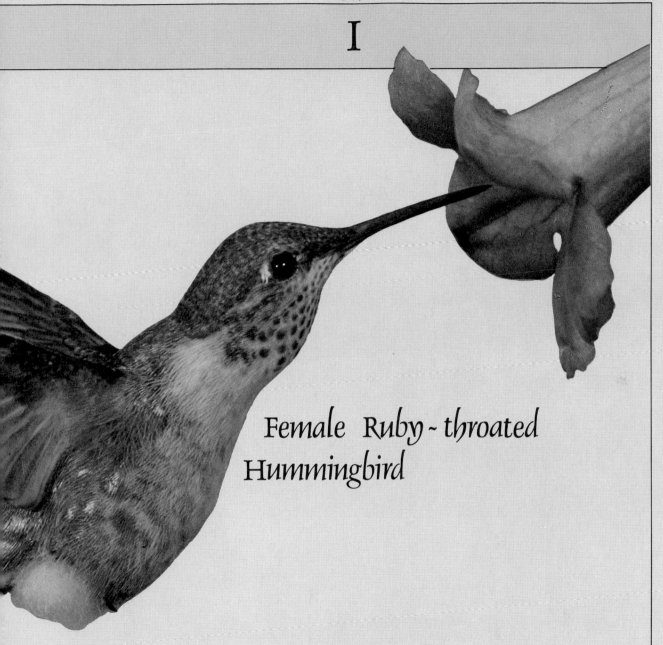

Female Ruby-throated
Hummingbird

Carl W. Rettenmeyer

If you examine the world around you, you will find it full of living things. Most easy to observe may be plants and animals, but other types of life are also present. Although the life forms seem very different, they have some things in common. All living things need food. From the food they get energy. How do living things such as these ants obtain and use energy? What is the major source of energy to the living things on Earth?

Introduction: There is no more exciting and logical starting point for your course in biology than having your students walk into a classroom that is alive. Prepare for your first class by stocking your classroom with a variety of living things which students can observe closely with the unaided eye or a microscope. Choose familiar specimens such as flowering plants in bloom, cacti, mosses, bread mold, fish, mice, worms, and frogs. Forms less familiar to most students that you might want to have in your room include cultures of protozoa, bacteria, and algae. Slime molds, lichens, hydras, Venus's-flytraps, and rotifers are other specimens you might want to include. A good way to begin is to ask students to identify the natural habitats of the specimens and to name other organisms that might live in those habitats. Ask students to name similarities and differences in the organisms. This approach will aid in teaching the concept that, although organisms may seem quite different, they all share the same, broad characteristics.

THE WORLD OF LIVING THINGS

Chapter 1 introduces the community level of organization and the major characteristics of living systems.

A general discussion of performance objectives and objectives for each chapter are listed in the Teacher's Guide.

You are about to begin a course in **biology,** the study of life. Naturally, you want to know what you will be learning. Your study will involve different kinds of **organisms** (living things). Part of the course will examine the major groups of organisms which exist today. You will learn about the physical characteristics which set one type of organism apart from others.

GOAL: You will gain an understanding of the basic features of life common to all organisms.

Biology is more than just a study which describes the many differences among living things. There are nearly two million known kinds of living organisms. You could not possibly learn about all or even most of them. Therefore, your study of life will focus on the similarities among organisms. These similarities most often involve the life processes of organisms—their activities and functions. By studying these processes, you will see that there are certain features common to all living things. By the time you complete the course, you will have a good understanding of what is meant by the word "life."

Biology is the study of life.

A living thing is called an organism.

Organisms are similar in their activities and functions.

THE COMMUNITY

1:1 Organisms

Have you ever had the chance to spend a day exploring the natural surroundings where you live? Perhaps you live in an area near a forest. Imagine that you are about to walk through the forest. As you near the edge of the forest, you see many things.

Major terms are printed in boldface next to their definitions. Italics are used for emphasis.

Teaching suggestion. Have students describe life forms in various communities. Emphasize that life although very diverse exhibits unity.

A community is a naturally occurring group of different kinds of organisms.

In phonetic pronunciations, accented syllables are printed in half-size capital letters. Refer students to the pronunciation key, page 742.

bacteria (singular, bacterium)

FIGURE 1-1. A forest community may include organisms such as (a) red fox and (b) orange Indian pipe.

At first you see plant life such as grasses, weeds, shrubs, and other plants. As you enter the forest, you are aware of the most striking forms of life, the trees.

You then see much more. There are other types of plants such as ferns and mosses growing on the forest floor. Leaves and fallen branches litter the earth. You look under them and find many kinds of animal life. Insects are plentiful. Ants scurry about, each doing its special job. You see spiders, worms, and many–legged creatures. Other animal life is also plentiful. Birds sing their songs and a rabbit bounds quickly out of sight. Perhaps you see a deer nibbling leaves or a snake sliding off into the undergrowth. You look more closely at the trees and find many other living things. Bees swarm around their hive. A small butterfly, almost the same color as the bark, clings to the trunk of a tree. You also see a caterpillar moving silently across a leaf, eating as it goes.

Your trip has been an eventful one. Yet you saw only a fraction of the living things in such a community. **A community** is a naturally occurring group of organisms living in a certain area. You missed the countless microscopic (mi kruh SKAHP ihk) organisms that live in the soil, in puddles of water, and inside other plants and animals. If you had taken a sample of soil or water, you would have found that it contains a vast amount of life. With a microscope, you would see many bacteria, very small living things. You might also have seen many other tiny creatures, larger than bacteria and more complex. These creatures include mites and insects and very small worms.

a

b

Gene Frazier　　　　　　　　*Richard Brommer*

Robert G. Bachard

Gerry Atwell/U.S. Fish and Wildlife Service

a

b

Maybe your surroundings are different. Perhaps you live near a grassland or desert. Perhaps you live near an aquatic (uh KWAHT ihk) community such as a pond, lake, or stream. No matter what type of community you study, each has its own kinds of living things.

From your study, one common feature of life becomes evident. Living things do not exist by themselves but exist in communities. Can you suggest some reasons? As you consider possible reasons, other common features of living things will become evident.

FIGURE 1-2. Organisms in different communities vary. (a) An ocean reef community may include sponges, fish, and other organisms. (b) A polar community may include organisms such as polar bears.

1:2 Food

Study of different communities reveals many kinds of animal life. One striking similarity among all animals is their need for food. Has it occurred to you that all animals must get their food from other living things? Some feed on other animals, some on plants, and some feed on both other animals and plants. However, in any community, there must be some organisms which can make their own food. These organisms are mainly the green plants. Most other members of the community depend directly or indirectly on green plants for food.

Green plants are not the only living things which are able to make food. Several other forms of life, such as certain algae (AL jee) and some bacteria, can also make food. Biologists refer to all living things which make their own food as **producers.** Most producers use sunlight to produce food by a process called **photosynthesis.** Photosynthesis means "put together with light."

Animals obtain food from other organisms.

Every community includes some organisms, mainly green plants, which can make food.

Another term for producer is autotroph (auto-, self). Another term for consumer is heterotroph (hetero-, other). These terms are presented in Chapter 18.

Producers manufacture food by the process of photosynthesis.

a　　　b　　　c

FIGURE 1-3.　(a) A tomato slug is a consumer, eating the tomato plant, a producer. (b) A shelf fungus on a live tree is a parasite. (c) Coral fungus lives on dead matter and is a saprophyte.

Consumers depend directly or indirectly on producers for food.

Parasites live in or on a host from which they obtain food.

Saprophytes feed on waste products of living things or upon dead organisms.

Energy is the ability to do work or cause motion.

The food manufactured by producers is used by the producer itself and by other members of the community. Living things unable to produce their own food are called **consumers.**

Some consumers cannot move around in search of food as most animals do. Many of them obtain food by other means. Some are **parasites,** organisms that live in or on another living thing. Parasites obtain their food from a **host** and usually harm the host. A heartworm is an animal that is a parasite inside another animal—a dog. A rust is a fungus and is an example of a plantlike parasite that grows on wheat. What are some other parasites and their hosts? tapeworm and human; flea and dog

Some consumers obtain their food from dead organisms or from waste products of living organisms. These consumers are called **saprophytes** (SAP ruh fitez). A mushroom is a saprophyte which obtains its food from materials in the soil. Some bacteria and other microorganisms are saprophytes, too.

The need for food is a basic feature of living things. But there is another question to be answered. Why do all living things need food? for energy

1:3 Energy

In many ways a living organism is similar to an automobile engine. Both a living thing and an engine are complex structures. Each consists of many parts which work together so the whole may function smoothly.

In an automobile engine, all the parts have certain jobs or functions to perform. In order for them to perform, they must have fuel. Fuels are sources of energy. **Energy** is the ability to do work or cause motion. You cannot see energy, but you can see its effects. Just as gasoline is the source of energy in automobile engines, food is the source of energy in living things.

In an engine, the energy of burning gasoline sets in motion a chain of events. The result is the movement of the various parts. The energy is transferred to the wheels of the automobile. As long as fuel is available, the engine will run. As soon as the fuel is used up, the engine will stop. Similarly, each living thing must be provided with fuel if it is to function. When the fuel supply runs out, the plant or animal will stop functioning.

Automobile engines can remain inactive for long periods of time. When provided with more fuel, an engine will run again. However, living "machines" need a continuous supply of fuel. If a plant or animal is deprived of fuel for long periods of time, its parts will die. No amount of fuel supplied later will restore its ability to function.

Life, then, suggests a picture of constantly working machinery. There is a continuous need for fuel (in the form of food) to keep a living thing functioning. Every living thing uses the energy of food for its biological work. Obtaining and using energy is a feature of all living things.

A continuous supply of food provides energy for biological work.

Although sugars are the major source for quick energy, fats and proteins may also be used as "fuels."

Sugar is the main food used by organisms.

1:4 Food Production and Energy Transfer

The type of food made by producers is sugar. It is not the same as the sugar you put on your cereal in the morning, but it is very similar. Sugar is the universal fuel for life.

Because the making of sugar involves work, energy is necessary. Most producers obtain energy for making food from sunlight. The energy of sunlight is used to combine water and a gas, carbon dioxide, to make sugar. A special substance,

FIGURE 1-4. In photosynthesis, carbon dioxide and water are combined in green plants to make sugar. Sometimes plants convert sugars to other forms such as starches which are stored in plant parts.

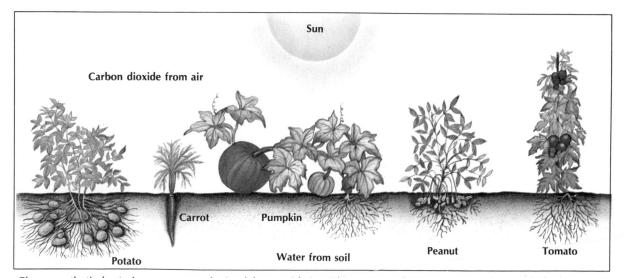

Chemosynthetic bacteria use energy obtained from oxidation of inorganic substances and produce carbohydrates.

Photosynthesis requires sunlight, carbon dioxide, water, and chlorophyll.

Suggested demonstration. You can easily illustrate the interrelationship of photosynthesis and cellular respiration by setting up a miniature community consisting of several sprigs of *Elodea* and a small fish. Place them in an Erlenmeyer flask and seal the flask. Under suitable illumination, both plants and animal will remain healthy.

Cellular respiration produces carbon dioxide and water, raw materials for photosynthesis.

FIGURE 1-5. **The processes of photosynthesis and cellular respiration contribute to the recycling of materials through a community.**

chlorophyll, is also needed. **Chlorophyll** is the substance that *traps* the energy of sunlight for use in making food. Water and carbon dioxide are obtained from the environment, but chlorophyll is made by the producer. Chlorophyll is the substance that makes plants green.

Thus, part of the sun's energy is transferred to and stored in the sugar. The sugar is later "burned" by a living thing. "Burning" of sugar is called **cellular respiration.** Cellular respiration transfers energy first produced by the sun. This energy can be used for work by a living thing.

Carbon dioxide and water are not in endless supply. How can you explain that they continue to be available to producers? During cellular respiration, sugar is broken down into carbon dioxide and water. Carbon dioxide and water are the same substances needed for photosynthesis. These substances are constantly being returned to the air. Water reaches the soil or bodies of water as rain, and carbon dioxide stays in the air or dissolves in water. These substances are used over and over again. Your body is "burning" sugar right now. The carbon in that sugar might long ago have been part of a giant fern or a dinosaur.

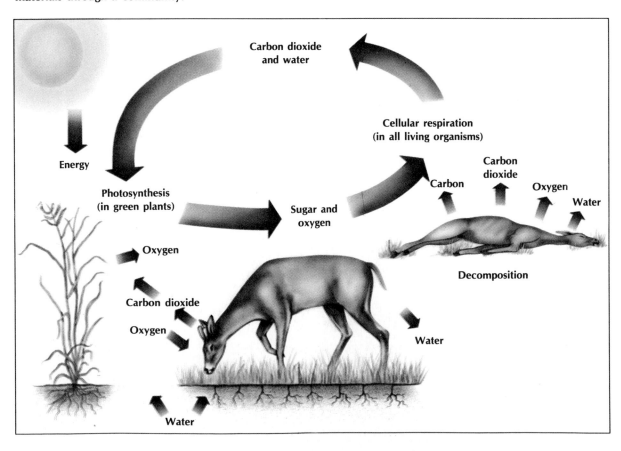

The "burning" process releases materials needed for photosynthesis—water and carbon dioxide. Photosynthesis, in turn, produces sugar and releases an important substance, oxygen. Oxygen is needed by most organisms to "burn" the sugar. Can you see that the "burning" process and photosynthesis are interdependent?

A producer, such as wheat, may "burn" sugar and use energy to do work. Or, a producer might be eaten by a consumer. Mice and deer, for example, are animals which feed on producers. Consumers "burn" the sugar in the producers they eat and use the energy for their own needs. A snake, in turn, may prey on (eat) the mouse, and a hawk may prey on the snake. Animals that prey on other animals are **predators** (PRED ut urz). The passage of energy from plants through a series of animals feeding on other animals and plants is a **food chain**. Wheat—mouse—snake—hawk is one food chain.

Living organisms constantly produce waste products. Eventually, the organisms die. Wastes and dead organisms are acted upon by other members in a food chain, the decomposers. **Decomposers** are organisms such as bacteria and fungi which cause decay. They are consumers. Decomposers obtain their needed energy from cellular respiration of the materials left in wastes or dead organisms. In so doing, they also release carbon dioxide and water which can be used by producers. Decomposers also return to the environment substances containing elements such as nitrogen, sulfur, and phosphorus. These elements will be used again by other living things. *Thus, in any community, the basic materials of life are recycled.*

In a food chain, energy is passed from one living thing to another. This energy is used for each organism's work. Once the energy is used for work, though, it cannot be used again. *Thus, energy cannot be recycled.* It must always be available in the form of food. There must be a constant source of energy for photosynthesis. That energy is sunlight. Without sunlight, life as we know it could not survive.

FIGURE 1-6. A food chain shows the direction energy moves from producer to consumers. Energy is not recycled in a food chain.

Energy is distributed to all organisms through food chains.

Materials are recycled through a community, but energy cannot be recycled.

REVIEWING YOUR IDEAS

1. Do all living things live in communities in nature? Why?
2. What is a producer? How are producers important to a community?
3. List several examples of consumers.
4. Why do living things need food?
5. What materials are necessary for photosynthesis? What does a producer need to combine these materials to form sugar?
6. What is a food chain? Why is it important? Give an example of a food chain involving yourself.
7. Compare what happens to the materials and the energy used by a community.

1. Yes. They depend on one another for materials and energy.
2. Producers manufacture food. All other organisms depend on producers for food.
3. insect, mushroom, fish, human, many bacteria
4. Food is a source of energy.
5. Carbon dioxide and water are needed for photosynthesis. Light energy and chlorophyll are necessary for the process to occur.
6. A food chain is the path of energy through a series of organisms. By food chains, all organisms obtain energy originally trapped by producers. Example: grass → cow → human.
7. Materials are recycled but energy is not.

THE USES OF ENERGY

Sugar is made by producers and "burned" by all organisms. Thus, the materials and energy needed for proper functioning are made available to living things. What are these functions? They can be grouped into four broad areas: growth and development, maintenance and repair, reproduction, and organization. These functions are important because they are common features of living things.

1:5 Growth and Development

Every living thing has some period of growth during its lifetime. The overall growth may be slight, as of a bacterium; or it can be large, as of a whale or elephant. Whether great or small, growth is a feature of every living thing. But, what is growth, and how does it occur?

Suppose you placed a wilted lettuce leaf in a bowl of water. After a period of time, the leaf would have increased in weight and volume. Is this growth? No, **growth** is an increase in the amount of living material in a plant or animal. The lettuce leaf has not added living material; it has just absorbed water.

Consider another situation. Suppose you placed a lettuce seed in some moist soil. In about a week, a lettuce plant would begin to appear. Water was again taken in, but this time also true growth has occurred. The basic difference is that the seed has used the water (with carbon dioxide and minerals) to form living materials. Water was not just soaked up, or absorbed, in a physical

Suggested demonstration. Show water absorption of wilted plants. Have students compare the process with plant growth.

Growth is an increase in the amount of living material.

FIGURE 1-7. Growth, an increase in the amount of living material, of (a) lions, can be shown (b) in a graph of increase over time.

a

b
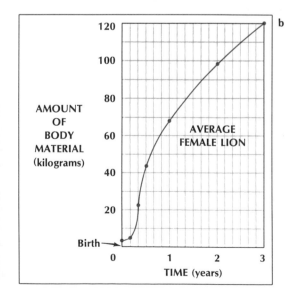

Grant Heilman

manner. It was put together with the other materials in a special way to become part of the living thing. Growth is not just an increase in amount. It is an increase in the amount of living material.

Not only did the lettuce seed grow, it became a certain kind of living thing. It became a lettuce plant with its specialized parts. How are materials put together in a lettuce seed to form a lettuce plant? Why does the seed not become a beet or carrot plant? The series of changes a living thing undergoes in reaching its final form is called **development.** The lettuce seed developed into a lettuce plant. Perhaps you know that development involves heredity (huh RED ut ee). **Heredity** is the transmission of features from one generation to the next. Later you will study both heredity and development.

1:6 Maintenance and Repair

Organisms are faced with many changes in the environment, including the activities of other organisms. Temperatures change during a day and from season to season, and the water and food supplies can also change. A resting animal suddenly may need to flee from a predator.

If an organism is to survive such changes, somehow its internal operation must be adjusted. When you are outside in cold weather, you might shiver. A bear hibernates in the winter. A plant conserves water in dry spells. The heartbeat and breathing rates of a running animal increase. All of these features help the living things survive in their environments. How?

These responses and activities use energy. They are controlled by the interaction of many parts and systems, such as chemicals, nerves, muscles, and the skeleton. Such responses maintain **homeostasis** (hoh mee oh STAY sus), balance of the internal operation of an organism regardless of external changes. If homeostasis did not occur, organisms would not be able to live very long. Maintenance is a continual process.

What are some possible dangers to living things? A list would be endless because of the great complexity of living things. Minor problems, such as cuts and scratches or infections, usually can be overcome by natural means. Scratches heal as a result of clotting blood which covers the wound and prevents infection while new skin is being formed. Special cells in an organism often attack and destroy bacteria in an infection. Sometimes repair of an injury can even involve replacement of body parts. A salamander can replace a lost limb, growing a new limb. It also can replace other body parts. A starfish can replace a lost "arm." Much energy goes into the repair and replacement of worn-out and damaged parts in living things.

White blood cells trap bacteria.

Muscle contractions during shivering increase body heat. The bear's energy demands are lowered during the period of inactivity. Conserving water prevents wilting and death. Increased heartbeat and breathing rates provide the cells with more food and oxygen.

Organisms respond to changes in the environment.

Homeostasis is the steady balance of the internal operation of an organism.

FIGURE 1-8. Monitors on this man's chest detect his heart's response to his changed level of activity. The heart's response is part of the body's mechanism to maintain homeostasis.

Hickson-Bender Photography

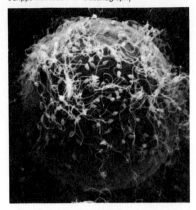

FIGURE 1-9. Coded instructions are passed in the sperm and egg from one generation to the next. A sea urchin egg covered with sperm is shown here magnified about 800 times.

During reproduction, a set of coded instructions is passed from one generation to the next.

DNA (Chapter 9) is the "master code."

Life is a continuous process.

Energy is needed for the parts of an organism to work together in an orderly way.

How is the degree of organization of your desk or locker related to the energy you expended in the organizing process?

1:7 Reproduction

Teaching suggestion. Point out that not all reproduction is sexual.

A feature which distinguishes living things from nonliving things is **reproduction** (production of offspring). Only living things can reproduce. New plants and animals have certain features that set them apart from other kinds of living things. Rabbits produce rabbits and oak trees produce oaks. "Like produces like" is a basic biological principle. Rabbits may differ in appearance, but most people would be able to identify a rabbit.

That all living things can reproduce poses new questions. Most plants and animals begin life as a small, fertilized egg. How do you explain that from this small structure a fully grown, complex oak tree (or octopus, or orangutan) is produced?

A fertilized egg does not contain a small form of the living thing. What does it contain? Analysis shows that a fertilized egg is composed of many chemicals but is mostly water. Some of these chemicals direct the putting together of other materials so that a distinct living thing forms. In other words, the fertilized egg contains a "master code" for life. Reproduction is the transfer of the coded instructions which direct the formation of the new organism. Living things pass to each generation a formula for continuing life.

In many organisms, tiny sperm and eggs are living "messengers" which unite to form a fertilized egg, the beginning of a new life. As "messengers," sperm and eggs link one generation to the next so that the process of life continues. Individual plants and animals die and many groups of organisms have become extinct, but life continues without interruption.

1:8 Organization

You have now looked at some ways in which energy is used by living things. Growth and development, maintenance and repair, and reproduction are all common functions of life which use energy. Although each has been discussed alone, all of them are ongoing processes in a living system. None of the functions of living things is isolated from the others.

A common feature of organisms is their precise organization. **Organization** is the orderly functioning of a living system. It involves the coordination of all the complex processes and activities of an organism. Organization can only be maintained if energy is available. It is the main result of energy use. Without a steady supply of energy, organization soon disappears. What happens to an organism's organization once it dies? Why?

Not only are the complex processes and activities of a living thing organized. Living things are physically organized also. An organism is composed of interworking parts which differ in complexity. Thus, scientists have defined levels of organization.

Organization disappears as decomposition proceeds. Energy is not available to maintain organization. Expenditure of energy counteracts entropy, leading to a more ordered state.

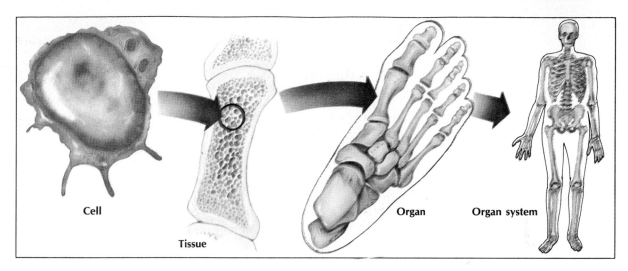

Cell

Tissue

Organ

Organ system

Most types of organisms are made of more than one kind of cell. You will study cells and their parts in Chapter 5. In organisms made of more than one kind of cell, similar cells are organized to do certain jobs. A group of cells having the same origin, structure, and function is called a **tissue.** Animal tissues include muscles, bones, skin, nerves, and blood. Plant tissues include protective areas such as bark and the outer surfaces of leaves, conductive tissue which transports water and food, and special regions of growth.

Groups of tissues are further organized into **organs.** The leaf of a plant, for example, is an organ of photosynthesis. It contains tissues for protection, water and mineral transport, food production, and transport of food. What are some other organs?

A group of organs working together is known as a **system.** The stomach is an organ which is only part of the entire digestive system. What other organs work with the stomach? What are some other animal systems and some plant systems?

The total organism represents the next higher level of organization, but organism is not the end point. Life is more than individual organisms. Higher levels of organization, involving groups of organisms, also exist. For example, you have already learned about a community, which is composed of many kinds of organisms. Later you will learn about other ways in which organisms are grouped.

FIGURE 1-10. Levels of biological organization include cells, tissues, organs, and organ systems.

Biological levels of organization: cell, tissue, organ, system, organism.

Higher levels of organization: population, community, biome, biosphere.

REVIEWING YOUR IDEAS

8. What is development? How does it differ from growth?
9. Why are maintenance and repair important to living things?
10. What is reproduction? What is passed on to each generation?
11. List the levels of biological organization through organism.

8. Development is the series of changes through which an organism goes in attaining its final form. It involves a special pattern of growth.
9. Maintenance and repair allow organisms to survive changes.
10. Reproduction is the production of offspring. The "master code" message is passed on to the next generation.
11. cell, tissue, organ, system, organism

ORGANISM AND ENVIRONMENT

1:9 Adaptation

When you think about a community, you naturally think about the organisms living in it. A lake is inhabited by fish, snails, and algae. Cactus plants, scorpions, and lizards live in a desert. Crabs, jellyfish, and whales are found in the ocean. Deer, birds, and maple trees live in a forest.

Has it occurred to you that organisms are suited to particular kinds of environments? A fish has gills that obtain oxygen from the water. A deer has teeth that grind plant material. Birds have wings. A cactus stores water. Maple trees have broad leaves which trap sunlight in photosynthesis.

Organisms are suited to particular environments.

These special parts and activities of organisms are examples of adaptations. An **adaptation** is a feature of a living thing which enables it to survive in its environment. Adaptations are another common feature of living things. You will learn more about adaptations in Chapter 11.

Adaptations promote survival.

1:10 Relationships Within the Environment

Each living thing is a complex organization of interacting parts. Without the proper working of all of its parts, the organism would be in trouble. So, too, the success of a community depends on the organisms in it. Living things do not exist alone; they live together and depend on each other. The study of the relationship between organisms and their environment is **ecology.** An ecologist wants to know how organisms live with each other and how they interact with the things around them.

Ecology is the study of the relationship between organisms and their environment.

FIGURE 1-11. (a) Water lilies and (b) a hermit crab have special adaptations which aid their survival. What are some of their adaptations?

a

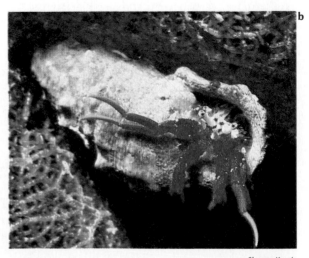
b

Richard Brommer

Sharon Kurgis

Teaching suggestion: Have students
suggest other ecological relationships.   Gene Frazier   1:10 RELATIONSHIPS WITHIN THE ENVIRONMENT   17

Don Nieman

a   b

A study of a community reveals many ways in which plants and animals interact. Many birds build nests in trees and other plants. Bees transfer pollen from flower to flower. Seeds of some plants are transported in the fur of mammals. Molds may grow on rotting wood, and some insects live under the bark of trees. Many organisms require mates in order to reproduce, and many young organisms must be cared for by their parents. The predator and prey relationship (Section 1:4) is another way organisms depend on each other.

Physical factors of the environment are also important to a community. Without water, carbon dioxide, and oxygen, most organisms could not live. The type of soil and amount of water determine the kinds of plants which can live and grow in a certain place. The amount of shade the plants provide affects temperature which in turn affects the kinds of plants and animals that can live there.

Can you see that a community, like an organism, is a well-organized system? Also, in nature the community is a feature of life because no organism, regardless of its adaptations and complexity, can exist by itself. In many ways humans depend on their environment. They also affect their environment in many ways. Explain. What do you think is the responsibility of humans concerning the environment?

FIGURE 1-12. Physical factors of the environment determine the kinds of organisms that can live in different places. (a) Trees cannot grow above a certain altitude mainly due to colder temperatures. (b) Due to the amount of water, hippos can live in areas where certain other organisms cannot.

Organisms depend on one another in many ways.

Physical factors of the environment determine the kinds of organisms living in a given community.

12. An adaptation is a characteristic which promotes survival in a particular environment. Examples include: hoof of a horse, beak of a bird, and hibernation of a squirrel.
13. An ecologist studies interactions of organisms with their living and physical surroundings.
14. Different organisms depend on one another for food, for homes, for reproduction, and in other ways. For example, many animals eat plants, some birds nest in trees, many animals disperse plant seeds, and bees transfer flower pollen.

REVIEWING YOUR IDEAS

12. What is an adaptation? List three animal adaptations.
13. What does an ecologist want to find out about a community?
14. List several ways in which organisms depend on one another.

CHAPTER REVIEW

SUMMARY

1. The nearly two million kinds of known living things share certain common features.
2. Organisms live together in communities.
3. All organisms need food. Producers make their own food while consumers depend on other living things for food.
4. The energy in food comes from sunlight through photosynthesis. "Burning" of food transfers energy.
5. Materials in a community are recycled. Because energy is not recycled, a community must have a constant supply of energy.
6. Energy from the "burning" of food is used for growth and development, maintenance and repair, reproduction, and organization.
7. Scientists have defined several levels of organization to describe living things—cell, tissue, organ, system, organism, and community. Higher levels also exist.
8. Organisms are adapted for life in particular environments. Organisms also interact in and with their environments.

Teaching suggestion. Remind your students that the summary is an excellent aid to chapter review.

LANGUAGE OF BIOLOGY

adaptation	homeostasis
biology	host
cellular respiration	organ
chlorophyll	organism
community	organization
consumer	parasite
decomposer	photosynthesis
development	predator
ecology	producer
energy	reproduction
food chain	saprophyte
growth	system
heredity	tissue

CHECKING YOUR IDEAS

On a separate paper, match each phrase from the left column with the proper term from the right column. Do not write in this book.

1. necessary for decay process
2. balance of internal processes
3. released during photosynthesis
4. characteristic promoting survival
5. interaction of organisms and environment
6. increase in living material
7. obtains food from host
8. necessary for work
9. substance "burned" by all organisms
10. Like produces like.
11. tissues working together
12. makes own food

a. adaptation
b. decomposer
c. ecology
d. producer
e. energy
f. growth
g. homeostasis
h. organ
i. oxygen
j. parasite
k. reproduction
l. sugar

EVALUATING YOUR IDEAS

1. Why is it difficult to define "life"? What is important to an understanding of "life"?
2. What are some similarities between an automobile engine and a living thing? What are some differences?
3. Distinguish between parasites and saprophytes. Are they producers or consumers?
4. What is energy? What is the source of energy in every community? How is it transferred to all members of a community? Is energy recyclable? Explain.
5. How are decomposers important to a community? What would happen to a community in which there were no decomposers? Why?

CHAPTER REVIEW

6. How are photosynthesis and cellular respiration important to each other?
7. What is homeostasis? Why is it important to living things?
8. What is meant by the phrase "like produces like"? Why does it occur?
9. Why is it possible to say that the process of life is continuous?
10. What is meant by "organization" of living things?
11. What is a tissue? What is an organ? What is a system? List some examples of each.
12. What is an adaptation?
13. What are some physical factors of the environment?

APPLYING YOUR IDEAS

1. List several types of communities. What do they have in common? How do they differ?
2. Indian pipe is classified as a green plant, but it lacks chlorophyll. Why is it able to survive on a forest floor better than green plants with chlorophyll?
3. Classify each of the following as a parasite or saprophyte.
   (a) tick on a dog
   (b) termites in dead wood
   (c) tapeworm in a cow
4. Give an example of a possible food chain in a lake and in a desert.
5. What would be the simplest possible food chain in a community? Explain.
6. A piece of potato immersed in water absorbs some of the water and swells. Has the potato grown? Explain.
7. How are availability of water, temperature, light, and type of soil important to a community?

8. List three adaptations of a tree. List three adaptations of a human. How do the adaptations you listed help the organism survive in its environment?
9. Why are there few producers at the bottom of a deep lake or ocean?

EXTENDING YOUR IDEAS

1. Search the area near your home for different kinds of organisms. Classify each one as either producer or consumer. Identify any parasites or saprophytes you find. Determine how each organism fits into food chains of the community. List several adaptations of each organism.
2. Create your own miniature community by setting up a freshwater aquarium or a terrarium.
3. Make a list of five specific ways in which your body uses energy.

SUGGESTED READINGS

Bauer, Erwin A., "How to Get Close to Wildlife." *National Wildlife*, October-November, 1981.

Deyrup, Mark, "Deadwood Decomposers." *Natural History*, March, 1981.

Feininger, Andreas, *Nature through the Seasons.* New York, Dover Publications, Inc., 1979.

Milne, Lorus J. and Margery, "The Social Behavior of Burying Beetles." *Scientific American*, August, 1976.

Smith, R. L., *Ecology and Field Biology.* New York, Harper and Row, 1980.

Way Things Work Book of Nature. New York, Simon and Schuster, Inc., 1980.

Additional student readings and suggested teacher readings are provided in the Teacher's Guide.

B iology is the branch of science in which living things are studied. To study something scientifically, a method must be followed and precise measurements must be made. Scientific research may be carried out both in the laboratory or in the field. Here a field biologist studies organisms living in the trees of the tropical rain forest. How is a scientific study done? What steps must be followed and what kinds of measurements are made?

Introduction: Begin this chapter with an inquiry approach by posing a scientific question of your choosing. The problem should be simple and one which can be investigated by experimentation. The problem may take the form of demonstration and should involve student participation. The experiment should be designed to evoke discussion of the methods of science and controlled experimentation, and if possible should involve quantitative data which can be integrated with your teaching of the International System of Measurement. Some possible problems for investigation are 1) Will production of starch by geranium leaves be affected by darkness? 2) What is the effect of diet on the weight of mice? 3) Can a small fish and green plant survive together in a sealed flask of water? 4) How is the rate of photosynthesis affected by differences in light intensity (*Applying Your Ideas*, question 1, page 35)?

Chapter

2

BIOLOGY AS A SCIENCE

Chapter 2 discusses the methods of science and presents the International System of Measurement.

Humans have always wondered about themselves, other organisms, their world, and space. They have sought to explain things and to make use of what they learned.

Early biology centered on studies vital to human life. Thousands of years ago humans learned about planting crops and taming animals. They were also concerned with the body and with health. Later, humans became curious about things other than their own needs.

Rather than question ideas themselves, most people relied on the beliefs of earlier scientists. Some of these beliefs were not correct. Thus, progress in biology (and other sciences) was slow. This pattern lasted until the 1500's. Then important findings based on new observations and study began to be made.

The late 1800's were an exciting time for biology. It was learned that all living things are made up of small units called cells, and that some cells called microbes can cause disease. It was shown that all life comes from life. The basic laws of heredity were discovered. These findings were important because they were general enough to apply to most organisms. Also, they provided a basis for later discoveries.

Today is an even more exciting time for biology. Diseases such as malaria and polio are now understood and can be prevented or treated. The structure of the "genetic message" has been worked out. Genes can be moved from one organism to another. Energy is being derived from many sources. Surgery now often includes the use of lasers. Crop yields are being improved. Computers are being used to gather, record, and analyze information.

Knowledge continues to grow at a rapid rate. Each year, new information is built on the foundation of prior knowledge. Much of this knowledge benefits humans and other organisms. How has science affected you personally?

GOAL: You will gain an understanding of how a scientist conducts an investigation and how to use the International System of Measurement.

Many so-called "truths" remained untested until the sixteenth century when scientists began to experiment for themselves.

During the late 1800's some important general discoveries about biology were made.

Teaching suggestion: Students should realize that certain discoveries in science, while extremely important, have had or could have deleterious effects if used without good foresight and judgement. Examples include use of pesticides and manipulation of genes. A class discussion concerning the social obligations of science could be lively and worthwhile.

METHODS OF SCIENCE

2:1 What Is Science?

Early scientists did not know *how* to solve their problems. Often they did not study all the facts. Many times they did not know what they were looking for. One of the most important factors in good science is asking the right questions. Many discoveries made in the last few hundred years are valid because the scientists who made them were good detectives.

The *methods* by which science is studied are unique. A scientist is a detective who must solve problems by asking questions and putting the answers together in a meaningful and conclusive way. Intelligent guessing is important to the scientist. But guessing alone is not enough. The guesses must be supported or rejected by evidence.

Science is a process which produces a body of knowledge about nature. Areas of study, such as art, music, or history, are no less scholarly than science because all of them involve creativity. But, the *manner* in which science studies nature makes it different.

Science is carried out because people want to learn more about nature. Applying the knowledge to real problems is **technology** (or applied science). For example, the science of heredity can be used to solve real problems. Plants that make more food and organisms that break down oil have been produced. What practical problems have these technological advances helped to solve?

Scientists can solve problems in many ways. Each "case" is different. Usually certain parts such as observation, interpretation, hypothesis (hi PAHTH uh sus) formation, and experimentation are included. The relative place of each of these in scientific investigations may vary. However, they interact and are necessary in solving a problem.

2:2 Observation

Careful **observation** is very important to a scientist. No matter what the problem, scientists must observe carefully all they can about it. Often this process includes reading what is known already about the subject or related subjects. Careful and confirmed observations become facts. **A fact** is something about which there is no doubt. It is a fact that this paper is white.

In science facts are often called **data.** A list of the measurements of the growth of a tadpole is a set of data. Also, the color and shape of a tadpole are data.

A scientist must be a good detective.

Science differs from other areas of study in the methods used.

Technology is the application of scientific knowledge in a practical way.

A scientist observes to determine what is fact.

Facts in science are called data (singular, datum).

James N. Westwater

David M. Dennis

Hickson-Bender Photography

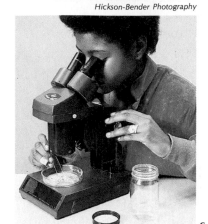

a

b

c

Scientists must be careful not to overlook facts. They must know the importance of what they observe. Sometimes an observation may seem unimportant. However, it may end up being valuable.

In 1928, the British scientist Sir Alexander Fleming (1881-1955) made such an observation. He was studying a certain type of bacteria, *Staphylococcus* (staf loh KAHK us), in his laboratory. The bacteria were grown in culture dishes. Fleming noticed that a mold called *Penicillium* (pen uh SIHL ee um) grew in some of the culture dishes. He might have thrown out these dishes, but he observed something else. Around the *Penicillium* was a clear zone (Figure 2-2). This area was clear because the bacteria which had grown there had died. In dishes without the mold, no clear zone appeared because bacteria continued to grow and reproduce.

2:3 Interpretation

This method of interpretation is called inductive reasoning.

This brief discussion of Fleming's discovery points out an important part of the scientific procedure. Observing that bacteria were killed, Fleming *reasoned* that the mold must be producing a substance, a chemical, which killed the bacteria. He *assumed* that the chemical moved from the mold throughout the clear zone. He could not observe a substance either being produced by the mold or killing the bacteria. But this idea was the most *logical* explanation he could make of the observed facts.

Such reasoning is a key part of scientists' investigations. They must be able to *interpret* their observations of nature. These interpretations and explanations may not always be correct. What may seem to be a logical explanation might turn out completely or partly wrong. Logical reasoning and interpretation are necessary to obtain a final answer to any scientific problem.

FIGURE 2-1. Observations can be made with all of the senses. (a) A biologist identifies a tree by its smell. (b) Bird songs are observed by hearing and are recorded for study. (c) A student observes traits of a starfish visually.

Culture dishes contain agar to which various nutrients have been added. Agar is a substance which gels the nutrient medium. Bacteria then are grown on the surface of the gelatinous medium.

Fleming made an unexpected observation which was the basis of an important discovery.

FIGURE 2-2. Penicillin from the soaked filter in the center of the dish produces a clear zone where no bacteria will grow. Notice the bacterial growth outside the clear zone.

C. Findel, J. Gnau, and A. Ottolenghi at O.S.U.

The clear zone is known as the "zone of inhibition."

2:4 Hypothesis

Facts have no meaning unless they can be tied together. A scientist must try to put together the pieces as if working a jigsaw puzzle without knowing what the total picture will look like.

If a scientist gains insight into the problem, he/she will develop an idea which may fit the pieces of the puzzle together. Such an idea or statement is called a **hypothesis.** The purpose of a hypothesis is to relate and explain observed facts. Fleming's reasoning about the action of *Penicillium* on bacteria could be stated as a hypothesis. Fleming's hypothesis was that some chemical produced by the *Penicillium* kills certain bacteria.

A good hypothesis not only *explains* the facts but also *predicts* new facts. Besides stating that a chemical killed the bacteria, Fleming also predicted that the certain chemical *alone* (not the entire mold) should be able to kill bacteria.

Forming a hypothesis is not the end of the problem. Many early scientists failed because they made a hypothesis their conclusion. A good hypothesis must be tested. Only if there is a test can a scientist be certain a hypothesis is correct. A hypothesis is a "tool" for further study of a problem.

2:5 Experimentation

Once a hypothesis has been presented, the next step is to test it. Such scientific testing is known as **experimentation.** You may have thought of experiments as involving smoking liquids in strange gadgets. Most experiments are fascinating but offer little of this type of excitement. Rather, they involve an orderly procedure and careful work. The excitement comes from finding a way to check a hypothesis.

A hypothesis relates and explains observations and predicts new facts.

A hypothesis which cannot be tested is of no value. Often testing of a hypothesis must wait until new techniques and/or equipment are developed. A hypothesis may require more than one test.

A hypothesis must lend itself to testing.

Experimentation is scientific testing.

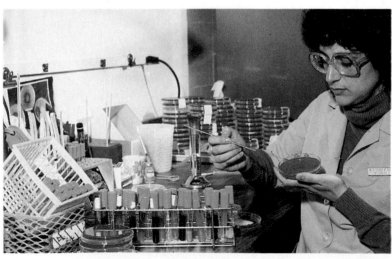

FIGURE 2-3. Experimentation is done to test hypotheses. This scientist is testing a hypothesis about the growth requirements of certain bacteria.

Doug Martin

Fleming had to isolate the substance he thought was killing the bacteria. Then he had to test the prediction that the substance would kill the bacteria. To do this test, he transferred some of the mold to nutrient broth solutions. Nutrient broth solutions contain the basic ingredients needed for the mold to grow and reproduce. Fleming assumed the mold would produce a chemical that would flow into the liquid broth. After he added the chemical and broth (minus the mold) to the bacteria, he observed that the bacteria were killed. Thus, he had isolated the chemical and also verified the prediction of his hypothesis. The chemical alone could kill the bacteria; the mold was not necessary. Has the hypothesis been verified beyond doubt? no

A scientist must be sure of the cause of a certain effect. Fleming, for example, believed that the chemical in the broth killed the bacteria, but how could he be sure? Something in the broth itself might have killed the bacteria. When a test of the broth alone showed that it did not kill the bacteria, the doubt was removed. The hypothesis was supported. Fleming named the chemical *penicillin.*

Scientists conduct their experiments in a carefully controlled manner. A **controlled experiment** is one in which all factors are the same except the one being tested. The factor being tested is called the **variable factor.** Suppose you were testing a substance suspected of killing bacteria. You would have to run a controlled experiment to verify your idea. You would need two groups of bacteria which would be the same in all ways except that one would be exposed to the new substance and the other would not. Thus, the substance is the variable factor between the two groups. The group which received the chemical is the **experimental group;** the other group is the **control group.** Use of controls and using only one variable factor at a time are common features of scientific investigation because they reduce uncertainty.

Fleming tested a variety of molds including other strains of *Penicillium.* He found no others that produced antibacterial chemicals. Since Fleming's time, penicillin has been found to interfere with bacterial cell wall production.

Scientists carry out controlled experiments in which there is only one variable factor.

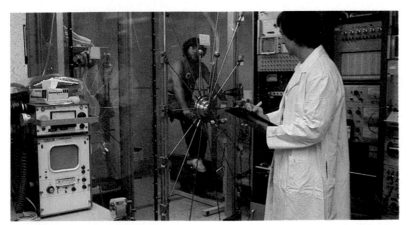

Tom Stack for Tom Stack and Associates

FIGURE 2-4. In this controlled experiment the man inside the chamber is undergoing a stress test in polluted air. The polluted air is the variable factor. All other factors are controlled.

An experiment may indicate that a hypothesis is not correct. If so, a scientist, like a detective, must either revise or develop a new hypothesis to explain the facts.

Experimental results must be reproducible.

antibiotic (anti-, against; bio-, life)

Many practical benefits result from the natural curiosity of scientists.

Science builds upon previous knowledge.

An experiment does not always support a hypothesis. Instead, it may show that the hypothesis was partly or totally wrong. When this result happens, the facts must be looked at again and interpreted in some other way. The hypothesis may need to be changed or a new hypothesis may need to be formed. The whole process may have to be repeated many times before a hypothesis is confirmed.

Fleming's work with penicillin arose by chance during other research and led to a major *practical* breakthrough. Fleming realized the future use of penicillin as a drug and studied its effect on many common disease-causing bacteria. Penicillin's discovery has caused a search for similar drugs. Many drugs have been discovered since that time which kill bacteria. These drugs, now called **antibiotics,** have been a great aid to modern medicine. Although many people take antibiotics for granted, it's not surprising that they were once called miracle drugs. Their use has saved millions of lives.

This example illustrates two important points. First, much scientific research is carried on because of the natural curiosity of humans. They want to know the "hows" and "whys" of the world. As a result, there have been many benefits, from microwave ovens to antibiotic drugs. Fleming did not set out to discover a drug to cure bacterial infections, but when the unexpected happened, he did not ignore it. Use of the drug in medicine came about only after he made his "accidental" discovery.

Second, scientific knowledge builds upon the foundations of previous findings. Once penicillin was discovered and its value shown, widespread interest arose. A single, important finding led to many related discoveries. This pattern has been repeated often in the history of science—an important hypothesis provides a basis for further work.

FIGURE 2-5. **Antibiotics are a great aid to modern medicine and are now mass-produced. This man is working with an antibiotic granulator.**

Courtesy of Eli Lilly and Co.

PEOPLE IN BIOLOGY

About the time of Fleming's discovery of penicillin, Dorothy Crowfoot was becoming interested in a then new technique called X-ray crystallography (krihs tuh LAHG ruh fee). This technique involves the use of X rays to determine the structure of substances.

In 1937, Hodgkin received her doctorate from Oxford University in England where she continued X-ray research begun as a student. During World War II, the demand for penicillin became great.

(1910 -   )

Dorothy Crowfoot Hodgkin

Penicillin could be made in large amounts if its structure were determined. Hodgkin set a goal to determine this structure. By 1948 she accomplished this goal. Through her work and that of her research team, the foundation was laid for mass production of antibiotics.

Among other accomplishments, Hodgkin has determined the structure of vitamin B_{12} and insulin. She has received many honors, including honorary degrees, the Royal Medal, and the Order of Merit. In 1964 she received the Nobel Prize in Chemistry for her contributions to biochemistry and medicine.

Hodgkin has three children and is now a grandmother, also. She lives in England with her husband and still works in her research lab in Oxford.

2:6 Theory

A theory is an explanation based on observation and experiments, and is still subject to revision. A law is a theory that has been tested many times and stays the same. A principle is a fundamental law or set of facts.

Scientists tend to shy away from the word "proof" in describing experimental results. It is possible that new data will cause revision of an accepted hypothesis.

In general, when a major hypothesis has survived testing, it is called a **theory.** Common usage of the word suggests an uncertainty, such as, "This is only a theory, but . . ." The opposite meaning is true in science. A theory is as close to a complete explanation as science has to offer and can be used to predict future outcomes.

All scientific theories are subject to revision and further analysis. New findings can alter an accepted explanation of observed facts.

1. Science differs in its methods.
2. A fact is something about which there is no doubt. It is based on observation. Data are scientific facts.
3. reasoning and logic
4. A hypothesis explains and relates facts and predicts new facts.
5. A controlled experiment is one in which all conditions are identical except for a single variable factor. Such an experiment reduces doubt about the effects of the variable factor.

REVIEWING YOUR IDEAS

1. Compare science to other areas of study.
2. What is a fact? What are data?
3. What elements are necessary for interpretation?
4. What are the functions of a hypothesis?
5. What is a controlled experiment? Why is it necessary?

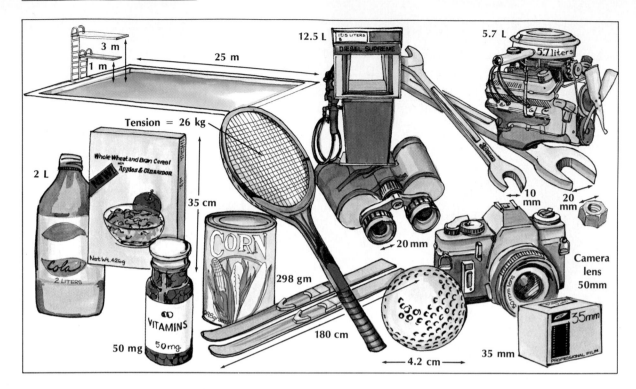

FIGURE 2-6. Measurements of many common items are made in SI units.

SI is a universal system of measurement.

SI stands for **Système Internationale** which is the French name for International System.

SI is based on tens and multiples or fractions of tens.

SCIENCE AND MEASUREMENT

2:7 International System

Because science is a worldwide study, discoveries made in one place are important to scientists around the world. The transfer of information is hindered by the many languages in the world. There is no special language in which to record and publish findings. Thus, reports must be translated in foreign journals to inform scientists worldwide of progress made. However, there is a special language of measurements and their symbols, the **International System of Measurement (SI).** SI is a modern form of the older metric system and is now used in most countries. What are some other advantages of converting to the International System of Measurement?

SI measurements may seem a bit foreign to you when you begin using them. However, you will soon see that there are advantages to using SI. One major advantage is that SI is a decimal system. It is based on tens, multiples of tens, and fractions of tens. Because it is a decimal system, SI is much easier to use. You need to know only a few major points. Did you ever stop to think that the English system of measurement is a lot less practical?

2:8 Linear Measurement

The basic unit of length in SI measurements is the **meter** (m). One meter is about as long as a golf club. The height of most doorways in a home is about 2 m. In SI, any measurement of length contains the word "meter." Measurements of lengths smaller or greater than a meter are indicated by a prefix and the word "meter." Each prefix stands for a multiple or a fraction of ten. The SI prefixes most important to you in this course are indicated in Table 2-1. According to this system, one hundredth of a meter is one centimeter, and a kilometer equals one thousand meters. What is a millimeter? 0.001 m

Length is expressed in meters in SI.

Prefixes are used to indicate fractions or multiples of each SI unit.

TABLE 2-1. IMPORTANT SI PREFIXES			
Prefix	Symbol	Meaning	Multiply basic unit by
kilo	k	one thousand	1000
centi	c	one hundredth	0.01
milli	m	one thousandth	0.001
micro	μ	one millionth	0.000 001
nano	n	one billionth	0.000 000 001

Bases are the meter, liter, and kilogram. Larger and smaller units of measurement in SI are obtained by multiplying or dividing the base unit by some multiple of ten. Multiply to change from larger units to smaller units. Divide to change from smaller units to larger units. For example, to change 10 kg to g, multiply 10 kg X 1000 (for kilo-) = 10 000 g. To change 10 g to kg, divide 10 g ÷ 1000 (for kilo-) = 0.01 kg.

Biologists often use the smaller units for microscopic work. The most common of these is the **micrometer** (μm) which is a unit of length equal to 0.001 mm or 0.000 001 m. Smaller measurements are recorded in nanometers. A **nanometer** (nm) is equal to 0.001 μm or 0.000 000 001 m. These measurements are commonly used to measure cells and cell parts.

The micrometer and nanometer are important in microscopic work.

Areas can be calculated using SI measurements. A rectangle measuring 5 cm by 3 cm has an area of fifteen centimeters squared (15 cm²). What is the area of this rectangle in millimeters squared? 1500 mm² Meters squared? 0.0015 m²

2:9 Volume

Units for solid volumes come from linear measurements. The measurements are cubed for volumes. For example, solid volumes can be expressed in centimeters cubed (cm³). A cube measuring two centimeters on each side has a volume of eight centimeters cubed. Express this amount in millimeters cubed (mm³). 8000 mm³

SI units of area and volume are derived from the meter.

Units for liquid and gas volumes come from linear measurements, too. One cubic centimeter equals one milliliter (mL). One thousand milliliters equals a **liter** (L), a unit for liquid or gas volumes. Scientists often work with small volumes, so use of the milliliter (or cubic centimeter) is common.

The liter is the basic SI unit for liquid and gas volumes.

FIGURE 2-7. Astronauts experience weightlessness at certain places in space.

NASA

2:10 Weight and Mass

Weight is the measure of gravitational attraction between two objects.

Suppose astronauts were to weigh an object before lifting off in a space shuttle and then weigh the same object again at various distances from the earth. They would find a decrease in **weight,** a measure of gravitational attraction between two objects. As the shuttle reaches a point where the earth has very little attraction for the object, the object (and the astronauts) would become essentially weightless. Its weight would be very small.

Mass is the measure of the amount of material in an object.

Before leaving Earth, suppose the astronauts measured the amount of material in the object. This measurement, called **mass,** would have been constant throughout their voyage.

Weight not only varies in space. Because points on Earth are not exactly the same distance from Earth's center, there are differences in the weight of an object on the earth at different places.

Mass remains constant. However, weight varies with the size of and distance between objects.

Mass and weight are often confused because many people incorrectly regard them as equal. *Mass is the amount of material of which something is composed. It does not change with location. Weight is a measure of gravitational attraction between two objects and varies with size of and distance between the objects.*

The basic unit of mass in SI is the **kilogram** (kg). One kilogram equals 1000 grams. The mass of two paper clips is about one gram. The same set of prefixes applies to this unit of measure as applies to the meter. Therefore, mass can be measured in units such as milligrams (mg) and micrograms (μg).

A scale is used to measure weight. Mass is measured by using an instrument called a **balance.** The object being massed is compared to an object of known mass, called a standard, on the balance.

2:11 Temperature and Time

Scientists also use the Kelvin scale.
(°K = °C + 273°)

Most scientists use the **Celsius** (SEL see us) scale to measure temperature. On this scale, the freezing point of water is zero degrees, and the boiling point is one hundred degrees. The temperature often is given in weather reports in degrees Celsius.

Another measurement important to scientists is time. The basic unit of time in SI is the **second** (s). SI prefixes are often used for very short time periods. For example, a millisecond is one thousandth of a second. Such exact measurements have become common in the study of some biological processes.

Some people have suggested changing the minute, hour, and day to new units based on multiples of ten. Do you think this should be done? Why or why not? What problems might the change cause?

FIGURE 2-8. Standards such as this kilogram mass are maintained by the National Bureau of Standards in Washington, DC, and by the International Bureau of Weights and Measures in Sèvres, France.

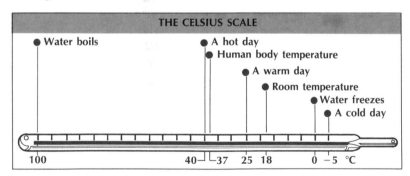

THE CELSIUS SCALE

- Water boils
- A hot day
- Human body temperature
- A warm day
- Room temperature
- Water freezes
- A cold day

100   40—37 25 18   0 −5 °C

FIGURE 2-9. The Celsius scale is used for scientific measurements of temperature. Some common temperatures are shown here.

REVIEWING YOUR IDEAS

6. What are some advantages of the International System of Measurement?
7. List the prefixes most commonly used with SI units. What does each prefix represent?
8. In SI, what is the basic or accepted unit of length? Mass? Volume? Time?
9. What are the freezing and boiling points of water on the Celsius scale?

6. SI is a universal system and is based on decimals.
7. kilo- (k) = 1000; centi- (c) = 0.01; milli- (m) = 0.001; micro- (μ) = 0.000 001; nano- (n) = 0.000 000 001
8. meter = length; kilogram = mass; liter = volume; second = time
9. Pure water freezing point = 0°C; pure water boiling point = 100°C.

Camera M. D. Studios, Inc.

FIGURE 2-10. The electron microscope is a valuable tool in many fields of biology.

A microscope's resolving power is its capability to distinguish two objects as separate.

The resolving power of the human eye is about 0.1 mm. The best electron microscopes have a resolving power of about 0.2 nm. Most atoms have diameters of 0.1 to 0.5 nm.

Light microscopes in your school may be equipped with oil immersion objectives which magnify about 90X giving a total magnification of about 900X.

FIGURE 2-11. Both the light microscope and the electron microscope direct a beam through a specimen, focus it with lenses, and enlarge the final image. They differ in that the light microscope focuses a beam of light with glass lenses whereas the electron microscope focuses a beam of electrons with magnets.

The compound light microscope is explained more fully in the Teacher's Guide and in the laboratory manuals that accompany this text.

ADVANCES IN BIOLOGY

2:12 Electron Microscopy

Observation is a key part of any scientific work. It is especially important to a biologist. Because the biologist may study extremely small objects—a tiny organism or the parts of a cell—observation often requires tools which magnify.

During your course in biology, you will use a compound light microscope. It works because light passes through the object being examined and is focused by glass lenses. Your microscope will magnify things about 450 times. The highest powered light microscopes can magnify as much as 2000 times. You could see a bacterium with the light microscope, but you could see little of its outer structure and none of its inner structure. Not only is magnification important, but resolving power also determines what can be seen with a microscope. **Resolving power** is the ability to distinguish two objects as two separate things. The resolving power of a light microscope is about 500 nm. Two objects closer together than 500 nm will be seen as one object with the light microscope.

For greater magnification and resolving power, many biologists rely on **electron microscopes.** Although electron microscopes are not new, their use has become increasingly important in many areas of biology. Electron microscopes typically magnify hundreds of thousands of times. The resolving power is about 0.5 nm. Two main types, the **transmission electron microscope (TEM)** and the **scanning electron microscope (SEM),** are used in modern research.

With the TEM, the sample to be studied is frozen and then sliced into very thin sections. Thus, living specimens cannot be

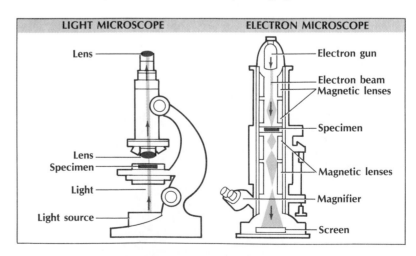

Hans Pfletschinger for Peter Arnold

David M. Dennis

David Scharf for Peter Arnold

a

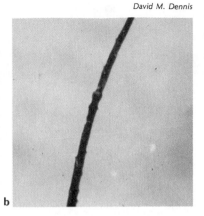

b

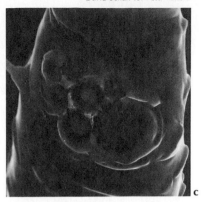

c

FIGURE 2-12. **(a) Aphids are small insects which can be seen with the unaided eye. Details of an aphid can be seen by use of microscopes. (b) The antenna can be seen enlarged with the light microscope and (c) sensors on the antenna can be seen with the electron microscope.**

viewed; only parts of structures can be seen. When the sample is put in the microscope, a beam of electrons passes through it. Focusing is done with magnets instead of glass lenses. The electrons form an image that can be seen on a screen. Photos of the sample also can be made. The TEM is very important in the study of the structures inside cells. It reveals fine details that aid in understanding how cells and cell parts function.

The SEM permits a view of surfaces not possible with the TEM. Although the SEM does not magnify as much as the TEM, the SEM produces a three-dimensional (3-D) image. Thin sections are not required because the beam of electrons does not pass through the specimen. Instead, the beam sweeps across and bounces off the object, causing electrons to be knocked loose from the object. These electrons produce light and dark patterns. An image is formed on a televisionlike screen. Because thin sections are not used, living organisms can be viewed and details about their surfaces can be learned. Knowledge of the surfaces of cells, for example, is important in studying cancer and other diseases. Interactions of cells with each other and with chemicals can be studied with the SEM.

The SEM produces a three-dimensional view of living specimens.

The maximum resolution of the SEM is about 5 nm, and of the TEM is about 0.2 nm. Another microscope, the scanning transmission electron microscope (STEM) was first available in the 1970's. It combines features of both the TEM and SEM, giving higher magnification and resolution, and producing a 3-D image. The STEM also has a different kind of electron gun.

a

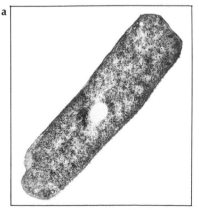

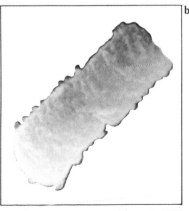

b

FIGURE 2-13. (a) The transmission electron microscope shows an image, in this case of a bacterial cell, that is two-dimensional. (b) The same kind of cell has a three-dimensional image when seen with the scanning electron microscope. Both cells are shown enlarged about 22 000 times.

John Hansen/OSU

John Hansen/OSU

CHAPTER REVIEW

SUMMARY

1. An interest in themselves and their world led humans to study nature.
2. Early attempts at science often were unsuccessful because inaccurate observations and poor logic were used. Untested conclusions were made.
3. Modern methods of science have been responsible for the vast new wealth of scientific information.
4. Scientific investigation usually includes observation, interpretation, hypothesis formation, and experimentation.
5. A controlled experiment is used to determine whether or not a hypothesis is correct. The experimental group is compared to the control group.
6. Scientists all over the world use the International System of Measurement, a system based on multiples of ten.
7. SI units include the meter (length), kilogram (mass), liter (liquid volume), Celsius degree (temperature), and second (time).
8. Biology as a science has advanced greatly due to the use of microscopes. Electron microscopes have yielded much information about the structure and functions of organisms and their parts.

CHECKING YOUR IDEAS

On a separate paper, complete each of the following statements with the missing terms. Do not write in this book.

1. A statement explaining and relating facts is called a(n) _____.
2. SI measurements are based on fractions or multiples of _____.
3. A controlled experiment has only one _____ factor.
4. In SI, the basic unit for length is the _____.
5. Applied science is also called _____.
6. One liter equals _____ milliliters.
7. _____ is the amount of material of which something is composed.
8. A major hypothesis which withstands the "test of time" is called a(n) _____.
9. Information gathered during an experiment is recorded. These recorded facts are also called _____.
10. The _____ electron microscope is used to view the surfaces of cells.
11. The _____ of a microscope is the closest two points can be and still be seen as separate.
12. Zero degrees is the temperature at which water freezes on the _____ scale.

LANGUAGE OF BIOLOGY

Celsius
controlled experiment
data
experimentation
hypothesis
International System
   of Measurement
kilogram
liter
mass
meter

observation
resolving power
scanning electron
   microscope (SEM)
second
technology
theory
transmission electron
   microscope (TEM)
variable factor
weight

EVALUATING YOUR IDEAS

1. Why did some of the unconfirmed conclusions of early scientists prevail for more than a thousand years?
2. List some of the major biological discoveries made since the late 1800's.
3. What makes a hypothesis good? Is a good hypothesis necessarily correct? Explain.
4. What hypothesis did Fleming attempt to test? How did he test it? What precaution

CHAPTER REVIEW

did he take to make certain that his hypothesis was correct?

5. What benefits were derived from Fleming's work? What point does this illustrate about science?

6. Why do scientists prefer not to use the word "proof"?

7. The milliliter and cubic centimeter are both units of volume. How do they differ?

8. What is the difference between weight and mass?

9. Express 50 cm in (a) meters and (b) millimeters.

10. Express 1.5 kg in (a) grams, (b) milligrams, and (c) micrograms.

11. Express 8 mL in liters. Express 800 L in milliliters.

12. Express the sum of 1.20 km + 844 mm + 125 cm in (a) meters, (b) centimeters, (c) millimeters, and (d) kilometers.

13. Express the sum of 2.2 L + 176 mL + 250 μL in (a) liters, (b) milliliters, and (c) microliters.

14. List some differences in light microscopes and electron microscopes.

15. Describe the purpose for which the TEM and SEM are used.

16. Distinguish between magnification and resolving power.

APPLYING YOUR IDEAS

1. How would you conduct an experiment to test the hypothesis that the rate of photosynthesis increases as the amount of available light increases?

2. How would you conduct an experiment to test a new dog food for "dog appeal"?

3. What would happen to your weight as you climbed a mountain? What would happen

to your mass? Are dieters really trying to lose weight or mass?

4. The micrometer and nanometer are units of linear measurement. Why are these units important to some biologists?

EXTENDING YOUR IDEAS

1. Prepare a report on several kinds of antibiotics. Include in your report the names of the organisms from which the antibiotics are prepared and the diseases against which they are useful.

2. Many molds growing in soil have antibiotic properties. Collect soil samples from different areas and place them on agar in different culture dishes. Transfer to agar plates on which bacteria are growing the different molds which appear. Determine whether any of these molds produce antibiotics.

SUGGESTED READINGS

Dolman, Claude E., "Reflections on Sir Alexander Fleming," *Chemistry*, September, 1978.

Dubos, Rene, *Louis Pasteur: Free Lance of Science.* New York, Charles Scribner's Sons, 1976.

"Educated Guess." *Sciquest*, April, 1981.

Goldstein, Thomas, *Dawn of Modern Science.* Boston, Houghton Mifflin Co., 1980.

"History of Science." *Sciquest*, October, 1980.

"Images." *Sciquest*, February, 1980.

Kauffman, George B., "The Penicillin Project: from Petri Dish to Fermentation Vat." *Chemistry*, September, 1978.

Kopp, Friedrich, *Electron Microscopy.* Carolina Biology Reader. Burlington, NC, Carolina Biological Supply Co., 1981.

Additional student readings and suggested teacher readings are provided in the Teacher's Guide.

Bicycles are assembled from many different, separate parts. The bicycle parts were made by processes that changed their shape and composition. The changes were both physical and chemical. In the same way, living things are composed of many different substances that go through similar physical and chemical changes. What are the different substances of which living things are made? How are the substances like those that form nonliving things?

Introduction and suggested demonstration: Partially fill one test tube with lead nitrate solution, $Pb(NO_3)_2$, and another test tube with potassium iodide solution, KI. (Both solutions can be 1M solutions and both will appear clear.) Do not reveal the contents of the tubes. Carefully set the tubes inside a large Erlenmeyer flask, taking care that the contents of the tubes do not spill and mix. Cork the flask and have a student determine and record the total mass. Then tip the flask so the contents of the test tubes spill and react. Lead iodide, a yellow precipitate (PbI_2) will form.

$$Pb(NO_3)_2 + 2KI \rightarrow 2KNO_3 + PbI_2$$

Ask your students to predict the mass of the flask again. (Some might think the mass will have increased because of the precipitate formation.) Then have a student mass the flask again to show there is no change. You may refer to this demonstration many times during the teaching of this chapter, such as when discussing chemical formulas and reactions, law of conservation of mass, ions and dissociation, and balancing chemical equations.

MATERIALS OF LIFE

Chapter 3 presents basic concepts of chemistry needed for understanding modern biology.

For a long time biology was just a description of living things. Organisms were grouped and named by their features. Early biologists were curious about the **anatomy** (study of internal and external structure) of organisms. They then became curious about *how* the parts worked. Study of how living things work is known as **physiology** (fihz ee ᴀʜʟ uh jee). The beating of the heart and the flowering of a plant are examples of physiological processes. How does a nerve transmit an impulse? What causes a muscle to contract? How are minerals moved from the roots of trees to the leaves?

Biologists realized that knowledge of chemistry and physics was needed because living things shared many features with nonliving things. Some principles about matter and its properties are presented in this chapter. Knowledge of these principles is needed for an understanding of many biological functions.

GOAL: You will gain an understanding of how chemistry relates to the study of living things.

Physiology is the study of the functions of living things.

An understanding of the properties of matter is needed for the study of physiology.

CLASSIFICATION OF MATTER

3:1 Atoms

Matter is anything which has mass and takes up space. All matter is composed of building blocks called **atoms.** Atoms are very small, most of them being from 0.1 to 0.5 nm in diameter. Today only the most powerful microscopes can photograph individual atoms. Much detail still cannot be seen.

Matter has mass and takes up space.

37

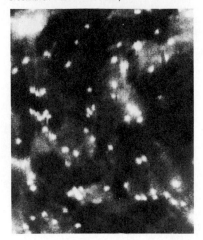

FIGURE 3-1. Because atoms are so small, not much detail can be seen in photographs of them. Uranium atoms are shown here magnified about 5.5 million times.

Electrons form electron clouds around the nucleus of an atom. Some electrons are farther from the nucleus than others.

Electrons are most often found at certain probable distances from the nucleus. The probable location of an electron is determined by quantum mechanics.

Different energy levels, when filled, have different numbers of electrons.

two in the first level, five in the second level

two in the first level, eight in the second level, eight in the third level

Figure 3-2 shows models of atoms. It is not meant to show actual size relationships between nucleus and electrons or actual position of electrons. Models such as these are useful in explaining how atoms and molecules combine but do not represent how the atom would look if it were visible.

FIGURE 3-2. Diagrams of a lithium atom and an aluminum atom show the energy levels at which electrons move around the nuclei of the atoms. The best description of the probable location of electrons in an atom is an electron cloud.

Atoms are composed of three major particles—protons, neutrons, and electrons. **Protons** and **neutrons** are bunched tightly together in the center to form the **nucleus** of an atom. Moving rapidly outside this nucleus are **electrons.** Protons are positively charged, neutrons have no charge, and electrons are negatively charged. Electrons are sometimes indicated as e⁻. In an atom, the number of protons equals the number of electrons. Therefore, the atom as a whole is neutral, has no electric charge.

Diagrams have been drawn based on information gathered about atoms. A diagram of an atom is just another way of showing its parts. Such diagrams show protons and neutrons as tightly packed particles at the center of the atom. Electrons move about the nucleus at certain *probable* distances from the center. The space which electrons fill forms an electron cloud around the nucleus. The **electron cloud** represents the space around the nucleus which the electrons *can occupy.*

Hydrogen, with one proton and one electron, is the simplest atom. A helium atom has two protons, two electrons, and two neutrons. In a helium atom, the two electrons are about the same distance from the nucleus. Lithium (Figure 3-2) has three electrons per atom. One of the electrons is usually farther from the nucleus than the other two.

The different regions in which electrons travel about the nucleus are called **energy levels.** The first energy level holds a maximum of two electrons. The second energy level has a maximum of eight electrons, and the third energy level has eighteen electrons. Aluminum (Figure 3-2) has thirteen electrons per atom. Electrons of each aluminum atom would usually be arranged as follows: two in the first level, eight in the second level, and three in the third level. How would electrons be arranged in an atom with seven electrons? Eighteen electrons?

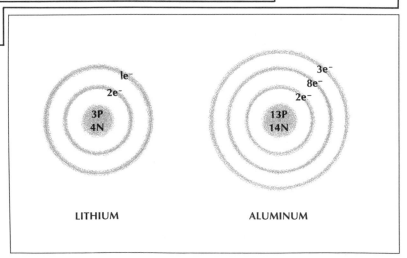

LITHIUM   ALUMINUM

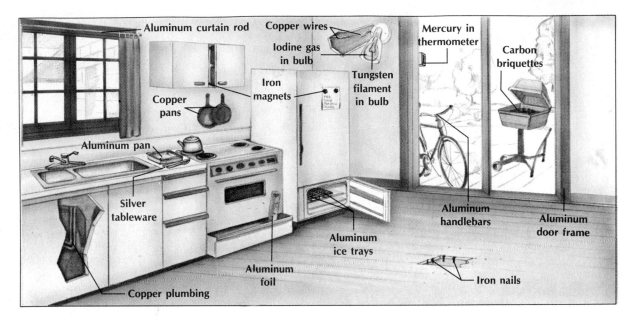

Aluminum curtain rod
Copper wires
Iodine gas in bulb
Mercury in thermometer
Carbon briquettes
Iron magnets
Tungsten filament in bulb
Copper pans
Aluminum pan
Silver tableware
Aluminum ice trays
Aluminum handlebars
Aluminum door frame
Aluminum foil
Iron nails
Copper plumbing

FIGURE 3-3. Many common objects are composed of one element each.

3:2 Elements

Hydrogen, helium, lithium, and aluminum are all **elements,** substances composed of only one type of atom. The number of protons in the nucleus determines the type of atom. For example, a piece of copper has only copper atoms. Each atom has the same number of protons, 29. Each iron atom has 26.

Any given proton, neutron, or electron in a substance is the same as in any other substance. The combination of these particles makes one kind of atom different from another. All copper atoms are identical to one another in the number of protons and electrons. But iron atoms differ from copper atoms in the number of protons and electrons each type has.

Atoms of the same element can differ in their number of neutrons. Such atoms are called **isotopes** (ɪ suh tohps) of each other. Atoms of hydrogen usually contain no neutrons, but one isotope (heavy hydrogen) has one neutron, and another isotope (heavy, heavy hydrogen) has two neutrons. All three isotopes of hydrogen have one proton and one electron.

All atoms of a given element have the same number of protons in their nuclei.

Heavy hydrogen is called deuterium. Heavy, heavy hydrogen is called tritium, a radioactive isotope often used as a tracer in research.

Isotopes are atoms which differ from other atoms of the same element only in the number of neutrons in their nuclei.

1. Matter is something that has mass and occupies space. It is composed of atoms.
2. Proton, in nucleus, positive; neutron, in nucleus, neutral; electron, around nucleus, negative
3. The number of protons and electrons is equal.
4. An element is a substance composed of only one kind of atom. Isotopes are atoms which differ only in their number of neutrons.

REVIEWING YOUR IDEAS

1. What is matter? Of what is matter composed?
2. List the three major kinds of particles of an atom. Where is each located and what is its charge?
3. Why does a free atom have no electric charge?
4. What is an element? What is an isotope?

3:3 Molecules

Although only eighty-eight elements exist naturally, there are thousands of different substances. Atoms combine with one another to form different substances. Often two or more atoms of the same element are combined. For example, the hydrogen atom never occurs alone in nature. It always combines with other atoms, including other hydrogen atoms.

Most atoms combine in such a way that their outer energy levels acquire a total of eight electrons. This principle is called the **octet rule.** (In the case of atoms with only one energy level, that energy level acquires a total of two electrons—the **duet rule.** For example, a hydrogen atom has only one electron in its outer level. In combining with other atoms, it must acquire one more electron.) An atom of nitrogen has five electrons in its outer level. When it combines with other atoms, it must acquire three more electrons.

Two hydrogen atoms can join by *sharing* their electrons (Figure 3-4) so that each hydrogen atom has two electrons in its outer energy level. When this sharing occurs, the electrons occupy the space between and around the two nuclei.

Atoms which have joined are held together by forces called *chemical bonds.* The forces involved in the sharing of electrons, such as between hydrogen atoms, are known as **covalent** (koh VAY lunt) **bonds.** Such a combination of two or more atoms joined by a covalent bond is called a **molecule.**

3:4 Compounds

Suppose you had a small, covered bottle of hydrogen gas (hydrogen molecules). The air in the room would contain oxygen molecules. Because the bottle is covered, the hydrogen and oxygen molecules cannot meet. If you removed the cover, oxygen would enter the bottle and mix with the hydrogen, but nothing would happen. However, if an outside source of energy is applied, drops of water would form on the inside of the bottle (Figure 3-5). What has happened?

The energy increased the force of collisions between the two kinds of molecules. Bonds between the atoms in hydrogen molecules and between the atoms in oxygen molecules broke. The atoms then recombined to form water.

In order to combine to form water, each hydrogen atom must obtain one electron, and each oxygen atom requires two electrons. The duet and octet rules are obeyed when two hydrogen atoms combine with one oxygen atom. Each hydrogen atom *shares* its electron with an oxygen atom. Thus, the oxygen atom gains the two electrons it needs—one from each hydrogen

When simple atoms combine, their outer energy levels acquire an outer octet of electrons.

FIGURE 3-4. Two hydrogen atoms join to form a hydrogen molecule by sharing electrons.

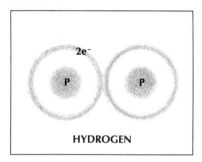

2e⁻

P   P

HYDROGEN

Energy increases the force of collisions between particles.

Teaching suggestion: Explain that the separate hydrogen and oxygen atoms exist as such for only a fraction of a second before they combine to form water.

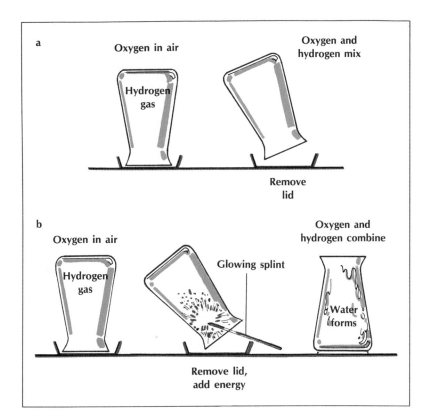

FIGURE 3-5. (a) Hydrogen and oxygen mix when no energy source is added. (b) With an added energy source, hydrogen and oxygen combine to form water.

Teaching suggestion: Point out that hydrogen and oxygen are both diatomic molecules in nature. However, when they combine only one atom of oxygen is used in the formation of one molecule of water. The number of atoms contributed by the elements is determined by the requirements of the duet and octet rules.

In water, covalent bonds exist between hydrogen and oxygen atoms.

FIGURE 3-6. A water molecule is formed and outer energy levels are filled when two hydrogen atoms and one oxygen atom share electrons.

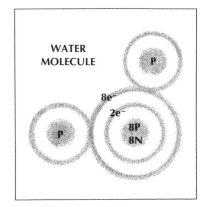

atom. Each hydrogen atom obtains its needed electron by sharing electrons with the oxygen atom. Thus, each atom obtains its required number of electrons by sharing. As a result, the atoms join to form a new substance. Because the bond is formed by sharing of electrons, it is a covalent bond.

This combination of two hydrogen atoms and one oxygen atom is also a molecule, a molecule of water. Water, salt, and sugar are substances made of two or more kinds of atoms. Substances composed of different kinds of atoms are known as **compounds.**

When atoms combine with one another, the new substances formed have a definite composition. A molecule of hydrogen always contains two hydrogen atoms. Water molecules always consist of two hydrogen atoms and one oxygen atom. Definite composition is explained by the octet or duet rule.

Biologists and biochemists are interested in the chemical reactions that occur in living things. Many of these reactions involve the synthesis (making) of compounds from atoms of other compounds or elements. The properties and processes of living things depend on the structures and reactions of compounds.

FIGURE 3-7. Sodium chloride forms when one electron is transferred from a sodium atom to a chlorine atom. The outer energy levels of both atoms are filled in this way.

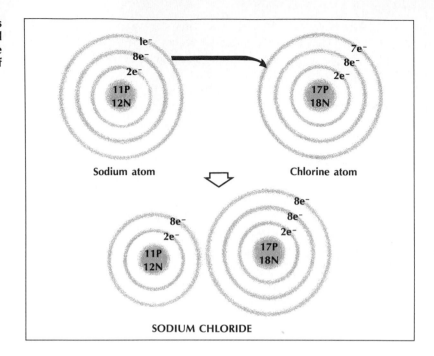

Sodium atom   Chlorine atom

SODIUM CHLORIDE

3:5 Ions

Teaching suggestion: Have students draw several atoms and the ions they form.

Some chemical bonds form by the transfer of electrons.

The -ide suffix distinguishes a negatively charged ion from a neutral atom. Example: chlorine and oxygen (neutral atoms), chloride and oxide (negatively charged ions).

Sometimes electrons are *transferred* to form an outer octet or duet of electrons. Compounds can be formed as a result of electrons being added or taken away from atoms. Two simple atoms, sodium and chlorine, can combine in this way (Figure 3-7). They combine to form the compound sodium chloride which is better known as table salt. A sodium atom has eleven electrons—two in the first energy level, eight in the second, and only one in its outer energy level. The outer level could be filled by "picking up" seven electrons or by "giving up" its one outer electron. Either way would give it an outer octet. A chlorine atom has seventeen electrons—two in the first energy level, eight in the second, and seven in the third. Because the atom has seven electrons in its outer energy level, it needs only one more. As sodium and chlorine atoms combine, each sodium atom "gives up" one electron which is "picked up" by a chlorine atom. In this way, each atom obtains an outer octet of electrons.

There is no clear cut division between ionic and covalent bonds. Most bonds have characteristics of both types. They are usually classified as one or the other based on which they resemble more.

A loss or gain of electrons results in an unbalanced electric charge on an atom. Because a sodium atom has eleven positively charged protons and ten negatively charged electrons after losing an electron, it is positive by one charge, $1+$. After gaining an electron, a charged chlorine atom has an excess of one negative charge, $1-$. Such charged atoms are known as **ions** (ɪ ahnz). The electrons of each ion move about the nucleus of that ion.

Ions are charged atoms or groups of atoms.

One positive ion would combine with two negative ions.

Because sodium and chloride ions are oppositely charged, they attract each other. The attraction between ions is called an **ionic bond.** The number and kind of charge on each ion determine the composition of a compound. In order for a compound to form ionic bonds, the positive and negative charges must balance each other so the net charge is zero. Because sodium ions have a 1+ charge and chloride ions have a 1− charge, one of each ion gives a neutral compound. How would ions with a 2+ charge combine with ions with a 1− charge? Could two positive ions combine? no

Instead of being called molecules, compounds of ions are called **ionic compounds.** Water is composed of water molecules in which each molecule contains two hydrogen atoms and one oxygen atom. However, a crystal of salt is made of a continuous network of alternating sodium and chloride ions. These ions are not paired with each other (Figure 3-8) to form a molecule. Salt is an ionic compound.

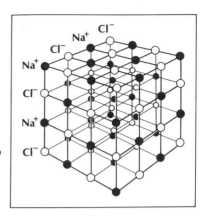

FIGURE 3-8. Ionic compounds do not exist as individual molecules. Salt, for example, is a crystal of alternating sodium and chloride ions.

3:6 Symbols and Formulas

Chemists have developed a shorthand system for representing elements. Each element is given a **symbol** agreed on by all scientists. This symbol consists of either one or two letters. Hydrogen has the symbol H, iron is Fe, and copper is Cu. Notice that when a symbol contains two letters, the second is not capitalized. In addition to hydrogen, the elements most commonly found in living systems are carbon (C), oxygen (O), and nitrogen (N). A list of the chemical symbols is included in Appendix D.

Ionic compounds are composed of positive and negative ions, not molecules (as in covalent compounds).

Each element can be represented by a symbol of one or two letters.

Carbon, hydrogen, oxygen, and nitrogen are the elements most abundant in organisms.

Many symbols are based on the Latin names for elements. Some elements were named to honor scientists.

Energy-storing compound in living things $C_{10}H_{16}N_5O_{13}P_3$
Blood chemical $(C_{738}H_{1166}FeN_{208}S_2)_4$
Air 77% N_2, 21% O_2, 0.03% CO_2, 1.97% other
Steel 98% Fe, 1% C, 1% other
Chlorophyll $C_{55}H_{72}MgN_4O_5$
Plant fiber $(C_6H_{10}O_5)n$
Water H_2O

Joseph F. Vieste/fpg

FIGURE 3-9. Chemical formulas can be written using chemical symbols for the atoms in the compounds and mixtures. Formulas of some of the items in this photo are shown. Those things that can vary in composition are written as percents.

Chemical formulas represent the number and kind of each atom in a compound.

A group of symbols, called a **chemical formula,** is used to show the number and kind of each atom in a compound. A molecule of water is composed of two hydrogen atoms and one oxygen atom. The chemical formula of water is H_2O. The subscript 2 refers to the element it follows. **Subscripts** in a formula represent the number of atoms of the element. When a symbol is not followed by a number, it is understood to represent one atom or ion.

In sodium chloride, the simplest ratio is one sodium ion to one chloride ion. Its formula is written NaCl. Notice that no subscripts are written because only one of each ion is involved.

A number before a chemical formula indicates the number of molecules or ionic units of a compound.

The formulas H_2O and NaCl represent one molecule of water and one unit of salt. Five water molecules would be indicated by a number in front of the formula. It would be written $5H_2O$.

15—

How many atoms are there in $5H_2O$? The 5 refers to the entire molecule, H_2O. Thus, there are 5 times 2 atoms of hydrogen and 5 times 1 atom of oxygen. The total atoms in $5H_2O$ is 10 + 5 = 15. How many atoms are there in 3NaCl? (3 X Na) + (3 X Cl) = 6 atoms

Chemical formulas are determined by the bonding requirements of the atoms of which the compound is composed.

Chemists determine formulas by analyzing substances in the laboratory. Some formulas are listed in Appendix D. You do not need to learn many formulas in this course, but you should remember that the formula of a compound is determined by the bonding requirements of its atoms. Each compound has a definite composition which does not vary. You will be seeing formulas of biological substances throughout your study of biology.

A solution can be any homogeneous combination of solids, liquids, and gases. For example, air is a solution of gases in gases, alloys are solutions of solids in solids, and a carbonated beverage is a solution of a gas (CO_2) in a liquid.

3:7 Solutions

Hydrogen molecules and compounds, such as water and salt, are examples of homogeneous (hoh muh JEE nee us) substances. **Homogeneous** means the same throughout. In a glass of water, each water molecule is the same as every other water molecule.

A homogeneous substance is the same throughout.

Compounds such as water are homogeneous materials with a definite composition. The composition is definite because chemical bonds form in definite ways. Thus, certain atoms can combine only in specific ways.

FIGURE 3-10. Potassium permanganate, $KMnO_4$, is a solute which can be dissolved in water, a solvent. An aqueous (water) solution of potassium permanganate results.

Some homogeneous materials do not have a definite composition. These materials are formed as a result of a physical combination of substances. Suppose you dissolved one gram of sugar (a compound) in 100 mL of water (a compound). You would obtain a material which would be the same throughout. It would be homogeneous. If you added two grams of sugar to another 100 mL of water, you would again get a homogeneous material. The two materials would be the same, sugar water, but they would differ in composition. The second sample would contain a greater amount of sugar in the same amount of water.

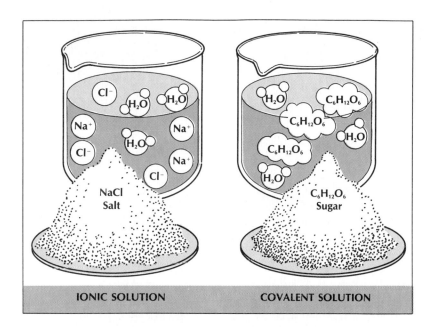

IONIC SOLUTION   COVALENT SOLUTION

FIGURE 3-11. In solution ionic compounds, such as salt, dissociate into ions. Covalent compounds, such as sugar, dissolve as separate molecules.

This type of homogeneous material is called a **solution.** True solutions are homogeneous, but they have variable compositions depending on how much of one substance is dissolved in the other. The portion of a solution in greater quantity is called the **solvent** (SAHL vunt); the part in lesser quantity is the **solute** (SAHL yewt). In the example, the solute, sugar, was dissolved in the solvent, water. In a water-alcohol solution in which there is more alcohol present than water, the alcohol is the solvent and the water is the solute.

Because sugar is a covalent compound, the sugar molecules separate when sugar crystals dissolve in water. The sugar molecules become dispersed (scattered) equally throughout the solvent. Ionic compounds do not behave in this way because they are not composed of molecules. When salt dissolves in water, the sodium and chloride ions separate by a process called **dissociation.** As a result, sodium and chloride ions move independently through the water. Therefore, a solution of sodium chloride in water consists of water molecules, sodium ions, and chloride ions (Figure 3-11).

Water is an excellent solvent. Because organisms are composed of about 70 percent water, dissociation of ionic compounds within living systems is common. Also, many ions which enter an organism are dissolved in water. Ions are important in many biological processes. For example, sodium (Na^+) and potassium (K^+) are essential to nerve conduction. Other ions are involved in processes such as muscle contraction. Ions are also parts of bone, blood, and other tissues.

A solution is a homogeneous substance which can have different compositions.

A solute dissolves in a solvent.

Covalent compounds dissolve as separate molecules.

When ionic compounds dissolve, their ions separate and move independently in the solution.

The polar nature of water molecules is responsible for the separation of ions. The positive end of the water molecule (H) exerts an attraction on negative ions while the negative end of the water molecule (OH) attracts the positive ions.

Water is an important solvent in living things.

Teaching suggestion: On the chalkboard, draw a molecule of water. Separate the proton of one hydrogen atom from the rest of the diagram. Its charge is 1+. The remaining combination of oxygen and hydrogen has a total of nine protons and ten electrons, a net charge of 1−.

Teaching suggestion: Consider covering this material with only the more capable students. The section should be treated as optional.

3:8 Acids and Bases

Each water molecule contains two hydrogen atoms and one oxygen atom. Very rarely (about two molecules per billion) one hydrogen atom breaks away from the rest of a molecule. The formation of a positively charged hydrogen ion (H^+) and a negatively charged hydroxide ion (OH^-) results.

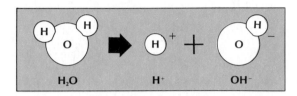

Therefore, in a given volume of water, most of the water exists as water molecules, but there are some hydrogen ions and some hydroxide ions. The number of hydrogen and hydroxide ions is equal because one of each kind of ion is produced from each water molecule that dissociates. A solution, such as pure water, in which the number of hydrogen ions equals the number of hydroxide ions is a **neutral solution.**

In a neutral solution, the hydrogen ions and hydroxide ions are equal in number.

Hydrogen chloride is a gaseous compound which dissolves in water to form hydrogen ions and chloride ions. Addition of hydrogen chloride increases the number of hydrogen ions in the water (Figure 3-12). If the number of hydrogen ions is greater than the number of hydroxide ions, the solution is called an **acid.** A solution of hydrogen chloride in water is called hydrochloric acid. Acid solutions have a sour taste. Lemons and grapefruit are sour because they contain citric acid.

In an acid solution, the number of hydrogen ions is greater than the number of hydroxide ions.

Acids give a "tangy" taste to many fruits. Apples contain malic acid; grapes have tartaric acid. Vinegar contains acetic acid.

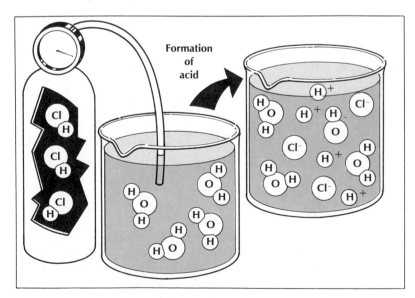

FIGURE 3-12. When an acid is formed, the concentration of hydrogen ions is greater than the concentration of hydroxide ions.

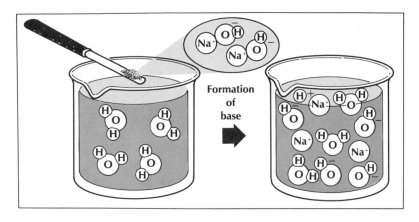

If the number of hydroxide ions in a solution exceeds the number of hydrogen ions, the solution is a **base**. Basic solutions have a sharp, bitter taste, and they feel slippery. In water, sodium hydroxide dissociates into a solution of sodium ions and hydroxide ions. The solution is basic because of an excess of hydroxide ions (Figure 3-13).

Chemists have devised a system for indicating the relative concentration of ions in acids and bases. The system is a scale of numbers, called the **pH scale.** The scale runs from 1 to 14 with 7 representing a neutral solution. Numbers below 7 represent acids. The lower the number, the greater the concentration of hydrogen ions and the more acidic the solution. A solution with a pH of 2 has more hydrogen ions and is more acidic than a solution with a pH of 6. Numbers above 7 represent bases. The higher the number, the greater the concentration of hydroxide ions and the more basic the solution. Therefore, a solution with a pH of 12 has more hydroxide ions and is more basic than a solution with a pH of 9.

FIGURE 3-13. When a base is formed, the concentration of hydroxide ions is greater than the concentration of hydrogen ions.

Suggested demonstration: Prepare a weak solution (0.1M) of sodium hydroxide. Add a few drops of bromthymol blue indicator. The solution will turn blue indicating the presence of a base. Using a straw, exhale repeatedly into the solution. The carbon dioxide will cause the solution to turn from blue to yellow indicating that the solution has become acidic. When CO_2 combines with H_2O, carbonic acid is formed, H_2CO_3. The acid exists as H^+ and HCO_3^- ions.

In a basic solution, the number of hydroxide ions is greater than the number of hydrogen ions.

Acid-base indicators are usually organic compounds which turn different colors in acidic or basic solutions. See *Extending Your Ideas,* number 5, page 57.

Concentrations of ions in acids and bases are represented by a set of numbers called the pH scale.

FIGURE 3-14. (a) When the pH of items is determined, it is a number between 1 and 14. (b) The pH can be determined with pH paper or with a pH meter. The pH paper changes color indicating pH. The pH meter indicates pH directly on a scale. Is the solution tested here acidic or basic? basic

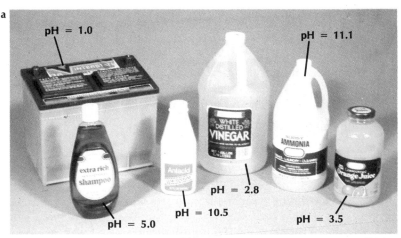

a

pH = 1.0

pH = 11.1

pH = 2.8

pH = 10.5

pH = 3.5

pH = 5.0

Lightforce

b

Herm Beck

TABLE 3-1. RELATIVE CONCENTRATIONS OF HYDROGEN AND HYDROXIDE IONS IN SOLUTIONS			
pH	Concentration of Hydrogen Ions	Concentration of Hydroxide Ions	Kind of Solution
1-7	Greater than concentration of hydroxide ions	Less than concentration of hydrogen ions	Acid
7	Equal to concentration of hydroxide ions	Equal to concentration of hydrogen ions	Neutral
7-14	Less than concentration of hydroxide ions	Greater than concentration of hydrogen ions	Base

The table above summarizes the meaning of pH scale measurements.

The pH of solutions is important to living systems. The pH of water determines which organisms will live in the water, and the pH of soil determines which organisms will grow in the soil. Also, the pH of solutions influences many of the chemical reactions which take place in organisms. For example, in order for digestion to occur properly, the pH of the stomach must be about 2. However, the pH of the intestine is about 8.

The rate at which enzymes operate is affected by pH.

pH influences the habitats and chemical reactions of organisms.

5. A molecule is two or more atoms joined by covalent bonds. A compound is two or more different atoms joined by chemical bonds.
6. Atoms are held together by chemical bonds. Covalent and ionic are two types of bonds.
7. A chemical formula tells the number and kinds of atoms in a molecule or compound.
8. A solution is a homogeneous substance with variable composition. The parts are solvent and solute.
9. In a neutral solution, the number of hydrogen and hydroxide ions is equal. An acid has an excess of hydrogen ions; a base has an excess of hydroxide ions. Relative strengths are indicated by the pH scale.

REVIEWING YOUR IDEAS

5. What is a molecule? A compound?
6. How are bonded atoms held together?
7. What information does a chemical formula provide?
8. What is a solution? What are the two parts of a solution?
9. What is a neutral solution? Compare an acid to a base. How is the relative strength of an acid or base indicated?

CHANGE IN MATTER

3:9 Properties of Matter

Each material has certain features or properties. A piece of wood has a definite mass, volume, shape, color, hardness, and texture. Such features which describe a piece of matter are called **physical properties.**

Physical properties and appearance may change. The size, shape, and mass of a piece of wood can be changed by sawing or carving it, but after it is sawed, it is still wood. Any change in the physical properties of a substance which does not change the substance is a **physical change.** Other examples of physical changes include stretching a rubber band and molding clay.

Physical properties describe the features of a substance.

In a physical change, the substance itself does not change.

What happens when you burn a piece of wood? Many of its properties are changed. When wood is burned completely, the only visible remains are ashes which do not resemble the wood.

Bruce Charlton   *Bruce Charlton*   *Allan Roberts*

a   b   c

FIGURE 3-15. (a) The physical properties of a wooden log are changed when (b) the wood is carved (a physical change). (c) When the wood is burned, the chemical properties are changed (a chemical change).

Burning is a **chemical change,** a change rearranging the atoms or molecules of the materials involved. A chemical change may involve the formation of new bonds between two or more substances or the breaking of bonds between atoms. When wood burns, it combines with oxygen in the air, and the carbon, hydrogen, and oxygen of the wood are rearranged to form new substances with new properties. The new substances formed are the invisible gases carbon dioxide and water vapor. Such a change is called a **chemical reaction.**

A property of the wood is that it can be burned—wood can combine with oxygen to form new substances. A **chemical property** is a property which depends on the substance's being changed into a new substance or substances. For instance, sodium atoms combine with chlorine atoms to form a new substance, sodium chloride (table salt). The properties of salt are entirely different from the properties of either sodium or chlorine.

A chemical change involves the rearranging of atoms or molecules as new substances are formed.

Chemical properties describe how a substance reacts with other substances.

Sodium is a silvery-white solid which reacts violently with water. Chlorine is a greenish-yellow gas. Both are poisonous.

3:10 Chemical Equations

By using chemical shorthand, you can show chemical reactions. When iron rusts, it reacts chemically with oxygen. The chemical reaction of iron and oxygen to form iron oxide can be expressed in words.

Write a word equation for the formation of table salt.

Iron plus oxygen yields iron oxide.

A + can be used for "plus" and an → can be used for "yields."

iron + oxygen ⟶ iron oxide

This reaction can also be shown using symbols and formulas rather than words to represent the elements and compounds involved in the reaction. A statement describing a chemical reaction with symbols and formulas is a **chemical equation.** All chemical reactions can be written as chemical equations. In the equation for the formation of iron oxide, iron and oxygen are called **reactants,** and iron oxide is the **product** of the reaction.

A chemical equation describes a chemical reaction.

Teaching suggestion: In an algebraic equation, each side of the equation represents the same quantity, but in a different form; e.g., 2 + 3 = 4 + 1. Relate a chemical equation to an algebraic equation. Each side of a chemical equation represents the same number of atoms, but in a different form.

The sum of each kind of atom is the same on both sides of a balanced equation.

10. Physical properties describe the features of matter. Change in physical properties is a physical change.
11. During a chemical change, chemical bonds are broken and formed and atoms are rearranged. After a chemical change, new materials are formed. After a physical change, the matter itself is not changed.
12. A chemical equation is a shorthand way to describe a chemical change. In a balanced equation, the number of each kind of atom is the same on each side of the equation. A balanced equation satisfies the law of conservation of mass.
13. A chemical equation describes a chemical reaction.

A chemical equation is like an algebraic equation in that both sides must represent the same quantity. *The number of atoms of each element on each side of the arrow must be equal.* The **law of conservation of mass** is followed: *during a chemical reaction, mass is neither created nor destroyed.* Therefore, a chemist would write the equation for the formation of iron oxide as follows:

$$4Fe + 3O_2 \longrightarrow 2Fe_2O_3$$

This statement is a **balanced equation** because the number of atoms of each element is the same on both sides. Four iron atoms must combine with three molecules of oxygen to produce two units of iron oxide.

REVIEWING YOUR IDEAS

10. What is a physical property? What is a physical change?
11. What occurs during a chemical change? How do physical changes and chemical changes differ?
12. What is a chemical equation? What is a balanced equation? Why must an equation be balanced?
13. How are chemical equations and reactions related?

BIOLOGICAL CHEMISTRY

3:11 Carbon Compounds

Biologists and chemists have been aware for many years of complex compounds being produced by living things. Because they were found in organisms, these substances were named **organic compounds.** At first scientists thought organic compounds could be produced only by living systems and not in the laboratory. Chemists have since learned to make them, but the name organic compound has remained.

Analysis of organic compounds shows that they all contain the element carbon. They now are also called **carbon compounds.** The study of these compounds is called **organic chemistry.**

Carbon atoms are relatively simple in structure with six electrons. Because carbon has four electrons in its outer level (Figure 3-16), a carbon atom "needs" four more electrons in forming bonds with other atoms (Section 3:3). Carbon atoms obtain these electrons by forming covalent bonds.

A carbon atom can join with other kinds of atoms and with other carbon atoms. The complex molecules found in living systems are composed of long chains of carbon atoms. Inorganic compounds (those not containing carbon) consist of small numbers of atoms. Carbon atoms also join to form cyclic and ring compounds.

FIGURE 3-16. An atom of carbon has four electrons in its outer energy level. It forms bonds by sharing electrons with other atoms.

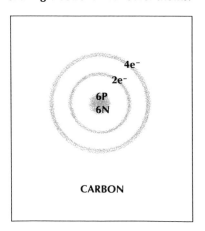

4e⁻
2e⁻
6P
6N

CARBON

3:12 Structural Formulas

Chemical formulas discussed so far are called **simple formulas.** The formula H_2O shows the kinds and number of atoms per molecule of water. However, organic compounds present a problem because they are complex. Because their properties are easier to understand if the arrangements of their atoms in space are known, organic compounds often are shown by **structural formulas.**

Methane is a compound composed of one carbon atom and four hydrogen atoms per molecule. Its simple formula is CH_4, but its structural formula shows more about the compound (Figure 3-17). The formula shows that each of the four hydrogen atoms is bonded to the central carbon atom. Each line drawn between atoms represents a covalent bond, the sharing of one pair of electrons. One line between two atoms is a single covalent bond (C—C). Two lines between two atoms is a double covalent bond (C=C), the sharing of two pairs of electrons. Three lines would be a triple bond (C≡C) in which three pairs of electrons are shared. Because a hydrogen atom shares only one electron, each hydrogen atom has only one bond.

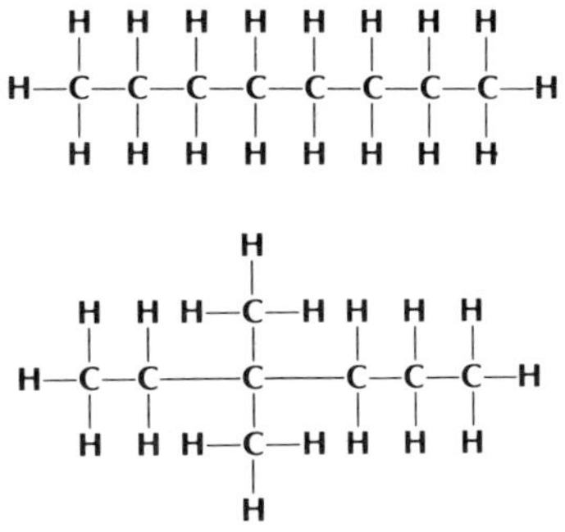

Figure 3-18 shows two possible structural formulas for C_8H_{18}. In each formula, each carbon atom has four bonds and each hydrogen atom has one bond as required by electron numbers. Compounds which have the same simple formula but different structures are called **isomers** (ɪ suh murz). The existence of isomers is one reason chemists prefer to use structural formulas to represent organic chemicals. With structural formulas, there is usually no doubt about which isomer is meant.

Isomers have different physical and chemical properties. For example, there are two isomers of the sugar lactose, commonly found in milk. Babies can readily digest only one form.

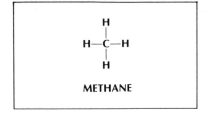

FIGURE 3-17. A structural formula of methane shows the arrangement of the atoms.

Structural formulas show the arrangement of atoms in space.

FIGURE 3-18. Each of these structures has the formula C_8H_{18}. Because the arrangement of the atoms differs, the structures are isomers.

REVIEWING YOUR IDEAS

14. How is the term "organic compound" defined today? How is this definition better than the original meaning?
15. What information is given by a structural formula that is not given by a simple formula?
16. Which type of formula, structural or simple, gives more information about a compound?
17. What is an isomer? Which of the following are isomers?

14. An organic compound contains carbon. This definition is better because organic compounds include substances other than those produced by organisms.
15. A structural formula shows the arrangement of atoms in space.
16. structural
17. Isomers are compounds with the same simple formula but different structures. Only b shows isomers.

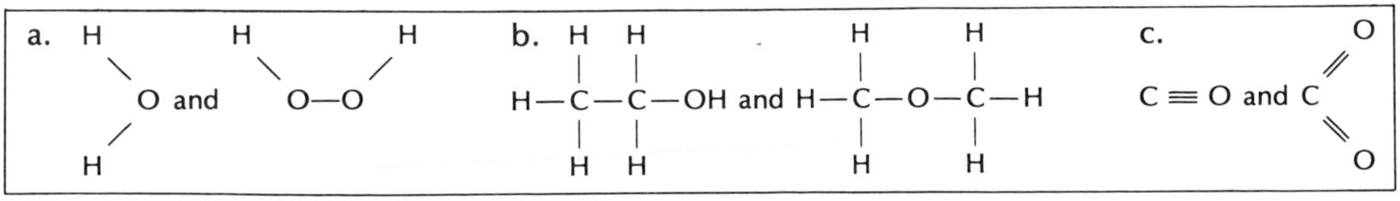

a. H   H   H   b. H   H   H   H   c.   O
    \   \   / | | | | //
     O and   O—O   H—C—C—OH and H—C—O—C—H   C ≡ O and C
    / | | | | \\
   H   H   H   H   H   O

FIGURE 3-19. Certain foods are high in carbohydrates, fats (lipids), and proteins.

Lightforce

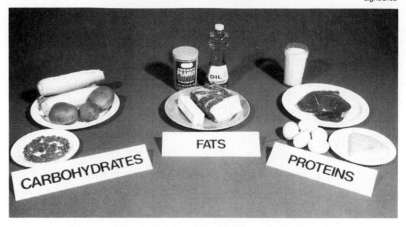

3:13 Carbohydrates

There would be no energy supply to sustain life.

One of the most important groups of organic compounds of living systems is the **carbohydrates.** Carbohydrates are composed of carbon, hydrogen, and oxygen with a ratio of two hydrogen atoms to one oxygen atom. Glucose, the sugar produced by plants, is an important carbohydrate (Figure 3-19). Glucose and most other carbohydrates are energy sources for organisms. What would happen if all plants suddenly stopped producing glucose?

Carbohydrates are composed of carbon, hydrogen, and oxygen.

Glucose, $C_6H_{12}O_6$, is an example of the simplest type of carbohydrate, a **monosaccharide** (mahn uh SAK uh ride), or single sugar. Monosaccharides are the building blocks of complex carbohydrates.

Monosaccharides are the basic building blocks of carbohydrates.

Two monosaccharides can join to form a **disaccharide,** or double sugar. Table sugar (sucrose) is a disaccharide formed from joining one molecule each of glucose and fructose (another monosaccharide). Maltose is a disaccharide formed from two molecules of glucose. Both of these disaccharides have the simple formula $C_{12}H_{22}O_{11}$. Lactose, another isomer, is formed from one molecule each of glucose and galactose.

Larger carbohydrate molecules, **polysaccharides,** are also found in living systems. The most complex of all carbohydrates, the **starches,** are composed of hundreds of monosaccharides linked together. Plants produce more sugar than they use. They "store" excess sugar in the form of starch. A potato, kernels of corn, and beans are mostly starch. This starch will be used as food for the new plants which grow from the potato and seeds. Some polysaccharides, such as **cellulose,** are used by plants for structural purposes. Cellulose is similar to starch. **Glycogen** (GLI kuh jun) is a starchlike carbohydrate in animals. When needed, glycogen is broken down into monosaccharides which are "burned" for energy. Cellulose, the constituent of plant and algal cell walls, differs from starch in that glucose units are bonded together in a different configuration. Glycogen, with yet another bonding pattern, is stored in the liver and in skeletal muscle.

FIGURE 3-20. The structural formula of glucose, a monosaccharide, shows a ring made of one oxygen and five carbon atoms.

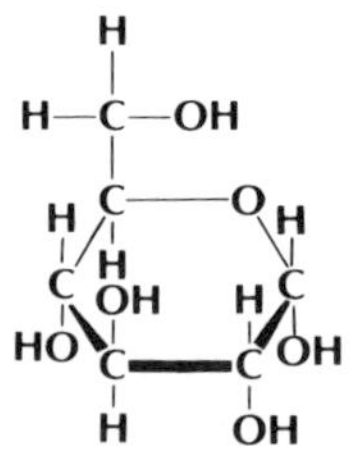

Glucose ($C_6H_{12}O_6$)

3:14 Lipids

The role of carbohydrates and lipids in nutrition will be discussed in Chapter 25.

Lipids are a class of organic compounds which includes fats, waxes, and oils. They are used for energy and often are stored as energy reserves. Usually, solid fats are produced by animals, and liquid oils are produced by plants. Waxes are produced by both plants and animals. Like carbohydrates, lipids are composed of carbon, hydrogen, and oxygen, but the number of carbon and hydrogen atoms per molecule is much greater than the number of oxygen atoms. Thus, most fats are more complex than carbohydrates.

A fat molecule (Figure 3-21) is formed from two less complex molecules: **fatty acids** and **glycerol** (GLIHS uh rawl). There are many different fatty acid molecules, but all of them have a certain part in common, a **carboxyl** (kar BAHK sul) **group** (—COOH). In the structural formula of a fatty acid (Figure 3-21), R represents a long chain of carbon and hydrogen atoms. The exact number, arrangement and bonding of these atoms accounts for the differences among fatty acids.

Notice that there is a double bond between the carbon atom and one oxygen atom. This double bond represents the sharing of two pairs of electrons (Section 3:12). A double bond occurs because each oxygen atom may share two pairs of electrons with the same atom in forming compounds. Also, carbon must share four electron pairs and hydrogen must share one electron pair. Check the general formula again to see whether all these requirements have been met.

3:15 Proteins

Proteins are the building blocks of living material. They make up much of the structure of living things. Proteins are important in the growth, maintenance, and repair of living material. Certain proteins are also essential in running the chemical reactions in living organisms (Section 4:3).

Like lipids and carbohydrates, proteins contain carbon, hydrogen, and oxygen; but, they also contain nitrogen. Proteins also can contain other elements such as sulfur. Proteins are much larger and more complex than either lipids or carbohydrates.

Proteins are made of compounds called **amino** (uh MEE noh) **acids.** Most of the twenty amino acids important to living things contain a central carbon atom to which is attached a carboxyl group (–COOH), a hydrogen atom, and an **amino group** (–NH₂). Also attached to the carbon atom is the rest of the molecule, the part that makes each amino acid different. It is represented by the letter R.

Another natural amino acid has recently been discovered. It is aminocitric acid, a constituent of ribonucleoproteins.

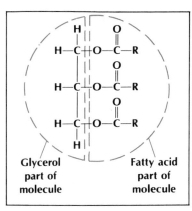

FIGURE 3-21. Glycerol, $C_3H_5(OH)_3$, combines with three fatty acids to form a molecule of fat.

Fats are composed of fatty acids and glycerol.

Saturated fats have no double bonds between carbon atoms; thus, each carbon is bonded to as many hydrogen atoms as possible. Unsaturated fats have double bonds.

FIGURE 3-22. (a) The general formula for an amino acid shows a central carbon atom to which are attached the amino group, the carboxyl group, and the R group. (b) Find each of these groups in valine.

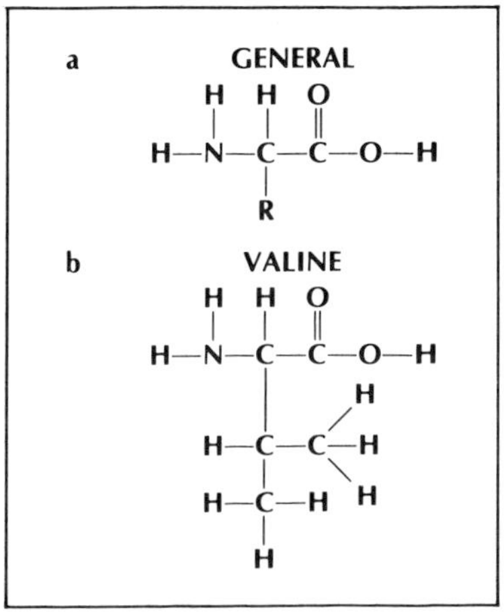

FIGURE 3-23. A protein is made of amino acids held together by peptide bonds. Proteins differ in the kind, number, sequence, and arrangement of amino acids.

FIGURE 3-24. A nucleic acid, DNA, from a virus is shown magnified 65 000 times.

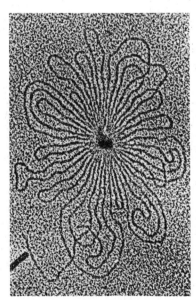

Science Photo Library International

Two amino acids are held together by a **peptide bond.** Two amino acids joined together by a peptide bond form a **dipeptide.** Many amino acids joined together form a **polypeptide.**

Polypeptides combine to form large protein molecules consisting of hundreds or thousands of amino acids. One protein differs from another in its kind, number, sequence, and arrangement of amino acids. Hair and fingernails are proteins that differ because of their amino acids. As the twenty-six letters of the alphabet form many words, the twenty amino acids can form an almost endless number of proteins. It is estimated that there are between 10 000 and 50 000 different kinds of human proteins.

TABLE 3-2. IMPORTANT BIOLOGICAL MOLECULES			
Compound	Elements Present	Building Blocks	Use
Carbohydrate	Carbon Hydrogen Oxygen	Monosaccharides	Energy
Fat	Carbon Hydrogen Oxygen	Fatty Acids Glycerol	Energy reserve
Protein	Carbon Hydrogen Oxygen Nitrogen Sulfur	Amino Acids	Building living material Regulating chemical reactions

3:16 Nucleic Acids

Nucleic (noo KLAY ihk) **acids** are the most complex of all biological compounds. They are extremely large molecules which may consist of hundreds of thousands of atoms. Two very important nucleic acids are **deoxyribonucleic** (dee AHK sih ri boh noo KLAY ihk) **acid** (DNA) and **ribonucleic** (ri boh noo KLAY ihk) **acid** (RNA) which control heredity. DNA is the material which usually contains the "genetic message." RNA works with DNA in carrying out the instruction of the DNA code. You will study this process in Chapter 9.

3:17 Reactions of Organic Compounds

You have seen that organic compounds may combine to form larger molecules. Also, large compounds can be changed to smaller ones. As in any chemical reaction, old bonds must be broken and new bonds formed.

Consider the linking of two amino acids to form a dipeptide. The bonds that are broken involve oxygen and hydrogen atoms.

DEHYDRATION SYNTHESIS

One hydrogen atom is removed from one amino acid. The other amino acid loses an oxygen atom and a hydrogen atom (Figure 3-25). These atoms always come from the same parts of the amino acids. When these atoms are removed, electrons become available for sharing and the two amino acids join together. The two hydrogen atoms and one oxygen atom removed during the reaction join to form a molecule of water. Because the new molecule is made by removing a molecule of water, the process is called **dehydration synthesis.**

Dehydration synthesis is common in all cells. It occurs in synthesizing fats from fatty acids and glycerol. It also occurs in constructing larger carbohydrate molecules from monosaccharides.

Dehydration synthesis is reversed when large molecules are split into smaller molecules. A bond holding the larger molecule together is broken, and a molecule of water is added to form two smaller molecules. This process is called **hydrolysis** (hi DRAHL uh sus) because water is added (Figure 3-26). Like dehydration synthesis, hydrolysis is a common type of cell reaction.

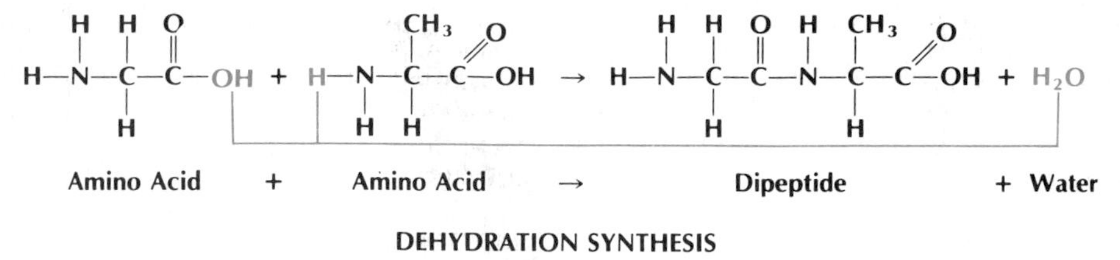

FIGURE 3-25. When water is removed (dehydration), a dipeptide is formed from amino acids by dehydration synthesis.

Large molecules commonly are made in a cell by dehydration synthesis.

FIGURE 3-26. Water is added in the breaking (hydrolysis) of a disaccharide into monosaccharides.

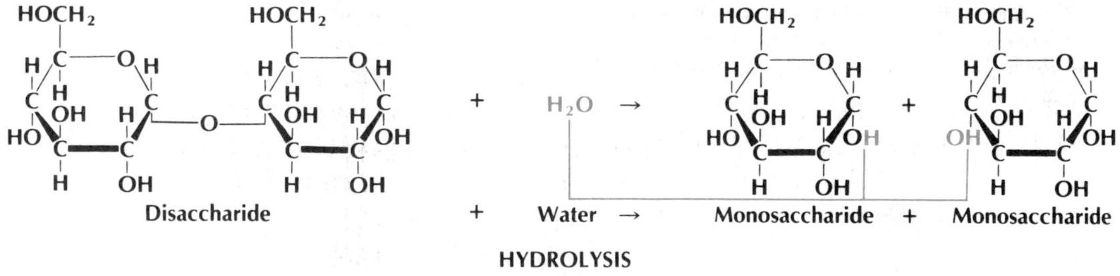

HYDROLYSIS

REVIEWING YOUR IDEAS

18. How are carbohydrates important to organisms?
19. What are lipids? How are fats used by living systems?
20. How are proteins used by organisms?
21. Name two nucleic acids. What are their functions?
22. Name a cellular process that breaks large molecules into smaller ones. Name a cellular process that builds.

18. Carbohydrates are the major energy sources of organisms.
19. Lipids are fats, waxes, and oils. Fats are energy reserves.
20. Proteins are used to build living material and to regulate chemical reactions.
21. DNA and RNA. They control heredity.
22. hydrolysis; dehydration synthesis

CHAPTER REVIEW

SUMMARY

1. Matter is composed of atoms which are made of protons, neutrons, and electrons.
2. Elements are substances composed of one type of atom. Molecules and ionic compounds form when atoms join by covalent or ionic bonds.
3. Ions form when atoms gain or lose electrons.
4. Solutions form when molecules dissolve and ionic compounds dissociate in a solvent.
5. The concentration of hydrogen ions in acids and bases is measured by the pH scale.
6. Matter has both physical and chemical properties and can undergo both physical and chemical changes.
7. Complex carbon-containing compounds are found in living systems.
8. Carbohydrates, lipids, proteins, and nucleic acids are the major groups of carbon compounds important to living systems.
9. Dehydration synthesis and hydrolysis are important reactions of organic compounds.

LANGUAGE OF BIOLOGY

acid	element	matter
amino acid	fatty acid	molecule
atom	formula	neutron
base	glycerol	nucleic acid
carbohydrate	hydrolysis	pH scale
compound	ion	protein
covalent bond	ionic bond	proton
dehydration	isomer	solution
synthesis	isotope	
electron cloud	lipid	

CHECKING YOUR IDEAS

On a separate paper, complete each of the following statements with the missing term(s). Do not write in this book.

1. In an atom with no overall charge, the number of protons equals the ____.
2. Ionic bonds result from the ____ of electrons.
3. ____ are the main building blocks of living material.
4. To show arrangement of parts, organic compounds are shown by ____ formulas.
5. A(n) ____ is a homogeneous material of a solute in a solvent.
6. The stretching of a spring is an example of a(n) ____ change.
7. A(n) ____ is composed of atoms joined by covalent bonds.
8. A total of ____ atoms is shown by $4H_2O$.
9. ____ and ____ are the main energy sources of living systems.
10. A molecule of fat is changed to fatty acids and glycerol by the process of ____.
11. A dipeptide consists of ____ amino acids.
12. Heredity is controlled by ____ and ____, two kinds of large organic molecules.
13. During a(n) ____ change, new substances with new properties are formed.
14. The part of an atom involved in bond formation is the ____.
15. Isotopes of an element have different numbers of ____.

EVALUATING YOUR IDEAS

1. Why is knowledge of chemistry and physics important to a biologist?
2. List the four elements most common in living things. What are their symbols?
3. What happens to the outer energy level when an atom joins with another atom?
4. Why must a molecule of water be composed of two hydrogen atoms and one oxygen atom?
5. What is the difference between a chlorine atom and a chloride ion?
6. How are ionic compounds different from molecular compounds?

CHAPTER REVIEW

7. What is meant by the expression $3H_2O$? How many atoms are there in $3H_2O$?

8. Describe the difference between a solution of sugar in water and a solution of salt in water.

9. Why is a solution of hydrogen chloride in water an acid? Why is a solution of sodium hydroxide in water a base?

10. A chemist tests two solutions. One has a pH of 6. The other has a pH of 2. Which is more acidic? Explain.

11. What properties of carbon make it suitable as a part of complex molecules?

12. What is a double bond? What is a triple bond? Why can't hydrogen form double or triple bonds?

13. What group of atoms is common to both fatty acids and amino acids?

14. What element found in proteins is not found in either lipids or carbohydrates?

15. How does one protein differ from another?

16. With what important biological function are the nucleic acids associated?

17. Classify each reaction below as either a hydrolysis or dehydration synthesis.
    (a) conversion of starch to glucose
    (b) synthesis of protein from amino acids
    (c) production of a disaccharide from monosaccharides
    (d) conversion of a protein to dipeptides
    (e) conversion of fats to fatty acids and glycerol

APPLYING YOUR IDEAS

1. A certain atom has 8 protons and 10 neutrons. How many electrons does it have? Draw a diagram of this atom.

2. One ion has a charge of $3+$. Another ion has a charge of $1-$. How would the two ions combine to form a neutral compound?

3. Helium, argon, and neon are atoms whose outer energy levels are filled. They are known as noble (inactive) gases. Why are they inactive?

4. Bromthymol blue is a substance which is yellow-green in the presence of an acid and blue in the presence of a base. When CO_2 is dissolved in water, an acid is formed. Suppose CO_2 is dissolved in water to which bromthymol blue has been added. What color is the water? What would happen to the color of the water if an aquatic green plant were placed in it? Why?

5. Which of the following changes are physical and which are chemical?
   (a) tearing a sheet of paper
   (b) melting of ice
   (c) joining of two monosaccharides

6. Butane, C_4H_{10}, is an organic compound containing single covalent bonds. Draw structural formulas of 2 isomers of C_4H_{10}.

7. Ecologists are concerned about the effects of acid rain. What pH range could acid rain have? How might acid rain affect the environment?

EXTENDING YOUR IDEAS

1. List ten common chemical changes.

2. How would you separate a mixture of sand and iron filings? Of sand and salt?

3. Using reference materials, determine how the pH of the blood is kept constant. What happens if the blood pH varies too much?

4. Prepare a report on cholesterol and its possible effects on humans.

5. Prepare a demonstration showing how various indicators are used to tell pH.

SUGGESTED READINGS

Baker, J.J.W. and Allen, G.E., *Matter, Energy, and Life: An Introduction for Biology Students.* Reading, MA, Addison-Wesley, 1975.

Rosenfeld, Albert, "The Great Protein Hunt." *Science 81*, January/February, 1981.

Additional student readings and suggested teacher readings are provided in the Teacher's Guide.

This phenomenon is called bioluminescence.

Living things need energy to maintain life processes. Energy must not only be present but it must be in a form usable within the cells of an organism. Here, chemicals within the tissues of the firefly release energy causing the firefly to glow. What types of energy changes occur in this process and other processes within living things? In what forms can energy exist? How is one form changed to another?

Introduction and suggested demonstration: To introduce the topic of cellular respiration, set up a series of fermentation tubes, each of which contains a different sugar in solution. Make each a 5% solution and use the same volume in each tube. Glucose (dextrose), fructose, galactose, sucrose, maltose, and lactose may be used. In a separate tube prepare a yeast suspension of either powdered dry yeast or cake yeast in water. Add an equal amount of the yeast suspension to each sugar solution and plug each tube with cotton. If the tubes do not have gradations, add them. Use a wax pencil to mark lines 5 mm apart. As the yeast respire, CO_2 is produced which displaces the liquid. The rates will vary depending on the sugar used. The rate of respiration can be measured indirectly by measuring the amount of liquid displaced per unit time. Besides stimulating a discussion of respiration in general, this demonstration can lead to the topic of enzymes. You might begin by asking students for evidence of chemical change. The rates at which different sugars are respired is related to the enzymes the yeast have.

Chapter

4

ENERGY FOR LIFE

Chapter 4 explores more deeply the role of energy in organisms. The functions of enzymes and ATP and the processes of aerobic and anaerobic respiration are discussed.

Living systems require a supply of energy for growth and development, maintenance and repair, reproduction, and overall organization. Without a constant input of energy, no single organism or community could long survive. Energy is necessary for life.

What is energy? The best way to define energy is to describe what it does. The movement of a car, the running of an air conditioner, and the changing of ice to water all require energy. Each of these examples involves motion and can be considered to be work. **Energy** is the ability to do work or cause motion.

In living things, energy is used for biological work or motion. Without energy muscles would not contract, certain particles would not move into or out of cells, and new living tissue would not be built. Can you think of other ways in which organisms use energy? conduction of nerve impulses; biosynthesis; bioluminescence

GOAL: You will gain an understanding of the need for and uses of energy and the process of cellular respiration.

Teaching suggestion: You might want to review with students the concepts about energy presented in Chapter 1 before beginning this chapter.

Energy is the ability to do work or cause motion.

Energy is used for biological work.

ENERGY AND REACTIONS

4:1 Changes in Forms of Energy

Consider a rock at the top of a hill. If the rock is pushed over the side, it will roll down the hill. As it is rolling, the rock could do work or cause motion such as knocking down trees on the hill. At the bottom of the hill, the rock stops rolling and can no longer do work.

Now think about burning wood. As the wood burns, heat and light (radiant energy) are released. The energy could be used for work. For example, the heat could be used to cook food or warm a room. Eventually, the wood will all be burned and no more work can be done.

Thomas Zimmerman/Alpha

Thomas Zimmerman/Alpha

a

b

FIGURE 4-1. (a) A bobsled team at the top of the run has high potential energy and low kinetic energy. (b) While on the run, the potential energy is converted to kinetic energy.

Potential energy can be converted to kinetic energy.

Some compounds, such as ATP, contain bonds which are easily broken and, in the process, provide the energy needed to force other reactions to occur. The energy, however, is not really *stored* in the bonds. The energy is released only when a bond is broken and a change to a specific substance of lower energy, such as ADP, occurs. Reactions take place because there is an overall decrease in free energy.

Energy is conserved as it changes form.

In cells, potential chemical energy is converted to kinetic energy used for work.

Both the rock at the top of the hill and the wood have high potential energy. **Potential energy** is energy of position or stored energy. As the rock rolls down the hill or as the wood is burned, the potential energy is converted to kinetic energy. **Kinetic energy** is energy of motion. The rock at the bottom of the hill and the products formed from burning the wood have low potential energy. The difference between the high and low potential energies equals the energy released.

Energy, either potential or kinetic, can be in many forms and can change from one form to another. The potential energy in the wood molecules is called **chemical energy.** That energy is "stored" in the bonds of the molecules in wood cells. (Where did that energy come from originally?) When wood is burned, old bonds are broken and new bonds are formed. The potential chemical energy is changed to heat and light (radiant energy).

Any time energy changes form, it is conserved so that the total amount of energy in a system is constant. For example, in the burning of wood, some energy is released and can be used for work. Some of the original energy exists in the bonds of the new compounds formed, carbon dioxide and water. The total amount of this energy is equal to the amount of energy in the wood and the oxygen with which it reacted. The **law of conservation of energy** is: *energy is neither created nor destroyed, but it can be changed from one form to another.*

Changes of energy are important to living things. *Cells depend upon potential chemical energy in the bonds of energy-rich molecules. When the bonds are broken, the potential energy is converted to kinetic energy which can be used by cells for biological work.*

4:2 Activation Energy

You know that sugar by itself in a dish will not burn. Even though oxygen molecules in the air are colliding with the sugar molecules, no reaction occurs. But if the sugar is heated, it will burn (combine with oxygen). A chemical reaction will occur. The energy boost needed to get the reaction started is called **activation energy.** In this case, the activation energy was the heat you added. Just as a push (activation energy) is needed to start the rock rolling, heat is needed to get the sugar burning.

Once the reaction starts, the activation energy can be removed and the reaction will continue. Energy in the form of heat and light will be released and carbon dioxide and water will be formed. The energy released during the burning of sugar was present *in* the sugar molecules. Some of this potential energy was transformed into radiant energy (heat and light) as the sugar burned. No energy was lost in the process; it only changed forms (Section 4:1).

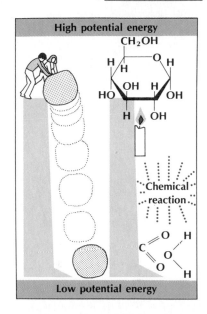

FIGURE 4-2. Activation energy is required to start a rock rolling down a hill and to start many chemical reactions. In both cases, potential energy is converted to kinetic energy as the processes occur.

REVIEWING YOUR IDEAS

1. Distinguish between potential and kinetic energy.
2. How do cells obtain their usable energy?
3. What is activation energy? What form of energy is often used to speed up chemical reactions in a chemistry lab?

1. Potential energy is stored energy. Kinetic energy is energy of motion.
2. Cells obtain usable energy when bonds of energy-rich molecules are broken.
3. Activation energy is the energy needed to start a reaction. Heat is a source of activation energy for reactions in a chemistry lab.

ENERGY FOR CELLULAR WORK

4:3 Enzymes

In some ways, the chemical reactions of living and nonliving things are alike. For example, sugar in a test tube burns by using up oxygen, and a mouse needs oxygen to burn its food in order to stay alive. But there are differences. The test-tube reaction gives off heat and light while the mouse gives off a little heat but no light. Burning in the test tube is "explosive"; the energy is released quickly. In the mouse, even though energy is released quickly, the "burning" of food is controlled.

Heat energy is the activation energy for the sugar in the test tube. But heat cannot be the activation energy for chemical reactions in organisms. The amount of heat needed to start most cellular reactions would be so great it would kill the cell. Even if heat could be used, it would cause most reactions to occur at the same time. For a cell to function smoothly, specific reactions must occur at definite times.

In a cell, sugar is "burned" so that energy is released slowly.

Heat is not a suitable source of activation energy for organisms.

Enzymes lower the activation energy necessary to start biological reactions.

Enzymes are used in some commercial products such as meat tenderizers and cleaning agents.

The first enzyme discovered was isolated from barley seeds by Payen and Persoz in 1833. The enzyme, called diastase, converts starch to sugar.

Enzymes are proteins. They are specific and reusable.

Enzyme function varies with temperature, pH, and substrate concentration. High temperatures denature proteins.

What is the name of the enzyme which breaks down sucrose?

sucrase

FIGURE 4-3. According to the lock and key hypothesis, an enzyme fits a specific substrate just as a key fits a specific lock.

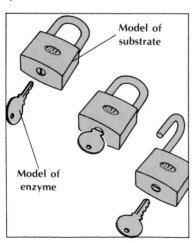

Model of substrate

Model of enzyme

If heat is not the source of activation energy in cells, how do cellular reactions get started? Cells contain special chemicals called enzymes (EN zimes). **Enzymes** are chemicals which *lower* the amount of activation energy required and allow reactions to occur at cellular temperatures. Thus, no additional heat is required. Without enzymes, the kinetic energy of particles at cellular temperatures would be insufficient to cause many reactions to occur at detectable rates.

4:4 Properties of Enzymes

Since the discovery of the first enzyme, many more have been found. All of these enzymes have certain properties. Each enzyme is specific in that it boosts only one or one type of a cell's many reactions. Also, enzymes themselves are not changed or used up during a reaction.

Enzymes are proteins, complex molecules made up of amino acids. Because the number of possible arrangements of amino acids is large (Section 3:15), it is not surprising that there are many different enzymes. Each enzyme has a unique three-dimensional shape. The substance upon which a certain enzyme acts is called a **substrate.**

An enzyme often is named by adding the suffix -ase to part of the name of the substrate. Thus, the enzyme which converts maltose to simpler sugars is called maltase. The enzymes which break down proteins are called **proteases** (PROHT ee ays uz). Some enzymes are named on the basis of their function. For example, an enzyme that removes hydrogen is called a dehydrogenase (dee hi DRAHJ uh nays). An enzyme that transfers an amino group is called a transaminase (tranz AM uh nays). Some names of enzymes, such as pepsin, do not end in -ase. These enzymes were named before the -ase system of naming was used, although some have been renamed since by the -ase system.

Teaching suggestion: Point out how the lock and key hypothesis uses elements of logic and creative thinking to explain the known facts about enzymes.

4:5 Lock and Key Hypothesis

How does an enzyme lower the activation energy needed to start a reaction? The properties of enzymes have been studied in detail. The **lock and key hypothesis** is one explanation of enzyme function. It explains some enzyme properties.

Every lock has a specific key which will open it. The shape of the key enables it to open a lock. The key is cut so that it matches the tumblers of the lock. Only if the two surfaces fit together will the lock open.

Each substrate can be acted upon only by a specific enzyme. Thus, the surface shapes of the enzyme and substrate must match each other and fit together. Biologists assumed that the enzyme has a special shape which would fit a part of the substrate.

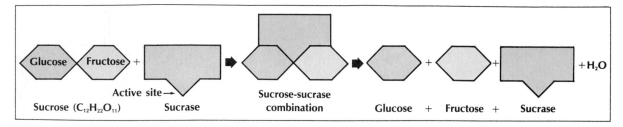

The parts would fit just as a key fits a lock or as two pieces of a jigsaw puzzle fit together. The part of the enzyme molecule which fits the substrate is called the **active site.** This idea explains the fact that each enzyme is specific for its substrate.

Sometimes, other substances alter the shapes of active sites (Section 4:6). In some cases the fit between enzyme and substrate is not exact, but when they join, the shape of the enzyme changes to make a better fit.

Now consider a common biological reaction. Sucrose (table sugar), a disaccharide, breaks down into two monosaccharides, glucose and fructose (Section 3:13). This reaction is a hydrolysis reaction (Section 3:17). It occurs in your intestine as you digest a meal. Although sucrose and water molecules collide, the force of such collisions is not great enough to cause the hydrolysis reaction to occur. The bond holding the two monosaccharides together is too strong.

Now suppose a molecule of sucrose collides with a molecule of the enzyme sucrase (Figure 4-4). According to the lock and key hypothesis, the active site of the sucrase molecule fits a certain part of the sucrose molecule. Thus, if the two molecules collide, they can join. While the sucrase and sucrose are joined, the bond holding the two monosaccharides together is somehow weakened and then broken. A molecule of water is added to complete the reaction. *When an enzyme and substrate are joined, the activation energy requirement is lowered. The reaction, therefore, occurs at cellular temperatures.* After the bonds between glucose and fructose are broken, the enzyme separates from the substrate. The enzyme is not used up or changed during the reaction and can be used over again.

Enzymes also can work in reactions that combine smaller molecules to form a larger molecule. Proteins are formed from amino acids (Section 3:15). To join two amino acids, an enzyme with two active sites is needed—one site fits each amino acid. As the two amino acids lie side by side on the surface of the enzyme, they are in a position which increases the chances for bonds to form between them. Again, while the enzyme and substrates are joined, the activation energy required is lowered. A molecule of water is removed in this dehydration synthesis (Section 3:17). A dipeptide is formed as the two amino acids join (Figure 4-5).

FIGURE 4-4. The enzyme sucrase is involved in the breakdown of sucrose. The active site of the enzyme fits the shape of the substrate (sucrose).

The active site is the "key" which fits the substrate "lock."

In general:
1. enzyme + substrate → enzyme-substrate complex
2. enzyme-substrate complex → products + enzyme

FIGURE 4-5. In the formation of a dipeptide, an enzyme with two active sites is involved.

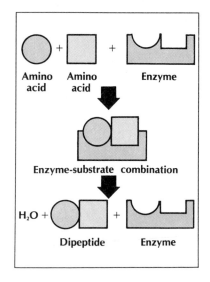

The lock and key hypothesis is supported by experimentation.

Many reactions are reversible. Often enzymes can catalyze reactions in either direction. The direction is determined by factors such as concentration of the reactants and products.

End products of reactions, when present in excess, may combine with and alter the active site of an enzyme, thus stopping the reaction until the concentration of end products decreases.

The shape of the active site may be altered when other molecules combine with the enzyme.

The lock and key hypothesis has been modified somewhat by the idea of "induced fit."

Some coenzymes change the shape of an enzyme's active site.

Coenzymes often act as transfer agents.

A well-balanced diet should provide all vitamins required as coenzymes or for the synthesis of necessary coenzymes.

FIGURE 4-6. These foods are high in vitamin B₁. A disease called beriberi can result if the diet does not include enough vitamin B₁.

Experimental evidence supports the lock and key hypothesis. If the active site of an enzyme is destroyed, the enzyme cannot direct its normal activities. However, if the active site remains and another region is destroyed, the enzyme can sometimes perform properly. Also, a substance with a shape similar to the normal substrate can compete with the substrate. It combines with some of the available enzyme molecules so that the enzyme cannot do its job. This process is called competitive inhibition.

Using computers, scientists are identifying the active sites of some enzymes. They have learned where enzymes combine with their substrates. The shape of the active sites of some enzymes may be altered by molecules which either produce the proper active site or distort it. Perhaps these molecules control when an enzyme operates.

4:6 Coenzymes

Some enzymes, during a reaction, join temporarily with other molecules, **coenzymes** (koh EN zimes). In many cases, a coenzyme alters the shape of the enzyme's active site. The enzyme then fits its substrate better and the reaction occurs.

Coenzymes are usually organic molecules, smaller than enzymes. Like enzymes, they are not consumed during a reaction and can be reused. Coenzymes often serve as transfer agents of atoms, parts of atoms, or groups of atoms during a reaction. For example, an enzyme might remove a hydrogen atom from a molecule. The coenzyme would pick up the atom and donate it to some other substance. The reaction could not occur without the coenzyme to accept the hydrogen.

Some essential coenzymes are made from vitamins or vitamin fragments. If an organism's diet does not include enough of a needed vitamin, the coenzyme cannot be made. Certain cellular reactions cannot occur and symptoms of a disease occur. For example, lack of vitamin B₁ causes beriberi. Beriberi involves weakening of the muscles and paralysis. Vitamin B₁ is needed to make an enzyme biologically active. The enzyme is involved in the process of "burning" food. Vitamin B₁ functions as a coenzyme.

Tim Dietz

Roger K. Burnard

Tim Courlas

a

b

4:7 ATP

Reactions both inside and outside of living things require activation energy to get started. Once started, some reactions release energy. A reaction that gives off energy is called **exergonic** (ek sur GAHN ihk). Burning wood (wood combining with oxygen) is an exergonic reaction. Activation energy (heat from a match) is required to start the wood burning. Then the wood continues to burn, giving off heat and light.

Some reactions once started use energy. Reactions that use energy are called **endergonic** (en dur GAHN ihk). Compresses sometimes used on sprained ankles contain chemicals that when mixed react with each other. The reaction uses up energy. As the chemicals react and the energy is used, the compress gets colder. Heat energy is absorbed.

Many cellular reactions are endergonic. They require an enzyme to lower the activation energy needed. But, they require more than this "spark" of activation energy. They need an additional energy source. The source of energy for most endergonic reactions in a cell is a special kind of molecule. The molecule is called **adenosine triphosphate** (uh DEN uh seen·tri FAHS fayt). This source of chemical energy is commonly called **ATP.** An example of an endergonic reaction using energy from ATP is the synthesis of starch from glucose.

ATP is a complex molecule which can be simplified as A—Ⓟ〰Ⓟ〰Ⓟ. The A stands for the adenosine part of the molecule, and the Ⓟ 's represent groups of atoms called phosphate groups. The wavy lines represent special bonds called **high-energy bonds** between phosphate groups. When these bonds are broken (and new bonds are formed), a large amount of chemical energy is released. The high-energy phosphate bonds liberate about twice as much energy as normal phosphate bonds. *This chemical energy is used in endergonic reactions.*

FIGURE 4-7. (a) The explosion of fireworks is an exergonic reaction. Heat and light are given off. (b) A cold compress has chemicals undergoing an endergonic reaction. Heat is being absorbed.

An exergonic reaction liberates energy.

An endergonic reaction requires energy.

ATP provides energy for most endergonic reactions in cells.

The terminology "high-energy phosphate bond" is really a misnomer. The term indicates a large free energy difference in the reactants and products, but this energy does not really reside in the phosphate bond. The terminology is used often, but it really means that a compound has high-phosphate transfer potential.

ATP contains high-energy bonds which, when broken, release chemical energy for endergonic reactions.

Approximate energy production from removing phosphate groups by hydrolysis:
ATP → ADP + Pi (30.6 kJ)
ADP → AMP + Pi (30.6 kJ)
AMP → adenosine + Pi (14.2 kJ)

ATP is used by cells along with enzymes for endergonic reactions. The energy in ATP is released after an enzyme breaks the bond holding the third phosphate group. Then the molecule contains only two phosphates and is called **adenosine diphosphate** (di FAHS fayt) or **ADP.** A high energy phosphate group, represented as ～ⓟ, is also a product. When the high-energy phosphate forms a bond with another substance, chemical energy is released and work is done. As the work is done, the high-energy phosphate is said to change to low-energy phosphate, —ⓟ (Figure 4-9).

ATP is used in many cellular jobs. For example, energy released from high-energy phosphate is necessary for contracting muscle fibers, lighting a firefly, or conducting nerve impulses. It also drives the many unseen chemical reactions necessary for other cellular activities.

Energy is needed to change ADP and low-energy phosphate to ATP.

Because cells do not have an endless supply of ATP molecules, there must be a way of making more ATP. When a molecule of ATP is used, a molecule of ADP and a low-energy phosphate group are produced and energy is released. ADP and low-energy phosphate can be rejoined to produce ATP. Energy is used in the production of ATP. This energy changes the low-energy phosphate to high-energy phosphate of ATP.

4. Enzymes are proteins. They are specific and reusable.
5. Enzymes are named based on their substrates and/or functions.
6. Coenzymes are organic molecules. Some are vitamins or vitamin fragments. Some coenzymes alter the shapes of enzymes; others act as transfer agents.
7. ATP is necessary because it is the energy source for many cellular reactions. ATP is a high-energy molecule; energy is released when its high-energy phosphate bonds are broken.

REVIEWING YOUR IDEAS

4. List three characteristics of enzymes.
5. How are enzymes named?
6. Of what are coenzymes made? How do they function?
7. Why is ATP necessary for many cellular reactions? What property of ATP makes it suitable for its function?

Teaching suggestion: Refer students to Appendix B for the details of respiration.

PRODUCTION OF ATP

Sugar can be "burned" to supply energy for living systems (Chapter 1). The sugar which organisms most commonly use as an energy source is glucose, $C_6H_{12}O_6$. It is the source of energy for making ATP. Why is glucose such a good energy source?

4:8 Respiration With Oxygen

Aerobic respiration requires oxygen.

The process in which a cell releases the energy of glucose is called **cellular respiration.** During this process, the energy is transferred to the ATP. Respiration in most cells makes use of oxygen and is called **aerobic** (er ROH bihk) **respiration.** ("Aerobic" means requiring oxygen.)

Thomas Zimmerman/fpg   *Thomas Zimmerman/fpg*

The process of aerobic respiration involves many separate chemical reactions which occur in a definite sequence. Each reaction requires an enzyme. Energy is released during certain of these reactions. The following equation summarizes the many reactions of aerobic respiration of glucose:

FIGURE 4-8. Oxygen taken in by the body is used in cellular respiration. During exercise, more oxygen is taken in.

$$C_6H_{12}O_6 + 6O_2 \xrightarrow[\text{2 ATP}]{\text{enzymes}} 6CO_2 + 6H_2O + \begin{matrix} \text{energy for} \\ \text{38ATP} \end{matrix}$$

In the series of steps glucose is converted to carbon dioxide and water. *Energy of glucose is released and is used in the formation of ATP from ADP and low-energy phosphate.* Thus, ATP contains energy originally in glucose.

Note that some ATP molecules are "invested" in the process. This "investment" is needed because certain early steps require energy. Enough energy, however, is released during later steps to make a large net yield of ATP molecules. The process as a whole is exergonic.

Why must the energy in glucose be transferred to ATP? ATP molecules are the major *usable* energy source in a cell. The step-by-step process of cellular respiration slowly releases the potential energy of glucose and transfers it to ATP. How does this energy release differ from that of the burning of glucose in a test tube? In a test tube, glucose burns rapidly as chemical energy of glucose is converted to heat.

During aerobic respiration, some of the energy in the bonds of glucose is transferred to the bonds of ATP.

ATP is the major usable energy source in a cell.

FIGURE 4-9. When ATP is converted to ADP and ⓟ, energy is released which is used in cells for different purposes.

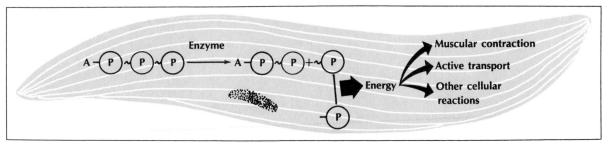

FIGURE 4-10. In cellular respiration, the energy of glucose converts ADP and (P) to ATP. The ATP is broken down later releasing energy that is used in cells.

RESPIRATION

$C_6H_{12}O_6$

ATP

Energy of respiration added to form ATP

Energy given off is used in cellular activities

$6 CO_2 + 6 H_2O$

ADP + (P)

Figure 4-10 summarizes the interrelationships among cellular respiration, ATP, ADP, and the work of the cell. This series of chemical events is called the ATP-ADP cycle. The cycle shows that during aerobic respiration, energy of glucose is released. This energy is used to join ADP and low-energy phosphate to form ATP which can then be used as an energy source for cellular work.

Anaerobic respiration occurs in the absence of oxygen.

4:9 Respiration Without Oxygen

Most cells undergo aerobic respiration, but may change to **anaerobic** (an uh ROH bihk) **respiration** if deprived of oxygen. ("Anaerobic" means not requiring oxygen.) In some cells, anaerobic respiration may occur even if oxygen is present, but some microbes cannot even live in the presence of oxygen. Thus, they rely only on anaerobic respiration for energy.

Most plant cells and microbes commonly undergo a type of anaerobic respiration called alcoholic **fermentation.** Glucose is broken down as shown in the following equation:

$$C_6H_{12}O_6 \xrightarrow{\text{enzymes}} 2C_2H_5OH + 2CO_2 + \underset{\text{(ethyl alcohol)}}{} \quad \underset{2ATP}{} \quad \underset{4ATP}{\text{energy for}}$$

FIGURE 4-11. (a) Anaerobic respiration of yeast produces carbon dioxide which makes bread rise. (b) Anaerobic respiration of certain bacteria causes fermentation of cucumbers in the production of pickles.

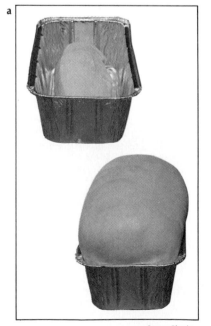

a

Bruce Charlton

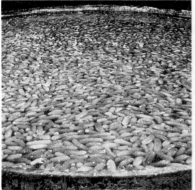

Open and closed pickle vats shown.

Heinz USA

b

Heinz USA

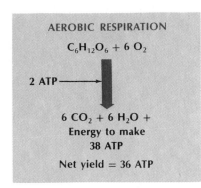

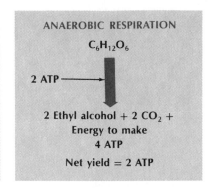

FIGURE 4-12. Aerobic respiration and anaerobic respiration both produce ATP. What are the main differences in these two processes?

Notice that no free oxygen is involved in the process. As in aerobic respiration, enzymes and a small amount of ATP energy are required. Energy is released for the formation of more ATP. However, in anaerobic respiration, glucose is not broken all the way down to CO_2 and water. Therefore, only a small amount of ATP is netted. The product, ethyl alcohol, has more chemical potential energy than the products of aerobic respiration. Thus, less energy was "released" in the form of ATP.

Yeasts are useful in industry because of their fermentation products—alcohol and carbon dioxide. Alcohol is used in some beverages. The carbon dioxide formed when yeast cells break down the carbohydrates in dough causes dough to rise. Thus, yeasts are used in the baking industry as well.

Many animals and some microbes carry on anaerobic respiration at certain times. For example, during times of heavy physical activity, oxygen may not be supplied fast enough to muscle cells for aerobic respiration to take place. When oxygen is low, the muscle cells "switch" to anaerobic respiration. At these times, glycogen (Section 3:13), which is stored in muscles, is converted to glucose. Glucose is then broken down without oxygen to produce lactic acid. Energy is released and used to form ATP molecules. Thus, energy is supplied for muscle contraction even in the absence of oxygen.

$$C_6H_{12}O_6 \xrightarrow[\text{2ATP}]{\text{enzymes}} \underset{\text{(lactic acid)}}{2CH_3CHOHCOOH} + \underset{\text{4ATP}}{\text{energy for}}$$

Figure 4-12 compares the events of aerobic and anaerobic respiration. Examine the figure closely.

REVIEWING YOUR IDEAS

---

8. What is cellular respiration? Why is it necessary? How is it related to breathing?
9. Contrast aerobic and anaerobic respiration.

Anaerobic respiration produces much less energy than aerobic respiration.

Fermentation is useful in the baking and brewing industries.

Lactic acid effects in muscle tissue are discussed in Chapter 28.

Muscle cells undergo anaerobic respiration when oxygen is unavailable.

Why would oxygen not be supplied quickly enough during heavy exercise?

8. Cellular respiration is the process by which the energy of glucose is transferred to molecules of ATP. Respiration is necessary so energy is made available in a usable form, namely ATP. Respiration is related to breathing in that the oxygen used is that taken in. Carbon dioxide is released, also.
9. Aerobic respiration uses oxygen, anaerobic does not. Aerobic respiration results in a greater production of ATP than anaerobic.

CHAPTER REVIEW

SUMMARY

1. Energy is the ability to do work or cause motion. In living things, energy is used for biological work or motion.

2. Organisms obtain usable energy by breaking down high-energy molecules. Chemical potential energy is converted to kinetic energy.

3. All chemical reactions require activation energy to get started. Enzymes lower the required activation energy in cells.

4. Each cellular reaction requires a certain enzyme. The lock and key hypothesis is one explanation of enzyme function and also explains some enzyme properties.

5. Coenzymes work along with many enzymes. A coenzyme may combine with an enzyme to alter the enzyme's active site. Coenzymes also act as transfer agents.

6. When the high-energy bonds of ATP are broken, energy is released for biological work. ATP is used in all cellular jobs.

7. Each time a molecule of ATP is used, the cell is left with a molecule of ADP and low-energy phosphate. ADP and low-energy phosphate can rejoin in a cell when energy is added.

8. Most cells break the bonds of glucose by the process of aerobic respiration. Much ATP results from the aerobic respiration of one glucose molecule. The process of aerobic respiration involves many separate chemical reactions which occur in a definite sequence.

9. Transfer of energy from glucose to ATP is necessary because ATP is the major usable energy source in cells.

10. Less ATP is formed from the anaerobic breakdown of one molecule of glucose than from the aerobic breakdown. Fermentation is a type of anaerobic respiration.

LANGUAGE OF BIOLOGY

activation energy
active site
ADP
aerobic respiration
anaerobic respiration
ATP
cellular respiration
chemical energy
coenzyme
endergonic
energy
enzyme
exergonic
fermentation
high-energy bond
kinetic energy
law of conservation
   of energy
lock and key
   hypothesis
potential energy
substrate

CHECKING YOUR IDEAS

On a separate paper, indicate whether each of the following statements is true or false. Do not write in this book.

1. Cellular respiration is an endergonic set of reactions.

2. Enzymes lower required activation energy in cells.

3. All cellular reactions require ATP.

4. Energy for making ATP can come from glucose.

5. The part of the enzyme which combines with the substrate is the active site.

6. More energy is released during anaerobic respiration than during aerobic respiration.

7. When energy changes form, some energy is lost.

8. Enzymes are reusable.

9. ATP is a usable source of chemical energy in cells.

10. A battery not being used has potential energy.

EVALUATING YOUR IDEAS

1. What are some forms which energy may take? Give an example of energy changing in form.

CHAPTER REVIEW

2. Which form of energy is most important to living things? Explain how it is used.

3. What is meant by "conservation of energy"? Give an example.

4. Why is heat not a suitable source of activation energy for organisms?

5. Describe the lock and key hypothesis. What traits of enzymes does it explain?

6. Using diagrams, show how an enzyme would operate in (a) the synthesis of a disaccharide and (b) the conversion of a dipeptide to two amino acids.

7. Distinguish between an endergonic reaction and an exergonic reaction.

8. How is ATP used in driving reactions?

9. What remains after a molecule of ATP has been used? What is needed to produce ATP?

10. What are the reactants and products of cellular respiration?

11. How efficient would cells be if the energy from glucose were not transferred to ATP?

12. Describe the ATP-ADP cycle.

13. How is cellular respiration similar to a rock on a hill? How is it different?

14. How is anaerobic respiration less "profitable" than aerobic respiration? Why?

15. How is fermentation in yeasts useful?

APPLYING YOUR IDEAS

1. Assume that the amount of enzyme in a reaction is kept constant. How would you expect the rate of a reaction to be influenced by adding more substrate? Why?

2. ATP may be considered as the "coins" which the cell uses to pay its debts. Using this analogy, how would you describe glucose? Why?

3. Yeasts can respire both with and without oxygen. Explain why yeasts respiring with oxygen grow and divide more rapidly than yeasts respiring without oxygen.

4. Which has the most potential energy—a diver on a high board, a diver on a low board, or a diver entering the water? Explain your answer in terms of kinetic energy.

5. Glucose is made by producers. How does the producer use that glucose?

6. How is photosynthesis an example of energy transformation (energy changing forms)?

EXTENDING YOUR IDEAS

1. Conduct an experiment to determine the effect of temperature or pH on the rate at which an enzyme operates.

2. Report to the class on several vitamin-deficiency diseases and their symptoms.

3. Some organisms are bioluminescent (by oh lew muh NEHS uhnt). That is, they produce "cold" light. Find out how these organisms produce light and how the light is useful to them.

4. Louis Pasteur was a versatile scientist. What role did he play in solving the problems of the wine industry?

5. Devise a class demonstration which shows the idea of alcoholic fermentation.

SUGGESTED READINGS

Baker, Jeffrey W. and Allen, Garland E., *Matter, Energy and Life: An Introduction for Biology Students*, 3rd ed. Reading, MA, Addison-Wesley Publishing Co., Inc., 1975.

Chappell, J. B., *The Energetics of Mitochondria*, 2nd ed. Carolina Biology Reader. Burlington, NC, Carolina Biological Supply Co., 1979.

Hollaway, M. R., *The Mechanism of Enzyme Action*. Oxford Biology Reader. London, Oxford University Press, 1976.

Additional student readings and suggested teacher readings are provided in the Teacher's Guide.

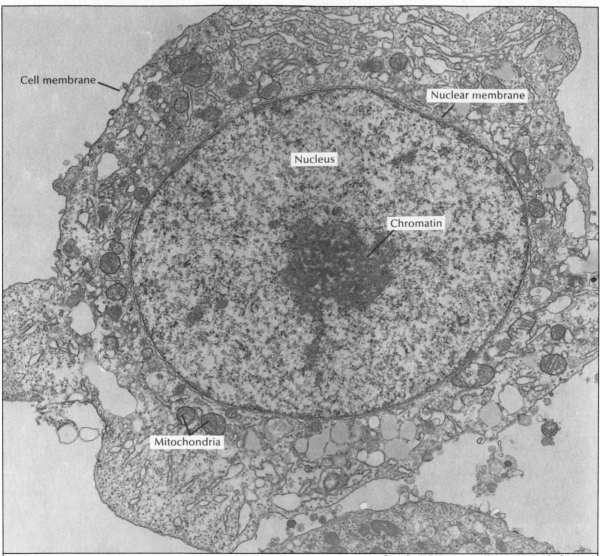

Cell membrane

Nuclear membrane

Nucleus

Chromatin

Mitochondria

Rat liver tumor cell

Dr. Judie Walton, Lawrence Livermore National Laboratory

The cell is the basic unit of life. Different cell parts function in different ways resulting in life processes such as fluid balance and protein production. This liver cell is shown magnified about 4000 times. What cell structures are present in this cell and in other cells? How do the cell parts function? How can cells and cell parts be studied?

Introduction and suggested demonstration: You may wish to begin your study with a demonstration of the principles of diffusion. Cut a 10-cm length of dialysis tubing (available from biological supply houses). Moisten the tubing under running water so that you can open it into a cylinder. Tie one end securely with a string or rubber band. Pour a solution of starch (use soluble starch in distilled water) into the tube and tie the open end securely. At the beginning of class, place the starch tube in a beaker of distilled water to which you have added a few drops of Lugol's (iodine-potassium iodide) solution. The particles of the Lugol's solution will move through the membrane of the tube, reacting with the starch and forming a blue-black color. Leave the tube in the beaker all period; the color will darken with time. Discuss the idea of selective permeability. Point out that the starch molecules are too large to move through the membrane. Therefore, there is no color change in the beaker.

CELL STRUCTURE AND FUNCTION

Chapter 5 presents the development of the cell theory and the structure and functions of cells.

In 1665, Robert Hooke, an English scientist, made important observations. Using an early microscope, he examined razor-thin slices of cork, a plant material. He saw that the cork is composed of many tiny units. Because they reminded him of a honeycomb, he named these units **cells.** Although Hooke did not realize it, he was the first to observe this feature of life.

GOAL: You will gain an understanding of the structure and function of the cell.

Robert Hooke, who first observed and named cells, saw only the walls of dead cork cells.

DISCOVERING CELLS

5:1 The Cell Theory

Hooke's discovery of cork cells was the foundation of a major biological theory. The development of that theory, however, took almost two hundred years. Study was limited by poor microscopes. Although later scientists reported finding cells in many plants and animals, they did not realize the importance of the observations. They made no general statements about cells.

When Hooke looked at cork, he saw only dead cells. Only the outer parts, or walls, of the cells were visible. He observed, then, only the borders of hollow compartments. There was certainly no hint that living cells are active and are composed of still smaller parts.

Later discoveries by a number of scientists led to a more accurate picture of a living cell. In the 1830's Robert Brown (1773–1858) determined that a cell contains a central part, or **nucleus** (NEW klee us). It was later reported that cells are not hollow structures. Cells are filled with a thick, jellylike fluid. Matthias Schleiden (SHLI dun) determined that all plants are composed of cells and that cells are the basis of an organism's function. A year later, Theodor Schwann (SHVAHN) determined the same things about animals. In 1858, Rudolf Virchow (FIHR koh) concluded that all cells come from other living cells.

In 1824, Dutrochet suggested that various parts of organisms are composed of cells but he made no broad generalization about the universality of cells as structural units of life.

A cell has a nucleus (or nuclei) and is filled with a jellylike fluid.

All organisms are composed of cells.

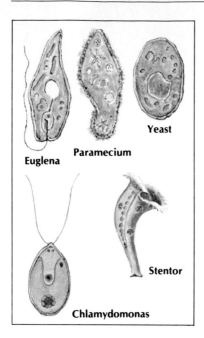

FIGURE 5-1. A unicellular organism is one cell. It performs all life functions. Many organisms are unicellular.

All cells perform similar, basic functions.

1. The cells Hooke saw were dead; only cell walls remained.
2. Schleiden first stated that all plants are composed of cells; Schwann, that all animals are composed of cells; and Virchow, that cells come from cells.
3. All organisms are composed of cells or cell fragments which are the basic units of structure and function. All cells come from cells.
4. Unicellular organisms are composed of only one cell, whereas multicellular organisms are composed of many cells.
5. Obtaining food and other materials, gas exchange, waste removal, synthesis of living material, regulation of water balance, reproduction.

The conclusions made by Schleiden, Schwann, and Virchow are extremely important because they apply to all living things and they have been supported by later findings. These statements form the basis of one of biology's most important concepts, the **cell theory.**

An example of cell fragments is platelets.

1. All organisms are composed of cells or cell fragments which are the basic units of structure and function.
2. All cells are produced from other cells.

The development of the cell theory is a good example of the interaction of careful observation, interpretation, and curiosity. Why is it called a theory rather than a hypothesis?

It applies to all organisms and has stood the test of time.

5:2 Characteristics of Cells

Cells exist in many shapes, such as spherical and cubical. Epithelial cells, cells found in protective layers, are cubical. Some cells, such as the amoeba, have shapes that will change. The surfaces of the cells vary too. Some have rough surfaces; some have extensions and other cell parts coming from their surfaces. A sperm cell has a "tail." Cells also vary in size. Ostrich eggs are as wide as 10 cm; other cells are smaller than half a micrometer. Regardless of shape, surface traits, and size, all cells are alive and are the basic units of life.

Many organisms such as bacteria, amoebae, certain algae, and yeasts are **unicellular** (composed of only one cell) organisms (Figure 5-1). More often, however, an organism is multicellular. A **multicellular** organism is composed of many cells. A full grown human contains trillions of these units of life. Both unicellular organisms and cells of multicellular organisms perform the following functions. Most cells get food for energy, rid themselves of wastes (dangerous by-products of chemical reactions), obtain oxygen, and synthesize (SIHN thuh size) (build up) new living material. They also get necessary chemicals, regulate water balance, react to changes in the environment, and produce other cells.

How are all these life activities and processes carried out? The answer can be found by examining the composition of cells and learning about those parts common to most cells.

REVIEWING YOUR IDEAS

1. Why did Hooke see only the outer walls of cells?
2. Describe the findings of Schleiden, Schwann, and Virchow.
3. State the cell theory.
4. Distinguish between unicellular and multicellular organisms.
5. List some functions of cells.

Dr. Judie Walton,
Lawrence Livermore National Laboratory

John Hansen/OSU

a

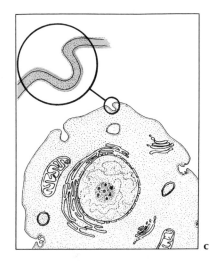

c

b

Chinese hamster ovary cells above

THE CELL AND ITS ENVIRONMENT

Each cell, whether an entire organism or a small part of a larger living system, is in an environment. An amoeba may be in a pond. A kidney cell may be surrounded by blood. Wherever the cell is, it must exchange materials with its moist environment.

5:3 Cell Membrane

Each cell has a boundary which separates it from neighboring cells or its environment. This boundary is called the **cell membrane.** The cell membrane holds the cellular contents together. It also determines the cell's shape and protects the cell.

With a light microscope, the cell membrane appears as a thin, single line. The electron microscope shows the membrane to consist of two layers (Figure 5-2). Analysis shows that the membrane is composed of proteins and lipids in roughly equal amounts. Studies suggest that some of the proteins are partly or totally embedded in the lipid portion. Other proteins seem to lie on the surface of the lipids (Figure 5-3). The position of the proteins and lipids may change slightly from time to time. This model of membrane structure is called the **fluid mosaic model.**

FIGURE 5-2. (a) A scanning electron micrograph of a hamster cell magnified 3500 times shows surface properties of the cell membrane. (b) Magnified 23 000 times, a cell membrane can be seen as two layers. (c) The two layers of the cell membrane are shown in relation to the cell.

A cell is enclosed by a cell membrane.

Folding of the plasma membrane results in increased surface area.

The cell membrane is composed of protein and lipid.

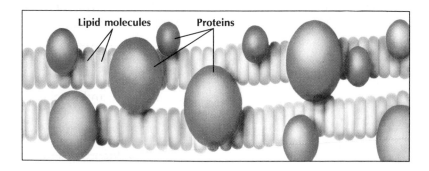

Lipid molecules   Proteins

FIGURE 5-3. The fluid mosaic model of membrane structure shows proteins which move in the layers of lipid molecules.

Membranes of many other cell parts have a structure similar to the cell membrane. The differences may be due to the kinds and locations of proteins in each membrane.

Proteins in the membrane play both a structural and functional role. Many of them are enzymes (Section 4:3). Some act as "markers" that are recognized by chemicals produced by other cells. Others help certain particles pass across the membrane. Some of the openings, or pores, in the membrane seem to be lined with protein.

The membrane is an active part of the cell. Membranes of many cells are very flexible and can change shape because the lipids and proteins of membranes can move. Movement can be studied and observed only with living cells. When cells are removed from an organism and stained for microscopic study, they die. Some cells you will see in the laboratory will be dead. Keep in mind that what is seen in prepared slides is somewhat artificial.

5:4 Diffusion

Besides being a structural boundary, the cell membrane is also the "gatekeeper" of a cell. Many cell functions (Section 5:2) are related to the cell's environment. For example, how do amino acids that the cell combines into protein get into the cell? What is the source of food molecules "burned" for energy within the cell? What happens to the carbon dioxide produced during the "burning" process? What happens to waste products? These and other materials must enter and leave cells through the cell membranes.

It is important that only *certain* materials pass through the cell membrane. Only those materials which must be exchanged with the environment should enter and leave. Unnecessary and harmful substances must be kept out. Important and needed substances must stay in if the cell is to survive. A membrane, such as the cell membrane, which allows only certain materials to pass through it is called a **semipermeable** (sem ih PUR mee uh bul) **membrane.** How do materials pass through a semipermeable membrane?

If you place some crystals of blue copper sulfate in a beaker of water, you will see evidence of an important physical process. At first, the water will be colorless and the crystals will settle to the bottom of the beaker. Several hours later you will see that the water has turned blue and the crystals have disappeared. What has happened?

When copper sulfate is placed in water, its ions begin to separate from each other. The ions have kinetic energy (energy of motion) (Section 4:1). They move about randomly. As a result,

Proteins in the cell membrane play both structural and functional roles.

Cell membranes are active and flexible.

The cell membrane is the "gatekeeper" of the cell.

Amino acids move through the cell membrane from the environment. Food molecules come from the environment. Carbon dioxide and other wastes are given off to the environment.

A semipermeable membrane sometimes is referred to as a selectively or differentially permeable membrane.

The cell membrane is semipermeable.

Suggested demonstration: Show the diffusion of copper sulfate by adding some crystals to a beaker of water. Prepare one beaker before the discussion begins. Compare it to another beaker set up in front of the class. Complete diffusion may require several days depending on amount of copper sulfate added and temperature of water. Set the beakers up where they will remain undisturbed.

Edwin Shay

FIGURE 5-4. Copper sulfate, a blue crystal, diffuses through water distributing copper and sulfate ions evenly throughout. The solution turns bluer as diffusion proceeds.

they collide with each other, the molecules of water, and the sides and bottom of the beaker. Each time a collision occurs, ions bounce off and move in new directions. Random movement results in a uniform distribution of ions throughout the water.

The water appears blue because there are equal numbers of copper ions in any given region at any given time. This random movement of ions (and other particles) caused by kinetic energy is called **diffusion** (dihf YEW zhun). Diffusion results in the spreading out of particles. The particles become distributed evenly in all the available space. After the ions become distributed evenly, they continue to move, but the same number of ions enters a certain area as leaves the area.

Suppose a cell is surrounded by oxygen molecules and the membrane is permeable to oxygen. Because the oxygen molecules are in random motion, they bump against each other and the membrane of the cell. The membrane is permeable to oxygen. Thus, the molecules can pass through it into the cell. As oxygen molecules enter the cell, their movement results in more collisions. Random movement across the membrane occurs in both directions. At first more oxygen molecules enter the cell than leave the cell. Later the oxygen molecules become distributed evenly inside and outside the cell. This balance is called a **dynamic equilibrium** (di NAM ihk·ee kwuh LIHB ree um). After dynamic equilibrium is reached, molecular motion continues, but the number of molecules entering and leaving the cell is equal.

This random movement of molecules shows the importance of diffusion in living systems. Some needed materials may enter a cell by diffusion. Also, as some by-products of cellular activities build up in a cell, their random motion may move them out. *In either case, a substance moves from a region of greater concentration to a region of lesser concentration.* Once equilibrium occurs, the substance remains in equal concentration on both sides of the membrane although movement still occurs.

FIGURE 5-5. Diffusion of oxygen molecules into a cell occurs as the oxygen molecules move from a region of greater concentration to a region of lesser concentration. Dynamic equilibrium results.

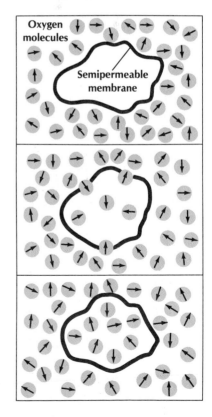

5:5 Osmosis

Water is important to living systems. Water makes up a great part of an organism's mass (seventy percent or more) and is also the major part of each cell's environment. Movement of water into and out of cells is so common that it is given a special name—osmosis (ahs MOH sus). **Osmosis** is the diffusion of water through a semipermeable membrane. Water can pass in either direction across the membrane.

Like diffusion, osmosis is the random movement of particles that results in a state of balance. Water molecules become balanced on both sides of a membrane. The water in a red blood cell is in dynamic equilibrium with the water in the bloodstream. However, if the cell is removed from the blood and placed in pure water, equilibrium is destroyed. The blood cell contains water and other substances, but the surrounding water has no other substances in it. Thus, the concentration of water inside the cell is less than the concentration of water outside the cell. As a result, more water molecules enter the cell than leave the cell. More molecules enter the cell because more hit the membrane from the outside than from the inside. Thus, the cell's water balance is achieved.

Water entering the red blood cell causes it to swell. If equilibrium is not reached, the cell will continue to swell. So much water may enter the cell that it bursts. Therefore, it is important that cells be in osmotic (ahs MAHT ihk) balance with their environment. **Osmotic balance** is a kind of dynamic equilibrium. It occurs when the amount of water entering and leaving a cell is equal.

Elodea (ih LOHD ee uh) is a freshwater plant often seen in home aquariums. The cells of *Elodea* contain water and dissolved materials, but the freshwater environment consists mainly of water molecules. Therefore, in its usual environment, water tends to enter the cells of this plant. Because the pressure of the cell wall balances the pressure of water inside the cell, osmotic balance is reached. Pressure is exerted by the cell wall because the wall is inflexible.

What would happen if an *Elodea* leaf were placed in a saltwater solution? The concentration of water molecules inside the cells would then be greater than outside the cells. Water molecules would leave the cells faster than they would enter. Such loss of water in a cell causes the cell contents to shrink (Figure 5-6) and is called **plasmolysis** (plaz MAHL uh sus). The Elodea plant would appear to be wilted because the cell walls cannot hold up the plant. Prolonged plasmolysis or a large water loss results in death to the cells and can result in death to the entire plant.

Diffusion of water through a semipermeable membrane is called osmosis.

Osmosis results in a state of balance.

FIGURE 5-6. (a) In fresh water, the *Elodea* cells are in osmotic balance with the environment. (b) In salt water, water moves out of the cells. As a result, the contents shrink to the center of the cell.

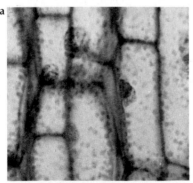

a

Ward's Natural Science Establishment, Inc.

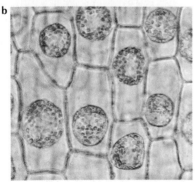

b

Grant Heilman

5:6 Passive Transport

Osmosis of water and diffusion of other particles are important for their passage across the cell membrane. Movement of these materials into and out of the cell is caused by their kinetic energy and random motion. The particles may move through pores in the membrane. The cell has no active role (does no work) in moving the particles. Because no extra energy is needed in diffusion or osmosis, this type of movement is called **passive transport.**

In some cases, even if a particle is in greater concentration on one side of the membrane than the other, it cannot easily cross the membrane by diffusion. It may be too large to get through the pores. Maybe it is not soluble in the lipid part of the membrane. Many such particles, sugars, for example, can move across the membrane by another form of passive transport.

Recall that some of the proteins in the cell membrane play a role in speeding the movement of particles across it (Section 5:3). The models used to explain the movement include proteins called carrier molecules. **Carrier molecules** combine with certain particles and help them to pass across the membrane. Exactly how this process occurs is not known. Evidence indicates that when the particle combines with the carrier, the carrier's shape is changed. The change in shape somehow "pushes" the particle across the membrane (Figure 5-8). Like diffusion, this process involves the movement of substances from regions of greater to lesser concentration. Because a carrier helps (facilitates) the process, it is called **facilitated diffusion.** Glucose enters red blood cells by facilitated diffusion.

Passive transport involves net movement of particles from a region of greater to lesser concentration. The kinetic energy of the particles determines the direction in which the particles move.

FIGURE 5-7. Glucose moves into muscle cells by facilitated diffusion, a kind of passive transport.

In passive transport, no added energy is used in exchanging materials.

Teaching suggestion: Remind students that the shapes of enzymes may change when the enzymes combine with other substances.

In facilitated diffusion, carrier molecules help move particles from a region of greater to lesser concentration.

Facilitated diffusion is sometimes called passive mediated transport or downhill active transport.

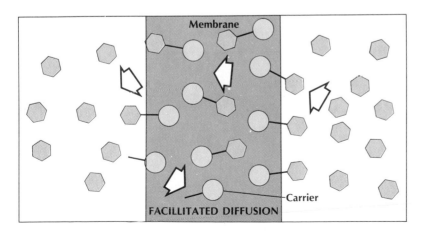

Membrane

Carrier

FACILLITATED DIFFUSION

FIGURE 5-8. In facilitated diffusion, carriers aid (facilitate) the movement of other molecules across the membrane. Here the molecules are being moved from right to left. The carriers then return to move other molecules across.

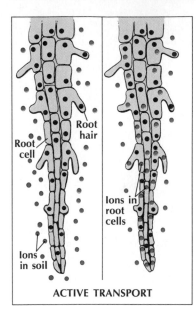

FIGURE 5-9. By active transport, root cells accumulate ions in concentrations greater than in the soil. Active transport requires energy.

Small particles pass through the cell membrane more easily than large particles.

Fat-soluble particles readily pass through the cell membrane.

Cells differ in their permeability.

5:7 Active Transport

Active transport is an "uphill" process in that it requires energy input; passive transport is a "downhill" process in that it does not require added energy.

Sometimes a cell must move particles from a region of lesser to greater concentration. The cell must use energy to counteract the kinetic energy of the particles. (The cell's energy causes the movement of the particles to be less random.) The cell plays an active role and does work. Because extra energy is required to move the particles, this type of movement is called **active transport.** The energy of ATP (Section 4:7) is used. Active transport also involves carrier molecules.

A cell can rid itself of harmful particles by active transport. For example, some cells of the kidney actively transport wastes out. Waste materials must be removed. Some wastes (even in small amounts) would poison an organism. Active transport maintains a greater concentration of the waste materials outside the kidney cells than inside the cells.

Active transport also may work to bring extra particles into the cell. For example, root cells of plants bring in and retain needed mineral ions from the soil. There are more ions in the root cells than in the soil, but ions continue to enter the cells by active transport. Use of energy by these cells prevents the natural diffusion of these ions out of the cells (Figure 5-9).

5:8 Factors of Permeability

The ideas of how transport occurs fit with the model of cell membrane structure (Section 5:3). You can see why membranes are semipermeable. In general, smaller particles pass through the membrane more easily than do large ones. These small particles may pass through the pores or through the spaces between lipid molecules. Substances which are soluble in fat pass through the cell membrane readily. Remember that the membrane contains lipid. Fat-soluble substances may slide between the protein molecules and then dissolve in the lipid portion of the membrane. Later they pass into (or out of) the cell.

Different cells are permeable to different particles. The structure of each type of cell membrane varies depending upon the proteins present. Size of pores may vary and different carriers exist. Also, a given cell may be more or less permeable to a certain particle at different times. Recall that the position of both proteins and lipids may change.

5:9 Endocytosis

Some materials which are too large to pass through the cell membrane by passive or active transport can enter a cell in another way. **Endocytosis** (en duh si TOH sus) is a process in which a cell uses energy to surround and take in large particles.

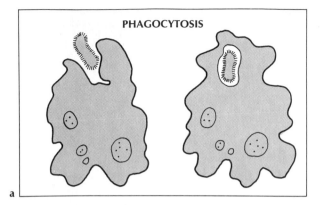

PHAGOCYTOSIS

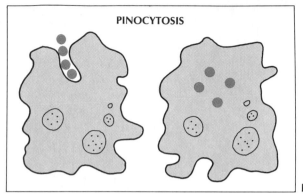

PINOCYTOSIS

a   b

Many unicellular organisms, such as an amoeba, depend on smaller organisms for food (Figure 5-10). After detecting food, an amoeba's cell membrane engulfs (flows over and encloses) the food organism. That portion of the membrane then breaks away and moves to the cell's interior. The food contained within it will later be digested (Section 5:13). The trapping of a solid in this way is called **phagocytosis** (fag uh si TOH sus). Phagocytosis requires energy because work is done in capturing the food and in "repairing" the cell membrane where the part pinched off.

Cells of multicellular organisms also use phagocytosis. For example, certain cells in your blood (white cells) are very much like amoebae. These cells engulf and digest bacteria and other foreign particles which invade the body. Thus, the white cells are a line of defense against disease.

Pinocytosis (pihn uh si TOH sus) is another type of endocytosis. Liquids and small particles are taken into a cell by pinocytosis. Pinocytosis involves the formation of channels through which the liquids and small particles enter a cell. The channeled substance then becomes surrounded by the membrane. The substance is later digested within the cell.

A reverse process is used to rid some cells of wastes or even useful substances needed elsewhere. The substances, enclosed in a membrane, move toward the cell membrane. The two membranes fuse and the materials are expelled from the cell. This process is called **exocytosis** (ek soh si TOH sus).

FIGURE 5-10. (a) In phagocytosis, the cell surrounds the particle or organism being taken in. (b) In pinocytosis, the cell forms channels through which liquids and small particles are taken in.

FIGURE 5-11. Exocytosis is a process in which substances are expelled from a cell.

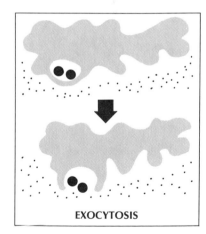

EXOCYTOSIS

REVIEWING YOUR IDEAS

6. What is the cell membrane? Of what is it composed?
7. What is diffusion? What is the name for the balance that results from diffusion?
8. What is osmosis?
9. Compare diffusion and facilitated diffusion.
10. Distinguish between passive and active transport.
11. Distinguish between endocytosis and exocytosis.

6. The cell membrane encloses the cell. It is composed of proteins and lipids.
7. Diffusion is the random movement of particles. Dynamic equilibrium results.
8. Osmosis is the diffusion of water across a semipermeable membrane.
9. Facilitated diffusion involves carrier molecules; diffusion does not. Both result in the movement of a substance across a semipermeable membrane.

10. Cells expend no extra energy in passive transport, but do so in active transport.

11. Large particles are taken into cells by endocytosis and leave by exocytosis.

INSIDE THE CELL

Once substances enter a cell, what does the cell do with them? How and where does the cell assemble new living materials or "burn" food for energy? Where in the cell do wastes arise? The answers are to be found in a study of the cell's interior.

5:10 Protoplasm

Protoplasm is a colloidal substance. That is, it is heterogeneous and contains large particles which are not dissolved but do not settle out.

Protoplasm is the living, jellylike portion of cells.

Two regions of protoplasm exist in most cells—cytoplasm and nucleoplasm.

The composition of protoplasm is constantly changing.

Metabolism is the total of a cell's chemical reactions.

The total of all anabolic reactions, those which involve the building of larger molecules from smaller ones,is called anabolism. The total of all catabolic reactions, those which involve the breaking down of substances,is called catabolism.

The "living stuff" of cells was first described in the 1830's (Section 5:1). Hooke did not see it because the cork cells he saw were not alive. This "living stuff" of cells, the thick, jellylike substance which makes up most of each cell, is **protoplasm** (PROHT uh plaz um).

Protoplasm consists of two regions. Inside the nucleus it is called **nucleoplasm** (NEW klee uh plaz um) and outside the nucleus it is called **cytoplasm** (SITE uh plaz um). These terms are based only on location in the cell.

Protoplasm is about 70 percent water and about 30 percent protein, fats, carbohydrates, and small amounts of mineral ions. The composition of protoplasm varies. Thousands of different substances are brought into or made by a cell and are changed from second to second. A molecule of sugar now existing in one of your cells easily could be converted to carbon dioxide by the time you finish reading this sentence. Protoplasm changes constantly. Chemical reactions within a cell both build up and tear down many complex molecules. The total of the reactions is called **metabolism** (muh TAB uh lihz um).

Metabolism involves a variety of reactions. Some of them, such as dehydration synthesis or hydrolysis (Section 3:17), occur in one step. Often a complex set of reactions is involved in a metabolic change. Think of the many separate steps of cellular respiration (Section 4:8). Photosynthesis (Chapter 21) is another complex set of reactions.

Not all the reactions of metabolism occur in the cytoplasm. Some take place in specialized structures within the cytoplasm.

FIGURE 5-12. An organism's proper functioning is the result of chemical reactions that take place in the protoplasm of the cells.

5:11 Organization in Cells

In Chapter 1, you learned how cells were organized into tissues and organs. But, for cells to perform their many functions, they too must be organized. Certain jobs are carried out by specific cell parts called **organelles** (or guh NELZ), located in the cytoplasm. An organization of parts each doing specific jobs is known as **division of labor**. Division of labor occurs among the cell's organelles. However, a cell survives only if all of its parts work together.

Much of what is known about cell structure has been learned from studies with the electron microscope (Section 2:12). Biochemical analysis also has been used to study the function of cell parts. The descriptions of cell parts given here are based on these methods. Keep in mind that many structures are either not clear or not visible with the light microscope. So do not expect to see all the parts described in this chapter when you view cells in the laboratory.

Organelles are specialized for cellular functions. Division of labor occurs among the organelles.

Division of labor is characteristic of other biological levels of organization.

PEOPLE IN BIOLOGY

As a teenager, Earnest Just left the South with few academic skills other than reading. He completed high school and college in New Hampshire, graduating with honors, and soon began teaching in Washington DC. His interests in cell biology led him to the University of Chicago, where he completed his doctorate in 1916. The rest of his life was devoted to both research in cell biology and embryology and to teaching.

In the 1920's and 1930's, Just took some unpopular stands concerning the roles of various cell parts. He thought that cell membranes were active parts of cells, not just coverings. He also felt that the cytoplasm was as important as the nucleus in determining the cell's activities. (Remember that much of the information we have today about cells was not known at that time.) Because of his unpopular views, even though later shown to be correct, Just and his work were not fully appreciated in his lifetime. He did, however, publish numerous articles and authored two books. In 1915, he was the first person to receive the NAACP Spingarn Medal for "highest achievement. . . . in an honorable field of human endeavor."

(1883-1941)

Earnest Everett Just

FIGURE 5-13. The biggest division among cells is between (a) eukaryotic cells, and (b) prokaryotic cells. Eukaryotic cells have nuclei and membrane-bound organelles. Prokaryotic cells lack these structures.

Audio-Visual Productions   *Carolina Biological Supply Co.*

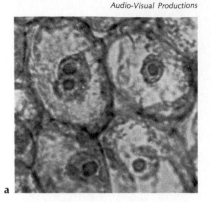
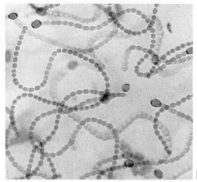

a   b

5:12 Cell Parts of Eukaryotes

Cells of all organisms fall into one of two broad groups. They are either eukaryotes (yew KER ee ohtz) or prokaryotes (proh KER ee ohtz). **Eukaryotes** are cells that are more complex and contain a distinct nucleus surrounded by a membrane. Eukaryotes also contain organelles enclosed by membranes. **Prokaryotes** lack nuclei and other membrane-bound organelles. Bacteria and blue-green algae are prokaryotes. All other cells are eukaryotic. Specialized cell parts presented in this section are parts of eukaryotic cells. Prokaryotes only have a few of these cell parts (with different structures). Structure of prokaryotes will be studied in Chapter 13.

Eukaryotic cells have nuclei and membrane-bound organelles. Prokaryotic cells lack nuclei and membrane-bound organelles.

Blue-green algae and bacteria are prokaryotes. All other cells are eukaryotes.

Mitochondria (singular, mitochondrion) are the "powerhouses" of the cell.

Mitochondria (mite uh KAHN dree uh) are organelles scattered through the cytoplasm. They vary in size, often are cigar-shaped, and have a double-layered membrane with the inner layer folded inward. The folds are called **cristae** (KRIS tee). The central cavity is filled with a fluid (Figure 5-14).

More mitochondria are found in cells requiring great amounts of energy than in other cells. Mitochondria are involved with energy. Because much of aerobic respiration occurs in the mitochondria, they often are called the "powerhouses" of the cell. They are the sites of production of most of the cell's ATP.

FIGURE 5-14. A mitochondrion is a double-membraned organelle which releases energy in a usable form (ATP) in a cell. This mitochondrion is shown magnified about 40 000 times.

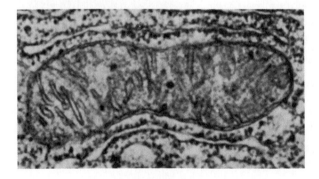

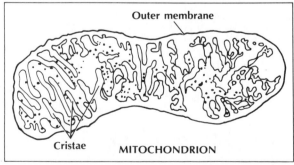

Outer membrane

Cristae   MITOCHONDRION

Endoplasmic reticulum (en duh PLAZ mihk · rih TIHK yuh lum) is a network of fluid-filled, tubelike structures found in most eukaryotic cells. It is often called ER. These tubes connect with one another, often ending in "blind alleys." In some cells, portions of the network are connected with the nuclear membrane. The endoplasmic reticulum acts as a cellular "subway" or "canal system" that transports materials within cells.

Some of the cell's ER has a smooth surface and is called *smooth ER*. The structure of the ER's membrane is similar to that of the cell membrane. Some of the proteins in smooth ER membrane function as enzymes needed for making lipids (Section 3:14). Ribosomes associate as polyribosomes or polysomes.

Ribosomes (RI buh sohmz) are tiny spherical organelles most often located on the surface of ER. (Such ER, because of its "bumpy" surface, is called *rough ER*.) Some ribosomes are scattered through the cytoplasm. These bodies, composed mainly of RNA, are the sites of protein synthesis. Proteins may pass from the surface of the ribosomes into the endoplasmic reticulum for transport within the cell.

Golgi (GAWL jee) **bodies** are structures in the cytoplasm that usually consist of a stack of flattened, slightly curved tubes with saclike ends. When seen in a section, Golgi bodies resemble ER except that the tubes of the Golgi do not appear to be connected to each other. Golgi bodies are involved in the storage and **secretion** (sih KREE shun) (pouring out) of chemicals from the cell. These chemicals may affect other parts of the body or other organisms. Digestive juices are cell secretions that affect other parts of the organism. A snake's venom is a secretion that affects another organism.

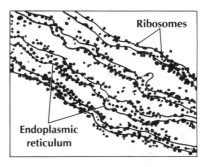

FIGURE 5-15. Cellular materials are thought to be transported in the tubes of endoplasmic reticulum. Proteins are synthesized on ribosomes. This ER is shown magnified about 40 000 times.

Golgi bodies function in the storage and secretion of cellular chemicals.

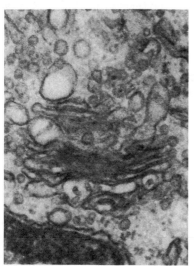

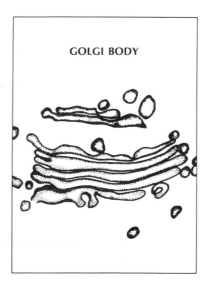

GOLGI BODY

FIGURE 5-16. Golgi bodies help manufacture and store molecules which later are secreted from cells. Golgi bodies are shaped like stacked plates. This Golgi body is shown magnified about 54 000 times.

FIGURE 5-17. (a) Most vacuoles function in storage. In this cell, one vacuole takes up most of the space inside. (b) Lysosomes contain chemicals which hydrolyze food molecules. These lysosomes are shown magnified 25 000 times.

Barbara Stevens

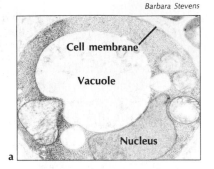

Barbara Stevens

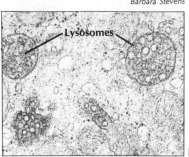

a

b

Vacuoles may be used for storage of materials.

Vacuoles (VAK yuh wohlz) are clear, fluid-filled sacs within cells. Many vacuoles are used for the storage of food, water, and minerals. In some plant cells the vacuole may be the prominent structure. Certain unicellular water organisms have vacuoles which serve as pumps for removing excess water. Such water-removing structures are called **contractile** (kun TRAK tul) **vacuoles** (Section 18:7).

Lysosomes contain enzymes which hydrolyze large molecules.

Lysosomes (LI suh sohmz) are small, spherical organelles that contain digestive enzymes. They are found mostly in animal cells. The enzymes break down large molecules brought into the cell by phagocytosis.

Lysosomes sometimes digest other cell parts. "Worn out" cell parts are broken down and removed from cells. Also, some parts may be digested to provide energy during starvation. If lysosomes break, the enzymes may even destroy the cell itself. "Worn out" cells may be removed in this way. Normally, the cell is protected from the digestive enzymes by the lysosome's membrane.

FIGURE 5-18. Microfilaments are threadlike structures composed of protein. These bundles of microfilaments are shown magnified about 11 500 times.

Microfilaments are long, thin threadlike structures that have been found in a variety of cells. They are composed of protein and are involved with movement. Contraction of skeletal muscle (Chapter 28) depends upon microfilament movement. They also function in other ways such as locomotion of an amoeba or in causing changes in a cell's shape.

Microtubules are long, thin structures that provide support and shape to the cell. They are hollow rods composed of protein. Often microtubules are found just beneath the cell membrane where they help maintain the cell's structure. Microtubules also help with the movement of cell parts within the cell. They are important structures in moving genetic material in cell division (Section 6:6) and also they are involved in locomotion of some cells (Section 5:14).

Some microtubules are permanent parts of cells. Most are built up from protein within the cell when needed. They are then torn down and their protein can be reused later in the formation of other microtubules. Microtubules are composed of a protein called tubulin. Their rapid assembly and breakdown account for quick changes in cell shape. In plant cells, microtubules control the orientation of cellulose fibers as new cell walls are built.

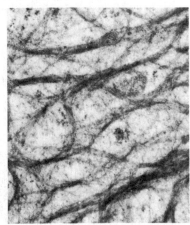

Dr. Judie Walton,
Lawrence Livermore National Laboratory

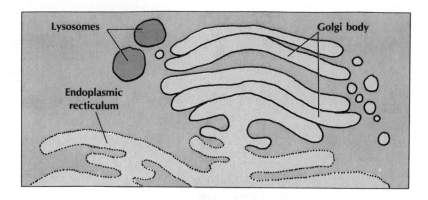

FIGURE 5-19. Because endoplasmic reticulum, Golgi bodies, and lysosomes work together, they are sometimes thought of as a complex.

5:13 Interaction of Cell Parts

Study of how lysosomes do their job shows the interdependence of cell parts. The enzymes in lysosomes are proteins and are manufactured on ribosomes. From there they may pass into the rough endoplasmic reticulum. From time to time, the endoplasmic reticulum may form temporary connections with the Golgi bodies. Thus, the enzymes can pass from the endoplasmic reticulum to the Golgi bodies. The enzymes accumulate in the ends of the Golgi body tubes which enlarge and pinch off as lysosomes.

Cell parts interact in carrying out cell processes.

Enzymes in lysosomes are manufactured on ribosomes. They travel to the Golgi bodies via the ER.

When a cell traps food by phagocytosis (Section 5:9), it enters the cell in a food vacuole. (The membrane of the vacuole came from the cell membrane.) The food vacuole may fuse with a lysosome and the enzymes in the lysosome digest the food into small molecules. The small molecules may then diffuse across the membrane of the vacuole into the cytoplasm. They can be used for energy or as building blocks of cell parts. Undigested particles remain in the vacuole and leave the cell by exocytosis (Section 5:9).

Secretion of chemicals from the cell also involves interdependence of cell parts. Many secretions are proteins which may come to the Golgi bodies from the ribosomes through the endoplasmic reticulum. In the Golgi body other chemicals such as carbohydrates may be added to the protein. These secretions then may be pinched off the ends of Golgi bodies in small packets. The packets then can fuse with the cell membrane and pour their contents out of the cell.

Packets of secretions are formed from the Golgi bodies.

5:14 Other Eukaryotic Cell Parts

The cell parts studied so far are found in most eukaryotic cells. Some other parts, though, are found in only some kinds of cells.

Grant Heilman

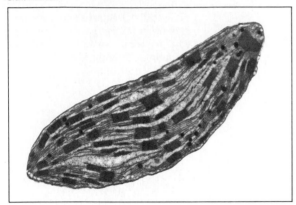

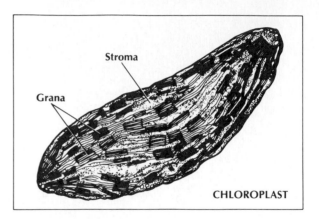

FIGURE 5-20. Chloroplasts are organelles that function in photosynthesis. This chloroplast is shown magnified about 25 000 times.

Photosynthesis occurs in chloroplasts.

Leukoplasts store starch. Chromoplasts contain pigments.

Cell walls support and give shape to cells of algae, fungi, and plants.

Centrioles function in the division of animal cells.

FIGURE 5-21. Centrioles are found mostly in animal cells and are involved in cell division. Centrioles exist in pairs. This pair of centrioles is shown magnified about 135 000 times.

Green plant cells and most algae contain structures called **plastids** (PLAS tudz). The most common plastids are **chloroplasts** (KLOR uh plastz) which contain the chlorophyll needed for photosynthesis. A chloroplast has many stacks of platelike structures called **grana** (GRAY nuh) (Figure 5-20) located in a liquid. The liquid is called **stroma**. Light energy for photosynthesis is trapped by the grana. Glucose is made in the stroma (Chapter 21).

Other types of plastids contain pigments which aid chlorophyll in trapping solar energy. Some plastids make and store starch and fats.

Cells of plants, fungi, and algae have a boundary, called the **cell wall,** outside the cell membrane. The cell wall is composed of cellulose or other carbohydrates (Section 3:13). A cell wall gives structure and shape to individual cells and helps support a plant so that it grows upright.

Cells of animals and of some algae and fungi contain a pair of organelles called **centrioles** (SEN tree olz) which play an important role in cell division. Centrioles come in pairs and are found near the nucleus. Each centriole is composed of nine sets of microtubules (Section 5:12) arranged to form a circle. Each set is

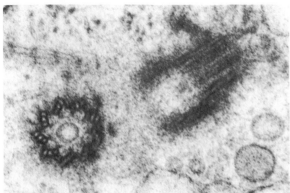

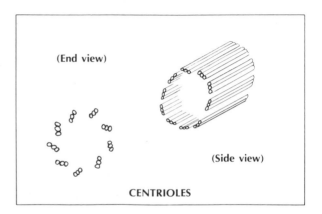

Carey Callaway/Center for Disease Control

Barbara Stevens

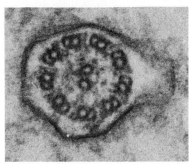

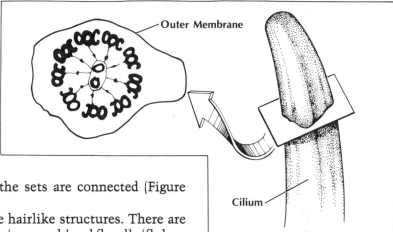

Outer Membrane

Cilium

composed of three tubules and the sets are connected (Figure 5-21).

Many cells have one or more hairlike structures. There are two kinds of these structures, cilia (SIHL ee uh) and flagella (fluh JEL uh). In general, **cilia** are much shorter than flagella and appear in greater numbers. **Flagella** are longer structures and usually appear singly or in pairs. Both cilia and flagella are similar in structure to a centriole except that they have two microtubules in the center of the circle. Also, each outer set contains only two tubules. An extension of the cell membrane forms the border of cilia and flagella. Cilia and flagella are attached to the interior of a cell by a **basal body** which has the same structure. New cilia and flagella are produced from the basal bodies after cell division occurs.

Movement of cilia and flagella by unicellular organisms results in locomotion of the organism. These structures also are present on some cells of plants and animals. A sperm cell, for example, moves by means of a flagellum. Also, cells lining your windpipe have cilia. The cells do not move but the movement of the cilia helps filter the air you breathe.

FIGURE 5-22. Cilia are movable hairlike structures that usually are smaller and exist in greater numbers than flagella. This cilium in cross section is shown magnified about 105 000 times.

Cilia and flagella aid locomotion in unicellular organisms and some specialized cells of multicellular organisms.

TABLE 5-1. EUKARYOTIC CELL STRUCTURES		
Structure	Found in Cells of	Main Functions
CELL WALL	Plants; algae; fungi	Support; protection
CELL MEMBRANE	All organisms	Boundary; "gatekeeper"
CYTOPLASM	All organisms	Site of most metabolism
CENTRIOLES	Animals; some algae and fungi	Cell reproduction
CHLOROPLASTS	Plants; algae	Photosynthesis
ENDOPLASMIC RETICULUM	All organisms	Intracellular transport
GOLGI BODIES	All organisms	Storage; secretion
LYSOSOMES	Mainly animals	Intracellular digestion
MICROFILAMENTS	All organisms	Movement
MICROTUBULES	All organisms	Support; movement
MITOCHONDRIA	All organisms	Cellular respiration
NUCLEOLUS	All organisms	Production of ribosomes
NUCLEUS	All organisms	Control; heredity
RIBOSOMES	All organisms	Protein synthesis
VACUOLES	All organisms	Storage

Barbara Stevens

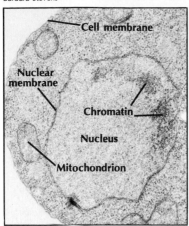

FIGURE 5-23. The nucleus is the cell's control center. It contains the cell's coded information. This cell has a large central nucleus.

12. Jellylike substance in cells. Cell reactions occur in constantly changing protoplasm.

13. Total of cell's reactions.

14. Each cell part has special functions. Yes, e.g., each organ has special functions.

15. Prokaryotes lack nuclei and membrane-bound organelles characteristic of eukaryotes.

16. The nucleus is the control center of the cell, separated by the nuclear membrane.

FIGURE 5-24. To separate cell parts, broken cells are put in tubes that are loaded into a special container called a rotor. The rotor is then put inside the centrifuge and spun at high speeds.

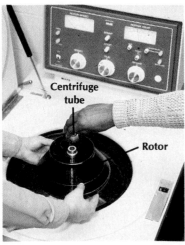

Lightforce

5:15 The Nucleus

Almost every kind of eukaryotic cell contains a central, spherical body called the **nucleus.** The nucleus is the control center of the cell. It is separated from the rest of the cell by a **nuclear membrane** which is a double membrane. Definite **pores** exist in this double membrane. Certain materials may pass through these pores when they travel between nucleus and cytoplasm. Other materials move from the nucleus to the cytoplasm by way of the endoplasmic reticulum or through the membrane. Inside the nuclear membrane is nucleoplasm (Section 5:10).

Within the nucleus of most cells are one or more smaller bodies called **nucleoli** (new KLEE uh li). Nucleoli are regions that make the RNA of ribosomes. The role of the nucleus in heredity will be studied in Chapter 6.

REVIEWING YOUR IDEAS

12. What is protoplasm? Why is it called "living stuff"?
13. What is metabolism?
14. How is division of labor in cells accomplished by cell parts? Is there division of labor in organisms other than that in cells? Explain.
15. How are prokaryotes and eukaryotes different?
16. What are the general functions of a nucleus? What separates the nucleus from the rest of the cell?

ADVANCES IN BIOLOGY

5:16 Cell Fractionation

Microscopes can give a picture of the structure of organelles, membranes and other cell parts. The functions of the cell parts are determined by biochemical tests performed on the separated cell parts. How are the parts of a cell separated?

Separation of cell parts, **cell fractionation**, is a process that makes use of the differences in cell parts. The most important differences in the parts are size and density.

To separate cell parts, whole cells or tissues are first ground up in a blender. This step breaks down the cell membranes (and cell walls, if present) releasing the inside cell parts. The cell parts and liquid are put in a tube that is spun at high speed in an instrument called a **centrifuge**. The spinning of the centrifuge puts a downward force on the cell parts within the tube. Depending on how fast the centrifuge is run, the force can be thousands of times the force of gravity. This spinning forces larger parts to the bottom of the tube; smaller parts remain higher in the tube. Certain parts can be removed in the liquid and spinning can be repeated at various speeds to separate other cell parts by size in this way.

Sometimes cell parts that need to be separated may be the same size. Particles that are the same size can be separated by their densities. **Density** is the amount of matter that something contains in a certain volume. Nuclei, for example, are more dense than mitochondria. They contain more matter per volume. A simple and rapid separation method makes use of the buoyant (floating) properties of these cell structures.

The principle can be shown very simply using materials in your home. Cooking oil, water, and syrup are liquids of different densities. The oil is the least dense; the syrup is the most dense. If oil and syrup are in a clear glass or tube, the oil will float on top of the syrup. The formation of the two layers is chiefly the result of their different densities. If water (colored with food coloring) is poured gently over the oil, it will sink to a position between the oil and the syrup. These liquids could mix with each other, but if each is carefully layered on the next, they will form separate bands according to their densities.

To separate cell parts by density, the parts are layered on top of a centrifuge tube that contains liquids of different densities in layers or steps. When the tubes are spun in the centrifuge, the cell parts move into the liquids stopping at the layer that is more dense than they are. For example, if nuclei and mitochondria are being separated, nuclei will sink to the bottom and mitochondria will float on top of the most dense layer. There are two different forces responsible for this separation. One force is gravitational force (enhanced by the spinning centrifuge) directed toward the bottom of the tube. The other force is upward buoyancy which causes the less dense cell parts to float. The spinning of the centrifuge speeds the cell part separation. Because the tube contains zones or steps of different density, the tube with the liquids is called a **step density gradient** (GRAYD ee unt).

Sometimes these methods are not adequate to separate cell parts having similar sizes and similar densities. For example, mitochondria and lysosomes differ only slightly in density and are similar in size. Another kind of gradient is used in these cases. A **linear density gradient** varies, increasing density from one end to the other, but not in discrete steps. Because each position in the tube has a different density, cell structures with different densities will end up at different positions in the tube after spinning. Each can be removed from the tube without mixing, and in this way, pure samples of cell parts can be obtained.

These techniques were developed in the 1950's and 1960's and are still vital to the study of cell parts. Once separated the cell parts can be analyzed by measuring the content of enzymes and other chemicals. Their reactions may be studied, also.

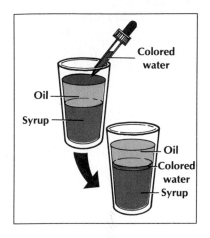

FIGURE 5-25. Liquids of different densities will form bands as they separate.

FIGURE 5-26. Step density gradients separate particles of similar size that have different densities. Linear density gradients separate particles of similar size and similar density.

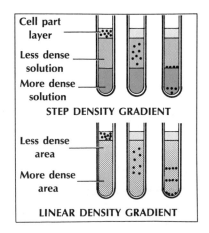

All Chapter Review answers and additional chapter teaching suggestions are provided in the Teacher's Guide at the front of this text.

CHAPTER REVIEW

SUMMARY

1. Beginning with Robert Hooke's discovery of the cell, other discoveries led to the development of the cell theory.
2. Cells can exist in many sizes and shapes and can exist independently as organisms or as parts of multicellular organisms.
3. Cells have a cell membrane which provides structure and regulates the passage of materials between the cell and its environment.
4. Water enters and leaves a cell by osmosis, a special type of diffusion. When dynamic equilibrium is reached, the number of molecules entering and leaving a cell is equal.
5. Materials can pass through a cell membrane by active or passive transport.
6. Size and solubility in fat are among the factors that influence whether particles will pass through a cell membrane.
7. Some cells obtain very large particles from their environment by endocytosis. Certain particles leave a cell by exocytosis.
8. Protoplasm is the site of much of a cell's metabolism.
9. Prokaryotes are cells that lack a definite nucleus and most of the special cell parts.
10. Specialized cell parts carry out most of the functions of eukaryotic cells.
11. Most eukaryotes have cell parts such as nuclei, mitochondria, endoplasmic reticulum, ribosomes, Golgi bodies, vacuoles, and lysosomes.
12. Cell parts not found in all eukaryotes are plastids, centrioles, cilia, and flagella.
13. The nucleus is the control center of the cell.
14. Various techniques of cell fractionation are used to separate cell parts. Once the parts are separated, their functions and other properties can be determined by biochemical methods.

LANGUAGE OF BIOLOGY

active transport
basal body
carrier molecule
cell
cell fractionation
cell membrane
cell theory
cell wall
centrifuge
centriole
cilia
density
diffusion
endocytosis
endoplasmic reticulum
eukaryote
exocytosis
facilitated diffusion
flagella
Golgi body
grana

linear density
    gradient
lysosome
metabolism
microfilament
microtubule
mitochondrion
nucleus
organelle
osmosis
passive transport
phagocytosis
pinocytosis
plastid
prokaryote
protoplasm
ribosome
step density
    gradient
stroma
vacuole

CHECKING YOUR IDEAS

On a separate paper, match the phrase from the left column with the proper term from the right column. Do not write in this book.

1. random movement of particles
2. specialization of parts
3. controls heredity
4. requires energy
5. semipermeable
6. engulfing of solid materials
7. diffusion of water
8. cell containing many organelles
9. total of cell's reactions
10. all organisms are composed of cells

a. active transport
b. cell membrane
c. cell theory
d. diffusion
e. division of labor
f. eukaryote
g. metabolism
h. nucleus
i. osmosis
j. phagocytosis

CHAPTER REVIEW

EVALUATING YOUR IDEAS

1. Why is the cell theory important?
2. Compare the functions of cells of unicellular and multicellular organisms.
3. How is the cell membrane important to the cell and its environment? What might happen to a cell if the membrane were permeable to all molecules?
4. Why is osmosis important to living things?
5. How does carbon dioxide travel between cells and blood?
6. How can a certain unicellular alga accumulate a concentration of potassium ions a thousand times greater than that of the surrounding water?
7. Why can passive transport be considered a "downhill" passage of materials? Why is active transport an "uphill" passage?
8. What are some factors that determine whether a particle will pass through a cell membrane?
9. Relate the structure of the cell membrane to the fact that cells differ in permeability.
10. Distinguish phagocytosis and pinocytosis.
11. Give the main functions of each of the following cell parts. Tell the kind of cell(s) in which they are usually found.
    - (a) cell wall
    - (b) centriole
    - (c) chloroplast
    - (d) cilia, flagella
    - (e) ER
    - (f) Golgi body
    - (g) lysosome
    - (h) microfilaments
    - (i) microtubules
    - (j) mitochondrion
    - (k) nucleolus
    - (l) nucleus
    - (m) ribosome
    - (n) vacuole
12. Why are chemicals inside a lysosome instead of being free in the cytoplasm?
13. Distinguish between rough and smooth ER.
14. Explain the means by which a substance might be produced, stored, and then secreted from a cell.
15. How are cell parts isolated for study? How are their functions determined?

APPLYING YOUR IDEAS

1. *Paramecium* is a single-celled, freshwater organism. Its cytoplasm contains water and many other substances. What "problem" does a paramecium have? What structure might a paramecium have to deal with this problem? What might happen to a paramecium in salt water? Why?
2. Oxygen from blood continually moves into cells by diffusion. What explains that the net movement of oxygen is always much greater into the cell? (Hint: What happens to the oxygen inside the cell?)
3. Why have scientists been unable to synthesize protoplasm in the laboratory?
4. Why are there many mitochondria in a muscle cell?
5. Hormones are chemicals secreted by specialized gland cells. Name a structure which would be abundant in these cells. Explain.

EXTENDING YOUR IDEAS

1. Prepare a report, with drawings, on five different specialized animal or plant cells.
2. Physicians often conduct a test called a basal metabolism test. What is the purpose of this test and how is it carried out?
3. Build a model of a "typical" cell. Is there really such a cell?

SUGGESTED READINGS

Allison, A. C., *Lysosomes*, 2nd ed., Carolina Biological Reader, Burlington, NC, Carolina Biological Supply Co., 1978.

Cook, G.M.S., *The Golgi Apparatus*, 2nd ed. Carolina Biological Reader, Burlington, NC, Carolina Biological Supply Co., 1980.

Dustin, Pierre, "Microtubules." *Scientific American*, August, 1980.

Additional student readings and suggested teacher readings are provided in the Teacher's Guide.

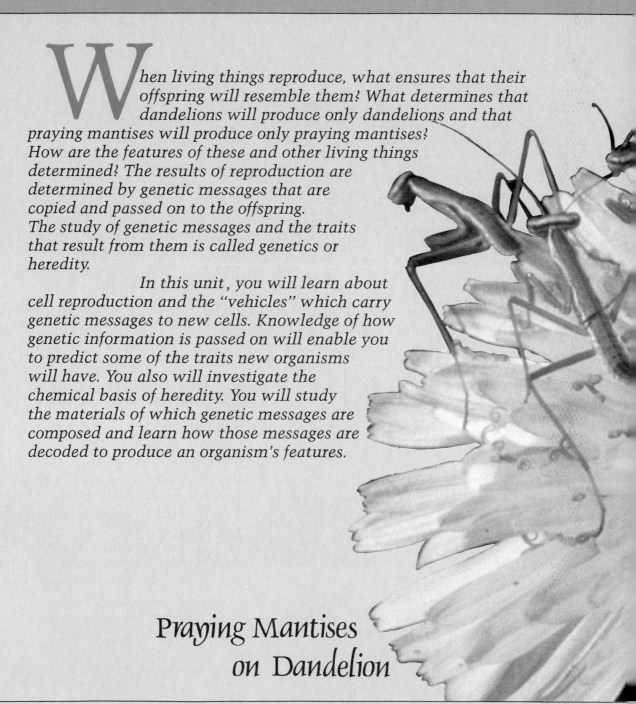

HEREDITY

When living things reproduce, what ensures that their offspring will resemble them? What determines that dandelions will produce only dandelions and that praying mantises will produce only praying mantises? How are the features of these and other living things determined? The results of reproduction are determined by genetic messages that are copied and passed on to the offspring. The study of genetic messages and the traits that result from them is called genetics or heredity.

In this unit, you will learn about cell reproduction and the "vehicles" which carry genetic messages to new cells. Knowledge of how genetic information is passed on will enable you to predict some of the traits new organisms will have. You also will investigate the chemical basis of heredity. You will study the materials of which genetic messages are composed and learn how those messages are decoded to produce an organism's features.

Praying Mantises
on Dandelion

Roger K. Burnard

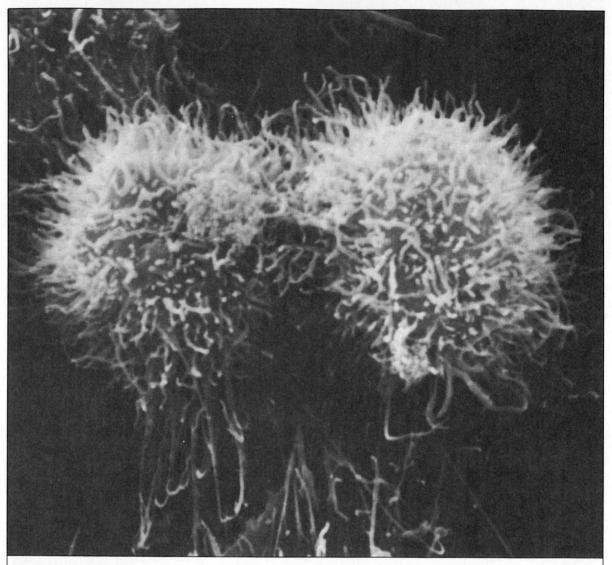

New cells are produced by other living cells. Dividing human body cells are shown here magnified about 6400 times. The projections on the cell surfaces are extensions of the cytoplasm. How do cells divide? Are all cells produced in the same way? How do body cells differ from sperm and eggs? Are all cells produced by cell division identical to the parent cell? What are some of the ways cell division is important in your body?

Introduction: As you begin this chapter, pose this question: Will microorganisms appear in a solution of sugar water? Divide the class into teams and challenge each team to predict the answer and to design an experiment to test their prediction. Then provide the sugar water and necessary equipment. Remind students about variable factors and controlled experiments. As the experiments are in progress, proceed with the chapter. Students may change their approach and/or their interpretation of the original question based on what they are learning. After several days of observation, have students report to the class on their experiments. Encourage them and other members of the class to be critical, but remind them that the debate about spontaneous generation lasted several hundred years.

THE CELLULAR BASIS OF HEREDITY

Chapter 6 treats the development of the theory of biogenesis and presents and analyzes mitosis, meiosis, and fertilization.

Aristotle (AR uhs taht uhl), 384-322 B.C., a Greek philosopher and scientist, often is called the "Father of Biology." He made important studies in anatomy and classification. Other scientists thought his reports to be true without questioning, but some of his findings and conclusions were not correct.

One of Aristotle's mistaken beliefs concerned the origin of organisms. He thought that some forms of life could be produced from nonliving sources. For example, Aristotle believed that eels came from the slime at the bottom of rivers or oceans. Other popular notions included the idea that maggots were produced from decaying meats and that a horse hair in water became a worm.

Today most people know that such beliefs are false. Why were they accepted as facts for so long? Careful observation and experimentation were not used to test these ideas. Eels were found in bodies of water and were slimy like the bottom of an ocean or river. But no one had ever studied their origin carefully. People just concluded that eels came from the slime.

GOAL: You will gain an understanding of past beliefs concerning how living things reproduce, and present knowledge of cellular reproduction.

Long ago, many biologists thought that some living things were produced from nonliving things.

Lack of experimentation led to false beliefs about reproduction.

LIFE FROM LIFE

6:1 Spontaneous Generation: Prologue

The concept that living things come from nonliving things is called **spontaneous** (spahn TAY nee us) **generation.** For hundreds of years, people believed that decaying meat produced maggots.

Spontaneous generation also is called abiogenesis.

Spontaneous generation is the idea that living things can come from nonliving things.

97

FIGURE 6-1. Redi showed in a controlled experiment that maggots are not spontaneously generated from decaying meat.

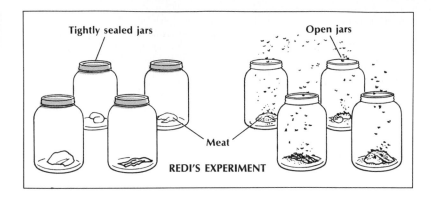

REDI'S EXPERIMENT

Teaching suggestion: Have students distinguish between the control group and experimental group in Redi's experiment.

Redi assumed that maggots are produced by flies.

A controlled experiment was done to learn about the origin of maggots.

Redi's experiment did not remove all doubt about spontaneous generation.

Francesco Redi (RAY dee), an Italian physician and biologist, was not convinced that spontaneous generation occurred. Thus, he tried to show that maggots come from other living things. In 1668, he performed a series of important experiments. Redi noticed that adult flies hovered over decaying meat. He assumed that the flies produced the maggots and that if the flies could be kept away from the meat, no maggots would appear.

To test his hypothesis, Redi prepared eight jars with various types of meat. He left four of the jars open and sealed the other four jars. After a few days, the open jars were covered with maggots and swarming with adult flies, but the sealed jars revealed no life at all! Redi then put some maggots in a container and observed them. He noted that each maggot went through a series of changes and turned into an adult fly.

What was the importance of Redi's investigations? By carrying out controlled experiments, Redi showed that maggots do not come from decaying meat. He did not, however, completely disprove the concept of spontaneous generation. His work was not enough to convince those who accepted the

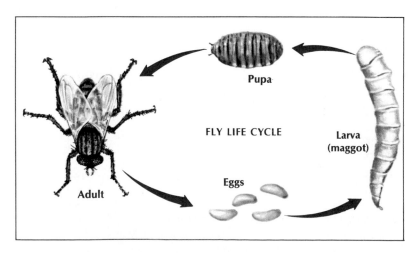

FLY LIFE CYCLE

Adult

Pupa

Larva (maggot)

Eggs

FIGURE 6-2. Maggots develop from fly eggs. The maggots go through a pupal stage during which they change. They emerge from the pupal stage as flies.

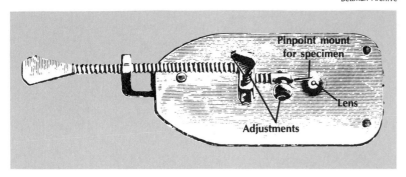

Bettman Archive

FIGURE 6-3. This paddlelike instrument is one of the many homemade microscopes made by Anton van Leeuwenhoek. Specimens were mounted on the pin-point and enlarged with the lens. This drawing is ⅓ larger than the actual microscope.

concept, but it began the downfall of the idea. Redi was the first to use experimental procedures to test the hypothesis. Thus, he opened the door for further investigation of the problem.

6:2 Convincing Evidence

The issue of spontaneous generation of maggots and other familiar organisms gradually became settled. But, in 1675, Anton van Leeuwenhoek (LAY vun hook) discovered the world of microorganisms. A major event in itself, this discovery renewed the battle between those who believed in spontaneous generation and those who did not. These small organisms had never been seen before, so many people were quick to conclude that they were spontaneously generated.

The debate continued for almost two hundred years. Some experiments seemed to favor spontaneous generation. Others did not. Many experiments tested whether microorganisms would appear in nutrient solutions called **infusions** (ihn FYEW zhunz). Slight differences in the experiments affected the results. If air were present in the flasks containing the infusions, microorganisms usually appeared after several days. If no air were present, no life appeared. Therefore, those who believed in spontaneous generation concluded that air was an essential ingredient in spontaneous generation. They would not accept the results of their opponents' experiments.

Louis Pasteur (1822-1895), a great French scientist, opposed spontaneous generation. From earlier experiments, he believed that microorganisms came from special cells called **spores**. He thought that these small spores were carried on dust particles in the air. He believed that spores were inactive in the air but became active when materials needed for life were available (as in an infusion).

To disprove spontaneous generation, Pasteur had to keep spores from entering his infusions. Pasteur's opponents insisted that air must be present. Thus, he was faced with the problem of letting air into an infusion but keeping spores out.

Pasteur's knowledge of microorganisms and spores came from his work with fermentation. Before these experiments, Pasteur already had learned to isolate and study spores from the air. He considered his important experiments concerning spontaneous generation a digression from his other research.

Leeuwenhoek's discovery of microorganisms revived the debate about spontaneous generation.

Teaching suggestion: You may wish to have students report to the class on the work of John Needham and Lazzaro Spallanzani. Needham and Spallanzani conducted experiments with contradictory results.

FIGURE 6-4. These spores from a fungus are cells carried in the air. The spores are shown here magnified about 1800 times.

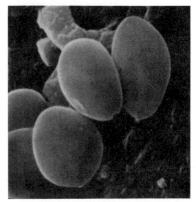

Dr. Judie Walton,
Lawrence Livermore National Laboratory

FIGURE 6-5. Pasteur used S-shaped flasks in his experiments to disprove spontaneous generation. Although air entered the flasks, spores were trapped in the curved neck. No growth occurred in the broth.

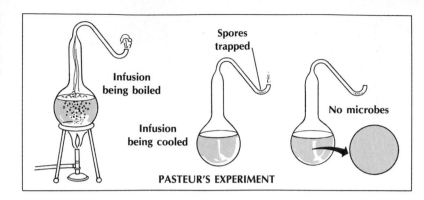

PASTEUR'S EXPERIMENT

In an earlier experiment, Pasteur exposed infusions to air at high altitudes and only one of 20 infusions showed life. However, his opponents argued that the infusions had not been continuously exposed to air.

Pasteur devised an experiment which allowed air to enter an infusion but kept spores out.

Pasteur devised an experiment which allowed infusions to be in contact with air. He prepared infusions and boiled them thoroughly in flasks. The flasks were specially made, and had long, S-shaped necks (Figure 6-5). The boiling killed any organisms which were present in the infusion. Also, the steam produced destroyed any spores clinging to the glass. Air entering the flask would contain dust and spores, but the spores would be trapped in the curved portion of the neck. Thus the infusion would remain **sterile**, free of life, for a long time.

Pasteur's prediction proved to be correct—the infusions remained clear. As a result, the major objection of his critics was overcome. He showed that microorganisms, like other organisms, did not come from nonliving things, and a belief held for over two thousand years was finally disproved.

Pasteur's experiment showed that microorganisms, like other organisms, are produced from other living things.

In this way, a principle which applied to all living things was established. Biologists refer to this idea as the **theory of biogenesis** (bi oh JEN uh sus): *at the present time and under present conditions on Earth, all living things are produced from other living things.*

The theory of biogenesis: Living things are produced only by other living things.

Pasteur's convincing evidence about the reproduction of living things appeared in 1864. Recall that the announcement came in 1858 that all cells come from other cells (Section 5:1). These two discoveries were each important as biological principles, but more important, they fit together. Cells are the basic units of structure and function, and all cells are reproduced from other cells. Thus, all life must come from living things.

The cell theory and the theory of biogenesis fit together.

1. The idea was not tested.
2. Open jars served as a control. Observations of fly development supported the idea that maggots come from flies, not decaying meat.
3. The S-shaped flask allowed air to enter but trapped spores.
4. At the present time and under present conditions, all living things are produced from other living things.

REVIEWING YOUR IDEAS

1. Why was the idea of spontaneous generation believed for a long time?
2. Why did Redi seal only some of the jars in his test? Why did he observe fly development?
3. Why did Pasteur use a flask with an S-shaped neck?
4. State the theory of biogenesis.

REPRODUCTION OF CELLS

6:3 Importance of the Nucleus

Facts being gathered about cells led biologists to believe that the cell is the basis of heredity. They correctly assumed that a study of cell reproduction would lead them to a better understanding of reproduction in general. The discovery of special dyes and stains aided microscopic study of cell division. Viewing of living cells became easier as better microscopes were made.

It soon was evident that the nucleus has a major role during cell reproduction. Almost every kind of eukaryotic cell contains a **nucleus** (Section 5:15). The nucleus is the control center of the cell. Prokaryotic cells, although they do not have nuclei, do have nuclear material.

The main substance located in the nucleus is called **chromatin** (KROH mut un). Although chromatin structure has been studied for many years, it is still a current area of biochemical research. Chromatin appears as a mass of material. However, during cell division, chromatin appears as distinct bodies called **chromosomes** (KROH muh sohmz). Chromosomes are composed of **nucleoprotein** (new klee oh PROH teen), a combination of nucleic acid (DNA) and protein. DNA is the material which carries the "genetic code." Therefore the nucleus is important in heredity.

Each time a cell divides, the chromosomes must be replicated and the copies must be distributed to each new cell. A process in eukaryotes in which chromosomes are replicated and distributed to new nuclei is called **mitosis** (mi TOH sus). Nuclear replication and division and cytoplasm division often occur at the same time. However, mitosis refers only to the replication and division of the nuclear material.

The nucleus is the control center of eukaryotic cells.

The term chromosome means "colored body," so named because of its appearance when stained.

When cells reproduce, chromatin can be seen as distinct chromosomes.

The term mitosis comes from the Greek word *mitos* meaning "thread."

Mitosis involves the replication of chromosomes and their equal distribution to new nuclei.

Sometimes mitosis is called karyokinesis. Cytokinesis is the term applied to the division of the rest of the cell.

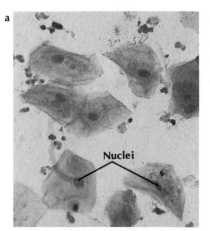

Nuclei

Tom Stack and Associates

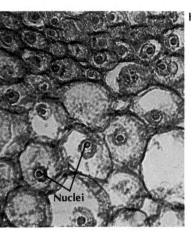

Nuclei

Audio-Visual Productions

Shown in photos: a) human cheek (squamous epithelial) cells b) parenchyma cells

FIGURE 6-6. (a) These animal cells and (b) plant cells show cell nuclei clearly. The main substance in a cell nucleus is chromatin.

Roger K. Burnard

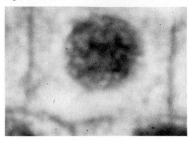

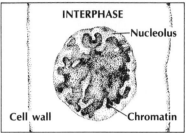

INTERPHASE

Nucleolus

Cell wall

Chromatin

FIGURE 6-7. Although they appear inactive, interphase cells are actively taking in and making materials. Chromosomes are not distinct in interphase but are undergoing duplication.

FIGURE 6-8. In prophase, the nuclear membrane disappears and chromosomes become visible.

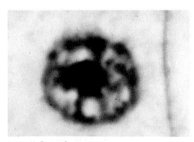

Roger K. Burnard

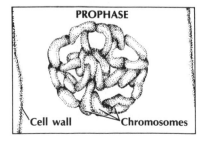

PROPHASE

Cell wall

Chromosomes

6:4 Interphase

On the average, a cell spends about 2/3 of its life cycle in interphase. Of course, this time varies with the type of cell being considered.

For most of its life, a cell appears to be in a state of little activity. This part of a cell's life cycle, called **interphase** (IHNT ur fayz), is the state before and after mitosis. When you observe living cells through a microscope, you most often see them in interphase.

During interphase, a cell nucleus is composed mainly of the membrane, a nucleolus or nucleoli, and chromatin. During interphase, the chromatin is long, thin, and intertwined and is not seen as distinct bodies. During cell division, the chromatin condenses into distinct chromosomes. It is thought that chromosomes are one or a few thin "threads" containing DNA, the material which carries the genetic message.

Although interphase cells appear to be inactive, they are active in receiving and making materials needed for growth, development, and maintenance. Also, they are making the substances needed for cell division.

Chemical tests show that *each chromosome replicates before mitosis begins*. The significance of this replication is great because chromosomes are the code carriers for proper cell functioning. Each new cell must have a complete and accurate copy of the code. Mitosis achieves this accurate copying and dividing of genetic information. When the cell divides, the new cells each get a complete copy of the code.

6:5 Mitosis

Teaching suggestion: The teaching of mitosis and meiosis will be facilitated greatly by audio-visual aids. See *Suggested Audio-Visuals* in the Teacher's Guide.

Although cell division is a continuous series of events, there are four main phases of mitosis. The four phases are **prophase** (PROH fayz), **metaphase** (MET uh fayz), **anaphase** (AN uh fayz), and **telophase** (TEL uh fayz). Each phase can be thought of as frames of a movie.

● **Prophase**. Prophase is a series of events which sets the stage for later events. Those events lead to the equal distribution of chromosomes to new nuclei. Prophase follows interphase. In early prophase, the nucleolus (or nucleoli) begins to disintegrate. Chromatin becomes thicker and shorter, but separate chromosomes are not clearly seen. By middle prophase, the nucleolus has disappeared completely. Chromosomes are clearly visible, and the nuclear membrane begins to break down. In animal cells, centrioles (Section 5:14) begin to separate and migrate toward opposite poles of the cell. Microtubules (Section 5:12) then form as tiny fibers between the poles.

By late prophase, the nuclear membrane is completely absent. Chromosomes appear even more distinct and can be seen to be replicated. They appear as double-stranded structures. Each

Together, the spindle, centrioles and asters are known as the mitotic apparatus. A centriole and aster are sometimes called the centrosome.

strand is called a **chromatid** (KROH muh tud). The chromatids of a chromosome are joined at a special region, the **centromeres** (SEN truh mihrz). Microtubules form an oval-shaped structure between the poles of the cell called the **spindle**. Other fibers, the **aster**, radiate outward from the centrioles in most animal cells. Most other eukaryotic cells lack centrioles and asters, but they do have spindles.

- **Metaphase**. During metaphase, a short stage, chromosomes move toward the center of the cell. The centromeres of each chromosome (2 chromatids) attach to a separate spindle fiber. They are attached near the center or "equator" of the cell. The rest of the chromatids may face in any direction.

- **Anaphase**. Separation of chromatids marks the onset of this stage. A chromatid of each pair is pulled to each pole of the cell. How the chromosomes move is not fully understood. The pull may occur as the microtubules break down and the fibers shorten.

At the end of anaphase, there is one set of single-stranded chromosomes at each end of the cell. The cell membrane of animal cells begins to pinch together at the cell's center. Microfilaments (Section 5:12) seem to be involved. In plants, the **cell plate** begins to appear midway across the cell. The cell plate may form from membranes of Golgi bodies or ER. The cell plate will become the membranes of the two new cells. Later new cell walls form between the membranes.

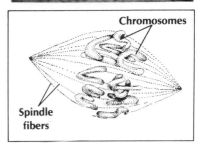

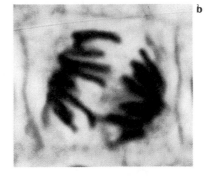

FIGURE 6-9. A spindle is an oval-shaped structure made of microtubules. Chromosomes attach to the spindle fibers.

By the end of anaphase, one set of single-stranded chromosomes has been pulled to each end of the cell.

Teaching suggestion: Emphasize that chromosomes are double-stranded only during late interphase and during prophase and metaphase of mitosis.

Roger K. Burnard

a

Roger K. Burnard

b
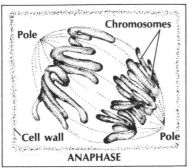

FIGURE 6-10. (a) During metaphase, chromosomes line up at the center ("equator") of the cell. (b) During anaphase, chromatids of each chromosome separate and begin moving to opposite ends (poles) of the cell.

Roger K. Burnard

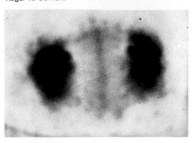

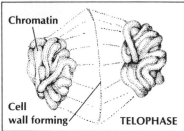

Chromatin

Cell
wall forming   TELOPHASE

FIGURE 6-11. During telophase, chromosomes finish moving to opposite poles of the cell and the formation of two daughter cells occurs.

Certain chromosomes or regions of chromosomes called nucleolar organizers cause the nucleolus to reform. The organizer consists of multiple copies of genes for the synthesis of ribosomal RNA.

- **Telophase.** Telophase ends mitosis with events opposite to those of prophase. The nucleolus reappears, and a nuclear membrane forms around each set of chromosomes. The nuclear membrane forms from ER. Meanwhile, chromosomes lose their distinct form so they once again appear as a mass of chromatin. In animal cells, when cell division is completed, the cell membrane pinches completely together so that the single cell is separated into two **daughter cells**. In plants, the cell plate is completed to form the daughter cells. Eventually cell walls will form between the plant cells. In late telophase of animal cells, the centrioles also replicate.

Each daughter cell has the same number and kinds of chromosomes as the parent cell which produced it. After mitosis, the daughter cells enter interphase. As they mature and grow, their single-stranded chromosomes eventually will be replicated. Then, mitosis can begin again.

Teaching suggestion: Remind students that mitosis is not limited to diploid cells. It can occur in cells that are monoploid or polyploid. In any case, the resulting daughter cells have the same number of chromosomes as the parent cell.

FIGURE 6-12. Mitosis ensures that each daughter cell has the same number and kinds of chromosomes as the parent cell. Follow the movement of the chromosomes through the stages of mitosis.

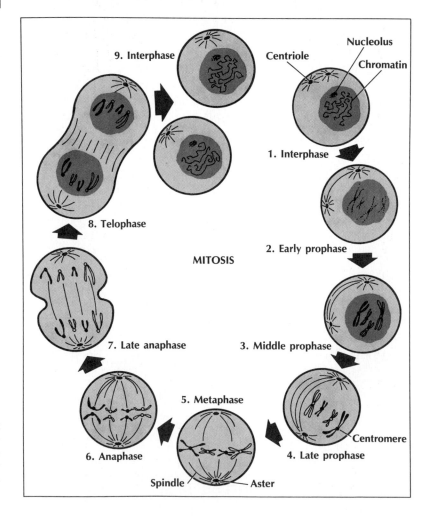

9. Interphase

Centriole   Nucleolus

Chromatin

1. Interphase

8. Telophase

2. Early prophase

MITOSIS

7. Late anaphase   3. Middle prophase

5. Metaphase

6. Anaphase   4. Late prophase

Centromere

Spindle   Aster

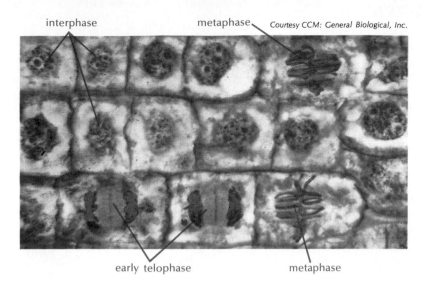

interphase   metaphase   *Courtesy CCM: General Biological, Inc.*

early telophase   metaphase

FIGURE 6-13. Stained cells from an onion root tip show different stages of mitosis. Which stages can you identify?

6:6 Analysis of Mitosis

Mitosis is a process which guarantees genetic continuity (kahnt un EW ut ee) when it occurs properly. **Genetic continuity** results in the reproduction of offspring with the same set of features as the parent.

Normally, a cell has one of each kind of chromosome during most of the cell's life. However, during interphase, each chromosome is replicated. Replication is necessary in order to give the same genetic message to each new cell. If exact replication fails to occur, the daughter cells will not receive the genetic message correctly. In this case, they probably would function improperly, or they might die.

Once the genetic message is replicated, exact separation of chromosomes also is necessary. During metaphase, each chromosome lines up on a *separate* spindle fiber. Thus, after separation, *one of each kind of chromosome* will be present in each new nucleus. What would happen if the chromosomes were to line up in a random fashion? Genetic continuity would be disrupted. There would be no way to ensure that one of each kind of chromosome would be present in each daughter nucleus.

Mitosis guarantees genetic continuity.

Replication of chromosomes during interphase is essential.

Because of how chromosomes line up at metaphase, each daughter cell has one of each kind of chromosome.

6:7 Chromosome Number

The number of chromosomes per cell varies from one kind of organism to another. Humans have forty-six chromosomes per cell and fruit flies have eight. The cell in Figure 6-12 has a total of four chromosomes. Some types of organisms have several hundred chromosomes per cell. Each cell of each kind of organism has a certain number of chromosomes, and each cell of an organism should have the same number and kinds of chromosomes. Also, a certain chromosome from one cell carries the same kind of information as its counterpart in another cell.

Each kind of organism has a specific number of chromosomes per cell.

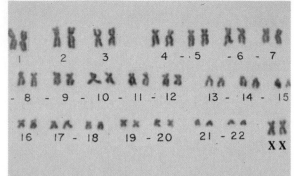

Thomas Russell

a

b

FIGURE 6-14. (a) Chromosomes can be photographed and then (b) paired in a karyotype. This karyotype shows the chromosomes of a normal human female. Humans have 23 pairs of chromosomes.

The monoploid number is the number of different pairs of chromosomes per cell *(n)*.

The term haploid often is used for monoploid.

The diploid number is the total number of chromosomes per cell *(2n)*.

The two chromosomes of each pair are called homologs.

5. Mitosis is the replication and equal distribution of chromosomes. It occurs in all body cells.

6. Chromatin is the main material of the nucleus. It appears as a mass of material. Chromatin is composed of DNA and protein.

7. Chromosomes replicate.

8. In early mitosis, chromosomes become visible as double-stranded structures. The strands of a chromosome are joined by a centromere.

9. The spindle is composed of microtubules between poles of a cell. The aster is made of fibers radiating out from centrioles in most animal cells.

10. Mitosis and cell division result in genetic continuity.

11. A karyotype shows the sizes, shapes, and number of chromosomes in a cell of an organism.

Chromosomes can be isolated and separated for detailed study of features. All of the features of the chromosomes, including size and number, make up a cell's **karyotype** (KER ee uh tipe). Karyotypes show that each cell of a certain kind of organism does have the same number and kinds of chromosomes and that *chromosomes of many organisms exist in pairs.* In humans there are twenty-three pairs, and in fruit flies there are four pairs per cell. The number of different pairs is given as n, which is the **monoploid** (MAHN uh ployd) **number** of chromosomes. In humans, $n = 23$. The total number of chromosomes per cell is $2n$ which is called the **diploid** (DIHP loyd) **number.** In humans, $2n = 46$. What are n and $2n$ in fruit flies? $n = 4; 2n = 8$

Each partner in a pair of chromosomes has the same basic shape and structure. The two chromosomes of each pair are said to be **homologous** (huh MAHL uh gus), and they are referred to as **homologs** (HOH muh lawgz). Each homolog carries information for the same hereditary trait as its partner, but the specific instructions may differ. For example, each homolog of a pair may carry a coded message for eye color. One chromosome's message may be for brown eyes, and the other chromosome's message may be for blue eyes. The combination of the two sets of instructions determines the result in the offspring. A single pair of homologs may carry information for several thousand hereditary traits.

REVIEWING YOUR IDEAS

5. What is mitosis? Where does it occur?

6. Distinguish between chromatin and chromosomes. Of what important chemical are they mainly composed?

7. What happens during interphase just before mitosis begins?

8. Describe the appearance of a chromosome early in mitosis.

9. Distinguish between a spindle and an aster.

10. What is the result of mitosis and cell division?

11. What does a karyotype show?

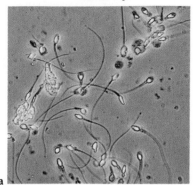

Manfred Kage for Peter Arnold

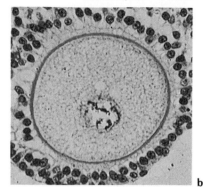

Manfred Kage for Peter Arnold

a

b

FIGURE 6-15. The products of meiosis are (a) sperm cells and (b) egg cells. (Only one egg cell is shown here.) A sperm and an egg each carry half the genetic message.

Human sperm and egg are shown here.

Teaching suggestion: Students need to understand the reduction of meiosis and the increase at fertilization so the work in genetics which follows will have more meaning. Spend as much time as is necessary on this topic.

Meiosis sometimes is called reduction division.

Gametes, eggs and sperm, contain only one member of each pair of chromosomes.

FIGURE 6-16. (a) In meiosis I, the members of each pair of chromosomes separate and move apart forming two cells. Chromosome pairs are shown lined up at the center of the cell. (b) In meiosis II, chromosomes line up at the center of each cell and the chromatids separate. Four cells result, each with half the chromosome number of the original cell.

6:8 Meiosis

What is the source of the two homologs of each pair of chromosomes in each cell? Development usually starts with a fertilized egg or **zygote** (ZI goht). Genetic information in the zygote guides development as mitosis produces a new multicellular organism. The zygote results from the union of two different kinds of cells, the sex cells. The sex cells, also called **gametes** (GAM eets), are a **sperm** from the male parent and an **egg,** or **ovum** (OH vum), from the female parent. Each sperm and egg contains only one member of each pair of chromosomes. Thus, one half of the diploid number in the zygote is from the male parent, and the other half is from the female parent.

Each sperm and egg cell contains only half the diploid number of chromosomes. Because mitosis yields daughter cells with the diploid number of chromosomes, production of sperm and eggs must involve a different process. Also, not just any half of the chromosomes will do because each sperm and egg must contain the *monoploid* number of chromosomes. Each sex cell must have *one member of each homologous pair.* The process by which the gametes are produced is called **meiosis** (mi OH sus). Correct meiosis ensures that the sex cells will have the right *number* and *kinds* of chromosomes. As a result, the zygote gets the proper *number* and *kinds* of chromosomes when fertilization occurs.

Meiosis occurs in certain tissues of an animal's reproductive organs and produces gametes. Meiosis also occurs in the life cycles of plants, algae, fungi, and some unicellular organisms. In plants and some algae and fungi, meiosis results in special cells called spores. Meiosis in unicellular organisms often produces monoploid nuclei rather than special cells. In any case, meiosis occurs in two major parts—**meiosis I** and **meiosis II**. Each stage of meiosis is labeled with a Roman numeral I or II.

Figure 6-16 shows stages of meiosis in the lily anther. The four cells resulting are called microspores which develop into pollen grains.

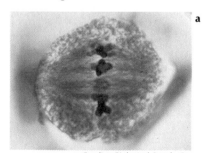

a

Carolina Biological Supply Co.

b

Carolina Biological Supply Co.

Dr. Judie Walton, Lawrence Livermore National Laboratory

FIGURE 6-17. Meiosis in males occurs in tubules in the testes. Part of one of the tubules is shown magnified about 1800 times. Cells near the outside of the tubule (left) move toward the tubule's center (right) as they undergo meiosis. The dark lines at the right are mature sperm.

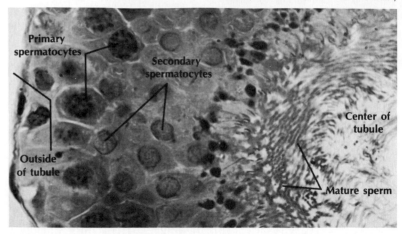

Not all organisms that undergo meiosis are diploid. For simplification in presentation, we are assuming that the adult organism undergoing meiosis is diploid. When meiosis occurs in a polyploid organism, just as in a diploid organism, the resulting cells have half the number of chromosomes as the parent cell.

Chromosomes replicate prior to meiosis I.

During prophase I, homologous chromosomes move close together.   Synapsis is important to the phenomenon of crossing-over (Section 8:6).

In metaphase I, tetrads attach to spindle fibers.

During anaphase I, one double-stranded chromosome of each tetrad is pulled to each pole.

In males, meiosis I produces two secondary spermatocytes, each of which is monoploid.

6:9 Meiosis in Males

The main events of meiosis as it occurs in a male animal are diagrammed in Figure 6-18. In early prophase of meiosis I, chromosomes do not appear to be double-stranded. However, studies show that the chromosomes are replicated during interphase (as in mitosis). In middle prophase I of meiosis, homologous chromosomes move close together by a process called **synapsis** (suh NAP sus). Not only do the chromosomes come together, but identical parts lie side by side. During this time the chromosomes may be wound around one another. Finally, in late prophase I, the replicated chromosomes are seen clearly. The cell now is called a **primary spermatocyte** (spur MAT uh site). Each pair of chromosomes is called a **tetrad** (TEH trad) because four strands (chromatids) lie close together.

While these chromosome activities are occurring, the cell undergoes some events similar to mitosis. The nucleolus (if present) and nuclear membrane disappear, the centrioles move apart, and the spindle and aster form. The major difference between this prophase and prophase of mitosis is that the homologous chromosomes are paired in meiosis I.

There is another main difference in mitosis and meiosis that occurs in metaphase I. Each chromosome does not attach to a separate spindle fiber in meiosis. Instead, each *tetrad*, or pair of chromosomes, attaches to a separate fiber. During anaphase I which follows, the spindle fibers contract, and *one pair of chromatids of each tetrad is pulled to each pole.*

Then, the cell membrane begins to pinch in and telophase I begins. The original cell is divided to form two **secondary spermatocytes** in which each cell has one member of each homologous pair (*n*). However, the chromosomes consist of two chromatids still joined together.

Meiosis II usually follows right after meiosis I. Meiosis II is much like mitosis. The secondary spermatocytes may skip prophase and go into metaphase directly (Figure 6-18).

Meiosis II is like mitosis.

TABLE 6-1. COMPARISON OF MITOSIS AND MEIOSIS		
	Mitosis	Meiosis
Occurs in	all body cells	certain cells of reproductive organs
Number of cells produced	two	four (3 may die)
Chromosome number of parent cell	diploid (2n)	diploid (2n)
Chromosome number of daughter cells	same as parent cell	monoploid (n)
Kind of cells produced	various body cells	gametes or certain spores
Function	genetic continuity from cell to cell	genetic continuity between generations; promotes variation

A total of four monoploid cells, called **spermatids,** are produced by meiosis II. A flagellum (Section 5:14) then forms from one of the centrioles of each spermatid. The spermatid with the tail becomes a sperm. The flagellum helps the sperm swim toward an egg aiding fertilization.

In males, four spermatids are produced from one primary spermatocyte.

6:10 Meiosis in Females

Production of eggs by meiosis in a female animal follows the same general pattern as sperm production, but there are interesting differences. Meiosis I in human females begins before birth! As early as the third month of development, **primary oocytes** (OH uh sites) begin to form in a female fetus. (Oocytes correspond to the spermatocytes of males.) Meiosis is stopped at this point until sexual maturity is reached many years later. At this point, on a cyclic basis, several primary oocytes continue meiosis I, but usually only one per cycle survives. A primary oocyte divides to produce two cells of unequal size. The larger cell is the **secondary oocyte,** and the smaller cell is the **first polar body.** The first polar body may divide again, but cells produced from the first polar body do not survive.

In females, meiosis I begins before birth.

A fetus is a developing organism.

Unequal cell division of a primary oocyte produces a secondary oocyte and the first polar body.

The secondary oocyte enters meiosis II and divides unequally to form a small **second polar body** and a large **ootid** (OH uh tihd). The polar body dies, but the ootid develops into a mature ovum (Figure 6-18).

Another difference in the making of the sperm and the egg is that the sperm must be in its final form before fertilization can occur. Oocytes can be fertilized before they are mature.

An ootid develops into a mature egg.

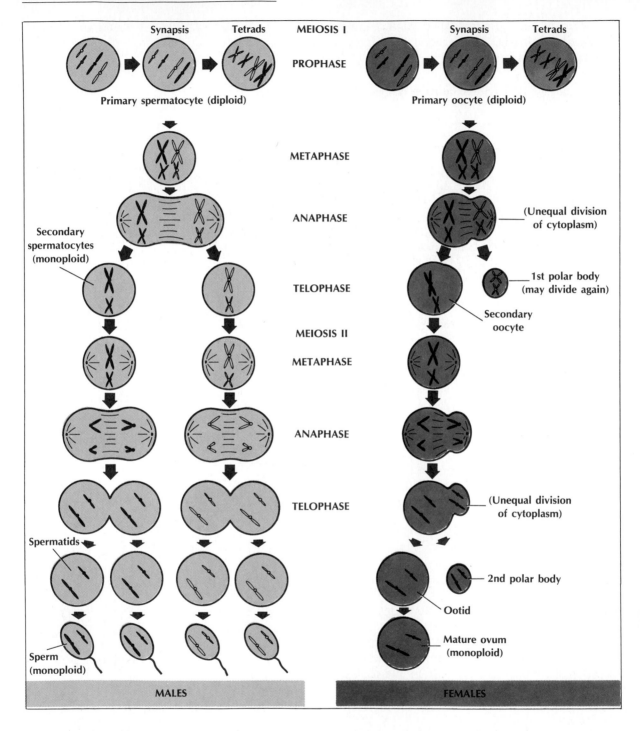

FIGURE 6-18. Meiosis yields cells with half the number of chromosomes as the parent cell. Compare and contrast meiosis in males with meiosis in females.

In a male, four sperm cells develop from each cell (primary spermatocyte) that undergoes meiosis. But, only one egg develops from each cell (primary oocyte) that undergoes meiosis in a female. Can you think of any way in which unequal cell division in a female is adaptive? Production of one large egg provides a storehouse of cytoplasm and nutrients for early development.

6:11 Importance of Meiosis

Meiosis assures that the genetic code of a certain kind of organism is passed to the next generation. This special means of reaching the monoploid number of chromosomes is necessary. If it did not occur, the next generation could not exist in the same form as its parents. Perhaps it could not exist at all.

Meiosis provides more than the continuing of the genetic code. Most organisms have some means of sexual reproduction. Meiosis and fertilization needed for sexual reproduction also provide the means for variation among offspring. Meiosis and fertilization have a special advantage for organisms. Reproduction by mitosis alone produces little variety in offspring.

In playing a game of cards, the deck is shuffled before each new hand is played. Shuffling rearranges the cards so you are dealt a new set of cards with which to play. Some hands are better than others; they are the winning ones. Other combinations are not so good, so sometimes you lose.

Meiosis is a process which reshuffles genetic information (chromosomes). In this case, the hands being played are the offspring produced as a result of the information they receive. In any population there are differences among the individuals caused by the variety of information possible.

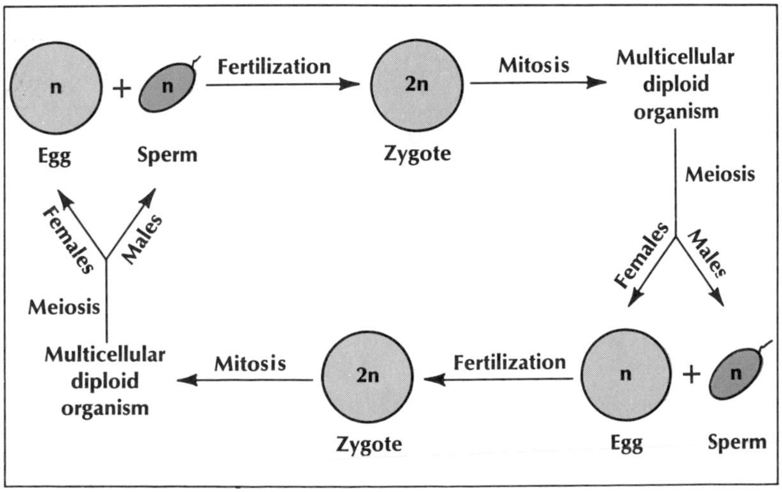

Meiosis assures that the genetic code is passed from one generation to the next.

Meiosis and fertilization contribute to variety among offspring.

FIGURE 6-19. Organisms develop by mitosis and produce offspring by the union of eggs and sperm. Eggs and sperm are produced by meiosis.

Variation is important for survival.

How is this variation important? *Variation promotes a better chance for survival of some offspring should changes in the environment occur.* By keeping many different "hands" in the game, nature decreases the chances of too many losers. Adaptation depends on variety.

6:12 Meiosis and Variation

How does meiosis increase variety? Recall that information for the same trait is carried on each member of a pair of chromosomes. An example of the variety of chromosome possibilities is diagrammed in Figure 6-20. The two pairs of chromosomes in the mother's cells are A and a, B and b. A and a are homologous chromosomes which represent two chromosomes carrying the same trait but with different information. B and b represent a different homologous pair for another trait. The chromosomes in the father's cells are the same. After meiosis, four possible combinations of chromosomes exist among the gametes—AB, Ab, aB, and ab.

The number of possible combinations of chromosomes in a gamete = 2^n where n = the number of chromosome pairs. In a human, $2^n = 2^{23} = 8\ 388\ 608$. The number of possible combinations of chromosomes in a zygote is represented by $(2^n)^2$.

Meiosis can produce gametes with new combinations of chromosomes.

The particular chromosomes in a gamete depend on how they line up at metaphase I. If both A and B chromosomes lie on the same side of the "equator," they will both be pulled to the same end of the cell. Chromosomes a and b will be pulled to the other end of the cell. As a result, two gametes produced will be AB and two will be ab. However, if A and b are on the same side, some gametes produced will be Ab, and the other gametes produced will be aB.

FIGURE 6-20. Chromosome combinations in gametes depend on how homologs line up during metaphase I of meiosis.

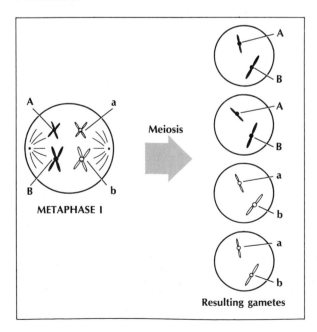

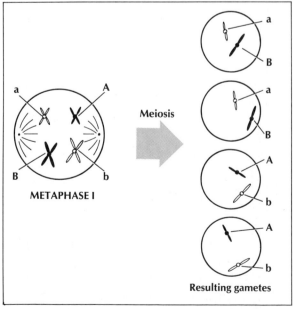

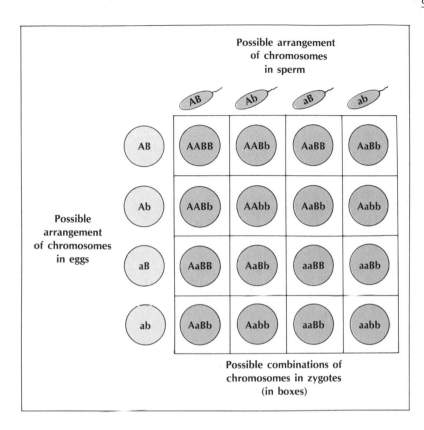

Possible arrangement
of chromosomes
in sperm

Possible
arrangement
of chromosomes
in eggs

Possible combinations of
chromosomes in zygotes
(in boxes)

FIGURE 6-21. When gametes contain different combinations of chromosomes, fertilization leads to genetic recombination and increases variety among offspring.

There are nine different combinations of a and b chromosomes possible in the zygote including *AABB*, *AaBb*, and *aabb* (Figure 6-21). Eight of these zygote combinations are different from the parental combination. Thus, different combinations of features may appear among the offspring. Some combinations may be more useful to an organism's survival than others. This reshuffling of genetic instructions is referred to as **genetic recombination** (ree kahm buh NAY shun). In meiosis, recombination between parts of certain chromosomes also occurs in prophase I and adds to variability (Section 8:6).

REVIEWING YOUR IDEAS

12. Distinguish between monoploid and diploid numbers. How do gametes differ from other body cells?
13. What is meiosis? Why is it necessary? Where does it occur?
14. What is synapsis? What is a tetrad?
15. How does meiosis differ in males and females?
16. How does meiosis differ from mitosis?
17. What is genetic variability? Why is it a benefit that meiosis promotes variability?

Zygotes usually contain combinations of chromosomes different from those in the cells of the parents.

12. The monoploid number is the number of pairs of chromosomes while the diploid number is the total number of chromosomes. Gametes are monoploid; body cells are diploid.

13. Meiosis is the process by which gametes are produced. As a result of the decrease in chromosome number in meiosis, each generation has the same number of chromosomes. Meiosis occurs in certain reproductive tissues.

14. Synapsis is the pairing of homologs during prophase I. A tetrad is a pair of double-stranded chromosomes as they appear during synapsis.

15. Meiosis in males results in four monoploid gametes, sperms. In females, as a result of unequal divisions only one gamete, an egg, is produced.

16. Meiosis produces cells with half the chromosome number of the parent cell. Cells produced by mitosis have the same number of chromosomes as the parent cell.

17. Genetic variability is the reshuffling of genetic information. It promotes survival should the environment change.

All Chapter Review answers and additional chapter teaching suggestions are provided in the Teacher's Guide at the front of this text.

CHAPTER REVIEW

SUMMARY

1. For several centuries, some biologists believed that certain living things were produced by spontaneous generation.
2. Redi showed that maggots are not spontaneously generated.
3. Leeuwenhoek's discovery of microorganisms caused the debate about spontaneous generation to continue.
4. Finally, in 1864, Pasteur conducted experiments that showed that microorganisms are not spontaneously generated, and that led to the theory of biogenesis.
5. Mitosis is the process which results in the replication and equal distribution of chromosomes to new nuclei.
6. Replication of chromosomes occurs during interphase, the period between mitoses.
7. The four phases of mitosis are prophase, metaphase, anaphase, and telophase.
8. Mitosis results in genetic continuity.
9. Each type of organism has a certain number of chromosomes.
10. Fertilization of an egg by a sperm results in the formation of a diploid zygote.
11. Meiosis is a process in which gametes having the monoploid number of chromosomes are produced. It occurs in two successive stages.
12. Meiosis and fertilization contribute to variation among offspring.

LANGUAGE OF BIOLOGY

anaphase	genetic	prophase
biogenesis	recombination	sperm
cell plate	homologs	spindle
centromere	interphase	spontaneous
chromatid	meiosis	generation
chromatin	metaphase	telophase
daughter cell	mitosis	tetrad
diploid	monoploid	zygote
gamete	ovum	

CHECKING YOUR IDEAS

On a separate paper, complete each of the following statements with the missing term(s). Do not write in this book.

1. Mitosis of a $2n$ cell results in the production of cells with a(n) _____ number of chromosomes.
2. Pasteur's experiments led to the theory of _____.
3. Meiosis in animals produces cells called _____.
4. Replication of chromosomes occurs during _____.
5. _____ of chromatids attach to spindle fibers.
6. During telophase a(n) _____ forms between the poles of plant cells.
7. Meiosis and fertilization promote _____ among organisms.
8. Cells produced from a $2n$ cell by meiosis have a(n) _____ number of chromosomes.
9. _____ is the idea that living things arise from nonliving things.
10. The chromosomes of a matching pair are called _____.

EVALUATING YOUR IDEAS

1. What was Aristotle's mistaken belief about where living things come from?
2. Did Redi disprove the theory of spontaneous generation? Explain. What important role did Redi play in the history of spontaneous generation?
3. Write an essay about Pasteur's experiment that disproved spontaneous generation. Discuss his equipment, the reasons for his procedure, and his results and their significance.
4. Why is the theory of biogenesis important?
5. How are the cell theory and the theory of biogenesis related?

CHAPTER REVIEW

6. Describe the events of mitosis: (a) interphase, (b) prophase, (c) metaphase, (d) anaphase, and (e) telophase.

7. How does mitosis in plant cells differ from mitosis in animal cells?

8. What is genetic continuity? How does mitosis contribute to genetic continuity?

9. What are homologous chromosomes? How are homologs the same? How are they different?

10. In a given organism, the diploid number of chromosomes is 12. How many chromosomes will a gamete produced by this organism contain? Explain.

11. What is the origin of each member of a homologous pair of chromosomes?

12. Why is it important that a human egg or sperm contain the monoploid set of chromosomes rather than just any 23?

13. Describe the events of meiosis: (a) prophase I, (b) metaphase I, (c) anaphase I, and (d) telophase I as they occur in a male.

14. Compare meiosis II with mitosis.

15. How does meiosis in a female differ from meiosis in a male?

16. In terms of genetic continuity, summarize the relationship among meiosis, fertilization, and mitosis.

17. How does meiosis contribute to genetic recombination?

18. Why does asexual reproduction (mitosis) offer little opportunity for variety among offspring? Can you think of ways in which there is variation in mitosis?

APPLYING YOUR IDEAS

1. Supporters of spontaneous generation claimed that air must be present for the process to occur. Do you think this idea was good science? Explain.

2. Explain how Redi's experiments made use of the elements of the scientific method.

3. Using the same procedure and equipment as Pasteur, what control could be used to show that spores are the "parents" of microorganisms?

4. Make a series of labeled drawings illustrating mitosis in a cell with a $2n$ of 6.

5. Make a series of labeled drawings illustrating meiosis in a male cell with a $2n$ of 6. Compare your drawings with the drawings in question 4.

6. How is the structure of a sperm cell adapted to its function? An egg?

7. List several examples of variations among organisms. Choose one feature and explain how a variation in this trait might be important in terms of a possible change in the environment.

8. Suppose a cell had four chromosomes of each type instead of two. How many chromosomes of each type would be in the daughter cells produced by mitosis?

EXTENDING YOUR IDEAS

1. Prepare your own mitosis slides from onion root tips which you grow.

2. Salivary glands of fruit flies have giant chromosomes. Describe the structure of these chromosomes either by using library sources or, preferably, by making and examining slides of them.

3. Design and conduct an experiment about spontaneous generation of microorganisms. Consider variable factors such as presence of air, thorough boiling of infusions, and types of nutrients.

SUGGESTED READINGS

Angyal, Jennifer, *Mitosis and Meiosis Illustrated*, Burlington, NC, Carolina Biological Supply Co., 1980.

Dubos, Rene, *Louis Pasteur: Free Lance of Science.* New York, Charles Scribner's Sons, 1976.

Additional student readings and suggested teacher readings are provided in the Teacher's Guide.

John Colwell for Grant Heilman

Offspring inherit traits from their parents. This inheritance of traits gives parents and offspring many features in common. Yet, no two living things are exactly alike. Differences exist among parents and offspring, between offspring, and between different types of organisms. How do organisms of the same type differ? How do you differ from your brothers and sisters, your cousins, or your friends?

Introduction and suggested demonstration: About ten days before you start this chapter, plant 100 corn seeds in moist soil. Save some seeds for later examination by students. The seeds used should be heterozygous, carrying the allele for albinism. Such seeds are available from biological supply houses. (Other seeds with known genotypes also may be available.) By the time you are ready to begin the study of genetics, seedlings will have appeared. Explain to your students what you did and have them examine some of the unplanted seeds. Ask your students to count the green and white seedlings (expected ratio = 3 green: 1 white). Once the data are tabulated, students should conclude that the difference among the seeds is genetic (no apparent differences in unplanted seeds). You can refer to this demonstration throughout the chapter. For example, ask students to compare the actual ratio to the expected (predicted) one and suggest reasons for differences. Ask also whether the albino seedlings will continue to live. The answer can lead to a discussion of lethal genes. Could a line of albino plants be created? Are all the green seedlings homozygous? How could these answers be determined?

PRINCIPLES OF HEREDITY

Chapter 7 presents the work of Mendel and a discussion of probability and introductory genetics.

Genetic information is passed from parents to offspring. How this process occurs was not known until this century. In 1866, Gregor Mendel (1822-1884) reported the results of eight years of study and thought. His work was ignored until 1900, but when discovered, it was seen as a breakthrough. The study of **genetics** (juh NET ihks), the science of heredity, as a distinct branch of biology resulted.

To appreciate genetics, it is helpful to learn how Mendel arrived at his conclusions. Keep in mind the steps of good science. All of them are shown in Mendel's creative work.

GOAL: You will gain an understanding of genetics and probability and learn to solve genetic problems.

DeVries, Correns, and Tschermak each discovered Mendel's principles in 1900.

ORIGIN OF GENETICS

7:1 Mendel's Experiments

Mendel worked with the common pea plant. Pea plants are grown easily and produce large numbers of offspring in a short time. Mendel found that traits (characteristics) are hereditary and that they are transmitted (passed) from generation to generation. He also found that many traits exist in either of two possible forms. For example, pea seeds are either round or wrinkled. The stems of pea plants are either tall or short. Mendel set out to determine how traits were transmitted from parents to offspring.

In pea plants, several traits exist in either of two possible forms.

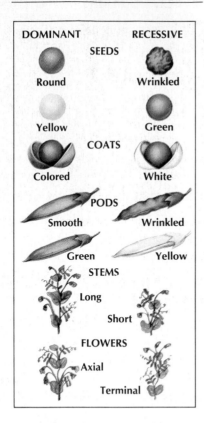

DOMINANT	RECESSIVE
SEEDS	
Round	Wrinkled
Yellow	Green
COATS	
Colored	White
PODS	
Smooth	Wrinkled
Green	Yellow
STEMS	
Long	
Short	
FLOWERS	
Axial	
Terminal	

FIGURE 7-1. Mendel worked with seven pea plant traits in his first experiments. Each trait could appear in one of two forms.

In the F_2 generation, a ratio of three round-seeded plants to one wrinkled-seeded plant appeared.

Mendel decided to use pea plants because the hybrids produced fertile offspring. Also, the structure of the sex organs precluded natural cross-pollination, but allowed him to use artificial pollination.

FIGURE 7-2. Mendel cross-pollinated pea plants by transferring the pollen from one plant to another plant. In this way, he could determine what types of offspring are produced from these parents.

It is a good thing that Mendel chose to work with a large number of plants. Perhaps he realized that the greater the number of plants, the greater the chances that his results would be more meaningful. He was looking for general trends because he wanted to make a basic set of rules about the transmission of traits. In all, Mendel worked with seven traits in his first experiments on the pea plants (Figure 7-1).

7:2 Mendel's Results

Pea plants reproduce sexually. Both male and female sex organs are in the same flower. Normally, male gametes fertilize eggs of the same flower. After many generations, offspring still have the same features as the parents. Such plants are said to be pure.

Mendel wished to cross a plant having one certain trait with a plant having the opposite trait. For example, he wanted to cross plants which produced round seeds with plants which produced wrinkled seeds. Therefore, he transferred the male gametes (pollen) of one plant to another plant (Figure 7-2).

In some cases, the pollen was obtained from round-seeded plants and transferred to wrinkled-seeded plants. The opposite combination also was done. Mendel found that in every case, the **parental cross** (P) yielded offspring which all had round seeds. The offspring of a parental cross are the first **filial** (FIHL ee ul), or F_1, **generation.**

Mendel was impressed that there were no wrinkled-seeded plants in the F_1 generation. He then allowed members of the F_1 generation to reproduce in the usual fashion.

The offspring of this cross are called the **second filial**, or F_2, **generation.** The results of this cross were very revealing. Of the 7324 offspring produced, 5474 plants had round seeds and 1850 had wrinkled seeds. These numbers give a ratio very close to three

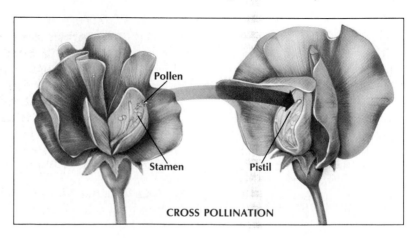

CROSS POLLINATION

round-seeded plants to one wrinkled-seeded plant. Mendel also repeated these experiments with the other pairs of traits and obtained a 3:1 ratio in each case.

Mendel noted that for each trait there is one form which "dominates" the other. On the basis of the results of the F_1 generation, the trait for round seeds is the **dominant** (DAHM uh nunt) **trait**. The other trait, wrinkled seeds, which disappears in the F_1 generation, is called a **recessive** (rih SES ihv) **trait**. Mendel generalized this idea in his **law of dominance** (DAHM uh nunts): *one form of a hereditary trait, the dominant trait, dominates or prevents the expression of the recessive trait.*

7:3 Mendel's Hypothesis

Mendel referred to "pollen cells" rather than sperm.

In Mendel's crosses the recessive trait disappeared in the F_1 generation but reappeared in the F_2 generation. To explain this result, Mendel made certain *assumptions*. Each pea plant is produced as a result of the union of a sperm and an egg. Thus, he reasoned that for every trait there must be two governing factors. One must come from the sperm and one must come from the egg. He called the factors **characters**, but we now call them **genes**. Mendel represented the genes by symbols. A dominant gene was represented by a capital letter. A recessive gene was represented by the same letter as the dominant gene but in lowercase. For example, if the gene for round seed shape (dominant) were R, then the gene for wrinkled seeds (recessive) would be r. The two genes combine in the fertilized egg so that each new pea plant contains two genes for each trait (Figure 7-3).

In Mendel's experiments, the pure parental plants each had the same genes. Round-seeded plants (dominant) were RR. Wrinkled-seeded plants (recessive) were rr. Mendel reasoned that the two genes segregate (separate) during gamete formation. Sperms and eggs would have just one gene for each trait. Thus, the gametes of round-seeded parents should have the R gene, and gametes of wrinkled-seeded parents should have the r gene. As a result, all F_1 plants should be Rr, the only possible combination. Because the R gene is dominant to the r gene, all F_1 plants would have round seeds.

If Mendel's assumptions were correct, all F_1 plants (Rr) should produce half their gametes with the R gene and half with the r gene. There would be three possible combinations in the F_2 generation—RR, Rr, and rr. The chances of R and r gametes combining would be twice as great as other possible combinations. These possibilities can be expressed as a ratio—1 RR : 2 Rr : 1 rr. Both RR and Rr plants will produce round seeds, while rr plants will produce wrinkled seeds. This result is a ratio of 3 round-seeded plants : 1 wrinkled-seeded plant.

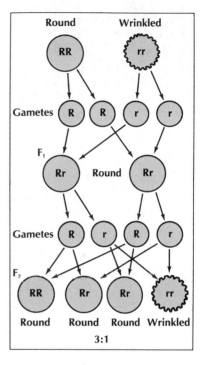

FIGURE 7-3. Mendel's analysis of his experimental results can be set up in a flow chart that shows parents, gametes, and possible offspring.

Mendel reasoned that the two genes governing each trait segregate from each other during gamete formation.

FIGURE 7-4. Combinations of characters among offspring can be determined by using Punnett squares. Sperm and egg possibilities are listed along the top and left side of the square. Possible offspring are shown inside the Punnett square.

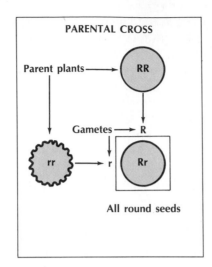
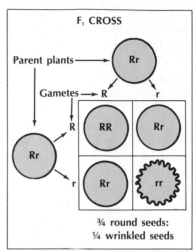

PARENTAL CROSS

Parent plants

Gametes → R

All round seeds

F₁ CROSS

Parent plants

Gametes → R   r

¾ round seeds:
¼ wrinkled seeds

Punnett squares can be used to solve genetics problems.

Teaching suggestion: Time spent on Punnett squares will be helpful throughout the discussion of genetics. Have students identify the gametes and possible offspring in several simple Punnett squares.

Law of segregation: During gamete formation, the pair of genes responsible for each trait segregate so that each gamete contains only one gene for each trait.

FIGURE 7-5. Mendel predicted the results of this cross (*Rr* × *rr*). His results matched his predictions and verified his assumptions.

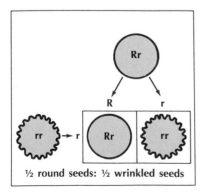

½ round seeds: ½ wrinkled seeds

Results of genetics problems can be shown with Punnett (PUN ut) squares (Figure 7-4). A **Punnett square** is a chart used to determine the possible combinations of characters among offspring. Across the top of the square are written the gametes produced by one parent. The gametes produced by the other parent are listed along the left side of the square. The square is then filled in by listing all the possible combinations of gametes. Each square in the chart represents a *possible* zygote.

7:4 The Test of Segregation

Mendel was able to explain what he observed in his experiments. His laws of dominance and his hypothesis of gene segregation into gametes grew from his experiments. Alone, these did not mean that his explanation was correct, so a test was needed to confirm his hypothesis. Mendel did this test after predicting the outcome of another cross.

If F₁ generation round-seeded plants were crossed with wrinkled-seeded plants, Mendel thought that he should get ratios different from the other ones. According to his hypothesis, F₁ round-seeded plants are *Rr* and wrinkled-seeded plants are *rr*. Round-seeded plants produce both *R* and *r* gametes while wrinkled-seeded plants produce only *r* gametes. Mendel predicted that the possible combinations would be *Rr* (round) and *rr* (wrinkled) and that the number of each should be the same (Figure 7-5). When Mendel performed the experiment, this result did occur. He obtained about half (50 percent) round-seeded and half (50 percent) wrinkled-seeded plants. The same ratio was observed when he used other traits.

As a result of his experiments, Mendel assumed his hypothesis was correct. His hypothesis led to the **law of segregation** (seg rih GAY shun): *during gamete formation the pair of genes responsible for each trait separate so that each gamete contains only one gene for each trait.* The gametes unite to produce predictable ratios of traits among the offspring.

7:5 Terminology

Mendel's "characters" may take different forms, such as dominant and recessive. These forms of genes for a trait are **alleles** (uh LEELZ). Thus, the trait expressed as seed shape is determined by two alleles, *R* and *r*. The combination of alleles which an organism has is called its **genotype** (JEE nuh tipe). The genotype for any trait includes both alleles. For seed shape in pea plants, the possible genotypes are *RR*, *Rr*, and *rr*. The physical or visible feature which each genotype determines is called the **phenotype** (FEE nuh tipe). Round seeds and wrinkled seeds are phenotypes determined by the alleles *R* and *r*. Round seeds is the phenotype determined by the genotypes *RR* and *Rr*. Wrinkled seeds is the phenotype determined by the genotype *rr*. Notice that different genotypes may result in the same phenotype.

When each cell of an organism contains two alleles that are the same, the organism is **homozygous** (hoh muh ZI gus) for that trait. *RR* and *rr* are both homozygous genotypes. To avoid confusion, the terms **homozygous dominant** and **homozygous recessive** are used. When each cell of an organism contains one of each kind of allele, it is **heterozygous** (het uh roh ZI gus). A plant with the genotype *Rr* is heterozygous. You should learn these terms for your work in genetics.

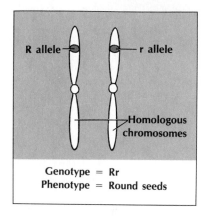

Genotype = Rr
Phenotype = Round seeds

FIGURE 7-6. Terminology: A genotype represents the alleles on homologous chromosomes that give a certain phenotype.

A genotype indicates the combination of alleles an organism has for a given trait.

A phenotype is the trait determined by a particular genotype.

REVIEWING YOUR IDEAS

1. What did Mendel notice about the appearance of hereditary traits? What did Mendel try to find? Did he succeed?
2. Why did Mendel transfer the male gametes of one plant to another plant?
3. State the law of dominance.
4. How are dominant and recessive traits represented?
5. What led Mendel to form his law of segregation? How did Mendel test the law of segregation?
6. Define allele, genotype, phenotype, homozygous, and heterozygous.
7. In a certain organism, the gene for tall, *T*, is dominant to the gene for short, *t*. Write the genotype and phenotype for an organism that is (a) heterozygous, (b) homozygous dominant, and (c) homozygous recessive.

1. He noticed that they occurred in two possible forms. He wanted to learn how traits are transmitted from parents to offspring. Yes, he succeeded.
2. He wanted to combine gametes of plants having opposite traits, and so he cross-pollinated them in this way.
3. One form of a hereditary trait, the dominant form, prevents the expression of the other, the recessive form of the trait.
4. by capital and lower case letters respectively
5. He reasoned that there must be two genes for each trait in an organism, one gene from each gamete. He performed a test cross to test the law of segregation.
6. allele: different form of a gene; genotype: combination of alleles for a given trait; phenotype: trait determined by a genotype; homozygous: having two of the same alleles for a trait; heterozygous: having one of each kind of allele for a trait
7. a) Tt, tall; b) TT, tall; c) tt, short

FIGURE 7-7. Each toss of a coin has a 50% probability of being a head (or a tail). To find the probability of combinations of tosses in a row, use the product rule. What is the probability of tossing a tail followed by a head?

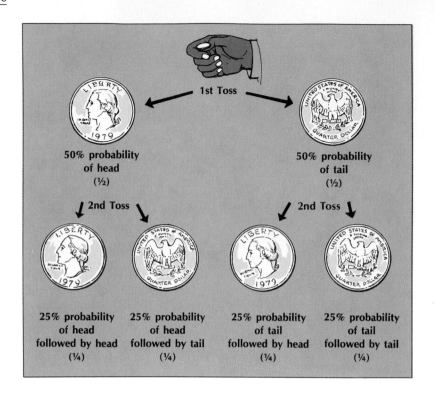

Teaching suggestion: You can show examples of probability using a deck of cards. Show students that the chance of drawing the ace of spades from a full deck is 1/52 (one card out of 52). You can break this probability down into the chance of drawing an ace (4/52 or 1/13) and the chance of drawing a spade (13/52 or 1/4). The probability of drawing the ace of spades is then the product of the two probabilities (1/13 X 1/4 = 1/52).

The product rule: The probability of two or more events occurring together is the product of the individual probabilities of each event occurring alone.

SOLVING GENETICS PROBLEMS

7:6 Probability

When you toss a coin, the chances are equal that you will get a head or a tail. Stated another way, there is a fifty—fifty chance of getting a head (or a tail). There is an equal **probability** of tossing either a head or a tail. This probability also can be written 1 head: 1 tail, or ½ heads: ½ tails. These expressions say the same thing. It is simply a matter of chance whether a head or a tail appears.

What are the chances of tossing two heads in a row? The answer is the product of (multiply) the individual probabilities. This rule is called the **product rule.** Each time the coin is tossed, the chance of getting a head is ½. To find the probability of tossing two heads in a row, multiply ½ times ½. The answer is ¼. *Previous tosses of the coin do not influence individual tosses.* Even if you tossed heads five times in a row, the chance that the next toss would be a head is still ½. But, what are the chances of tossing five heads in a row? Using the product rule, the answer is ½ × ½ × ½ × ½ × ½ or ¹⁄₃₂.

Probability is important in genetics and in solving genetics problems. The law of segregation states that alleles separate during gamete formation. Each gamete gets its allele for a trait purely by chance. Consider the F_1 generation in Mendel's experiments in which each plant had the genotype Rr. Gametes produced by these plants must have had either the R or r allele. Like a two-sided coin, the chances are equal for R and r to appear in a gamete so the ratio of alleles produced by the F_1 plants should be ½ R: ½ r. One half the gametes, by chance, will contain the R allele and one half will contain the r allele.

How can this idea be used to predict the results of breeding plants or animals? Consider ½ R and ½ r as the chances of the gametes being produced by parents with the Rr genotype. The ratios of genotypes and phenotypes of their offspring can be determined by using the product rule. The possible combinations of the alleles in the next generation can be found in the following way:

(1) Probable distribution of alleles:
½ R + ½ r (for both parents)
(2) Probable combinations of alleles:

$$
\begin{array}{r}
½\ R\ +\ ½\ r \\
\times\ ½\ R\ +\ ½\ r \\
\hline
+\ ¼\ Rr\ +\ ¼\ rr \\
¼\ RR\ +\ ¼\ Rr \\
\hline
¼\ RR\ +\ ½\ Rr\ +\ ¼\ rr
\end{array}
$$

(3) Genotypes:
¼ RR + ½ Rr + ¼ rr
(4) Phenotypes:
¾ round: ¼ wrinkled

This answer is the same ratio which Mendel obtained. Do you see why it was good that he worked with many plants? For example, suppose Mendel had only examined four offspring of the Rr by Rr cross. It is possible that the four offspring would have all been rr, all wrinkled. This answer would have been as far as possible from the expected 3:1 ratio. As the number of offspring examined increases, the chance that the results will vary from the expected decreases. Mendel examined hundreds of offspring to get his results. Segregation and combination occur by chance so the larger the number of offspring observed, the closer the result will be to the 3:1 ratio.

Compare this method with the Punnett square method. Listing the possible gametes across the top and side of the square is like following the rules of probability. By using the Punnett square method, you actually are multiplying probabilities (the product rule).

The laws of probability are used widely in the study of genetics.

Students may also solve genetics problems by the Punnett square method. The method shown in the text, however, emphasizes probability.

Note that the genotypes RR and Rr produce the same phenotype, round seeds.

Both the genotypic ratio and the phenotypic ratio should add up to a total of one. Check your work.

Expected results are more likely to be obtained when large numbers of individuals are considered.

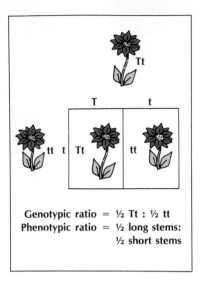

Genotypic ratio = ½ Tt : ½ tt
Phenotypic ratio = ½ long stems:
½ short stems

FIGURE 7-8. In this Punnett square solution to Sample Problem 1, notice that half the possible offspring are *Tt* and half are *tt*.

As students become familiar with genetics problems, they may be able to give the genotypic ratios for single traits from memory. An able student could then omit steps 2, 3, and 4.

7:7 Ratios

Often a geneticist (juh NET uh sust) is interested in finding probable ratios of the genotypes and phenotypes among the offspring of a cross with one trait. The **genotypic** (jee nuh TIHP ihk) **ratio** is the result obtained by the product rule. The **phenotypic** (fee nuh TIHP ihk) **ratio** is found by interpreting the genotypes. Study the following sample problem.

Sample Problem 1: In a certain plant, tall stems (*T*) are dominant to short stems (*t*). A farmer crosses a short-stemmed plant with a heterozygous long-stemmed plant. What are the expected genotypic and phenotypic ratios?

Solution:
(1) Write the genotype of each parent.
   short stem: *tt*
   long stem: *Tt*
(2) Determine the probable distribution of alleles in the gametes.
   short = *tt* → 1/1*t*
   long = *Tt* → ½*T* + ½*t*
(3) Using the product rule, multiply to find the probable combination of alleles (genotypic ratio).

$$\frac{\begin{array}{r} ½\,T + ½\,t \\ \times\ ^{1\!/_1}\,t \end{array}}{½\,Tt + ½\,tt}$$

(4) Interpret the genotypes to find the phenotypic ratio.
   ½ *Tt* = long stems
   ½ *tt* = short stems
Therefore, the phenotypic ratio is ½ long stems: ½ short stems.

Figure 7-8 shows the solution to this problem by the Punnett square method.

REVIEWING YOUR IDEAS

8. What is the probability of tossing a coin and getting heads three times in a row?
9. What is the chance that the next toss will be heads? What is the chance that the next toss will be tails?
10. What is the probable ratio of alleles produced in the gametes of an organism with the genotype (a) *MM*, (b) *Mm*, and (c) *mm*?
11. Why was it good that Mendel worked with large numbers of plants?

8. ½ X ½ X ½ = ⅛
9. ½ ; ½
10. a) All gametes are M; b) ½ M and ½ m; c) All gametes are m.

11. He got a result close to that predicted by probability.

12. In a certain plant, yellow fruit, *Y*, is dominant to white fruit, *y*. A heterozygous plant with yellow fruit is crossed with a plant with white fruit. Find the probable genotypic and phenotypic ratios resulting from this cross.
13. Find the probable genotypic and phenotypic ratios expected from crossing two heterozygous plants of Problem 12.

12. Genotypic ratio = ½ Yy : ½ yy; Phenotypic ratio = ½ yellow : ½ white
13. Genotypic ratio = ¼ YY : ½ Yy : ¼ yy; Phenotypic ratio = ¾ yellow : ¼ white

a

b

FIGURE 7-9. (a) In four o'clocks, the gene for red flowers is incompletely dominant over the gene for white flowers. (b) The heterozygote has pink flowers.

7:8 Incomplete Dominance

Sometimes heterozygous alleles result in a phenotype between the dominant and recessive traits. For example, in some flowers, the alleles for red and white produce pink flowers when heterozygous. This phenomenon is called **incomplete dominance**. To solve a genetics problem involving incomplete dominance, proceed in the same manner as the sample problem. However, the heterozygous condition results in a new trait.

In incomplete dominance, the heterozygous condition is intermediate between or different from the dominant and recessive traits.

FIGURE 7-10. The Punnett square solution to Sample Problem 2 illustrates incomplete dominance.

Sample Problem 2: In four-o'clocks the genes for red flowers, *R*, and white flowers, *r*, are incompletely dominant to one another. The heterozygous condition results in pink flowers. A gardener crosses a red four-o'clock with a white one. What are the expected genotypes and phenotypes of the offspring?

Solution: (1) The parental genotypes must be *RR* for the red flower and *rr* for the white. Why? (2) The *RR* flowers produce all *R* gametes and the *rr* flowers produce all *r* gametes. (3) Therefore, the genotype is all *Rr*. The genotype interpreted as phenotype gives all pink flowers.

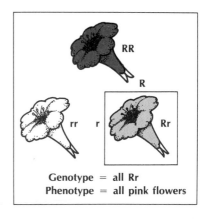

Genotype = all Rr
Phenotype = all pink flowers

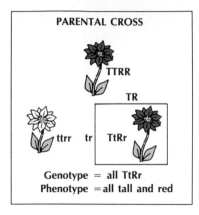

FIGURE 7-11. The F₁ generation of a parental cross involving two traits is shown in this Punnett square.

Teaching suggestion: Had Mendel worked with two pairs of genes on the same chromosome, he would not have attained the 9:3:3:1 ratio. (Section 8:5). He would have obtained 3 tall, red : 1 short, white. You may want to work this problem out for your more advanced students.

7:9 Two Traits

After Mendel's first set of experiments, he studied the inheritance of two traits at once. For example, what types of plants would develop from a cross between a tall, red-flowered plant (*TTRR*) and a short, white-flowered plant (*ttrr*)? Remember, *each gamete must contain one allele for each trait* (law of segregation). Therefore, the gametes of the tall, red parent should have the alleles *T* and *R* and the short, white plant should produce gametes with *t* and *r* alleles. If they do, F₁ plants would all have the genotype *TtRr* and the phenotype tall and red (Figure 7-12). Mendel found these results.

The F₁ cross presented another problem to Mendel. The F₁ plants had the genotype *TtRr*. He knew that gametes produced by these plants must contain one of each kind of allele. But, do the alleles segregate independently of one another during gamete formation? Or do they stay in the same combination (*TR* or *tr*)? Mendel hypothesized that they segregate independently so that the possible gametes would be *TR*, *Tr*, *tR*, and *tr*. The F₂ generation should show a phenotypic ratio of 9:3:3:1 (Figure 7-13). Again, experiments verified this prediction. The **law of independent assortment** states that *alleles segregate independently during gamete formation.*

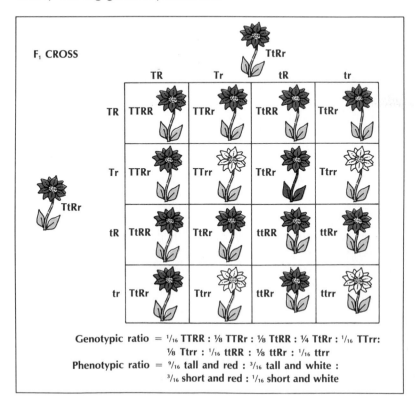

FIGURE 7-12. The F₂ generation of an F₁ cross involving two traits is shown in this Punnett square. You can see how Punnett square solutions become more involved as more traits are considered in a cross.

Genotypic ratio = ¹/₁₆ TTRR : ⅛ TTRr : ⅛ TtRR : ¼ TtRr : ¹/₁₆ TTrr: ⅛ Ttrr : ¹/₁₆ ttRR : ⅛ ttRr : ¹/₁₆ ttrr

Phenotypic ratio = ⁹/₁₆ tall and red : ³/₁₆ tall and white : ³/₁₆ short and red : ¹/₁₆ short and white

Grant Heilman

FIGURE 7-13. Guinea pigs are animals in which different observable traits, such as coat color, can be studied.

Because alleles are sorted in this manner, genetics problems involving two traits are solved easily. The problem is a little longer, but no more difficult. Each trait is treated separately. Then, using the product rule again, the probabilities of all four alleles combined can be determined.

Sample Problem 3: In guinea pigs, rough coat (R) is dominant to smooth coat (r). Black color (B) is dominant to albino (b). A heterozygous black, smooth male is bred to a heterozygous black, heterozygous rough female. What are the probable genotypic and phenotypic ratios among their offspring?

Solution:

(1) Genotypes:

$$\text{male: } Bbrr$$
$$\text{female: } BbRr$$

(2) Gametes produced for color (B and b alleles):
$$\text{male} = Bb \rightarrow \tfrac{1}{2}B + \tfrac{1}{2}b$$
$$\text{female} = Bb \rightarrow \tfrac{1}{2}B + \tfrac{1}{2}b$$

(3) Multiply to find the probable combinations of B and b alleles among offspring.

$$
\begin{array}{r}
\tfrac{1}{2}B + \tfrac{1}{2}b \\
\times\ \tfrac{1}{2}B + \tfrac{1}{2}b \\
\hline
\tfrac{1}{4}BB + \tfrac{1}{4}Bb \\
\tfrac{1}{4}Bb + \tfrac{1}{4}bb \\
\hline
\tfrac{1}{4}BB + \tfrac{1}{2}Bb + \tfrac{1}{4}bb
\end{array}
$$

FIGURE 7-14. A cell that is heterozygous for two traits could produce four different gamete types depending on how the chromosomes assort.

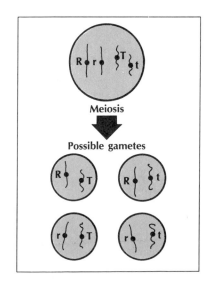

Use the product rule for the second trait.

(4) Repeat steps 2 and 3 for the other trait (R and r alleles).

$$\text{male} = rr \rightarrow \tfrac{1}{1}r$$
$$\text{female} = Rr \rightarrow \tfrac{1}{2}R + \tfrac{1}{2}r$$
$$\begin{array}{r} \tfrac{1}{2}R + \tfrac{1}{2}r \\ \times\ \tfrac{1}{1}r \\ \hline \tfrac{1}{2}Rr + \tfrac{1}{2}rr \end{array}$$

Use the product rule again to determine the probable combinations of all four alleles.

(5) Multiply each of these products to find the probable combinations of all four alleles (genotypic ratio).

$$\begin{array}{c} \tfrac{1}{4}BB + \tfrac{1}{2}Bb + \tfrac{1}{4}bb \\ \times\ \tfrac{1}{2}Rr + \tfrac{1}{2}rr \\ \hline \tfrac{1}{8}BBRr + \tfrac{1}{4}BbRr + \tfrac{1}{8}bbRr + \tfrac{1}{8}BBrr + \tfrac{1}{4}Bbrr + \tfrac{1}{8}bbrr \end{array}$$

If a Punnett square is used, identical genotypes will appear at various places in the square. These must be combined to determine the genotypic ratio. Using the probability method, students obtain the genotypic ratio directly from multiplication.

(6) Interpret genotypes to find the phenotypic ratio.

$\tfrac{1}{8}BBRr$ = black and rough
$\tfrac{1}{4}BbRr$ = black and rough
$\tfrac{1}{8}bbRr$ = albino and rough
$\tfrac{1}{8}BBrr$ = black and smooth
$\tfrac{1}{4}Bbrr$ = black and smooth
$\tfrac{1}{8}bbrr$ = albino and smooth

The phenotypic ratio is $\tfrac{3}{8}$ black and rough: $\tfrac{1}{8}$ albino and rough: $\tfrac{3}{8}$ black and smooth: $\tfrac{1}{8}$ albino and smooth. Check the accuracy of the phenotypic ratio by adding the fractions. The sum should equal one: $\tfrac{3}{8} + \tfrac{1}{8} + \tfrac{3}{8} + \tfrac{1}{8} = \tfrac{8}{8} = 1$.

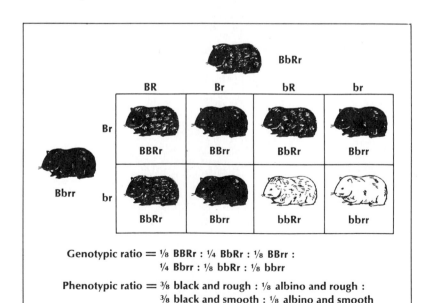

FIGURE 7-15. The Punnett square solution to Sample Problem 3 shows the genotypes of a cross involving two traits. The phenotypes can be determined from the genotypes.

7:10 Multiple Alleles

— Type AB blood is an example of incomplete dominance.

Often two alleles act together to produce a trait in an organism, but many traits are governed by more than two alleles, **multiple alleles**. Human blood type, for example, is controlled by three alleles, I^A, I^B, and I^O. The possible genotypes involving these alleles are $I^A I^A$, $I^B I^B$, $I^O I^O$, $I^A I^B$, $I^A I^O$, and $I^B I^O$. Both I^A and I^B are dominant to I^O. However, neither I^A nor I^B is dominant over the other. Therefore, four blood types are possible: A, B, AB, and O. These are the phenotypes. The genotypes that produce the blood types are listed in Table 7-1.

TABLE 7-1. BLOOD TYPES	
Phenotype	Genotype
A	$I^A I^A$, $I^A I^O$
B	$I^B I^B$, $I^B I^O$
AB	$I^A I^B$
O	$I^O I^O$

Sample Problem 4: A woman who is known to have type B blood marries a man who has type A blood. They have five children, all with type AB blood. What are the most *probable* parental genotypes?

Solution: Consider the genotype of the children. Each of them has type AB blood. Therefore, their genotype must be $I^A I^B$. Now consider the parental possibilities. The mother could be either $I^B I^B$ or $I^B I^O$. The father could have the genotype $I^A I^A$ or $I^A I^O$. That all their children have $I^A I^B$ indicates that both parents are probably homozygous. If either of the parents were heterozygous, then some other blood types would probably occur among the five children. The mother's genotype is probably $I^B I^B$ and the father's is probably $I^A I^A$.

If these parents have a sixth child whose blood type is O ($I^O I^O$), would you change your answer? Why or why not? ———— Yes, the parents would have to be $I^B I^O$ and $I^A I^O$.

More than two alleles for a trait may be present in a population but an individual diploid organism has only two alleles for the trait.

Some students will solve this type of problem intuitively. Others will find it necessary to first determine all the possibilities, then match the problem with the correct solution.

REVIEWING YOUR IDEAS

14. In four-o'clocks the genes for red flowers, R, and white flowers, r, are incompletely dominant to one another. The heterozygous condition results in pink flowers. A gardener crosses two red four-o'clocks. What are the expected genotypes and phenotypes of the offspring?
15. State the law of independent assortment.
16. What are multiple alleles?

14. Genotypes = all RR; phenotypes = all red.
15. Alleles segregate independently during gamete formation.
16. three or more alleles in a population governing a single trait

---

CHAPTER REVIEW

SUMMARY

1. The science of genetics began with the discovery in the early 1900's of Gregor Mendel's work.

2. Mendel studied the transmission of traits in pea plants and was the first to note that traits can exist in two possible forms. His work led to a statement of three main laws of inheritance.

CHAPTER REVIEW

3. The three main laws of inheritance coming from Mendel's work are the laws of dominance, segregation, and independent assortment.

4. The law of dominance states that one form of a hereditary trait, dominant, prevents the expression of another form, recessive.

5. The law of segregation states that alleles separate in gamete formation and go to different gametes.

6. Alleles determine genotypes and phenotypes.

7. Laws of probability can be used to solve genetics problems.

8. Incomplete dominance occurs when one gene is not dominant over another.

9. The law of independent assortment says that segregation of alleles occurs independently of segregation of other alleles.

10. Incomplete dominance and multiple alleles are some ways in which genetic transmission can be complex.

LANGUAGE OF BIOLOGY

alleles
dominant
gene
genotype
heterozygous
homozygous

incomplete dominance
law of dominance
law of independent assortment
law of segregation
multiple alleles
phenotype
Punnett square
recessive

CHECKING YOUR IDEAS

On a separate paper, indicate whether each of the following statements is true or false. Do not write in this book.

1. Each gamete contains only one allele for each trait.

2. If the gene for yellow seeds, Y, is dominant to the gene for green seeds, y, then an organism which is Yy will have green seeds.

3. The organism described in question 2 is heterozygous.

4. Alleles segregate independently during gamete formation.

5. Actual results obtained from a cross are always the same as expected results.

6. By chance, one fourth of the gametes of an Aa organism will contain an A allele.

7. If two heterozygotes are crossed, half their offspring are expected to be heterozygous.

8. If an organism, BB, is crossed with an organism, Bb, all the offspring should be homozygous.

9. If two heterozygotes are crossed and one allele is dominant to the other, then one-half the offspring are expected to have the dominant trait.

10. The chances of tossing three coins and getting all heads is $\frac{1}{6}$.

11. A gamete produced from an organism $AABB$ contains two A genes and two B genes.

12. If two organisms with the genotype $AaBb$ are crossed, a 9:3:3:1 phenotypic ratio is expected.

13. Parents with the genotype I^AI^O and I^BI^B can produce a child with type O blood.

14. Type AB blood results because the genes I^A and I^B show incomplete dominance.

15. If multiple alleles are present, an organism must contain three alleles for each trait.

EVALUATING YOUR IDEAS

1. How were the results of Mendel's parental crosses unusual? How did Mendel interpret these results?

2. What happened when Mendel crossed members of the F_1 generation?

3. Why did Mendel assume that each organism has two characters for each trait?

4. How did Mendel test segregation?

5. Distinguish among the laws of dominance, segregation, and independent assortment.

CHAPTER REVIEW

APPLYING YOUR IDEAS

1. In a certain animal, black fur, *B*, is dominant to white fur, *b*. Determine the expected genotypic ratios and phenotypic ratios resulting from crosses between (a) homozygous black × white, (b) two heterozygous blacks, and (c) heterozygous black × white.

2. Suppose that in outer space there exist creatures whose traits are inherited by Mendel's laws. You find that purple eyes, *P*, are dominant to yellow eyes, *p*. Two purple-eyed creatures mate and produce six offspring. Four of them have purple eyes and two have yellow eyes. What are the genotypes of the parents? The phenotypes? What are the genotypes of the offspring?

3. In fruit flies, long wing, *L*, is dominant to short wing, *l*. Two long-wing flies produced 49 short-wing and 148 long-wing offspring. What were the probable genotypes of the parents? What proportion of the long-wing offspring should be heterozygous?

4. In humans, brown eyes, *B*, are dominant to blue eyes, *b*. A brown-eyed man marries a blue-eyed woman. They have eight children, all are brown-eyed. What are the possible genotypes of each person in the family?

5. In Andalusian fowl, *B* is the gene for black plumage. Small *b* is the gene for white plumage. The genes show incomplete dominance. The heterozygous condition results in blue plumage. List the genotypic and phenotypic ratios expected from the crosses (a) black × blue, (b) blue × blue, (c) blue × white.

6. In cattle, black coat color is dominant to white coat color. A farmer has a black male of undetermined genotype. How can the farmer determine the genotype of the male?

7. A black, smooth guinea pig was mated with an albino, rough guinea pig. Their offspring were black rough and black smooth. These were the only types produced over a period of years in a number of matings. What was the probable genotype of each parent?

8. What is the probable genotypic ratio among children born to a mother having the genotype $I^A I^O$ and a father with type AB?

9. One parent has type A blood and the other parent has type B blood. What are their genotypes if they produced a large number of children whose blood types were (a) all AB, (b) ½ AB and ½ B, (c) ½ AB and ½ A, and (d) ¼ AB, ¼ A, ¼ B, ¼ O?

10. A woman with blood type B has a child with blood type O. What are the genotypes of the mother and child? Which genotypes could the father not have?

EXTENDING YOUR IDEAS

1. An organism *AaBBCcDd* is crossed with an organism *AaBbCcDD*. Without working out the entire cross, find the expected frequency of an offspring with the genotype *aaBbCcDd*.

2. A plant is wanted which has the genotype *AAbb*. Given parental strains *AABB* and *aabb*, outline the methods you would use to obtain such a plant. How would you test the genotype of the plant once you think you have obtained it?

3. Radishes may be long, round, or oval. Crosses of long and oval gave 159 long and 156 oval. Crosses of oval and round produced 203 oval and 199 round. Crosses of long and round gave 576 oval. Explain.

SUGGESTED READINGS

Bornstein, Jerry and Bornstein, Sandy, *What Is Genetics?* New York, Messner Pub., 1979.

Raab, Carl and Raab, Joan, *The Student Biologist Explores Genetics.* New York, Rosen Press, 1979.

Additional student readings and suggested teacher readings are provided in the Teacher's Guide.

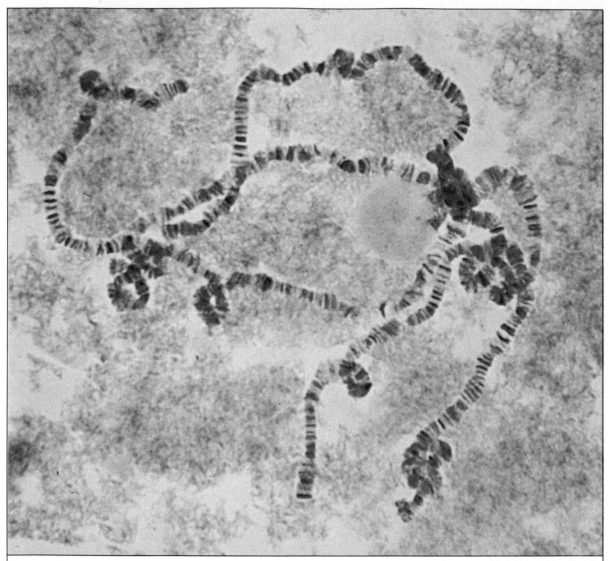

Giant chromosomes from *Drosophila* salivary gland

Harris Biological Supplies Ltd.

Within each cell of your body are structures called chromosomes that contain thousands of genes. The genes of the <u>Drosophila</u> chromosome above are responsible for the development of specific fruit fly traits. How do genes control development of traits? What can happen if chromosomes are not replicated normally during cell division? How can abnormal genes and chromosomes be detected in humans?

Introduction: Much of the material presented in this chapter centers around the pioneering work in genetic research which made use of the fruit fly as an experimental organism. An exciting introduction to the chapter is the film *The Fruit Fly: A Look at Behavior Biology* (CRM/McGraw Hill Films, 110 15th St., Del Mar, CA 92014). The film explains the features which make fruit flies such excellent specimens for study and shows a wide variety of mutants. In addition, it focuses on the work of Seymour Benzer and his associates who have used mutant strains of flies to study behavior. Thus, the film explores the role of the gene in an area of which many students are unaware. The film should certainly provoke discussion about the possibility of a genetic basis of human behavior.

GENES AND CHROMOSOMES

Chapter 8 discusses genetics in the twentieth century, the relationship between genes and chromosomes, and human genetic diseases.

The early 1900's showed a burst of research in the field of genetics. Important observations seemed to link events of meiosis (Section 6:9) with some of Mendel's laws. It was noted that homologous chromosomes separate during gamete formation. A fertilized egg has both homologs of each chromosome pair (the diploid pair). It was reasoned that each cell that is formed from the zygote by mitosis has pairs of homologous chromosomes.

As a result of observations and reasoning, a hypothesis that genes are located on chromosomes was made. One gene for a trait is carried on one homolog and the other gene is on the other homolog. Later this hypothesis was verified.

GOAL: You will gain an understanding of how genes and their locations on chromosomes affect the phenotypes of humans and other organisms.

In the early 1900's, it was hypothesized that genes are located on chromosomes.

THE CHROMOSOME THEORY OF HEREDITY

8:1 Sex Determination

Drosophila melanogaster (droh SAHF uh luh • mel uh NOH gas tur), fruit flies, are often used in genetic studies. They are small (about 2 mm in length), easily handled, and they produce many offspring in two weeks.

In *Drosophila* cells, Thomas Hunt Morgan (1866-1945) first noted a difference in the chromosomes of females and males. Female flies have four pairs of homologous chromosomes, but males have three homologous pairs plus one pair of two different chromosomes (Figure 8-1). One of the two chromosomes looks like those of the fourth pair of female chromosomes. It is called the **X chromosome.** The other chromosome which has a different shape is called the **Y chromosome.** The female fruit fly has two X chromosomes while a male has one X and one Y chromosome.

FIGURE 8-1. Male and female *Drosophila* have eight chromosomes. Three pairs are autosomes. The other two chromosomes are sex chromosomes. Females have two X chromosomes. Males have one X and one Y.

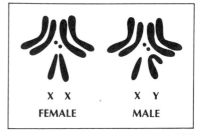

X X
FEMALE

X Y
MALE

FIGURE 8-2. This Punnett square shows that half the possible offspring are female and half are male.

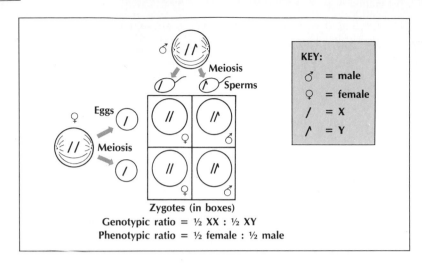

Zygotes (in boxes)
Genotypic ratio = ½ XX : ½ XY
Phenotypic ratio = ½ female : ½ male

KEY:
♂ = male
♀ = female
/ = X
/\ = Y

Because the X and Y chromosomes are related to sex, they are called **sex chromosomes.** The other chromosomes are called **autosomes** (AWT uh sohmz). Thus, both female and male *Drosophila* have three pairs of autosomes and one pair of sex chromosomes. A female normally has three pairs of autosomes and two X chromosomes. A male normally has three pairs of autosomes, an X chromosome, and a Y chromosome.

Cells of *Drosophila* have three pairs of autosomes and one pair of sex chromosomes. X and Y are the sex chromosomes.

All the gametes produced by the female will contain an X chromosome. The male fruit fly's X and Y chromosomes are not homologous, but they behave as a homologous pair during meiosis. They are separated from each other in gamete formation. Half the male's gametes will contain the X chromosome and half will contain the Y chromosome. The possible combinations of X and Y chromosomes among offspring can be determined like other traits (Figure 8-2). By probability, half the offspring would have the genotype XX (female). The other half would have XY (male).

Teaching suggestion: A brief review of meiosis might be useful here.

By probability, half of the *Drosophila* offspring are male and half are female.

Such a pattern of sex determination is evident in many organisms, including humans. However, the pattern is different in some organisms. For example, in grasshoppers, there is no Y chromosome. Females have two X chromosomes; males have only one X chromosome.

8:2 Morgan's Discoveries

In 1910, Morgan made an unexpected discovery in the eye color trait of his fruit flies. He found a male with white eyes. These flies were from a pure line having only red eyes.

He decided to breed this white-eyed male to red-eyed females assuming that red eye color was dominant to white eye color. Morgan expected to find all red-eyed offspring in the F_1

generation. He also expected the F_1 flies, when interbred, to produce a ratio of three red-eyed flies to one white-eyed fly. He did get these results.

Morgan also noted that all the white-eyed flies in the F_2 generation were *males!* There were no white-eyed females. Because white eye color seemed to be linked with sex, it is called a **sex-linked characteristic.**

Morgan's hypothesis was that the alleles for eye color are carried only on the X chromosomes, and that there are no alleles for eye color on the Y chromosome. Thus, the parental cross was between red-eyed females (X^RX^R) and white-eyed males (X^rY) (Figure 8-3). X and Y represent the sex chromosomes. R represents the red eye color allele, and r stands for the white eye color allele. The results of the cross (F_1 generation) were red-eyed males (X^RY) and red-eyed females (X^RX^r). The F_2 generation (Figure 8-3) would have been red-eyed females (X^RX^R or X^RX^r), red-eyed males (X^RY), and white-eyed males (X^rY). Morgan's hypothesis explained his previous data by showing how all males are white-eyed in the F_2 generation.

But, a hypothesis should predict new facts. Morgan predicted that he could produce white-eyed females by breeding an F_1 red-eyed female (X^RX^r) with a white-eyed male (X^rY). When such a cross was done, Morgan's prediction was confirmed. There were white-eyed females among the offspring. This evidence was also important in supporting the hypothesis that genes are carried on chromosomes.

All of Morgan's F_2 fruit flies with white eyes were males.

Traits inherited with sex are called sex-linked characteristics.

Morgan hypothesized that alleles for eye color in *Drosophila* are carried on the X chromosome but not on the Y chromosome.

Some traits are sex-limited as opposed to sex-linked. Human baldness, for example, appears more frequently in men, but the genes for baldness are not carried on the sex chromosomes. The expression of the baldness phenotype is influenced by hormones. Baldness is a dominant trait. All homozygous dominant individuals are bald, but of the heterozygotes only males are bald.

FIGURE 8-3. Assuming eye color is sex-linked, results predicted with Punnett squares agree with Morgan's experimental results. The parental and F_1 crosses he did are shown.

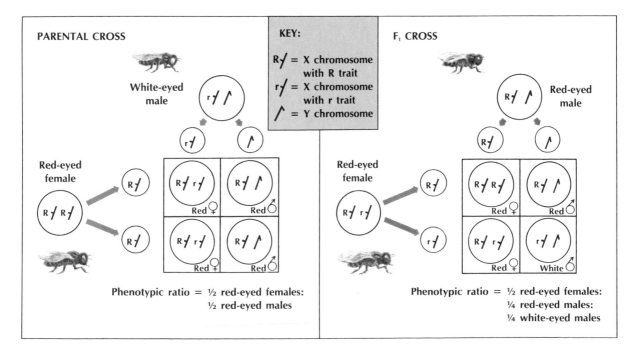

PEOPLE IN BIOLOGY

In 1970, in front of a small group of scientists gathered at the University of Wisconsin, Har Gobind Khorana announced that he and his research team had made the first synthetic gene. This announcement was the result of many years of research in chemical genetics.

(1922-   )

Details of what genes are chemically and how they function are presented in Chapter 9.

Har Gobind Khorana

Khorana was born and reared in India. After he earned his degrees at Punjab University, he moved to England where he began his life-long study of nucleic acids and proteins. From there his research led him to a post in Canada. Later he became Co-director of the Institute for Enzyme Research at the University of Wisconsin. It was here that Khorana began to decipher the genetic code of yeast. In 1968 he received the Nobel Prize for Medicine for interpreting the code and explaining how genes determine the function of cells. Only two years later, Khorana reported his synthesis of a yeast gene.

Dr. Khorana, who has been an American citizen since 1966, now lives in Massachusetts with his wife. He has three children, and in his spare time he enjoys hiking, swimming, and listening to music.

8:3 Solving Problems

Problems with sex-linked traits can be solved in the same way you solve other genetics problems.

Sample Problem 1: In a certain animal, the gene for black coat color *(B)* is dominant to the gene for orange coat color *(b)*. The characteristic is sex-linked. Determine the probable genotypic and phenotypic ratios among the offspring produced by a heterozygous female and a black male.

Include the alleles and the chromosomes in problems involving sex-linked traits.

Consider each chromosome and its allele as a unit.

Solution:

(1) Write the genotype of each parent.

$$\text{female: } X^B X^b$$
$$\text{male: } X^B Y$$

(2) Determine the probable distribution of chromosomes and alleles in the gametes.

$$\text{female} = X^B X^b \rightarrow \tfrac{1}{2}\,X^B + \tfrac{1}{2}\,X^b$$
$$\text{male} = X^B Y \rightarrow \tfrac{1}{2}\,X^B + \tfrac{1}{2}\,Y$$

Teaching suggestion: Remind students that in step 4 below, carrier females and normal females are not distinguished in the phenotypic ratio. They have the same phenotype.

(3) Using the product rule, multiply to find the possible combination of chromosomes and alleles (genotypic ratio).

$$\frac{\frac{1}{2}\ X^B + \frac{1}{2}\ X^b}{\times\ \frac{1}{2}\ X^B + \frac{1}{2}\ Y}$$
$$\frac{1}{4}\ X^BX^B + \frac{1}{4}\ X^BX^b + \frac{1}{4}\ X^BY + \frac{1}{4}\ X^bY$$

(4) Interpret the genotypes to find the phenotypic ratio.

$\frac{1}{4}\ X^BX^B$ = black female $\frac{1}{4}\ X^BY$ = black male

$\frac{1}{4}\ X^BX^b$ = black female $\frac{1}{4}\ X^bY$ = orange male

Therefore, the phenotypic ratio is $\frac{1}{2}$ black females: $\frac{1}{4}$ black males : $\frac{1}{4}$ orange males.

The Punnett square answer to Sample Problem 1 is shown in Figure 8-4.

Sample Problem 2: What genotypes and phenotypes must each parent have to produce an orange female?

Solution: The genotype of the orange female must be X^bX^b because the gene for orange is recessive. One of the X chromosomes is received from the mother. The other is received from the father. Therefore, the father's genotype must be X^bY. He is orange. The mother must have the genotype X^BX^b (black) or X^bX^b (orange).

8:4 Nondisjunction

Calvin Bridges (1889-1938) made another unexpected discovery working with fruit flies. He found female flies which had two X chromosomes and a Y chromosome. Also, some male flies had just an X chromosome and no Y chromosome at all. These unusual patterns occurred because the homologous sex chromosomes of the parents failed to segregate properly during meiosis (Figure 8-5). He called this process **nondisjunction** (nahn dihs JUNK shun). Nondisjunction of autosomes can also occur. Bridges' discovery of nondisjunction was associated with abnormal genetic results and was important evidence of the **chromosome theory of heredity:** *genes are located on chromosomes.*

Bridges' discovery of nondisjunction changed the concept of sex determination. It had been thought that the presence of the Y chromosome in fruit flies determined sex. Bridges found that in *Drosophila* the chromosome arrangement XXY will produce a female and a single X will produce a male. Thus, it is now known that the presence of *two* X chromosomes produces females and the absence of the second X chromosome produces males. Sex in fruit flies is determined by the number of X's.

In humans, unlike fruit flies, the Y chromosome determines sex. If a Y chromosome is present, a male will be produced no matter how many X chromosomes there are. Cells such as X,

Bridges hypothesized nondisjunction to explain the occurrence of unexpected phenotypes. His hypothesis was confirmed by observing the cells of the unexpected offspring.

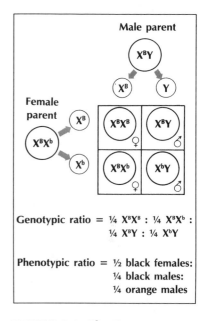

Genotypic ratio = $\frac{1}{4}\ X^BX^B$: $\frac{1}{4}\ X^BX^b$: $\frac{1}{4}\ X^BY$: $\frac{1}{4}\ X^bY$

Phenotypic ratio = $\frac{1}{2}$ black females: $\frac{1}{4}$ black males: $\frac{1}{4}$ orange males

FIGURE 8-4. The Punnett square solution to Sample Problem 1 shows the inheritance of coat color which, in this example, is sex-linked.

Teaching suggestion: Explain to students that the best clue for solving a problem like *Sample Problem 2* is the presence of the recessive offspring. For their presence, each parent must have at least one recessive allele.

FIGURE 8-5. Nondisjunction, failure of homologous chromosomes to segregate properly, explains the rare occurrence of white-eyed females and red-eyed males in *Drosophila.*

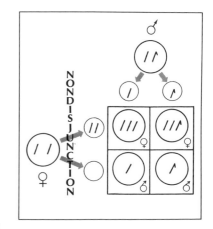

In birds and some insects, the female determines the sex of the offspring. The female's sex chromosomes are designated ZW. The male is ZZ.

Some genes are carried on the Y chromosome, but not the X chromosome.

1. *Drosophila* are handled easily and produce large numbers of offspring within two weeks.
2. Females have three pairs of autosomes and a pair of X chromosomes whereas males have three pairs of autosomes and an X and a Y chromosome.
3. Female gametes all contain an X chromosome. Half the male gametes are X and half are Y.
4. All the white-eyed flies were males.
5. Nondisjunction is the failure of homologous chromosomes to segregate properly during meiosis.

Many genes are located on a single chromosome.

FIGURE 8-6. The Punnett square results involving two traits that are linked show that linked genes do not assort independently.

XX, and XXX produce females while combinations such as XY, XXY, and XXXY produce males.

The human Y chromosome seems to carry genes for male sex. The Y chromosomes also carry other genetic information. Some Y chromosome genes do not have corresponding genes on the X chromosome. For example, the gene which causes the rims of the ears to be hairy is on the Y chromosome only.

REVIEWING YOUR IDEAS

1. Why are *Drosophila* useful for genetic studies?
2. Describe the chromosomes of male and female *Drosophila*.
3. Why are the chances of a couple having a girl 50:50?
4. What was unusual about Morgan's F_2 3:1 ratio?
5. What is nondisjunction?

OTHER GENETICS CONCEPTS

8:5 Gene Linkage
Teaching suggestion. Sections 8:5-8:7 should be reserved for more advanced students.

Today it is known that the total number of genes in a cell is much greater than the total number of chromosomes. Thus, each chromosome must contain many different genes. Each gene influences certain traits. Genes which occur on the same chromosome are said to be linked. This phenomenon is called **gene linkage.**

Think of the cross of tall, red-flowered plants, *TTRR*, and short, white-flowered plants, *ttrr*. A 9:3:3:1 ratio occurs in the F_2 generation (Figure 7-13). The expected results would be different if the genes were linked (Figure 8-6).

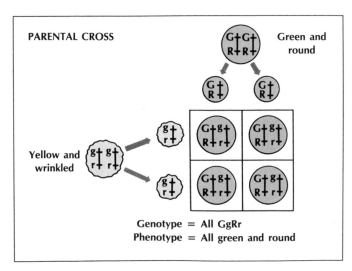

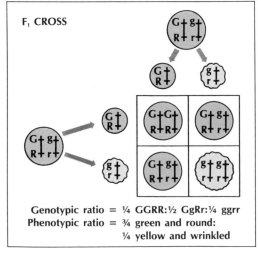

Assume in a certain plant that green seeds, *G*, are dominant to yellow seeds, *g*, and that round seeds, *R*, are dominant to wrinkled seeds, *r*. Also assume that the alleles are on the same pair of homologous chromosomes. As a result, they do not assort independently (Section 7:9) during meiosis. They stay together and enter the gametes in the same combinations each generation.

When *GGRR* and *ggrr* are crossed, the F₁ offspring have green, round seeds *(GgRr)*. These results are the same as those produced when genes are not linked. But, there are only three possible genotypes among the F₂ offspring—*GGRR*, *GgRr*, and *ggrr*. The phenotypic ratio is three green, round to one yellow, wrinkled. Without gene linkage, the F₂ phenotypic ratio is 9:3:3:1 because of independent assortment. *Thus, gene linkage reduces the chances for genetic recombination and variety among offspring.*

If genes are linked, they do not assort independently.

Teaching suggestion: Make certain that students understand that the 9:3:3:1 ratio discussed here applies only to a dihybrid cross.

Gene linkage reduces variety among offspring.

8:6 Crossing-Over

Suppose all linked genes in a population remained in their parental combinations. The variety among organisms would be reduced. Geneticists have come to realize that linked genes can be separated by crossing-over. **Crossing-over** is an exchange of segments of chromosomes between two homologous chromatids (Figure 8-7). Crossing-over may occur at more than one place along a chromosome.

Crossing-over occurs during prophase I of meiosis and may continue into metaphase I (Section 6:10). When homologous chromosomes pair, the four chromatids lie side by side. They are

Crossing-over is only apparent when it is between non-sister chromatids in the tetrad.

Crossing-over, exchange of alleles between homologous chromosomes, separates linked genes.

FIGURE 8-7. The differences in the genetic makeup of gametes produced with no cross-over, a single cross-over, and a double cross-over can be easily compared.

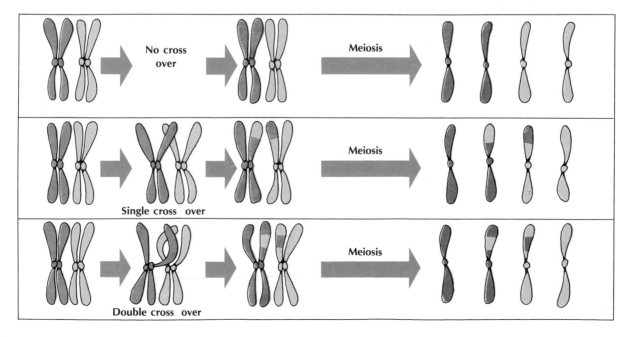

No cross over   Meiosis

Single cross over   Meiosis

Double cross over   Meiosis

0.0	Yellow body
1.5	White eyes
7.5	Ruby eyes
20.0	Cut wing
33.0	Vermillion eyes
36.1	Miniature wing
51.5	Scalloped wing
57.0	Bar eye
66.0	Centromere

FIGURE 8-8. A genetic map of the *Drosophila* X chromosome shows the linear arrangement of genes. Many of the genes that have been mapped were omitted from this drawing for simplification. The numbers indicate relative distances between genes.

Frequency of crossing-over is an indication of the distance between genes on a given chromosome.

positioned so that alleles of one chromosome are beside alleles for the same trait on the other chromosome. When the homologous pairs are pulled apart in meiosis I, the chromatids can have different combinations of genes as a result of exchange.

Crossing-over has survival value for a population. Most gametes will have the parental combination of linked genes, but some are different as a result of crossing-over. These gametes are called **recombination gametes.** The union of these gametes with other gametes results in offspring with a wider variety of traits which helps a population survive over long periods of time in a changing environment. These traits could be important if changes in the environment favored new features (Section 6:13).

Crossing-over can be used as a tool to learn the location of genes on chromosomes. When genes are known to be linked, expected phenotypic ratios can be determined. Variations from the expected ratios show how often two genes on homologous chromosomes cross-over. The frequency or amount of cross-over can then be used to determine where the genes are on the chromosomes.

The linear arrangement of genes on chromosomes has been worked out for many oganisms. The location of genes on a chromosome is called a **genetic map.** The genetic map is determined by the amount of crossing-over between different genes. The farther apart two genes are, the greater the chance of their crossing-over. Why?

As an example, it was determined that in *Drosophila* the ruby-eye gene was farther from the bar-eye gene than it was from the cut-wing gene (Figure 8-8). More crossing-over occurred between the ruby-eye and bar-eye than between the ruby-eye and cut-wing genes. The distances between the genes are given in genetic map units, shown as numbers on Figure 8-8. Genetic map units indicate the amount of crossing-over between genes. One unit equals 1% crossing-over. Why is it important to learn where genes are on chromosomes? What are the advantages of making genetic maps of human chromosomes?

FIGURE 8-9. Chromosomes in bacteria are circular. This genetic map of the *E. coli* chromosome, a bacterial chromosome, shows some of the genes whose locations are known. Many genes were omitted from this drawing for simplification.

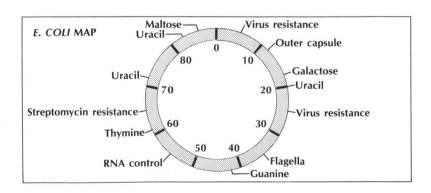

8:7 Many Genes—One Effect

The hereditary traits studied so far are explained by Mendel's laws in which single pairs of genes operate by complete or incomplete dominance (Section 7:8). Examples are red flowers or white flowers, normal color vision or color blindness, and round seeds or wrinkled seeds. They are determined by the combination of two alleles on a single pair of chromosomes.

However, Mendel's laws do not explain all genetic traits. For example, there is a wide range of ear lengths in corn. Ears of corn are not just long or short. Long and short are limits between which many lengths exist. If length were controlled by a single pair of genes showing incomplete dominance, there would be only three lengths—long, medium, and short.

Many ear lengths in corn is an example of **continuous variation.** Continuous variation can be explained by assuming that more than one pair of genes is involved. Suppose that two pairs of genes (*A* and *a*, *B* and *b*) are responsible, and they are on different pairs of homologs. Suppose also that *AABB* represents the genotype of the longest ears of corn, and *aabb* represents the genotype of the shortest ears of corn. A cross between *AABB* and *aabb* parents results in F_1 offspring which are *AaBb* (intermediate length) (Figure 8-10).

If these F_1 organisms are interbred, a broad range of genotypes and phenotypes is produced in the F_2 offspring (Figure 8-11). The genotype *AaBb*, medium length ears of corn, is the one most often produced. *AABB* (longest) and *aabb* (shortest) are very seldom produced. The rest of the genotypes produce the other lengths.

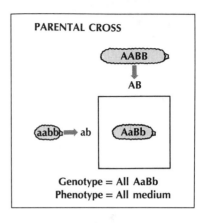

PARENTAL CROSS

Genotype = All AaBb
Phenotype = All medium

FIGURE 8-10. This Punnett square shows a parental cross of corn in which two pairs of genes determine one trait, ear length.

The range of phenotypes seen in continuous variation is controlled by several pairs of genes.

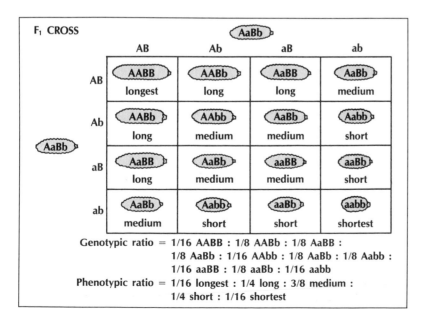

F_1 CROSS

Genotypic ratio = 1/16 AABB : 1/8 AABb : 1/8 AaBB :
1/8 AaBb : 1/16 AAbb : 1/8 AaBb : 1/8 Aabb :
1/16 aaBB : 1/8 aaBb : 1/16 aabb
Phenotypic ratio = 1/16 longest : 1/4 long : 3/8 medium :
1/4 short : 1/16 shortest

If A and B were genes controlling two different traits, a 9:3:3:1 ratio would be expected.

FIGURE 8-11. When two pairs of genes determine a trait, many different phenotypes (continuous variation) are possible in the F_2 generation.

Allan Roberts

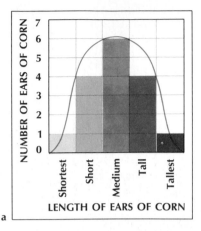

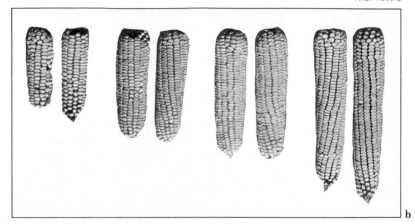

a   b

FIGURE 8-12. (a) A graph of the distribution of ear lengths in corn shows continuous variation. The distribution is bell-shaped with medium length ears occurring most often. (b) The continuous variation in length can be seen in the corn ears.

Continuous variation is determined by multiple genes.

Teaching suggestion: Be sure students do not confuse the term *multiple genes* with the term *multiple alleles* (Section 7:10).

Expression of genes may depend on environment.

Some are longer than medium; some are shorter than medium. When graphed, these results show a distribution such as that in Figure 8-12. When these crosses are made, the results agree with those predicted by the Punnett square. Geneticists explain many such traits in terms of **multiple genes** or **multiple factors** in which many genes may affect a single trait. Human skin color is among other traits thought to be determined by multiple genes.

8:8 Heredity and Environment

Genes are the carriers of hereditary information. But, will the same genes produce the same features under all conditions? The answer is often no. In most cases, the expression of a gene depends on the environment in which the organism is developing. For example, a person might have genes for brown hair, but exposure to the sun might turn the hair blond.

In fruit flies, the gene for curly wings is expressed differently at different temperatures. Curly-winged flies bred at 25°C will have offspring with curly wings. But at 16°C, the offspring will have straight wings. Both sets of offspring, if interbred at 25°C, will produce curly-winged flies.

FIGURE 8-13. (a) Curly-winged *Drosophila* bred at 16°C will produce (b) straight-winged offspring. Temperature is an environmental factor that influences the final traits of this organism.

a

b

Carolina Biological Supply Co.   *Carolina Biological Supply Co.*

USDA

Steve Lissau

a

USDA

b

FIGURE 8-14. Environmental factors influence traits in many ways. (a) A soybean plant with ample iron (above) grows much better than an iron-deficient soybean plant (below). (b) Sun exposure can darken skin color and lighten hair color.

One way of determining the effects of environment on traits is to study identical twins. Identical twins have exactly the same genotype because they are produced as a result of the dividing of one zygote. Identical twins separated at birth and raised in *different* environments usually have some different traits such as height, weight, and even intelligence. Thus, different environments can cause different expressions of the genotype. How might environment affect intelligence?

In general, the development of any organism is affected by the environment. A given genotype may be for long ears of corn. But, the soil in which the corn is growing may be poor, or there may be a drought during the growing season. Each of these may affect the phenotype so that there may be short ears of corn or even no ears. The phenotype depends on the environment as the source of needed materials and energy. An organism which cannot get the proper energy and materials will not develop properly no matter what its genetic message.

Environment may affect phenotypes.

REVIEWING YOUR IDEAS

6. What is gene linkage?
7. Why does each chromosome contain many genes?
8. How does gene linkage affect variety among offspring? Why?
9. What is crossing-over? How does it affect variety among offspring?
10. How is crossing-over useful in constructing genetic maps?
11. What is continuous variation? How is it explained?
12. How are heredity and environment related?

6. Gene linkage is a term that describes the condition in which genes are located at different places on the same chromosome.
7. The total number of genes is greater than the total number of chromosomes.
8. Gene linkage reduces variety because linked genes do not assort independently; they move together at meiosis.
9. Crossing-over is the exchange of segments of chromosomes (between two homologous chromatids) when the chromosomes pair in meiosis. Crossing-over increases variety.

10. Frequency of crossing-over indicates relative distances between genes.

11. Continuous variation is a genetic pattern characterized by a range of phenotypes. It is explained by multiple genes.

12. Environment may affect the expression of hereditary information — the genes.

See the Teacher's Guide for addresses to write for additional information.

HUMAN GENETIC DISEASE

Genetic disease affects many humans in a variety of ways.

Humans inherit traits in the same manner as other organisms. In some cases, humans develop diseases which are genetic in origin. Genetic disease is not really rare; many people are affected by genetic diseases. It is estimated that in the United States, genetic disease is the cause of about 40% of all miscarriages and 40% of all infant deaths. It is also thought about 80% of all mentally retarded people and about ⅓ of all children that are in hospitals have problems that are genetic in origin. You can see why there is great concern about the prevention and treatment of genetic disease.

Genetic counseling can help couples weigh the risks of having children.

Genetic counseling is now available to prospective parents such as those from families with a history of hereditary disease. In counseling sessions, genetic counselors discuss with the couples their chances of having children with certain genetic diseases. The counselors may discuss results of tests with the prospective parents. They also help the couples make decisions about having children in situations where children with serious genetic defects are likely. As a result of genetic counseling, some couples may choose not to have children.

Some genetic diseases are caused by the presence of certain alleles. Others may result from an abnormal inheritance of chromosomes. Examples of both of these types of genetic disease are given here.

FIGURE 8-15. (a) Normal red blood cells are disc-shaped. (b) Red blood cells of a person with sickle-cell anemia are distorted sickle shapes. These cells are shown magnified about 2200 times.

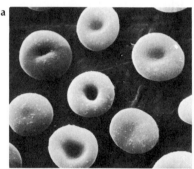

Kessel/Shih, Springer-Verlag ©1976

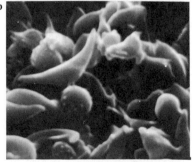

SEM Laboratory, Morris Brown College

8:9 Problem-Causing Genes

Genes may exist in two or more forms or alleles. It is possible that one allele for a particular trait may be harmful or even lethal. A **lethal gene** causes death. It is estimated that every person has five to eight dangerous genes. Yet, most people show no signs of disease. Usually the harmful alleles are recessive, and their effects are masked by dominant alleles. When a person is homozygous for the recessive allele for a disease, the symptoms appear. Some examples of human diseases due to gene defects are discussed below.

● **Sickle-Cell Anemia.** This disease affects mostly black people. A person with the disease most often is homozygous recessive for a gene which makes hemoglobin. Hemoglobin is a protein in red blood cells which combines with oxygen and transports it to the cells. In persons with sickle-cell anemia, hemoglobin is abnormal, and the red cells are a sickled shape (Figure 8-15). Normal red cells are disc-shaped. Analysis shows that normal and abnormal hemoglobin differ in only one of the nearly six hundred amino acids that make up the molecule.

Teaching suggestion: Be sure students do not get the impression that all genetic diseases are caused by recessive genes. For example, polydactyly, presence of extra fingers or toes, is the result of the presence of a dominant gene.

Although tested on animals for 5 years, the sickle-cell machine was first used on humans in 1980.

Doug Martin

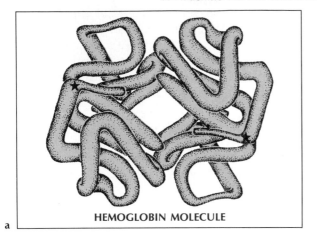

HEMOGLOBIN MOLECULE

a

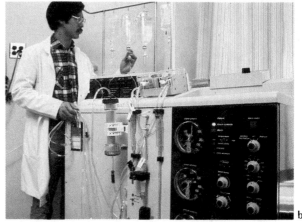

b

FIGURE 8-16. (a) Sickle-cell hemoglobin differs from normal hemoglobin by only one amino acid—valine appears instead of glutamine. A representation of hemoglobin is shown with the stars marking the locations of the sickle mutations. (b) A new machine, similar to a kidney machine, is being used successfully to treat sickle-cell patients.

Sickled cells carry less oxygen and can block small blood vessels.

This slight difference prevents abnormal hemoglobin from carrying enough oxygen to cells. The red cells change to a sickled-shape in the blood vessels. Because capillaries are of small diameter, the sickled cells do not easily pass through. The sickled cells clog the vessels. Thus, body cells do not get needed oxygen. As a result, the person might die.

Several promising treatments of sickle-cell anemia are being used. Different chemicals are being used that, among other things, help hemoglobin to hold more oxygen. Many sickled red cells will return to their normal shape when carrying a lot of oxygen.

A blood test can be used to determine whether parents are carriers of genes for sickle cell. Carriers are heterozygotes; they have one gene for the sickled-cell trait. If both parents are carriers, they might choose not to have children.

● **Galactosemia** (guh lak tuh SEE mee uh). People who have this disease have two recessive genes for this trait. They cannot manufacture a certain enzyme. The enzyme is necessary for metabolism of a simple sugar, galactose. Galactose is part of lactose, a sugar found in milk. The galactose cannot be converted to glucose because the needed enzyme is missing. The galactose instead is converted to another compound. As that compound builds up, damage to the nervous system results. The damage can lead to an early death. Fortunately, the problems can be avoided by early detection and by a diet which contains no galactose.

● **PKU.** The dangerous recessive allele which causes this rare disease is carried by about one in every hundred thousand persons. PKU results from a missing enzyme and leads to severe mental retardation. An abnormal compound can be found by testing the urine of an infant and thus, the disease can be detected. Symptoms of PKU are prevented by a special diet early in life.

In PKU (phenylketonuria), the amino acid phenylalanine cannot be converted to tyrosine. An alternate pathway changes phenylalanine to phenyl-pyruvic acid, which is excreted in the urine.

FIGURE 8-17. Most states now screen newborn babies for PKU as well as other diseases. Blood taken from the heel and collected on a card like this one is tested. If a positive test for PKU results, the baby can be treated with a special diet.

Lightforce

FIGURE 8-18. Information about Tay-Sachs disease is available from the National Tay-Sachs & Allied Disease Association.

Diabetes may be caused by both genetic and environmental factors.

If both parents are heterozygous, the chances are one in four. If one parent is heterozygous and the other homozygous dominant, the chances are zero.

Diabetes mellitus has been called a "geneticist's nightmare" because it appears that many factors are involved and the disease onset is influenced by many different factors such as weight, age, diet, etc. See Chapter 29.

Principle: The reagent patch of the test strips contains the enzymes glucose oxidase, peroxidase and color indicators. D-glucose is oxidized and the hydrogen peroxide that results from this reaction oxidizes the indicators. The intensity of the color formed is proportional to the glucose concentration in the specimen.

FIGURE 8-19. Diabetics can monitor their own blood sugar level by (a) putting a small amount of blood on a special chemical-treated strip which (b) is read in a glucose determinator. The glucose value for this sample is 146 mg/dL.

The enzyme missing in Tay-Sachs is one involved in glycolipid metabolism. Fatty substances accumulate in cells of the nervous system. The gene for Tay-Sachs is ten times more prevalent in Jews of central and eastern European origins than in other people.

● **Tay-Sachs** (TAY saks) **Disease.** This disease occurs most often in Jewish people and is caused by a recessive gene. A child with this disease begins life normally, but the nervous system fails to develop properly. An important enzyme is missing that breaks down a kind of fat. The child loses ability to move normally, eventually becoming inactive. Death usually occurs by the age of two or three.

There is no cure for Tay-Sachs disease. However, parents in the high-risk group can have a blood test to determine whether they carry the allele. It is then their decision whether to have children. Blood tests can also be done on fetuses to see if they have Tay-Sachs.

What would be the chances of producing a child with Tay-Sachs disease if both parents were heterozygous? What if one parent were heterozygous and the other homozygous dominant?

● **Diabetes Mellitus** (MEL ut us). This disease is believed to be caused by several recessive genes. Factors such as age, weight, diet, and environment also influence the time of onset of the disease. Some persons with diabetes cannot produce enough insulin, the substance necessary for the transfer of sugar. As a result, sugar collects in the blood. Not enough sugar gets into the cells where it can be used as an energy source. Complications such as blindness, kidney disease, and heart disease may develop. There is no cure for the disease, but many people are treated by injections of insulin.

Diabetics find that by monitoring the level of sugar in the blood, the sugar level can more easily be kept within the normal range. If the blood sugar level is very high, the kidneys remove the excess sugar and it appears in the urine. When blood sugar is monitored, high sugar levels can be remedied before the kidneys overwork in removing the excess sugar. A diabetic determining that his or her blood sugar level is high would immediately take some insulin. Low sugar levels can also be determined, and in those cases, the diabetic would immediately eat something to raise the blood sugar level to normal.

a 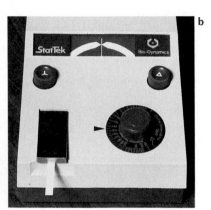 b

Tim Courlas   Tim Courlas

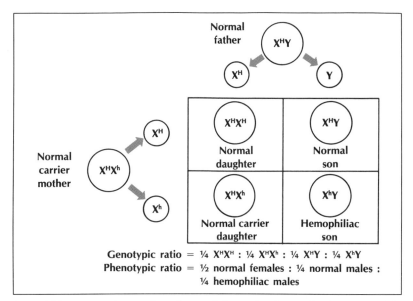

Genotypic ratio = ¼ X^H X^H : ¼ X^H X^h : ¼ X^H Y : ¼ X^h Y
Phenotypic ratio = ½ normal females : ¼ normal males : ¼ hemophiliac males

FIGURE 8-20. A cross of parents with normal blood clotting shows the probability of hemophiliac offspring if the mother carries the hemophilia gene. A female hemophiliac is rare because she must receive a hemophilia gene from each parent. Why is the probability of this occurrence low?

It would be extremely rare for a hemophiliac to be the mother because of the low incidence of female hemophilia. If the mother were just a carrier, it would still be rare for her to marry a hemophiliac because the probability of such a marriage is not high and because most hemophiliacs (in this case the father) do not live to reproduce.

8:10 Sex-linked Diseases

Sex-linked diseases are those diseases with genes that are carried on the sex chromosomes. Therefore, they will appear more often in one sex. These diseases, just as those discussed earlier, are caused by abnormal alleles.

● **Hemophilia** (hee muh FIHL ee uh). In persons with hemophilia, the blood will not clot properly. The disease is the result of a sex-linked recessive gene. The alleles for hemophilia and normal blood clotting are carried on the X chromosome. The Y chromosome carries no matching alleles. Thus, a male is more likely to get the disease than a female. His cells only need one gene for the disease trait to appear. The chances of getting one recessive allele are greater than the chances of getting two recessive alleles. If a male gets the one recessive allele, his blood will not clot properly. The recessive gene results in the failure to make a substance which must be in the blood for clotting to occur.

There is no cure for hemophilia. People with the disease lose large amounts of blood from events that are minor to most people. Usual treatment consists of blood transfusions. Clotting factors, chemicals that help clot blood, are also given to hemophiliacs.

● **Colorblindness.** Some humans do not see red or green. Instead, anything that is red or green appears as gray. These people have red-green color blindness, a sex-linked trait. The genes for color vision are located on the X chromosome. As in other sex-linked traits, a male is more likely to have the defect. Females are often carriers.

FIGURE 8-21. (a) Charts are used to detect red-green color blindness. Persons with normal vision can see a number in the top chart. What is the number? (b) To someone who is red-green color-blind, the chart appears as tones of gray.

The number is 97.

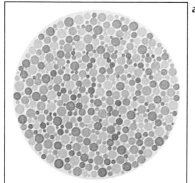

a

Russ Kinne for Photo Researchers

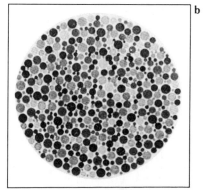

b

Russ Kinne for Photo Researchers

Department of Pediatrics, Children's Hospital, Columbus, OH

Medical Genetics Laboratory, Children's Hospital, Columbus, OH

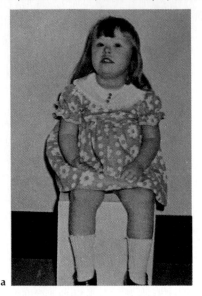

a

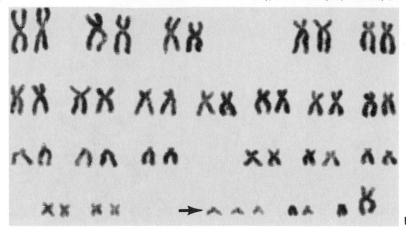

b

FIGURE 8-22. (a) A child with Down syndrome has (b) a karyotype that shows three chromosomes (arrow) for one of the pairs.

Down syndrome is sometimes called trisomy 21 because of the presence of three number 21 chromosomes.

Down syndrome may be caused by nondisjunction.

In Turner syndrome, a female has one X chromosome and no other sex chromosomes.

A person with Klinefelter syndrome is a male with two X chromosomes and one Y chromosome.

13. Answers will vary. In general diseases are caused by abnormal alleles or abnormal inheritance of chromosomes.

14. It results in the presence of an extra chromosome or the absence of a chromosome.

8:11 Chromosome Problems

● **Down Syndrome.** Nondisjunction (Section 8:4) can cause a variety of human defects. One cause of a disease called Down Syndrome is the nondisjunction of autosomes. A person with Down Syndrome caused in this way has one extra chromosome in the cells. Recall that when chromosomes are identified, they are numbered. A Down Syndrome cell has three number 21 chromosomes.

Symptoms of this disease include mental retardation, abnormal facial traits, short arms and legs, and internal defects. At present, there is no treatment for the disorder.

Defects can occur from chromosome abnormalities other than an incorrect chromosome number. Sometimes, parts of an entire chromosome can become attached to other chromosomes. Another cause of Down Syndrome results from this process. Also, a fragment of a chromosome may be missing in some cases.

● **Turner Syndrome** results from nondisjunction of the sex chromosomes. The person has one X chromosome and no Y chromosome. Because there is no Y chromosome, the person is female. However, she fails to develop normal characteristics and is sterile. A person with Turner Syndrome is usually short and sometimes has below average intelligence.

● **Klinefelter Syndrome** results in an XXY chromosome pattern. Those with this disease are males. They fail to develop normal sex characteristics and are usually sterile. They also have very long arms and legs and below average intelligence.

REVIEWING YOUR IDEAS

13. List several human genetic diseases and their causes.
14. How can nondisjunction cause genetic disease?

ADVANCES IN BIOLOGY

8:12 Detecting Human Genetic Disease

More than 200 000 babies each year in the United States are born with genetic disorders or birth defects. Although many of them are minor, others cause severe health problems. Some cause death. Several techniques allow physicians to detect dangerous problems in the fetus (unborn child).

Amniocentesis (am nee oh sen TEE sus) is a process in which a sample of fluid surrounding the fetus is withdrawn through a long, thin needle. The fluid can be analyzed for the presence or absence of certain chemicals which indicate genetic disease. Examples of diseases detected are hemophilia, some forms of muscular dystrophy, Tay-Sachs disease, and sickle-cell anemia.

Some diseases are detected by studying fetal cells found in the fluid that is withdrawn in amniocentesis. The chromosomes in these fetal cells can be studied. Recall that the chromosomes, when photographed and paired, are called a karyotype. Karyotypes of cells can reveal if the fetus has certain diseases, such as Down Syndrome. Other examples of diseases that show in karyotypes are Turner and Kleinfelter Syndromes. (Sex of the fetus may also be determined this way.)

Amniocentesis can be used to determine if a fetus has certain genetic diseases.

Amniotic fluid is usually withdrawn during the 14th-15th week of pregnancy.

FIGURE 8-23. In amniocentesis, fluid from the amnion is withdrawn. The fluid contains some of the unborn baby's cells. The cells are grown and their chromosomes are analyzed. Certain diseases can be determined from this procedure.

AMNIOCENTESIS

Amniotic fluid

Amnion

Uterine wall

Placenta

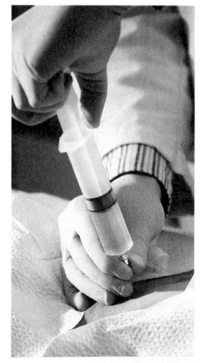

Kenneth Garrett

Gerard Photography

Kenneth Garrett

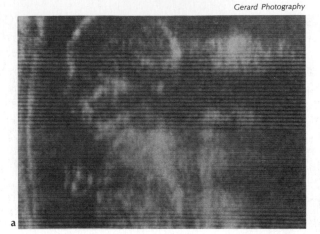
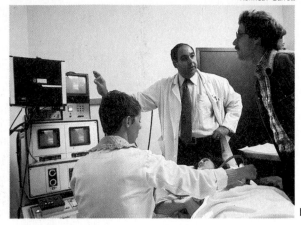

a

b

FIGURE 8-24. (a) This echogram shows the head and shoulders of an unborn baby. (b) Sound waves emitted from the probe at the mother's abdomen "echo" back from the fetus resulting in the production of the image on the screen.

Certain physical abnormalities can be detected using ultrasonography.

Direct observation of a fetus may be made using an endoscope.

Ultrasonography is used in a variety of ways other than fetal examination. For example, it is used to detect location of clogs in blood vessels, such as those in the neck.

A technique called **ultrasonography** (ul truh suh NAHG ruh fee) can be used to determine the position and anatomy of a fetus. An ultrasound probe is passed over the mother's abdomen. It emits high frequency sound waves which "echo" from the tissues of the fetus. Different tissues send back different waves which, together, form an image on a screen. By studying these images, called echograms, physicians can spot abnormalities such as certain forms of heart disease. Ultrasound is also used prior to amniocentesis. Its use ensures that the needle is inserted such that the fetus is not harmed.

Fetoscopy (fee TAHS kuh pee) allows direct observation of the fetus and surrounding tissues. After using ultrasound to determine the position of the fetus, a device called an **endoscope** is used. The endoscope is inserted through a small incision in the mother's abdomen. The fetus is viewed directly through the endoscope tube. An image of the fetus is seen on a screen, too. Using other tools inserted into the endoscope, small samples of skin or blood may be withdrawn for study. These may reveal abnormalities.

For the most part, these techniques are used to determine whether disease exists, not to cure the disease. In some cases, physicians can be prepared for treatment or surgery as soon as the infant is born.

Endoscopes are used in a variety of ways to detect or treat disease in humans other than fetuses.

FIGURE 8-25. An endoscope is an instrument used for seeing inside the body. They are used to examine internal organs and fetuses. Some surgery can be done through an endoscope.

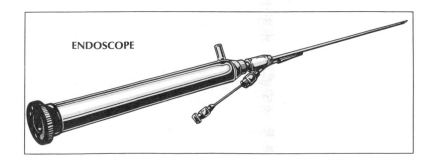

ENDOSCOPE

Yale University, School of Medicine

Yale University, School of Medicine

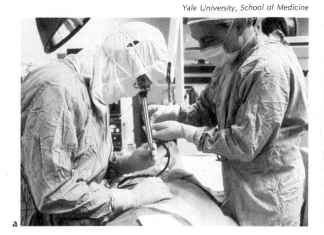

a

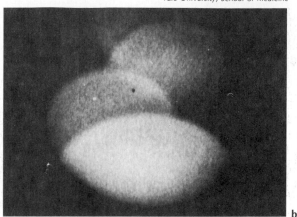

b

Certain problems, though, can be treated before birth. Fetoscopy has been used to give a transfusion to a fetus. It has also been used to remove excess fluid from around a fetus' brain. Recently, an operation was done that temporarily solved a problem in the urinary system of a fetus. The outlook for fetal medicine is bright. It is hoped that a greater number of diseases will be detected, and that more fetuses will benefit from early medical treatment.

FIGURE 8-26. (a) Fetoscopy is a procedure of inserting an endoscope into the abdomen to examine or medically treat the fetus. (b) This picture shows the bottom of the toes of a fetus as seen through an endoscope.

In some cases fetoscopy can be used to treat a fetus.

CHAPTER REVIEW

SUMMARY

1. The movements of chromosomes during meiosis fit with Mendel's Laws about the activities of genes. Alleles are carried on homologous chromosomes.

2. Thomas Hunt Morgan discovered that certain traits are sex-linked. Alleles for these traits are carried on the X chromosomes but not on the Y chromosomes.

3. Bridges' discovery of nondisjunction in *Drosophila* confirmed that genes are located on chromosomes—the chromosome theory of heredity.

4. Bridges' work also revealed the basis for sex determination in *Drosophila*. Later work showed that the basis for sex determination in humans is slightly different.

5. Genes located on the same chromosome are said to be linked. Because linked genes do not assort independently during meiosis, gene linkage reduces the chances for genetic recombination and variety among offspring.

6. Crossing-over is an exchange of the same segments of chromosomal material between two strands of a tetrad. Crossing-over tends to increase variety among offspring by recombining linked genes.

7. The frequency of crossing-over between linked genes can be used in making genetic maps. The more crossing-over that occurs between two genes, the farther apart the genes are.

8. Certain traits show continuous variation. Multiple genes probably control the expression of these traits.

9. Environment may affect the expression of genes.

All Chapter Review answers and additional chapter teaching suggestions are provided in the Teacher's Guide at the front of this text.

CHAPTER REVIEW

10. Genetic abnormalities may result in a variety of human diseases. These diseases may be caused by the presence of alleles for the disease or by an abnormal number of chromosomes.

11. Certain genetic diseases are sex-linked because the genes for the traits are present on the X chromosome.

12. Amniocentesis, ultrasonography, and fetoscopy are methods used to detect human genetic disease of a child before its birth. Treatment is sometimes given before birth.

LANGUAGE OF BIOLOGY

amniocentesis
autosomes
chromosome theory of heredity
continuous variation
crossing-over
fetoscopy
gene linkage
genetic map

hemophilia
lethal gene
multiple genes
nondisjunction
sex chromosomes
sex-linked characteristic
ultrasonography

CHECKING YOUR IDEAS

On a separate paper, complete each of the following statements with the missing term(s). Do not write in this book.

1. Expression of some genes depends upon the organism's _____ .

2. _____ are located on chromosomes.

3. _____ is the failure of chromosomes to separate properly during meiosis.

4. A couple has three sons. The chance that their next child will be a boy is _____ .

5. People with sickle-cell anemia have red cells which do not carry enough _____ .

6. If a color-blind man marries a woman heterozygous for normal color vision, _____ of their offspring are expected to be color-blind.

7. Genes located on the same chromosome are said to be _____ .

8. In order for a white-eyed female fruit fly to be produced, both parents must carry a (n) _____ gene.

9. A human with an XXXY chromosome pattern would be a(n) _____ .

10. Linked genes may be separated by _____ .

EVALUATING YOUR IDEAS

1. Did observation of meiosis verify that genes are carried on chromosomes? Explain.

2. How many pairs of autosomes does a human cell contain?

3. A couple has five daughters. What are the chances that their next offspring will be female?

4. How did Morgan test his hypothesis about sex-linked characteristics?

5. Did the results of Morgan's test (Question 4) verify that genes are carried on chromosomes? Explain.

6. How is nondisjunction explained?

7. State the chromosome theory of heredity.

8. In a certain organism, one chromatid contains the genes *A* and *b*. Its homologous chromatid contains *a* and *B*. What combinations of genes would be found in gametes of this organism if no crossing-over occurs? What combinations of genes might be found in the gametes if crossing-over does occur?

9. Several plants of the same kind vary in height from 15 to 30 cm. How can this be explained?

10. Explain how the cells of a human might contain two X chromosomes and one Y chromosome. What sex is the person?

11. Why are identical twins useful for studying effects of environment on development?

12. In *Drosophila*, the gene for red eyes, *R*, is dominant to the gene for white eyes, *r*. This trait is sex-linked. Determine the probable

CHAPTER REVIEW

genotypic and phenotypic ratios expected from a cross between (a) a heterozygous female and a red-eyed male, (b) a heterozygous female and a white-eyed male, (c) a homozygous dominant female and a red-eyed male, and (d) a homozygous dominant female and a white-eyed male.

13. In humans, the gene for normal blood clotting, H, is dominant to the gene for hemophilia, h. The trait is sex-linked. A woman with normal blood clotting has four children. They are a normal son, a hemophiliac son, and two normal daughters. The father has normal blood clotting. What is the probable genotype of each member of the family?

14. In humans, the gene for normal color vision, C, is dominant to the gene for red-green color blindness, c. The trait is sex-linked. The gene for brown eyes, B, is dominant to the gene for blue eyes, b. Calculate the probable genotypic and phenotypic ratios of the children born to a blue-eyed woman who is heterozygous for color vision and a heterozygous brown-eyed man who is color blind.

15. Explain why blue eyes and blond hair or brown eyes and brown hair are commonly inherited together.

16. List several factors which cause human genetic disease. Give several examples of diseases caused by each factor.

17. Discuss several techniques which are used to detect genetic diseases in human fetuses.

APPLYING YOUR IDEAS

1. Alleles A, B, and C are known to be linked. A crosses over with B ten percent of the time. A crosses over with C twenty percent of the time. Genes B and C cross over ten percent of the time. What is the sequence of the genes on the chromosome?

2. In a certain plant, tall, T, is dominant to short, t. Red flowers, R, are dominant to white flowers, r. A gardener crosses a $TtRr$ plant with a $ttrr$ plant. Seeds from this cross produce 52 plants which are tall and red and 48 plants which are short and white. Explain these results.

3. What would be the result if chromosome parts crossed over between the two chromatids of a chromosome?

EXTENDING YOUR IDEAS

1. Determine the heights of a large number of your classmates. Draw a graph comparing the number of people versus heights. What genetic pattern does the graph suggest?

2. Conduct an experiment with *Drosophila* to show the inheritance of linked genes and the concept of crossing-over.

3. Obtain some tobacco plant seeds. Allow the seeds to germinate under normal lighting conditions. Calculate the phenotypic ratio of leaf color among the seedlings. Repeat the procedure but this time vary lighting conditions to include darkness, normal light, and bright light. Compare your data with those from your first experiment.

SUGGESTED READINGS

Free, Helen M., "Inborn Errors of Metabolism." *Sciquest*, July/August, 1980.

Hendrin, David, and Marks, Joan, *The Genetic Connection: How to Protect Your Family Against Hereditary Disease*. New York, William Morrow and Co., 1978.

Langone, John, "Treating the Littlest Patient." *Discover*, January, 1981.

Singer, Sam, *Human Genetics*. San Francisco, W. H. Freeman and Co., 1978.

"The New Gene Doctors." *Newsweek*, May 18, 1981.

Willis, Judith, "Genetic Counseling: Learning What to Expect." *FDA Consumer*, September, 1980.

Additional student readings and suggested teacher readings are provided in the Teacher's Guide.

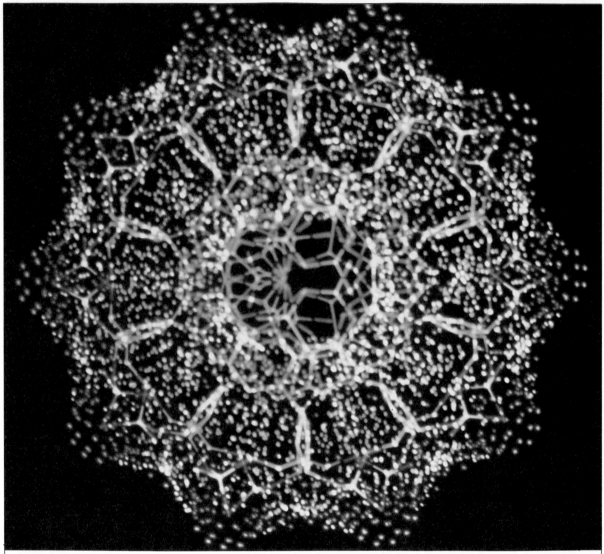

DNA computer rendering above shows structure as viewed from one end looking down the center of the spiral. Color coding: Carbon, green; nitrogen, blue; oxygen, red; and phosphorus, yellow.

UCSF/Rainbow

Generation after generation, genes are replicated and passed on to offspring, and the gene products result in certain traits. How is genetic information passed on in such exact form? A chemical called DNA is responsible. Shown here is a computer drawing of DNA, viewed as you would see it if you were looking down the center of the molecule. DNA directs replication of cells and functions as the chemical of heredity. How does DNA control heredity?

Introduction: This chapter can be introduced with the filmloop *DNA Transformation Experiment*, Holt, Rinehart, and Winston. It illustrates a technique used to "repeat" the classic experiment conducted by Fred Griffith in 1928 (Section 9:1). Two strains of bacteria are used, one of which has a mutation which prevents its synthesizing an amino acid from a minimal growth medium. DNA is extracted from the normal strain and incorporated into some cells of the mutated strain. Students will observe that these cells are then able to grow and reproduce on a minimal medium, indicating a change in the genetic instructions in the cells. The film not only relates the original insight about the role of DNA, but also reviews and applies controlled experimentation.

THE GENETIC CODE

Chapter 9 presents evidence for DNA as the hereditary material and describes the role of DNA in protein synthesis.

The gene is the unit of heredity. Combinations of genes produce certain, predictable features among offspring. What is a gene? Of what materials are genes composed? How does a gene duplicate? How does it regulate the activities of cells?

GOAL: You will gain an understanding of the chemical basis for the transmission of traits, and of the features of genes and their chemical structure.

STRUCTURE OF DNA

9:1 Bacterial Transformation

Experiments with the bacterium *Pneumococcus* (new muh KAHK us) helped answer some of these new and challenging questions. Several strains or varieties of this bacterium are known. (Strains differ genetically.) One strain consists of cells which are enclosed within a capsule. This strain is referred to as "smooth." Another strain has cells not enclosed by a capsule. It is referred to as "rough." Smooth cells cause the disease pneumonia, but rough cells do not.

In 1928, Fred Griffith injected a mixture of heat-killed, smooth cells and living, rough cells into healthy mice. Griffith expected the mice to remain healthy because rough cells do not cause pneumonia and because the smooth cells were dead.

Smooth and rough are forms of *Pneumococcus* controlled by different genes.

Smooth and rough refer to the appearance of colonies. Cells in smooth colonies are capsulated. Cells in rough colonies are not capsulated.

FIGURE 9-1. (a) Injected smooth cells kill mice; rough cells or dead smooth cells do not. (b) When dead smooth cells and rough cells are mixed, bacterial transformation occurs. The injected mixture kills mice.

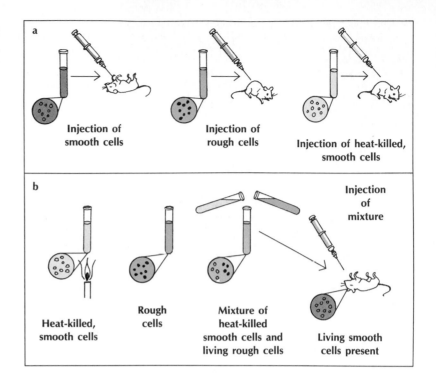

a

Injection of smooth cells

Injection of rough cells

Injection of heat-killed, smooth cells

b

Injection of mixture

Heat-killed, smooth cells

Rough cells

Mixture of heat-killed smooth cells and living rough cells

Living smooth cells present

However, some of the mice died of pneumonia. On examining the blood of the dead mice, Griffith made an unexpected observation—living, smooth *Pneumococcus* cells were present (Figure 9-1)! Had the dead cells returned to life? Of course not.

One strain of cells altered the heredity of the other strain.

There was one reasonable explanation—the dead, smooth cells must have directed the rough cells to become smooth. A hereditary trait of the rough cells must have been changed. This kind of change of trait in bacteria is called a **bacterial transformation.**

It was assumed that a chemical was responsible for the bacterial transformation.

How could such a change in traits occur? Scientists suspected that something, most likely a chemical, in the dead, smooth cells caused the change. If a chemical did cause the change, then that chemical alone could cause a change in heredity.

To test this hypothesis, colonies of smooth cells were grown on a nutrient medium in culture dishes. When enough colonies had formed, they were ground up to release the chemicals from the cells. The chemicals were removed, or extracted, from the cells. The solution of the removed chemicals was called an **extract.** The scientists thought that a chemical in the extract would cause transformation.

The extract was absorbed from the medium by some of the rough cells as they reproduced.

The extract from the smooth bacteria was added to the culture medium in each plate of another set of culture dishes. These plates were then inoculated with rough cells only. When many colonies had formed, cells were isolated for study. On observation many of the cells were smooth! Also, the new smooth cells produced more smooth cells. When injected into healthy mice, the new smooth cells caused pneumonia (Figure 9-2). Controls to which no extract was added showed no bacterial change. They did not cause pneumonia when injected into mice.

The extract had changed the heredity of the rough cells just as the hypothesis had predicted. A chemical in the extract was involved in heredity. It had changed the form of the one strain and had affected the cells' offspring. This chemical was called the **transforming principle.**

The transforming principle was not easy to identify. But in 1944, it was identified as **deoxyribonucleic acid (DNA)** (Section 3:16). DNA was discovered in 1871, but it was not thought to be involved in heredity until this work was done.

Identification of DNA as the transforming principle was made by Oswald Avery, Colin McLeod, and Maclyn McCarty. In 1952, Alfred Hershey and Martha Chase showed that DNA controls viral reproduction. By this time it was becoming evident that DNA is the material of which genes are composed.

9:2 A Model

Other research supported DNA as the chemical of heredity. Biochemists found that DNA is a complex molecule composed of three smaller parts. The parts are a sugar (deoxyribose), phosphate groups, and compounds called bases. The three parts combine to form subunits called **nucleotides** (NEW klee uh tidez). Many nucleotides joined together form a DNA molecule.

In DNA, there are four different bases. They are **adenine** (AD un een), **guanine** (GWAHN een), **thymine** (THI meen), and **cytosine** (SITE uh seen). In Figure 9-3, the chemical structure of each base is shown. Note that each base contains nitrogen. Sometimes the bases in nucleic acids are called nitrogen bases. The chemical structure of each base is shown in the figure on top of a colored shape. Each shape refers to that specific base in the figures that follow. You will easily be able to tell what chemicals are being shown in the drawings if you keep in mind what the shapes represent as you examine the other figures in this chapter.

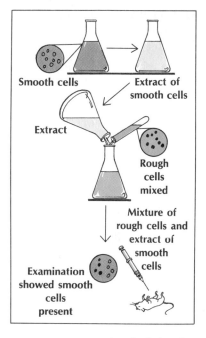

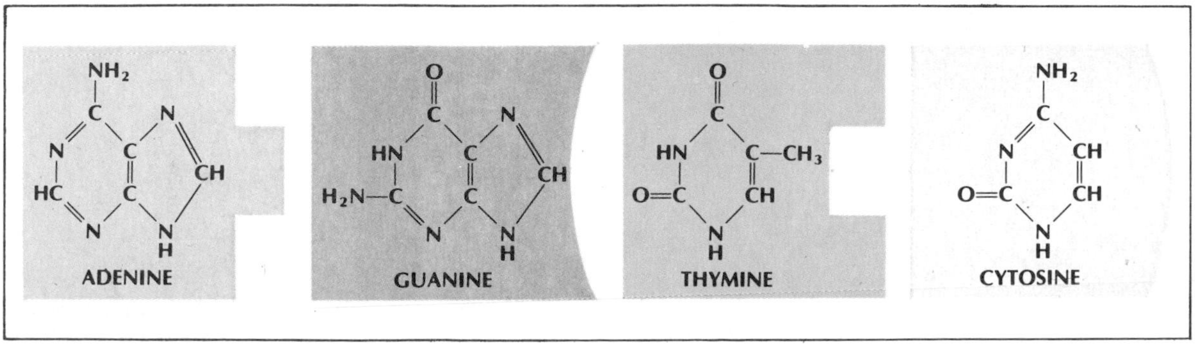

FIGURE 9-2. A chemical in the extract prepared from smooth bacteria caused some rough cells to become smooth.

DNA contains the bases adenine, guanine, cytosine, and thymine.

FIGURE 9-3. The four bases of DNA all contain nitrogen. They are shown on colored shapes that will be used throughout the chapter to represent these chemicals.

ADENINE

GUANINE

THYMINE

CYTOSINE

FIGURE 9-4. The structural formula of an adenine nucleotide shows a molecule of deoxyribose, a phosphate group, and adenine. They are shown on colored shapes that will be used throughout the chapter to represent these chemicals.

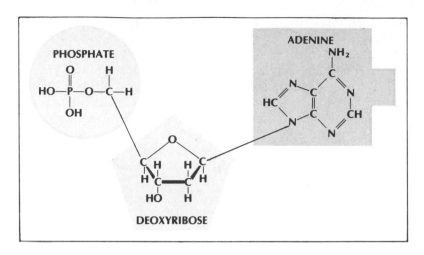

Wilkins used X-ray diffraction to elucidate the spiral structure of DNA. (See *Extending Your Ideas*, question 2 in Teacher's Guide.)

A nucleotide is named for the base which it contains.

A model of DNA, to be of value, must explain how copies of DNA are made.

FIGURE 9-5. (a) In the ladder model of DNA structure, the uprights are the sugar and phosphate molecules. The rungs are the matched base pairs. **(b)** In a 3-D model with colored balls for atoms, the twist of the DNA ladder can be seen. **(c)** A computer drawing of DNA also shows the twist in the ladder.

Each nucleotide is named for the base it contains. Adenine nucleotide contains adenine. Figure 9-4 shows the arrangement of the three parts of a nucleotide. Note again the color shapes that will be used in the figures to follow.

James Watson and Francis Crick combined the results of their own research with the results of other scientists. Much of the experimental work was done by Maurice Wilkins. Watson and Crick presented a model of DNA in 1953. A model is a description that helps you picture something. A model can be used to explain known facts. If the model does not explain the facts, it is of little use. The structural model of DNA had to explain how new cells get exact copies of DNA.

The Watson and Crick DNA model is built like a ladder (Figure 9-5) made of two chains of nucleotides joined together. The uprights of the ladder are composed of the sugar and phosphate parts of the nucleotides. The rungs are made up of the

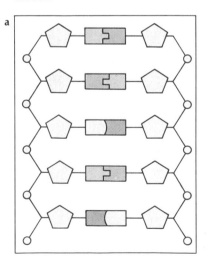

a

b

Ira Wyman/Sygma
Color coding of space-filling model above: C, black; N, blue; O, red; P, yellow; and H, white.

c

McCoy/Langridge, UCSF-Rainbow
Color coding of computer rendering above: C, green; N, blue; O, red; and P, yellow.

nitrogen bases of the nucleotides. Bases have shapes that fit together only in certain ways, much like an enzyme and a substrate fit (Section 4:5). *Adenine nucleotides always join with thymine nucleotides and guanine nucleotides always join with cytosine nucleotides.* Adenine fits thymine and guanine fits cytosine. Notice that the chains of nucleotides are twisted around each other to form a double spiral or double helix (HEE lihks). Watson and Crick included as part of their model this twisting of DNA because the helix is the most stable form possible.

In DNA, adenine nucleotides join with thymine nucleotides, and guanine nucleotides join with cytosine nucleotides.

DNA is in the form of a double helix.

9:3 Replication of DNA

The Watson and Crick model of DNA structure explains the models of the mechanism of DNA **replication** (duplication). Of particular importance to replication is the pairing of bases. By this model of replication, the DNA molecule first unwinds from its twisted form. It then "unzips." That is, weak bonds that hold the bases of the nucleotides together break and the two strands separate. As the separation occurs, the bases of the nucleotides become exposed to the contents of the nucleus. In the nucleus there are many nucleotides which already have been formed. *These nucleotides join the exposed bases only in certain ways (adenine with thymine, guanine with cytosine).* The nucleotides added to one strand of the original DNA molecule form a sequence exactly like that of the other strand. Eventually, joining of new nucleotides to the exposed bases is completed. The nucleotides are joined to each other. The result is two DNA molecules exactly like the original molecule (Figure 9-6). This entire process proceeds by the action of several enzymes and the energy of ATP. For example, DNA polymerase is needed for the synthesis of new nucleotide chains.

As the DNA molecule "unzips," nucleotides present in the nucleus join with the exposed nucleotides; A with T, and G with C.

FIGURE 9-6. Exact duplication of a DNA molecule involves specific base pairing. The two resulting molecules are identical.

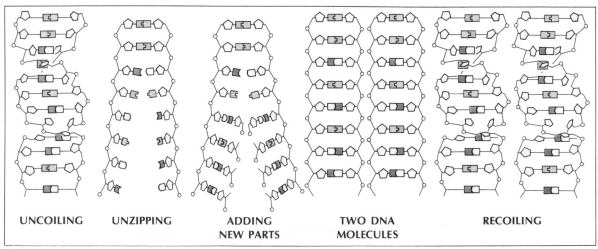

| UNCOILING | UNZIPPING | ADDING NEW PARTS | TWO DNA MOLECULES | RECOILING |

This DNA copying is called semiconservative replication because one strand of each molecule is conserved with each replication. Messelsohn and Stahl first confirmed semiconservative replication.

The structure and replication of DNA fit together with the processes of mitosis and meiosis in eukaryotic cells. DNA is the material which makes up genes and thus, chromosomes. Chromosomes replicate prior to mitosis and meiosis. As a result, new cells and new organisms have the proper genetic instructions. This replication of chromosomes is essentially a replication of DNA molecules. The number of DNA molecules per chromosome is uncertain. Regardless of the number, each DNA molecule must be replicated.

There are models other than the one presented to explain DNA replication. All of them involve proper base pairing. It is certain that much is yet to be learned about this process.

REVIEWING YOUR IDEAS

1. Define the transforming principle. Why is it so named?
2. What compound is the transforming principle?
3. What is a nucleotide? Of what is it composed? How is a nucleotide named?
4. Explain the pairing of nucleotides in the DNA molecule.
5. Compare the DNA molecule to a ladder.
6. Briefly describe a model for DNA replication.

Replication of chromosomes during mitosis and meiosis is essentially a replication of DNA.

1. Transforming principle is the chemical that changed the heredity of rough cells. It was so named because the change was a transformation.
2. DNA
3. A nucleotide is a subunit of a DNA molecule composed of deoxyribose, a phosphate group, and a base. It is named for the base it contains.
4. Because of matching shapes, A pairs with T and C pairs with G.
5. The uprights of the ladder are composed of sugars and phosphates; the rungs consist of paired bases.
6. The two strands of DNA "unzip." Nucleotides in the nucleus join only with the proper nucleotides along each strand. The process results in two DNA molecules which are replicas.

THE ROLE OF DNA

9:4 Proteins in Cells

Mendel first suggested hereditary units (genes) in 1866. Almost a century later genes were found to be made of DNA. The next logical question was how do the genes, regions of DNA molecules, work? What does DNA do?

You recall that proteins are unique organic molecules (Section 3:15) composed of different combinations of about twenty amino acids. A protein may consist of hundreds, even thousands, of amino acids. A certain amino acid may appear many times in a protein. The order of amino acids varies greatly from protein to protein.

Besides the order of amino acids, other factors also make one protein different from all others. The long chains of amino acids are coiled and folded. Thus, the protein has a specific, three-dimensional shape.

As an example, the structure of the protein hemoglobin is that of four chains together. A representation of the 3-D shape of hemoglobin was shown in Figure 8-16. In Figure 9-7, the chains of the molecule are shown folded and coiled as they would be in the final molecule. Remember that each chain is made of a specific sequence of amino acids.

FIGURE 9-7. Hemoglobin is a blood protein made of two α chains and two β chains of amino acids. The chains are coiled and folded in a specific 3-D shape.

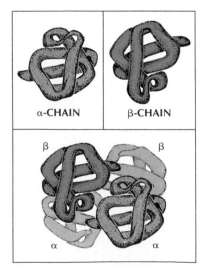

α-CHAIN   β-CHAIN

β   β

α   α

The linear sequence of amino acids is the primary structure of a protein. The coiling is the secondary structure and the folding is its tertiary structure. The arrangement of specific chains (of those proteins that have more than one chain) is called the protein's quaternary structure.

Proteins have specific jobs in cells. Each cell contains thousands of different protein molecules. Many of these are enzymes. The three-dimensional nature of proteins gives each enzyme a specific shape. Its shape "fits" only certain substrates (Section 4:5).

Think of a cell as a constantly working factory into which raw materials are always being brought. These materials will be used in certain ways according to the enzymes present. Each cell is what it is because of its enzymes. Cells differ because each cell's enzymes are different and so their chemical reactions are different. The raw materials are about the same for most cells, but the ways the materials are used are different. Thus, each type of cell is different.

Many proteins are not enzymes. They function in many other ways in cells. They can be parts of cellular structures such as the plasma membrane, chromosomes, and organelles. Some are carrier molecules (Section 5:6) and some have other functions (Sections 19:11 and Chapter 29.

Enzymes control a cell's metabolism. Uniqueness of cells is due to the combination of enzymes at work in them.

Not all proteins are enzymes. Some have other roles.

Some proteins are hormones, toxins, etc. Some proteins are antibodies, highly specific chemicals which protect the body against antigens, foreign materials (mainly other specific proteins).

9:5 Genes and Proteins

Might there be a relationship between genes and proteins? Proteins are unique and genes are unique. Perhaps the role of DNA (the genes) is to guide the synthesis of proteins. This idea could explain, for example, the difference between healthy people and those with sickle-cell anemia. Perhaps the difference in their hemoglobins is caused by a difference in their genes.

Athough the explanations were logical, there was no experimental evidence for them. In 1941, such evidence was provided. It was shown that genes work by forming enzymes.

Today, it is known that genes control the synthesis of every type of protein, not just enzymes. Also, a gene may be responsible for the synthesis of only a single polypeptide (a part of a protein). Hemoglobin is made up of two different pairs of polypeptides that are formed by two different genes. After they are made, they join with one another to form the hemoglobin molecule.

This work, done by George Beadle and Edward Tatum, resulted in what is known as the "one gene — one enzyme hypothesis."

Genes control the synthesis of proteins and polypeptides.

J. Gnau, A. Ottolenghi, G. Marzluf/OSU

FIGURE 9-8. Initial experiments showing that genes function by producing proteins were done with this mold, *Neurospora crassa*. The mold is shown here growing inside a flask.

TABLE 9-1. AMINO ACIDS AND SOME mRNA CODONS

Amino Acid	Codons		
Alanine	GCU	GCC	GCA
Arginine	CGU	CGC	CGA
Asparagine	AAU	AAC	
Aspartic acid	GAU	ACG	
Cysteine	UGU	UGC	
Glutamic acid	GAA	GAG	
Glutamine	CAA	CAG	
Glycine	GUG	GGC	GGA
Histidine	CAU	CAC	
Isoleucine	AUU	AUC	
Leucine	UUA	UUG	CUU
Lysine	AAA	AAG	
Methionine	AUG		
Phenylalanine	UUU	UUC	
Proline	CCU	CCC	CCA
Serine	UCU	UCG	
Threonine	ACU	ACC	ACG
Tryptophan	UGG		
Tyrosine	UAU		
Valine	GUU		

Anticodons of tRNA would be the complements of mRNA codons shown above.

Three bases in a row, a codon, represent one amino acid.

Figure the possible combinations by using 4^n, where 4 = no. of bases and n = the no. of nucleotides in a sequence. Thus, $4^2 = 16$ and $4^3 = 64$.

RNA contains ribose and uracil. It is single-stranded.

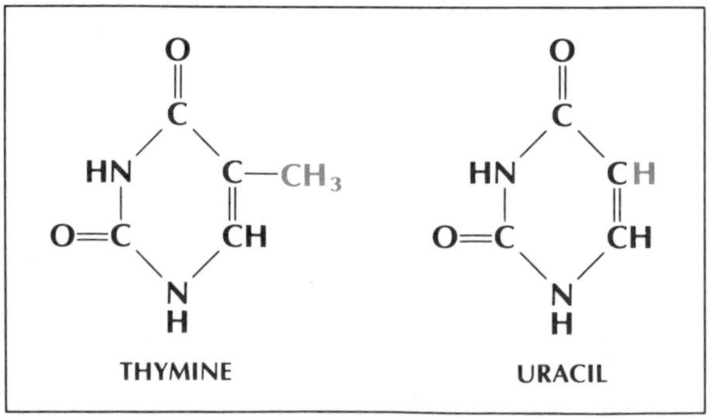

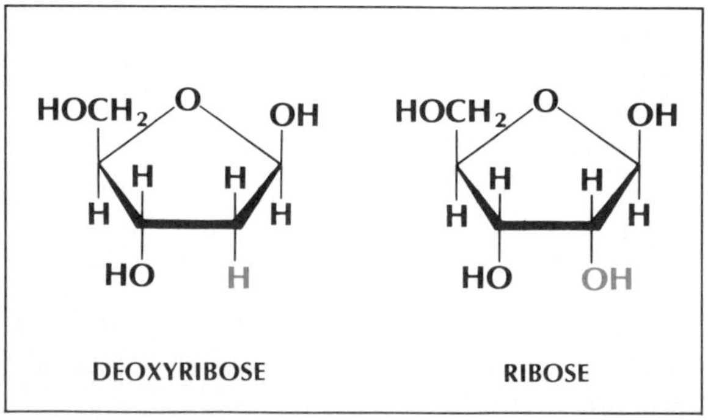

FIGURE 9-9. Uracil has a structural formula much like that of thymine. Deoxyribose is much like ribose. Uracil and ribose in RNA take the places of thymine and deoxyribose respectively in DNA.

9:6 DNA Code

The single DNA molecule of *E. coli* is approximately 3 million nucleotide pairs long (codes for about 3000 proteins).

DNA contains information for protein synthesis. The information is in a code. The sequence of base pairs from the top to the bottom of the "ladder" makes one DNA molecule different from another. It seems reasonable that this sequence of bases is the code.

Recall proteins are composed of amino acids. The order and arrangement of amino acids make each protein different. There are twenty amino acids but only four kinds of bases in DNA. A single base cannot represent an amino acid. Also a combination of two bases in a row along the DNA ladder cannot represent an amino acid. There are only sixteen possible combinations of the four bases two at a time. Three bases in a row, however, give more than the twenty combinations needed. In fact, it provides sixty-four possible code "words." Experiments have shown that three bases in a row do act as the code for amino acids. The three bases representing an amino acid are known as a **codon** (KOH dahn). Some amino acids have more than one codon. In other words, you can get the same amino acid in more than one way (Table 9-1).

The DNA of the cell's nucleus does not leave the nucleus during protein synthesis. However, protein synthesis occurs on ribosomes (Section 5:12) which are located in the cell's cytoplasm.

Different kinds of another nucleic acid, **ribonucleic acid (RNA)** (Section 3:16), are found in the nucleus, the cytoplasm, and the ribosomes. RNA is a chemical similar to DNA. But RNA contains ribose, rather than deoxyribose, as its sugar (Figure 9-9). Also, instead of the base thymine, T, it contains **uracil** (YOOR uh sihl), U. The other three bases—guanine, G; cytosine, C; and adenine, A—are the same as in DNA. RNA is often a single-stranded molecule as opposed to DNA's being double-stranded. What is the relationship between DNA, RNA, and protein synthesis? How is the DNA code passed from the nucleus to the cytoplasm? How is the code "transferred" from DNA to proteins?

THYMINE
URACIL

DEOXYRIBOSE
RIBOSE

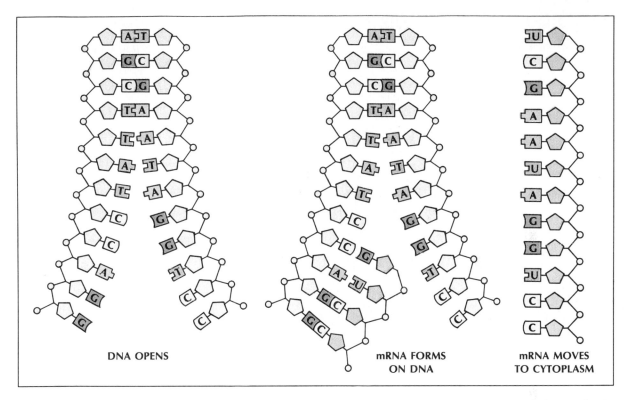

DNA OPENS

mRNA FORMS
ON DNA

mRNA MOVES
TO CYTOPLASM

9:7 Protein Synthesis: Transcription

Protein synthesis begins as a DNA molecule "unzips" (Figure 9-10). As the double-stranded DNA molecule unwinds, the exposed bases of one strand match up with RNA nucleotides. The RNA parts then attach to each other to form an RNA strand. After synthesis of the RNA is completed, it breaks away from the DNA strand. The two DNA strands then rejoin.

An RNA molecule is a single strand of nucleotides. *It has a specific sequence of bases determined by the sequence of DNA bases.* RNA has the code of the DNA strand from which it was made. If a DNA segment contains the nucleotide sequence AGC TTA TCC AGG, it would be changed into the RNA sequence UCG AAU AGG UCC. This sequence contains four codons. Notice that U takes the place of T in RNA. This RNA is called **messenger RNA (mRNA).** The process of transferring the code from DNA to RNA is called **transcription** (trans KRIHP shun). DNA codons are transcribed into mRNA codons.

After the mRNA is made, enzymes "snip" out certain regions that are broken down. The remaining pieces of the mRNA rejoin. The mRNA then leaves the nucleus and becomes associated with the ribosomes.

FIGURE 9-10. Protein synthesis begins when a DNA molecule opens. mRNA is formed on the DNA and moves to the cell's cytoplasm. The process of forming the mRNA is transcription.

During transcription, genetic information is transferred from DNA to RNA.

For simplification of the transcription presentation, the mRNA has had no sequences removed in Figure 9-10. The regions of mRNA removed are formed on the DNA introns. The "snipping out" and rejoining (RNA splicing) is thought to be involved in genetic control in eukaryotic cells (Section 9:13).

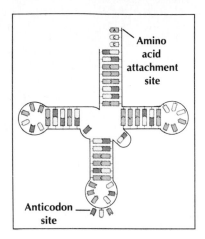

Amino
acid
attachment
site

Anticodon
site

FIGURE 9-11. Transfer RNA is a cloverleaf-shaped molecule, a single strand of RNA. tRNA molecules have different anticodons. tRNA molecules join with certain amino acids and bring them to the site of protein synthesis.

Because tRNA anticodons fit only with specific mRNA codons, amino acids are joined in the proper sequence.

Certain mRNA codons act as "punctuation marks" which signal the end of the message.

After several copies of a protein are made, the mRNA breaks down.

Teaching suggestion: Because protein synthesis is often confusing for students, you might want to summarize the events: 1) DNA code is translated into mRNA; 2) mRNA moves to cytoplasm to ribosomes; 3) tRNA combines with amino acids; 4) tRNA-amino acids attach to mRNA; 5) amino acids attach to each other to form protein.

The sequence of steps during protein synthesis maintains genetic continuity.

Ribosomes are made of a third kind of RNA called ribosomal RNA (rRNA).

9:8 Protein Synthesis: Translation

Certain genes produce another type of RNA called **transfer RNA (tRNA).** Each tRNA is composed of nucleotides arranged somewhat like a cloverleaf (Figure 9-11). The tRNA's combine with amino acids and bring them to the mRNA. There are as many different kinds of tRNA molecules as there are mRNA codons. *Each tRNA combines with only one type of amino acid.* One end of the tRNA molecule combines with the amino acid. This attachment requires an enzyme and ATP. The other end has a set of three exposed bases called an **anticodon.** Each type of tRNA has a different anticodon. In Figure 9-12, the tRNA's are shown as small cloverleaves with their anticodons showing.

When protein synthesis begins, mRNA has become associated with the ribosomes. A ribosome moves along the mRNA strand. As it does so, a tRNA molecule carrying its certain amino acid approaches. The anticodon of each tRNA molecule fits only with a certain codon of mRNA (Figure 9-12a). There is little chance for mistake because of shape requirements for joining. As another tRNA comes along, it "finds" its appropriate codon. Its amino acid links to the previous amino acid with a peptide bond. The first tRNA is then freed to work again. In this way a chain of amino acids is linked together in a specific sequence.

At the end of the mRNA strand is thought to be one of three codons—UAG, UAA, or UGA—which stops the message. Special tRNA molecules that carry no amino acids fit with these codons. So, there is nothing for the chain of amino acids already formed to join. The chain breaks away as a completed polypeptide or protein with a three dimensional shape. The protein is then ready for use in the cell. Several copies of a protein are made from one mRNA molecule. Then the mRNA breaks down. The interaction of mRNA, tRNA, and ribosomes to form a protein is called **translation.** Several enzymes are involved in this process.

The steps of protein synthesis do not occur one at a time. The process is rather a continuous synthesis, different parts of which may happen at once. For example, one end of the mRNA can be read while the other end of the same molecule is still being produced.

Protein synthesis is a remarkable adaptation. The genetic code is stored in the DNA of each cell. It is replicated during each mitosis and later it is transcribed to mRNA molecules. Protein formation results from the translation of the mRNA. This process is very important in maintaining genetic continuity. The chances for mistakes are small because tRNA's only match with certain amino acids and tRNA anticodons only match with certain codons.

Knowledge about genes has increased greatly since Mendel's time. Just how far genetics has progressed is shown by the fact

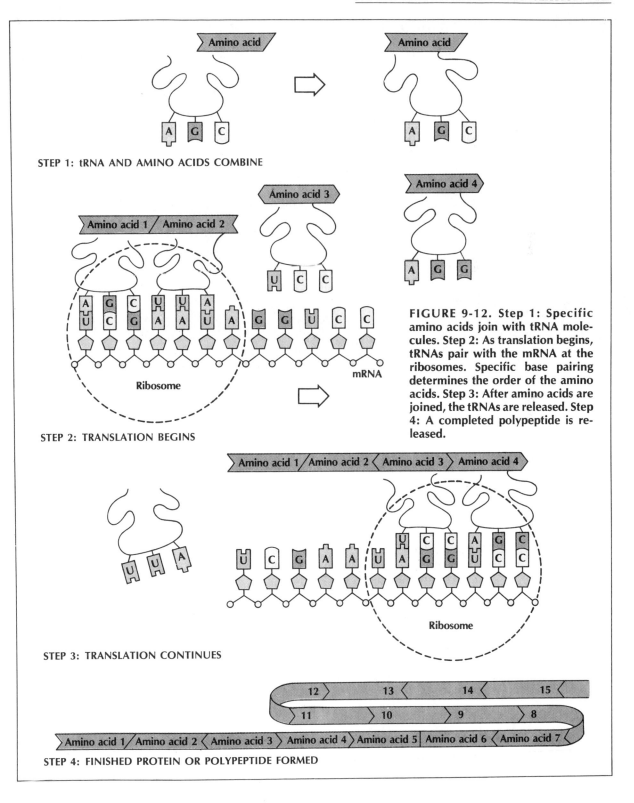

STEP 1: tRNA AND AMINO ACIDS COMBINE

STEP 2: TRANSLATION BEGINS

FIGURE 9-12. Step 1: Specific amino acids join with tRNA molecules. Step 2: As translation begins, tRNAs pair with the mRNA at the ribosomes. Specific base pairing determines the order of the amino acids. Step 3: After amino acids are joined, the tRNAs are released. Step 4: A completed polypeptide is released.

STEP 3: TRANSLATION CONTINUES

STEP 4: FINISHED PROTEIN OR POLYPEPTIDE FORMED

that artificial genes have been synthesized. Some genes can be artificially moved around, also. More recently it has been confirmed that certain genes move around on chromosomes and from one chromosome to another naturally.

A current major area of research involves genetic engineering. **Genetic engineering** is the experimental manipulation of DNA that results in genetic recombination (Section 6:12). Using a technique of moving genes from one organism to another (often a bacterium), scientists can learn a great deal about how genes work to produce proteins and how they work with one another. This technique is discussed in Chapter 13 as an example of the importance of microorganisms to humans.

Techniques of genetic engineering are important in learning about the functions of genes.
7. proteins
8. A codon is three bases of mRNA in a row representing an amino acid. An anticodon is three exposed bases of a tRNA molecule which match a particular codon.
9. RNA has uracil instead of thymine, ribose instead of deoxyribose, and is single-stranded rather than double-stranded.
10. During transcription, the DNA code is transferred to mRNA. During translation, proteins are synthesized according to the mRNA code.
11. Transcription occurs in the nucleus; translation in the cytoplasm.
12. Messenger RNA carries the DNA code. Transfer RNA joins with specific amino acids and carries them to the mRNA at the ribosomes.
13. Genetic engineering is a technique of manipulating genetic information of organisms.

REVIEWING YOUR IDEAS

7. Genes (DNA) control the synthesis of what other chemicals?
8. What is a codon? Anticodon?
9. Compare the structure of RNA to that of DNA.
10. Distinguish between transcription and translation.
11. Where do transcription and translation occur?
12. Distinguish between mRNA and tRNA.
13. What is genetic engineering?

PEOPLE IN BIOLOGY

The process she originally described is called transposition. It was not until almost forty years after Barbara McClintock first discovered the "jumping gene" that the scientific community recognized its importance to genetic theory. McClintock began her research in the 1940's by studying the effects of crossing corn plants that had different kernel colors and textures. She observed kernel color patterns that could not be explained by the genetic principle popular at the time. This principle stated that genes were fixed structures laid out in a line. The results of McClintock's experiments led her to conclude that genes, instead of being fixed, move around on a chromosome, affect each other's functionings, and cause massive mutations. Scientists are just now beginning to realize how important this discovery is and how "jumping genes" bring diversity to a species.

Dr. McClintock is still researching corn genetics at Cold Spring Harbor, Long Island, where she has been for the past forty years. The recognition of the importance of her discovery has led to her receiving many awards, including the National Medal of Science in 1970 and the Rosensteil Award in 1978. In 1981, she became the first Prize Fellow Laureate of the John D. and Catherine T. MacArthur Foundation.

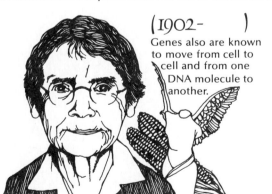

(1902-   )
Genes also are known to move from cell to cell and from one DNA molecule to another.

Barbara McClintock

The genetics with which your students are familiar to this point are based on the idea that genes do not move around. But, as McClintock showed, some genes do. Her work with corn, largely unappreciated at the time, preceded by 30 years work done with bacteria showing transposable elements (transposons).

Tom McHugh for Photo Researchers

Grant Heilman

Larry Hamill

Lightforce

a   b   c

FIGURE 9-13. (a) A white gorilla is a mutant of the normal black gorilla. (b) The legs of the bassett hound are a mutant form of the normal longer legs of dogs. (c) Seedless fruit, such as grapefruit and grapes, are mutant forms of fruit.

EXPRESSION OF GENES

9:9 Mutation

The mechanisms that control the transfer of hereditary traits usually produce normal results. But, sometimes changes, **mutations,** occur. Mutations can occur as a result of changes in either chromosomes or genes (DNA).

Chromosome mutations may occur in many ways. For example, parts of chromosomes can be dropped off or lost during crossing-over (Section 8:6) and at other times. Sometimes these "lost" parts rejoin the chromosome, but they may attach backwards or at the wrong end. Also, they may attach to the wrong chromosome. All these changes can result in abnormal information in the genetic code.

Changes in chromosome number also may occur. In nondisjunction (Section 8:4), gametes with extra or missing chromosomes can be formed. Sometimes a chromosome may fail to attach to a spindle fiber also resulting in abnormal gametes.

Many things result in gene mutations. Some mutations are the result of leaving out a nucleotide or adding an extra one when a new DNA strand is being built. If a nucleotide is left out or added, the remaining codons read improperly.

The rate at which mutations occur varies. A recessive allele that results from mutations causes hemophilia (Section 8:9). Such mutations occur about once in each 50 000 X chromosomes. It is estimated that in *Drosophila*, some gene mutations occur about once in 200 000 gametes. Some occur more often.

Mutations are mistakes in the genetic message resulting from changes in either chromosomes or genes.

Chromosome mutations may occur during meiosis.

Gene mutations often involve the adding or leaving out of a nucleotide during DNA replication.

It is estimated that as high as 10% of human infants have at least one notable mutation. The actual rate of mutation may be higher considering those fetuses which do not complete development. Spontaneous abortion (sometimes called miscarriage) of a pregnancy reduces the frequency of undesirable genes in the population.

Janet L. Adams

Janet L. Adams

CAUTION—MICROWAVES

Do not attempt to operate this oven with the door open. Do not allow soil to accumulate on sealing surfaces. Consult the service manual for precautions to be taken to avoid possible exposure to extensive microwave energy.

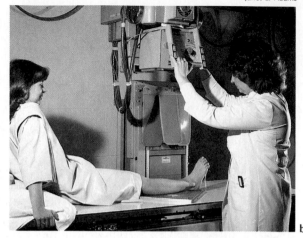

FIGURE 9-14. Because radiation is a mutagen, certain precautions must be taken. (a) Microwave ovens are labeled with warnings about microwave exposure. (b) A lead apron is worn to prevent X-ray exposure of body parts other than the ankle being X-rayed.

They are not passed to successive generations.

Mutations arising in sex cells may spread throughout a population.

FIGURE 9-15. The petite mutation in yeast shows when the cells form small white colonies instead of the normal larger tan colonies. The petite mutation is a mutation in mitochondrial DNA.

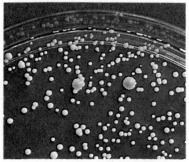

Richard Brommer

Radiation and high temperature are examples of external causes of mutations. Mutation producing agents are called **mutagens** (MYEWT uh junz). Some chemicals such as formaldehyde (for MAL duh hide) are mutagens, too. Mutagens may cause bond breaking in DNA. Mutagens can be used to increase mutation rates.

Regardless of their causes and rates, genetic mutations can be copied as if the code were unchanged. If they occur in a body cell of an organism, they are not important to the species as a whole. Why? But, mutations in the sex cells may affect an entire population of organisms because the information can be passed from one generation to the next. Will mutations be copied if they are very harmful? Explain.

Some mutations may have little effect or even be helpful. Others may be harmful or lethal, resulting in diseases such as sickle-cell anemia, PKU, and Tay-Sachs disease (Section 8:9). Nonlethal mutations may be important for the future by providing a "storehouse of variety" for a population. If a mutation were very harmful, the organism carrying it might not live to pass it to offspring.

9:10 DNA Outside the Nucleus

Most genetic information is probably transmitted according to the scheme discussed in this chapter. But, DNA in a eukaryotic cell is sometimes found outside the nucleus. Eukaryotes have organelles such as mitochondria and chloroplasts that contain DNA. This DNA is called **organelle DNA.** Also, these organelles contain mRNA, tRNA, and ribosomes and carry on some protein synthesis.

Organelle DNA is known to code for tRNAs, RNA of ribosomes, and some other substances involved in photosynthesis and cell respiration. Nuclear DNA is thought to control the synthesis of the outer protein part of these organelles, proteins of For at least one enzyme involved in CO_2 fixation and for a number of polypeptides of the respiratory chain.

ribosomes, and enzymes needed for organelle protein synthesis. Things made in the cell cytoplasm from nuclear DNA instructions can migrate into the organelles.

9:11 DNA and Genetics

What you have learned about DNA and protein synthesis can explain some ideas of genetics. As an example, consider flower color in a plant. Red flowers *(R)* are dominant to white flowers *(r)*. Plants having the genotype *RR* or *Rr* will be red. Plants with the genotype *rr* will be white. How can these patterns be explained?

Genes are DNA, and DNA codes for specific proteins. Suppose the *R* allele (DNA) carries a code that directs the synthesis of a particular enzyme. (Enzymes are proteins.) That enzyme converts a substance in the cells of flowers to a red pigment. The *r* allele (DNA) is a mutant form of the *R* allele. Its nucleotide sequence (and so its code) is slightly different. Because of the difference, the enzyme needed to make red pigment is not produced properly. Thus, a flower which is *RR* or *Rr* will be able to make the red pigment. Its phenotype will be red. But an *rr* flower cannot make any pigment. Its phenotype will be white.

Phenotypes are really the results of *which* enzymes (or other proteins) are produced by certain combinations of alleles. All phenotypes have a chemical basis. An organism is a set of thousands of phenotypes, each of which is based on the synthesis of proteins. Not all the phenotypes that an organism has can be seen. The presence of some, such as type B blood or abnormal hemoglobin, can be determined in ways other than by *seeing* the phenotype.

9:12 A Genetic Control System Optional

What is a gene? The study of protein synthesis shows one way to define a gene—part of a DNA molecule that directs the synthesis of a protein or polypeptide. This type of gene is called a **structural gene.** You know that genes cannot all be making proteins all the time. What controls when genes are active? What controls which proteins are made within cells at certain times?

Much of the current knowledge of genes comes from research with bacteria, prokaryotic cells (Section 5:12). These cells have no true nuclei but they do have DNA like the DNA of eukaryotic cells. Studying of bacteria shows that several types of genes exist for these cells. Some genes control the synthesis of proteins by structural genes. Therefore, they are called **regulator genes.** Like structural genes, regulator genes synthesize mRNA. The mRNA in turn synthesizes special proteins called **repressors.** Repressors determine whether a structural gene will synthesize a protein or not.

Knowledge of DNA and protein synthesis can be related to ideas of genetics.

Phenotypes result from the combination of proteins produced by a given set of alleles.

Teaching suggestion: This section specifically describes an inducible system in a prokaryote. Make sure students realize that this section applies to only prokaryotes, that other systems exist in prokaryotes, and that control in eukaryotes (Section 9:13) is different.

Structural genes direct the synthesis of proteins.

Regulator genes produce repressors which control the activity of structural genes.

FIGURE 9-16. (a) When no inducer is present, (b) repressor molecules bind to the operator gene and prevent synthesis of the enzyme. (c) When inducer molecules are present, they combine with the repressor. (d) Thus, the operator gene is not blocked and the mRNA specific for making the enzyme is produced.

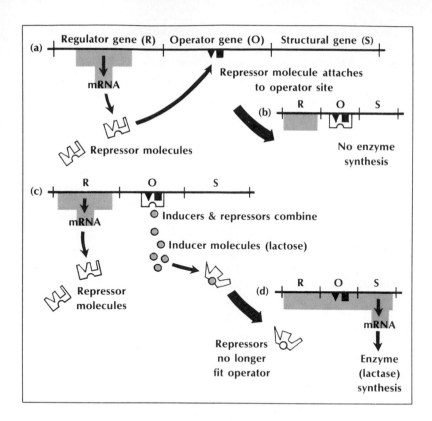

Mechanisms also exist for repression of enzyme production. For example, if some amino acids are added to a culture medium, the cells will stop synthesizing the enzymes necessary for the synthesis of these amino acids.

In enzyme induction, a substrate causes a cell to begin making the enzyme associated with it.

Repressors may combine with the operator genes, blocking the synthesis of an enzyme.

Bacteria called *E. coli* thrive on a culture medium containing glucose. Glucose is their normal energy source. Therefore, the cells constantly produce the enzymes needed to break down glucose. Lactose, a disaccharide, is not normally used as an energy source. The bacteria can be grown on a culture medium with lactose instead of glucose. The bacteria begin to produce the enzyme lactase. Lactase enables the cells to convert lactose to monosaccharides which can be broken down. The monosaccharides can then be used as energy sources. This process in which a substrate (lactose) entering a cell causes the cell to begin producing an enzyme is called **enzyme induction.** The chemical causing induction is an **inducer.** If lactose is removed, lactase production stops.

Enzyme induction depends on regulator genes and repressors. The regulator genes synthesize repressors. The repressors, in turn, combine with a region of DNA called the **operator gene.** The operator is located ahead of the structural gene for lactase. This blocks the enzyme which "unzips" the DNA of the structural gene. Thus, no mRNA can be formed and no lactase can be produced. However, when lactose enters the cell, it combines with the repressor molecule and changes its shape. Then the operator is no longer blocked, mRNA can be formed, and lactase can be produced (Figure 9-16).

What is the advantage of enzyme induction? It results in the production of certain enzymes *only when they are necessary.* In this way, the cell conserves both materials and energy by not producing unnecessary enzymes. Research with other enzymes and with other prokaryotes shows that enzyme induction is common. But, various other control systems have been described for prokaryotes.

Control systems other than enzyme induction also exist in prokaryotes.

REVIEWING YOUR IDEAS

14. What is a mutation?
15. Where is most of a cell's DNA located? Where else is it found?
16. How is DNA related to the expression of a phenotype?
17. Distinguish between a structural gene and a regulator gene in a bacterium.

---

14. A mutation is a mistake in the genetic message
15. Most of a cell's DNA is in the nucleus. Some is found in certain organelles, such as mitochondria and chloroplasts.
16. DNA controls the synthesis of enzymes and/or other proteins which determine a given phenotype.
17. A structural gene controls the synthesis of a protein. A regulator gene controls the activity of a structural gene.

ADVANCES IN BIOLOGY

9:13 Genetic Control in Eukaryotes

With the discovery of gene regulation systems in prokaryotes, biologists assumed similar systems would be found in eukaryotes. It is now known that gene control in eukaryotes is much more complex. As in prokaryotes, the activity of eukaryotic genes seems to depend upon the presence or absence of different chemical substances. Several events being studied occur between a gene and expression of its product.

DNA in eukaryotes has both more and more kinds of proteins bound to it than does DNA in prokaryotes. Most likely some of those proteins are involved in gene regulation, probably at the level of transcription (Section 9:7). (This control is the major kind that occurs in prokaryotes.) Most of the protein molecules bound to eukaryotic DNA are histones. Histones are very basic proteins that play an important role in chromosome structure. However, they probably do not take part directly in gene control. Other proteins (non-histone proteins) are present in smaller amounts and are suspected to be very important in gene activity. In controlling transcription a protein may inactivate a gene by binding to it. Another protein may expose the gene and make it active by removing a bound protein. Certain chemical regulators, hormones, affect cells by "switching on" genes (Section 29:8). It is known that hormones bind to specific sites on DNA, probably directly to proteins located at those sites.

Certain proteins are suspected to be involved in eukaryotic gene control.

The presence of methyl groups bonded to DNA seems to affect gene activity. A **methyl group** is a carbon atom bonded to three hydrogen atoms ($-CH_3$). For reasons that are not yet understood genes that have more such groups seem to be more active in transcription. Inactive genes may become active by the

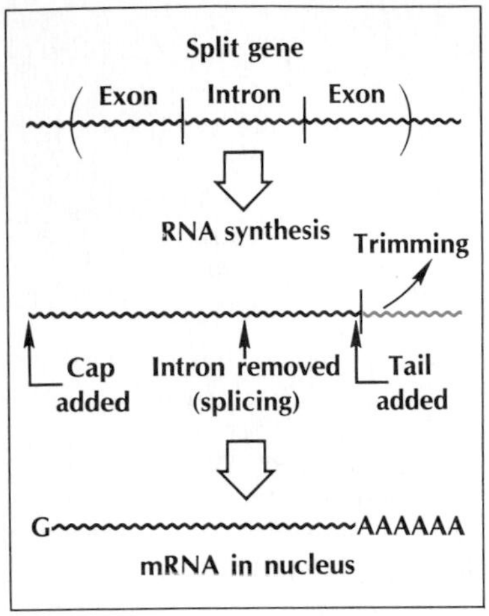

FIGURE 9-17. Splicing, capping, and tailing of mRNA are events which can be involved in gene expression in eukaryotes. These events occur in the cell nucleus.

Proper splicing can control gene expression.

In growing cells, a mRNA molecule may exist for only a few minutes or hours and then is degraded and replaced with a new one.

Some messages are "masked" for years in the cytoplasm.

addition of methyl groups, a process called **methylation**. Or, active genes may become inactive by their removal. Some researchers propose that methyl groups affect gene activity by changing the structure of the DNA. Others suggest that they determine which proteins bind to DNA or how tightly they bind.

Whether or not a gene is active, there are events after transcription is completed that can determine if the product of the gene is made. These events are called "post-transcriptional" events. One class of such events occurs in the nucleus and is called **RNA processing**. mRNA differs from other RNA molecules in certain ways. For example, at one end of the mRNA there is a quanine "cap." At the other end of the mRNA is a long "tail" of adenine molecules. The cap and tail are added in the nucleus after the RNA is made. These changes of the RNA seem to make it bind more easily to ribosomes and be more stable. The functional mRNA is also much shorter than the RNA originally made in the nucleus. Extra parts at the beginning and end are removed in the nucleus in a process called trimming. The pieces of RNA removed are usually unstable and are broken down.

Many genes of complex organisms are called **split genes**. They contain sections of DNA called **exons** that contain the information that codes for the protein product of the gene. RNA copies of exons are present in the mRNA. In split genes, however, the exons are separated by other DNA sequences called **introns** that do not code for the protein. Transcription of a split gene produces a long RNA molecule in the nucleus that contains copies of exons and introns. There are enzymes in the nucleus that remove the RNA copies of introns and splice together the exons so that the continuous set of exon information needed to make the protein is formed. If splicing does not occur properly, mRNA will not form and the gene will not be expressed.

Even after the exons are spliced together and cap and tail added, the mRNA cannot be used for protein synthesis until it is moved from the cell nucleus to ribosomes in the cytoplasm. Very little is known about the steps required to move the mRNA. It is clear that new mRNA in the cytoplasm is associated with proteins. It is likely that those proteins are involved in the transport process.

In most growing cells, once mRNA reaches the cytoplasm, it is used for protein synthesis. However, in some cell types, RNA molecules are stored in the cytoplasm for use later. Stored or "masked" messages are coated with proteins and remain in the cytoplasm until they are "unmasked." The existence of masked messages was first discovered in frog eggs and has been studied there in detail. In egg cells, masked messages can last for years.

After the protein product is made, there are still a number of steps where the product's function can be controlled. Some proteins carry out reactions that occur in a different place in the

For example, histones are proteins of the nucleus; they are made in the cytoplasm but move to the nucleus where they remain. Also, proteins that function inside mitochondria must cross at least two

9:13 GENETIC CONTROL IN EUKARYOTES 173

membranes to reach their site of action.

cell from where they are made or even outside that cell. These proteins must move to their places of action and that movement involves crossing one or more membranes. Most of these proteins are made with extra amino acids that help them cross membranes. The extra amino acids are removed.

Many proteins require the post-translational addition of other chemicals, such as sugars. Sugar molecules are added to proteins in Golgi bodies. Finally, many proteins require activation as a final step.

In this section you see that there are many control steps between a gene and the expression of its phenotype in eukaryotes. They include control of transcription, RNA processing, RNA transport, translation and protein processing and movement. Not all of these control steps are unique to eukaryotes. Bacteria do not, however, have split genes, do not "cap" and "tail" their mRNAs, and do not have to transport mRNA from the site of transcription to the site of translation. A great deal more must be learned about the details of each type of regulation and how all the types work together. Many researchers throughout the world have devoted their lives to unraveling these complex processes.

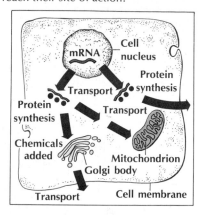

FIGURE 9-18. Genetic control in eukaryotes occurs at many levels between a gene and the expression of its product in a phenotype. These events include transport of mRNA out of the nucleus, RNA unmasking, protein movement to site of action, and addition of other chemicals.

CHAPTER REVIEW

SUMMARY

1. DNA was discovered in 1871. However, its role as the genetic message was not suspected until Griffith's experiments.

2. Watson, Crick, and Wilkins developed the double helix model of DNA in 1953. The "ladder" in this model has uprights composed of alternating sugars and phosphates. The rungs are pairs of nitrogen bases.

3. During DNA replication, the strands of the helix make new strands. Each new molecule contains one original strand of DNA and one new strand.

4. Many proteins are enzymes that control a cell's chemistry. Other proteins may have other functions.

5. Genes code for synthesis of proteins or polypeptides. In this way, genes determine a cell's features.

6. DNA is a genetic code. Bases in groups of three, codons, code for specific amino acids.

7. During transcription, the DNA code is transcribed into messenger RNA. During translation, transfer RNA molecules bring specific amino acids to the messenger RNA on the ribosomes. There the amino acids are assembled in the proper sequence to form a polypeptide or protein.

8. Mutations, genetic changes, may occur in both genes and chromosomes. Some may occur during replication. Others are caused by external factors. Mutations can be harmless, but often they are harmful or lethal.

9. Organelles such as mitochondria and chloroplasts contain DNA and the machinery necessary for protein synthesis. They are known to synthesize certain compounds.

10. Phenotypes result from the synthesis of certain proteins.

11. Study of bacteria (prokaryotes) has shown that enzyme induction can occur and that structural, regulator, and operator genes are present. There are other systems of gene control in prokaryotes, and eukaryotes have different systems, too.

CHAPTER REVIEW

12. Gene control in eukaryotes involves a variety of events. Expression of genes may be regulated during transcription, before mRNA leaves the nucleus, or after a protein has been synthesized.

LANGUAGE OF BIOLOGY

anticodon
bacterial
  transformation
codon
DNA
enzyme induction
exons
inducer
messenger RNA
methylation
mutagen
mutation

nucleotide
operator gene
organelle DNA
regulator gene
replication
repressor
split genes
structural gene
transcription
transfer RNA
transforming principle
translation

CHECKING YOUR IDEAS

On a separate paper, match each phrase from the left column with the proper term from the right column. Do not write in this book.

1. organelle where protein synthesis occurs
2. has an anticodon
3. genetic mistake
4. transcription occurs in this cell part
5. represents an amino acid
6. contains nonnuclear DNA
7. carries DNA code to ribosomes
8. material of which genes are made
9. four kinds in DNA
10. later discovered to be DNA

a. codon
b. DNA
c. mitochondrion
d. mutation
e. mRNA
f. nucleotide
g. nucleus
h. ribosome
i. transforming principle
j. tRNA

EVALUATING YOUR IDEAS

1. How did Griffith explain that living, smooth *Pneumococcus* cells were in the blood of mice?
2. How was Griffith's hypothesis tested? What control was used?
3. What is a model? What facts did Watson and Crick hope to explain by constructing a model of DNA? Did they succeed?
4. Sketch a segment of a molecule of DNA which is six base-pairs long. Show how this segment of a DNA molecule probably replicates.
5. What happens to DNA during interphase? Why is this process necessary? What would happen during mitosis if this process did not occur?
6. Genes direct the synthesis of what kind of large molecules?
7. Why is a codon composed of three nucleotides? What does a codon represent?
8. Using the DNA model of question 4, assume that one strand of the segment served as a pattern for the formation of a segment of a molecule of mRNA. Sketch the segment of the mRNA molecule that would be formed. What information would be contained in this segment of mRNA?
9. How many kinds of tRNA molecules are there? Why?
10. By using diagrams, describe the translation phase of protein synthesis.
11. A certain protein is composed of 1500 amino acids. How long is the gene responsible for its synthesis?
12. How are gene mutations caused? How can a mutation be passed to future generations?
13. How can chromosome mutations occur?
14. Why are mutations which occur in a body cell of an organism not important to the entire species? How may mutations in the sex cells be important to the entire species?

CHAPTER REVIEW

15. Give examples of DNA located outside the nucleus. What are some functions of organelle DNA?

16. A certain bacterium normally does not use sucrose. However, if sucrose is available it begins to manufacture the enzyme sucrase. How is this process controlled? How is it adaptive?

17. Explain several ways in which genes of eukaryotes are controlled.

APPLYING YOUR IDEAS

1. Suppose a gene contains the code for synthesis of an enzyme. During replication of the gene a mutation occurs so that one of the nucleotides is left out. Will the enzyme produced more likely be close to "normal" if the deleted base occurs near the beginning or the end of the gene? Explain.

2. How does the knowledge that mitochondria and chloroplasts have their own DNA systems support a hypothesis that these organelles might actually be descendants of what were once free-living organisms?

3. In a certain flower, the genes red, R, and blue, r, are incompletely dominant. The heterozygous condition produces purple flowers. Using your new knowledge of DNA and protein synthesis, explain why:
   (a) the genotype RR produces red flowers
   (b) the genotype rr produces blue flowers
   (c) the genotype Rr produces purple flowers

4. A dominant allele results in the production of normal hemoglobin. The recessive allele results in abnormal hemoglobin. Using your knowledge of sickle-cell anemia, predict what the red cells of a heterozygous person would look like.

EXTENDING YOUR IDEAS

1. Build a set of models to represent a DNA molecule, the mRNA made from it, several tRNA molecules, and amino acids. Use the model to illustrate the process of protein synthesis.

2. Maurice Wilkins used X–ray diffraction to analyze the shape of the DNA molecule. Learn about this technique.

3. The experiments of Meselson and Stahl and of Taylor, Woods, and Hughes established that DNA replicates according to the Watson-Crick hypothesis. Both experiments made use of isotopes. Prepare a report on each of these experiments and explain how they verified the hypothesis.

4. Prepare a report on radiation as a cause of mutation.

5. Certain strains of *Paramecium aurelia* exhibit a "killer" trait. This trait seems to be determined by cytoplasmic rather than nuclear inheritance. Using library resources, research and prepare a report on this phenomenon.

SUGGESTED READINGS

Frankel, Edward, *DNA: the Ladder of Life*, 2nd ed. New York, McGraw Hill Book Co., 1979.

"Genetic Repair." *Sciquest*, January, 1981.

Jinks, J. L., *Cytoplasmic Inheritance*, 2nd ed. Carolina Biology Reader. Burlington, NC, Carolina Biological Supply Co., 1978.

Milunsky, Aubrey, M.D., *Know Your Genes.* Boston, Houghton Mifflin, 1977.

Patrusky, Ben, "The New Gene." *Sciquest*, February, 1980.

"Selfish DNA." *Sciquest*, March, 1981.

Silverstein, Alvin and Silverstein, Virginia, *The Genetics Explosion*. New York, Four Winds Press, 1980.

Travers, A. A., *Transcription of DNA*, Oxford Biology Reader, 2nd ed. London, Oxford University Press, 1977.

Winter, Charles A., *Opportunities in Biological Sciences Careers*. Louisville, KY, Vocational Guidance Manuals, Inc., 1976.

Additional student readings and suggested teacher readings are provided in the Teacher's Guide.

CHANGES

Nearly two million kinds of organisms are known to live on Earth today. However, these same types of organisms have not always lived here. Over time environments have changed and with changing environments, the types of organisms have changed.

Organisms must be adapted to their environments or they may become extinct. Shown here are fossils of ammonites, sea animals that lived about 150 million years ago. These fossils were found in southern England, which at that time was covered by warm seas. Ammonites were once well adapted to their environment but after their environment changed, they became extinct. Information about them comes from study of their fossils and from study of their present-day relatives, squids and nautiluses.

How did living things originate? What has caused the changes among some organisms and the extinction of others? What information do we have about organisms no longer living? Biologists attempt to answer these and related questions using scientific methods. In Unit III, you will study some of the evidence that has been gathered and some of the conclusions that have been made. You also will study how living things are classified.

Fossil Ammonites

Fossils are remains or evidence of things which were once alive. They can be found in almost every part of the world. Special techniques are used to dig up and preserve these remains for study. Here, workers in South Dakota are digging up the remains of mammoths. Mammoths are animals that lived several thousand years ago and resemble elephants. How is the age of a fossil determined? What kinds of information are obtained from fossils?

Introduction: The idea of evolution is introduced in this chapter by exploring the evidence behind the theory. One line of evidence is the fossil record. Student interest can be stimulated by the opportunity to examine a variety of fossils. If your school does not have a collection, you can start one by purchasing specimens from suppliers of earth science materials. Also, *Voyage to the Enchanted Isles* is an outstanding film which recounts Charles Darwin's findings on the Galapagos Islands. This film combines excellent footage of the diversity of unique plant and animal life examined by Darwin with an explanation of heredity and adaptive change by natural selection. The film can be rented from University of Illinois Film Center, 1325 South Oak Street, Champaign, IL 61820.

CHANGE WITH TIME

Chapter 10 introduces the evidence for the theory of evolution and the origin and explanation of Lamarckian and Darwinian theories of evolution.

The earth is thought to be nearly five billion years old. Biologists estimate that life first appeared on Earth more than three billion years ago. Both the earth and the organisms inhabiting it have changed during that time. The change in organisms over a period of time is called **evolution.**

Different explanations have been given to explain how evolution occurs. Some of these explanations will be studied later in this chapter. First, it is helpful to study evidence that living things change.

GOAL: You will gain an understanding of evolution (changes in living things) and the evidence supporting the theory of evolution.

The theory of evolution is the most widely accepted scientific explanation of the origin of life and changes in living things. You may wish to investigate other theories.

Teaching suggestion: If some students have fossil collections, you might want to encourage them to share the collections with the class.

EVOLUTION: EVIDENCE

10:1 Fossils: Formation and Dating

Any part of or trace of a once living organism is called a **fossil.** A fossil may be all, part, or an imprint of an organism. Some entire organisms have been found frozen in ice or enclosed in amber. But this type of fossil is rare. When most organisms die, they are quickly decomposed (Section 1:4), so no record of their life is left. In order for a fossil to form, something must happen to prevent the organism or part of it from decaying. A hard part of an organism, such as a bone or a tooth, may be preserved if it is surrounded and compressed by clay or sand soon after the organism dies. The surrounding sediments prevent decomposition. Then, as the sediments turn to rock over long periods of time, the part of the organism is preserved.

Fossils formed in sedimentary rock are the most common fossils. Sedimentary rocks form by particles settling on top of each other. Layers of the particles are built up. When the layers

FIGURE 10-1. The impression of a fern leaf in rock is a fossil formed when the leaf is pressed into mud that hardens. The leaf decomposes leaving the impression.

University of Houston

Frank Balthis

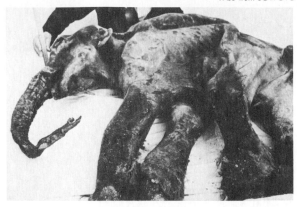

a

b

FIGURE 10-2. Parts of animals and whole animals have been found preserved. (a) Bones of dinosaurs and other animals have been uncovered in excavations at Dinosaur National Monument, Utah. (b) This baby mammoth was unearthed from frozen ground in the Magadan territory of Russia.

Half-life is the time necessary for one half of a radioactive sample to disintegrate.

FIGURE 10-3. (a) Undisturbed sedimentary rock shows flat layers of deposits. Fossils found in lower layers of undisturbed sedimentary rock are older than fossils found in top layers. (b) When sedimentary rock is disturbed, age of fossils is sometimes harder to determine.

are undisturbed, the lower layers are the oldest and the upper layers are the newest. As an analogy think of this situation. If you stacked up newspapers adding the current paper each day to the top, as long as the stack was undisturbed, the oldest paper would be on the bottom and the newest paper would be on the top. Fossils found in undisturbed lower layers of rock are of organisms older than those whose fossils are found in upper layers. The relative time of appearance and disappearance of many organisms can be determined from this layering.

There are more accurate methods of dating organisms. These methods are based on the use of isotopes. Recall that isotopes (Section 3:2) are atoms that differ in the number of neutrons they have. Some isotopes have unstable nuclei and are called **radioactive isotopes.** The unstable nuclei break down and give off particles. You may be familiar with Geiger counters. Geiger counters are instruments that detect those particles. Energy is also given off. When radioactive isotopes decay, matter changes to energy at known rates. The **half-life** of an isotope is the time needed for one half of the radioactive material to decay. Carbon 14 is a radioactive isotope with a half-life of 5730 years. After 5730 years, half of an original carbon-14 sample will have changed to energy.

a

b

Michael Collier

Larry Roberts

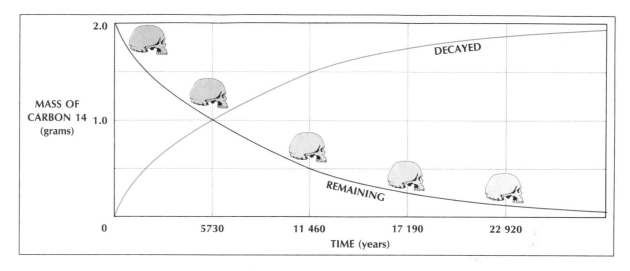

All living things contain some radioactive isotopes. During photosynthesis, plants take in radioactive carbon from the air. The carbon is in the form of $^{14}CO_2$. This carbon enters all organisms through food chains (Section 1:4). A given mass of living tissue contains a certain amount of radioactive carbon. Scientists compare the amount of radioactive carbon remaining in a fossil with the amount in the same mass of living tissue today. By using the half-life, they can approximate the age of the fossil. This method is known as radiocarbon dating and gives results valid for fossils up to about 20 000 years old.

Ages of older fossils can be estimated by studying surrounding rock samples for other radioactive elements such as uranium and potassium. These elements have a much longer half-life than carbon 14. Thus, they can be used for dating fossils millions of years old.

FIGURE 10-4. Radioactive decay of carbon 14 is the principle behind radiocarbon dating. The age of a fossil is determined by comparing amounts of carbon 14 present in living organisms with the amount remaining in the fossil. For example, if a fossil contained 0.5 g carbon 14 and living specimens contained 2 g, the fossil would be about 11 460 years old. In this time three-fourths of the carbon 14 decayed.

Some fossils can be dated by studying radioactive decay in rock samples.

Teledyne Isotopes Radiocarbon Laboratory

FIGURE 10-5. In the process of radiocarbon dating, carbon dioxide gas is purified in this apparatus prior to its analysis for carbon-14 content.

10:2 Fossil Record: Interpretation

Earth's history can be divided into **eras** and subdivided into **periods.** Table 10-1 gives a brief account of the earth's history and the major life forms of each period. Much information about life in the past comes from the fossil record.

What general facts come from the study of fossils? Many fossils give information about types of organisms no longer living on Earth. Such organisms are said to be **extinct.** Extinct organisms are studied in terms of what is known about the environment at the time and place the organisms lived. It seems that organisms were adapted to their environments. But, environments change. If a kind of organism is to survive, it must "fit" the new environment. Many organisms did not "fit," so they became extinct.

In order to survive in a changing environment, organisms must adapt.

TABLE 10-1. GEOLOGIC TIMETABLE AND MAJOR LIFE FORMS				
Era	Period	Epoch	Age (years ago)	Representative Life Forms
CENOZOIC	Quaternary	Recent	100 000	Humans; modern forms of plants and animals
		Pleistocene	1 000 000	Extinction of many mammals; primitive humans; grasslands
	Tertiary	Pliocene	10 000 000	Early humans; other mammals; herbs
		Miocene	30 000 000	Mammals; grasses
		Oligocene	40 000 000	Primates and other mammals; forests common
		Eocene	60 000 000	Primitive horse; other mammals; flowering plants
		Paleocene	75 000 000	Mammals predominant; more modern flowering plants
MESOZOIC	Cretaceous		135 000 000	Extinction of giant reptiles; birds and insects; flowering plants
	Jurassic		165 000 000	Dinosaurs dominant; primitive birds and mammals; earliest flowering plants
	Triassic		205 000 000	Dinosaurs and other reptiles; early mammals; primitive seed plants
PALEOZOIC	Permian		230 000 000	Rise of insects; early reptiles
	Carboniferous		280 000 000	Insects and amphibians; mosses and ferns
	Devonian		325 000 000	Age of fishes; early amphibians; early bryophytes; ferns
	Silurian		360 000 000	Club mosses; insects and other invertebrates
	Ordovician		425 000 000	Primitive mollusks and fish; algae
	Cambrian		500 000 000	Protists; sponges; jellyfish; spore-producing plants
PRECAMBRIAN			5 000 000 000	Monerans; simple protists; fungi; simple invertebrates

Studies of fossils also indicate that older organisms (found in lower layers) are generally less complex than newer ones (found in upper layers). Thus, biologists have concluded that simpler forms of life existed first. These simpler forms of life were gradually added to or replaced by more complex forms.

From looking at the fossil record as a whole, the number of early forms of organisms was small. The number of forms increased more and more rapidly as time progressed. Earliest fossils represent aquatic organisms. Later fossils indicate that organisms began to live on land.

The fossil record is not perfect. Many fossils linking one organism to another have not been discovered. However, it seems to indicate that life forms on Earth have changed.

Simple forms of life appear to have existed before complex forms.

Fossil records indicate that life today is different from that of the past.

10:3 Comparative Anatomy

Study of the structures of different organisms is called **comparative anatomy.** Figure 10-6 shows the legs of several familiar animals. Note that the bones are similar but slightly different in structure. Each animal has a leg structure which is a variation of a common pattern.

The legs of these animals are all used in walking, but the actual method of walking varies. The different bone structures

Comparative anatomy is the study of structures of different types of organisms.

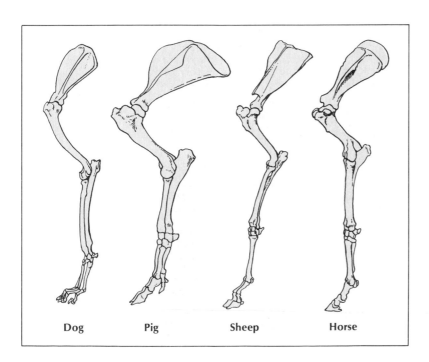

Dog Pig Sheep Horse

FIGURE 10-6. The leg and foot structures of many vertebrates appear similar in the number and locations of the bones. Each, however, is slightly different.

FIGURE 10-7. These limb structures are homologous. Although their functions are different, their structure and origin are similar. Is an insect wing homologous with these structures?

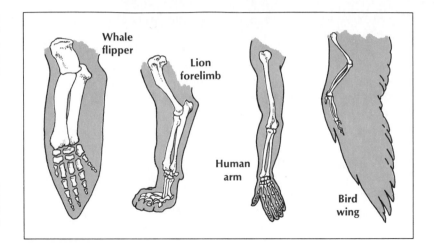

Bird and insect wings, parts with similar functions, are examples of analagous structures. Analagous structures result from convergence (Section 11:8).

Homology is the basis for classifying organisms (Section 12:3). Homologous structures are those with a common embryological origin.

The cat and dog have more homologous structures than the cat and giraffe and so are more closely related.

Homologous parts indicate common ancestry among organisms.

FIGURE 10-8. The two small toes on the pig's foot and the human appendix are examples of vestigial structures. They have no apparent function.

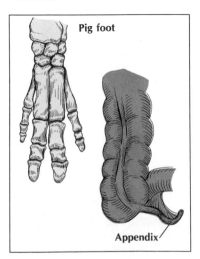

are suited to the particular way each animal walks. This similarity suggests that the animals are all related. Their ancestors had the same basic leg structure seen in each of them. Over many years, each animal's leg structure evolved "fitting" its way of life.

These structures often have the same basic structure because they developed in similar ways. Structures that are similar in structure and origin, such as the leg bones of these animals, are said to be **homologous.** Their presence is considered evidence of evolution from a common ancestor. The fewer the number of homologous structures shared by organisms, the less closely related the organisms must be.

Both birds and insects have wings. The wings of the two organisms have the same function but their structures are quite different, and they develop in entirely different ways. Therefore, their wings are not homologous. Birds and insects are not closely related and fossil evidence supports this assumption. Do you think a cat is more closely related to a dog or to a giraffe? Why? Do you think two animals are more closely related than an animal and a plant?

Certain structures have no known functions and are called **vestiges** (VES tih juz) or **vestigial** (veh STIHJ ee ul) **organs.** The pig's two small toes (Figure 10-8) are vestigial because they are not used. The human appendix, a small sac connected to the large intestine, is also a vestige. Why is it there? At one time in the past, perhaps some ancestor of humans may have had an appendix with some major function. It may have functioned in digestion. As humans evolved, the basic body plan of their ancestors remained the same. They inherited the appendix as part of that body plan, but it may no longer have the same function as before. Thus, presence of vestigial structures is considered as evidence of evolution.

10:4 Other Comparisons

Organisms can be compared in other ways, giving more evidence for evolution. **Comparative embryology** is the study of the development of different organisms. A developing organism is sometimes called an embryo. Similarities and differences can be seen in embryos of different organisms. These comparisons can show relationships.

It would be difficult for you to tell an early human embryo from an early pig embryo. Why are they so much alike? It is thought that humans and pigs are related. The more alike the embryos and development patterns of two organisms are, the more closely related the organisms are thought to be. Maybe the human and the pig have inherited the same basic body plan from a common ancestor and begin their development in the same way. But although they are similar, they have changed from the ancestor into their present development patterns.

Often biologists compare organisms on a biochemical level. **Comparative biochemistry** also supports the theory of evolution. For example, the hemoglobin of a chimpanzee and of a human are similar. They are more similar than the hemoglobin of a human and a dog, or of a dog and an earthworm. Again, the greater the similarity, the greater the assumed relationship between the organisms. A human and a chimpanzee are much more closely related than are a human and a dog. One possibility for the similarity between them is that they might have a more recent common ancestor. In a broad sense, chemical similarities are homologous just as development or parts of organisms are homologous. Thus, the human, the chimpanzee, the dog, and the earthworm have changed from the ancestors into present forms.

Comparative embryology is the study of embryos of different types of organisms.

Parts of closely related organisms have similar patterns of development.

Comparative biochemistry is a study of various organisms on a chemical level.

FIGURE 10-9. Stages of embryonic development are similar in closely related animals. The early embryos of certain animals look so much alike that it is difficult to distinguish among them. Only in later stages do they become easily recognizable.

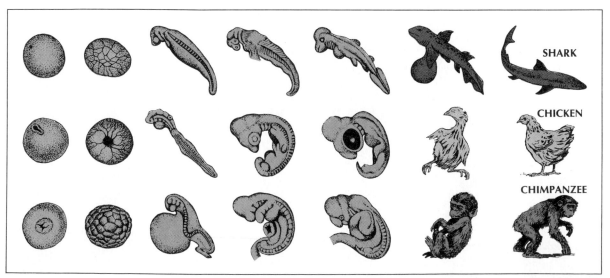

SHARK

CHICKEN

CHIMPANZEE

Teaching suggestion: You might want to point out that common ancestry is a better explanation for homologies than assuming that similar features evolved independently over and over again.

10:5 Genetics

Evidence so far presented is further strengthened by genetics. Genes can change as a result of mistakes in DNA replication or from external causes (Section 9:9). Also, the chromosomes can change through mistakes in mitosis and meiosis. New alleles of genes occur through the mutation of existing alleles, and changes in genotypes can cause changes in phenotypes. Also, meiosis reshuffles genes, or sorts them into new combinations. Thus, the genetic codes for the features of organisms can change.

Genetics explains the origin of change in organisms.

Organisms do not remain the same because mutation and genetic recombination (Section 6:12) are among the factors which increase variability in populations. Thus, *mutation and genetic recombination could be called the "raw materials" of evolution*. It is reasonable to assume that genetic information has been changing for many years.

Mutation and recombination lead to variability in populations.

For thousands of years humans have made use of the fact that genetic information changes. Perhaps they did not think of plant and animal breeding as a *form* of evolution, but it is. The development of crops of wheat and corn from plants different from the new ones is an example of evolution. Plants with the "best" traits were selected and bred with one another so the traits would be passed on to the offspring. The techniques were used for ornamental plants as well as for crop plants. These practices are called **selective breeding.**

Selective breeding is a form of evolution controlled by humans.

Recombinant DNA will be discussed further in Section 13:19.

The same technique was used in the taming of animals such as dogs, cats, cattle, and horses. These domestic animals are descendants of wild animals. They are the products of selective breeding.

FIGURE 10-10. Plants have been selectively bred (a) for better fruits and (b) as ornamentals. Some animals have been selectively bred (c) as work animals.

Hickson-Bender Photography

L and M Photo

Robert Mischka

10:6 Evolution Observed

Evidence for evolution so far presented is indirect. "Evolution in action" has not been shown. Most evolutionary changes occur gradually over such a long period of time that they cannot be observed. Changes may occur over thousands of years. However, some changes occur rapidly. Rapid changes provide direct evidence of evolution.

Penicillin kills many kinds of bacteria. Where the bacteria are killed by the drug, a clear zone forms (Section 2:2). Usually no bacteria survive in the clear zone. Sometimes, however, a few bacteria survive the penicillin treatment. They live to form colonies of bacteria that are resistant to penicillin. If some of the surviving bacteria are transferred to another culture containing penicillin, they continue to produce more bacteria resistant to penicillin.

The millions of bacteria in each colony are offspring of a single bacterium which happened to be resistant to penicillin. When penicillin was added (a change in the environment), resistance became very important for survival. All the bacteria which were not resistant died. Those that were resistant survived to reproduce. Thus, the population of bacteria evolved because all the organisms living after the change in the environment are adapted to the new environment.

Bacteria cause many diseases in humans and animals (Chapter 19). Therefore, evolution of bacterial resistance to penicillin and other antibiotics is a serious problem. When some resistant forms of bacteria cause disease, the drugs will not kill them. For this reason, scientists continually search for new antibiotics to treat bacterial diseases.

Teaching suggestion: Show the film loop *Adaptation of Bacteria by Natural Selection* as you teach this section. It is available from Encyclopedia Brittanica Educational Corp., 425 N. Michigan Ave., Chicago, IL 60611.

Bacteria resistant to penicillin produce offspring which also resist penicillin.

Industrial melanism (Section 11:3) provides another example of direct evidence of evolution.

In an environment of penicillin, only resistant bacteria survive and reproduce.

Because bacteria become antibiotic resistant, scientists search for new, effective antibiotics.

REVIEWING YOUR IDEAS

1. What is the theory of evolution?
2. What is a fossil? Give three examples of different kinds of fossils.
3. How is the relative time at which organisms lived on Earth determined?
4. How is an understanding of radioactive decay of isotopes useful in determining the age of certain fossils?
5. What is radiocarbon dating?
6. What does extinct mean?
7. What does the fossil record indicate about complexity of organisms and the position of their fossils in rock?
8. What are homologous structures?
9. What does comparative anatomy reveal about the relationships among organisms? Comparative embryology? Comparative biochemistry? Genetics?

1. It is the explanation of changes in organisms with time.
2. A fossil is any remains or evidence of a once living thing. Examples may include parts of organisms, whole organisms, tracks or prints of organisms, and so on preserved in stone, amber, ice, etc.
3. by studying the layers of sedimentary rock in which the fossils appear
4. It leads to a method for determining age of fossils.
5. Radiocarbon dating is a method of fossil dating based on comparison of the amount of radioactive carbon found in a fossil with the amount found in the same mass of living tissue.
6. Extinct refers to types of organisms which are no longer living.
7. Older organisms are generally less complex than newer ones. Fossils found in lower layers are generally less complex than those found in upper layers.

8. structures with a common origin and similar structure

9. Comparative studies show relationships and common ancestry. Genetics explains the sources of genetic change.

EVOLUTION: SOME EXPLANATIONS

10:7 Lamarck

Lamarck thought of evolution in terms of independent lines rather than common descent. Moreover, each line originated by spontaneous generation. He thought that organisms had an inner drive for perfection. Lamarck's insight into evolution originated with his work on classification.

Many biologists believed that evolution occurs, but very few of them gave explanations of *how* it occurs. In 1809, a French naturalist, Jean Baptiste de Lamarck (luh MARK), published a book called *Zoological Philosophy*. The ideas about evolution in the book are known as Lamarckism (luh MAR kihz um).

Lamarck had studied evolution and was certain of its existence and importance. He saw evolution as a "ladder of life" from the simplest to the most complex animals, with humans as the top rung of the ladder. Lamarck did little in the way of explaining the origin of this ladder, but he did offer an explanation for the origin of adaptations.

Lamarck's thinking revolved around two basic assumptions. The first of these was the **law of use and disuse.** According to Lamarck, an organism could change certain body features during its lifetime. He thought that by using a certain part of its body, an animal could change the part to better fit the environment. On the other hand, by disuse, a body part would begin to disappear. In either case, the changed feature was called an **acquired characteristic.** The feature was acquired during the organism's life.

Lamarck thought that characteristics could be obtained or lost as a result of use or disuse.

Lamarck's second assumption was the **inheritance of acquired characteristics.** He thought that acquired characteristics were passed on to (inherited by) the offspring of that individual and would occur generation after generation. Gradually a group of organisms better able to survive would evolve.

Often used to illustrate Lamarck's hypothesis is the giraffe's long neck. Lamarck assumed that long-necked giraffes evolved from short-necked ancestors. He would explain the phenomenon in this way. The short-necked ancestors could graze on grasses, but the grasses began to disappear (a change in the environment) so the only remaining food source was the leaves of trees. According to Lamarck, each short-necked giraffe would try to reach the leaves of trees and thus would stretch its neck. As these individuals reproduced, the results of neck stretching (an acquired characteristic) would be passed on to the offspring which would be born with slightly longer necks than those of their parents. Thus, long-necked giraffes gradually evolved.

Lamarck's hypothesis can be criticized on several points. The law of use and disuse is a poor idea because it implies that an organism can sense its needs and physically change to meet the needs.

FIGURE 10-11. Lamarck would have explained the evolution of the giraffe's long neck by saying that individuals stretched their necks. The longer necks were then passed on to future generations.

Pangenesis was an explanation which attempted to explain the transmission of information from body cells to gametes. Pangenes were supposedly produced by body cells, poured into the bloodstream, and sent to the sex organs. There they entered the gametes.

10:8 DARWIN: GATHERING EVIDENCE   **189**

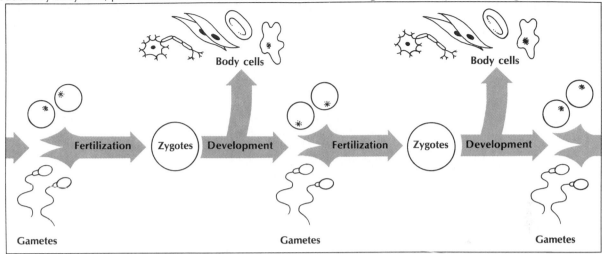

Body cells

Fertilization — Zygotes — Development — Fertilization — Zygotes — Development

Gametes   Gametes   Gametes

Inheritance of acquired characteristics suggests that these changes (in body cells) can be passed to offspring. It is known that genetic information is passed from generation to generation in the gametes (Section 6:9). If inheritance of acquired characteristics were true, the changing body cells would need to have a way of "informing" the sex cells about the change. However, information "flows" from the zygote to the body cells. There is no way for it to "flow" from body cells to the gametes (Figure 10-12). Thus, even if changes could occur by use and disuse, they could not be passed to offspring. If inheritance of acquired characteristics were true, a person with well-developed muscles would produce a child with well-developed muscles, but such is not the case. Also, it is known that a mutation in a body cell does not change the genes in sex cells (Section 9:9).

Another criticism of inheritance of acquired characteristics is that there has never been an experiment which supports it. To be accepted, a hypothesis must be confirmed by experiments (Section 2:5). Because all attempts to confirm this hypothesis have failed, it should be regarded as invalid. Lamarck did offer an explanation for the means by which evolution occurs even though there is no evidence to support his hypothesis.

The leading Russian biologist, Lysenko, was a modern adherent of Lamarckism. In 1965, Lysenko was ousted after Soviet genetics was found to be behind the times.

FIGURE 10-12. Genetic information is passed from one generation to the next in the gametes. Changes in the body cells are not transmitted to future generations.

Inheritance of acquired characteristics implies that genetic change can occur in body cells and then be transmitted to sex cells. Modern genetics shows this idea to be false.

The idea of inheritance of acquired characteristics has never been confirmed by experiments.

In one experiment, mice tails were removed for over twenty generations. Each succeeding generation of mice was born with tails.

10:8 Darwin: Gathering Evidence

Charles Darwin (1809-1882) became ship's naturalist aboard the H.M.S. *Beagle* in 1831. The *Beagle* was destined for a five-year around the world cruise. Darwin was interested in nature, and so he welcomed the chance to study living things in their natural habitats.

FIGURE 10-13. (a) The scarlet crab, (b) Galapagos tortoise, (c) red-footed booby, and (d) marine iguana are animals found on the Galapagos Islands.

Bertram G. Murray Jr./Animals Animals

Virginia Crowl

a

b

William Ferguson/Nature Photography

George C. Harrison for Grant Heilman

c

d

Darwin suspected that if the earth has changed, then the organisms must also have changed.

When the trip began, Darwin had little interest in or real knowledge of evolution, but during the cruise he read a book about the earth's history. The book presented the idea that the earth was very old and had undergone great change. These ideas turned Darwin's attention to evolution. He knew that organisms are suited for special environments. If the environments change, do the organisms which live in them also change? If organisms change, what causes this change?

During the voyage, Darwin made discoveries similar to those discussed earlier in this chapter. He noted that living things change with time and that they show close relationships with one another.

Observations of Galapagos organisms supported Darwin's conclusion that evolution occurs.

Of special interest to Darwin were the Galapagos (guh LAHP uh gus) Islands (about 970 km) west of South America at the equator . There, he studied some forms of life, such as huge turtles and swimming lizards, not found anywhere else in the world. Despite their uniqueness, Darwin saw that these animals were similar to more common forms. The similarities convinced him that the Galapagos animals were related to more common turtles and lizards. By the end of the trip, Darwin believed that evolution was true—that one form of life could have evolved into another. However, he had not developed an explanation to account for it.

Darwin was the first to offer a plausible explanation of evolution based on observation and insight. Darwin's grandfather, Erasmus, thought that evolution occurred but offered no explanation of its mechanism.

10:9 DARWIN'S EXPLANATION: NATURAL SELECTION   191

10:9 Darwin's Explanation: Natural Selection

During the next twenty years, two kinds of evidence seemed to explain some of the things Darwin saw on his trip. The first was an essay about population growth by Thomas Malthus. Malthus stated that the human population was growing faster than the food supply needed to feed it (Figure 10-14). This essay started Darwin thinking about all forms of life. He realized that in nature there is an over-production of organisms in which many of the offspring die. Therefore, he reasoned that there must be a *struggle for existence* among organisms. Darwin envisioned many kinds of struggles such as competition for food, escape from predators, and ability to find shelter. Only part of all the organisms born can survive.

The second line of evidence was selective breeding. Darwin knew that breeders could "create" desirable plants and animals by selecting parents which *already* had the desired traits. He knew that in any population, organisms have *variations which can be inherited.* Features such as color, size, mass, and number of seeds vary in plants. Cows vary in amount of milk produced. Breeders selected variations in parents and obtained large numbers of offspring with the same features. Organisms with less desirable features were not used as parents. Darwin wondered if there were some force in nature similar to this *artificial selection* used by breeders.

Pieces of the puzzle began to fall into place. Variations exist among all organisms. Those organisms with variations that help them "cope" with their environment have a better chance of surviving and thus, they leave more offspring. The offspring often have the same variations and are also suited to the environment. Organisms with variations not suited to their environment leave

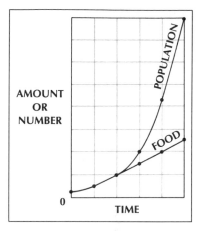

FIGURE 10-14. Malthus noted that population size increases faster than the food supply needed to support it. The result is a struggle for existence.

FIGURE 10-15. The tendency among organisms is for overreproduction. (a) Maple trees produce hundreds of seeds each year in bunches like this one. (b) Frogs lay and fertilize eggs in large masses. (c) When cut open, fruits like this melon show many seeds. Although many seeds are produced or eggs fertilized, only a few survive.

a

Raymond A. Mendez/Earth Scenes

b

Z. Leszczynski/Animals Animals

c

Lightforce

By natural selection, better adapted organisms leave more offspring than other organisms.

Teaching suggestion: To aid student understanding, it is good to emphasize the word *natural* in natural selection.

Evolution is a result of the interaction of organisms and their environments.

A favorable variation is said to be "selected for" and an unfavorable variation is "selected against."

few, if any, offspring. They "lose" in the struggle for existence. Darwin called this idea **survival of the fittest,** which is really a kind of **natural selection.** The best-adapted organisms (those most fit) survive and produce more offspring while the least-adapted may produce fewer offspring and may also die sooner.

According to Darwin's theory, *evolution is an interaction of organisms and environment.* Natural selection is not a conscious force working here and there. Chance variations either fit or do not fit the environment. Suitable variations are passed on; others are not. Darwin's concept of evolution can be summarized as follows.

(1) In nature there is a tendency toward overproduction.
(2) Not all organisms survive.
(3) Variations exist in any population.
(4) Variations are inherited.
(5) Those organisms with variations which are suitable for their environment will survive. Thus, these variations will tend to be passed on to the next generation. Unsuitable variations may be eliminated.
(6) The population as a whole will become better "fit" for its environment.

Darwin drew up his theory of evolution by natural selection over a period of many years. In 1859, Darwin published a book entitled *The Origin of Species* which described his evidence supporting the theory of evolution by natural selection.

10:10 Darwin and Lamarck Compared

How would Darwin have explained the giraffe's long neck? According to Darwin, the population of giraffe ancestors would have included animals with many neck lengths. As long as grass was plentiful, neck length was not important, but if grass became scarce, long necks would be important. Animals with long necks would be able to graze on the leaves of the trees. Thus, taller giraffes would have a better chance of surviving and reproducing.

Because long necks were a variation, many of the giraffe offspring would also have long necks. Darwin would have said that animals with longer necks were naturally selected. Animals whose necks were not long would be less likely to survive because they would be unable to eat tree leaves when grass became scarce. They would leave fewer offspring. This pattern would repeat itself over many generations. After a long period of time, there would be no short-necked animals. The entire giraffe population would have longer necks. Would they all be the same length? What might be another explanation for the giraffe's long neck? No, the giraffe's necks would not all be the same length. Students may want to discuss Biblical or other explanations with which they may be familiar that have been given to explain the traits of organisms.

FIGURE 10-16. Darwin would have explained the evolution of long necks in giraffes by saying that variations in neck length were originally present. Those with longer necks were better suited to the environment and survived.

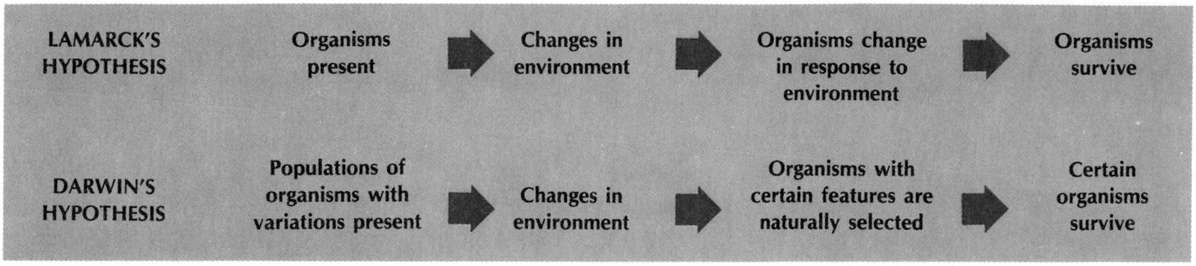

LAMARCK'S HYPOTHESIS	Organisms present		Changes in environment		Organisms change in response to environment		Organisms survive
DARWIN'S HYPOTHESIS	Populations of organisms with variations present		Changes in environment		Organisms with certain features are naturally selected		Certain organisms survive

A major difference between Lamarck's and Darwin's ideas concerns *when* a variation appears. Lamarck thought that organisms improved or lost structures *after* the environment changed. That is, a change in the environment caused a change in the organism. Darwin believed that a variety of features is present in a population *before* the environment changes. When a change occurs, some of the organisms may be able to survive. Lamarck saw evolution in terms of *individuals*, but Darwin realized that *populations* are important.

Darwin did not know that variations result from mutation and genetic recombination or that they are inherited as a result of mitosis and meiosis. It is to his credit that modern knowledge of genetics strengthens his theory of evolution by natural selection.

FIGURE 10-17. How do Lamarck's and Darwin's ideas about the origin of features differ?

Lamarck believed that variations began to occur after the environment changed.

Darwin believed that variations occur at random, in many cases before the environment changes.

REVIEWING YOUR IDEAS

10. What are the two assumptions behind Lamarck's theory of the evolution of adaptations?
11. How was the book of Earth history important to Darwin's thinking?
12. What is artificial selection? How has selective breeding been used?
13. What is natural selection? Is natural selection occurring today?
14. How did Darwin's work differ from that of Lamarck's? Compare their ideas about when a variation appears. Which of them saw evolution in terms of individuals of a population rather than in terms of the whole population?

10. the laws of use and disuse and inheritance of acquired characteristics
11. It caused him to think that organisms must adapt to changing environments.
12. Artificial selection is the choosing by humans of desirable traits in other organisms for breeding. Selective breeding has been used to produce better crop plants, certain ornamental plants, and certain traits in animals. Students may give other examples.
13. Natural selection is the selection for the more "fit" and against the less "fit" organisms. The more fit leave more offspring. Yes, it is occurring today.
14. Unlike Lamarck, Darwin thought that variations occur randomly, prior to changes in the environment. Lamarck saw evolution in terms of individuals.

ORIGIN OF LIFE

10:11 Formation of Organic Compounds

Have you ever wondered how life began? Because biologists are concerned with this question, many hypotheses have been proposed to explain how life began. One was proposed in 1936 by a Russian scientist, Alexander Oparin (oh PAH rihn). Other scientists have continued to test and alter this hypothesis.

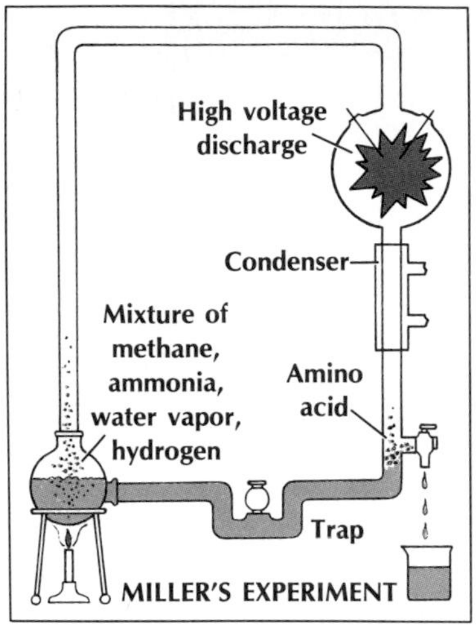

FIGURE 10-18. Miller showed that organic compounds (amino acids) can be produced when an inorganic mixture is exposed to an electric charge. He speculated that amino acids may have been formed this way in the earth's primitive atmosphere many years ago.

Teaching suggestion: Point out that Miller's experiment is based on certain assumptions and that it shows only what might have occurred.

Teaching suggestion: Some students may object to this account of the origin of life. Point out that the hypothesis discussed here is the best that *science* has to offer. It may be helpful to review the elements of scientific methods (Chapter 2). Also, point out that a scientific explanation does not necessarily preclude other explanations.

Complex organic compounds may have collected in the early oceans and become surrounded by a membrane.

The first organisms may have been prokaryotes with anaerobic respiration.

Scientists agree that the atmosphere of the early Earth was far different from what it is now. Some feel that it consisted of the gases methane (CH_4), ammonia (NH_3), and water vapor (H_2O). Others think it was composed of carbon monoxide (CO), carbon dioxide (CO_2), hydrogen (H_2), and nitrogen (N_2). Note that the main elements of organic compounds—carbon, hydrogen, oxygen, and nitrogen—were present. Also, Earth was probably being bombarded by ultraviolet radiation (UV) and lightning. These energy sources may have changed some of the existing chemical bonds. Thus, new, *organic* compounds may have formed.

In 1953 Stanley Miller circulated gases thought to be part of the early atmosphere throughout a chamber (Figure 10-18). He subjected them to electric discharges. The discharges represented the energy sources (lightning bolts and UV) of the early atmosphere. Water vapor condensed and settled into a trap at the bottom of the chamber. At the end of one week, water in the trap was studied and found to contain amino acids (organic compounds)! Therefore, it *is possible* that organic compounds could have been produced in a similar manner in the early atmosphere of Earth. Later experiments like this one have shown that other kinds of organic compounds can be formed from four main elements. Sugars, fatty acids, and nitrogen bases have been produced in the laboratory.

10:12 The First Organisms

These aggregates of chemicals are called coacervates.

Simple organic molecules produced in the ancient atmosphere could have fallen to Earth during heavy rains. It is hypothesized that they then reacted to form more complex compounds such as fats, proteins, and nucleotides. They then were washed into newly-formed oceans. In the oceans, groups of these molecules could have come together. Some kind of membrane might have formed that kept them separated from the surrounding water. The chemicals surrounded by the membrane might have looked like a primitive cell.

Other organic molecules not inside the membrane may have been brought into this simple "chemical machine." Some proteins may have served as enzymes. Sugars might have been used as energy sources. Because no free oxygen was present, early respiration was probably anaerobic. With energy from respiration came better organization. Nucleic acids eventually took over control of the activities (including reproduction) of these first, true organisms. The first organisms were probably prokaryotes.

As the primitive population grew, it is thought that there was competition for energy sources. This struggle for existence may have led to the evolution of the first producers. These organisms used photosynthesis to make their own food and provided food for the earlier organisms, consumers. Photosynthesis would have led to the production of free oxygen. Oxygen could then be used in aerobic respiration. As a result, more energy would be available for various functions.

Competition for food may have led to the evolution of the first producers.

REVIEWING YOUR IDEAS

15. Describe the atmosphere which might have existed on early Earth.
16. What energy sources might have been present on early Earth?
17. What factors might have caused a struggle for existence among the first cells?

---

15. CH_4, NH_3, H_2O, CO, CO_2, H_2, N_2
16. Energy in the form of lightning and UV may have been present.
17. There may have been a competition for energy sources.

ADVANCES IN BIOLOGY

10:13 Origin of Eukaryotic Cells

Most biologists agree that the first cells were prokaryotes, cells with simple structure and no nuclei (Section 5:12). Among the millions of organisms alive today, only two groups, bacteria and blue-green algae, are prokaryotes. Cells of all other organisms are eukaryotic. If the first cells were prokaryotes, how did eukaryotes arise?

One model proposed to explain how eukaryotes arose is called the **symbiotic** (sihm bee AHT ihk) **theory. Symbiosis** (sihm bee OH sus) is a relationship in which two organisms live in close association and in general, both benefit from the relationship. There are many examples of symbiosis in nature. For example, certain fish live among other animals called sea anemones. The anemones have stinging cells but do not sting the fish. Instead, the fish are protected by the anemones. In turn, food particles dropped by the fish are eaten by the sea anemones. Both fish and anemone benefit from the association.

In the symbiotic theory of the origin of eukaryotes, it is suggested that certain prokaryotes "took up residence" inside other prokaryotic cells. Either the larger cell took in the smaller ones or the smaller ones invaded the larger. Their association became helpful to both organisms (symbiotic). This kind of "internal resident" is known to occur in many symbiotic relationships. Green algae are known to exist inside certain protozoa. Certain microbes called normal flora and fauna live inside your respiratory and digestive systems.

In the symbiotic model, it is assumed that the prokaryotes that formed the association had different traits. The traits contributed to the success of the resulting organism. Suppose a prokaryote, such as a bacterium, with aerobic respiration

FIGURE 10-19. A clown fish lives in a symbiotic relationship with the sea anemone. Both animals benefit from the association.

Tom Stack for Tom Stack and Associates

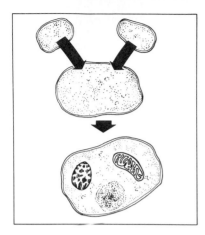

FIGURE 10-20. The symbiotic theory of the origin of eukaryotes states that certain prokaryotes took up residence inside other prokaryotes. The result was a symbiotic relationship and the resulting cell eventually evolved into a eukaryotic cell.

FIGURE 10-21. Support for the symbiotic theory comes from the similarities between certain organelles and certain prokaryotic cells. (a) A chloroplast resembles (c) blue-green algae in that both contain chlorophyll. (b) A mitochondrion is similar to (d) certain bacteria. Although most bacteria do not have membraneous structures, this photo of *Nitrosococcus oceanus* magnified about 29 500 times shows membranes clearly.

(Section 4:8) invaded a prokaryote that carried on only anaerobic respiration. The anaerobic cell would then have the advantage of obtaining more energy from its food. Suppose a prokaryote such as a blue-green alga took up residence inside a bacterium. The association would enable a bacterial cell that had been a consumer to carry on photosynthesis. These events are what is proposed in the symbiotic theory (Figure 10-20).

Although a few biologists claimed all of the internal parts of eukaryotic cells resulted from symbiosis, most did not. Most biologists focused the arguments for the symbiotic theory on their study of certain cell structures, namely chloroplasts and mitochondria. Many years ago it was noted that blue-green algae resemble chloroplasts and some bacteria resemble mitochondria (Figure 10-21). More recently it was determined that chloroplasts and mitochondria have their own DNA, RNA, and ribosomes. Both of these organelles can also carry on their own protein synthesis. This protein synthesis is different and separate from the protein synthesis that is carried on in the cytoplasm of eukaryotic cells under the direction of the cell nucleus. These similarities of the organelles and prokaryotes are considered the best evidence for the symbiotic theory.

Until the early 1970s the symbiotic theory was widely accepted and went essentially unchallenged. Researchers since then have been doing very detailed studies of both chloroplasts and mitochondria. Many feel that while the symbiotic theory may make a neat story, information obtained about mitochondria in particular does not support it. This new information indicates many significant differences between mitochondria and prokaryotes and suggests another model for the origin of eukaryotes. In this **nonsymbiotic model**, prokaryotes are thought to have evolved directly into eukaryotes with organelles. This process is thought to have occurred as cells became larger.

a

Grant Heilman

b

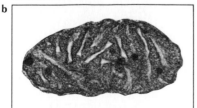

Dr. Judie Walton,
Lawrence Livermore National Laboratory

c

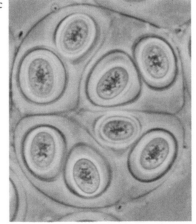

Ward's Natural Science Establishment

d

Dr. Stanley Watson/
Woods Hole Oceanographic Institution

The presence of DNA in mitochondria does make mitochondria somewhat like bacteria. However, mitochondrial DNA has a genetic code that is different from that of both prokaryotic and eukaryotic cells, and this code varies among mitochondria. Although the mitochondrial code resembles the "universal" code of cells, it is not the same and not prokaryotic in nature.

Also the DNA required for the assembly of mitochondria is present in the cell nucleus, not in the DNA of mitochondria themselves. Thus, if symbiosis is the case, the relationship must be very close. In fact, there would have had to have been a large scale transfer of genes from the mitochondria to what became the DNA of the cell nucleus. How this gene transfer occurred is hard to picture, and evidence does not support its having happened.

Mitochondria are different from prokaryotes in other ways, too. For example, mitochondria contain chemicals called cytochromes (SITE uh krohmz) that function in aerobic respiration. These chemicals are different from bacterial cytochromes and do not respond to bacterial cytochrome enzymes. Differences are also apparent in structures. Different eukaryotes have mitochondrial ribosomes of various sizes. Some are larger than bacterial ribosomes while others are smaller. Neither kind of mitochondrial ribosome can be considered typically "bacterial." Findings such as these led to the idea of a nonsymbiotic origin of eukaryotes, with organelles (mitochondria, at least) being produced by specialization of the original cell rather than by a symbiosis (Figure 10-22).

Evidence indicates that eukaryotes arose by both processes. Chloroplasts seem to have arisen from a symbiosis whereas research indicates that mitochondria did not.

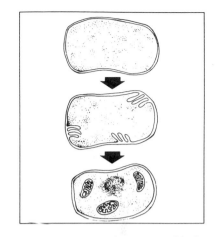

FIGURE 10-22. The nonsymbiotic theory states that eukaryotic cells formed as prokaryotes gradually evolved. No symbiosis of prokaryotes is involved.

Which of the two models do you prefer? Why? Is it possible that in the origin of eukaryotes both processes occurred? In what other way may eukaryotes have arisen?

CHAPTER REVIEW

SUMMARY

1. Information from many sources suggests that organisms change with time. That is, they evolve.

2. The fossil record provides evidence of evolution. Study of fossils shows that simple organisms appeared first and that more complex organisms appeared later. The record also shows that many organisms are now extinct.

3. The theory of evolution is supported by comparative anatomy, embryology, biochemistry, and genetics. These suggest common ancestors that changed into present day forms.

4. Sources of change among organisms include mutation and genetic recombination.

5. Resistance of bacteria to penicillin and other drugs is direct evidence of evolution.

6. According to Lamarck, organisms acquire new characteristics by use or disuse. These acquired characteristics were thought to be inherited by offspring.

7. Modern genetics shows that acquired characteristics, even if they occurred, could not be inherited. Also, there is no experiment to support Lamarck's ideas.

8. Charles Darwin, while serving on the H.M.S. *Beagle*, gathered many lines of evidence which suggested that evolution occurs. Later studies of population size and

CHAPTER REVIEW

selective breeding suggested an explanation of how it occurs.

9. According to Darwin, some inheritable variations exist in all populations. Those organisms with variations best suited to their environment seem to be naturally selected while others are eliminated. Thus, with time, the entire population becomes better fit for the environment.

10. Darwin realized that the source of change, variation, is present before the environment changes. He also recognized that it is the population which evolves, not individuals as Lamarck thought.

11. Biologists attempt to explain the origin of life on Earth by using the methods of science. They believe that the first organisms were probably heterotrophs. Autotrophs probably evolved later as competition for energy sources among heterotrophs increased.

12. Two theories are predominant today in explaining the origin of eukaryotic cells.

LANGUAGE OF BIOLOGY

acquired characteristic
comparative anatomy
comparative
  biochemistry
comparative
  embryology
evolution
fossil
half-life
homologous

inheritance of
  acquired charac-
  teristics
law of use and disuse
natural selection
radioactive isotope
selective breeding
symbiosis
vestigial organs

CHECKING YOUR IDEAS

On a separate paper, indicate whether each of the following statements is true or false. Do not write in this book.

1. The front leg of a dog and the arm of a human are homologous.

2. Acquired characteristics can be inherited.

3. More organisms are produced than can survive.

4. Domesticated animals were produced by selective breeding.

5. Closely related organisms have similar patterns of development.

6. Lamarck's conclusions are supported by knowledge of genetics.

7. Earlier organisms were simpler than later organisms.

8. The giraffe's long neck probably evolved according to the law of use.

9. Mutation and genetic recombination explain the variations among a population of organisms.

10. Evolution always produces organisms which can survive changes in the environment.

EVALUATING YOUR IDEAS

1. How is a fossil usually formed?

2. In general, what does the fossil record reveal? How do scientists interpret these findings?

3. What conclusions can be drawn from studying structures such as the legs of different animals?

4. How are homologous structures useful in the study of evolution?

5. Explain how comparative embryology, comparative biochemistry, and modern knowledge of genetics support the idea of evolution.

6. Explain how development of resistance to drugs by bacteria offers direct evidence of evolution.

7. Criticize each of Lamarck's assumptions about evolution of adaptations.

8. Summarize the evidence Darwin used to conclude that evolution occurs.

CHAPTER REVIEW

9. How did Darwin arrive at his explanation of evolution?

10. Outline Darwin's theory of evolution by natural selection.

11. Does Miller's experiment indicate that organic compounds were produced spontaneously in the primitive atmosphere? Explain.

12. Outline the steps leading to the evolution of the first true organisms.

13. What primary advantage would have resulted from the evolution of producers? What secondary advantages would result?

14. Why do you think it is more logical to assume that the evolution of producers followed, rather than preceded, the evolution of consumers?

APPLYING YOUR IDEAS

1. In studying a fossil, a scientist determines that only one-quarter of the original carbon 14 remains. How old is the fossil?

2. Indicate which of the following are examples of homologous structures:
   (a) leg of frog and leg of grasshopper
   (b) oak leaf and pine needle
   (c) ribs of dog and ribs of cat
   (d) human eye and horse eye

3. What would you conclude about the relationship between two organisms which produce many of the same enzymes?

4. A population of insects is characterized by a color which enables them to blend with their environment. The insects evolved this color over a long period of time. How would Lamarck have explained this? How would Darwin have explained it?

5. What possible harm could come from people taking antibiotic drugs when they are not absolutely needed?

6. Darwin recognized the existence of variations and the fact that they are inherited.

However, he knew nothing about genetics. How do (a) Mendel's work, (b) events of mitosis, meiosis, and fertilization, (c) mutation and crossing-over, and (d) role of DNA support his theory? *Chapters 8 and 9

EXTENDING YOUR IDEAS

1. Prepare a report on the extinct flying organism, *Archaeopteryx*.

2. Prepare a report on the results of selective breeding in various plants and animals.

3. Charles Darwin made contributions to biology other than the theory of evolution by natural selection. Use library sources to learn about his other biological work. Report to the class on his accomplishments.

4. Prepare a report on life on the Galapagos Islands.

5. Investigate some "living fossils" such as the *Ginkgo* tree (Section 14:9). Find out what they are and their histories.

6. Find out what a paleontologist does.

SUGGESTED READINGS

Asimov, Isaac, *In the Beginning*. New York, Crown Publishers, 1981.

Ayala, Francisco J., "The Mechanisms of Evolution." *Scientific American*, September, 1978.

Darwin, Charles with R. E. Leakey, *The Illustrated Origin of Species*. New York, Hill and Wang, 1979.

Keen, A. Myra, "Paleontological Hoaxes." *Natural History*, May, 1977.

Langston, Wann, Jr., "Pterosaurs." *Scientific American*, February, 1981.

Racle, Fred A., *Introduction to Evolution*. Englewood Cliffs, NJ, Prentice-Hall, Inc., 1979.

Volpe, E. Peter, *Understanding Evolution*. Dubuque, IA, William C. Brown, Publishers, 1977.

Additional student readings and suggested teacher readings are provided in the Teacher's Guide.

Teiji Saga for Photo Researchers

Organisms are adapted to their particular environments. An adaptation is a trait which improves chances for survival and reproduction. These whooper swans have several adaptations that help survival in exteme cold. A gland near the tail secretes oils which the swans work into their feathers, providing an insulating layer. The swans also huddle together. What special adaptations do you have that help you survive in your environment?

Introduction: You might want to begin this chapter by discussing with your students the adaptations of a particular animal. A variety of organisms could be considered but for this discussion the frog is ideal because students are familiar with its adaptations and one can be observed easily. Get the discussion started by having students think about the frog's environment. Have them put together a list of morphological adaptations such as webbed feet for swimming, powerful hind limbs for jumping, or streamlined body shape. A discussion of the tongue's being adapted for catching insects can lead, in turn, to analysis of physiological adaptations, such as those involved in digestion. Behavioral adaptations may be introduced as a result of suggesting a variety of stimuli to which a frog responds.

ADAPTATION AND SPECIATION

Chapter 11 explores the evolution of adaptation, the origin of species, and the evolution of humans.

Darwin's theory of evolution by natural selection helps explain change in organisms and accounts for the diversity within a group of similar organisms. Also, it can explain the origin of new groups of organisms. That a *population* of organisms evolves is an important point in Darwin's theory. An individual is born with, lives with, and dies with the same genes. But in a population, there is variation in the genes. **A population** is a group of organisms which naturally interbreed. The sum of all the genes of a population is called a **gene pool.** Thus, it is a pool of genetic information which will be passed to each new generation. *The gene pool is what evolves.* Keep this idea in mind as you study the theory of evolution. Darwin's ideas become most useful when they are put into modern terms.

GOAL: You will gain an understanding of how the principle of natural selection can be used to explain the evolution of adaptations and of new groups of organisms.

The gene pool of a population evolves.

Students often see evolution in terms of adaptation. It is important that they also understand the theory as it applies to speciation.

ADAPTATION

11:1 Origin of Adaptations

An **adaptation** is an *inherited* trait or set of traits which helps the chances of survival and reproduction of an organism. The source of new adaptations is variation. Variations which help survival will be selected and will spread through a population. Remember, organisms with suitable variations have the best chance of reproducing (Section 10:8). After many generations, each member of the population will have the variation. At that point, it can be called an adaptation.

Adaptations promote survival and reproduction.

Variation does not equal adaptation. Those variations which promote survival and reproduction may become adaptations.

201

FIGURE 11–1. A tiger's stripes camouflage this animal by breaking up the outline of the body, making the tiger more difficult to see. This adaptation aids the tiger in food getting.

Teaching suggestion: Point out that evolution is an essentially irreversible process. If a structure has been modified, it does not later evolve back to its original form. It may, of course, be further modified.

A complex adaptation evolves over a long period of time.

FIGURE 11–2. The complex structure of the human eye may be the product of millions of years of evolution.

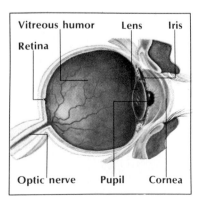

Vitreous humor   Lens   Iris

Retina

Optic nerve   Pupil   Cornea

The concept of end-directed or guided evolution embraces the idea of teleology. Students may feel that each adaptation must have been "designed" with a goal in mind. This teleological viewpoint is not a scientific explanation of adaptation.

A trait is an adaptation only if it improves the chances of survival *and* reproduction. A feature such as gills (an adaptation for fish) would be useless to a land animal. It would not aid survival or reproduction and would not be an adaptation to a land animal.

No trait, however useful it might be in survival, will be selected if it in any way prevents reproduction. For example, an organism might receive genetic information which gives it an edge in escaping predators. If this information also interferes with its ability to reproduce, it would not be selected and would not spread throughout the population.

11:2 Adaptations Evolve Gradually

Adaptations rarely occur "overnight" by means of a single change in the genetic message. Natural selection operates with what is available; it cannot "invent." *It can only affect what is already there.*

As clay can be molded into many forms, a living population can be changed in form through natural selection. But with natural selection, there is no final mold. It changes occur which improve the chances of survival, then by natural selection the features will be continued. The population will change as new genes spread throughout the population.

Complex eye structure may be the result of millions of years of slow evolution. Each step probably gave organisms slightly better vision. Perhaps this organ began only as an area which could distinguish light and dark. This feature would improve the chances of survival and reproduction. Organs that could see light and dark were adaptive. What advantages could they give? The organ may have then evolved into an eye with a primitive lens that gave blurred vision. This change also gave an advantage. Seeing any image is better than seeing no image at all. Later changes may have led to a sharpening of focus. Eventually, eyes that could clearly see things evolved. Each step along the way was adaptive. It improved the chances of survival and reproduction of the organisms. Natural selection has slowly changed these organs by selection of structures already present. Processes like this one take millions of years.

Is it hard for you to imagine how these factors could have produced the many organisms alive today? If it is, think about the length of time evolution has been going on. According to the theory of evolution, natural selection has been at work for more than three billion years! How big is three billion? Suppose you had three billion dollars and you spent a dollar a second, day and night. It would take you over 95 years to spend all the money.

11:3 Evolution of Adaptation Observed

Evolution and adaptation do not always take long periods of time. In Chapter 10, you studied how bacterial resistance to penicillin can occur quickly. The few bacteria that can live in the presence of penicillin reproduce. As a result, many bacteria that are resistant to penicillin are produced.

This example is important for two reasons. First, it shows that evolution is an interaction of organism and environment. Second, it points out that evolution and natural selection work on the basis of genetic change within a population. What was the source of the change? Did the resistance to penicillin originate in response to the change in the environment? Lamarck would have said yes, but according to Darwin's ideas, the answer is no! The allele for resistant bacteria already was present in the gene pool, but it was quite rare. It was not until the environment changed that bacteria resistant to penicillin became more numerous. Natural selection removed the bacteria that were not resistant. The number of alleles in the gene pool for resistance increased.

Observable evolution does not only occur in bacteria. Another example of observable evolution occurred in England around 1850. At this time, almost all peppered moths in England were very light in color. Black moths with a pigment called **melanin** (MEL uh nun) were rare. During the day, the moths rest on tree trunks. At one time the trunks were very light in color, so the light-colored moths blended with their environment (Figure 11-3a). Birds which fed on peppered moths had a hard time locating light-colored moths, but dark moths were easily seen and eaten. Thus, the light-colored moths had an adaptive advantage and produced more offspring.

Evolution of resistance to penicillin is extremely rapid because it involves only one allele and asexual reproduction. Thus, all surviving organisms inherit the favorable variation. Those organisms lacking the variation are quickly eliminated by natural selection.

Natural selection depends on genetic change within a population.

Teaching suggestion: Make certain that students understand the origin of the term "industrial melanism" and that it applies only to this particular example of evolutionary change.

FIGURE 11–3. (a) Before industrialization, tree bark was light in color. Light-colored moths were camouflaged and dark moths were easily seen. (b) After industrialization, tree bark was dark. Dark moths were camouflaged and light moths were visible.

a

James A. Bishop

b

James A. Bishop

As industry in England increased, the tree trunks became black with soot and smoke. Then, the mutant, black forms of the peppered moth had an adaptive advantage. On the dark tree trunks, birds could not see them, but light-colored moths became easier prey. During the last 100 years, the gene pool has changed so that today, over 90 percent of the peppered moths are black. This change is called **industrial melanism** (MEL uh nihz um).

Industrial melanism shows again that evolution is an interaction of organism and environment. It shows that the population change involved was genetic, too. How would Lamarck have explained what happened to the moths? How would Darwin have explained it?

When did the allele for black color originate? It may have been long before the environment changed. Many mutations which arise are neutral; they neither hinder nor help organisms when they first appear. Very few mutations are useful to a population right away, but a neutral mutation may become important later when the environment changes. This type of mutation is probably what happened in peppered moths.

Industrial melanism illustrates the relationship between organisms and environment as well as the role of natural selection in the process of evolution.

Lamarck would have said the organisms changed color to match the trees. Darwin would have said the dark moths were selected for and the light moths were selected against once the trees became darkened by the soot.

Neutral mutations may accumulate in a population and may become important if the environment changes.

11:4 Types of Adaptations

Organisms as they are today are adapted to their environments. If they were not, they could not survive and reproduce. Adaptations can be grouped into three major types—morphological (mor fuh LAHJ ih kul), physiological (fihz ee uh LAHJ ih kul), and behavioral (bih HAY vyuh rul).

Morphological adaptations are those which involve the structures of organisms (their anatomy). These adaptations are the most obvious of the three types, such as the structure of the bones of the hand, the beaks of birds, or the hoofs of horses. How is each of these structures adapted for its function?

Many interesting morphological adaptations in animals are for obtaining food. A woodpecker's tongue is narrow and very long. It can probe small openings in trees which have been pecked

The hand can grasp objects. Beaks of birds aid in obtaining food. Horses' hooves contribute to support of body weight and rapid locomotion.

Morphological adaptations involve body structures.

FIGURE 11–4. Adaptations can be morphological, physiological, and behavioral. (a) A woodpecker's sharp beak and long tongue are morphological adaptations. (b) Secretion of venom by a snake is a physiological adaptation. (c) A plant's bending toward the light is a behavioral adaptation.

a

b

c

Ward's Natural Science Establishment, Inc.

Tom McHugh for Photo Researchers

Robert Neulieb

Breck P. Kent/Animals Animals

Z. Leszczynski/Animals Animals

a

b

away by the bird's sharp beak. Insect larvae living beneath the bark are picked out by the tongue and eaten by the woodpecker. An anteater's sticky tongue inserted into an anthill attracts ants as it moves. If the ants touch the tongue, they stick to it. When the anteater pulls its tongue in, the ants are trapped easily.

Tongues are not the only adaptation for food getting. Protruding from the top of the angler fish's skull is a long filament (Figure 11-5b) that is broad and flat at its tip. It hangs in front of the fish's mouth and attracts prey much like a fishing lure. When the prey "bites" at the lure, the fish sucks the prey into its mouth. Some deep-water angler fish of the North Atlantic have modified fins. Part of a fin glows in the dark waters and attracts prey. The prey then can be easily trapped and swallowed.

Physiological adaptations are involved with the metabolism of organisms (Section 5:10). The enzymes needed for digestion, clotting of blood, or muscular contraction in animals all have a physiological basis. Secretion of a poison venom by a snake is another example. Protein materials in a spider's web are made chemically. An enzyme released by sperm cells enables them to break down the outer wall of an egg. These adaptations are physiological.

Organisms have many **behavioral adaptations,** those involving reactions to the environment. Migration of birds, hunting and storing of nuts by squirrels, and tracking abilities of hunting dogs are all behavioral adaptations. They all improve the chances of survival as well as reproduction. Plants, too, have certain behavior even though they have no nerves. Their behavior is controlled by hormones (Section 22:9). The bending of a plant toward light is an example of plant behavior.

FIGURE 11–5. Many adaptations are related to food getting. (a) The anteater's long snout and sticky tongue are adaptations for eating ants. (b) The filament protruding from the angler fish's skull is an adaptation that serves as a lure in attracting prey.

Physiological adaptations include biochemical features.

Behavioral adaptations govern an organism's reactions to the environment.

Teaching suggestion: Adaptations also can be considered as broad or narrow. A narrow adaptation is a characteristic suited to a highly specialized way of life. A broad adaptation applies to many organisms. Ask students about some of the broad and narrow adaptations of a particular organism. Cellular respiration and the ability to reproduce are among the broadest adaptations.

a

b

FIGURE 11–6. Cryptic coloration makes animals more difficult to see. (a) A frog blends in well with the sand. (b) A Carolina anole changes colors and matches its background.

Some organisms gain cryptic coloration by changing color.

Shape and behavior, as well as color, may be important in camouflage.

Of course, these adaptations are artificially grouped. Any one type of adaptation depends on other types. For example, the behavioral adaptation of bird migration depends on morphological adaptations such as feathers, lightweight bones, and strong muscles. Also, nerve and muscle coordination and energy production are among the physiological adaptations involved.

11:5 Camouflage and Other "Tricks"

Adaptations involving deception and camouflage are widespread in nature. Camouflage is a kind of "disguise" that blends with the environment. The color of peppered moths is a type of camouflage in which the moths blend with their environment. Thus, it is hard for predators to see them. This type of protection is called **cryptic** (KRIHP tihk) **coloration.**

Camouflage not only serves the hunted but can also help the hunter. A tiger's stripes break up the general body outline of the animal so that another animal may not see a tiger approaching.

Many animals can change colors in different environments (Figure 11-6b). They can change colors because they have special cells called **chromatophores** (kroh MAT uh forz) which are cells filled with one or more pigments. When the pigment spreads throughout the entire cell, one color pattern is seen. When the pigment shrinks to one part of the cell, another color is seen. These changes are probably triggered by the action of nerves and chemicals. Vision and other senses may be involved. A chameleon (kuh MEEL yun) is a reptile that can change colors. The coloration pattern is determined by the interaction of three pigments—black, yellow, and red.

In addition to camouflage by color, some animals "hide" by means of their shape and behavior. The dead-leaf butterfly and many other insects have wings shaped like leaves (Figure 11-7a). The veins within the wings have a central vein from which many smaller veins branch like the veins of leaves. Also, the insect may remain very still. Pipefish (Figure 11-7b) can resemble the algae

Point out that not all animals having protective coloration and/or shape are actually protected. The population, however, profits.

a

FIGURE 11–7. (a) The deadleaf butterfly resembles a dead leaf when its wings are closed. It is more easily visible when its wings are open. (b) Pipefish can swim in an upright position. Thus, they resemble plants and are hidden.

b

Robert Fridenstine

J.R. Schnelzer

FIGURE 11–8. Warning coloration announces the presence of an organism. (a) Certain moths and (b) larvae have spots that have the appearance of eyes.

among which they live by swimming in an upright position. Many insects look like the twigs of plants upon which they rest. In all these cases, the combination of color, shape, and behavior provides protection. How would Lamarck have explained the origin of these adaptations? How can they be explained using Darwin's theory of evolution?

Warning coloration involves a display of bright colors and patterns which announce rather than hide animals. The yellow and black stripes of a bumblebee warn predators that the bee is distasteful and can sting. A predator which once ate a bumblebee or got stung would learn to avoid bumblebees later. Often, behavioral adaptations are important in warning coloration. Some animals show their presence by sudden movements or changes in position.

Mimicry (MIHM ih kree) is a type of deceptive adaptation. In mimicry, organisms have evolved a color pattern like that of harmful or distasteful organisms. The robber fly (Figure 11-9) is a *mimic* of the bumblebee which is called a *model*. The two insects are not closely related, but their likeness in color deceives predators. As a result, predators ignore the mimic just as they do the model.

Some distasteful or harmful organisms advertise their presence by warning coloration.

This type of adaptation is Batesian mimicry. In Mullerian mimicry, two or more distasteful or harmful species resemble one another.

FIGURE 11–9. Examples of mimicry are prevalent among the insects. Each mimic gains some protection because it resembles a model.

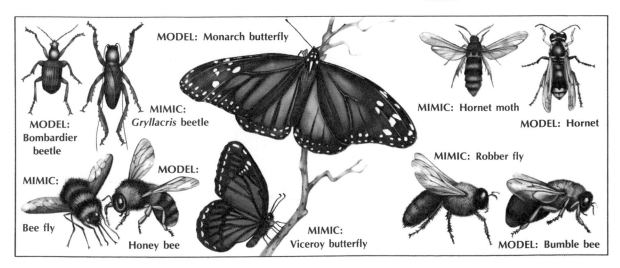

MODEL: Monarch butterfly

MODEL: Bombardier beetle

MIMIC: *Gryllacris* beetle

MIMIC: Bee fly

MODEL: Honey bee

MIMIC: Viceroy butterfly

MIMIC: Hornet moth

MODEL: Hornet

MIMIC: Robber fly

MODEL: Bumble bee

1. Morphological, physiological, and behavioral. Student examples will vary, but might include things such as: Morphological—grasping hand, upright posture. Physiological—digestive processes, control of heartbeat. Behavioral—baby's crying, blinking reflex.

2. Cryptic coloration is coloration of an organism that matches its environment.

3. In warning coloration, an organism is brightly colored and advertises its presence. In mimicry one nonharmful species has a color pattern similar to a harmful or distasteful organism.

The origin of all these adaptations is genetic. By chance, variations occur which cause one group of organisms to survive better. Organisms which have the variation are less likely to be eaten, so they will survive to produce offspring with the same adaptations. This process occurs gradually with each change being adaptive.

REVIEWING YOUR IDEAS

1. What are the three types of adaptations? Give a human example of each type.
2. What is cryptic coloration?
3. Distinguish between warning coloration and mimicry.

ORIGIN OF NEW GROUPS

11:6 Evolution of Species

When Darwin visited the Galapagos Islands, he noticed that there were many kinds of birds. He found one group, the finches, very interesting. There were thirteen forms of finches on the islands. They were similar in many ways, but there were enough differences to make each of them a distinct species.

What is a species? A **species** is a group of organisms which normally interbreed *in nature* to produce *fertile offspring*. Many organisms can be crossbred when removed from their natural environment. A lion and a tiger can be crossed in captivity to produce a "liger" (or tiglon), but this probably would never occur in nature. Also, a horse and a donkey can mate and produce a mule. Because male mules are not fertile, two mules cannot mate to produce more mules. Thus, horses and donkeys are not the

These finches have come to be known as "Darwin's finches." A fourteenth species of finch is found on the Cocos Islands (970 km from the Galapagos Islands). It is sometimes considered as one of the Galapagos species.

A species is a group of organisms which normally interbreed in nature to produce fertile offspring.

FIGURE 11–10. (a) A horse and (b) a donkey are each members of distinct species which can mate. (c) A hinny is the offspring of a male horse and a female donkey. A hinny, except for rare cases, is infertile.

a

Jean Wentworth

b

M.A. Chappel/Animals Animals

c

Grant Heilman

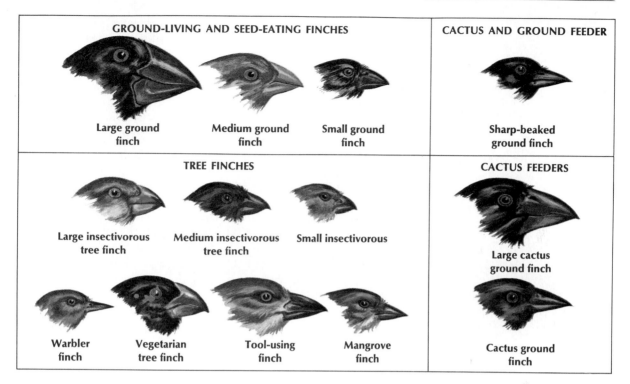

GROUND-LIVING AND SEED-EATING FINCHES

Large ground finch

Medium ground finch

Small ground finch

CACTUS AND GROUND FEEDER

Sharp-beaked ground finch

TREE FINCHES

Large insectivorous tree finch

Medium insectivorous tree finch

Small insectivorous

Warbler finch

Vegetarian tree finch

Tool-using finch

Mangrove finch

CACTUS FEEDERS

Large cactus ground finch

Cactus ground finch

same species. Species also can be defined as a closed gene pool into which "foreign" genes cannot enter by normal mating.

Because the Galapagos finches share so many features, Darwin thought they must have had a common ancestry. It is thought that the ancestor of the island finches was from the South American mainland. It was probably a ground-living, seed-eating species. Today's species of Galapagos finches differ mainly in their beak structures and their sizes. They consist of three species which live on the ground like the ancestor and eat seeds. Also, there are two cactus feeders, one cactus and ground feeder, and seven tree finches (Figure 11-11). How might these species have evolved?

In order for a new species to evolve, biologists feel that there must be a division that isolates a population. The division is often caused by a large barrier such as a river, canyon, or mountain. This type of separation is known as **geographic isolation.** The gene pools of two groups become isolated by a barrier and can no longer interbreed. As time goes on, each gene pool evolves in response to its environment. Each group adapts to the environment in which it is living. Mutations and genetic recombinations in each gene pool would be different because they arise by chance. Eventually the two groups have their own sets of traits. If the barrier were removed, they could still interbreed to produce fertile offspring. Thus, they are still the same species, but because of their different traits, they are classified as subspecies.

FIGURE 11–11. Each of these Galapagos finches is a distinct species evolved from a single species. They have adapted to several different environments.

Geographic isolation may be the starting point for speciation.

Subspecies have differences but they are capable of interbreeding.

Paul Nesbit

Harry Crocket from National Audubon Society

FIGURE 11–12. (a) The Albert squirrel and (b) the Kaibab squirrel probably evolved from the same population of squirrels. As a result of geographical isolation by the Grand Canyon, the original population evolved into separate species.

Teaching suggestion: Stress that isolation between islands and on the same island caused the speciation. Also, point out that many species live side by side now because of reproductive isolation.

If isolation persists and further changes occur, eventually the two groups might not be able to interbreed, even if they could get together. At this point, the two groups are separate species (Figure 11-13). Evolution of a new species is called **speciation** (spee shee AY shun).

This sequence of events may have occurred with the Galapagos finches. Somehow some finches got to the islands. As a result, they became isolated from others of their species by 600 miles of ocean. The two environments were different, so island birds would have evolved differently from mainland birds. Further isolation occurred between each island and also between birds on each island. As a result, many gene pools would have evolved independently of one another. In this way, the thirteen species presently living on the islands could have come about. The evolution of a species into two or more species with different characteristics is called **divergence** (di VUR junts).

The gene pool of one species is separated from all other species. The result of any barrier to interbreeding is called **reproductive isolation.** Because their gene pools are different, distinct species cannot produce offspring. Many factors may contribute to reproductive isolation, such as differences in mating habits, inability of sperms to fertilize eggs, physical impossibility of mating, and seasonal differences in mating. If zygote formation does occur, chromosome differences (genes) are often so great that the embryo may not develop normally or at all.

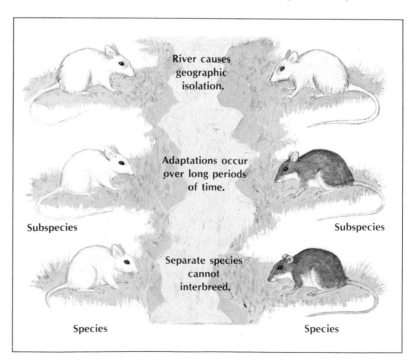

River causes geographic isolation.

Subspecies

Adaptations occur over long periods of time.

Subspecies

Separate species cannot interbreed.

Species

Species

FIGURE 11–13. Speciation can result when a geographic barrier such as a river isolates organisms. The groups of organisms then evolve separately.

Why is reproductive isolation important? Recall that each species has its own set of chromosomes with specific alleles, and each species is adapted to a certain environment. Suppose that species could interbreed freely and randomly. The resulting zygotes would receive "nonsense" genetic messages. Even if they could develop, they would probably not be suited to their environment.

11:7 Adaptive Radiation

Evolution of the Galapagos finches is an example of **adaptive radiation,** the evolution of many new species from a common ancestor in a new environment. For adaptive radiation to occur, several conditions must be met. (1) There must be a way for the ancestral form to reach the new environment. (2) The ancestral form must have some basic adaptations which are suited to its new habitat. (3) The new environment must be free from competition with similar, better adapted species.

The ancestor of the island finches is thought to have met these conditions. Because they could fly, finches could get to the new environment. They had basic adaptations because the islands' environment was not too different from the mainland. Also, there was no competition. Very few species of birds were already on the islands, and they occupied different ecological niches (NIH chuz). An **ecological niche** is the specific role an organism plays in a community.

Once on the islands, the ancestral species could evolve rapidly. Because similar types of bird life were rare, the birds were free from environmental pressures on the islands. Food was plentiful, competition for food was slight, and the islands formed a chain in which each island was isolated. Thus, there were many ecological niches to be filled.

One type of finch filled the ecological niche of a woodpecker. A normal woodpecker has strong neck muscles, a hard, sharp beak, and a narrow, very long tongue. Although the "woodpecker finch" has a short tongue (a long tongue never evolved), the finch adapted in another way. Once it pecks a hole, it picks up a cactus thorn or twig in its beak and probes the hole with it. Insects caught on the thorn or twig provide food for the "woodpecker finch" (Figure 11-14).

This adaptation shows that evolution works by selecting what is already present. Beak variations, chosen by natural selection, permitted drilling of holes. Beak variations were already present in the population. The behavioral variation, namely using the twig, was also already present in the population. This behavioral variation was naturally selected, too. It also shows that evolution does not "invent."

Adaptive radiation is the evolution of several new forms from a common ancestor.

The factors necessary for adaptive radiation illustrate the role of chance in evolution.

For adaptive radiation to occur, a variety of ecological niches must be available.

FIGURE 11-14. One type of Galapagos finch is adapted to fill the ecological niche of a woodpecker. The woodpecker finch picks insects from trees with a cactus thorn.

In convergence, distantly related species produce descendants which have similar features.

Evolution of marsupial and placental mammals is an example of convergence involving a large number of organisms.

Convergence may occur when organisms evolve in similar environments.

4. A species is a group of organisms which interbreed to produce fertile offspring in nature. Horses and donkeys can interbreed but do not produce fertile offspring.
5. Divergence is the evolution of organisms with different traits, whereas convergence is the evolution of organisms with similar traits.
6. interbreeding
7. An ecological niche is an organism's specific role in a community.

FIGURE 11–15. (a) The ring-tail lemur and (b) the racoon show convergence in their coat markings. (c) The dolphin's flipperlike structures and (d) the fish's fins also show convergence.

11:8 Convergence

Structures arising from convergence, e.g., bird wing and insect wing, are said to be analogous.

Most often, evolution results in new species which are different from one another (divergence). Sometimes, though, convergence (kun VUR junts) occurs. **Convergence** is a process in which species which are not closely related produce offspring with similar traits.

Think about fish and dolphins. The ancestor of fish is thought to be a simpler marine (sea living) organism. Dolphins are descendants of a land mammal. Thus, ancestors of fish and dolphins are not closely related. But, in some ways, fish and dolphins are similar. Both have a streamlined shape for swimming. Fish have fins; the limbs of dolphins have been modified to form flipperlike structures.

The similarities between fish and dolphins can be explained in terms of their environment. Both organisms evolved in water. In each organism, natural selection favored variations suited for an aquatic environment. But the organisms did not undergo convergence in all their traits. For example, the fish has gills, but the dolphin has lungs. Each can live in water with these organs, but the dolphin must come to the surface for oxygen. Can you think of other differences in these sea animals? means of reproduction and development, differences in behavior, etc.

REVIEWING YOUR IDEAS

4. What is a species? Why are horses and donkeys two species?
5. What is divergence? What is convergence?
6. What does reproductive isolation prevent?
7. What is an ecological niche?

J. Stevenson/Animals Animals

Alvin E. Staffan

Frank Balthis

Joey Jacques

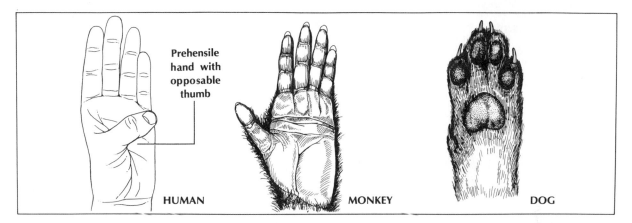

HUMAN   **MONKEY**   **DOG**

HUMAN ORIGINS

What place do humans have in nature? They gather food and plant crops. They breed animals to use for work, food, and protection. Humans build shelters, cities, roads, and factories. They create masterpieces of art and write poetry. When you think of human activities, you probably picture the type of things mentioned here. Many of these are unique features of human life.

11:9 Unique Human Traits

What traits do humans have that make them unique? The first ones may seem obvious to you. Humans have upright posture and **bipedal** (bi PED ul) **locomotion**, locomotion on two feet. Most other animals do not walk around on their back legs. Humans are called bipeds because of this locomotion pattern.

A second unique feature of humans is **prehensile** (pree HEN sul) **hands**. Prehensile hands are hands that can grasp or wrap around objects. Humans can grasp mainly because the thumb on the human hand opposes (moves in a direction opposite) the fingers. Each finger of the hand can be touched to the thumb. Compare the human hand, the dog paw, and the monkey paw shown in Figure 11-16.

Humans also have three-dimensional vision. They can perceive depth as well as width and height. Many animals see things only in two dimensions, width and height.

Humans are indeed unique, but because they are also organisms, many scientists believe that humans have an evolutionary history. In 1871, Charles Darwin published *The Descent of Man*. In this book, Darwin presented the evidence which led him to his conclusions about humans. He believed that humans were the product of biological evolution and that they descended from primitive primates. Primates are a group of

FIGURE 11–16. Although the human hand and monkey paw are both prehensile (able to grasp), the human hand has an opposable thumb and the monkey paw does not. The dog paw is not prehensile. Also, the structure on the dog paw equivalent of the thumb is reduced.

Humans are unique organisms.

Humans have upright posture and bipedal locomotion.

Prehensile hands permit humans to grasp objects.

Three-dimensional vision allows for depth perception.

Teaching suggestion: Make certain that students understand that humans are not descendants of any primate living today. It may be helpful to review the principles of speciation studied earlier.

The common ancestor might be the ape *Dryopithecus* which lived 20 million years ago. A later ape, *Ramapithecus*, might be a direct ancestor of the hominid line.

FIGURE 11–17. Early humans made many types of primitive tools from stone, wood, and bones. Some of these tools were used for hunting. Other tools were used for things such as preparing animal hides.

Hominids lived in areas where fossils were not readily formed.

animals that includes monkeys, great apes, and humans (Section 16:14). *This theory did not state that humans are descended from any of the great apes. Apes and humans are contemporary organisms. Both types of animals are believed to be descendants of some common primate ancestor which lived millions of years ago. This common ancestor is now extinct.* Two lines of evolution arose from this ancestor. One led to the modern apes, and the other led to modern humans. In the process, many species evolved and became extinct. They form the fossil record giving insight into the evolution of humans.

How could the development of the unique human traits have been important in human evolution? When early human ancestors moved from trees to the ground, adaptations for the new environment became important. In walking upright, the hands of these human ancestors were freed from any role in locomotion. Hand-eye coordination became possible with prehensile hands and three-dimensional vision. **Hand-eye coordination** is the ability to use sight and touch together for delicate movements. Objects could be grasped and used as tools and weapons. Eventually, humans were able to live successfully with other animals. With high intelligence came other human adaptations. These adaptations include language and speech, emotions, and personality. These adaptations form the basis for complex human societies.

11:10 African Origins

Fossils of human ancestors are rare. Early humans, or **hominids**, lived in tropical or subtropical regions which are not well suited for fossil formation (Section 10:1). In warm areas, the rate of decay and decomposition of dead organisms is high. Thus, there is little chance of sediment covering an organism before it decays. It would be good to have more evidence, but some fossils have been found which offer an exciting, yet somewhat limited, glimpse into the past.

FIGURE 11–18. (a) Humans probably originated in East Africa. (b) Eight spots on the map mark sites of major archeological finds.

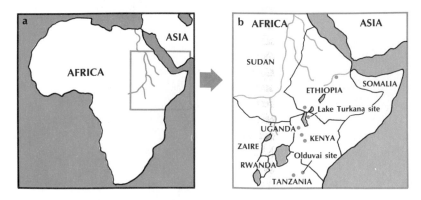

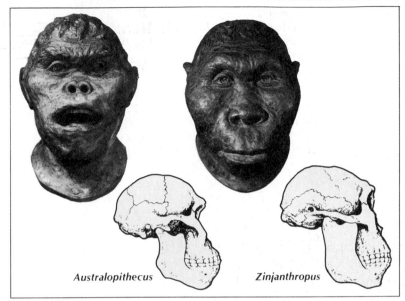

American Museum of Natural History

Australopithecus   Zinjanthropus

FIGURE 11–19. By making casts from the fossil skulls found, reconstructions of the head and facial features can be made. The earliest fossil showing human traits is *Australopithecus*. Another early hominid is *Zinjanthropus*. Both have smaller brain capacities and more prominent brow ridges than modern humans.

In 1924, Raymond Dart, a South African anthropologist, discovered some skull fragments embedded in rocks. The fossil was of a child which had features never before discovered. Dart named this fossil creature *Australopithecus africanus* (aw stray loh PIHTH uh kus • af ruh KAHN us).

Dart's fossil had both apelike and humanlike features. The organism was bipedal and had teeth more like those of humans than of apes. But, its skull structure was more like that of apes.

Since Dart's first finds, hundreds of fossils of similar organisms have been uncovered. All these fossils are thought to be Australopithecines. In general, these organisms had a brain capacity of about 500 cm³, slightly larger than that of a modern gorilla. However, scientists believe that their brain structure was more like that of a human than of an ape. Most forms were about 1.0 to 1.5 m tall with a mass of about 50 kg.

Many of the important discoveries of human origins have been the work of the remarkable family of Louis (1903-1972) and Mary (1913-   ) Leakey. In 1959, while working in Olduvai (OHL duh vi) Gorge, a canyon in East Africa, Mary discovered the skull of a prehuman dated at more than 1.75 million years old. They named the fossil prehuman *Zinjanthropus* (zihn JAN thruh pus), now thought to be an Australopithecine.

In 1974, Donald Johanson and Maurice Taieb made an important discovery in Ethiopia. They found a remarkably complete skeleton of a twenty-year-old female Australopithecine who lived between 3 and 4 million years ago! Findings such as this one have shown that hominids are much older than was thought before. This fossil, known as Lucy, may represent a third species, *Australopithecus afarensis*.

Teaching suggestion: This account of human evolution includes some scientific names. You may wish to introduce the idea of binomial nomenclature that will be presented in Section 12:2.

Features of *Australopithecus* indicate that these organisms were more like humans than apes.

Zinjanthropus is thought to be a member of *Australopithecus robustus*, a larger, stockier species.

In 1975, what is believed to be a family of 13 individuals was found.

Australopithecines may have lived as long as four million years ago.

11:11 Earliest Humans

Other discoveries have revealed another important fact—other groups of hominids were living at the same time as *Australopithecus*. In 1961, Jonathan Leakey (1940-   ), the Leakeys' son, discovered a fossil which was 1.8 million years old. It was more humanlike than *Australopithecus* and had a larger brain (700 cm³). Because this organism was more like a true human, it is classified by some as *Homo*. It was not a modern human but was a separate form, *Homo habilis*. It is thought that *Homo habilis* was a toolmaker because many pebble tools were found in the area where the fossil was discovered.

In 1972, Richard Leakey (1944-   ), another of the Leakeys' sons, discovered skull fragments in the Lake Turkana region of Kenya. This skull has been dated at 2.0 million years old and had a humanlike brain with a capacity of 800 cm³. Some scientists feel that this fossil should also be classified as *Homo habilis*. Others argue that these hominids are more primitive than *Homo* and that they are Australopithecines. This disagreement shows the difficulty in determining classification from incomplete fossil data.

Fossils of ancient humans had been found before the African discoveries. One finding occurred in 1889 in Java. The fossils found were of **Java** people and showed that these people, more modern than *Homo habilis*, lived about 500 000 years ago. This early human is classified as *Homo erectus*.

Very similar to the Java people are the **Peking** people, also classified as *Homo erectus*. A fossil of a Peking person was discovered in 1929, near Peking, China. Java people and Peking people may represent varieties of the same hominid. Both forms had a skull with features like those of apes—heavy, large brow ridges, a receding chin, and protruding jaws and teeth. But both walked erect, used tools, and had brain capacities of about 1000 cm³. Discovery of hearths in caves indicates that the Peking people used fire.

Homo habilis means "handy man," so named because of the tool-making abilities.

The earliest human may have been *Homo habilis* who lived two million years ago.

These findings may mean that *Australopithecus* was not an ancestor of true humans and that *Homo habilis* may be.

Because of the initial discovery of Java (and later Peking) fossils, it was long assumed that humans had an Asian, rather than African, origin.

Java people and Peking people are both classified as *Homo erectus*.

FIGURE 11–20. Because of similarities in the fossils found and the similar ages of these fossils, both (a) Java people and (b) Peking people are considered in the group *Homo erectus*.

a
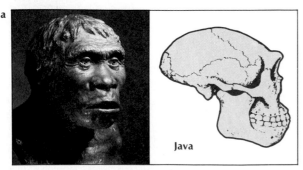

Java

Courtesy of the American Museum of Natural History

b
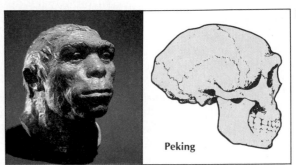

Peking

Reconstruction by Harry Shapiro, American Museum of Natural History

PEOPLE IN BIOLOGY

Margaret Mead began observing people when she was ten years old and her grandmother taught her to record the actions and reactions of her brother and two sisters. The techniques of observation she developed at home served her throughout her career studying primitive cultures on South Pacific islands.

The first anthropologist to study cultures by living among the people and adopting their customs, Dr. Mead studied traits that the modern world considered "inborn" in people such as aggression, competition, and the "desire" for war. Dr. Mead discovered that these traits do not exist in all cultures and concluded that they must be the result of the training children receive and environment in which children grow up.

Throughout her career, Dr. Mead wrote many books and articles describing her experiences among primitive cultures. Her first book, *Coming of Age in Samoa*, was written in a language that everyone, not just scientists, could understand, and it made anthropology a recognized social science. Dr. Mead also pioneered the use of photography to document cultural research when she wrote *Balinese Character: A Photographic Analysis* with her husband. She received many awards for her research including the President's Freedom Medal, awarded to her after her death.

(1901 - 1978)

Margaret Mead

A skull found in Africa in 1975 and dated at 1.5 million years old has a brain capacity of 900 cm³. The features are similar to those of the Peking people. Thus, it is possible that *Homo erectus* is much older than had been thought and could have also lived in Africa at the same time as *Australopithecus*. It is also possible that *Homo erectus* might have replaced *Homo habilis* and led to the extinction of *Australopithecus*.

11:12 Modern Humans

Remains of a more modern human were discovered in 1856 in the Neander Valley near Düsseldorf, Germany. This human, called **Neanderthal** (nee AN dur thawl), lived from 35 000 to 100 000 years ago and was more advanced than *Homo erectus*. Remains indicate that the people were short and quite strong.

Neanderthals lived during the last glacial period. Some biologists believe that the tough, strong appearance of this organism evolved in response to the harsh conditions of this period.

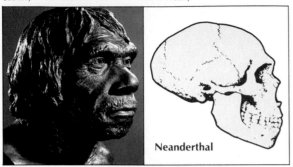

Neanderthal

a

Cro-Magnon

b

FIGURE 11–21. (a) Neanderthals and (b) Cro-Magnons are the most recent of fossil hominids. These are classified, along with modern humans, as *Homo sapiens*.

Neanderthals were excellent tool makers and they had some form of religion.

Cro-Magnons lived from 20 000 to 50 000 years ago.

Also, facial features were less like those of apes. Brain size was about equal to that of modern humans (about 1450 cm³). Evidence indicates that Neanderthals made excellent tools and were good hunters. Sometimes they buried their dead with sacrifices. Many authorities classify Neanderthals as *Homo sapiens*, the same classification used for modern humans. The features of the two groups are slightly different. Thus, if Neanderthals were alive today, they would be members of a race of humans.

Another type of modern humans (*Homo sapiens*) was found in France and was named **Cro-Magnon** (kroh MAG nun). Physically, they were as human as you. They lived from 20 000 to 50 000 years ago and were excellent toolmakers and artists. Artwork has been found on the walls of caves where these humans lived.

This drawing is located in Lascoux, France.

FIGURE 11–22. Artwork has been found on walls of caves where early humans lived. Artwork, done mostly by Cro-Magnons, is the earliest known step in the development of writing.

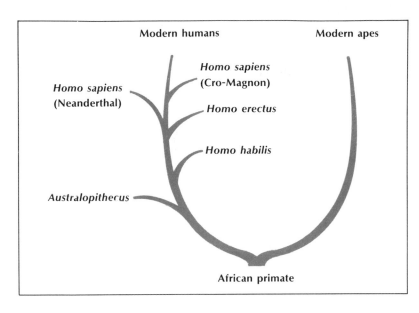

FIGURE 11–23. This evolutionary tree shows one possible set of relationships among early hominids. Other trees have been proposed.

Because the fossil evidence for humans is limited, human evolutionary progress is not definitely known. But, the evolution of humans probably took place like the evolution of other organisms. As a result of natural selection, humans evolved from African primate ancestors. Figure 11-23 shows a possible path based on fossil evidence. What other ways have you heard that humans might have originated?

REVIEWING YOUR IDEAS

8. Why are human fossils rare?
9. Why have biologists concluded that *Australopithecus* was more like humans than apes?
10. Why are *Homo habilis*, Java people, Peking people, and modern humans all classified as *Homo*? Why do modern humans belong to a different group than Java people and Peking people?
11. Compare the classification of modern humans and Neanderthals. Explain this classification.

---

8. Hominids were probably rapidly decomposed before they were covered by sediments.

9. *Australopithecus* walked erect and had teeth and brain structure like those of humans.

10. These forms all have human features. Modern humans have features such as larger brain size and different facial traits.

11. Both forms are *Homo sapiens*. If Neanderthals were alive today, they would be a race of humans. The features are similar to modern humans.

CHAPTER REVIEW

SUMMARY

1. An adaptation is an inherited feature which aids survival and reproduction in a certain environment. Adaptations arise from the natural selection of suitable variations that are present.

2. Adaptations evolve gradually as natural selection modifies existing structures.

3. Adaptations can be grouped as morphological, physiological, or behavioral, but adaptations may fit in more than one category.

4. Industrial melanism shows evolution as an interaction of organisms and environment.

CHAPTER REVIEW

It shows that in a population, variations exist which may become important should the environment change. Neutral mutations are often important long after they first appear.

5. Adaptations involving camouflage and deception are common. Cryptic coloration, warning coloration, and mimicry are special adaptations which "confuse" predators or prey. These adaptations involve color, shape, and behavior. They can be explained using Darwin's ideas.

6. Speciation occurs as a result of geographic isolation and the evolution of separate gene pools. Each gene pool evolves in response to its own environment. Speciation usually results from divergence.

7. Gradually, separated gene pools evolve into subspecies and then into distinct species. A species is a group of organisms with a closed gene pool. Reproductive isolation results from any factor which keeps the gene pool closed by preventing interbreeding.

8. Adaptive radiation occurs when many new species evolve from a common ancestor in a new environment. This process happens when there is little competition, and the ancestor is already adapted for life in new surroundings.

9. Convergence is a type of evolution in which different forms of life come to resemble one another. It results from different organisms living in similar environments.

10. Among unique human traits are upright posture, bipedal locomotion, prehensile hands, and three-dimensional vision.

11. *Australopithecus* was a form of humanlike animals which lived in Africa between 1.5 and 3.5 million years ago.

12. The earliest humans were *Homo habilis* and *Homo erectus*. More modern humans include the Neanderthals and Cro-Magnons, *Homo sapiens*.

LANGUAGE OF BIOLOGY

adaptation
adaptive radiation
behavioral adaptation
bipedal locomotion
convergence
cyptic coloration
divergence
ecological niche
gene pool
geographic isolation
hominid
industrial melanism
mimicry
morphological adaptation
physiological adaptation
prehensile
reproductive isolation
species
warning coloration

CHECKING YOUR IDEAS

On a separate paper, complete each of the following statements with the missing term(s). Do not write in this book.

1. Similarities in the leg of a grasshopper and a frog show the pattern of evolution known as _____.

2. Speciation begins as a result of _____ isolation.

3. _____ is the general term given to early humans.

4. Migration of birds is an example of a(n) _____ adaptation.

5. Every organism occupies a special _____ in its environment.

6. _____ is any barrier to interbreeding.

7. _____ may occur when many species evolve from a common ancestor in a new environment.

8. Java, Neanderthal, and modern humans are all classified as _____.

9. In mimicry, the _____ is distasteful or harmful.

10. Protection by camouflage is called _____.

EVALUATING YOUR IDEAS

1. Explain: The measure of a population's success is its ability to reproduce.

CHAPTER REVIEW

2. Explain industrial melanism as it occurred in peppered moths. Why is it evolution?
3. Give three examples for each of the three kinds of adaptation. How is each adaptive?
4. How might the eye have evolved?
5. How is geographic isolation important?
6. Why do isolated gene pools evolve differently from one another?
7. When does one species become two?
8. Explain the conditions necessary for adaptive radiation to occur. How were they met by Darwin's finches?
9. How are tools extensions of body strength and physical adaptations?
10. How might a large brain have evolved? Would it have evolved if the ancestors of humans remained in the trees? Explain.
11. Describe the features of *Australopithecus*. When and where did this animal live?
12. Why is *Homo habilis* considered more humanlike than *Australopithecus*? When and where did it live?
13. What effect might early *Homo erectus* have had on *Homo habilis* and *Australopithecus*?
14. How are Neanderthals different from Java people and Peking people?
15. What do scientists call the first modern humans? What was unique about these humans?

APPLYING YOUR IDEAS

1. Learning is a type of behavior in complex animals. For example, a dog can learn a trick. Should learning be considered a behavioral adaptation? Would it be better to say that the basis for learning is an adaptation? Explain.
2. Human eye color and human blood types are examples of inherited traits. Do you think that these traits are adaptations? Can you offer a hypothesis to explain that all humans have these traits?

3. Recent evidence suggests that pollution in England is decreasing. How do you think decreasing pollution is affecting the peppered moth populations?
4. Both monarch and viceroy butterflies have orange and black markings. How can this similarity be explained? How could you test your hypothesis?
5. Do you think tiger and zebra stripes are the same type of cryptic coloration? Explain.
6. Why did none of the Galapagos finches evolve into a cat or a dog?
7. Using modern ideas about speciation, explain the fact that two closely related species of fish inhabit the same lake.
8. Why are tooth type and structure useful clues in determining human evolution?

EXTENDING YOUR IDEAS

1. Find out about the Irish elk and the possible causes for its extinction.
2. Prepare a report on the evolution of the small bones of the mammalian ear.
3. Carefully study the external and internal anatomy of an animal, such as a frog or grasshopper. Prepare a list of its morphological adaptations. Explain how the organism's structures suit their functions.
4. Do you think humans are still evolving? If so, what changes do you think might occur?

SUGGESTED READINGS

Dean, Anabel, *Animal Defenses*. New York, Julian Messner, 1978.

Guring, Joel, "In the Beginning." *Science 80*, July-August, 1980.

Hutchins, Ross E., *Nature Invented It First*. New York, Dodd Mead and Co., 1980.

Johanson, Donald C., and Edey, Maitland, A., "Lucy." *Science 81*, March, 1981.

Rohrmann, George F., "Misleading Mantids." *Natural History*, March, 1977.

Additional student readings and suggested teacher readings are provided in the Teacher's Guide.

If the art piece shown here were in a group of art pieces, how could you classify it? Using different traits, you could classify it in several different ways. For example, you might classify it as biological art, as sculptured art, as turquoise art, or as Aztec Indian art. In the same way, living things are classified by different traits. Systems to classify living things vary based on the classifying traits used. How can living things be classified?

Introduction: It is important that students understand that a classification system must have a logical basis so that, once established, it will be both useful and consistent. To emphasize this point, assign teams of students to work out classification systems for a variety of items. Each team should consist of several students so that they can work together in reasoning out the best approach. Things such as vehicles, schools, sports, or tools can be classified. Have each team construct a system which first establishes "kingdoms" and then categories within each kingdom. These should lead from general to specific. Have each team "test" its system by classifying examples of the item. Once the students have completed their classification systems, have one member of each team report briefly to the class. Follow this discussion by asking students how they would classify living things.

CLASSIFICATION

Chapter 12 introduces the principles and theory of taxonomy.

Many human activities involve organizing and classifying sets of objects. For example, if you had a coin collection, you would arrange and store your coins for easy reference. In setting up your collection, you might classify the coins by any one of a number of features. You might choose to use the size of the coins, their color, their value, or the country from which they came. Once you have set up your system of classification, new coins could easily be added to the proper spot.

Biologists have long been interested in classifying organisms. There are nearly two million known species of organisms, and new species continue to be discovered. Thus, a good system of classifying organisms is important. The science of classifying living things is **taxonomy** (tak SAHN uh mee).

GOAL: You will gain an understanding of the development and use of the universal system of classification.

Taxonomy is the science of classifying organisms.

THEORY OF CLASSIFICATION

12:1 The Need for Classification

Rather than dealing individually with millions of different organisms, biologists place them in major groups. Each group has a certain set of features. When a new organism is discovered, its characteristics are studied, and it is then added to the proper group. If its features are unique, it may lead to the formation of an entirely new group.

Taxonomy enables biologists to study and identify organisms more easily.

223

Teaching suggestion: You might ask students to make a list of organisms that are different from the living things their names imply.

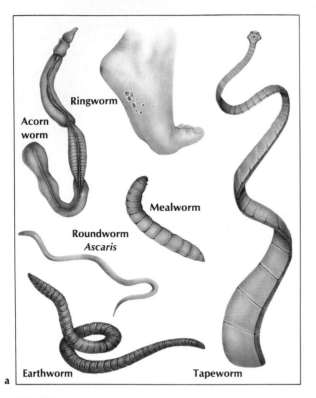

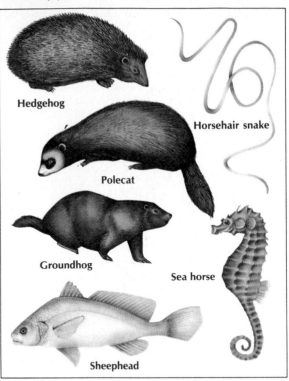

a

b

FIGURE 12–1. Common names are confusing for scientific work. (a) A common name, such as worm, may have many different meanings. (b) Some organisms have common names which include common names of other, totally different organisms.

Classification results in precise names of organisms.

Common names for organisms can be confusing.

Teaching suggestion: As another example of the problems of common names, use the term "fish." Consider, for example, that jellyfish (coelenterate), cuttlefish (mollusk), and silverfish (arthropod) are not really fish.

What are some of the reasons for classifying living things? One reason is the need for order and organization. You know it would be difficult to find a certain book in a disorganized library. The same is true for organisms. It would be difficult to find information about a certain organism if organisms were not in some order. Because they are put in an order, information about similar organisms is also easier to find.

Another reason to classify organisms is that a logical means for naming organisms is needed. Common names are inadequate for use in a uniform classification system. The word *frog*, for instance, suggests a certain mental image to you, but it is inaccurate as a scientific label. What kind of frog is it? Is it a grass frog, a tree frog, or a toad? Consider also the common word *worm*. To you, this name probably suggests an animal which is cylindrical, slimy, and soft; but biologists are familiar with many worms such as roundworms, flatworms, and segmented worms. Also, there are organisms such as ringworms, mealworms, and acorn worms which are not worms. A ringworm is a fungus, a mealworm is an insect stage, and an acorn worm is a simple relative of the vertebrates.

Also, common names vary country to country and language to language. They even vary region to region. Consider that puma, cougar, and mountain lion refer to the same organism.

12:2 Binomial Nomenclature

Many early biologists devised classification schemes. Aristotle divided organisms into two groups—plants and animals. Plants were classified on the basis of structure and size—herbs, shrubs, and trees. Animals were subdivided on the basis of habitat—air, land, and sea. A classification system should have the same basis for all groupings. In the eighteenth century, Carolus Linnaeus (luh NAY us) developed a classification system based only on structural features of organisms. According to Linnaeus, each type of organism was a distinct species. If organisms had the same set of features, they were the same species.

Linnaeus' decision to group organisms on the basis of structure was important. Many of his groupings are still used today. His species concept was based on the concept of structure in that a species has certain features. In his classification, Linnaeus put close together those species with close similarities.

Linnaeus introduced a two-term naming system, **binomial nomenclature** (bi NOH mee ul • NOH mun klay chur), for classifying organisms. Each organism is given a two-word Latin name. The first word, often a noun, is the **genus** (JEE nus) to which an organism belongs. Its first letter is a capital. The second word, an adjective, represents the **species**. Its first letter is not a capital. For example, many cats belong to the genus *Felis* (FEE lus), but there are many species of cats. An African lion is *Felis leo*, a tiger is *Felis tigris*, and a house cat is *Felis domesticus* (doh MES tih kus). Oak trees belong to the genus *Quercus* (KWUR kus). A red oak is *Quercus rubra* and a white oak is *Quercus alba*. Note that in print these names usually are italicized. In handwriting the names should be underlined. Sometimes the genus name is abbreviated by using only the first letter. *Felis leo* is sometimes written as *F. leo*.

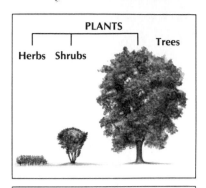

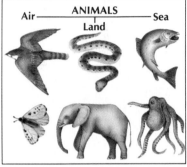

FIGURE 12–2. Aristotle divided organisms into plants and animals. He classified plants on the basis of structure and animals on the basis of habitat.

Some sources classify the lion and tiger in genus *Panthera* rather than genus *Felis*.

In binomial nomenclature, each organism is named by genus and species.

Leonard Lee Rue III from National Audubon Society

Don C. Nieman

FIGURE 12–3. Scientific names list the genus and species of organisms. Although both are considered wildcats, (a) the tiger, *Felis tigris,* and (b) the cheetah, *Acinonyx jubatus,* are classified in different genera. What is the genus of each?

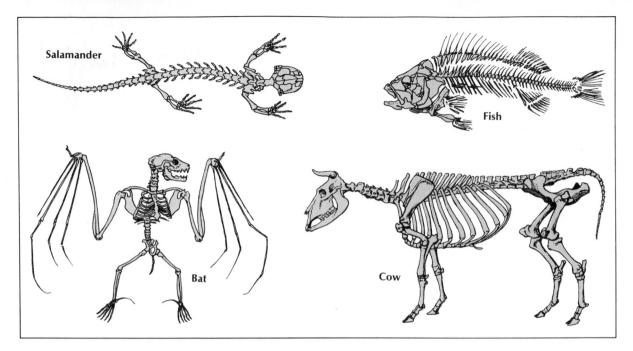

FIGURE 12–4. Similarity in structures is a basis for classification. These animal skeletons show many homologous structures.

Homologous structures are often the basis for classification.

FIGURE 12–5. The horseshoe crab, *Limulus polyphemus,* (bottom view shown) is not a true crab, but a relative of the spider. Comparative studies of the blood of these organisms have caused the reclassification of horseshoe crabs with spiders.

Carolina Biological Supply Co.

12:3 Bases for Classification

As the theory of evolution became more widely understood, biologists noted many bases for classification. Many of the ideas which support the theory of evolution are used in grouping organisms. The major basis of classification is homologous structures (Section 10:3). Like Linnaeus, modern taxonomists examine the structures of organisms when studying them in order to determine similarities. According to the theory of evolution, homologous structures indicate a common ancestry. Therefore, they are valuable clues to a biologist attempting to classify organisms.

Comparative biochemistry (Section 10:4) can be used to solve many problems in classification, because similarities at this level may be more important in classification than similarity in structures. For example, the horseshoe crab (Figure 12-5) was thought to be like "true" crabs as the common name indicates. But, studies of the blood of this crab show that it is more like spiders. As a result, the horseshoe crab's classification has been changed so it is included as a relative of spiders.

Modern genetics is another basis of taxonomy. For example, two organisms which have similar numbers and kinds of chromosomes may be closely related. Also, the DNA of different organisms can be studied biochemically. The amount of each type of base (adenine, cytosine, guanine, thymine) can be determined. Organisms with similar amounts of the bases are thought to be more closely related. Also, by matching single strands of DNA with known mRNA molecules, sequences in different species can be compared. More similar species have more similar sequences in specific regions of DNA. The greater the similarity of DNA among organisms, the more closely related the organisms are thought to be.

Analysis of nucleic acids can be useful in determining relationships among organisms.

REVIEWING YOUR IDEAS

1. What is taxonomy? What might have been the result if organisms were not classified?
2. How did Aristotle classify organisms?
3. What is binomial nomenclature?
4. Why is Linnaeus' system better than Aristotle's system?
5. Upon what important biological theory is modern taxonomy based?

1. Taxonomy is the science of classifying organisms. Without a classification system, there is a lack of organization, and confusion about names of organisms could result.
2. He classified plants on the basis of structure and animals on the basis of habitat.
3. It is a two term (genus and species) naming system.
4. Linnaeus used structure as the basis for classifying all organisms.
5. the theory of evolution

PEOPLE IN BIOLOGY

William Montague Cobb has spent most of his life studying the structural features of humans. He has been an anatomist for fifty-one years at the Howard University Medical School. Dr. Cobb founded a comparative anatomy museum to assist his students in studying the relationships between many different organisms and their structures. He has also made a collection of over 600 human skeletons to research the effects of aging on the skeletal system.

(1904 -   )

William Montague Cobb

Besides his work in anatomy, Dr. Cobb has also done research in physical anthropology, public health, and medical education. He has published papers and articles in all these fields and has become especially well known for his work on the growth and development of American Blacks.

Dr. Cobb has received many honors for his work. He was the first Black president of the American Association of Physical Anthropologists, and he served as editor of the *Journal of the National Medical Association* for 28 years. He has received the Distinguished Service Medal of the National Medical Association and the U. S. Navy Distinguished Public Service Award. Dr. Cobb was married in 1929, has two daughters, and now lives in Washington, D.C.

W. H. Hodge for Peter Arnold

W. H. Hodge for Peter Arnold

FIGURE 12–6. (a) The paper birch, *Betula papyrifera,* and (b) the yellow birch, *Betula alleghaniensis,* are members of the same genus.

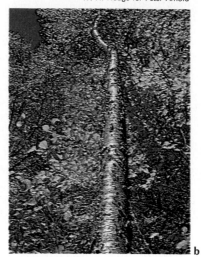

a

b

SYSTEM OF CLASSIFICATION

12:4 Classification Groups

Using the evidence discussed in Section 12:3, a system of classifying living things has been devised. Each organism is given a two-word name (binomial nomenclature) which is its genus and species. This name is used because it is the most specific. Each species is a distinct form of life.

However, species have traits in common with other organisms and so there are other, broader levels, or groups, of classification into which species fall. In the complete classification of an organism the groups are **kingdom, phylum** (FI lum), **class, order, family, genus,** and **species.**

A complete classification includes increasingly specific groups.

Each group from kingdom to species becomes more specific as each step narrows the number of organisms of the previous group. A kingdom represents all the organisms of a large group such as plants. Animals are another example of a kingdom. Phylum represents one group of the kingdom. Finally, at the end of the classification, all the organisms of a kingdom are divided into species, each species being one certain type of organism.

As presented, the sequence is in its simplest form. Classification is often more complex because each of these major groups may be subdivided. For example, a single species may be made up of several subspecies. Subspecies (Section 11:6) are sometimes called varieties or races. The various breeds of dogs are all subspecies.

12:5 Some Examples

Consider the complete classification of a common house cat. Because it is an animal, it is placed in Kingdom Animalia (an uh MAY lee uh). The decision to classify a cat as an animal is based on the very broad features of all animals. A cat eats rather than makes its own food. A cat also moves around and has a nervous system.

Kingdom is the broadest classification group. Because of certain other features, a cat is then put into Phylum Chordata (kor DAHT uh). An important subphylum of Chordata is Vertebrata (vurt uh BRAHT uh), animals with backbones. The complete classification of a common house cat appears in Table 12-1. Each group represents a more specific set of features than the previous group. Notice that in writing the species names, the genus is repeated.

Compare the classification of a cat to that of a dog (Table 12-1). Because cats and dogs share the same broad features, they are in the same kingdom, phylum, subphylum, class, and order. At the family level, the classification differs because a dog's features are distinct from those of a cat. Each of the remaining groups is, of course, also different from the others.

Now compare the cat and dog to humans (Table 12-1). How closely do humans seem to be related to dogs and cats? How many groups do humans have in common with dogs and cats? At what level do the classifications differ? ————————————————

Finally, compare these three animals to the common American grasshopper (Table 12-1). The only common group among the grasshopper, cat, dog, and human is kingdom—all are animals. What are some of the features of the grasshopper which cause biologists to classify it in a phylum different from that of the cat, dog, and human?

Henry Ausloos/Animals Animals

FIGURE 12–7. The zebras and gazelles shown here are in separate orders of the same class, Mammalia. The birds are in a separate class, Aves. The grasses are classified in a different kingdom, the plants.

Cats and dogs have many features in common. However, they belong to different families.

Dogs and cats are related through the order level. Humans have kingdom, phylum, subphylum, and class in common with dogs and cats. The classifications differ at the order level.

Traits of arthropods will be discussed in Chapter 16. Some students, however, may be familiar with some of the phylum traits of arthropods, such as external skeleton and segmentation, which would put them (e.g. grasshoppers) in a phylum different from chordates (e.g. cats, dogs, humans).

TABLE 12-1. CLASSIFICATIONS OF SOME ANIMALS				
Division	House Cat	Dog	Human	Grasshopper
KINGDOM	Animalia	Animalia	Animalia	Animalia
PHYLUM	Chordata	Chordata	Chordata	Arthropoda (ar THRAHP uh duh)
SUBPHYLUM	Vertebrata	Vertebrata	Vertebrata	
CLASS	Mammalia (muh MAY lee uh)	Mammalia	Mammalia	Insecta (ihn SEK tuh)
ORDER	Carnivora (kar NIHV uh ruh)	Carnivora	Primates (PRI may teez)	Orthoptera (or THAHP tuh ruh)
FAMILY	Felidae (FEE luh dee)	Canidae (KAN uh dee)	Hominidae (hoh MIHN uh dee)	Locustidae (loh KUS tuh dee)
GENUS and SPECIES	*Felis domesticus*	*Canis familiaris*	*Homo sapiens* (HOH moh • SAY pee unz)	*Schistocerca americana* (shis tuh SUR kuh)

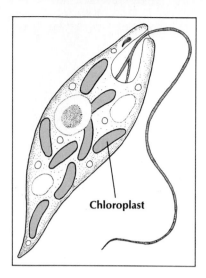

FIGURE 12–8. Classification of organisms such as *Euglena* poses special problems. *Euglena* moves like an animal but can make its own food like a plant.

Many organisms cannot be easily grouped as either plants or animals.

Many biologists now use a five-kingdom system of classification: monerans, protists, fungi, plants, and animals.

12:6 The Kingdom Problem

For many years all organisms were classified as either plants or animals. This two-kingdom scheme was reasonable for most familiar, multicellular organisms. However, the later discovery of microscopic organisms posed a problem. Some unicellular forms were easily put in one kingdom or the other. Those which were autotrophs were classified as plants. **Autotrophs** are organisms which make their own food. **Heterotrophs**, organisms which depend on other living things for food, were classified as animals. But many one-celled organisms did not fit neatly with either group. For example, *Euglena* (yoo GLEE nuh) has features of both kingdoms. *Euglena* is mobile like an animal and autotrophic like a plant. Also, at certain times it may lose its chlorophyll and become heterotrophic.

There are other problems with a two-kingdom system. For example, how should fungi such as mushrooms and molds be classified? They are like plants in structure, and they do not move. But they are heterotrophic like animals. Sponges are heterotrophic, but they do not move around and they show little response to changes in their environment.

To solve some of these problems many biologists today use a five-kingdom classification system. This system is based on current ideas about evolutionary relationships among organisms. The five kingdoms and their characteristics are listed below.

● **Kingdom Monera** (muh NIHR uh). This is a small kingdom composed of two main groups—the bacteria and blue-green algae. Monerans (members of the Kingdom Monera) are a separate kingdom because they are all prokaryotes (Section 5:12).

● **Kingdom Protista** (pruh TIHS tuh). Included in this kingdom are protozoa (animal-like forms) and certain simple algae. Protists are usually unicellular. Some are heterotrophic; others are autotrophic.

● **Kingdom Fungi**. Organisms in this kingdom are mostly multicellular. Fungi are heterotrophic and absorb small food molecules.

● **Kingdom Plantae.** Plants are multicellular, autotrophic organisms. They generally have a complex structure. Certain complex algae also are included in this group.

● **Kingdom Animalia.** Animals are multicellular organisms that are usually mobile. They are heterotrophic and ingest their food. **Ingestion** is the taking in of bits of food not yet digested. Also, except for sponges, animals have nerve cells.

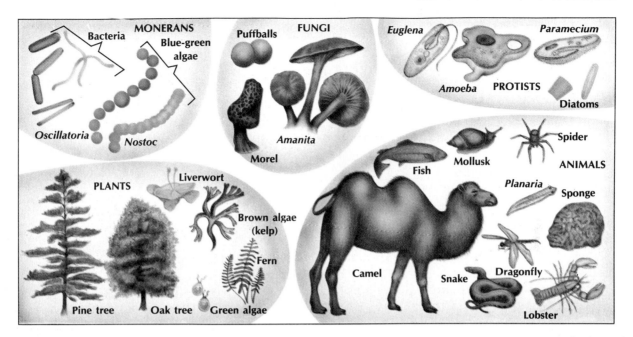

FIGURE 12–9. The classification system used in this text has 5 kingdoms of organisms.

Other classification systems have been proposed. As a result, names and groupings differ slightly from scheme to scheme. Remember taxonomy is an invention of humans, not of nature. There are still many unanswered questions, and future discoveries may lead to further changes. A classification system based on five kingdoms is presented in Appendix A. Use this system as a reference.

In the next unit you will study the major phyla and some classes of organisms in detail. You will learn about the features which determine each group's classification. This study will illustrate the great diversity of life forms. But recall that even though organisms differ in physical characteristics, they have certain functions in common (Chapter 1). For example, organisms reproduce and most require oxygen. In Chapters 17 through 30 you will study these and other common functions. You will compare how these functions are carried out by the various forms of life—monerans, protists, fungi, plants, and animals. The similarities in life processes among organisms will become apparent.

Teaching suggestion: Some biologists today use a four-kingdom system in which fungi and all algae are considered protists. Stress that classification schemes change as more is learned about evolutionary relationships.

Although organisms differ in physical characteristics, they have many functions in common.

REVIEWING YOUR IDEAS

6. What are the major classification groups from broadest to most specific? Which of the groups are used in the scientific name of an organism?

7. Why do many biologists use a five kingdom system of classification?

6. Kingdom, phylum, class, order, family, genus, species. Genus and species are used in the scientific name.

7. Use of a five kingdom system aids in solving some problems of classifying simple organisms.

CHAPTER REVIEW

SUMMARY

1. Taxonomy is the study of classification of organisms. Classification brings order to the great variety of organisms alive today.

2. Precise classification of organisms is necessary so that each living thing has a name recognizable to biologists everywhere.

3. Linnaeus devised a system of classification based on structural similarities. His system of binomial nomenclature is still used today.

4. Modern taxonomy depends on the theory of evolution. Classification is based on factors such as homologous structures, biochemical similarities, and genetics.

5. The classification categories, from general to specific, are kingdom, phylum, class, order, family, genus, and species. Each of these major categories may be subdivided.

6. Many systems of classification use a five-kingdom plan: monerans, protists, fungi, plants, and animals.

7. Monerans are prokaryotes—bacteria and blue-green algae. Protists include unicellular organisms such as protozoa and simple algae. Fungi are multicellular heterotrophs which absorb their food.

8. Plants are multicellular, autotrophic organisms with a generally complex structure.

9. Animals are complex, multicellular organisms. They are heterotrophic and ingest their food. Except for sponges, they are coordinated by nerve cells.

LANGUAGE OF BIOLOGY

autotroph
binomial
  nomenclature
class
family
fungi
genus

heterotroph
kingdom
order
monerans
phylum
protists
taxonomy

CHECKING YOUR IDEAS

On a separate paper, match each phrase from the left column with the proper term from the right column. Do not write in this book.

1. mostly multicellular; heterotrophic

2. 1st classification category smaller than class

3. broadest classification category

4. means obtaining food from other organisms

5. eukaryotes; both autotrophic and heterotrophic forms

6. multicellular; ingest food; most have nerves

7. most specific classification category

8. prokaryotic

9. means making its own food

10. autotrophic; complex structure

a. animals
b. autotrophic
c. fungi
d. heterotrophic
e. kingdom
f. monerans
g. order
h. plants
i. protists
j. species

EVALUATING YOUR IDEAS

1. Why is it necessary to classify and clearly name living things?

2. Why was Aristotle's basis for classifying plants better than his basis for classifying animals?

3. Upon what did Linnaeus base his system of classification? Why is his system better than Aristotle's? What modern theory might have been helpful to him?

4. Is there any relationship between the words species and specific? Explain.

5. Why are the many lines of evidence of evolution also used in classifying organisms?

CHAPTER REVIEW

6. What structural features of humans put them in the same kingdom, subphylum, phylum, and class as cats and dogs? Why are humans in a different order from cats and dogs?

7. Give several reasons why a two-kingdom system of classification is not satisfactory.

8. What are the major characteristics of the kingdom of plants? The kingdom of animals?

9. Name three kingdoms other than plants and animals. What are the major characteristics of each of these kingdoms of organisms?

APPLYING YOUR IDEAS

1. Both cats and dogs are grouped into the same kingdom, phylum, subphylum, class, and order. List their common structural features. Cats and dogs belong to different families, genera, and species. Therefore, they must have some different structural features. List some of the ways in which they differ.

2. Based on your own knowledge of their characteristics, set up a scheme to place the animals listed below in groups and subgroups. No scientific terms are needed.

   (a) baboon   (j) jellyfish
   (b) bear   (k) lobster
   (c) cheetah   (l) mosquito
   (d) clam   (m) ostrich
   (e) earthworm   (n) panther
   (f) frog   (o) planaria
   (g) fruit fly   (p) robin
   (h) horse   (q) turtle
   (i) human

3. How can the similar features of two different species (such as tiger and cheetah) be explained by the theory of evolution?

4. Two groups of salamanders resemble each other very closely. One group lives in northeastern United States. The other group lives in southeastern United States. A biologist discovers that the southeastern group mates in April, and the northeastern group mates in June. How would you classify the two groups? Why? Would the two groups interbreed if brought together? Explain.

5. Many common names of organisms have come from their scientific names. What is the common name of each of these organisms?

   Rattus norvegicus   *Gorilla gorilla*
   Equus zebra   *Pinus ponderosa*
   Elephus maximus   *Camelus bactrianus*

EXTENDING YOUR IDEAS

1. Domesticated dogs are classified as *Canis familiaris.* Using library resources, prepare a report on ten subspecies of this species.

2. Obtain a classification key to woody plants. Use the key to identify woody plants near your home.

3. Use a classification key to identify protists from a pond, lake, or mud puddle.

4. Study the various classification systems. Discuss the pros and cons of each.

5. Obtain a culture of *Euglena.* Subdivide the culture among 4 containers. Leave one culture exposed to light at room temperature as a control. Place another culture in a dark area at room temperature. Place a third in the light but in a warm environment. If available, add streptomycin (an antibiotic) to another culture (in light, room temperature). Note the effect of darkness, heat, and streptomycin on the color of *Euglena.*

SUGGESTED READINGS

Gould, Stephen Jay, "This View of Life; the Five Kingdoms." *Natural History,* June-July, 1976.

Haas, George H., "What's in a Name?" *National Wildlife,* December 1, 1977.

Valentine, James W., "The Evolution of Multicellular Plants and Animals." *Scientific American,* September, 1978.

Additional student readings and suggested teacher readings are provided in the Teacher's Guide.

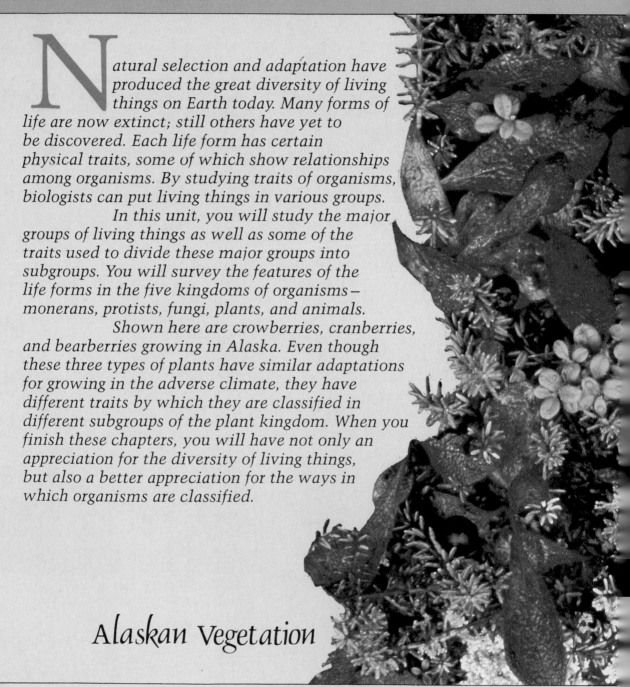

DIVERSITY

N atural selection and adaptation have produced the great diversity of living things on Earth today. Many forms of life are now extinct; still others have yet to be discovered. Each life form has certain physical traits, some of which show relationships among organisms. By studying traits of organisms, biologists can put living things in various groups.

In this unit, you will study the major groups of living things as well as some of the traits used to divide these major groups into subgroups. You will survey the features of the life forms in the five kingdoms of organisms— monerans, protists, fungi, plants, and animals.

Shown here are crowberries, cranberries, and bearberries growing in Alaska. Even though these three types of plants have similar adaptations for growing in the adverse climate, they have different traits by which they are classified in different subgroups of the plant kingdom. When you finish these chapters, you will have not only an appreciation for the diversity of living things, but also a better appreciation for the ways in which organisms are classified.

Alaskan Vegetation

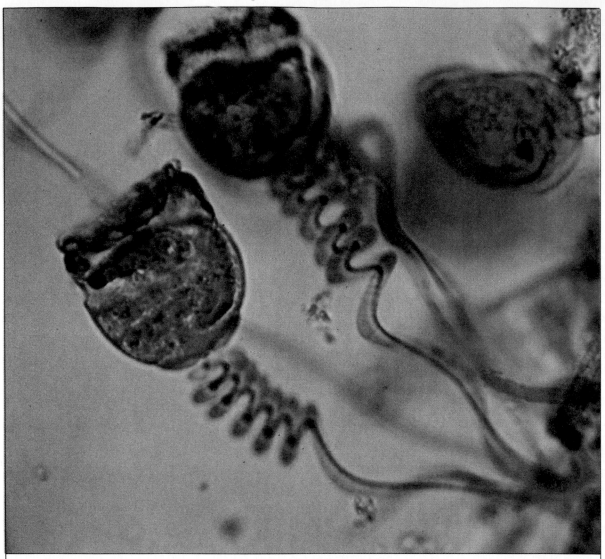

Carolina Biological Supply Co.

Some organisms cannot be classified in either the plant or the animal kingdom. These organisms fall into three other kingdoms—monerans, protists, and fungi. *Vorticella* is a microscopic protist, shown here magnified about 1400 times. *Vorticella*, like many other simple organisms, lives in water. Some simple organisms, such as some fungi, live in damp places. What are the main traits of some of the simple organisms? How are simple organisms important, both economically and ecologically?

MONERANS, PROTISTS, FUNGI, AND VIRUSES

Chapter 13 presents general characteristics of three kingdoms of organisms—the monerans, protists, and fungi—and the characteristics of viruses.

Introduction: Cultures may be obtained from biological supply houses or, depending upon your location and the season, collected by you and your students. If you purchase cultures, consider including slime molds. They can be ordered already growing in culture or as part of a kit to culture in the classroom. You can also obtain living cultures of algae, bacteria, and protozoa. Molds can be easily cultured on bread, fruits, and vegetables.
GOAL: You will gain an understanding of what the moneran, protist, and fungi kingdoms include and learn the basic features of the major groups of organisms in these kingdoms. You will also learn about viruses.

In the two-kingdom system of classification, many organisms were considered as either plants or animals even though their features do not really match those groups. One major problem was that these organisms are quite simple in structure. Many are unicellular. All lack the complex structure of true plants and animals. Many have features of both kingdoms. For these reasons, relationships could not be easily determined.

The gradual change to a five-kingdom system has solved many of these problems. These simple organisms are now classified as members of three new kingdoms—monerans, protists, and fungi. Although simple in structure and less familiar than plants and animals, these organisms play important roles in nature. Their activities affect all natural communities and the lives of humans and other organisms.

Monerans, protists, and fungi play important roles in nature and affect the lives of many organisms.

KINGDOM MONERA

13:1 Prokaryotes

Kingdom Monera includes two main groups of organisms— blue-green algae and bacteria. These organisms (monerans) are grouped together because they are all prokaryotes (Section 5:12). They may be descendants of the first types of cells to have lived on Earth.

algae (singular, alga)

A prokaryote has no true nucleus or nuclear membrane. It usually contains one circular chromosome composed of DNA, but no protein. Small ribosomes are present, but most of the other cell parts found in eukaryotes are absent. There are no mitochondria; cellular respiration occurs on the inner surface of the cell membrane. Chlorophyll may be present, but there are no chloroplasts. The cell wall is composed of a material called **murein** (MYOOR ee un). If flagella are present, they do not contain microtubules. Table 13-1 summarizes the main differences between prokaryotes and eukaryotes.

A prokaryote lacks a true nucleus and membrane-bound organelles.

237

TABLE 13-1. DIFFERENCES BETWEEN PROKARYOTES AND EUKARYOTES	
Prokaryotes	Eukaryotes
no true nucleus or nuclear membrane	true nucleus and nuclear membrane
single, circular chromosome of DNA	several, linear chromosomes of DNA and protein
small ribosomes	large ribosomes
no mitochondria, ER, Golgi bodies, lysosomes	mitochondria, ER, Golgi bodies, lysosomes
chlorophyll, if present, not in chloroplasts	chlorophyll, if present, in chloroplasts
cell wall present containing murein	cell wall, if present, does not contain murein
no microtubules in flagella	microtubules in flagella

13:2 Blue-Green Algae

The red pigment is phycoerythrin.

Blue-green algae belong to the phylum **Cyanophyta** (si uh NAHF uh tuh). All forms are autotrophic; that is, they make their own food. They have a blue pigment called **phycocyanin** (fi koh sɪ uh nun) which, along with chlorophyll, gives many of these algae their blue-green color. Yellowish pigments called **carotenes** (KER uh teenz) are also present. Some forms also contain a red pigment which, with the other pigments, can cause a purple-black color.

The color of blue-green algae is determined by several pigments.

Blue-green algae are among the least complex organisms living on Earth (Figure 13-1). Some forms exist as single round or oval cells. In other species, cells may be arranged in chains, small colonies, or filaments. However, there is little, if any, division of labor. Each cell of the "multicellular" forms is almost the same. Sometimes these organisms are enclosed within a jellylike layer. Blue-green algae have no flagella, but some forms can move. How they move is not known.

Blue-green algae exist as single cells, chains, filaments, or colonies.

Although the art appears to show nuclei in some of the cells, these areas are actually condensed chromatin.

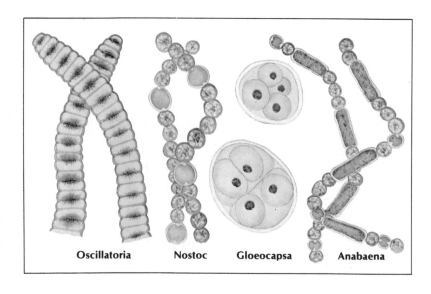

FIGURE 13-1. Blue-green algae can be single cells or cells grouped in colonies or filaments. The cells are prokaryotic, lacking nuclei and membrane-bound organelles.

Oscillatoria   Nostoc   Gloeocapsa   Anabaena

Within the cells of blue-green algae, the pigments are scattered throughout the cytoplasm, sometimes attached to membrane fragments. These membrane fragments appear similar to those found in chloroplasts of eukaryotes (Section 5:12). The thick cytoplasm sometimes contains storage granules of a starchlike substance.

Sexual reproduction is unknown in this phylum. Reproduction is asexual (ay SEK shul). **Asexual reproduction** is the production of one or more offspring from a single parent. New cells may be formed along a chain or filament by simple cell division. Sometimes filaments are broken apart, and each section produces a new series of cells.

Blue-green algae are important as producers in aquatic communities. They are common in ponds, lakes, puddles, streams, and even moist places on land. Many forms are important in recycling nitrogen (Section 33:5).

In hot weather, they multiply rapidly and often cause the bad odor of stagnant bodies of water. Public water supplies are checked and treated often during this season to prevent a rapid reproduction of blue-green algae and other microorganisms. Often, small amounts of copper sulfate are added to the water to destroy algae.

Blue-green algae have no chloroplasts. Photosynthesis occurs on membrane fragments found throughout the cytoplasm.

Reproduction in blue-green algae is asexual.

Blue-green algae are producers in aquatic communities.

Rapid multiplication of algae is an algal bloom. Algal blooms may cause stagnation by consuming large quantities of oxygen needed by other organisms (Section 35:7).

13:3 Bacteria

Bacteria, phylum **Schizomycophyta** (skihz uh mi KAHF uh tuh), are everywhere—in air, food, and soil and on almost anything you touch. Many live in or on other organisms. Three million bacteria could fit side by side across this page.

Most bacteria have one of three shapes. Spherical bacteria are called **cocci** (KAHK si), rod-shaped ones are **bacilli** (buh SIHL i), and spiral-shaped ones are called **spirilla** (spi RIHL uh). Bacteria are unicellular but many exist in pairs, clusters, or chains with each cell of such a group as an independent organism. The average diameter of a coccus bacterial cell is only about one micrometer.

Bacteria are classified by shape: spherical (cocci), rod (bacilli), and spiral (spirilla).

FIGURE 13-2. The three basic shapes of bacteria are (a) spherical, the cocci, (b) rod-shaped, the bacilli, and (c) spiral shaped, the spirilla.

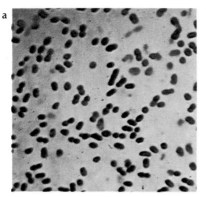
a

Rasulo Graphic Service

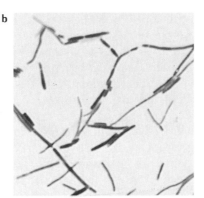
b

Runk/Schoenberger for Grant Heilman

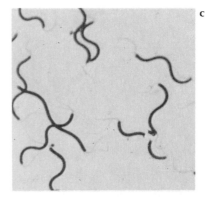
c

Runk/Schoenberger for Grant Heilman

FIGURE 13-3. The flagellated bacterium, *Proteus vulgaris,* shows many of the bacterial cell parts. This cell is shown magnified 21 000 times.

American Society for Microbiology

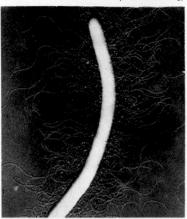

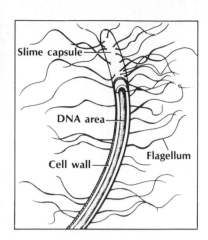

Slime capsule

DNA area

Cell wall

Flagellum

The bacterial cell wall is important in maintaining an osmotic balance between the cell and the environment.

Most bacterial cells are enclosed by a cell wall. This wall protects the cell and helps maintain an osmotic balance (Section 5:5) between the bacterium and its environment. Penicillin is effective against many bacteria because it hinders the production of murein needed to make new cell walls. Thus, the bacteria cannot reproduce. Often the cell wall is surrounded by an outer slime capsule which may protect the cell. Some bacteria have flagella and can move by "wiggling."

Besides the main chromosome, bacteria have small segments of DNA called plasmids.

This replication in the presence of antibiotics is a feature that is taken advantage of in recombinant DNA experiments (See section 13:19).

Each bacterium has one main chromosome. In addition, bacteria contain smaller, circular segments of DNA called **plasmids**. Replication of plasmids is independent of the main chromosome. Sometimes part of a plasmid may become part of the chromosome. Then it replicates along with the chromosome. Other plasmids never join with the chromosome. Many of these plasmids carry genes which make the bacterium resistant to antibiotics. When the cell in which they are located comes into contact with an antibiotic, these plasmids may replicate many times. This replication aids the survival of the bacterium.

Despite their small size and simple structure, bacteria can survive in a wide variety of environments. One reason for their success in many places is that they vary in their metabolic reactions. Most bacteria require oxygen and carry on aerobic respiration. Some can carry on anaerobic respiration, and so, they can live without oxygen. Others cannot live in the presence of oxygen and carry on only anaerobic respiration.

Bacteria obtain energy from a variety of sources.

Another reason for the success of bacteria in many places is that they differ in how they get or make food. Many bacteria are consumers, but some are producers.

Most bacteria are heterotrophic and live as parasites or saprophytes. The bacteria that live inside other organisms often cause disease. Some bacteria that live inside other organisms are necessary for the health of the organism. You could not survive without some of the bacteria in your body.

Biophoto Associates

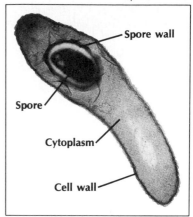

Some forms of bacteria are photosynthetic. These bacteria contain a form of chlorophyll not found in other autotrophs. Also, they do not use water or give off oxygen in their making of food. They contain no true chloroplasts.

Another group of bacteria can derive energy from inorganic materials such as iron, sulphur, and nitrogen compounds. The energy is used to make carbohydrates. The process is called **chemosynthesis** (kee moh SIHN thuh sus).

Bacteria are also successful in different environments because they can exist in two forms. One form is the active cell which reproduces. Usually bacteria reproduce asexually by simple cell division, but sexual reproduction also occurs. The other form in which bacteria exist is the dormant spore. When living conditions are unfavorable, some bacteria form protective walls. Such an organism is an inactive, highly resistant structure called an **endospore**. Bacteria can withstand temperature extremes when endospores are formed. They can survive temperatures from about −250°C to over 100°C.

An **autoclave** is a kind of equipment used in labs and hospitals to kill bacteria. It sterilizes glassware and other utensils by exposing them to steam under high pressure. The temperature of the steam under pressure is raised higher than 100°C and so most spores are killed. Some spores are not killed in an autoclave. To kill these bacteria, the process must be repeated several times. Each time the spores that have germinated are killed.

FIGURE 13-4. Certain bacteria, such as *Clostridium,* shown here magnified about 25 000 times, form spores that enable them to withstand conditions that would kill a normal active cell. When conditions are right, the spore germinates, giving rise to normal bacterial cells by cell division.

FIGURE 13-5. Bacteria are used in many processes in the dairy industry. *Lactobacillus bulgaricus* is a bacterium commonly used in the production of yogurt.

13:4 Beneficial Bacteria

Bacteria have important roles in nature and in human economy as well. Most decomposers are bacteria which break down the organic material of dead organisms and organic wastes into its basic inorganic parts. Carbon dioxide, water, and nitrogen and sulfur compounds are some of the most important materials returned to the soil and atmosphere (Section 33:4). These materials form organic material once again in other organisms. Such cycling of materials could not occur in the absence of certain bacteria.

Bacteria are used in many processes in the dairy industry. Products such as yogurt and buttermilk are made by adding certain bacteria to milk. The bacteria thrive and multiply rapidly in the milk and secrete substances which flavor the milk. Production of cheese depends on bacteria which cause the milk products to turn to solids. Cream is converted to butter as a result of bacterial action. Cream is soured by a type of bacteria, then churned into solid form, butter. The flavor of butter results from chemicals produced by other bacteria. Bacteria are also indirectly involved in the production of milk in the cow. These bacteria

Lightforce

Dannon Yogurt

The making of many dairy products requires bacteria of the genus *Lactobacillus*. These bacteria produce lactic acid as a metabolic by-product. Lactic acid sours milk.

James N. Westwater

Courtesy of Eli Lilly and Co.

a

b

FIGURE 13-6. (a) Bacteria are used in sewage treatment. In large tanks open to the air, several kinds of aerobic bacteria break down the sewage. (b) Bacteria also are used industrially in many processes. Several kinds of bacteria are involved in the commercial production of amino acids.

Bacteria are important in a variety of industrial processes.

A major new use of bacteria involves production of compounds by recombining bacterial DNA with DNA from other organisms.

1. They are both prokaryotes.
2. Blue-green algae contain chlorophyll and phycocyanin.
3. Blue-green algae exist as single cells, chains, colonies, or filaments.
4. Bacteria may be spherical (cocci), rod-shaped (bacilli), or spiral (spirilla).
5. Bacteria exhibit a variety of metabolic processes.
6. Bacteria play a role in recycling materials. They are important in the dairy industry and in other industries, such as those involved in production of vinegar, certain fibers, and some antibiotics.

grow in the rumen of the cow and help break down plant material from which the cow gets its requirements.

Bacteria also are used in other industries. Bacteria can convert alcohol to vinegar. Alcohol is changed to acetic acid which gives vinegar its odor. Some bacteria are used to break down the material holding together fibers of cellulose in plants such as flax and hemp. The fibers can then be used in making linen or rope. Preparing skins for making leather also involves bacteria. Many of today's antibiotics are produced by bacteria. These antibiotics are used to kill other bacteria.

One of the most important and promising uses of bacteria today is in the field of genetics. Using techniques that recombine DNA from different sources, bacteria have been produced that can make a variety of compounds. This topic is presented in Section 13:18.

While many bacteria are very helpful, still others are harmful and dangerous. The role of bacteria in disease is discussed in Chapter 19.

REVIEWING YOUR IDEAS

1. Why are blue-green algae and bacteria classified in the same kingdom?
2. Why are blue-green algae blue-green in color?
3. Describe different kinds of blue-green algae.
4. What are the three main shapes of bacteria? Describe each.
5. Why can bacteria survive in such a variety of environments?
6. How are bacteria important in communities of organisms? In industry?

KINGDOM PROTISTA

Kingdom Protista includes simple, eukaryotic organisms. Most forms are unicellular, but some are very simple multicellular organisms with little division of labor. Some protists are autotrophic, some are heterotrophic, and some may obtain food either way. The protists include simple algae, protozoa, and a group called slime molds.

Protists are simple eukaryotes which may be unicellular or simple multicellular organisms.

The algal protists are mostly unicellular producers. Their chlorophyll and other pigments are located in chloroplasts. They are mostly aquatic, living in fresh water, salt water, and moist places on land. They are classified into phyla on the basis of color and structure.

Algal protists are aquatic producers and are classified on the basis of color and structure.

Protozoa are unicellular, animallike organisms. Most of them can move and are classified into phyla based on how they move. They are heterotrophs, and many have special features for obtaining food. Some actively trap food, while others are parasites. They undergo both sexual and asexual reproduction.

Protozoa are unicellular heterotrophs, classified on the basis of how they move.

Slime molds have a unique life cycle with features of both protozoa and fungi. Some stages are unicellular, while others are multicellular.

13:5 Euglenoids

Euglenoids (yew GLEE noydz), phylum **Euglenophyta** (yoo gluh NAHF uh tuh), are unicellular algae. Many forms are autotrophic, but some are heterotrophic. Some may live as animal parasites.

Euglenoids are motile, having a long flagellum (or two) to propel them. They have no cell walls. They are mostly aquatic, usually freshwater forms. All forms reproduce asexually by mitosis. No means of sexual reproduction is known.

Euglena is an interesting genus of organisms. *Euglena* contain chlorophyll, and when they are present in high concentration, the water they are in appears green. These photosynthetic organisms swim swiftly through water, occasionally changing from cigar shape to round shape. A *Euglena* (Figure 13-7) has a reddish–orange eyespot or **stigma** near the base of its flagellum. The stigma is sensitive to light. Thus, the *Euglena* can respond and move to a source of light. How is this behavior adaptive? A **contractile vacuole** (Section 5:12) pumps out water maintaining water balance in the cell. Excess food is stored in a structure called the **pyrenoid** (pi REE noyd). Pyrenoids are located on the chloroplasts. *Euglena* is an example of euglenoid that may lose its chloroplasts and become heterotrophic. The loss of chloroplasts results from prolonged darkness.

Euglena can move by flagellar motion or by alternately contracting and expanding. The latter is known as euglenoid motion.

FIGURE 13-7. The euglenoids include *Euglena,* a single-cell organism with certain plant and animal traits.

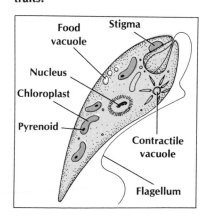

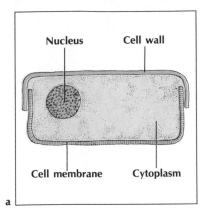

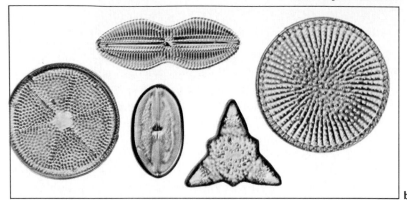

a

b

FIGURE 13-8. (a) The shell of a diatom, a golden alga, consists of one part that overlaps the other and is made of a glasslike material. (b) The beautiful forms diatoms take are many and varied. The diatoms shown are magnified about 2000 times.

FIGURE 13-9. (a) Representative dinoflagellates show that each has a pair of flagella for locomotion. (b) A "red tide" is the result of rapid reproduction of certain dinoflagellates.

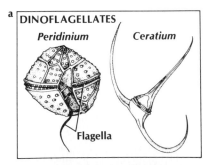

a DINOFLAGELLATES
Peridinium   *Ceratium*

Flagella

b

13:6 Golden Algae

The **golden algae**, phylum **Chrysophyta** (kruh SAHF uh tuh), are mostly unicellular. Their colors may range from a yellow-green to golden-brown depending on the carotenes they contain. Most common and best known of this phylum are the **diatoms** (DI uh tahmz). Diatoms inhabit both fresh water and salt water. They are the most numerous of the many small producers which float on the surface of the sea. Thus, they are important marine producers.

Diatoms are unicellular and have many shapes and colors making them some of nature's most beautiful organisms (Figure 13-8). Each diatom is composed of a two-part outer shell in which one part of the shell overlaps the other like a lid and box. The shell of a diatom is the cell wall covered with a glasslike material. When diatoms die, the cell walls collect producing huge deposits of this material, known as **diatomaceous** (di ut uh MAY shus) **earth**, which is useful to people. Among its uses are as a filtering agent for juices and other liquids and as an ingredient in scouring powders, cosmetics, and toothpaste.   silicon dioxide

13:7 Dinoflagellates

Dinoflagellates are members of the smallest phylum of algae, **Pyrrophyta** (puh RAHF uh tuh). These unicellular forms are found in both fresh water and salt water and are food for aquatic heterotrophs. Each cell has two flagella for locomotion (Figure 13-9a). Certain species sometimes produce a red pigment and can color the water to produce "red tides" when they multiply rapidly. During "red tides," substances produced by the algae may be poisonous to fish. During the summer, red tides can cause the death of thousands of organisms along coasts of the United States (Figure 13-8b). They do not occur every summer but kill or damage seafood when they do occur.

13:8 Sarcodines

One of the simplest and most often studied protozoa is the **amoeba** (Figure 13-10). Amoebae are **sarcodines** (SAR kuh dinez), phylum **Sarcodina** (sar kuh DI nuh), which move by means of extensions of the cytoplasm called **pseudopodia** (sewd uh POHD ee uh) (false feet). Such movement is called **amoeboid** (uh MEE boyd) **motion**. An amoeba can form pseudopodia because of its flexible plasma membrane and its constantly moving and changing cytoplasm. The cell membrane extends as the cytoplasm flows toward it. The shape of the amoeba changes as new pseudopodia are formed and others disappear.

Pseudopodia are used in both moving and food-getting. Pseudopodia engulf particles of food by phagocytosis (Section 5:9). The food particle enters the cytoplasm within a vacuole and is digested there. These food vacuoles are often visible in an amoeba.

The type of amoeba often studied is commonly found in ponds and other bodies of water. It is a harmless form, but some others are quite dangerous to humans. One causes the disease amoebic dysentery (DIHS un ter ee) which is common in areas where unsanitary conditions prevail.

Two marine forms of sarcodines are well-known. One type, the *Foraminifera* (fuh ram uh NIHF ra), or forams, have an outer, protective skeleton composed of calcium carbonate. The second group, the *Radiolaria* (rayd ee oh LER ee uh), have an internal skeleton which contains a glasslike material. In some radiolarians the skeleton may protrude outward from the cytoplasm forming spines which can be moved or withdrawn. Both forams and radiolarians live in the ocean and are eaten by larger consumers.

Skeletons of forams have formed much of the limestone and chalk on Earth, including the white cliffs of Dover, England. Radiolarian skeletons form a rock called chert.

FIGURE 13-10. The amoeba, *Chaos chaos,* is a sarcodine. It moves with pseudopodia, extensions of the cytoplasm.

Pseudopodia (singular, pseudopodium) function in locomotion and food-getting.

Forams and radiolarians are eaten by larger ocean dwellers.

FIGURE 13-11. (a) Two marine forms of sarcodines, Radiolarians and Foraminiferans, have skeletons. (b) Foram skeletons have formed much of the white cliffs of Dover, England.

a
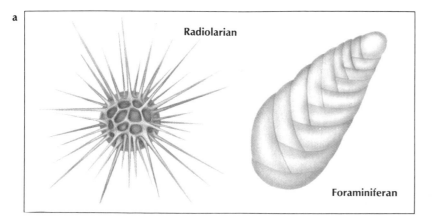

Radiolarian

Foraminiferan

b

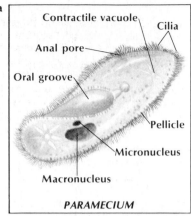

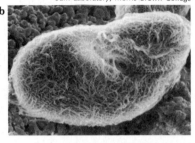

SEM Laboratory, Morris Brown College

FIGURE 13-12. (a) *Paramecium* is a ciliate commonly studied by biology students. (b) The cilia, the hairlike structures on the surface, show clearly in this photo magnified about 775 times.

Ciliates have two types of nuclei.

Most flagellates are parasites.

FIGURE 13-13. *Trypanosoma* is a flagellate that causes African sleeping sickness and is transmitted by the tsetse fly.

13:9 Ciliates

In general, ciliates have the most complex division of labor found among unicellular organisms.

Ciliates (SIHL ee ayts), phylum **Ciliophora** (sihl ee AHF uh ruh), have many hairlike **cilia** on their surfaces. These cilia are used for obtaining food and for locomotion. Like sarcodines and most other protozoa, ciliates are unicellular. Unlike amoebae, they have a definite shape because they have a rather stiff covering called a **pellicle** (PEL ih kul) which borders the cell.

Genus *Paramecium* (Figure 13-12) is the group of ciliates most often studied by biology students. A paramecium is a complex organism with division of labor. For example, food enters through the **oral groove**. The contractile vacuole helps pump out excess water, and undigestible materials leave through the **anal pore**.

Movement is accomplished by the coordinated beating of the cilia which surround the cell. Usually a paramecium rotates as it glides rapidly through water. If disturbed, a paramecium may curl up and suddenly reverse its direction.

Ciliates have two types of nuclei within a single cell. A large **macronucleus** controls the basic activities of the cell. The smaller **micronucleus** is involved in reproduction. Some ciliates have many micronuclei. It is thought by some that two kinds of nuclei are needed because the cells are highly specialized.

13:10 Flagellates

Protozoa which move by means of flagella are called **flagellates** and belong to the phylum **Mastigophora** (mas tuh GAHF uh ruh). Some flagellates are free-living organisms in both freshwater and saltwater habitats. Most forms, though, live within other organisms.

One species is a parasite which causes African sleeping sickness. This organism, a member of the genus *Trypanasoma*, is transmitted to humans by the tsetse (SEET see) fly. It lives in the blood and releases a poisonous substance that attacks the nervous system causing weakness and then death.

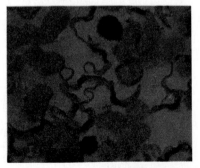

Roger K. Burnard

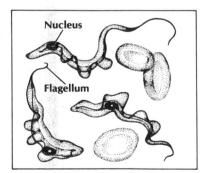

Another flagellate lives in the gut of termites. It secretes enzymes that digest the wood termites eat. Thus, both the flagellate and the termite benefit. A relationship in which two organisms live in close association and benefit each other is called **mutualism** (MYEW chuh lihz um) (Section 33:6).

Flagellates living within termites is an example of mutualism.

13:11 Sporozoans

Sporozoans (spor uh ZOH unz), phylum **Sporozoa** (spor uh ZOH uh), include protozoa that have no means of moving and that reproduce by means of sporelike structures. Since they have no way to move, they cannot actively obtain food. They are parasitic and depend on their hosts for food. As parasites, some cause disease in humans and many animals.

Sporozoans cannot move. They reproduce by spores and are parasites.

Most dreaded of the sporozoans are members of the genus, *Plasmodium*. They are responsible for malaria, a disease which has caused millions of deaths. Even today in tropical regions, at least a million persons per year die of malaria. This disease is discussed in Section 19:8.

Malaria is caused by the sporozoan *Plasmodium* and is transmitted to humans by the female *Anopheles* mosquito.

13:12 Slime Molds

Slime molds, phylum **Myxomycota** (mihks uh mi KOH tuh), are one of the most fascinating groups of protists. In some species the life cycle begins as a **plasmodium** (plaz MOHD ee um), a yellowish, slimy mass of material composed of many nuclei but no cell walls. Note that the plasmodium stage of a slime mold is not the same as the name of the organism that causes malaria. A slime mold plasmodium very slowly "crawls" and oozes on the forest floor over rotting logs and other decaying materials. The plasmodium takes in organic materials by phagocytosis.

As a plasmodium creeps along the forest floor, it may slow down and undergo an amazing change. The plasmodium develops into many fruiting bodies which produce spores by mitosis and then release them. The spores develop into flagellated swarm

a

Carolina Biological Supply Co.

b

Runk/Schoenberger for Grant Heilman

FIGURE 13-14. (a) The plasmodium, a slimy mass of protoplasm, is a stage in the life cycle of a slime mold. (b) Fruiting bodies develop from the plasmodium. The fruiting bodies are spore-producing structures.

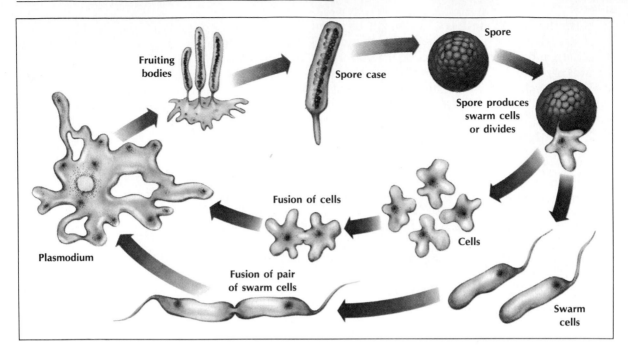

FIGURE 13-15. The life cycle of a slime mold includes many changes in form. Notice that swarm cells resemble flagellates and the plasmodium resembles amoeboid sarcodines.

Cellular slime molds have a different life cycle than that described here for true slime molds.

During its life cycle, the slime mold changes form several times.

cells which can join if moisture and food are available. These cells are attracted to each other by a chemical which they secrete. Swarm cells fuse to form a zygote which loses its flagella and begins to move like an amoeba. Mitosis and growth occur, but no cell division occurs, to produce a new plasmodium. Sometimes several small plasmodia fuse to form a larger plasmodium.

Features of slime molds are interesting to biologists because the life cycle involves many changes in form. These different forms resemble other forms of life. Spore production is like that of fungi. Individual, flagellated swarm cells are like protozoa. Biologists are studying slime mold development to try to better understand the development of more complex organisms.

7. Algal protists are classified on the basis of color and structure.
8. *Euglena* is an oval, green cell with a single flagellum. It is autotrophic like a plant, but motile like an animal.
9. Euglenophyta, Chrysophyta, and Pyrrophyta are the three phyla of algal protists.
10. Certain dinoflagellates cause red tides which kill marine organisms.
11. Protozoa are classified on the basis of locomotion. The phyla are Sarcodina, Ciliophora, Mastigophora, and Sporozoa.
12. Pseudopods and cilia are both used for locomotion and food-getting.

REVIEWING YOUR IDEAS

7. On what basis are the algal protists subdivided?
8. Describe the structure of *Euglena*. What features of this organism make it difficult to classify?
9. What are the three phyla of algal protists?
10. How may certain dinoflagellates be harmful?
11. On what basis are the protozoa subdivided? List the name of each phylum of protozoa.
12. Describe the uses of pseudopodia and cilia.
13. How do sporozoans obtain food? Can they obtain food in other ways? Why?
14. How are slime molds similar to other simple forms of life?

13. Sporozoans are parasites. Because they cannot move, they cannot obtain food in other ways.

14. Different stages of the slime mold's life cycle have features of other life forms, such as protozoa and fungi.

KINGDOM FUNGI

Fungi are plantlike in that many are stationary. However, they are heterotrophic; they do not have chlorophyll. Because they cannot move to capture food, fungi are either parasites or saprophytes. They absorb small molecules of food from a host or the environment.

Most true fungi have filamentous stalks called **hyphae** (HI fee). In some fungi, each hypha is a mass of cytoplasm containing many nuclei and no cell walls. In others, the hyphae are composed of definite cells. A mass of hyphae is called a **mycelium** (mi SEE lee um). The cell walls of most fungi are composed of **chitin** (KITE un), a carbohydrate material. Some forms are unicellular and lack hyphae.

Fungi reproduce by forming spores and by other means. Thickened walls of the hyphae and spores are adaptations which permit fungi to live on land. *Fungi are classified on the basis of their spore-producing structures.*

fungi (singular, fungus)

Fungi are heterotrophs which obtain nourishment by absorbing small food molecules.

hyphae (singular, hypha)

mycelium (plural, mycelia)

Fungi are adapted for life on land.

13:13 Sporangium Fungi

The common bread mold (Figure 13-16), *Rhizopus* (RI zuh pus), is a member of the phylum **Zygomycota** (zi goh mi KOH tuh), or sporangium fungi. In this phylum, spores are produced in **sporangia**. Sporangia are structures located at the tips of certain hyphae. The hyphae are called **sporangiophores** (spuh RAN jee uh forz). They stick up above the food source giving the fungus a fuzzy appearance. Other hyphae called **stolons** (STOH lunz) spread along the surface of the food supply, or substrate (SUB strayt). In addition to asexual reproduction by means of spores, bread mold can also reproduce sexually (Section 17:6).

The common bread mold, *Rhizopus*, is an example of a sporangium fungus.

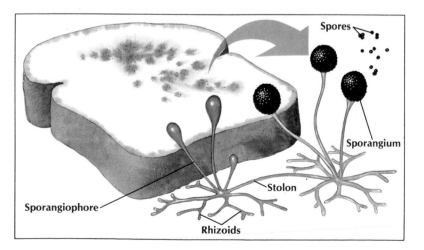

FIGURE 13-16. The black dots of common bread mold, *Rhizopus nigricans*, are sporangia. The mold can reproduce asexually by releasing spores from the sporangia.

FIGURE 13-17. (a) Downy mildew, *Peronospora manshurica*, shown here growing on a soybean plant, is a parasitic fungus. (b) Its rhizoids penetrate and digest the tissues of the host plant.

Don Durovich for Photo Researchers

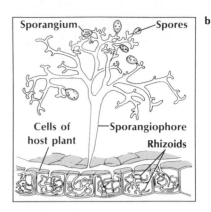

Rhizoids anchor fungi and digest and absorb food.

A downy mildew was responsible for the infamous potato blight in Ireland in the nineteenth century.

Many sporangium fungi are important saprophytes, but some are dangerous parasites.

Still other hyphae, **rhizoids** (RI zoydz), anchor the fungus to the food source. Thus, rhizoids resemble roots in function. Rhizoids enter the substrate and secrete enzymes which break the food molecules into simpler molecules. The simple molecules diffuse into the rhizoids and throughout the mold.

Most relatives of the bread mold are saprophytes which decompose dead organisms for their food. As a result, valuable materials are returned to the soil and atmosphere. However, some species such as the downy mildews are parasites which cause disease by feeding on many plants, including potatoes and cereal grains. They produce rhizoids which penetrate the tissues of the host plant and "rob" it of nutrient materials.

13:14 Club Fungi

Club fungi produce spores in basidia (singular, basidium).

Mushrooms are a class of fungi which have club-shaped, spore-producing structures called **basidia** (buh SIHD ee uh). The phylum is **Basidiomycota**, or **club fungi**. Also in this phylum are shelf fungi, rusts, smuts, and puffballs (Figure 13-18).

Mushrooms are important because many of them are edible. The edible part of a mushroom is only the reproductive part of the organism. Underground is a branching network of hyphae which obtain nourishment in much the same way as does bread mold.

FIGURE 13-18. Club fungi include (a) mushrooms, (b) shelf fungi, and (c) puffballs. Club fungi have spore-producing structures called basidia.

Ward's Natural Science Establishment, Inc.   *James N. Westwater*   *Alvin E. Staffan*

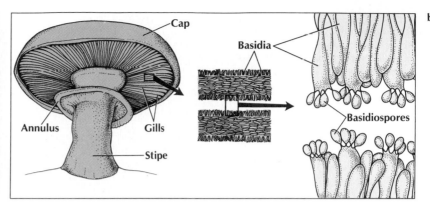

FIGURE 13-19. (a) *Amanita verosa*, the "destroying angel," is a poisonous mushroom. (b) Mushroom basidiospores are produced on the gills.

The button portion of the mushroom develops as a small outgrowth of the mycelium in the soil which pushes through the soil and develops into a stalklike section, the **stipe**, and an umbrellalike **cap**. Beneath the cap are spokelike **gills** on which basidia are located. Each basidium produces four spores which can be dispersed by the wind.

Poisonous mushrooms are commonly called toadstools. Toadstools can cause illness and some, such as a few *Amanita* (am uh NITE uh) species, can even cause death if eaten (Figure 13-19a). *Therefore, an untrained person should not eat mushrooms found growing wild.*

Toadstools commonly are considered poisonous mushrooms.

Whereas mushrooms are valuable to humans, many fungi in this class are harmful. Mycelia of rusts, for example, invade the internal parts of wheat, oats, and rye. In this way, they can destroy entire crops of these and other plants. Geneticists have developed some strains of plants which are resistant to these parasites.

Some club fungi cause extensive crop damage.

13:15 Sac Fungi

Yeasts, cup fungi, and powdery mildews are all members of phylum **Ascomycota**, the **sac fungi**. In each of these organisms, the zygote develops into a saclike structure, the **ascus.** Spores are produced in the ascus.

In sac fungi, spores are produced in the ascus (plural, asci).

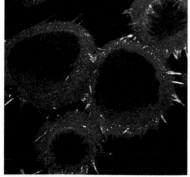

FIGURE 13-20. (a) Cup fungi and (b) powdery mildew (shown growing on leaf litter) are examples of sac fungi. They produce spores in structures called asci.

FIGURE 13-21. (a) *Penicillium* mold, shown here growing in a Petri dish, is a sac fungus that produces the antibiotic penicillin. (b) Morels are edible sac fungi that resemble mushrooms.

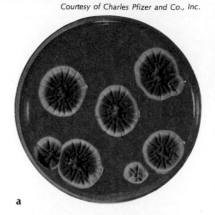

a

b

Yeasts are unusual fungi in that they are unicellular. Recall that they are important in both the brewing and baking industries (Section 4:9). They are also very important in research because they are simple eukaryotes.

Other types of sac fungi are also important. One species of *Penicillium* mold is used to produce penicillin (Section 2:5). Other species of *Penicillium* are used in making cheeses such as Roquefort (ROHK furt) and Camembert (KAM um ber) in which enzymes produced by the molds give the cheeses their flavors. Morels (Figure 13-21) are sac fungi that resemble mushrooms and are edible.

While some sac fungi are useful, many others cause disease in a variety of plants. For example, Dutch elm disease results from invasion by a sac fungus which destroys the tree's conductive tissues. The fungus is transmitted by bark beetles. It has been responsible for the death of millions of elm trees. Biologists are working to control the disease by using bacteria which inhibit growth of the fungus. Another approach involves the use of natural chemicals to attract the beetles to traps.

Dutch elm disease is caused by a sac fungus.

13:16 Lichens

Found in some of the most desolate regions are organisms called **lichens**. Lichens are not single organisms with a separate

FIGURE 13-22. Lichens take various forms and can live in barren places.

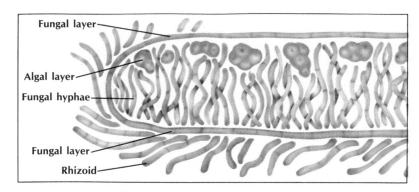

James N. Westwater

FIGURE 13-23. A lichen is an association of an alga and a fungus. The alga produces food; the fungus may provide protection and moisture.

classification. Rather, they are a combination of two different organisms, a fungus and an alga (Figure 13-23). The alga is either a blue-green or green species. *Nostoc* (Section 13:2) is commonly found as part of lichens. The alga is surrounded by the mycelium of the fungus. Lichens grow on soil, rocks, and trees throughout the United States. Some lichens grow flat and close to the surface while others grow upward and may appear shrublike.

Lichens can grow in barren places such as on bare rock or on the ice of the Arctic. Neither the fungus nor the alga could survive in such places alone. How do they live together? The alga is autotrophic so it provides food by photosynthesis for itself and probably for the fungus. The fungus is not a parasite because it does not harm the alga. Exactly how the fungus aids the alga is not clear. Perhaps the fungus provides protection and moisture for the alga. It may also be a source of inorganic materials. A lichen is another example of mutualism.

Reproduction of lichens is not fully understood. Some new lichens may develop from pieces of old lichens. Others produce grains of powder containing an algal cell and a hypha of the fungus. In some lichens, the fungi release spores which must associate with the "right" alga in order for the lichen to form.

Lichens may serve as food for animals, such as reindeer "moss" which is eaten by reindeer and caribou. Also, lichens serve another important ecological function. Fungi secrete acids which begin the breakdown of rock into particles of soil (Section 34:1). Also, when lichens die, they decompose, enriching the soil. Gradually more complex plants can grow in these regions and small animals may also be able to flourish.

Lichens are combinations of two organisms—an alga and a fungus.

In a lichen, the alga produces food for the fungus.

The fungus may provide protection and moisture for the alga.

Lichens may serve as a food source for animals. They are also important in the process of soil formation.

15. Fungi are classified on the basis of their spore-producing structures.
16. Mushroom—basidium; *Rhizopus*—sporangium; yeast—ascus
17. A bread mold consists of sporangiophore hyphae bearing sporangia at their tips. Stolons run along the substrate and rhizoids penetrate the substrate.
18. Most of the mycelium of a mushroom is in the soil. The portions above the soil are the stipe (stalk) and cap. Basidia are located on gills on the underside of the cap.
19. A lichen is a mutualistic association of an alga and a fungus. The alga provides food for the fungus while the fungus may provide moisture and protection for the alga. The association allows for life in barren places.

REVIEWING YOUR IDEAS

15. How are fungi classified?
16. What is the spore-producing structure of a mushroom? Of *Rhizopus*? Of yeast?
17. Describe the structure of bread mold.
18. Describe the structure of a mushroom.
19. What is a lichen? Why can lichens live in barren places?

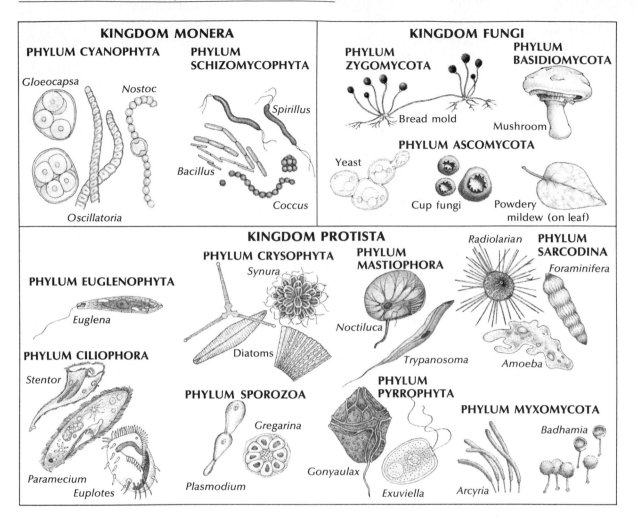

TABLE 13-2. SUMMARY OF MAJOR CHARACTERISTICS OF MONERANS, PROTISTS, AND FUNGI

Kingdom	Phylum	Common Name	Structure	Nutrition	Examples
Monera	Cyanophyta	Blue-Green Algae	Prokaryotic; Mostly Unicellular	Autotrophic	*Nostoc*
	Schizomycophyta	Bacteria	Prokaryotic; Unicellular	Mostly Heterotrophic	*Diplococcus*
Protista	Euglenophyta	Euglenoids	Unicellular	Autotrophic	*Euglena*
	Chrysophyta	Golden Algae	Mostly Unicellular	Autotrophic	diatoms
	Pyrrophyta	Dinoflagellates	Unicellular	Autotrophic	*Gonyaulax*
	Sarcodina	Sarcodines	Unicellular	Heterotrophic	*Amoeba*
	Ciliophora	Ciliates	Unicellular	Heterotrophic	*Paramecium*
	Mastigophora	Flagellates	Unicellular	Heterotrophic	*Trypanasoma*
	Sporozoa	Sporozoans	Unicellular	Heterotrophic	*Plasmodium*
	Myxomycota	Slime Molds	Unicellular and Multicellular stages	Heterotrophic	*Physarum*
Fungi	Zygomycota	Sporangium Fungi	Multicellular	Heterotrophic	*Rhizopus*
	Basidiomycota	Club Fungi	Multicellular	Heterotrophic	mushroom
	Ascomycota	Sac Fungi	Multicellular	Heterotrophic	cup fungus

Dr. Judie Walton,
Lawrence Livermore National Laboratory

a

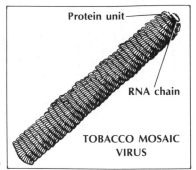

b

Protein unit

RNA chain

TOBACCO MOSAIC
VIRUS

Dr. C. Wayne Ellet, Professor Emeritus/OSU

c

FIGURE 13-24. (a) The tobacco mosaic virus (TMV), shown here magnified about 590 000 times, is rod-shaped and has (b) an RNA center surrounded by a protein coat. (c) When TMV infects a tobacco plant, the plant leaves become mottled and wilted.

VIRUSES

Monerans, protists, and fungi are simple organisms compared to plants and animals. However, there are even simpler "organisms" in nature. They are the viruses. Because their characteristics are unique, they are not classified in a kingdom. As you study their features, try to decide whether viruses are organisms or particles of chemicals.

Viruses are not assigned to a kingdom of organisms.

13:17 Characteristics

For many years scientists knew of diseases which were not caused by any known living thing. Such an agent of disease was called a **virus** which means poison. One of the many organisms affected by a virus is the tobacco plant. Because the leaves of an infected plant become mottled and take on a mosaic (moh ZAY ihk) pattern (Figure 13-24c), the disease was named tobacco mosaic disease.

In 1935, the tobacco mosaic virus was isolated in crystal form. Since then, many other viruses have been isolated. Although viruses cannot be seen with a light microscope, much has been learned about them by using electron microscopes and biochemical analysis.

Viruses have several shapes such as spherical, needle-like, cubical, and many-sided (Figure 13-25). Each virus particle

The existence of viruses was known before they were actually discovered.

In the laboratory, viruses must be cultured in living tissue. Some animal viruses are cultured in chick embryos.

A virus is composed of a nucleic acid surrounded by protein.

FIGURE 13-25. (a) T₄ bacteriophage, shown magnified about 150 000 times, is a DNA virus that infects bacterial cells. (b) Adenovirus, shown magnified about 500 000 times, is a DNA virus that infects animal cells.

a

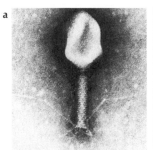

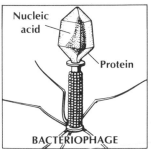

Nucleic acid

Protein

BACTERIOPHAGE

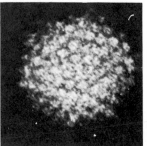

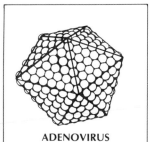

ADENOVIRUS

b

Science Photo Library International   *Center for Disease Control*

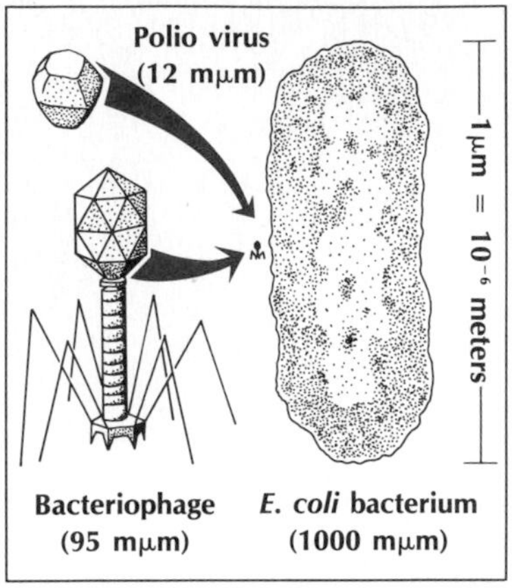

Polio virus
(12 mμm)

1 μm = 10⁻⁶ meters

Bacteriophage
(95 mμm)

E. coli bacterium
(1000 mμm)

FIGURE 13-26. Viruses, though they vary in size and shape, are all much smaller than bacteria.

A virus requires a specific host for reproduction.

Viruses may be descendants of more complex organisms.

20. A virus is a nucleic acid core surrounded by a protein coat.
21. Viruses can be crystalized and in that way are like nonliving substances. However, viruses can infect and reproduce inside living cells.

FIGURE 13-27. Human growth hormone produced by recombinant DNA techniques is packaged for shipment.

Steve Northrup/TIME Magazine

consists of an outer coat of protein and an inner part of nucleic acid. The nucleic acid can be either DNA or RNA depending on the type of virus. A virus does not have even a cellular level of organization. Viruses are so small that a bacterium seems huge in comparison. For example, the virus which causes polio is only 25 nanometers in diameter. Food is not metabolized for energy and no organelles or membranes are present. The only life function a virus carries out is reproduction which it cannot do by itself. To reproduce, it requires a specific host cell. How a virus reproduces is discussed in Section 17:7.

13:18 Some Questions

Is a virus alive? This question is debatable. In terms of the basic features of life discussed in Chapter 1, viruses do not seem to qualify as living things. However, viruses can reproduce, which is the most universal function of living things.

Another question that may be more important than whether or not viruses are alive is the question of the possible origin of viruses. Viruses may have evolved from a simple structure without an enzyme system. Or, viruses may have had these enzymes but lost them and became dependent on true cells. Most biologists today agree that viruses are probably products of what is called **degenerative** (dih JEN uh ruh tihv) **evolution**. That is, they probably are descendants of a more complex living system. In becoming parasitic, viruses may have lost some features. What is left is the chemical basis for reproduction, the genes.

REVIEWING YOUR IDEAS

20. Describe the structure of a virus.
21. Why is it difficult to decide whether or not viruses are alive?

ADVANCES IN BIOLOGY

13:19 Recombinant DNA

Since the DNA structure model was first proposed, much has been learned about genes, their functions, and their manipulation. Certain methods, called **recombinant DNA techniques,** have been developed which combine information about the traits of certain organisms and about what proteins certain genes code for. Recombinant DNA experiments result in the creation of a cell that can make a certain protein. This result is obtained by combining genes from two different kinds of organisms.

Most recombinant DNA experiments use the bacterium, *E. coli,* because the genetics of this organism have been studied in detail. Certain *E. coli* have **plasmids,** rings of DNA separate

The technology may be used in the distant future to modify higher eukaryotic organisms, but current work is mostly with prokaryotes, lower eukaryotes, and higher eukaryotic cells in culture.

The procedure is sometimes called gene splicing.—
from the main chromosome. The plasmids are the structures into which the genes of other organisms are inserted.——

Consider the hormone insulin, a substance needed by the body for normal sugar metabolism. Persons that lack insulin have diabetes mcllitus (Section 8:9), and often arc treated with injections of insulin from pigs or cattle. Some diabetics, however, cannot use pig or cattle insulin. Human insulin can now be made using recombinant DNA techniques. The procedure followed has these main steps. 1) A single gene, in this case the gene for insulin production, is obtained from a human source cell. The gene usually is obtained using enzymes; the reactions are carried out in test tubes. 2) The gene, once obtained, is inserted into the *E. coli* plasmid. The plasmid is treated with an enzyme that breaks it at a specific place. The exposed bases of the plasmid's DNA match those of the human gene to be inserted. Using another enzyme, the DNA of the organisms is joined. The resulting plasmid has recombinant DNA—DNA from the bacterium and the newly inserted human DNA (the gene for insulin production). 3) The recombined *plasmids* reproduce within the *E. coli* cell, making copies. Also, the *cells* can be reproduced making even more copies of the human gene. Plasmids may carry genes for drug (antibiotic) resistance. Therefore, if the human gene is inserted into a plasmid that is also drug resistant, the *E. coli* cells can be multiplied in the presence of the drug. Other cells, lacking resistance, will not reproduce. This procedure ensures that many cells with the human gene are produced. 4) Finally, the structure of the resulting gene is verified, and the protein product made. The protein is then purified, and its identity is verified before it is mass produced. The product in this case is *human* insulin. A variety of other products have been made using recombinant DNA techniques and the list of products is only beginning. In 1981, an effective vaccine against foot-and-mouth disease (a highly contagious animal disease) became the first vaccine to be produced by recombinant DNA techniques.

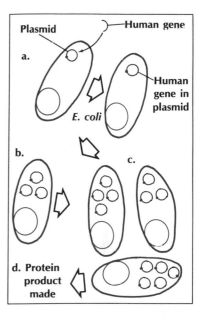

FIGURE 13-28. By recombinant DNA techniques, human insulin can be produced by bacteria. (a) The human gene is inserted into a bacterial plasmid. (b) The plasmid replicates inside the bacterial cell. (c) The bacterial cell with the inserted gene is replicated. (d) After many gene copies are made, the protein of the gene is produced and purified.

The human insulin produced is identical to that produced by the human body.

CHAPTER REVIEW

SUMMARY

1. Prokaryotes are cells which lack true nuclei They also have no membrane-bound organelles.

2. Monerans include blue-green algae and bacteria, organisms which are prokaryotes.

3. Blue-green algae are autotrophic and contain pigments. Most forms are unicellular, but some are filaments, chains, or colonies.

4. Most bacteria are one of three shapes. Most are heterotrophic, but some are autotrophs.

5. Bacteria are important in nature and to humans. They are helpful in recycling materials. They are essential in some industrial processes.

6. Protists are simple, eukaryotic organisms. Most are unicellular. The kingdom includes both autotrophic and heterotrophic forms.

7. Algal protists are mostly unicellular autotrophs. They are mostly aquatic and are producers for freshwater and marine communities. They are classified on the basis of color and structure.

CHAPTER REVIEW

8. Slime molds have a unique life cycle involving unicellular and multicellular stages. The cycle includes stages characteristic of other life forms.

9. Fungi are heterotrophic. They absorb their food as parasites or saprophytes. Most forms are multicellular and have hyphae. They are classified on the basis of their spore-producing structures and means of sexual reproduction. Common fungi are bread mold (sporangium fungus), mushroom (club fungus), and yeast (sac fungus).

10. Lichens are combinations of two organisms — a blue-green or green alga and a fungus. The organisms are mutualistic.

11. Protozoa are heterotrophic, unicellular, animallike protists. They are classified on the basis of the way they move: sarcodines, pseudopodia; ciliates, cilia; flagellates, flagella; and sporozoans, no movement.

12. Viruses are composed of a protein coat and a nucleic acid core. They have no cellular structure and reproduce only in living host cells.

13. Viruses may be descendants of a more complex living system which underwent degenerative evolution.

14. An important beneficial use of bacteria is in recombinant DNA research. With special DNA techniques, bacteria are used in both pure and applied research.

LANGUAGE OF BIOLOGY

asexual reproduction	chitin	plasmodium
ascus	cocci	protozoa
autoclave	diatoms	pyrenoid
bacilli	endospore	rhizoid
basidium	hypha	spirilla
cap	lichen	sporangium
carotenes	murein	stipe
chemosynthesis	mycelium	stolon
	plasmid	

CHECKING YOUR IDEAS

On a separate paper, complete each of the following statements with the missing term(s). Do not write in this book.

1. _____ are cells which have no true nuclei.

2. A relationship in which two organisms live closely together and benefit each other is called _____.

3. Fungi have filaments called _____.

4. Protozoa are classified on the basis of their means of _____.

5. Yeasts and mushrooms belong to the _____ kingdom.

6. Kingdom _____ includes both autotrophic and heterotrophic eukaryotes.

7. Each virus has an inner part that is made up of _____.

8. A rod-shaped bacterium is called a(n) _____.

9. Spore-producing structures are a feature of Kingdom _____.

10. Many bacteria withstand harsh conditions by producing _____.

11. In bacteria, _____ is carried out on the inner surface of the cell membrane.

12. _____ algae have no chloroplasts.

13. Presence of two types of nuclei in a cell is a characteristic of the _____.

14. The plasmodium is a stage in the life cycle of the _____.

15. Red tides may be caused by certain _____.

EVALUATING YOUR IDEAS

1. Compare prokaryotic and eukaryotic cells in terms of:
   (a) nucleus and nuclear membrane
   (b) composition of the cell wall
   (c) kinds of organelles
   (d) structure of flagella
   (e) location of chlorophyll
   (f) chromosome number and structure

CHAPTER REVIEW

2. Where does photosynthesis take place in blue-green algae? Why?

3. What are plasmids? How may certain plasmids be important to bacteria?

4. Describe the various ways in which bacteria obtain nourishment.

5. What are some ways that bacteria are beneficial to humans?

6. Describe the characteristics of the protists. What groups of organisms are included in this kingdom?

7. Describe the features of the algal protists.

8. How are diatoms important to humans?

9. List the main characteristics of protozoa.

10. Describe food-getting and locomotion in an amoeba and a paramecium.

11. Why do some scientists think that two nuclei are necessary in ciliates?

12. Describe the life cycle of a slime mold.

13. List the characteristics of fungi.

14. How are fungi adapted for life on land?

15. In general, how do fungi reproduce?

16. What are the three main phyla of fungi? Name an organism belonging to each one.

17. How are the algae and fungi of lichens mutualistic?

18. What is degenerative evolution? How is this concept useful in explaining the possible origin of viruses?

19. Describe the technique for producing recombinant DNA.

20. Why are plasmids bearing drug-resistant genes used in gene splicing?

APPLYING YOUR IDEAS

1. Why are endospores not considered reproductive cells?

2. Do you think heterotrophic euglenoids have a stigma? Explain.

3. How do you think protozoa and fungi were classified in the two-kingdom system of classification? Why? *Chapter 12

4. Consider the life cycle of a slime mold (Figure 13-15). Which stages are animal-like? Plantlike? Explain.

5. Some biologists have made the statement that a virus is much like a eukaryotic chromosome. What do you think they mean by that statement?

6. Could something like today's virus have been the first living thing? Explain.

EXTENDING YOUR IDEAS

1. Prepare a report on the uses of bacteria in the dairy industry.

2. Prepare a report on the life cycle of a parasitic fungus such as wheat rust or corn smut.

3. Test the effect of various disinfectants and "germ killers" on bacteria.

4. Expose various foods such as fruits, bread, and potatoes to dark, moist conditions. Later, check these foods for presence of fungi. Where did the fungi come from?

5. Prepare a report on the factors governing changes in form in slime molds.

SUGGESTED READINGS

Anderson, Lucia, *The Smallest Life Around Us.* New York, Crown Publishers, 1978.

"Beneficial Bacteria." *Sciquest*, May/June, 1981.

Bonner, John T., "Slime Molds." *Natural History*, December, 1978.

Hopkins, Harold, "Danger Lurks Among the Molds." *FDA Consumer*, Dec. 1980– Jan.1981.

Kaufman, Wallace, "Mycologists Have More Fungi." *Nat. Wildlife*, Oct.-Nov., 1981.

Kriss, Ronald P., "Paul Berg and the Ultimate Technology." *Discover*, January, 1981.

Litten, Walter, "The Most Poisonous Mushrooms." *Scientific American*, March, 1975.

Menosky, Joseph A., "The Gene Machine." *Science 81*, August, 1981.

Additional student readings and suggested teacher readings are provided in the Teacher's Guide.

Green plants are organisms that manufacture their own food. Plants can be found in almost every environment on Earth. However, different types of plants are found in different environments. What are some adaptations of plants that enable them to live in different environments? How do humans depend on plants? What new uses are being found for plants?

Introduction: In addition to presenting features of algal and land plants, this chapter centers around the adaptations which land plants have for carrying out common life functions in a terrestrial environment. You can lead your class to identify some of these functions by beginning this chapter with observations of various plants. Set up a variety of specimens around the classroom or laboratory area. Include bryophytes, ferns, and seed plants. (Or, if possible, observe such plants in nature.) Have all students observe the specimens. As they do so, ask them to begin compiling a list of functions for life on land common to all plants. Then conduct a class discussion based upon their conclusions. Hopefully, the class will formulate a set of functions similar to those discussed in Section 14:4.

PLANTS

Chapter 14 presents the characteristics of major groups of algal and land plants.

In the five kingdom classification system used in this text, plants are nonmotile, autotrophic organisms. Almost all are multicellular, and they have cell walls made of cellulose. The plant kingdom is composed of five phyla, three of which are algae. These algae are included here because they have a more complex structure than the algae of the moneran and protist kingdoms (Chapter 13).

Plants occupy a wide variety of habitats. Many forms live on land, but others live totally or partly in water. Regardless of their environment, plants are the producers of their communities.

GOAL: You will gain an understanding of what organisms the plant kingdom includes and learn the basic features of the major groups of organisms in this kingdom.

ALGAE

Those algae classified as plants are mostly multicellular organisms. Most of them have no true tissues or organs, but they do exhibit some division of labor. The entire body of an alga is called a **thallus**. In some complex algae, the shape of the thallus varies, but in most forms, it is a flattened structure. Development in these algae occurs in the water. The developing organisms are not protected by the parent plant. As with the algal protists, algal plants are subdivided on the basis of color and structure.

Algal plants are classified on the basis of color and structure.

14:1 Green Algae

Cells of **green algae**, phylum **Chlorophyta** (kloh RAHF uh tuh), closely resemble cells of true plants. It is believed that complex plants came from these algae. Chlorophyll is the major pigment in green algae, but yellow carotenes (Section 13:2) add to the color of the cells. When the amount of carotene is high, algae have a light, yellowish-green color.

Green algae contain chlorophyll and carotenes.

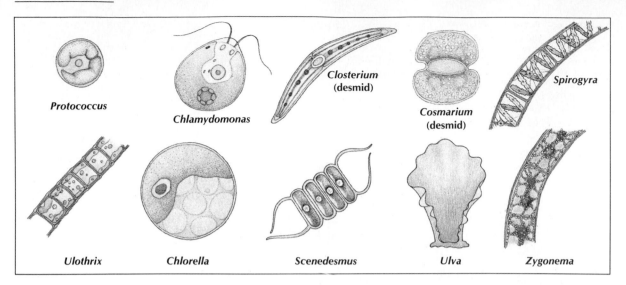

Protococcus

Chlamydomonas

Closterium
(desmid)

Cosmarium
(desmid)

Spirogyra

Ulothrix

Chlorella

Scenedesmus

Ulva

Zygonema

FIGURE 14-1. Green algae exist as single cells, filaments, and colonies.

Some green algae are unicellular.

Green algae are usually found in fresh water, but some live in the sea. *Protococcus* (proht uh KAHK us) can grow on the bark of trees when enough moisture is present.

Many green algae are filamentous, colonial, or multicellular. Thus, they seem more like other plants. Some forms, though, are unicellular. *Protococcus* is unicellular. *Chlamydomonas* (klam ud uh MOH nus) is also a one-celled green alga.

Chlamydomonas has a single large chloroplast and moves with two flagella (Figure 14-1). It may seem to you that classification systems do not make much sense because *Chlamydomonas* in many ways is similar to *Euglena* (Section 13:5), a protist. Both carry on photosynthesis and move with flagella. *Chlamydomonas*, however, has other traits that cause it to be classified as a plant. You can see that no system solves all problems of classification.

Desmids (DEZ mids) are one-celled green algae which have interesting and often beautiful forms. A desmid is composed of two halves connected by a narrow section in which the nucleus is located. Desmids float freely in water. Desmid cells can join to form colonies or filaments.

Spirogyra and *Ulothrix* are filamentous green algae in which most cells are alike.

Examples of filamentous algae are *Spirogyra* (spi ruh JI ruh) and *Ulothrix* (YEW loh thrihks). *Spirogyra* is commonly found in ponds where many filaments may grow together forming a dense mat. Individual filaments look like very thin threads. Each filament contains many identical cells. The chloroplasts are ribbon-shaped structures which form spirals throughout each cell. *Ulothrix* usually grows in fresh water where it is anchored by a special cell called a holdfast. The other cells of the filament are all alike. Any one of them may produce spores which may develop into a new filament.

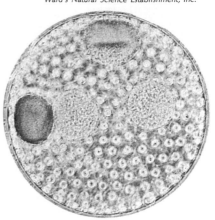

Ward's Natural Science Establishment, Inc.

Volvox (VAHL vahks) is a colonial green alga. *Volvox* cells, which resemble *Chlamydomonas* cells, form a hollow sphere. The colony has a slight amount of specialization. For example, some cells are sensitive to light. Reproductive cells divide to form daughter colonies which can be seen in the hollow cavity of the parent colony. The parent colony will burst to free the daughter colonies. A colonial form such as *Volvox* may represent a middle form of life between unicellular and multicellular organisms.

14:2 Brown Algae

Brown algae, phylum **Phaeophyta** (fee AHF uh tuh), are complex multicellular algae, almost all of which are found in salt water. They contain chlorophyll and a special carotene which gives them their brown color. Many forms grow in cool water along rocky coasts where they are anchored by holdfasts. These forms often become visible during low tide. Some grow unattached in warmer waters. One such form is *Sargassum* which grows so densely that it covers much of the surface water of the Atlantic Ocean near Bermuda. This area, called the Sargasso Sea, covers millions of square kilometers.

Brown algae are commonly called seaweeds or kelps. They may be as long as 50 m. Many forms have a thickened thallus with specialized parts. Sometimes the thallus is branched and "treelike." *Fucus* (FYEW kus), or rockweed, is a brown alga that has air-filled bladders which act as floats (Figure 14-3). Some branches of the thallus have receptacles which contain sex organs. The thallus of *Laminaria* (lam uh NER ee uh), a kelp, has a holdfast, a stemlike portion, and a leaflike region. It also has a variety of primitive tissues for protection, conduction of food, and storage. These forms are among the most complex algae.

FIGURE 14-2. The colonial green alga *Volvox* is a group of many cells forming a sphere. Four reproductive cells can be seen in the center of this colony. The colony is shown here magnified about 190 times.

Brown algae are a source of iodine. Kelps can be used as fertilizer and as a source of algin which is used in making a variety of foods, such as ice cream.

Brown algae are complex, having specialized tissues.

a

Mrs. Eileen Tanson for Photo Researchers

b

Tom Stack for Tom Stack and Associates

FIGURE 14-3. (a) Seaweed and (b) kelp are brown algae, some of which grow up to 50 m long.

Ward's Natural Science Establishment, Inc.

FIGURE 14-4. The red algae *Poly-siphonia* is red due to the presence of the pigment phycoerythrin.

14:3 Red Algae

Red algae, phylum **Rhodophyta** (roh DAHF uh tuh), are similar to brown algae. They are multicellular and more complex than the other phyla of algae. The red color is due to the pigment **phycoerythrin** (fi koh ER ih thrun). Their color and feathery structure make many red algae beautiful.

They also contain a special form of chlorophyll which can trap light at greater depths in the ocean. Thus, many forms can live deeper in the ocean than other groups of algae. Other red algae live anchored in mud along coasts.

Red algae are used in various ways. *Chondrus crispus* (KAHN drus • KRIHS pus), commonly called Irish moss, is used by some people for food. Agar is a substance made from various red algae and is used to make culture media gel. Substances from red algae are also used in making ice cream, puddings, and icings.

1. Green algae contain chlorophyll and carotenes.
2. Green algae may be unicellular, filamentous, or colonial.
3. Brown algae are generally larger than green algae and many forms have specialized tissues.
4. Some red algae are used as food. Substances from red algae are used to make agar, puddings, and ice cream.

REVIEWING YOUR IDEAS

1. What pigments are found in green algae?
2. Describe the various forms which green algae may take.
3. Compare the structure of brown algae to the structure of green algae.
4. What are some uses of red algae?

LAND PLANTS

14:4 From Water to Land

Unlike cells of most land plants, cells of algae are in close or direct contact with the environment, thus facilitating exchange of materials.

Land plants are adapted for life in a dry environment.

Algae are well adapted for life in water. They can easily obtain materials needed for photosynthesis. Most live in or near surface waters where light is present. Almost all cells of the thallus carry out photosynthesis. Thus, each cell can survive independently of other cells.

Many lines of evidence suggest that land plants resulted from changes in some form of green alga. During this process, land plants probably became well adapted for life in a dry environment. Their adaptations involve ways of:

(1) obtaining water and dissolved minerals,
(2) distributing water and dissolved minerals to all tissues,
(3) distributing food to cells which cannot make their own,
(4) preventing evaporation of water,
(5) obtaining carbon dioxide from air,
(6) supporting tissues that grow into the air,
(7) increasing the chances of fertilization, and
(8) protecting the developing plant.

You will study such adaptations among the major groups of land plants alive today.

On the basis of the presence or absence of vascular (vas kyuh luhr) tissue, land plants are classified into two major phyla—Bryophyta (bri AHF uh tuh) and Tracheophyta (tray kee AHF uh tuh). **Vascular tissue** transports food, water, and minerals throughout the plant. Bryophytes (BRI uh fites) do not have this tissue so they are called **nonvascular plants**. Tracheophytes (TRAY kee uh fites) have vascular tissue so they are called **vascular plants.**

Land plants are classified according to the presence or absence of vascular tissue.

Bryophytes lack vascular tissue.

Tracheophytes have vascular tissue.

14:5 Bryophytes

Phylum Bryophyta includes two major plant groups—**liverworts** and **mosses.** The major features of this phylum are (1) small size, (2) lack of specialized tissues for transport of materials, and (3) lack of true stems, roots, or leaves. Both groups are widely distributed, and almost all bryophytes live in a moist environment.

Mosses and liverworts are bryophytes.

Bryophytes number between 20 000 and 25 000 species.

Liverworts have "leathery" photosynthetic structures that lie flat upon the water or soil in which they grow. Liverworts are so named because the thin "leaves" are often liver-shaped (Figure 14-5a). Mosses are somewhat more complex than liverworts in that their "leaflets" are attached to upright stalklike structures (Figure 14-5b). In both groups of bryophytes, the familiar, predominant stage of the life cycle is the monoploid phase. The diploid phase is small, nonphotosynthetic, and lasts only a short time (Section 20:4).

In bryophytes, the monoploid phase of the life cycle is predominant.

Some bryophytes are useful to people. *Sphagnum* is a moss which grows in lakes and bogs in the form of floating mats. As *Sphagnum* decomposes, it forms peat moss which is commonly used as a fertilizer to improve soil quality in gardens. Mosses are often an early invader of new environments. Their decay results in the formation of rich soil suitable for other plants.

a

Alvin E. Staffan

b

Ruth Dixon

FIGURE 14-5. (a) A liverwort has a flat leaflike photosynthetic structure. (b) Mosses have leaflike structures attached to stalks. Liverworts and mosses are bryophytes.

FIGURE 14-6. A liverwort shows several adaptations for life on land. This section of the leaflike structure shows pores, rhizoids, and cutin.

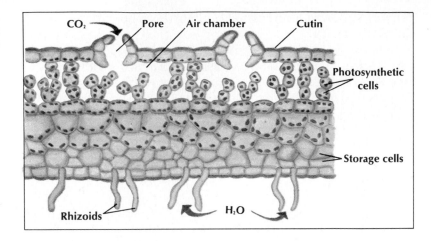

Adaptations for land life among the bryophytes can be seen by studying the structure of a liverwort. Figure 14-6 shows a cross-section of such a plant.

The source of water for most land plants is the soil. Bryophytes have no roots, but they do have rootlike **rhizoids** (RI zoydz) which anchor the plants. Rhizoids extend into the moist soil where they obtain water by osmosis and dissolved minerals by diffusion.

Bryophytes obtain water through rhizoids.

Because bryophytes have no vascular (conductive) tissues, water moves from cell to cell by osmosis. This process is slow but it works because the plant is small. Also, food made by photosynthesis is transported by diffusion.

In bryophytes, water is distributed by osmosis and food is distributed by diffusion.

A plant on dry land loses water by evaporation. **Cutin,** a waxy covering found on the outer surfaces of bryophytes and most other land plants, helps prevent excess water loss by forming a watertight seal. The single, thin "leaf" of liverworts is also helpful in water conservation. Because the surface area is small, the amount of water loss will be small.

Water loss from leaves is reduced by the presence of cutin.

Plants that live in water take in carbon dioxide dissolved in the water. Land plants get this gas from air. The atmosphere contains only 0.03 percent carbon dioxide, so land plants have adaptations for getting enough carbon dioxide. Bryophytes have **pores,** small openings in "leaves." Air enters a plant through these pores. In order to be absorbed by plants, gases must first be dissolved in water. Land plants have evolved in such a way that the cells are surrounded by a thin film of water. Thus, carbon dioxide entering a plant through the pores dissolves in the water and then diffuses into the cells.

Carbon dioxide enters bryophytes through pores. Inside the plant it dissolves in water before diffusing into the cells.

Part of the life cycle of liverworts and mosses involves sexual reproduction. Sperms produced by the male plant swim, by means of flagella, to the eggs of the female plant. This reproduction can occur only if bryophytes live in a *moist* environment.

In reproduction of bryophytes sperm swim to the eggs of the female.

Roger K. Burnard

SEM Laboratory, Morris Brown College

a

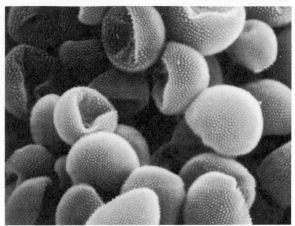
b

The bryophyte life cycle also includes spore production. Spores are an adaptation for land life in that their walls are tough and resist evaporation. When spores settle upon moist land, they may germinate into a new monoploid plant.

In both liverworts and mosses, the zygote is formed within the female part. The female part provides a sterile, moist environment for the zygote and early embryo. Therefore, there is less chance of their being destroyed.

Adaptations for support are not found in bryophytes. In more complex plants, vascular tissue provides support, but bryophytes do not have vascular tissue. Thus, they grow very close to or directly upon the ground.

Although adapted for life on land, bryophytes are not as common as some other plants. They need large amounts of water. Because adequate water is not available everywhere, the range of bryophytes is limited. Also bryophytes are small plants. Their size is limited because transport occurs by diffusion.

FIGURE 14-7. (a) Moss plants produce spore capsules from which (b) spores are released. The moss spores shown are magnified 3150 times.

In bryophytes fertilization occurs within the female reproductive structure.

Bryophytes have no adaptations for support.

Although most bryophytes inhabit moist environments, some species are found in areas, such as rocks, where moisture is only occasionally available.

Bryophytes, because of their need for water, are limited in size and distribution.

14:6 Characteristics of Tracheophytes

Plants of the phylum **Tracheophyta** have vascular tissue and (in most forms) true roots, stems, and leaves. In general, they do not have to live as near to water as bryophytes. The diploid stage of tracheophytes is predominant. Included in this phylum are early forms found mostly in warm, tropical climates. Modern groups are well distributed over the earth. The most widespread of these plants are those that reproduce by seeds.

Ancestors of today's tracheophytes were the major plant forms during the Carboniferous (kar buh NIHF rus) Period about 280 million years ago (Table 10-1). This period is so named because the plants living then have formed the vast coal (carbon) deposits.

Most tracheophytes have true roots, stems, and leaves. The diploid stage of the life cycle is predominant.

Vascular tissue is present only in the diploid phase of the life cycle.

FIGURE 14-8. (a) A club moss and (b) horsetail are primitive tracheophytes. Club mosses and horsetails reproduce by spores.

a

b

The conelike structures of club mosses and horsetails are called strobili.

14:7 Club Mosses and Horsetails

Club mosses (Figure 14-8a) are primitive tracheophytes. They are so named because of their resemblance to true mosses. Club mosses have true roots, stems, and leaves. They grow close to the ground. Most forms live in damp woods, but some grow in deserts and on mountains. These plants produce spores in conelike structures. Club mosses were very prominent at one time, some species being as large as trees.

Club mosses are small, primitive tracheophytes which produce spores in cones.

Horsetails (Figure 14-8b) are also simple tracheophytes. They grow in moist, sandy areas. *Equisetum* (ek wuh SEET um) is the only genus which exists today. It includes twenty-five species. Most forms are small with a slender stem. Groups of small, wedge-shaped leaves are arranged at several points along the stem. Some stems are reproductive and release spores. Other stems possess no reproductive organs. Horsetails are commonly called scouring rushes because they have been used to scour utensils. At one time these tracheophytes were widespread.

FIGURE 14-9. Ferns have true leaves, stems, and roots. The leaves, sometimes called fronds, often are branched and appear lacy.

14:8 Ferns

Modern **ferns,** class **Filicineae** (fihl uh SIHN ee ee), range in size from quite small to as large as trees. Large forms in the tropics reach a height of ten to fifteen meters. In temperate areas, ferns often grow as low shrubs on the damp, forest floor. Some forms float in water or are rooted in mud, and some live in very dry areas such as on cliffs. Species living in dry regions are dormant when moisture is not available but resume life activities when water is present.

Harry Ellis for Tom Stack and Associates

P. Hurd Fernbank Science Center

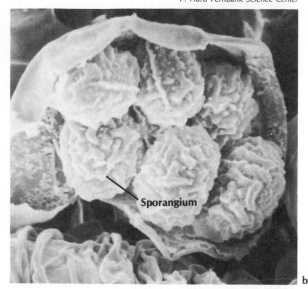

a

b

The diploid phase is the major form in the life cycle of ferns. The diploid fern has leaves and a **rhizome** (RI zohm), an underground stem from which roots and leaves develop (Figure 14-9). In tree ferns, an upright stem develops as a separate, aboveground structure, but in most ferns, only the rhizome exists. Leaves, sometimes called **fronds,** are usually highly branched and often have a lacy appearance.

On the underside of the leaves of some species of ferns are **sori** which contain sporangia. Sori often appear as dark, circular dots. In other species of ferns, sporangia are located on separate, reproductive structures. A spore produced in a sorus develops into a monoploid form called a **prothallium** (proh THAL ee um). The prothallium is nonvascular and produces sperms and eggs for sexual reproduction.

Ferns have some adaptations not in the bryophytes. For example, the diploid forms have vascular tissues which transport water and food between leaves and roots. The presence of vascular tissue permits larger size. Also, specialized cells in the stem provide support for these plants and water loss is reduced by cutin on the leaves and the presence of special cells which control the size of pores (Section 21:1).

Like mosses and liverworts, ferns are limited to a moist environment because the sperms require a thin film of moisture to swim to the eggs. Also, the prothallium has no vascular tissue so water absorbed through rhizoids moves by osmosis to other cells. Ferns must live in a moist area to obtain enough water.

As in bryophytes, fertilization occurs within the female and development of the embryo begins there. However, the young plant is soon "on its own" because the parent dies.

FIGURE 14-10. (a) The underside of a fern frond shows sori. A sorus contains spores. (b) Magnified about 540 times, the sori of the fern *Hypolepis tennifolia* show as clusters of sporangia.

In most ferns, roots and leaves develop from an underground stem, the rhizome.

sori (singular, sorus)

Spores are produced in sori in ferns.

The prothallium is the nonvascular, monoploid phase in the fern life cycle.

Compared to bryophytes, ferns have larger size, a means of support, and conserve more water.

Like bryophytes, ferns are limited to a moist environment.

Most ferns are perennials, new leaves being produced from the rhizome each growing season.

Paul Steucke, U.S. Forest Service

William J. Jahoda for Photo Researchers

Russ Kinne for Photo Researchers

The *Ginkgo* is a deciduous gymnosperm without cones.

a

b

c

FIGURE 14-11. (a) Pine trees, (b) redwoods, and (c) *Ginkgo biloba* are examples of gymnosperms. Pines and redwoods are conifers whereas the *Ginkgo* is in a separate order and does not produce cones.

Gymnosperms and angiosperms reproduce by seeds.

Gymnospermae means "naked seeds."

In most gymnosperms, gametes are produced in cones.

In both gymnosperms and angiosperms, there is no multicellular monoploid phase in the life cycle.

Unlike bryophytes and ferns, conifers do not require water for reproduction.

Conifers are supported by wood.

14:9 Gymnosperms

There are two major classes of seed plants—**Gymnospermae** (jihm nuh SPUR mee) and **Angiospermae** (an jee uh SPUR mee). Most **gymnosperms** living today have seeds which develop uncovered on the scales of cones. These cone-producing gymnosperms are commonly called **conifers**.

In gymnosperms the diploid phase is dominant; the monoploid phase is reduced to only a few cells (Section 20:6). Separate male and female cones each produce gametes. Male gametes are contained in pollen grains. When the gametes fuse, the seeds are formed.

Most gymnosperms are trees, but shrubs and even vinelike forms exist. Familiar forms include the evergreens, such as pines, firs, and spruces, which have needlelike leaves. *Sequoia* (sih KWOY yuh) is a conifer which may reach a height of more than 100 meters and an age of more than 4000 years (Figure 14-11b). Conifers are distributed over most of the earth, and large forests once were common in temperate regions. Today, they are found mainly in northern latitudes. These forests provide most of the lumber for commercial use.

Conifers are well-adapted for living on land. Unlike bryophytes and ferns, they do not require water for the gametes. Pollen grains resist evaporation and provide protection. Seeds protect the delicate embryos during their early development.

Conifers can grow as large as they do because of large amounts of wood which supports the plants. Gymnosperms have adaptations, such as bark on the stems and cutin and special cells on the leaves, which reduce water loss.

An unusual relative of the conifers is the *Ginkgo* (GING koh) tree of China (Figure 14-11c). Because *Ginkgo* is the only living member of an order of gymnosperms which was common at one time, it is called a "living fossil." Only one species now exists, *Ginkgo biloba* (BI loh buh). It is grown in the United States mainly as an ornamental tree.

The species name, *biloba*, was given to *Ginkgo* because the leaves have two lobes. Leaves grow in clusters along the branches and conelike structures form on short branches of the tree. Each tree has either male or female structures. Pollen is transported from male trees to female trees by wind. Ginkgo seeds are spherical and soft on the outside. Although they look like fruits such as cherries, they are not true fruits. Plants like *Ginkgo* were probably the earliest seed producers.

14:10 Angiosperms

More than 250 000 species of **angiosperms,** flowering plants, are known. They grow in almost all types of climates. Angiosperms are adapted for life at the equator as well as the arctic regions. Most of the plants you see everyday are flowering plants.

Flowering plants have some of the same basic features as conifers. However, the organ of reproduction in angiosperms is the **flower.** The angiosperms are a more successful group than the gymnosperms due to differences in reproduction. Angiosperms have better means of pollination and well protected seeds. Also the seeds are dispersed in more ways.

Like gymnosperms, angiosperms produce pollen. Also, water is not required for transfer of pollen. In gymnosperms, pollination occurs mainly by wind. Pollination in angiosperms may also involve wind, but often involves animals. Thus, the chance of pollination is greater than in gymnosperms and more offspring can be produced.

The flower is the reproductive organ of angiosperms.

Angiosperms produce pollen.

FIGURE 14-12. (a) Angiosperms, flowering plants, may have obvious flowers, as this water lily shows. Other examples of flowering plants have inconspicuous or modified flowers. (b) The maple tree and (c) wheat, a grass, (not shown here when flowering) are examples.

a

Alvin E. Staffan

b

James N. Westwater

c

USDA

FIGURE 14-13. Some plants have complex flower-insect relationships to help ensure pollination. The European orchid resembles a female wasp. Male wasps attracted by the orchid's appearance transfer pollen from one flower to another.

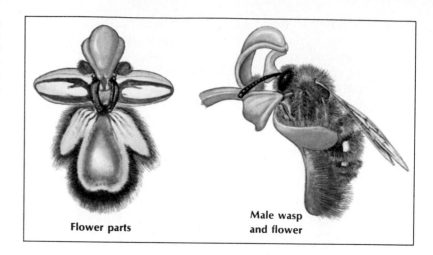

Flower parts

Male wasp and flower

Some intricate insect-flower relationships have evolved for pollinating flowers. One relationship involves a species of wasp and the European orchid in which the flower parts look like a female wasp. In attempting to mate with the "female," a male wasp picks up pollen and transfers it to the next flower it visits. As a result, pollination is quite likely to occur.

After pollination and fertilization, an embryo forms within the flower (Section 20:9). As in gymnosperms, the zygote develops into an embryo within a seed which protects the embryo from the dry environment. The seeds of angiosperms are enclosed within a **fruit** which protects the seed and aids in its dispersal (Section 20:10). Thus, the chance for survival of the new angiosperm plant is good. In gymnosperms, the seeds are less protected and dispersal is mainly by the wind so embryos are less likely to find a suitable place to begin and complete their development.

Angiosperms have many sizes, shapes, and forms. Some have no chlorophyll and are, therefore, saprophytes. Indian pipe is an albino plant which grows in damp forest soil. Mistletoe is a green plant which lives as a parasite on other plants but which also can produce food by photosynthesis.

Seeds of flowering plants are protected within the fruit. The fruit also aids in seed dispersal.

14:11 Monocots and Dicots

Angiosperms are classified as either **monocots** (MAHN uh kahts) or dicots (DI kahts). **Monocots** are plants whose seeds have one **cotyledon** (kaht ul EED un), a food-storing structure. Seeds of **dicots** have two cotyledons.

In addition to the difference in number of cotyledons per seed, monocots and dicots differ in other ways. In monocots, **vascular bundles,** groups of conductive tissue, are scattered

Two types of angiosperms are monocots and dicots.

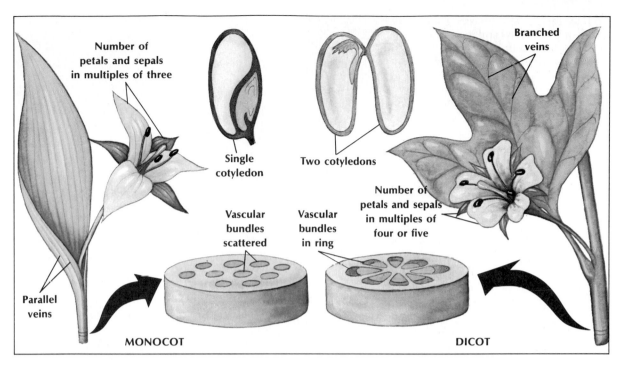

throughout the stem, but in dicots, they are arranged in a circle. Monocots have long, narrow leaves with parallel veins. Dicot leaves are broad with branched veins. Flower parts of monocots are arranged in threes or multiples of threes, but flower parts of dicots are arranged in fours or fives or multiples of four or five. Common monocots include plants of great value to humans, such as bananas and cereals such as corn, wheat, rice, and barley. Ornamental flowers which are monocots include tulips, orchids, and lilies. Beans, carrots, peas, and potatoes are dicots. The number of species of dicots is much greater than the number of species of monocots. Internal structures of monocots and dicots will be studied in Unit VI.

FIGURE 14-14. Monocots and dicots differ in seed structure, stem structure, vein pattern, and number of flower parts.

REVIEWING YOUR IDEAS

5. Distinguish between vascular and nonvascular plants.
6. Why do bryophytes need a lot of water?
7. Name the three main classes of tracheophytes.
8. Which phase is dominant in each of the three main classes of tracheophytes?
9. What are the reproductive structures of gymnosperms and angiosperms?
10. Explain how monocots and dicots differ. Describe the cotyledons, vascular bundles, leaf veins, and flower parts of both monocots and dicots.

5. Vascular plants have conductive tissue; nonvascular plants do not.
6. Bryophytes require water for reproduction. They lose water through pores.
7. The classes of tracheophytes are Filicineae (ferns), Gymnospermae, and Angiospermae.
8. The diploid phase is dominant in tracheophytes.
9. gymnosperms — cones; angiosperms—flowers
10. Monocots have one cotyledon per seed, vascular bundles scattered through the stem, narrow leaves with parallel veins, and flower parts in threes or multiples thereof. Dicots have two cotyledons per seed, vascular bundles arranged in an outer circle in the stem, broad leaves with branching veins, and flower parts in fours or fives or multiples thereof.

FIGURE 14-15. (a) A fibrous root system has many secondary roots. (b) A taproot system has one large primary root with a few secondary roots.

Allan Roberts

Bruce Charlton

a

b

FEATURES OF ANGIOSPERMS

Most of the plants that you see around you are angiosperms, the major plant form on Earth today. Because of their wide distribution and importance, it is useful to learn more about them. Other than flowers, the three major organs of angiosperms are the root, stem, and leaf. In this chapter, you will study the external features of these organs. In later chapters, you will learn about their internal structures and functions.

14:12 Root Types

Roots anchor plants, store food, and absorb water and minerals.

Humans use root cuttings to propagate certain plants (e.g., sweet potatoes). Plant reproduction is discussed in Chapter 20.

Major functions of roots are anchorage, food storage, and absorption of water and minerals from the soil. The role of roots in absorption of water and minerals will be studied in Chapter 22. Most woody plants have a **fibrous** (FI brus) **root system** which consists of many secondary roots and root hairs (Figure 14-15a). The secondary roots are branches of the primary root which first develops during early development.

Other plants have a **taproot system** which has one large, long primary root with a few secondary roots (Figure 14-15b). Carrot and beet plants are examples of plants with a taproot system. In these examples, the taproot is a food storage organ and is an edible portion of the plant.

14:13 The Stem

A stem supports a plant and is a transport link between roots and leaves.

A plant has no skeletal system but is supported by the stem. Also, the stem is a transport link between the roots and the leaves, and some stem cells store food. The involvement of the stem in transport will be studied in Chapter 22.

Stems are either herbaceous (hur BAY shus) or woody. **Herbaceous stems** are soft, green, and often juicy, with very little or no woody tissue. Plants which live for a single growing season are usually herbaceous. A plant with a herbaceous stem is supported by the pressure of water in the cells of the stem. This pressure causes **turgidity** (tur JIHD ut ee), or stiffness, which causes the plant to stand upright. In the event of a water shortage, the stem loses turgidity (wilts) and bends down. **Woody stems** are composed mainly of certain tough, dead cells. These cells support the plant. Figure 14-16 illustrates the external structures of woody stems.

Buds are protected, dormant tissue which may develop into new stems, flowers, or leaves. During winter, buds are protected by modified leaves called **bud scales. Terminal buds** are buds at the tips of branches which are responsible for lengthening stems during each growing season. **Lateral buds** are along the sides of branches and give rise to new branches. Lateral buds are often smaller than terminal buds.

Nodes are places on a stem where leaves develop. The space between two nodes is called the **internode** (IHNT ur nohd). **Leaf scars** are the marks left on a stem after leaves fall off. The leaf scar pattern on a twig indicates the arrangement of leaves. If there is one leaf scar (or leaf) per node, leaves are arranged in an *alternate* pattern on the twig. If there are two leaf scars (or leaves) per node, leaves are arranged in an *opposite* pattern. Presence of three or more leaf scars (or leaves) at the node indicates a *whorled* arrangement of leaves.

Flower scars and **fruit scars** can also be found on the stems of flowering plants. **Bud scale scars** may also be found on stems. Bud scale scars mark the places where bud scales surrounded a bud. Because most bud scales form around terminal buds, the age of a twig can be determined by counting the bud scale scars of previous terminal buds. Amount of growth can be determined by measuring the distance between the bud scale scars.

On young stems, porous regions, or **lenticels** (LENT uh selz), are easily seen. Exchange of gases between the stem and the atmosphere occurs through the lenticels.

14:14 The Leaf

Flowering plants exhibit a diversity of leaf types and forms. Although the details of leaf structure vary, the main function of leaves is the same in all plants. The leaf is the major organ of photosynthesis (Section 21:1).

A leaf is attached to the stem by a slender stalk, the **petiole** (PET ee ohl). The expanded part of a leaf is the **blade.**

In leaves with branching veins, several vein patterns called **venation** (ve NAY shun) can be observed. A feathery pattern in which veins branch from a central vein, or midrib, is called

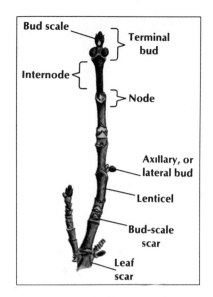

FIGURE 14-16. The external structure of a woody stem shows buds and scars which can be used to identify different kinds of stems.

FIGURE 14-17. The leaf is the main photosynthetic organ of a plant. Externally, the leaf is composed of a blade (where most photosynthesis occurs) and a petiole, or stalk, which attaches the blade to the stem.

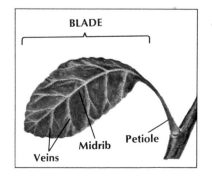

Kodansha

Grant Heilman

Photo Researchers

Robert Ashworth
for Photo Researchers

a

b

c

d

FIGURE 14-18. Leaf shape and vein patterns vary among the many species of plants and can be used in plant identification. (a) A simple leaf with pinnate venation, (b) a simple leaf with palmate venation, (c) a palmately compound leaf, and (d) a pinnately compound leaf are shown.

pinnate (PIHN ayt) **venation** (Figure 14-18a). This pattern is found in oaks and elms. In trees such as the maples, many large veins originate at and spread out from the point where the petiole is attached to the blade. This pattern is called **palmate** (PAL mayt) **venation** (Figure 14-18b).

If a leaf is composed of one blade, it is a **simple leaf.** However, when the blade is subdivided into distinct parts, called **leaflets,** it is a **compound leaf.**

Patterns in compound leaves correspond to venation patterns. Leaves are said to be **palmately compound** when the leaflets are all attached to the petiole at a central point (Figure 14-18c). Clover is a common example of a palmately compound leaf. When leaflets branch out along different points of the petiole, they are said to be **pinnately compound** (Figure 14-18d). Leaves of the rose bush and walnut tree have this pattern.

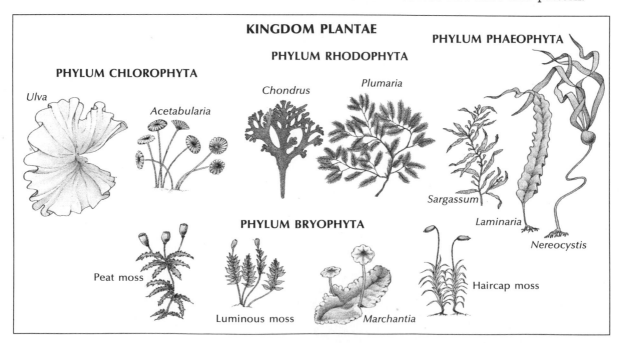

KINGDOM PLANTAE

PHYLUM PHAEOPHYTA

PHYLUM RHODOPHYTA

PHYLUM CHLOROPHYTA

Ulva

Acetabularia

Chondrus

Plumaria

Sargassum

Laminaria

Nereocystis

PHYLUM BRYOPHYTA

Peat moss

Luminous moss

Marchantia

Haircap moss

11. Roots anchor plants, store food, and absorb water and minerals.

REVIEWING YOUR IDEAS

11. What are the major functions of a root?
12. What are buds? What are terminal and lateral buds?
13. What is the main function of a leaf?
14. What traits are used to describe leaf differences?

12. Buds are dormant tissues which may develop into new stems, flowers, or leaves. Terminal buds add to length of stems and lateral buds produce new branches.
13. photosynthesis
14. patterns of venation and leaf arrangement

		Vascular		
Classification	Common Name	Tissue	Structure	Habitat
Phylum Chlorophyta	Green algae	Absent	Unicellular and multicellular; little division of labor	Water
Phylum Phaeophyta	Brown algae	Absent	Multicellular; tissues in some forms	Water
Phylum Rhodophyta	Red algae	Absent	Mostly multicellular	Water
Phylum Bryophyta	Mosses/Liverworts	Absent	Multicellular; no true roots, stems, or leaves	Moist areas on land
Phylum Tracheophyta Subphyla Lycopsida and Sphenopsida	Club mosses/Horsetails	Present	Multicellular; true roots, stems, and leaves	Moist areas on land
Phylum Tracheophyta Subphylum Pteropsida Class Filicineae	Ferns	Present	Multicellular; true roots, stems and leaves, develop from rhizome	Moist areas on land
Phylum Tracheophyta Subphylum Pteropsida Class Gymnospermae	Conifers	Present	Multicellular; true roots, stems and leaves	Land
Phylum Tracheophyta Subphylum Pteropsida Class Angiospermae	Flowering plants (Monocots and dicots)	Present	Multicellular; true roots, stems and leaves	Land

TABLE 14-1. SUMMARY OF MAJOR CHARACTERISTICS OF PLANTS

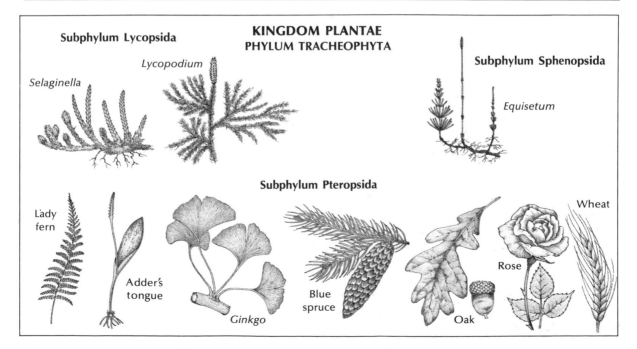

KINGDOM PLANTAE
PHYLUM TRACHEOPHYTA

Subphylum Lycopsida

Selaginella

Lycopodium

Subphylum Sphenopsida

Equisetum

Subphylum Pteropsida

Lady fern

Adder's tongue

Ginkgo

Blue spruce

Oak

Rose

Wheat

All Chapter Review answers and additional chapter teaching suggestions are provided in the Teacher's Guide at the front of this text.

CHAPTER REVIEW

SUMMARY

1. Plants are nonmotile, mostly multicellular, autotrophic organisms. They have cell walls composed of cellulose. Most plants have a life cycle involving diploid and monoploid phases.

2. The plantlike algae are mostly multicellular with some division of labor. They are subdivided on the basis of color and structure.

3. All land plants have adaptations for life out of water.

4. Plants are classified on the presence or absence of vascular tissue. Bryophytes lack vascular tissue and tracheophytes have vascular tissue.

5. Bryophytes include mosses and liverworts which are small plants with no true roots, stems, or leaves. They are probably descendants of certain green algae.

6. Bryophytes are limited in size because of lack of vascular tissue and in habitat because of their need for moisture for fertilization.

7. Tracheophytes include plants with true roots, stems, and leaves. They have vascular tissue and are better adapted for life on land than the bryophytes.

8. Club mosses and horsetails are primitive tracheophytes which reproduce by spores.

9. Ferns consist of an underground rhizome from which roots and leaves develop. They are larger than bryophytes but, like them, require moisture for fertilization.

10. Gymnosperms are seed plants, mostly conifers, in which seeds are formed on the underside of the scales of cones and are dispersed by wind. Because they require no water for fertilization, they are widely distributed.

11. Angiosperms, flowering plants, are best adapted for life on land. Animals often are involved in pollination, making the chances of fertilization greater than in gymnosperms. Also, the fruit better protects the seeds and aids in their dispersal. These factors make flowering plants the most abundant forms.

12. Angiosperms are divided into monocots and dicots. These groups differ in number of cotyledons per seed, number of flower parts, shapes of leaves, vein patterns, and arrangement of vascular bundles.

13. Roots anchor a plant, absorb water and minerals, and store excess food. Both fibrous and taproot systems are found among angiosperms.

14. The stem is an organ of support and transport. Stems are either woody or herbaceous. The external structure of a stem is characterized by buds, nodes, and scars.

15. Leaves are the organs where most photosynthesis occurs.

16. Leaves can be characterized by their vein patterns, by whether they are simple or compound, and by their arrangement.

LANGUAGE OF BIOLOGY

angiosperm	flower	rhizome
bryophyte	fruit	taproot system
bud	gymnosperm	thallus
conifer	herbaceous	tracheophyte
cotyledon	stem	vascular tissue
cutin	lenticel	woody stem
dicot	monocot	
fibrous root	prothallium	
system	rhizoid	

CHECKING YOUR IDEAS

On a separate paper, indicate whether each of the following statements is true or false. Do not write in this book.

1. All land plants have vascular tissue.

2. The body of algae is called the thallus.

3. Vascular bundles have conductive tissue.

CHAPTER REVIEW

4. No gases are exchanged by the stems of plants.
5. Land plants must have adaptations for conserving water.
6. Food storage is a major function of most stems.
7. Pollen is produced by all land plants.
8. A fibrous root system has one large root often used for food storage.
9. Most algae have no true tissues.
10. Bryophytes are restricted to moist habitats.

EVALUATING YOUR IDEAS

1. Describe the traits of the algal plants.
2. Why do some biologists think that an organism like *Volvox* might represent an intermediate form of life between unicellular and multicellular organisms?
3. In what ways do some brown algae resemble land plants?
4. Why can red algae live deeper in the ocean than other algae?
5. List the functions which are carried out by land plants.
6. How do bryophytes carry out these jobs?
7. How are bryophytes limited? Explain.
8. Describe the structure of club mosses and horsetails.
9. How are ferns better adapted for land life than mosses? How are ferns limited?
10. Compare conifers to ferns in terms of support and sexual reproduction.
11. How are angiosperms better suited for life on land than gymnosperms?
12. Distinguish among pollen, seed, and fruit.
13. Distinguish between a fibrous root system and a taproot system.
14. What are buds? Into what may they develop?
15. What structures leave scars on stems?
16. Describe venation and leaf forms.

APPLYING YOUR IDEAS

1. Compare the plantlike algae to moneran and protistan algae. *Chapter 13
2. How do plants differ from fungi? *Chapter 13
3. Embryos of land plants have some protection from the parent plant. Algal embryos develop in the water. Explain the reasons for this difference.
4. Complex brown algae have tissues for conduction and support. Land plants also have these tissues. Do you think this is an example of convergence or of homologous structures? Explain. *Chapters 10 and 11
5. How would you explain the origin of Indian pipe, a heterotrophic angiosperm? *Chapter 11
6. What are some advantages of a fibrous root system? A taproot system?
7. Why do you think there are usually longer branches low on a tree?
8. How might venation and leaf patterns be useful to a biologist?

EXTENDING YOUR IDEAS

1. Make a collection of leaves of many woody plants near your home. Use a classification key to identify each plant. Also record the venation and leaf pattern of each plant. Put your specimens in a plant press and then mount each one on colored paper. Record the information for each plant on the sheet.
2. Find out what you can about Spanish moss. Is it really a moss?

SUGGESTED READINGS

Bold, Harold C., and Hundell, C. L., *The Plant Kingdom*. Englewood Cliffs, NJ, Prentice-Hall, Inc., 1977.

Elias, Thomas S., and Irwin, Howard S., "Urban Trees." *Scientific American*, Nov., 1976.

Eshleman, Alan, *Poison Plants*. Boston, Houghton Mifflin Co., 1977.

Additional student readings and suggested teacher readings are provided in the Teacher's Guide.

Geri Muphy

Even simpler animals have adaptations which help them survive in their environments. Here, serpulid worms, segmented aquatic worms, produce water currents with their ciliated filaments. The currents bring food particles into their mouths. What kinds of simple animals are there? What kinds of adaptations do these less complex animals have? Are any of their adaptations similar to adaptations you have?

Introduction: Because animals in this chapter will be less familiar to your students, filmloops and films are valuable in surveying the simpler invertebrates. See *Suggested Audio-Visuals* in the Teacher's Guide. A collection of preserved specimens also is useful. Encourage your students to bring in samples they may have, such as sponge remains and mollusk shells. If live specimens (worms, snails, etc.) are brought in, require that they be properly cared for. You also may wish to order cultures of simple forms, such as *Hydra* and *Planaria,* for student observation.

Chapter

15

ANIMALS: SPONGES THROUGH MOLLUSKS

Chapter 15 presents the characteristics of the major groups of less complex invertebrates.

Many characteristics of animals are related to their heterotrophic way of life. Features such as movement, support systems, sensory equipment, and nervous control work together to help an animal obtain food. These features depend upon specialized tissues, organs, and systems not found in other organisms.

Animals can be divided into two groups—the **invertebrates** (ihn vURT uh brayts) which do not have backbones and the **vertebrates** (vURT uh brayts) which do have backbones. Invertebrates are classified into more than ten distinct phyla; vertebrates make up only one *subphylum* of animals. In this chapter, you will study the major features of the less complex invertebrates. In Chapter 16, you will learn about the complex invertebrates and the vertebrates.

GOAL: You will gain an understanding of the basic features of some of the major groups of organisms in the animal kingdom.

Vertebrates have backbones; invertebrates do not.

Teaching suggestion: Emphasize how many invertebrates there are relative to vertebrates.

THE SIMPLEST ANIMALS

Unlike animals with which you are familiar, many of the simplest animals do not move or actively search for food. They lack the higher levels of organization seen in more complex animals. However, they do have adaptations for the heterotrophic way of life.

281

Carolina Biological Supply Co.   *Courtesy CCM: General Biological, Inc.*   *Joey Jacques*

FIGURE 15-1. Sponges, the simplest animals, have incurrent and excurrent pores. The animals vary in size, shape, and color.

15:1 Sponges

Simplest of all animals now living is a group called sponges, phylum **Porifera** (puh RIHF uh ruh). They are so named because they have many openings, called **incurrent pores,** through which water enters. The body of a sponge has one or a few large openings called the **oscula** (AHS kyuh luh), or **excurrent pores.** Water leaves a sponge through the oscula.

Most sponges are marine. Often they are part of a colony and individual organisms cannot be seen easily. They have two tissue layers—**ectoderm** (outer layer) and **endoderm** (inner layer). Between these layers is a jellylike substance containing unspecialized cells which may specialize during the life of the sponge.

Mature sponges remain attached in one spot for most of their life cycle. An attached organism is said to be **sessile** (SES ul). Sponges are attached to rocks or the ocean floor. In some sponges, there are cells that can contract, or shorten. Some movement can be detected in these cells. However, there is no evidence of any true locomotion in adult sponges.

Sponges feed on microscopic organisms in the water and gases are exchanged with the water. Wastes are poured into the water, too.

Sponges do not have bony skeletons. However, they are supported by structures called **spicules** (SPIHK yewlz) made of different substances. Spicules stick out from the jellylike layer between the ectoderm and endoderm.

Sponges are grouped into three classes on the basis of the minerals in their spicules. One class has calcium carbonate spicules. One class, known as glass sponges, has silica spicules. Their skeletons, when dry, have a beautiful, glasslike appearance. Another class has members with no spicules but with an elastic substance. These sponges are dried and sold as bath sponges. Are most commercially sold sponges now really animal remnants?

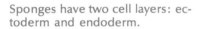

Many students may be unaware that most commercially sold sponges are synthetic and not remnants of animals.

Sponges have two cell layers: ectoderm and endoderm.

Mature sponges have no locomotion.

Sponges are supported by structures called spicules.

Sponges with calcium carbonate are the calcareous sponges. The elastic fiber of some sponges is called elastin.

A sponge does not have a nervous system. Any responses are made by individual cells being directly stimulated. Other animals have some kind of nervous system.

A sponge does not have a nervous system.

Sexual reproduction occurs in sponges. Some of the cells in the jellylike layer become modified as eggs or sperm. In some species, individuals are hermaphrodites (hur MAF ruh dites). **Hermaphrodites** are animals which produce both sperms and eggs. In other species, separate sexes exist. Fusion of sperms and eggs produces zygotes. Zygotes develop into free swimming, immature organisms which eventually attach to the ocean bottom and develop into new sponges.

Asexual reproduction also occurs in sponges. Sometimes a new sponge begins to grow from the parent and then breaks away. Sometimes a piece of a parent sponge may break away and then develop into a new sponge. Some sponges produce branches which develop into new sponges. Others asexually produce flagellated embryos which swim away and attach to form new sponges. These processes give rise to colonies of sponges. At times, gemmules (JEM yewlz) form. **Gemmules** are groups of cells that have become enclosed by a tough outer covering. They are resistant to both dryness and cold temperatures. When conditions become favorable, such as after a drought or winter, the cells leave the gemmule, come together, and form a new sponge.

Sponges reproduce both sexually and asexually.

Sponges are the least complex animals. They do have specialized cells, but the cells are not really organized into tissues (Section 1:8). Because they have no nerve cells, there is no coordination between parts. If one dissociates (separates) the cells of a sponge, they move back together and form a sponge again. In many respects, a single sponge is not much more complex than a colonial organism.

Sponge cells are specialized but are not organized into tissues.

FIGURE 15-2. (a) In commercial sponge-fishing, sponges brought up by divers are hung up to allow the living part of the sponges to decay. (b) Sponge culturing (growing) has replenished some areas that have been depleted by too much sponge-fishing. Fragments of sponges, attached to tiles, are lowered to the bottom. Under good conditions, they grow quickly into sponges like the one shown.

Florida Department of Commerce

Lightforce

Courtesy CCM: General Biological, Inc.

Sharon Kurgis

a

b

FIGURE 15-3. (a) The sea anemone and (b) white coral are examples of coelenterates. Coelenterates have two tissue layers—ectoderm and endoderm.

Coelenterates have two tissue layers.

Nerves and other tissues are found in coelenterates.

Tentacles are used in trapping food.

Polyps are sessile forms of coelenterates. Medusae are motile.

15:2 Coelenterates

More complex than Porifera are organisms of phylum **Coelenterata** (sih len tuh RAH tuh). This phylum includes organisms such as jellyfish, *Hydra*, corals, and sea anemones (uh NEM uh neez). **Coelenterates** (sih LENT uh raytz) have two tissue layers with a jellylike layer called the **mesoglea** (mez uh GLEE uh) between them. The mesoglea contains some unspecialized cells.

Coelenterates, unlike sponges, have true tissues. A major difference is the presence of nerve cells which form a network throughout the organism. Although simple, this network coordinates movements, but there is no brain as found in more complex animals. No specialized tissues for gas exchange or excretion are present either.

Coelenterates have a hollow body with one opening, the mouth. Around the mouth is a ring of **tentacles** (TENT ih kulz). **Nematocysts** (nih MAT uh sihsts), sometimes called "stinging cells," are special capsules on the tentacles which "shoot out" poisonous filaments that paralyze the prey. The tentacles then surround the food and transfer it to the mouth.

Coelenterates have two body forms. The **polyp** (PAHL up) form has a cylindrical body which is usually sessile. The mouth faces upward. Hydras are examples of polyps. The other form of coelenterate is called a **medusa** (mih DEW suh). A medusa is a free-swimming form with the characteristic jellyfish shape which has the mouth facing downward.

Some coelenterates are colonial and have specialized polyps and medusae. For example, *Stephallia* has both of these body forms at the same time. The Portuguese man-of-war is a floating,

The polyp constricts to form a vertical group of saucerlike portions, each of which can develop into a medusa. *Aurelia* is a member of class Scyphozoa.

Obelia polyp

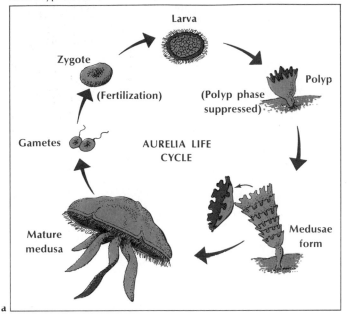

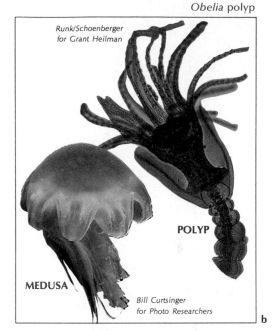

FIGURE 15-4. (a) The life cycle of *Aurelia* shows an alternation of two body forms. (b) The body forms of a coelenterate are the polyp and medusa.

colonial coelenterate composed of a float and trailing specialized polyps. Its tentacles can paralyze large animals such as fish. Its stings at times have led to the deaths of humans.

Many coelenterates have a life cycle which alternates between polyps and medusae. *Aurelia* is an example of such an organism. As a polyp, it is sessile and reproduces asexually. The top of the polyp may transform into medusae. The medusae reproduce sexually. The fertilized eggs develop into attached polyps (Figure 15-4).

Many coelenterates have a life cycle including both polyp and medusa forms.

George Marler for Bruce Coleman

Animals Animals

FIGURE 15-5. (a) The Portuguese man-of-war, *Physalia physalis*, is a colony of polyps which float due to the gas-filled chamber on the water surface. (b) The cigar jellyfish is a medusa that moves by contraction of muscles.

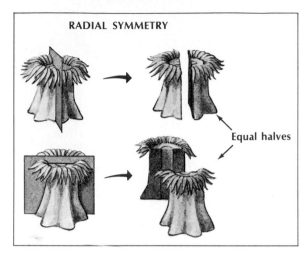

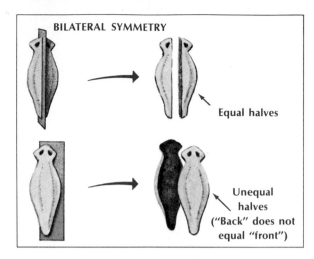

FIGURE 15-6. (a) A radially symmetric animal can be cut lengthwise through the center in any direction, and the result is two equal halves. (b) A bilaterally symmetric organism can only be cut lengthwise through the center in only one place to give equal halves.

FIGURE 15-7. Names of areas of a bilaterally symmetric animal, a snail, are shown. These names are used to accurately give locations of body parts.

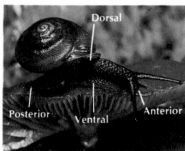

Alvin E. Staffan

15:3 Symmetry

Suppose an anemone were cut in half lengthwise. The two halves produced would be identical (Figure 15-6). It would make no difference in what direction across the diameter the lengthwise cut was made. An anemone has the same features all around its cylindrical body. This body plan is called **radial symmetry** (RAYD ee ul • SIH muh tree). It is a feature of coelenterates, some sponges, and several other animal groups.

Animals with a specific direction of locomotion have a different body pattern. It is called **bilateral** (bi LAT uh rul) **symmetry.** One side of such an organism is a mirror image of the other. One cut down the midline of an animal from head to tail would result in identical halves (Figure 15-6). Other lengthwise cuts would not produce identical halves.

In bilaterally symmetrical organisms, definite areas can be labeled with respect to their position in the organism. There is a definite front, or **anterior** (an TIHR ee ur) end. Also, there is a hind, or **posterior** (pah STIHR ee ur) end. There is a top, or **dorsal** (DOR sul) side, and a bottom, or **ventral** (VEN trul) side. There are also definite sides or lateral areas (Figure 15-7). Which side is your dorsal side? Your anterior end? Head end

Back side

REVIEWING YOUR IDEAS

1. invertebrates and vertebrates
2. Sponges have many pores.
3. A coelenterate has nerves throughout the body, but no brain.
4. A polyp is usually sessile. A medusa is motile.
5. Coelenterates have specialized tissues, mesoglea, tentacles, nerve nets, and most forms can move about. Sponges have none of these.

1. Name the two major divisions of animals.
2. Why are sponges called Porifera?
3. Describe the coelenterate nervous system.
4. Distinguish between polyp and medusa.
5. How are sponges and coelenterates different?
6. Distinguish between radial and bilateral symmetry. Distinguish between dorsal and ventral, and anterior and posterior.

6. An animal with radial symmetry has the same features all around. In bilateral symmetry, one side of the animal is the mirror image of the other. Dorsal is the top or back side; ventral is the bottom or belly side. Anterior is the front end; posterior is the hind end.

WORMS AND MOLLUSKS

Although most worms and mollusks may not be very familiar to you, they are ecologically important. Certain worms play an important role in decomposition and recycling of materials. Some land mollusks cause damage to plants. Mollusks such as clams, oysters, and squid are human foods.

Worms and mollusks are more complex than the animals you have studied so far. They have characteristics such as true muscles, simple organs for locomotion, specialized systems, and primitive brains.

15:4 Flatworms

Flatworms, phylum **Platyhelminthes** (plat ih hel MIHN theez), are aquatic or semiaquatic animals, the simplest animals with bilateral symmetry. Figure 15-8 shows a type of free-living flatworm called planaria (pluh NER ee uh). Flatworms have three tissue layers. Between the ectoderm and endoderm is **mesoderm.** With bilateral symmetry and mesoderm, there is also a greater degree of differentiation.

Unlike sponges and coelenterates, flatworms have definite organs. Nervous tissue (brain) and sensory organs are concentrated at the anterior end of these organisms as seen, for example, in planarians. A planaria has a digestive system with a mouth and intestine. As in coelenterates, the flatworm mouth is also the anus. Specialized parts for other functions such as excretion of excess water are also present. Muscles aid locomotion. There are no specialized tissues or organs for gas exchange, waste removal (other than excess water), or transport of materials. They obtain dissolved oxygen from the water by diffusion.

Flatworms have three tissue layers: ectoderm, endoderm, and mesoderm.

Flatworms have specialized tissues and organs for some, but not all, life functions.

Sensory apparatus includes eyespots (which detect light intensity but no images) and sensory lobes which detect touch.

FIGURE 15-8. *Planaria* **is a nonparasitic flatworm which has nervous and sensory tissue concentrated at its anterior end.**

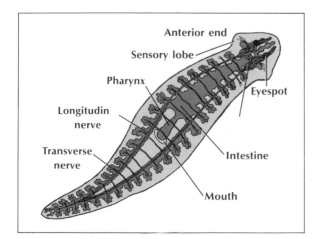

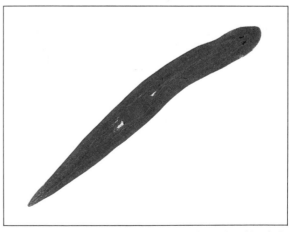

Carolina Biological Supply Co.

Planarians may reproduce sexually or asexually.

Planarians are hermaphrodites though they do not self-fertilize. Instead, one planarian exchanges sperm with another. Asexual reproduction may also occur when part of the planaria breaks off. Both parts may regrow missing tissues, thus producing two planarians.

In addition to free-living forms such as planaria, this phylum includes many parasitic animals. The parasitic forms include the flukes and tapeworms.

Often, the parasites have a complex life cycle involving two or three different hosts. The Chinese liver fluke, for example, spends part of its life in a snail, a fish, and a human. The dog tapeworm spends part of its life in dog fleas and lice, and part of its life in dogs. These parasites do not exhibit the same features as their free-living relatives. Instead, they have specialized adaptations related to the kinds of hosts they invade and live inside.

PEOPLE IN BIOLOGY

(1888 - 1969)

Libbie Henrietta Hyman

Growing up in a poor family in Fort Dodge, Iowa, Libbie Hyman never imagined that she would one day be the foremost expert on invertebrates in the Western Hemisphere. Libbie Hyman developed her interest in zoology while earning her B.A. and Ph.D. degrees at the University of Chicago. After graduating, Dr. Hyman stayed at the university as a research assistant and wrote two textbooks still in use today: *A Laboratory Manual for Elementary Zoology* and *A Laboratory Manual for Comparative Vertebrate Anatomy.*

In 1931 Dr. Hyman moved to New York City and began work on a treatise on invertebrates. At first Dr. Hyman thought the book would take two volumes. She soon discovered that to cover the one million classified invertebrates, she would need to write ten. Because she had no money to hire an artist, Hyman drew all her own pen and ink illustrations for each volume.

After only three volumes had been published, Dr. Hyman was awarded the Daniel Giraud Medal of the National Academy of Science. She also received the Gold Medal of the Linnaen Society of London. Hyman went on to write three more volumes before her death.

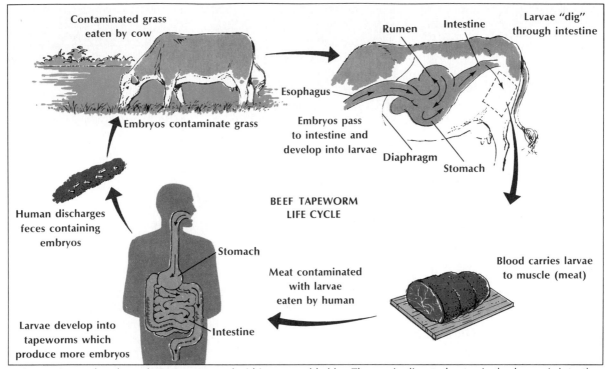

Contaminated grass eaten by cow

Rumen

Intestine

Larvae "dig" through intestine

Esophagus

Embryos contaminate grass

Embryos pass to intestine and develop into larvae

Diaphragm

Stomach

Human discharges feces containing embryos

BEEF TAPEWORM LIFE CYCLE

Stomach

Meat contaminated with larvae eaten by human

Blood carries larvae to muscle (meat)

Larvae develop into tapeworms which produce more embryos

Intestine

In the cow's muscles, the embryo is protected within a sac or bladder. The sac is digested away in the human's intestine, at which point the head attaches to the intestinal wall.

FIGURE 15-9. The life cycle of the beef tapeworm, *Taenia saginata*, alternates between cattle and human hosts.

15:5 The Tapeworm: A Parasitic Flatworm

A tapeworm lacks a mouth and a digestive system. Tapeworms get food by diffusion. Figure 15-9 shows the life cycle of a beef tapeworm. A cow grazing on grass contaminated with tapeworm embryos may eat some of them. The capsules around the embryos are digested in the cow's intestine. Then the embryos grow, change form, "dig" through the wall of the intestine, and enter the bloodstream. Then, they can enter the cow's muscles.

Cows may eat tapeworm embryos on grass.

If a human eats beef that contains developing tapeworms which is not well cooked, the worms may not be killed. Thus, some may reach the human intestine. In the intestine, the adult worm forms. It attaches to the intestinal wall by a head which has suckers and/or hooks. It lives on the host's digested food.

FIGURE 15-10. Tapeworms have suckers and hooks, adaptations for attachment, on their heads.

Tapeworms are highly specialized for sexual reproduction. The body of the tapeworm is composed of a series of flat sections produced from the neck. Each section contains reproductive organs. Sperm fertilize eggs (often from a different section) and a capsule forms around each zygote. The sections of the worm then fall off full of these fertile eggs. The zygotes develop into embryos that pass out of the host's intestine along with wastes. Human wastes with these embryos can then contaminate grass. What conditions promote the life cycle of the beef tapeworm?

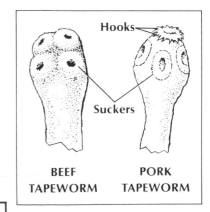

Hooks

Suckers

BEEF TAPEWORM

PORK TAPEWORM

The body sections, proglottids, of a tapeworm are not true segments.

unsanitary conditions; conditions of poor waste (especially feces) removal

Edward J. Webster *Lester V. Bergman and Associates* *Carolina Biological Supply Co.*

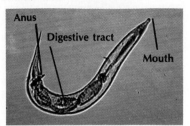

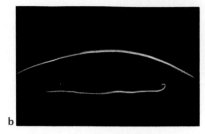

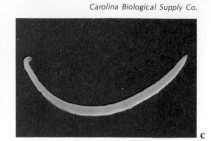

FIGURE 15-11. (a) Roundworms have two body openings. The mouth and anus are at opposite ends of the digestive tract. (b) Roundworms have separate sexes; female (larger) and male *Ascaris* are shown. (c) Many roundworms are parasites. The hookworm is a parasite of humans.

Many roundworms are parasites.

Filaria worms cause swelling by blocking lymph vessels.

Roundworms, unlike flatworms, have two body openings.

15:6 Roundworms

Members of phylum **Nematoda** (nem uh TOH duh), the **roundworms** (Figure 15-11), are found almost everywhere. This group includes some free-living forms which live in soil and water. However, most nematodes are parasites. At least fifty species are parasites of humans alone!

Ascaris (AS kuh rus) is a parasite which can live in the intestines of humans and most other mammals. It "robs" the host of digested food, and, if enough worms are present, they may block the intestine, which could kill the host.

The hookworm is a parasite of humans which attaches to the wall of the intestine and sucks blood. This loss of blood may lead to a lack of energy in the host. Outside the bodies of their hosts, hookworms need warm soil temperatures. Therefore, they are common in southern parts of the United States. They can enter the human body through bare feet.

Filaria (fuh LER ee uh) worms cause the disease elephantiasis (el uh fun TI uh sus). In this disease, enormous swelling of tissues occurs. Filaria are transmitted by a certain species of mosquito and their occurrence is rare in the United States.

Trichinella worms spend part of their life cycle in muscles of hogs. If a human eats infected pork which is not thoroughly cooked, these worms may not be killed. They enter the human's intestine, reproduce, and eventually spread to the muscles. The result is a painful, sometimes fatal, disease called trichinosis. Trichinosis can be prevented by thorough cooking of pork.

Unlike sponges, coelenterates, and flatworms, nematodes (NEM uh tohdz) have two body openings. Food is taken in through the mouth. Undigested materials are egested (ih JEST ud), or removed, through the anus (AY nus). The mouth and anus are openings at opposite ends of the digestive tract.

Unlike flatworms, which are hermaphrodites, roundworms are either male or female. Sex organs are located in the space between the outer muscle layer and the digestive tube. Fertilization is internal; it occurs within the female. Development is external. Fertilized eggs are deposited in a host or other suitable place.

Allan Roberts

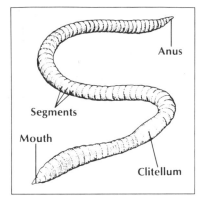

FIGURE 15-12. The earthworm is a common annelid which plays a role in soil ecology. Annelids have easily visible segments.

15:7 Segmented Worms

Members of phylum **Annelida** (uh NEL ud uh) are the **segmented worms.** The common earthworm, *Lumbricus* (LUM bruh kus), is an example. The cylindrical bodies of these worms are segmented. Each segment, or unit, is distinct and visible on the outside of the worm. Most segments contain the same internal structures. The common earthworm usually has around one hundred segments (Figure 15-12). Giant earthworms of Australia can be three meters long.

Earthworms play an important role in soil ecology. As they tunnel through soil, earthworms make a network of spaces which help aerate the soil and improve water drainage. They eat a lot of dirt in this process and then undigested materials, mostly soil, pass through the worms and are deposited on the surface as **castings.** In this way, earthworms are constantly turning over the soil and enriching it with their waste materials. All these factors improve growing conditions for plants. Thus, earthworms have been called "nature's plows."

Although the earthworm is the annelid most familiar to you, most annelids are aquatic. *Nereis* (NIHR ee us) (Figure 15-13a) is an ocean dweller which lives near the coastline, sometimes in burrows in the mud. On each segment (except the first and last) are a pair of paddlelike **parapods** (PER uh pahdz) which aid in locomotion. Parapods also help in gas exchange. *Nereis* has separate sexes and external fertilization; fertilization occurs outside the organism. The young develop in the water. In earthworms, there are no parapods, fertilization is internal, and fertilized eggs are sealed in a capsule and deposited in the soil. An earthworm develops without a larval stage.

Leeches are a group of annelids most of which are both aquatic and parasitic (Figure 15-13b). They have suckers at both ends of their bodies. The posterior sucker attaches to a host. Sometimes the host is a human; often the hosts are fish.

Segmentation is internal as well as external. Each segment contains many of the same structures. This arrangement is called serial homology.

Earthworms enrich and aerate soil.

FIGURE 15-13. (a) *Nereis* **is a segmented worm with parapods. (b) A leech is a parasitic segmented worm.**

a

Robert Dunne for Photo Researchers

b

J. Howard for Photo Researchers

Sharp teeth in the anterior sucker puncture the skin. Then, the leech sucks the blood of its host. A leech can store blood in special pouches. Thus, a single feeding can last a leech for several months.

An annelid has a circulatory system.

An important adaptation in segmented worms is a circulatory system. A series of **hearts** pumps blood throughout the organism in a system of closed tubes. Blood carries food molecules, gases, and certain wastes.

Another feature not present in the previous phyla is a body cavity, or **coelom** (SEE lum). The coelom is the space between the outside body wall and the digestive tract. Within this cavity are the major organs. The coelom is usually lined with a thin sheet of tissue called the **peritoneum** (per ut un EE um).

An annelid has a digestive system and excretory system but has no gas exchange system.

Segmented worms, like roundworms, have two body openings to the digestive tract. But the digestive systems of segmented worms are more complex. Also, segmented worms have a simple excretory system which removes nitrogen wastes. However, no specialized gas exchange system is present, and so gases are exchanged by diffusion through moist skin. Muscles aid locomotion in annelids as well as in the nematodes.

Figure 15-14 compares in cross section the general body plan of a hydra, a planarian, a nematode, and an earthworm. How many cell layers does each have? Which have digestive tubes rather than just digestive cavities? Which has a circulatory system? Which have some kind of a body cavity, or coelom?

A nematode has a pseudocoelom (a remnant of the blastocoel) which is not entirely surrounded by mesoderm. A true coelom is entirely surrounded by mesoderm.

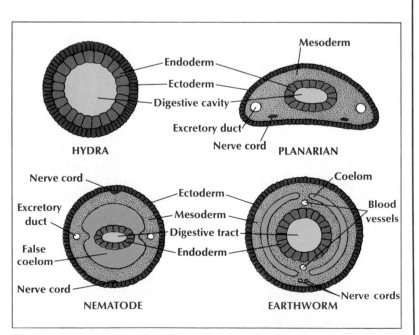

FIGURE 15-14. Cross sections of the bodies of a hydra, planarian, nematode, and earthworm show increasing complexity.

Planarians, nematodes, and earthworms all have three cell layers. Hydras have only two cell layers. Nematodes and earthworms have muscular body walls and digestive tubes. An earthworm has a circulatory system and coelom.

Gene Frazier

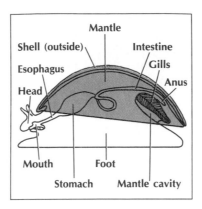

Mantle

Shell (outside)

Intestine

Esophagus

Gills

Head

Anus

Mouth

Foot

Stomach

Mantle cavity

FIGURE 15-15. A snail is a univalve, a mollusk with one shell. Mollusks use the thick, muscular foot for locomotion.

15:8 Mollusks

Mollusks (MAHL usks), members of phylum **Mollusca** (mah LUS kuh), are animals with soft bodies. They are usually enclosed within a hard outer shell. Mollusks commonly have a **mantle**, a folded tissue, covering the internal organs. They move by means of a thick, muscular organ called a **foot.** Most species of mollusks are marine. However, they also live in fresh water and on land. They have highly specialized systems for circulation, digestion, gas exchange, and excretion. Reproduction is sexual.

Like worms, mollusks have three cell layers. A coelom is also present. However, the anatomy of members of this group of animals is quite different. On the basis of both internal and external features, adult mollusks do not seem to be closely related to annelids. However, comparative embryology (Section 12:4) indicates a close similarity between these phyla.

There are three main classes of mollusks. **Univalves** (YEW nih valvz) are mollusks, most of which have one shell. The shells of mollusks are also called **valves.** This group includes snails (Figure 15-15) and slugs. Although most are aquatic, many snails and slugs are land forms. They have tentacles which are used as sensory organs. Snails have a coiled shell. Although classified as univalves, slugs have no shell at all. Both forms have a mouth structure called the **radula** (RAJ uh luh). The radula looks like a tongue covered with toothlike structures. Univalves feed by rubbing the radula against the surface of plants. Pieces of the plant break off and are eaten. Snails often are added to an aquarium where they scrape algae from the glass.

Bivalves (BI valvz) are those forms with two shells. Members of this group include clams, oysters, scallops, and mussels (Figure 15-16). Oysters and mussels are sessile—they remain attached to rocks and other surfaces during their lifetimes. They filter food from the water (Section 25:1).

Mollusks have soft bodies, usually enclosed in a hard shell.

Mollusks and annelids are closely related.

Both mollusks and marine annelids produce trochophore larvae which resemble each other.

FIGURE 15-16. Mussels are bivalves, mollusks with two shells. Mussels are sessile (non-moving) and are filter feeders.

Ward's Natural Scientific Establishment, Inc.

Head-foot mollusks are active predators. Their shells are either absent or greatly reduced.

7. The hosts are cows and humans.
8. Flatworms are hermaphrodites and have only one body opening; round-worms have separate sexes and two body openings.
9. A coelom is a body cavity.
10. Annelids and mollusks both have three cell layers — endoderm, mesoderm, and ectoderm.
11. A mollusk has a soft body, hard outer shell (usually), a mantle enclosing internal organs, and a muscular foot, an organ of locomotion.

FIGURE 15-17. Head-foot mollusks include (a) the octopus, (b) squid, (c) cuttlefish, and (d) chambered nautilus. These organisms have eyes and are more active than other mollusks.

Most mollusks are slow-moving organisms. But the squid and octopus, called **head-foot mollusks,** are active predators (Figure 15-17). The foot has been modified into several arms, or tentacles, originating at the head region. Also included in this group are the cuttlefish (KUT ul fihsh) and chambered nautilus (NAHT ul us). Head-foot mollusks have eyes which may aid them in being more active than other mollusks. The similarities of vertebrate eyes and mollusk eyes may be the result of convergence (Section 11:8). A squid has a reduced internal shell and an octopus has no shell. Squids measuring over seventeen meters and octopuses of about ten meters in length have been found. These are some of the largest invertebrates.

REVIEWING YOUR IDEAS

7. What are the two usual hosts in a beef tapeworm's life cycle?
8. How are flatworms and roundworms different?
9. What is a coelom?
10. Compare the cell layers in annelids and mollusks.
11. What are the distinguishing features of mollusks?

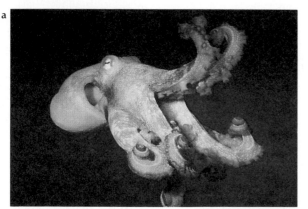

a

Geri Murphy

b

Peter David for Photo Researchers

c

Tom McHugh for Photo Researchers

d

Tom McHugh for Photo Researchers

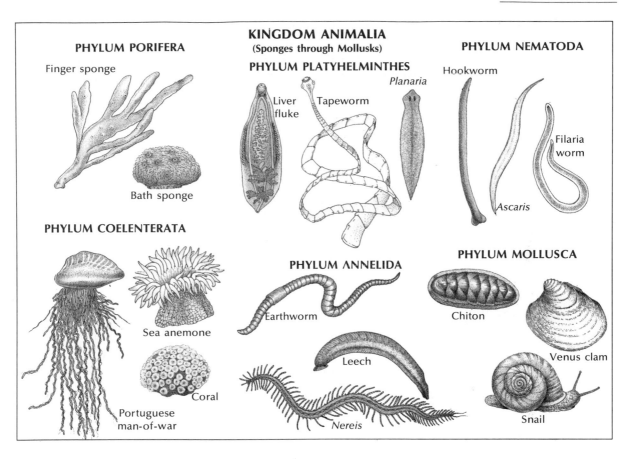

KINGDOM ANIMALIA
(Sponges through Mollusks)

PHYLUM PORIFERA

Finger sponge

Bath sponge

PHYLUM PLATYHELMINTHES

Liver fluke — Tapeworm — *Planaria*

PHYLUM NEMATODA

Hookworm

Filaria worm

Ascaris

PHYLUM COELENTERATA

Sea anemone

Coral

Portuguese man-of-war

PHYLUM ANNELIDA

Earthworm

Leech

Nereis

PHYLUM MOLLUSCA

Chiton

Venus clam

Snail

TABLE 15-1. SUMMARY OF MAJOR CHARACTERISTICS OF SIMPLE INVERTEBRATES						
PHYLUM	Porifera	Coelenterata	Platyhelminthes	Nematoda	Annelida	Mollusca
COMMON NAME	sponges	colenterates	flatworms	roundworms	segmented worms	mollusks
LOCOMOTION	none	mostly sessile; free-floating	muscles; cilia	muscles	muscles	muscles
SYMMETRY	none or radial	radial	bilateral	bilateral	bilateral	bilateral
NUMBER OF BODY OPENINGS	one	one	one	two	two	two
NUMBER OF CELL LAYERS	two	two	three	three	three	three
NERVOUS SYSTEM	none	present	present	present	present	present
DIGESTIVE SYSTEM	none	present	present	present	present	present
EXCRETORY SYSTEM	none	none	present	present	present	present
CIRCULATORY SYSTEM	none	none	none	none	present	present
RESPIRATORY SYSTEM	none	none	none	none	none	present
SKELETAL SYSTEM	spicules, no true system	none	none	none	none	hard outer shell

CHAPTER REVIEW

SUMMARY

1. Most of the features of animals can be related to their heterotrophic way of life. Most animals have mobility, a nervous system, and sense organs. They must digest food and excrete wastes. Animals can be subdivided into two groups—invertebrates and vertebrates.

2. Sponges are the least complex animals. They lack true tissues and are sessile.

3. The coelenterates have a nerve net and other tissues. The body has only one opening and may be either a polyp or medusa form.

4. Coelenterates and some sponges have radial symmetry.

5. Flatworms include free-living and parasitic forms. They have one body opening, three cell layers, organs, and a primitive, central nervous system. The tapeworm is an example of a parasitic flatworm.

6. The roundworms have two features not seen in less complex animals—two body openings and separate sexes. Many forms are parasites.

7. The segmented worms have systems for transport and excretion. Most forms are aquatic.

8. Mollusks have soft bodies and often hard, mineral shells. Major groups include bivalves, univalves, and head-foot mollusks.

LANGUAGE OF BIOLOGY

anterior	incurrent pore	posterior
bilateral	invertebrate	radial
symmetry	mantle	symmetry
coelom	medusa	segmented
dorsal	mesoderm	sessile
ectoderm	mesoglea	tentacles
endoderm	nematocyst	valves
excurrent pore	osculum	ventral
gemmules	parapods	vertebrate
hermaphrodite	polyp	

CHECKING YOUR IDEAS

On a separate paper, match the phrase in the left column with the proper term in the right column. Do not write in this book.

1. simplest phylum of animals with two body openings
2. simplest phylum with three tissue layers
3. side of an animal
4. one form of coelenterate
5. characterized by many pores
6. same features on all sides
7. have two tissue layers and a mesoglea
8. front of an animal
9. soft body and hard shell
10. simplest phylum with a circulatory system

a. anterior
b. coelenterates
c. flatworms
d. lateral
e. medusa
f. mollusks
g. radial symmetry
h. roundworms
i. segmented worms
j. sponges

EVALUATING YOUR IDEAS

1. Explain how several animal features are related to an animal's heterotrophic way of life.

2. Why do you think sponges are classified as animals?

3. What is the highest level of organization in sponges?

4. Describe the various ways in which sponges reproduce.

5. In what ways are coelenterates more complex than sponges?

6. How do coelenterates obtain food?

7. Describe the life cycle of *Aurelia*.

8. How many cell layers do flatworms have? What kind of symmetry and levels of organization do flatworms have? Give examples.

CHAPTER REVIEW

9. Flatworms do not have specialized organs for gas exchange and waste removal. How do these processes occur?

10. Describe the life cycle of a beef tapeworm.

11. How many body openings does a roundworm have?

12. Distinguish between reproduction in roundworms and reproduction in flatworms.

13. What are some diseases caused by roundworms?

14. What systems are present in segmented worms? What systems do segmented worms lack?

15. How are earthworms important in soil ecology?

16. Is an earthworm a land animal? Explain.

17. How do aquatic annelids reproduce? How does the earthworm reproduce? What might be an explanation for the differences?

18. List some unique characteristics of mollusks.

19. What is the basis for dividing mollusks into three groups?

20. Compare methods of food getting among mollusks.

6. Can you explain why, long ago, sick people were treated by attaching leeches to their skin?

7. Consider the three major classes of mollusks. Relate their locomotion to differences in their structure.

8. In what ways are bivalve mollusks similar to sponges?

9. How is the obtaining of food different in animals and fungi? *Chapter 13

10. What ecological approach could be used to eliminate tapeworms?

EXTENDING YOUR IDEAS

1. Use library resources to prepare a report on the development of mollusks and annelids. Explain the assumption that mollusks and annelids are closely related.

2. Prepare a report on several of the animal parasites mentioned in this chapter. Include the life cycle of each form.

3. Write a report comparing and contrasting flukes and leeches.

4. Find out about comb jellies and brachiopods. What other kinds of animals do they resemble?

APPLYING YOUR IDEAS

1. In what ways are animals similar to protozoa? How are they different? *Chapter 13

2. Why do you think that some biologists suggest that sponges be classified as protists? *Chapter 13

3. How is radial symmetry an advantage to sessile animals?

4. What adaptations must tapeworms have to be able to live in a digestive organ like the intestine? (Hint: What kinds of chemicals are present?)

5. Most hermaphrodites mate with other hermaphrodites. Why do tapeworms fertilize themselves?

SUGGESTED READINGS

Buchsbaum, Ralph, *Animals Without Backbones*, rev. 2nd ed. Chicago, University of Chicago Press, 1975.

Hansen, James, ''Leeches, Lancets, and Fleams.'' *Science 81*, October, 1981.

Patent, Dorothy H., *The World of Worms*. New York, Holiday House, 1978.

Schaefer, Jack, *An American Bestiary*. Boston, Houghton Mifflin Co., 1975.

Sumich, James L., *An Introduction to the Biology of Marine Life*, 2nd ed. Dubuque, IA, William C. Brown Co., 1980.

Yonge, C. M., ''Giant Clams.'' *Scientific American*, April, 1975.

Additional student readings and suggested teacher readings are provided in the Teacher's Guide.

Like simple animals, more complex animals have adaptations that help them survive and reproduce in a variety of environments. What types of adaptations help these tropical rabbit-fish survive in their warm, aquatic environment? How are these fish different from other types of fish? How are they different from land animals? You are classified in the same phylum with these fish. What traits do you have in common with them?

Introduction: You may wish to encourage a variety of related projects such as setting up and maintaining aquaria or terraria or collection of insects. (See Extending Your Ideas, numbers 2 and 3, in the Teacher's Guide.) Some students will be interested in observing a variety of animals in the lab; e.g., hermit crabs, salamanders, turtles, snakes, and small mammals. Care *must* be taken to treat these animals properly with arrangements made for times when school is not in session. If at all possible, also coordinate the teaching of this chapter with a trip to a zoo or museum. Consider the use of selected films or other media which bring the chapter to life. (See *Suggested Audio-Visuals* in the Teacher's Guide.)

ANIMALS: ARTHROPODS THROUGH VERTEBRATES

Chapter 16 presents the characteristics of the major groups of complex animals.

Study of the characteristics of simple invertebrates (Chapter 15) reveals a variety of animal adaptations. Each phylum of organisms has particular features which make it unique. Yet, the animals have much in common as they carry out the same basic life functions. Their adaptations enable them to survive and reproduce in a variety of habitats. In this chapter, you will study three other phyla of animals—arthropods, echinoderms, and chordates. They, too, have a variety of adaptations and particular features which make each group unique. The arthropods and vertebrates have complex adaptations which make them the most successful of the animal phyla.

GOAL: You will gain an understanding of the basic features of the major groups of complex organisms in the animal kingdom.

Arthropods and vertebrates are the most successful animal phyla.

ARTHROPODS AND ECHINODERMS

Arthropods (AR thruh pahdz) are the most advanced invertebrates. This phylum has more living members than all other phyla combined. In this sense, these animals are the most successful. They are found almost everywhere. The many species illustrate the diversity of adaptations which have come about in living systems.

Echinoderms (ih KI nuh durmz) are less complex and diverse than arthropods. They are slow-moving organisms with a body plan different from other animals. However, they seem to be more closely related to the chordates than any other animal phylum.

Arthropods are the most abundant of all animals.

FIGURE 16-1. *Peripatus*, a primitive arthropod, has features common to both annelids and arthropods.

phylum Onychophora

16:1 Arthropods

Arthropods, phylum **Arthropoda** (ar THRAHP uh duh), have segmented bodies and seem to be close relatives of annelids (Section 15:7). *Peripatus* (puh RIHP ut us) is an example of an animal which has features common to both annelids and arthropods (Figure 16-1). *Peripatus* often is classified in a small phylum separate from both annelids and arthropods. Sometimes people classify *Peripatus* in a class of arthropods instead of in a separate phylum.

Modern arthropods have the following features:
(1) segmented body covered by an **exoskeleton** (ek soh SKEL ut un), or external skeleton
(2) pairs of jointed **appendages** (uh PEN dihj uz), such as limbs and antennae
(3) well-organized muscles with definite points of attachment to the exoskeleton
(4) body segments in most forms fused into distinct body regions—**head; thorax,** or chest; and **abdomen**
(5) highly developed, specialized **mouthparts**
(6) highly developed, specialized **sensory organs**

Arthropods have well organized muscles.

Study of these and other features can show why arthropods are adapted to many environments. An exoskeleton, jointed appendages, and a developed muscular system allow greater mobility for arthropods than worms have. For example, consider the jumping of a grasshopper or the scurrying of a millipede. The exoskeleton gives body support. Muscles are arranged in special ways and are attached to definite points on the exoskeleton (Section 28:1). This arrangement permits movement of certain parts as well as movement of the entire organism. Without a support system and appendages, animals are limited to either crawling or floating. In addition, the exoskeleton provides some protection of the arthropod from predators.

The exoskeleton provides support and protection and improves locomotion.

Because they live in many environments, arthropods have various diets. Several types of mouthparts have evolved. Some mouthparts are toothed and are used for chewing. Others help hold and transfer food to the mouth.

In most arthropods, body segments are fused into distinct regions.

Fusion of segments into distinct body sections (compartments) is another kind of specialization. The arrangement of the body into compartments provides definite areas for organs and certain functions. This system is more advanced than those found in less complex invertebrates.

Arthropods are bilaterally symmetrical. As in annelids, the nervous system occupies the ventral portion of the body. Reproduction in arthropods is mostly sexual.

The compound eye of an arthropod is composed of individual tubes called ommatidia, each with its own lens.
David Scharf for Peter Arnold

Mrs. George T. Butts

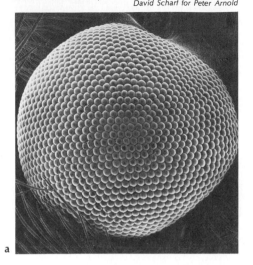

a

b

Also, sensory organs are present in arthropods. **Antennae** function in hearing, tasting, feeling, and smelling for different arthropods. Arthropods also have complex eyes.

FIGURE 16-2. Arthropods have highly developed, specialized sensory organs. (a) The compound eye and (b) antennae (here, of a moth) are adaptations which help arthropods survive in many environments.

16:2 Centipedes and Millipedes

Five important classes of arthropods presently live on Earth. Two classes are **Chilopoda** (ki LAHP uh duh), the centipedes or "hundred leggers," and **Diplopoda** (duh PLAHP uh duh), the millipedes or "thousand leggers." Both are wormlike organisms. Both forms have head regions but the rest of their bodies are made up of separate (unfused) segments.

A centipede has a pair of antennae on the head and mouthparts called mandibles. **Mandibles** are adapted for biting and chewing. Centipedes are land dwellers and carnivores. The

Some taxonomists refer to these two classes jointly as Myriopoda.

a

b

FIGURE 16-3. (a) A millipede, class Diplopoda, has two pairs of legs per segment. (b) A centipede, class Chilopoda, has one pair of legs per segment.

Alvin E. Staffan   *Ward's Natural Science Establishment, Inc.*

Most segments of a centipede bear one pair of walking legs.

Millipedes have two pairs of walking legs on most segments.

Crustaceans breathe by gills and live in aquatic or moist environments.

FIGURE 16-4. (a) Shrimp and (b) crayfish are common crustaceans that, like most animals in this class, breathe by means of gills. (c) Sow bugs are among the few crustaceans that live on land. They have simple tracheal systems.

first pair of body appendages contain **poison claws** through which poison can be injected into prey. The claws are not jaws; they are modified appendages. Centipedes hunt at night. Their diet includes insects, earthworms, and slugs. Sometimes they eat small reptiles or mammals.

Each of the body segments of a centipede, except for the first one and last two, has one pair of walking legs. The total number of legs ranges from as few as thirty to more than three hundred. Centipedes exchange gases with the atmosphere by means of special tubes called **tracheae** (TRAY kee ee) which open through the exoskeleton to the outside of the body (Section 27:3).

Millipedes also have one pair of antennae and mandibles. They are not carnivorous but feed on decaying plant material. They have no poison claws. Each of the first four body segments has one pair of walking legs. The rest of the body has two pairs of walking legs per segment. Like centipedes, millipedes exchange gases by means of tracheae.

16:3 Crustaceans

Class **Crustacea** (krus TAY shee uh) is a diverse group of arthropods with a variety of adaptations. They have mandibles, two pairs of antennae, and breathe by means of gills. Their body forms vary a great deal. Most crustaceans live in the sea, but others are found in fresh water and moist places on land.

Most familiar to you are large crustaceans such as the lobster, shrimp, and crab. Commonly called shellfish, these animals are a major part of the seafood industry. Red tides (Section 13:7) may cause severe economic loss by poisoning or killing these animals.

The lobster, like most other forms, has two body sections, the **cephalothorax** (sef uh luh THOR aks), a fusion of head and

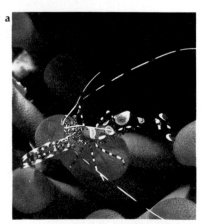
a

b

c

Chris McLaughlin   Alvin E. Staffan   Michael DiSpezio

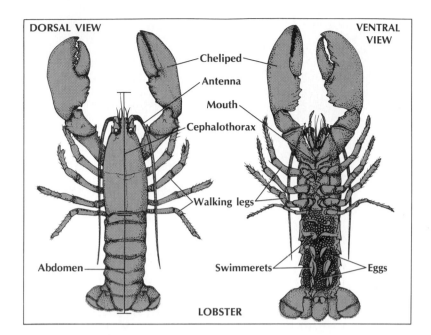

DORSAL VIEW

VENTRAL VIEW

Cheliped

Antenna

Mouth

Cephalothorax

Walking legs

Abdomen

Swimmerets

Eggs

LOBSTER

FIGURE 16-5. The lobster has two body sections, the cephalothorax and the abdomen. Swimmerets can be seen on the ventral side.

thorax, and the **abdomen**. It also has five pairs of legs on the cephalothorax. The first pair is modified as claws called **chelipeds** (KEE luh pedz) and is used in trapping food and for defense. One cheliped is larger than the other and is used for crushing prey. The smaller cheliped is used for holding and tearing food. The other four pairs of legs are walking legs.

The lobster's abdomen has one pair of appendages on every segment except the last. These appendages are used for swimming and are called **swimmerets**. The first pair in males is specialized for transferring sperm to the female. Fertilized eggs are attached to some of the female's swimmerets during early development. The last pair of abdominal appendages is fused with the last segment to form a flipper. The appendages of the lobster are shown in Figure 16-5. By studying the diagram, you can see how different appendages are specialized for many functions—sensing, feeding, locomotion, and reproduction.

An example of a crustacean living on land is the sowbug. This animal, whose small size is like that of most crustaceans, has gills. It lives under logs or stones and stays moist.

Although most crustaceans are motile, adult barnacles (Figure 16-6) are sessile. They are marine forms which may be attached to other animals, to rocks, or to bottoms of ships. The pattern of the barnacles is sometimes used to identify sea animals, such as whales, to which they attach. Barnacles secrete mineral shells which surround their bodies. Their jointed appendages may reach out of the shell and trap small animals for food.

Most crustaceans have two body sections, cephalothorax and abdomen.

FIGURE 16-6. Barnacles secrete shells in which they live, remaining sessile. Barnacle patterns are sometimes used to identify whales. Barnacles are shown here attached to a gray whale.

James C. Simmons for Tom Stack and Associates

FIGURE 16-7. Insects are not only the most numerous type of arthropod, but with over 800 000 species, they are also the most numerous type of animal.

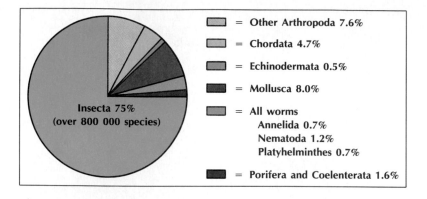

= Other Arthropoda 7.6%

= Chordata 4.7%

= Echinodermata 0.5%

= Mollusca 8.0%

= All worms
    Annelida 0.7%
    Nematoda 1.2%
    Platyhelminthes 0.7%

= Porifera and Coelenterata 1.6%

Insecta 75%
(over 800 000 species)

16:4 Insects

The largest group of arthropods is class **Insecta** (ihn SEK tuh). Insects are widely distributed. With the exception of salt water, insects have successfully invaded a wide variety of habitats and ecological niches. Their large numbers, high reproduction rate, and diversity of adaptations have made many of them pests to humans. Beetles, earwigs, and locusts are insects which eat crops and garden plants. Thus, they compete with humans for food. Termites destroy wood both in living trees and in houses. Gypsy moth caterpillars can strip trees bare as they eat leaves. Lice and fleas are parasites of a variety of animals. Certain mosquitoes and flies transmit disease. Moths may damage clothing. Other insects are beneficial to humans and in nature. They may prey on harmful insects, pollinate flowers, or make things such as honey or silk.

Insects have three body regions—head, thorax, and abdomen. The head has one pair of antennae and a pair of mandibles. The mandibles and other mouthparts of insects are specialized for many different ways of feeding. Consider a caterpillar chewing a leaf or a mosquito piercing your skin and sucking blood. Insects have three pairs of legs, one pair on each thoracic segment. In most forms, the second and third segments of the thorax also each have a pair of wings. The abdomens of some insects have small, vestigial appendages or appendages used in reproduction. Insects breathe by means of tracheae. Oxygen enters the tracheae through small openings located between abdominal segments.

Many insects have complex behavior (Section 31:10). Some forms including ants, termites, and bees live in colonies. The colonies show division of labor in that different insects have special roles. These roles are genetically determined.

The diversity of adaptations is a reason for the success of insects in various environments. Some of the major orders of insects are described in Appendix A. Representative examples from the orders are pictured on page 305.

Insects are adapted for a great variety of environments.

Insects have three body sections and, in most forms, two pairs of wings.

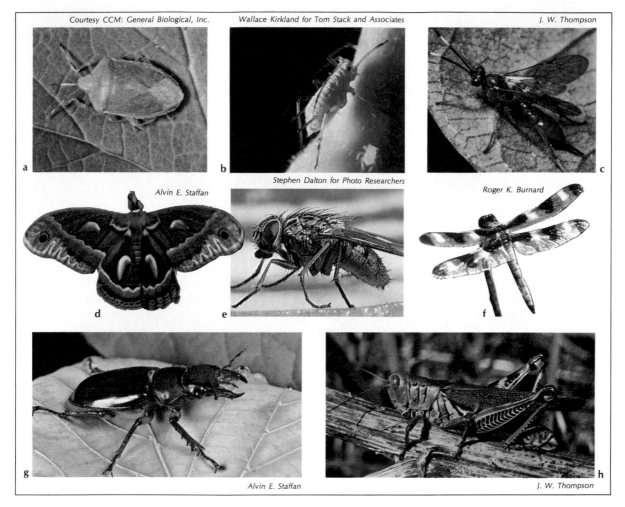

Courtesy CCM: General Biological, Inc.
Wallace Kirkland for Tom Stack and Associates
J. W. Thompson
Alvin E. Staffan
Stephen Dalton for Photo Researchers
Roger K. Burnard
Alvin E. Staffan
J. W. Thompson

16:5 Arachnids

Class **Arachnida** (uh ʀᴀᴋ nuh duh) is a group which includes spiders, ticks, mites, and scorpions. **Arachnids** (uh ʀᴀᴋ nuhdz) have two body sections—cephalothorax and abdomen. Unlike other classes of arthropods, they have no antennae. Also, they have chelicerae (kih ʟɪʜs uh ree) instead of mandibles. **Chelicerae** are either fanglike or pincerlike mouthparts. Spiders have fanglike chelicerae which transfer poison that paralyzes their prey. Some spiders, such as the black widow and brown recluse, produce a poison which may be fatal to humans. Posterior to the chelicerae are a pair of **pedipalps** which hold and tear apart food. Behind the pedipalps are four pairs of walking legs. These six pairs of appendages are all located on the cephalothorax. The abdomen usually has no appendages.

FIGURE 16-8. These insects, (a) stinkbug, (b) aphid, (c) wasp, (d) cecropia moth, (e) housefly, (f) dragonfly, (g) stag beetle, and (h) grasshopper, are representatives of different orders of the class Insecta.

Arachnids have two body sections and no antennae. Unlike other arthropods, they have chelicerae rather than mandibles.

Teaching suggestion: Point out that more spiders are beneficial to humans than are harmful. Spiders are an important natural control of numerous insect pests.

Arachnids have four pairs of walking legs.

Stephen J. Krasemann/DRK photo   *Courtesy CCM: General Biological, Inc.*   *Michael DiSpezio*

a   b   c

FIGURE 16-9. Class Arachnida includes (a) the giant hairy scorpion, (b) tarantula, and (c) dog tick. Arachnids have four pairs of legs.

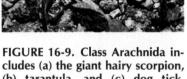

Spiders' webs are devices for trapping prey.

Scorpions are active predators.

Most arachnids exchange gases by means of tracheae. Others have special structures called **book lungs** for exchanging gases. These structures are so named because they resemble an opened book in appearance.

Many spiders, as you know, spin webs to catch prey. The webs are made from threads of silk which leave the spider's body through **spinnerets** located at the tip of the abdomen. Insects become trapped in the sticky threads of the web and thus, become food for the spider.

Scorpions are common in the southwest United States. They are inactive during the day but search for insects and spiders at night. A scorpion has a poisonous stinger at the end of the abdomen. Prey is held by pincerlike chelicerae while the poison from the stinger is injected into it. The sting of a scorpion may be painful to a human, but it rarely causes death. It usually causes some illness.

TABLE 16-1. SUMMARY OF CHARACTERISTICS OF ARTHROPODS

Class	Examples	Body Sections	Antennae	Mouthparts	Number of Walking Legs	Gas Exchange
Chilopoda	centipedes	head and body segments	1 pair	mandibles	1 pair per segment	tracheae
Diplopoda	millipedes	head and body segments	1 pair	mandibles	2 pair per segment	tracheae
Crustacea	lobster, crab, shrimp	cephalothorax and abdomen	2 pair	mandibles	5 pair in most forms	gills
Insecta	wasp, beetle, mosquito	head, thorax, and abdomen	1 pair	mandibles	3 pair	tracheae
Arachnida	spider, tick, scorpion	cephalothorax and abdomen	none	chelicerae	4 pair	tracheae; book lungs

Ward's Natural Science Establishment, Inc.

Geri Murphy

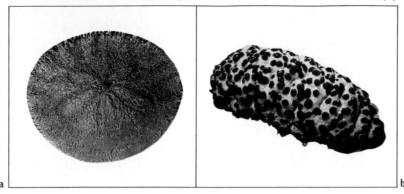

a

b

Geri Murphy

c

FIGURE 16-10. (a) The sand dollar, (b) sea cucumber, and (c) brittle starfish are representative echinoderms. Echinoderms have radial symmetry as adults.

16:6 Echinoderms

Most animals in phylum **Echinodermata** (ih ki nuh dur MUH tuh) are spiny skinned. Plates of minerals with projecting spines are embedded in the soft tissues of the body. The starfish, sea urchin (UR chun), and sand dollar are members of this phylum. All echinoderms live in salt water.

Starfish are the most familiar echinoderms. A starfish has an **endoskeleton** (en doh SKEL ut un), or internal skeleton, composed of spines. In a starfish is a **central disc** from which "arms" (usually five) stick out. These arms provide a means of movement and food getting. The slow movement is controlled by a special water-pumping system (Section 28:7). water vascular system

A starfish has a spiny skin and an internal skeleton.

In a starfish, materials are distributed within the fluid of the coelom. Gases are exchanged through gill-like structures. Simple nervous and sensory systems are present. There is no excretory system. Reproduction involves external fertilization.

Adult echinoderms are radially symmetrical. However, young developing echinoderms have bilateral symmetry. A comparison of certain developing echinoderms to developing forms of some chordates suggests a close relationship between the phyla. Evidence from comparative biochemistry also supports this idea.

Echinoderms and chordates seem to be closely related.

REVIEWING YOUR IDEAS

1. What is an exoskeleton? What are appendages?
2. List the five major classes of arthropods. Give an example of each class.
3. What are the three body regions of an arthropod?
4. Why are echinoderms called "spiny-skinned" animals?
5. Why do some biologists believe echinoderms and chordates are closely related?

1. An exoskeleton is an external skeleton. Appendages are structures such as limbs and antennae.
2. Chilopoda—centipede; Diplopoda—millipede; Crustacea—lobster; Insecta — grasshopper; Arachnida — spider.
3. head, thorax, and abdomen
4. Echinoderms have plates of minerals with projecting spines embedded in their soft tissues.
5. The two forms have some similarities in development and biochemistry.

CHORDATES

You are a **chordate** (KOR dayt), a member of phylum **Chordata** (kor DAHT uh). All chordates, at some stage of their lives, have a stiff rod of cartilage called a **notochord** (NOHT uh kord). The notochord runs along the dorsal side of the organism. Your notochord has become your backbone.

A chordate, at some stage of life, has a notochord and gill pouches. It also has a dorsal nerve cord and ventral heart.

Chordates also have gill pouches, a dorsal nerve cord, and a ventral heart. Gill pouches, like the notochord, do not remain in all chordates through their entire lives. Often, they are present only in the early embryo.

16:7 Characteristics of Chordates

All vertebrates (animals with backbones) are chordates, but not all chordates are vertebrates. Chordates that are not vertebrates are the tunicates (TEW nuh kayts), and lancelets (LAN sluts). They are marine dwellers. Most tunicates are sessile and grow singly or as colonies attached to rocks. They have a tough body wall in which there are two openings. When the body contracts suddenly, water is forced out of the openings. For this reason, tunicates are known as sea squirts. Tunicates obtain food from water which passes into the body through numerous gill slits.

Tunicates and lancelets are nonvertebrate chordates.

Lancelets more closely resemble vertebrates. *Amphioxus* (am fee AHK sus) (Figure 16-11b) is a small lancelet which you might mistake for a fish. Its body is pointed at each end and is streamlined. Although it can swim, it usually lives partly buried in sand. It feeds on microorganisms in water drawn into its mouth.

Acorn worms (not really worms) are quite primitive and have no definite notochord. They do have other chordate features. At one time they were considered to be a subphylum of chordates, but now they are classified in a separate phylum. Acorn worms are so named because their body is wormlike and, at one end, has

FIGURE 16-11. (a) Tunicates and (b) a lancelet are chordates that are not vertebrates. (c) Acorn worms, shown as they live burrowed in sand, were once thought to be invertebrate chordates. Now, they are classified in a separate phylum, the Hemichordata.

a

Geri Murphy

b

Michael DiSpezio

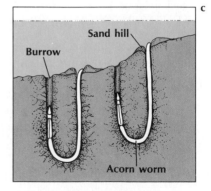
c

Sand hill

Burrow

Acorn worm

a structure resembling an acorn. These animals burrow in sand and take sand into their bodies. Organic particles in the sand are used as food. Study of early development of acorn worms suggests that they are closely related to echinoderms.

Vertebrates are in the subphylum **Vertebrata** (vurt uh BRAHT uh). In vertebrates, the notochord is replaced by bony structures, the **vertebrae** (VUR tuh bray), for which the group is named. Vertebrae connect to form the spinal column, or backbone. The following features are common to all vertebrates:

(1) internal skeleton of bone and/or cartilage
(2) specialized muscle system
(3) advanced centralized nervous system with a true brain and spinal cord
(4) complex sensory equipment
(5) dorsal nervous system and a ventral heart
(6) complex **integumentary** (ihn teg yuh MENT uh ree) system (outer covering)
(7) paired appendages for locomotion (never more than two pairs)

An internal skeleton provides excellent protection and support. Specialized bones have shapes that suit their function. Muscles are larger and provide vertebrates with greater speed and agility than found in many invertebrates. Because vertebrates have large, specialized brains, they often have more complex behavioral patterns. A well-developed nervous system controls the smoothly coordinated movements of vertebrates. In general, sensory organs are much more complex and effective in this group of animals than in any other.

Various vertebrates have outside coverings such as scales, thin skin, "armor," feathers, and hair. As a result of these and other adaptations, vertebrates occupy a wide range of habitats. Seven classes of vertebrates exist today.

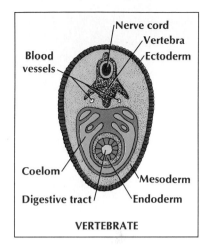

FIGURE 16-12. The cross section of the body of a generalized vertebrate shows the vertebra, bone that replaces the notochord.

Vertebrates have a variety of complex adaptations.

FIGURE 16-13. (a) Feathers, (b) fur or hair, and (c) scales are three types of integumentary adaptations.

a

b

c

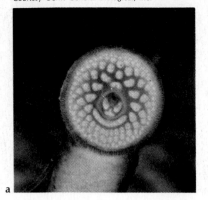

a

b

FIGURE 16-14. (a) The lamprey's sharp teeth aid (b) its attachment to other fish. Two lampreys are shown attached to a carp, feeding on its tissues and blood.

Fish have gills, limbs in the form of fins, and are ectotherms. Most fish have scales.

Placodermi is an extinct class of fish characterized by armorlike plates.

An agnathan has a slimy skin without scales, a skeleton of cartilage, and a permanent notochord.

Agnatha are jawless fish which prey on other fish.

16:8 Jawless Fish

Three classes of vertebrates are fish. Fish exchange gases by means of gills, and most have scales. Their limbs are in the form of fins. Like all other animals studied so far, their body temperature changes with that of the environment. For example, when the environment is cold, the body becomes cold. Such animals are called **ectotherms** (EK tuh thurmz).

The most primitive fish belong to the class **Agnatha** (AG nuh thuh). At one time, these fish were a very diverse group whose bodies were covered with armorlike plates. Today, this small class is composed of two groups, lampreys and hagfish. Lampreys inhabit both fresh water and salt water. Hagfish live in salt water.

These fish have a slimy skin with no scales. They lack paired fins, and their gill openings are not covered. They have a skeleton of cartilage and retain a notochord as adults. The notochord is not replaced by vertebrae, but these animals are still considered vertebrates. You can again see difficulties in making a classification scheme.

Instead of hinged jaws, an agnatha has a sucker-shaped mouth. Thus, agnatha are called **jawless fish**. The fish's mouth is lined with sharp teeth. The lamprey catches prey such as trout or other fish and hooks onto it. Then, with its toothed tongue, it rasps a hole and feeds on the blood or tissues of its host. Sometimes the attack is fatal to the host. However, many fish survive and have scars which indicate previous lamprey attacks. Lampreys can cause great economic loss by destroying fish. In the Great Lakes, for example, lampreys have destroyed many trout.

Hagfish are eel-like and live in deep parts of cold water. A hagfish often lies buried in the sand except for its head. Most hagfish are not parasites. They feed upon invertebrates or dead animals. They often attack fish caught in nets. They may bore into the bodies of these fish, eating the fish from inside. Thus, hagfish can also cause economic loss.

16:9 Cartilage Fish

Like the agnatha, members of class **Chondrichthyes** (kahn DRIHK thee eez) have skeletons composed of cartilage. These **cartilage fish** include sharks, skates, and rays (Figure 16-15). They have a skin covered with toothlike scales, two pairs of fins for locomotion, and hinged jaws. Their gill openings are not covered. These fish are unusual in that most have internal fertilization.

Sharks range in size from pigmies, which may be only 0.6 m, to whale sharks, which may be 15 m long with a mass of several thousand kilograms. The dogfish shark is common along both the Atlantic and Pacific coasts. It is about 1.0 m long and has a mass of 3.5 kg. Other sharks include the hammerhead and white shark.

Almost all sharks are meat eaters. Their diet includes fish, squid, crustaceans, jellyfish, sea turtles and even sea lions. Most sharks have mouths lined with rows of sharp teeth slanted backwards to hold their prey in the wide mouth. Often, these teeth are replaced when lost. Their sense of smell, swimming ability, and size make sharks excellent predators. Although the shark is feared by many humans, shark attacks are quite rare. The forms most dangerous to humans are the white, hammerhead, tiger, and sand shark. The whale shark, largest of all, is harmless to humans. It engulfs small animals as it swims along.

Sharks are commercially important in several ways. Shark liver oil is a source of Vitamin A and is used for tanning leather, in preserving wood, and as a lubricant. Shark skin can be made into leather. The meat of some sharks is eaten by humans and is a good source of protein. Shark fin soup also is eaten.

Rays and skates have flattened bodies. Some, like the stingray, are dangerous. They have a barbed tail which secretes a venom. When stepped on, the ray lashes its tail inflicting a very painful wound. Both rays and skates are bottom dwellers in coastal waters. They usually feed on mollusks.

A cartilage fish has a skeleton of cartilage, scaly skin, paired fins for locomotion, and hinged jaws. Most have internal fertilization.

The male's pelvic fins are modified for injecting sperm into the female.

Sharks are well adapted for a predatory way of life.

FIGURE 16-15. (a) A white tip shark and (b) a stingray are fish with skeletons made of cartilage.

a

b

Don and Valerie Taylor for Tom Stack and Associates

Geri Murphy

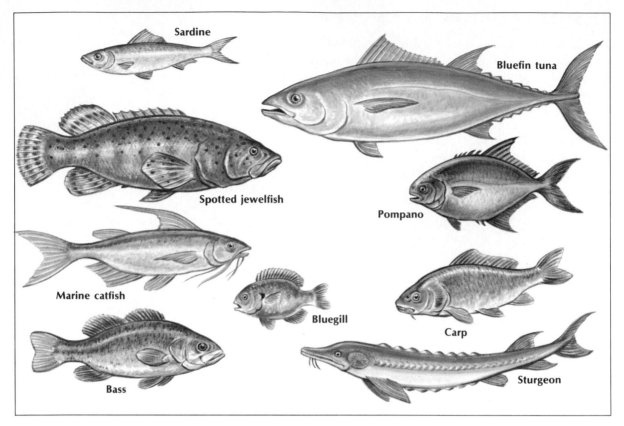

FIGURE 16-16. Bone replaces cartilage in the skeletons of bony fish, members of the class Osteichthyes.

16:10 Bony Fish

Modern **bony fish** belong to the class **Osteichthyes** (ahs tee IHK thee eez). They are the most diverse group of fish and live in both fresh water and salt water. A few can even live on land for short periods of time.

Although many bony fish have a similar appearance, there are a variety of unique adaptations and forms. Eels, for example, are snakelike in appearance, often lacking one or both of the pairs of fins found in most bony fishes. The electric eel and some other fish have a specialized organ which can generate as many as 400 volts of electricity for several milliseconds. This adaptation enables the animal to stun or kill small fish.

Bony fish exhibit a variety of unique adaptations.

In certain angler fish (Section 11:4) and other fish, a glowing structure lures prey into the fish's mouth. Luminescence may also aid some fish in finding mates in dark waters. Often, the light is actually produced by luminescent bacteria which live under the skin of the fish. In some cases, though, light is produced during chemical reactions within special organs of the fish.

As their name implies, bony fish have a skeleton made of bone. They have hinged jaws. Also, they have two pairs of lateral fins as well as a tail fin, two dorsal fins, and a ventral or anal fin. These fins are used for both locomotion and balance. Some may also aid in defense. These fish have scales made of flat discs of bone which grow as other bones do. The slimy body aids in swimming and offers protection. The gills are covered and protected by a hard plate, the **operculum** (oh PUR kyuh lum). You can see the operculum open and close as a bony fish exchanges gases with the water. As in all vertebrates, reproduction is sexual. In most cases, fertilization is external.

A bony fish has a skeleton of bone, hinged jaws, paired fins for locomotion, and scaly skin. The gills are covered by opercula.

REVIEWING YOUR IDEAS

6. List two kinds of chordates that are not vertebrates.
7. What structure is replaced by vertebrae in vertebrates?
8. What is an ectotherm?
9. List distinguishing features of jawless, cartilage, and bony fish.

6. Tunicates and lancelets are nonvertebrate chordates.
7. the notochord
8. An ectotherm is an animal whose body temperature changes with the environment.
9. Jawless fish—no hinged jaws, slimy skins with no scales, no paired fins, permanent notochord; cartilage fish—skeleton of cartilage, scales, paired fins for locomotion, hinged jaws; bony fish—skeleton of bone, scales, paired fins for locomotion, gill cover

16:11 Amphibians

Amphibians, class **Amphibia** (am FIHB ee uh), may be related to an extinct group of fish with lungs. As a class of animals, amphibians were the first vertebrates to live on land. Modern amphibians include frogs, toads, newts, salamanders, and apodes. Newts are small salamanderlike animals. Apodes are limbless, blind, burrowing animals.

In most amphibians, fertilization and development occur in water. Thus, they are "chained" to the water of streams and ponds. They have adaptations for life on land, but most return to water to reproduce. Some species live exclusively in water.

Although external fertilization is the rule, some species have internal fertilization. For example, some male salamanders deposit sperm clumps called spermatophores on the ground near or on twigs in water. The sperm clumps are taken into the

Amphibians are adapted for life on land.

FIGURE 16-17. Amphibians include (a) toads, (b) frogs, and (c) salamanders. As a class, amphibians were the first animals to live on land.

Courtesy CCM: General Biological, Inc.

Gene Frazier

J. R. Schnelzer

External gills

FIGURE 16-18. Some salamanders such as the tiger salamander have external gills as adults. The feathery structures at the sides of the head are the gills.

female's reproductive system where internal fertilization occurs. Although external development occurs in most amphibians, some have internal development. Some frogs are mouth breeders. The male stuffs fertilized eggs into his vocal sacs where they develop into young. In a certain type of Australian frog, fertilized eggs are kept in a dorsal brood pouch on the female. Young frogs are "born" from the pouch.

In stages of development, amphibians have gills that obtain oxygen. In most forms, gills are replaced by lungs as the organism develops into adult form. Also, as an adult, an amphibian has a thin, moist skin which contains a rich supply of blood vessels. Oxygen taken in through the skin adds to the amount obtained by the lungs. In one kind of aquatic frog, the male has hairlike filaments on its legs. These "hairs" contain blood vessels and aid in getting oxygen.

Some salamanders, such as the mud puppy, retain gills as adults, even though they also develop lungs. The gills of a mud puppy are external, projecting out in front of the front legs. Axolotls, another type of salamander, retain some characteristics of developing salamanders throughout their lives and reproduce without ever becoming "mature" adults. Retaining immature traits indefinitely in the "adult" form is called **neoteny** (nee AHT un ee).

Amphibians move in a variety of ways.

Amphibians are adapted for both swimming and locomotion on land. When moving quickly on land, salamanders and newts slither along the ground with their legs hardly touching the ground. This movement is a sort of "swimming on land." When moving more slowly, salamanders and newts walk on their four feet. Frogs and toads are adapted for jumping, which they can do quickly and to large distances. Certain "flying" frogs can jump 12 to 15 meters. Tree frogs are adapted for climbing in trees. In these frogs, toe discs or digital pads help them climb. These pads are covered with a sticky mucus which helps the frog cling to the tree.

16:12 Reptiles

Reptiles have internal fertilization and can inhabit a variety of ecological niches.

Dinosaurs, once the largest and most dominant reptiles, lived about two hundred million years ago. Today's **reptiles**, class **Reptilia** (rep TIHL ee uh), include snakes, turtles, lizards, and alligators. All have a means of internal fertilization and most of the young develop in shelled eggs. The shelled egg (Section 24:4) is a moist, protected environment for development. Therefore, reptiles do not need to reproduce in water as amphibians do. This adaptation has allowed reptiles to occupy a variety of niches on land, but some species, such as the sea tortoises, do live in water.

  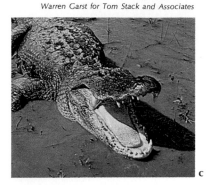

a   b   c

Except for snakes, these animals have limbs that are located toward the ventral side of the body. Thus, the body is lifted off the ground, an adaptation for locomotion on land. Claws are present on the feet.

Throughout life, reptiles breathe by means of large lungs. They are protected by a dry, scaly skin which prevents water loss by evaporation. Lungs and scales are among the important adaptations for land life. Reptiles are ectotherms.

Lizards are a diverse group of reptiles which live in a variety of habitats including the Arctic, the tropics, and the desert. Geckos are small lizards only 3 cm long with a mass of a few grams. Geckos have toes with special pads for climbing and even walking on ceilings. The largest lizards are the monitors which may be three meters long with a mass of 150 kg. Most lizards move on four legs though some have no limbs and are snakelike.

Most lizards eat insects and small rodents. In some parts of the world, small lizards, such as geckos, are welcome in and around homes because they prey on these pests. Most lizards are harmless to humans. But a few forms, such as Gila (HEE luh) monsters, are poisonous. Gilas release venom from poison glands in the mouth. The poison affects breathing. Gilas will attack humans if provoked.

A variety of adaptations for defense and escape are found among lizards. Sometimes a predator may catch a lizard by the tail. There are certain planes within the tail at which it will break. The lizard's tail breaks off and the lizard escapes. The missing part of the tail is usually regrown. Some lizards have spiny tails which they use as defense weapons. Others have tissues around the throat which enlarge and scare off a predator. Many lizards can change color to blend with the environment (Section 11:5).

Crocodiles and alligators live in shallow waters of tropical environments. Both types of these ancient-looking reptiles are meat eaters. The eyes, ears, and nostrils are located on the top of the head and remain above water while the rest of the body floats beneath the surface hiding the animal from its prey. They feed on

FIGURE 16-19. (a) The snake, (b) turtle, and (c) alligator are representative reptiles. Reptile skin is dry and scale-covered, an adaptation that aids survival on land.

Reptiles are ectotherms, breathe by lungs, and have a dry, scaly skin.

FIGURE 16-20. An adaptation for quick escape of lizards is a tail that breaks off at certain caudal (tail) planes. When a lizard tail regrows, the place where it broke off can be seen because the new growth looks different from the old part of the tail.

Caudal plane

FIGURE 16-21. Snakes molt, shed their skins, several times a year. This red rat snake is crawling from its old skin.

Poisonous snakes inject venom through their fangs.

FIGURE 16-22. The fossil bird *Archaeopteryx* has features of both reptiles and birds. Reptile features include teeth, solid bones, and a long tail.

fish, small mammals, and birds. Occasionally, they have been known to attack deer, cattle, and humans. Their strong jaws and sharp teeth make them good predators.

Turtles live on land, in fresh water, and in the sea. These reptiles are protected by a shell of plates and bones. The shell also slows their movement. Most turtles are small animals, but the Atlantic leatherback may grow to nearly four meters long with a mass of 60 kg. Turtles live longer than any other vertebrates. Some have lived for 150 years.

The diet of turtles includes worms, insects, and other small animals. Large aquatic turtles eat fish, birds, and small mammals. Some turtles can go weeks without eating. The alligator snapping turtle of the southern United States has a lure on the floor of its mouth. The lure attracts prey into the mouth.

Both turtle meat and eggs are eaten by humans. The shells of many species are prized as ornaments. Because turtles have been killed in large numbers by poachers, some forms are now protected by law.

Snakes are legless reptiles which occupy both aquatic and land habitats. In a process called **molting**, snakes shed their outer skin layer of scales. Molting may occur several times each year. During molting, the old layer begins to loosen. The snake then crawls out of its old skin.

Very few snakes are poisonous. They have fangs with which they inject venom. Venom of snakes such as cobras and rattlers can be fatal to humans. The poisons in snake venom may act either on the nervous system or circulatory system of the prey. Those that affect the nervous sytem interfere with nerves controlling breathing and the heartbeat. Poisons affecting the circulatory system may destroy red blood cells and the walls of blood vessels. Antidotes to snake venom are prepared from venom "milked" from the fangs. Because of the danger of the few poisonous species, many people fear snakes.

16:13 Birds

Birds, class **Aves** (AY vayz), represent animals which probably arose as an early branch of the reptile group. *Archaeopteryx* (ar kee AHP tuh rihks) is a fossil bird with several features of reptiles. Today's birds have many features similar to those of reptiles. If you examine the legs of a bird, you will see that they are covered by scales and have claws. Like some reptiles, birds have a tough beak. Birds also develop in shelled eggs like reptiles.

Modern birds have a constant body temperature and are called **endotherms** (EN duh thurmz). They are covered with feathers which help to insulate the bird and maintain a constant

Larry Roberts

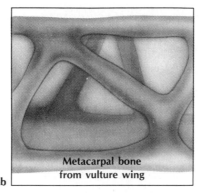

Metacarpal bone
from vulture wing

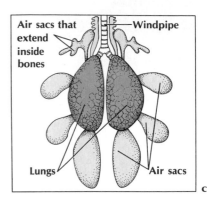

Air sacs that extend inside bones — Windpipe

Lungs — Air sacs

FIGURE 16-23. (a) Birds are well adapted for flight, as the ringbilled gull shows. (b) Bones within bird wings are hollow with braces crossing them. The bones are therefore light and strong. (c) The lung system has extra air sacs that fill spaces in the body and even within some bones. The sacs are part of a highly specialized respiratory system and they help make the animal lighter.

body temperature. Most birds gradually molt (replace old feathers) once a year. Many birds molt seasonally.

Although some birds such as penguins and ostriches do not fly, most birds are well adapted for flight. The forelimbs are modified as wings, the shape of which is important to flight. The bird's skeleton is composed of thin, lightweight bones that contain hollow cavities. Some of these hollow bones contain small extensions of bone that cross the internal cavities and serve as braces adding strength. Many of the skeletal bones are fused and reduced. The breastbone is large providing an attachment site for flight muscles. Movement of the wings downward is accomplished by contraction of the large pectoralis muscles which can make up as much as twenty percent of the total body weight of the bird.

Not only are the skeletal and muscular systems adapted for flight, but other body parts are as well. Feathers play an important role in balance and flight. Those few birds that lose all their feathers at one time in molting remain flightless until new feathers grow. The respiratory system is also adapted for flight. A system of **air sacs** connects with the lungs. The air sacs extend into the body cavity and even into some of the bones. The air sacs, as well as the lungs, fill with air. They also empty more completely when the bird exhales. The red blood cells in the bird's blood carry more hemoglobin, and thus, more oxygen. A large amount of oxygen needs to be supplied to the flight muscles for cell respiration during flight.

The bird's skeleton is also well adapted for walking. The entire body weight of a bird is on the legs when the bird is on the ground. The pelvis bones and muscles are adapted to this form of locomotion.

Bill (beak) structure is one of the many variations seen in birds. For example, cardinals are seed eaters and have crushing bills; pelicans have bills adapted for "fishing." Bill structure, along with other traits such as plumage color, foot structure, and behavior, is used to classify birds.

The limbs and bones of birds are adapted for flight.

A bird's respiratory system delivers a plentiful supply of oxygen to the flight muscles.

Endothermy and the bird's four-chambered heart are also important adaptations for its high energy demands. The latter ensures that blood leaving the heart is fully oxygenated.

TABLE 16-2. SUMMARY OF CHARACTERISTICS OF VERTEBRATES

Class	Examples	Integument	Body Temperature	Limb Structure	Gas Exchange	Fertilization
Agnatha	lamprey, hagfish	slimy skin	ectotherm	no paired limbs	gills	external
Chondrichthyes	shark, skate, ray	scales	ectotherm	2 pair of fins	gills	internal
Osteichthyes	perch, bass, trout	scales and slimy skin	ectotherm	2 pair of fins	gills	external
Amphibia	frog, toad, salamander	slimy skin in most forms	ectotherm	2 pair of legs; no claws	gills; lungs	external
Reptilia	turtle, lizard, snake, alligator	dry; scaly	ectotherm	2 pair of legs; claws	lungs	internal
Aves	robin, eagle, pelican	feathers; scales on legs	endotherm	1 pair of wings; 1 pair of legs with claws	lungs	internal
Mammalia	bear, whale, kangaroo	hair	endotherm	2 pairs of legs; claws in most forms	lungs	internal

16:14 Mammals

Mammals are the most complex vertebrates.

Development in mammals includes shelled eggs and partial or complete internal development.

FIGURE 16-24. The three main groups of mammals are represented by (a) the duck-billed platypus, a monotreme, (b) the Tasmanian devil, a marsupial, and (c) the field mouse, a placental.

Mammals, class **Mammalia** (muh MAY lee uh) are the most complex and most successful group of vertebrates living today. They are adapted for life in a variety of ecological niches from land to water. Why are mammals so successful?

Most of the mammals with which you are familiar bear their young alive. The young develop completely within the female and are then born. These mammals are called **placentals**. In mammals called **monotremes**, young develop in shelled eggs. The spiny anteater and duckbill platypus are monotremes. Pouched mammals, called **marsupials**, have partial development within the female. In these animals, such as the kangaroo and opossum, the young leave the mother's body before development

a

b

c

Tom McHugh for Photo Researchers

Schmidecker/fpg

Alvin E. Staffan

is complete. They complete development within a pouch on the mother's abdomen.

Mammals care for their young until they are able to survive on their own. This caring gives added protection for the newborn animal and ultimately for the species. Young are fed milk from mammary (MAM uh ree) glands. Development of mammals will be studied in Chapter 24.

Mammals are endotherms. Their bodies are covered with hair or fur, and they breathe by means of lungs. The nervous system of mammals is the most advanced of all animals. They have more complex behavior (Chapter 31) and greater intelligence than other animal groups. There are many orders of mammals. Appendix A summarizes the features of some of them.

Mammals are named for the presence of mammary glands.

Mammals are covered with hair, breathe with lungs, and are endotherms.

FIGURE 16-25. Mammals are a diversified class of animals adapted to many environments. Included are (a) the camel, (b) raccoon, (c) orangutans, (d) deer, (e) killer whale, (f) bat, and (g) opossums.

Leonard Lee Rue III from National Audubon Society

Alvin E. Staffan

Tom McHugh for Photo Researchers

a

b

c

d

e

Marineland of the Pacific

f

Toni Angermayer for Photo Researchers

g

Alvin E. Staffan

Leonard Lee Rue III for Photo Researchers

The order to which you belong is the primates. Primates also include the lemurs, monkeys, and great apes. The great apes are the orangutan, gibbon, chimpanzee, and gorilla. Most primates are adapted to an arboreal environment.

The great apes, family **Pongidae** (PAHN juh dee) have no tails. Many spend at least part of their lives on land where they walk, sometimes on their back feet. The gorilla is almost entirely a land-dweller, returning to the trees only to sleep. The great apes have large brains and appear to be the most intelligent of the nonhuman primates.

Humans are the only living members of the family of primates called Hominidae.

Humans are members of a family of primates called **Hominidae** (hoh MIHN uh dee). Modern humans are the only living member of this family. They belong to the genus and species *Homo sapiens* (HOH moh • SAY pee unz).

Humans are distinctive in certain respects. For example, their offspring have a long childhood in which they develop both physically and mentally. This period of time allows for training and learning. In most human societies, pair-bonds are formed; that is, a male mates with a single female. Thus, the family is the basic unit of most human societies. Mating can occur at any time instead of during a specific breeding season as in other animal species. A major human feature is a high degree of intelligence. This ability permits humans to learn and to apply their knowledge to the world around them (Section 32:11).

A high degree of intelligence enables humans to learn and apply their knowledge.

10. amphibians — frogs, toads, salamanders, newts, apodes; reptiles —snakes, turtles, lizards, alligators.
11. hollow bones, feathers, wings, air sacs that fill the body cavity and enter some bones, large flight muscles
12. Placentals have complete internal development. Monotremes lay eggs. Marsupials have partial development inside the mother, then the young move into the pouch where they complete development.
13. Hominidae
14. *Homo sapiens*
15. long childhood, pair-bonds, no particular breeding seasons, high intelligence

REVIEWING YOUR IDEAS

10. What are the major groups of amphibians? Of reptiles?
11. List several adaptations of birds for flight.
12. Distinguish among placentals, monotremes, and marsupials.
13. To which family group of mammals do you belong?
14. What is the genus and species of humans?
15. List some distinctive human adaptations.

TABLE 16-3. SUMMARY OF MAJOR CHARACTERISTICS OF HIGHER ANIMALS

PHYLUM	Arthropoda	Echinodermata	Chordata
Common name	arthropods	echinoderms	chordates
Locomotion	muscles, appendages	water pumping system	muscles, limbs
Symmetry	bilateral	radial	bilateral
Number of body openings	two	two	two
Number of cell layers	three	three	three
Nervous system	present	present	present
Digestive system	present	present	present
Excretory system	present	present	present
Circulatory system	present	present	present
Respiratory system	present	present	present
Skeletal system	external	mineral deposits	internal

KINGDOM ANIMALIA
(Arthropods through Vertebrates)

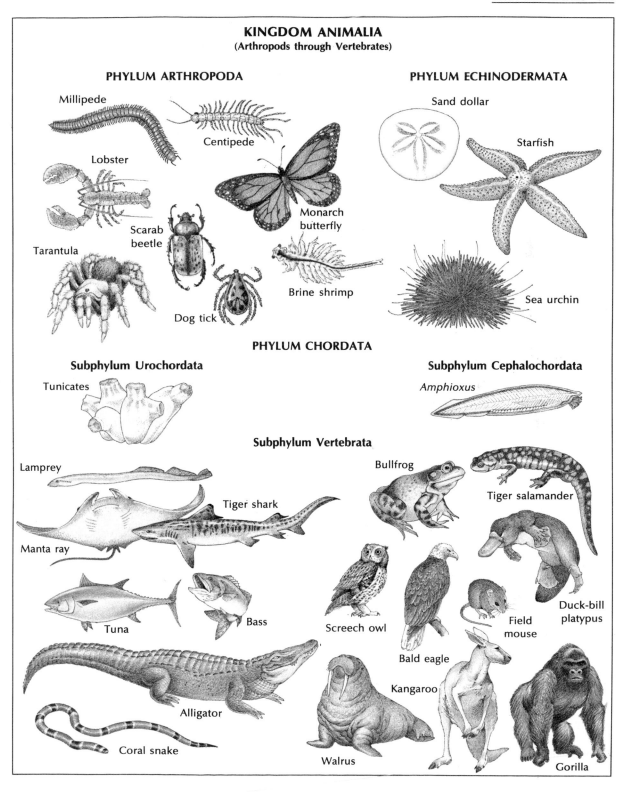

PHYLUM ARTHROPODA

Millipede

Centipede

Lobster

Monarch butterfly

Scarab beetle

Tarantula

Brine shrimp

Dog tick

PHYLUM ECHINODERMATA

Sand dollar

Starfish

Sea urchin

PHYLUM CHORDATA

Subphylum Urochordata

Tunicates

Subphylum Cephalochordata

Amphioxus

Subphylum Vertebrata

Lamprey

Bullfrog

Tiger salamander

Tiger shark

Manta ray

Duck-bill platypus

Tuna

Bass

Screech owl

Field mouse

Bald eagle

Alligator

Kangaroo

Walrus

Gorilla

Coral snake

CHAPTER REVIEW

SUMMARY

1. Arthropods are the most numerous animals and are adapted to more habitats than other invertebrates.

2. Class divisions of arthropods are based on the number of body sections, number of pairs of appendages, and type of mouthparts. Classes of arthropods include centipedes, millipedes, crustaceans, insects, and arachnids.

3. All echinoderms live in the ocean and most have spiny skins. Echinoderms are closely related to chordates.

4. Every chordate has a notochord and gill pouches at some time in its life. A chordate also has a dorsal nerve cord and a ventral heart.

5. The biggest subphylum of chordates is the vertebrates. Members of this subphylum have vertebrae.

6. The classes of vertebrates are based mainly on breathing mechanisms, integument, and means of reproduction. The classes are jawless fish, cartilage fish, bony fish, amphibians, reptiles, birds, and mammals.

7. Primates are an order of mammals that include lemurs, monkeys, great apes, and humans.

LANGUAGE OF BIOLOGY

air sacs	exoskeleton
central disc	mandible
cephalothorax	molting
chelicera	notochord
cheliped	operculum
ectotherm	pedipalp
endoskeleton	spinneret
endotherm	swimmeret

CHECKING YOUR IDEAS

On a separate paper, indicate whether each of the following statements is true or false. Do not write in this book.

1. Reptiles are well adapted for life on land.

2. All chordates are vertebrates.

3. Arthropods have jointed appendages and an external skeleton.

4. Salamanders develop in shelled eggs.

5. Spiders and ticks are in the class Insecta.

6. Echinoderms are the closest relatives of chordates.

7. Reptiles live only on land.

8. Insects and spiders have the same kind of mouthparts.

9. Most primates are adapted for an arboreal environment.

10. Lizards and snakes are amphibians.

EVALUATING YOUR IDEAS

1. What are some reasons why arthropods are a successful group of animals?

2. Annelids and arthropods are both segmented. How are the segments different?

3. Compare the classes of arthropods in terms of number of body sections, kind of mouthparts, number of walking legs, and means of gas exchange.

4. What are the functions of chelipeds and swimmerets?

5. In what ways are insects pests to humans? How are they beneficial?

6. How are chordates different from all other animals?

7. What kinds of animals are chordates but not vertebrates? Where do they live? How do they obtain food?

8. Compare the location of the circulatory systems and nervous systems of vertebrates and invertebrates.

CHAPTER REVIEW

9. What are integumentary systems? Give examples from different classes of vertebrates.

10. How would you tell the difference between agnathans and all other fish?

11. How do lampreys and hagfishes interfere with the fishing industry?

12. How would you distinguish between cartilage and bony fish?

13. Why are most amphibians "chained" to the water?

14. Describe the various ways by which amphibians obtain oxygen.

15. List some ways in which reptiles are adapted for life on land.

16. How do the venoms of poisonous snakes affect animals?

17. How is beak structure important to birds? Give some examples.

18. Distinguish molting in reptiles from molting in birds.

19. What are three means of development among mammals? Give an example of each type.

APPLYING YOUR IDEAS

1. Why might a barnacle be incorrectly classified as a mollusk? *Chapter 15.

2. Why do you think most barnacles are hermaphrodites?

3. How would you explain the fact that many birds eat quite frequently?

4. Why do many ectotherms migrate or hibernate?

5. Suggest some reasons why arthropods and vertebrates are the most successful animals. Are there ways in which they are similar?

6. Placentals and marsupials live in different parts of the world, yet many forms resemble one another. How can the similar features of these two groups be explained? *Chapter 11

Occasionally questions are added to the *Applying Your Ideas* that require students to use information they have learned from previous chapters. Those questions are marked with asterisks and chapter references.

EXTENDING YOUR IDEAS

1. Collect sowbugs from a damp area such as the forest floor. Examine the structure of these crustaceans with a hand lens or binocular microscope. Describe their response to light and touch.

2. If you have a terrarium, add several spiders to it. Observe the spiders' feeding habits by providing small insects for food. Also, observe web-building activities.

3. Make a collection of insects. Trap insects in a net and transfer them to a killing jar. Use a classification key to identify the order to which each insect belongs and to study its features. Use insect pins to mount each insect inside an empty shoe box or cigar box.

4. With what kinds of animals is each of the following branches of biology concerned: ichthyology, entomology, herpetology?

SUGGESTED READINGS

Appleby, Leonard G., "Snakes Shedding Skin." *Natural History*, February, 1980.

Colbert, Edwin H., *The Year of the Dinosaur.* New York, Charles Scribner's Sons, 1977.

Ellis, Richard, "The Rarest Large Animal." *Science 80*, September-October, 1980.

Gorman, James, "Elephant Watching." *Discover*, April, 1981.

Helfman, Gene S., "Coconut Crabs and Cannibalism." *Natural History*, November, 1979.

Jenkins, Marie M., *Kangaroos, Opossums, and Other Marsupials.* New York, Holiday House, 1975.

Otte, Daniel, "Beetles Adorned with Horns." *Natural History*, August, 1980.

Patent, Dorothy H., *Reptiles and How They Reproduce.* New York, Holiday House, 1977.

Wiewandt, Thomas A., "La Gran Iguana de Monera." *Natural History*, December, 1979.

Additional student readings and suggested teacher readings are provided in the Teacher's Guide.

SIMPLE ORGANISMS

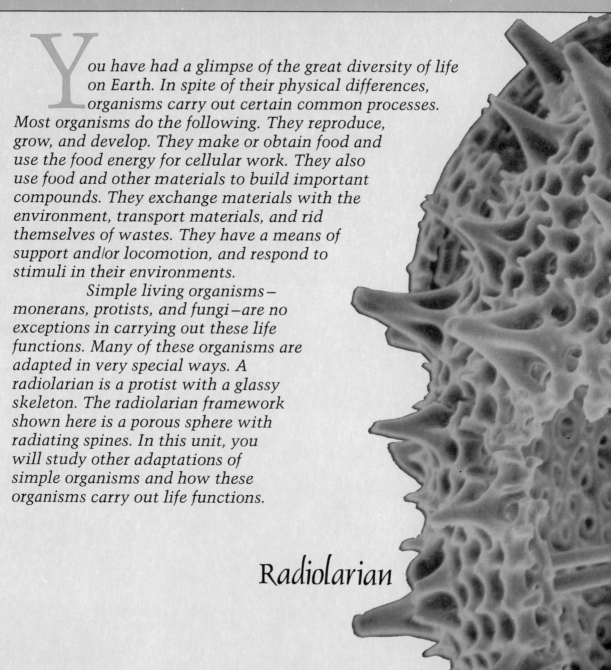

You have had a glimpse of the great diversity of life on Earth. In spite of their physical differences, organisms carry out certain common processes. Most organisms do the following. They reproduce, grow, and develop. They make or obtain food and use the food energy for cellular work. They also use food and other materials to build important compounds. They exchange materials with the environment, transport materials, and rid themselves of wastes. They have a means of support and/or locomotion, and respond to stimuli in their environments.

Simple living organisms— monerans, protists, and fungi—are no exceptions in carrying out these life functions. Many of these organisms are adapted in very special ways. A radiolarian is a protist with a glassy skeleton. The radiolarian framework shown here is a porous sphere with radiating spines. In this unit, you will study other adaptations of simple organisms and how these organisms carry out life functions.

Radiolarian

Simple organisms often are grown in the laboratory for research. You might think of this reproduction as always occurring in a test tube or Petri dish. However, sometimes biologists need large numbers of these organisms. Here, a fermenting machine incubates reproducing bacteria. The bacteria are grown in the steel containers. The colored valves control nutrients. How do bacteria reproduce? How is their reproduction different from that of other simple organisms?

Introduction: *Suggested Audio-Visuals* in the Teacher's Guide lists a variety of filmloops covering reproduction in algae, mushrooms, yeasts, *Paramecium*, *Rhizopus*, and viruses. These aids are valuable in helping students understand and visualize the processes discussed in this chapter. Prepared slides, available from biological supply houses, are also useful. Cultures of reproducing organisms can be obtained for observation. Also, you can get strains of different mating types of algae and fungi, mate them in the class, and have students observe.

Chapter

17

SIMPLE ORGANISMS: REPRODUCTION

Chapter 17 presents various forms of reproduction in monerans, protists, fungi, and viruses.

Genetic information is present in the DNA of a cell. You learned that it is transcribed into RNA and translated in the making of proteins in a cell. Transmission of the code occurs when the cells divide, each new cell getting an exact copy of the code. Chromosomes are the means by which DNA is moved from cell to cell and from one generation to the next.

The processes just described are similar in many organisms and ensure that the genetic code is passed to offspring when living things reproduce. The ways that organisms reproduce, however, vary. In this chapter, you will learn about the kinds of reproduction found in the simplest organisms—monerans, protists, fungi, and viruses.

GOAL: You will gain an understanding of the various ways in which monerans, protists, fungi, and viruses reproduce.

ASEXUAL REPRODUCTION

Asexual reproduction is the production of one or more offspring from *one parent*. It occurs in simple organisms in several ways, but each time it occurs, an identical set of genes is formed from one set. Therefore, each offspring has the same genotype and phenotype as its parent. Asexual reproduction is adaptive because it passes the *same* genes to the offspring. Because the offspring gets the same set of genes as its parent, the offspring is suited to its environment, just as the parent was. The only source of variation is mutation. Is variation helpful or harmful to a group of organisms? How good is asexual reproduction in a *changing* environment? Variation generally is helpful to a population. If the environment changes, all members of a population with no variation could die. Asexual reproduction may not be very good in a changing environment, because asexual reproduction does not increase variety.

Offspring produced by asexual reproduction are genetically identical.

FIGURE 17-1. Bacteria can reproduce asexually by fission. First the chromosome duplicates and then the cell wall lengthens and pinches in forming two cells.

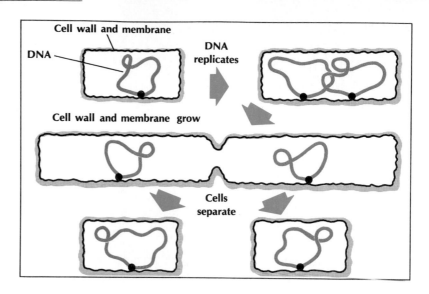

17:1 Fission in Monerans

In fission, one organism is split into two or more offspring of equal size.

In prokaryotes, fission does not involve mitosis.

This process is known as transverse or binary fission.

Fission (FIHSH un) is the splitting of a cell into two smaller cells (offspring) that are equal in size. Monerans, blue-green algae and bacteria, reproduce by fission. These organisms are prokaryotes (have no true nuclei), and so they do not undergo mitosis. Recall that mitosis is a process that occurs only in cells with nuclei. A moneran cell has one circular chromosome made of DNA. As cell fission begins, the chromosome attaches to the inside of the cell membrane and a duplicate is formed (Figure 17-1). The new chromosome also attaches to the cell membrane at a point near the first chromosome. While this attachment occurs, a new cell membrane and cell wall form, and the cell gets longer. At the center of the cell, more new membrane and cell wall form and begin to push inward. As the new membrane and wall grow inward, the two chromosomes become separated. Two separate daughter cells are formed, each with the same genetic material.

Fission is the most important form of reproduction in the blue-green algae. Bacteria most often reproduce asexually by fission, but other forms of reproduction are also possible (Section 17:5). Under ideal conditions, some bacteria can reproduce by fission every twenty minutes.

17:2 Fission in Eukaryotes

Fission in eukaryotes involves mitosis.

Eukaryotic cells have true nuclei and reproduce by mitosis. Mitosis results in the production of the cells of a multicellular organism. It is also the process that occurs during fission in unicellular forms such as *Amoeba*, *Euglena*, *Paramecium*, some fungi, and many one-celled algae.

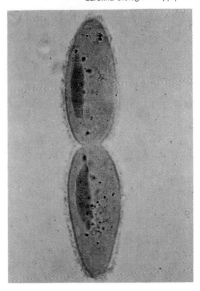

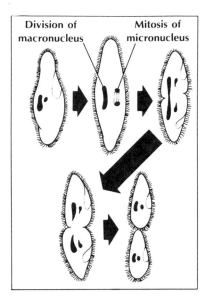

Division of macronucleus   Mitosis of micronucleus

FIGURE 17-2. When *Paramecium* reproduces asexually by fission both macronucleus and micronucleus divide, the micronucleus dividing by mitosis.

In organisms such as *Amoeba* and *Euglena*, fission may occur as often as once each day. Chromosomes replicate, become attached to spindle fibers, and identical sets are pulled to each end of the cell. The cell membrane then pinches in to form two distinct offspring.

Fission in *Paramecium* is more complex. This organism contains a macronucleus and one or more micronuclei (Section 13:9). As reproduction occurs, the chromosomes of both nuclei replicate. The division of the macronucleus does not involve mitosis. It appears to "stretch out" and pull apart into two equal-sized parts. The micronucleus divides by mitosis. Its chromosomes are pulled to opposite poles of the cell. The cell membrane pinches in midway along the length of the cell, and two daughter cells are produced. Each new *Paramecium* has one of each type of nucleus (Figure 17-2).

Paramecium is a complex cell with specialized parts such as the oral groove and contractile vacuoles. As fission occurs, the oral groove disappears. New oral grooves begin forming at each end of *Paramecium* before the original cell has finished its division. At the same time, new contractile vacuoles begin to form in each half of the parent cell. Both the oral grooves and contractile vacuoles are fully formed by the time the daughter cells separate.

17:3 Budding and Fragmentation

Budding is a type of asexual reproduction in which an outgrowth forms on the parent organism. This outgrowth eventually breaks off, and the "bud" then grows into a complete organism.

Teaching suggestion: You may find it necessary to review mitosis with your students.

In *Paramecium*, the macronucleus divides without mitosis, but mitosis occurs in the division of the micronucleus.

New specialized cell parts of *Paramecium* form as the cell divides.

In budding, an outgrowth develops on and then breaks away from the parent organism.

FIGURE 17-3. Yeast cells reproduce asexually by budding, a process in which outgrowths of the cell, buds, grow and eventually break away. The photo shows a budding yeast cell magnified about 3600 times.

Barbara Stevens

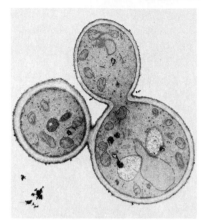

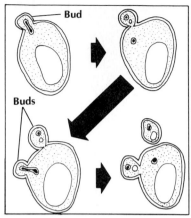

Budding can occur in both unicellular and multicellular organisms. Because it occurs with mitosis, offspring have the same traits as the parent. Yeast, a unicellular fungus, may reproduce asexually by budding (Figure 17-3). In a yeast cell, a portion of the cell wall grows out to form a bud. When the nucleus replicates, one of the nuclei remains in the parent cell and the other one moves to the bud. The new cell may give rise to a chain of buds or may be pinched off. Yeasts can also reproduce in other ways (Sections 17:2 and 17:6).

In fragmentation, a piece of an organism breaks off and becomes a new organism.

Breaking off of large parts of an organism can lead to another form of asexual reproduction called **fragmentation**. For example, certain blue-green algae such as *Nostoc* may break apart into two or more smaller filaments. The breaks usually occur at a heterocyst. **Heterocysts** (HET uh roh sihsts) are special cells in the filament that have thick walls, no DNA, and that appear empty. After fragmentation, each filament adds new cells by fission.

17:4 Spore Formation

Some organisms develop asexually from spores. Each **spore** is a specialized cell that contains DNA and a small mass of cytoplasm enclosed within a tough outer wall. The wall protects the spore until conditions are favorable for development.

Anabaena is a filamentous blue-green alga. Along the filament are special oval cells with thick walls. These cells are spores. Because of their thick walls, these spores can resist harsh winter conditions. They may remain dormant in a pond during the winter and begin their development the next spring.

Endospore formation in bacteria (Section 13:3) is not a form of asexual reproduction. It is an adaptation that allows survival of adverse conditions, but does not result in propagation of new bacteria.

One phylum of protozoans, Sporozoa (Section 13:11), reproduces by spores. The nucleus of the parent cell undergoes mitosis many times to form the spores. The parent cell later bursts, releasing the spores which develop in a particular host. *Plasmodium*, which causes malaria (Section 19:8), is an example of a sporozoan.

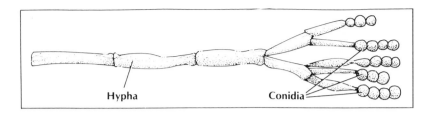

Hypha   Conidia

FIGURE 17-4. *Penicillium* **mold produces conidia at the ends of the hyphae. The brush shape of the hyphae with conidiospores gave rise to the mold's name. The Latin word for small brush is** *penicillus.*

Asexual reproduction by spores occurs in different ways in many types of fungi. The common bread mold, *Rhizopus* (Section 13:13), produces thousands of spores by mitosis in each **sporangium**. The sporangium breaks open, releasing the spores which may be carried by wind or animals. If a spore lands in a suitable environment, it will develop into new hyphae.

Fungi reproduce asexually by spores.

Penicillium molds may also reproduce asexually by spores. These molds have hyphae called **conidiophores** (kuh NIHD ee uh forz). They are so named because by mitosis chains of spores called **conidia** (kuh NIHD ee uh) form at their tips (Figure 17-4). Each spore may develop into a new mold.

REVIEWING YOUR IDEAS

1. What is asexual reproduction?
2. How do asexually reproduced offspring compare genetically with their parent and one another?
3. Distinguish between fission in prokaryotes and eukaryotes.
4. Distinguish between budding and fragmentation.
5. What is a spore?

1. Asexual reproduction is the production of one or more offspring from a single parent.
2. They are all identical.
3. Fission in prokaryotes does not involve mitosis, whereas fission in eukaryotes does.
4. In budding, a new organism forms on the parent and then breaks away. In fragmentation, a piece of the parent breaks off and then becomes a new organism.
5. A spore is a specialized reproductive cell containing DNA and cytoplasm and enclosed by a tough outer wall.

SEXUAL REPRODUCTION

Asexual reproduction is a *division* process which involves one parent. However, the opposite is true of sexual reproduction. **Sexual reproduction** is the *fusion* (union) of two sets of DNA which usually come from different parents.

Sexual reproduction is the union of two sets of DNA.

Fusion of different sets of DNA results in genetic recombination (Section 6:12) and variety among offspring. Variety in offspring shows as new features. Because of this variety, *sexually reproducing organisms can adapt to changing environments.* This advantage explains the fact that almost all types of organisms have some means of sexual reproduction in their life cycles.

Sexual reproduction provides variety among offspring.

In simple organisms, conjugation is a common form of sexual reproduction. **Conjugation** (kahn juh GAY shun) is the fusion of nuclear material of two cells. Unlike sexual reproduction in more complex organisms, simple conjugation does not involve gametes.

Conjugation involves fusion of nuclear material but does not involve gametes.

FIGURE 17-5. When bacteria conjugate, genes move from the F⁺ cell into the F⁻ cell. Conjugating bacteria are shown magnified about 21 000 times.

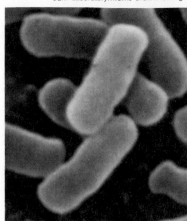

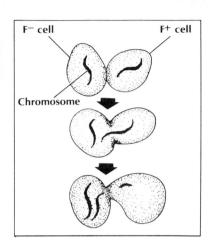

17:5 Conjugation and Transformation in Bacteria

Although bacteria usually reproduce asexually by fission, they may also reproduce sexually by conjugation. Bacteria have no distinct sexes, but different mating types do exist. One is called F⁺. *F* stands for **fertility factor.** F⁺ bacteria have this factor. It is located on a plasmid (Section 9:1). The other type, F⁻, has no fertility factor.

During bacterial conjugation, genes are transferred from F⁺ to F⁻ bacteria.

Only F⁺ and F⁻ bacteria can conjugate. During conjugation, bridges of cytoplasm form between bacteria. The plasmid of the F⁺ type moves through the bridge and into the F⁻ cell. The F⁻ cell then contains its own DNA plus DNA from another cell.

Not only the fertility factor, but other genes on the plasmid also are transferred. Recall that some of these genes make bacteria resistant to antibiotics. An F⁻ bacterium with no resistance to antibiotics could become resistant as a result of conjugation. This resistance results from genetic recombination.

Bacterial recombination may also occur as a result of transduction (Section 17:8).

In bacteria, recombination can result from transformation.

Another form of genetic recombination also occurs in bacteria. **Transformation** (Section 9:1) occurs when one bacterium breaks open and part of its DNA enters another bacterium. Recall that transformation occurred in *Pneumococcus* cells. It caused a change in the genotype and phenotype of rough cells. The rough cells, which did not cause pneumonia, were changed to smooth cells that did cause the disease.

17:6 Conjugation in Other Organisms

In addition to asexual reproduction by means of spores, bread mold may reproduce sexually by a conjugationlike process. This process involves different types of hyphae, called *plus* and *minus*. Branches grow from each of these hyphae and meet. The tip of each branch becomes a separate cell and acts as a "gamete." The

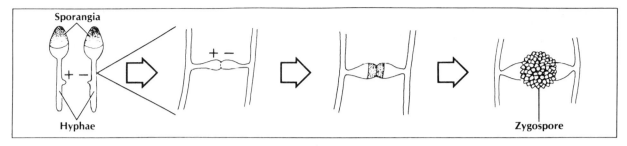

"gametes" fuse to form a resistant zygote called a zygospore (Figure 17-6). The zygospore goes through a dormant period. Later, the zygospore grows, meiosis occurs, and new hyphae develop from the spores produced.

Other fungi also undergo sexual reproduction. In yeasts, individual cells can fuse to form a zygote. The zygote can bud or it can undergo meiosis to form four spores. The zygote is modified into an ascus (Section 13:15) which holds the spores. Spores are then freed and develop into separate cells. Figure 17-7 shows the entire life cycle of the yeast.

In club fungi such as mushrooms, different types of underground hyphae fuse and produce the rest of the mycelium. Cells of the basidia (Section 13:14) contain two nuclei. These nuclei fuse to form a zygote. The zygote then undergoes meiosis to produce four spores. Each spore may develop into a new underground mycelium.

FIGURE 17-6. Bread mold reproduces sexually by a conjugationlike process. A resistant zygote called a zygospore results.

Conjugation is common in many fungi.

REVIEWING YOUR IDEAS

6. What is sexual reproduction?
7. How do sexually reproduced offspring compare genetically with their parents and one another?
8. What is conjugation? Name several organisms in which it occurs.
9. What is transformation?

6. Sexual reproduction is the fusion of two sets of DNA.
7. They are genetically different.
8. Conjugation is the fusion of the nuclear material of two cells after formation of a conjugation tube. It occurs in bacteria. A conjugationlike process also occurs in certain fungi.
9. Transformation occurs when one bacterium breaks open and part of its DNA enters another bacterium.

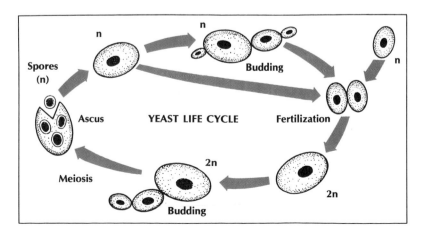

FIGURE 17-7. Both monoploid and diploid cells exist in the life cycle of yeasts. The life cycle shows asexual and sexual reproduction.

PEOPLE IN BIOLOGY

It was not until after he studied astronomy and physics in college that Max Delbrück found a scientific "home" in biology. In 1937, Delbrück left his German homeland and moved to the California Institute of Technology (Caltech). There, Delbrück became fascinated with viruses and their method and rate of reproduction. Very little was known at this time about viral reproduction, except that a virus invades a bacterium, reproduces at a fast rate, and then the offspring explode from the bacterial cell. Dr. Delbrück wanted to see if different types of viruses could reproduce inside a single bacterial cell. He injected two different types of viruses into one bacterium, and then he examined the offspring. Delbrück found viruses like the two he had injected. He also found new viruses which had been produced by a recombination of DNA from the two viruses that had been injected into the bacterial cell. Delbrück had shown that two viruses, if present in the same bacterial cell, could exchange DNA when reproducing. For this discovery, and for his other work on viruses, Max Delbrück was awarded the Nobel Prize in 1969.

As physics instructor at Vanderbilt University and biology professor at Caltech, he was a model for many scientists doing research. Besides the Nobel Prize, Dr. Delbrück received the Kimber Genetics Award in 1965 and was elected to the National Academy of Sciences in 1949.

(1906 - 1981)

Max Delbrück

FIGURE 17-8. Viruses can reproduce only by infecting living cells. Bacteriophages, shown magnified about 31 000 times, are shown infecting a bacterium.

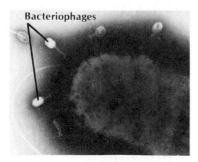

Bacteriophages

Barbara Stevens

REPRODUCTION IN VIRUSES

Viruses (Section 13:17) are unique particles which have no cellular structure or metabolism. In fact, their only lifelike characteristic is their ability to reproduce. Even their reproduction can only occur within a *specific* host cell. As "reproductive parasites," viruses may cause illness in or death to their hosts.

17:7 Bacteriophage Life Cycles

A virus which attacks a bacterium is called a **bacteriophage** (bak TIHR ee uh fayj), or simply a **phage**. Like all viruses, phages have an outer coat of protein. Inside the phage is a core of DNA. The phage has a tail-like portion by which it attaches to a bacterial cell. It "recognizes" a specific host because the bacterium has special receptors in its wall. It is thought that a protein in the tail reacts with the receptor. Part of the tail pierces the cell wall, and the phage's DNA is injected into the bacterium. The viral DNA takes over the bacterial cell and uses the bacterium's materials, enzymes, ATP, and cell parts to reproduce. How this process occurs is not completely understood.

Within a very short time, the bacterium splits open releasing many new virus particles (Figure 17-9). This breaking open of bacteria or other cells by viruses is called **lysis** (LI sus). The viral life cycle causing lysis is called the **lytic cycle**. The new phages continue the cycle by attacking other bacteria.

Sometimes a phage infects a host cell but does not destroy it. The DNA of the phage becomes part of the bacterium's DNA and is replicated right along with the bacterial DNA when the bacterium reproduces (Figure 17- 9). This viral life cycle is called the **lysogenic** (li suh JEN ihk) **cycle**. A virus which has become part of its host's DNA is called a **provirus**. The provirus may even cause some phenotypic changes among the resulting bacteria. Also, the viral genes prevent other viruses from infecting the bacteria. Eventually, certain changes occur and the bacterial cells begin making new phages. The bacteria then lyse and release the phages. It is thought that many organisms, including humans, have proviruses in their cells. Genes of the proviruses may affect the phenotypes of the host organism. In time, changes within the body of the host or from outside sources may affect proviruses and trigger them to become active again. Some diseases may occur as proviruses change to active forms and destroy their host cells.

Phage DNA makes use of bacterial materials to direct the production of more phages.

In the lytic cycle, viruses reproduce, destroy host cells, and then attack other host cells.

In the lysogenic cycle, the viral DNA becomes part of and replicates along with the host cell's DNA.

FIGURE 17-9. Phage DNA enters a host cell. It may take over the host's metabolic "machinery" to produce new phages (shown on left). Or it may attach to the host's DNA, divide when the host cell divides (shown on right), and then take over the "machinery." Many phages are released when the host cell lyses.

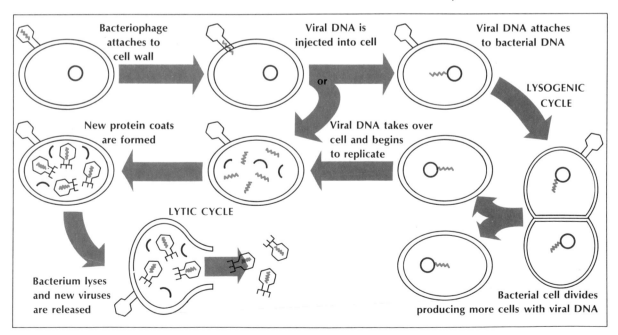

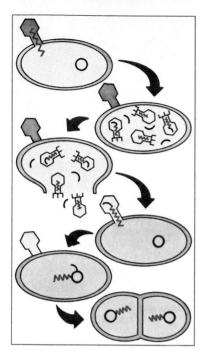

FIGURE 17-10. In transduction, a newly formed virus picks up part of the bacterial chromosome. The bacterial chromosome is then transferred to another bacterium when the virus infects it. Here part of the chromosome of the yellow cell is transferred to the green cell by the virus, and the chromosome part becomes incorporated and reproduced by the green cell.

Whether viruses cause tumors in humans is still controversial.

Some tumor viruses have RNA, rather than DNA.

The life cycles of bacteriophages are generally similar to those of other viruses which attack other kinds of cells. Nonbacterial viruses may enter their host cells whole. But, like phages, only their nucleic acid is important for reproduction. Sometimes the nucleic acid is RNA. Many plant viruses are carried by insects which may inject them through the tough walls of plant cells.

17:8 Transduction

Because viral DNA can combine with bacterial DNA, sometimes a new phage is formed that contains a small portion of the chromosome of the bacteria. If this phage then attacks a different bacterium, it will inject this portion of the first host's chromosome into the second host. This process is known as **transduction** (trans DUK shun) (Figure 17-10). Transduction is a source of variety among bacteria.

Transduction can be used to learn about the genes of bacterial cells. Some geneticists feel that a transduction process might be a method of introducing a normal gene into a person lacking that gene.

REVIEWING YOUR IDEAS

10. What is required for a virus to reproduce?
11. What is a bacteriophage?
12. What part of a virus is involved in its reproduction?

10. A virus needs a specific host cell to reproduce.
11. A bacteriophage is a virus which attacks bacteria.
12. The nucleic acid of a virus is involved in its reproduction.

ADVANCES IN BIOLOGY

17:9 RNA Tumor Viruses

Many viruses have been suspected of causing cancer (Section 19:13) in certain animals. One group of viruses, however, is known to cause tumors in animals. These viruses are interesting because their hereditary material and life cycle are unusual variations of the pattern shown for other viruses in this chapter. The process of tumor formation is complicated, but there is hope that the study of RNA tumor viruses will aid in the development of methods to prevent cancer.

Some tumor viruses are quite similar to other DNA viruses, but those discussed here have RNA as their genetic material. RNA tumor virus particles contain a coat of protein around the genetic material. The virus core, RNA and protein coat, is surrounded by a lipid envelope that resembles the outer membrane of the cell that produced the virus. As you will see, the virus structure is largely explained by its life cycle.

RNA tumor viruses seem to defy the principles that describe the replication of genetic material (Chapter 9). Their life cycle is different in that it requires an extra step. The extra step is essential because of the kind of genetic material they have. The RNA that is present in these viruses is single-stranded and so it requires a step that changes it into a form that can be replicated.

The life cycle begins when a virus particle infects a living cell. The virus envelope fuses with the cell membrane and the inner core enters the cell in a process that resembles pinocytosis (Section 5:9). The RNA comes out of the protein coat in a process called **uncoating.** These steps are similar to the general steps for other animal viruses up to this point.

Once free RNA is inside the infected cell, it is copied by an enzyme called reverse transcriptase to form a double-stranded molecule. One strand of this molecule is the infecting RNA and the other is the newly-made DNA strand. The formation of this DNA/RNA molecule is an essential step in the life cycle and is unique to RNA viruses. This copying resembles transcription (Section 9:7) but is called **reverse transcription** because an RNA master is used to make a DNA copy. The RNA strand is then replaced by a DNA and the resulting double-stranded DNA molecule becomes circular. The DNA contains all of the genetic information of the infecting virus.

The DNA enters the cell nucleus and becomes a provirus, part of the DNA of the infected cell. From the nucleus of the infected cell, the viral genes are expressed in a way much like the other genes of the cell are expressed.

The steps above of reverse transcription and provirus formation are needed so that many copies of the viral RNA can be made. These steps are essential to this life cycle. The RNA copies then are used to program the making of proteins for the new coats and to become new RNA strands for inside the new viruses. When viruses are assembled, they move to the inner side of the cell membrane where they are enveloped in cell membrane as they leave the infected cell. The exit process is similar to the entry process but in reverse.

While some viruses disrupt normal cell functions and kill the infected cells, RNA tumor viruses do not kill the cells. In this way, an infected cell can produce many new viral particles. The new viruses can infect other cells and produce still more viruses. While some viruses completely assembled within the cell break the cell open (Section 17:7) when they leave, RNA tumor viruses exit the infected cells without breaking them.

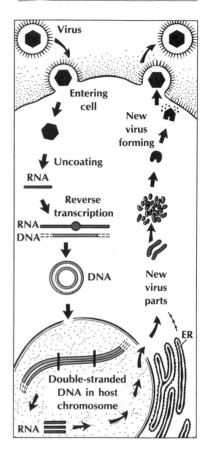

FIGURE 17-11. An RNA tumor virus enters a cell and undergoes reverse transcription. The DNA becomes incorporated in a host cell chromosome and new viral parts are made. The viruses are assembled within the host cell and exit without breaking the cell open.

After reverse transcription, RNA copies direct the synthesis of proteins and more RNA needed for the production of more viruses.

RNA tumor viruses do not destroy host cells as they leave them.

CHAPTER REVIEW

SUMMARY

1. Asexual reproduction involves the production of one or more offspring from a single parent. Since all offspring are genetically identical, asexual reproduction does not increase variety.

2. Asexual reproduction in simple organisms is by fission, budding, and fragmentation.

3. Spore formation is a means of asexual reproduction involving the production of special reproductive cells.

4. Sexual reproduction is the fusion of two sets of DNA. It results in genetic recombination and variety among offspring.

5. Most sexual reproduction in simple organisms occurs by conjugation, the fusion of nuclear materials of two cells.

6. Transformation is a possible source of genetic recombination in bacteria.

7. Viruses reproduce only at the expense of a specific host cell. The life cycle of a virus may be either lytic or lysogenic.

8. During transduction, a portion of one bacterial chromosome may be injected into another bacterium. This process gives another source of variety among bacteria.

9. RNA tumor viruses have a unique form of reproduction in which DNA is made from RNA. The DNA then enters the nucleus of the infected cell.

LANGUAGE OF BIOLOGY

asexual reproduction	lysogenic cycle
bacteriophage	lytic cycle
budding	provirus
conidia	reverse transcription
conidiophore	sexual reproduction
conjugation	sporangium
fertility factor	spore
fission	transduction
fragmentation	transformation
heterocyst	uncoating

CHECKING YOUR IDEAS

On a separate paper, complete each statement by filling in the blank with the best term. Do not write in this book.

1. Sexual reproduction involves the fusion of two sets of _____.

2. Most sexual reproduction in simple organisms occurs by _____.

3. Blue-green algae have only _____ reproduction.

4. During _____, DNA of one bacterium moves into another bacterium.

5. _____ reproduction results in genetic recombination.

6. During conjugation in bacteria, _____ _____, as well as plasmid genes, is transferred from one bacterium to another.

7. In a certain form of asexual reproduction called _____, an outgrowth forms on the parent organism.

8. Fission in prokaryotes does not involve the process of _____.

9. A virus which attacks a bacterium is called a(n) _____.

10. During the _____ cycle of viruses, the host cell is destroyed.

EVALUATING YOUR IDEAS

1. Describe the process of fission among monerans.

2. How is fission in eukaryotes different from that in prokaryotes? Describe fission in *Paramecium*.

3. How does asexual reproduction occur in yeasts?

4. Compare asexual reproduction by spores in *Rhizopus* and *Penicillium*.

5. How are the tough outer walls of spores adaptive?

CHAPTER REVIEW

6. How is sexual reproduction more advantageous than asexual reproduction?
7. Describe conjugation in bacteria.
8. Discuss two ways other than conjugation which may lead to genetic recombination in bacteria.
9. Describe sexual reproduction in *Rhizopus*.
10. Compare sexual reproduction in yeasts and mushrooms.
11. Describe the process by which a bacteriophage reproduces.
12. Do viruses always destroy their host cells? Explain.
13. List two ways RNA tumor viruses differ from other viruses.
14. What is reverse transcriptase? What does it do in the viral reproduction process?

APPLYING YOUR IDEAS

1. Consider the complete life cycle of *Rhizopus* and yeast. Which structure(s) is (are) monoploid? Which is (are) diploid?
2. Normal bacteria can synthesize substances A, B, C, and D from a basic growth medium. These substances are essential for life. Two mutants are found. One cannot synthesize A and B. The other cannot synthesize C and D. The two mutants are transferred to a basic medium. Soon a few colonies of bacteria occur. How might this result be explained?
3. Why were the mutants in question 2 above not able to synthesize certain substances?
4. After conjugation, what is the mating type of the original F⁻ bacterium? Explain.
5. Why can asexual reproduction be called "multiplication by division"?
6. Explain why viruses usually cause disease in their hosts.
7. How is it adaptive that RNA tumor viruses do not lyse their host's cells?

EXTENDING YOUR IDEAS

1. Start a yeast culture by adding either powdered or cake yeast to a solution of sugar water. Take samples from the culture and prepare wet mount slides. Observe the yeast cells for signs of budding. Does the amount of budding vary in different sugar solutions?
2. Using library sources, find out about "high frequency recombination" (Hfr) bacteria. Compare their means of conjugation with that which occurs between F⁺ and F⁻ bacteria.
3. Examine bread mold or mold growing on fruit with a binocular microscope or hand lens. Identify and describe spore-producing structures which you may observe. If necessary, transfer a small portion of the mycelium to a clean slide, prepare a wet mount, and observe under high and low power of a compound microscope.
4. You have learned that asexual reproduction in *Paramecium* is a complex process. Find out how *Paramecium* reproduces sexually.

SUGGESTED READINGS

Campbell, Allan, "How Viruses Insert Their DNA into the DNA of the Host Cell." *Scientific American*, December, 1976.

Dixon, Bernard, *Magnificent Microbes*. New York, Athenum, 1976.

Gibbons, Don L., "Closing in on the Virus-Cancer Link." *Sciquest*, April, 1981.

Levine, Arnold J., "Cancer and Viruses." *Chemistry*, May, 1977.

Sanders, F. Kingsley, *Viruses*, 2nd ed. Burlington, NC, Carolina Biological Supply Co., 1981.

Weiner, Jack, *Microorganism Control*. Appleton, WI, Institute of Paper Chemistry, 1977.

Additional student readings and suggested teacher readings are provided in the Teacher's Guide.

Ann Kramer

Simple organisms carry out life functions other than reproduction. They must obtain and digest food, eliminate wastes, and distribute needed materials within and among cells. How is this fungus obtaining food? How is the food distributed from cell to cell in the fungus? How do other simple organisms carry out other life functions?

Introduction and suggested demonstration: Most functions of simple organisms are not readily observable because of the organisms' small sizes and lack of specialized structures. However, response to chemicals can be demonstrated using various protozoa. For example, *Paramecium* swims toward food. To study the effect of chemicals, add a drop of hydrochloric or acetic acid to the edge of a coverslip covering a wet mount of *Paramecium*. The *Paramecium* should be seen moving away from the incoming acid and may discharge trichocysts as well. The demonstration can lead to a discussion introducing life processes other than reproduction in simple organisms.

Chapter

18

SIMPLE ORGANISMS: OTHER LIFE FUNCTIONS

Chapter 18 presents nutrition, transport, gas exchange, excretion, locomotion, and responses in simple organisms.

In Chapter 17, you learned how the simplest organisms reproduce. In this chapter, you will study how these simple living things carry out other vital functions. To survive, they must carry out the same functions that more complex organisms do. Yet, most of these organisms are one-celled, and all lack true tissues and organs. Each function they have involves interaction with the environment in some way.

GOAL: You will gain an understanding of the life functions of monerans, protists, and fungi.

NUTRITION

Chemicals within cells constantly react to form new substances. Some new substances are being built while others are being torn down. Where do these substances come from?

Each cell gets what it needs from its environment. Once the needed substances are inside the cell, they can be used as is or rearranged to form other substances. For example, glucose may be used as an energy source in cell respiration or may become part of a larger molecule that is stored. In general, materials required by cells are called **nutrients** (NEW tree unts). Nutrients may be complex or simple compounds, or mineral ions.

Each cell obtains needed materials from its environment.

18:1 Nutrient Requirements

You learned in Chapter 12 that autotrophs are organisms that make their own food, and heterotrophs are organisms that feed on other living or once-living things. Autotrophs and heterotrophs have different nutrients that they need.

Teaching suggestion: Stress the fundamental difference between autotrophs and heterotrophs before proceeding. Be certain that students understand the need for digestion in heterotrophs. Heterotrophs ingest complex, organic molecules that must be broken down to enter cells.

TABLE 18-1. MAJOR FOOD SOURCES AND THE PRODUCTS OF DIGESTION	
Food Type	Digestive Products
Carbohydrates	Simple sugars
Fats	Fatty acids, glycerol
Proteins	Amino acids

Teaching suggestion: You may want to review with students the above macromolecules and the simpler molecules of which they are made.

Chemical digestion involves hydrolysis reactions.

Heterotrophs require water, minerals, and vitamins.

Essential nutrients are those which must be obtained from the environment.

Autotrophs need carbon dioxide and water which they make into sugar. Sugar may be changed to starch, fat, or other compounds. Autotrophs need things other than carbon dioxide and water, too. For example, to make amino acids calls for nitrogen and sometimes sulfur, and to make chlorophyll calls for magnesium. *In general, autotrophs take in simple nutrients and change them to complex substances.*

Heterotrophs cannot make their own food and thus, *they ingest or absorb complex, organic molecules.* These molecules are too big to pass through cell membranes; they first are broken into small molecules. The process by which an organism breaks large molecules into smaller ones is called **digestion**. Small molecules can pass through cell membranes, and then once inside the cells, they can be used.

Digestion involves chemical changes caused by enzymes in the breakdown of large molecules. Hydrolysis is the breaking down of large molecules into small ones by adding water (Section 3:17). Table 18-1 lists the major food types and the forms into which they are digested.

Heterotrophs require water and small amounts of minerals and vitamins just like autotrophs do. Minerals are ingested as ions in foods or water. Although they may be complex, vitamins are easily absorbed and need not be broken down. Many vitamins are known to be coenzymes (Section 4:6).

In general, simple heterotrophs can make more of their needed substances than more complex organisms can. Bacteria, for example, can synthesize needed materials from a very few basic nutrients. The nutrients which an organism must obtain from its environment are called **essential nutrients**. Sugar is an essential nutrient for most heterotrophs.

18:2 Digestion Within Simple Autotrophs

Organisms such as blue-green algae, euglenoids, diatoms, dinoflagellates, and some bacteria are autotrophs. They take in *small*, inorganic molecules and mineral ions by passive or active transport. By photosynthesis they make organic molecules such as glucose, amino acids, and ATP.

Digestion does occur in these organisms, too. For example, starch is a complex molecule made from excess glucose and stored in cells. When the supply of glucose is decreased, enzymes in the cells hydrolyze the starch to glucose molecules. Then the glucose can be "burned" for energy. The breakdown of molecules in these organisms occurs inside the cells and is called **intracellular** (in truh SEL yuh lur) **digestion**. To some extent, intracellular digestion occurs in all organisms.

Digestion within cells is called intracellular digestion.

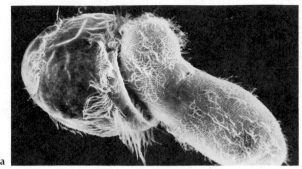

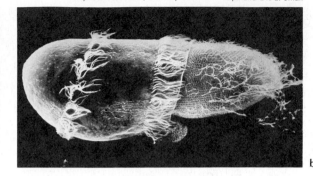

a

b

18:3 Digestion Within Simple Heterotrophs

Digestion is intracellular in protozoa. Because these organisms live in water, their food supply often surrounds them. They have many adaptations which help their chances to obtain food. Amoebae trap and ingest food by phagocytosis (Section 5:9) and the food is enclosed within a **food vacuole** (Figure 18-2). The food, which may be other small protozoa or algae, is digested within the vacuole. Enzymes for digestion are within lysosomes (Section 5:12) which fuse with the food vacuole. The food that is digested into small molecules can diffuse across the vacuole membrane and into the amoeba's cytoplasm. Undigested food remains in the vacuole. This food leaves the cell by exocytosis (Section 5:9). In general, elimination of undigested food is called **egestion**.

In *Paramecium* (Figure 18-2), currents caused by the beating of cilia draw food into the **oral groove**. The food is swept down the groove where it collects. A food vacuole forms around it. As in *Amoeba*, food vacuoles fuse with lysosomes and digestion occurs. As a vacuole moves slowly through the cytoplasm of the *Paramecium*, small molecules diffuse out across the vacuole membrane. Movement of the vacuole allows distribution of digested food to all parts of this cell. Undigested food remains in the food vacuole until the vacuole fuses with the **anal pore** where egestion occurs.

FIGURE 18-1. *Didinium,* a ciliate (a) captures and (b) ingests whole another ciliate, *Paramecium*. The organisms, shown magnified about 500 times, are both simple heterotrophs.

Many protozoa digest food in special food vacuoles.

Lysosomes fuse with food vacuoles and provide the enzymes necessary for digestion.

Egestion is the elimination of undigested food.

Food is drawn into the oral groove of a *Paramecium* by the action of cilia.

FIGURE 18-2. (a) *Amoeba* traps and ingests food by phagocytosis. (b) *Paramecium* draws food into the oral groove by beating cilia.

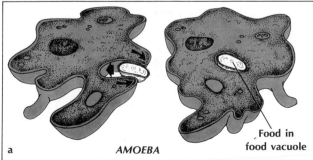

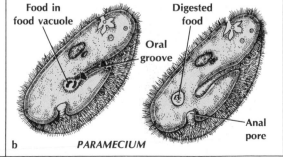

a   AMOEBA   Food in food vacuole

Food in food vacuole   Digested food   Oral groove   Anal pore

b   PARAMECIUM

Teaching suggestion: Explain to students that leaf litter that they might see in a forest has cottonlike fibers running through it. These fibers are mycelium of fungi.

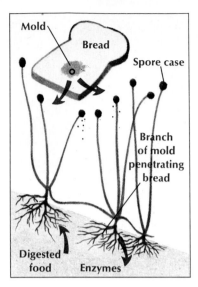

FIGURE 18-3. Enzymes secreted from rhizoids of bread mold digest starch in the bread. Glucose molecules then are absorbed.

FIGURE 18-4. Some fungi have adaptations allowing them to capture nematodes. This fungus, *Arthrobotrys oligospora*, forms hyphal rings in which worms, in this case *Ditylenchus dipsaci*, become trapped. The fungus then digests the worm and absorbs the food.

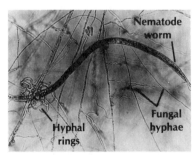

Courtesy of USDA, Beltsville, MD

1. Nutrients are materials required by cells.
2. Digestion involves the breakdown of large molecules to smaller ones. Intracellular digestion occurs in cells, whereas extracellular digestion occurs outside cells.
3. Intracellular digestion occurs in most autotrophs, bacteria, and protozoa. In general, fungi have extracellular digestion and absorb simple molecules.

18:4 Digestion by Fungi

Fungi must obtain food from their hosts or substances upon which they live. Unlike protozoa (or animals), fungi do not ingest chunks of food and then digest it. Instead, they first digest food outside their cells, a process called **extracellular** (ek struh SEL yuh lur) **digestion**. After it is digested, the food is absorbed by the fungus.

As an example of extracellular digestion in fungi, consider *Rhizopus* (Figure 18-3), common bread mold. *Rhizopus* usually obtains nourishment from bread. Because carbohydrates in bread are in starch form, they must be digested. Enzymes which change the starch to glucose are secreted from the rhizoids of the mold into the bread. Rhizoids absorb the glucose, and it is then moved to the rest of the plant.

Other saprophytic fungi, such as mushrooms or cup fungi (Section 13:14), digest and absorb food as bread mold does. Recall that these fungi have a large underground mycelium. These hyphae secrete enzymes into the soil or decaying material. Digestion of organic materials is extracellular. Small molecules are absorbed by the hyphae and then pass to other cells by diffusion.

Many fungi are parasitic, obtaining nutrients from plant or animal hosts. In so doing, they may cause disease and economic loss. For example, fungi cause damage to crops such as wheat (Section 19:4).

Some small fungi live within individual cells of their host and may directly absorb food without digestion. Other forms send hyphae into or between cells of the host. The hyphae secrete enzymes, digest food, and then absorb the digested food, which passes to other cells by diffusion.

Some fungi have adaptations for trapping small animals, such as nematode worms (Section 15:6). The hyphae of some of these fungi are sticky. Nematodes stick to the hyphae and become trapped. Other "predator" fungi have hyphae which form a ring of cells. If a nematode enters the ring, the cells swell and trap the worm. In either case, other hyphae penetrate the worms. Digestion and absorption of digested food then occur as in other fungi.

REVIEWING YOUR IDEAS

1. What are nutrients?
2. What is digestion? Distinguish between intracellular and extracellular digestion.
3. Which type of digestion occurs in autotrophs? In bacteria? Protozoa? Fungi?

OTHER LIFE PROCESSES

In addition to nutrients, organisms must obtain other materials from their environment and distribute them within cells or from cell to cell. Waste materials are deposited in the environment. Also, many living things must have a way of moving in their environment. Finally, they must be able to respond to their environment.

18:5 Transport

Organisms transport or move materials within a cell or between cells. The transported substances include gases, such as oxygen and carbon dioxide. They also include food molecules and certain wastes. Because monerans, protists, and fungi are unicellular, or composed of relatively few cells, substances within them do not have to be transported very far.

In unicellular forms, such as bacteria, simple algae, and protozoa, materials are often distributed by diffusion. Also, the cytoplasm of most cells flows in movements called **cytoplasmic streaming.** Streaming helps to distribute larger substances such as food. It moves materials more quickly than diffusion.

Although some simple organisms have more than one cell, the organisms still are usually small. Also, in many forms, such as filamentous blue-green algae, each cell is independent. That is, it acts almost like a separate "organism." Therefore, transport in these forms occurs as it does in unicellular organisms. Fungi are larger organisms, but they have no special tissues for transport. They, too, distribute materials by diffusion and streaming.

Diffusion and cytoplasmic streaming help to move materials within cells.

No specialized transport tissues exist in simple organisms.

18:6 Gas Exchange

Oxygen and carbon dioxide are gases important to almost all living systems. In autotrophs, carbon dioxide is a raw material of photosynthesis, and oxygen is given off as a by-product. Most heterotrophs and autotrophs require oxygen to "burn" food for energy in the process of cellular respiration (Section 4:8). All organisms obtain needed gases from and release others to the environment. In general, this movement of oxygen and carbon dioxide between organisms and their environment is called **gas exchange**.

In order for gases to pass into or out of cells, they must be dissolved in water or another liquid. Thus, moisture is needed for gas exchange to occur. Most simple organisms live in water or a moist environment in a host. Fungi live on land, but only in damp areas.

Gas exchange is the movement of oxygen and carbon dioxide between organisms and their environments.

Gas exchange depends upon moisture.

FIGURE 18-5. Simple organisms that exchange gases solely by diffusion live in wet environments. The gas exchange in organisms such as these fungi depends on moisture.

Cells of simple organisms exchange gases directly with the environment.

In unicellular organisms, gases are exchanged by diffusion across the cell membrane. Diffusion accounts for gas exchange in simple multicellular organisms, too. In filamentous blue-green algae, each cell is in direct contact with the environment. Thus, each cell can exchange gases directly. Sometimes an organism is several cells thick, and diffusion can still serve as the means of gas exchange. Each cell is close enough to the external environment.

18:7 Excretion

Because metabolism occurs constantly within all living systems, cells produce many needed products and by-products. Often, the by-products are harmful and must be removed from the organism. The release and removal of by-products, or waste materials, is called **excretion** (ek SKREE shun).

Excretion is the removal of metabolic by-products.

Many chemicals are included as waste material, but what may be a waste material in one organism may not be a waste in another. Carbon dioxide is such a substance. In protozoa, carbon dioxide is a dangerous waste material, but in algae, it is a reactant in photosynthesis.

Elimination of undigested food (egestion) is not considered excretion because it does not involve removal of metabolic by-products.

Protozoa produce ammonia (NH_3) as a waste product. It is formed during the breakdown of proteins. Because it contains nitrogen, ammonia is called a **nitrogenous** (ni TRAHJ uh nus) **waste**. Ammonia is poisonous and must be removed. Protozoa are in direct contact with water. Thus, ammonia can diffuse directly into the water. It is removed without a special system.

Ammonia is a nitrogenous waste produced by protozoa.

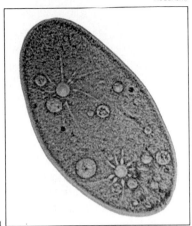

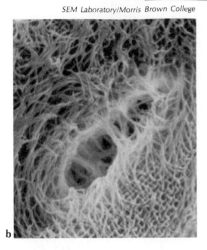

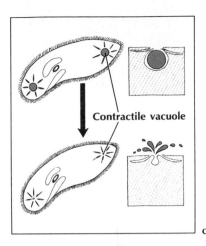

a   b   c

Contractile vacuole

FIGURE 18-6. (a) **Protozoa such as** *Paramecium* **have contractile vacuoles that remove excess water. (b) The opening of a contractile vacuole of a ciliate at the cell surface is shown magnified about 3000 times. (c) When contractile vacuoles fill, they contract, forcing water out the opening.**

Although water is not a waste product, its level must be carefully controlled by all organisms. In some cases, water must be stored, while in others, it must be removed.

Simple marine organisms have little trouble keeping a proper water balance with their environment. The salt water in which they live is like the contents of their cells. Therefore, water enters and leaves by osmosis in equal amounts.

In simple freshwater organisms, the fluid of the cells and the surrounding water are not balanced because there are more dissolved substances inside the cells. As a result, water molecules enter the cells by osmosis. Constant osmosis of water into these organisms could cause the cells to swell and burst (Section 5:5). Therefore, water must be removed.

Paramecia and many other protozoans have **contractile vacuoles** (Section 5:12) which remove water. Water entering a paramecium cell fills canals which surround these vacuoles. The water slowly passes from the canals into the vacuole. When a vacuole is full, its membrane contracts forcing the water from the vacuole and through the plasma membrane. This process requires energy.

In simple freshwater organisms, water enters the cells by osmosis.

Many protozoans have contractile vacuoles that remove excess water.

18:8 Locomotion: Amoeboid Motion

Many protozoans actively get food. To trap food, they must be able to move. Movement is also involved as they respond to their environment.

An amoeba moves by forming extensions of cytoplasm called pseudopodia (Section 13:8). This motion, **amoeboid motion**, involves cytoplasmic streaming. If you examined a living amoeba under a microscope, you would see that some of its cytoplasm flows. As it flows, it causes the membrane ahead of it to bulge outward.

Amoeboid motion involves cytoplasmic streaming.

Carolina Biological Supply Co.

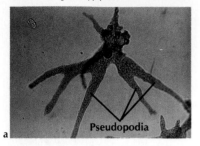

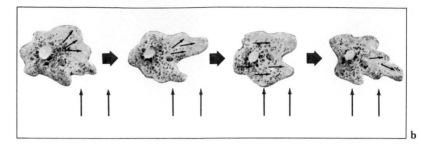

FIGURE 18-7. (a) *Amoeba proteus* **moves by (b) formation of pseudopodia. Sol-gel transformations occur as the pseudopodia form.**
Teaching suggestion: To aid students in visualizing sol-gel transformations, have students relate what happens when making gelatin. You can demonstrate the effect with warm agar in a Petri dish. Point out that the amoeba makes the changes in seconds and the changes do not involve heating/cooling.

Pseudopodia are formed by sol-gel changes in the cytoplasm.

Not all the cytoplasm in an amoeba flows freely. At certain times, part of the cytoplasm is in a more fixed, jelly-like state known as a **gel**. At other times, the cytoplasm is more like a fluid and is known as a **sol** (SAHL). Amoeboid motion depends upon changes between the sol and gel states of cytoplasm. Cytoplasm in the sol state flows toward a part of the membrane which begins to bulge out and form the pseudopodium. The cytoplasm then moves to the other side of the amoeba where it changes to a gel. The gel again changes to sol which flows toward the pseudopodium. The flow of cytoplasm is controlled by contraction of microfilaments (Section 5:12). As they contract, the microfilaments are thought to push the cytoplasm out and toward the pseudopodium.

18:9 Locomotion: Ciliary and Flagellar Motion

Many protists have either cilia or flagella (Section 5:14) for locomotion. *Paramecium* (Section 13:9) has hundreds of tiny cilia while *Euglena* (Section 13:10) moves by means of a single flagellum. Locomotion by cilia is called **ciliary** (SIHL ee er ee) **motion**, and by a flagellum it is called **flagellar motion**. ATP is a necessary energy source for this work.

Exactly how cilia and flagella operate is not known. However, the hundreds of oarlike cilia on a cell work together. Like coordinated movements of the oars of a rowboat, cilia cause motion in a certain direction.

FIGURE 18-8. Cilia beat together in a coordinated fashion moving a cell. A cilium is thought to alternate power strokes and recovery strokes in the process.

Cilia and flagella have microtubules (Section 5:12) which can contract. According to one hypothesis, contraction of certain microtubules results in their sliding over other microtubules, causing the cilium or flagellum to bend forward in a power stroke. A recovery stroke follows the power stroke. While some microtubules contract, other relax. Alternation of power strokes and recovery strokes causes locomotion (Figure 18-8).

Many bacteria also move by means of flagella. However, the flagella do not contain microtubules. Movement is not so smooth as in protozoa. The means of flagellar movement in bacteria is not known.

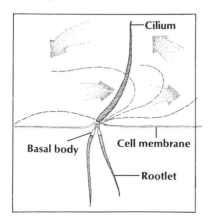

18:10 Response to Environment

All cells can respond to stimuli. If an amoeba is touched with a needle, it curls up into a ball. Somehow the stimulus is transmitted by the protoplasm. This property of cytoplasmic response is called **basic irritability**.

Some simple organisms have specialized parts for response to the environment. *Euglena* has a stigma (Section 13:10) which can detect light. Some ciliates have **neurofibrils** (noor oh FIBE rulz) which transmit impulses. In *Euplotes* (yoo PLOHD eez) the neurofibrils are connected to a control center (Figure 18-9). The control center and neurofibrils coordinate the movement of large bundles of cilia called **cirri** (SIHR i).

Response to the environment may involve a means of protection. *Paramecium* has special structures called **trichocysts** just inside the cell membrane. Certain chemical changes in the environment cause the trichocysts to discharge long threads of cytoplasm. The paramecium then has a "fuzzy" appearance. It is thought that these threads work something like spears and protect the organism.

Paramecium can also respond to objects in its way. Suppose a *Paramecium* is moving freely through a drop of water and comes into contact with an object. It will reverse the beating of its cilia and back away from the object. Then it turns at an angle of about 30° and continues to move forward. These responses continue to be made until the *Paramecium* passes by the object (Figure 18-10). The *Paramecium* does not "choose" to turn 30°. A "goal" is not involved in this behavior, but rather the protist merely "carries out" its genetic instructions for dealing with objects in its path.

4. gases and food molecules

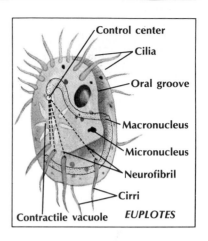

FIGURE 18-9. In the ciliate *Euplotes* neurofibrils transmit impulses from the control center to the cirri.

Paramecium can respond to objects in its path by reversing its motion and turning.

FIGURE 18-10. (a) A protective adaptation of *Paramecium* is the discharging of trichocysts, the threadlike structures at one end of the organism. (b) Each trichocyst, drawn here enlarged about 9 000 times, is shaped like a spear. (c) *Paramecium* also exhibits specific turning behavior when it runs into objects in its path.

REVIEWING YOUR IDEAS

4. What are some materials which must be transported by organisms?

5. What is gas exchange?

6. What is excretion? What substance is excreted by protozoa?

7. List two types of locomotion in protozoa.

8. What is basic irritability? Give an example.

5. movement of oxygen and carbon dioxide between cells and their environments

---

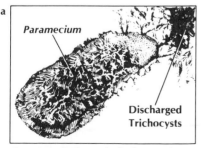

6. removal of metabolic by-products; ammonia

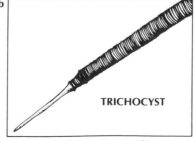

7. amoeboid motion, ciliary and flagellar motion

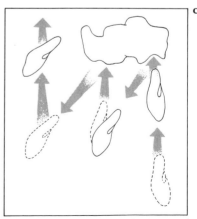

8. response of protoplasm to a stimulus; curling of amoeba when touched

CHAPTER REVIEW

SUMMARY

1. Each cell gets nutrients from its environment. Autotrophs require simple substances which are then built into complex organic compounds. Heterotrophs take in some simple materials and large, complex molecules.

2. Large molecules must be digested, or broken down, so that they can pass into the cells.

3. Autotrophs carry on intracellular digestion, digestion within the cells. Protozoans digest food in this way, too.

4. Fungi carry on extracellular digestion, digestion outside the cells. They absorb small molecules from their host or environment.

5. Organisms must transport materials within and between cells. In simple organisms, such as *Amoeba* and *Paramecium*, transport occurs by diffusion and cytoplasmic streaming.

6. Gas exchange occurs between organisms and their environment. For gas exchange to occur, moisture is needed.

7. In simple organisms, most cells are in direct or close contact with moisture. They exchange gases directly with the environment by diffusion.

8. Excretion is a process which removes nitrogenous wastes. The amount of water in living organisms also must be controlled.

9. Excretion in protozoa occurs by diffusion. Many protozoa have contractile vacuoles that maintain water balance by excreting excess water.

10. Locomotion in protozoa may occur by amoeboid, ciliary, or flagellar motion.

11. Simple organisms respond to their environment in a variety of ways. Among the things that they react to are light, touch, food, and chemicals.

LANGUAGE OF BIOLOGY

amoeboid motion
anal pore
basic irritability
ciliary motion
contractile vacuole
cytoplasmic streaming
digestion
egestion
essential nutrient
excretion
extracellular

digestion
flagellar motion
food vacuole
gas exchange
gel
intracellular digestion
nitrogenous waste
nutrient
oral groove
sol
trichocyst

CHECKING YOUR IDEAS

On a separate paper, match the phrase from the left column with the proper term from the right column. Do not write in this book.

1. process that transports faster than diffusion
2. elimination of dangerous products
3. involves pseudopodia
4. movement of oxygen and carbon dioxide
5. cannot be synthesized by an organism
6. digestion in protozoa
7. hydrolysis reaction
8. involves microtubules
9. fuses with lysosomes during digestion
10. digestion in fungi

a. amoeboid motion
b. ciliary motion
c. cytoplasmic streaming
d. digestion
e. essential nutrient
f. excretion
g. extracellular digestion
h. food vacuole
i. gas exchange
j. intracellular digestion

EVALUATING YOUR IDEAS

1. What kinds of nutrients are required by autotrophs? By heterotrophs? Explain the differences.

CHAPTER REVIEW

2. Why is digestion necessary?

3. Why is digestion in autotrophs different from that in heterotrophs? Do autotrophs digest molecules? Explain.

4. By what chemical process are molecules digested?

5. Describe ingestion, digestion, and egestion in *Amoeba* and *Paramecium*. How are they similar? How are they different?

6. Discuss several ways in which fungi obtain and digest food.

7. Explain how transport occurs in simple organisms.

8. Why must gas exchange occur in a moist environment? How do simple organisms exchange gases?

9. How does excretion occur in protozoa?

10. Why do many salt water protists have little trouble maintaining proper water balance?

11. How does a paramecium rid itself of excess water?

12. Explain how amoeboid motion occurs.

13. How are ciliary and flagellar motion thought to occur?

14. How does *Paramecium* protect itself? How does it react to objects in its path?

APPLYING YOUR IDEAS

1. How is extracellular digestion in fungi adaptive?

2. How is digestion in fungi important to community life?

3. What organelle functions in intracellular transport?

4. Explain several ways in which protozoa are more complex than other simple organisms. Can you suggest a reason for the complexity of protozoa?

5. Certain bacteria are able to synthesize a great variety of substances. How is this capability of producing substances adaptive?

6. Explain the different responses to the environment made by *Euglena* and *Paramecium*. How does each organism detect changes in the environment? How is each type of response adaptive?

EXTENDING YOUR IDEAS

1. Remove a drop from a paramecium culture, make a wet mount and observe it under a microscope. Add a drop of iodine or vinegar to the slide. Observe the discharge of trichocysts.

2. Place another drop from a paramecium culture on a clean slide. Add a few threads of cotton and a coverslip. Describe the response of a paramecium when it bumps into a thread.

3. Remove a drop from an amoeboid culture, make a wet mount, and observe it under a microscope. Describe the movement of the amoeba and the streaming motion of its cytoplasm.

SUGGESTED READINGS

Anderson, Lucia, *The Smallest Life Around Us.* New York, Crown Publishers, Inc., 1978.

Dixon, Bernard, *Magnificent Microbes.* New York, Athenum, 1976.

Heinrich, Milton R., ed., *Extreme Environments: Mechanisms of Microbial Adaptation.* New York, Academy Press, Inc., 1976.

Jahn, Theodore L. and Jahn, Francis F., *How to Know the Protozoa*, 2nd ed. Dubuque, IA, William C. Brown Co., 1979.

Rossmoore, Harold W., *Microbes, Our Unseen Friends.* Detroit, MI, Wayne State University Press, 1976.

Additional student readings and suggested teacher readings are provided in the Teacher's Guide.

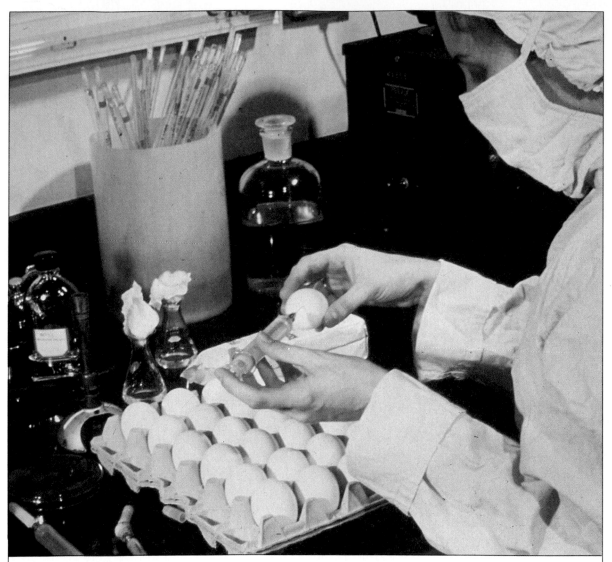

Although many simple organisms are beneficial to humans and the environment, others are harmful and cause disease. Plants and animals including humans are affected by these disease organisms. Many methods of detecting and fighting these organisms have been developed. Here, a scientist injects eggs with a kind of virus to determine if the viruses cause disease. What are some disease causers? How does your body defend against disease organisms?

Introduction: Because of its relevance to their lives, students are especially interested in the subject matter presented in this chapter. They often want to know more about the detection, symptoms, and treatment of certain infectious diseases. Arrange to have a guest speaker such as a physician, pharmaceutical researcher, or public health officer visit your class. If you can arrange for such a speaker, you may wish to have students prepare and submit questions beforehand, so that the speaker will know what to expect. Also, a variety of excellent teaching aids are available on this topic. See *Suggested Audio-Visuals* in the Teacher's Guide.

SIMPLE ORGANISMS AND DISEASE

Chapter 19 presents an overview of infectious diseases, the immune system, and modern methods of prevention and treatment of disease.

Many simple organisms play important, beneficial roles in nature and in human activities. Algae are producers in their aquatic communities. Certain fungi and bacteria decompose organic material and help in the recycling of materials. A variety of forms are used in producing foods and other substances for human use.

Although many simple organisms are helpful or useful, others are quite harmful. They are **pathogens** (PATH uh junz) or disease-causing organisms. Pathogens cause disease in plants, animals (including humans), and in other organisms. Their activities may result in illness, death, and destruction of crops. Diseases caused by pathogens are called **infectious diseases.** Infectious diseases can be spread from one organism to another.

GOAL: You will gain an understanding of how simple organisms cause disease and the means by which humans prevent and treat some diseases.

Pathogens are agents of infectious disease.

BACTERIAL AND VIRAL DISEASE

19:1 Koch's Postulates

Many of the infectious diseases with which you are familiar are caused by bacteria. However, the role of bacteria as agents of disease was not well understood until the end of the 19th Century. At that time, Louis Pasteur proposed the **germ theory of disease**. That theory states that bacteria can cause disease.

Bacteria cause many infectious diseases.

353

At about the same time, a German physician, Robert Koch, identified two pathogenic bacillus bacteria. One bacillus causes the disease anthrax (AN thraks) which affects sheep, cattle, horses, and humans. The other causes tuberculosis in humans. The methods by which Koch determined that a bacterium causes a specific disease are known as **Koch's postulates**. They are as follows:

Koch's postulates provide a method for identifying pathogens.

(1) The organism suspected of causing the disease must be present in the diseased host and isolated from it.
(2) The organism must then be grown in a pure culture.
(3) Organisms taken from that pure culture and injected into a healthy host must cause the disease in the host.
(4) The organism must be isolated from the new diseased host, grown in pure culture, and compared to the original culture.

Since Koch's time, these same rules have been and still are being used by many others. Use of the rules has led to the discovery of many bacterial pathogens. Use of Koch's postulates has also led to the discovery of nonbacterial pathogens. The procedure of isolation and reinfection has become standard in determining the cause of infectious disease regardless of what kind of organism is the cause.

Teaching suggestion: Remind students that many diseases are genetic in origin (Chapter 8). Others result from infestation; e.g., tapeworm and elephantiasis (Chapter 15).

19:2 Bacterial Disease and How It Is Spread

Many bacteria have been found to cause infectious diseases in humans and other animals. Among the diseases caused are bacterial pneumonia, bubonic plague, pertussis (whooping cough), strep throat, and meningitis. Several sexually transmitted (venereal) diseases, such as syphilis and gonorrhea, are also caused by bacteria.

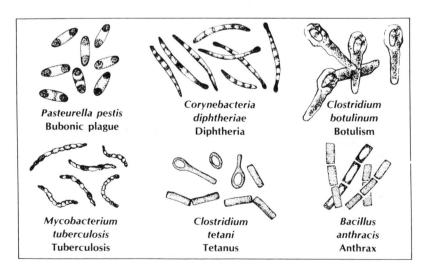

Pasteurella pestis
Bubonic plague

Corynebacteria diphtheriae
Diphtheria

Clostridium botulinum
Botulism

Mycobacterium tuberculosis
Tuberculosis

Clostridium tetani
Tetanus

Bacillus anthracis
Anthrax

FIGURE 19-1. Many bacteria cause diseases. Six such organisms are shown with the disease each causes listed below it.

a

b

FIGURE 19-2. Some types of bacteria cause plant diseases. (a) The large tumor, called a Crown gall tumor, on this *Euonymous* plant, is the result of the presence of the bacterium, *Agrobacterium tumefaciens*. (b) Wilts are common diseases of plants caused by bacterial infections. The cucumber bacterial wilt shown is caused by *Erwinia tracheiphila*.

Bacteria also cause some plant diseases, such as pear blight and fire blight. Bacteria may cause the rotting or wilting of a variety of plants. Some cause galls, abnormal swellings, to occur in plant tissues.

Infectious disease may spread from one organism to another in several ways. Some diseases are airborne. Microorganisms are carried through the air on small droplets produced when an infected organism sneezes or coughs. Other diseases are waterborne. They spread by the drinking of water contaminated by sewage containing human wastes. Still other diseases are spread by direct contact with an object or living thing in or on which microorganisms are located. Sexually transmitted diseases are spread by sexual intercourse. Some microorganisms are transmitted by arthropods such as lice, flies, ticks, and mosquitoes. For example, bubonic plague is transmitted by rat fleas. Often the microorganism enters the body when the arthropod bites or pierces the skin of an animal.

Bacteria may cause disease in plants as well as in humans and other animals.

Infectious organisms may be air-borne, water borne, or spread by direct contact.

FIGURE 19-3. Transmission of disease organisms occurs in several ways. (a) *Pneumococcus* bacteria responsible for pneumonia are airborne organisms. (b) *Neisseria gonorrhea*, bacteria that cause the disease gonorrhea, are transmitted by sexual contact. (c) Human plague organisms, *Yersinia pestis*, are transmitted by arthropods.

a

b

c

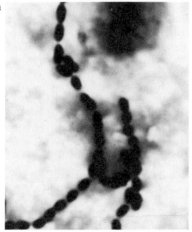

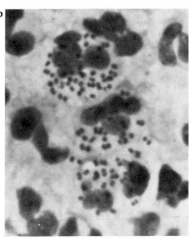

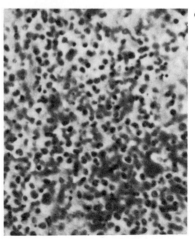

19:3 How Bacterial Diseases Occur

When pathogens enter the body, they may cause disease in several ways. Many bacteria produce poisonous chemicals called **toxins** (TAHK sunz). **Exotoxins** are released by living bacteria. They travel through the bloodstream and affect particular tissues. For example, one species of genus *Clostridium* (klah STRIHD ee um) causes tetanus (lockjaw). It secretes a toxin that stimulates certain nerves causing some muscles to remain contracted. As a result, the condition can be very painful and may cause death. The bacterium which causes diphtheria secretes a toxin which may damage the heart, kidneys, and nerves. Although it is not known how toxins produce harmful effects, most of these diseases can now be either prevented or cured.

Exotoxins are secreted by living bacteria and damage particular tissues in the body.

Endotoxins remain in the bacteria cytoplasm. When bacteria die and break open, the endotoxins are released. Endotoxins are the causes of diseases such as cholera, tuberculosis, and bubonic plague.

Clostridium tetani is a saprophytic anaerobe. It can live only in dead tissues in the absence of oxygen. These conditions mainly result from deep puncture wounds.

Bacteria may cause disease in other ways. As they invade tissues, they may reproduce in such great numbers that they may alter the host's metabolism. Sometimes the reaction of a host, as it responds to the foreign invader, causes changes in the host's cells. The cells may become less active as chemical changes occur within them. Chemical changes can interfere with respiration or upset the osmotic balance between cells and their fluid environment. These abnormalities may lead to the death of the cells.

Endotoxins are released when bacteria die.

As bacteria reproduce, they may affect the host's metabolism.

19:4 Food Poisoning

Another undesirable action of bacteria is food spoilage. Spoilage is counteracted by modern methods of canning, refrigeration, and freezing. If spoiled food is eaten, the result can be food poisoning. Food poisoning is not an infectious disease; it is not passed from one organism to another. However, in food poisoning, bacterial toxins have some of the same effects on the host as they do in infectious diseases.

The sometimes fatal disease botulism (BAHCH uh lihz um) can result from improperly canned food. The food must be completely sterilized or spores of another species of *Clostridium* can become active. As they metabolize the food, they produce a colorless, tasteless exotoxin. If the food is eaten, the toxin affects the nervous system causing problems in vision, paralysis, and often death.

A clue to whether canned food may be contaminated is the presence of a bulge at the top of the can. This bulge is due to the presence of gas released as the bacteria metabolize the food. *Should you find such a can, do not eat its contents.* Also, some

Spores of *Clostridium botulinum* are heat resistant. They are commonly found in soil.

FIGURE 19-4. Home canning must be carefully controlled and done at the proper temperatures so that microorganisms, such as those which cause botulism, are killed.

Elaine Comer

bacteria may enter a sealed can that is cracked as a result of a dent. These bacteria may cause other kinds of food poisoning. Although not all food poisoning is as dangerous as botulism, food from these damaged cans should also be avoided.

Pasteurization of milk and other foods ensures the killing of dangerous bacteria. The substance to be pasteurized is heated and then cooled rapidly. Heating kills most of the bacteria, and cooling retards the growth of those bacteria remaining. Why does milk "sour" as it ages? Will it sour if it is unopened after pasteurization?

Freezing of foods is another method of preventing bacterial contamination. Although the food, when frozen, may contain bacteria, the cold temperature reduces their activity. As the food thaws, the bacteria become more active, but they are usually destroyed in cooking.

Bacteria may cause various forms of food poisoning.

Pasteurization kills many of the bacteria in milk and other foods.

Milk sours as bacteria reproduce and metabolize the milk. Yes, eventually it will sour.

Freezing reduces the activities of bacteria in food.

Teaching suggestion: Tell students about polio epidemics in years past. They may be surprised to learn how recently these epidemics threatened human life. In some countries polio is still a problem.

The effect of a virus depends on the kind of tissue it invades.

19:5 Viruses and Disease

Viruses were not isolated until 1935. Since that time, a great many viruses have been discovered. Although some are harmless to humans, many are pathogenic. Human diseases caused by viruses include polio, smallpox, influenza, measles, mumps, rabies, and viral pneumonia. One form of herpes virus causes a sexually transmitted disease. Other species of herpes virus cause infectious mononucleosis and cold sores. Other diseases caused by viruses include distemper in dogs and cats, foot and mouth disease in cattle, and swine influenza in pigs.

Viral diseases are transmitted in the same ways as bacterial diseases. But, control of viral diseases is more difficult because viral particles often mutate (change forms) and so there are problems in developing effective vaccines. Influenza is an example of a viral disease that is difficult to control for this reason.

Usually there is only one kind of host in a viral disease. But, some viruses which affect humans also occur in other animals. Encephalitis, an inflammation of the brain, is a disease of humans and horses. Viruses sometimes spread from one kind of host to another. Rabies can be spread among animals such as raccoons, dogs, and humans.

The symptoms of viral disease vary with the virus and the tissues "under attack." Viruses reproduce in specific tissues or organs. For example, polio virus attacks nerves in the brain and spinal cord. As polio viruses reproduce, they destroy nerve cells. Destruction of nerve cells may lead to paralysis and, in some cases, even death. The effects of other viruses are also related to the part of the host which is invaded by the virus.

FIGURE 19-5. Rabies vaccination of pets is required by law in many areas. The virus cannot be transferred to vaccinated animals.

Carolyn Russell

Gerard Photography

19:6 Rickettsia and Viroids

Rickettsias are parasites which cause certain diseases.

Two other groups of disease-causing organisms are **rickettsia** (rihk ET see uh) and viroids. These pathogens are neither bacteria nor viruses and are difficult to classify.

Rickettsia are all parasites. They cannot live except in other cells. In this way, rickettsia are like viruses. But in structure, rickettsia are more like bacteria. Certain rickettsia cause diseases in humans and other animals. Epidemic typhus fever, which is transmitted by body lice, and Rocky Mountain spotted fever, which is transmitted by dog ticks, are examples of rickettsial diseases.

Viroids are known to cause some plant diseases.

Recently, unique structures called viroids have been discovered. **Viroids** are small segments of RNA now known to cause disease in a variety of plants, including potatoes and tomatoes. They may cause disease by regulating the host's genes in an abnormal manner. The origin, transmission, and effect of viroids must be studied further. Their name suggests that they are related to viruses, but that idea is not fact.

1. disease-causing organism
2. diseases caused by pathogens and spread from one organism to another
3. Answers will vary. Examples given might be tuberculosis, bacterial pneumonia, strep throat, and bubonic plague.
4. poisonous chemical, exotoxins and endotoxins
5. Answers will vary but might include measles, mumps, influenza, and polio.

REVIEWING YOUR IDEAS

1. What is a pathogen?
2. What is an infectious disease?
3. List some diseases caused by bacteria.
4. What is a toxin? What are the two types of toxins?
5. List some diseases caused by viruses.

FIGURE 19-6. (a) *Rickettsia prowazekii,* **which causes epidemic typhus fever, is shown magnified about 46 000 times. (b) The life cycle of** *Rickettsia typhi,* **the organism that causes endemic typhus fever, shows how fleas transmit the disease.**

a

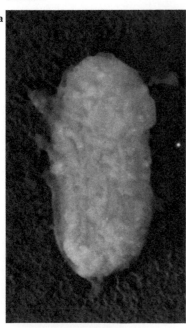

American Cyanamid Company

b

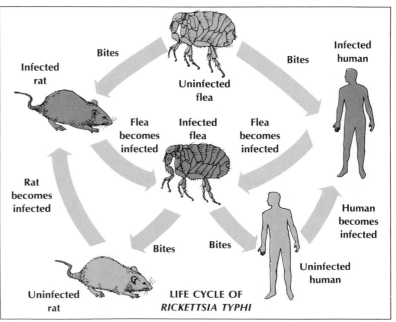

LIFE CYCLE OF *RICKETTSIA TYPHI*

Centers for Disease Control

Lightforce

a

b

FIGURE 19-7. Histoplasmosis is a disease caused by the fungus *Histoplasma capsulatum*. Air-borne spores cause infections primarily in the lungs. (a) White spots on lung X rays are used to diagnose the disease. These spots are sores hardened with calcium deposits. (b) *Histoplasma* spores often are found in abundance in nests of certain birds and in the ground beneath the nests.

OTHER AGENTS OF DISEASE

19:7 Fungal Diseases

Fungi are heterotrophs and many are parasites. As many fungal parasites obtain food, they cause disease in their host. Thus, some fungi are pathogens.

Some fungi cause disease in animals and humans. Often, the fungi invade the skin. Ringworm (a disease of the scalp, skin, or nails) and athlete's foot are human fungal infections. Both of these diseases involve the cracking and scaling of the skin and the formation of small blisters. These symptoms occur as the hyphae invade the skin.

Some fungi cause disease in animals as they invade the skin.

Sometimes, fungi attack internal organs such as the lungs where they may cause serious disease. Thrush is a fungal disease in infants. The fungus invades and causes soreness of the mouth, throat, and tongue. Histoplasmosis is a fungal disease which affects the mouth, throat, and lungs of humans. Found mostly in the United States, it results from spores entering the body from the air. These spores are often found in birds' nests.

Fungi cause several respiratory diseases in humans.

Rusts and smuts are club fungi (Section 13:14) which cause disease in a variety of plants. Many parasitize grains such as wheat, barley, oats, and corn. They spread rapidly through a dense crop of such plants and cause the loss of millions of dollars in ruined crops each year.

a

b

Corn smut can be controlled by destroying the fungus directly; i.e., burning diseased plants.

FIGURE 19-8. Rusts and smuts are plant diseases caused by parasitic fungi. (a) Blackberry rust and (b) corn smut cause extensive damage to crops.

Allan Roberts

David M. Dennis

Dr. C. Wayne Ellet, Professor Emeritus/Ohio State University

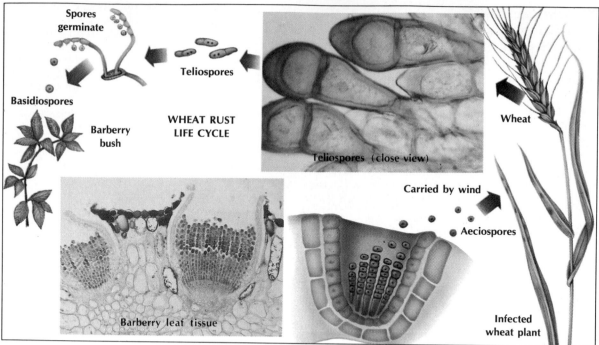

Spores
germinate

Teliospores

Basidiospores

Barberry
bush

WHEAT RUST
LIFE CYCLE

Teliospores (close view)

Wheat

Carried by wind

Aeciospores

Barberry leaf tissue

Infected
wheat plant

E. J. Cable for Tom Stack and Associates

FIGURE 19-9. Life cycle of wheat rust fungus *Puccinia graminis* involves both barberry and wheat hosts.

Wheat rust can be controlled by indirect means—removal of the barberry bush host.

Wheat rust has a life cycle involving two hosts.

In order to deal with diseases caused by some fungi, it is necessary to study the life cycles of the fungi. Wheat rust has a complex life cycle involving two hosts—wheat and the barberry bush. The fungus attacks and damages the stem and leaf cells of young wheat plants (Figure 19-9). Spores produced at this time invade other, healthy wheat plants. Different spores are produced later. After a dormant period during the winter, the spores invade the barberry bush. In the bush, more spores are produced. They attack young wheat plants to complete the cycle.

19:8 Protozoan Diseases

Some human diseases are caused by protozoa. African sleeping sickness (Section 13:11) is caused by a flagellate. Amoebic dysentery is a disease caused by a certain species of amoeba. It is a serious, and often long-lasting, infection of the large intestine.

Malaria is caused by the protozoan *Plasmodium*.

One of the most lethal diseases in human history is malaria, caused by *Plasmodium*, a sporozoan. *Plasmodium* is transmitted to humans by female *Anopheles* (uh NAHF uh leez) mosquitoes. If this insect bites a person with malaria, some parasites are sucked up in the human's blood cells that the mosquito takes in. These then pass along with blood into the mosquito's stomach where they grow and reproduce. Some of them pass into the mosquito's bloodstream and eventually reach the salivary glands.

An organism such as the *Anopheles* mosquito, which transmits a parasite, is called a vector.

When the mosquito bites a healthy person, some parasites enter the human's blood through the skin. The parasites enter the blood and travel to the liver where they develop for about eight days. Then they reenter the human's bloodstream and invade the red blood cells. The red cells provide an oxygen-rich environment and a food source for the parasites. In each blood cell, many parasite spores form. Eventually the red cells burst releasing the spores which then enter other red cells. These cells later burst and a regular cycle of bursting develops. Cells usually burst every twenty-four or forty-eight hours.

Each time cells burst in large numbers, the host has chills, headache, high fever, and heavy sweating. These symptoms result from the parasites' waste products being emptied into the blood. During the time between the bursting of red cells, the host may feel well, although weak.

In some kinds of malaria, the cycle may continue for several weeks and then seem to disappear. But, the symptoms may suddenly come back months later. In another form of malaria, death may result within several hours after the onset of symptoms. The type of disease depends on the species of *Plasmodium* which infects the person.

After developing in the liver, malarial parasites travel to the red blood cells where they produce and release spores.

Symptoms of malaria occur when the red blood cells burst.

Quinine was originally used to treat malaria. Today, synthetic drugs are used.

6. Answers will vary, but may include athlete's foot, ringworm, and histoplasmosis.
7. As plant parasites, fungi cause millions of dollars in damage each year. The fungi destroy crops such as corn, wheat, and oats.
8. Malaria is caused by *Plasmodium*, transmitted by the female *Anopheles* mosquito.

REVIEWING YOUR IDEAS

6. What human diseases are caused by fungi?
7. How is agriculture affected by fungi?
8. What organism is responsible for malaria? How is it transmitted?

FIGURE 19-10. Malaria is caused by the protist *Plasmodium malariae*, and is transmitted by female *Anopholes* mosquitoes.

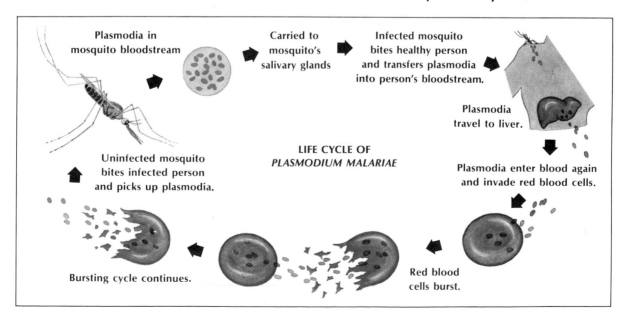

Plasmodia in mosquito bloodstream

Carried to mosquito's salivary glands

Infected mosquito bites healthy person and transfers plasmodia into person's bloodstream.

Plasmodia travel to liver.

Uninfected mosquito bites infected person and picks up plasmodia.

LIFE CYCLE OF
PLASMODIUM MALARIAE

Plasmodia enter blood again and invade red blood cells.

Bursting cycle continues.

Red blood cells burst.

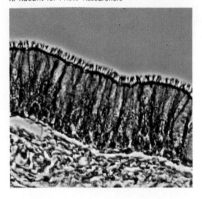

FIGURE 19-11. Cilia lining the windpipe are a barrier to entry of pathogens. These cilia, from a cat windpipe, are shown magnified about 330 times.

Adaptations which destroy or prevent entry of microbes into the body include the skin, filtering of air, trapping in mucus, and action of acids and enzymes.

DEFENDING AGAINST DISEASE

19:9 Barriers to Pathogens

Even though pathogenic microbes may be present, they often do not cause disease. For disease to occur, pathogens must first gain entry to the cells and tissues of the body. Several factors act to keep pathogens out.

A major barrier to the entry of pathogens is the skin. The outer layer of skin is made of dead cells which microbes cannot penetrate. When the skin is broken, pathogens can enter the host.

Openings in the body, such as the nostrils and mouth, are points at which microbes may enter. However, other adaptations usually inhibit entry of the microbes. Hairs in the nose filter air, preventing many microbes from going further. Mucus in the lining of the nose traps and destroys microbes. The lining of the windpipe and smaller tubes leading to the lungs contains cells with many cilia. The cilia move mucus from the lungs to the mouth. As air moves down toward the lungs, microbes are trapped in the mucus. Action of the cilia and mucus prevents respiratory infection. You can see how damaging these cilia with cigarette smoke hurts one of the body's natural defenses.

Acids and enzymes in the body kill organisms that may enter openings. The digestive organs have substances which kill microbes. An enzyme in tears kills bacteria that may enter the tear ducts of the eyes. That enzyme breaks down the cell walls of the bacteria. Lysozyme is the enzyme in tears.

Although the body has many barriers to entry of pathogens, sometimes the microbes still get in. The immune system (next two sections) responds if microbe entry occurs.

19:10 The Immune System: Structures

Attacks by pathogens are often serious and sometimes fatal. Yet, in many cases, the host survives and regains its health. How does the diseased organism fight off the pathogens? A branch of biology called **immunology** studies how the body protects itself from pathogens. It explains defense of the body against certain foreign chemicals and particles. Immunology also explains why transplanted organs are often rejected by the patient's body.

Early in development, an embryo detects a difference between the embryo's own chemicals and those which are foreign to it. In general, any foreign chemical (protein, carbohydrate, nucleic acid) is called an **antigen.** An antigen may be a protein in the membrane of a bacterium or virus or a chemical secreted by another organism.

An antigen is any foreign chemical or substance.

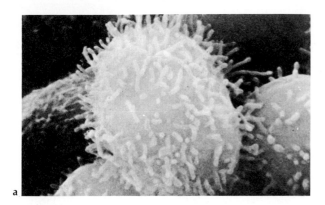

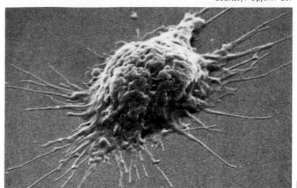

Courtesy: Upjohn Co.

a

b

The immune response involves two parts. First, the body must recognize the antigen and next, it must get rid of it. Both of these steps involve certain types of white blood cells. **Lymphocytes** (LIHM fuh sites) are white blood cells produced by bone marrow, the tissue in the hollow parts of some bones. Lymphocytes are also produced by the **spleen,** a small abdominal organ. Lymphocytes enter the blood and the lymph nodes. **Lymph nodes** are structures that filter a type of tissue fluid called **lymph** and are located at various points. Some of the lymphocytes first pass through the **thymus** gland, a small gland located beneath the breastbone. Lymphocytes (Figure 19-12) which pass through the thymus are called **T-cells** while others are called **B-cells.** **Macrophages** (MAK ruh faj uz) are another kind of white blood cell involved in immunity. These cells and tissues make up the body's immune system.

FIGURE 19-12. (a) A lymphocyte (shown magnified about 30 000 times) and (b) a macrophage, are two important cell types involved in the immune response.

One of the earliest clues to the involvement of the thymus in immunity was the discovery that the thymus is very prominent in young children but later shrinks in size.

The immune system is composed of lymphocytes, other blood cells, the spleen, thymus, and lymph nodes.

19:11 The Immune System: Functions

The number of possible antigens is huge. How do lymphocytes recognize them? Both B-cells and T-cells have protein molecules called **antibodies** (ANT ih bahd eez) on their surfaces. Different lymphocytes have different antibodies, each unique because of the order of the amino acids it contains. Thus, thousands of different kinds of antibodies can be made. It is thought that each type of antibody molecule has a shape which matches a specific antigen molecule. The antibody matches an antigen in much the same way that an enzyme fits a substrate (Section 4:5).

Bacteria have antigen molecules on their surfaces. When bacteria enter the body, macrophages change the bacteria slightly and present them to the lymphocytes. Lymphocytes have antibodies that match the bacterial antigens. The antigens and antibodies join.

Once the antibody of a B-cell is linked to an antigen, the B-cell becomes activated and begins to enlarge. This large B-cell divides to form a clone of cells called **plasma cells.**

An antibody is a specific protein which matches a certain antigen.

FIGURE 19-13. Antibodies produced by a clone of B-cells attach to the antigens of invading bacteria, making the bacteria more susceptible to macrophage attack.

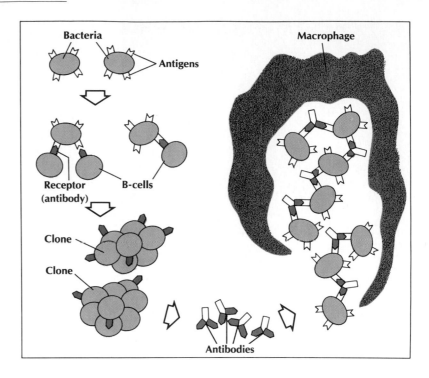

B-cells give rise to a clone of plasma cells which produce antibodies.

FIGURE 19-14. Macrophages attack foreign matter other than bacterial cells. Here a macrophage attacks a tumor cell. Holes have appeared in the tumor cell's membrane due to the macrophage's attack.

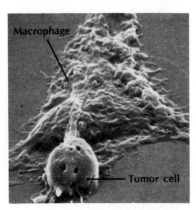

Courtesy: Upjohn Co.

A **clone** is a group of genetically identical cells. Each clone of plasma cells produces only one kind of antibody. The antibodies are just like those on the surface of the B-cell. These antibodies are poured into the blood and other tissues. These free antibodies attach to bacterial antigens.

It is thought that some T-cells help stimulate B-cells to grow and produce antibodies. T-cells also have antibodies on their surfaces. Entire T-cells can attach to antigens. Some T-cells seem to attach to antigens which are bound to foreign cells such as whole bacteria or cells which are part of a transplanted organ.

The combination of antibody and antigen can have several results. The antibodies may make viruses or bacteria more susceptible to attack by macrophages. Macrophages engulf the microbes by phagocytosis. The digested microbes enter the lymph and are destroyed by white cells in the lymph nodes. Sometimes the antibody causes microorganisms to clump together making them inactive. The toxins that some bacteria secrete are antigens which, when combined with the antitoxin (antibody), are destroyed or made inactive.

Complement, a chemical part of blood serum, is also involved in immunity. Through a series of reactions, it binds to foreign cells, such as bacteria. The reactions occur in two ways. One way involves the presence of antibodies and the other does not. Both result in the breaking open of the foreign cells. Much is yet to be learned about complement and its functions.

19:12 Immunity and Treatment

Not all plasma cells produce antibodies. Some become "memory" cells. Long after an antigen has been defeated or destroyed, the "memory" cells remain in the blood. Suppose the same antigen should appear again later. A larger supply of antibodies will be formed in a short time. They will attack the antigen before it does much harm. The presence of "memory" cells explains why an adult who had measles as a child will not get the disease again. This example shows **active immunity** (ihm YEW nut ee). Active immunity is immunity or disease resistance resulting from production of antibodies by the host.

Memory cells provide immunity.

Active immunity results from antibodies produced by the host.

These principles of active immunity may be used to prevent certain diseases from occurring. Solutions of antigens of weakened or dead microorganisms or toxins called **vaccines** (vak SEENZ) can be prepared. Vaccines injected into a healthy person do not cause the disease but do cause antibody formation. The person may suffer mild discomfort from the vaccine, but the antibodies give protection from the disease organisms or the toxin when the body is later exposed. This process makes use of active immunity.

Active immunity resulting from exposure to disease is called natural active immunity whereas active immunity resulting from vaccinations is called artificial active immunity.

Many vaccines have been developed. Among them are polio, measles, mumps, some forms of influenza, tetanus, diphtheria, and bubonic plague vaccines. When someone receives a vaccination, the person is said to become immunized against the disease. Without these vaccines, exposure to many of these diseases could be fatal. Children are required to receive certain vaccinations before entering school. Because some diseases such as polio are less common now, some people are neglecting to have their children vaccinated. Why is this practice dangerous?

FIGURE 19-15. Chickens are vaccinated for Marek's disease before they hatch. Often they are exposed to the disease virus immediately after hatching. Therefore, vaccinations given after hatching are too late to give immunity.

Often when a person becomes infected, the body cannot produce antibodies fast enough to fight the disease. A vaccination of weakened or dead organisms also would not result in production of antibodies rapidly enough to fight the disease. In these cases (such as tetanus), a person may receive antibodies made by an animal. The antibodies are extracted from the animal's blood. The solution of antibodies and blood serum is called an **antiserum.** Injection of an antiserum provides "borrowed" antibodies to fight off a disease. Because the person is not making antibodies, this process results in what is called **passive immunity.** Passive immunity works more quickly than active immunity, but its effects last for a shorter time.

Vaccines which produce either active immunity or antisera that give passive immunity can prevent a variety of diseases. People can recover from some diseases as a result of their immune responses. But the immune system may not always work quickly or efficiently enough to fight off a disease. If only the immune system were at work, many diseases could be fatal.

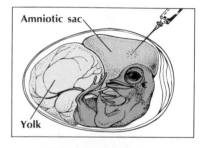

USDA

Bacterial diseases can be treated with antibiotics.

Modern medicines are used to *treat* many diseases. Bacterial diseases are treated with antibiotics (Section 2:5). These drugs work along with the immune system in destroying bacteria and restoring health. Each kind of antibiotic has a specific kind of effect. Some work on many kinds of bacteria, others work only on certain types. Because some people are allergic to certain antibiotics, these drugs should never be taken unless they are necessary and prescribed by a physician. Many people have become allergic because of overuse of antibiotics.

No drugs are available for destroying viruses.

There are no drugs which destroy viruses. Symptoms of viral diseases can be treated with other drugs, but they do not affect the virus. Also viral vaccines have been developed to combat certain viruses. Resistance to some viral diseases lasts longer than resistance to most bacterial diseases. It is rare that a person gets a second case of measles, mumps, or chicken pox.

19:13 Interferon

Protection from a first attack by a virus does not seem to come from antibodies produced during the infection. Instead, a different kind of protein is involved. The protein is produced by a host cell under viral attack and plays an important role in defense. This protein protects other cells from the virus. Because it interferes with the virus, the protein was named **interferon** (ihnt ur FIHR ahn). Interferon leaves a diseased cell and travels to a healthy cell nearby. There it causes the synthesis of another protein which protects the cell. The protein produced by the healthy cell interferes with the reproduction of any viruses that may enter it.

Since the discovery of interferon in 1957, scientists have been hoping to use it in the treatment of viral diseases. Some feel that interferon may be a useful treatment for some forms of cancer (Section 19:14). Until recently, research has been limited, because it is difficult and expensive to extract interferon from cells. Now, though, interferon is being produced by recombinant DNA techniques (Section 13:19). Larger quantities of less expensive interferon are becoming available for study. Much more interferon will be available to give to patients.

In a recent test, interferon was shown to be helpful in the treatment of multiple sclerosis (MS). It does not seem to be a cure, but it may slow the progress of the disease, which leads to the destruction of the nervous system, paralysis, and, sometimes, death. The fact that interferon seems to help MS patients suggests that MS might be caused by a virus. Perhaps the potential of interferon as an antiviral or anticancer drug will soon be known.

PEOPLE IN BIOLOGY

Medicine was a family tradition in Jane Wright's family—both her father and grandfather were doctors—so it surprised no one when she decided to go to medical school after graduating from Smith College. She received her M.D. in 1945 from the New York Medical College and began to specialize in cancer research, especially chemotherapy. Chemotherapy is the use of chemicals, often injected into the bloodstream, to treat disease. She succeeded her father as head of the Harlem Hospital Cancer Research Foundation in 1949. In 1955 she joined the New York University Medical School as an instructor in research surgery, and later became director of cancer chemotherapy there. In 1967 Dr. Wright was appointed dean and professor of surgery at the medical school—the highest post ever held at that time by a Black woman in an American medical school.

(1919 -   )

Jane C. Wright

Dr. Wright is most noted for her work in finding drugs and surgical procedures effective against cancer. In 1975 she was honored by the American Association for Cancer Research for her contributions to research in clinical cancer. The mother of two daughters—a doctor and a clinical psychologist—Jane Wright also enjoys swimming, mystery novels, and painting watercolors.

19:14 Cancer

Cancer is a disease in which there is uncontrolled production of certain body cells. The causes of cancer are not fully understood. Some cancers are caused by viruses (Section 17:9), although it is not certain whether any human cancers are viral.

Viruses cause some types of cancer.

Experiments suggest that proteins on the membranes of cancer cells are different from the proteins of the body's normal cells. Thus, they are antigens and the body detects these antigens as "nonself." Some of these abnormal cells might be destroyed by the body's immune system. But, in a cancer patient, there seems to be a breakdown in the immune system. Cancer cells then may spread throughout the body. Death often results when cancer cells spread throughout the body.

The immune system of a patient with cancer does not function properly.

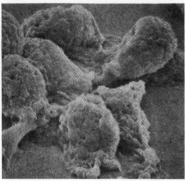

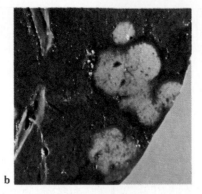

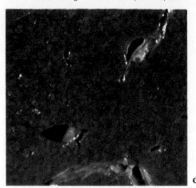

a

b

c

FIGURE 19-16. (a) Cancer cells have surface properties different from other cells. The cells tend to pile up. (b) Cancerous liver tissue has areas of uncontrolled cell production (yellow areas) whereas (c) healthy liver tissue is pink and uniform.

9. An antigen is any foreign chemical. Antibodies are proteins which recognize and help destroy antigens.
10. Both B-cells and T-cells are lymphocytes. T-cells pass through the thymus but B-cells do not.
11. active and passive
12. A vaccine is an injection which causes the body to produce antibodies. An antiserum is an injection which contains antibodies produced by an animal.
13. Interferon is a protein produced by cells that have been attacked by viruses. It helps protect healthy cells from viral attack.
14. Cancer is a disease characterized by uncontrolled production of body cells. People with cancer seem to have a poorly functioning immune system.

Synthetic vaccines have been made from parts of antigen molecules.

Persons with cancer seem to have a poorly working immune system. If something could be done to "recharge" the immune system, then, perhaps, the cancer cells could be destroyed. Biologists and physicians are exploring ways of "recharging" the system. They have had some success in animals such as mice, but cancer in humans has not yet been overcome. Further knowledge of the immune system may bring with it a cure for this dreaded disease.

REVIEWING YOUR IDEAS

9. What is an antigen? What is the relationship between antigens and antibodies?
10. Distinguish between B-cells and T-cells.
11. What are the two forms of immunity?
12. Distinguish between a vaccine that produces active immunity and an antiserum.
13. What is interferon?
14. What is cancer? How is it related to the immune system?

ADVANCES IN BIOLOGY

19:15 New Ways to Produce Antibodies

Two new methods for producing antibodies are being used and may have many applications. Among the applications are the treatment of diseases, diagnosis of abnormal conditions, and knowledge of basic life functions.

One method produces synthetic vaccines. Most vaccines are produced from inactive or weakened microbes or toxins. However, the entire organism is not really important. A specific antigen is what is recognized and fought off by the host. **Synthetic vaccines** are made from pure antigens. They contain only the outer part of the antigen molecule—the part attacked by the antibody.

These outer parts of antigens have been synthesized and injected into rabbits which then produce antibodies against them. Thus, injections of a small portion of an antigen can act like a vaccine and induce active immunity. Synthetic vaccines against viral hepatitis and influenza are being developed and tested.

Synthetic vaccines have several advantages over vaccines produced from whole cells or viruses. They are less expensive to make. Also, they are pure, containing no unwanted chemicals or live organisms. Other vaccines sometimes have side effects, some of which are occasionally fatal. Another advantage is the possibility of producing a single synthetic vaccine that would provide immunity against a combination of many diseases.

A second method provides large amounts of pure antibodies for a variety of uses. In this method, a mouse is injected with a bacterium, virus, or chemical. Lymphocytes in the mouse's spleen respond by making antibodies against the antigens present in the injection. Each lymphocyte makes only one kind of antibody.

The lymphocytes are then removed from the spleen and fused with certain cancer cells. This step is done because the cancer cells divide over and over again in culture. Each fused cell, or hybridoma (hy bre DOH ma), is cultured and forms a clone. Each clone is made of many cells that make only one kind of antibody. Antibodies produced by this procedure are called **monoclonal antibodies.**

After the antibody produced by each clone is identified, the clones can be separated and grown. As they grow, they produce one kind of pure antibody. Even greater quantities of pure antibody can be obtained by injecting a mouse with the hybridomas. The hybridomas form a tumor which produces a large amount of the antibody. The antibody is later filtered from the mouse's body fluids.

Monoclonal antibodies might be used in many ways. Each way makes use of the fact that each antibody is unique. They might provide another type of vaccine. They could be used to diagnose pregnancy or a variety of diseases, including cancer. This use is possible because in pregnancy, as in infectious disease, antigens are present. If the pure antibody is injected and a certain reaction occurs, then the antigen must be in the body. Biologists also see a role for monoclonal antibodies in research. They may be useful in learning about the nature of the proteins in the cell membrane. This information could lead to better "matches" in organ transplants. Development of embryos may involve differences in membrane proteins. By using monoclonal antibodies, more may be learned about how development occurs.

FIGURE 19-17. Antibody-producing lymphocytes are fused with cancer cells so they are multiplied rapidly in culture. After screening, selected hybridomas are injected into different mice and specific antibodies are formed in quantity.

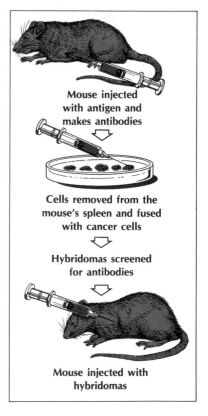

Mouse injected with antigen and makes antibodies

Cells removed from the mouse's spleen and fused with cancer cells

Hybridomas screened for antibodies

Mouse injected with hybridomas

CHAPTER REVIEW

SUMMARY

1. Many simple organisms are pathogens and are sources of infectious disease. The idea that microorganisms can cause disease was proposed by Louis Pasteur in the germ theory of disease.
2. Many pathogens have been discovered using Koch's postulates.
3. Bacterial pathogens may be airborne or waterborne, or spread by direct contact.
4. Many pathogenic bacteria produce toxins which affect certain parts of the body. Both exotoxins and endotoxins are produced. Other pathogenic bacteria affect metabolism or destroy tissues. Some bacteria cause food poisoning.
5. Many viruses cause diseases such as polio, flu, common cold, measles, and mumps.
6. Fungi may cause disease in humans, plants, and animals. Great economic loss can occur as a result of fungal disease in crops.
7. Barriers of the body to pathogen entry include skin, hair, mucus, cilia, digestive juices, and enzymes in liquids such as tears.
8. Malaria, a disease responsible for millions of human deaths, is caused by the protozoan, *Plasmodium*.
9. The immune system includes the blood, lymph, and other tissues. Antigens are recognized by lymphocytes which produce antibodies to destroy or inactivate them.
10. Protection against pathogens may result from active or passive immunity.
11. Many bacterial diseases are treated with antibiotics that kill the bacteria. There are no known virus-killing drugs used to treat patients.
12. Interferon is a protein produced by cells attacked by viruses. It protects healthy cells from being attacked by the viruses.
13. Cancer is a disease which involves abnormal cell growth. Viruses are known to cause cancer in some animals.
14. Two ways of producing antibodies involve synthetic vaccine and monoclonal antibody techniques. Antibodies produced by these methods may be used in the treatment or detection of disease and in learning about life processes.

LANGUAGE OF BIOLOGY

active immunity
clone
endotoxin
exotoxin
germ theory of disease
immune system
immunology
infectious disease
interferon
lumph
lymph node
lymphocyte
macrophage
monoclonal antibody
pathogen
spleen
synthetic vaccine
thymus
toxin
vaccine
viroid

CHECKING YOUR IDEAS

On a separate paper, indicate whether each statement is true or false. Do not write in this book.

1. The skin is a barrier to pathogen entry.
2. An antigen is matched by a specific antibody.
3. Exotoxins remain in bacterial cells until the cells die.
4. Viruses can be successfully treated with antibiotics.
5. Malaria is transmitted by a mosquito.
6. The germ theory of disease was first stated by Koch.
7. Interferon is a natural means of protection against viruses.
8. Memory cells are important in long-lasting immunity.
9. Infectious diseases may be spread from one organism to another.
10. The common cold is caused by a bacterium.

CHAPTER REVIEW

EVALUATING YOUR IDEAS

1. What is the germ theory of disease?
2. Explain the procedure for determining whether a given microorganism causes a certain disease.
3. Explain four ways in which infectious disease may be spread.
4. Name two sexually-transmitted diseases. How are they transmitted?
5. Distinguish between exotoxins and endotoxins. What are some diseases caused by each type of toxin?
6. Explain how botulism occurs and its symptoms.
7. What is pasteurization? Why is it needed?
8. What are viroids? How are they thought to cause disease?
9. Give the stages in the wheat rust life cycle.
10. Describe the stages in the life cycle of *Plasmodium*. Relate the stages to the symptoms of malaria.
11. How do pathogens enter their hosts?
12. Explain how pathogens are prevented from entering a host's cells and tissues.
13. Explain how antigens are recognized.
14. Discuss the steps which occur after an antigen is recognized.
15. What function do lymph nodes have?
16. What is active immunity? List two ways in which active immunity may develop.
17. What is passive immunity? In what way does a person get passive immunity?
18. Compare active and passive immunity in terms of long-lasting effects.
19. How are bacterial diseases often treated? Viral diseases?
20. Explain how interferon helps to fight off viruses. How might interferon be useful?
21. How are synthetic vaccines made? What are the advantages of synthetic vaccines?
22. What are monoclonal antibodies? How might they be used?

APPLYING YOUR IDEAS

1. Why do you think that autotrophs are not pathogens?
2. What is an indirect way of eliminating the wheat rust fungus?
3. Many vaccinations require later "booster" shots. Why are they necessary?
4. What problem usually follows an organ transplant?
5. Why does a physician usually examine the lymph nodes during a physical examination?
6. What else causes disease besides pathogens?
7. Bed rest, aspirin, and drinking of fluids are often "prescribed" for a cold or flu. Does this treatment destroy the pathogens which cause the disease? Explain. *Chapters 8 and 15

EXTENDING YOUR IDEAS

1. How important are tonsils? Study the pros and cons of tonsil removal.
2. Prepare a report on the Salk polio vaccine.
3. Find out what Jenner and Lister contributed to knowledge of infectious disease.
4. Choose several diseases mentioned in this chapter. Find out the details of the causes of the diseases and their cures (if any).
5. What does a public health officer do?

SUGGESTED READINGS

Epps, Garrett, "The Amazing, All New, All-Purpose Vaccine." *Science 81*, April, 1981.

Epps, Garrett, "Viroids Among Us." *Science 81*, September, 1981.

Hecht, Annabel, "Battling Resistant Bacteria." *FDA Consumer*, April, 1978.

"The Big IF in Cancer." *Time Magazine*, March 11, 1980.

Van Gelder, Richard, "Malaria Safari." *Natural History*, May, 1980.

Additional student readings and suggested teacher readings are provided in the Teacher's Guide.

PLANTS

lants may seem like inactive organisms to you because they have no adaptations for locomotion. However, plants carry out the same basic functions as other forms of life. They reproduce and develop in cycles involving both monoploid and diploid forms. They make their own food, and a few plants trap insects which become food. Plants transport water, minerals, and food, they exchange gases, and release or store wastes. Although plants do not move, they have parts that move. These movements are a plant's response to stimuli in the environment. In addition, many plants have a means of support.

VI

Desert plants are adapted to dry environments with high
and low temperatures. With an average 17.8 cm rainfall each year,
these cacti growing in the southwest United States survive temperatures as high as about 50°C and as low as about −10°C. Yet
desert plants carry out the same basic life functions as plants that
live in a tropical rain forest. In this unit, you will learn about
plant life functions and how plants are adapted
to carry out these functions.

Desert Plants

L ike other living things, plants reproduce and develop. Both asexual and sexual reproductive patterns are found among plants. The flower is the structure of sexual reproduction in most plants. Here, male and female parts of a lily flower are visible. What are the parts? How does fertilization in a flower occur? How do nonflowering plants reproduce? What is involved in plant development?

Introduction and suggested demonstration: Vegetative propagation can be easily demonstrated by you or as projects assigned to students. Cuttings of geranium stems or sweet potato can be rooted in moist sand or water, and leaves of *Bryophyllum* will root if placed flat on moist sand. You might also plant some bulbs in vermiculite. The bulbs can be removed easily for observation during the development process. Prepared slides are available for studying the life cycle of algae like *Spirogyra*, or of land plants such as mosses and ferns. Preserved specimens may also be useful; e.g. a gametophyte moss with attached sporophyte or fern prothallia. A local florist or greenhouse might be willing to provide a variety of flowers for class examination.

PLANT REPRODUCTION AND DEVELOPMENT

Chapter 20 discusses patterns of asexual and sexual reproduction among algal and land plants.

Although you may not realize it, evidence of plant reproduction and development is common. Seeds, cones, flowers, and fruits are plant reproductive structures with which you are familiar. If you have hay fever, you know that your symptoms may be due to a reaction to certain types of pollen in the air. You may have seen seeds or bulbs develop into plants. What is involved in plant reproduction and development?

Plant life cycles include stages in which the cells of the organism are monoploid. Plant gametes are produced by *mitosis* from monoploid cells. Fertilization, or fusion of gametes, results in a diploid stage in the life cycle. The diploid stage, in turn, produces monoploid spores by *meiosis*. The monoploid and diploid stages in plants follow one another in an **alternation of generations** in which each generation depends on the other.

Each plant life cycle involves both asexual and sexual means of reproduction. Recall that asexual reproduction results in genetically identical offspring. The sexual phase of the life cycle ensures variation among a population of plants.

GOAL: You will gain an understanding of patterns of reproduction found among plants.

Alternation of generations is a life cycle in which the diploid and monoploid generations follow one another.

LIFE CYCLES OF ALGAE

20:1 Spirogyra

Spirogyra is a filamentous green alga (Section 14:4). The cells of a filament are identical. The asexual phase of *Spirogyra's* life cycle is reproduction by fragmentation. New cells are formed along a new filament as a result of mitosis and cell division.

Spirogyra reproduces asexually by fragmentation.

FIGURE 20-1. *Spirogyra* reproduces sexually by conjugation. The contents of cells adjoined by a conjugation tube fuse.

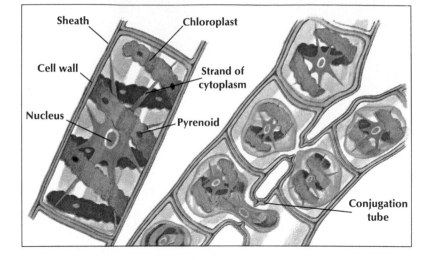

Teaching suggestion: Stress that conjugation and subsequent meiosis create variety among offspring.

FIGURE 20-2. *Ulothrix* life cycle involves both asexual and sexual reproduction. Asexual reproduction occurs by fragmentation and zoospore formation. Sexual reproduction involves fusion of gametes.

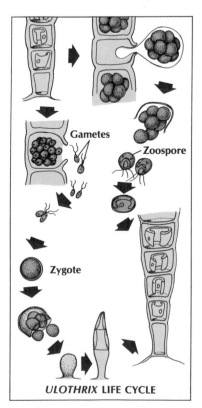

ULOTHRIX **LIFE CYCLE**

Sexual reproduction in *Spirogyra* occurs by conjugation. Bridges of cytoplasm form between adjacent cells of two monoploid filaments lying side by side (Figure 20-1). The cell contents from one filament pass through the bridges into the cells of the other filament. There the contents of the cells fuse to form diploid zygotes.

Many zygotes can be seen along a filament after conjugation. Each zygote develops a tough outer "shell" and is called a **zygospore.** A zygospore is a *diploid* spore. When conditions are favorable, the zygospore divides by meiosis to form four monoploid cells. Three of the cells die, but the surviving cell divides by mitosis to form a new *Spirogyra* filament thereby completing the cycle.

20:2 Ulothrix

The life cycle of *Ulothrix*, another green alga, also includes asexual and sexual reproduction. However, the means of reproduction are different from those in *Spirogyra*. Sometimes, asexual reproduction occurs by fragmentation if a portion of the filament breaks off. More often, though, asexual reproduction involves production of special cells, **zoospores.** Zoospores are produced by mitosis from **sporangium** cells located along the monoploid filament. The zoospores have four flagella. They actively swim through the water for a while, settle down, divide by mitosis, and develop into a new filament.

At certain times, sexual reproduction occurs. Certain cells produce gametes having two flagella. These gametes fuse to form a diploid zygote. The zygote later undergoes meiosis to produce four monoploid spores. Each spore then can develop into a new filament by mitosis. Figure 20-2 illustrates the life cycle of *Ulothrix*.

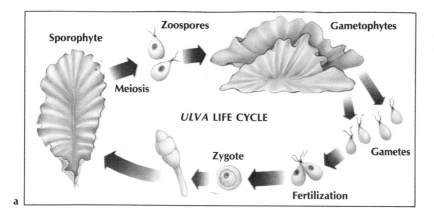

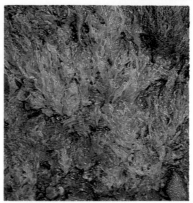

FIGURE 20-3. (a) The life cycle of *Ulva* involves both zoospore and zygote formation. (b) The "leafy" appearance of the diploid sporophyte has given this plant the common name sea lettuce.

20:3 Ulva

Both *Spirogyra* and *Ulothrix* have life cycles in which all structures except the zygote are monoploid. The zygote undergoes meiosis to produce spores which develop into new monoploid plants. There is no *multicellular*, diploid stage.

Ulva, or sea lettuce, is a green alga in which the life cycle includes multicellular stages in each generation. The diploid and monoploid stages look the same in *Ulva*. Sporangia of *Ulva* in the diploid stage undergo meiosis to produce spores which develop into multicellular monoploid plants. Certain cells of a monoploid *Ulva* produce gametes by mitosis. These gametes fuse to form a zygote which develops into a multicellular diploid plant.

Like *Ulva*, most complex plants have a life cycle with multicellular stages in each generation. The multicellular monoploid stage is called the **gametophyte** (guh MEET uh fite) **generation.** It produces gametes and reproduces sexually. The multicellular diploid stage is called the **sporophyte** (SPOR uh fite) **generation.** It produces spores and reproduces asexually. Figure 20-3 shows this pattern.

Notice that both the sporophyte and gametophyte may undergo asexual reproduction in addition to sexual reproduction by alternation of generations. The relative importance of gametophyte and sporophyte generations varies from one type of plant to another. An examination of the major groups of land plants illustrates the differences in life cycles.

The life cycle of *Ulva* includes both monoploid and diploid multicellular stages.

Life cycles of some brown algae are characterized by a predominant sporophyte phase, much like land plants.

A gametophyte plant is monoploid and produces gametes by mitosis. A sporophyte plant is diploid and produces spores by meiosis.

REVIEWING YOUR IDEAS

1. What is alternation of generations?
2. What kind of reproductive cells are made by monoploid plants? By what process?
3. What kind of cells are made by diploid plants?
4. Is the monoploid or diploid stage predominant in green algae?
5. Distinguish between sporophyte and gametophyte.

1. Alternation of generations is a plant life cycle in which monoploid and diploid stages follow one another.
2. Monoploid plants produce gametes by mitosis.
3. Diploid plants produce spores by meiosis.
4. monoploid
5. Sporophytes are diploid plants which produce spores. Gametophytes are monoploid and produce gametes.

LIFE CYCLES OF HIGHER PLANTS

20:4 Mosses

Mosses are among the simplest true land plants. A moss plant has multicellular sex organs in the gametophyte generation which protect the gametes—sperm and eggs.

Each gametophyte, male and female, makes many monoploid gametes by mitosis. Sperm which are made by the **antheridium** (an thuh RIHD ee um), the male sex organ, must swim through a film of moisture to the egg. The egg stays in the female sex organ, the **archegonium** (ar kih GOH nee um), where fertilization and zygote formation occur. The diploid zygote, still embedded, then begins to divide by mitosis to become a sporophyte. The sporophyte is not photosynthetic. It obtains nourishment by growing from the female gametophyte. When mature, the sporophyte produces many spores by meiosis. If conditions are favorable, each spore develops into a small structure, the **protonema** (proht uh NEE muh) which grows into a mature gametophyte.

Gametophyte moss plants produce sperm and eggs.

Sperm swim to the eggs which are in the archegonia.

FIGURE 20-4. The gametophyte generation is predominant in the life cycle of a moss. The sporophyte (which cannot live alone) grows from the female gametophyte.

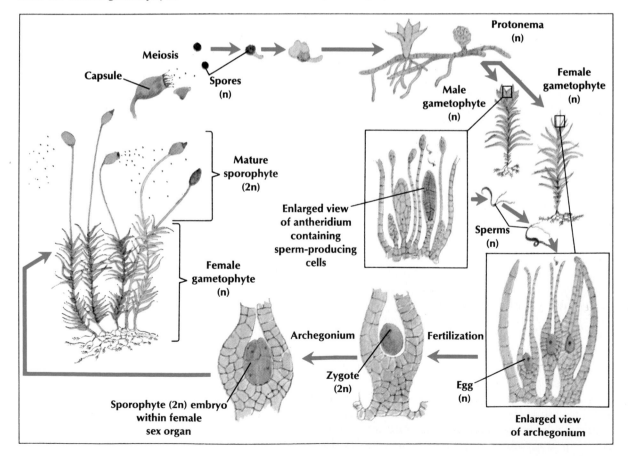

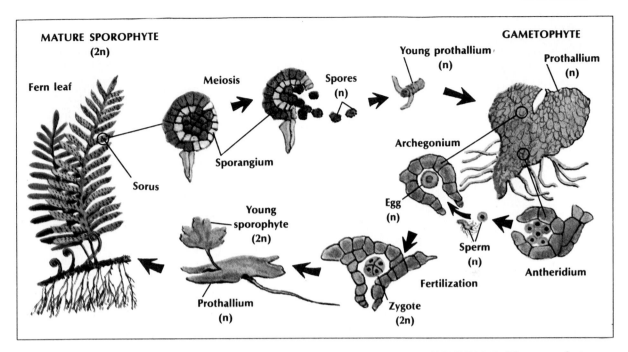

MATURE SPOROPHYTE (2n)

Fern leaf

Meiosis

Spores (n)

Sporangium

Sorus

Young sporophyte (2n)

Prothallium (n)

GAMETOPHYTE

Young prothallium (n)

Prothallium (n)

Archegonium

Egg (n)

Sperm (n)

Antheridium

Fertilization

Zygote (2n)

FIGURE 20-5. The sporophyte generation is predominant in the life cycle of a fern. However, a distinct gametophyte generation, the prothallium, also exists. The young sporophyte begins its development on the prothallium.

20:5 Ferns

Unlike mosses, ferns have a predominant sporophyte generation. The gametophyte is very small and lives for only a short time. The plant which you would recognize as a fern is the sporophyte. By meiosis, the sporophyte produces many monoploid spores. Spore cases can be seen on the underside of the fern fronds. These structures are clustered in groups called **sori** and contain the monoploid spores.

Each spore may develop into a tiny, heart-shaped gametophyte called the **prothallium** (proh THAL ee um). This tiny structure is about 2 cm in diameter and contains both archegonia and antheridia (Figure 20-5). It has no vascular tissue. The archegonia produce eggs and the antheridia produce sperm. The sperm swim to the eggs in the archegonia and fertilize them. The zygote begins its development within the archegonium, but it soon grows systems of its own and separates from the gametophyte to become an independent plant, which is the sporophyte. The gametophyte then dies. The sporophyte has become independent of the gameotphyte in this group of plants, and the monoploid generation is reduced greatly.

Ferns and mosses are not very plentiful. Because sperms must swim to the eggs, water is needed. Thus, these plants are restricted to moist environments. Also, the fern gametophyte is fragile and easily damaged. Should anything happen to the gametophyte, the sporophyte could not develop.

In ferns, the sporophyte is dominant.

A spore develops into a distinct gametophyte, the prothallium.

Ferns, like mosses, are restricted to a moist environment.

FIGURE 20-6. Developing embryos of conifers are protected in seed cones.

Spores produced by female cones are modified to form eggs.

The seed of a conifer contains an embryo sporophyte and a food source.

20:6 Conifers

Plants which reproduce by seeds are the most abundant on Earth today. In one group of these plants, the conifers, seeds are produced in structures called **cones** (Section 14:8). Conifers have two kinds of cones, male and female. Female cones are larger than male cones. In most conifers, male and female cones are found on separate branches of the same tree.

Seed plants have a dominant sporophyte generation. The gametophyte consists of only a few cells. In mosses and ferns, spores develop into gametophyte plants which then produce gametes. In seed plants, spores develop directly into gametes, skipping the separate gametophyte plant.

Figure 20-7 shows the life cycle of the pine, a typical conifer. In the spring, certain diploid cells in the male cones produce monoploid spores by meiosis. The spores become **pollen grains** which are carried by the wind to female cones on the same or a different tree. Pollen grains have tough outer walls which resist evaporation. The process by which pollen reaches the female cone is called **pollination.** After releasing pollen grains, the male cone falls off the tree.

Certain diploid cells in the female cone undergo meiosis to produce monoploid spores. The spores are later modified to form eggs. When pollination occurs, a monoploid sperm cell is produced within the pollen grain. The sperm fertilizes an egg within the female cone. Fertilization results in a diploid zygote, the beginning of a new sporophyte generation.

The zygote develops into an embryo, and a hard covering forms around the embryo forming a seed. A **seed** contains an embryo and a food source for early development. A single female cone may bear many seeds, each partly protected by the overlapping scales of the cone. Each seed develops a "wing"

FIGURE 20-7. The life cycle of the pine involves fertilization of cells within the female cones by pollen produced in the male cones.

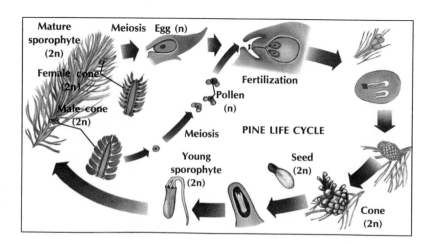

Mature sporophyte (2n)

Female cone (2n)

Male cone (2n)

Meiosis   Egg (n)

Fertilization

Pollen (n)

Meiosis

Young sporophyte (2n)

PINE LIFE CYCLE

Seed (2n)

Cone (2n)

which aids in the dispersal of the seeds by wind. The time between pollination and seed formation is often longer than a year. Female cones remain on the plant much longer than male cones.

The life cycle of the conifers shows several adaptations not seen in mosses and ferns. Water is not needed for fertilization. Sperm cells are carried to eggs in pollen grains. Thus, the sperm does not dry out, and conifers are not restricted to a moist habitat. Also, the embryo is protected by the outer seed coat and by the cone in which the seed is formed. These adaptations are also seen in the flowering plants.

Conifer seeds are dispersed by wind.

Unlike mosses and ferns, conifers are not restricted to a moist habitat.

20:7 Flowering Plants: Reproductive Structures

Most numerous of the seed plants are the flowering plants. The reproductive structures of flowering plants are the flowers. A flower and its parts are diploid. Both male and female organs may be located within a single flower, or they may be in separate flowers. Flowers with both male and female organs are said to be *perfect* while those with only male or female organs are said to be *imperfect*.

The female organ of a flower is a long, vase-shaped structure called the **pistil** (PIHS tul). A pistil is divided into three parts. The top is a sticky, structure called the **stigma** (STIHG muh). The stalklike portion is the **style,** and the swollen, lower region of the style is the **ovary.** Within the ovary are one or more **ovules** (OHV yewlz), female sporangia.

The male organ of a flower is the **stamen** (STAY mun). The stalklike portion of a stamen is called the **filament.** At the tip of the filaments are **anthers** (AN thurz) which contain **pollen sacs,** male sporangia.

Flowers are the reproductive structures of flowering plants.

The pistil is the female organ of a flower.

FIGURE 20-8. The reproductive structure of flowering plants is the flower. (a) Pollen is transferred from the male part, the stamen, to the female part, the pistil. (b) Pollen is adapted for adhering to the stigma. Notice the edges on the Lamb's quarter pollen shown here magnified about 1450 times.

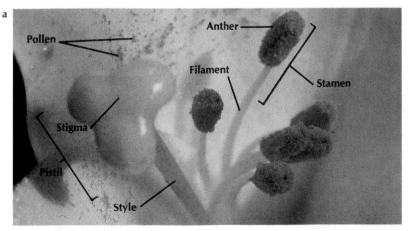

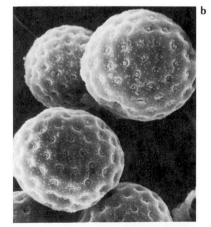

Larry Hamill

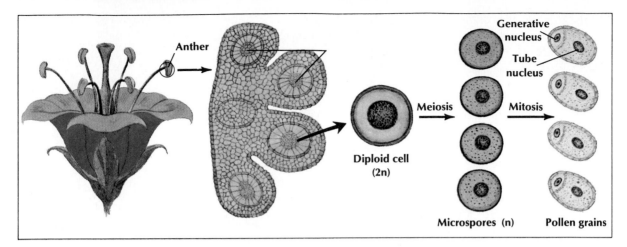

FIGURE 20-9. Pollen grains are produced by meiosis within the pollen sacs of the anther.

Teaching suggestion: Have students examine pollen with a microscope, using high power.

Within diploid pollen sacs, meiosis occurs producing monoploid microspores which develop into pollen grains.

Certain diploid cells within the ovule undergo meiosis producing a monoploid megaspore which gives rise to the egg and polar nuclei.

FIGURE 20-10. After meiosis and several mitoses, an egg and two polar nuclei are formed within an ovule. The other monoploid cells that result from this process do not survive.

20:8 Flowering Plants: Sporophyte to Gametophyte

Sexual activities begin within the ovules and anthers of a flower. Diploid cells in the pollen sacs undergo meiosis (Figure 20-9) to produce four monoploid cells known as **microspores** (small spores). Each microspore nucleus divides by mitosis to form two monoploid nuclei, the **tube nucleus** and the **generative nucleus.** When the outer wall of the microspore hardens, the structure becomes a **pollen grain.**

A similar type of activity takes place within each ovule (Figure 20-10). Certain cells of the ovule undergo meiosis to produce four monoploid cells of which only one survives. This surviving cell is called a **megaspore** (MEG uh spor), which means large spore. The megaspore nucleus divides by mitosis to form two monoploid nuclei, and each of these nuclei divides two or more times to produce a total of eight monoploid nuclei. These nuclei and the cytoplasm around them represent the entire female gametophyte generation. Of the eight nuclei produced, only three are important in reproduction, two **polar nuclei** in the center of the ovule and the true egg at one end. The remaining five monoploid nuclei die.

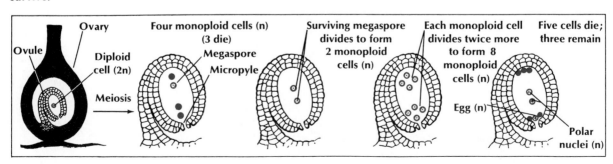

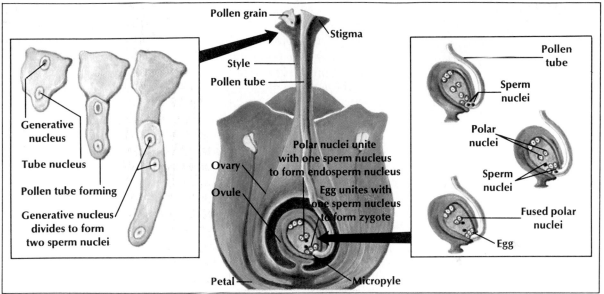

The green, leaflike structures beneath the petals are known as the sepals. Collectively, the sepals form the calyx. The stalk of the flower is the pedicel. Collectively, the petals are called the corolla.

20:9 Flowering Plants: Fertilization and Seed Formation

When and if a pollen grain reaches the pistil (pollination), it sticks to the surface of the stigma (Figure 20-11). There the tube nucleus causes a **pollen tube** to form and "dig" its way down through the style. It eventually reaches a small opening in the ovule called the **micropyle** (MI kruh pile). Meanwhile, the generative nucleus divides (by mitosis) to produce two monoploid sperm nuclei which are carried down the pollen tube into the ovule. (The nucleus of the pollen tube and the two sperm nuclei make up the male gametophyte generation.)

Within the ovule, one of the sperm nuclei joins with the two polar nuclei to form a triploid (TRIHP loyd), or 3n, structure called the **endosperm** (EN duh spurm) **nucleus.** The other sperm nucleus fertilizes the egg to form the diploid zygote. Fertilization and zygote formation mark the beginning of a new sporophyte generation.

After fertilization, the zygote begins some early stages of development. The endosperm nucleus divides many times to form a mass of tissue called **endosperm.** Endosperm is the food source for the developing plant. The outer covering of the ovule hardens into a protective device, the **seed coat.** The ovule is now a seed. *Within each seed is the developing plant and a food source.*

In summary, a flowering plant has a life cycle in which the sporophyte is predominant. Within a seed is a diploid embryo. The embryo grows and develops into a multicellular sporophyte and produces flowers. By meiosis, diploid cells within the ovules

FIGURE 20-11. When pollen lands on the stigma, a pollen tube forms and begins growing down to the ovule (left insert). After the tube reaches the ovule, one sperm nucleus fuses with the egg forming the zygote, and one fuses with the polar nuclei forming the endosperm nucleus (right insert).

Sperm nuclei are produced by mitosis from the generative nucleus.

In fertilization, one sperm nucleus fuses with the two polar nuclei to form the triploid endosperm nucleus. The other sperm nucleus fertilizes the true egg to form the diploid zygote.

The union of sperm nuclei with the egg and polar nuclei is called double fertilization.

After fertilization, the ovule becomes the seed containing the developing plant and a food source.

Cereal grains such as corn and wheat are rich in endosperm but not all seeds have endosperm.

Teaching suggestion: Point out that some fruits contain only one ovule (peach, olive). Others have two or more ovules (bean pod, grape). Have students think of other examples. Point out that although only one pollen grain fertilizes each ovule, many ovules may be fertilized within the same flower.

Allan Roberts

FIGURE 20-12. Fruits have a variety of forms. These walnuts are one example of a fruit.

The ovary becomes the fruit of the plant.

Fruit functions in the dispersal of seeds.

FIGURE 20-13. Seeds may be dispersed in many ways, including wind, water, and animals. Some plants have pods which burst open, dispersing seeds.

produce megaspores, and cells within anthers produce monoploid microspores. These structures are the beginning of a gametophyte generation. Cells derived from the megaspores and microspores undergo mitosis to become eggs and sperms. Fertilization results in the formation of a diploid zygote, marking the beginning of a sporophyte generation and completing the life cycle.

20:10 Flowering Plants: Fruit Formation and Seed Dispersal

While the seed coat develops, other activities are taking place. Most of the flower parts begin to die, but the ovary (in which the seeds are located) enlarges rapidly. An enlarged ovary becomes a **fruit.** You are familiar with fleshy, sweet fruits such as oranges, grapes, and peaches. Also, many "vegetables" such as tomatoes, beans, peas, and kernels of corn are really fruits. Many kinds of nuts and grains are fruits, too.

Once formed, fruit plays an important role in the reproductive process of flowering plants. Each fruit contains one or more seeds, and each seed contains an embryo. In addition to protecting the seeds, a fruit has another important function; it aids in **seed dispersal** (dihs PUR sul), the scattering of seeds. If seeds are to **germinate** (JUR muh nayt), begin development, they must land where there is a suitable environment. They cannot all grow well in the shadow of their parents because they could not compete for light and water. For this reason, it is essential that some get away from the parent plant.

Because of the good taste of many fruits, they are eaten by animals. The seeds of the fruit pass through the digestive systems of the animals and are usually deposited at a distance from the parent plant. If conditions are favorable, they will germinate.

Not all fruits are tasty. Cockleburs are inedible fruits, but they stick easily to the fur of animals and may be transported in that manner. Other fruits, such as those of maples and elms, which are "winged," may be carried great distances by the wind. Coconuts and other seeds float and may be dispersed by water.

Seeds that pop from plants

Seeds carried by wind

Seeds carried by water

Seeds carried by humans and other animals

20:11 Success Story

There are many reasons why seed plants are so plentiful on Earth. Methods of reproduction are more specialized than in mosses and ferns. Also, water is not important as a means of sperm transport. The male and female organs are close together, and there are various ways pollination occurs.

A plant which has flowers with both male and female sex organs can be pollinated within itself. This process, called **self-pollination,** can result from physical contact between the stamens and the pistil in which pollen is transferred. Self-pollination can also occur between different flowers of the same plant. When pollination occurs between flowers of separate plants, the process is called **cross-pollination.** In both self- and cross-pollination, pollen may be transferred by the wind, insects, or small birds. Many of the elaborate colors and scents of flowers are adaptations that attract these pollen-transferring animals, and thus, increase the chance of fertilization. Pollination in the conifers occurs mostly by wind transfer of pollen.

The seed plants have other adaptations not found in mosses and ferns. The embryos that they produce are protected within seeds. Also, seeds are adapted in various ways for a variety of methods of dispersal.

Plants are more specialized from mosses, to ferns, to conifers, to flowering plants. As plants become more specialized, the diploid phase of the life cycle is more predominant. Seed plants, almost totally diploid, are the dominant group of land plants. All the plants studied have the capability for sexual reproduction and the variety it produces. Why, then, is there this trend in more complex plants to have more predominant sporophytes (diploid phases)? What is adaptive about the predominant sporophyte stage?

The answer is that the monoploid organism has only one possible allele for each trait while diploid organisms have two. The presence of two alleles offers a better chance of survival because the chances of harmful traits or mutations appearing in an organism are reduced. A harmful allele may be masked by another allele in a diploid organism.

FIGURE 20-14. One reason for the success of flowering plants is that pollination is aided by insects and birds. Notice the yellow pollen covering this bee.

Pollination is aided by wind and animals.

Cross pollination provides greater variety among offspring.

Teaching suggestion: You may need to review briefly with your students the life cycles of mosses, ferns, conifers, and flowering plants to make this point.

The presence of two alleles for each trait reduces the probability of expression of a harmful trait.

Having two alleles per trait also increases the number of possible phenotypes.

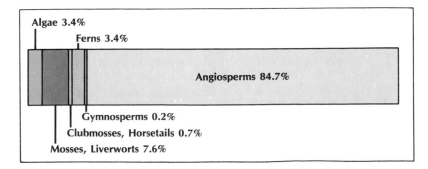

Algae 3.4%

Ferns 3.4%

Angiosperms 84.7%

Gymnosperms 0.2%

Clubmosses, Horsetails 0.7%

Mosses, Liverworts 7.6%

FIGURE 20-15. Flowering plants make up the majority of all plants. Their success is due in part to the removal of dependence on water for sperm transport and the development of various methods of pollination.

Herm Beck

Grant Heilman

Hickson-Bender Photography

FIGURE 20-16. (a) Many plants can be grown vegetatively from bulbs they form. (b) Strawberry plants reproduce from runners. (c) Potato "eyes" are buds, each of which can produce a new plant.

In vegetative propagation a new organism is produced from a nonsexual part of the parent.

Runners, buds, and bulbs are means of vegetative propagation in plants.

Vegetative propagation produces offspring which are genetically identical to the parent organism.

20:12 Vegetative Propagation

Recall that life cycles of plants may include asexual reproduction. **Vegetative propagation** (VEJ uh tayt ihv · prahp uh GAY shun) is another name for asexual reproduction in plants. It refers to reproduction (propagation) of an organism from a nonsexual (vegetative) part of the parent organism. This form of reproduction may occur in either the gametophyte or sporophyte stage, depending on the plant. It also may occur in nature or can be artificially carried out on plants by humans.

Examples of vegetative reproduction in nature are numerous. Strawberry plants develop outgrowths of stems called runners. These grow outward along the ground. At points along the runners, new strawberry plants develop. Bud formation is a form of vegetative reproduction in potatoes. The part of the potato plant which you eat is a swollen underground stem call a tuber. The "eyes" of the potato are buds which can develop into a complete plant. A short underground stem surrounded by many scales (modified leaves) is called a **bulb.** Daffodils, irises, and tulips are examples of garden plants grown vegetatively from bulbs.

Artificial vegetative propagation is carried out in several ways. One way involves cuttings from a plant stem. The cuttings, or cut pieces of stem, are removed from a plant and placed in moist sand. Special **adventitious** (ad ven TIHSH us) **roots** grow from the stems, and the stems grow into mature plants. Other vegetative parts, such as roots and leaves, can be used for cuttings. Because mitosis is involved, artificial vegetative propagation preserves the genetic traits of plants. As a result, gardeners and nursery people can preserve suitable types of plants for generations.

Fruit crops are artificially propagated in another way. In this process, buds are removed from one plant and grafted to the stem of another plant. The grafted buds later produce new shoots on which fruit develop. Apples, pears, and peaches are examples of fruits produced this way. Why would orchard keepers prefer to propagate crops by artificial vegetative propagation?

Grafting is a method of artificial vegetative propagation.

REVIEWING YOUR IDEAS

6. Which stage of the life cycle is predominant in mosses? In ferns? In conifers? In flowering plants?
7. What are the reproductive structures of a conifer?
8. What are the sex organs of a flower?
9. Distinguish between seed and fruit. Distinguish between pollen and seed.
10. Distinguish between self- and cross-pollination.
11. Name several means of vegetative propagation in plants. Give an example of each.

6. The gametophyte is predominant in mosses. The sporophyte is predominant in ferns, conifers, and flowering plants.
7. cones
8. pistils and stamens
9. A seed contains an embryo and a food source. A fruit contains seeds. Pollen contains monoploid cells, whereas seeds contain diploid cells (embryo).
10. Self-pollination may occur within a single flower or between flowers on the same plant. Cross-pollination occurs between flowers on separate plants.
11. Budding — potatoes; runners — strawberries; bulbs — tulips. Examples may vary.

DEVELOPMENT IN FLOWERING PLANTS

20:13 Germination

Some plants, such as mosses, undergo internal development. In these organisms, sporophytes often develop within the female gametophyte. However, seed-producing plants develop externally. After the zygote has been formed, it develops by repeated mitosis into a seed.

The seed then enters a period of inactivity, or **dormancy** (DOR mun see), which is necessary before development can continue. During the dormant period, chemical changes occur which prepare the embryo for further change. Then, when a seed is planted (or otherwise reaches a suitable environment), the embryo within the seed resumes its development, or germinates. Sprouting occurs. Germination can occur if conditions, which include enough oxygen, moisture, and a suitable temperature, are right. Each type of seed has its own moisture and temperature requirements. Oxygen is needed because respiration occurs rapidly to provide the growing embryo with enough energy.

Within a seed are structures which will develop into a mature plant. The **radicle** (RAD ih kul) is the first part of the embryo to emerge from the seed. It becomes the primary root of the new plant. Above the radicle is the **hypocotyl** (HI puh kaht ul) which becomes part of the root and part of the stem of the plant. The top part of the embryo, the **epicotyl** (EP ih kaht ul), is a pair of small leaves which will open early in development. The epicotyl will give rise to the rest of the stem and leaves of the plant.

Teaching suggestion: Have students bring fresh fruits such as tomatoes, apples, or cucumbers to class. Dissect out the seeds, and plant them. Seeds that do not have a dormancy period may germinate within a week.

FIGURE 20-17. As a corn seed germinates, food in the seed is used.

Grant Heilman

FIGURE 20-18. (a) Dicot seeds, such as beans, each have two cotyledons. One seed half has been removed here showing the embryonic plant inside. (b) Monocot seeds, such as corn, each have one coytledon.

Kodansha   *Kodansha*

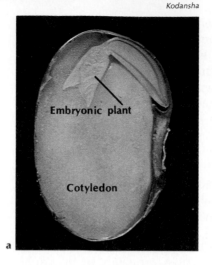
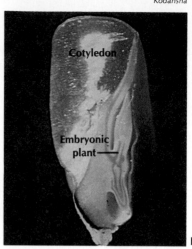

a   b

In some seeds, cotyledons provide the food source for germination.

The seed also contains cotyledons (Section 14:11), or seed leaves, which store food. The young plant uses this food until it can make its own food. Plants such as beans are dicots and have two cotyledons per seed. Corn is an example of a plant which is a monocot; it has one cotyledon per seed. In some seeds, the cotyledons contain endosperm (Section 20:9). In other seeds, the endosperm and cotyledons are separate food sources (Figure 20-18). In either case, food stored in seeds provides a source of energy during early development.

FIGURE 20-19. Cell division occurs in meristematic regions, such as the root tip. Behind the cell division region are regions of elongation and maturation.

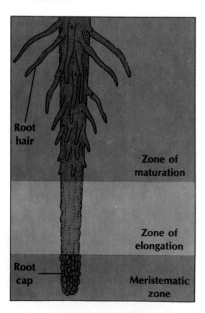

Root hair

Zone of maturation

Root cap

Zone of elongation

Meristematic zone

20:14 Further Development

As an example of plant development, consider the growth of a young tree root (Figure 20-19). The tip of the growing root has an outer **root cap** composed of protective cells. Cells in the root cap are scraped off as the root tip pushes downward through the soil. However, new cap cells are produced by the apical meristem. A **meristem** (MER uh stem) is a plant growth tissue. Cells of meristems actively divide at certain times. **Apical meristems** are located at the tips of roots and stems. Other new cells are produced further from the root tip on the other side of the apical meristem. They form the **elongation region.** Cells in this area grow only in length adding to the total length of the young root, and helping push it deeper into the soil. On the other side of the region of elongation is the **maturation region.** Cells here are even larger and develop into different types of specialized tissue. Changes in cells which result in the formation of specialized parts are called **differentiation** (dihf uh ren chee AY shun). In a young root, early differentiation results in the formation of different types of tissues for conduction of water and food, storage of food, protection, and uptake of water and minerals. Later differentiation produces a meristem called the **vascular cambium** located near the center of the root. All of these types of cells develop from cells produced by the meristem. You will study the details of root structure in Chapter 22.

The events described so far lead to an increase in the length of the root. Once the vascular cambium is formed, an increase in diameter also occurs. This increase occurs as the vascular cambium undergoes mitosis to provide many cells which form conductive tissues. Cells on the inside of the vascular cambium differentiate into tissue which transports water. On the outside, new cells develop into tissue which transports food. Each year the vascular cambium produces new conductive tissues and moves farther away from the center of the root. This pattern results in the increase of thickness of the root.

The pattern of growth and differentiation in a root is similar to that in other plant parts. Meristems in stems and buds produce cells which become specialized for particular functions. Some seed plants live for many years. During their lives, they continue to produce new tissues and organs year after year; for example, cones, leaves, and flowers. How does the development of a plant such as an oak tree compare to your development?

The root's vascular cambium is a meristem which gives rise to cells which become conductive tissues.

Meristems in stems and buds produce cells which develop into specialized tissues.

REVIEWING YOUR IDEAS

12. What is germination? What conditions are necessary for it to occur?
13. List the various parts of a seed.
14. What are the regions of a developing root?

12. Germination is the resumption of development by a seed. It requires proper temperature and adequate moisture and oxygen.
13. A seed contains one or two cotyledons, a radicle, hypocotyl, and epicotyl.
14. A developing root contains a root cap, apical meristem, and elongation and maturation regions.

CHAPTER REVIEW

SUMMARY

1. Plants have a life cycle in which there is an alternation of generations—a diploid, spore-producing stage and a monoploid, gamete-producing stage.
2. *Spirogyra* and *Ulothrix* have life cycles with no multicellular diploid stage.
3. In *Ulva* and most complex plants, the life cycle includes a multicellular monoploid stage, the gametophyte, and a multicellular diploid stage, the sporophyte.
4. Mosses have a life cycle with a predominant gametophyte generation. Ferns have a pre-dominant sporophyte but have a distinct, though small, multicellular gametophyte. Conifers and flowering plants have a pre-dominant sporophyte and no distinct, multicellular gametophyte.

5. The major events of reproduction in flowering plants are pollination (self- or cross-pollination), fertilization, and seed and fruit formation.

6. Seed plants are diploid so they have two genes for each trait. Having more than one gene for each trait reduces the expression of harmful traits and produces a greater variety of phenotypes.

CHAPTER REVIEW

7. Seed plants develop externally as opposed to mosses and ferns which develop in archegonia. The embryo within a seed contains structures which form the first roots, stem, and leaves of the plant.

8. Many plants have a continuous pattern of development throughout their lives. New tissues and organs are produced each year.

LANGUAGE OF BIOLOGY

alternation of
  generations
anther
antheridium
apical meristem
archegonium
cone
differentiation
elongation region
epicotyl
filament
fruit
gametophyte
germination
hypocotyl
maturation region
ovary

ovule
pistil
pollen grain
pollen sac
pollination
prothallium
protonema
radicle
seed
sporangium
sporophyte
stamen
stigma
style
vascular cambium
vegetative
  propagation

CHECKING YOUR IDEAS

On a separate paper, complete each of the following statements with the missing term(s). Do not write in this book.

1. In plants, gametes are produced by the process of _____.

2. Sporophytes contain the _____ number of chromosomes.

3. The _____ of a seed develops into the primary root.

4. The _____ develops from the ovary of a flower.

5. _____ have no independent multicellular gametophyte stage.

6. Pollination between flowers on the same plant is _____ pollination.

7. Fruits aid in the dispersal of _____.

8. _____ is another name for asexual reproduction in plants, reproduction from a nonsexual plant part.

9. Describing chromosome number, each pollen grain contains two _____ nuclei.

10. In mosses, the _____ generation is the predominant form.

EVALUATING YOUR IDEAS

1. Compare sexual reproduction in *Spirogyra* and *Ulothrix*. How are they different?

2. What stage of *Ulva's* life cycle is not part of the life cycle of *Spirogyra* and *Ulothrix*?

3. Describe a generalized plant life cycle.

4. Describe the life cycle of a moss.

5. In terms of reproduction, how have mosses adapted to life on land?

6. Why are mosses less abundant than other land plants?

7. Describe the life cycle of a fern. How are ferns limited?

8. Describe the life cycle of a conifer. What adaptations in a conifer's life cycle are not present in the life cycles of mosses and ferns?

9. How is a pollen grain formed?

10. Describe the activities within an ovule.

11. How does fertilization occur within flowering plants?

12. What is the major role of the fruit in the life cycle of flowering plants? Describe how this function is accomplished. Why is it necessary?

13. Why are seed plants the most common plants? Why are flowering plants even more successful than conifers?

14. Describe the structures of the embryo within a seed. List the functions of the structures.

15. What is the function of cotyledons during germination? Which structures take over the function of cotyledons?

16. How does a root increase in length? What tissues develop during this period?

17. How does an increase in the thickness of a root occur?

18. How is artificial vegetative propagation advantageous?

APPLYING YOUR IDEAS

1. How might a tree be "produced" that has both plums and peaches on separate branches?

2. Why would you not expect to see a moss growing in an open field?

3. Find out if the following are flowering plants:
   (1) saguaro cactus   (7) palm tree
   (2) maple tree   (8) yucca tree
   (3) pine tree   (9) bamboo
   (4) cotton plant   (10) wheat
   (5) redwood tree   (11) mustard
   (6) blueberry bush   (12) grass

4. In what way is a plant produced by vegetative propagation a clone?

5. Many of the events of the development of a stem are like those of a root. What differences are there in the development of these two organs?

6. What kind of tissue allows plants to develop new structures over and over again?

7. What features of development of a woody root would not be a part of the development of a tomato root? Explain.

EXTENDING YOUR IDEAS

1. Using library resources, prepare a report on methods of artificial vegetative propagation.

2. Use reference materials to study the life cycles of *Chlamydomonas*, *Oedogonium*, and *Fucus*. How do these life cycles compare to those of land plants (mosses, ferns, and seed plants)?

3. Trace the events which occur when a sweet potato is placed in water. What kind of reproduction is this plant formation?

4. Conduct an experiment to determine the rate of growth of a seedling during germination. Use ten seeds. Measure the mass of each seed before it is planted. Record the height of each seedling daily. At the end of the experiment, pool your results and prepare graphs of (a) total height each day, (b) increase in height each day, and (c) increase in height each day expressed as a percentage of the previous day's height. Measure the mass of the seedings at the end of the experiment and record the increase in mass. Analyze your results.

5. Using the experiment described in Extending Your Ideas 4 as a control, repeat the experiment using a variable factor such as amount of light or amount of water. Compare and analyze your data.

SUGGESTED READINGS

Cook, Robert Edward, "Long-Lived Seeds." *Natural History*, February, 1979.

Mulcaky, David L., "Rise of the Angiosperms." *Natural History*, September, 1981.

Patent, Dorothy, *Plants and Insects Together*. New York, Holiday House, 1976.

Spencer, Patricia W., "Roses Are Red, White, Yellow, Pink . . ." *Natural History*, June-July, 1977.

Additional student readings and suggested teacher readings are provided in the Teacher's Guide.

Roger K. Burnard

Plants are the producers in almost every community on Earth. Through the process of photosynthesis, plants convert the energy of sunlight to chemical energy of glucose. How does photosynthesis occur? What is required? What properties of light are important in the process? In what other ways do plants get nutrients?

Introduction and suggested demonstration: Sprigs of actively growing *Elodea* plants from an aquarium can be used to indirectly show the uptake of carbon dioxide during photosynthesis. Exhale through a straw into a dilute solution of bromthymol blue in aquarium water until the solution turns yellow. This breathing introduces carbon dioxide into the solution, forming carbonic acid which is responsible for the color change from blue to yellow. Now add the yellow solution to a test tube containing a sprig of *Elodea* and expose to sunlight (or another light source). As *Elodea* undergoes photosynthesis, it uses carbon dioxide, and the solution returns to a blue color as its pH increases. As a control, prepare a second test tube in the same way, but keep it in the dark. The solution will remain yellow.

PLANT NUTRITION

Chapter 21 explores the process of photosynthesis and discusses plant digestion and nutrition.

Plants are essential members of every type of community. In oceans, lakes, forests, and deserts, algae or more complex plants are producers. All other forms of life depend, directly or indirectly, on plants for food.

In Chapter 4, you learned how all organisms obtain usable energy from food by cellular respiration. The food most often used by living things is glucose. Glucose is important because it has chemical potential energy. Only autotrophs, mostly green plants, can make glucose. They trap light energy and change it to chemical energy. In this chapter, you will study how glucose is made and how plants get their nutrient requirements.

GOAL: You will gain an understanding of food production and nutrition in plants.

Autotrophs convert radiant energy of sunlight to the chemical energy of glucose.

TRAPPING ENERGY

21:1 The Leaf: Internal Structure

Photosynthesis can occur in all plant cells containing chlorophyll. In complex plants, most photosynthesis occurs in one special organ, the **leaf.**

A leaf is composed of several distinct cell layers. The upper layer of a leaf is called the **upper epidermis** (ep uh DUR mus). Its main function is to protect the other layers of the leaf. Epidermis is classified as a protective tissue in plants. Beneath the epidermis is a layer of palisade (pal uh SAYD) cells. **Palisade cells** are long cells arranged vertically. These cells, along with the **spongy layer** beneath them, contain chlorophyll. Photosynthesis occurs in these cells of a leaf.

Leaves are the major sites of food production in plants.

Photosynthesis occurs in the palisade and spongy layer cells of a leaf.

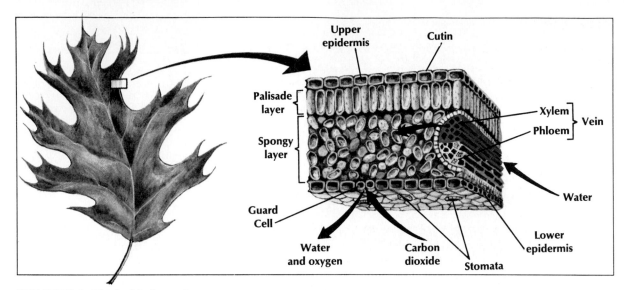

Upper epidermis

Cutin

Palisade layer

Spongy layer

Xylem

Phloem

Vein

Guard Cell

Water

Water and oxygen

Carbon dioxide

Stomata

Lower epidermis

FIGURE 21-1. The leaf is the major organ of photosynthesis. Photosynthesis occurs within palisade and spongy layer cells.

Guard cells regulate the opening and closing of stomata.

Regulation of stomata is discussed in Section 22:6.

A general biological principle: structure is related to function.

How does a leaf illustrate the relationship between structure and function?

Shape and arrangement of leaves are adaptations for trapping light energy.

Running through a leaf are two types of vascular (conductive) tissue, xylem and phloem. **Xylem** (ZI lum) cells carry water and minerals. **Phloem** (FLOH em) cells carry food. The veins of the leaves connect with the veins of the stem which are continuous with those of the roots. Through the veins, water and minerals move from roots to leaves, and food is carried from leaves to other parts of the plant.

The lower layer of a leaf is the lower epidermis. It contains guard cells. **Guard cells** surround and regulate the opening and closing of pores called **stomata** (STOH mut uh).

Both the upper and lower epidermis of a leaf are covered by cutin (Section 14:4). In the leaves of some plants, such as ivy, cutin is especially thick and gives the leaf a shiny appearance.

All the materials necessary for glucose production enter the leaves. Carbon dioxide from the atmosphere enters a leaf through the stomata and is dissolved in the watery film surrounding the cells. Water enters the leaf through xylem vessels which originate in the roots of the plant. Thus, *the leaf structure is adapted for photosynthesis.*

A leaf also provides for the distribution of glucose. Once glucose has been produced, it is distributed by the phloem. Phloem cells transport glucose to all parts of the plant which cannot produce glucose. Other products of photosynthesis, water and oxygen, escape from the leaf through the stomata.

Structure of a plant as a whole is also related to function. Besides the materials needed for photosynthesis, energy is needed to put the materials together. This energy is sunlight. At the ends of branches, leaves receive more sunlight than if they were shaded from the sun. Also, leaves are often flat and broad. These are adaptations for greater exposure to sunlight. What effects does air pollution have on photosynthesis? It slows photosynthesis by decreasing the amount of light available to plants.

21:2 Light

To understand how radiant energy is used to make glucose, you must learn about light. Light is a form of radiant energy. All radiant energy travels in waves. The distance between consecutive crests of the waves is called **wavelength** (Figure 21-2). The human eye is sensitive to radiant energy with wavelengths of about 400 to 700 nm. This portion of radiant energy is called **white light.**

When white light is passed through a prism, several different colors can be seen. As it passes through the prism, the light spreads because each wavelength of light is bent at a different angle. As a result, white light is separated into a band of colors known as the **visible spectrum** (SPEC trum). The colors of the different wavelengths are red, orange, yellow, green, blue, and violet. Red light has the longest wavelength of the visible spectrum, and violet light has the shortest wavelength. Ultraviolet and infrared wavelengths, on the ends of the visible spectrum, are invisible to humans.

Have you ever worn a dark blue or black sweater on a spring day? If you have, you know that after a short period of time, you begin to feel quite warm. Why? Molecules of dye in the sweater absorb certain wavelengths of light energy. As the light energy is absorbed, it is changed into heat which you feel. Whenever light energy is absorbed, it is changed to another form of energy. A solar cell traps light energy and changes it to electric energy.

Not all light is absorbed when it strikes an object. A dark blue sweater appears blue because its molecules reflect mostly the blue portion of the spectrum. The portion of the spectrum reflected is the color of an object. A blue object reflects blue light; a red object reflects red light. Window glass and cellophane are common objects which transmit light. Reflection and absorption of light are important concepts in understanding the trapping of light in photosynthesis.

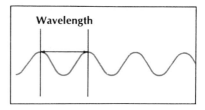

FIGURE 21-2. Light travels in waves. One wavelength is the distance between two consecutive crests. Light of different wavelengths is different colors.

Visible light is a small portion of the electromagnetic spectrum, which includes gamma and X rays ($\lambda \approx 10^{-16}$ to 10^{-9}m), ultraviolet ($\lambda \approx 10^{-9}$ to 10^{-7}m), infrared ($\lambda \approx 10^{-6}$ to 10^{-2}m), microwaves ($\lambda \approx 10^{-3}$ to 10^0m), and radio waves ($\lambda \approx 10^0$ to 10^5m).

White light is composed of many wavelengths.

When light energy is absorbed, it is changed to another form of energy.

Colors that you see are wavelengths reflected from an object.

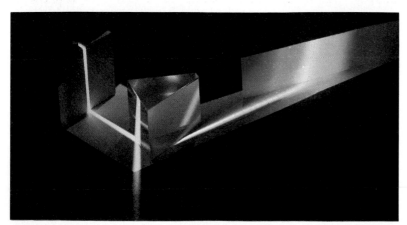

Eastman Kodak Co.

FIGURE 21-3. When white light is passed through a prism, light of different wavelengths is separated, producing a spectrum. The visible light spectrum includes wavelengths of 400 nm (violet) to 700 nm (red).

The absorption spectrum of chlorophyll closely parallels the action spectrum of photosynthesis.

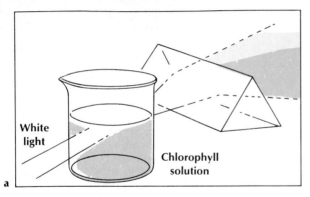

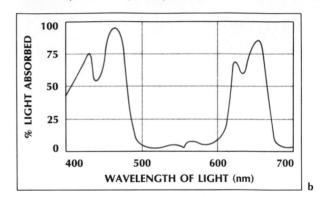

a

b

FIGURE 21-4. (a) When white light passes through a chlorophyll solution, only yellow-green light is transmitted. Other colors are absorbed. (b) A graph of the absorption spectrum of chlorophyll shows that green and some yellow light are reflected, while other colors are absorbed.

Suggested demonstration: Over a hot plate, boil several ground up leaves in alcohol until the solution turns dark green. Spinach and geranium leaves work well. Remove the leaf remnants and add an equal volume of petroleum ether. Then pour the mixture in a separatory funnel. Shake the mixture and then let it settle. Different pigments will separate into clearly visible layers.

Chlorophyll absorbs certain wavelengths and transforms them into chemical energy.

In eukaryotes, chlorophyll is located in chloroplasts. Prokaryotes have no chloroplasts.

Carotenes, another class of pigments in plants, aid in absorbing light energy for photosynthesis.

Teaching suggestion. Emphasize that only the portion of light absorbed by chlorophyll is significant. The absorbed light is transformed into chemical energy.

21:3 Chlorophyll and Other Pigments

Organisms which make glucose have a pigment called **chlorophyll** (Section 1:4) which *traps light energy which it changes to chemical energy.* These organisms include green plants, algal protists, blue-green algae, and certain bacteria. They appear green because chlorophyll reflects mostly the green portion of the spectrum. The other wavelengths of light are absorbed or reflected. A spectrum of chlorophyll is obtained by passing white light through a solution of chlorophyll and then through a prism. When this spectrum is compared to the spectrum of white light, differences are seen (Figure 21-4). Because certain wavelengths are either reduced or absent in the chlorophyll spectrum, it is called an **absorption** (ub SORP shun) **spectrum.** Violet, blue, orange, and red wavelengths are almost totally absorbed by chlorophyll. When light energy is absorbed, it is changed in form. Thus, chlorophyll absorbs violet, blue, red, and orange wavelengths and changes light into chemical energy.

There are several types of chlorophyll, but they are very similar in structure and properties. The most common types are chlorophyll *a* and chlorophyll *b*. The formula of chlorophyll *a* is $C_{55}H_{72}O_5N_4Mg$, and the formula for chlorophyll *b* is $C_{55}H_{70}O_6N_4Mg$. Chlorophyll is found in organelles called **chloroplasts** (Section 5:14) in eukaryotes. The chlorophyll of blue-green algae is attached to membranes in the cytoplasm. In autotrophic bacteria, chlorophyll is located in chromatophores.

Chloroplasts also may contain yellow and orange pigments called **carotenes** (Section 13:6). They aid chlorophyll in trapping light energy for photosynthesis. Carotenes and other pigments are also present in other parts of a plant. These yellow, orange, and red colors are most often seen in flowers and fruits. Carotenes and other pigments in leaves often are masked by chlorophyll. In northern latitudes, the manufacture of chlorophyll slows down in autumn. With less chlorophyll present, the carotenes and other pigments become visible so the leaves turn from green to yellow, orange, and red.

Alvin E. Staffan

Alvin E. Staffan

a

b

FIGURE 21-5. Plants contain pigments other than chlorophyll. (a) In some plants, such as the coleus, these pigments are visible. (b) In many trees, pigments other than chlorophyll become more obvious in autumn.

REVIEWING YOUR IDEAS

1. What is the chief function of leaves?
2. Why is glucose important to cells?
3. What is light? How does it travel?
4. What happens to light when it is absorbed?
5. Why is chlorophyll green? Why do green leaves turn orange or yellow in autumn?

---

1. photosynthesis
2. Glucose is an energy source.
3. Light is a form of radiant energy. It travels in waves.
4. When light is absorbed, it is changed to another form of energy.
5. Chlorophyll reflects mostly green wavelengths. In autumn, chlorophyll production ceases, and carotenes become visible.

PHOTOSYNTHESIS

21:4 The Light Reactions

Photosynthesis is a complex process by which an autotroph makes food. Like cellular respiration, photosynthesis is a set of many separate reactions. *It is the process by which light energy is absorbed and then converted to the chemical energy of glucose.* Because energy (light) is absorbed, photosynthesis is an endergonic process (Section 4:7).

The many reactions of photosynthesis are summarized by the following equation:

$$6CO_2 + 6H_2O \xrightarrow[\text{light energy}]{\text{enzymes, chlorophyll}} C_6H_{12}O_6 + 6O_2$$

Biologists now know that there are two main sets of reactions in photosynthesis. They are known as the light reactions and the dark reactions.

In photosynthesis, light energy is converted to the chemical energy of glucose.

Teaching suggestion. For honors or advanced classes, consider studying the details of photosynthesis as presented in Appendix B.

The **light reactions** involve a series of changes dependent on light. They occur in the grana (Section 5:14) of chloroplasts of eukaryotes. During these reactions, light is absorbed by chlorophyll and carotene molecules. These molecules trap the energy of light and pass it to a special chlorophyll molecule. Then, by a series of steps, the light energy is converted to the chemical energy of ATP molecules.

Another part of the light reactions involves the water used in photosynthesis. The water molecules are split into hydrogen ions and oxygen. The oxygen is given off as a by-product. The hydrogen ions are used in later steps of photosynthesis.

Note that the light reactions do not involve carbon dioxide, and no glucose is produced. See Appendix B for more details about the light reaction. In summary, the light reaction involves two main events.

1. Light energy is trapped and converted to chemical energy in the bonds of ATP.
2. Water is split into hydrogen ions and oxygen.

PEOPLE IN BIOLOGY

Charles French became fascinated with photosynthetic reactions as a college sophomore. Using simple, precise measurements of light absorption, gas exchange, and growth rate of photosynthetic cells, French has researched the process of photosynthesis. Dr. French has spent much of his life trying to concentrate the photochemically active parts of chloroplasts to learn how each part works. To aid him in his research, Dr. French invented several scientific instruments. These instruments include one which disintegrates chloroplasts and one that records the fluorescence (energy given off as light) of plant pigments. Using these and other instruments, French confirmed that the extra pigments in a plant cell such as chlorophyll-*b* and carotenoids absorb energy from light and then transfer the energy to chlorophyll-*a* for use by the cell. Since his retirement in 1973, Dr. French has been measuring the wavelengths of light used in some of the reactions that occur in photosynthesis.

For his work on photosynthesis, Dr. French was elected to the National Academy of Sciences and the American Academy of Arts and Sciences in 1963 and has received several honorary doctorates.

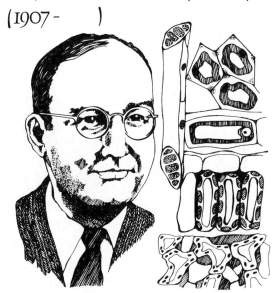

(1907-)

Charles Stacy French

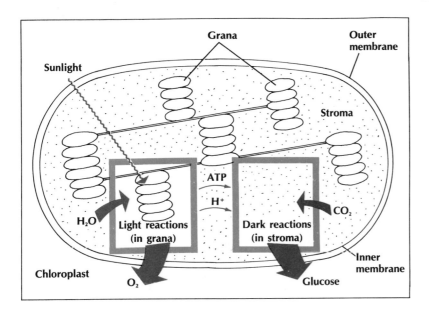

FIGURE 21-6. Photosynthesis can be broken into the light reactions, which require light, and the dark reactions, which do not require light.

21:5 The Dark Reactions

The events of the light reactions are a preparation for the dark reactions. Synthesis of glucose occurs during the **dark reactions.** The dark reactions do not have to occur in the dark; they simply do not require light.

Synthesis of glucose occurs during the dark reactions.

The dark reactions occur in the stroma (Section 5:14) of chloroplasts in eukaryotes. During these reactions, carbon dioxide is converted to glucose. These changes require energy. Also, hydrogen must be added to the carbon dioxide. (Each glucose molecule contains 12 hydrogen atoms.) The energy comes from ATP. The hydrogen comes from water molecules. Both the ATP and hydrogen used in the dark reactions come from the light reactions. See Appendix B for more details about the dark reactions. Figure 21-6 shows the relationship between the light and dark reactions of photosynthesis.

The ATP and hydrogen atoms needed in the dark reactions come from the light reactions.

Although glucose is the main product of photosynthesis, other important compounds are also made. Some of the glucose can be converted to fats and amino acids (Chapter 3), and some is used directly as an energy source. Glucose transported to other areas of a plant can be stored as starch or converted to cellulose, the substance contained in cell walls.

Glucose produced in photosynthesis may be converted to other compounds.

21:6 Energy Relationships

In some ways, photosynthesis is the opposite of respiration. The reactants (raw materials) and end products are different, and respiration is exergonic while photosynthesis is endergonic.

TABLE 21-1. COMPARISON OF PHOTOSYNTHESIS AND RESPIRATION		
	Photosynthesis	Respiration
REACTANTS	CO_2 and H_2O	$C_6H_{12}O_6$ and O_2
PRODUCTS	$C_6H_{12}O_6$ and O_2	CO_2 and H_2O
ENERGY	Endergonic	Exergonic
EQUATION SUMMARY	$6CO_2 + 6H_2O \rightarrow$ $C_6H_{12}O_6 + 6O_2$	$C_6H_{12}O_6 + 6O_2 \rightarrow$ $6CO_2 + 6H_2O$

Photosynthesis and respiration are interdependent.

Glucose provides energy for the plant in which it was produced and for any animal which eats the plant.

Teaching suggestion: Stress that both autotrophs and heterotrophs rely on glucose for energy.

6. Photosynthesis is the process by which light energy is trapped and converted to the chemical energy of glucose.
7. carbon dioxide and water
8. light and dark reactions; chloroplasts; The light reactions occur in the grana and the dark reactions occur in the stroma.
9. Photosynthesis is endergonic whereas respiration is exergonic. The reactants of one are the products of the other.
10. Carbon dioxide and water produced during respiration are necessary reactants in photosynthesis. The glucose and oxygen produced during photosynthesis are necessary for respiration.
11. Glucose is high in potential chemical energy. Carbon dioxide and water are low in potential chemical energy.
12. Photosynthesis requires energy. Light is the energy source.

Photosynthesis and cell respiration depend on each other. Through photosynthesis, cells make glucose which can be broken down in respiration to produce energy. Carbon dioxide and water are low in chemical energy. During photosynthesis, the energy of sunlight is changed into chemical energy as the carbon dioxide and water combine to form glucose (Table 21-1). Once formed, glucose is a source of potential energy.

Glucose can be used by the plant which produced it or be passed along a food chain (Section 1:4). It is passed along the food chain when another organism eats the plant.

In the cells, glucose is broken down by respiration. In this way, what was originally the sun's energy is transferred to ATP. The energy is available to the cells through respiration for the many activities an organism performs. The products of aerobic respiration, carbon dioxide and water, are low in potential energy. They are then available for buildup into glucose by photosynthesis again. Because it has energy that is available to cells, glucose is one of the most important organic compounds.

REVIEWING YOUR IDEAS

6. What is photosynthesis?
7. What are the reactants of photosynthesis?
8. What are the two main sets of reactions in photosynthesis? In what organelle do they occur in eukaryotic cells? Where does each set of reactions occur within that organelle?
9. In what ways is photosynthesis the opposite of cellular respiration? Compare the two processes in terms of reactants, products, and energy.
10. In what ways is photosynthesis dependent on cellular respiration? How does cellular respiration depend on photosynthesis?
11. Compare the potential chemical energy of glucose with that of carbon dioxide and water.
12. Why is photosynthesis an endergonic process? What is the source of energy for photosynthesis?

DIGESTION IN PLANTS

21:7 Insectivorous Plants

Although most plants do not take in food and digest it, large molecules of starch, stored in roots or seeds, may be digested by enzymes. The digestion is intracellular. Digestion of starch results in glucose molecules which can be used as energy sources.

Some autotrophic plants, although capable of photosynthesis, take in food in an organic form. They are called **insectivorous** (in sek TIHV uh rus) **plants** because they "eat" insects. These plants usually live in soil low in nitrogen and sometimes other elements, such as soil in a bog. Insects are an added source of these elements for the plants. Because insectivorous plants can synthesize food, they do not require insects as food for their survival.

One type of insectivorous plant is Venus's-flytrap (Figure 21-7). The upper part of a leaf of this plant is bordered by spines and is hinged along a midrib. There are sensory hairs on the upper surface of each lobe of a leaf. When these hairs are stimulated by the touch of an insect, the leaf quickly closes and traps the insect. Then, digestive enzymes are secreted into the hollow formed by the lobes, and extracellular digestion of the insect takes place. The digested molecules are absorbed and transported throughout the plant.

Other insectivorous plants include the sundew plant and the pitcher plant. Sundew plants trap insects differently from Venus's-flytraps. Long "tentacles" extending from the leaves secrete a sticky substance which traps small insects. Then, the "tentacles" bend inward toward the center of the leaf where the insect is digested. Pitcher plant leaves form pitcherlike structures. Insects are attracted to the pitchers and fall into the traps where they are digested by enzymes.

Intracellular digestion occurs in roots and seeds of plants.

Insectivorous plants trap and digest insects. The insects provide nitrogen and other elements for the plants.

Stimulation of the sensory hairs results in a loss of turgidity in certain sensitive cells and a subsequent closing of the leaf.

FIGURE 21-7. (a) The Venus's flytrap, (b) sundew plant, and (c) pitcher plant have adaptations that aid in catching insects. Insectivorous plants get nitrogen and other nutrients from insects.

Carolina Biological Supply Co.

Roger K. Burnard

Roger K. Burnard

21:8 Plant Nutrients

Water and carbon dioxide are materials necessary for photosynthesis. Carbon dioxide enters a plant from the surrounding environment. Water enters through roots of land plants or by osmosis in algae.

Plants require a variety of essential nutrients.

In addition, plants require a variety of other essential nutrients (Section 18:1). For example, magnesium is needed because it is a part of chlorophyll. Nitrogen is needed for the production of ATP, the nitrogen bases of nucleic acids, and amino acids. Sulfur is also a part of several amino acids. Other important nutrients in plants include iron, phosphorus, potassium, and calcium.

These essential nutrients enter a plant in the form of ions (Section 3:5) dissolved in water. They pass into algae and mosses by passive or active transport. In higher plants, they are absorbed by roots and move through the stem to the leaves (Section 22:4) in special cells.

13. Insectivorous plants are those having adaptations for trapping and digesting insects. The insects contain nitrogen and other nutrients not readily available from the soil.
14. Plant nutrients include nitrogen, sulfur, magnesium, iron, and phosphorus. They enter a plant as ions in water.

REVIEWING YOUR IDEAS

13. What are insectivorous plants? Why are insects important to them?
14. List five nutrients required by plants. How do these nutrients enter a plant?

ADVANCES IN BIOLOGY

21:9 Fuel from Plants

Coal, oil, and natural gas are fossil fuels.

Nearly all the energy used in the highly industrialized countries of Western Europe, the United States, and Japan comes from fossil fuels. **Fossil fuels** (coal, oil, and natural gas) are made deep within the earth from the remains of plants and animals and take millions of years to form. Fossil fuels are also called hydrocarbons because they are made up of hydrogen and carbon. These fuels not only run cars and produce electricity and heat, but extracts from the fuels, called **petrochemicals** (peh troh ᴋᴇᴍ ih kulz) are used to make plastics, drugs, pesticides, and many other products. In the face of increasing energy demands and decreasing supplies of fossil fuels, scientists are looking for other ways to produce fuels and petrochemicals similar to those derived from fossil fuels. Some scientists are looking to plants as a possible solution to energy problems.

With increasing energy demands and decreasing supplies of fossil fuels, scientists are looking for ways to produce fuels.

During photosynthesis, plants use sunlight, water, and carbon dioxide to make carbohydrates (Section 3:13). Some plants, such as sugarcane and corn, are very efficient in making large amounts of sugar. In order to make fuels, these sugars are fermented. In this process, microorganisms attack the sugars, take out some of the oxygen, and make alcohol. Alcohol can be mixed with gasoline to produce **gasohol** (GAS uh hahl) which will fuel a standard car. If the engines are slightly changed, cars will run on alcohol and water (95% alcohol, 5% water). In Brazil, alcohol is being distilled further to produce substances similar to petrochemicals to be used in manufacturing. Because these fuels are made by artificial processes, they are called **synfuels** (SIHN fyewlz).

Dr. Melvin Calvin of the University of California, Berkeley, is experimenting with plants of the Euphorbiaeceae (yew for bee AY see uh) family to try and produce synfuels. These plants, which include the rubber tree and gopher plant, take photosynthesis one step further and produce actual hydrocarbons. In the past, these hydrocarbons, in the form of latex, have been used to make rubber for tires. By using different species of *Euphorbias* (yoo FOR bee uz), Calvin has been able to produce a sap composed of about one third hydrocarbon that he believes can be used as a petroleum substitute.

In Brazil, Calvin has discovered a tree, the copa-iba tree, which produces an oily sap which can be used as diesel fuel without having to be processed. Calvin has germinated over 2000 trees to be cultivated in an experimental plantation to try and "grow" oil. A company in Japan is also trying to "grow" oil. By planting a *Euphorbia* in specially treated soil, they expect to produce between five and ten barrels of oil per acre per year. Some other species are expected to yield between ten and twenty barrels of oil per year.

Some people are concerned about the use of plants for fuel. They feel that using plants that are normally used to feed people and livestock for fuel may bring on an increase in world hunger. Also, land and oil may be depleted by overfarming of the fuel crops which take vital nutrients from the soil. If demand for fuel crops becomes high, marginal land which is not very productive for farming may be used to grow crops.

These problems have been recognized by scientists doing synfuels research, and some answers are being found. Many of the *Euphorbia* species currently being tested grow only in semiarid regions, so more productive land can be used for food crops. Dr. Calvin is experimenting with an artificial membrane which would work like plant membranes in converting the sun's energy to fuel. Instead of producing sugars, these membranes would make hydrogen and hydrocarbons. Using these artificial membranes would decrease or eliminate the need for using farmland to produce fuel.

Production of alcohol for use in gasohol involves fermentation of sugars from sugarcane or corn.

Certain species of plants may be useful in producing hydrocarbons which may be used as a petroleum substitute.

Certain plants produce oily substances that can be used as fuels. These plants are being experimentally cultivated.

FIGURE 21-8. *Euphorbia villosa* is an oil producing plant.

Euphorbia villosa

CHAPTER REVIEW

SUMMARY

1. When light strikes an object, certain wavelengths may be absorbed and the energy form changed.

2. Chlorophyll reflects mostly the green portion of the spectrum. The other wavelengths are absorbed and the light is changed to chemical energy. Carotenes aid in the absorption of light energy.

3. During photosynthesis, radiant energy is trapped and converted to chemical energy.

4. During the light reactions of photosynthesis, light energy is converted to chemical energy of ATP. Water is split into hydrogen and oxygen. The oxygen is released.

5. In the dark reactions of photosynthesis, the ATP and hydrogen from the light reactions are used in the synthesis of glucose.

6. Glucose made in photosynthesis may be used in respiration or converted to fats, amino acids, starch, or cellulose.

7. Photosynthesis and respiration are interdependent reactions. During photosynthesis, energy is used to produce glucose from carbon dioxide and water. During respiration, energy is released as glucose is converted to carbon dioxide and water.

8. In photosynthesis, light energy is changed to the chemical energy of glucose. During respiration, energy from glucose is changed to the chemical energy of ATP. ATP energy is used for work.

9. Most plants undergo intracellular digestion as they convert starch to glucose. Insectivorous plants obtain needed nitrogen and other nutrients by the extracellular digestion of insects.

10. In addition to carbon dioxide and water, plants require essential nutrients such as nitrogen, magnesium, sulfur, potassium, phosophorus, calcium, and iron.

11. Experimental work is being done to derive fuels from plants.

LANGUAGE OF BIOLOGY

absorption spectrum
carotene
chlorophyll
dark reactions
fossil fuels
guard cell
insectivorous plant
light reactions
palisade cells
phloem
photosynthesis
spongy layer
stomata
synfuels
visible spectrum
wavelength
xylem

CHECKING YOUR IDEAS

On a separate paper, indicate whether each of the following statements is true or false. Do not write in this book.

1. Chlorophyll absorbs mostly wavelengths of light in the green part of the spectrum.

2. Overall, the reactions of photosynthesis are endergonic.

3. Synthesis of glucose occurs in the dark reactions.

4. The products of respiration are the reactants of photosynthesis.

5. Hydrogen in a glucose molecule comes from water.

6. Light energy is changed to chemical energy of glucose during the light reactions.

7. Carbon dioxide and water are the only essential nutrients of plants.

8. Digestion is extracellular in most plants.

9. Carotenes are present in leaves only during autumn.

10. Oxygen given off during photosynthesis comes from carbon dioxide.

EVALUATING YOUR IDEAS

1. List the parts of a leaf and give the function of each.

2. In terms of energy, why is photosynthesis so important to all living things? How does photosynthesis affect you?

CHAPTER REVIEW

3. What does an absorption spectrum reveal about chlorophyll? What is the significance of the absorption spectrum of chlorophyll?

4. What are carotenes? When are they visible in leaves?

5. What are the reactants and products of photosynthesis?

6. Describe the major events of the light reactions.

7. Explain how the light reactions and dark reactions are related.

8. Once glucose is produced in photosynthesis, what are some ways in which it is used by the plant?

9. How is photosynthesis the opposite of respiration?

10. How is the chemical energy produced during photosynthesis used? What happens to some of the chemical energy?

11. Write an essay about the interdependence of photosynthesis and respiration. Your essay should include a discussion of both materials and energy.

12. How does a Venus's-flytrap trap and digest insects?

13. Explain how magnesium, nitrogen, and sulfur are used by plants.

14. Explain several ways in which photosynthesis might be used to provide new fuels.

APPLYING YOUR IDEAS

1. Relate the events of photosynthesis to the structure of the leaf.

2. What would the absorption spectrum of carotenes be like? Explain.

3. Why are fertilizers often used in growing plants?

4. Explain how photosynthesis and respiration result in the recycling of materials.

5. From where does the oxygen necessary for aerobic respiration come?

6. Trace the "flow of energy" from light to energy used for work. Is energy recycled? Explain.

7. Nitrogen is important to plants. From where does it come? How is it made available to plants?

8. What is phosphorus used for in plants?

EXTENDING YOUR IDEAS

1. Using reference materials, prepare a brief report on the contributions of van Helmont, Priestley, and Ingen-Housz to our understanding of photosynthesis.

2. Will a developing plant grown in the dark produce chlorophyll? Conduct a controlled experiment to determine the answer. As a follow up, test other developing plants using different colored lights. Does any particular color seem to favor chlorophyll production?

3. Conduct an experiment to determine the effect of different wavelengths of light on the rate of photosynthesis.

4. Find out how Spanish moss, which grows on the branches of trees, obtains its nutrients.

5. Grow two groups of insectivorous plants during the school year. Keep all conditions for both groups the same except that group A is fed insects and group B is not. Compare the growth and appearance of the two groups.

SUGGESTED READINGS

Bold, Harold C., and Hundell, C. L., *The Plant Kingdom*, 4th ed. Englewood Cliffs, NJ, Prentice-Hall Inc., 1977.

Slack, Adrian, *Carnivorous Plants*. Cambridge, MA, M.I.T. Press, 1980.

Whittingham, L. P., *Photosynthesis*, 2nd ed. Carolina Biology Reader. Burlington, NC, Carolina Biological Supply Co., 1977.

Additional student readings and suggested teacher readings are provided in the Teacher's Guide.

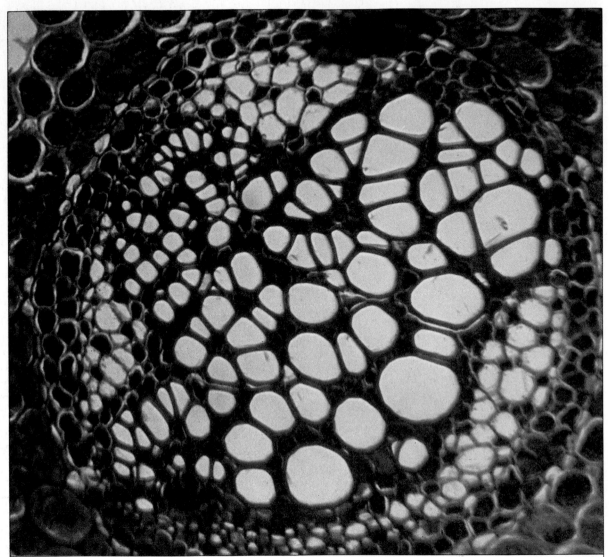

P lants use glucose they make in carrying out their life functions. These functions include transport, gas exchange, and response to the environment. The rhizome, a rootlike structure, of a fern transports materials within the plant. Pictured here is a cross section of a fern rhizome. How is the rhizome adapted for transport? What other structures of plants transport materials? How do plants exchange gases and respond to the environment?

Introduction: Because plants are not "active" organisms, students do not usually think of them as performing functions other than photosynthesis. They are often especially surprised by the idea that plants respond to their environment. You might want to begin this chapter by viewing films or filmloops which use time lapse photography to show phenomena such as tropisms, apical dominance, flowering, and regular movements of leaves and flowers. Students will also enjoy having access to specimens of plants such as *Mimosa* and Venus's-flytrap, which respond to touch. Consider assigning teams of students to investigate various phenomena discussed in the chapter. For example, you might ask some students to initiate projects to demonstrate tropisms, photo-periodism, abscission, and apical dominance (see Extending Your Ideas, numbers 1 and 2 in the Teacher's Guide). Auxins, gibberellins, and other plant hormones are available from biological supply houses.

PLANTS: OTHER LIFE FUNCTIONS

Chapter 22 presents the anatomy of angiosperm roots and stems, and discusses transport, gas exchange, and responses of these plants.

Green plants produce glucose by photosynthesis. The energy stored in glucose is then used for a variety of life processes. One use of energy is reproduction and development (Chapter 21). In this chapter, you will learn about other activities which plants carry out—transport, gas exchange, and response to factors of the environment.

GOAL: You will gain an understanding of the life functions of plants.

STRUCTURE OF ANGIOSPERMS

Recall from Chapter 14 that the plant kingdom includes certain algae and the land plants. Algae have a simple structure. Most land plants are more complex, having tissues, organs, and systems.

Land plants can be grouped as nonvascular, those without special transport cells, and vascular, those with special transport cells. The nonvascular plants include liverworts and mosses. Vascular plants include club mosses, horsetails, ferns, gymnosperms, and angiosperms. Of the vascular plants, the angiosperms, flowering plants, are predominant. Therefore, it is important to your understanding of plant functions that you have a knowledge of the internal structures of angiosperms. You learned about angiosperm leaf structure in Chapter 21. Root and stem structure are presented here.

Liverworts and mosses are nonvascular. Other land plants are vascular.

Teaching suggestion: In the sections that follow, stress the complementarity of structure and function.

22:1 Roots: Internal Structure

The outer part of an angiosperm root is the **epidermis** which protects the root. **Root hairs** are outgrowths of the epidermis. Much of a root is **cortex** which is used for storage. Within the cortex is a central cylinder called the **stele** (steel). The stele of the

FIGURE 22-1. Cross sections of dicot and monocot roots show that both have a central cylinder composed of xylem and phloem. However, the arrangements of xylem and phloem differ.

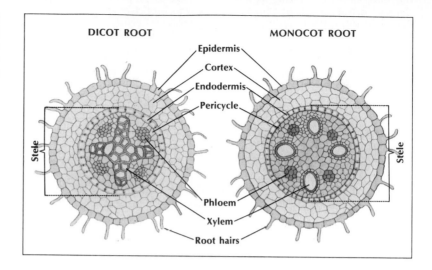

root is surrounded by a layer of cells called the **endodermis** (en duh DUR mus). The outer tissue of the stele is a layer of cells called the **pericycle** (PER uh sy kuhl). The pericycle is a kind of meristem (Section 20:14). Branch roots originate in the pericycle. The inner part of the stele is composed of the vascular tissues—xylem and phloem.

Xylem cells carry water and minerals from the roots to the leaves of the plant. These cells are thick-walled and dead. They are hollow cylinders arranged end to end to form a tube. In cross section, they appear as empty circles. Phloem cells carry food made by the leaves to other parts of the plant. These phloem cells are also cylindrical but are not dead. They contain cytoplasm and have a smaller diameter than xylem cells.

Xylem cells transport water and minerals. Phloem cells transport food.

In a dicot root, xylem tissue is usually arranged in a star-shaped pattern with phloem vessels between the arms of the star (Figure 22-1). In a monocot root, the stele is somewhat larger than that of the dicot. It contains a great deal of **pith** tissue in the center. Pith aids in storage of food and water. Large xylem vessels are arranged in a circle around the pith with phloem vessels between them (Figure 22-1).

22:2 Stems: Internal Structure

A plant has no skeletal system but is supported by the **stem.** Also, the stem is a transport link between the roots and the leaves, and some stem cells store food.

Stems are either herbaceous (hur BAY shus) or woody. **Herbaceous** stems are soft, green, and often juicy, with very little or no woody tissue. Plants which live for a single growing season are usually herbaceous. A plant with a herbaceous stem is supported by the pressure of water in the cells of the stem. This

Plants which live for a single growing season (e.g., beans, lettuce, peas) are called annuals. Biennials (e.g., carrots, cabbage, and beets) live for two growing seasons. Biennials develop roots, stems, and leaves the first year. During the second year they produce flowers and seeds. Perennials (e.g., asparagus and lilies) live longer than two years. Stems of herbaceous perennials die each year and are renewed from underground structures the next year. Stems of woody perennials (e.g., shrubs and trees) do not die and produce new structures each year.

Herbaceous stems are soft and green.

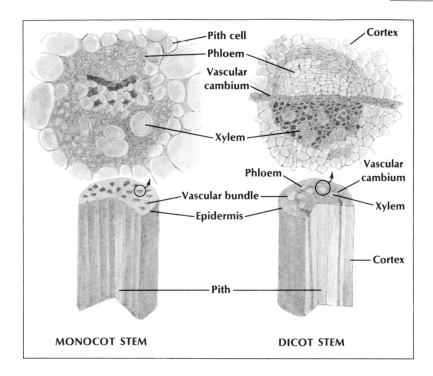

Pith cell
Phloem
Vascular cambium
Xylem

Cortex

Phloem
Vascular bundle
Epidermis

Vascular cambium
Xylem

Cortex

Pith

MONOCOT STEM

DICOT STEM

FIGURE 22-2. Herbaceous mono-cot and dicot stems both have vascular bundles. In monocots, the bundles are scattered throughout the stem. In herbaceous dicots, they are located close to the edge of the stem in a ring.

pressure causes **turgidity,** or stiffness, which causes the plant to stand upright. In the event of a water shortage, the stem loses turgidity (wilts), and bends down.

As in roots, there are slight differences between monocot and dicot stems. In herbaceous monocots, vascular bundles are scattered throughout the stem. In herbaceous dicots, they are located close to the edge of the stem, and there is a layer of vascular cambium between phloem and xylem. The vascular cambium is a meristem (Section 20:14) which produces cells that later develop into new xylem and phloem tissue. Both stem types contain pith for food storage. Also, the dicots have cortex. Some cortex tissue stores food, but other cortex contains chloroplasts and makes food.

A **woody stem** is more complex than a herbaceous stem. The outermost part of the stems of trees or woody shrubs is called **outer bark.** It is composed of special cells called cork which is produced from cork cambium, the deepest layer of outer bark. Cork cells are coated with an oily material called **suberin** (SEW buh run) which protects the cells against water loss. Inside the outer bark lies a region of **inner bark** made up of cortex and phloem tissue. This cortex is a food storage layer.

Next to the inner bark is the vascular cambium. This cambium produces new xylem and phloem cells each growing season. Phloem cells are formed toward the bark side. Xylem cells are formed toward the center of the stem.

Herbaceous stems lack cambium and do not produce additional xylem and phloem on a yearly basis.

Vascular bundles of dicots contain a vascular cambium, a meristem which gives rise to new xylem and phloem cells.

The outer bark protects the stem of woody plants and helps prevent water loss.

FIGURE 22-3. A woody stem cross section shows that much of the stem is made up of xylem, the wood of a tree.

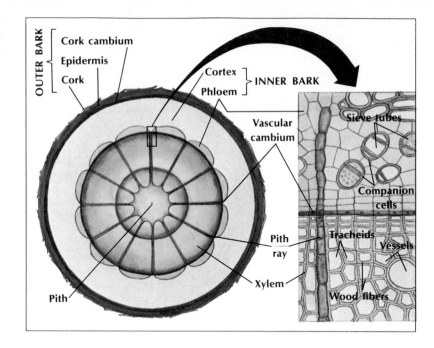

Woody stems are composed mostly of xylem tissue. Xylem is the wood of a tree.

Tracheids are tapered at the ends and often pitted. They function in both transport and support. Vessels function in transport and their walls are often reinforced with rings or spirals.

Spring wood is the lighter colored rings of a tree. Summer wood is the darker colored rings.

Annual rings, lines of growth, are a means of determining the age of a tree.

The bulk of a woody stem is xylem, the wood of a tree. It is located inside the cambium layer. Closest to the cambium is active, or new, xylem tissue which transports water and minerals up the stem. This xylem is composed of two kinds of cells called **tracheids** (TRAY kee udz) and **vessels.** Closer to the center of the stem are old xylem cells filled with waste matter. Old xylem makes up most of the xylem. Cells closest to the center of a stem are the oldest because new cells are produced from the cambium. Wood produced in the spring, **spring wood,** is mostly large xylem vessels. **Summer wood** is composed of vessels of smaller diameter. In a cross section of a woody stem, lines are visible between layers of cells. These circular lines are the **annual rings** which represent growth during a year. Annual rings provide a means of determining the age of a tree.

FIGURE 22-4. (a) Annual rings of a woody stem indicate the age of the tree. How old is this tree? (b) Core samples can be taken from a tree so that the age can be determined without cutting the tree down to count rings. The number of bands on the core sample indicate the tree's age.

12 years

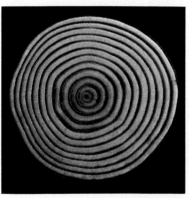

Weyerhauser Co.

Hickson-Bender Photography

The center of a woody stem is composed of pith cells. Pith occupies a large part of young, woody stems. Because it is not produced by the cambium, pith does not enlarge as the tree grows, and so it becomes a smaller part of the stem. **Pith rays** extend from the central pith cylinder outward to the inner bark region. These are conductive cells that transport materials horizontally between pith, wood, and bark. Pith rays are easily seen between vascular bundles.

Careful study of a cross section of a woody stem shows that structure and function complement each other. A stem transports materials and also supports a plant. Cells and tissues are adapted for these functions. For example, the "pipeline" structure of active xylem vessels transports water. Dead xylem fibers closely packed are tough materials which support the stem as it grows upright.

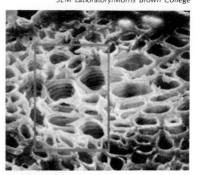

SEM Laboratory/Morris Brown College

FIGURE 22-5. Xylem tissue of a woody stem magnified 250 times shows xylem vessels as connected tubes. Xylem transports water in plants.

REVIEWING YOUR IDEAS

1. What is the stele of a root? What kind of tissues are located in the stele?
2. Distinguish between herbaceous and woody stems.
3. Compare the location of vascular bundles in monocot and dicot stems.
4. What are annual rings?
5. How are structure and function of stem parts related?

1. The stele is the central portion of a root and is composed of xylem and phloem.
2. Herbaceous stems are soft and green. Woody stems are more complex, containing wood and other tissues. They are usually hard.
3. In monocots, vascular bundles are scattered throughout the stem. In dicots they are located near the edge of the stem.
4. Annual rings are visible layers of cells in woody stems cut in cross section.
5. In general, the structures of stems are suited for transport of water and food and for support and protection.

TRANSPORT AND GAS EXCHANGE

22:3 Simple Plants

The major materials transported within plants are water, dissolved minerals, and food. Oxygen and carbon dioxide are exchanged directly with the environment. In algae, there are no specialized tissues for transport or gas exchange. Most cells of algae act independently. Each is in direct or very close contact with the environment. Water, minerals, and gases enter each cell directly from the water. Also, most cells make food by photosynthesis. Thus, food "transport" is limited to within the cell and occurs by diffusion or cytoplasmic streaming.

Liverworts and mosses are more complex than algae. However, they are small plants which can distribute materials without specialized transport tissues. Water enters the rhizoids and is transported to other cells by osmosis. Food moves to all cells from photosynthetic cells by diffusion (Section 14:15). Gases are exchanged through pores.

Algae have no specialized tissues for transport or gas exchange.

In liverworts and mosses, transport occurs by diffusion or osmosis and gases are exchanged through pores.

Kodansha

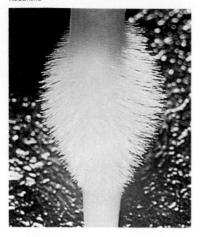

FIGURE 22-6. Root hairs increase surface area over which water can pass. Water moves into root hairs by osmosis.

FIGURE 22-7. Root pressure may contribute to the transport of water through stems. Root pressure can support a column of water as shown. However, there is not enough pressure to account for transport over long distances.

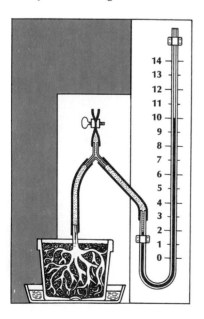

22:4 Uptake of Water and Minerals in Vascular Plants

Water is important to plants because it is necessary for cell metabolism, including photosynthesis. Most vascular plants live on land and obtain water from the soil through their roots (Section 22:1).

Water moves from the spaces between soil particles into root hairs by osmosis. The millions of tiny root hairs together have a large surface area for absorbing these materials. Minerals in the soil often move into root hairs by active transport. The water passes by osmosis from the root hairs, across the cell layers of the root, and into the xylem by a process called **successive osmosis.** Xylem is composed of dead, hollow cells with no end walls. The cells are joined end to end to form a continuous tube. This "pipeline" structure is an adaptation for the water transport function.

The xylem of the roots extends into the stem and then the leaves of a vascular plant. As in the roots, the xylem cells form a tube for water transport. Water travels through the xylem to the leaves. The vascular bundles of stems also contain phloem, cells which transport food.

22:5 Transpiration-Cohesion Theory

Water entering the xylem in roots must travel through the stem to the leaves. Sometimes this movement involves a distance greater than one hundred meters. How can this process occur?

As a result of osmosis, water enters a root and passes into the xylem of the stele. The water in the xylem exerts a pushing force called **root pressure.** Perhaps you have seen the effects of root pressure. Sometimes, when root pressure is high, water is forced out of the end of leaf veins. The water forms droplets around the edges of the leaf, a process known as guttation.

Root pressure can also be shown by an experiment. Suppose a piece of tubing is attached to the cut stem of a plant whose roots are immersed in water. Water will rise in the tube (Figure 22:7). Root pressure alone does not cause water to rise in stems of plants, but it may be involved with starting transport.

Most biologists favor another explanation, called the **transpiration** (trans puh RAH shun)–**cohesion** (koh HEE zhun) **theory** for water transport through a stem. According to this theory, water is pulled up the stem. In order for such a pull to occur, water must form continuous columns from roots to leaves. Two properties of water, cohesion and adhesion (ad HEE zhun), make this water movement possible. **Cohesion** is the clinging together of the same kind of molecules, and **adhesion** is the

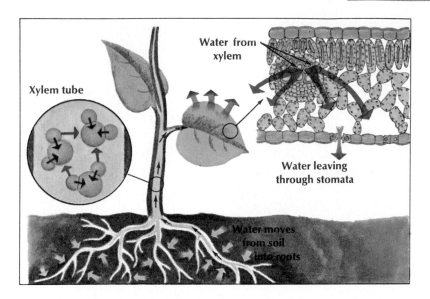

Xylem tube

Water from xylem

Water leaving through stomata

Water moves from soil into roots

FIGURE 22-8. Movement of water in tree stems is explained by the transpiration-cohesion theory. Cohesion among water molecules in a xylem vessel makes the water a continuous column. Transpiration from leaves exerts a "pull" on the dense columns of water in xylem tubes.

This explanation for the movement of water from roots to leaves was first proposed near the turn of the century by H.H. Dixon and J. Joly and is sometimes called the Dixon-Joly theory.

attraction of unlike molecules. Water molecules cling to one another and adhere to the walls of the xylem tissues. *In these very narrow tubes*, the combination of cohesion and adhesion gives a column of water the properties of a metal wire—continuous and very dense. This assumption is important to the theory.

What causes the pull? Water constantly is leaving the leaves of plants through the stomata (Section 21:1). This water loss is called **transpiration.** As water molecules leave, other water molecules from the xylem vessels of the leaf replace them. Because of cohesion, this movement creates a *tension, or pull*, called **transpiration pull** on the rest of the water column. This pull can be thought of as a "stretching" effect. The "stretching" force extends all the way to the roots. The faster water is lost, the faster it is pulled up through the plant. As the water in the root xylem is pulled up, more water moves into the xylem from the surrounding root cells. The water comes from spaces in the soil.

Transpiration pull is not the same as drawing a liquid through a straw. Even a vacuum pump could not lift water to the height it travels in tall trees. The pull occurs only because the column of water is continuous and dense. Without cohesion and adhesion of water in the narrow xylem tubes, transport could not occur. The combination of these properties produces an unbroken column of water that can be pulled.

It is important that no air gets into a column of water. Air bubbles would break the continuous column of water. Thus, they would prevent an effective tension on the water column.

There is experimental evidence to support this theory. But, scientists think that although this explanation is the best available, it is not the complete story. Transpiration pull is probably only one of several forces involved.

Suggested demonstration: Show the spontaneous rise of water with capillary tubes and a colored water solution. This phenomenon, capillary action, alone cannot explain transport over a long distance.

Because of cohesion and adhesion, water in xylem vessels forms a dense column.

Transpiration creates a pull on the water columns in xylem and water is "stretched" from roots to leaves.

A vacuum pump could raise water only to a height of about ten meters. Such a column of water would balance the pressure of one atmosphere.

Air bubbles in a xylem vessel would prevent transpiration pull on the water.

Teaching suggestion: Ask students what happens when air gets into a drinking straw.

Kodansha

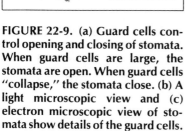

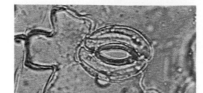

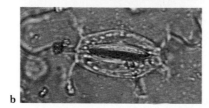

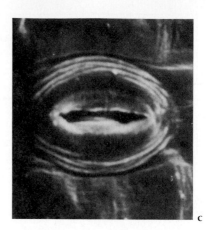

a

b

c

Stoma open

Chloroplasts

Nuclei

Stoma closed

FIGURE 22-9. (a) Guard cells control opening and closing of stomata. When guard cells are large, the stomata are open. When guard cells "collapse," the stomata close. (b) A light microscopic view and (c) electron microscopic view of stomata show details of the guard cells.

During the day, stomata are large, permitting carbon dioxide to enter and water to escape.

22:6 Control of Stomata

Loss of some water by transpiration is important for upward transport of water from the roots. However, if too much water escapes, a plant will die. An adaptation involving guard cells and stomata prevents excess water loss.

During the day, carbon dioxide enters a leaf, so the stomata must be open. Guard cells have chlorophyll and undergo photosynthesis when light is available. As photosynthesis occurs, guard cells swell, their shape changes, and the size of the space (the stoma) between them is increased (Figure 22-9). Carbon dioxide can then enter the leaf. However, water also escapes from the stomata during the day. Transpiration is this loss of water from stomata.

Decrease in the size of stomata at night reduces water loss.

At night, because light is not present, no photosynthesis occurs in the guard cells. The guard cells collapse, their shape changes, and they move together, reducing the size of the stomata between them. As stomata become smaller, loss of water is decreased. In summary, this adaptation prevents excess water loss. Some water escapes during the day when the stomata are fully open. However, at night the openings become smaller, so less water escapes.

22:7 Transport of Food

In vascular plants, phloem tissue transports food.

Food is transported by phloem cells located in the vascular bundles. Like xylem tissue, phloem forms a continuous "pipeline" from leaves to roots. Because phloem cells do not lose their cytoplasm as they mature, the pipeline they form is not hollow.

The end wall of each phloem cell is perforated so it resembles a sieve. Therefore, phloem tubes are called **sieve tubes.** The sidewalls of phloem cells have small holes, and strands of cytoplasm pass horizontally between phloem cells.

Although the cytoplasm remains in mature phloem cells, the nucleus dies. Smaller **companion cells,** which have nuclei, often lie next to sieve tubes. Perhaps they control the cytoplasm of sieve tubes.

As food is made within a leaf, it is dissolved in water. Dissolved food enters the phloem cells of the veins (Section 21:1). From here, food may be transported in any direction within the plant. The transport of food within a plant is called **translocation** (trans loh KAY shun). Usually, food moves downward through the phloem of the stem into the roots where it enters the cortex. In the cortex, simple sugars are converted to starch and stored. Food also may be transported laterally through the strands of cytoplasm between cells.

Exactly what causes the transport of food within phloem is not known. Food probably enters the cytoplasm of the phloem. Observations indicate that strands of cytoplasm can move through the continuous sieve tubes. The cytoplasm probably carries the food with it.

One hypothesis suggests that food moves through the phloem as a result of pressure. As sugar enters cells of sieve tubes in a leaf, water enters from other leaf cells by osmosis. The entrance of water increases the pressure inside the sieve cell. Because of this pressure, the sugar and water are forced into the next sieve cell where pressure is lower. These differences in pressure in sieve cells from leaves to roots may account for the downward movement of food. At the roots, both sugar and water leave the sieve cells. Thus, pressure remains lower in the roots. This explanation is known as the **pressure-flow hypothesis.** Further testing is needed to determine whether it is correct.

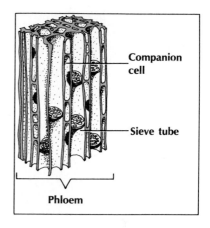

FIGURE 22-10. Sieve tubes, the conductive parts of phloem tissue, are in close association with companion cells. Food moves through plants in the phloem.

Pressure differences between sieve cells may move food through phloem.

22:8 Gas Exchange

In plants, carbon dioxide is a raw material for photosynthesis, and oxygen is given off as a by-product. Therefore, you may think of gas exchange in plants as an inward movement of carbon dioxide and an outward flow of oxygen. This exchange occurs only in photosynthetic tissues when light is present. However, all plant tissues, both photosynthetic and nonphotosynthetic, take in oxygen for cellular respiration and give off carbon dioxide.

Within roots, cells obtain minerals from the soil by active transport. Energy needed for active transport and other processes comes from cellular respiration. The oxygen needed for respiration is in the air spaces between soil particles. Oxygen from the air dissolves in the moisture of the soil and then diffuses into the

Root cells exchange gases with soil.

Alvin E. Staffan

a

Carolina Biological Supply Co.

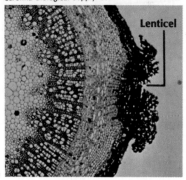

b

FIGURE 22-11. (a) Lenticels are visible as white dots on this twig. (b) A cross section of a stem through the lenticel shows the lenticel as an opening in the tissue.

Both oxygen and carbon dioxide may be used by leaves.

6. Plants transport water, minerals, and food.
7. In simple plants, materials are transported within cells by diffusion or streaming and between cells by diffusion.
8. Root hairs absorb water and minerals.
9. Xylem transports water and dissolved minerals. Phloem transports food. Xylem is composed of dead cells, but phloem cells contain cytoplasm.
10. Successive osmosis is the passage of water from root hairs, across cell layers, and into the xylem of a root.
11. transpiration-cohesion theory
12. Cohesion is the clinging together of the same kind of molecules. Adhesion is attraction between unlike molecules.

root hairs. Then it is distributed by diffusion to other root cells such as the cortex. As respiration occurs within the root cells, carbon dioxide is produced as a by-product. This carbon dioxide diffuses from the root cells to the root hairs and then from the root hairs into the soil.

Most of a woody stem is composed of dead cells (Section 22:2). However, cells of the outer and inner bark region are alive so they need oxygen for respiration. The combination of dead cork cells and suberin forms a continuous protective layer around the stem. Oxygen enters and carbon dioxide leaves the stem through tiny openings called **lenticels** (Section 14:13). Lenticels also are found on large roots lacking root hairs. These roots, like stems, are covered by a layer of cork.

As photosynthesis occurs, carbon dioxide enters and oxygen is given off. The cells in a leaf where photosynthesis occurs are surrounded by a thin film of moisture. Carbon dioxide in the air enters a leaf through stomata (Section 22:6). The carbon dioxide dissolves in the thin film of moisture and then diffuses into the cells. Oxygen, a by-product of photosynthesis, diffuses from the cells and dissolves in water. The flat shape of leaves, the large number of leaves per plant, and the position of the leaves on the plant provide a large surface area for gas exchange and for sunlight exposure for photosynthesis.

Because cells in the leaf also undergo respiration, some of the oxygen from photosynthesis may be used for respiration. Also, some of the carbon dioxide from respiration may be used in photosynthesis. At night, only cellular respiration occurs in leaves. At that time, there is an intake of oxygen, and carbon dioxide is released. Photosynthesis does not occur at night because the light reactions require energy of sunlight.

REVIEWING YOUR IDEAS

6. What are the major materials transported in plants?
7. How are materials transported in simple plants? How do the materials enter simple plants?
8. What is the function of root hairs?
9. Distinguish between xylem and phloem. What does each of them carry?
10. What is successive osmosis?
11. What theory accounts for the transport of water and materials in vascular plants?
12. Distinguish between cohesion and adhesion.
13. What hypothesis explains the translocation of food in vascular plants?
14. What is the function of guard cells?
15. How do guard cells work?

13. pressure flow hypothesis
14. Guard cells regulate the size of stomata.

15. When guard cells swell, stomata open. When guard cells shrink, stomata close. Guard cells work by changing shape.

RESPONSE TO ENVIRONMENT

Plants are not active organisms, but they do respond to changes in the environment. Plants respond to certain stimuli such as light, water, and gravity. A **stimulus** is anything that causes an activity or change in an organism. Plant responses to stimuli often involve movement. Unlike animals, plants usually respond slowly, and their movement often is not noticed. Control of plant responses is chemical.

Plant responses are controlled chemically and occur slowly.

22:9 Discovery of Auxins

Many plants respond to stimuli by movements called tropisms (TROH pihz umz). A **tropism** is a plant growth response caused by unequal stimulation on opposite sides of a plant. Growth of a plant part toward the stimulus is a positive tropism. Growth away from the stimulus is a negative tropism. One part of a plant may have a positive tropism to a certain stimulus. But, another part of the plant may have a negative tropism to the same stimulus. For example, the shoot of a plant has negative **geotropism** (jee oh TROH pihz um), or response to gravity, but the roots have positive geotropism.

Plants exhibit positive and negative tropisms.

Biologists have long been interested in these plant responses. Plants show positive **phototropism** (foh toh TROH pihz um), a response of growing toward light. How is growth toward light adaptive? What is the mechanism?

It provides more surface area exposed to sunlight, an aid to photosynthesis.

If a young oat seedling is exposed to a light source from one side, the leafy tip of the seedling, called the **coleoptile** (KOH lee AHP tul), bends in the direction of the light. But, if the tip is covered with an opaque substance, such as foil, no bending occurs. Also, no bending occurs if the tip is removed (Figure 22-12). Thus, the tip must be involved in positive phototropism, but what role does it play in this response?

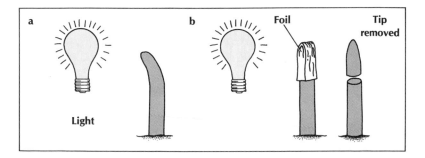

FIGURE 22-12. (a) A seedling coleoptile bends toward a light source. (b) If the tip is covered with foil or removed, no bending occurs.

FIGURE 22-13. Experiments with seedlings indicate that a chemical in the coleoptile is involved in phototropism. (a) The chemical cannot pass through mica, so no bending occurs, (b) but can pass through or (c) into and out of agar blocks. (d) The unequal distribution of the chemical causes the bending.

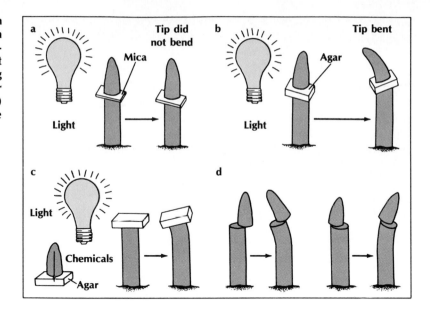

The tip of a coleoptile is involved in positive phototropism of the shoot.

Suppose a chemical is secreted from the tip. To test this hypothesis, experiments were done in which different materials were placed between the tip and the shoot. In one experiment, a piece of mica (MI kuh) was inserted between the tip and the shoot. (Chemicals cannot diffuse through mica.) The plant was exposed to a light source from one side. If the assumption were correct, the plant should not bend toward the light. In the experiment, the plant did not bend (Figure 22-13a).

In a second experiment, a piece of agar was placed between the tip and shoot. (Chemicals can diffuse through agar.) This plant responded positively to the light (Figure 22-13b). The scientists concluded that a chemical produced by the tip is necessary for positive phototropism.

Knowing that a chemical was involved, the scientists experimented further. Tips were removed and placed upon agar blocks. They assumed that the chemical would diffuse into the blocks. These blocks alone were then placed on the rest of the shoot, and the plants bent in the direction of the light source (Figure 22-13c).

In another experiment, tips were put on the shoot in an off-center manner (Figure 22-13d). The plants grew away from the side with the tip on it. This result occurred even in complete darkness! Thus, unequal chemical concentration on the two sides of the shoot must be responsible for the bending. Also, agar blocks containing the chemical were placed on one side of the shoot. The same effect was obtained, the plants grew away from the side with the tip on it, even in darkness.

In 1928, the chemical responsible for positive phototropism was isolated. The chemical is one of a group of plant hormones known as **auxins** (AWK sunz). A **hormone** is a chemical regulator that is produced in one part of the organism and affects other parts. This particular auxin causes the lengthening of cells and is called indoleacetic (IHN dohl uh seet ihk) acid (IAA).

Auxin, a plant hormone, causes phototropism.

Suppose a stem or shoot is exposed to a light source from only one side. *Auxin migrates away from the lighted side of the plant, and thus, more auxin is concentrated in the shaded side than in the side exposed to the light.* The cells in the shaded side grow faster than the cells on the lighted side because auxin increases the rate of growth of cells. Because of the unequal growth rates of the sides of the stem, the stem or shoot grows (bends) in the direction of the light source.

The degree of bending (due to lengthening of cells) is proportional to the amount of auxin.

Unequal auxin concentrations are responsible for unequal cell growth resulting in phototropism.

PEOPLE IN BIOLOGY

(1888 - 1969)

Henrik Gunnar Lundegardh

Although most of his research concerned absorption and accumulation of salts in plant roots, Henrik Lundegardh spent more than ten years studying plant tropisms. Working at the laboratory of plant physiology in Lund, Sweden, Lundegardh published a series of papers on plant movements. Geotropism, the effect of gravity on plants, and phototropism, the reaction of plants to light, were studied and reports were presented to groups of plant physiologists. Dr. Lundegardh's research led to the use of film as a scientific method of documenting and recording the movements of plants under varying conditions. Even though Lundegardh did his work before the discovery of auxins (plant hormones that affect movement), his research illustrated the movements and effects of auxins within a plant.

Dr. Lundgardh was a professor of plant physiology and botany at several universities and institutions in Sweden. In 1947 Lundgardh built a private research laboratory to study the chemical reactions of photosynthesis. Dr. Lundgardh was elected a foreign member of the American Academy of Arts and Sciences in 1950 and of the U. S. National Academy of Sciences in 1964.

FIGURE 22-14. In a demonstration of positive geotropism, (a) a root is positioned horizontally. (b) Lower root cells (those closer to the earth) accumulate auxin which inhibits their growth. Thus, the top layer of cells lengthens more rapidly and the root grows downward.

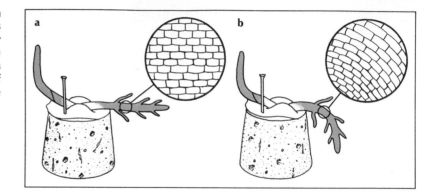

22:10 Other Effects of Auxins

Auxins are responsible for a variety of plant responses.

Since 1928, many auxins have been discovered. Many of them cause growth and are responsible for other tropisms. For example, positive geotropism of a root also may be caused by unequal auxin concentration.

Suppose a plant is placed sideways. Mainly because of gravity, more auxin would collect in the lower side of the root than in the upper side. On the basis of knowledge from the experiments with phototropism, this should cause the root to curve upward because the lower cells would grow more quickly. However, root cells react differently to auxin than do stem cells. The type of reaction depends on the *concentration* of auxin. In a stem, a high concentration of auxin stimulates cells to elongate, but in roots, a high concentration of auxin inhibits elongation of cells. Thus, the root cells with less auxin (upper surface) will elongate more than the cells with more auxin (lower surface). The result is that the root bends downward (Figure 22-14). The target organ, not the hormone, determines the response. How would a stem placed on its side react? Why?

The target organ, not the hormone, determines the response.

It would bend upward because auxin accumulates on the lower side of the stem and causes the cells there to lengthen.

Auxin produced by the apical bud inhibits development of lateral buds.

Auxins also cause **apical** (AY pih kul) **dominance** in plants. The apical bud is meristem tissue (Section 14:13) at the tip of a shoot. When present, it produces auxin. The high concentration of the auxin stimulates the stem cells to elongate, but it inhibits much of the growth of lateral buds. Thus, the lateral buds near the top of the stem (where auxin concentration is highest) do not develop into branches. Those farther from the apical bud can develop because the concentration of auxin is lower at those points. This results in a few, small branches near the top and more, larger branches near the bottom.

If the apical bud is removed, auxin production ceases. The lateral buds near the top can grow because they are not inhibited by high concentrations of auxin. As a result, the plant becomes bushier. Many gardeners produce bushy plants by "pinching off" the apical buds.

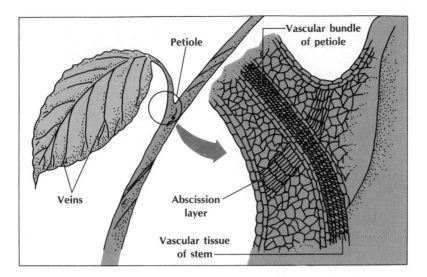

FIGURE 22-15. Decreased auxin production causes an abscission layer to form across a leaf petiole. The cells weaken in this area and the leaf eventually falls off.

Synthetic auxins are sometimes applied to potatoes to prevent the growth of the buds. Buds are the "eyes"; they tend to sprout with age. The high concentration of auxin inhibits the growth of the buds, and the potatoes may be stored for longer periods of time.

Abscission (ab SIHZH un), the falling of leaves from trees, is caused by a decreased auxin amount. During the growth season, leaves produce auxin constantly, but as the leaves begin to die, auxin production decreases. A group of cells, called the **abscission layer,** forms where a petiole is attached to the stem. The abscission layer weakens this area, and eventually the leaf falls from the plant.

Practical applications have come from this knowledge. Spraying plants with the proper auxins can delay the falling of leaves and fruits from a tree. The falling of fruits before they are fully developed and ready for eating is prevented.

Auxins can also be used to cause fruit formation in certain plants. Normally, fruits are formed *after* pollination has occurred because the seed produces an auxin. But, if auxin is added to the pistils of some flowers *before* pollination, the ovary will develop into a fruit. The fruits produced in this way look like those produced by pollination. However, the seeds cannot be used to produce new plants. Why? They are not fertilized.

Auxins can be used to prevent potatoes from sprouting.

Decrease in auxin production by leaves causes the formation of an abscission layer across the petiole.

Many people associate frost with leaf fall. Frost on a leaf adds mass to the leaf, and causes the leaf to break at the weakened abscission layer.

Addition of auxin can cause some fruits to form without pollination.

22:11 Gibberellins

A group of chemical regulators in plants was discovered in Japan. For years, rice farmers had noticed many young, unusually tall, rice plants in their crops. These tall plants did not live to maturity, and thus, were ignored as being of no practical importance. In 1926, it was discovered that these tall plants were

FIGURE 22-16. Gibberellic acid increases plant growth. The plant on the right was supplemented with gibberellic acid.

Lightforce

parasitized by a fungus called *Gibberella* (jihb uh REL uh). Later, a substance called **gibberellin** (jib uh REL un), which causes healthy rice seedlings to grow very rapidly, was isolated from the fungus.

Since the original discovery of gibberellin, other similar compounds have been isolated from fungi and plants. They are all known as gibberellins, and some seem to play a role in cell elongation. **Gibberellic** acid is a gibberellin often used experimentally. When applied artificially, it causes growth in some types of plants (Figure 22-16). Such treatment often is used to produce large seedless grapes and large, tender stalks of celery. Germination of many seeds and development of buds also are speeded up by gibberellins. In nature, gibberellins work with auxins and other plant hormones to control the growth of plants.

Gibberellins cause cells of some plants to elongate.

22:12 Control of Flowering

In angiosperms, flowers develop from buds. The time of year during which flowers develop varies, depending on the plant. Some plants flower only in the spring, some only in summer, and some only in autumn or winter. Other plants have no definite flowering season.

Botanists have been studying the causes of flowering since about 1920. They first learned that flowering in many plants depends on the relative amounts of exposure to day and night in a 24-hour period. Plants such as chrysanthemums and ragweed, which flower in autumn, are called **short-day plants** because they flower when the day length is less than some critical period. Clover and beets, which flower in summer, are called **long-day plants** because they flower only when the day length exceeds some critical value. Plants such as sunflower and tomato are examples of **day-neutral plants** because their flowering does not depend on day length.

Plants may be short-day, long-day, or day-neutral.

M. E. Warren for Photo Researchers   John Henry Sullivan Jr. for Photo Researchers

a

b

FIGURE 22-17. Poppy flowers (a) before and (b) after opening show a plant response not yet fully understood. Temperature and hormones seem to be factors involved.

Although plants are grouped in terms of day length, further work has shown that it is not really the amount of light that determines time of flowering. Rather, it is the amount of continual darkness. A short-day plant is really a long-night plant, and a long-day plant is really a short-night plant. The response of flowering plants to light and dark conditions is known as **photoperiodism.**

Once it was established that flowering in some plants depends on relative amounts of light and darkness, botanists then wondered *how* a plant responds to day and night length and what causes the flowering. A series of experiments have suggested that the detection of light and darkness occurs in the leaves, not in the flower buds. It is thought that the leaves contain a pigment, called **phytochrome** (FITE uh krohm), which is sensitive to light. Somehow the time when flowering should occur is detected. Many lines of evidence suggest that the leaves then produce and secrete a hormone which travels through the phloem to the flower buds. There it causes the buds to flower. Although the hormone has not been isolated, it has been given the name **florigen** (FLOR uh jen). Further work is needed to determine how the amount of darkness is detected and how it is related to production of florigen. Also, florigen must be isolated. Other factors such as temperature and other hormones, especially gibberellins, seem to be involved.

Time of flowering is determined by the amount of continuous darkness to which a plant is exposed.

Leaves contain phytochrome, a pigment sensitive to light.

Flowering may be controlled by a hormone, florigen, produced in the leaves.

REVIEWING YOUR IDEAS

16. What is a tropism?
17. Distinguish between positive and negative tropisms.
18. What controls tropisms?
19. What are some plant responses other than tropisms?
20. What effect do gibberellins have?
21. Distinguish among short-day, long-day, and day-neutral plants.

16. A tropism is a plant growth response caused by unequal stimulation on opposite sides of a plant.
17. Positive tropisms are growth toward a certain stimulus. Negative tropisms involve growth away from a stimulus.
18. Auxins control tropisms.
19. Abscission of leaves and fruits and apical dominance are other plant responses.
20. Gibberellins play a role in cell elongation.
21. Short-day plants flower when the day length is less than some critical period. Long-day plants flower when the day length exceeds some critical period. Flowering in day-neutral plants does not depend on day length.

CHAPTER REVIEW

SUMMARY

1. Roots are composed of tissues which function in the absorption of water and minerals and in the storage of food.
2. Stem tissues function in transport of water, minerals, and food as well as in support.
3. Transport in simple plants occurs by diffusion or cytoplasmic streaming.
4. Complex plants are too big to transport materials solely by diffusion or osmosis. Instead, they have a specialized transport system which links their cells with the environment.
5. In vascular plants, transport occurs within different sets of tubes. Water and minerals are pulled through the xylem from roots to leaves. Sugars are transported from the leaves to other tissues of the plant through the phloem.
6. The transport of water through a stem is explained by the transpiration-cohesion theory. Translocation of food is explained by the pressure-flow hypothesis.
7. Guard cells control the size of stomata, thus regulating water loss.
8. Exchange of oxygen and carbon dioxide in plants is needed for both photosynthesis and cellular respiration.
9. Gas exchange in plants occurs directly with the environment. In vascular plants, gases are exchanged mainly at the root hairs, lenticels, and stomata.
10. Plant tropisms are controlled by hormones called auxins.
11. Auxins also affect apical dominance, leaf abscission, and fruit formation.
12. Gibberellins are hormones found in some fungi and plants. They affect many processes, including cell elongation, seed germination, and bud development.
13. Flowering in many plants depends on the relative amounts of light and darkness and seems to be controlled by florigen.

LANGUAGE OF BIOLOGY

abscission
apical dominance
auxin
cortex
day-neutral plant
florigen
gibberellin
herbaceous stem
hormone
lenticel
long-day plant
pericycle
photoperiodism
pressure-flow
  hypothesis
short-day plant
stele
stimulus
translocation
transpiration-cohesion
  theory
tropism
woody stem

CHECKING YOUR IDEAS

On a separate paper, complete each of the following statements with the missing term(s). Do not write in this book.

1. Chemicals that affect certain target organs and control plant responses are called _____.
2. Gas exchange in stems occurs through openings called _____.
3. _____ is the response of flowering plants to light and dark conditions.
4. Transport of food is explained by the _____.
5. In a root, vascular tissue is located in the central cylinder called the _____.
6. Roots have _____ geotropism.
7. _____ is the falling of leaves and fruits from trees.
8. Transport of water is explained by the _____ theory.
9. Water travels from soil to xylem cells in the roots by _____.
10. Transport of food in plants is called _____.

EVALUATING YOUR IDEAS

1. List the functions of the tissues of a root. How do monocot and dicot roots differ?

CHAPTER REVIEW

2. Compare the structure of herbaceous monocots and herbaceous dicots. What is the function of each structure in these stems? Is a woody plant a monocot or a dicot?

3. Distinguish between the inner and outer bark regions of a woody stem.

4. How would you distinguish between spring wood and summer wood?

5. How are materials transported in algae and mosses? How are gases exchanged?

6. How is a transport system in vascular plants adaptive?

7. How does water enter a vascular plant?

8. Describe successive osmosis.

9. Explain the transpiration-cohesion theory.

10. How do guard cells control the size of stomata? How is this control adaptive?

11. How is food transported in plants?

12. Why do plants not need special gas exchange systems?

13. Why do root cells require oxygen? How do they obtain it?

14. What are lenticels? What is their function?

15. How are gases exchanged in leaves?

16. How did biologists discover the role of auxins in plant behavior?

17. How does auxin cause a plant to grow toward a light source?

18. What causes a root to exhibit positive geotropism?

19. What practical benefits have come from knowledge of abscission?

20. What are the functions of gibberellins? What practical use is made of gibberellins?

21. Explain the means by which some plants are thought to detect the relative amounts of light and darkness and to control flowering.

APPLYING YOUR IDEAS

1. How is the shape of a plant, caused by apical dominance, adaptive?

2. How could you show that flowering depends on darkness rather than on light?

3. How might you conduct an experiment to cause a short-day plant to flower in July?

4. Why are the movements of plants so much slower than those of animals? *Chapters 15 and 16

5. Compare transport and gas exchange in algae with those functions in monerans, protists, and fungi. *Chapter 18

6. How might the size of stomata change if light intensity is increased? How might it change if the amount of available CO_2 is decreased? Explain.

7. What would happen to a leaf if its lower surface were covered with a film of petroleum jelly? Why?

8. Where would the stomata on a lily pad be located? Why?

EXTENDING YOUR IDEAS

1. Obtain a healthy coleus plant. With a razor blade, remove only a leaf blade. Apply auxin to the cut end of the petiole. Remove another leaf blade. Leave the petiole untreated. Compare the times necessary for abscission of the petioles.

2. Design an experiment to illustrate the role of auxins in apical dominance. (See *Extending Your Ideas* 1.)

3. Using library resources, find out about the role of the plant hormones cytokinin and ethylene.

SUGGESTED READINGS

Galston, Arthur W., *The Life of the Green Plant*, 3rd ed. Englewood Cliffs, NJ, Prentice-Hall, Inc., 1980.

Norstog, Knut, and Long, Robert W., *Plant Biology*. Philadephia, W.B. Saunders, 1976.

Wooding, F. B. P., *Phloem*, 2nd ed. Carolina Biology Reader. Burlington, NC, Carolina Biological Supply Co., 1978.

Additional student readings and suggested teacher readings are provided in the Teacher's Guide.

ANIMALS

In general, animals are more complex than other forms of life. This complexity is related to their heterotrophic (food getting) nutrition and active way of life. They have many adaptations related to food getting. The lionfish shown here is adapted in several ways to obtain food and to prevent its being food for other animals. Its feathery fins can help it corner smaller fish for food. Its camouflage coloration helps hide it from its prey and its potential predators. The lionfish also has a dorsal fin that is modified into poisonous spines that protect it from predators.

Food getting, however, is only one of the many life functions of animals. Like other organisms, animals reproduce, develop, transport materials, exchange gases, and remove wastes. Most animals have skeletal systems and a means of locomotion. They have chemical and nervous control systems that coordinate their activities and responses. In this unit, you will learn about the life processes of animals and how animals are adapted to carry on these activities.

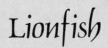

Lionfish

Michael DiSpezio   **427**

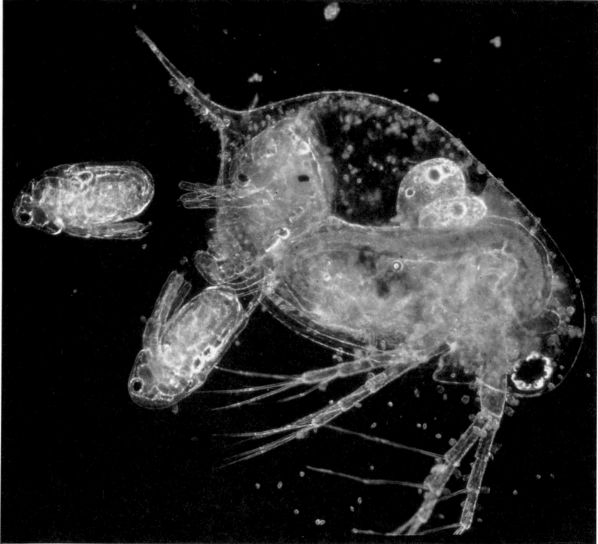

These young were produced by parthenogenesis.

Certain animals, such as the water flea, can reproduce both sexually and asexually. Here, a water flea gives birth to young which developed inside her from eggs that were not fertilized. This development is the result of asexual reproduction. At other times, water fleas develop from fertilized eggs—from sexual reproduction. What conditions must be met for animals to reproduce successfully? How do reproductive patterns vary among animals?

Introduction: Begin this chapter by involving teams of students in exercises which illustrate modes of asexual reproduction in animals. Possible activities include regeneration in planarians or earthworms and observations of budding hydras (the latter available from biological supply houses). Have students observe their specimens daily as you proceed with the chapter and later ask a member of each team to share his or her observations and conclusions with the class. In teaching human reproduction, consider using the set of filmloops *Human Reproduction and Birth* available from Holt, Rinehart and Winston. These filmloops combine photography and animation to present reproductive anatomy and physiology as well as development and birth, topics presented in the next chapter.

Chapter

23

ANIMAL REPRODUCTION

Chapter 23 presents patterns of asexual and sexual reproduction among animals.

In simple organisms such as monerans, protists, and fungi, asexual reproduction is common. Sexual reproduction, if it occurs, is accomplished by simple processes such as conjugation. Plant life cycles include both asexual and sexual phases, and plants have specialized reproductive tissues or organs. In animals, sexual reproduction is predominant, and most animals have complex reproductive systems. In this chapter, you will study the processes of reproduction found among animals.

GOAL: You will gain an understanding of patterns of reproduction found among animals.

PATTERNS OF DEVELOPMENT

23:1 Asexual Reproduction

Some animals may reproduce asexually. Figure 23-1 illustrates **budding** (Section 17:3) in a hydra. The bud forms as a small group of cells on the side of the parent animal. After all the specialized cells and tissues have developed, the young hydra breaks away, settles in a new location, and leads a separate life.

Fragmentation is another form of asexual reproduction in animals. In fragmentation, pieces split off from the parent and then grow into new organisms. This type of reproduction often occurs in sponges and coelenterates.

Fragmentation may also occur in the flatworm planaria. If the worm is cut in half (fragmented), each half will regrow the missing parts. The process of regrowing missing parts is called **regeneration** (rih jen uh RAY shun). The head end develops a new tail, and the tail end regenerates a new head. Even if a planarian is cut into four sections, each section is capable of regeneration.

FIGURE 23-1. *Hydra* produces asexually by budding. The bud grows and breaks away as a small hydra.

Runk/Schoenberger for Grant Heilman   **429**

Because new organisms can be formed in this way, sometimes it is said that the animals can reproduce by regeneration. In nature, planaria are not cut into pieces. However, they may twist around and break into a front and tail end.

Recall that asexual reproduction results in genetically identical offspring. Both hydras and planarians may also reproduce sexually, resulting in variety among their offspring. Asexual reproduction is common in less complex animals such as sponges, coelenterates, and flatworms.

Some insects, such as aphids and honeybees, reproduce asexually by means of parthenogenesis. **Parthenogenesis** is the development of an unfertilized egg into an adult. In honeybees, the queen lays both fertilized and unfertilized eggs. The fertilized eggs develop into females, mostly workers. The unfertilized, monoploid eggs become males called drones.

23:2 Sexual Reproduction: Animal Life Cycles

Animal life cycles are similar to plant life cycles in that both involve monoploid and diploid stages. But, they are different in that in the lower animals there is no predominant *multicellular* stage as there is in the lower plants. Recall that in moss and fern life cycles there are multicellular, monoploid structures. In most animals, only the gametes are monoploid. The gametes are produced by meiosis of diploid cells. Once the gametes are produced, fertilization occurs and the resulting offspring are again diploid.

In animals, gametes are produced from diploid cells by meiosis.

Animal and plant life cycles also differ in another way. In plants, the sporophyte gives rise to the gametophyte by asexual means, the production of spores. The gametophyte produces the sporophyte by sexual means, fertilization of gametes. Each complete plant life cycle thus involves both asexual and sexual reproduction. Most animals have a life cycle involving only sexual reproduction. Although asexual reproduction may occur in some animals its occurrence is not usually necessary for sexual reproduction to occur. However, in some animals the life cycle does involve both an asexual and a sexual stage. *Aurelia*, (Section 15:2) for example, has an asexual polyp and a sexual medusa stage. Although both of these structures are diploid, the fact that one stage must follow the other makes this life cycle similar to that of plants.

The life cycle of many animals involves only sexual reproduction.

Almost all sexual reproduction in animals involves separate males and females which have sex organs, or **gonads** (GOH nadz). Sperm are produced in the male gonads, the **testes** (TES teez), and eggs are produced in the female gonads, the **ovaries** (OHV reez).

Sex of animals is determined by the presence of ovaries (female) or testes (male).

The clitellum, the thickened region, secretes a mucus "cocoon." Sperm from each worm are deposited in the cocoon and travel through it to the other worm. Sperm are stored and fertilization of eggs occurs later.

FIGURE 23-3. Eggs formed in frog ovaries are stored in the ovisacs after passing through the oviducts. How are conditions for fertilization met in frogs?

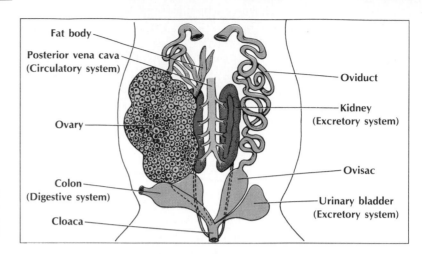

Fat body

Posterior vena cava (Circulatory system)

Ovary

Colon (Digestive system)

Cloaca

Oviduct

Kidney (Excretory system)

Ovisac

Urinary bladder (Excretory system)

In both types of fertilization, four conditions must be met. They are (1) proper timing of release of gametes so both sperm and eggs are present at about the same time, (2) protection of the gametes, (3) a pathway for sperm to reach eggs, and (4) a liquid medium in which sperm can swim to the eggs.

23:4 External Fertilization

Frogs have external fertilization.

Frogs are animals with external fertilization. In females, eggs develop in ovaries. As the eggs grow, they burst from the ovaries into the coelom (body cavity). The eggs then enter two long, coiled tubes, the **oviducts** (OH vuh dukts). The opening of each oviduct is funnel-shaped and located toward the anterior end of the abdomen. Action of cilia which line the oviducts pushes the eggs to the back of the frog where the eggs are covered by a jellylike coat and stored in the **ovisac** (OH vuh sak). In males, sperm are produced in the testes and travel, via tubes, to the kidneys. Figure 23-3 shows the reproductive organs of frogs.

During the breeding season, a female frog is stimulated by bodily contact with the male. At this time, her eggs leave the ovisac, pass into the **cloaca,** a body chamber that receives wastes as well as gametes, and then enter the water. In the male, sperm travel through ducts to the cloaca and are deposited into the water at the same time as the eggs leave the female's body.

FIGURE 23-4. Amplexus of frogs is an adaptation ensuring fertilization of eggs. The clasping behavior results in proper timing in the release of sperm and eggs.

Rannels for Grant Heilman

In the case of frogs, the timing condition is met by behavioral patterns. The clasping of the female by the male results in the gametes' being released at the same time. This clasping is called **amplexus** (am PLEX us) (Figure 23-4). Some other aquatic animals go through elaborate **courtship patterns.** Courtship involves complex behavior which stimulates both sexes to deposit eggs and sperm at about the same time. Proper timing is important because gametes have short life spans in which to unite.

The condition of protection of the gametes is not so easily met. The environment in which the eggs have been deposited (water) is hazardous. The eggs may be eaten by other animals. Also, physical factors, such as water temperature and the amount of oxygen, are important. Frogs (and many other aquatic animals) deposit thousands of eggs at one time. There is "safety in numbers" in that at least some of the eggs will be fertilized and some of the fertilized eggs will survive. The jellylike layer around the eggs also protects them from predators and harsh conditions.

Producing many eggs and many sperm at once also helps meet another condition. Because both eggs and sperm are deposited in water, there is no direct pathway to the eggs for sperm to follow. A lake or a pond is a huge volume of water, and the lifetime of the gametes is short. Although gametes are released at about the same time and in the same place, the chances for sperm and eggs uniting are increased further by their large numbers.

Because fertilization occurs in water, the water serves as a liquid medium in which sperm can swim. The water also provides moisture which keeps the gametes from drying out. Thus, animals with external fertilization are "chained" to the water. Any attempt at fertilization on dry land would fail.

External fertilization requires the production of large numbers of gametes.

External fertilization requires water.

23:5 Internal Fertilization

The grasshopper is an example of an animal with internal fertilization. Eggs are produced in the female's ovaries and enter the oviducts. Sperm are produced in the male's testes, then travel to the **sperm duct** where fluids are added. During mating, the sperm and fluids pass out of the **penis** and enter the **vagina** (vuh JI nuh). The vagina is the organ in the female that receives sperm from the male. The sperm are stored in a special sac, the **sperm receptacle,** attached to the vagina (Figure 23-5). During late summer, the eggs move along the oviduct where yolk and a shell are added. Fertilization occurs as the eggs pass through the vagina. A small pore in the shell allows sperm to enter. The posterior abdominal segments of the female form two pairs of pointed structures. These structures, called **ovipositors,** are used to tunnel into the soil. Fertilized eggs leave the vagina and are deposited in the soil. There the eggs remain until the following spring.

Because fertilization occurs internally, the dangers of predators and a harsh environment for the gametes are removed. Sperm and eggs pass through specific reproductive structures which provide a direct pathway for gametes and increase the chances of fertilization. Protection and a pathway are provided by the internal organs. Large numbers of eggs are not produced. Also,

FIGURE 23-5. Sperm are deposited inside the female grasshopper and are stored in the sperm receptacle. Fertilization occurs as eggs pass through the vagina. Fertilized eggs are deposited in the soil.

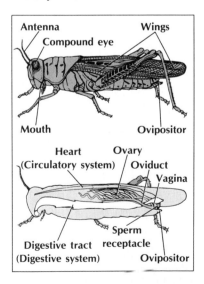

FIGURE 23-6. As part of the court-ship ritual of frigate birds, the male bird puffs up his red throat sac and extends his wings, attracting the female.

Animals which have internal fertil-ization are not restricted to a wet habitat.

The estrous cycle is an excellent example of the interaction of mor-phological, physiological, and behav-ioral adaptations (Chapter 11).

Estrous cycles ensure that mating occurs when mature eggs are ready for fertilization.

a liquid accompanies the sperm, meeting the condition of a liquid medium. As a result, these animals are not "chained" to water as are frogs. The final condition, timing, is met by storage of sperm by the female grasshopper. The sperm are kept alive until the eggs are ready for fertilization.

Proper timing may occur in other ways in animals with internal fertilization. In many cases, the female "informs" the male that she is ready to mate. Certain hormones cause the start of the estrous (ES trus) cycle in the female. The **estrous cycle** is a series of chemical and physical changes leading up to the production of mature eggs. It occurs in mammals such as dogs and cats. When the female is in estrous, or "heat," she undergoes physical and behavioral changes that coincide with the matura-tion of eggs within the ovary. Because the male recognizes and interprets these changes as her readiness for mating, the female only mates when mature eggs are present.

Courtship patterns also exist among animals with internal fertilization. **Courtship patterns** are signals used by animals to identify members of their own species ready for mating. These signals include sounds, dances made up of intricate movements and body postures, and other displays. These mechanisms ensure proper timing so sperm and eggs can unite.

5. External fertilization occurs outside the female. Internal fertilization occurs within the female's body.
6. In frogs, fertilization occurs in wa-ter. Fertilization in grasshoppers occurs internally as eggs pass through the vagina.
7. A courtship pattern is a display that involves signals which identify animals of the same species ready for mating.
8. Storage of sperm is an adaptation which keeps sperm alive until eggs are ready to be fertilized.

REVIEWING YOUR IDEAS

5. Distinguish between external and internal fertilization.
6. Where does fertilization occur in frogs and grasshoppers?
7. What is a courtship pattern?
8. How is storage of sperm by some female animals important?
9. What is an estrous cycle?

9. An estrous cycle is a series of phys-ical, chemical, and behavioral changes leading to the production of mature eggs.

HUMAN REPRODUCTION

23:6 Structures and Functions

In mammals (Section 16:14), fertilization is internal. Study of human reproduction shows the basic pattern found among mammals in general.

Figure 23-7 shows the human female reproductive system. On each side of a female's abdominal cavity is one ovary. Within the ovary are groups of cells called **follicles** (FAHL ih kulz). Eggs begin to form from cells that divide by meiosis within the follicles of the ovary. oogonia

Very close, but not attached, to each ovary is a tube called the oviduct, or **Fallopian** (fuh LOH pee un) **tube.** Because the oviduct is not attached to the ovary, the end can move around the ovary somewhat. When an immature egg is released from a follicle, it is pulled into the oviduct by the action of tiny cilia which line the tube and its opening.

The two oviducts join to a thick-walled, muscular organ called the **uterus,** or womb. The hollow uterus narrows to a small opening called the **cervix** (SUR vihks) which leads to the vagina. The vagina is a canal which has an external opening separate from the **urethra** (yoo REE thruh), the opening through which urine is excreted.

Eggs are produced within follicles of the ovary.

An egg travels to the uterus via the oviduct.

FIGURE 23-7. In humans, usually one egg is released from an ovary and passes down the Fallopian tube to the uterus.

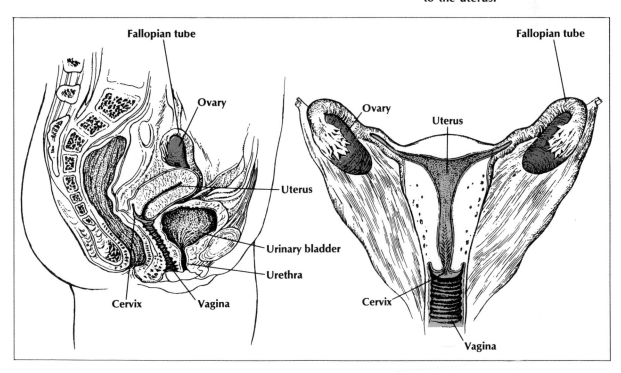

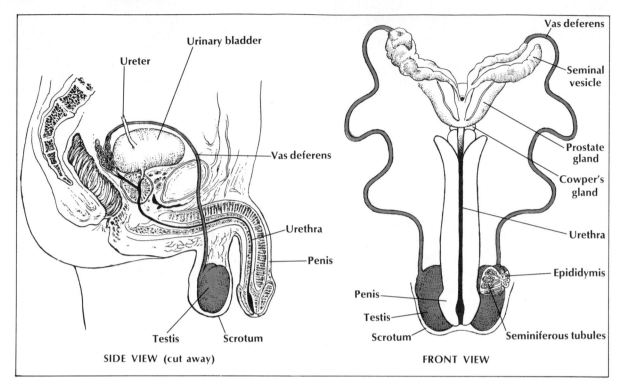

Urinary bladder

Ureter

Vas deferens

Urethra

Penis

Testis   Scrotum

SIDE VIEW (cut away)

Vas deferens

Seminal vesicle

Prostate gland

Cowper's gland

Urethra

Epididymis

Penis

Testis

Scrotum

Seminiferous tubules

FRONT VIEW

FIGURE 23-8. Sperm are produced in the testes. Fluid from the seminal vesicle, prostate gland, and Cowper's gland is added to the sperm, aiding their movement.

Testes develop in the abdominal cavity. Rarely, one or both fail to descend into the scrotum. When this occurs, sperm die from body heat. The scrotum provides a cooler environment because in it, the testes are located outside the body cavity.

Sperm are produced in the testes.

Semen is a combination of sperm and fluids.

Fertilization usually occurs in the oviduct.

The testes of the male are two oval structures within an external sac called the **scrotum** (SKROHT um). In many animals, the testes are within the abdomen. But, in humans and some other mammals, sperm require a temperature slightly lower than body temperature. Thus, the suspension of the testes in an "external" structure is adaptive (Figure 23-8). spermatogonia

Sperm are produced by meiosis in special cells of the testes and transferred along a series of highly coiled tubes. As sperm leave these tubes, they pass three structures which add fluids that help sperm swim. Sperm have long tails, or flagella, adaptations for swimming. The combination of sperm and the fluids is called **semen** (SEE mun). Semen leaves the body through the urethra of the penis.

During sexual intercourse (mating), semen is forcefully ejected from the male's urethra into the female's vagina. Although millions of sperm may enter the vagina, only a few thousand of them pass through the cervix into the uterus. Still fewer enter the oviduct where fertilization usually occurs and only one fertilizes an egg.

In order for fertilization to occur, the sperm must penetrate the egg. The sperm secretes an enzyme which helps form an entryway in the outer zone of the egg. Once this secretion occurs,

Dr. Judie Walton, Lawrence Livermore National Laboratory

Carolina Biological Supply Co.

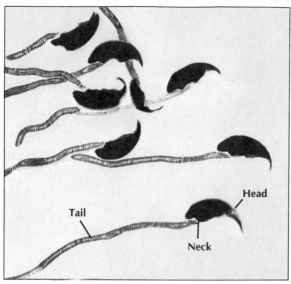

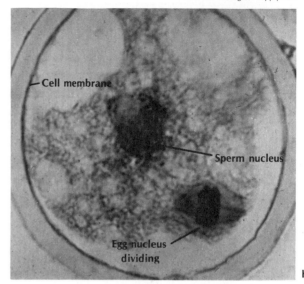

FIGURE 23-9. (a) Adaptations ensuring fertilization include sperm with tips aiding their entry. Mouse sperm have pointed heads. (b) An *Ascaris* egg shows completion of meiosis after sperm penetration. Human sperm and eggs have similar adaptations.

the outer zone becomes changed so that no other sperm can enter the egg. Why is this adaptation of one sperm per egg important? Penetration of the egg by the sperm triggers the immature egg to complete meiosis II, and the second polar body is discarded (Section 6:10). Then the monoploid nuclei of sperm *(n)* and egg *(n)* combine to form the zygote *(2n)*.

If a zygote is formed, it moves downward toward the uterus where development occurs. The zygote becomes embedded in the uterine wall which has been thickened and enriched with blood vessels.

23:7 Menstrual Cycle

Human females do not undergo a seasonal estrous cycle as dogs or cats do. Instead, an egg (secondary oocyte) is released from an ovary about once every twenty-eight days. At the same time, certain uterine changes occur to prepare for a possible pregnancy. This monthly egg maturation and uterine preparation, called the **menstrual** (MEN strul) **cycle,** occurs in four distinct phases. Menstrual cycles begin around age twelve and continue until around age fifty. Ending of the menstrual cycle in the later years of life is called **menopause.**

During the menstrual cycle, an egg matures and the uterus is prepared for a possible pregnancy.

Activities of the ovary and the uterus are controlled by an interaction of hormones. **Follicle-stimulating hormone** (FSH) is produced by the **pituitary** (puh TEW uh ter ee) **gland** located at the base of the brain. The hormone is secreted into the blood and travels throughout the body but affects only the ovaries. FSH causes primary oocytes in some follicles to complete meiosis I

In males, FSH is involved in production of sperm.

Estrogens are responsible for secondary sexual characteristics in females.

During the follicle stage, an egg matures and the uterine lining becomes thicker.

In males, LH stimulates the production of androgens which produce secondary male sexual characteristics.

LH causes ovulation and the conversion of the follicle to the corpus luteum.

Progesterone also prevents the contraction of uterine muscle.

LH causes the corpus luteum to produce progesterone, the hormone which maintains the uterus for pregnancy.

If fertilization does not occur, the corpus luteum disintegrates and the uterine lining breaks down.

10. Sperm are produced in the testes; eggs in the ovaries.
11. oviduct
12. The menstrual cycle is the monthly maturation of an egg and preparation of the uterus. Menopause is the ceasing of the menstrual cycle in later years.
13. pituitary gland, hypothalamus, ovaries, corpus luteum, uterus

and form secondary oocytes. Only one of these usually survives per menstrual cycle. FSH, along with another pituitary secretion, **leutenizing** (LEW teen i zing) **hormone** (LH), causes the ovaries to produce a hormone of its own called estrogen (ES truh jun). Estrogen causes the tissues of the uterus to thicken and the blood supply to increase. This series of changes lasts for about ten days and is called the **follicle stage.**

As the level of estrogen in the blood increases, it is detected by a structure near the pituitary gland called the **hypothalamus** (hi poh THAL uh mus). It directs the pituitary gland to decrease production of FSH and to increase production of LH. The increase in LH causes **ovulation** (ahv yuh LAY shun), bursting of a follicle and release of an egg. This is a very short stage in the menstrual cycle.

LH also causes the ruptured follicle to change to a yellowish body called the **corpus luteum** (KOR pus · LEWT ee um). Under the influence of LH, the corpus luteum produces some estrogen and a hormone called **progesterone** (proh JES tuh rohn). Progesterone further prepares the uterus for pregnancy. This stage of the cycle lasts about two weeks and is called the **corpus luteum stage.**

If an egg has been fertilized, it begins to undergo cell division. By the end of the first week of life, the zygote has developed into a ball of cells and has become embedded in the uterine lining (Section 24:6). Some of these cells produce a hormone similar to LH which "informs" the corpus luteum to keep producing progesterone. Thus, the uterine conditions necessary for pregnancy are maintained. After about five weeks, the embryo itself will produce progesterone to maintain the uterus throughout pregnancy. human chorionic gonadotropin (HCG)

If a fertilized egg does not become implanted in the uterus, the corpus luteum begins to break down and progesterone production ceases. As the progesterone level decreases, the uterine lining begins to break down and bleeding results. Blood, some uterine tissue, and the unfertilized egg pass from the vagina. This tissue loss is called the menstrual flow. This stage, called **menstruation** (men STRAY shun), lasts three to five days. It marks the beginning of a new menstrual cycle. As menstruation is proceeding, a new egg is already beginning to mature within the ovary. Figure 23-10 summarizes the events of the menstrual cycle and the hormones which control these events.

REVIEWING YOUR IDEAS

10. Where are human eggs and sperm produced?
11. Where does fertilization occur in humans?
12. What is the menstrual cycle? What is menopause?
13. List the important structures involved in the menstrual cycle.

MENSTRUAL CYCLE

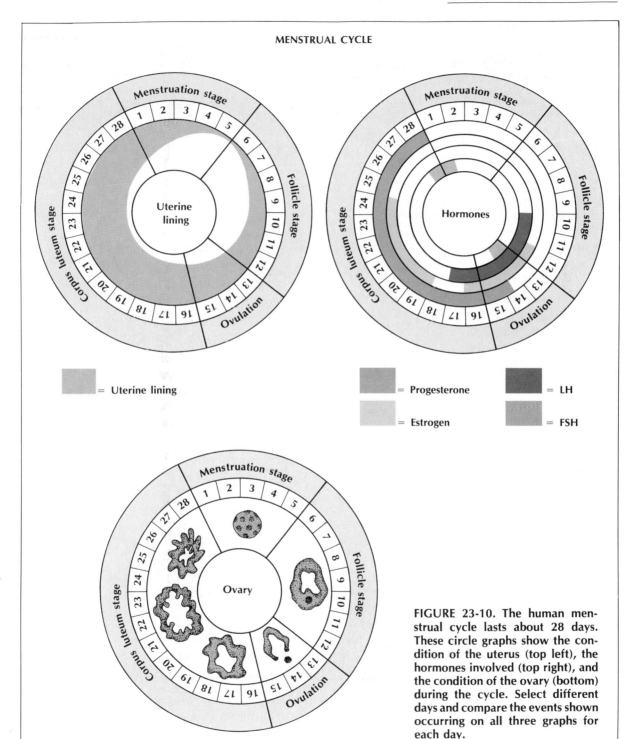

= Uterine lining

= Progesterone

= Estrogen

= LH

= FSH

FIGURE 23-10. The human menstrual cycle lasts about 28 days. These circle graphs show the condition of the uterus (top left), the hormones involved (top right), and the condition of the ovary (bottom) during the cycle. Select different days and compare the events shown occurring on all three graphs for each day.

CHAPTER REVIEW

SUMMARY

1. Asexual reproduction in animals may occur by budding, fragmentation, or parthenogenesis. Sexual reproduction is more common in animals.
2. Animal life cycles involve monoploid and diploid stages. Gametes are monoploid.
3. Fertilization in animals can be external or internal. Conditions for fertilization are proper timing of release of gametes, protection of gametes, a pathway for sperm to reach eggs, and a liquid medium in which sperm can swim to eggs.
4. Frogs have a reproductive system based on external fertilization. The reproductive system of grasshoppers is specialized for internal fertilization. Animals have adaptations that meet the fertilization conditions.
5. Human fertilization occurs internally. During sexual intercourse, semen is injected into the vagina. Fertilization usually occurs within the oviduct.
6. Human females undergo a monthly cycle of events called the menstrual cycle. The cycle is controlled by hormones produced by the pituitary gland, ovaries, and the corpus luteum.

LANGUAGE OF BIOLOGY

amplexus
cervix
cloaca
corpus luteum
estrous cycle
Fallopian tube
follicle
gonad
hypothalamus
menopause
menstrual cycle
ovary
oviduct
ovipositor

ovulation
parthenogenesis
pituitary gland
regeneration
scrotum
semen
sperm duct
sperm receptacle
testes
urethra
penis
uterus
vagina

CHECKING YOUR IDEAS

On a separate paper, match each phrase from the left column with the proper term from the right column. Do not write in this book.

1. produces hormones which control menstrual cycle
2. release of egg from follicle
3. produced from ruptured follicle
4. place of sperm production
5. organ in which a human develops
6. organ where sperm are deposited
7. place of egg production
8. cycle leading to proper timing
9. sperm and fluid
10. cycle involving maturation of an egg and preparation of uterus for pregnancy
11. development of an unfertilized egg
12. regrowth of missing parts
13. behavioral pattern in frog reproduction
14. means of asexual reproduction in hydra
15. male grasshopper reproductive structure

a. amplexus
b. budding
c. corpus luteum
d. estrous cycle
e. menstrual cycle
f. ovaries
g. ovulation
h. parthenogenesis
i. pituitary gland
j. regeneration
k. semen
l. sperm duct
m. testes
n. uterus
o. vagina

EVALUATING YOUR IDEAS

1. Explain how asexual reproduction may occur in planaria.
2. How does the life cycle of animals differ from that of plants?
3. Describe sexual reproduction in earthworms.

CHAPTER REVIEW

4. What conditions are necessary for successful fertilization in animals?

5. List the reproductive structures of male and female frogs. What is the function of each?

6. How arc the conditions of fertilization met in frog reproduction?

7. Why are courtship patterns necessary in some animals?

8. Describe reproduction of grasshoppers.

9. How are the conditions of fertilization met in grasshopper reproduction?

10. List the reproductive structures of the human male and female. What is the function of each?

11. Describe the events of the four stages of the menstrual cycle assuming
    (a) no pregnancy occurs
    (b) pregnancy occurs

12. Explain the chemical control of the menstrual cycle.

APPLYING YOUR IDEAS

1. Can you suggest a reason why most animals undergo sexual reproduction?

2. Internal fertilization offers protection of and a pathway for sperm. Despite these adaptations, animals produce millions of sperm. Explain why production of so many sperm is adaptive.

3. Why do you think that animals which are parasites are often hermaphrodites?

4. Why do many hermaphrodites exchange sperm rather than fertilize their own eggs?

5. The conditions for fertilization met in animal reproduction must be met in plant reproduction. How are these conditions met in moss reproduction? In flowering plant reproduction? *Chapter 20

6. Which plants undergo external fertilization? Internal fertilization? *Chapter 20

7. In artificial insemination, semen from selected bulls is stored at a very cold temperature. Later, it is injected into cows. Why would the semen be stored at cold temperatures? Why would only certain bulls be selected as sperm donors?

8. Can you think of examples of regeneration that do not involve the reproduction of an animal?

EXTENDING YOUR IDEAS

1. Carry out an experiment to demonstrate fragmentation and regeneration in planaria. Keep records of the appearance of each section right after cutting and each day until regeneration is complete.

2. Prepare a report on various courtship patterns in birds.

3. Use library sources to learn about fertilization of human eggs in the laboratory.

4. Find out how oral contraceptives are related to the events of the menstrual cycle.

SUGGESTED READINGS

Fraser, J. T. "Delightful Early Clockshops: When Time and Life Began." *Science Digest*, June 3, 1980.

Grobstein, Clifford, "External Human Fertilization." *Scientific American*, June, 1979.

Gwynne, D. T., "Sexual Difference Theory: Mormon Crickets Show Role Reversal in Mate Choice." *Science*, August 14, 1981.

Ilmensee, K., "On the Way to a Clone: Research on Mice." *Science News*, July 28, 1979.

Netboy, Anthony, "Those Salmon Keep Butting Those Dams." *Natural History*, July 1980.

"Ready Clone: Zebra Fish by the Hundreds," *Science News*, June 13, 1981.

Smolensky, M., "To Everything There Is a Season." *Science News*, September 6, 1980.

"Test Tube Calf: Food and Fertility." *Science News*, July 4, 1981.

"Tide of Life" *Science Digest*, August 1981.

Additional student readings and suggested teacher readings are provided in the Teacher's Guide.

The series of changes which occurs as a living thing reaches its final form is called development. These chicks went through many changes during their development before they hatched. They will continue to change as they develop into adult flamingos. What changes have you gone through during the course of your development? Are you still going through the developmental process? What determines the length of the developmental period?

Introduction: The film *Development and Differentiation* combines animation and direct observation to illustrate development through the gastrula stage and formation of tissue layers. The film relates the process of development to the role of DNA and this serves as a good link to material previously studied. Another film, *Prenatal Development*, combines an outline of human development with a study of various factors which may affect the physical and behavioral characteristics of the fetus and young infant. These factors include diet, drug use, and psychological state of the mother. Both films may be rented from CRM/McGraw-Hill Films, 110 15th St., Del Mar, CA, 92014.

Chapter

24

ANIMAL DEVELOPMENT

Chapter 24 compares patterns of development among animals and presents an analysis of the mechanisms involved.

Most animals reproduce sexually; two sets of DNA fuse to form a zygote. The zygote receives a complete set of instructions which control its **development,** the series of changes a zygote undergoes in becoming an adult. As it is developing, a new organism is called an **embryo.** The study of development is called **embryology.**

Embryos are alive and have the same basic functions as any other living animal. They must secure food, obtain oxygen, rid themselves of wastes, and respond to their environment.

In Chapter 23, you learned that some animals have external fertilization and others have internal fertilization. Also, there are different types of development found among animals. In this chapter, you will study external and internal development and the various patterns of development among animals.

GOAL: You will gain an understanding of embryology and the changes through which animals go to attain a final form.

A living embryo performs the same functions as a mature animal.

Animals undergo external and internal development.

FIGURE 24-1. Frog eggs are protected by a jelly coat that swells when the eggs are deposited in water.

PATTERNS OF REPRODUCTION

24:1 External Development: Adaptations for Protection

Animals which are produced by external fertilization also develop externally. Just as protection is important for an unfertilized egg (Section 23:4), it is also important for an embryo. Animals have a variety of adaptations for protecting fertilized eggs and embryos.

Fertilized frog eggs are surrounded by a jellylike layer which protects the eggs, insulates them, and helps them adhere to objects. The jellylike layer is added to the eggs as they pass through the oviducts. The layer swells when the eggs are deposited in water.

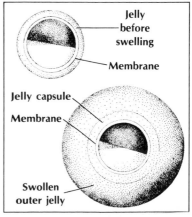

Jelly
before
swelling

Membrane

Jelly capsule

Membrane

Swollen
outer jelly

FIGURE 24-2. (a) The color pattern of frog eggs may be a protective adaptation. (b) A protective adaptation involving the parents is the behavior of stickleback fish, in which the male guides the female into the nest for egg laying.

Teaching suggestion: Frog eggs can be placed in preservative and used each year to show the poles and jellylike layer.

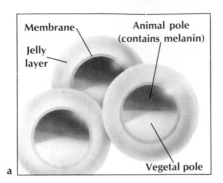

Membrane

Jelly layer

Animal pole (contains melanin)

Vegetal pole

a

b

The vegetal pole of the frog's egg contains yolk. The animal pole contains cytoplasm.

Coloration may also be protective. The bottom half of an egg, the **vegetal** (VEJ ut ul) **pole,** is light-colored because it contains yolk. The top half, the **animal pole,** is composed of living cytoplasm which has a dark pigment. Because the vegetal pole is more dense than the animal pole, it faces the bottom of a pond or stream. This pattern of coloration may blend well with the aquatic environment. Predators swimming above the eggs see a dark color which may blend with the bottom of the stream or pond. A fish swimming below an egg mass sees a light color.

Parents may help to protect eggs and embryos.
Experiments indicate that some male mouthbreeders will not abandon their young even if offered food, especially when a predator is nearby.

A tissue called a pseudoplacenta, spongy and rich in blood vessels, forms in the pouch. Developing embryos use their own yolk supply but are nestled in the pseudoplacenta. After a month of development, the pouch opens and young are expelled over a period of several days.

Some protective adaptations involve the parents. In stickleback fish, the male builds a nest and guides the female to it. She lays eggs and is then driven away by the male. He enters the nest and deposits sperm on the eggs. The male protects the developing eggs from predators and "fans" them with water currents to provide oxygen.

Many species of fish are "mouthbreeders." Fertilized eggs are picked up by one of the parents and held in its mouth. The parent carries the eggs in its mouth until the eggs hatch and the young are able to live alone. During this period of development, which may last for many weeks, the parent does not eat.

Sea horses are an unusual type of fish (Figure 24-3). A female transfers unfertilized eggs to a pouch on the male's abdomen. The male then releases sperm into the pouch. He carries the fertilized eggs in the pouch until they have hatched and the young are released.

FIGURE 24-3. (a) The cichlid is a mouthbreeding fish. Fertilized eggs are incubated in the mouth of the adult. (b) Male sea horses are adapted with pouches in which eggs are fertilized and incubated.

a

b

Francois Gohier for Photo Researchers

Sharon Kurgis

24:2 External Development: Metamorphosis of a Frog

Animals which develop outside the female (or male) usually go through a series of changes in structure. These changes help the young to survive apart from the parents as the young mature. After hatching from the egg, many animals develop into a **larva,** an immature animal which can live on its own. Larval forms are common in animals in which external fertilization occurs. The change of an immature animal to an adult is called **metamorphosis** (met uh MOR fuh sus). The organisms going through metamorphosis obtain food and oxygen and get rid of wastes independent of the parents.

A frog's development from egg to adult is one type of metamorphosis (Figure 24-4). Fertilized frog eggs develop for one or two weeks within their jellylike blanket, obtaining energy from the yolk, exchanging gases, and getting rid of wastes by diffusion. At the end of this time, the eggs hatch and tadpoles emerge. A very young tadpole is inactive, but soon changes begin to occur. A long, tapering tail and three pairs of external gills develop. Gills pick up oxygen which is dissolved in the water. Gills also release carbon dioxide into the water. The tadpole is then a free-living, larval form of frog. Although it has no yolk remaining as a food source, it can reach and feed on algae and plant matter. It has small horny teeth which scrape plant matter.

As a tadpole grows, further changes occur. First, the hind legs, then the front legs begin to appear. Internally a pair of lungs develop, and the circulatory system becomes coordinated with the lungs and skin. Eventually, the lungs and skin can obtain oxygen directly from the air and can get rid of carbon dioxide. Other wastes are excreted from special organs. As teeth develop within the tadpole's mouth, the tadpole's diet changes from plants to insects. The tail is resorbed by the animal; the materials of which it is composed are taken into the body. Many of the materials are used as an additional energy source for the developing frog. This entire series of events takes about three months in the common leopard frog (Figure 24-4), but the exact time length may depend on the temperature of the water.

A larva is immature but independent.

Metamorphosis is a series of changes in the development of an immature animal into an adult.

Teaching suggestion: Stress that metamorphosis of a tadpole involves changes in all the body systems.

A tadpole is adapted for exchanging gases and obtaining food.

Tadpole teeth are scraping edges that help get algae for food. The vomerine teeth of a frog help the frog hold prey in its mouth before the prey is swallowed whole. Neither tadpoles nor frogs chew food.

Changes prepare a developing frog for life on land.

FIGURE 24-4. Among the many changes that occur in frog metamorphosis, (a) free swimming larvae (b and c) develop limbs. Eventually the tail is resorbed and the tadpole becomes a frog.

Harry Rogers for Photo Researchers

Harry Rogers for Photo Researchers

Harry Rogers for Photo Researchers

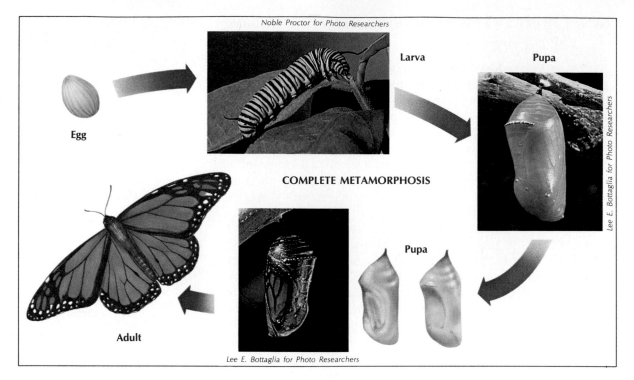

Noble Proctor for Photo Researchers

Egg

Larva

Pupa

COMPLETE METAMORPHOSIS

Lee E. Bottaglia for Photo Researchers

Pupa

Adult

Lee E. Bottaglia for Photo Researchers

FIGURE 24-5. Complete metamorphosis in insects is shown by the development of a monarch butterfly. The egg undergoes changes becoming a larva and then a pupa. The adult emerges from the pupa.

24:3 External Development: Metamorphosis in Insects

Insects undergo metamorphosis after internal fertilization has occurred. Fertilized eggs are deposited by the female in places such as water, soil, plants, or other animals where they develop externally. The young embryo obtains food from yolk and exchanges gases and gets rid of wastes by diffusion.

Metamorphosis may occur in either three or four stages, depending on the type of insect. **Complete metamorphosis** occurs in four stages—egg, larva, pupa (PYEW puh), and adult.

Complete metamorphosis: egg, larva, pupa, adult.

A fertilized egg first develops into a wormlike larva such as a maggot (housefly) or caterpillar (butterfly or moth). An insect larva, like a tadpole, is free-living and secures its own food. This food is needed as an energy source for the larva and is important for the changes which follow. The larva becomes inactive and changes to a **pupa.** The pupa is usually enclosed within some type of protective shell or case. During the pupal (PYEW pul) stage, the tissues of the animal are completely reorganized. The energy needed for this change is provided by burning food eaten during the larval stage. After a period of time, an adult emerges from the pupa case. A pupa from a maggot becomes a housefly, and a pupa from a caterpillar becomes a moth or butterfly (Figure 24-5).

During the pupal stage, a complete change of form occurs.

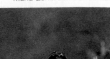

Maria Zorn/Animals Animals

William Ferguson/Nature Photography

William Ferguson/Nature Photography

a b c

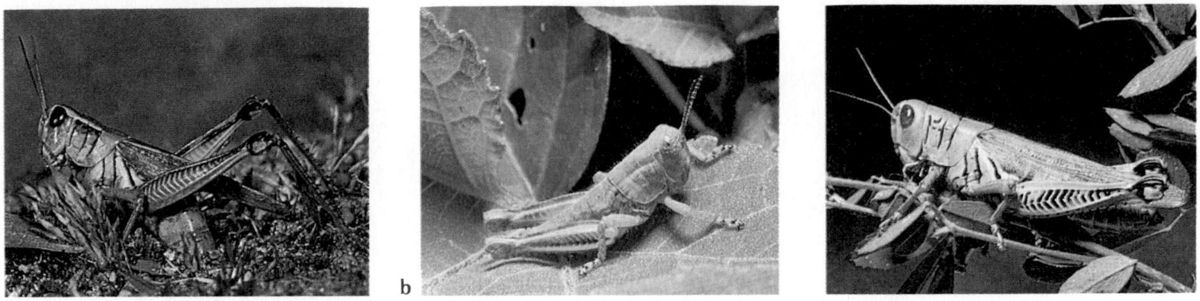

FIGURE 24-6. Grasshoppers show incomplete metamorphosis. (a) A female deposits fertilized eggs in the ground. (b) A nymph is a young animal which resembles (c) the adult.

Incomplete metamorphosis occurs in three stages—egg, nymph (NIHMF), and adult. An egg hatches into a **nymph** which closely resembles the adult but is smaller and often wingless. A nymph grows and usually wings develop. A reproductive system also develops. Grasshoppers undergo incomplete metamorphosis (Figure 24-6).

The nymph grows by a series of molts (Section 29:9).

24:4 The Shelled Egg

Reptiles and birds reproduce by internal fertilization. After fertilization, the zygote travels down the oviduct. As the zygote travels, a shell develops around it. In reptiles, the shell is tough and leathery; in birds, it is brittle and porous.

The **shelled egg** is an important adaptation because it permits reptiles and birds to live and reproduce away from water. If an embryo is to develop successfully upon land, it must be kept moist. Because the waterproof shell of reptile and bird eggs prevents evaporation, the developing embryo will not dry out.

The shelled egg retains moisture necessary for development on land.

Shelled eggs of reptiles and birds are complete environments for the embryos. They provide needed moisture and food and a means for gas exchange. Bird eggs require heat to develop. Birds are endotherms (Section 16:13). How is the heat provided? Reptile eggs are usually deposited in sand or soil and left alone. Temperature is not as important because reptiles are ectotherms. They assume the temperature of the surroundings.

Body heat is usually provided by the parents.

Shortly after fertilization, the nucleus of the zygote is at one end of the yolk. It then divides to form a disc of cells. Later, four membranes develop from the embryo. Beneath the porous shell lies a very thin membrane called the **chorion** (KOR ee ahn) which encloses the other three membranes. Attached to the developing digestive system of the embryo is the **yolk sac,** a membrane which encloses the yolk. The yolk (mainly fat), along with the white of the egg (protein), is a food source for the developing embryo. The yolk sac contains blood vessels through which the food passes to the embryo's cells.

FIGURE 24-7. Reptiles lay shelled eggs, an adaptation for life on land. The young turtle has just emerged from the egg.

Carolina Biological Supply Co.

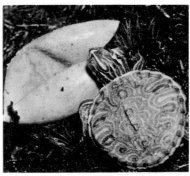

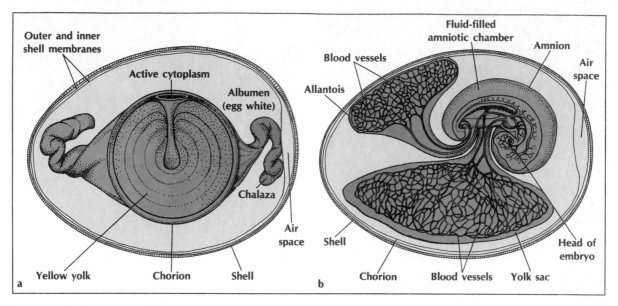

Outer and inner shell membranes

Active cytoplasm

Albumen (egg white)

Chalaza

Air space

Yellow yolk

Chorion

Shell

a

Fluid-filled amniotic chamber

Amnion

Air space

Blood vessels

Allantois

Shell

Head of embryo

Chorion

Blood vessels

Yolk sac

b

FIGURE 24-8. A shelled egg provides protection, a food source (yolk), and a means of gas exchange and waste removal. (a) Egg parts before fertilization and (b) after development has begun are shown.

The allantois functions in waste removal and gas exchange.

The embryo is kept moist in the fluid-filled amnion.

FIGURE 24-9. The spiny anteater is a monotreme. Spiny anteaters live in parts of Australia, New Guinea, and Tasmania.

Australian Tourist Office

Also connected to the digestive region of the embryo is a membrane sac called the **allantois** (uh LANT uh wus). Waste products collect in this sac. Carbon dioxide in the blood vessels of the allantois passes by diffusion through the shell and into the environment. Oxygen diffuses in the other direction. Part of the allantois lies close to the chorion. Later the allantois acts with the chorion in gas exchange.

Surrounding the entire embryo is a fluid-filled sac called the **amnion** (AM nee ahn). The fluid cushions the delicate embryo and keeps it moist.

Near the end of their development period, birds obtain additional oxygen from air trapped in an area near the blunt end of the egg. Using this air, the bird's lungs start working. A short time later, the bird begins to break open its shell and breathes air from outside.

Shelled eggs are also produced by a group of primitive mammals called **monotremes**. Only two groups, the spiny anteater and duckbill platypus, are alive today. These animals, now protected in Australia, have features of both reptiles and mammals and may be very much like the earliest mammals.

The duckbill platypus has fur and produces milk from glands similar to the mammary glands of other mammals, but without nipples. It also has a ducklike bill and webbed feet. The female produces several eggs which she keeps warm in a nest she builds. After the young hatch, they feed by licking milk from the mother's fur around the glands.

Shelled eggs are adaptive. Far fewer eggs are produced by animals with shelled eggs than are produced by insects and

Monotreme eggs have a large supply of yolk; marsupial eggs have a small supply.

J. W. Thompson

Allan Roberts

a

b

FIGURE 24-10. Shelled eggs provide the embryo a favorable environment until it exists independently. (a) Avocet bird eggs and (b) blacksnake eggs give the young of these species a better chance to survive than embryos which must develop without the protection of a shelled egg.

aquatic animals. Because fertilization occurs internally in animals with shelled eggs, the chances of fertilization are great. Shelled egg membranes provide an embryo with a favorable environment until it is ready to exist independently. These adaptations give an embryo within a shelled egg a better chance to survive than an embryo which must develop without the protection of a shelled egg.

Shelled eggs provide an embryo with a favorable environment for development.

24:5 Partial Internal Development: The Marsupials

Although shelled eggs provide an improved method for development, there are other patterns. Development in most mammals occurs either partially or totally within the mother's body. Partial internal development occurs in a group of pouched mammals called **marsupials** (mar sew pee ulz). These mammals, such as kangaroos, live mainly in Australia. Opossums are marsupials found in North America.

FIGURE 24-11. (a) After birth, small baby opossums complete their development within their mother's pouch. (b) A young kangaroo "rides" in its mother's pouch where mammary glands are located. Opossums and kangaroos are marsupials.

a

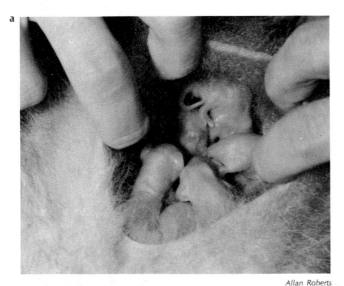

b

Allan Roberts

Opening the pouch does not harm the opossum. The pouch is a fold of skin that covers the mammary glands.

Australian News and Information Bureau

A marsupial begins developing within the mother's uterus and finishes developing in the mother's pouch after birth.

In all marsupials, eggs are fertilized internally, and the embryos begin development within the mother's uterus. The same four membranes that are in bird and reptile eggs develop from the embryo. The embryo receives some nourishment from the mother while in the uterus, but the tiny young are soon expelled from the uterus. They crawl into a pouch on the female's abdomen where mammary glands are located. The young secure milk through the nipples of the mammary glands. When they leave the uterus, young kangaroos are only a few centimeters long. Further development and growth of the embryo occurs in the pouch.

Complete internal development requires methods for food supply, gas exchange, and waste removal.

One reason marsupial embryos are limited to partial development within the mother is that they become too large for the uterus. Also, they may not be able to get enough food and oxygen while in the uterus. And, they may not be able to get rid of wastes effectively. If complete internal development is to occur, there must be methods for a continuous food supply, gas exchange, and waste removal. These methods are found in another group of mammals.

The expression "complete internal development" does not include the sexual development of the offspring. Secondary sex traits develop later.

24:6 Complete Internal Development: The Placentals

Placental mammals undergo complete internal development.

Complete development of embryos within the mother occurs in mammals called **placentals** (pluh SENT ulz). In these mammals, a special structure, the **placenta,** is formed in the uterus from the embryo's and the mother's tissues. Exchange of gases between the embryo and the mother occurs in the placenta. Also, the placenta is the site where food is obtained and wastes are removed. Humans, dogs, rats, horses, and deer are examples of placental mammals.

FIGURE 24-12. (a) Elephant seals and (b) African elephants are examples of placental mammals. Young develop within the mother's uterus and are nourished through the placenta during development.

Development of a human embryo is an example of placental development. Prior to fertilization, the uterus becomes thickened, and its blood supply increases during the menstrual cycle (Section 23:7). Fertilization often occurs within the oviduct.

a

Frank Balthis

b

Leonard Lee Rue III from National Audubon Society

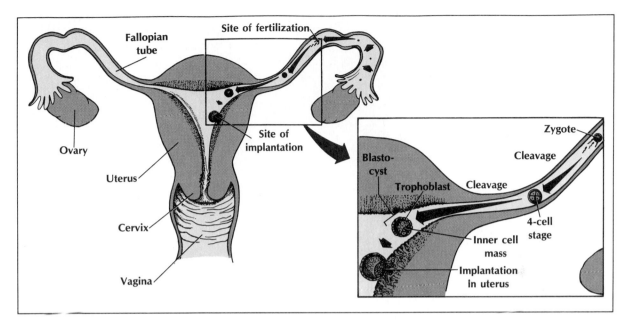

FIGURE 24-13. Usually fertilization occurs in the Fallopian tube. A zygote then begins development before implantation in the uterus.

After fertilization, the zygote begins to divide and forms a ball of cells called a **blastocyst** which travels down the oviduct to the uterus. Two regions of cells form as the cells divide. One is an outer layer of cells called the **trophoblast**; the other is called the **inner cell mass.** The embryo develops from the inner cell mass. During this time, the embryo obtains food from the small amount of yolk. On the sixth or seventh day after fertilization, the blastocyst attaches to the spongy wall of the uterus. During this process, cells of the trophoblast produce enzymes that digest some of the uterine cells. The embryo then embeds in the uterine wall. This process of attaching and embedding of the embryo within the uterus is called **implantation.** Implantation marks the start of pregnancy.

As implantation occurs, the amnion begins to form around the embryo. Soon the trophoblast and embryo are connected to the uterine wall by a part called a **body stalk.**

In addition to the amnion, the other membranes found in bird, reptile, and marsupial embryos develop. But in placental mammals, some of the membranes have different functions and complete internal development is, therefore, possible. Many branches form from the chorion and become embedded in part of the uterine wall. In these branches, small blood vessels, capillaries, develop from the allantois and become part of the placenta. The rest of the placenta is made of uterine tissue. The capillaries of the placenta are part of the embryo's circulatory system. As these capillaries form, the embryo's heart and circulatory system are also developing. In humans, these changes occur during the fourth week of development.

The human develops from the inner cell mass of the blastocyst.

The trophoblast secretes estrogen which prepares the uterine tissue for implantation.

Pregnancy begins when the fertilized egg is implanted in the spongy uterine wall.

Branches formed from the chorion become embedded in the uterine wall. Capillaries which develop in the branches become part of the placenta.

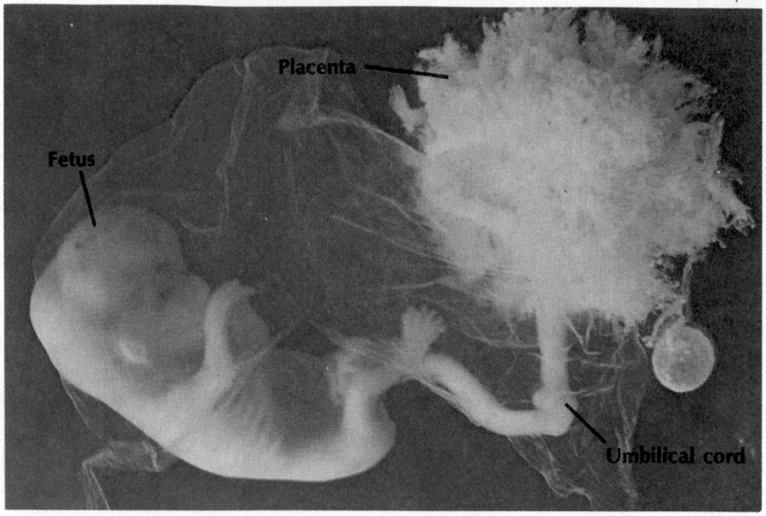

FIGURE 24-14. A human embryo at six weeks of development has a well developed umbilical cord and placenta.

Alpha

Placenta

Fetus

Umbilical cord

The umbilical cord contains two umbilical arteries which take blood to the placenta and an umbilical vein which returns blood to the embryo.

The umbilical cord contains blood vessels that link the embryo and the placenta.

Identical twins share a single placenta.

Blood of the embryo does not mix with the mother's blood.

The embryo is connected to the placenta by the **umbilical** (um BIHL ih kul) **cord** which contains large blood vessels that transport blood between the embryo and the placenta. These blood vessels also are formed from the allantois. The cord itself develops from the body stalk. There is a separate placenta and umbilical cord for each developing embryo.

Blood pumped by the embryo's heart enters the vessels of the umbilical cord and circulates through the capillaries of the placenta. The blood comes into close contact with the blood in the mother's uterine wall. The two blood supplies normally do not mix together, but they are close enough so that certain

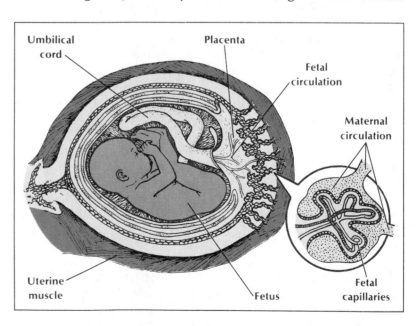

Umbilical cord

Placenta

Fetal circulation

Maternal circulation

Uterine muscle

Fetus

Fetal capillaries

FIGURE 24-15. Needed materials and wastes are exchanged between embryo and mother through the placenta.

materials diffuse between them. The mother's blood carries food molecules digested by her system and oxygen taken in by her lungs. Some of these molecules diffuse from her blood into the blood in the capillaries of the placenta. Water and vitamins also pass from mother to embryo. The blood then goes back to the embryo through the umbilical cord. From here it circulates through the embryo's blood vessels. The oxygen and food then diffuse from the blood into the embryo's body cells. At the same time, carbon dioxide leaves the embryo's cells and enters its blood. At the placenta, the carbon dioxide diffuses into the mother's blood and is exhaled by her lungs. Excretory products are also transferred to the mother at the placenta and are excreted by the mother. Inside the mother's body, the embryo is well protected from the harsh environment (Figure 24-17). Also, the amniotic fluid helps cushion the embryo and keep it moist. Everything the developing embryo needs is supplied to it. Thus, its chances of survival are very good.

Oxygen and digested food pass from mother to embryo via placental blood.

FIGURE 24-16. (a) A six week old human fetus shows paddles for hands and feet on the limb buds, and a large head with forming eyes and ears. (b) At eight weeks facial features become more obvious and hands and feet more developed. (c) At eleven weeks, fingers and toes are clearly visible, and the rib cage can be seen just beneath the elbow. (d) At seven months, a human fetus is well-developed and grows rapidly. If born prematurely at this time, however, it can survive only with special care.

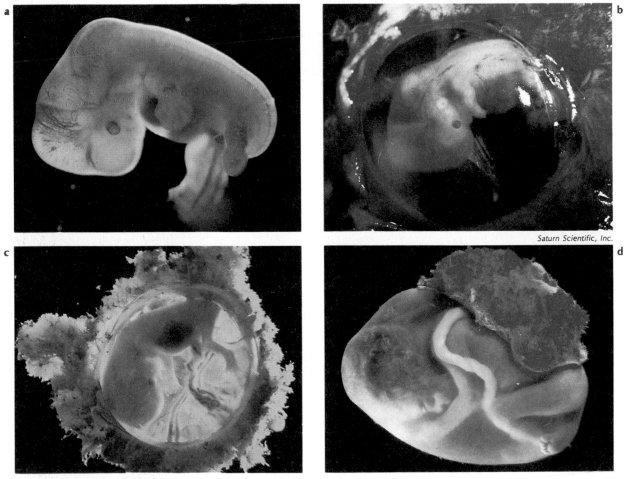

Saturn Scientific, Inc.

Lennart Nilsson, *A Child is Born*, US Delacorte Press/Seymour Lawrence—photos a, c, and d

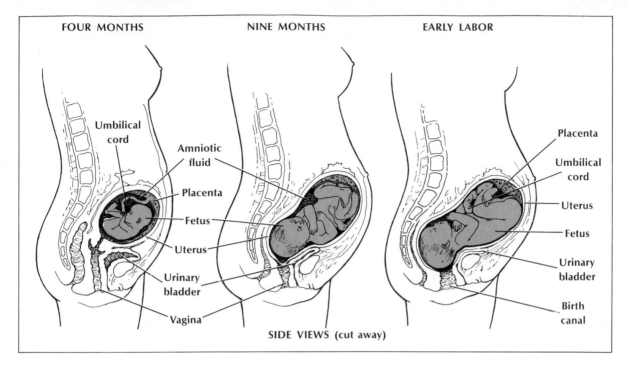

FIGURE 24-17. The fetus is protected within the uterus during its development. Before birth, the baby usually turns and is born head first.

24:7 Birth

As development proceeds, the embryo grows and causes the uterus to expand. After about eight weeks, the embryo is called a fetus (FEET us). Humans have a gestation (jeh STAY shun) period of about 280 days (a little over nine months). **Gestation period** is the length of pregnancy.

At the end of the gestation period, certain hormones start **labor,** a series of contractions of the uterine muscles. The amniotic sac, or "bag of waters," bursts and the cervix and vaginal opening (Section 23:6) enlarge. As contractions become more frequent and intense, the child is pushed to the bottom of the uterus. Usually the child is in a headdown, facedown position. Further contractions push the child headfirst out of the mother's body through the vagina. This expulsion of a baby from the uterus is called **birth.** A little later, a final series of contractions expels the placenta, or **afterbirth.** In humans, the umbilical cord is tied and cut. The remainder of the cord falls off the baby after several days. The **navel** (NAY vul) is the place where the umbilical cord was attached to the baby's body.

After a mammal is born, a period of care is needed. The young is fed milk (nursed) from the mother's mammary glands until it can eat other things. The mother (and sometimes the father) serves as a teacher for the young mammal. The nursing, training, and parental care periods vary from mammal to mammal.

Labor is initiated by a posterior pituitary hormone, oxytocin.

Contraction of uterine muscles during labor forces the child out of the mother's body through the vagina.

Different mammals need various amounts of parental care after birth.

Stephen J. Krasemann/DRK Photo

Mac Albin

a

b

FIGURE 24-18. Parental care is important in animals other than humans. (a) Mountain lions and (b) cedar wax wings are among animals that provide food and protection for their young.

The number of eggs produced by placental mammals at one time is relatively small. But, the chances for survival of young are good. Because a small number of offspring are produced, the parent or parents can better care for the young. In humans, the infant is extremely helpless, and the parental care period is long. Usually one child is born at a time. As a result, the parents can better aid the survival of each child. What do you think would be the ideal length of time between children in a family?

REVIEWING YOUR IDEAS

1. Distinguish between the vegetal pole and the animal pole of a frog egg.
2. What is metamorphosis?
3. Distinguish among larva, pupa, and nymph.
4. What is the major advantage of shelled eggs?
5. Distinguish between a marsupial mammal and a placental mammal.
6. What factors are necessary for complete internal development?

1. The vegetal pole contains yolk and is light in color while the animal pole contains cytoplasm and pigment and is dark colored.
2. Metamorphosis is the changes of an immature animal to an adult.
3. A larva is an immature animal which looks different from the adult and can live independently. A pupa is a stage of insect development during which the tissues are reorganized. A nymph is a young insect resembling an adult but lacking reproductive organs and, often, wings.
4. Shelled eggs allow animals to reproduce and develop on land.
5. A marsupial has partial internal development whereas a placental has complete internal development.
6. There must be a continuous food supply and methods for gas exchange and waste removal.

MECHANISM OF DEVELOPMENT

24:8 Cleavage

These topics (Sections 24:8-24:12) are optional and should be covered only with advanced students.

Embryologists are interested in learning how a zygote develops into a complete, recognizable form. The first studies of animal development were made with animals which develop in water. Frogs, starfish, and sea urchins are favorite specimens for study because they are easy to raise and observe. Later, it became possible to study both shelled and mammalian embryos. Also, methods for fertilizing eggs in culture media and watching their development have been devised.

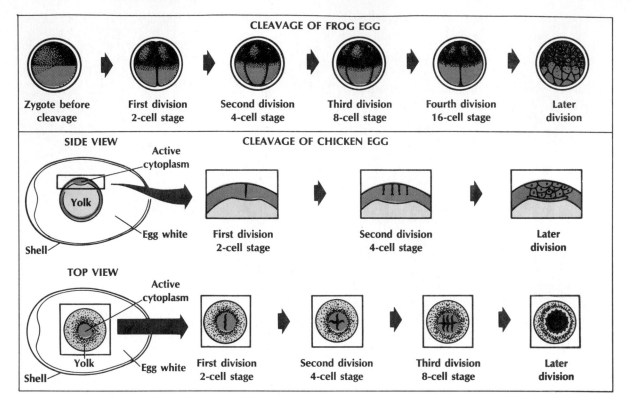

CLEAVAGE OF FROG EGG

Zygote before cleavage | First division 2-cell stage | Second division 4-cell stage | Third division 8-cell stage | Fourth division 16-cell stage | Later division

CLEAVAGE OF CHICKEN EGG

SIDE VIEW

Active cytoplasm · Yolk · Egg white · Shell

First division 2-cell stage | Second division 4-cell stage | Later division

TOP VIEW

Active cytoplasm · Yolk · Egg white · Shell

First division 2-cell stage | Second division 4-cell stage | Third division 8-cell stage | Later division

FIGURE 24-19. Cleavage in frog and chick eggs produces blastulas. Amount of yolk in the eggs influences the cell divisions. Notice that the part of the chicken egg that divides is just a small area on top of the yolk.

The zygote divides into numerous smaller cells during cleavage.

Early stages of development are similar in all animals.

Cleavage results in a hollow ball of cells, the blastula.

Differences in early development are found among animals, but there is a general scheme. Development begins with a series of many cell divisions called **cleavage** (KLEE vihj). Figure 24-19 shows the stages of cleavage as they occur in a frog and a chick. Notice that the pattern differs between the two animals. The difference is due to the location and amount of yolk in each kind of egg. In a frog egg, the yolk is found throughout the cytoplasm, but there is more yolk in the vegetal pole than in the animal pole. As a result, cells of the animal pole divide more rapidly and become more numerous than those of the vegetal pole. In the chick egg, the cytoplasm is a small area on top of the yolk. Cleavage does not cut through the yolk. A disc of cells is formed as the nucleus and cytoplasm divide on top of the yolk.

In an animal embryo, cleavage produces a mass of cells which form a new, multicellular animal. Notice that there has been little growth up to this point. The large zygote has merely been subdivided into many smaller cells. These cells form a hollow ball called the **blastula** (BLAS chuh luh). The blastula consists of one layer of cells called the **ectoderm** (EK tuh durm). Inside the blastula is a cavity called the **blastocoel** (BLAS tuh seel) which is filled with fluid. The shape of the blastula allows for further rearrangement of cells in later stages of development.

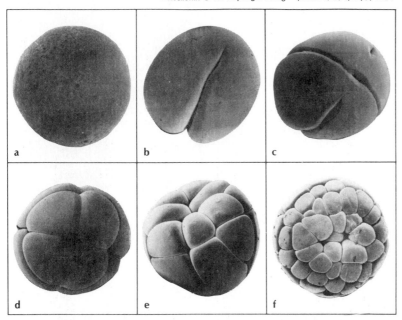

FIGURE 24-20. Frog egg cleavage results in smaller cells at one end. More yolk is present in the end with the larger cells.(a) Zygote,(b) 2-cell,(c) 4-cell, (d) 8-cell, (e) 16-cell, and (f) many - celled stages are shown. From zygote to 16 - cells usually takes about five hours.

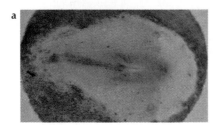
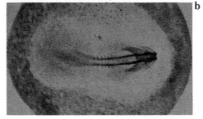

Chicken egg cleavage (shown in Figure 24-19) has occurred prior to photo a in this series. These photos show later chick development.

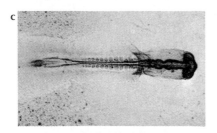
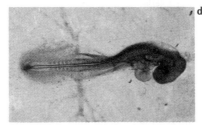

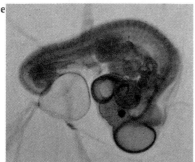
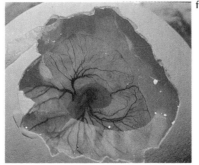

FIGURE 24-21. After cleavage in a chicken egg, continued divisions and cell movements result in the formation of a recognizable embryo. (a) 18 hour, (b) 24 hour, (c) 33 hour, (d) 56 hour, and (e) 96 hour developing chickens are shown. (f) The developing chicken can be seen inside the egg.

Courtesy CCM: General Biological, Inc.
—photos a,b,c,d, and e

Roger K. Burnard

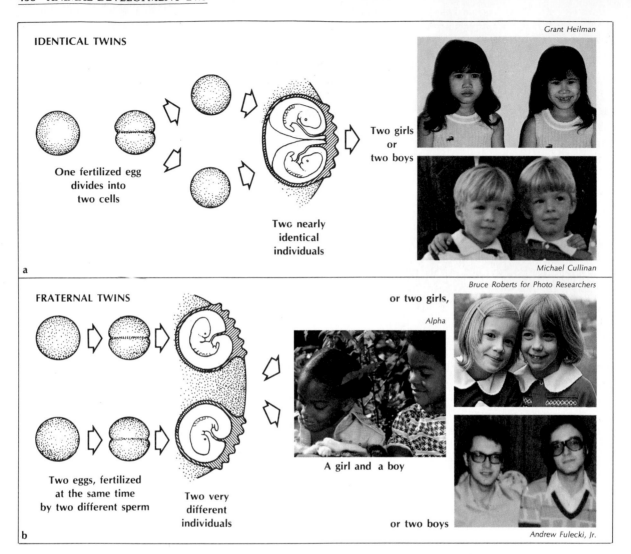

FIGURE 24-22. (a) Identical twins develop from a single fertilized egg which divides into two cells. (b) Fraternal twins develop from two fertilized eggs. Identical twins must be the same sex. Fraternal twins do not have to be the same sex. Why?

Identical twins have the same genotypes.

Fraternal twins have different genotypes.

Sometimes in the division at the two-cell stage the embryo divides into two separate cells. Each cell can develop into a new animal so that two animals are produced. They have the same genotype and are physically identical because they have the same sets of DNA. These two animals are **identical twins.**

Fraternal (fruh TURN ul) **twins** are not identical because they develop when each of two different eggs is fertilized by a different sperm. Each zygote begins life with a different set of DNA instructions. Therefore, fraternal twins are no more alike than any brothers or sisters. Fraternal twins are not common in humans because females normally produce only one egg each menstrual cycle. Must fraternal twins be the same sex? Must identical twins be the same sex? Why?

⌐No.

⌐Yes. ⌐They have the same sex chromosomes.

24:9 Morphogenesis

Following formation of the blastula in a frog, a small indentation forms near the vegetal pole. Some cells from the outside surface of the blastula move inward through this indentation and a curved groove, the **blastopore** (BLAS tuh por) is formed in this region. The upper part of the groove is called the **dorsal lip.** This rearrangement of cells is called **gastrulation** (gas truh LAY shun) (Figure 24-23).

Certain cells migrate through the blastopore to form a second layer of cells called the **endoderm** (EN duh durm). This stage of the developing embryo is called the **gastrula.** You can picture a gastrula by thinking how an inflated balloon (the blastula) would look with your thumb stuck into one end. When pushed in, the outer "skin" of the balloon presses against itself to form two "skin" layers. The endoderm cells continue to move inward and upward to form an internal cavity called the **archenteron** (ar KENT uh rahn). This cavity will later develop into the digestive system of the frog.

Later in gastrulation, a third layer of cells, called the **mesoderm** (MEZ uh durm), forms between the ectoderm and the endoderm. Mesoderm forms in different ways in different animals. In frogs, mesoderm forms from cells which migrate inward through the blastopore. After gastrulation is completed, the blastopore is reduced in size and will become the anus (AY nus) of the frog. The anus is the opening through which undigested food is expelled.

During gastrulation, cells of the ectoderm migrate inward through the blastopore.

The archenteron gives rise to the digestive organs.

FIGURE 24-23. Gastrulation of a developing frog embryo involves morphogenetic movement of cells. Notice the formation of the archenteron as cells push in.

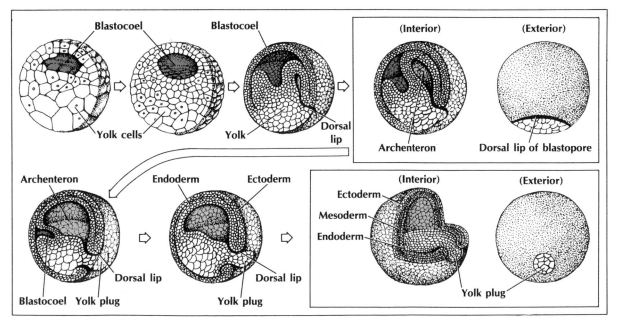

As the archenteron is formed, the blastocoel is obliterated.

TABLE 24-1. MAIN TISSUES PRODUCED BY THE THREE CELL LAYERS			
Cell Layer	Ectoderm	Mesoderm	Endoderm
Tissues Produced	Brain Spinal cord Nerves Skin (outer layer) Eye cup and lens Nose and ears	Skeleton Muscles Gonads Excretory system Skin (inner layer)	Pancreas Liver Lungs Lining of digestive system

Morphogenesis is the creation of shape or form.

The series of changes of the blastula from a hollow, one-cell thick sphere to a three-layered ball is the beginning of **morphogenesis** (mor fuh JEN uh sus). The term morphogenesis means the creation of shape or form. Formation of the three cell layers is necessary for later development.

At this point, there is no visible evidence of any differences in the cells of the embryo. The cells are merely rearranged into three layers. Formation of ectoderm, mesoderm, and endoderm occurs in all the multicellular animals except in sponges and the jellyfish group. Each of these cell layers gives rise to certain tissues during further development. Table 24-1 lists some tissues which develop from each of these layers.

PEOPLE IN BIOLOGY

James Bonner broke family tradition when he became a biologist. Although both of his parents were chemists, and he, along with his five brothers and one sister, majored in chemistry, Bonner has spent his life researching development in cells. He was fascinated by differentiation, the process by which similar cells change to cells that are different from one another. Bonner experimented to find out what controlled differentiation. By studying genes on chromosomes, Dr. Bonner discovered that not all of the genes were working; some of the genes were repressed. Repressed genes are those genes which have their genetic information "turned off" and are not functioning in the cell. The repressed genes were found to be covered with a protein. When the protein was removed, the repressed genes "turned on" and functioned in the cell.

Bonner also did research on hormones as antirepressors for genes while a staff member at the California Institute of Technology. He wrote and coauthored several books, including *The Molecular Biology of Development*. For his work in development and differentiation, Dr. Bonner was elected to the National Academy of Sciences in 1950.

(1910 -   )

James Frederick Bonner

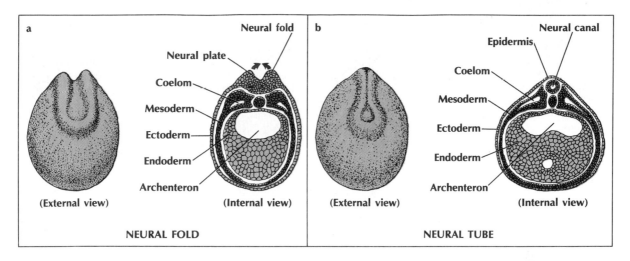

FIGURE 24-24. Formation of the neural tube begins (a) as neural folds form which (b) meet to form a tube. The brain and spinal cord form from the neural tube.

24:10 Differentiation and Growth

After the three cell layers form, changes occur which result in the formation of the many body parts. This series of changes is called **differentiation** (dihf uh ren chee AY shun). Morphogenesis proceeds as cells and tissues differentiate.

Differentiation is the formation of specialized parts.

One of the earliest visible signs of differentiation occurs on the surface of the gastrula. Ectoderm cells along the top of the embryo divide rapidly to form a flat **neural** (NOOR ul) **plate** (Figure 24-24). Then the sides of this plate rise up (buckle) in two folds along the entire length of the embryo. The raised cells form **neural folds** which gradually fuse together to form a hollow groove beneath them called the **neural tube.** The brain and spinal cord will form from the neural tube. Figure 24-24 shows the neural tube as a circle because the figure shows a section through the embryo.

Formation of the neural tube is an early sign of differentiation.

During further development, all the parts of the embryo develop. At the same time, the embryo is also growing. Growth is an increase in the amount of living material (Section 1:5). Earlier stages of development involved dividing of the large zygote into a number of smaller cells. These cells then were arranged in a specific pattern, but no growth had occurred. During gastrulation, cell division becomes less rapid and the cells grow. In the case of the frog, the embryo soon becomes recognizable as a tadpole (Section 24:2). Even at this point, though, further differentiation is necessary.

Growth adds living matter to the organism.

In animals which form shelled eggs and in mammals, much differentiation is completed before the young animal is hatched or born. After that, mostly growth occurs. The period of growth varies from animal to animal. In humans, it lasts for about eighteen to twenty-one years.

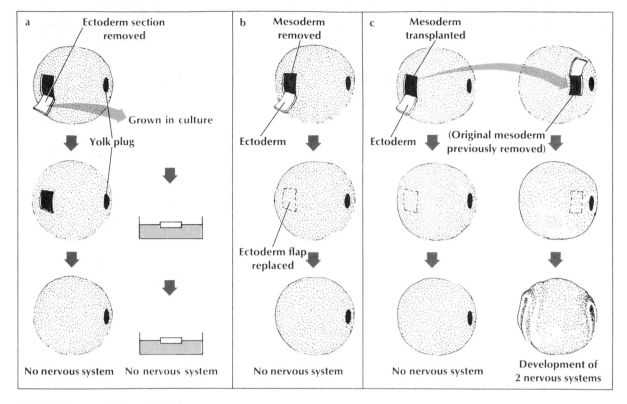

FIGURE 24-25. Embryonic induction experiments, (a) removing a portion of ectoderm, (b) removing a portion of mesoderm, and (c) transplanting a portion of mesoderm, show that mesoderm influences development of the ectoderm.

by Hans Spemann and Hilde Mangold

A certain portion of the ectoderm is necessary for proper development of the nervous system.

Both ectoderm and mesoderm must be present for the nervous system to develop.

24:11 Embryonic Induction

Much has been learned about the sequence of changes which occur during development, but scientists do not fully understand *how* development occurs or what causes it. The question commonly asked is, "What causes each area of the embryo to differentiate into a certain part?" Experiments performed in the 1920's on salamanders helped answer this question.

Sections of ectoderm were removed from salamander embryos and placed in separate culture dishes. The ectoderm section used was that which would develop into the neural tube (nervous tissue). The result of this surgery was that the embryos developed either a defective nervous sytem or no nervous system at all. Also, the pieces of ectoderm in culture failed to differentiate.

A separate experiment was done to determine if the mesoderm, the layer beneath the ectoderm, was involved in the differentiation of the ectoderm. A flap of ectoderm was cut, mesoderm was removed from beneath it, and the ectoderm flap was returned to its original position. The embryo that developed failed to form a nervous system. In other words, even with ectoderm present, no nervous system formed without the presence of the mesoderm.

Teaching suggestion: Make certain that students understand that embryonic induction applies to different parts of the embryo, not just the nervous system.

24:12 CONTROL SYSTEM: A HYPOTHESIS **463**

Alvin E. Staffan

A third experiment was done, this one to determine for sure if the mesoderm was involved in the nervous system differentiation. A piece of mesoderm from the same region as before was removed and transplanted to a second embryo but at a point exactly opposite from where the neural tube normally develops. (The original mesoderm from this site had been removed.) The second gastrula developed a normal nervous system in the expected manner and location. It also developed a second one where the mesoderm had been transplanted (Figure 24-25). These results led to the development of the concept of embryonic induction. **Embryonic induction** occurs when one part of an embryo somehow influences, or induces, the development of another part of the embryo.

Differentiation is a step-by-step process in which one layer of tissue induces another to differentiate. Chemicals are thought to pass from one tissue to another causing differentiation to occur. At least two different substances seem to be involved in embryonic induction. Both are thought to be proteins. These substances are more concentrated in certain regions of the embryo. Thus the location of certain embryonic layers in relation to inducing tissues is very important. Biologists think that the different chemical and physical factors in various parts of the embryo cause parts to develop differently. But, how do these substances cause differentiation of other cells?

FIGURE 24-26. The development of many structures is induced by other tissues near the structures. Formation of the frog tympanic membrane is induced by the cartilage beneath it.

FIGURE 24-27. Transplantation of diploid blastula nuclei into eggs from which the nuclei have been removed results in development of the tadpole. The blastula nuclei have the information necessary for total development.

24:12 Control System: A Hypothesis

Discovery of the existence of embryonic induction answered some questions but caused many more. These unanswered questions involve the how of differentiation. Each cell of a developing embryo contains exactly the same DNA (due to mitosis). Then how are different types of cells produced from this same set of information?

One explanation is that not all genes are active in all cells at the same time. If they were, all cells would develop in the same way. Somehow during development, certain genes must be "switched off." "Switching off" would result in the synthesis of only certain enzymes which would "direct" the development of specific traits.

Experiments conducted with frogs support the inactive gene idea. Nuclei from blastula cells, gastrula cells, and intestinal cells of an adult frog were transferred to unfertilized eggs from which the nuclei were removed. Since the nuclei were already diploid, the eggs did not have to be fertilized. Many of these eggs developed into normal tadpoles and adults. These offspring were clones (Section 19:11) because they were genetically identical to their parents. This experiment showed that *the nuclei of cells in various stages of development still have the full DNA code.*

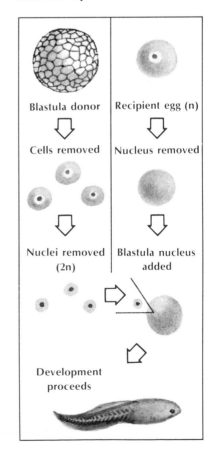

Blastula donor | Recipient egg (n)

Cells removed | Nucleus removed

Nuclei removed (2n) | Blastula nucleus added

Development proceeds

Experiments suggest that the nucleus of a specialized cell retains the genetic code necessary for the development of a new organism.

During development, genes are switched on and off.

7. Cleavage is a series of cell divisions of the zygote resulting in a ball of cells, the blastula. The blastula contains a cavity, the blastocoel.
8. A blastula becomes a gastrula as a result of inward migration of ectoderm cells.
9. ectoderm, endoderm, and mesoderm
10. The neural tube is a canal along the dorsal side of the embryo. From it will form the brain and spinal cord.
11. Embryonic induction is the development of one part of an embryo under the influence of another part.

FIGURE 24-28. Research on aging is aimed at increasing the useful life span of humans. Here a chronologically older person is an active fisherman.

Joey Jacques

Since the same DNA was present in the nuclei when they were parts of blastula, gastrula, or intestinal cells, some of it must not have been operating. But, when the nuclei were placed in the egg cells, the DNA was "switched on" again.

Other experiments involving cloning support this hypothesis. For example, a single, fully differentiated cell from a carrot or tobacco plant can be placed in a special culture medium. At first, the cell divides by mitosis to form an unorganized mass of cells. Later, the mass of cells becomes organized and develops into an entire new plant. This process shows that a mature cell has all the DNA necessary to produce a new organism.

Scientists are working to understand what causes genes to be switched on and off (Section 9:11). This switching on and off of genes probably is involved in many developmental processes. How is a salamander limb regenerated? How do cells become changed in cancer? These processes are some being studied that are thought to be the result of different genes switching on and off. Thus, these problems are important challenges of modern biological research.

REVIEWING YOUR IDEAS

7. What is cleavage? Describe an embryo after cleavage.
8. How is a blastula transformed to a gastrula?
9. What are the three cell layers formed during morphogenesis?
10. What is the neural tube and what does it form?
11. Explain the term embryonic induction.

ADVANCES IN BIOLOGY

24:13 Aging

Aging is a life process that you can see in the people around you. The most obvious signs of aging are some of the problems that often appear late in life such as loss of sight or hearing, arthritis and heart disease.

Aging is a very complex process. It occurs at different rates in different people. Children with a disease called progeria (proh JER ee uh) age physically very rapidly while other processes, such as growth and learning, are not accelerated. By the time they are eight or ten years old, they have the physical features and problems normally found only in very old people. You are aware that under even normal circumstances some old people look and act much older than others of the same age.

Many researchers are trying to understand the aging process in the hope of controlling its rate. They hope to increase the useful life span of humans. Aging is a more significant issue for human beings today than it was for our great-grandparents. Their life expectancy was much lower than is ours because the chance of death from causes such as childhood diseases was so great 100 years ago. Fewer people lived long enough to experience aging.

Important knowledge about aging can come from studies of age-related changes in cells. Some years ago a scientist named Leonard Hayflick discovered that certain human cells called fibroblasts (skin cells) grown in the laboratory will divide only a limited number of times. (When the number of fibroblasts in a culture dish has doubled, one population doubling has occurred.) He also found that while fibroblasts from embryos can undergo 40 to 70 doublings, those from old people can double, but not as many times. As an organism ages, its fibroblasts lose more and more of their potential for division. His studies led to the idea that aging at the cellular level may be a normal part of life.

Researchers have tried to identify biochemical differences in cells from young and old animals that might explain the differences in the potential for cell division. Old cells seem to have more defective proteins than do young ones. Those defects may occur from random mistakes during protein synthesis. Some errors can be tolerated but if the translation machinery becomes more error-prone as cells age, then the amount of defective proteins made will increase in older cells. At some point, there will be so many that needed cellular functions are affected and the cell dies. This process has been called the **error catastrophe theory of aging**. Errors accumulate until a catastrophe occurs.

You know that the processes of DNA replication, RNA synthesis and protein synthesis are not perfect. Mistakes are made. Cells do have correction mechanisms for repairing newly-made mistakes before there are problems. But those correction mechanisms involve enzymes. If there are more mistakes in proteins with age, then the correction mechanism does not work as well in old cells. These processes are probably more important in some tissues than in others. Our skin cells are dying all of the time and dead cells are naturally replaced by new, living ones. However, in some tissues, such as brain and heart, there is no cell division and so every cell that dies cannot be replaced. Eventually an organ may fail because cells have died.

Faulty proteins occur in various ways. Cells contain some chemicals called **free radicals** that are very reactive. Free radicals can cause DNA mutations and result in the synthesis of faulty proteins. They can also inactivate proteins directly. Cells have several mechanisms to protect against the effects of free radicals, some of which involve enzymes. As an organism ages, those defenses may become less effective. Some free radicals are produced inside cells from compounds that enter from the environment (in food or from the air and water). Since humans can control parts of their environment and diet to reduce the amounts of chemicals that can become free radicals, they already know one way to increase life expectancy.

Researchers are trying to understand the aging process to control its rate and increase the length of useful life span.

Oddly enough, cancer is a disease that disrupts that program. Cancerous fibroblasts can divide many more times than can normal ones. Under favorable conditions cancerous cells seem to be able to divide forever.

Aging may be a normal and programmed feature of the life process.

In the error catastrophe theory of aging, errors in proteins accumulate until a catastrophe occurs.

Proteins that are inactivated by a chemical do not usually cause other faulty proteins to be made.

Free radicals that are made in cells or enter cells can cause mutations and inactivate proteins directly.

Some racial or cultural groups eat special foods or foods prepared in special ways that increase or decrease the intake of chemicals that can lead to free radicals. Also, since in different cities or countries environmental sources of chemicals that can become free radicals vary widely, this aspect of the aging process varies.

All Chapter Review answers and additional chapter teaching suggestions are provided in the Teacher's Guide at the front of this text.

CHAPTER REVIEW

SUMMARY

1. A developing animal must obtain food, exchange gases, and expel wastes. A means of protection is also important.

2. Many animals which develop externally undergo metamorphosis. Often the immature form is a larva. A larva can live apart from its parents.

3. Some animals with internal fertilization develop within a shelled egg. Reptiles, birds, and monotremes lay shelled eggs.

4. Marsupials have internal fertilization and partial internal development. After birth, development is completed within the mother's pouch where milk is available.

5. Complete internal development occurs within placental mammals. Exchange of materials between mother and embryo through the placenta and protection of the embryo occur in complete internal development.

6. At the end of the development period, placental mammal young are pushed from the uterus.

7. Development in animals includes cell division (cleavage), morphogenesis, differentiation, and growth.

8. Differentiation of structures depends on location in the embryo. In embryonic induction, one area causes a neighboring area to differentiate. Proteins are thought to be involved in this process.

9. All cells of an embryo have the same genes. During development, certain sets of genes are probably "switched off." The active genes would then determine the cells' chemical reactions. Different sets of reactions would cause development of different features.

10. Scientists are investigating the process of aging in an effort to increase the useful lifespan of humans. Several theories of aging are being studied.

LANGUAGE OF BIOLOGY

allantois
amnion
blastocyst
blastual
body stalk
chorion
cleavage
development
differentiation
ectoderm
embryo
embryonic induction
endoderm
error catastrophe
free radical
gastrula
gestation period

implantation
inner cell mass
labor
larva
marsupial
mesoderm
metamorphosis
monotreme
morphogenesis
nymph
placenta
placental
pupa
shelled egg
trophoblast
umbilical cord
yolk sac

CHECKING YOUR IDEAS

On a separate paper, complete each of the following statements with the missing term(s). Do not write in this book.

1. A developing animal is called a(n) _____.

2. In shelled eggs, wastes are removed by the _____.

3. The process of the developmental change of an immature animal to an adult is _____.

4. _____ is the stage of development marked by rapid cell division.

5. Blood travels from an embryo, through the _____, to the placenta.

6. An embryo of a bird, reptile, or mammal is surrounded by a fluid-filled sac, the _____.

7. _____ are mammals with partial internal development.

8. In placentals, food passes from the mother to the embryo's capillaries at the _____.

9. Bird and reptile embryos obtain most nourishment from the _____.

10. _____ describes one part of an embryo causing a neighboring part to differentiate.

Occasionally questions are added to the *Applying Your Ideas* that require students to use information they have learned from previous chapters. Those questions are marked with asterisks and chapter references.

467

CHAPTER REVIEW

EVALUATING YOUR IDEAS

1. How are fertilized frog eggs protected?
2. Describe the changes which take place in the metamorphosis of a frog. Relate the structures which develop to the environment in which the frog is living.
3. What are the adaptive advantages of the presence of a larval stage?
4. What are the adaptive advantages of internal development?
5. What are the four membranes which develop from the embryo in a shelled egg? What are their functions?
6. Describe development in marsupials. Why are marsupials limited to partial internal development?
7. Describe the implantation of an embryo of a placental mammal and the formation of the placenta and umbilical cord.
8. How is the placenta important?
9. Describe the birth process in humans.
10. Why is the number of mammals born at one time usually relatively small?
11. Explain how the volume of material in a blastula compares with the volume of material in a zygote.
12. Explain two ways in which cleavage is important for the rest of development.
13. How is the formation of fraternal and identical twins different? Compare their genotypes and phenotypes.
14. How is the archenteron formed? Into what major structures will it develop?
15. What is differentiation? What is embryonic induction?
16. Why must it be assumed that some genes are "switched off" during development?
17. Explain the experimental evidence that supports the hypothesis of question 16.
18. What is the error catastrophe theory?
19. Give two ways in which free radicals might be involved in the aging process.

APPLYING YOUR IDEAS

1. Compare the time when yolk and shell are added to bird and reptile eggs with the time they are added to grasshopper eggs.
2. Sometimes a hen's egg is found containing two yolks. How might this egg be formed?
3. In human females, ovulation usually does not occur during the time a mother is nursing a baby. Can you think of adaptive advantages of the lack of ovulation at this time?
4. A human embryo could be considered as "foreign" to its mother. What system of the mother adjusts to presence of the embryo to avoid recognition of the embryo as foreign?
5. How does a mammal develop after birth? *Chapter 19
6. In what ways are animal and plant development similar? How are they different?
7. Why do most animals with external development develop in water or moist areas?
8. Compare aging in plants and animals. Do you think that unicellular organisms can be said to age? Explain.

EXTENDING YOUR IDEAS

1. Abnormal development may result from environmental factors. Give effects of drugs and/or diseases on development.
2. Use library sources to learn about methods of cloning mammals. How do these methods compare to cloning of plants such as carrots?

SUGGESTED READINGS

Gould, Stephen Jay, "This View of Life: Human Babies as Embryos." *Nat. Hist.*, Feb., 1976.

Hayflick, Leonard, "The Cell Biology of Human Aging." *Scientific American*, January, 1980.

Hopson, Janet L., "A Queer Animal of Ducklike Bill and Reptilian Walk." *Smithsonian*, January, 1981.

Jenkins, Marie M., *Embryos and How They Develop*. New York, Holiday House, 1975.

Additional student readings and suggested teacher readings are provided in the Teacher's Guide.

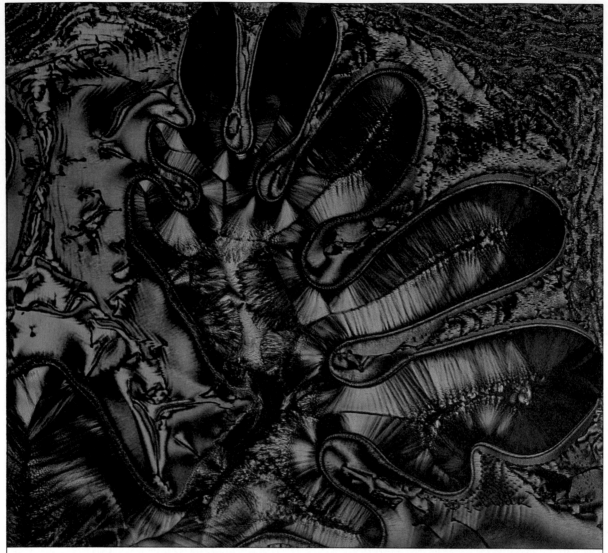

Manfred Kage for Peter Arnold

To maintain life processes, animals take in and digest various nutrients. Vitamins are one type of nutrient needed for life. Vitamin C, shown here as crystals photographed in a special way, is needed for proper muscle development. For what processes are other vitamins needed? What other nutrients besides vitamins do you need? What would happen if you were deprived of any of these nutrients?

Introduction: This chapter is the first in a sequence of six which focuses on animal life functions. Attention in each chapter is given to a variety of animals with emphasis on humans. These chapters can be introduced by showing the film *Man: The Incredible Machine.* The film uses a variety of techniques which include sight and sounds within the body. Covered are the heart, blood vessels, trachea, and ear. It also focuses on the muscular and skeletal systems, brain function, and vision. The photography and choice of topics should create a great deal of enthusiasm and excitement among your students. The film, produced by *National Geographic* can be rented from Modern Film Rentals. See *Audio-Visual Suppliers* in the Teacher's Guide for a list of distributors.

Chapter

25

FOOD GETTING AND DIGESTION

Chapter 25 presents digestive systems of representative animals and discusses the processes involved in digestion.

Like other heterotrophs, animals take in complex, organic molecules. These molecules are too large to pass through cell membranes. They must be digested, or broken down, in order to enter and be used by cells.

Digestion in animals involves both physical and chemical processes. Chewing and grinding are physical processes which reduce the size of pieces of food. Churning food and moving it from place to place within the animal are other physical aspects of digestion. As in other organisms, chemical digestion in animals occurs by hydrolysis reactions (Section 3:17).

GOAL: You will gain an understanding of how animals obtain food and how the food is changed in the process of digestion.

Digestion may include both physical and chemical processes.

PATTERNS OF DIGESTION

25:1 Filter Feeding

Sponges (Section 15:1) cannot move; they must extract food from the water around them. This method of obtaining food is called **filter feeding** because food is filtered from surrounding water. To filter feed, a sponge draws water into its hollow body through many incurrent pores. Lining the endoderm layer are cells called **collar cells.** These cells have flagella surrounded by collars of protoplasm. Movement of the flagella sets up currents of water into the sponge. A sponge's diet is mostly microorganisms. Food is trapped when the microorganisms stick to the collar as water enters the cell. The food travels to the base of the collar and is engulfed. Digestion can occur within vacuoles of the collar cells.

Sponges obtain food by filter feeding.

Flagella of collar cells set up currents of water into the sponge.

Water passes through slits in the collars, but food particles adhere to the outside of the collars.

469

FIGURE 25-1. A sponge obtains food by filtering small organisms from the water which passes through it. The collar cell flagella set up currents of water into the sponge.

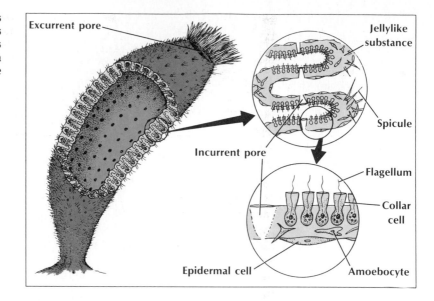

Digested food is distributed by diffusion in sponges.

FIGURE 25-2. Cells on the tentacles of *Hydra* have nematocysts which are discharged from the stinging cells into prey.

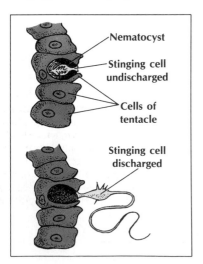

Food also enters the jellylike layer and is engulfed and digested by cells, called **amoebocytes** (uh MEE buh sites), that resemble amoebae. As amoebocytes move through the sponge, they distribute digested food to other cells by diffusion. Waste materials and excess water in the hollow body constantly are expelled from the cavity through the osculum. An animal such as a sponge, which has this method of obtaining food, is called a **filter feeder.**

Filter feeding is found in other sessile animals and in some unattached animals. Oysters, for example, also are filter feeders. Like sponges, they do not actively seek out food. An oyster is much more complex than a sponge, but the food-getting method is similar. Cilia on the surface of the gills draw water into the oyster. Microscopic food particles stick to the gill surfaces and eventually are passed to the mouth to start through the digestive system. It may surprise you to learn that some whales are filter feeders! These whales have "teeth" which strain small organisms from the water they take into their mouths.

25:2 Two-Way Traffic: Hydra

A hydra (an aquatic animal of phylum Coelenterata) also obtains its food from the water in which it lives. A hydra does not swim around in search of food, but has structures for trapping food which comes close to it. When a living animal passes close to a hydra, the hydra extends its tentacles toward it. When a nematocyst (Section 15:2) is stimulated by the touch of a small organism, the filament, which is coiled inside, uncoils and is forcefully ejected. Some nematocysts have filaments which wrap around and trap prey. Others are barbed, stick into the prey like fishhooks, and prevent the prey from escaping. Poison which either paralyzes or kills the prey is injected into it through the filament. Then the prey is drawn to the mouth of the hydra and into the body cavity. Because hydras take in large bits of food, they are called **chunk feeders.** Most animals are chunk feeders.

There are no special regions for digestion in the cavity of a hydra. This cavity is called the **gastrovascular** (gas troh vas kyuh lur) **cavity.** It is really part of the water environment. Lining the cavity are many gland cells which secrete digestive enzymes into the cavity. These enzymes break large molecules of food into small molecules. This process, because it occurs outside of the body cells, is called extracellular digestion (Section 18:3).

Other endoderm cells then take in these molecules by phagocytosis and diffusion. Once inside the cells, digestion continues in food vacuoles. This process, because it occurs within the body cells, is called intracellular digestion (Section 18:3). Digested food passes out of the food vacuoles and into the surrounding cytoplasm. Because the animal is only two cell layers thick, digested food readily can pass into the outer (ectoderm) layer of cells from the inner (endoderm) layer of cells.

Hydras have only one body opening, so both incoming food and outgoing waste materials must pass through the mouth. There is a "two-way traffic" in which food and wastes move in opposite directions through the same opening. The digestive system of *Hydra* is not very specialized.

Nematocysts help hydra to trap food.

Hydras are chunk feeders.

In hydras, digestion begins in the gastrovascular cavity.

The gastrovascular cavity is so named because it serves both digestive and transport functions.

Both extracellular and intracellular digestion occur in hydra.

Teaching suggestion: Have students suggest ways in which "two-way traffic" is less specialized than "one-way traffic."

FIGURE 25-3. *Hydra* **takes prey into its mouth and extracellular digestion begins in the gastrovascular cavity. Intracellular digestion follows.**

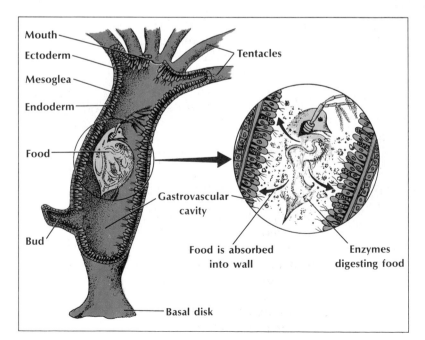

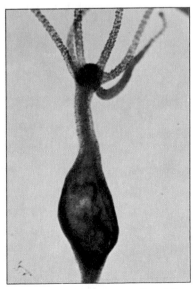

Carolina Biological Supply Co.

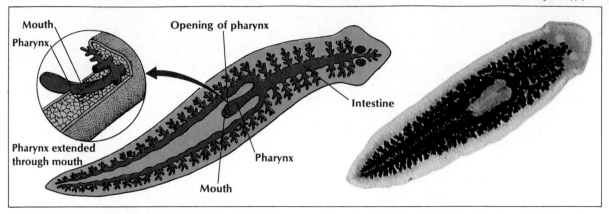

FIGURE 25-4. Extracellular digestion is carried on in the hollow of a planarian's intestine. Some intracellular digestion occurs within cells of the intestinal lining. The branching digestive system clearly is visible in the stained specimen at the right.

In planarians, food is digested in the hollow of the intestine and in cells of the intestinal lining.

Because the intestine of planarians is branched and spreads throughout the body, digested food can diffuse to all cells.

Suggested demonstration: Students can easily observe feeding in planarians. Add a small amount of hard boiled egg yolk to a shallow dish containing a worm and view with a binocular microscope or hand lens. Remove uneaten yolk to prevent bacterial contamination.

Some food reaches the cells of flatworms by active transport, but the general principle remains the same.

Organisms with two body openings have more specialized digestive systems.

25:3 Two-Way Traffic: Planaria

A "two-way traffic" system is also found in other simple animals. A planarian has only a single opening on its ventral (belly) side. When an animal comes into contact with a suitable food source, a tube called the **pharynx** (FER ingks) protrudes through the opening. Food enters the pharynx and the pharynx is withdrawn into the animal. The food moves into another tube called the **intestine** where some of the food is digested (extracellular). Digestion of the remaining food occurs in cells of the intestinal lining (intracellular).

As in *Hydra*, digested food reaches the body cells by diffusion. Although a planarian has three cell layers, diffusion can transport food to all the cells because the intestine is branched throughout the animal! No cell is very far from the intestine and digested food (Figure 25-4).

In more complex animals, direct diffusion from digestive organs to body cells is impossible because too many cells are too far from the food. In these animals, digested food is transported to body cells by blood.

25:4 One-Way Traffic: Earthworm

In most of the other animal phyla, there are two body openings, the mouth and the anus, in the digestive system. In such a system there is "one-way traffic." Food is ingested through the mouth, passed posteriorly during digestion, and waste material is egested (expelled) through the anus. *With this plan there is differentiation of digestive organs. The organs are specialized. Each organ has a certain function.*

In general, food passes through a long, hollow tube called the **alimentary** (al uh MEN tree) **canal.** Different areas of the tube have

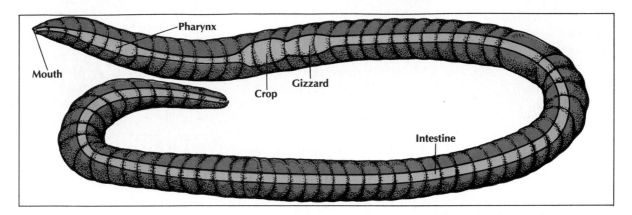

Pharynx

Mouth

Crop

Gizzard

Intestine

certain shapes and features. Usually one section can clearly be distinguished from another.

In earthworms, food enters the anterior end of the alimentary canal through the mouth (Figure 25-5). From the mouth, the food is moved by muscle contractions into a thickened area, the **pharynx** and then to a tube called the **esophagus** (ih SAHF uh gus). The thin esophagus pushes the food onward into the first of two round organs, the **crop,** where it is stored until it can be pushed to the second round organ, the **gizzard.** In the gizzard the food is ground up with the aid of coarse soil particles ingested by the worm. After this physical digestion, food passes into a long, thin tube called the intestine. This organ is lined with gland cells which pour enzymes into the cavity. The enzymes break the food into small molecules which enter the cells of the intestinal wall. These small molecules are picked up by the blood and transferred to all parts of the body where they diffuse into the body cells. Undigested materials are pushed through the intestine and finally are expelled through the **anus** (Figure 25-5). Because digestion occurs within the cavity of the alimentary canal and not in the body cells themselves, digestion is extracellular.

25:5 One-Way Traffic: Other Invertebrates

Arthropods have a digestive system similar to the earthworm's. Arthropod mouthparts are well developed for obtaining, chewing, and grinding food. These mechanical processes prepare the food for compact storage and further digestion.

Mouthparts of all arthropods are adapted for obtaining their certain foods. Butterflies have a tubelike **proboscis** (pruh BAHS kus), or snout, which is used to suck nectar from flowers. Female mosquitoes have mouthparts adapted for piercing skin and sucking blood. A housefly's mouthparts sponge, or suck, food through a small opening (Figure 25-6).

The grinding action in the gizzard is analogous to the chewing activities of more complex animals. Birds, which also lack teeth, grind food in a gizzard.

FIGURE 25-5. The earthworm, having both mouth and anus, has a "one-way" digestive system. Notice the digestive system is more specialized than that of less complex animals.

Along the esophagus are three pairs of calciferous glands. By excreting calcium carbonate into the esophagus, these glands rid the worm of excess calcium.

FIGURE 25-6. Arthropods have specialized mouth parts. A housefly sucks liquid food through an opening in the labellum.

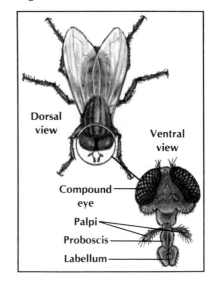

Dorsal view

Ventral view

Compound eye

Palpi

Proboscis

Labellum

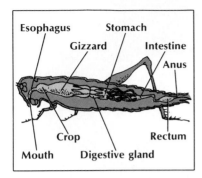

FIGURE 25-7. A "one-way" digestive system is present in a grasshopper. Digestive glands secrete enzymes into the alimentary canal.

1. Filter feeding is the extraction of food from water passing through an animal. It occurs in sponges, oysters, and some whales.
2. Hydras obtain food by discharging harpoonlike filaments which trap and sometimes poison the prey.
3. In "two-way traffic" animals have only one body opening. Animals with "one-way traffic" have two body openings.
4. diffusion
5. The alimentary canal is the series of organs through which food passes as it is digested.
6. blood
7. mostly extracellular

FIGURE 25-8. The starfish turns its stomach outward into the clam and begins digestion of the clam tissues.

Besides the organs of the alimentary canal, arthropods have other organs which aid in digestion. Food does not pass directly through these other organs, but these organs are important because they produce enzymes and other materials which are secreted into the alimentary canal. For example, a grasshopper has many digestive glands which surround the alimentary canal near the crop and stomach (Figure 25-7).

The starfish also has a digestive system with two body openings. The starfish moves along the floor of the ocean by using a type of water pressure system in which suction cups on the underside of each arm can attach to objects. This suction also can be used to obtain food. Using the suction cups, a starfish can pry apart the two shells of a clam. The starfish then sticks its stomach through its mouth which is located on the lower surface of its body. The stomach secretes enzymes which partially digest the clam. Then the partially digested food passes from the stomach to digestive glands located in each ray (arm) where digestion is completed. A small amount of undigestible material is egested through the anus located on the upper body surface. Small food molecules are carried by a fluid in the coelom (Section 15:7).

REVIEWING YOUR IDEAS

1. What is filter feeding? In what kinds of animals is it found?
2. How do hydras obtain food?
3. Distinguish between "two-way traffic" and "one-way traffic" digestive systems.
4. How is digested food distributed in hydras and planarians?
5. What is an alimentary canal?
6. How is digested food distributed in earthworms?
7. Is digestion in a starfish intracellular or extracellular?

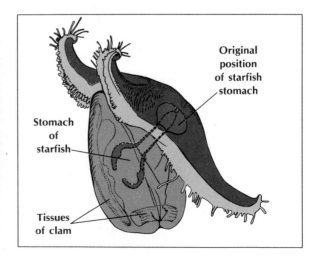

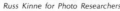
Russ Kinne for Photo Researchers

DIGESTION IN HUMANS

25:6 Nutrition

Before studying the digestive system of humans, it is important to consider human nutrition. **Nutrition** is the study of foods and how they are used by the body. Like other organisms, humans require certain nutrients (Section 21:8). Nutrients are used in two main ways—as sources of energy and as sources of molecules needed for growth and maintenance. Energy in food is commonly measured in units called Calories. Some nutrients are complex molecules—carbohydrates, fats, and proteins. These are large molecules which must be digested.

Although you may not think of it as such, water is an essential nutrient in the diet. Water is necessary for a variety of functions. It is a solvent for many cellular substances. It is also the major component of protoplasm and blood. Hydrolysis reactions and other metabolic processes use water. Water evaporating from the skin helps to cool the body and maintain constant temperature. Some of the water that is used or lost is replaced by water produced in dehydration synthesis and cellular respiration. However, to maintain enough water in the body, water must be taken in as part of foods and beverages.

Minerals, another group of essential nutrients, are ingested as ions in food or water. They serve a variety of important metabolic functions and are parts of molecules such as hemoglobin, ATP, and DNA. Table 25-1 lists some important minerals and their functions.

Nutrients are used as energy sources or as molecules used in growth and maintenance.

Water is an important nutrient used in a variety of ways.

A Calorie is the amount of heat needed to raise the temperature of one kilogram of water one Celsius degree. A Calorie is not an SI unit of measurement but it is commonly used in referring to the amount of energy in foods. The SI unit of energy is the joule.

Minerals function in metabolism.

TABLE 25-1. SOME IMPORTANT MINERALS		
Mineral	Sources	Needed For
Calcium	Milk, cheese, meats, vegetables, whole-grain cereals	Blood clotting, muscle contraction, bone and tooth formation
Iron	Liver, leafy vegetables, meats, raisins	Production of hemoglobin, part of molecules used in respiration
Iodine	Seafood, iodized table salt	Part of hormone which controls rate of metabolism
Magnesium	Leafy vegetables, meats, potatoes	Proper functioning of some enzymes
Phosphorus	Milk, meats, eggs, vegetables	Bone and tooth formation, part of ATP and nucleic acids
Potassium	Vegetables, bananas	Conduction of nerve impulses
Sodium	Table salt, vegetables	Conduction of nerve impulses, maintaining osmotic balance

TABLE 25-2. SOME IMPORTANT VITAMINS		
Vitamin	Sources	Deficiency Symptoms
A	Green and yellow vegetables; eggs; fruits; liver	Night blindness; dry skin
B_1	Whole-grain cereals; liver; other meats; nuts; most vegetables	Weak muscles; paralysis (beriberi)
B_2	Milk; cheese; eggs; liver; whole cereals	Poor vision; sores in and around mouth
B_{12}	Liver; other meats; eggs; milk products	Anemia
C	Citrus fruits; tomatoes; some vegetables	Loose teeth; bleeding gums; swollen joints; poor muscle development (scurvy)
D	Milk; egg yolk; fish liver oil; (also made in skin)	Soft bones; deformed skeleton (rickets)
K	Green vegetables; liver; (also made by intestinal bacteria)	Slow blood clotting

Another group of vital nutrients, **vitamins,** are present in many foods. They may be complex molecules, but are easily absorbed. Many vitamins are needed to make coenzymes (Section 4:6). Table 25-2 lists some vitamins important to humans and what foods are good sources of them. The diseases that result when the vitamins are not available in the diet in proper amounts are also given. These diseases are called vitamin-deficiency diseases. For example, if a young person's diet does not include enough vitamin D, bones and muscles will not develop properly—a disease called rickets. Lack of vitamin A results in night blindness.

Vitamin deficiencies may result in disease.

FIGURE 25-9. A balanced diet includes foods from each of the four basic food groups.

25:7 Diet and Health

A balanced diet consists of proper amounts of foods from four major groups—dairy products, breads and cereals, fruits and vegetables, and meats. A person eating a variety of foods from each group each day receives enough of all nutrients. Eating a proper, balanced diet is an important part of maintaining good health.

MEAT   FRUIT AND VEGETABLE

Gerard Photography

DAIRY   CEREAL

Gerard Photography

Some sources list a fifth basic food group by separating foods such as oils, dressings, desserts, and certain condiments into a separate category.

If one or more essential nutrients are missing from a person's diet over a period of time, **malnutrition** will occur. Malnutrition can lead to a loss of weight and a variety of health problems. For example, in children, a protein deficiency can lead to weight loss, liver damage, and anemia.

Many people today have a diet which includes too many "junk foods." Junk foods include many foods eaten as snacks. These foods provide quick energy sources (carbohydrates, sugars, and fats) and are high in Calories, but provide few other nutrients. A diet made up to a large extent of these foods and few others may cause a person to suffer from malnutrition or obesity. Obesity, an overweight condition, occurs when more food is consumed than is burned up by the body. Obesity can lead to severe health problems. Extra weight increases the chance of developing high blood pressure by two to three times. High blood pressure may lead to heart disease or stroke. The chances of developing high blood cholesterol levels or diabetes are also greater for overweight people. The only known "cure" for obesity is a lowered Calorie intake. A lower Calorie intake should be accomplished while still eating a balanced diet. Foods from all four food groups should be selected, but portions should be smaller. Removing high Calorie foods such as junk foods from the diet and increasing the amount of daily exercise are also helpful in controlling weight.

> Junk foods provide sources of energy but often few other nutrients.

> High blood pressure and heart disease are discussed in the next chapter. Diabetes is discussed in Chapter 29.

PEOPLE IN BIOLOGY

A Mohawk Indian raised by her Quaker grandparents, Rosa Minoka-Hill made up her mind early in life to help needy Indians. On a primitive farm on the Oneida Indian Reservation in Wisconsin, Dr. Minoka-Hill carried out that decision. Accepting everything in payment from chickens to a day's work on her farm, Rosa Minoka-Hill delivered babies, treated diseases, and ran a "kitchen clinic" stocked with herbals (plants used for medical treatment) and medicines provided by the doctors in Green Bay

(1876 - 1952)

Lillie Rosa Minoka-Hill

for the people of the reservation. Dr. Minoka-Hill also spent much of her time teaching the Indians about good nutrition and eating habits to try and relieve their ever present problem of malnutrition.

In addition to her medical practice, Dr. Minoka-Hill reared her six children and ran her farm alone after the death of her husband in 1916. Because of her dedication, the Oneidas adopted her into their tribe and gave her the name "you de gent"—"She who serves." Rosa Minoka-Hill was also named outstanding American Indian of the year in 1947 by the Indian Council Fire in Chicago, and was given an honorary membership to the State Medical Society of Wisconsin.

Hickson-Bender Photography

FIGURE 25-10. Much is learned about the nutritional value of foods, what additives are present, and the relative amounts of ingredients present by carefully reading food labels.

Excess sugar and salt may be harmful.

An excess of some nutrients may also be harmful to the body. Many people eat an excess of sugar and salt. Besides adding these two nutrients to food during cooking and at the table, many people consume large quantities of them in packaged foods. Some "ready-to-eat" processed foods have large amounts of sugar and salt added. Excess sugar contributes to obesity, may promote tooth decay, and has been linked to hyperactivity in children. Excess salt contributes to high blood pressure and heart disease, and may cause the body to retain water, thus adding to body weight.

In recent years, consumers have become more aware of the substances added to many foods. Food companies now list product ingredients on the label in the order of the amount of each ingredient present. The ingredient present in the greatest amount is listed first, second greatest second, and so on. This type of labeling helps consumers to choose products carefully.

25:8 Mouth, Pharynx, and Esophagus

In humans, food is ingested through the **mouth,** or **oral cavity.** The major function of this organ is physical digestion; teeth grind and tear food into chunks small enough to be swallowed. The grinding action of teeth also increases the surface area of food. With more surface area, enzymes can work more effectively.

Besides being physically broken down in the mouth, food also is moistened by **saliva** (suh LI vuh), the liquid secretion of three pairs of **salivary** (SAL uh ver ee) **glands.** Saliva contains a substance called **mucin** (MYEWS un) (mucus) which makes food slippery so it can be swallowed easily. Also, the water in saliva makes the food a thin paste.

FIGURE 25-11. Both physical and chemical digestion begin in the mouth. The esophagus transports food from mouth to stomach.

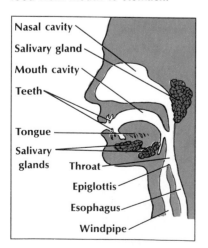

Nasal cavity
Salivary gland
Mouth cavity
Teeth
Tongue
Salivary glands
Throat
Epiglottis
Esophagus
Windpipe

Saliva also contains an enzyme called **salivary amylase** (AM uh lays) which begins the chemical digestion of food. This enzyme breaks starch into molecules of maltose, a disaccharide (Section 3:13). No digestion of fats or proteins occurs in the mouth.

The three pairs of salivary glands are the sublingual (under the tongue), submaxillary (rear lower jaws), and parotid (below and in front of the ears).

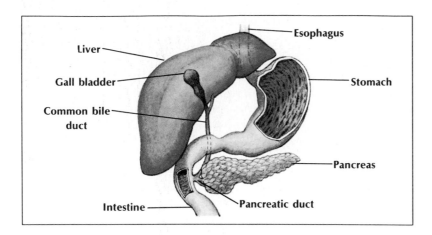

FIGURE 25-12. Food is liquefied in the stomach. Both the liver and pancreas produce substances necessary for digestion in the small intestine.

From the mouth, the moistened, slightly digested food passes through the pharynx (throat) to a long, slender tube, the esophagus. No chemical digestion occurs in the esophagus; it transports the food and adds mucus to it. Food is moved by a series of alternating muscular contractions and relaxations called **peristalsis** (per uh STAHL sus). Peristalsis also occurs along the rest of the alimentary canal. The muscle action moves and churns food and controls the rate of passage of food material.

Peristalsis helps food pass through the esophagus and other organs of the alimentary canal.

25:9 Stomach

Food leaves the esophagus through a muscular ring called the **cardiac sphincter** (KARD ee ak · SFINGK tur) and enters a large hollow organ, the **stomach.** Normally, the cardiac sphincter prevents food from passing back to the esophagus. When does food go from the stomach to the esophagus? during regurgitation

Protein digestion begins in the stomach. Lining the stomach wall are **gastric** (GAS trihk) **glands** which secrete a fluid called **gastric juice** into the stomach. Release of gastric juice is stimulated by a hormone called **gastrin** (GAS trun). When food enters the stomach, certain stomach cells release gastrin into the bloodstream. Gastrin travels throughout the body but affects only the gastric glands by stimulating these glands to secrete gastric juice.

Gastric juice contains hydrochloric acid and a protein called **pepsinogen** (pep SIHN uh jun). Hydrochloric acid gives gastric juice a pH of between one and two (Section 3:8). This acidic pH is necessary to change pepsinogen to the enzyme **pepsin.** Pepsin hydrolyzes proteins into long chains of amino acids called polypeptides. The activities of these chemicals are aided by a churning motion of the stomach. (Churning of an empty stomach is felt as hunger pangs.) By the time this phase of digestion is completed, food that is in the stomach is an acidic liquid called **chyme** (KIME).

The stomach lining is normally protected against the action of hydrochloric acid. However, in some persons, this protection breaks down and an open sore, an ulcer, develops. This painful condition can occur in the stomach (peptic ulcer) or duodenum (duodenal ulcer). It sometimes can be cured by special, bland diets, but surgery may be required.

Gastrin stimulates release of gastric juice from the stomach.

In the stomach, proteins are hydrolyzed into polypeptides.

25:10 Small Intestine

Chyme passes in small spurts through the **pyloric** (pi LOR ihk) **sphincter** of the stomach into the **small intestine.** Thus, the stomach regulates the flow of food into the intestine. The first part of the small intestine is the **duodenum** (dew uh DEE num), which, in an adult human, is about 25 cm long. Next the food passes into a section called the **jejunum** (jih JEW num). From the jejunum, food moves into the last and longest portion of the small intestine called the **ileum** (IHL ee um). The total length of the coiled small intestine is about seven meters in an adult human.

Two organs which are not part of the alimentary canal are very important in digestion of food in the small intestine. The **liver** produces a greenish substance called **bile.** Bile is stored in the **gall bladder,** an organ which lies beneath the liver. From the gall bladder, bile moves through a tube called the **common bile duct** to the duodenum. Bile is not an enzyme, but it contains **bile salts** which break up fat globules in the intestine. This process is called **fat emulsification** (ih mul suh fuh KAY shun) and it helps speed up the rate of enzyme action on the fat by increasing fat surface area. This aspect of fat digestion is physical digestion.

The other organ, the **pancreas** (PAN kree us), lies behind and partially below the stomach. Certain cells of the pancreas secrete enzymes which are transported by the **pancreatic** (pan kree AT ihk) **duct.** This duct merges with the common bile duct from the gall bladder and empties into the duodenum.

The pancreas secretes several important enzymes. **Lipase** (LI pays) breaks fat molecules into fatty acids and glycerol. **Pancreatic amylase** changes starch to maltose. Several proteases (PROH tee ay suz), called **trypsins** (TRIHP sunz), hydrolyze polypeptides and proteins not digested in the stomach. The polypeptides are broken into smaller polypeptides. Each trypsin breaks bonds between certain amino acids.

Also released by the pancreas is **sodium bicarbonate** (bi KAR buh nayt) which neutralizes the acidity of the chyme and raises its pH to about eight (slightly basic). Pancreatic enzymes do not work effectively in an acid environment. Stimulation of the pancreas to release digestive materials is controlled by hormones.

Fingerlike projections called **villi** (VIHL i) on the intestinal lining extend into the hollow of the small intestine. Villi greatly increase the surface area for absorption of digested food. Disaccharides and small polypeptides in the intestine are actively transported across the membranes into the villi. Cells in the villi contain enzymes needed to complete digestion of these molecules. Several enzymes called **peptidases** (PEP tuh days uz) convert small polypeptides to amino acids. Other enzymes

Most digestion and absorption occurs in the jejunem and duodenum.

Bile is secreted by the liver and stored in the gall bladder.

Bile is channeled to the small intestine where it breaks up fat globules.

FIGURE 25-13. (a) Villi contain blood vessels which pick up absorbed food molecules. (b) Shown magnified about 15 000 times, the large number of villi greatly increases the surface area of the small intestine available for absorption.

a
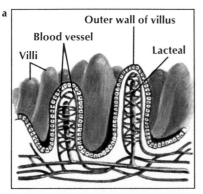

Outer wall of villus

Blood vessel

Villi

Lacteal

b

Kessel/Kardon © 1979,
W. H. Freeman and Company

TABLE 25-3. SUMMARY OF DIGESTION IN HUMANS		
Digestive Organ	Major Physical Aspects	Major Chemical Aspects
Mouth	Chewing Grinding Moistening	$\text{Starch} \xrightarrow{\text{salivary amylase}} \text{maltose}$
Esophagus	Moistening, Peristalsis	
Stomach	Moistening Churning Peristalsis Some absorption	$\text{Proteins} \xrightarrow{\text{HCl Pepsin}} \text{polypeptides}$
Small intestine	Peristalsis Fat emulsification Most food absorption (villi)	$\text{Starch} \xrightarrow{\text{pancreatic amylase}} \text{maltose}$ $\text{Proteins} \xrightarrow{\text{proteases, eg. trypsins}} \text{polypeptides}$ $\text{Polypeptides} \xrightarrow{\text{peptidases}} \text{amino acids}$ $\text{Fats} \xrightarrow{\text{lipases}} \text{fatty acids \& glycerol}$ $\text{Disaccharides} \xrightarrow{\text{maltase, lactase, sucrase}} \text{monosaccharides}$
Large intestine	Most water absorption Peristalsis Waste elimination	

convert disaccharides to monosaccharides. **Maltase** (MALT tays) breaks down maltose left over from previous digestion; **sucrase** (SEW krays) breaks down sucrose, or table sugar; and **lactase** (LAK tays) breaks down lactose, or milk sugar. Because these activities occur within the cells of the villi, digestion in humans is partly intracellular.

In the small intestine, all complex food molecules are converted to simple forms. Proteins are broken into amino acids, fats are split into fatty acids and glycerol, and carbohydrates are hydrolyzed into simple sugars, or monosaccharides. These small molecules can pass through cell membranes. Table 25-3 summarizes the major events of digestion.

25:11 Absorption of Food

Most absorption of the digested molecules into the blood occurs in the small intestine through the villi. The villi contain many small blood vessels called **capillaries.** Glycerol, amino acids, simple sugars, vitamins, and minerals enter these

Teaching suggestion: Emphasize that the small intestine is the major organ of digestion, not the stomach.

Lactose is converted to glucose and galactose; maltose to two molecules of glucose; and sucrose, to glucose and fructose.

Intestinal enzymes are responsible for the hydrolysis not only of small polypeptides to amino acids, but also of lactose, maltose, and sucrose to monosaccharides.

Amino acids, monosaccharides, fatty acids, and glycerol are absorbed through cell membranes and then circulated through the organism.

Teaching suggestion: In stressing the importance of food absorption, you may want to tie the topic to the subject of weight control. For example, students may be unaware that in extreme cases of overweight, radical surgery sometimes is performed to reduce the length of the small intestine. If the intestine is shortened, the area over which absorption of food can occur is decreased. When less food is absorbed, more stored body reserves are used.

A portal system is one that begins and ends in capillaries.

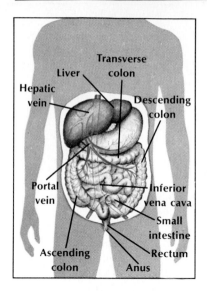

FIGURE 25-14. Blood which picks up food molecules in the small intestine passes through the liver where harmful substances are removed and the sugar level is monitored. Then the blood moves to the rest of the body.

capillaries. The capillaries of the villi merge to form the **hepatic** (hih PAT ihk) **portal vein** which carries blood to the liver. The liver detects the level of food molecules in the blood. After circulating through the liver, blood enters other blood vessels which carry food to all body cells. When the blood reaches capillaries throughout the body, sugars, amino acids, vitamins, minerals, and other substances leave it and enter the cells.

Glucose content of blood must be within a certain range. After digestion of a meal, blood coming to the liver from the small intestine has more than the normal amount of glucose. The liver detects this glucose and removes some of it from the blood. After being converted, the glucose is stored in the liver as **glycogen,** an animal starch. Later, when the glucose content in blood begins to fall, the liver converts stored glycogen back to glucose. The glucose then enters the blood and it restores the glucose level to normal.

Fatty acids are absorbed by another kind of vessel in the villi called **lacteals** (LAK tee ulz). Lacteals are part of a special transport system, the lymphatic (lihm FAT ihk) system. This system is discussed in Section 26:8. Fatty acids and glycerol are transported throughout the body to tissues by the lymphatic system.

25:12 Large Intestine

Undigested materials and water are passed from the small intestine to the **large intestine,** or **colon** (KOH lun). The large intestine forms a loop around and partly covers the small intestine. The large intestine is divided into three sections—the **ascending colon** (to which the appendix is attached), **transverse colon,** and **descending colon.** No digestion occurs in the large intestine.

The major function of the large intestine is to absorb the water from undigestible or undigested materials. Thus, water is conserved in the body. Absorption of water out of the waste matter causes the wastes to become a solid. Solid waste, called **feces** (FEE seez), is stored in the **rectum** (REK tum) and is egested through the **anus.**

In the large intestine, undigestible materials become solid as water is absorbed from them.

In addition to food remnants, feces contain many bacteria which live in the intestine. Some of these bacteria make vitamin B_{12} which the body needs. A deficiency of this vitamin results in abnormal red blood cell and hemoglobin production (Table 25-2). The existence of these intestinal bacteria and humans together is an example of mutualism (Section 13:10) because bacteria and host benefit each other. Other bacteria in the large intestine are harmless parasites.

8. study of foods and their uses in the body; carbohydrates, fats, proteins, water, minerals, and vitamins

9. A balanced diet includes foods from each of four groups — dairy products, breads and cereals, fruits and vegetables, and meats.

10. a series of muscular contractions and relaxations which moves food along the alimentary canal, occurring in the esophagus, stomach, small and large intestine

11. The alimentary canal consists of mouth, esophagus, stomach, small intestine, large intestine, and rectum. The salivary glands, liver, gall bladder, and pancreas are also important in human digestion.

12. Villi are fingerlike projections on the intestinal lining. They increase the surface area for absorption of digested food.

REVIEWING YOUR IDEAS

8. What is nutrition? What are the six kinds of nutrients required by humans?
9. What is needed for a balanced diet?
10. What is peristalsis? In what organs does it occur?
11. List the organs of the human alimentary canal. What other organs are important in human digestion?
12. What are villi? How are they important in absorption?
13. What is the function and importance of the large intestine?
14. Is human digestion mainly intracellular or extracellular?

13. The large intestine absorbs water from undigestible materials, thus conserving water.

14. extracellular

CHAPTER REVIEW

SUMMARY

1. Sessile animals are often filter feeders, but some other animals are filter feeders, too. Most animals are chunk feeders.

2. Coelenterates and flatworms have only one body opening and "two-way traffic" with little specialization of digestive organs. Both have a combination of extracellular and intracellular digestion.

3. Most other animal groups have two body openings, "one-way traffic," specialization of digestive organs, and more efficient digestion. Food passes through an alimentary canal and digested food is transported by blood or other fluids throughout the body.

4. Nutrients are used as energy sources and to build materials for growth and maintenance.

5. In humans, most digestion is extracellular. Digestion begins in the mouth where food is made ready for swallowing and where carbohydrate digestion begins.

6. Food then passes to the stomach via the esophagus. It is pushed along by peristalsis. In the stomach, food is churned and protein digestion begins.

7. Bile from the liver and enzymes from the pancreas pour into the small intestine where most chemical digestion takes place. The small intestine itself produces some necessary enzymes for this process. Chemical digestion also occurs in the villi.

8. Amino acids and monosaccharides are absorbed by the capillaries of the villi and are transported to the body cells by the bloodstream. Fatty acids enter lacteals in the villi and are distributed by the lymphatic system.

9. In the large intestine, water is absorbed from undigested materials. Feces are solidified, stored in the rectum, and egested through the anus.

LANGUAGE OF BIOLOGY

alimentary canal	lacteal
amoebocyte	large intestine
anus	malnutrition
bile salts	minerals
chunk feeder	nutrition
collar cell	pancreas
crop	peristalsis
esophagus	pharynx
filter feeder	rectum
gall bladder	small intestine
gastric juice	stomach
gastrovascular cavity	villi
gizzard	vitamin

CHAPTER REVIEW

CHECKING YOUR IDEAS

On a separate paper, indicate whether each of the following statements is true or false. Do not write in this book.

1. Filter feeding occurs in animals with two body openings and not in animals with one body opening.
2. Digestion in *Hydra* begins in the nematocysts.
3. Clams and sponges are chunk feeders.
4. The planaria has a digestive system with "one-way traffic."
5. In some animals, grinding of food occurs in the crop.
6. In an earthworm, digested food is transported to body cells by diffusion.
7. Substances such as iron, calcium, and sodium are nutrients.
8. Villi absorb digested food in the human's intestine.
9. Most chemical digestion in humans occurs in the large intestine.
10. Digestion in humans is mainly extracellular digestion.

EVALUATING YOUR IDEAS

1. Explain food getting and digestion in sponges.
2. Compare digestion in the coelenterate *Hydra* and the flatworm *Planaria*.
3. Why are the digestive systems of hydras and planarians not very specialized?
4. What is the adaptive advantage of a digestive system with two openings—a mouth and an anus?
5. How is digestion in an earthworm different from digestion in a planarian?
6. Why must digested food molecules be distributed by blood in earthworms and many other animals?
7. How does a starfish obtain and digest food?

8. What are the two main ways in which nutrients are used?
9. How is water important in the body? How is it lost? How is it replaced?
10. List several ways in which minerals are used in the body. Why are vitamins important?
11. Discuss the possible effects of obesity. How may obesity be avoided?
12. How may an excess of sugar and salt in the diet be harmful?
13. How is chewing important to human digestion? What other physical processes occur in the mouth? What might result if these processes did not occur?
14. What are the functions of the esophagus?
15. How is gastrin important to digestion in the stomach?
16. Why is hydrochloric acid necessary for digestion in the stomach?
17. Is bile an enzyme? Explain. How is bile important in digestion?
18. Why must carbohydrates, fats, and proteins be broken down? What are the products of their digestion?
19. What structures in humans secrete enzymes necessary for digestion? Does food pass through all of them? Explain.
20. In which organs of the alimentary canal does actual chemical digestion occur?
21. How are villi important in digestion?
22. What happens to digested food after it is absorbed by the villi?
23. How is the large intestine important?
24. How are bacteria of the large intestine important?

APPLYING YOUR IDEAS

1. In what way(s) is digestion in *Paramecium* similar to digestion in a complex animal? Why? *Chapter 18

CHAPTER REVIEW

2. What characteristic of a planarian enables it to distribute digested food by diffusion?

3. Birds have a gizzard. How is this adaptive?

4. In what way might regurgitation be adaptive?

5. Why is the diet of a person whose gall bladder has been removed restricted in fat intake?

6. Have you ever seen commercials about "acid indigestion"? What causes acid indigestion? Why would medicines containing sodium bicarbonate be useful to relieve it?

7. The inner surface of the intestine of a shark is coiled. How is a coiled intestine adaptive?

8. How is digestion in animals different from digestion in most plants? Are there any plants with digestion similar to digestion in animals? *Chapter 21

9. Compare food getting and digestion in *Planaria* and a tapeworm. *Chapter 15

10. Why are many nutrients needed in greater amounts by children and teenagers than adults?

11. Vitamins and minerals are available in tablets, capsules, and liquids. Do you think most people need to take these nutrients in this form? Explain.

12. When you swallow food, some salivary amylase enters the stomach. Does that enzyme "work" in the stomach? Explain.

13. Compare the taking in of food in fungi and animals. *Chapter 18

14. Why may fad diets be a danger to health? Do you think people who lose weight on these diets usually keep it off? Explain.

EXTENDING YOUR IDEAS

1. Conduct a survey among classmates to determine whether each is eating a balanced diet.

2. Prepare a report on the digestive system of a cow. What is the rumen?

3. In 1822 Alexis St. Martin received a wound which resulted in a hole leading into his stomach. Use library sources to learn about the experiments which were carried out on St. Martin.

4. Find out about different kinds of food additives. Why are they used? What are the possible side effects of some of them? Are many of these additives necessary?

5. Find out about careers in nutrition. What do nutritionists do? What do dietitians do? Why are many of them hired by institutions such as schools and nursing homes?

6. Using library sources, research the different names used for sugar and salt on food labels. Use this information to survey the items in your home pantry. How much "hidden" sugar and salt does your family consume?

SUGGESTED READINGS

Glick, Nancy, "Food Terminology: What It Says Is Not Always What It Is." *FDA Consumer*, June, 1979.

Hecht, Annabel, "Vitamins Over the Counter: Take Only When Needed." *FDA Consumer*, September, 1979.

Jones, Jack C., "The Feeding Behavior of Mosquitoes." *Scientific American*, June, 1978.

Keen, Sam, "Eating Our Way to Enlightenment." *Psychology Today*, October, 1978.

Lehmann, Phyllis E., "Food Additives: A Double-Edged Sword." *Sciquest*, April, 1980.

Lehmann, Phyllis E., "Vitamin Facts and Fads." *Sciquest*, May/June, 1980.

Levitsky, David A. "Ill-Nourished Brains." *Natural History*, October, 1976.

McMinn, R. M. H., *The Human Gut*, 2nd ed. Carolina Biology Reader. Burlington, NC, Carolina Biological Supply Co., 1977.

Additional student readings and suggested teacher readings are provided in the Teacher's Guide.

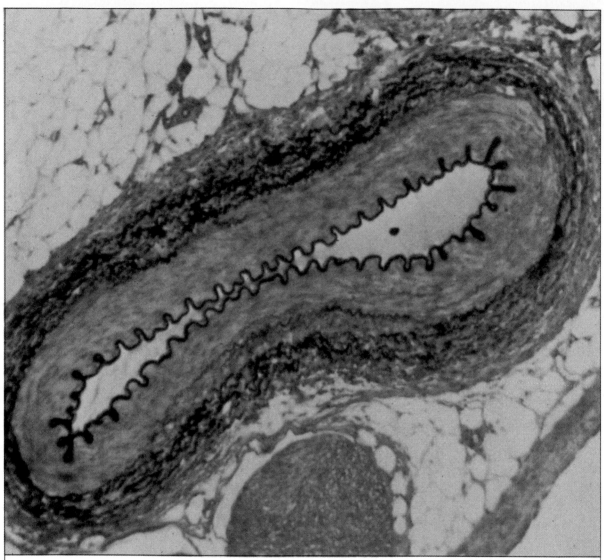

Most complex animals have systems which transport materials throughout their bodies. These systems have some kind of liquid to carry materials and points where the materials can be exchanged with the environment. The liquid in the transport system often moves through tubelike structures like the human artery shown below in cross section. How are materials transported through your body? Where are materials exchanged?

Introduction: To begin this chapter, have students locate their pulses in either the radial artery of the wrist or the carotid artery of the neck. Record each student's resting pulse rate on the board. Then have students run in place for ten seconds and take their pulses again. After recording these data, have your students (sitting once again) relocate their pulses and determine the rates at rest once more. Record the data in a third column and average each column. The data should show how heartbeat rate varies depending on activity. Encourage discussion about the reasons for this phenomenon and lead your students to the idea that blood is bringing food and oxygen to the cells and removing carbon dioxide.

TRANSPORT

Chapter 26 presents circulation in animals, the structure and functions of blood, and also discusses heart disease.

Animals such as sponges, coelenterates, and flatworms are composed of cells only a few layers thick so each cell can exchange materials directly with the environment. In larger, more complex animals, many individual cells cannot exchange materials directly with the environment because they are too far from it. In these animals, materials enter and leave at certain points and are carried to and from these points by some kind of liquid. The liquid is part of a transport system, a link between the cells of an animal and the environment. Because exchange of materials occurs between cells and the transport fluid, the fluid often is called the "internal environment" of the animal.

GOAL: You will gain an understanding of what transport is and how it occurs in animals.

Cells of simple animals can exchange necessary materials directly with the environment.

Larger, more complex animals have transport systems which link cells and the environment.

Teaching suggestion: Students should see the diversity of circulatory adaptations among animals. Caution them about using words like "better" to compare systems or organisms. Each species is adapted to its own particular way of life.

In complex animals, blood is the agent of exchange between cells and the external environment.

CIRCULATORY SYSTEMS

In animals with transport systems, a pump circulates a liquid throughout the animal. The pump is a **heart** and the liquid is **blood.** The contents and functions of blood vary in different animals. In general, blood carries materials needed for metabolism and waste materials. Thus, blood is the exchange agent between internal tissues and the environment. Blood and the structures through which it passes are known as the **circulatory** (SUR kyuh luh tor ee) **system.**

26:1 Annelids

Segmented worms are the least complex animals to have a true circulatory system. This system is very simple in structure, but it permits rapid and efficient exchange of materials. In an earthworm, blood is transported through two major blood vessels—the **dorsal blood vessel** and the **ventral blood vessel.**

Teaching suggestion: Emphasize the transport system as a link between the body cells and the external environment. The latter serves as a source of necessary materials and a depository for wastes.

Carolina Biological Supply Co.

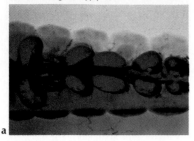

a

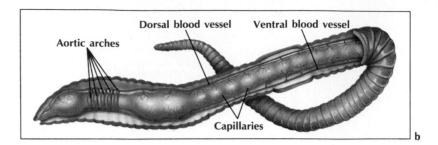

b

FIGURE 26-1. (a) Five pairs of aortic arches pump blood through (b) the closed circulatory system of an earthworm.

Teaching suggestion: An analogy between the circulatory system and a railroad illustrates the differences between larger blood vessels (arteries and veins) and capillaries. Passengers are "exchanged" at the stations (capillaries). The rails between stations (arteries and veins) move the passengers rapidly to their destinations (exchange points).

Exchange of materials between cells and blood occurs through capillaries.

In a closed circulatory system, blood is always in the blood vessels.

These two vessels are connected near the anterior end of the worm by a series of five pairs of enlarged tubes called **aortic** (ay ORT ihk) **arches** which function as hearts. As the aortic arches contract, blood is pumped through the body (Figure 26-1).

Blood flows in the dorsal blood vessel from body tissues to the aortic arches where it is pumped into the ventral blood vessel. The blood flows posteriorly in the ventral blood vessel. Other vessels in almost every segment send blood from the ventral to the dorsal blood vessel. These vessels are not the sites of exchange between blood and cells; they are merely tubes to transport the blood.

Exchange between blood and cells takes place in small branches of the major vessels called **capillaries.** Capillaries have thin walls so materials pass easily into and out of them. Capillaries extend all over the body of a worm. Food molecules enter the blood in the region of the intestine and oxygen enters the capillaries near the skin. These materials are transported through the body to each cell. Capillaries are so numerous that no cell is far from the blood and so each cell is "linked" with the external environment.

In an earthworm, blood is always in the blood vessels. For this reason, this system is known as a **closed circulatory system.** A closed system is present in several animal phyla.

26:2 Arthropods

Arthropods have a circulatory system in which blood is not always in the blood vessels. Such a system is called an **open circulatory system.**

A grasshopper has a dorsal, segmented heart (Figure 26-2) which pumps blood anteriorly into a single blood vessel, the **aorta** (ay ORT uh). Blood empties from the aorta into a body cavity called the **hemocoel** (HEE muh seel) which is composed of spaces, or **sinuses** (SI nus uz), through which blood passes. While in the sinuses, the blood bathes the cells directly. Blood is circulated in the sinuses by muscular movements of the grasshopper. Eventually the blood collects in a sinus surrounding the heart and enters the heart through tiny openings called **ostia** (AHS tee uh).

FIGURE 26-2. A grasshopper has an open circulatory system. Blood passes through the hemocoel rather than remaining inside blood vessels all the time.

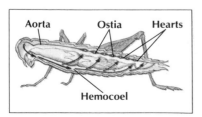

The open circulatory system of the grasshopper may seem less efficient than a closed system. In insects the major function of the circulatory system is to carry food to and wastes away from cells. Oxygen and carbon dioxide are transported by a series of tubes separate from the circulatory system. Thus, blood flow is not as rapid and ordered as it is in a system where blood carries these gases.

Some arthropods, such as spiders and crayfish, have open systems in which the blood does carry oxygen and carbon dioxide. In crayfish, blood bathes the gills as it moves through the sinuses. In the gills, oxygen enters the blood and carbon dioxide is removed.

In insects, gases are transported by means other than by blood.

26:3 Fish

Every vertebrate has a closed circulatory system made up of a single heart and three types of blood vessels. The heart has two kinds of chambers—atria and ventricles. (An atrium is sometimes called an auricle (or ih kul).) An **atrium** receives blood coming to the heart and a **ventricle** pumps blood away from the heart. The three types of blood vessels are arteries, veins, and capillaries. **Arteries** carry blood away from the heart to the body; **veins** carry blood to the heart from the body; and **capillaries** connect arteries and veins. Materials exchange in the capillaries.

A vertebrate has a closed circulatory system composed of a single heart, arteries, veins, and capillaries.

atrium (plural, atria)

In fish, the heart has only two chambers—one atrium and one ventricle. Blood from the body collects in a saclike structure, the **sinus venosus** (si nus · vih NOH sus). From there, blood enters the atrium and is forced into the ventricle. Contractions of the ventricle pump the blood into a large artery, the **ventral aorta.** The blood is under much pressure as it leaves the ventricle. Smaller arteries branch from the ventral aorta and lead to gills where the arteries are subdivided into capillaries. As blood passes through capillaries in the gills, oxygen is taken in and carbon dioxide is given off. The gill capillaries merge to form arteries leading to the **dorsal aorta.** The dorsal aorta is subdivided into smaller arteries which lead to all parts of the body. Exchange of materials occurs in the capillaries. Blood returns in veins.

Fish have two-chambered hearts. Oxygen and carbon dioxide are exchanged at the gills after the blood leaves the heart.

FIGURE 26-3. In fish, blood is oxygenated in the gills after leaving the heart. Fish have two-chambered hearts. Each heart has one atrium and one ventricle.

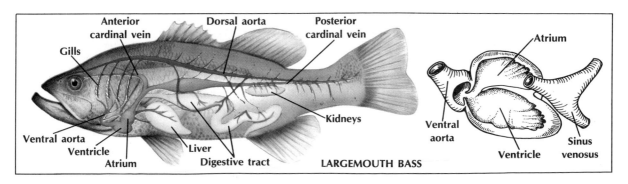

Anterior cardinal vein   Dorsal aorta   Posterior cardinal vein   Atrium

Gills

Ventral aorta

Kidneys

Ventral aorta
Ventricle
Atrium   Liver   Digestive tract   LARGEMOUTH BASS

Ventricle   Sinus venosus

The blood pressure to force blood through the fish's body is lowered in the gills.

For a fish, this type of circulatory system is adaptive. But, compared to more complex vertebrates, blood circulation is slow. As blood leaves the gill capillaries, its pressure is reduced. There is less pressure to force blood to the rest of the body.

26:4 Amphibians and Reptiles

In amphibians, the heart has three chambers—two atria and one ventricle. Deoxygenated blood (blood from the body which does not have oxygen) enters the right atrium from the sinus venosus. Oxygenated blood (blood with oxygen) from the lungs enters the left atrium through the **pulmonary** (PUL muh ner ee) **veins.** Blood from both atria enters the one ventricle so there is some mixing of blood with and without oxygen. In general, arteries from the ventricle take blood to the body, lungs, and skin. The arteries end in capillary networks where exchanges take place. The capillaries merge to form veins which return blood to the heart (Figure 26-4).

Amphibians have three-chambered hearts. Gases are exchanged at the skin and lungs. Oxygenated and deoxygenated blood are mixed in the ventricle.

In frogs, oxygenated blood returns to the heart before going to the body. Therefore, there is not the great loss of blood pressure as there is in fish. By going back to the heart after being oxygenated, the blood is under the full force of the ventricle as it enters the arteries to the body. Thus, blood is pumped twice in a complete circulation of the body. It is pumped to the lungs and then again to the rest of the body.

In amphibians, blood reenters the heart after being oxygenated. Thus, there is more pressure to force this blood to the rest of the body.

Although blood from both the lungs and the body enters the ventricle, blood from the left atrium (oxygen-rich blood) is deflected so that it is pumped to the body. Blood from the right atrium (deoxygenated) passes into the ventricle and is pumped to the lungs and skin to pick up oxygen. Although some of the blood going to the body is not oxygenated, enough oxygen is present for the body cells. Oxygenated and deoxygenated blood are separated somewhat by grooves in the ventricle.

FIGURE 26-4. Amphibians have three-chambered hearts. Each heart has two atria and one ventricle. A portion of the blood is oxygenated in the lungs before entering the heart. Partially mixed oxygenated and deoxygenated blood is pumped from the ventricle.

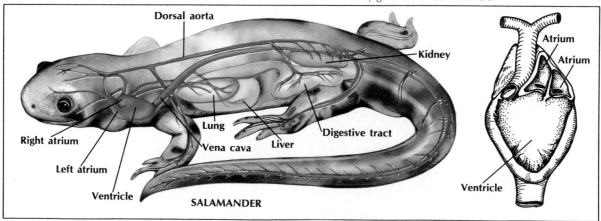

Dorsal aorta
Kidney
Atrium
Atrium
Lung
Digestive tract
Vena cava
Liver
Right atrium
Left atrium
Ventricle
Ventricle
SALAMANDER

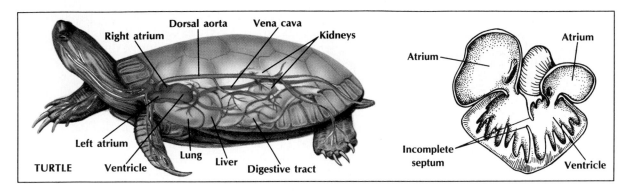

Like amphibians, most reptiles have three-chambered hearts. However, the ventricle is partly divided by a wall of muscle called a **septum** (SEP tum). This wall keeps oxygenated and deoxygenated blood almost completely separated. Therefore, deoxygenated blood is directed only to the lungs and oxygenated blood is directed to all other tissues (Figure 26-5).

FIGURE 26-5. In reptiles, oxygenated blood in the heart is directed to the body. Reptiles have three-chambered hearts. The ventricle is partly divided.

Most reptiles have three-chambered hearts.

26:5 Birds and Mammals

In birds and mammals, the heart has four chambers. These are the **right** and **left atria** and **right** and **left ventricles.** Two ventricles are present because the septum is complete (Figure 26-6). A four-chambered heart prevents deoxygenated blood from going to the body cells. The circulatory system of humans is typical of the system in birds and mammals.

Blood from the body enters the right atrium which contracts and forces blood into the right ventricle. Contraction of the right ventricle forces blood into the **pulmonary artery.** A branch of this artery goes to each lung where oxygen is picked up and carbon dioxide is removed from the blood.

Birds and mammals have four-chambered hearts.

Deoxygenated blood enters the right side of the heart in humans.

FIGURE 26-6. In mammals, blood moving from the heart to the body is fully oxygenated. Mammals have four-chambered hearts. Each heart has two atria and two ventricles.

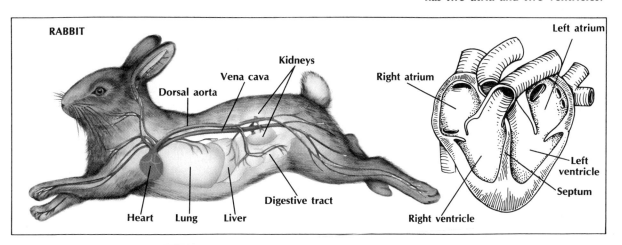

Blood from the lungs travels to the left atrium through the **pulmonary veins.** As the left atrium contracts, blood is forced into the left ventricle. A powerful contraction of the left ventricle forces blood into the **aorta,** the large artery from the heart. The aorta forms an arch which bends behind the heart. Smaller arteries branching from the aorta direct blood to all parts of the body. The arteries further divide into capillaries which merge to form small veins. These veins merge to form the large veins which bring blood to the right atrium.

The human heart contains valves between the atria and ventricles and at the entrances of the arteries from the ventricles. These valves allow blood to flow only in one direction. Why do you think blood flow in one direction is important? Between the right atrium and right ventricle is the **tricuspid** (tri ᴋᴜs pud) **valve.** Between the left atrium and ventricle is the **bicuspid** (bi ᴋᴜs pud) **valve.** At the entrances of the arteries from the ventricles are **semilunar** (sem ih ʟᴇᴡ nur) **valves.**

The bird and mammalian circulatory systems are more complex than those of other vertebrates. In birds and mammals, all blood travels through the heart twice during each circulation around the body. By going through the heart twice and being pumped both to the lungs and the body, blood circulation is efficient. (The entire trip takes about one minute in humans.) Because there are two ventricles, a complete separation of oxygenated and deoxygenated blood is assured as well. Blood from the left ventricle for general circulation to body cells is fully oxygenated so all tissues get the needed oxygen. Blood from the right side of the heart lacking in oxygen is sent to the lungs where oxygen is picked up.

Contraction of the left ventricle forces blood out through the aorta and to the body cells.

Heart valves prevent blood from flowing backward.

Birds and mammals have the most highly developed circulatory systems.

FIGURE 26-7. The human heart contains valves which keep the blood moving in one direction.

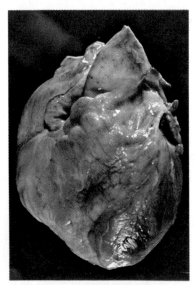

Dr. N. Baba, Department of Pathology/OSU

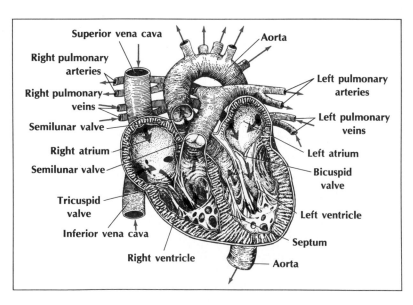

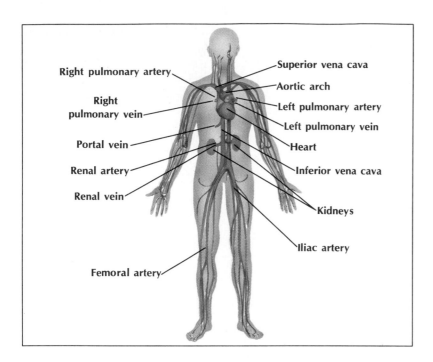

Right pulmonary artery

Right pulmonary vein

Portal vein

Renal artery

Renal vein

Femoral artery

Superior vena cava

Aortic arch

Left pulmonary artery

Left pulmonary vein

Heart

Inferior vena cava

Kidneys

Iliac artery

FIGURE 26-8. The right side of the heart pumps blood to the lungs. There it is oxygenated and returned to the heart. The left side of the heart pumps blood to the body. Oxygen moves from the blood into body cells, and carbon dioxide is picked up from the body cells by the blood.

PEOPLE IN BIOLOGY

In the late 1800's, most American medical schools admitted and trained only men. Into this male-dominated field came Florence Rena Sabin, one of the first women to be accepted at the Johns Hopkins Medical School. Sabin was well prepared to enter the medical world. While earning her B.S. in Zoology and teaching at Smith College, she had shown an exceptional ability for accurate and original observations in her laboratory work.

(1871 - 1953)

After graduating with her M.D. in 1900, Dr. Sabin became the first woman faculty member at Johns Hopkins where she did important research on the lymphatic system. Using pig embryos, Sabin was able to describe the origins and development of the lymphatic system. Later, she did similar research on blood vessels, and finally, at the Rockefeller Institute for Medical Research, studied the body's immunity to tuberculosis.

Dr. Sabin's research brought her many awards in her lifetime including the M. Carey Thomas Prize in Science, 1935, and the Lasker Award, 1952. But Dr. Sabin's interests went beyond the medical laboratory. She enjoyed reading, cooking, and collecting Oriental art.

Florence Rena Sabin

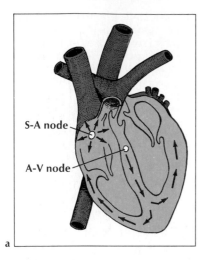

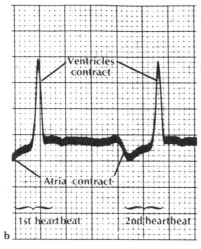

FIGURE 26-9. (a) Currents from the S-A node cause the atria to contract. These currents stimulate the A-V node which causes the ventricles to contract. (b) An electrocardiogram showing two normal heartbeats has a characteristic shape. (c) A computerized pulse readout shows contraction of the valves. Each green line describes the volume of a heartbeat. Readouts such as these are used to diagnose heart disease.

FIGURE 26-10. An artificial pacemaker may be implanted in the chest if the natural pacemaker is failing. Much like the natural pacemaker, the artificial one sets up electric currents.

26:6 The Heartbeat

In a developing chick embryo, there is at first a slight twitching of an incomplete heart. Later, the twitching becomes a definite, rhythmic beating. This heartbeat becomes more and more regular and will continue to beat steadily for the remainder of the animal's life. The source of each and every heartbeat is from within the heart itself!

The human heartbeat originates in a small bundle of tissue located in the right atrium. This bundle is called the **pacemaker,** or **sinoatrial** (si noh AY tree ul), or S-A, **node.** In the S-A node, a flow of ions sets up a current which travels quickly across the muscle fibers of the atria and causes the atria to contract. The current then reaches another small bundle, the **atrioventricular** (ay tree oh ven TRIHK yuh lur), or A-V, **node** located between the atria and ventricles. From here the current sweeps outward and downward along the muscle walls of the ventricles causing them to contract (Figure 26-9). The heart of a resting adult human beats about seventy times per minute.

As a result of technology, artificial pacemakers have been made. These devices allow people with a damaged natural pacemaker to survive. An artificial pacemaker uses small batteries as its power source and sets up electric currents in much the same way as the natural pacemaker does. Some pacemakers can even be implanted within the body.

Control of the heartbeat is a part of maintaining homeostasis, a constant internal environment despite external change (Section 1:6). Blood is part of the internal environment of humans. Enough blood must reach all body cells under all conditions to supply needed materials and carry away wastes. At rest, a heartbeat rate of seventy beats per minute is adequate, but during heavy exercise cells need more oxygen and glucose. Also, the cells yield more wastes. Blood must bring in and take away these materials quickly in order to keep the body cells healthy. How is this change in heart rate accomplished?

Although each heartbeat begins at the S-A node, the heartbeat *rate* is controlled by two pairs of nerves. The nerves begin in a part of the brain called the **medulla oblongata** (muh DUL uh · ahb long GAHT uh) (Section 30:10). There are two nerve centers in the medulla oblongata—an **acceleration center** and an **inhibition** (ihn uh BIHSH un) **center.** When the acceleration center is stimulated, impulses are sent to the S-A and A-V nodes along the accelerator nerves. The right and left accelerator nerves stimulate the heart to beat faster, thus the heartbeat rate is increased. Several factors can cause increased heartbeat rate. Among these are heavy muscular activity and build-up of carbon dioxide in the blood.

When the inhibition center is stimulated, impulses are sent to the S-A and A-V nodes along the **vagus** (VAY gus) nerves. The right and left vagus nerves slow the heartbeat. Lowered carbon dioxide content of the blood is one thing that results in stimulation of this center. How are these changes involved in homeostasis?

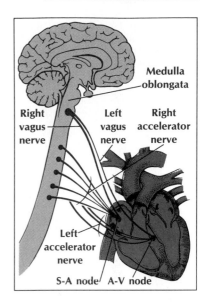

FIGURE 26-11. Vagus and accelerator nerves originate in the medulla oblongata of the brain and control heartbeat rate.

26:7 Blood Pressure

Each heartbeat consists of two phases. The forceful, muscular contraction of the ventricles is called **systole** (SIHS tuh lee). During systole, blood is pumped into the aorta. Systole is followed by a short period of "rest" called **diastole** (di AS tuh lee). During diastole, the atria and ventricles fill with blood.

Each heartbeat consists of two phases, systole and diastole.

As blood is pumped, it exerts a pressure on the walls of blood vessels. Because systole is a contraction of the ventricles, pressure during systole is greater than during diastole. **Blood pressure** is the ratio of systolic to diastolic pressure and is measured with a special gauge. It is usually measured in the arm because the pressure drops as blood flows farther from the heart. The two pressures are measured in millimeters of mercury and expressed as a fraction such as 120/80. (This fraction represents a systolic pressure of 120 and a diastolic pressure of 80, normal for a healthy adult.)

Blood pressure is the ratio of systolic to diastolic pressure.

Blood pressure is typically measured in mm of Hg, although mm of Hg is not an SI measurement of pressure. The SI measurement unit for pressure is pascals.

Blood pressure affects heartbeat rate. Low blood pressure can stimulate the accelerator center, increasing the rate. As the rate increases, blood pressure rises. High blood pressure can stimulate the inhibition center, decreasing heartbeat rate and lowering blood pressure.

Blood pressure is a factor influencing heartbeat rate.

In general, blood pressure increases gradually with age, but unusually high blood pressure, or **hypertension,** is a dangerous condition. Hypertension has been referred to as the "silent killer"

FIGURE 26-12. Blood pressure, which is measured with a special gauge, should be checked periodically. High blood pressure is a sign of something wrong with the body.

The device for measuring blood pressure is called a sphygmomanometer.

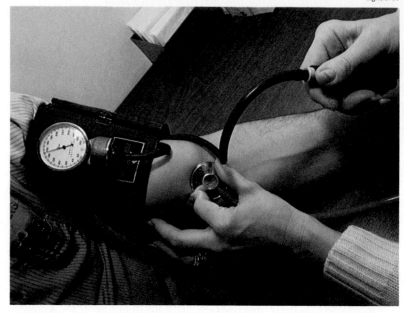

Lightforce

Hypertension may lead to a variety of illnesses and even death.

because it has no obvious symptoms that can be recognized by a person with the condition. Prolonged hypertension may lead to enlargement of and damage to the heart, shortness of breath, kidney failure, heart failure, and death. Hypertension may also be related to **atherosclerosis** (ath uh roh skluh ROH sus). Atherosclerosis is a condition in which the arteries become lined with fatty deposits. These deposits make the arterial walls thicker, reduce blood flow, and further elevate blood pressure. Regular measurements of blood pressure are important in the diagnosis and control of this condition. Should hypertension exist, it can be treated with special drugs that reduce the blood pressure. Early detection and use of these drugs can prevent the harmful, long range effects of this disease.

26:8 Lymphatic System

Capillaries are the sites of exchange, but not all materials are exchanged directly between the body cells and the blood in the capillaries. (Carbon dioxide and oxygen probably are.) As blood passes through the capillaries, pressure is exerted on the capillary walls. The pressure is greatest at the arterial end of the capillary. This pressure forces some water and small dissolved particles out of the capillaries and into the tissues. The water and particles are called **tissue fluid.** Large molecules, such as proteins, remain in the capillaries. At the venous end of the capillary, blood pressure is lower, so some tissue fluid returns to the capillary by osmosis. Osmosis occurs because there is a larger amount of protein and a smaller amount of water in the capillaries than in the surrounding tissue fluid.

Tissue fluid is composed of water and dissolved particles derived from blood.

The thoracic duct is the terminal duct for 3/4 of the body. Lymph from the upper right part of the body drains into the right lymphatic duct.

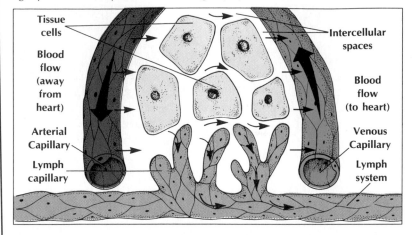

FIGURE 26-13. Blood pressure forces some of the fluid portion of blood out of the capillaries. The tissue fluid that does not return to the capillaries but rather enters the lymphatic system is called lymph.

Some less complex vertebrates have lymph hearts which help lymph return to the bloodstream. The lymph vessels of humans have valves such as those found in veins.

FIGURE 26-14. The lymph system consists of vessels that run throughout the body and groups of lymph nodes which are located in specific places.

Tissue fluid is an important agent in the exchange of materials with cells. Materials such as nutrients and ions actually enter cells from the tissue fluid. Also, wastes and secretions such as hormones enter the tissue fluid from cells. Thus, tissue fluid is a vital part of the internal environment.

Not all tissue fluid returns to capillaries by osmosis. Some of the fluid enters a special network of **lymph vessels.** Fluid which enters this network is called **lymph.** Lymph vessels also carry fats which enter the lacteals of the small intestine (Section 25:10). There is no "pumping action" for lymph circulation, but random body movements force the lymph to a major collecting tube, the **thoracic duct,** located near the heart. The thoracic duct empties lymph into a large vein. In this way, the liquid portion of the blood lost at the capillaries is restored.

Scattered throughout the lymphatic system are special structures called **lymph nodes** (Section 19:15). They contain cells which engulf and destroy bacteria and dead cells. Lymph nodes also remove and store small particles. Where are some of your lymph nodes? Have you ever experienced swelling in these lymph nodes? What does this swelling indicate?

1. blood and the structures through which it passes

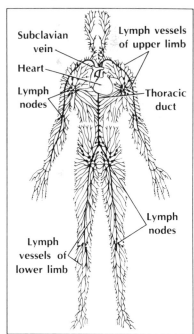

REVIEWING YOUR IDEAS

1. What is a circulatory system?
2. What is the function of a heart?

2. A heart pumps blood through the body.

3. Distinguish between a closed circulatory system and an open circulatory system.
4. Distinguish among arteries, veins, and capillaries.
5. Distinguish between atria and ventricles.
6. Compare the hearts of fish, amphibians, reptiles, birds, and mammals.
7. What is the pacemaker?
8. What is blood pressure? How is it measured?
9. How is tissue fluid important to circulation?

3. In a closed system, blood remains in vessels. In an open system, it does not.
4. Arteries carry blood away from the heart and veins return blood to the heart. Capillaries link arteries and veins and are the sites of exchange of materials with cells.
5. Atria are heart chambers which receive blood from the body. Ventricles are chambers which pump blood to the body.
6. Fish have two-chambered hearts, amphibians and reptiles have three-chambered hearts, and birds and mammals have four-chambered hearts.
7. The pacemaker is the bundle of tissue in which each heartbeat originates.

8. Blood pressure is a measure of the force blood exerts in the blood vessels. It is measured in the arm with a special gauge and expressed in mm Hg as a ratio of systolic and diastolic pressure.

9. Tissue fluid is the liquid with which cells exchange most materials.

THE BLOOD

Blood transports materials, repairs wounds, fights infection,
and helps maintain body temperature.

Teaching suggestion: Point out that
blood is a liquid tissue. You may
choose to introduce the term plasma,
the liquid in which the formed elements (blood cells and platelets) are
contained.

As your internal environment, blood functions in the homeostasis of your body. Your cells get needed materials from the blood. Oxygen, digested food such as glucose and amino acids, mineral ions, and vitamins are transported by blood (Section 25:11). Waste products including urea and carbon dioxide are dumped into the blood. Blood has protective functions including **repair of wounds and defense against disease.** Blood also has a part in maintaining body temperature and other body functions. The materials in blood are listed in Table 26-1.

TABLE 26-1. BLOOD CONTENTS	
Substance	Characteristics
Erythrocytes (red blood cells)	biconcave, disc-shaped cells with no nuclei; transport oxygen and some carbon dioxide
Leukocytes (white blood cells)	many types with round shape; all have nuclei; "fight off" bacteria and produce antibodies
Platelets	cell fragments which liberate materials necessary for clotting activities
Proteins	some involved with clotting activities; some are antibodies; some have other functions
Hormones	chemicals secreted by glands and transported to specific areas where they perform specific functions
Urea	waste product formed by liver; transported to kidneys where it is filtered out
Glucose, amino acids, vitamins, minerals, lipids, salts	transported from intestine to all cells and tissues

FIGURE 26-15. Red blood cells function in gas transport. Red blood cells contain hemoglobin, a protein that carries oxygen.

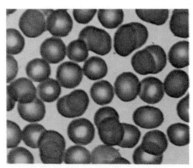

Phillip Harris Biological Inc.

26:9 Gas Transport

A microscope shows that a drop of human blood is packed with disc-shaped cells. These cells are indented on each side and they have no nuclei (Figure 26-15). There are about 5 million of them per cubic millimeter of blood. These cells are called **red cells** or **erythrocytes** (ih RIHTH ruh sites).

Red blood cells are important in the transport of gases. Red blood cells contain a pigmented molecule called **hemoglobin** (HEE muh gloh bun). Hemoglobin is a complex protein which contains iron and can carry oxygen. In the lungs, oxygen combines readily with hemoglobin to form the compound **oxyhemoglobin** (ahk sih HEE muh gloh bun), making the blood bright red. From the lungs, oxyhemoglobin goes to the heart and then to the body cells. In the capillaries, oxyhemoglobin breaks down into hemoglobin

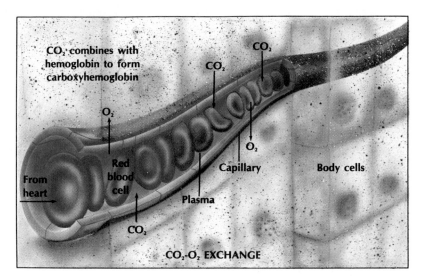

FIGURE 26-16. In capillaries, oxygen is given off and carbon dioxide is picked up by red blood cells.

The blood of some crustaceans and mollusks has a protein, hemocyanin, which contains copper instead of iron. The pigment of these animals is carried in the plasma and is blue in color.

and oxygen. The oxygen diffuses from the red blood cells to the body cells. After losing oxygen, blood is dark red.

While oxygen diffuses to body cells, carbon dioxide leaves the body cells and enters the blood. Some of the carbon dioxide ionizes in the watery portion of the blood. Another portion of the carbon dioxide combines with hemoglobin to form a complex molecule called **carboxyhemoglobin.** The remaining carbon dioxide combines with the liquid in the red blood cells. The carbon dioxide is exchanged for oxygen in the lungs by the blood.

Carbon dioxide diffuses from the body cells to the blood.

and is transported in the form of H^+ and HCO_3^- ions

Red blood cells cannot reproduce. Why? Instead, they are made constantly by **bone marrow,** the tissue in the hollow part of a bone. A young red blood cell has a nucleus which disappears as it matures. Red blood cells live for about three months. Dead cells constantly are filtered from blood and destroyed by the liver and spleen (Section 19:10). The spleen is also a blood reservoir.

They have no nuclei.

Red blood cells are formed in the marrow of certain bones.

Production of new red blood cells sometimes does not equal the number being destroyed. The result is a type of **anemia** (uh NEE mee uh), a disease which usually results in dizziness, weakness, pale color, and lack of energy. Anemia may also be caused by lack of iron or hemoglobin in blood or by low blood volume. Foods rich in iron or injections of iron-containing drugs may help correct certain forms of anemia.

26:10 Protection Against Injury and Infection

Most people assume that a cut or bruise will heal quickly. But, a cut blood vessel would be fatal if there were no way to stop the blood flowing from it. Repairs of cuts and bruises occur by the clotting of blood. Clotting of blood involves **platelets** (PLAYT luts),

Phillip Harris Biological Inc.

E. Bernstein and E. Kairinen, Gillette Research Institute, Rockville, MD

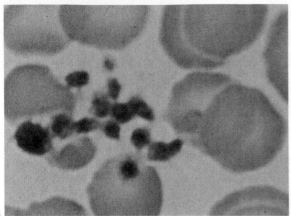

a   b

FIGURE 26-17. (a) Platelets are cell fragments that function in blood clotting. (b) A red blood cell, shown magnified 8000 times, is caught in fibers which form the beginning of a blood clot.

Platelets release chemicals which trigger reactions leading to the formation of a blood clot.

certain cell fragments lacking nuclei (Figure 26-17). Platelets arise from the breaking apart of very large cells produced by bone marrow. Platelets are colorless, disc-shaped, and live for only about ten days. A cubic millimeter of blood contains about 250 000 platelets.

When an injury occurs, blood platelets release chemicals which trigger a set of reactions in the blood. Calcium ions and other chemicals are needed for these reactions to occur. These reactions produce a protein called **fibrin** (FI brun).

$$\text{PLATELETS} \rightarrow \underset{\text{from platelets}}{\text{Chemicals}} + \underset{\text{in blood}}{\text{Chemicals}} \rightarrow \text{Thromboplastin}$$

$$\text{Prothrombin} \xrightarrow{\dfrac{\text{Thromboplastin}}{\text{Ca}^{++}}} \text{Thrombin}$$

$$\text{Fibrinogen} \xrightarrow{\text{Thrombin}} \text{Fibrin}$$

Fibrin is insoluble, so it settles out of the blood as long strands which form a tangled network of fibers. This network of fibers traps other blood parts and forms a **blood clot** which covers the wound and prevents excessive loss of blood.

Vitamin K is also essential for blood clotting.

White cells, or leukocytes, protect against infectious disease.

Protection against infectious disease involves white blood cells or **leukocytes** (LEW kuh sites). Leukocytes are also produced by bone marrow. Although there are several types of leukocytes, they are all colorless, larger than other blood cells, and they all have distinct nuclei.

Leukocytes play essential roles in the body's immune system (Section 19:15). Leukocytes are involved in recognizing antigens, producing antibodies, and destroying pathogens. Normally, a cubic millimeter of blood contains about 8000 leukocytes. However, during infection, the number may be as

Mononucleosis is associated with an abnormally large number of leukocytes called monocytes.

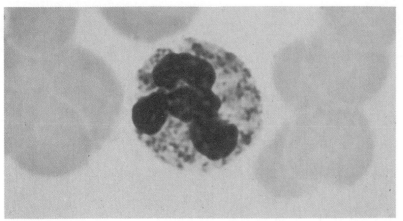

William Patterson for Tom Stack and Associates

FIGURE 26-18. White blood cells function in protection against disease. They play essential roles in the immune system of the body. A type of white blood cell, a neutrophile, is shown magnified about 5 400 times.

Leukocytes increase as a response to the infection. The white cells "fight" the infection.

great as 25 000. Why? A collection of dead bacteria and white cells in an infected area is called pus. During infection, certain areas may be full of these materials.

26:11 Major Blood Types

Blood type is genetically determined. The four major blood types determined by three possible alleles (Section 7:10) are A, B, AB, and O. Differences in blood type involve antigens on the surface of red cells. Type A blood has A antigens and type B has B antigens. Type AB blood has both A and B antigens and type O blood has neither antigen (Table 26-2).

Teaching suggestion: Blood typing kits are available from biological supply houses. Many students are interested in typing their own blood, if it is permitted in your school. Be sure to follow safety guidelines carefully.

Antigens (proteins on the surface of red cells) are responsible for the different blood types.

TABLE 26-2. BLOOD TYPES AND TRANSFUSION POSSIBILITIES				
Type	Antigens	Antibodies (Agglutinins)	Can Receive	Can Donate to
A	A	anti-B	O, A	A, AB
B	B	anti-A	O, B	B, AB
AB	A, B	none	all	AB
O	none	anti-A anti-B	O	all

Blood plasma of type A blood contains an antibody called **anti-B agglutinin** (uh GLEWT uh nun). This antibody, a chemical formed in response to foreign elements in the blood, attacks type B antigens so anti-B agglutinins link with the type B antigens. Thus, if type B blood is injected into a person with type A blood, red cells will clump together. This process is called **agglutination** (uh glewt un AY shun), a type of antigen-antibody reaction which has undesired effects. The reverse is also true. That is, type B blood has **anti-A agglutinin** so type A blood in a type B bloodstream will clump, too. Type AB blood has neither anti-A nor anti-B agglutinins; type O has both.

Agglutination results from the action of certain antigens and agglutinins (antibodies).

Cliff Beaver

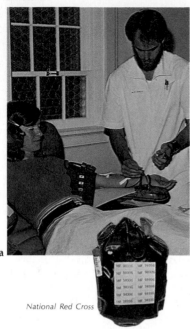

National Red Cross

FIGURE 26-19. (a) Donated blood can be stored in bags and refrigerated for later use. (b) Before it is used, blood is carefully typed. Blood test cards for the ABO blood types are shown. Clumping shows as dotted areas, whereas blood that does not clump remains smooth looking when mixed with anti-sera on the cards.

Blood must be cross matched before a transfusion is performed.

Rh factors are another group of proteins in the blood.

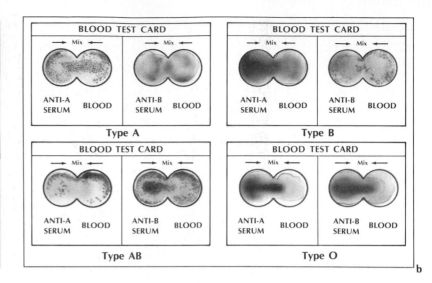

People with type AB blood could receive any blood type because no clumping will occur. For this reason, a person with type AB blood is called a **universal recipient.** A person with type O blood is called a **universal donor** because the red cells have no antigens. Type O blood cells will not be attacked by agglutinins.

Transfusions of incorrect blood types result in agglutination (Figure 26-19) which can be fatal. When performing transfusions, foreign antigens must not be introduced. Introduction of foreign agglutinins (antibodies), however, is not so serious. They are rapidly diluted by the watery part of the recipient's blood so there is little chance of agglutination. This dilution explains why type O blood is a universal donor. The anti-A and anti-B agglutinins will not cause clumping because there are so few of them. However, before any transfusion is made, the blood of the donor and the recipient should be cross matched. Matching will indicate the presence of other antigens which might cause agglutination.

26:12 Rh Factor

Other proteins called **Rh factors** may also be present on red blood cells. Rh comes from "rhesus" (REE sus) because these antigens were first discovered in the blood of rhesus monkeys. About 85 percent of the people in the United States have the Rh factor and are Rh positive. The remaining 15 percent do not have the Rh factor and are Rh negative.

Suppose Rh positive blood is given to a person with Rh negative blood. Antibodies against the foreign blood may form. The result will be agglutination. A person with Rh positive blood can safely receive Rh negative blood. Why? Rh negative blood contains no Rh antigens.

Rh factors can harm a developing embryo if the child is Rh positive and the mother is Rh negative. A few blood cells may pass from the child through the placenta into the mother's circulatory system near the end of pregnancy. In response to these foreign blood cells, the mother produces antibodies which may pass back across the placenta into the embryo's bloodstream. The baby's blood would be foreign protein to the antibodies. Anemia in the child or even death could result. Rh incompatibility is rarely dangerous during a mother's first pregnancy. Usually, the quantity of antibodies in her blood formed is small and they do not form until late in the pregnancy. However, the antibodies are retained in the mother's blood, so their number may increase with each pregnancy. A chemical is available to help solve this problem. It is injected into an Rh negative mother shortly after she delivers an Rh positive child. The chemical prevents the mother's immune system from recognizing that the child's red blood cells (those passed to the mother) are Rh positive, so no antibodies are built up. The foreign red blood cells which have entered her blood eventually are destroyed along with the mother's own red blood cells by the liver. The injection procedure must be repeated each time the mother delivers an Rh positive child. If the chemical is not taken, later pregnancies involving Rh positive babies will cause problems.

The allele for Rh positive is dominant. Thus, the father, in this case, must be Rh positive.

This condition is called erythroblastosis fetalis. Amniocentesis can be used to diagnose the seriousness of the disease.

The danger of problems from Rh incompatibility increases with each pregnancy.

FIGURE 26-20. If an Rh⁻ mother becomes pregnant with an Rh⁺ child, often a little of the child's blood enters the mother during delivery of the baby. A chemical can be injected into the mother that prevents her body from making antibodies that would cause incompatibility with future Rh⁺ children.

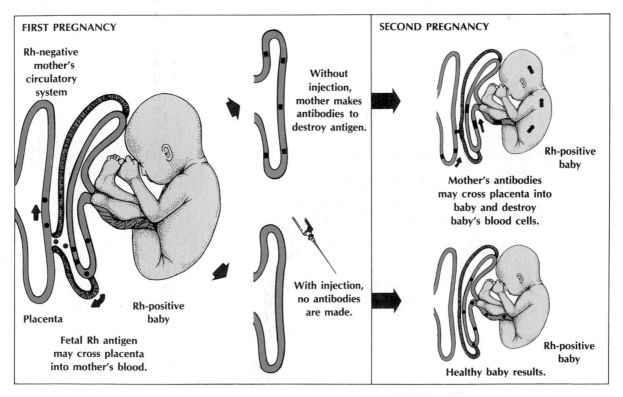

FIRST PREGNANCY

Rh-negative mother's circulatory system

Without injection, mother makes antibodies to destroy antigen.

Placenta

Rh-positive baby

Fetal Rh antigen may cross placenta into mother's blood.

With injection, no antibodies are made.

SECOND PREGNANCY

Rh-positive baby

Mother's antibodies may cross placenta into baby and destroy baby's blood cells.

Rh-positive baby

Healthy baby results.

HEART DISEASE

26:13 Causes, Treatments, and Preventions

Most heart disease results from damage to heart muscle.

Heart disease is the leading cause of death in the United States. Many coronary (heart) problems arise as heart muscle becomes damaged. Heart muscle can be weakened or even killed by a variety of factors. Prolonged hypertension (Section 26:7) can damage the lining of the coronary arteries and can also cause heart muscle to become thickened and overworked. This strain on the heart may lead to abnormal pumping action which interferes with normal blood flow and leads to death by heart failure.

A clot lodged in a coronary blood vessel may lead to death of a part of the heart muscle—a heart attack.

In some cases, a blood clot may form or become lodged in the coronary blood vessels. The clot may block a vessel, stopping the flow of blood (and oxygen) and causing a portion of the muscle to die. This series of events leads to a heart attack. Heart attacks are sometimes quickly fatal because the heartbeat control system breaks down, and the rhythm of the heartbeat cannot be controlled. In persons suffering from atherosclerosis (Section 26:7), clots are more easily trapped because the arteries are clogged with fatty deposits. Most people who have heart attacks also have atherosclerosis.

Treatment of heart disease varies. Treatment may involve reduced physical activity and the use of drugs, or surgery may be performed. In one type of surgery, heart valves may be repaired or artificial valves installed. In other surgical procedures, veins from other parts of the body are grafted onto diseased coronary arteries so that blood can bypass the damaged vessels.

FIGURE 26-21. (a) Body scanners sometimes are used to diagnose heart disease. The three scans inset on this photo show the heart muscles at work. (b) Artificial heart valves can be put surgically into the heart, replacing damaged valves. This valve is being used experimentally in pigs.

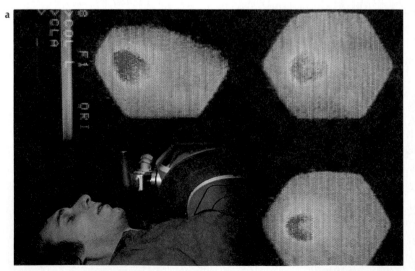

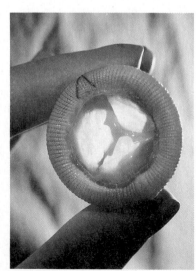

Bill Pierce from Rainbow

Timothy Eagan for Woodfin Camp and Associates

Steve Lissau

Janet Adams

Certain forms of heart disease are preventable. Eating the proper diet is one way heart disease may be prevented. Avoiding large amounts of fats, especially animal fats and those in dairy products such as butter, cream, and whole milk reduces the risk of heart disease. These substances add cholesterol to the blood, which some physicians think may contribute to atherosclerosis. Obesity can also lead to heart disease and put a strain on the heart. Such strain results from the heart's having to work harder in an overweight person to supply blood to all the tissues. Obesity may also lead to accumulation of fatty deposits in blood vessels. Also, fat builds up around the heart.

Other personal habits besides diet affect the chances of getting heart disease. Cigarette smokers run a greater risk than nonsmokers of getting heart disease. Nicotine in cigarette smoke constricts blood vessels and causes the heart to beat more quickly than normal. Smoking also seems to increase the chances of developing atherosclerosis.

Exercise is also important in maintaining a healthy heart. Just as exercise may strengthen other muscles, it can also improve the efficiency of the heart. In a person who exercises regularly, the heartbeat rate is lower and more blood is pumped to the body with each beat. Thus, the heart does not work as hard in getting an adequate supply of food and oxygen to the body tissues. Swimming and bicycling are excellent forms of exercise for maintaining a healthy heart and circulatory system.

FIGURE 26-22. Regular exercise is important in preventing heart problems. Exercise programs should begin slowly and build up gradually.

Cholesterol is also produced by the body. Some forms of cholesterol may not be dangerous and, in fact, may help prevent clogging of vessels.

High density lipoprotein (HDL) has been found to increase during exercise. HDL is thought to help prevent heart disease.

A proper diet may help to prevent heart disease.

Regular exercise strengthens the heart.

Riverside Methodist Hospital

FIGURE 26-23. During heart transplants or other kinds of heart surgery, the patient's blood is oxygenated by a heart-lung machine, shown here in the foreground.

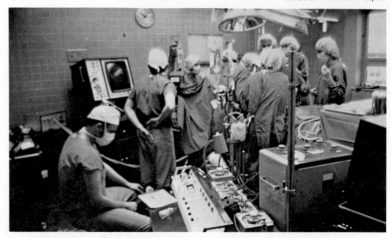

Teaching suggestion: The subjects of heart transplants and artificial hearts would be good research or debate topics. These subjects may be sensitive subjects for some students to discuss. Respect a student's right to privacy in any assignment.

Use of the heart-lung machine enables surgeons to operate on the heart.

Implantation of a foreign organ causes the recipient to manufacture antibodies against the organ as foreign protein.

26:14 Heart Transplants

In rare cases when heart disease is most severe, a heart transplant may be done. During a heart transplant, the patient's blood bypasses the heart and lungs and circulates through a heart-lung machine. This machine pumps the blood, oxygenates it, and removes carbon dioxide from it (Figure 26-23). Meanwhile the damaged heart is removed and the new heart is attached to the major blood vessels. Once the operation is completed, blood is no longer circulated through the machine but is channeled through the lungs and the new heart of the patient.

Although this type of surgery is possible, there are problems involved. An organ contains the proteins of the body in which it developed. To the person receiving a donor organ, these proteins are antigens. The receiver's immune system begins producing antibodies and cells to destroy the antigens. Eventually the foreign organ may be rejected (destroyed).

Other organs which can be transplanted include kidneys, eyes, lungs, liver, and testicles.

FIGURE 26-24. Some people carry Uniform Donor Cards, which indicate their wish to donate body organs in the event of death. In some states, these cards are attached to drivers' licenses.

UNIFORM DONOR CARD

OF_____
<small>Print or type name of donor</small>

In the hope that I may help others, I hereby make this anatomical gift, if medically acceptable, to take effect upon my death. The words and marks below indicate my desires.

I give: (a) _____ any needed organs or parts

          (b) _____ only the following organs or parts

_____
<small>Specify the organ(s) or part(s)</small>

for the purposes of transplantation, therapy, medical research or education;

          (c) _____ my body for anatomical study if needed.

Limitations or
special wishes, if any :_____

Drugs have been developed which combat the natural tendency of the body to protect itself, that is, make antibodies. Many such drugs currently are being tested. These drugs have permitted organ transplants from donors not related to the patient. (Often the organ comes from a person killed in an accident.) There is a danger in using these drugs because they will cause the recipient to be defenseless against other diseases or infections. Often a transplant is surgically successful, but the patient dies of other causes as a result of weakened body defenses. By using monoclonal antibodies (Section 19:15), physicians can learn how well the drugs are combating the immune system. The dosage of the drug can then be adjusted as needed.

Medication has been developed to help eliminate the rejection of transplanted organs.

Meanwhile, physicians compare the tissues of donor and recipient by matching tissues much like blood types are matched for a transfusion. Whenever possible they transplant organs from donors who have proteins similar to those in the recipient. The closer the tissues match, the less the chance that the organ will be rejected.

REVIEWING YOUR IDEAS

10. What are the functions of blood?
11. What are the two types of blood cells? What are platelets? List the functions of each.
12. What is hemoglobin?
13. What causes anemia?
14. Why is clotting of blood important?
15. What are the four major blood types? How do they differ?
16. What is the Rh factor? What can be done if an Rh⁻ mother has an Rh⁺ child to avoid problems in later pregnancies?
17. What is a heart attack? In what ways can certain heart problems be prevented?
18. Why are heart transplants risky?

10. Blood transports needed materials such as foods, minerals, vitamins, and hormones, and wastes such as carbon dioxide and urea. It also functions in clot formation and defense against disease.
11. Blood cells are red (erythrocytes) which function in gas exchange, and white (leukocytes) which function in body defense. Platelets are cell fragments involved in clotting.
12. Hemoglobin is a protein in red blood cells which carries oxygen and carbon dioxide.
13. Anemia is caused by a lower than normal number of red cells.
14. Clotting prevents excess loss of blood.
15. The four major blood types, A, B, AB, and O, differ in the antigens they contain.
16. The Rh factor is a protein on the surface of red cells. A certain chemical can be given to the mother to prevent her forming antibodies to the baby's blood.
17. A heart attack results from the death of part of the heart muscle. Certain heart problems can be prevented by careful control of diet and avoidance of smoking. Exercise is also vital to a healthy heart.
18. The transplanted organ may be rejected.

ADVANCES IN BIOLOGY

26:15 Artificial Hearts

Heart transplants are expensive, the number of donor hearts available is very small, and rejection of the new heart is a major problem. For many years, physicians and scientists have been working to avoid some of these problems by developing an artificial heart. One type of artificial heart was implanted in a human in 1969. It worked successfully for 65 hours, but was removed when a donor heart for transplantation became available. Another kind of artificial device does not replace the heart, but takes over for the heart until it recovers. The device is

Development of an artificial heart may eliminate the problems associated with heart transplants.

then removed. This device is called a **left ventricular assist device** (LVAD). LVAD's have been in use since the 1970s. In 1981, a new kind of artificial heart was implanted in a human. It kept the patient alive for 54 hours before being replaced by a donor heart.

In severe heart disease, the ventricles become weakened. Today's "generation" of artificial hearts consists of two chambers which replace the ventricles. The artificial heart is grafted to the patient's atria and to the pulmonary artery and aorta. In one model, the ventricles have an aluminum base and the rest of each chamber is composed of a meshlike material. Inside the device is a flexible membrane which separates blood from the base. Attached to the base of each chamber is a tube which passes out of the chest wall and is connected to an external air compressor. As air is pumped into the ventricle, it pushes against the membrane, forcing blood up and out into the arteries. When compression stops a moment later, the membrane falls back, and blood enters from the atria. This "on and off" pumping of air keeps blood moving through the heart and circulating to the lungs and body.

Right now, the artificial heart is seen as a temporary measure to be used until a donor heart becomes available. Some people argue that there will never be enough donor hearts available for all those who need them. They see the artificial heart as a permanent solution. But many problems remain if the artificial heart is to be used for a long period of time. Because the artificial heart is driven by an outside source (the compressor), a person is not able to move around freely. Research is underway to develop a smaller, portable compressor that would allow a more normal life-style. Even if a person could move freely, the rate at which

Some artificial hearts consist of chambers which replace damaged ventricles.

Air from a compressor forces blood from the artificial heart to the arteries.

FIGURE 26-25. (a) This artificial heart replaces (b) the ventricles (shaded area) when implanted. Air from a compressor outside the body moves diaphragms in the heart and pushes the blood. A rhythmical pulse of air keeps the heart beating.

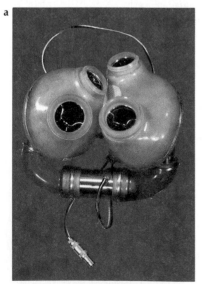

a

Hank Morgan / Rainbow
Jarvik -7 heart shown.

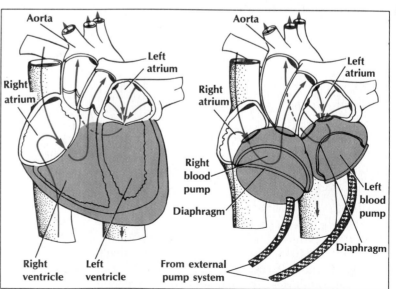

b

Hank Morgan/Rainbow

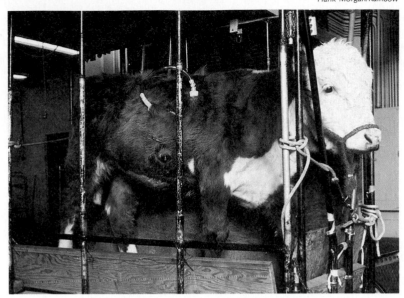

FIGURE 26-26. At the University of Utah, artificial hearts have been tested experimentally in calves.

blood is pumped from the heart is limited. This rate would limit the patient's activities. Why? Another problem is infection in the areas where the air tubes enter the body. It may be many years before these problems are solved and the role of artificial hearts is established.

CHAPTER REVIEW

SUMMARY

1. Complex animals have specialized circulatory systems which link their cells with the environment.

2. An animal's circulatory system includes a fluid, pipelines, and a pump. The system may be open or closed.

3. Annelids have a closed circulatory system and arthropods have an open system.

4. All vertebrates have closed circulatory systems. Fish have two-chambered hearts, amphibians and most reptiles have three-chambered hearts, and birds and mammals have four-chambered hearts.

5. Each heartbeat originates within the S-A node. However, the speed at which the heart beats is influenced by the accelerator and vagus nerves.

6. Blood pressure is the ratio of systolic pressure to diastolic pressure. Hypertension, high blood pressure, is a serious disease which can be treated with drugs.

7. Tissue fluid directly bathes the tissues. Many substances are exchanged between cells and tissue fluid. Lymph reenters the circulatory system at the thoracic duct.

8. Red blood cells are important in transport of gases. Hemoglobin combines with oxygen and transports it to body cells. Carbon dioxide also may combine with hemoglobin or ionize in the watery part of blood.

9. Blood platelets are important in blood clotting. After an injury, they release chemicals which set off a chain of reactions

510

All Chapter Review answers and additional chapter teaching suggestions are provided in the Teacher's Guide at the front of this text.

CHAPTER REVIEW

resulting in the formation of a protective clot.

10. White cells play important roles in defense against infectious diseases.

11. Blood types differ in the types of antigens present on the surface of the red cells. Transfusion of incorrect blood types results in agglutination.

12. The Rh factor can cause problems during pregnancy if the mother is Rh negative.

13. Heart disease may be brought on by hypertension, blood clots, and atherosclerosis. Proper diet and exercise are factors which may prevent certain types of heart disease.

14. Transplanting organs can have effects similar to those of incorrect blood transfusions. The recipient can produce antibodies and reject the protein of the foreign organ.

15. Artificial hearts are being developed. These devices may be used until a heart for transplantation becomes available or they may be permanently implanted.

LANGUAGE OF BIOLOGY

agglutinin
aorta
artery
atherosclerosis
atrium
blood
blood clot
blood pressure
capillaries
circulatory system
closed circulatory
  system
diastole
heart
hemocoel
hemoglobin
leukocyte

lymph
lymph node
lymph vessel
open circulatory
  system
pacemaker
platelet
red cell
Rh factor
sinus venosus
systole
thoracic duct
tissue fluid
universal donor
universal recipient
vein
ventricle

CHECKING YOUR IDEAS

On a separate paper, match each phrase from the left column with the proper term from the right column. Do not write in this book.

1. receives blood from left ventricle
2. liquid which exchanges materials with cells
3. heart of fish
4. combines with oxygen in blood
5. heart of bird or mammal
6. red blood cell
7. carries blood toward heart
8. source of heartbeat
9. white blood cell
10. heart of amphibian

a. aorta
b. erythrocyte
c. four-chambered
d. hemoglobin
e. leukocyte
f. pacemaker
g. three-chambered
h. tissue fluid
i. two-chambered
j. vein

EVALUATING YOUR IDEAS

1. Why must complex animals have a transport system?
2. What is the "internal environment" of an organism?
3. How is circulation in an earthworm different from circulation in a grasshopper?
4. How is a grasshopper able to live with an open circulatory system which does not transport oxygen and carbon dioxide?
5. Compare the circulatory systems of fish and frogs.
6. Why is a fish's blood circulation slow?
7. What accounts for the high pressure of the blood going through a frog's body?
8. How is a reptile's heart different from a frog's heart? How is this heart difference adaptive?
9. Trace a drop of blood through the human circulatory system beginning at the right atrium.

CHAPTER REVIEW

10. How are the valves of a human heart important?

11. Name some adaptive advantages of the mammalian circulatory system. How do you think these adaptations benefit mammals? Why is this system of blood circulation efficient?

12. What is the source of the heartbeat? Why do you think you feel your heartbeat on the left side of your chest?

13. Why must the heartbeat rate vary? How is the heartbeat rate controlled?

14. What is hypertension? What are some possible effects of hypertension? How can these effects be avoided?

15. How are tissue fluids, lymph, and the lymphatic system important?

16. How are oxygen and carbon dioxide transported by red blood cells?

17. How does blood clot?

18. Explain what can happen if an embryo with Rh positive blood is developing within a mother with Rh negative blood.

19. Explain what causes some heart failure and heart attacks. What can be done to prevent heart attacks?

20. How are the dangers of organ transplants lessened?

21. Explain how an artificial heart works. How might such a device be used? What problems exist?

APPLYING YOUR IDEAS

1. Diameter of capillaries is controlled by nerves. How might the diameter be important in regulation of body temperature?

2. Because all capillaries in the body are not open at one time, it is not wise to go swimming after eating. Why? Which capillaries would be open if an injury occurred that resulted in internal bleeding? Why?

3. Why would a hole in the septum between atria be a dangerous birth defect?

4. Why are high blood pressure and lowered carbon dioxide content of blood signals to reduce heartbeat rate?

5. What might happen if a blood clot formed inside a blood vessel?

6. What would happen if a person with type B blood received a transfusion of type A?

7. What would happen if a person with type AB blood received a transfusion of type A?

8. What would you predict about the resting heart rate of an athlete? Why?

9. How is transport in animals different from transport in vascular plants? *Chapter 22

EXTENDING YOUR IDEAS

1. Obtain a beef heart from a butcher shop. Locate the major veins and arteries leading to and from the heart. Use a glass rod to probe the vessels. Notice the coronary arteries and veins on the surface of the heart. Make a lengthwise incision through the heart. Describe its internal structures.

2. William Harvey played a significant role in early studies of circulation. Use library resources to learn about his hypotheses.

SUGGESTED READINGS

American Heart Association, *Heartbook*. New York, E. P. Dutton and Co., 1980.

Franklin, Kenneth J., *William Harvey: The Circulation of the Blood*. New York, E. P. Dutton and Co., 1979.

Grady, Denise, "The Plug-in Artificial Heart." *Discover*, April, 1981.

Jarvik, Robert K., "The Total Artificial Heart." *Scientific American*, January, 1981.

Kluger, Matthew J., "The History of Bloodletting." *Natural History*, November, 1978.

Mayer, Robin, "Blood Without Donors." *Science 81*, June, 1981.

"Taming the No. 1 Killer." *Time*, June 1, 1981.

Additional student readings and suggested teacher readings are provided in the Teacher's Guide.

Animals exchange oxygen and carbon dioxide with the environment during respiration. Animals also rid their bodies of harmful by-products of metabolism by excretion. Complex animals have specialized systems for carrying out these processes. This whale is exhaling carbon dioxide through its blowhole. The blowhole is connected to its lungs and is part of the whale's respiratory system. What adaptations do other aquatic animals have for gas exchange and excretion? What adaptations do land animals have for gas exchange and excretion?

Introduction and suggested demonstration: Prepare or obtain a solution of lime-water which is tightly sealed to prevent reaction with carbon dioxide. Prior to class, dispense equal volumes of the limewater into Erlenmeyer flasks or other containers. Distribute a supply of drinking straws and flasks to groups of students. Have a student in each group exhale into the limewater solution. The students should observe the solution turn milky which indicates a reaction between carbon dioxide and limewater (formation of calcium carbonate). The amount of carbon dioxide exhaled in a given time can be determined quantitatively by passing the milky solution through filter paper and then finding the mass of the precipitate. Encourage students to plan experiments which will measure the carbon dioxide output under varying circumstances. Discuss the results of these experiments, pointing out that the carbon dioxide output is a measure of cellular respiration and that specialized respiratory systems are adaptations for gathering oxygen from and dumping carbon dioxide into the environment. Variations in breathing rate can also be related to variation in heartbeat rate studied in the previous chapter.

RESPIRATION AND EXCRETION

Chapter 27 presents the anatomy and physiology of animal respiration and excretion.

Gas exchange in animals involves taking in oxygen and giving off carbon dioxide. This exchange is called **respiration.** There are two types of respiration, internal and external. Cellular respiration is a form of **internal respiration.** Internal respiration is the exchange of oxygen and carbon dioxide within the body of an animal. Oxygen enters the cells from either blood, lymph, or water; carbon dioxide diffuses into the same liquids. In **external respiration,** the exchange of gases occurs between the circulating fluid and the external environment. In sponges, coelenterates, and flatworms, external respiration occurs directly between body cells and the watery environment. However, complex animals have special systems for this external gas exchange.

Recall that gases must be dissolved in water before they can pass across cell membranes. Therefore, animals living on land must have adaptations for keeping the exchange surface that comes in contact with dry air moist. There must also be a large surface area for respiration so that enough gas can be obtained for all the animal's cells. Keep the need for moisture and large surface area in mind as you study and compare respiratory systems in different kinds of animals. You will see that the *type of respiratory system is related to the environment in which an animal lives.*

GOAL: You will gain an understanding of the processes of respiration and excretion as they occur in animals.

Teaching suggestion: Stress that external respiration is a prelude to and does not take the place of internal respiration.

In external respiration, oxygen and carbon dioxide are exchanged between the animal and environment.

Gas exchange requires a large, moist surface area.

FIGURE 27-1. Gas exchange in planarians occurs directly between body cells and surrounding water by diffusion.

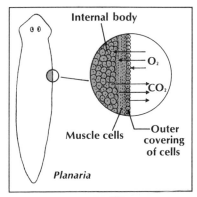

Internal body

O_2

CO_2

Muscle cells

Outer covering of cells

Planaria

RESPIRATION IN WATER

27:1 Annelids

Complex aquatic animals have systems for external respiration. Most cells in these complex animals are not close to oxygen in the surrounding environment. Thus, even if exchange of gases could occur across outer membranes, the gases could not diffuse

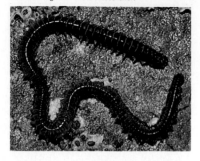

FIGURE 27-2. Gas exchange in *Nereis* occurs by diffusion in the parapods. The parapods are the bristled paddles on the sides of the worm.

In earthworms, gases dissolve in the moisture on the skin. Oxygen diffuses inward to the blood. Carbon dioxide diffuses outward from the blood through the skin and into the soil.

from cell to cell quickly enough to sustain life. Instead, special regions for gas exchange and methods of transporting gases have resulted. These parts make up the **respiratory system.**

Most annelids live in water. *Nereis* is an example of a marine annelid. *Nereis* has rows of parapods (Section 15:7), paired, bristled paddles that extend from the worm's segments, along the length of the body. These parapods are rich in blood and are quite thin. Oxygen in the water diffuses across the surface of the parapods and into the blood. The blood then transports the oxygen to body cells. Carbon dioxide diffuses from the blood in the parapods to the water.

Earthworms are annelids that live on land. But an earthworm is "aquatic" in that it can survive only in *moist* soil. Moist soil is needed for gas exchange because an earthworm does not have a respiratory system. A thin film of moisture covering the earthworm is enough to dissolve needed gases. These gases then diffuse inward and finally reach the earthworm's blood. In the blood, oxygen is transported throughout the body. Carbon dioxide diffuses into the blood from the body cells and is given off in the opposite direction. The surface area for gas exchange is large because the gas exchange process occurs all over the body.

An earthworm cannot live very long outside its dark, moist environment. However, when heavy rains fall, worms must come up to the surface or drown in the excess water in their burrows. You probably have seen dead earthworms on the ground after such a rainfall. These worms, unable to get back into the soil quickly enough after the rain ended, died from lack of oxygen and exposure to ultraviolet radiation from the sun.

27:2 Animals With Gills

Gills are the organs of respiration in several groups of complex aquatic animals.

In mollusks, some aquatic arthropods, fish, and some other aquatic animals, **gills** are the respiratory organs. Gills are located close to the outside or on the outside of the body. This location is

FIGURE 27-3. Most mollusks have respiratory organs called gills. (a) An exception is the nudibranchs, most of which lack gills. The extra folds of tissue on the body serve as added surface area over which diffusion occurs. (b) The gills of the oyster can be seen as rows of tissue just inside the opened shell.

a

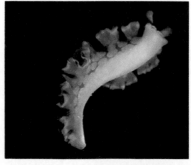

b

Grant Heilman

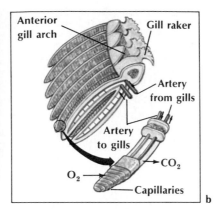

Anterior gill arch

Gill raker

Artery from gills

Artery to gills

O_2

CO_2

Capillaries

a

b

FIGURE 27-4. (a) In bony fish, the gills are covered by opercula. The operculum is raised on this fish showing gills beneath. (b) As water passes over the gills, oxygen enters blood in the capillaries and carbon dioxide diffuses into the water.

Jawless and cartilaginous fish lack opercula.

adaptive; the gills are kept moist by direct contact with the surrounding water.

In fish, water, which contains oxygen, enters through the mouth and passes back to the pharynx. From the pharynx, the water goes to the **gill chamber.** As water is taken into the mouth, the operculum (Section 16:10) of the gill chamber closes. Contraction of the pharynx forces water over the gills, the operculum opens, and water is expelled.

Each gill is made up of a **gill arch,** a structure made of cartilage which supports the respiratory tissues. These tissues, called **gill filaments,** protrude from each arch and increase the surface area for gas exchange. Gill filaments are double rows of thin-walled tissue through which capillaries pass. The circulatory system is very closely associated with the respiratory system in these gill filaments.

Attached to the gill arches are gill rakers which trap food and debris.

Gills provide a large surface area for gas exchange.

In fish, blood without oxygen leaves the heart and travels to the gill capillaries. As water passes over the gills, oxygen enters blood in the capillaries and carbon dioxide leaves the gills and enters the water. Blood with oxygen is then transported from the gills to all parts of the body. Internal respiration occurs between the blood and the body cells.

Gases are exchanged as water passes over gill capillaries.

REVIEWING YOUR IDEAS

1. Distinguish between internal and external respiration.
2. What two requirements are necessary for gas exchange?
3. Describe external respiration in simple aquatic animals.
4. Describe respiration in the earthworm. How does this process compare to that of *Nereis?*
5. Why do complex aquatic animals need a respiratory system?
6. In what sense are earthworms "aquatic" organisms?
7. What are gills? In what kinds of animals are they found? How do they work?

1. Internal respiration is the exchange of oxygen and carbon dioxide within the body. External respiration is the exchange of these gases between the animal and its environment.
2. Gases must be dissolved in water and there must be a large surface for gas exchange.
3. In simple aquatic animals, most cells exchange gases by diffusion with the water.
4. In both animals, oxygen diffuses in and is carried by blood to body cells. In earthworms, there are no special respiratory structures, diffusion occurring across the skin. *Nereis* has parapods.
5. They are too large for all cells to directly exchange gases with the environment.
6. Earthworms must be surrounded by moisture for gas exchange to occur.

7. Gills are respiratory organs found in aquatic animals such as mollusks, arthropods, and fish. Gases are ex-

changed with blood as water passes over the gills.

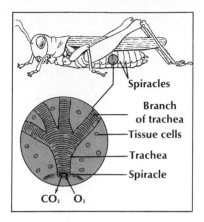

FIGURE 27-5. A grasshopper has a specialized respiratory system composed of spiracles and tracheae.

In insects, gases are dissolved in the moisture of the tracheoles. Diffusion of gases occurs between the tracheoles and body cells.

Spiracles are located in soft tissue between the segments of the exoskeleton. A grasshopper has ten pairs of spiracles. The tracheae are strengthened by an internal cuticle.

FIGURE 27-6. Although adult *Xenopus laevis* frogs breathe with lungs, much gas exchange occurs through the thin membranes of their hind feet. As a result, these frogs can stay underwater for long periods of time.

Peter Arnold

RESPIRATION ON LAND

27:3 Tracheal System

Teaching suggestion: Remind students that aquatic arthropods respire by means of gills.

Most land animals exposed to the dry air cannot undergo gas exchange on their body surfaces; there is not enough moisture to dissolve the needed gases. Instead, *dry air is brought into moistened areas within the body.*

In some land arthropods (insects and their relatives), air enters the animals through small openings called **spiracles** (SPIHR ih kulz). Spiracles are located along the sides of the body and are the external openings of tubes called tracheae (Section 16:1). Tracheae branch and rebranch within an animal, the smallest branches ending in tiny air sacs called **tracheoles** (TRAY kee ohlz), which contain water (Figure 27-5). Spiracles, tracheae, and tracheoles make up the **tracheal** (TRAY kee ul) **system.**

Air is circulated through a tracheal system either by simple diffusion, or, as in large insects, by muscular contractions. Oxygen in the air dissolves inside the moist tracheoles and passes directly to the cells. Carbon dioxide from the cells passes to the tracheoles and is expelled through the spiracles. The system works because no cell is very far from a tracheole. The large number of tracheoles provides a large surface area for gas exchange. In an animal with a tracheal system, the respiratory system is not related to the circulatory system. Blood does not transport gases; its main function is to transport nutrients and wastes.

27:4 Lung System

Most amphibians and all reptiles, birds, and mammals have another system for external respiration. Like insects, these animals have moist internal areas for gas exchange, but they are located in two organs, the **lungs.** Also, the respiratory system is linked to the circulatory system. Gases are transported between cells and the external environment by blood.

In many amphibians, gills are present in the larval stages but are replaced by lungs as the animals mature. Most amphibians lead a partly aquatic life; they live where moisture is plentiful. Frogs and some salamanders have lungs, but much oxygen also diffuses through the moist skin and enters the blood in the many capillaries on the inner surface of the skin. This oxygen adds to the oxygen taken in by the small lungs. The thin skin of the feet has many blood vessels. Like the outer skin, the lining of the

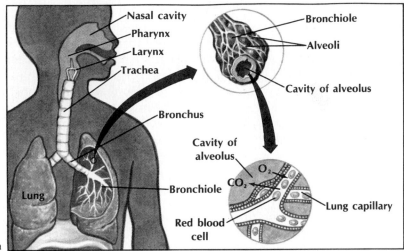

The visible rings on the trachea are cartilage which prevent collapse of the tube.

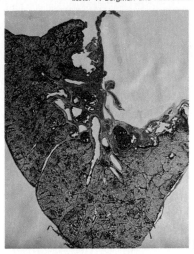

FIGURE 27-7. (a) Oxygen moves into the blood in capillaries that surround the alveoli. (b) A section of a human lung shows the spongy nature of the tissue.

frog's mouth is moist and rich in blood vessels. These adaptations provide another means of gas exchange. In fact, more oxygen is obtained through the mouth lining than the lungs. Why do you think the lungs are small?

In birds and mammals, exchange cannot occur through the skin. In humans, oxygen (as part of the air) enters the nose or mouth, passes to the **pharynx,** and then moves downward into the windpipe, or **trachea.** The opening of the trachea is protected by a structure called the **epiglottis** (ep uh GLAHT us). While breathing, the trachea is open. When a person swallows food, the epiglottis closes over the top of the trachea so food goes down only the esophagus. Have you ever choked from talking while eating? Choking occurs when the epiglottis fails to close properly and food starts into the trachea.

The epiglottis prevents food from entering the trachea.

Branching from the trachea are two large tubes called **bronchi** (BRAHN ki). The bronchi branch into many smaller **bronchial tubes** which further branch into **bronchioles** (BRAHN kee ohlz) within the lungs. Bronchioles end as many small, moist sacs called **alveoli** (al VEE uh li) (Figure 27-7). Gas exchange occurs in the alveoli. Like the filaments of gills, groups of alveoli greatly increase the surface area of the lungs for gas exchange.

Gas exchange occurs in the alveoli of the lungs.

Recall that hemoglobin is the pigment in red blood cells which combines with oxygen (Section 26:9). Carbon dioxide is transported in both red cells and in the liquid portion of blood. Blood reaches the alveoli via capillaries which branch from the pulmonary arteries. This blood is rich in carbon dioxide and poor in oxygen. In the alveoli, the level of carbon dioxide is low and the level of oxygen is high. Under these conditions, the carbon dioxide diffuses from the blood into the alveoli and is exhaled. At the same time, oxygen diffuses from the alveoli into the blood and

In the lungs, carbon dioxide passes from blood to the alveoli from which it is exhaled.

In the tissues, oxygen passes from blood to cells and carbon dioxide diffuses from cells to blood.

combines with hemoglobin to form oxyhemoglobin. The oxygenated blood is returned by the pulmonary vein to the left side of the heart from which it is pumped throughout the body.

At the body tissues, the levels of carbon dioxide and oxygen are reversed from the levels in the lungs. The tissues are rich in carbon dioxide and poor in oxygen. Under these conditions, oxyhemoglobin readily breaks down into hemoglobin and oxygen, and the oxygen diffuses from the blood to the tissues. Carbon dioxide diffuses from the tissues to the blood and is carried back toward the heart and lungs.

27:5 Control of Breathing

Breathing is controlled by the action of the diaphragm and rib muscles.

Suggested demonstration: To show the events of breathing, place a two-holed rubber stopper in an opening at the top of a bell jar. Working from the inside of the jar, insert two bent pieces of glass tubing up through the stopper holes as shown below. The bent parts should face in opposite directions. Attach a small balloon to each piece of tubing to represent the lungs. Fasten a piece of balloon rubber to the bottom and make it taut. Pulling down on the piece of rubber simulates the movement of the diaphragm during inhalation and the balloons will expand. The reverse simulates exhalation.

Movement of air into and out of the human respiratory system is called **breathing.** Breathing involves the action of the ribs, rib muscles, and a large muscular sheet, the **diaphragm** (DI uh fram), which separates the chest from the abdomen. During **inspiration** (taking air in), the diaphragm moves down and the ribs move up and out. This increases the size of the chest cavity and decreases the inside pressure. As a result, air from the atmosphere rushes into the lungs. About 500 mL of air are brought into the lungs in a normal inspiration.

When the lungs are full, an opposite set of movements occurs. During **expiration** (expelling of air), the diaphragm moves up and the ribs move in and down. This decreases the size of the chest cavity and increases the inside pressure. As a result, air is forced out of the lungs through the trachea.

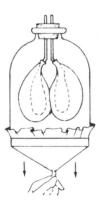

FIGURE 27-8. When the diaphragm moves down, air is taken into the lungs. When the diaphragm moves up, air is expelled. Rib muscles also play an important role in this process.

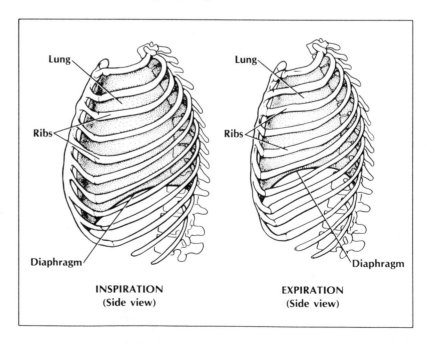

INSPIRATION (Side view)   EXPIRATION (Side view)

At rest, an adult breathes about fifteen times per minute. Normal breathing is controlled by nerves on the surface of the lungs. Filling the lungs with air stimulates the nerves sending impulses to the **breathing center** of the medulla oblongata (Section 30:10). The medulla stops sending messages to the diaphragm and rib muscles. As the muscles relax, air is forced from the lungs, and the nerves are no longer stimulated. Thus, they do not send impulses to the medulla. The medulla once again sends messages to the rib muscles and diaphragm, which contract, causing air to enter the lungs, and the cycle to repeat again. Why is it important that the breathing rate be controlled?

The breathing rate can change according to the needs of the body. Cells in the breathing center analyze the carbon dioxide content of the blood. If the carbon dioxide content is high (a sign of increased cellular respiration), nerves carry impulses from the breathing center to the muscles of the ribs and the diaphragm. The muscles are stimulated to contract and relax quickly so that the breathing rate increases. More air and oxygen are brought into the lungs so more oxygen reaches the cells. At the same time, more carbon dioxide is exhaled. This process is important because excess carbon dioxide is dangerous.

When the carbon dioxide level in the blood is low, the breathing center is inhibited. The nerves transmit fewer impulses to the muscles of the ribs and diaphragm. As a result, contractions and relaxations slow down and the breathing rate decreases. Changes in the breathing rate maintain homeostasis by adjusting the rate of gas exchange to the needs of the cells. When would an increase in breathing rate occur? Why? —————— during exercise or activity; Cells use more oxygen at these times.

Continuous alternation of inspiration and expiration is controlled by nerves located on the surface of the lungs.

As the carbon dioxide content of the blood increases, the breathing rate increases.

Teaching suggestion: Ask students what finally happens when they try to hold their breath. Carbon dioxide builds up and eventually causes resumption of breathing.

A low level of carbon dioxide in the blood inhibits the breathing center.

27:6 Respiratory Disease

The respiratory system is a vital part of the body that, when working properly, is taken for granted. However, if you ever have had an illness which interferes with your breathing, you know how frightening and uncomfortable having a respiratory disease may sometimes be.

Because the respiratory system is in contact with the environment, its parts may be invaded easily by microbes. Although many microbes are destroyed by the body's natural defenses (Chapter 19), some of them may grow and reproduce in respiratory tissues, thus causing disease.

Influenza is a viral disease which can affect various parts of the respiratory system. Influenza viruses seem to reproduce in the alveoli, but they also affect the bronchi and trachea. Many influenza deaths result from complications due to secondary bacterial infections of the respiratory system. Today, there are

Respiratory organs sometimes are easily reached by microbes.

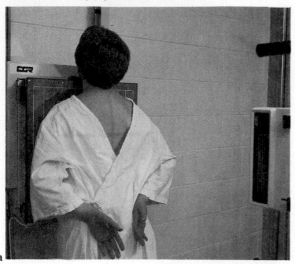

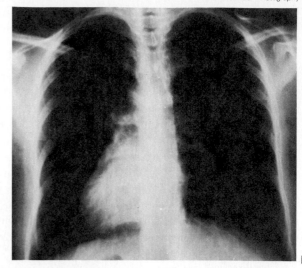

a

b

FIGURE 27-9. (a) Chest X rays can be used to diagnose certain respiratory diseases. (b) This X ray shows healthy lungs.

Many respiratory diseases are caused by bacteria.

Teaching suggestion: You might want to have students report to the class on cystic fibrosis, a genetic respiratory disease, or other respiratory ailments.

In asthma, the diameter of the bronchial passages is reduced, making breathing difficult.

vaccines which prevent many forms of influenza. If influenza and secondary bacterial infections occur, they can usually be treated by antibiotics. Influenza and its complications remain dangerous to young children and the elderly.

Bronchitis is another respiratory disease. Bronchitis may be caused by a virus or as a result of exposure to chemicals such as sulfur dioxide. Bronchitis is an inflammation of the bronchi and results in congestion in the bronchi and in coughing. It is usually over in several days.

A variety of respiratory diseases are caused by bacteria. Bacterial pneumonia, strep throat, and tuberculosis are examples of this type of respiratory disease. Before the discovery of antibiotics, these diseases were often fatal, because they cause damage not only to the respiratory system, but also to other parts of the body. Today, though, these diseases can usually be cured. Vaccines have also been developed for some of these diseases such as pneumonia.

Some respiratory problems result from allergies. Hay fever, caused by a reaction to certain types of pollen, affects the nose and sinuses. Hay fever results in irritation of the membranes, sneezing, and itching, watery eyes. A more serious respiratory problem is asthma. The exact causes of asthma are not known, but it is thought that it may result from an allergic reaction to some foods. Asthma attacks may also result from emotional causes. During the attack, which may come on suddenly, the muscles of the bronchial system contract, reducing the diameter of the air passages. As a result, breathing becomes more difficult. An asthma attack is usually treated by inhaling a medicine which helps increase the diameter of the bronchial passages and eases breathing.

27:7 Smoking and Its Effects

The respiratory disorders so far discussed result from natural biological causes. In many cases, they are not easily avoided. However, there are certain respiratory diseases which may be avoided. These diseases are ones known to be associated with smoking.

Recall that smoking affects the heart, causing it to beat faster (Section 26:13), and that smoking also increases the chances of heart attacks and atherosclerosis. Data collected over many years show that smoking also increases the chances of certain respiratory diseases. Smoking may not be the only cause of these diseases (other factors such as pollution may contribute), but studies clearly show that people who smoke run a much greater risk of developing these diseases than nonsmokers.

Smokers run a higher risk of developing certain respiratory diseases than nonsmokers.

Cigarette smoke contains hundreds of different compounds. With time, these compounds build up on the linings of the bronchial tubes and lungs. The cilia lining the respiratory passages stop moving and are eventually destroyed. When the cilia are not operating, mucus cannot be swept up toward the mouth. Coughing may occur, and the respiratory system becomes more likely to be infected because its defenses against disease are not working correctly.

Smoking may destroy cilia in the respiratory tract.

Smoking is known to contribute to a long-lasting form of bronchitis. This form of bronchitis may develop over many years and lead to blockage of the bronchioles. Shortness of breath develops, and exchange of oxygen and carbon dioxide in the lungs becomes difficult. Oxygen and carbon dioxide levels in the blood become abnormal, and body tissues become deprived of oxygen.

Emphysema is another disease linked to smoking. In emphysema, the bronchioles become inflamed. Also, the alveoli become scarred and eventually break. When the alveoli break, air

In emphysema, bronchioles and alveoli are damaged.

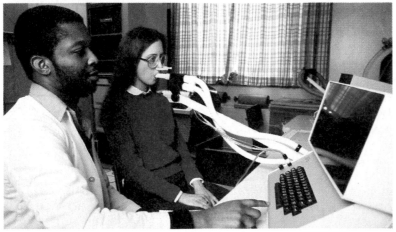

Kevin Fitzsimons

FIGURE 27-10. This patient is being given a test for emphysema. The exhaled air is tested for contents and measured for volume.

FIGURE 27-11. Respirators are used to aid breathing of people who cannot breathe on their own. The device maintains artificial respiration by forcing oxygen into the lungs.

Kevin Fitzsimons

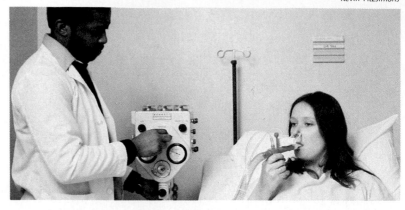

can escape from the lungs, so less oxygen moves into the bloodstream and less carbon dioxide is removed. Breathing may become very difficult and a heavy cough may develop. The heart becomes strained as it beats faster to force more blood to the lungs. Death may result from damage to the heart and lungs.

Most serious of all smoking-related diseases is lung cancer. At least fifteen of the compounds found in cigarette smoke are known to cause cancer in laboratory animals. Studies have also shown that a person who smokes a pack of cigarettes each day is twenty times more likely to die of lung cancer than a nonsmoker. Smoking pipes or cigars does not seem as risky as smoking cigarettes, but pipe and cigar smoke is also harmful.

As in other forms of cancer, lung cancer cells reproduce abnormally fast, crowding out and destroying healthy cells. Lung cancer is especially dangerous because it is often not detected until it has spread to other parts of the body. Even when it is detected early, it often causes death. Less than twenty percent of those persons diagnosed with lung cancer survive for more than five years.

Chances of getting these respiratory diseases can be reduced by not smoking. Studies have also shown that the chances of getting these diseases are reduced if a person who has smoked quits. Some of the damage done to both the circulatory and respiratory systems by smoking can be healed over a period of time. The longer one has smoked, the longer the healing period. Think about these facts. Is smoking a reasonable habit to have?

Cigarette smoking greatly increases the chances of lung cancer.

Some damage can be repaired after a person stops smoking.

8. Tracheae are air passages in insects.
9. Lungs are the respiratory organs of adult amphibians, reptiles, birds, and mammals.
10. Respiration is exchange of gases with blood or the environment. Breathing is the method by which air moves in and out of the body. Inspiration and expiration are the two phases of breathing.
11. influenza, bronchitis, pneumonia, strep throat. Answers may vary.
12. Asthma is a disease characterized by constriction of bronchial passages.
13. A form of bronchitis, emphysema, and lung cancer are associated with smoking.

REVIEWING YOUR IDEAS

8. What are tracheae? In what kinds of animals are they found?
9. What are lungs? In what kinds of animals are they found?
10. Distinguish between respiration and breathing. What are the two phases of breathing?
11. List some respiratory diseases caused by microbes.
12. What is asthma?
13. What respiratory diseases seem linked to smoking?

EXCRETION

Most waste products in animals are the chemicals produced from the breakdown of proteins. These substances, which are poisonous, contain nitrogen and are called **nitrogenous wastes.** Waste products of most animals are transported by body fluids and blood in the circulatory system to the excretory system where wastes are removed. As waste products are removed from these fluids, osmotic balance between the fluids and cells is restored. Thus, in many animals, the **excretory system** not only filters wastes, but also maintains water balance.

27:8 Planaria

Simple marine animals keep a proper water balance with their environment by osmosis. The salt water in which they live is the same as the contents of their cells. Therefore, water enters and leaves in equal amounts and osmotic balance is maintained.

Water balance is achieved in a different way by simple fresh water animals. Because the animal's cells contain many dissolved substances as well as fresh water, the fluid of the cells and the surrounding water are not in balance. As a result, water molecules enter the cells by osmosis. If not controlled, this constant osmosis could cause the cells to swell and burst (Section 5:5).

A planarian is a fresh water animal which has evolved a special system to maintain its water balance. A planarian has no circulatory system to transport wastes and excess water to a collecting site. Instead, a system of **excretory canals** and **flame cells** is found throughout the animal. Each flame cell has several flagella, the movement of which reminded scientists of candle flames, thus the name flame cells. Excess water is drawn into the flame cells where movement of the flagella sets up a current. This current moves the water into and along the excretory canals. At certain places, the canals branch into excretory ducts which open as pores on the surface of the planarian. Water is given off from a planarian through these pores. Energy is needed to actively remove the water.

Ammonia (NH_3) is the nitrogenous waste excreted by planaria. Ammonia is poisonous and can cause death if it accumulates, but is soluble in large amounts of water. Because cells of planaria are in direct or very close contact with water, ammonia diffuses into the water without a special system. More complex land animals do not excrete ammonia. Instead, they excrete other nitrogenous compounds which are less poisonous and require less water for removal.

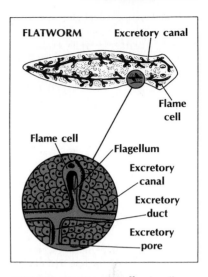

FIGURE 27-12. Flagella in flame cells of *Planaria* draw excess water from the body. The water collects in ducts and moves out of the body through pores.

In simple freshwater animals, water enters the cells by osmosis.

In planarians, water is collected in special channels and expelled through pores.

Planarians release ammonia by diffusion into the surrounding water.

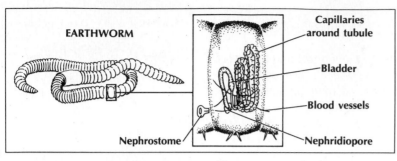

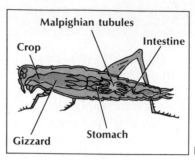

a   b

FIGURE 27-13. (a) In an earth-worm, wastes are separated in the nephridia and excreted through nephridiopores. Certain materials are reabsorbed by tubules and passed to capillaries for recircula-tion. (b) In a grasshopper, Malpigh-ian tubules absorb uric acid and water from blood. Water is reab-sorbed but uric acid is passed to the intestine and excreted through the anus.

An earthworm has excretory units called nephridia (singular, nephridium).

In each nephridium, harmful ma-terials are separated from neces-sary materials.

In aquatic arthropods like the crayfish, nitrogenous wastes are col-lected from the blood by a pair of green glands which open to the out-side at the base of the second an-tennae.

Insects conserve water by excret-ing a solid nitrogenous waste, uric acid.

Earthworms have a second "excretory system." Certain cells pick up wastes from the blood. These cells are later trapped by amoeboid cells which move to the body wall. The amoeboid cells break down, freeing the wastes which remain as pigment.

There are no nephridia in the first three segments and the last segment.

27:9 Earthworm and Grasshopper

Excretion in an earthworm is more complex than in planarians. Pairs of excretory units called **nephridia** (nih FRIHD ee uh) are found in almost every segment of an earthworm. Each nephridium is made up of a funnel-shaped **nephrostome** (NEF ruh stohm) which narrows into a tubule. The tubule passes into the next segment and widens into a **bladder.** The bladder ends as a **nephridiopore** (nih FRIHD ee uh por), a small opening to the outside.

Lymph in the body cavity of an earthworm contains both useful and waste materials. Lymph enters the nephrostome and is passed along the tubule by the action of cilia and muscular contractions. Certain cells of the tubule absorb the useful materials from the lymph. These substances pass from the tubule cells into the many capillaries of the tubule. Thus, useful materials are not lost. However, wastes remain in the tubule and enter the bladder. The wastes are then channeled to the outside through the nephridiopore.

This general filtering plan is found in most complex animals. The systems include filtering a liquid to remove wastes and the returning of usable substances to circulation. *The purpose of this system is separation of harmful from useful materials.*

Insects such as the grasshopper have a limited water supply so their bodies must conserve water. Rather than excrete nitrogenous wastes in the form of ammonia, they produce a waste compound called **uric acid.** Uric acid is not as poisonous as ammonia because it is in the form of insoluble crystals. Little water is required for excretion of solid uric acid. Ammonia excretion requires a large amount of water to dilute ammonia enough for safe removal.

Attached to the intestine of a grasshopper (Figure 27-13) is a group of stringlike structures called **Malpighian** (mal PIHG ee un) **tubules.** The free ends of these tubules lie in the hemocoel (Section 26:2). Nitrogenous wastes and water pass from the blood into the cells of the tubules where water is resorbed. The uric acid crystals are passed on to the intestine and later out the anus as solid material. Thus, wastes are removed and water is conserved.

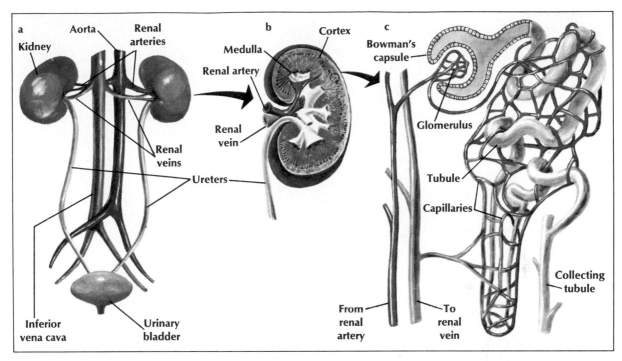

a Kidney Aorta Renal arteries Renal veins Ureters Inferior vena cava Urinary bladder

b Medulla Renal artery Cortex Renal vein Ureters

c Bowman's capsule Glomerulus Tubule Capillaries Collecting tubule From renal artery To renal vein

27:10 Humans

In vertebrates, the main excretory organs are two **kidneys.** Human kidneys remove nitrogenous wastes and unnecessary materials such as salts from the blood. Kidneys also maintain proper water balance in the body. Kidneys are fist-sized, bean-shaped organs (Figure 27-14) which lie near the dorsal abdominal wall. There is one kidney on each side of the body. The outer part of a kidney is called the **cortex,** the inside is the **medulla,** and the central, hollow cavity is called the **pelvis.**

Each kidney is composed of about a million tiny units called **nephrons** (NEF rahnz) which are similar to the nephridia of an earthworm. Each nephron is made up of a cup-shaped **Bowman's capsule** which narrows into a long, coiled **tubule.** In the center of each Bowman's capsule is a mass of capillaries called the **glomerulus** (gluh MER uh lus). Other capillaries from the glomerulus surround each tubule (Figure 27-15). A glomerulus begins as small arteries which branch from the **renal** (REEN ul) **arteries,** the blood vessels which bring blood to the kidneys. These arteries branch many times to form the capillaries of the glomerulus and those which surround each tube. The capillaries which surround the tubule merge to form small veins. These small veins merge to form the renal veins, which return purified blood to the general circulation.

FIGURE 27-14. (a) The human excretory system includes kidneys, ureters, and the urinary bladder. (b) The main organ, the kidney, is composed of (c) many filtering units called nephrons.

In addition to the kidneys, the human skin serves as an agent for expulsion of salts and water. Loss of water from the skin also is involved in body temperature regulation.

FIGURE 27-15. Inside the Bowman's capsule of each nephron is a glomerulus, a tight ball of capillaries, shown here magnified about 270 times. When blood enters the kidneys, much of the contents of the blood is forced from the glomeruli into the Bowman's capsules.

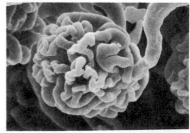

Dr. Judie Walton,
Lawrence Livermore National Laboratory

Kevin Fitzsimons

Dr. Stephen Ash and Mr. Jan Jackson,
St. Elizabeth Hospital Medical Center, Lafayette, IN

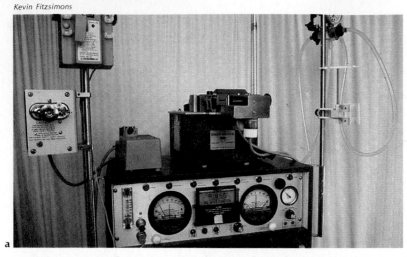

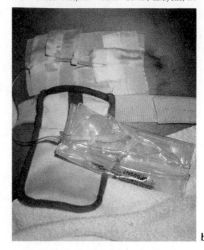

a   b

FIGURE 27-16. Persons with failing kidneys must have their blood cleaned on a regular basis. (a) A kidney dialysis machine is used to filter blood and return it to the body. (b) More recently a few patients have been "adapted" with sterile bags with which they add solutions to the body. Later, they drain away the solution and the wastes. Using bags, the patient is not restricted to kidney machine use and has more freedom.

Glucose in urine is indicative of diabetes mellitus. Protein in urine may indicate a form of nephritis. Presence of blood cells may be an indication of urinary tract infection or dysfunction.

In the nephrons, needed materials and most of the water are reabsorbed into the blood.

Urine is a combination of urea, excess salts, and water.

As blood travels through the body, it picks up **urea** (yoo REE uh), a nitrogenous waste produced in the liver. Excess salts and ions also collect in the blood.

Blood passing through the renal arteries is channeled into smaller and smaller arteries of the kidneys which lead to each glomerulus. Pressure forces most of the water and other contents of blood into the Bowman's capsule of the kidneys. The continuous flow of blood into the kidneys forces the liquid from the Bowman's capsules into the tubules which filter the liquid. Cells lining the tubule actively transport needed materials such as some food molecules, hormones, and ions out of the liquid passing through. These materials then pass from the tubule cells to the surrounding capillaries. Also, almost all the water moves by osmosis from the tubules back to the blood. The cleansed blood travels to the renal veins and back to the general circulation.

Urea, excess salts, and sometimes other substances, along with a small amount of water, are not resorbed but remain in the tubules. The combination of these materials is called **urine.** Table 27-1 compares the contents of urine with the contents of blood. Urine passes from the tubules into the **collecting ducts** in the medulla and on to the kidney pelvis.

Urea is produced in the liver. As a result of the catabolism of proteins, ammonia is produced. Because ammonia is very toxic, it is quickly converted, by a series of reactions involving the addition of CO_2, to urea. Uric acid is also produced, but as a result of nucleic acid metabolism. Accumulation of uric acid in the joints produces the disease called gout.

TABLE 27-1. COMPARISON OF URINE AND BLOOD		
Substance	In Blood	In Urine
Urea	small amount	large amount
Water	large amount	small amount
Salts	some	more
Glucose	present	usually absent
Amino acids	present	usually absent
Proteins	present	usually absent
Blood cells	present	usually absent

Leading from the pelvis of each kidney is a tube called the **ureter** (YOOR ut ur). The ureter transports urine to a hollow storage area called the **urinary bladder.** When the bladder becomes filled, a muscular valve relaxes which causes urine to be forced out through the **urethra.**

Besides filtering wastes from blood, the kidneys regulate the amounts of water, salts, and other materials in the body. The water content of tissue fluid must be the same as that of the cells. The entire volume of blood in the body passes through the kidneys about once every thirty minutes. In an average size person, about 185 liters of blood are filtered per day. However, usually only about one to two liters of urine are excreted per day. About 99 percent of the fluid is resorbed! The kidneys extract all the fluid and return most of it! They return an amount useful to the animal and remove the rest. This system is an amazing adaptation; it keeps the contents of blood and lymph fairly constant, regardless of diet, activity, or any of the other factors which affect an animal.

Urine is collected in the kidneys and transferred to the urinary bladder for storage until release from the body.

27:11 Control of Water Balance

A person's need for water may vary greatly under different conditions. A thirsty person, one who is perspiring freely, or one who has become dehydrated, needs to save water. A person who has drunk a large amount of liquid may need to get rid of more water than usual. Thus, a system is needed to control water content. Water balance is controlled by a hormone, **vasopressin** (vay zoh PRES un), secreted by the pituitary gland (Section 29:7).

Cells in the hypothalamus region of the brain (Section 29:6) detect the amount of water in the blood. If the water level is too low, the hypothalamus stimulates the pituitary gland to secrete vasopressin. Vasopressin enters the bloodstream and travels to the kidneys where it causes the tubules and collecting ducts to resorb more water. The greater the need for water, the more water resorbed, and thus, urine becomes more concentrated.

The opposite occurs when too much water is present in the blood. The hypothalamus detects the excess water and does not stimulate the release of vasopressin. Therefore, the kidney tubules and collecting ducts resorb little water and dilute urine is made.

During heavy exercise, much water is lost in perspiration. Perspiration also contains many important salts (ions). Loss of excess water and salts can be dangerous, because it can upset the osmotic balance in the body. A sharp decrease in the loss of certain ions can also affect the muscles, causing cramps or spasms. For these reasons, athletes often drink beverages containing salts during heavy exercise. These beverages, as well as the body's natural adjustments, help restore osmotic balance.

Vasopressin is also known as antidiuretic hormone (ADH).

FIGURE 27-17. Vasopressin regulates water balance in the body by controlling the water content of urine. The secretion of vasopressin by the posterior pituitary gland is controlled by the hypothalamus.

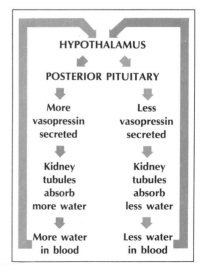

HYPOTHALAMUS

POSTERIOR PITUITARY

More vasopressin secreted	Less vasopressin secreted
Kidney tubules absorb more water	Kidney tubules absorb less water
More water in blood	Less water in blood

Mac Albin

FIGURE 27-18. Freshwater fish, such as this rainbow darter, have kidneys adapted to resorb very little water. Large volumes of urine are excreted in maintaining water balance.

Some marine birds drink seawater and excrete salty solutions from special salt glands in their heads.

Saltwater fish drink large amounts of water and excrete very little urine. Excess salt is actively removed through the gills or by salt glands.

Amphibian kidneys are adapted for life on land and in water.

Birds and reptiles conserve water by excreting uric acid.

Teaching suggestion: Tie together the circulatory system with the digestive, respiratory, and excretory systems. Students should master the essential relationships between the blood and these other systems. Review these relationships as they apply to humans and other animals.

27:12 Other Vertebrates

All vertebrates have kidneys which are adapted for the animal's way of life. Kidney structure is similar in all vertebrates, but kidney function varies in different groups.

In aquatic vertebrates, kidneys are more important for maintaining water balance than for excreting wastes. In freshwater fish, water enters the animal by diffusing through the gill membranes. Thus, excess water must be removed from the fish's body. The kidneys of freshwater fish are adapted to resorb mostly salts but very little water. So much salt is resorbed by the kidneys that the urine becomes very watery or dilute, and large amounts of urine are excreted. Most of the water which diffuses into a freshwater fish's blood is removed by the kidneys. Also, the salt content is kept constant by the kidneys. To reduce the intake of water from the environment, freshwater fish are adapted to drink very little water.

Because marine fish lose water by osmosis, their bodies must conserve water. Why? To maintain water balance, marine fish are adapted to conserve water. They drink large amounts of water. However, the water contains salt, and build up of salt is dangerous because salt build up might cause dehydration of body cells. This excess salt is actively transported from the surface of the gills to the water. Because very little water actually enters the kidneys, water is further conserved. Urea is absorbed by the tubules directly from the surrounding blood vessels. As a result, very little urine is excreted. Some marine animals have salt glands to remove excess salts.

Amphibians live in two environments, water and land. Thus, their kidneys are adapted to the conditions of each environment. On land, water must be conserved because it escapes to the dry environment. In water, excess water enters by osmosis. Thus, the kidneys must rid the animal of excess water. The nitrogenous waste product of amphibians is urea.

Birds and reptiles conserve water by excreting solid uric acid. Insects also excrete nitrogen in this form, but the systems of these two groups are not homologous (Section 12:3). Birds and reptiles have kidneys; insects do not. Bird and reptile kidneys resorb almost all the water from the tubules. Uric acid is excreted in pastelike form. Reptiles have no urinary bladders. The uric acid passes from the kidneys to a region called the cloaca (Section 23:4), a region which also collects undigestible food and serves as a reproductive opening. The uric acid and other wastes are excreted from the cloaca.

Excretion in mammals already has been described with reference to humans. Mammals excrete urea dissolved in water (urine). The kidney tubules recover most of the water that passes

Ward's Natural Science Establishment, Inc.

FIGURE 27-19. The kangaroo rat, a desert animal, excretes highly concentrated urine and thus, conserves water. This animal can get enough water from food and its metabolic reactions to survive without drinking water.

through the kidneys. Some desert mammals, such as the kangaroo rat (Figure 27-19), produce urine much more concentrated than that of humans. Their kidney tubules resorb most of the water which passes through them. So efficient are its kidneys that a kangaroo rat can survive without drinking water. Kangaroo rats obtain enough water from the food they eat and as by-products of metabolism.

Some desert mammals produce a very concentrated urine by reabsorbing a great amount of water in the kidneys.

REVIEWING YOUR IDEAS

14. What is excretion?
15. Why do planarians not swell and burst from water intake in their environment?
16. Why must nitrogenous wastes be removed? What is the source of nitrogenous wastes?
17. How is ammonia excreted from planaria?
18. What is the general function of excretory systems in the earthworm and most complex animals?
19. What nitrogenous waste product is excreted by land insects?
20. What are the organs of excretion in humans? What are the functions of these organs? Compare these organs to the excretory systems in earthworms and insects.
21. Why must water content be controlled in the body? What might happen if your kidneys removed too much water?

14. Excretion is the removal of nitrogenous wastes.
15. Their flame cell system removes excess water.
16. Nitrogenous wastes are poisonous. They arise from breakdown of proteins.
17. Ammonia diffuses from body cells to the water.
18. Excretory systems separate necessary and harmful materials from body fluids.
19. uric acid
20. Kidneys are the organs of excretion. They filter blood, retaining water and necessary materials and ridding the body of wastes. Although the structure of kidneys is different from nephridia and Malpighian tubules, the functions of all three are similar.
21. The water content of tissue fluid must be the same as that of body cells. The body might become dehydrated if too much water were removed.

CHAPTER REVIEW

SUMMARY

1. External respiration occurs between animals and their environment. For gas exchange to occur, moisture and a large surface area are needed. The type of respiratory system is related to the animal's environment.

2. In simple animals, most cells are in direct or close contact with moisture. Thus, the cells exchange gases directly with the environment.

3. Complex animals have specialized respiratory systems for gas exchange.

4. Earthworms exchange gases through their skin. In order for respiration to occur,

CHAPTER REVIEW

earthworms must remain in the soil where moisture is available.

5. Many aquatic animals have gills for gas exchange. Oxygen diffuses from surrounding water across the gill filaments and into the blood. Carbon dioxide diffuses in the opposite direction.

6. In most land animals, respiratory organs are in the body where moisture is available.

7. In insects, air enters the body through a tracheal system. Oxygen dissolves in moist tracheoles and diffuses directly to body cells. Carbon dioxide diffuses from cells to tracheoles.

8. The lungs are the organs of respiration in humans. Oxygen passes from the alveoli of lungs to the bloodstream, and carbon dioxide passes in the opposite direction.

9. Breathing is controlled by nerves which cause the diaphragm and rib muscles to contract and relax. Breathing rate is monitored by the breathing center in the medulla oblongata.

10. Many respiratory diseases are caused by microbes. Some respiratory disorders result from allergic reactions.

11. Cigarette smoking damages the lining of respiratory organs and has been linked to disorders including bronchitis, emphysema, and lung cancer.

12. Excretion is a process which removes nitrogenous wastes. Water balance also is maintained through excretion in more complex animals.

13. In simple animals, maintaining water balance and excretion of nitrogenous wastes are separate processes.

14. In earthworms, nephridia filter lymph and excrete nitrogenous wastes. Insects excrete uric acid which is collected by Malpighian tubules.

15. Kidneys are the main excretory organs of humans and other vertebrates. In humans, the kidneys extract urea and form urine.

16. Human kidneys also maintain balance of water in the body.

17. Kidneys of other vertebrates are adapted for the animal's environment.

LANGUAGE OF BIOLOGY

alveolus
diaphragm
excretion
expiration
flame cell
gill
glomerulus
inspiration
kidney
lung
Malpighian tubule

nephridium
nephron
respiration
spiracle
trachea
urea
ureter
urethra
urinary bladder
urine

CHECKING YOUR IDEAS

On a separate paper, complete each of the following statements with the missing term(s). Do not write in this book.

1. _____ respiration is the exchange of oxygen and carbon dioxide with the environment.

2. In vertebrates, nitrogenous wastes are filtered by organs called _____.

3. Breathing involves muscles of the ribs and the _____.

4. Insects have a _____ system for respiration.

5. Respiratory surfaces must be kept moist and have a large _____.

6. In earthworms, gas exchange with the environment occurs through the _____.

7. Most complex aquatic animals exchange gases at organs called _____.

8. _____ is the nitrogenous waste excreted by humans.

9. In planaria, excess water from the body is drawn into _____ cells.

10. Each kidney is composed of millions of filtering units called _____.

Occasionally questions are added to the *Applying Your Ideas* that require students to use information they have learned from previous chapters. Those questions are marked with asterisks and chapter references.

531

CHAPTER REVIEW

EVALUATING YOUR IDEAS

1. Compare respiration in *Nereis* and an earthworm. How are the means of respiration in each related to their different environments?

2. Describe the structure and operation of gills in fish. How is the gill system related to the circulatory system?

3. Describe respiration in a grasshopper. Why does the respiratory system not have to be linked with the circulatory system?

4. Describe respiration in humans.

5. How does breathing occur in humans?

6. Explain how the breathing rate in humans is controlled.

7. Explain the effect of cigarette smoking on the cilia lining respiratory organs. How does this effect interfere with normal respiratory functions?

8. What happens to respiratory tissues in emphysema and lung cancer?

9. Why do simple marine organisms have little water balance problem?

10. How do planarians rid themselves of excess water?

11. Why is ammonia not excreted by most complex animals?

12. Describe the excretory system of an earthworm.

13. How do land insects excrete wastes? Why do land insects excrete uric acid?

14. Describe the structure of a human kidney.

15. Explain the operation of a human kidney.

16. How is the amount of water excreted by the human kidney controlled?

17. How do freshwater fish rid themselves of excess water?

18. How do marine fish maintain a water balance?

19. How can a kangaroo rat live without drinking water?

APPLYING YOUR IDEAS

1. Why do most annelids live in water?

2. How is the respiratory system of humans similar to that of the grasshopper? How are the systems different?

3. Why do you suppose that the level of carbon dioxide in the blood is a signal for both breathing rate and heartbeat rate?

4. How might production of uric acid by birds and reptiles be an adaptation for development in shelled eggs? *Chapter 24

5. Would urine be more or less concentrated in a mammal on a hot day? Explain.

6. To a human afloat on an ocean, the ocean is a desert. Explain.

EXTENDING YOUR IDEAS

1. Use library resources to learn about the operation of gills in crustaceans. Compare this system to the gills in fish.

2. Design an experiment with several of your classmates to test the effect of exercise on breathing rate. Also determine the time needed for breathing rate to return to normal.

3. Skin is an excretory organ in humans. Use library sources to determine the roles of skin in excretion.

4. Find the cause of and treatment for "bends."

SUGGESTED READINGS

Hughes, G. M., *The Vertebrate Lung*, rev. ed. Carolina Biology Reader. Burlington, NC, Carolina Biological Supply Co., 1979.

Madison, Arnold, *Smoking and You*. New York, Julian Messner, 1975.

Moffat, D. B., *The Control of Water Balance by the Kidney*, 2nd ed. Carolina Biology Reader. Burlington, NC, Carolina Biological Supply Co., 1978.

Additional student readings and suggested teacher readings are provided in the Teacher's Guide.

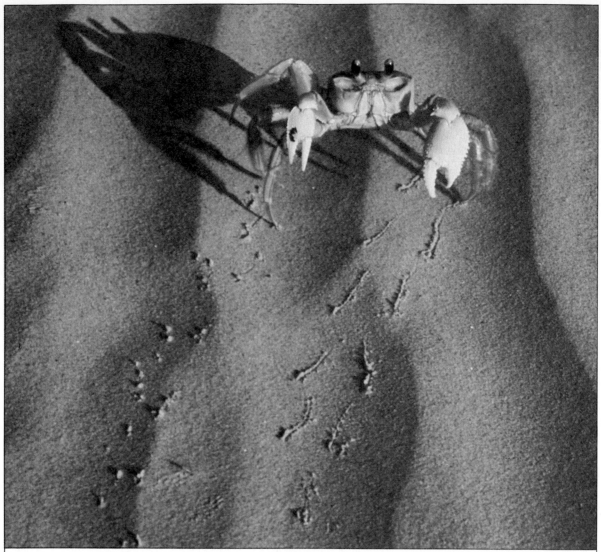

Stephen J. Krasemann/DRK Photo

M ost animals have some means of supporting their body weight. Often this support is in the form of an internal or external skeleton. Interactions between muscular and skeletal systems make most animals capable of locomotion. The muscles and external skeleton of this ghost crab work together in moving the crab across the sand. How do your bones and muscles work together?

Introduction: If your school has a human skeleton (or model of one), use it to begin your teaching of this chapter. Also, bring in bones from meats (e.g., chicken, fish, beef) found in the grocery. You can clean these bones by boiling the meat away and they then can be used for examination. Begin by having students explain how bones are specialized for particular functions. Introduce students to the various kinds of joints. Comparisons can be made between the meat bones and the human skeleton. These vertebrate skeletons or parts can also be compared to skeletal parts from animals of other phyla. For example, a lobster exoskeleton can be obtained in a grocery. Have students compare the skeletons in terms of how they contribute to protection, movement, and support.

SUPPORT AND LOCOMOTION

Chapter 28 presents the structures, roles, and interdependence of skeletal and muscular systems.

Without some kind of support, an animal would be little more than a jellylike mass. An animal without support would collapse from its own weight. Many complex animals have a system for support called a **skeletal system.**

The need for support is not as great in aquatic animals as it is in land animals. Water gives external support to aquatic animals. Land animals need more support because air provides much less external support than water. Are there any land animals lacking skeletal systems? Where do they live, and what are their features?
Yes; earthworm, other worms, and slugs, for example. They live in or on the soil. They are not very active organisms.

GOAL: You will gain an understanding of the structure and function of skeletal and muscular systems and their relationships to protection, support, and locomotion.

A skeletal system provides support.

SKELETAL SYSTEMS

Skeletal systems are absent in some phyla of animals. Sponges and echinoderms have skeletons made of mineral deposits which provide some support. Most mollusks have a hard outer shell for protection, but they have no skeletal system. Coelenterates, flatworms, roundworms, and segmented worms also lack skeletal systems.

Consider the features of these animals. Almost all of them live in water; they are limited to an environment in which they are supported by water. Some have muscle tissue, integument, and other body tissues which give added support. Many of these animals are sessile or slow moving.

The two most active groups of animals, arthropods and vertebrates, do have skeletal systems. Such systems provide support and protection, and aid movement.

Animals lacking skeletal systems are aquatic and either sessile or slow moving.

Skeletal systems provide protection and support and also aid in movement.

533

a   b

FIGURE 28-1. Arthropods have exoskeletons and periodically molt. (a) The exoskeleton of a beetle is a hard outer covering. (b) The tarantula at the right has just crawled from its old covering at the left.

Arthropods have an exoskeleton and flexible joints.

An exoskeleton limits size and movement.

FIGURE 28-2. Flexible joints allow for movement of arthropod body parts. The joints of praying mantis legs are shown.

28:1 The Exoskeleton

Arthropods have a hard outer layer made up of protein and a carbohydrate material called chitin (Section 16:1). This external skeleton is called an **exoskeleton** (Figure 28-1). An exoskeleton is a tough, rigid structure that is subdivided by soft, flexible **joints.** Joints are located between body segments, at the base of appendages, and between segments of appendages. Without joints, movement of body parts and of the entire animal would be difficult. Though protected, the arthropod would be a "prisoner" in its own "armor."

An exoskeleton has certain disadvantages. The exoskeleton limits the total adult size and movement of an arthropod. Because a very heavy outer skeleton needed to support a large arthropod would seriously limit land movement, most adult land arthropods are small. Flying would be impossible for a large insect.

Growth is also limited in arthropods. Once the exoskeleton is made by an animal, the skeleton's size cannot be changed. Instead, as the animal grows, it sheds its outer skeleton and makes a new, larger one. This process of shedding the skeleton is called **molting,** and is controlled by hormones (Section 29:9). Molting may occur as many as six times before an arthropod reaches its final adult size. After each molt, the new skeleton is soft, making an arthropod easy prey for predators. The animal has neither its armorlike protection nor the ability to move rapidly. Land arthropods also lose more water when molting.

Despite the limitations on size and growth, the exoskeleton is adaptive. The external "armor plate" provided by the exoskeleton shields the animal against physical and living factors in the environment. The exoskeleton also allows movement and supports the animal. More species of arthropods exist than have been discovered in all the other animal phyla combined. This great "success" of arthropods is due in part to the exoskelton.

Teaching suggestion: Freshly molted mealworms are a good organism to show the soft body beneath the hardened exoskeleton. A mealworm culture will have numerous "shed skins" on top. Students can see the flexible joints in these exoskeletons.

28:2 The Endoskeleton

In vertebrates, the skeleton lies within the soft tissues of the body rather than outside the body. Such an internal skeleton is called an **endoskeleton.** Because an endoskeleton and an exoskeleton are different in development and structure, the two systems are not homologous (Section 10:3). However, both types of skeleton provide support and protection, and aid movement.

An endoskeleton is subdivided into many distinct parts called **bones.** Bones provide more specialization than parts of an exoskeleton do. Each bone is adapted for certain functions and types of movements. Some bones are protectors. Skull bones, ribs, and the breastbone protect the brain, lungs, and heart. The column of vertebrae forms a protective hollow tube through which the spinal cord passes. The shape of the vertebral column is unique in humans. Humans have upright posture and locomotion. The double "s" curve of the vertebral column helps distribute and support body weight, making bipedal locomotion possible. Other bones also function in support. The long, dense thighbone supports the mass of the body and helps provide speed and strength for movement. Some bones such as the delicate finger bones help provide agility for precise small movements. Think about the nimble movements involved in playing the piano. All 206 bones in the human body have specific functions.

Internal skeletons protect the internal organs of the body but give little external protection. Some animals have skeletal adaptations that give more external protection. For example, turtles are covered by a shell made of bony plates. The shell includes both a dorsal part called a carapace and a ventral part called the plastron. The plates are made of bone covered by a horny material that is like the scales of reptiles. The plates are attached to the ribs of the endoskeleton but do not come from the ribs in their development.

Vertebrates have internal skeletons, or endoskeletons.

Bones are specialized and have different roles.

Suggested demonstration: To show vertebral bending, thread a piece of yarn through eight or ten empty thread spools. Tie the yarn to the top and bottom spools. Bend the spools sideways. Students will see how the vertebral column can bend and how its bending is limited.

Teaching suggestion: You might want to discuss scoliosis, a lateral curvature of the spine, with your students. Many areas require students be screened for scoliosis.

Many vertebrates have adaptations for external protection.

FIGURE 28-3. The turtle has an internal skeleton. It also has a shell (carapace and plastron) that adds protection.

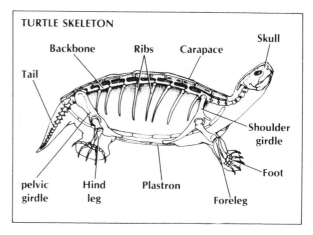

TURTLE SKELETON

Tail · Backbone · Ribs · Carapace · Skull · Shoulder girdle · Foot · pelvic girdle · Hind leg · Plastron · Foreleg

Animals with endoskeletons have other body parts that provide external protection, also. Hair, quills, feathers, and skin are nonskeletal parts that protect animals from cold, predators, radiation, and other things such as dehydration and invasion by microorganisms.

Although limited size and growth are the main disadvantages of an exoskeleton, size and growth are not as limited with an endoskeleton. Because bones can grow, there is no loss of protection or support as the animal grows. Figure 28-4 shows the human skeletal system.

Size and growth are not as limited in vertebrates.

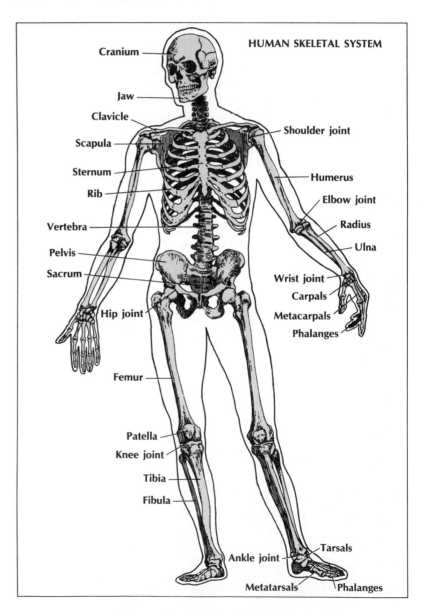

HUMAN SKELETAL SYSTEM

Cranium
Jaw
Clavicle
Scapula
Sternum
Rib
Vertebra
Pelvis
Sacrum
Hip joint
Femur
Patella
Knee joint
Tibia
Fibula

Shoulder joint
Humerus
Elbow joint
Radius
Ulna
Wrist joint
Carpals
Metacarpals
Phalanges

Tarsals
Ankle joint
Metatarsals
Phalanges

FIGURE 28-4. The human skeletal system is composed of about 206 separate bones. Sixty-four bones are in the hands and arms alone.

J. Gennaro for Photo Researchers

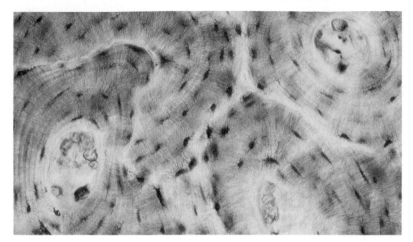

FIGURE 28-5. Bone tissue in cross section shows canals. Around each canal are the osteocytes, the bone cells.

28:3 Development of Bone

Because bone is made up of minerals and is hard, many people think that it is not living material. But a bone in a living animal is a living tissue. Within the minerals of a bone are living cells called **osteocytes** (AHS tee uh sites).

In a fetus, most of the skeleton is made up of **cartilage** (KART ul ihj), a tough, flexible tissue which has no minerals. As the fetus grows, osteocytes slowly replace cartilage cells and ossification (ahs uh fuh KAY shun) starts. **Ossification** is the changing of cartilage to bone by the addition of minerals such as calcium compounds. By the time an animal is born, many of the bones have been at least partly ossified. Because the bones are not completely ossified, a child cannot walk until it is about a year old. By this time, leg bones are strong enough to support the child's body weight.

Calcium compounds must be present for this process to take place. Osteocytes do not make these minerals, but must take them from the blood and deposit them in the bone. Because this process starts in the fetus, the mother must supply the minerals from her blood through the placenta. Thus, it is important that the mother eat a well balanced diet, taking in the proper amounts of nutrients.

Because bones grow after the birth of an animal, ossification continues and calcium compounds are still needed. Milk is a good source of calcium compounds and so it is a vital part of a child's diet. Vitamin D is also needed for proper bone development because it is necessary for calcium absorption from blood. Rickets (RIHK uts) is a disease that results from inadequate amounts of calcium or vitamin D and results in severe bone deformities (Section 25:6).

FIGURE 28-6. As an embryo develops, cartilage is replaced by bone. This skeleton is partly cartilage and partly bone. The bones are red in this photo.

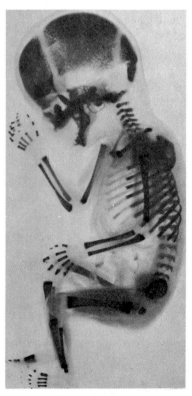

Carolina Biological Supply Co.

Some bones are not formed by ossification of cartilage. The flat bones of the face and skull and a part of the collarbone develop from membranes. These membranes are ossified by a process different from that which occurs in cartilage, but they still change into bone.

Not all cartilage is changed to bone. In some vertebrates, such as sharks, the whole skeleton remains cartilage throughout the life of the animal. However, in most animals only a few parts remain as cartilage. What parts of the human body are cartilage? What might result if these parts were bone? Explain.

In vertebrates, most, but not all, cartilage is changed to bone.

The outer ear and nasal septum are cartilage. They would lack flexibility if they were bone.

28:4 Structure of Bone

A bone is composed of both living and nonliving substances (Figure 28-7). The minerals which make a bone hard and strong are not living. The other parts of a bone are living, and are supplied with blood vessels and nerves.

Suggested demonstration: To emphasize the importance of minerals in bone, the mineral content of a bone can be removed by soaking the bone for several days in vinegar (weak acetic acid). At the end of this time, the bone will be flexible.

Bones contain bone cells, blood vessels, and nerves.

All bones are enclosed by an outer layer called the **periosteum** (per ee AHS tee um). Muscles are attached to the periostea of bones. Lying beneath this layer is the **bony layer** which contains the minerals. The bony layer is spongy near the ends of bones and hard in the midregion of a bone. Many channels called **Haversian** (huh VUR zhun) **canals** run throughout the bony layer. Inside the canals are blood vessels and nerves which supply the osteocytes.

Haversian canals contain blood vessels which nourish bone tissue.

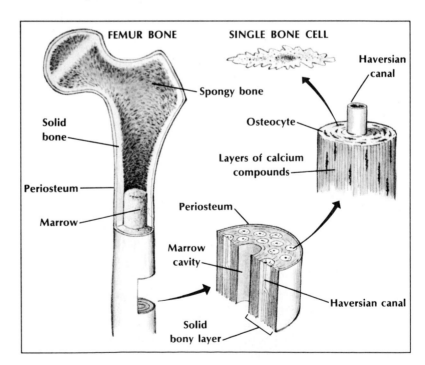

FIGURE 28-7. The human femur (upper leg bone) shows the parts of bone. All parts of the bone are living except the calcium deposits in the bony layer. Blood vessels and nerves fill the marrow cavity. Find the canals shown in Figure 28-5 in this drawing.

Some bones such as the sternum (STUR num) and the long bones of the arms and legs have central hollows filled with blood vessels and nerves. The tissue in the hollows of the bones is called **marrow.** Marrow may produce red and white blood cells and platelets or store excess fat. Marrow also functions in formation of bone cells. Bones without marrow, such as the small bones of the wrist, ankle, and toes, are solid throughout.

Blood cells are produced in red marrow located in the ribs attached to the sternum and in the ends of some long bones. Fat is stored in yellow marrow in the central areas of long bones.

28:5 Joints

The point at which bones connect with one another is called a **joint.** Most joints are movable and aid the movement of an animal and its parts. Movable joints are held together by connective tissue called **ligaments** (LIHG uh munts). Ligaments are made of flexible and elastic fibers. Movable joints of vertebrates are much more specialized than joints of arthropods, and joints fit together in several ways.

One of the most flexible of all joints is the **ball and socket joint** (Figure 28-8). In humans, this type of joint is found where the upper end of the femur (FEE mur) (thighbone) joins the pelvis (hipbone). The end of the femur is rounded into a knob which fits into a depression in the pelvis. The femur can rotate as well as move from front to back or side to side. Are there other ball and socket joints in the human body? If so, where? yes; shoulder joint

Hinge joints exist in many places within the human body, such as the knee. Rotation of a hinge joint is not possible; movement occurs in only one direction.

The elbow joint is similar to the knee joint, except that the elbow can be rotated. Thus, the elbow is a **pivot joint.** The cranium (KRAY nee um), or skull, is connected to the spine by a pivot joint. With this joint, the head can turn, as well as move up and down. Vertebrae are linked by **gliding joints.** In gliding joints, the bones move easily over one another in a back and forth manner. Gliding joints help make the backbone flexible.

In adults, the individual bones of the skull are held together by **fixed joints.** In fixed joints, the bones are fused together and do not move. These joints are not connected by ligaments. In babies and children, the skull bones are not fused together but rather have soft spots between them. Why is it important that the skull bones of young children not be fused? growth

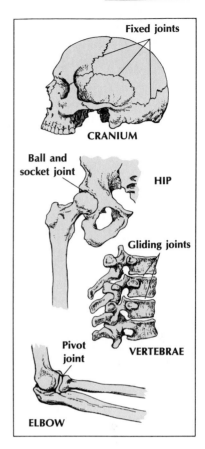

FIGURE 28-8. Bones of the skeleton are connected by different kinds of joints. Only fixed joints do not move.

Bones connected by fixed joints do not move.

1. support, protection, locomotion
2. An exoskeleton is external. An endoskeleton is internal.
3. Both bone and cartilage are parts of an endoskeleton. Bone is hard and contains minerals but cartilage is flexible and lacks minerals. Joints are points at which bones connect. Some bones are joined by ligaments, connective tissue fibers.

REVIEWING YOUR IDEAS

1. List three functions of a skeletal system.
2. Distinguish between exoskeleton and endoskeleton.
3. Distinguish between bone and cartilage, ligament and joint.

LOCOMOTION

Except for sponges, all animal phyla include adult animals which can move about. Most animals have muscle tissue, but some lack true skeletal systems. Animals move in many ways, each related to the animal's environment.

Most animals can actively secure food and escape from predators. These and other activities require movement of both individual body parts and the total animal. Movement of the total animal is called locomotion. In some invertebrates, movement is slow, although some mollusks such as the squid and octopus can move quickly. Arthropods and vertebrates are the most active of all animal forms.

Arthropods and vertebrates are the most active animals.

Arthropods and vertebrates can move easily and quickly, mainly because of their skeletal and muscular systems. A skeleton provides points of attachment for muscles. Thus, muscles and the skeleton work together to form a lever system which moves body parts and the whole body.

28:6 Locomotion: Simple Animals

Coelenterates exist in two forms, polyp and medusa (Section 5:2). *Hydra* is often a sessile polyp which can move by somersaulting (Figure 28-9). Medusas, such as jellyfish, float freely in the water or move by contracting their muscle cells, forcing water from the mouth to create a jet propulsion effect. The jellyfish moves in the direction opposite to that of the expelled water.

Earthworms are adapted for locomotion in soil. Their movement is controlled by two sets of muscles. One set shortens the body; the other set lengthens the body. Interaction of these two sets of muscles causes movement. In addition, bristles called **setae** (SEE tee) extend from each segment of an earthworm. With setae a worm "grasps" the soil, resulting in better movement. Some aquatic annelids such as *Nereis* use their **parapods** (Section 15:7) for locomotion.

FIGURE 28-9. (a) *Hydra* can "somersault," placing tentacles down and lifting the body. (b) Setae extend from the segments of the earthworm. They aid in locomotion.

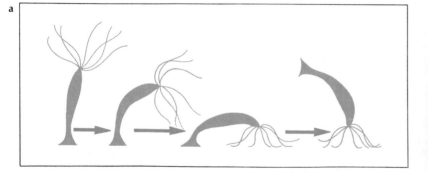

a

b

Runk/Schoenberger for Grant Heilman

Em Ahart for Tom Stack and Associates

Al Grotell

FIGURE 28-10. (a) Mollusks, in this case a clam, move on a muscular foot. (b) Echinoderms such as the starfish move with tube feet.

a

b

28:7 Locomotion: Mollusks and Echinoderms

Other means of locomotion in water occur in mollusks and echinoderms. For example, clams have a muscular foot which can be extended between the shells. To move, a clam extends the foot and anchors it in the mud. As the muscles in the foot contract, the clam is pulled forward.

In starfish, movement is controlled by a **water-vascular system** (Figure 28-11). Water is drawn into the animal through a small opening in the central disc and is passed to canals running along each "arm." Along each canal are hollow, muscular **tube feet** that open on the underside of the starfish. The bottom part of each tube foot is a sucker. The upper part of the tube foot is a bulb-shaped **ampulla.** The ampulla contains water which comes from the canal. When the ampullas contract, water is forced down, the tube feet lengthen, and the suckers attach to an object. When muscles in the walls of the tube feet contract, the feet shorten, the starfish moves forward, and water is forced back into the ampullas. Using its hundreds of tube feet, a starfish can creep along rocks and other solid objects. The water vascular system is also important in obtaining food (Section 25:5).

Starfish move by means of a water-vascular system.

FIGURE 28-11. (a) The water-vascular system controls movement of a starfish. Muscle contraction and water pressure cause the tube feet to act as suction cups. (b) Notice the many tube feet that cover the animal's ventral side.

a

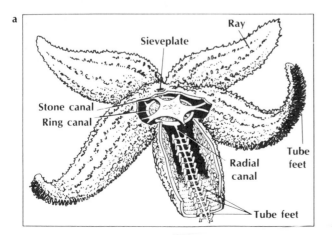

Ray

Sieveplate

Stone canal

Ring canal

Radial canal

Tube feet

Tube feet

b

Tube feet

Brian Parker for Tom Stack and Associates

FIGURE 28-12. Movement in vertebrates and arthropods is controlled by muscles that work in pairs. Contraction of the biceps muscle bends the elbow joint. Contraction of the triceps straightens the arm. While one muscle is contracted, the other is relaxed.

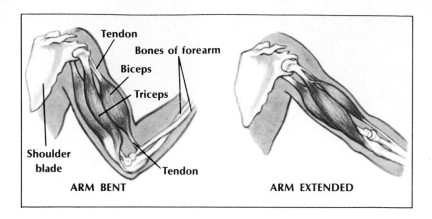

28:8 Locomotion: Vertebrates and Arthropods

Muscles and skeleton work together to provide movement.

Muscles are specialized tissues which can contract. Because certain muscles in vertebrates and arthropods are attached to the skeleton, locomotion in these animals is caused by the interaction of the muscular and skeletal systems.

Most muscles attached to bones have a point of origin and a point of insertion.

In vertebrates, most muscles are attached to bones by tough connective tissues called **tendons** (TEN dunz). The muscles are attached to bones at two different sites. During contraction, one end of the muscle and what it is attached to do not move. This attachment site is called the **point of origin.** The other end of the muscle and what it is attached to move when the muscle contracts. This attachment site is called the **point of insertion.** Attachment of a muscle to two sites is necessary for movement.

Muscles that cause locomotion work in pairs in vertebrates. For example, in humans the biceps (BI seps) and triceps (TRI seps) muscles work together. One end of the biceps muscle is attached to the top of the humerus (HYEWM uh rus), the upper arm bone (the point of origin). The other end of the biceps is attached to the radius (RAYD ee us), the larger of the two lower arm bones (the point of insertion). The biceps is called a **flexor** (FLEK sor) because it causes the bending (flexing) of a joint. When the biceps contracts, a force is exerted across the pivot joint of the elbow which causes the arm to bend. In order for the arm to bend, the triceps must relax or extend.

A flexor is a muscle which bends a joint.

To straighten the arm, the process is reversed. The triceps muscle links the back of the humerus with the ulna (UL nuh), the smaller of the lower arm bones. As the triceps contracts, it pulls the ulna, and at the same time the biceps relaxes and the arm straightens (Figure 28-12). The triceps is called an **extensor** (ihk STEN sur) because it causes the straightening (extension) of a joint. What are the points of origin and insertion of the triceps?

An extensor is a muscle which straightens a joint.

point of origin—humerus; point of insertion—ulna

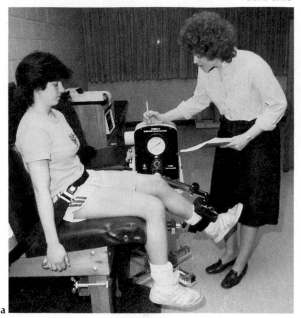

a   b

Other pairs of skeletal muscles in the body result in the movement of individual parts. Coordinated movement of several bones results in locomotion of the animal.

Besides bending or straightening a joint, paired muscles are important in another way. No muscle is ever completely relaxed; both muscles of a pair are always slightly contracted whether or not a movement is taking place. This condition results in **muscle tone** which provides enough contraction of the muscles to support the body. Also, muscle tone keeps the muscles ready for quick contractions. Tetanus (TET nus) is a disease in which some body muscles are in complete and continuous contraction (Section 19:2).

The strength and size of skeletal muscles may be increased by physical training. Greater strength develops as the mass of muscles increases and nervous control of the muscles improves. Strengthening seems to depend upon how much tension is placed on muscles during exercise. Increase in size of muscles depends upon repeated contractions of a muscle. The "pumping" action involved in weight training leads to an increase in the size of muscles. Are large muscles important in all sports?

In arthropods muscles are attached to the inside surface of the exoskeleton. Their muscles work in opposition to one another as in vertebrates. Contraction of one muscle exerts a pull on the exosksleton which results in the bending of a joint and a movement. When this muscle relaxes and the opposing muscle contracts, an opposite movement occurs.

FIGURE 28-13. (a) Physical training can increase muscle strength. Here an athlete is having her leg strength measured. (b) Conditioning also adds to muscle tone and flexibility.

FIGURE 28-14. In arthropods, pairs of muscles are attached to the interior surface of the exoskeleton. As in vertebrates, arthropod muscles work in opposition to bend and extend joints.

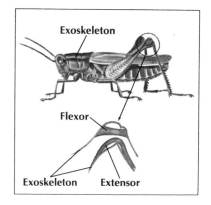

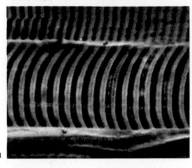 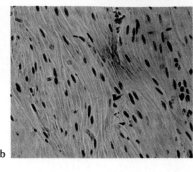 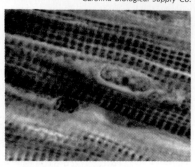

a   b   c

FIGURE 28-15. The three types of vertebrate muscle are (a) striated, (b) smooth, and (c) cardiac.

28:9 Types of Vertebrate Muscles

Of the three types of vertebrate muscles, the most important in terms of locomotion is **striated** (STRI ayt ud) **muscle** (Figure 28-15). Striated muscles are so named because of their striped appearance when viewed with a microscope. Separate striated muscle cells and their membranes are not easily visible. Each cell is called a **fiber** and contains many nuclei. Striated muscles are often called **skeletal muscles** because they are attached to the bones. Striated muscles are the muscles which move the body, Also, they are **voluntary muscles** because they can be controlled at will.

A skeletal muscle cell is stimulated by one nerve. A nerve impulse causes the muscle cell to respond. When the impulse stops, the muscle cell relaxes.

As well as muscles for locomotion, vertebrates have muscles for other functions. **Smooth,** or **nonstriated muscle,** moves many of the internal parts of the body. Smooth muscle is made up of visible, tapered cells, each with a nucleus. Smooth muscles are called **involuntary muscles** because an animal cannot control the activities of these muscles at will. Smooth muscles make up the walls of the hollow organs of the body, such as those of the alimentary canal (Section 25:4). Blood vessels also have a layer of smooth muscle. Contraction and relaxation of these muscles can regulate the diameter of the organs or vessels. Peristalsis (Section 25:8) is caused by smooth muscle contractions.

Smooth muscle cells are controlled by a pair of nerves (Section 30:12). One nerve causes contraction; the other nerve causes relaxation. Smooth muscles contract less forcefully and somewhat more slowly than skeletal muscles and are not involved in locomotion.

Cardiac (KAHRD ee ak) **muscle** makes up the heart. Cardiac muscle is similar to striated muscle in that both have striped fibers. However, its fibers, unlike those of striated muscle, are branched. Cardiac muscle is similar to smooth muscle in that it is an involuntary muscle and it is controlled by two nerves.

Striated muscles move the bones and are voluntary.

A skeletal muscle cell is stimulated by one nerve.

Smooth muscles move many of the internal parts of the body and are involuntary.

Smooth muscle is controlled by a pair of nerves.

The heart is composed of cardiac muscle.

28:10 Contraction of Vertebrate Skeletal Muscle

The fibers of a skeletal muscle are closely packed together, and separate cells are not easily seen. Each cylindrical fiber is made up of smaller units called **fibrils** (FIBE rulz). Fibrils are composed of **microfilaments** (Section 5:12), more simply called **filaments** (Figure 28-16). The arrangement of filaments gives striated muscle its striped appearance. There are two kinds of filaments. The thicker filaments are made of the protein **myosin** (MI uh sun), and the thinner ones are made of **actin** (AK tun). The myosin filaments have bridges that may link the two kinds of proteins together. Actin is attached to crossbands called **Z-lines.**

Electron microscope studies and experiments have led to a hypothesis to explain striated muscle contraction. This hypothesis is called the **sliding filament hypothesis** (Figure 28-17). A fiber receives a nerve impulse which begins a series of changes. ATP binds with myosin, and the bridges of myosin "hook" into special sites on the actin filaments. Calcium must be present for the bridges to "hook" onto the actin. The chemical energy of the ATP is then transformed to mechanical energy which moves the

Striated muscle is composed of fibers which are, in turn, composed of fibrils. Fibrils are composed of filaments containing actin and myosin.

Fibers are surrounded by a cell membrane called the sarcolemma. The unit of muscle between Z-lines is a sarcomere.

Skeletal muscular contraction is explained by the sliding filament hypothesis.

The outside of a muscle fiber has a high concentration of calcium ions and is positive with respect to the inside. Nerve stimulation results in an influx of calcium ions which are distributed through the fiber by a network of tubules. The influx results in a reversal of polarity necessary for contraction of the fibrils in a fiber.

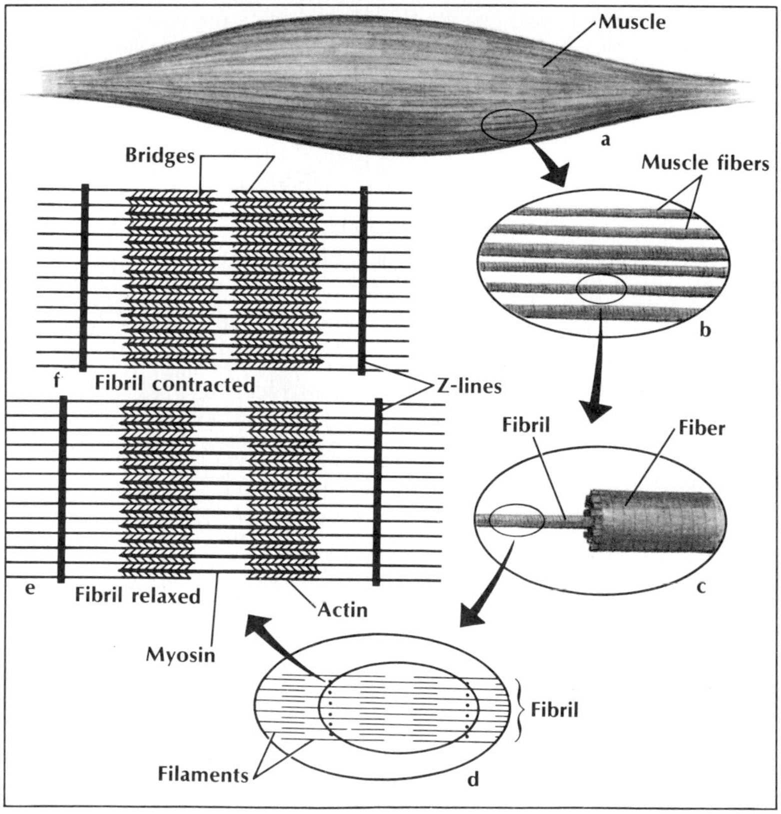

FIGURE 28-16. (a) Striated muscle is composed of (b) fibers that are made up of (c) fibrils. (d) Fibrils are made of two different kinds of filaments—actin and myosin. (e and f) In muscle contraction, filaments slide over each other.

actin filament. After moving the actin, the bridges break and reform at other places on the actin. A series of these small moves causes the actin and myosin filaments to slide over one another. The filaments themselves do not contract, but the filaments sliding over each other causes the muscle fiber to shorten.

During contraction, actin and myosin slide over one another.

Once an impulse reaches a muscle fiber there is an **all-or-none response.** That is, either the muscle fiber contracts fully or it does not contract at all; there is no partial contraction for a given fiber. Also, all contractions are of the same intensity. How, then, can a muscle contract to a greater or lesser degree? The number of fibers which contract at one time determines the strength of the contraction of the whole muscle. The greater the number of fibers which contract, the greater the contraction of the muscle as a whole.

Strength of a muscular contraction depends on the number of fibers contracting at one time.

The all-or-none response can also explain muscle tone. The nervous system constantly sends out messages of which you are not aware. These messages keep some fibers in each muscle "ready to go" (relaxed), and some fibers contracted. A muscle fiber must undergo a short recovery period after it contracts before it can contract again. The nerves constantly cause different fibers to contract so that while some fibers are contracting, others are recovering. Thus, some fibers will always be able to contract, and the muscle as a whole is always prepared for a complete contraction. Why is constant readiness of a muscle for contraction important? It is protective in terms of quick responses to stimuli.

Relaxation of fibers involves the joining of additional ATP to the actin-myosin complex. In death, this ATP is not available. The muscles remain in a contracted state, rigor mortis.

28:11 Energy for Skeletal Muscle Contraction

Energy is required for the contraction of muscles. The energy needed for muscle contraction is made available in several ways, depending on muscle activity.

During rest or very light activity, ATP is produced in muscle cells by aerobic respiration. Some of the ATP being produced this way is immediately used for muscle contraction. The remaining ATP is stored in the muscle cells either as ATP itself or as another compound, creatine phosphate (KREE uh teen · FAHS fayt) (CP), that can be converted to ATP quickly. CP is formed when molecules of ATP "donate" high-energy phosphate groups to molecules of a compound called creatine. As muscles become more active, the energy stored in CP can be used. CP changes to creatine and the high-energy phosphate produced combines with ADP to form ATP. The energy in the ATP can then be used for muscle contraction.

During prolonged or heavy exercise, the supplies of stored energy (both ATP and CP) are quickly used. Even though the heartbeat and breathing rates are increased during heavy exercise, not enough oxygen is delivered to muscle cells for aerobic respiration to continue. When not enough oxygen is present, the

FIGURE 28-17. ATP produced in muscle cells can be used or stored as ATP itself, but most of it is stored as creatine phosphate, CP. ATP can be produced quickly from the CP when needed (shown in red).

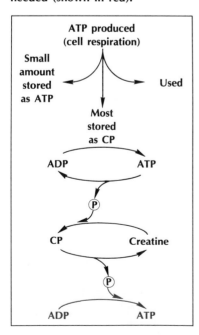

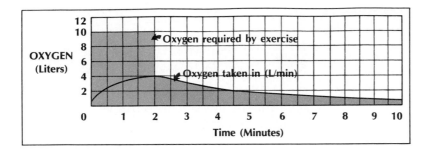

FIGURE 28-18. When more oxygen is used than is available, the result is "oxygen debt." This graph shows the oxygen required by two minutes of heavy exercise (blue) and the amount taken in during the two minutes (the amount under the black line). The green portion shows the "oxygen debt," the amount required after exercise has stopped to return the body to normal.

muscle cells switch to anaerobic respiration. During anaerobic respiration, glycogen stored in muscles is converted to lactic acid, and ATP is produced in the process (Section 4:9). Thus, energy is available for muscle contraction from anaerobic respiration.

After strenuous activity stops, heavy breathing continues. When enough oxygen is present, aerobic respiration can begin again. Some lactic acid in muscles is converted to carbon dioxide and water by this aerobic respiration. The amount of oxygen needed to remove the lactic acid from muscle cells is known as the "oxygen debt." The more lactic acid present, the greater the oxygen debt.

The lactic acid in muscle cells that is not aerobically broken down moves into the blood and is carried to the liver. In the liver it is converted to glycogen using ATP energy in the process.

Muscles switch to anaerobic respiration during heavy exercise.

The oxygen debt is "repaid" as lactic acid is converted to carbon dioxide and water.

REVIEWING YOUR IDEAS

4. What is locomotion?
5. What is muscle? Distinguish between voluntary and involuntary muscles.
6. List three kinds of muscles.
7. What is the name of the hypothesis which explains how muscles contract?
8. List three ways in which energy becomes available for muscle contraction.

4. Locomotion is the movement of the entire animal.
5. A muscle is a tissue specialized for locomotion. Voluntary muscles can be controlled; involuntary cannot.
6. striated, smooth, cardiac
7. sliding filament hypothesis
8. Energy is made available from ATP produced by aerobic respiration, from creatine phosphate, and from anaerobic respiration.

CHAPTER REVIEW

SUMMARY

1. In many animals, skeletal systems provide support, protection, and locomotion.

2. Arthropods have a rigid exoskeleton subdivided by soft joints.

3. Partly because they have exoskeletons, the growth and size of arthropods are limited.

4. Vertebrates have an endoskeleton composed of cartilage and/or bone.

5. Bones are specialized for support, protection, and movement.

6. Vertebrates are not as limited in growth and size as are arthropods.

7. Bone is a living tissue hardened by calcium compounds. Bone replaces cartilage or other tissues.

All Chapter Review answers and additional chapter teaching suggestions are provided in the Teacher's Guide at the front of this text.

CHAPTER REVIEW

8. Many bones are held together by ligaments at the joints. There are different kinds of joints. Most joints are specialized for certain types of movement.

9. Most animals lacking a skeletal system live in water, and many move slowly.

10. In arthropods and vertebrates, skeletal and muscle systems work together to cause locomotion. Muscles work in pairs to move the skeleton. When one muscle of a pair contracts, the other relaxes.

11. The three kinds of vertebrate muscle are striated, smooth, and cardiac. Striated muscle is important in moving skeletal parts.

12. The sliding filament hypothesis explains how striated muscles might contract.

13. ATP for muscle contraction may be produced by aerobic or anaerobic respiration. Energy in muscle cells is stored in ATP and creatine phosphate. CP can be used in the formation of ATP because CP changes to creatine and the high-energy phosphates produced in this process combine with molecules of ADP.

LANGUAGE OF BIOLOGY

actin
all-or-none response
ampulla
bone
cardiac muscle
cartilage
endoskeleton
exoskeleton
extensor
flexor
joint
ligament
marrow
molting
muscle

muscle tone
myosin
ossification
osteocyte
point of insertion
point of origin
skeletal system
sliding filament
  hypothesis
smooth muscle
striated muscle
tendon
tube feet
water-vascular
  system

CHECKING YOUR IDEAS

On a separate paper, indicate whether each of the following statements is true or false. Do not write in this book.

1. Bone contains living cells.
2. An exoskeleton limits an arthropod's size.
3. Skeletal muscles are involuntary muscles.
4. Both mollusks and echinoderms have a water-vascular system.
5. The knee is a pivot joint.
6. Muscles are attached to bone by ligaments.
7. Most bones form from cartilage.
8. A flexor bends a joint.
9. During heavy exercise, skeletal muscles undergo anaerobic respiration.
10. When skeletal muscle contracts, actin and myosin filaments get shorter.

EVALUATING YOUR IDEAS

1. Why do aquatic animals have less need for support than land animals?
2. What are the advantages and disadvantages of an exoskeleton?
3. Why are joints necessary in animals with an exoskeleton?
4. How do bones provide greater specialization than an exoskeleton?
5. How are the problems of size and growth in arthropods overcome by vertebrates?
6. How are bones formed?
7. Describe the internal parts of bones and the function of each part.
8. Distinguish between the types of human joints. Why do you think the skull has several bones joined by fixed joints rather than just one bone?
9. Explain locomotion in a jellyfish, earthworm, clam, and starfish. How does locomotion in these animals compare with locomotion in insects and vertebrates?

CHAPTER REVIEW

10. How are most muscles attached to bones? Distinguish between point of origin and point of insertion.

11. Explain how the human arm is bent and straightened.

12. What is muscle tone? Why is muscle tone necessary?

13. Distinguish among the three types of vertebrate muscles. Where is each located?

14. Explain the sliding filament hypothesis.

15. What is the all-or-none response? How can muscles be contracted to a greater or lesser degree?

16. How is creatine phosphate produced in skeletal muscle? When is it used?

17. When is anaerobic respiration used to provide energy for contraction of skeletal muscle? Why?

18. What is an oxygen debt?

Occasionally questions are added to the *Applying Your Ideas* that require students to use information they have learned from previous chapters. Those questions are marked with asterisks and chapter references.

APPLYING YOUR IDEAS

1. Why do you think animals without skeletal systems are small?

2. Why do you think arthropods are the largest phylum of animals?

3. What adaptive features do the bones of birds have? Why are these adaptive?

4. Explain why the femur is thick whereas foot bones are thin.

5. Knee injuries are common in football players. Explain why these injuries often occur.

6. How is the slow contraction of smooth muscle tissue adaptive?

7. Compare the amount of ATP energy produced by aerobic and anaerobic respiration in skeletal muscle. *Chapter 4

8. How does locomotion in animals differ from locomotion in protozoans? *Chapter 18

9. Why can skeletal muscles be controlled by just one nerve rather than two?

EXTENDING YOUR IDEAS

1. After studying the procedure from library sources, mount the bones of a small animal to make a complete skeleton.

2. Muscles can become fatigued. Place your hand on a flat surface, fingers separated in a comfortable position. Begin tapping your index finger quite rapidly. Continue for as long as possible. What happens?

3. Investigate the processes involved in bone repair after fractures occur.

4. Find out about a molecule called myoglobin and its role in muscles.

SUGGESTED READINGS

Angier, Natalie, "How Fast? How High? How Far?" *Discover*, November, 1981.

Buller, A. J. and N. P. Buller, *The Contractile Behavior of Mammalian Skeletal Muscle*, 2nd ed. Oxford Biology Reader. London, Oxford University Press, 1980.

Harrington, W. F., *Muscle Contraction.* Carolina Biology Reader. Burlington, NC, Carolina Biological Supply Co., 1981.

Hecht, Annabel, "Hocus Pocus As Applied to Arthritis." *FDA Consumer*, September, 1980.

Lenihan, John, *Human Engineering: The Body Re-examined.* New York, George Braziller, Inc., 1975.

Pritchard, J. J., *Bones.* Carolina Biology Reader, Rev. ed. Burlington, NC, Carolina Biological Supply Co., 1978.

Ryder, Henry W., et al., "Future Performance in Foot-racing." *Scientific American*, June, 1976.

Additional student readings and suggested teacher readings are provided in the Teacher's Guide.

Many functions of animals are controlled by chemicals. The chemicals are transported throughout the body by blood or other fluids. Milk production is one function under chemical control in mammals. Prolactin, a chemical produced by a gland near the brain of the mother dog stimulates the production of milk for these pups. How is the making of chemicals controlled? What might happen if a chemical imbalance occurred?

Introduction and suggested demonstration: An excellent project to accompany this chapter is testing the effect of thyroxine on tadpole metamorphosis. Prepare a stock solution of thyroxine by dissolving 10 mg of thyroxine in 5 mL of 10% sodium hydroxide and diluting to a volume of 1 L with distilled water. This solution is a concentration of 1:100 000. Refrigerate the stock solution until needed, at which time the stock can be diluted to make solutions from 1 part per million to 1 part per ten million. Obtain tadpoles in the early hind limb stage. House tadpoles in bowls or flasks containing thyroxine solutions of varying concentration. One set of tadpoles should be kept in water without thyroxine as a control. Tadpoles should be fed every other day hard boiled egg yolk or partly cooked lettuce or spinach. Remove uneaten food to prevent bacterial contamination. Change the solution of all tadpoles once a week. Have students record data about length of hind limbs and tail, time of appearance of forelimbs, and changes in body shape. As an alternate to thyroxine, iodine solution can be used. Prepare a stock solution of 0.1 mg crystalline iodine dissolved in 5 mL of 95% alcohol and dilute to 1 L with distilled water (1:10 000). Prepare further dilutions and proceed as above.

Chapter

29

CHEMICAL CONTROL

Chapter 29 explores the action of hormones in humans and other animals.

Animals are adapted for life in certain environments. But, no environment stays the same all the time. The most successful animals are those able to make the proper responses to stimuli.

Stimuli may come from outside or inside the body. For example, outside stimuli include a sudden drop in temperature or a baseball speeding toward you. You may respond by shivering or ducking your head. Internal stimuli include hunger pangs or a high level of carbon dioxide in the blood. Responses to these stimuli include eating and a speeding up of the heartbeat and breathing rates.

Often, stimuli and responses are not obvious. You may not be aware of many changes, especially internal ones. Some responses, such as growth, occur over a long period of time.

All these responses involve the smooth coordination of the many systems of the body. All body systems working together result in homeostasis (Section 1:6), the balance of the internal operation of an organism, regardless of external changes. In this way, an organism can survive when the environment changes.

Control of responses in animals may be chemical or nervous. The effects of chemical control are discussed in this chapter. Nervous control is discussed in Chapter 30.

GOAL: You will gain an understanding of chemical control systems and how they direct many body functions of animals.

Animals may respond to changes in their environment.

Chemical and nervous control systems regulate responses to stimuli.

ROLES OF HUMAN HORMONES

Most often, chemical control is directed by complex molecules called **hormones** (Section 22:9). Some hormones are made up of proteins, polypeptides, or amino acids. Others are made up of certain lipids called **steroids** (STIHR oydz). Hormones are transported throughout the body by blood or other fluids and stimulate organs to respond in certain ways.

Steroids have in their structure a series of interlocking carbon rings. Besides certain hormones, cholesterol, bile salts, and vitamin D are steroids. Students may be familiar with the controversy surrounding the use of anabolic steroids by athletes.

551

FIGURE 29-1. Locations of the major human endocrine glands are shown for males and females.

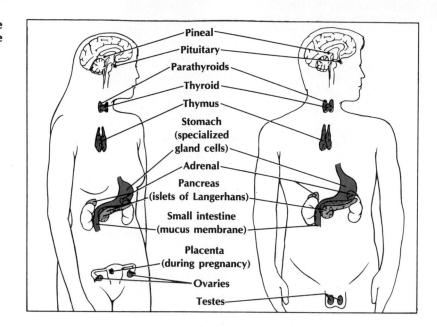

Pineal
Pituitary
Parathyroids
Thyroid
Thymus
Stomach (specialized gland cells)
Adrenal
Pancreas (islets of Langerhans)
Small intestine (mucus membrane)
Placenta (during pregnancy)
Ovaries
Testes

Hormones are usually produced by and secreted directly from endocrine glands.

In complex animals, hormones usually are produced by **endocrine** (EN duh krun) **glands.** Endocrine glands are ductless, so they pour their secretions directly into blood. (Other kinds of glands, such as salivary glands, have ducts.) The study of endocrine glands and hormones is called **endocrinology** (en duh krih NAHL uh jee). Humans have many endocrine glands which produce hormones that regulate their body functions. Information on some of the endocrine glands and the hormones they secrete follows.

29:1 Islets of Langerhans

Glucose travels through the bloodstream to all the cells of the body and is used as an energy source. Proper health depends on a regulated amount of glucose in the blood. A person with too much glucose in the blood may have **diabetes mellitus** (Section 8:9). Persons with diabetes often are very thirsty, and they urinate frequently. So much glucose passes through the kidneys that all the glucose cannot be returned to the blood. Thus, diabetics when untreated excrete a lot of glucose in their urine. Physicians can diagnose diabetes by analyzing urine for glucose.

In diabetes mellitus, there is too much sugar in the blood.

by Frederick Banting and C.H. Best

It was learned in the late 1800's that removal of the pancreases of dogs causes diabetes. Because the digestive functions of the pancreas were already known (Section 25:10), biologists realized that the pancreas must have more than one role. Microscopic study of the pancreas showed two different types of cells. One type, greater in number, secretes digestive enzymes. The other cells had an unknown function and were named the **islets** (I lutz) **of Langerhans** (LAHNG ur hahnz).

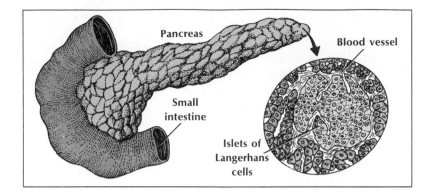

FIGURE 29-2. Islet cells in the pancreas secrete insulin which controls blood sugar level.

Scientists thought that islet cells might affect the glucose content of the blood by secreting a hormone into the bloodstream. This belief was proven correct when a chemical made by the islet cells, a protein called **insulin,** was taken from animal pancreases. When insulin was injected into dogs whose pancreases had been removed, the symptoms of diabetes disappeared. Insulin is produced only by one type of islet cell, the **beta cells.**

The islet cells of the pancreas produce insulin.

Insulin controls the level of sugar in blood. After a meal, insulin causes excess blood glucose to change to glycogen in the liver and muscle cells. Insulin also causes some excess glucose to be changed to fats and increases the permeability of cell membranes to glucose. These processes reduce the blood sugar level.

Insulin regulates the level of sugar in the blood.

One form of diabetes occurs when beta cells become destroyed and not enough insulin is produced. Without enough insulin, excess glucose cannot be changed to glycogen or fats, and glucose cannot be moved out of the blood effectively. This form of diabetes usually develops in people under twenty years of age. Recent studies suggest that a virus may destroy the beta cells, especially in people with certain harmful alleles (Section 8:9). People with this form of diabetes take regular injections of insulin obtained from animals. The animal insulin is slightly different in chemical structure from human insulin, but it works in reducing the level of glucose in human blood. Human insulin, which can be produced by recombinant DNA techniques (Section 13:19), may eventually be used instead of animal insulin. In either case, injections of insulin do not cure diabetes, but they prevent some of its symptoms.

In one form of diabetes, beta cells are destroyed and not enough insulin is produced.

This form is known as juvenile-onset diabetes and accounts for less than 10% of all cases.

Another form of diabetes usually occurs in people who are over forty years old and overweight. This type is the more common form. The beta cells are not destroyed and enough insulin is produced. However, glucose does not easily pass through the membranes of the muscle and liver cells, and thus, builds up in the blood. Diet, exercise, and certain drugs have been shown to improve uptake of glucose by muscle and liver cells and reduce the level of glucose in the blood.

This form, maturity-onset diabetes, develops slowly. The problem seems to arise from defects in target organs; i.e., abnormality in receptors which facilitate entry of glucose.

In the more common form of diabetes, enough insulin is produced but glucose does not easily pass into liver and muscle cells.

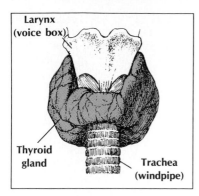

FIGURE 29-3. The thyroid gland is located on the trachea just below the voice box. The thyroid gland secretes thyroxine.

Iodine is an essential part of thyroxine.

29:2 Thyroid Gland

On the trachea in the neck region of humans is a small, butterfly-shaped structure called the **thyroid** (THI royd) **gland** (Figure 29-3). This gland secretes a hormone called **thyroxine** (thi RAHK sun). Thyroxine is secreted from the thyroid gland into the bloodstream and is carried to all body cells. In the cells, thyroxine speeds up the rate of metabolism. Too little thyroxine decreases the metabolic rate. Decreased metabolism may lead to obesity (Section 25:7). Too little thyroxine can cause several diseases. If this deficiency occurs in early childhood, a disease called **cretinism** (KREET un ihz um) results. The child develops into a malformed, mentally retarded dwarf called a **cretin.** Cretinism can be avoided by supplying thyroxine during childhood.

A disease related to the thyroid gland is goiter. **Goiter** is an enlargement of the thyroid gland itself and results in an increase in the size of the entire throat and neck. In one form of goiter, thyroid glands become enlarged because of a lack of iodine in the diet. Iodine is an important part of thyroxine. When little or no iodine is present, the thyroid gland cannot produce thyroxine. The lack of thyroxine affects cell metabolism.

In the past, certain geographic regions seemed to be "goiter belts." Many cases of goiter developed in these areas because food there was low in iodine. Persons living close to coastal areas usually did not get goiters because their diet included fresh seafood, rich in iodine. Today, iodized salt is sold. This salt provides enough iodine for normal production of thyroxine. As a result, this form of goiter is rare now in the United States.

Production of too much thyroxine results in rapid metabolism and can cause diseases also. Symptoms may include weight loss, irritability, protruding eyes, and nervousness. These symptoms can sometimes be corrected by removing or destroying part of the thyroid gland.

FIGURE 29-4. (a) Using radioactive iodine tracers, scans of the thyroid can be done to detect thyroid disease. (b) A scan of a healthy thyroid gland shows a small gland (dotted areas) whereas (c) the scan of the diseased thyroid shows a much enlarged gland.

a

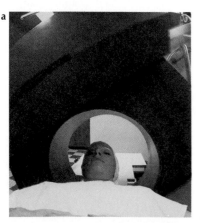

Dan McCoy from Rainbow

b

Medical Center Hospital, Chillicothe, Ohio

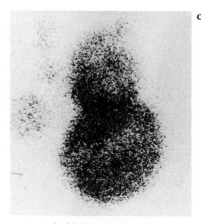

c

Medical Center Hospital, Chillicothe, Ohio

Increased blood pressure and faster heartbeat provide the tissues with a greater supply of food and oxygen. Increased blood sugar provides a greater source of potential energy. Increased metabolic rate accelerates energy production.

29:3 Adrenal Glands

On top of each kidney is a small **adrenal** (uh DREEN ul) **gland.** The outer part of this gland is the **adrenal cortex.** It differs in both structure and function from the inner part, the **adrenal medulla.**

The main hormone of the adrenal medulla is called **adrenaline** (uh DREN ul un), or **epinephrine** (ep uh NEF run). When the body is under stress, adrenaline helps it respond and be ready for most any activity. Adrenaline increases the heartbeat rate and blood pressure. It also causes blood sugar level to rise and metabolism to occur more rapidly. More blood is sent to critical places such as the brain, heart, lungs, and skeletal muscles. How is each response adaptive?

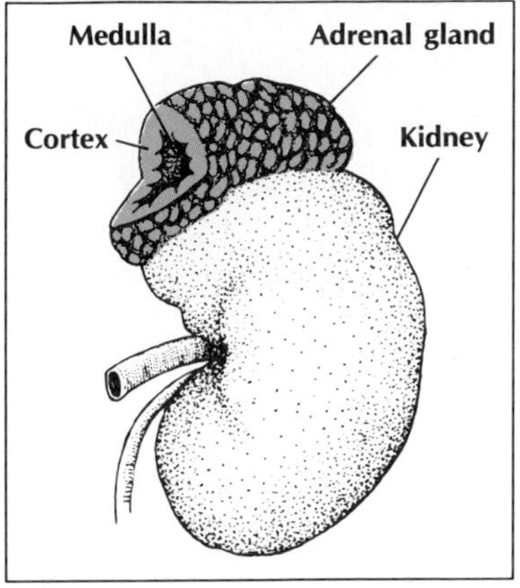

These activities are important during stress situations, but a person can live without an adrenal medulla. These same reactions can be caused by the nervous system. Also, cells which make up the adrenal medulla are more like nerve cells than gland cells. *These facts show a close relationship between the endocrine system and the nervous system.*

The adrenal cortex is truly an endocrine structure and, unlike the medulla, is needed for life. The cortex secretes several steroid hormones. **Aldosterone** (al DAWS tuh rohn) controls the salt level in blood by affecting absorption of sodium and potassium ions in the kidney. **Cortisol** (KORT uh zawl) causes the change of fats and proteins to glucose, which helps keep the right level of sugar in the blood. Cortisol and **cortisone** (KORT uh zohn) prevent inflammation. Cortisone in synthetic form is sometimes given to reduce the pain and swelling caused by diseases and injuries. These hormones also have a role in dealing with stress. They seem to take over after adrenaline has been secreted.

The adrenal cortex also secretes sex hormones in very small amounts. The majority of these hormones are **androgens** (AN druh junz), or male sex hormones. However, some **estrogens,** female sex hormones, are also produced.

FIGURE 29-5. The adrenal glands are located on top of the kidneys. The two parts of the adrenal gland, the medulla and cortex, secrete different hormones.

The effects of adrenaline can be duplicated by the nervous system.

Hormones from the adrenal cortex control salt balance and sugar level in the blood and prevent inflammation.

Other adrenal cortex hormones are androgens and estrogens.

The normal ranges are shown in parentheses.

DATE/TIME			DATE/TIME		
Na (136-145)	138.	meq/L	Na (136-145)	129.	meq/L
K (3.5-5.0)	4.5	meq/L	K (3.5-5.0)	6.1	meq/L
Cl (96-106)	104.	meq/L	Cl (96-106)	86.	meq/L
CO₂ (24-30)	25.	meq/l	CO₂ (24-30)	11.	meq/L

Kevin Fitzsimons   *Kevin Fitzsimons*

FIGURE 29-6. A kind of common adrenal gland malfunction called Addison's disease results in an imbalance of electrolytes (salts) in the body. (a) A printout of tests of normal blood shows sodium (Na), potassium (K), and chloride (Cl) all within normal ranges. (b) A printout of tests on blood from an Addison's patient shows an elevated potassium and lowered sodium and chloride levels.

a   b

FIGURE 29-7. Secondary sex traits can easily be seen in the plumage of birds. (a) Immature white ibis and (b) adult white ibis have very different plumage. The black wing tips of the male birds develop as the birds mature.

Estrogens start buildup of uterine tissue during the menstrual cycle and are responsible for secondary sexual characteristics in females.

Testosterone, an androgen, causes secondary sexual characteristics in males.

29:4 Gonads

Sex hormones are produced in large amounts by the **gonads,** the ovaries and testes. Follicle cells of the ovary release estrogens which start the buildup of uterine tissue during the menstrual cycle (Section 23:7). Estrogens also stimulate the development of secondary sexual characteristics in the female, such as enlargement of the breasts, broadening of the pelvis, and hair growth around the external reproductive organs and in the armpits. The onset of menstruation and the development of these secondary sex traits is called **puberty** (PYEW burt ee). During menopause (Section 23:7), the production of estrogens (and progesterone) decreases and menstrual cycles stop.

Androgens are secreted by the testes of a male. **Testosterone** (teh STAHS tuh rohn) and other androgens stimulate the formation of secondary sexual characteristics in males. At puberty, the external genitals enlarge and several other changes occur. The voice becomes deeper, and hair grows around the reproductive organs, in the armpits, and on the face. Fat formation decreases, and the body looks leaner. Lack of enough androgens may result in improper development of these secondary characteristics.

1. chemical and nervous
2. Hormones are regulator molecules produced in endocrine glands and transported by the blood.
3. An endocrine gland is ductless. Other kinds of glands have ducts.
4. thyroid — neck, thyroxine; islets of Langerhans — pancreas, insulin; adrenal cortex — on kidney, aldosterone, cortisol and cortisone; adrenal medulla — on kidney, adrenaline; ovaries — abdomen, estrogens; testes — scrotum, androgens

---

REVIEWING YOUR IDEAS

1. What two basic types of control systems are found among organisms?
2. What are hormones? Where are they produced in complex animals? How are they transported?
3. Distinguish between an endocrine gland and other glands.
4. Give the location of the following endocrine glands and list the hormone(s) which each produces: thyroid, islets of Langerhans, adrenal cortex, adrenal medulla, ovaries, and testes.

ENDOCRINE CONTROL

29:5 Pituitary Gland: Anterior Lobe

Located at the base of the brain is a tiny, three-lobed structure called the **pituitary gland.** The two major lobes are known as the **anterior pituitary** and the **posterior pituitary.** Many of the hormones produced by the anterior pituitary control the secretion of hormones from other endocrine glands and affect other body parts.

Two of the anterior pituitary hormones control the menstrual cycle in females. They are follicle-stimulating hormone (FSH) and leutenizing hormone (LH). FSH stimulates the ripening of eggs within the follicle of the ovary and causes the ovaries to secrete estrogen. LH starts ovulation and the conversion of the follicle to the corpus luteum. LH also causes the corpus luteum to secrete estrogen and progesterone.

FSH and LH also are produced by the pituitaries of males. In males, FSH stimulates production of sperm cells, and LH causes the release of androgens from the testes.

FSH and LH are chemically the same whether produced by males or females. However, they have different effects in males and females. These different results are due to the type of cell or tissue on which the hormone is acting, the **target organ** . Other evidence of the importance of the target is that most hormones work only on certain types of cells in the body. The same kind of hormone may be produced by different types of animals with different effects in each of them. *Therefore, the target organ is very important in determining the response.*

Anterior pituitary hormones affect other endocrine glands around the body. For example, the thyroid is controlled by a hormone called **thyroid-stimulating hormone (TSH).** The level of

The pituitary is also called the hypophysis. The anterior lobe is the adenohypophysis and the posterior lobe is the neurohypophysis.

The anterior pituitary gland secretes hormones, many of which control the activities of other endocrine glands.

FSH and LH control the menstrual cycle in females.

In males, FSH stimulates production of sperm cells, and LH causes the testes to release androgens.

The target organ is very important in determining a response.

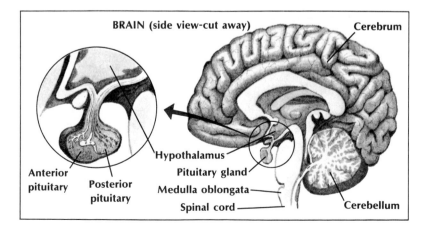

BRAIN (side view-cut away)   Cerebrum

Anterior pituitary   Posterior pituitary

Hypothalamus
Pituitary gland
Medulla oblongata
Spinal cord
Cerebellum

FIGURE 29-8. The pituitary gland is attached to the brain and is under the control of the hypothalamus. Many hormones secreted by the anterior lobe regulate functions of other endocrine glands.

FIGURE 29-9. (a) HGH deficiency in early childhood can result in dwarfism. (b) Excess HGH in childhood can result in giantism. This man is about 250 cm tall.

a

b

TSH controls the amount of thyroxine secreted by the thyroid.

TSH in the blood affects the amount of thyroxine secreted by the thyroid (Section 29:6). Another anterior pituitary hormone controls the adrenal cortex.

HGH influences the total growth of the body.

Excess HGH in adults causes acromegaly. This disease is characterized by an abnormal enlargement of the hands, feet, bones, and internal organs.

Some anterior pituitary hormones affect more than just a specific endocrine gland. For example, **human growth hormone (HGH)** influences the total growth of the body. Lack of enough HGH in early childhood can result in dwarfism or retarded growth (Figure 29-9). If too much HGH is made in childhood, giantism may result (Figure 29-9).

In 1970, scientists first made HGH in the laboratory. HGH is now being produced by recombinant DNA techniques. Soon, enough HGH may be available to treat children who do not produce enough of it, allowing these children to grow normally. HGH has other effects on the body and might also be used in other ways, including treatment of burns.

29:6 Feedback

The discovery of brain proteins over the past 20 years is making great changes in the study of brain chemistry (Section 30:14).

The hypothalamus secretes hormones which control the pituitary.

Because many pituitary hormones control other endocrine glands and body parts, the pituitary was once called the "master gland." Now it is known that the pituitary itself is under the control of hormones from the **hypothalamus,** a part of the brain near the pituitary. *This fact shows another close relationship between the endocrine system and the nervous system.*

Interaction of pituitary hormones with other endocrine glands usually involves a **feedback mechanism.** Control over other glands depends on information received from them. Control of the menstrual cycle (Section 23:7) is based on such a feedback mechanism.

Control of thyroxine production is another example of a feedback mechanism. Thyroxine circulates throughout the body in the bloodstream and reaches many tissues, including the hypothalamus. The hypothalamus contains cells sensitive to the amount of thyroxine in the blood. If the thyroxine level falls below normal, the hypothalamus secretes a hormone called a **releasing factor.** The releasing factor travels in the blood to the anterior pituitary and stimulates the anterior pituitary to secrete TSH. TSH is secreted into the blood and reaches the thyroid gland where it stimulates thyroxine production. If there is too much thyroxine in the blood, the hypothalamus stops secreting the releasing factor and the anterior pituitary decreases production of TSH (Figure 29-10). Thus, thyroxine production is decreased.

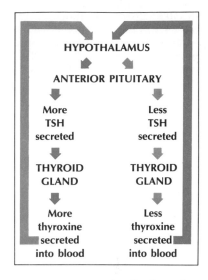

FIGURE 29-10. A feedback mechanism regulated by the hypothalamus maintains a certain amount of thyroxine in the blood.

C.H. Li discovered beta-lipotropin in 1964. Discoveries by Li and other researchers since the middle 1970s have shown that segments of beta-lipotropin are pharmacologically active. Endorphins and enkephalins (Section 30:14) are included among these active molecules.

PEOPLE IN BIOLOGY

In the 1930's, Chinese-born Choh Hao Li began the study of the chemistry and biology of anterior pituitary hormones. Throughout his years of research at the University of California, Berkeley, Li and his co-workers were either the first or among the first to isolate and identify the eight hormones secreted by the anterior pituitary.

(1913 -   )

Choh Hao Li

In more recent years, Dr. Li has concentrated on researching human growth hormone (HGH). In 1956, Li isolated HGH and later disclosed its complete structure. His research set the foundation for further research by other scientists into the use of HGH in helping children who lack the hormone to grow normally.

Li, who became an American citizen after receiving his Ph.D. at the University of California, Berkeley, is now the Director of the Hormone Research Laboratory of the University of California. He has won many awards and honors for his research including the National Award of the American Cancer Society (1971) and the Nichols Medal of the American Cancer Society (1979).

FIGURE 29-11. The posterior pituitary secretes vasopressin, which helps control water balance and blood pressure, and oxytocin, which causes labor contractions.

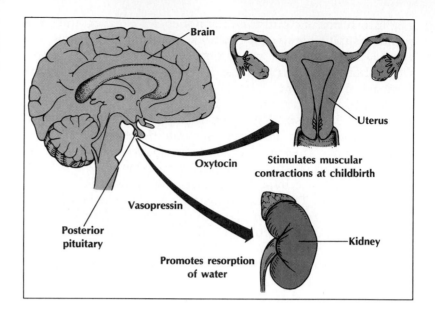

FIGURE 29-11. The posterior pituitary secretes vasopressin, which helps control water balance and blood pressure, and oxytocin, which causes labor contractions.

29:7 Pituitary Gland: Posterior Lobe

Oxytocin stimulates the contraction of uterine muscle during labor.

The posterior pituitary secretes two hormones, neither of which controls other endocrine glands. **Oxytocin** (ahk sih TOHS un) stimulates the contraction of uterine muscles and is secreted prior to childbirth. Oxytocin causes labor contractions (Section 24:7) and is sometimes injected to begin this process artificially.

Vasopressin regulates water balance control by the kidneys.

Vasopressin is a hormone which is involved in control of water balance by the kidneys (Section 27:11) and blood pressure. If too much vasopressin is present, the kidney tubules resorb too much water. The weight of the body becomes greater as more water is conserved. A lack of vasopressin prevents kidney tubules from resorbing water. As a result, the person urinates often and is always thirsty. This disease is known as **diabetes insipidus** (ihn SIHP ud us). It is named diabetes because of the frequent urination and thirst symptoms that it has in common with diabetes mellitus (Section 29:1). But in diabetes insipidus, there is no abnormal blood sugar level. The two diseases are related to two different hormones.

The endocrine system and nervous system are closely related.

Neither oxytocin nor vasopressin is produced by the posterior pituitary; they are only stored there. Both hormones are formed by the hypothalamus in the brain. In addition, cells of the posterior pituitary are more like nerve cells than endocrine cells. The production of hormones by the nervous tissue of the hypothalamus again is evidence of the *close link between the endocrine system and the nervous system*. You have seen many such lines of evidence in this chapter. Perhaps chemical and nervous control should not be considered as two separate systems. It might be better to think of chemical and nervous control as two divisions of the same system. In general, responses controlled by the endocrine system occur more slowly than those controlled by the nervous system. Table 29-1 lists the activities of many human hormones.

TABLE 29-1. SOME HUMAN HORMONES AND THEIR MAIN FUNCTIONS			
Hormone	Source	Location	Functions
THYROXINE	Thyroid gland	Neck	Regulates metabolic rate of body cells
PARATHORMONE	Parathyroid gland	On thyroid	Regulates calcium balance
INSULIN	Islets of Langerhans (beta cells)	Pancreas	Regulates level of sugar in blood
GLUCAGON	Islets of Langerhans (alpha cells)	Pancreas	Regulates level of sugar in blood
ADRENALINE	Adrenal medulla	On kidneys	Prepares body to cope with stress
ALDOSTERONE	Adrenal cortex	On kidneys	Regulates salt level in blood
CORTISOL	Adrenal cortex	On kidneys	Regulates level of sugar in blood Prevents inflammation
CORTISONE	Adrenal cortex	On kidneys	Prevents inflammation
ANDROGENS	Testes	In scrotum	Causes secondary sexual characteristics in males
ESTROGENS	Ovaries	In abdomen	Causes secondary sexual characteristics in females Prepares uterus for pregnancy
PROGESTERONE	Corpus luteum	In abdomen	Maintains uterus during pregnancy
FSH	Anterior pituitary	Base of brain	Causes maturation of egg in females Stimulates sperm production in males
LH	Anterior pituitary	Base of brain	Causes ovulation in females Causes release of androgens in males
TSH	Anterior pituitary	Base of brain	Stimulates thyroxine production
ACTH	Anterior pituitary	Base of brain	Stimulates release of adrenal cortex hormones
HGH	Anterior pituitary	Base of brain	Regulates growth of body
PROLACTIN	Anterior pituitary	Base of brain	Stimulates milk production
OXYTOCIN	Posterior pituitary	Base of brain	Stimulates contraction of uterine muscles
VASOPRESSIN	Posterior pituitary	Base of brain	Regulates water balance by kidneys
GASTRIN	Stomach cells	Stomach	Stimulates release of gastric juice
SECRETIN	Intestinal cells	Intestine	Stimulates release of pancreatic juice

29:8 Hormone Action

How hormones control metabolism is not completely understood. As hormones circulate in the blood, they pass by many types of tissues. Yet, most hormones cause a change in only one type of tissue. How does the hormone "know" its target organ? Once it has "spotted" the target organ, how does the hormone cause a change? Biologists have begun to make some progress in answering these questions.

Cell membranes are thought to have **receptors** on their outside surfaces. Different tissues have different receptors. Most hormones seem to "recognize" only certain receptors. Thus, each hormone can "identify" its target organ. Once the target organ is identified, the hormone exerts its effect.

A hormone identifies its target organ by recognizing a specific receptor on the cell membrane.

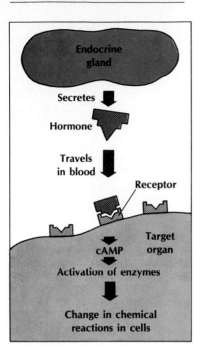

FIGURE 29-12. Some hormones act by causing the production of a second messenger, such as cyclic AMP (cAMP), which causes changes in a cell's reactions.

Steroid hormones are thought to cause changes by activating genes in the target cells.

Prostaglandins may play a role in regulating responses to other hormones.

The second messenger hypothesis resulted mainly from work done by Earl Sutherland, Jr.

A hormone does not cause its change directly. Rather, it causes chemical changes within the target cell which result in some effect. Some hormones composed of amino acids or proteins are thought to change cell enzyme activity and cause production of a **second messenger** compound in the target cell. (The hormone itself is the first messenger.) This compound does the work of the hormone by causing changes within the cell. This idea is called the **second messenger hypothesis.**

The second messenger hypothesis resulted from the study of the effects of adrenaline on glycogen stored in the liver. It was known that adrenaline causes glycogen to be converted to glucose. The glucose then can be used to provide a "burst of energy." Scientists found that adrenaline causes the formation of **cyclic AMP** (cAMP), a compound made from ATP. Cyclic AMP is a second messenger that causes reactions which lead to the formation of several enzymes. One of these enzymes begins the breakdown of glycogen.

It is now known the cAMP is a second messenger in many types of tissues and that several hormones cause cAMP to be produced. *The effect of cAMP depends on the type of cell in which it is formed.* For example, cAMP causes synthesis of certain steroid hormones in the adrenal cortex. In the kidneys, cAMP affects water transport. It also affects the breakdown of fatty acids in the liver and muscle cells. Second messengers other than cAMP are now thought to exist.

A steroid hormone does not cause formation of a second messenger. Instead, it combines with a receptor inside the cell and moves into the nucleus. There, it is thought to "switch on" a gene which has been inactive (Section 9:12). When the gene becomes active, it guides the formation of a protein which changes the cell's chemistry. The type of change depends on the hormone and the cells of the target organ.

Most animal tissues produce substances called prostaglandins. **Prostaglandins** are a special group of hormones. They are made from fatty acids (Section 3:14) and have many effects in the body. Some prostaglandins seem to play a role in how much cAMP is produced by target cells. After a hormone has combined with receptors on a target cell, the target cell releases more prostaglandins. The prostaglandins, in turn, may increase or decrease the production of cAMP. Thus, prostaglandins, as well as other hormones, may play a role in the target organ's response.

Activity of prostaglandins may occur outside the cells in which they are produced. Many travel in the blood to other tissues. Prostaglandins are involved in a variety of activities, such as controlling smooth muscle contraction, regulating pulse rate and blood pressure, causing swelling, and making the body aware of pain. One of the reasons aspirin relieves swelling and pain is that it decreases production of prostaglandins.

George Porter for Photo Researchers

Alvin E. Staffan

a

b

Robert Fridenstine

Roger K. Burnard

c

d

FIGURE 29-13. Thyroxine is the main hormone responsible for salamander metamorphosis from (a) larva to (b) adult. Metamorphosis in insects, such as the Cecropia moth, involves ecdyson and juvenile hormone. (c) Larvae and (d) adult moth are shown.

29:9 Hormones and Metamorphosis

Chemical control by means of hormones is not unique to humans. Many of the hormones discussed in this chapter are produced by other vertebrates. Invertebrates also produce hormones.

Hormones influence metamorphosis, change in form, in animals such as amphibians. For example, thyroxine causes many changes which transform a tadpole into an adult frog. You can carry out a simple experiment by treating tadpoles with varying concentrations of thyroxine. Additional thyroxine will greatly increase the rate of metamorphosis.

> Thyroxine plays a role in controlling metamorphosis of a frog.

During their development, insects also go through metamorphosis (Section 24:3). **Metamorphosis** includes a series of molts as either the larva or nymph grows into an adult. The molting process (Section 28:1) is controlled by hormones.

> Other insect hormones have been discovered. Among them are those with homeostatic functions; e.g., regulation of blood sugar, water balance, and protein metabolism.

In order for molting to occur, the brain secretes a hormone which causes the secretion of another hormone, **ecdyson** (EK duh sahn), that actually controls molting. After a certain number of molts, the nymph becomes an adult or the larva becomes a pupa. No further molting occurs after adulthood is reached.

> Molting is controlled by the action of two hormones. One is produced in the brain, and the other, ecdyson, is produced in the thorax.

What causes the final transition to the adult form? A third hormone, **juvenile hormone,** is involved. Juvenile hormone is constantly produced by a pair of glands, the corpora allata (KOR pruh · uh LAHT uh), located in the brain. Juvenile hormone and ecdyson together cause an insect to molt and grow. As the larva or nymph goes through its series of molts, the output of juvenile

> Juvenile hormone level decreases as molting proceeds.

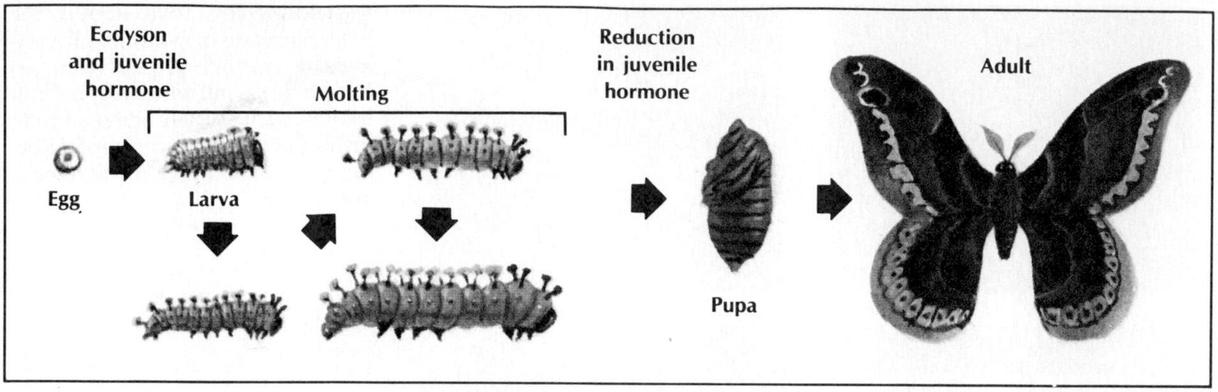

FIGURE 29-14. Insect metamorphosis includes a series of molts in which the larva becomes a pupa. The changes are the result of certain levels of hormones.

hormone decreases. This hormonal decrease causes the larva to enter the pupa stage or the nymph to enter its final molt. Absence of juvenile hormone results in no further molting (Figure 29-14). Can you think of any practical way in which juvenile hormone might be used? Juvenile hormone could be used to prevent the maturation and, therefore, the reproduction of insect pests.

REVIEWING YOUR IDEAS

5. Where is the pituitary gland located? What are its two main parts?
6. What is a feedback mechanism?
7. What is the hypothalamus? What might happen if your hypothalamus were removed?
8. What is the second messenger hypothesis?
9. What are prostaglandins?
10. Name a process in insects and frogs that is controlled by hormones.

5. The pituitary gland is located at the base of the brain. Its two main parts are the anterior and posterior lobes.
6. A feedback mechanism is a means of using information from a gland or body part to control the activities of that gland or body part.
7. The hypothalamus is a part of the brain near the pituitary. Its removal would disrupt hormonal control.
8. According to the second messenger hypothesis, some hormones cause in a target cell the production of a chemical which causes changes in the cell.
9. Prostaglandins are hormones which regulate responses of target organs and affect a variety of body functions.
10. metamorphosis

ADVANCES IN BIOLOGY

29:10 Insulin Pumps

Diabetics in whom the beta cells of the pancreas are destroyed do not produce enough insulin. To add to their own supply, they usually take injections of animal insulin (Section 29:1) one or more times daily.

Although the injection of insulin has been successful in saving lives, problems remain. In a healthy person, insulin is released constantly and in small amounts by the beta cells, not in large, sudden "spurts." Also, the beta cells detect the level of glucose in the blood and adjust the amounts of insulin they secrete. In this way, more insulin is released when needed, such as after a meal or during heavy exercise, keeping the level of glucose in the blood at normal levels. When insulin is taken by injection, its level cannot be so precisely adjusted. Between

Insulin is normally released constantly and in different amounts depending on the needs of the body.

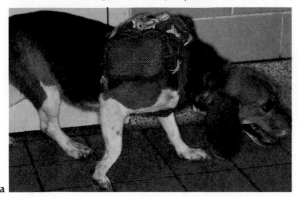

a

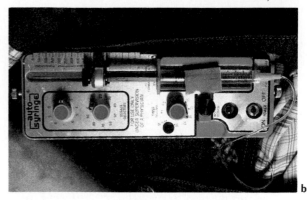

b

injections, the glucose level increases to a point above normal. Prolonged high levels of glucose in the blood cause many of the complications of diabetes, such as blindness and kidney failure.

Devices known as **insulin pumps** may solve the problems associated with insulin taken by injection. One kind of pump is powered by batteries and is strapped to the waist. Insulin enters the blood from the pump through small needles implanted under the skin. The insulin is released constantly at a certain rate. By pushing a button, the patient can increase the amount of insulin.

An implantable insulin pump has also been developed. This small, lightweight device is placed under the skin and is completely invisible. A tube from the pump delivers a steady flow of insulin into a vein. The pump can be refilled with insulin.

Both the external and internal insulin pumps help keep the glucose level of the blood closer to normal, and both free the patient from taking several insulin injections each day. Neither pump, though, can "mimic" the ability of normal beta cells to detect the level of glucose in the blood. To be most effective, a pump must be designed which can do this detection and automatically increase or decrease the amount of insulin needed. A pump with these capabilities has been developed, but because it is large, it is not portable. Research is underway to develop an implantable pump with a microcomputer which can sense and respond to the level of glucose in the blood.

FIGURE 29-15. (a) Insulin pumps have been tested experimentally on dogs. (b) The insulin pump for a human is a small device which may be strapped to the waist or worn on the belt.

Insulin pumps deliver a steady, constant supply of insulin.

The most effective device would be a pump which could vary insulin output as needed.

CHAPTER REVIEW

SUMMARY

1. Animals must constantly respond to stimuli, both external and internal.

2. In animals, chemical control is carried out by hormones, some of which are produced by endocrine glands.

3. Hormones are transported in blood and affect certain target organs.

4. Some of the main endocrine hormones in humans are secreted by the pancreas (insulin), thyroid (thyroxine), adrenals (adrenaline and cortisone), and the gonads (estrogens and androgens).

All Chapter Review answers and additional chapter teaching suggestions are provided in the Teacher's Guide at the front of this text.

CHAPTER REVIEW

5. The anterior pituitary secretes several hormones which control the activities of other endocrine glands. Interaction of these hormones, the hypothalamus, and glands involves feedback mechanisms.

6. The posterior pituitary gland secretes hormones which are produced in the hypothalamus.

7. In several ways, the endocrine and nervous systems are closely related.

8. The effect of a hormone depends in large part on the target organ.

9. Many protein-type hormones exert their effect according to the second messenger hypothesis.

10. Steroid hormones are thought to cause changes by activating certain genes in cells of the target organ.

11. Prostaglandins, a group of hormones, have many effects in the body and play a role in the amount of cAMP produced by target cells.

12. Hormones are produced by many animals. These hormones control such processes as metamorphosis.

13. Insulin pumps are being designed to solve problems of taking insulin by injection and to prevent some of the complications of diabetes mellitus.

LANGUAGE OF BIOLOGY

adrenal cortex
adrenaline
adrenal medulla
androgen
anterior pituitary
beta cells
cortisone
cyclic AMP
endocrine gland
estrogen
feedback mechanism
gonads
hormone

hypothalamus
insulin
islets of Langerhans
juvenile hormone
posterior pituitary
prostaglandin
releasing factor
second messenger
   hypothesis
steroids
target organ
thyroid
thyroxine

CHECKING YOUR IDEAS

On a separate paper, match the phrase from the left column with the proper term from the right column. Do not write in this book.

1. secretes HGH
2. mechanism controlling hormone production
3. involved in diabetes mellitus
4. male sex hormone
5. located on membrane of target organ
6. increases in response to stress
7. produces hormones released by posterior pituitary
8. involved in insect metamorphosis
9. contains iodine
10. female sex hormone

a. adrenaline
b. androgen
c. anterior pituitary
d. estrogen
e. feedback
f. hypothalamus
g. insulin
h. juvenile hormone
i. receptor
j. thyroxine

EVALUATING YOUR IDEAS

1. Describe the causes and symptoms of diabetes mellitus.

2. What is the role of insulin?

3. What are some functions of thyroxine?

4. What is the relationship between iodine and goiter?

5. What happens to adrenaline secretion during times of stress? What are the effects of adrenaline secretion?

6. How do adrenaline and the cells of the adrenal medulla indicate a close relationship between the endocrine system and the nervous system?

7. What are the functions of the adrenal cortex hormones?

8. How are hormones important in animal reproduction?

CHAPTER REVIEW

9. How are the effects of FSH and LH different in females and males? What do these effects indicate about how hormones work?

10. Distinguish between the effects of excess HGH and a deficiency of HGH.

11. How is thyroxine production controlled?

12. What are the functions of oxytocin and vasopressin? Where are these hormones made?

13. How do the structures and functions of the hypothalamus and posterior pituitary support the idea of a close relationship between the endocrine system and nervous system?

14. Explain how some hormones composed of protein or amino acids recognize their target organs and how they exert their effects in those organs.

15. How are steroid hormones thought to work?

16. List some effects of prostaglandins.

17. How are metamorphosis and molting controlled in insects?

18. What problems are associated with taking insulin by injection?

19. How do insulin pumps work? What must an insulin pump be able to do to be more effective in controlling diabetes?

APPLYING YOUR IDEAS

1. Insulin is a protein. Why must it be taken by injection rather than orally?

2. Oxytocin and vasopressin are peptides composed of eight amino acids, only two of which differ. How can their different actions be explained?

3. How would the size of an adult insect be affected if the corpora allata were removed in an early molt? Explain. How would the size of the insect be affected if juvenile hormone were added to a larva about to undergo its final molt? Explain.

4. Before insulin can become active, an enzyme must first remove certain parts of the molecule. How might the change from inactive to active insulin be adaptive as a control process?

5. What are some advantages of using insulin produced by recombinant DNA methods rather than insulin obtained from animals?

6. The effects of some hormones are balanced by the effects of other hormones. Glucagon is a hormone that balances insulin. What does glucagon do?

7. An enzyme in cells converts cAMP to a slightly different compound. How is this change a necessary reaction? (Hint: What might happen in a cell if cAMP built up?)

8. Compare chemical control in animals and plants. *Chapter 22

EXTENDING YOUR IDEAS

1. Histamine is a chemical that works like a hormone. Find out about its effects on the body. What is an antihistamine? When is it taken? Why?

2. The menstrual cycle involves the anterior pituitary gland and the hypothalamus. The menstrual cycle is controlled by a feedback mechanism. Find out how the hypothalamus "signals" the anterior pituitary during the cycle.

3. Find out about a condition called hypoglycemia. How is it caused and treated?

SUGGESTED READINGS

"Diabetes." *Sciquest*, October, 1980.

O'Malley, Bert W., and Schrader, William T., "The Receptors of Steroid Hormones." *Scientific American*, February, 1976.

Nourse, Alan E., *Hormones*. New York, Franklin Watts, Inc., 1979.

Silverstein, Alvin, and Silverstein, Virginia, *The Sugar Disease: Diabetes*. New York, J. B. Lippincott, 1980.

Additional student readings and suggested teacher readings are provided in the Teacher's Guide.

This microchip receives information, processes it, and relays messages. Similarly, your brain receives information from your body, interprets the information, and relays the proper messages. In "action," the microchip can control large complicated systems such as phone systems; the brain can control the large number of complicated responses of your body. What is involved in the movement of messages in the nervous system? What kinds of responses are made in the body?

Double pith a frog and place it, ventral side up, in a dissecting pan. Cut through the skin layer of the abdomen and thorax. Then cut through the muscle layer, exposing the still-beating heart. Using a dropper, flood the heart with amphibian Ringer's solution to maintain an environment similar to that of body fluids. Have a student determine the frog's heartbeat rate under these conditions. Next, add several drops of a solution of adrenaline to the heart. The heartbeat rate should increase. Rinse the heart again with Ringer's solution and add several drops of acetylcholine. The heartbeat rate should decrease. Class discussion based on this demonstration can be related to material presented in previous chapters, such as the role of the pacemaker and of the accelerator and vagus nerves (Chapter 26). Remind them also of the role of adrenaline discussed in Chapter 29.

Chapter
30

The fact that chemicals are associated with the nervous system will be more fully appreciated as you teach about synapses and neurotransmitters. This demonstration will emphasize the close relationship between chemical and nervous control systems.

NERVOUS CONTROL

Chapter 30 explores the structure and function of neurons and compares nervous systems of a variety of animals.

Many animal responses are chemically controlled by hormones (Chapter 29). Chemical control is efficient and needed for certain activities, but it is a slow process. Consider the responses which must be made to stimuli such as a fast car or a hot stove. In terms of "survival," reactions to these stimuli must be made quickly. These and many other responses are controlled by the nervous system. Recall that chemical and nervous control are closely linked. You will see further evidence of this close relationship in this chapter.

Three elements are needed for a nervous system response to occur. First, there must be a means of detecting a change in the environment (a stimulus). In most animals, stimuli are detected by structures called **receptors** (rih SEP turz). Can you name some receptors? Second, after the stimulus is received, it must be transmitted. A stimulus is transmitted as an impulse along a network of conductors. **Conductors** also transmit impulses to the third necessary element, the effectors (ih FEK turz). **Effectors** are the responding parts. Effectors carry out the correct responses to the stimuli. Muscles and glands are examples of effectors.

eyes, ears, nose, taste buds, and nerve endings for touch, pain, pressure, and temperature

GOAL: You will gain an understanding of the structure and functions of nervous systems in various animals.

Rapid responses to stimuli are made by the nervous system.

Receptors, conductors, and effectors are necessary for a nervous system response to occur.

CONDUCTION

30:1 Neurons

The conductors of a nervous response are specialized cells called **neurons** (NOO rahnz). There are three types of neurons in complex animals. Neurons differ in structure and in the direction in which they carry impulses. **Sensory neurons** transmit incoming impulses from receptors to a coordinating center, usually the brain or spinal cord. **Motor neuróns** transmit

FIGURE 30-1. A nervous response requires a receptor, conductor, and effector. Notice that the stimulus causes impulses that pass from sensory neuron to association neuron to motor neuron where a muscular response takes place.

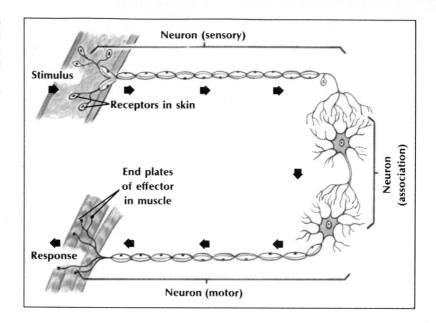

The three types of neurons are sensory, association, and motor.

FIGURE 30-2. (a) The cell body of a neuron contains the nucleus and most of the cytoplasm. (b) A typical motor neuron is composed of a cell body, an axon, dendrites, and end brushes. Motor neurons transmit impulses to effectors.

outgoing impulses from the brain or spinal cord to the effectors. These two types of neurons are joined in the brain and spinal cord by **association neurons.** In simple animals, association neurons may not be involved. A sensory neuron may stimulate a motor neuron directly. In some cases, a single neuron may detect a stimulus and conduct an impulse directly to an effector.

The structure of a typical vertebrate motor neuron is adapted for a special function—transmitting impulses (Figure 30-2). A neuron looks like a cell that has been drawn out into a long, fine fiber. These fibers are often grouped together to form a nerve. The portion of a neuron most resembling other kinds of cells is the **cell body** which contains a nucleus and cytoplasm. The long part of a neuron which transmits impulses *away* from the cell body is the

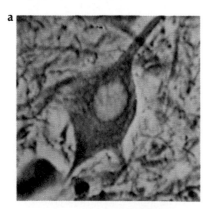

Roger K. Burnard

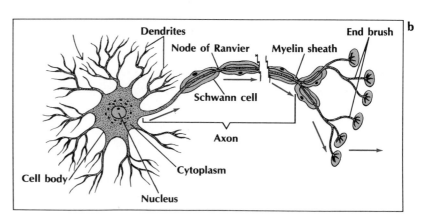

axon (AK sahn). The end of the axon is subdivided into many filaments, forming the **end brush.** The other end of a neuron is highly branched into structures called **dendrites** (DEN drites). Impulses are conducted *toward* the cell body from the dendrites. Thus, an impulse flows in a neuron from dendrite to cell body to axon. Then the impulse is transmitted to the dendrite of another neuron or to an effector.

Often, the axon of a neuron has an outer layer, the fatty **myelin** (MI uh lun) **sheath.** The myelin sheath comes from the cell membranes of **Schwann cells** which wrap around the axon. Schwann cells aid in the nutrition and regeneration of axons. Between Schwann cells are points where the axon is not covered, the **nodes of Ranvier** (RAHN vyay). Both the myelin sheath and the nodes of Ranvier are important in determining the speed with which impulses are conducted. Neurons lacking these features transmit impulses much more slowly than cells with a myelin sheath. Also, neurons with larger diameters conduct impulses more rapidly than those with smaller diameters.

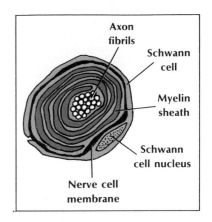

FIGURE 30-3. Cross section of a nerve axon shows wrapping of myelin sheath and Schwann cells.

PEOPLE IN BIOLOGY

Although trained as a doctor, biophysicist, and cell biologist, Humberto Fernandez-Moran's first love is neurology and neuropathology—the study of the nervous system and its diseases. Growing up in Venezuela, Fernandez-Moran developed an interest in the brain and central nervous system when

(1924-)

Humberto Fernandez-Moran

he saw the misery caused by tropical diseases that affect the central nervous system. Using electron microscope techniques which he developed, Dr. Fernandez-Moran discovered new brain and nerve traits. One of his main discoveries was that the myelin sheath, the fatty outer layer of some axons, acts much like a semiconductor, a material that can pass along an electrical charge. This idea helps explain why axons with myelin sheaths transmit impulses much more quickly than those without.

Fernandez-Moran has received many awards for his work, including the John Scott Award for inventing the diamond knife, used to slice samples for microscopic study, and the Venezuelan Medalla Andres Bello, the highest award granted to a Latin American Scholar. He now works at the Research Institute at the University of Chicago.

Many neurons are long, thin, delicate cells, but neuron length varies considerably. A single neuron may extend from the spinal cord to the foot of a person, a distance of about a meter. In the brain and spinal cord, the association neurons are very short and densely packed. The amount and length of dendrites and axons varies with the type and function of the neurons. However, regardless of these differences, an impulse is conducted in about the same way in all neurons.

The shape, size, and arrangement of neurons varies with their functions.

30:2 Membrane Potential

A resting neuron is polarized—there is a charge outside the membrane different from inside the cell. What causes this difference in charge? One factor is the number of sodium ions (Na^+) and potassium ions (K^+). Outside the cell, the number of sodium ions is high and the number of potassium ions is low. Inside the cell, the number of potassium ions is greater than the number of sodium ions. This difference in number of ions is due to what is called the cell's **sodium-potassium pump.** ATP energy is used to actively transport ("pump") sodium ions out of and potassium ions into the cell. Three sodium ions are pumped out for every two ions that enter the cell. As a result of the pump, more positive ions exist outside the cell (sodium) than inside (potassium). Thus, the outside of the cell is *more* positive than the inside.

The sodium-potassium pump contributes to the polarization of neurons.

Other factors play a role in polarization. Besides sodium and potassium, there are other ions inside the cell. Many of these ions have a negative charge. Because the cell membrane is permeable to potassium, some potassium moves outward from inside the cell. The membrane is not permeable to sodium, so it stays outside. As a result, the number of positive ions outside the cell increases. The negatively charged ions remaining inside the cell make the inside negative. All of these factors cause the outside of the cell to become positive with respect to the inside of the cell (Figure 30-4).

The interior of a neuron is negative with respect to the exterior.

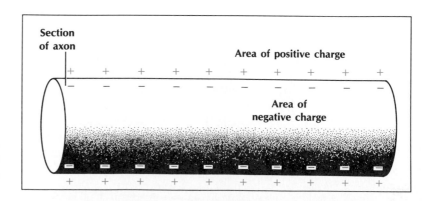

FIGURE 30-4. Unequal distribution of ions inside and outside its membrane polarizes a neuron. A section of an axon is shown.

The resting potential is about minus 70 millivolts.

This difference in charge and concentration in a resting neuron is called **membrane potential** or **resting potential.** Membrane potential is common to all cells. However, a neuron membrane potential is special.

30:3 Action Potential

When an axon is excited by things such as light, pressure, chemicals, or an electric current, changes take place. *A stimulus alters the permeability of the cell membrane.* The membrane changes and sodium ions can move quickly into the cell, causing a change of polarity. The inside of the cell is now positive with respect to the outside. After the sodium ions rush into the cell, the membrane changes again to allow potassium ions to move through, but it stops sodium ions. Potassium ions move from the inside of the cell to the outside very quickly. The polarity change and flow of ions caused by a stimulus results in a current and is called the **action potential.** The action potential shows that an impulse, which can be detected by electrical equipment, is being sent along a neuron. A neuron can send 500 to 1000 action potentials per second.

An action potential in one region of a neuron causes a change of polarity in the next region. In this way, action potentials (current) move along the whole length of the axon (Figure 30-6). A series of action potentials sweeping down an axon is a **nerve impulse.** In some large neurons, impulses may be sent at the rate of one hundred meters per second.

After a region of a neuron has been stimulated, it cannot immediately respond to another stimulus. A short period of time, the **refractory** (rih FRAK tree) **period,** which lasts for about 1.0 to 1.5 milliseconds, is needed to restore the resting potential. After a nerve impulse has been completed, the sodium-potassium pump moves sodium ions out of and potassium ions into the axon restoring the resting polarity and concentration differences of the neuron.

Transmission of a nerve impulse differs from an electric current in a wire. An electric current travels close to the speed of light and involves the flow of electrons along a wire. Current in a nerve impulse is caused by the flow of ions across the cell membrane. Thus, a nerve impulse is an electrochemical reaction. A nerve impulse is like the sputtering of a burning fuse in that it "jumps" along the neuron.

Muscle cells also have electrochemical activities. For example, the S-A node (Section 26:6) starts contraction of heart muscle. Polarity changes occur in the S-A node which cause changes in nearby muscle cells. As a result, the atria contract. The A-V node causes polarity changes in the muscle cells of the ventricles which also contract.

If an isolated axon is stimulated midway along its length by an electrode, the action potential sweeps out in both directions. In most living systems propagation occurs in only one direction.

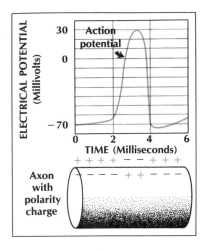

FIGURE 30-5. An action potential is an electrical change in the membrane that can be measured and graphed. It corresponds to the place on the axon where the polarity change is located.

FIGURE 30-6. Transmission of an impulse occurs as the action potential (polarity change) moves along an axon.

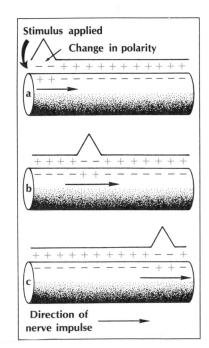

30:4 All-or-None Response

A stimulus must have a certain intensity in order for an impulse to result.

A nerve impulse is an "all or none" response.

All stimuli do not cause action potentials (impulses). A weak stimulus might generate some changes in a neuron, but unless polarity is changed, there would be no nerve impulse. A stimulus must have a certain intensity to change polarity in a neuron and start an impulse. This level of intensity is called the **threshold.** The threshold is reached when a stimulus causes a change in membrane permeability and sodium ions rush into the axon. Because of these needs, a nerve impulse is an **"all-or-none" response.** The impulse is either sent or not sent. Once the threshold is reached, an impulse will be sent.

A stimulus stronger than threshold level will produce the same kind of impulse as a stimulus just at the threshold level. The impulse will travel at the same speed and in the same way no matter how strong the stimulus is. How then, do you detect different strengths of stimuli? This detection depends on the number of impulses carried along a neuron in a given period of time and the number of the same kind of neurons carrying the impulse.

Responses to stimuli depend on what receptors pick up stimuli and the target to which impulses are sent, not the nature of the impulse.

How do you interpret *what* the stimulus is? How do you know whether you are being stimulated by light or noise or touch? The impulses are all essentially the same! The answer is that what you interpret and respond to depends on the pathway of the nerves and the *target* reached by the impulse. Once a certain pathway begins to carry an impulse, the result will be the same. What happens when you close your eyes and gently tap one eyelid? Do you see that the type of stimulus does not determine the way you interpret it?
You should see light.

FIGURE 30-7. A synapse between an axon and a muscle cell (effector) is shown. Acetylcholine is released from vesicles in the end of the axon into the synapse in transmitting the impulse.

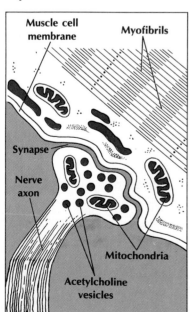

Muscle cell membrane
Myofibrils
Synapse
Nerve axon
Mitochondria
Acetylcholine vesicles

30:5 Synapse

Action potentials do not cease at the end of a single neuron but may be passed on to another cell. This cell is either another neuron or an effector. There is always a small space called a **synapse** (SIHN aps) between any two such cells. An action potential must cross a synapse and can cross in one direction only. A fiber which carries an impulse toward a synapse is a **presynaptic** (pree suh NAP tihk) **fiber.** A fiber which receives the impulse after it crosses the synapse is a **postsynaptic** (pohst suh NAP tihk) **fiber.** How does an impulse cross a synapse?

Certain chemicals called **neurotransmitters** are stored in sacs called vesicles at the ends of presynaptic axons. As an action potential sweeps toward the end of an axon, calcium ions enter it from outside the membrane. Entry of calcium causes the vesicles to release the neurotransmitter. The chemical diffuses toward the postsynaptic fiber where it combines with receptor molecules. The combination of neurotransmitter and receptor may cause the

Usually, a single action potential in the presynaptic fiber will not be carried across a synapse. Several presynaptic action potentials, however, will result in postsynaptic action potentials. This phenomenon is known as summation. It is adaptive in that "irrelevant" information can be reduced. An "important" impulse (one which is repeated) will get through.

membrane of the postsynaptic fiber to become permeable to sodium. If the fiber becomes permeable, sodium ions rush across the postsynaptic fiber's membrane starting an action potential. In this case, the neurotransmitter *excites* the next nerve cell (Figure 30-8).

In some cases, a neurotransmitter *stops* the sending of an impulse in a postsynaptic fiber. The chemicals released make the membrane less permeable to sodium so that no nerve impulse is sent. **Acetylcholine** (uh seet ul ĸoh leen), secreted by the vagus nerve which leads to the heart, stops the sending of an impulse and causes the heartbeat rate to slow down.

One other common neurotransmitter is **noradrenaline** (nor uh ᴅʀᴇɴ ul un), which is like adrenaline. This likeness shows how the endocrine and nervous systems are the same in some ways as both work by secreting chemicals.

The effects of a neurotransmitter depend on the postsynaptic fiber. Acetylcholine checks heart muscle impulses, but it starts them in the alimentary canal and skeletal muscles. Noradrenaline gives rise to impulses in heart muscle, but it checks them in the alimentary canal and makes no change in skeletal muscles. It is the target, not the chemical, which "decides" the response. Often, thousands of presynaptic axons, each with its own set of chemicals, lead to one postsynaptic fiber. Whether the fiber is excited or not depends on the net effect of all the chemicals.

Neurotransmitters are suppressed soon after they are released so that the postsynaptic fiber is not always excited. Acetylcholine is changed by an enzyme called cholinesterase (koh luh ɴᴇs tuh rays) that breaks it into two smaller molecules which have no effect on postsynaptic fibers. Noradrenaline is not chemically changed but is "recaptured" by the presynaptic fiber which released it.

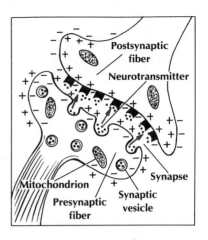

FIGURE 30-8. In transmission from nerve to nerve, neurotransmitter released at the synapse causes a polarity reversal in the second neuron. Thus, the impulse is started in the second neuron.

The effect of a neurotransmitter depends on the postsynaptic fiber.

Neurotransmitters are inactivated shortly after they are released.

The first indication of chemical involvement was demonstrated by Otto Loewi in 1921. The vagus nerve of a frog's heart produced a chemical which Loewi transferred to a second heart. The second heart stopped beating. Loewi named the chemical "vagusstuff" (acetylcholine).

30:6 Effects of Drugs and Other Chemicals

Drugs and other chemicals have come to play an important role in maintaining both physical and mental health. When used properly, these substances, among other things, cure or treat diseases and relieve discomforts such as pain. However, if not used properly, these substances may cause severe harm and even death.

How many chemicals affect living things is not known, but research has shown that certain ones work by affecting the central nervous system (CNS)—the brain and spinal cord. **Depressants** are a major group of drugs which reduce the reactions of the CNS. Tranquillizers have this effect on the body and are often used as calming medicines. These depressants have chemical structures very similar to some brain neurotransmitters and often work by blocking impulses in the brain. Some

Depressants reduce activities of the central nervous system.

Kevin Fitzsimons

Kevin Fitzsimons

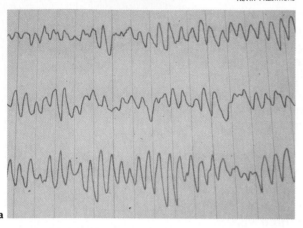
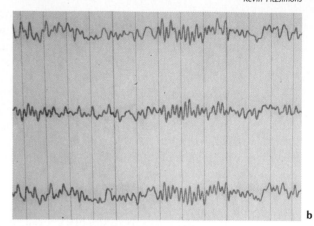

a

b

FIGURE 30-9. Electroencephalograms (EEG) give a means to measure brain function. (a) Normal traces are much different from (b) those of a patient taking stimulant drugs.

Barbiturates are used to induce sleep.

Pain killers are potentially addictive.

Stimulants increase activity in the central nervous system.

Some drugs exert their effects at synapses.

tranquillizers decrease transmission at synapses. Others block receptors so the number of impulses transmitted is lowered. The effect of these drugs is a calming one.

Barbiturates are the most powerful and most often abused depressants. These drugs can be used to make a person sleep. By first blocking brain impulses and then blocking impulses throughout the body, these drugs reduce thought, memory, and awareness of light and sound.

Other drugs that dull the senses are morphine, codeine, heroin, and alcohol. Morphine is a pain killer that is thought to reduce the amount of neurotransmitters released at synapses. Codeine is widely used in cough syrups; it reduces the cough reflex. Heroin, a drug made from morphine, dulls pain, but because it is addictive, it is seldom used in medicine. Alcohol (C_2H_5OH) is a depressant which interferes with transmission at synapses.

Stimulants, another major group of drugs, work by increasing the amount of activity in the CNS and are used to make a person more alert, to prevent sleep, and to control appetite or depression. Caffeine, found in coffee, tea, and cola drinks, is a stimulant that raises motor activity. Nicotine is a stimulant found in cigarette smoke (Section 26:13). Amphetamines (am FET uh meenz) are stimulant drugs at times given to obese people for appetite control but are often abused.

Other drugs also affect the nervous system. Marijuana leaves contain drugs which change the amounts of neurotransmitters in the brain. Nervous system enzymes and electrical activities are affected by marijuana use. LSD resembles a certain brain neurotransmitter. LSD acts like this chemical in the brain but cannot forward signals as the real neurotransmitter can. Thus, impulses are blocked and sensory perception is distorted when LSD is used. Curare is a muscle relaxant that combines with receptors for acetylcholine on muscle cells. Because receptors are blocked, impulses cannot move and muscles are not stimulated.

Teaching suggestion: Aspirin is America's most widely used drug. You might want to remind students that the use of even potentially helpful drugs can be abused.

Some scientists are researching drugs that affect the nervous system to determine how they might be used to fight diseases. The effects of some drugs are being studied to help understand mental disorders. For example, users of LSD sometimes show symptoms similar to those shown by people with schizophrenia, a mental disorder. Amphetamine users may also show this same effect.

Interactions of drugs and neurotransmitters need to be better understood to learn how to treat certain conditions. While drug misuse and abuse must be avoided, medical use of drugs can be very beneficial. The proper use of drugs has allowed physically and emotionally ill persons to lead nearly normal lives.

REVIEWING YOUR IDEAS

1. List the three elements needed for a nervous response.
2. List the three types of neurons and their functions.
3. Distinguish between axon and dendrite.
4. How do neurons become polarized?
5. Distinguish between action potential and nerve impulse.
6. What is a synapse? What kinds of chemicals are secreted at a synapse?
7. Distinguish between stimulants and depressants.

1. receptor, effector, conductor
2. Sensory neurons transmit impulses from receptors to the brain and spinal cord, motor neurons carry impulses to effectors, and association neurons link sensory and motor neurons in the brain and spinal cord.
3. Dendrites carry impulses toward the cell body whereas axons transmit impulses away from the cell body.
4. Neurons become polarized as a result of the sodium-potassium pump and the unequal accumulation of ions inside and outside the cell.
5. An action potential is a polarity reversal in a stimulated neuron. A series of action potentials along a neuron is a nerve impulse.
6. A synapse is the gap between a neuron and another cell; neurtransmitters.
7. Stimulants activate the central nervous system; depressants reduce activity in the central nervous system.

NERVOUS SYSTEMS

30:7 Invertebrates

In *Hydra,* nerve impulses can travel in either direction. Thus, the transmission of impulses may be more random.

Coelenterates such as *Hydra* have randomly scattered neurons which form a system called a **nerve net** (Figure 30-10). All the neurons are short and similar. Because neurons are short, an impulse must cross many synapses. In a coelenterate, impulses can travel in either direction across synapses. But, transmission is slow. Only strong stimuli cause impulses that are easily sent across many synapses. The impulses of many weak stimuli do not travel very far in a hydra. Other coelenterates have more complex nerve nets.

Sometimes responses are made by the whole animal. For example, a hydra can contract into a ball if disturbed. But more often, only single body parts such as tentacles are moved.

Planarians and other flatworms have more complex systems. At the anterior end of a planarian are two bundles of neuron cell bodies called **ganglia** (GANG glee uh) which act like the brain of more complex animals. Two major nerve cords from the ganglia run the length of the body, and connecting nerves join the main cords. Smaller neurons branch from the nerve cords and act much like a nerve net. Some biologists refer to this arrangement of nerves as a **ladder-type nervous system** (Figure 30-10).

FIGURE 30-10. (a) *Hydra* **has a nerve net nervous system. (b)** *Planaria* **has a ladder-type nervous system with the beginnings of central control in the ganglia of the head region.**

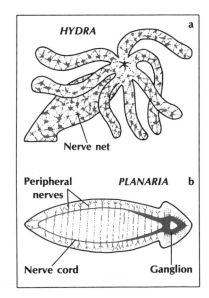

The nervous system of planarians is similar to the nervous systems in more complex animals. These animals have both a central and a peripheral (puh RIHF rul) nervous system. The ganglia (brain) and the connected nerve cords of planarians make up the **central nervous system.** The ganglia control the entire nervous system. The **peripheral nervous system** is made up of sensory and motor neurons connected with the ganglia. Thus, the peripheral nervous system is made up of nerves which join the central nervous system with the receptors and effectors.

More complex animals have these basic features, but the systems are more complex. Annelids and arthropods have brains, but the degree to which the brain controls responses varies. Destruction of an earthworm's brain does not cause death, but more complex animals cannot live without a brain.

30:8 Vertebrates

In vertebrates, the major nerve cord is along the dorsal (back) side of the animal. Annelids and arthropods have two ventral (front) nerve cords. The major nerve cord in vertebrates is called the **spinal cord** and is surrounded and protected by vertebrae. The spinal cord is an extension of the brain; together they make up the central nervous system. The peripheral nervous system of vertebrates is made up of sensory and motor neurons which carry impulses to and from the central nervous system. In humans, the peripheral nervous system is composed of twelve pairs of **cranial nerves** (attached to the brain) and thirty-one pairs of **spinal nerves.**

The spinal cord is involved in many responses, but the brain is the major coordinating center in vertebrates. Vertebrate brains differ in appearance (Figure 30-11), but each has three general

Most complex animals have a central nervous system and a peripheral nervous system.

A vertebrate has a brain and a dorsal spinal cord.

The human peripheral nervous system is composed of cranial and spinal nerves.

FIGURE 30-11. Although all of these vertebrate brains have the same three regions (forebrain, midbrain, and hindbrain), the regions have different features and functions.

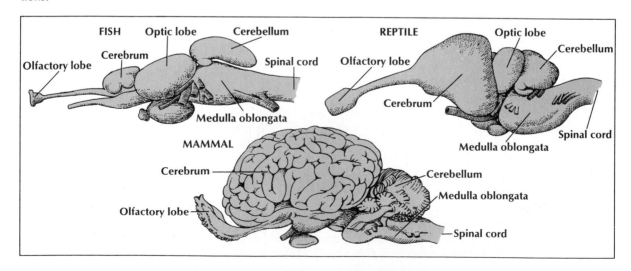

areas—**forebrain, midbrain,** and **hindbrain.** Each area of the brain controls certain functions. The functioning of the brain is very complex and not completely understood. Much is yet to be learned about how the brain controls the body and about the exact functions of the many parts of the brain. The following sections discuss the human nervous system.

The vertebrate brain is composed of three regions: forebrain, midbrain, and hindbrain.

In addition to a central nervous system, the planarian has the rudiments of other characteristics seen in more complex animals. Among them are cephalization and concentration of sensory "equipment" at the anterior end.

REVIEWING YOUR IDEAS

8. Compare the nervous systems of hydra and planaria.
9. What are the two divisions of the nervous system in complex animals?
10. Compare the location of the nerve cord in vertebrates and invertebrates.
11. What parts make up the central nervous system of vertebrates?
12. How are the brains of vertebrates similar to one another?

8. *Hydra* has a nerve net with no central control center. *Planaria* has a ladder type system with a primitive brain.
9. central nervous system and peripheral nervous system
10. The nerve cord is dorsal in vertebrates and ventral in invertebrates.
11. brain and spinal cord
12. Vertebrate brains consist of three parts — forebrain, midbrain, and hindbrain.

30:9 Forebrain

A human brain is protected by the cranium and three membranes called the **meninges** (muh NIHN jeez). These membranes protect and nourish both the spinal cord and brain. Between the inner two meninges is **cerebrospinal** (suh ree broh SPINE ul) **fluid.** This clear fluid cushions the brain against shock, but a severe shock can sometimes damage the brain. A concussion is a brain injury resulting from a severe blow to the head. Cerebrospinal fluid is also in the ventricles (VEN trih kulz) (cavities) of the brain. Capillaries in the walls of the ventricles exchange materials with the fluid which, in turn, exchanges materials with the brain cells. As in all vertebrates, the human brain is composed of a forebrain, midbrain, and hindbrain.

The human brain is protected by the cranium and meninges.

Cerebrospinal fluid cushions the brain. It is an exchange medium between brain cells and blood.

FIGURE 30-12. (a) Scanners such as this one are used to do brain scans to detect brain disfunction. **(b)** This scan is a cross sectional view of the brain of a stroke patient. The red area of the scan is an area of the brain with poor circulation.

a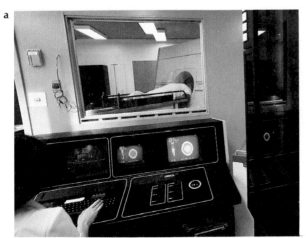

b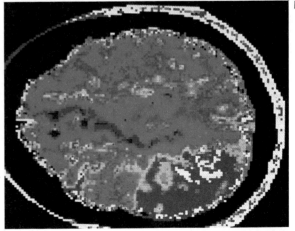

Dan McCoy from Rainbow

Courtesy of Physics Today

FIGURE 30-13. (a) The human brain is composed of three major regions—forebrain, midbrain, and hindbrain. (b) The forebrain, or cerebrum, has four lobes.

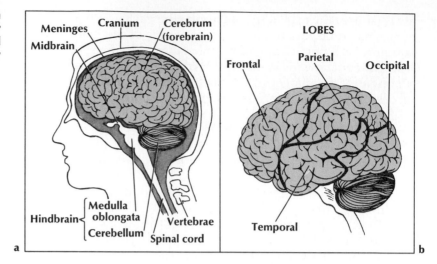

The cerebrum occupies most of the human forebrain.

The cerebrum functions in speech, reasoning, emotions, and personality.

The thalamus and hypothalamus are part of the forebrain.

The forebrain of humans includes the **cerebrum** (suh REE brum). The cerebrum is divided into two parts or hemispheres. Each hemisphere consists of four sections or lobes (Figure 30-13). The surface of the cerebrum, the **cerebral cortex,** has many folds called **convolutions** (kahn vuh LEW shunz). The cortex is made up of cell bodies which together are known as **gray matter.** Convolutions are thought to provide a greater surface area for the nerve cell bodies. The great number of cell bodies is important in complex behavior and intelligence. The interior of a human brain is **white matter** made up of axons with myelin sheaths.

Many human abilities are related to the very large cerebrum. Speech, reasoning, emotions, and personality are all jobs of this area of the brain. The cerebrum also interprets sensory impulses and starts motor impulses (Table 30-1).

Also in the forebrain are the thalamus and hypothalamus. The thalamus helps sort sensory information. The hypothalamus has many roles such as control of hunger, body temperature, and aggression. It also plays an important role of endocrine control.

A third section of the hindbrain, the pons, lies above the medulla oblongata. Through it, nerves pass from the cerebrum to the cerebellum.

TABLE 30-1. MAJOR PARTS OF THE HUMAN BRAIN AND THEIR MAIN FUNCTIONS	
Section	Functions In
FOREBRAIN (Cerebrum)	
Temporal lobe	Taste and smell, hearing, learning and memory
Parietal lobe	Sensory input, touch
Occipital lobe	Vision, motor output, speech
Frontal lobe	Personality, learning, thought, speech
MIDBRAIN	Relay center
HINDBRAIN	
Cerebellum	Coordinating impulses, posture and balance, motor coordination, muscle tone
Medulla Oblongata	Heartbeat rate and other internal control

30:10 Midbrain and Hindbrain

In less complex vertebrates, the midbrain is prominent. But in humans and other mammals, it mainly functions as a message station between the forebrain and hindbrain. The midbrain also is involved in some sight, hearing, and orientation responses.

There are two distinct areas of the hindbrain—the cerebellum (ser uh BEL um) and the medulla oblongata (muh DUL uh · ahb long GAHT uh). The **cerebellum** is a region lying at the back of the head below the cerebrum. Like the cerebrum, the cerebellum has convolutions. Its outer surface is made up of gray matter, and the inside is white matter. The cerebellum coordinates impulses sent out from the cerebrum. It receives sensory impulses from certain receptors. If the sensory information and cerebral impulses do not agree, the cerebellum sends messages to the cerebrum and the cerebral impulses change. The cerebellum also controls posture and balance and maintains muscle tone (Section 28:8).

Extending down from the center portion of the brain is the **medulla oblongata.** The medulla controls many involuntary responses of the internal organs. For example, the breathing rate and heartbeat rate, peristalsis, and some gland secretions are controlled by this part.

> The human midbrain functions mainly as a message center.

> The cerebellum, like the cerebrum, is subdivided into hemispheres.
>
> In humans, the cerebellum coordinates impulses leaving the cerebrum and controls posture, balance, and muscle tone.

> The medulla oblongata controls the involuntary responses of internal organs.

30:11 The Spinal Cord

Extending down from the medulla oblongata is the long spinal cord with a fluid-filled central canal. The spinal cord is surrounded and protected by the meninges (Section 30:9) and a series of vertebrae. Like the brain, the spinal cord is composed of white and gray matter (Figure 30-14). The outer part of the spinal cord is white matter, and the inner part is gray matter, an arrangement opposite of that in the brain.

> The spinal cord is protected by vertebrae and meninges.

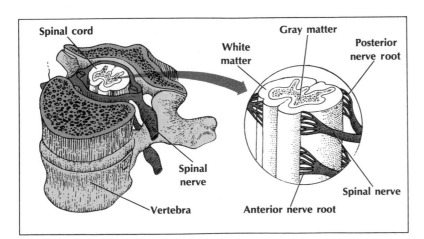

Spinal cord

Gray matter

White matter

Posterior nerve root

Spinal nerve

Vertebra

Anterior nerve root

Spinal nerve

> Because they contain both motor and sensory neurons, spinal nerves are called mixed nerves. In humans, they enter the spinal cord via a posterior nerve root and exit in an anterior nerve root.

FIGURE 30-14. This section of spinal cord shows its location relative to the vertebra and spinal nerves. Spinal nerves bring sensory information to the spinal cord and carry information for motor responses to the effectors.

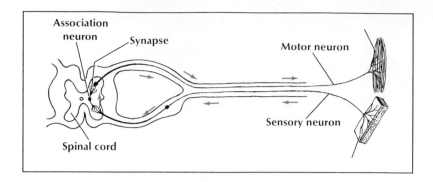

The spinal cord is a relay station between the brain and the peripheral nervous system.

In humans, the spinal cord is a major connection center between the brain and the peripheral nervous system. The spinal nerves are part of the peripheral system. They connect the body parts with the spinal cord. Spinal nerves enter and leave the spinal cord through nerve roots. Spinal nerves contain both sensory and motor neurons. Impulses reach the spinal cord from receptors and internal organs via sensory neurons and then travel to association neurons in the spinal cord. The impulses are usually transferred to the brain for interpretation. Impulses are then sent to the internal organs and the skeletal muscles by motor neurons.

Certain responses are made without involvement of the brain. In these cases, the spinal cord acts as the control center. Such a response is a reflex. (Some reflexes may involve the brain and not the spinal cord.) A **reflex** is a simple response which involves no conscious control. For example, consider the response made to the stimulus of stepping on a sharp rock while walking barefoot. Before you are aware of what has happened, certain leg muscles have contracted, lifting your foot from the rock. How is this response made?

A reflex involves no conscious control.

Reflex behavior is discussed in Section 31:2.

Receptors in the skin of the foot are activated by the pressure of the rock and the pain it causes. Each receptor stimulates a sensory neuron and causes an impulse to travel to the spinal cord via a spinal nerve. The sensory neuron enters the spinal cord (Figure 30-15) and crosses a synapse to an association neuron. The impulse travels along the association neuron and then passes across a synapse to a motor neuron. The motor neuron leaves the spinal cord and branches to form synapses with several muscle cells. Acetylcholine is released across the synapses. Polarity of the muscle cells is changed and the muscle contracts.

A reflex arc is the path of an impulse during a reflex.

The path of the impulse in a reflex is called a **reflex arc.** A reflex arc includes five parts—receptor, sensory neuron, association neuron, motor neuron, and effector (Figure 30-15).

The reflex just studied takes place within a fraction of a second and is not controlled by the brain. However, some association neurons synapse with other neurons leading to the brain, and the brain becomes aware of what has happened. Then

Yes, consider a "cry" of pain from a dog or cat.

secondary responses occur. A loud "Ouch" would be a common secondary response to the stimulus of the sharp rock.   Do other animals make secondary responses? Can reflexes be modified? yes Consider the blinking response. How can you modify this response? by conscious effort

30:12 Peripheral Nervous System

The sensory and motor neurons of the spinal and cranial nerves are part of the human's peripheral nervous system. Some neurons of spinal and cranial nerves carry impulses from receptors, to the brain and spinal cord, and to the skeletal muscles. They form a part of the peripheral system called the **sensory-somatic system.** Both reflex and voluntary responses are part of this system.

The sensory-somatic system controls impulses between receptors, the central nervous system, and the skeletal muscles.

Other neurons of spinal and cranial nerves control responses of the internal body organs. These neurons form a division of the peripheral system called the **autonomic system.** Autonomic responses are involuntary and involve smooth muscle, cardiac muscle, and glands.

The autonomic nervous system control involuntary responses of the internal organs.

The autonomic system is further subdivided into two other systems—the sympathetic (sihm puh THET ihk) system and the parasympathetic (per uh sihm puh THET ihk) system. The **sympathetic system** often begins responses which prepare the body for "emergencies." These responses are similar to those resulting from secretion of adrenaline. That is, these responses speed up or strengthen body functions. The accelerator nerves to the heart are sympathetic nerves. Other sympathetic nerves cause the adrenal medulla to secrete adrenaline, the pupils to become larger, and glycogen to be changed to glucose. Sympathetic nerves start in the spinal cord and also form synapses with chains of ganglia which lie outside the spinal cord.

Nerves of the sympathetic system cause responses which prepare the body for emergencies.

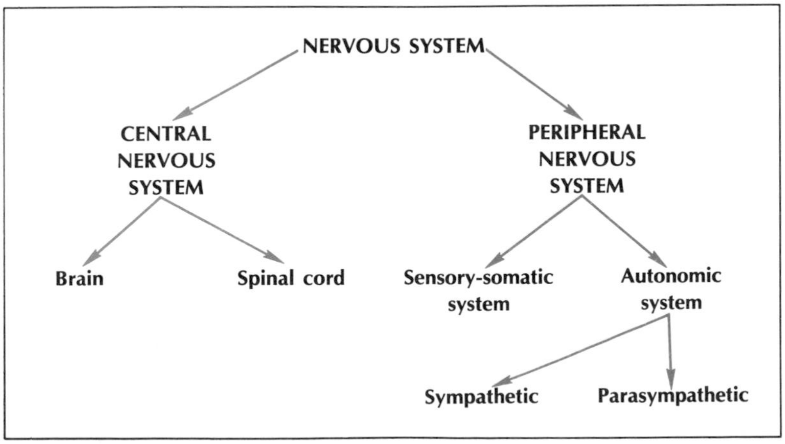

Both motor and sensory neurons are present in the autonomic system. Motor neurons run from the central nervous system to the viscera. Sensory neurons run to the central nervous system from the viscera.

FIGURE 30-16. Division of the nervous system helps in identifying particular nerves and responses.

FIGURE 30-17. The autonomic nervous system controls involuntary responses. Sympathetic nerves prepare the body for emergencies whereas parasympathetic nerves counteract these effects. Those processes that sympathetic nerves speed up, parasympathetic nerves slow down.

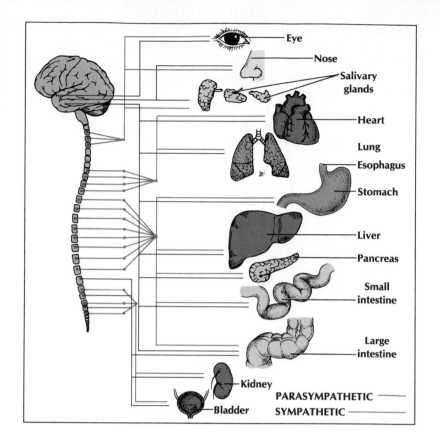

Nerves of the parasympathetic system cause impulses which balance the effects of the sympathetic system.

Responses made by the sympathetic system are balanced by the **parasympathetic system.** Impulses carried by parasympathetic nerves counteract the effects of the sympathetic nerves. This process of action-counteraction is important because the body must return to normal after an "emergency." Most parasympathetic nerves branch from the vagus nerve. The vagus nerve (a cranial nerve) originates in the medulla oblongata. The branch of the vagus nerve which reaches the heart slows down the heartbeat rate. Thus, the vagus nerve balances the effects of the accelerator nerve. Other branches of the vagus nerve stimulate peristalsis, the flow of saliva, and the release of bile. Balancing of the effects of sympathetic and parasympathetic nerves is important in maintaining homeostasis.

30:13 The Senses

Humans are adapted for sensing a variety of stimuli.

Animals are constantly bombarded by stimuli from their environment. Detecting and reacting to stimuli are important for an animal's survival. Humans have adaptations to sense a variety of stimuli. These adaptations include nerve endings, special cells in contact with nerves, and complex sense organs.

There are five major human senses—vision, hearing, smell, taste, and touch. Touch is a general term which also includes several related senses including pain, pressure, heat, and cold. Each of these "touch" senses is detected by separate skin receptors. Each kind of receptor detects only one sense. The number and location of touch receptors around the body varies. For example, there are more cold receptors than heat receptors, and there are more touch receptors in the fingertips than in the legs. Whether detected by a simple nerve ending or neurons in a complex organ, sensory information causes action potentials in neurons. Each receptor or sense organ sends impulses to particular parts of the brain where they are interpreted. Correct responses can then be made.

As an example of how a sense organ works, consider the ear. The ear consists of three areas—outer ear, middle ear, and inner ear. The outer ear consists of the outer flap, the auditory (hearing) canal, and the eardrum or **tympanic membrane.** The middle ear begins on the inner side of the eardrum and consists of a chain of three small bones called the hammer, anvil, and stirrup (so named because of their shapes). The stirrup contacts a second membrane called the **oval window.** Also in the middle ear is the **eustachian tube,** a canal which connects the middle ear to the nasal passages and throat. The eustachian tube contains air and maintains equal air pressure between the middle and outer ear. The inner ear contains two sets of fluid-filled canals. One set controls the sense of balance and is not involved in hearing. The other, the **cochlea,** is involved in hearing. Part of the cochlea is in contact with the oval window. The cochlea contains special hair cells that make up the organ of Corti. These hair cells are each connected to fibers of the auditory nerve.

How does hearing occur? Sound waves, vibrations of air molecules, enter the outer ear, pass through the auditory canal, and cause the eardrum to begin vibrating. The vibrations are picked up by the middle ear bones which amplify the vibrations and transfer them to the oval window. The oval window then

The five senses are vision, hearing, smell, taste, and touch.

Pain, pressure, heat, and cold are detected by different touch receptors.

The outer ear consists of the outer flap, auditory canal, and tympanic membrane.

The middle ear contains the hammer, anvil, and stirrup bones, the oval window, and the eustachian tube.

The cochlea is a fluid-filled chamber in the inner ear.

Sound waves cause the eardrum to vibrate. The middle ear bones and oval window then vibrate.

The semicircular canals function in balance. Loss of balance may occur during an inner ear infection.

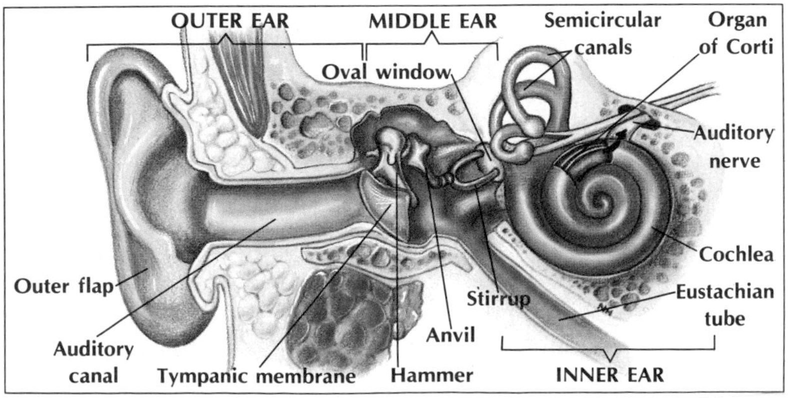

FIGURE 30-18. The human ear is a complex sense organ which receives impulses and passes them to the brain for interpretation.

Movement of fluid in the cochlea causes the hair cells to bend, setting off nerve impulses which travel to the brain.

vibrates, causing the fluid in the cochlea to move. Movement of the fluid within the cochlea causes the sensitive hairs to bend. When the hairs bend, action potentials are created in the auditory nerve fibers. Impulses are sent along the auditory nerve to the temporal lobe of the cerebrum where they are interpreted as sound. The particular sound you hear depends on the frequency of the vibrations entering the ear, the number of vibrations, and the number and position of hairs stimulated in the cochlea.

REVIEWING YOUR IDEAS

13. Cerebrospinal fluid surrounds the brain and spinal cord. It cushions these structures and is an exchange medium between blood and nervous tissue.

14. The cerebrum is part of the forebrain. Each hemisphere has four lobes.

15. White matter is made of myelinated axons. Gray matter is composed of cell bodies.

16. cerebellum and medulla oblongata

17. A reflex is a response involving no conscious control. A reflex arc is the nerve pathway followed during a reflex.

18. The sensory-somatic system controls reflexes and voluntary responses involving skeletal muscle. The autonomic system controls involuntary responses of smooth muscle and glands.

19. vision, hearing, taste, touch, and smell

13. What is cerebrospinal fluid? What are its functions?
14. What is the cerebrum?
15. Distinguish between white matter and gray matter.
16. What are the two major divisions of the human hindbrain?
17. Distinguish between reflexes and a reflex arc.
18. What are the two divisions of the peripheral nervous system?
19. What are the five major senses of humans?

ADVANCES IN BIOLOGY

30:14 Neuropeptides

In the last 20 years, great advances have been made in the study of the chemistry of the brain. The discoveries made make the links between the endocrine and nervous systems more definite. They also give insight into the nature of several mental disorders and provide possible means of treating these disorders.

The discoveries are those of brain proteins which are called neuropeptides. **Neuropeptides** are chains of amino acids of varying lengths that are made in the hypothalamus and pituitary. The brain proteins are found in tissues of the nervous system, and have been tied to various functions. Some are believed to be involved in memory, concentration, pleasure, water balance, learning, anxiety, depression, and pain relief.

Neuropeptides involved in pain relief, first discovered in the mid-1970's, are of particular interest to researchers attempting to understand pain causes and pain relief. Many people with diseases such as arthritis and terminal cancer suffer chronic pain. Other problems, such as broken bones, migraine headaches, toothaches, and back problems, result in pain that, although temporary or periodic, can be severe. Study of neuropeptides involved in pain and pain relief may result in pain treatments better than the drugs now given. Certain neuropeptides would be "natural" drugs in pain relief treatment in that they would be the same chemicals that the brain produces.

The term endorphin is short for "endogenous morphine."

Pain neuropeptides fall into two main groups—**endorphins** (en DOR fihnz) and **enkephalins** (en KEHF lihnz). Much of the work

Indications are that beta-endorphin can counter depression in humans.

There is some evidence that too few brain opiates causes mental illness. There is also some evidence that excess brain opiates causes mental illness. done shows that α- and β-endorphin reduce sensitivity to pain and tranquilize animals. Enkephalins are the brain's own pain relieving chemicals, and are referred to as "natural opiates."

Evidence shows that endorphins and enkephalins increase in the cerebrospinal fluid of patients during acupuncture. Acupuncture is a pain relieving technique that involves inserting pins at certain points in the body. Pain relieving peptides also have been shown to decrease in the fluid during migraine headaches. Other tests have linked endorphins to the **placebo** (pluh SEE boh) **effect.** Often symptoms of pain disappear when patients are given placebos, pills that look like medicine but contain nothing that will actually treat the symptom itself. Experiments have shown that when patients are unaware that they are receiving placebos, their endorphins increase and they really do experience less pain. Endorphins and enkephalins have been implicated in many other things too, such as the euphoric "runner's high" experienced by long distance runners, and the relief that heat treatments give to painful body areas.

The chemical structures of the pain relief neuropeptides also have been studied in detail, in attempts to understand their chemical origins. For example, β-endorphin contains the peptide methionine enkephalin (Figure 30-19) although it has been found that the enkephalin is not produced from the endorphin. Information of this kind is proving useful in synthetically making **analogs,** structures similar to the peptides. The analogs may be useful as drugs for patients experiencing pain.

The discovery and study of neuropeptides clearly is only beginning. The information being learned not only is useful in understanding and treating diseases and symptoms, but also is showing that the brain is far more complex than was once thought .

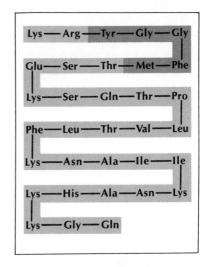

FIGURE 30-19. A model of enkephalin is shown with the larger molecule, endorphin, that contains it. Enkephalins have been found to counteract pain.

Endorphin and enkephalin analogs are being synthesized and some presently are being tested in humans.

CHAPTER REVIEW

SUMMARY

1. A nervous response involves receptors, conductors, and effectors.

2. Conductors are of three types—sensory, association, and motor.

3. During the resting potential, the outside of the membrane is positive with respect to the inside.

4. Nerve impulses result from a reversal of polarity and a current caused by a series of action potentials.

5. A nerve impulse is an all-or-none response.

6. Response to and interpretation of an impulse depends on the target organ, frequency of stimulation, the number of neurons carrying the same kind of impulse, and the kind of neurotransmitter acting.

7. Neurotransmitters are needed for transmission of an impulse across a synapse. They may either cause or check impulses.

8. Many drugs and other chemicals interfere with the normal activities at synapses.

9. Some invertebrates have a central nervous system composed of one or more simple ganglia (as a brain) and one or more ventral nerve cords, and a peripheral system.

CHAPTER REVIEW

10. Vertebrates have a central nervous system (brain and spinal cord). Cranial and spinal nerves make up the peripheral system.

11. The large human cerebrum controls traits such as speech, reasoning, and emotions.

12. The human midbrain serves mainly as a relay station between brain parts. The human hindbrain consists of the cerebellum, which coordinates voluntary muscle activity, and the medulla oblongata, which regulates many involuntary responses of internal organs.

13. The spinal cord is a link between the brain and the peripheral nervous system.

14. The sensory-somatic system controls voluntary responses and some reflexes. The autonomic nervous system controls involuntary responses.

15. Stimuli are detected by receptors and specialized sense organs.

16. Study of neuropeptides and their functions is giving insight as to how the brain works.

LANGUAGE OF BIOLOGY

action potential
all-or-none response
association neuron
autonomic nervous
  system
axon
central nervous system
cerebellum
cerebrum
cochlea
conductor
dendrite
depressant
effector
endorphin
enkephalins
eustachian tube
medulla oblongata
motor neuron
nerve impulse
nerve net
neuron
neuropeptide
neurotransmitter
oval window
peripheral nervous system
receptor
reflex
reflex arc
resting potential
sensory neuron
sensory-somatic system
stimulant
synapse
threshold
tympanic membrane

CHECKING YOUR IDEAS

On a separate paper, complete each of the following statements with the missing term(s). Do not write in this book.

1. Involuntary responses of internal organs are controlled by the _____ nervous system.

2. A postsynaptic fiber is affected by _____ released from presynaptic fibers.

3. In humans, the _____ is the part of the brain which controls intelligence.

4. Coelenterates have a nervous system called a(n) _____.

5. During an action potential, _____ ions rush into a neuron.

6. _____ neurons carry impulses toward an effector.

7. _____ are drugs which increase central nervous system activity.

8. The brain and spinal cord make up the _____ nervous system.

9. Stimuli are detected by _____.

10. In humans, the _____ coordinates impulses and maintains balance and muscle tone.

EVALUATING YOUR IDEAS

1. How are the nervous system and endocrine systems different and alike?

2. Explain functions and interrelationships of receptors, conductors, and effectors.

3. How is the structure of a motor neuron suited to its function?

4. In what direction do impulses travel along a vertebrate neuron?

5. How do the myelin sheath and nodes of Ranvier affect nerve transmission?

6. Describe how a neuron carries an impulse.

7. What is the refractory period? Why is the refractory period necessary?

8. Compare a nerve impulse to an electric current in a wire.

Occasionally questions are added to the *Applying Your Ideas* that require students to use information they have learned from previous chapters. Those questions are marked with asterisks and chapter references.

589

CHAPTER REVIEW

9. Explain the nerve all-or-none response.

10. Explain the factors which determine how you interpret the strength of a stimulus.

11. How does an impulse cross a synapse to a postsynaptic fiber?

12. Do neurotransmitters always cause an action potential in the postsynaptic fiber? Explain and give an example.

13. How do neurotransmitters show the relationship between the endocrine system and the nervous system?

14. How are neurotransmitters inactivated?

15. Explain several ways that chemicals and drugs affect synapses.

16. Describe the nervous system of *Hydra*.

17. How is the human brain protected?

18. Describe the functions of the human cerebrum.

19. What is the function of the human midbrain?

20. What are the roles of the cerebellum and medulla oblongata?

21. How is the spinal cord protected?

22. What are reflexes? How are they adaptive?

23. What are the roles of the sensory-somatic system?

24. What does the autonomic nervous system control? What are the two subdivisions of this system?

25. What senses are considered "touch"?

26. Discuss how hearing occurs in humans.

27. What are neuropeptides?

28. What are the functions of endorphins and enkephalins? How might these substances be used as drugs?

APPLYING YOUR IDEAS

1. How is the carrying of impulses in only one direction adaptive?

2. In a laboratory, an isolated neuron stimulated midway along the axon has action potentials sweep outward in both directions. Why does this moving in both directions not happen inside the animal?

3. Usually a stimulus must be repeated before neurotransmitters are secreted across a synapse. How is this delay adaptive?

4. Describe the reflex arc responsible for jumping up quickly after sitting on a pincushion full of pins.

5. Distinguish between the all-or-none response in nerves and muscles. *Chapter 28

6. Internal organs are stimulated by both sympathetic and parasympathetic nerves. Why does the same organ respond differently to these nerves? *Chapter 15

7. What animals lack nervous systems?

8. Why can plants survive without nervous systems? *Chapter 22

EXTENDING YOUR IDEAS

1. Have a classmate sit on the edge of a table or stool with legs crossed. Using the side of your hand, strike the knee just below the kneecap. Note the response. Can the subject prevent this response?

2. You can use many animals to test reflexes. Experiment with animals such as hydras and planarians and with more complex animals such as frogs. Expose them to several stimuli and note responses.

SUGGESTED READINGS

Baumann, Gilbert, "The Cell Membrane—Ready for Action." *Chemistry*, Dec., 1978.

Gurin, Joel, "Chemical Feelings." *Science 80*, Premier Issue, 1980.

Hecht, Annabel, "Tranquilizers: Use, Abuse, and Dependency." *FDA Consumer*, Oct., 1978.

Nicar, Michael J., "Marijuana Use and Abuse." *Chemistry*, January, 1979.

Postonik, Pauline, "Drugs and Pregnancy." *FDA Consumer*, October, 1978.

Additional student readings and suggested teacher readings are provided in the Teacher's Guide.

ENVIRONMENT

Organisms do not live in isolation. They interact with other organisms and with their physical surroundings. For example, the environment provides stimuli to which an organism responds. In Unit VIII, you will study the responses (behavior) of organisms.

Availability of food and other resources affects growth and size of populations and distribution of organisms. Geography, soil conditions, and amount of light are other conditions involved. Communities change with time, too. In this unit, you will learn about populations, communities, and how communities change.

Humans have affected other organisms and the environment in many ways. Some of the effects of humans have been negative; others have been positive. Shown here are birds and the habitat in which they live in the Hawaiian Islands. These birds and their habitat are protected in a bird sanctuary. You will conclude your study of environmental interactions by examining the role of humans in the environment.

Bird Sanctuary In Hawaiian Islands

VIII

Behavior can be classified as either innate (genetically determined) or learned. These carp are showing a type of learned behavior. Because people have walked to the edge of the pond and fed the carp many times, the carp now come to the surface whenever a human approaches, whether or not the human has food. This type of learned behavior is called a conditioned response. What other conditioned responses have you observed? What other kinds of behavior are there?

Introduction: National Geographic has produced a set of excellent films, any of which will provide a stimulating introduction to this chapter. *Invertebrates: Conditioning or Learning?* shows experiments with learning in simple animals. Experiments deal with such diverse organisms as planarians, honeybees, and dragonfly larvae. *Konrad Lorenz: Science of Animal Behavior* focuses on the pioneering work by Lorenz in the area of imprinting in young geese. It also concentrates on research involving social hierarchies in geese and the idea that geese inherit their mother's rank in the pecking order. *Do Animals Reason?* explores experiments devised to determine learning abilities in triggerfish, starlings, and dolphins. *The Tool Users* discusses this unique behavior in carpenter ants, woodpecker finches, and chimpanzees. Each film is fourteen minutes long and can be rented from Modern Film Rentals. See *Audio-Visual Suppliers* in the Teacher's Guide.

BEHAVIOR

Chapter 31 compares and contrasts different forms of innate and learned behavior.

Organisms respond to stimuli in their environment. The pattern of activities of an organism in reacting to stimuli is called **behavior.** The stimuli which cause behavior are both external and internal. External stimuli include things such as a change in temperature, a light, or a noise. Some internal stimuli are hunger and thirst. Although internal stimuli may result in behavior, internal functions such as beating of the heart are usually not considered to be behavior. Obtaining food or playing a violin is behavior.

Behavior varies among organisms. An organism's behavior is limited by the organism's biological "equipment." The complexity of the nervous and endocrine systems is very important in determining the behavior of a living thing, but all the systems of an organism affect behavior. For example, behavior often is involved with movement. Thus, the complexity of the muscular and skeletal systems adds to an animal's responses. In general, organisms with the most complex systems have the most complex behavior; thus, *behavior has a biological basis.* The types of systems an organism has, of course, depend on its genetic code. A mammal's behavior is more complex than that of a fish which in turn is more complex than that of an earthworm. All these animals have more complex behavior than plants.

GOAL: You will gain an understanding of the patterns of responses made by organisms to stimuli from their environment.

Behavior is the pattern of activities of an organism in response to its environment.

The terms ethology, psychology, and psychobiology are sometimes used for behavior.

An organism's behavior is limited by its biological "equipment."

INNATE BEHAVIOR

Part of every organism's behavior is innate. **Innate behavior** is inherited behavior. An organism's genotype (Section 7:5) determines how it reacts to given stimuli in certain, predictable

Teaching suggestion: You may want to review with students the concept of behavioral adaptations (Section 11-4).

Innate behavior is under direct genetic control.

Predictability is a key aspect in classifying behavior. An innate response can be predicted and is characteristic of each member of a species. For this reason, innate behavior is often called stereotyped behavior.

ways. Like other inherited features, innate behavior is adaptive; it promotes survival and reproduction. The curling of an amoeba when poked with a needle and the growth of a plant toward light are examples of innate behavior patterns. Each is adaptive and each is predictable. Neither the amoeba nor the plant can "choose" responses to these stimuli. Rather, the responses are "programmed."

31:1 Plant Behavior

To think about behavior in plants may seem strange, but plants do respond to stimuli. Most plant responses are controlled by hormones. For this reason, most plant behavior occurs slowly and is not easily seen. For example, a tropism (Section 22:9) may take hours or days to occur. Plant tropisms involve growth in a certain direction as a result of some external stimulus. You may notice that a plant stem is bent toward a light source or that roots bend downward, but you probably cannot see the plant stem bending or the roots growing down.

Tropisms are controlled by hormones and occur slowly.

Some plant responses do occur rapidly enough to be seen. Such behavior is not controlled by hormones. The snapping shut of a Venus's-flytrap is a rapid plant response (Section 21:7). Certain species of *Mimosa* (muh мон suh) plants also respond to touch. When the leaflets of this plant are touched they fold together and droop (Figure 31-1).

Rapid plant responses often are controlled by changes in water pressure.

Responses in both of these plants are controlled by changes in water pressure, or turgidity (Section 14:13). In *Mimosa*, certain areas at the bases of the leaflets contain very sensitive cells. When touched, these cells lose water, causing the leaflets to fold. Stimulation of the sensory hairs of the Venus's-flytrap also results in a loss of turgidity, causing the leaf to spring shut.

FIGURE 31-1. (a) A *Mimosa* plant before being touched has open leaflets. (b) After being touched, the leaflets close and droop.

a

William Huber

b

William Huber

Yeager and Kay for Photo Researchers   Alvin E. Staffan

a   b

FIGURE 31-2. The response of the pupils to light is a reflex. (a) In bright light the pupils close. (b) In less light, the pupils open allowing more light to enter the eyes.

31:2 Animal Behavior: Reflexes

At least some part of animal behavior is controlled by reflexes. A **reflex** is an innate behavior pattern resulting from the fixed pathways of the nervous system (Section 30:11). A certain stimulus is detected by a receptor. An impulse is transferred by neurons to a certain effector so that the same response always occurs.

Reflexes are found in all animals, including humans. They probably play a major role in the behavior of simple animals. For example, if a planarian receives an electric shock, it contracts. If it is exposed to a bright light, it glides away. The planarian always reacts the same way to these stimuli.

You already know some examples of reflexes in humans. Your hand is rapidly jerked away from a hot stove, and your foot is quickly lifted from a sharp rock. Both of these responses are reflexes (Section 30:11). You may think about the responses later, but the responses are made before you are aware of what has happened. Reflex behavior occurs more rapidly than responding after thinking, and thus is protective.

In a reflex, impulses normally travel over fixed pathways, but a reflex may be altered with practice and effort. If you touch a hot stove accidentally, by reflex you will probably remove your hand. However, you might be able to keep your hand on the stove by thinking about it. Changing of reflexes in humans involves different neurons from those involved in the reflex.

Because some reflexes can be altered, there is no clear cut division between innate behavior and learned behavior. The terms *innate* and *learned* are human inventions for the purpose of studying behavior. In reality, animal (including human) behavior is a combination of innate and learned responses.

Teaching suggestion: You may want to review the reflex arc (Section 30:11) with students.

Reflexes are determined by the fixed pathways of the nervous system.

Suggested demonstration: Place a bright light beside a culture dish that contains planaria. Turn the light off for several minutes, stir the culture, and turn the light on again. The planaria will move quickly from the lighted side.

Certain reflexes may be modified with practice and effort.

There is no clear division between innate and learned behavior.

In general, the less complex the animal, the greater its innate behavior.

FIGURE 31-3. Migration of birds involves complex, instinctive behavior. Some birds migrate thousands of miles.

31:3 Animal Behavior: Instincts

One of the most fascinating types of innate behavior is instinct. **Instinct** is behavior which involves a set of complicated responses to a stimulus or stimuli. Usually, it occurs in complex invertebrates and in vertebrates. These patterns are not limited to a single response but may involve many continued activities. Some activities of an instinct depend on previous responses. In other words, one activity triggers another.

Migration of birds is an example of behavior which is mostly instinctive. The activities involved in migration are complex. Thus, it may be hard to see how these activities could be innate responses, but at least some are. Biological "time-telling" (Section 31:5) seems to be a part of this instinct. Birds involuntarily respond to many environmental stimuli. For instance, it has been shown that their gonads respond to periods of daylight and darkness. As seasons change, the ratio of daylight to darkness hours changes. Also the air temperature varies. These changes affect the birds' hormone production, fat deposits, and metabolic rate. Exactly which of these stimuli, if any, starts migration is still a matter of research and debate.

How do migrating birds know where they are going? Young birds may follow more experienced birds, but studies have shown that this following does not seem to occur. In some species, young birds who have never migrated before can find their way even if the young birds have been isolated from older birds of their species. Birds may navigate by using the angles between the sun or stars and the horizon. Using birds in an enclosed pen with an artificial sky, it has been shown that starlings use a sun compass. Some birds may be able to detect and use the earth's magnetic field to navigate. Certain pigeons have been found to have a magnetic mineral in their heads. Further research is needed to learn whether this mineral is used for navigation and, if so, how.

Instinct is innate behavior involving a set of complicated responses.

Bird migration depends on responses to periods of light and darkness.

The positions of sun and stars are cues used in bird migration.

Many birds travel great distances to nearly the same place year after year. Kirtland's Warblers nest only in north central Michigan and winter in the Bahamas. The American golden plover travels from north Alaska through Nova Scotia to Argentina and back each year. Birds probably learn the features of their own nesting area. Thus, the instinct to migrate may be combined with learning.

Many factors seem to be involved in the migration behavior. Some of these factors are not understood and some probably are yet to be found.

Teaching suggestion: If space permits, show a map of the flyways of North America. Many migrating birds use the same route each year.

Many factors appear to be involved in bird migration.

31:4 Courtship Behavior

Courtship behavior is another example of a complex instinct in animals. Courtship is a series of ordered stimuli and responses between male and female prior to mating. The three-spined stickleback fish has a detailed courtship pattern (Section 24:1). Courtship behavior in the great crested grebe, a large water bird, involves a series of dives to the bottom of a pond or lake. During each dive, the grebe gathers weeds for nest building. The male and the female alternate dives. After each dive, the grebes face each other, stretch, shake their heads, and often touch. Time out for swimming may be taken between dives. Finally, mating occurs.

Because similar species often live together in a community (Section 1:1), it is important that each individual mate only with a member of its own species (Section 11:6). Certain kinds of "signals" ensure that appropriate mating will happen. For instance, the males of different species of fiddler crabs wave their claws and move their bodies in slightly different ways. Only a female of the same species will respond to a certain male and mate. Also, in each species of firefly, the pattern of flashes by the male is different. Bird songs and cricket chirps also vary with each species.

Courtship behavior maintains reproductive isolation (Section 11:6).

Courtship patterns are examples of complex innate behavior.

Courtship "signals" ensure that an animal mates with a member of its own species.

FIGURE 31-4. A bower bird builds a nest to attract a mate and then decorates it with shiny or bright objects. By contortions of his body and by tossing around the prized objects, he attracts the female. This courtship behavior is instinctive.

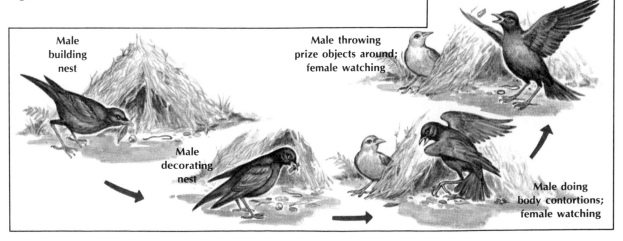

Male building nest

Male decorating nest

Male throwing prize objects around; female watching

Male doing body contortions; female watching

31:5 Biological Clocks

Behavior of many organisms occurs in a 24-hour cycle.

Activities with 24-hour cycles are called circadian rhythms.

Response to stimuli associated with time is probably an adaptation of all organisms. Most of these responses have about 24-hour cycles. Many flowers regularly open and close at certain times of the day. Honeybees must "keep track" of time in order to inform other bees about food sources (Section 31:10). Mice in cages show increased activity on running wheels at certain times of the night. Even some activities within organisms may occur in 24-hour cycles. Body temperature and enzyme activity vary with the time of day. The rate of photosynthesis in plants also varies.

Biological clocks control activities related to time.

Organisms are said to have **biological clocks** which control these activities. What is the clock? The answer is not known. The clock may involve some cellular or chemical mechanism. In complex animals, it may involve some control in or near the brain. Many hypotheses are being investigated.

Some scientists are researching the effect of cycles on manic and depressed mental states of humans. Their hypothesis is that these altered mental states are the result of not being on a sleep-wake cycle that is 24 hours long.

Clocks may be "set" according to environmental stimuli.

There is strong evidence that the clock can be "reset" according to stimuli from the environment. People who have flown great distances across many time zones experience "jet lag." For a day or two, the traveler's activities are out of phase with other people. They are hungry or sleepy while others on local time are not. Gradually, a traveler's clock is "reset" and activities are readjusted to local times.

1. Behavior is the pattern of activities of an organism in reacting to environmental stimuli.
2. Innate behavior is genetically controlled. It occurs in all animals.
3. A reflex is a simple form of innate behavior governed by the fixed pathways of the nervous system. An instinct is more complex innate behavior involving a set of responses.
4. Courtship behavior is a series of ordered stimuli and responses between a male and female prior to mating.
5. A biological clock controls activities related to time.

REVIEWING YOUR IDEAS

1. What is behavior?
2. What is innate behavior? In what kinds of animals is it found?
3. Distinguish between a reflex and an instinct.
4. What is courtship behavior? Give an example of courtship behavior.
5. What does a biological clock do?

Learned behavior is behavior that can be changed.

LEARNED BEHAVIOR

Learned behavior is behavior that can be changed. Unlike innate behavior, learning involves some choice of responses to a given stimulus. Also, learning is not *directly* controlled by genes. It depends on the animal's physical traits which are controlled by genes. Animals with the greatest intelligence or capacity for learning are those with complex nervous systems. The more complex the brain, for example, the wider the range of possible learned behaviors. Factors other than the animal's physical traits also influence learning. For example, diet may influence how an animal learns.

31:6 Trial and Error

At one time, scientists thought that only very complex animals could learn. Now, however, experiments suggest that simple forms of life can also learn. How much simple animals can learn in nature is unknown. However, simple animals can learn to change their behaviors in the laboratory.

A simple method of testing learning ability is to use a maze. The simplest type of maze is called a **T-maze.** It is shaped like a T so an animal has a choice of one of two turns. If an earthworm is placed in a maze like the one shown in Figure 31-5, it will learn to avoid the chamber in which it receives an electric shock. The worm will learn to enter the dark, moist chamber in which it finds food. Many trials are necessary before the worm learns which chamber to choose. But the point is that the worm can learn. There is no innate mechanism which tells the worm to turn right or left at the end of a T-maze. The worm must learn which way to turn as a result of its own experience.

Simple learning such as in the earthworm is by **trial and error.** By repeatedly trying a task, the animal learns by its mistakes. In the case of the earthworm, it learns to go into the moist chamber.

Motivation (moht uh VAY shun) is needed for the learning process of most animals. In animals, motivation usually involves satisfying a need, such as hunger or thirst. Learning in a maze can only occur if the animal is motivated. For example, the animal usually must be hungry to respond to food. Usually an animal must be thirsty to respond to water.

However, motivation alone does not ensure learning. Other factors are also important. An earthworm in a T-maze has two choices. One involves **punishment,** the shock; while the other results in a **reward,** the moist chamber containing food. The choice resulting in a reward satisfies the motivation. The punishment does not. The earthworm learns to avoid the shock and get the reward.

Human learning is also the product of motivation, reward, and punishment. In formal education, some students are motivated by the desire to do well. The reward may be a good grade, a feeling of pride, or use of the learned material later. Failure to learn and its consequences may be punishment. These same factors contribute to the learning that occurs outside the classroom throughout life. What motivates people to learn to drive cars? What motivates someone to practice playing the piano? Do you recall the experiences you had in learning to tie your shoelaces or to write your name as a young child? What was the motivation involved in those cases?

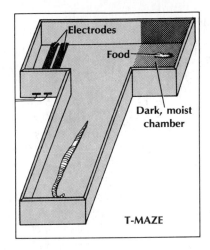

FIGURE 31-5. By trial and error, an earthworm will learn to enter the dark, moist chamber of a T-maze.

Trial and error is a simple form of learning.

Suggested demonstration: Demonstrate trial and error learning in earthworms by constructing a T-maze. One chamber should contain a supply of moist soil. The other should contain a "punishment" such as paper soaked in weak acid, a bright light, or a weak electric current. Use several worms, identifying each with colored markings. Repeat trials daily until the worms learn to find the soil and avoid the punishment.

Motivation, reward, and punishment are important aspects of the learning process.

31:7 Conditioned Response

In one kind of conditioning, the animal involuntarily learns an association of a response and a stimulus which does not normally cause that response.

This kind of conditioning is classical conditioning. The behavior is *elicited* from the animal. The response is involuntary.

Ringing a bell does not normally cause the response of salivating. Thus, salivating is a conditioned response.

Another type of learning is known as **conditioning.** There are two kinds of conditioning. In one kind, the *conditioned response is a response to a stimulus which does not normally cause that response.*

A Russian biologist, Ivan Pavlov (1849-1936), was the first to show such a learning mechanism. Pavlov knew that if a dog smelled food, it would begin to salivate. This response seemed to be an innate one. Pavlov began to ring a bell at the same time he gave a dog its dinner. Each time, the dog's saliva would begin to flow. After a while, ringing of the bell alone caused the dog's saliva to flow. The dog was conditioned (had learned) to respond to the bell as it did when fed. The response in this case is involuntary. Under normal conditions, the bell would not cause saliva flow. This response is learning because it involves *association and change of behavior.*

Another example of this kind of conditioning is shown by planaria. The normal (innate) response of a planarian is to glide away from a bright light. Also, it curls up when electrically shocked (Section 31:3). If a bright light is closely followed by an electric shock, the planarian curls up. Eventually the worm learns to associate the light with the shock, and the light alone will cause the curling up response. Such behavior is a conditioned response. The behavior of the planarian has been involuntarily changed by its experience (Figure 31-6).

FIGURE 31-6. (a) A dog can be conditioned to salivate at the sound of a bell if the bell has been rung in the past when the dog received food. (b) A planarian can be conditioned, associating a bright light with an electric shock.

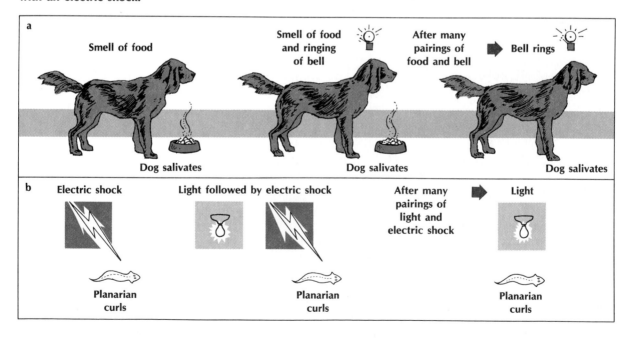

Smell of food	**Smell of food and ringing of bell**	**After many pairings of food and bell** → **Bell rings**
Dog salivates	Dog salivates	Dog salivates

Electric shock	**Light followed by electric shock**	**After many pairings of light and electric shock** → **Light**
Planarian curls	Planarian curls	Planarian curls

FIGURE 31-7. Animals can be taught tricks by a kind of conditioning in which the animal voluntarily does certain behaviors which get the desired effect (reward).

The other kind of conditioning involves trial and error learning. This type of conditioning is often used to teach animals to do tricks, such as teaching a dog to roll over. By rewarding the dog for doing the trick, the probability that the dog will repeat the trick is increased. Also, the dog learns by being punished for not doing the trick. (Punishment may be the absence of reward.) In this kind of conditioning, *the conditioned, or learned, response is that behavior which gets the desired effect* (in this case, the reward). Commands and gestures can be cues for the dog's behavior, but the dog has learned that the reward goes with certain behaviors. Learning in this case is the result of the animal's own activities. Can you think of examples of both kinds of conditioning in humans?

In the second kind of conditioning, the animal learns a voluntary response that gets a desired effect.

This kind of conditioning is operant conditioning. The animal *emits* the behavior. The reward or punishment increases or decreases respectively the probability that the animal will repeat the behavior.

31:8 Imprinting

Imprinting is a simple, very rapid, irreversible form of learning. Imprinting fills the gap between innate behavior and learning. Many birds, such as ducks and geese, follow their mothers after hatching. It was concluded that birds have the innate behavior (instinct) to follow something they see at a certain critical time shortly after hatching. Normally, the thing the young imprint on is the mother. Young birds learn to recognize the mother rapidly. This behavior is clearly adaptive.

However, the young can imprint on another object or animal if that object or animal is substituted and is what the young see at the critical time. The young birds will then follow the substitute. The young birds have the innate behavior to follow but learn to

Imprinting is a form of learning related to instinctive behavior.

Young birds normally imprint on their mother.

Alvin E. Staffan

FIGURE 31-8. These young Canada geese have imprinted on their mother. Imprinting is a following response and a form of learned behavior.

recognize the substitute. Young geese seeing a human at the critical time will imprint on that person. In one experiment, geese that imprinted on a human would not follow their natural mother when she was returned to them. The preference they formed for the human was permanent; the geese as adults still preferred the human over other geese.

Experiments with many birds have shown that birds will imprint on one of several types of objects. Exactly what certain birds will follow depends on the species. Many will follow a mechanical model. The number of species that follow a mechanical model increases if a rhythmic sound is added. Some species will respond to the stimulus of sound alone. The period of time in which birds can be imprinted is only a few days after they hatch. After this time, imprinting can no longer occur.

PEOPLE IN BIOLOGY

(1903 -   )

Konrad Zacharias Lorenz

Konrad Lorenz's lifelong interest in animal behavior grew out of his boyhood pastime of collecting, observing, and caring for animals. The first person to study animals in their natural habitat instead of in the laboratory, Lorenz founded modern ethology, the study of animal behavior. Working mainly with geese, Lorenz developed the concept of imprinting, the process by which a young animal learns to identify its mother. He also discovered that the birds could be made to imprint on a human instead of their mother, and he became famous for his substitute "mother-goose" role as he was seen being followed by young geese. More recently, Lorenz has been studying territoriality and aggression in animal species, including humans.

Konrad Lorenz was one of the first researchers to state that many behaviors were genetically determined, not learned. For his work in animal behavior, Lorenz shared the 1973 Nobel Prize for physiology and medicine with two other ethologists, and he has earned many other degrees and honors. His research has been published in several popular books, including *On Aggression* and *King Solomon's Ring*.

FIGURE 31-9. (a) The chimpanzee first attempts to reach the bananas by jumping. (b) It then stacks boxes and (c) stands on them to reach the fruit. Insight is involved in the chimp's behavior.

31:9 Insight

Suppose a chimpanzee is placed in a large cage containing several boxes. Bananas have been hung from the top of the cage well out of the chimp's reach. At first, the chimp begins to jump for the bananas, but it cannot reach them. Later, instead of jumping, the chimp gathers the boxes, stacks them, and crawls up the stack of boxes reaching the bananas (Figure 31-9).

No past experience provided the chimpanzee with a "plan of attack." Somehow it was able to "think" out the fact that stacking the boxes would allow it to reach the bananas. The chimp had insight to solve the problem. **Insight** is the ability to correctly plan a response to a new situation. This type of behavior eliminates some of the trial and error learning.

Insight eliminates some trial and error learning.

The chimpanzee formed a **concept**, or idea. The chimpanzee's concept was that added height would allow it to reach the bananas. This type of behavior is different from trial and error learning. Both forms involve experience, but insight or reasoning enables the animal to "plan."

In humans, reasoning, insight, and concept forming are involved in behavior. Thus, learning in humans is very complex. Learning in early life is often by trial and error or imitation. However, as humans get older, they rely more on reasoning, insight, and abstract idea formation. Humans draw on their own past experiences as well as those of others.

6. Learned behavior is behavior which can be changed. It occurs mostly in animals with more complex nervous systems.

7. Motivation is needed for learning to begin.

8. Punishment and/or reward are also necessary for learning.

9. Both kinds of conditioning change an animal's normal behavior and involve association. In one form of conditioning, an animal responds to a stimulus which ordinarily does not cause that response. In the other, trial and error learning is involved, and the conditioned response brings a desired effect such as a reward.

10. Imprinting is a form of learning in which an animal learns to recognize an object shortly after birth.

11. Insight learning is the planning of a response to a new situation.

Communication is an adaptation in many animals.

REVIEWING YOUR IDEAS

6. What is learned behavior? In what kinds of animals is it found?

7. How is motivation involved in learning in animals?

8. What other factors, besides motivation, are necessary for learning?

9. How are both kinds of conditioning learned behavior? How do the kinds of conditioning differ?

10. What is imprinting?

11. What is insight learning?

COMMUNICATION

Animals have a variety of ways of exchanging information. Communication is essential within species of animals. Communication among members of a species helps in activities such as locating food, reproduction, and defense against other animals. Courtship behavior (Section 31:4) involves communication such as visual displays and sounds. In the sections that follow, you will study some other examples of animal communication.

31:10 Honeybee "Talk"

Societies are common in some insects. The honeybee society has been studied carefully. One of the most important activities of bees is making honey from the nectar of flowers. As in all societies, a division of labor exists within a busy beehive (Figure 31-10). Activity centers around a single **queen bee** who mates only once and produces thousands of offspring. Most numerous are the **worker bees,** bees that do most of the work needed to maintain the hive. They feed larvae, produce honey, remove dead bees from the hive, and protect the hive from intruders. Worker bees are sterile females.

Division of labor exists within a society.

FIGURE 31-10. (a) A bee society is made up of (b) different kinds of bees with different roles.

National Audubon Society for Photo Researchers

Drones are male bees which develop from unfertilized eggs. Several drones mate with a queen during her single mating flight. A drone mates with only one queen bee and then dies.

Karl von Frisch (1886-), a German scientist, experimented to learn if bees can communicate. He believed that a bee can "inform" other bees of the location of food. Von Frisch had observed that a bee, after finding a supply of food, returned to the hive; soon after, hundreds of bees swarmed to the food supply. Von Frisch assumed that the first bee had "informed" the other bees of the location of the food.

In order to study bees, von Frisch marked some bees and made a glass-walled hive. To attract bees, he set out containers of sugar water.

How a bee informs other bees depends on distance. Suppose a bee discovers a food source at a distance of less than one hundred meters from the hive. The bee returns to the hive and performs what von Frisch calls a **round dance** on the inside wall of the hive. The bee circles first in one direction and then in the other (Figure 31-11). Soon other bees leave the hive, return shortly, and perform the same dance. Later, almost all the bees are aware of the distance to the food. The round dance must mean, "There is food somewhere within a radius of one hundred meters."

No directions are given during a round dance. Von Frisch determined this fact by placing the food source at various points around a one-hundred-meter circle. Regardless of the direction of the food, the dance was the same. How do the bees locate the food source? By using their antennae, they detect the scent of the food source on the dancer bee. The bees then seek the same scent when they leave the hive.

For distances greater than one hundred meters, a two-part dance called the **waggle dance** is performed by the bees. A bee returning from a food source begins the waggle dance on the wall of the hive. The bee does "figure eights" while wagging its abdomen. *Distance* from the hive is given by the number of complete cycles of the dance per fifteen-second time interval. The farther the food source from the hive, the fewer the number of figure eights. Sounds made by the dancing bee may also provide information about distance.

The waggle dance also gives the *direction* of the food. The angle (in comparison with an imaginary vertical line on the wall of the hive) at which each figure-eight dance is performed is the key. The vertical line represents the *present* direction of the sun. The angle from the vertical is the angle of the food source from the sun. If a bee begins its dance pointing 30° right of vertical, it means that the food source is 30° to the right of the sun (Figure 31-12).

ROUND DANCE

FIGURE 31-11. A round dance by one bee "tells" other bees that a food source is within 100 meters of the hive.

Different "languages" are found in different species of bees.

FIGURE 31-12. A waggle dance by one bee "tells" other bees both the direction of a food source and its distance from the hive. The angle of the dance with respect to a vertical corresponds to the angle of the food source from the sun. Frequency of the figure-eight movements indicates distance.

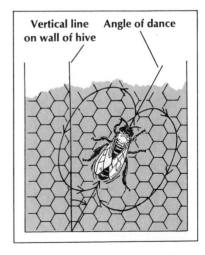

Vertical line on wall of hive   Angle of dance

In a society, innate behavior patterns are important to the entire species.

Round dances and waggle dances are complex instincts. These activities are governed by genes and are the products of natural selection. This type of innate behavior benefits the entire species. After returning to its hive, a bee does not dance for its own pleasure. The dance is rather a means of informing other bees of a food source.

31:11 Pheromones

Pheromones are chemical signals.

Communication by dancing is only one way that information is passed along in animal societies. Another means of communication is by secretion of chemicals called **pheromones** (FER uh mohnz). Pheromones are chemicals which can be detected by their odor.

Some pheromones attract animals for mating.

One use of pheromones is for attraction of mates. In some species of insects, the female releases a pheromone so strong that it can be detected by a male more than a kilometer away. The male follows the scent and, as he gets closer, the scent becomes stronger. Thus, he can locate the female and mate with her. Some female mammals secrete pheromones which inform the males that they are in "heat" (Section 23:5) and are receptive to mating.

In ant societies, some pheromones are used to inform others about the location of food. As an ant returns to its nest with food, it lays a trail of pheromone along the ground. Ants from the nest follow the scent to the food source and deposit their own trail as they return to the nest. Ants which do not find food do not release pheromones. In this way, there is no confusion about the location of food.

Other pheromones are also produced by ants. One is a compound released by decomposing ants. The pheromone acts as a signal to other ants to remove the dead ant from the nest.

Some pheromones affect behavior over a long period of time. Male mice secrete a pheromone which is needed for the start of the female's estrous cycle. This cycle involves a series of changes in hormone levels and behavior. In some insect societies, pheromones eaten by the insects determine the insects' roles in the society, including their reproductive abilities. In honeybees, the queen bee passes a pheromone orally to worker bees. The pheromone inhibits ovarian development and the behavior needed to make a queen cell in the hive.

FIGURE 31-13. The queen honeybee passes out pheromone to worker bees. It inhibits their developing into queen bees.

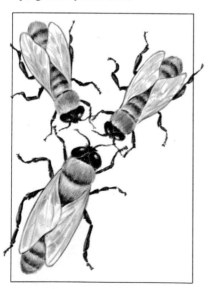

The search for a specific, single pheromone in humans is underway. Results of tests already carried out are unclear. However, human pheromones are thought to be involved in human behavior as male-female attractants and as attractants between mothers and their babies.

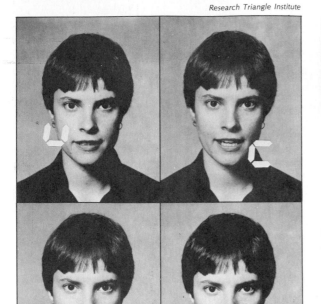

a

b

31:12 Language

Most scientists agree that language is a form of communication in which symbols are used to represent ideas. Human language involves both verbal and written symbols. Both spoken and written language provide young humans with the basics for survival and reproduction. Humans have available to them a record of the experiences of all those who lived before them. Thus, humans do not have to experience everything themselves but can benefit from what others have learned. Humans can use that accumulated knowledge as a basis for their personal discoveries. In this way, knowledge keeps building upon itself and the species as a whole benefits.

Language can occur only in animals with complex nervous systems, memory, and insight. Chimps cannot speak words, but they can use symbols to communicate. Their language, though, is much simpler than that of humans. Chimp language does not seem to involve the many complex thought processes that are common to human language. It is difficult to tell whether all or part of a chimp's language is really just a form of learning for rewards—a kind of trick. Whether chimps communicate by a form of language in nature must also be determined.

FIGURE 31-14. Special devices are being developed which help persons with hearing or sight problems communicate more easily. (a) An aid to persons with hearing problems, the computerized "auto-cuer," contained in special eyeglasses, "listens" to speech and displays cues that aid in lipreading. The photos show what the wearer would see as the girl pictured says, "He can go." (b) The Kurzweil reading machine reads typed text aloud, speaking in a clear voice that simulates human speech, and has been a great aid to blind persons.

Chimps can be taught to use symbols to communicate.

FIGURE 31-15. The gorilla, Koko, uses a keyboard to communicate. The scientist who taught Koko to use the keyboard is one of a group who argues that apes are capable of communication much like humans.

12. Bees communicate by "dancing."
13. Pheromones are chemicals produced by animals and serve as signals for communicating information.
14. Language is a form of communication in which symbols are used.

In experiments in which scientists study ape language, a computer and a keyboard with symbols are used. The apes recognize the symbols. By pushing different keys, they can put words together to make simple sentences. In some cases, they have put symbols together in new combinations to make meanings other than those they were taught. Some chimps and gorillas have been taught sign language of the deaf. They can express many words and simple thoughts.

Marine mammals such as whales, dolphins, and porpoises are intelligent animals. Many studies show that they make a variety of sounds. Some of the sounds are used to help the animals navigate and locate objects by means of echoes. Other sounds, including moans, whistles, and barking noises, may be a form of communication. The sounds made by some whales can travel as far as a distance of 80 km. Most "talkative" of all these mammals is the humpback whale. It produces a great variety of sounds, and the sounds alternate between whales, suggesting a "conversation." Although there has been much work done, scientists do not know what these sounds represent.

REVIEWING YOUR IDEAS

12. How do bees communicate?
13. What are pheromones?
14. What is language?

SOCIAL BEHAVIOR

Communication is one form of behavior which is important in animal societies. A **society** is a group of animals of one species living together in an organized way. Other behavior patterns are also found in many societies. Like communication, these other kinds of behavior are important to the organization of the society and the survival of its members.

31:13 Social Hierarchies

A social hierarchy is composed of all levels of authority.

Another example of social behavior involves a pecking order, or **social hierarchy** (HI rar kee). Much human life involves this aspect of behavior. A social hierarchy is composed of all levels of authority. Social hierarchies are present in most organizations such as an army, a school, or a business. Such a chain of command provides order and organization within a group of people. Thus, a social hierarchy eliminates confusion and promotes efficiency of the organization.

In many respects, the same patterns exist in animal societies. The term "pecking order" resulted from studies of animal dominance. A society of chickens forms a hierarchy by "pecking" at each other. Two chickens approach each other and may either fight or one may peacefully give way to the other (Figure 31-16). In either case, a dominance relationship results between these two chickens.

Dominance in animals is an authority relationship. Similar contacts occur throughout a flock so that a total hierarchy emerges. One chicken becomes dominant to all the others. Another chicken may be dominant to all but the first one, and so on. Once the order is decided, it remains constant. Sometimes a chicken with lower status challenges a more dominant one, but these encounters rarely change the pecking order. This type of hierarchy occurs in many groups of animals such as birds, some reptiles, and nonhuman primates.

What are the factors involved in establishing a hierarchy? In general, males dominate females. Beyond this, the strong dominate the weak, and the old dominate the young. Size and other factors may be involved. Strangers usually lose to animals in familiar territory.

Why is a hierarchy adaptive? A hierarchy promotes survival in several ways. The overall result of dominance is increased order and reduced aggression throughout the society. After the first pecking is over, the less dominant learns to "accept its fate." There is less fighting over food and mates. Therefore, if conditions are such that not every individual can eat and mate, then at least the more dominant ones will be able to do so. A social hierarchy is good insurance that the "best" genes are the ones passed on, and it prevents overbreeding. In any event, the pecking order promotes coordination and unity among the members of a society. Therefore, it is adaptive to the total group of animals.

FIGURE 31-16. Social hierarchy in chickens is established as a result of "conflicts" or pecks between members of the flock. A "pecking order" results.

Once a pecking order is established, order is increased within the society.

Roger K. Burnard

Stephen J. Krasemann/DRK Photo

FIGURE 31-17. (a) Impalas and (b) walruses combat in establishing social order in their groups.

Fran Allan/Animals Animals

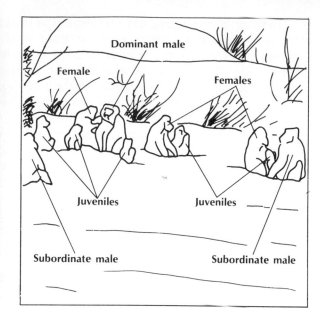

FIGURE 31-18. A troop of Anubis baboons shows a social hierarchy in which there is one dominant male, several females and their offspring, and subordinate males. Subordinate males work with the dominant male to provide defense for the troop.

Territoriality involves the occupation and defense of definite areas.

Territoriality often enables a male to attract a mate.

31:14 Territoriality

Many animals occupy and defend specific territories. This concept, known as **territoriality** (ter uh tor ee AL ut ee), was first seen in birds. The songs of many male birds announce that their home has been established. The song tells other birds to stay away, and it informs females of the species that a male has staked out his territory. Because having a territory "improves the status" of a male, territoriality is important in mating.

Studies of other kinds of animals in nature have shown many examples of territoriality. For example, howler monkeys travel in clans. They defend their territory against rival clans by howling accompanied by bluffs of fighting. Rarely is anything more serious needed. The intruding clan realizes that it is not on safe ground and usually retreats peacefully.

What is the advantage of having a territory? What does a territory do for an individual or, more importantly, for a society? Territoriality, like a social hierarchy, promotes survival. Possession of a territory by a bird helps attract a mate. Those that are most "fit" (best adapted) are those that win a territory and mate. Thus, their genes are most likely to be passed to the next generation. The weaker members of the group, with no territory, rarely pass their genes on because usually they do not mate. In many primate societies, mateless males live on the edges of the territories of other males. These males enjoy none of the pleasures of having a territory. Thus, territoriality is related to hierarchy.

Territoriality spreads the members of a group over a large area. Wide spacing ensures a better food supply for all members. Overbreeding and overcrowding are dangerous to a species. With given areas in which to live (eat, breathe, mate), conflicts are reduced and survival is ensured. Thus, the society (and species) benefits.

Several biologists question whether territoriality exists in humans. However, because many animals exhibit territoriality, it seems reasonable to assume that humans might have this trait also. More research is needed to determine if humans are territorial. Perhaps a keener understanding of human biological nature will reveal some of the reasons for human behavior. How might such knowledge be useful?

FIGURE 31-19. The male wolf in the foreground defends a territory against another male wolf.

REVIEWING YOUR IDEAS

15. What is a society?
16. What is a social hierarchy?
17. What is territoriality? How is territoriality related to social hierarchy?

15. A society is a group of animals of one species living together in an organized way.
16. A social hierarchy is a social relationship involving levels of authority.
17. Territoriality is the occupation and defense of a particular area. Both territoriality and social hierarchy promote survival and the passing on of "successful" genes.

CHAPTER REVIEW

SUMMARY

1. Behavior is the entire pattern of responses made by an organism to its environment.

2. Complexity of behavior is related to an organism's physical traits.

3. Innate behavior is genetically controlled. Innate behavior is predictable and adaptive.

4. Plant behavior includes such things as tropisms and responses to touch.

5. Reflexes are behavior patterns involving fixed pathways of the nervous system.

6. Instincts are complex patterns of innate behavior involving a set of responses. Examples of instinct are bird migration and courtship behavior.

7. Behavior associated with time is thought to be controlled by biological clocks.

8. Learned behavior is behavior that can be changed.

9. Motivation, reward, and punishment are often necessary factors for learning.

10. Trial and error is a simple form of learned behavior.

11. There are two kinds of conditioned responses. One kind of conditioned response is behavior in which an animal involuntarily learns to associate a response with a stimulus which does not normally cause that response. In the other kind of conditioning, a conditioned response is that behavior which the animal voluntarily does to get the desired effect (such as a reward or no punishment).

12. Imprinting fills in the gap between learning and innate behavior.

13. Complex learning can involve insight and concept formation.

14. Information about food sources in some honeybees is passed along by dancing.

15. Pheromones are chemical signals important in many animal societies.

16. Human language is written and spoken. It enables humans to learn from the experience of other humans. Other complex

CHAPTER REVIEW

animals, such as chimps and whales, may have a form of language.

17. A social hierarchy promotes survival in several ways including reduced aggression and increased order.

18. Territoriality also promotes survival. For example, it is important in mating, in even distribution of members of a society, and in reducing conflicts.

LANGUAGE OF BIOLOGY

behavior
biological clock
conditioning
imprinting
innate behavior
insight
instinct
learned behavior
motivation

pheromone
punishment
reflex
reward
social hierarchy
society
territoriality
trial and error learning

CHECKING YOUR IDEAS

On a separate paper, indicate whether each of the following statements is true or false. Do not write in this book.

1. Learning is behavior that can be changed.

2. A dog may learn a trick by conditioning.

3. A bee's waggle dance only gives information about distance of a food source from the hive.

4. Behavior has a biological basis.

5. Migration of birds is an example of learned behavior.

6. Insight enables an animal to plan a response to its environment.

7. Once "set," a biological clock cannot be "reset."

8. A reflex is a type of innate behavior.

9. Plant behavior occurs more slowly than animal behavior.

10. A newly hatched duckling will follow nothing but its mother.

EVALUATING YOUR IDEAS

1. What determines the variety of an organism's behavior?

2. Why is innate behavior considered an adaptation? Why is innate behavior predictable?

3. Explain the reaction to touch of *Mimosa* plants. What causes the reaction?

4. How are reflexes important to humans? List some human reflexes.

5. Why is bird migration considered an instinct?

6. What are some of the factors involved in navigation by birds?

7. How are migration and courtship adaptive?

8. Describe several examples of activities probably controlled by biological clocks.

9. What feature of the nervous system may be important for learning?

10. How is the learning process of an earthworm in a T-maze trial and error learning?

11. How did Pavlov demonstrate conditioning in dogs?

12. Describe imprinting behavior in young ducks and geese. How is imprinting an adaptive behavior?

13. How does insight differ from trial and error learning?

14. How does a bee inform other bees of a food source within 100 m of the hive?

15. Describe the waggle dance of bees. What information does it contain?

16. How are pheromones important in mating? In locating food?

17. How is language important to human learning?

18. Do animals such as chimps and whales have a language? Explain.

19. How is a social hierarchy formed in chickens? How is a hierarchy adaptive?

20. How is territoriality advantageous?

Occasionally questions are added to the *Applying Your Ideas* that require students to use information they have learned from previous chapters. Those questions are marked with asterisks and chapter references.

613

CHAPTER REVIEW

APPLYING YOUR IDEAS

1. List several examples of trial and error learning in humans.

2. A certain dog licks a person's face. The person in pushing the dog back rubs the dog's belly. The dog and the person then both repeat the behaviors many times. The dog gets the "belly rub" reward for face licking; the person gets the "dry face" reward for rubbing the dog's belly. Is the dog or the person conditioned in this example? Explain.

3. Is imprinting a type of learning in humans? Explain.

4. Compile a list of some of the unique advantages of human learning.

5. How might pheromones be used to control insect pests?

6. Why is defense of territory usually limited to gestures, bluffs, or loud noises?

7. Sometimes a queen bee leaves her old hive to start a new one. Why can a new queen then develop in the old hive?

8. How is reflex behavior related to a reflex arc? *Chapter 30

9. Why might certain medicines be more effective at specific times of the day?

10. A *Paramecium* bumps into an object. What kind of behavior is shown by the response of the *Paramecium*?

11. Why do plants not have learned behavior? *Chapter 22

EXTENDING YOUR IDEAS

1. Obtain a culture of the ciliated protozoan *Stentor*. Use a microscope to observe its behavior. Then, use a pipette to scatter India ink on the *Stentor*. Notice its response. Repeat several times. Does *Stentor* always respond in the same way? Explain.

2. Expose a pill bug to a light source from one side. Note the reaction of the bug. Is the bug exhibiting a tropism? (Review the definition of tropism and the kind of organism in which it occurs.) How can you explain this reaction of a pill bug?

3. Construct a maze to test learning in white mice or white rats. Keep a record of the number of trails necessary for the animals to learn the maze.

4. Using library sources, learn about the social structure of a baboon troop. How does this society compare to an insect society? How does the baboon society compare to a human society?

5. Place two sets of white mice which have been reared in separate cages together in another cage. Note any signs of a social hierarchy being formed.

6. Take your temperature at different times of the day. Is it always the same? Explain.

SUGGESTED READINGS

Bertram, Brian C. R., "The Social System of Lions." *Scientific American*, May, 1975.

Burgess, J. Wesley, "Social Spiders." *Scientific American*, March, 1976.

Eaton, G. Gray, "The Social Order of Japanese Macaques." *Sci. American*, October, 1976.

Gould, James L., "Do Honeybees Know What They Are Doing?" *Nat. His.*, June-July, 1979.

Gould, James L., and Carol G. Gould, "The Instinct to Learn." *Science 81*, May, 1981.

Harding, Robert S. O., and Strum, Shirley C., "The Predatory Baboons of Kekopey." *Natural History*, March, 1976.

Hilts, Philip, "The Clock Within." *Science 80*, December, 1980.

Lore, Richard, and Flannelly, Kevin, "Rat Societies." *Scientific American*, May, 1977.

Palmer, John D., "Biological Clocks of the Tidal Zone." *Scientific American*, February, 1975.

Patent, Dorothy Hinshaw, *How Insects Communicate*. New York, Holiday House, 1975.

"The Language Barrier." *Sci. News.*, May 10, 1980.

Additional student readings and suggested teacher readings are provided in the Teacher's Guide.

Several factors affect the sizes of populations of organisms. Some of these factors are the availability of food and space, and the presence of disease organisms. What are some of the factors which might limit the population of these chinstrap penguins? What factors might limit the populations of other organisms? What factors limit the human population?

Introduction: If possible, begin this chapter with a trip to a natural community—forest, field, or pond. Assign teams of students to make population counts of different types of plant and animal life. For example, in a forest, determine the number of trees, ferns, or insects in a small area.
As they locate organisms, students should also make note of any patterns, such as whether the organisms are randomly or nonrandomly dispersed throughout the area. If organisms are clustered, what factors seem to favor them in these areas? Where the organisms are sparse, what may be limiting them? Do any organisms appear to be overcrowded? Encourage students to consider both biotic and abiotic factors. Group discussion of findings should provide a sound basis for your study of population biology. Such discussion should lead to the ideas of limiting factors and their effects on population growth.

Chapter

32

POPULATION BIOLOGY

Chapter 32 discusses the growth of populations and the factors which limit that growth.

A population (Section 11:6) is a group of organisms that naturally interbreed. As reproduction occurs over a period of time, population size increases. **Population size** is the number of organisms in the population. As populations live and reproduce, they interact with their environment. In this chapter, you will study ways in which the environment affects population size.

GOAL: You will gain an understanding of the factors which affect growth and changes of populations.

Environment affects the size of a population.

GROWTH OF POPULATIONS

32:1 Biotic Potential

Under ideal conditions, the size of a population of organisms would continue to increase. Ideal conditions are those in which nothing limits the growth of the population—there is plenty of food, space, and other needed things for all organisms. For example, under ideal conditions, a population of bacteria doubles in size every twenty minutes. The highest rate of reproduction of a population under ideal conditions is called the **biotic** (bi AHT ihk) **potential.**

Populations of organisms tend to increase maximally under ideal conditions. If no factors limited population growth, starting with one bacterium, the earth would be covered with bacteria 30 cm deep in just 36 hours! Even organisms that you usually think of as reproducing slowly have a high biotic potential. It has been estimated that if no factors limited population growth, starting with one pair of elephants, there would be over 19 000 000 elephants in only 750 years!

However, factors exist which limit populations. Species do not reproduce to this maximum, and thus, the earth is not overrun with bacteria, elephants, or other organisms. The factors which hold the biotic potential in check are called **limiting factors.**

FIGURE 32-1. Under ideal conditions, a population would continue to increase. The increase can be shown graphically.

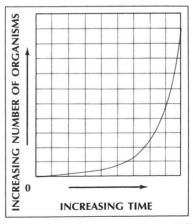

615

TABLE 32-1. GROWTH OF A YEAST POPULATION		
Population Age (h)	Number of Cells	Increase in Cell Number
0	10	
2	29	19
4	71	42
6	175	104
8	351	176
10	513	162
12	595	82
14	641	46
16	656	15
18	662	6

Thomas Malthus' essay about population growth is described in Section 10:9.

With time, population growth levels off.

Teaching suggestion: Make certain students understand that the rate of growth decreases when the population is in the top half of the "S". The population is increasing but at a decreasing rate.

32:2 Population Growth Curves

Population growth is the increase in the size of a population with time. Growth of some populations can be studied in the laboratory. To study the population growth of yeast cells, a culture medium can be inoculated with a few yeast cells. Counting the yeast cells at regular time intervals would give data much like that shown in Table 32-1. Note that the size of the population increases slowly at first. This period of slow growth is followed by a period of rapid growth and then slowed growth. Eventually, a point is reached when the population does not grow anymore. At this point, the population size remains stable.

Growth of the yeast population can be graphed (Figure 32-2). The graph of such growth is called a **population growth curve** or **S-shaped curve.** Growth of the yeast population is similar to the growth of many other populations. Up to a point, the population size increases. The increase is slow at first, and then it becomes faster. However, after a certain amount of time, the population growth in any real population levels off due to limits. Can you think of what some of these limits might be?

Rate of growth of a population can also be graphed (Figure 32-3). This graph, called a **population growth rate curve,** is a graph of *rate of increase* of a population per unit of time. It

a

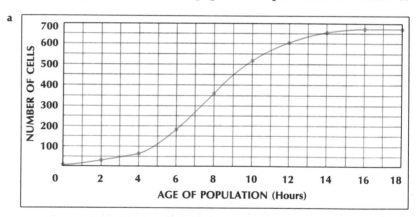

b

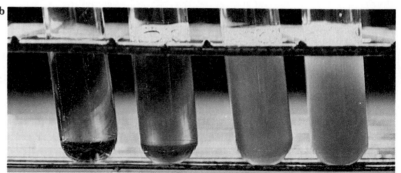

FIGURE 32-2. A yeast population can be grown under laboratory conditions. (a) When the growth is graphed, an S-shaped population growth curve results. (b) The liquid medium in which the yeast are grown becomes cloudy as the number of cells increases. The tube on the left corresponds to a population on the left side of the growth curve. The tube on the right corresponds to a population on the right side of the growth curve.

Richard Brommer

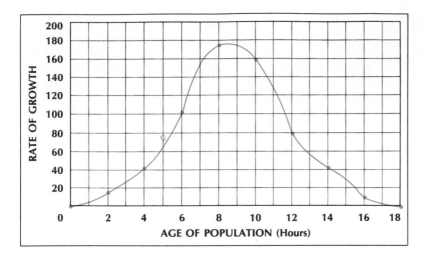

FIGURE 32-3. The growth rate of a population can be graphed. This growth rate curve is for a yeast population.

shows that up to a point, the size of a population increases. Then, the *rate* of increase slows down. The number of organisms still increases, but the rate of growth decreases. When the population growth levels off (the flat part of Figure 32-3), the population growth rate has returned to zero.

As a population grows, the rate of increase begins to decrease.

When a population reaches the point at which it is no longer increasing, it has reached the **carrying capacity** of the environment. The carrying capacity is the number of individuals which an environment can support. At the carrying capacity, the number of organisms born or produced, the **birthrate,** balances the number which die, the **death rate.** At this point, the size of the population remains fairly stable.

Carrying capacity is the number of organisms which can survive in a particular environment.

An environment includes physical and biological limiting factors, both of which are subject to change. Thus, the carrying capacity is also subject to change. Different environmental factors produce different carrying capacities for a given population. The sum of the limiting factors of a population is called **environmental resistance.** The size of a population is determined by a balance between biotic potential and environmental resistance. Environmental resistance is the difference between the biotic potential and the actual size of a population.

Biotic potential is limited by environmental resistance.

REVIEWING YOUR IDEAS

1. What is biotic potential? How do biologists know it is not reached by most organisms? What checks biotic potential?
2. Describe the growth of a yeast population. Distinguish a population growth curve from a population growth rate curve.
3. Distinguish between birthrate and death rate.
4. What is carrying capacity?
5. What is environmental resistance?

1. Biotic potential is the highest rate of reproduction of a population under ideal conditions. The fact that it is not reached is shown by calculations. Biotic potential is checked by limiting factors.
2. The population begins to grow slowly, then grows rapidly, slows again, and finally levels off. A population growth curve shows the increase in size of a population with time. A population growth rate curve shows the rate of increase of a population per unit time.
3. Birthrate is the number of organisms born or produced. Death rate is the number which die.

4. Carrying capacity is the number of organisms an environment can support.

5. Environmental resistance is the sum of limiting factors acting on a population.

a

b

FIGURE 32-4. Both (a) animal populations, such as gannets and (b) plant populations, such as phlox, have limiting factors. Limiting factors affect population of organisms other than animals and plants, also.

LIMITING FACTORS

Limiting factors, both physical and biological, control population size and growth. However, at any given time, only one factor limits a population. Limiting factors can change depending on environmental conditions. Factors affecting a population may be related to **population density,** the number of organisms per given area. Such factors are called density-dependent. Other factors not related to population density are called density-independent.

Many limiting factors are density-dependent.

32:3 Space and Food

Amount of physical space can be a limiting factor for some organisms. Many plants and protists must live attached to a substrate (substance on which an organism lives). These organisms cannot move and must occupy a given area. A plant's roots must extend far enough into the soil to obtain nutrients. In addition, its leaves must be exposed to sunlight in order for photosynthesis to occur. Only a certain number of plants can occupy a certain space. Therefore, the size of a plant population may be limited by space.

Space is an important limiting factor for some plants and protists.

Animals do not seem to be limited directly by space because most of them can move. Usually other factors, such as food, predators, or disease, limit an animal population before space does. However, many of these other factors are space related.

Emigration is one way in which population size and density are decreased in some animal populations. For example, many kinds of locusts swarm to new areas when overcrowding occurs. Some of the locusts remain in their original environment. They are able to survive in an environment of reduced population size and density.

Emigration is a means of decreasing population size and density.

The amount of food available may limit the size of a population. Suppose a population of one thousand animals lives in a community and feeds on certain plants. Because the plant and animal populations are in balance, the animals do not eat the plants faster than the plants can reproduce themselves. Thus, there is a constant food supply. However, if the animal population is doubled and the plant population is not, the plants would be eaten so quickly that they would have no time to reproduce. As a result, the animals would starve to death. Situations like this example are avoided by a wider spacing, or lower population density of animals. Thus, space and population density are related to another limiting factor—food availability.

32:4 Predation

Predation (prih DAY shun), the feeding of one organism on another, is another environmental factor that may limit the size of a population. Almost every organism is preyed on by some other organisms. It is often hard to find out if predation is a limiting factor, but the size of most populations is at least partly checked by predators.

Predation is a density-dependent factor. If at one time all the prey for a certain predator were eaten, all the predators would soon die. Rather, in a predator-prey relationship, each population continually determines the size of the other. An abundance of prey in an area leads to an increase in the number of predators. As predators feed on the prey, the number of prey begins to decline. The number of predators also declines because their food supply (prey) is reduced. As the number of predators decreases, the number of prey increases. This predator-prey interaction creates a cycle (Figure 32-5). The populations of both predator and prey change depending on the size of the other. But, the increase in numbers does not occur at the same time in both. One follows the other.

Food may be a density-dependent limiting factor.

A predator population can improve a prey population. For example, wolves often feed on caribou but prey mostly on the sick, deformed, young, and old. Thus, wolves act as a selective agent on the caribou population by maintaining a high percentage of healthy caribou of reproductive age. Inferior phenotypes (and genotypes) are eliminated.

FIGURE 32-5. (a) Predator-prey cycles can be represented graphically. After the prey increase, the predators increase, and after the prey decrease, the predators decrease. (b) A fox is a predator on rabbits (the prey). (c) Ants are predators on this grasshopper (the prey).

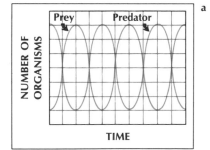

Allan Roberts

David M. Dennis

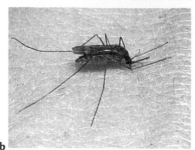

Ken Brate for Photo Researchers

a

b

c

FIGURE 32-6. (a) Ticks are parasites on various animals. Here two are shown on a dog. Ticks live on blood sucked from the host. (b) A mosquito is a parasite living on blood from its host. (c) These parasitic mites have killed the host beetle on which they were living.

Parasitism can be a limiting factor when the number of parasites carried by a host becomes too large.

The greater the population density, the more likely that parasitism will limit the population size.

Suggested demonstration: Examination of the organs of a pithed frog will reveal a diversity of parasites, such as lung flukes.

32:5 Parasitism

Parasitism (PER uh suh tihz um) can be a limiting factor. In a parasitic relationship (Section 1:2), one organism (the parasite) lives in or on another organism (the host), which is usually harmed by the parasite. Almost all organisms have some parasites but the parasites usually do not cause death because death of the host would result in death of the parasites. However, if a host has too many parasites, the host might die. Thus, the limitation is the *number* of parasites that a host is carrying.

This limitation is density-dependent. Parasitism usually causes death only when the parasites are in very dense host populations. The possibility that parasites will be passed from one organism to the next is greater in a dense host population. As the rate of transfer increases, the number of parasites in each host also increases. Too many parasites on one host may cause death by interfering with the host's nutrition or metabolism. The parasites may also reduce fertility of the host. As a result, the size and density of the host population decreases. Host organisms then have more space available to them, and transfer of parasites is less frequent. Since hosts have fewer parasites, the host population can survive and increase in number again. Thus, the cycle continues.

Disease is a density-dependent limiting factor.

DDT (Section 35:2) has played an important role in suppressing the *Anopheles* mosquito. In many areas, however, the mosquito has become resistant to DDT.

32:6 Diseases and Populations

Population density is closely related to the spread of certain diseases. For example, malaria results from a parasitic relationship between *Plasmodium* and humans (Section 19:8). Malaria is density-dependent in that the denser the human population, the greater the chance of the disease being passed to others. *Plasmodium* is carried by female *Anopheles* mosquitoes and transferred to humans by the bites of these mosquitoes. Thus, the spread of this disease is also dependent on the mosquito population density.

Paul Steuke, U. S. Forest Service

FIGURE 32-7. This dense population of trees is more subject to a severe attack by parasites than a scattered population would be.

Malaria can be treated with certain drugs, but the best solution to malaria is prevention of the disease by population control of the mosquitoes. Population control has been carried out in many places by destroying the swampy breeding grounds of *Anopheles.*

Sometimes disease spread can be used to control the size of certain animal populations. The disease can spread rapidly in a dense population and kill many organisms in a matter of days. For example, rabbits are not native to Australia; they were brought there by humans. The result was nearly a disaster. Because there were no predators, the size of the rabbit population increased rapidly. Soon rabbits began competing with sheep for food. In order to reduce the rabbit population and preserve the sheep population, biologists injected some rabbits with a lethal virus — which spread rapidly, killing large numbers of rabbits. The virus did not kill all the rabbits because disease spread is density-dependent. The virus was transferred directly from rabbit to rabbit. As the number of rabbits decreased, the rate of transfer also decreased. As a result, the smaller population size became stable.

Killing pests by using disease-causing organisms must be carefully controlled. Care must be taken that only the pest population is affected. If other organisms were killed, the natural ecological balance could be upset, causing even more harm (Chapter 35).

The size of pest populations may be decreased by the spread of disease.

In many urban areas, the control of animals, such as rats, that are disease carriers is a major factor in disease control efforts.

The viral disease is myxomatosis.

Pest control is discussed in Section 35:14.

32:7 Interspecific Competition

Suppose a certain factor limits one population and two populations compete for it. The competition itself may then become a limiting factor. In the laboratory, two populations can be made to compete for the same limiting factor. As a result, one population always dies. This fact led to the formulation of the **competitive exclusion principle;** *complete competitors cannot coexist.* This principle means that two populations cannot occupy the same ecological niche, or place in nature.

Two populations cannot occupy the same ecological niche.

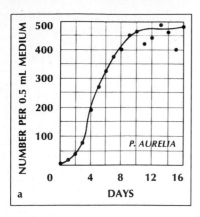
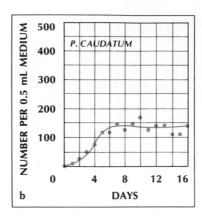
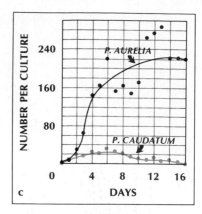

FIGURE 32-8. (a) A population growth curve shows *Paramecium aurelia* grows to a higher density than (b) *Paramecium caudatum* before leveling off. (c) When the two are grown together, interspecific competition occurs and *P. aurelia* survives while *P. caudatum* dies.

In an experiment, two species of paramecia were introduced into separate culture media. These species were *Paramecium caudatum* (kaw DAYT um) and *Paramecium aurelia* (aw REEL yuh). The food source in both media was a species of bacterium. The growth rate of each population was recorded (Figure 32-8a,b). The graphs showed that the biotic potential of *P. aurelia* is greater than that of *P. caudatum*.

Next, the two species of paramecia were placed in the same culture medium. The same species of bacteria was used as the only food source. Thus, both species of paramecia competed for the same food source. As a result of the competition, *P. caudatum* died while *P. aurelia* survived (Figure 32-8c). Each species survived on the food source when in separate cultures. However, when the two species are together, the competition for food limits the population. Such competition between populations of different species is called **interspecific** (ihn tur spih SIHF ihk) **competition** and is density-dependent.

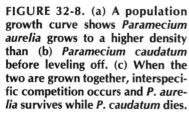
Interspecific competition is competition between populations of different species.

In this example, neither paramecium species harmed the other. *P. caudatum* died off because it was more sensitive to wastes produced by the bacteria. *P. aurelia* was better adapted to living among the bacterial wastes, and it survived. In similar experiments using other food sources, *P. caudatum* is better adapted and becomes the surviving species.

32:8 Intraspecific Competition

Intraspecific competition occurs between members of the same species. It is density-dependent.

Teaching suggestion: Ask students to suggest examples showing how competition within a species can be beneficial.

Competition between members of the same species is called **intraspecific** (ihn truh spih SIHF ihk) **competition.** It is the most severe competition and is also density-dependent. The greater the population density, the greater the chance for competition because there are more contacts among organisms. Some degree of competition is good for a species because by natural selection the "more fit" survive. But too much competition is not good. Does intraspecific competition occur among humans? Explain.

Excess intraspecific competition is avoided in many ways. Life cycles may be such that competition is avoided within a species. For example, adult frogs do not compete with tadpoles because the habitats and foods of frogs and tadpoles are different. The life span of an organism may also reduce competition. In many animals, adults die shortly after the young are born. Thus, old and young do not compete for food or space. In animals in which the parent does not die after the young are produced, maternal care is common. This avoids competition because the offspring depend on the mother. In plants, dispersal of spores and seeds by plants also prevents competition between members of the same species.

Life cycles of plants and animals may prevent intraspecific competition.

In social animals, social hierarchies (Section 31:13) and territoriality (Section 31:14) reduce conflict. Once a social hierarchy is set up, competition for food, mates, and space is reduced. Also, nonproductive activity is reduced so animals have more time and energy to "make a living." After a male bird sets up a territory, he is able to attract a female. The male's territory also provides enough space and food for supporting the "entire family."

Social hierarchies and territoriality reduce the chances for intraspecific competition.

Societies in which members have definite roles also have reduced intraspecific competition. In insect societies such as bees, ants, and termites, roles are somewhat genetically determined. Usually there is one queen which produces all new members of the society. Other members of the society may have roles as workers, soldiers, or foragers. Spreading out the work and activities reduces conflict and competition among the members of the society.

Existence of different roles among members of a society reduces intraspecific competition.

Overcrowding can lead to behavioral and physiological changes among members of the same species. If rats are overcrowded and cannot escape, the amount of aggressive behavior may increase resulting in more deaths than usual. Also,

Overcrowding can lead to stress, intraspecific competition, and abnormal behavior, all of which tend to lower population size.

Keith H. Murakami for Tom Stack and Associates

FIGURE 32-9. The social hierarchy established by confrontations of elephant seals is a form of intraspecific competition. Once established, the hierarchy reduces conflict.

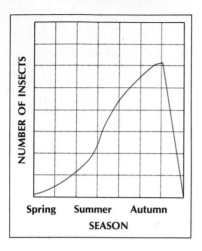

FIGURE 32-10. An insect population in the temperate zone increases each spring and summer and dies rapidly with the freezing weather of late fall.

Temperature may be a density-independent limiting factor.

A decrease in oxygen supply can affect many species in an aquatic community.

See Section 35:7 for a discussion of thermal pollution of water.

nests may be poorly built or not built at all. Hormonal changes resulting from stress may cause a reduction in litter size. In some cases, no young are produced. Sometimes the young are abandoned or eaten by the parents.

As a result of these behavioral and physiological changes, birthrate decreases and death rate increases. The result is reduction of the population size to a number the environment can support. Thus, a population is not only controlled by external forces but by internal changes also.

32:9 Other Limiting Factors

Populations may be limited by a variety of factors. In fact, *almost anything affecting the lives of organisms could act to limit a population's size*. Often these factors are not density-dependent. Temperature and oxygen supply are two examples.

Temperature often is a factor which limits the size of insect populations. In temperate zones, the population size begins to grow slowly in late spring and then more rapidly through the summer. But if the growth of such a population were graphed, it would be different from an S-shaped graph (Section 32:2). Like the S-shaped graph, it would start slowly and then rise rapidly. But instead of leveling off, the graph would show a sharp decline in population size because the adults rapidly die in autumn as freezing weather begins (Figure 32-10). Before they die, the insects deposit their fertilized eggs in some "safe" place. The following spring, the young adults emerge and begin another population "explosion."

Amount of oxygen can be a limiting factor in aquatic communities (Section 35:7). Oxygen is needed for respiration by almost all organisms. If the oxygen level drops too low, many animals cannot survive. Drop in oxygen content of the water can be caused by pollution. For example, improper sewage treatment can result in the dumping of much organic material into the water. Decomposition of this material by bacteria consumes huge amounts of oxygen. As a result, many animals die. When their dead bodies decay, the oxygen level is lowered further. This lack of oxygen can affect an entire aquatic community.

Oxygen content of water also is temperature related. More oxygen can dissolve in cold water than in warm water. Sometimes hot water is released into rivers, streams, or lakes from factories or power plants. The hot water may raise the temperature of the water to which it is added and cause the oxygen content to be lowered. Fish and other animals may not be able to survive.

THE HUMAN POPULATION

Complex intelligence and behavior of humans have had a major impact on all organisms, including humans themselves. Unlike other organisms, humans have learned to control the environment to some extent and can also alter it according to their own needs. Advances in two main areas, agriculture and technology, have been especially important. These areas are related to the size and growth of the human population.

32:10 Agriculture

Development of agriculture probably took place between 10 000 and 15 000 years ago. This development was one of the most profound steps in human progress. Crops were planted where they did not grow naturally; new strains of plants such as corn, wheat, and rye were developed. As a result, humans added variety to their diet and extended their range of habitats. Growing of crops reduced competition for food, and thus, population size increased and permanent homes could be established.

6. Population density is the number of organisms per given area.
7. Factors may limit only populations with a high population density.
8. Predation is the feeding of one organism on another. Yes, humans are predators.
9. Parasitism may be a limiting factor if a host has too many parasites.
10. Interspecific competition occurs between different species. Intraspecific competition occurs among members of the same species.

Humans control and alter their environment.

Agriculture added variety to the human diet, increased population size, and made a more permanent home possible.

FIGURE 32-11. Advances in how land is farmed have influenced the size and structure of the human population. This aerial view of farmland shows the large scale on which farming takes place today.

Aerial Photo by Collier/Condit

Agriculture remained the central feature of human society for thousands of years, and all human societies still depend on agriculture. In the past, everyone lived directly "off the land," and farming is still the major way of life in many countries. But some people gradually began to live in towns and villages. Division of labor increased as people began to make their livings in other ways besides farming. From the smaller population centers emerged larger cities and a more complex society.

32:11 Technology

As curious animals, humans investigate nature. The discovery of natural laws has enabled humans to become productive, and they have learned to make many things with the help of simple tools and machines. Since the beginning of the Industrial Revolution in the nineteenth century, society has become more technological than agricultural.

The products made by today's society have become important parts of our daily lives. Some advances add to our comfort. Others directly affect our health, and thus, our population. Technological advances have had a direct bearing on the size and growth of the human population.

Advances in sanitation have prevented many lethal diseases. For example, bubonic plague is a disease carried by rat fleas. In the 14th century, one-fourth of the population of Europe died of this disease! Proper sanitation procedures have prevented recent outbreaks of diseases such as plague. Modern sewage treatment is an important technological advance in sanitation.

Technological advances have also improved agriculture (Chapter 35). Crop yields have been improved and more nutritious foods have been produced. These advances affect populations in reducing the death rate and in lengthening life span of the population members.

Human curiosity has led to the development of a technological society.

Proper sanitation has prevented the spread of many diseases.

FIGURE 32-12. (a) Sewage treatment plants that clean area water supplies have greatly reduced water pollution. (b) A worker tests a water sample for chlorine, a chemical added to water to inhibit the growth of harmful bacteria.

Lightforce

Lightforce

a

b

Advances in medicine and surgery have also played a major role in decreasing the death rate and increasing life span. Many diseases which long ago might have resulted in an early death can now be treated or cured. Also, technological advances in disease detection have resulted in early treatment of some diseases and thus have increased the number of survivors. Medical advances have been especially important in reducing infant mortality. Survival of infants is a major way in which death rate has been reduced and by which the size of the human population has increased.

FIGURE 32-13. Medical advances in both patient care and professional training and in getting aid to patients have greatly influenced the survival rate of humans. (a) A surgical operation is shown on closed circuit television as a method of training new doctors. (b) A mobile cancer therapy unit reaches areas of a New Mexico Indian reservation where patients are long distances from professional medical care.

32:12 The Population Explosion

It is estimated that humans numbered about 0.25 billion in the year 1 A.D. By 1650, world population doubled. It took 200 more years to reach the billion mark. The population doubled again in the period between 1850 and 1930. In 1970, the world's population was about 3.5 billion. Thus, the length of time it takes for the population to double is continuing to decrease (Figure 32-14).

The time required to double the human population is decreasing.

FIGURE 32-14. The growth of the world's human population can be shown graphically. The dotted portion of the curve represents projected future growth.

EPA/Documerica

Edward Hutchins

FIGURE 32-15. Much of the world's human population is crowded together in cities. Crowding can have harmful effects.

The human population explosion has been caused by a decrease in the death rate.

The present ecological problems are compounded by the rapid rate of human population growth.

Family planning methods are a means of reducing birthrate.

Various contraceptive methods are discussed in the Teacher's Guide.

Information on family planning is now available in many countries throughout the world.

In 1970, the average rate of world population increase was about 2.1 percent per year. By 1980, the rate of increase had declined somewhat to 1.7 percent, with a world population estimated at more than 4 billion. Although growing more slowly, the world population is *still increasing*. It is estimated that world population will reach 6 billion by the year 1990.

Two factors are important in the rate of increase in population—birthrate and death rate. An increase in birthrate has not caused the human population explosion. Instead, the death rate has decreased. Because more people are born than die in a given year, the net result is an increase in population. The declining death rate is due primarily to improvements in sanitation, medicine, and food production.

The human population, like all other populations, interacts with its environment. It cannot continue to expand indefinitely because a point is reached in any population at which the environment cannot support additional growth. Most ecologists think that this point will be reached by humans. What do you think?

Most natural checks of population growth are increases in the death rate. The other alternative would be to decrease the birthrate. Decreasing the birthrate can be done as part of family planning methods. Biologists and physicians have developed several artificial ways of preventing pregnancy based on the biological aspects of reproduction. Natural methods to prevent pregnancy have also been learned.

Many countries around the world educate their citizens about family planning. Many people are using some family planning methods. Which, if any, family planning method is used depends on several factors, such as physical, emotional, religious, and moral factors. The results of this education may be a factor in the recent decline in population growth rate.

An average of 2.1 births/family could lead to zero population growth because not all females born survive to reproductive age.

The birthrate in the United States has dropped from a peak of 3.5 births per woman of reproductive age in the late 1950's to 1.8 in 1980. However, the size of the population is still increasing. A rate of 2.1 births per woman for many generations is necessary to attain zero population growth. **Zero population growth** is a condition in which the birthrate equals the death rate, so the rate of population growth equals zero. Because of the large proportion of young people now in the United States, even a birthrate of 1.8 would cause the 1980 United States population of 222.5 million to double in 99 years.

Teaching suggestion: Emphasize that zero population growth does not mean zero births.

In zero population growth, the birthrate equals the death rate.

11. Agriculture provided a greater variety of foods, reduced competition for food, and extended the range of possible habitats.
12. Technology adds to human comfort and convenience and extends life span.
13. The human population has grown from about 0.25 billion to more than 4 billion. This growth is due mostly to a decrease in the death rate resulting from improvements in sanitation, medicine, and food production.
14. Zero population growth is the point at which birthrate and death rate are equal.

REVIEWING YOUR IDEAS

11. How did agriculture affect early humans?
12. How do modern humans depend on technology?
13. How has the size of the human population changed during the last 2000 years? Is the birthrate or the death rate responsible for this change? Explain.
14. What is zero population growth?

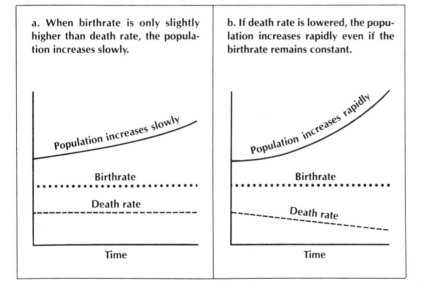

a. When birthrate is only slightly higher than death rate, the population increases slowly.

b. If death rate is lowered, the population increases rapidly even if the birthrate remains constant.

FIGURE 32-16. Birthrate and death rate together determine how fast a population grows. (a) A population can increase slowly or (b) rapidly. What happens to population growth if birthrate and death rate are equal?

CHAPTER REVIEW

SUMMARY

1. All organisms have biotic potentials. Biotic potential is checked by limiting factors.
2. The size of most populations usually increases rapidly and then levels off, producing an S-shaped population growth curve.
3. When birthrates and death rates are equal, no further increase in population size occurs. This point is the carrying capacity of the environment.
4. Limiting factors may be either density-dependent or density-independent.
5. Predator-prey relationships often follow a cycle in which changes in the size of one

CHAPTER REVIEW

population are followed by similar changes in the size of the other.

6. Parasitism is a density-dependent factor which may be limiting depending on the number of parasites a host is carrying.

7. Disease may be a density-dependent limiting factor.

8. Competition between two species for a requirement may itself be a limiting factor.

9. Competition within a species may promote natural selection. Too much competition may be avoided by such things as life cycles and territoriality.

10. Physical aspects of the environment, such as temperature and oxygen supply, can be density-independent factors limiting population size.

11. Development of agriculture and technology are two examples of major advances by humans.

12. The human population is exploding as a result of a decrease in the death rate. One way of checking human population growth is by decreasing the birthrate.

LANGUAGE OF BIOLOGY

biotic potential
birthrate
carrying capacity
competitive ex-
   clusion principle
death rate
environmental
   resistance
interspecific
   competition
intraspecific
   competition
limiting factor
population density
population growth rate
   curve
population size
predation
S-shaped curve
zero population growth

CHECKING YOUR IDEAS

On a separate paper, complete each of the following statements with the missing term(s). Do not write in this book.

1. The _____ is the number of individuals which an environment can support.

2. An S-shaped curve is a graph which shows _____.

3. Experiments with *P. caudatum* and *P. aurelia* illustrate how _____ competition may be a limiting factor.

4. Parasitism is a density-_____ limiting factor.

5. _____ is the number of organisms in a population.

6. _____ is the number of organisms in a given area.

7. A social hierarchy is a way of reducing _____ competition.

8. _____ is the condition in which the birthrate equals the death rate.

9. _____ is the highest rate of reproduction of a population under ideal conditions.

10. The sum of limiting factors of a population is called _____.

EVALUATING YOUR IDEAS

1. Compare the growth of a yeast population with limits to its growth to a yeast population with no limits.

2. Why does the population growth rate of an organism eventually decrease?

3. How is the size of a population determined?

4. Distinguish between biotic potential and carrying capacity.

5. Explain how space may be a limiting factor of a plant population. How are animal populations limited by space?

6. How may availability of food be related to population density?

7. Describe the interaction of a predator population and its prey population.

8. How is parasitism related to population density?

9. Why did the introduction of a lethal virus into the Australian rabbit population not kill all the rabbits? What would happen if the rabbit population again increased?

10. Explain competitive exclusion.
11. What happens when *Paramecium caudatum* and *Paramecium aurelia* are grown in the same culture medium? Why?
12. Why is some degree of intraspecific competition good for a species? Why would too much be harmful?
13. How do the life cycles of some organisms reduce intraspecific competition?
14. How do social hierarchies and territoriality reduce intraspecific competition?
15. Describe the effects of overcrowding in rats.
16. Discuss two examples of density-independent limiting factors.
17. How have agriculture and technology helped increase the human population size?

APPLYING YOUR IDEAS

1. Why is it important that all organisms have high biotic potentials?
2. Assuming that a human female has a "reproductive life span" of 30 years, how many offspring could a couple hypothetically produce during that time? If half of the offspring were females, how many children could they produce? What does this example indicate about the biotic potential of humans?
3. Do you think humans could be limited by space? Explain.
4. Explain how changes in overcrowded rat populations might be considered adaptive.
5. Discuss several ways in which technology has resulted in harmful effects on the environment.
6. The average height of Americans has increased several centimeters since the beginning of the twentieth century. How can this increase be explained? Is increased height an adaptation? Why?
7. Suggest some reasons why a very low population density might be harmful to a population.

EXTENDING YOUR IDEAS

1. Place several male and female *Drosophila* into a vial containing a food source. Plug the vial with sponge rubber or cotton. Count new flies as they emerge each day. (Dispose of flies once they have been counted.) Prepare a population growth graph and a population growth rate graph of your data.
2. Conduct a class discussion on the limiting factors of the human population. Should the population be allowed to increase unchecked? How might it be controlled?
3. Conduct a class discussion on the good and bad effects of our technology.
4. Use library resources to learn about the rate of population growth in other countries. Which countries seem to face the most severe problems? What is the standard of living in these countries?
5. Write a story about humans in the year 2050. Assume that the problems of pollution and population have not been solved.
6. How would you design an experiment to determine the population size of a given animal over a period of time?

SUGGESTED READINGS

Cherfas, Jeremy, "The Population Bomb Revisited." *Science 80*, November, 1980.
Desowitz, Robert S., "How the Wise Men Brought Malaria to Africa." *Natural History*, October, 1976.
Hauser, Philip M., "The Census of 1980." *Scientific American*, November, 1981.
Kormondy, Edward J., *Concepts of Biology*, 2nd ed. Englewood Cliffs, NJ, Prentice-Hall, Inc., 1976.
Odum, Eugene P., *Ecology*. New York, Holt, Rinehart and Winston, Inc., 1975.
Rhodes, Philip, *Birth Control*, 2nd ed. Oxford Biology Reader. London, Oxford University Press, 1976.

Additional student readings and suggested teacher readings are provided in the Teacher's Guide.

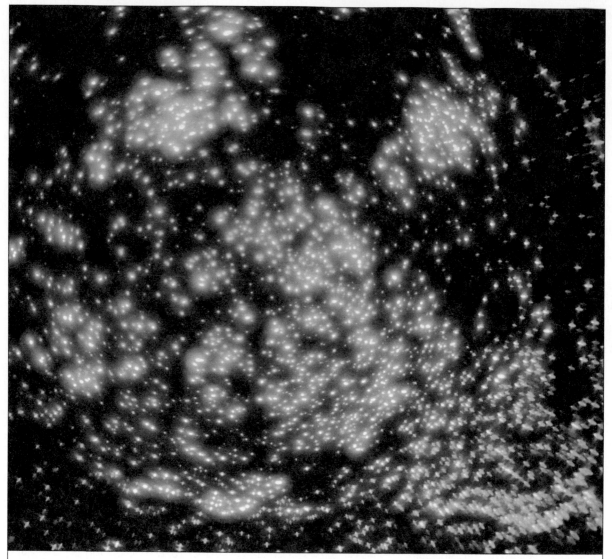

Organisms in an ecosystem interact with the physical environment and with one another. These glow worms on a New Zealand cave ceiling depend on living and nonliving factors of the environment. The worms (firefly larvae) spin filaments which trap insects that breed in water in the cave. The insects are attracted to the light of the glow worms. How do organisms in other places interact with their physical environment and with other organisms?

Introduction: To supplement this chapter, visit a natural area several times. The area should be diverse in both species and topography. Assign teams to study certain things. One team should map the topography of the area (or sections of it). They should pay attention to location of slopes, gulleys, or other signs of erosion, drainage, and streams or ponds. Another team should describe and analyze the soil (including types of organisms living within it). Other teams should identify major plant and animal forms, physical factors such as amount of light, humidity, and temperature, and evidence of pollution or other disruptions of natural processes. In each case, findings should be accurately recorded and, at the end of the study, a composite map can be constructed. From this extended and cooperative effort should emerge a real feeling for ecological relationships. Your students will have "real data" that will enhance their understanding of community life.

THE ECOSYSTEM

Chapter 33 surveys the role of biotic and abiotic factors in ecosystems.

Populations live together in communities (Section 1:1). A community is a group of populations living in the same area. The structure of a community is based on all the organisms living together. Within a community, living things interact with members of their own species and with other species, and they interact with their physical environment. Interaction of a community with its environment is an ecological system, or **ecosystem** (EE koh sihs tum). Interactions between the living and nonliving parts of an environment are the functions of a community. Ecologists study a community in terms of its functions.

These functions are "give-and-take" relationships. Living things "take" from the environment materials and energy needed for life. As they use these materials and energy, organisms "give," or transfer, materials and energy back to the environment. In a normal ecosystem, most materials are constantly recycled. But, energy cannot be recycled (Section 1:4). If an ecosystem is to survive, energy must be added constantly. The source of this energy is the sun. Energy is needed to maintain the organization of individuals and entire ecosystems. The importance of sunlight is also discussed in Chapters 1 and 21. Any living system, from cell to biosphere, requires a continual energy supply. Without energy, structure and function break down and randomness (entropy) results.

GOAL: You will gain an understanding of biotic and abiotic factors which affect an ecosystem.

An ecosystem is a community interacting with its physical environment.

Teaching suggestion: Point out that an ecosystem, like any other living system, is a level of biological organization.

Organisms take energy and materials from their environment and release energy and materials back to the environment.

Materials can be recycled, but energy cannot.

BIOTIC FACTORS
OF ENVIRONMENT

Many relationships exist among organisms. These relationships are called **biotic** (bi AHT ihk), or living, **factors** of the environment. In a normal ecosystem there is a delicate balance among the many forms of life.

Biotic factors are relationships among organisms.

Roger K. Burnard

Warren Garst for Tom Stack and Associates

G. C. Kelley for Tom Stack and Associates

Don C. Nieman

a

b

c

d

FIGURE 33-1. (a) Autotrophs, such as these grassland plants, are producers and make up the first feeding level of an ecosystem. (b) Organisms such as the tapir that are herbivores are called first-order consumers. (c) An otter eats sea urchins and thus is a second-order consumer. (d) Top level carnivores include animals such as tigers.

In an ecosystem, materials and potential energy are transferred along a series of feeding levels.

First-order consumers are also called herbivores. Herbivores eat plants.

Carnivores eat meat.

Second-order and third-order consumers are carnivores.

33:1 Feeding Levels

Energy enters an ecosystem as sunlight. This solar energy can be directly used only by autotrophs such as grasses, trees, or algae (Section 1:2). In photosynthesis, autotrophs trap light energy and use it to make sugars and other organic compounds. Light energy is changed to chemical energy in these compounds.

Because only autotrophs can trap and change light energy to chemical energy, all other organisms depend on them. Thus, a series of **feeding levels,** or steps, results. Materials and potential energy are transferred within an ecosystem through the feeding levels. Autotrophs make up the first feeding level, the producers, of an ecosystem. Feeding levels also are called trophic levels.

In order for an ecosystem to function, materials and energy must pass from producers to consumers. A consumer which feeds directly on a producer is called a **first-order consumer.** First-order consumers are also called **herbivores** (HUR buh vorz), or plant eaters. A cow grazing on grass, a deer browsing on foliage, and a tadpole eating algae are herbivores. Herbivores make up the second feeding level in ecosystems.

Consumers which feed on other consumers are called **carnivores** (KAR nuh vorz), or meat eaters. A mouse is a herbivore preyed on by snakes. Therefore, a snake is a carnivore and a **second-order consumer.** An owl which eats the snake is a **third-order consumer.** Second-order and third-order consumers make up higher feeding levels.

Each time an organism feeds on another living thing, there is a transfer of materials and potential energy. The transfer from organism to organism (feeding level to feeding level) forms a series called a **food chain** (Section 1:4). A food chain is represented using arrows.

Materials and potential energy are transferred along a food chain.

plant → mouse → snake → owl
(producer) (first-order (second-order (third-order
            consumer)   consumer)   consumer)

Teaching suggestion: Have students suggest several possible food chains and then construct a food web for a particular ecosystem.

A food chain represents *one* possible route for the transfer of materials and energy through an ecosystem. Many other routes exist. In an ecosystem, many species are found at each feeding level, and one species does not always feed on the same food source. A snake may also eat a lizard or a toad; an owl may feed directly on a mouse. In addition, some animals are **omnivores** (AHM nih vorz), organisms that eat both plants and animals. Humans are omnivores. All the possible feeding relationships in an ecosystem make up a **food web** (Figure 33-2).

Many interrelated food chains make up a food web.

FIGURE 33-2. A food web describes all the feeding relationships within an ecosystem. Some organisms can occupy various levels.

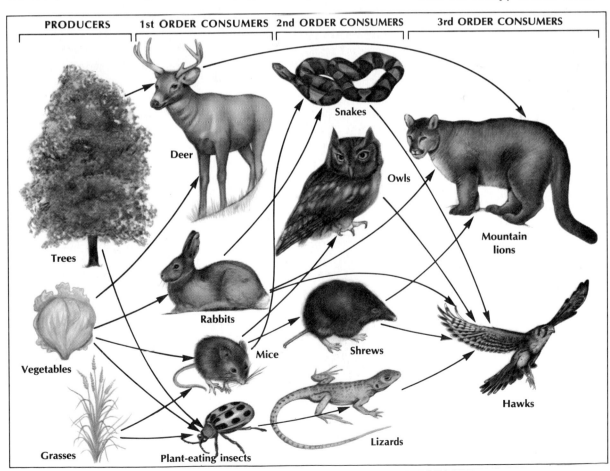

PRODUCERS   1st ORDER CONSUMERS   2nd ORDER CONSUMERS   3rd ORDER CONSUMERS

Snakes

Deer

Owls

Mountain lions

Trees

Rabbits

Mice   Shrews

Hawks

Vegetables

Lizards

Grasses   Plant-eating insects

FIGURE 33-3. A pyramid can be drawn to show the energy levels within an ecosystem. Less energy is available at the top of the pyramid because some is lost at each level. Both numbers of organisms and biomass of an ecosystem also can be drawn as a pyramid.

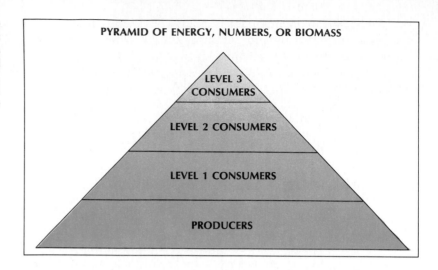

PYRAMID OF ENERGY, NUMBERS, OR BIOMASS

LEVEL 3 CONSUMERS

LEVEL 2 CONSUMERS

LEVEL 1 CONSUMERS

PRODUCERS

33:2 Pyramid of Energy

All foods have chemical potential energy. Thus, a food chain shows the transfer of potential energy. A food chain is needed in order for all organisms to obtain their share of the energy entering the ecosystem.

Energy is lost between each link in a food chain. The amount of energy actually transferred at each level depends on the ecosystem. Accurate data are difficult to obtain because of variables such as season, age and size of organisms, and amount of sunlight. A study of a river ecosystem in Silver Springs, Florida, was made by Howard Odum. It showed that only 17 percent of the potential energy in producers was transferred to herbivores. Second-order consumers obtained only 21 percent of the potential energy in herbivores. Only about 5 percent of the energy in second-order consumers was transferred to third-order consumers. The third-order consumers received only about 0.1 percent of the potential energy originally available in the producers. A graph of data such as these has a pyramid shape (Figure 33-3). Thus, ecologists refer to the transfer of energy as a **pyramid of energy.**

What happens to the energy in producers? Some of the potential energy which enters a food chain is used as each organism carries out its life functions. More than half of the potential energy of each food molecule is lost as heat during respiration. The usable energy from cellular respiration is used for life functions of growth and development, maintenance and repair, organization, reproduction, and catching food. During these functions, chemical energy is transformed to heat and is lost. This energy cannot be used again. Much of the potential

Loss of energy between each link in a food chain results in a pyramid of energy.

Chemical energy from cellular respiration is used for life functions, but some energy is lost as heat.

energy at each level never reaches the next level. Some organisms die and are acted on by decomposers. Also, members of a higher feeding level cannot consume every part of an organism. For example, only a small fraction of the organic material in a tree is consumed by herbivores. Not all parts of the material eaten by an organism are digested. For all these reasons, each link in the food chain has less potential energy available to it than the previous link. How does this energy loss affect humans?

The pyramid of energy explains why an organism feeds on certain other organisms. A lion preys on large animals. It gets more energy from a large animal than from a small animal. The lion might use more energy catching a rodent than it would get by eating the rodent. Lions hunt and eat zebras, for example. One chase results in an energy "profit" for the lion.

FIGURE 33-4. A timber wolf is at the "top of the pyramid." Top level consumers have less energy available to them than organisms at lower levels. Also, the number of wolves and their biomass is less than the number and biomass of animals on which they prey.

33:3 Pyramids of Numbers and Biomass

Loss of energy in a food chain explains several ecological principles. A food chain rarely includes more than four links. So much energy is lost at each level that usually not enough energy remains to support fourth- and fifth-order consumers. The loss of energy also explains why there are fewer organisms in each higher feeding level than in the previous level. For example, there are more mice than there are snakes which feed on mice. This relationship is known as the **pyramid of numbers.** Each higher feeding level has fewer organisms than the previous feeding level. A pyramid of numbers could be drawn in the same way as a pyramid of energy.

Research has shown an expected relationship in the biomass in an ecosystem. **Biomass** (BI oh mas) is the total mass of dry organic matter per unit of area. Table 33-1 shows the amount of biomass in each feeding level in the Silver Springs, Florida, ecosystem. These data show a **pyramid of biomass** in the ecosystem. A pyramid of biomass can be drawn in the same way as the other pyramids. Each higher feeding level contains less biomass than the previous feeding level. The pyramid of biomass also results from the loss of energy along a food chain.

Because of energy loss along a food chain, each level has fewer organisms than the preceding level.

Each level of a food chain has less biomass than the preceding level.

TABLE 33-1. BIOMASS IN AN ECOSYSTEM		
Feeding Level	Biomass (g/m²)	Percent of Biomass Compared to Previous Level
Producers	809	—
Herbivores	37	4.6
Second-order consumers	11	29.7
Third-order consumers	1.5	7.3

FIGURE 33-5. (a) The caracara and (b) the hyena are scavengers. Scavengers help recycle materials in an ecosystem by feeding on dead animals.

a

b

FIGURE 33-6. In an ecosystem, materials are constantly recycled. However, energy is lost and must be replaced.

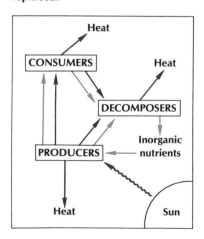

33:4 Recycling of Materials

Although energy is lost as it is transferred through an ecosystem, it is replaced by energy of sunlight. But the amount of *matter is limited* and it must be recycled. Carbon, hydrogen, and oxygen are made available by the processes of photosynthesis and cellular respiration (Section 1:4). These materials are also released during the burning of fossil fuels such as coal and oil. But sooner or later organisms die. If the matter in dead organisms could not be recycled, all available matter would one day be used up. This problem does not occur; instead the matter in dead organisms and in waste materials can be and is recycled in the ecosystem.

Decomposers (Section 1:4), mainly bacteria and fungi, release the materials in dead organisms and waste materials and these materials can be used again. Scavengers (SKAV un jurz) assist decomposers in this important function. **Scavengers** are animals such as buzzards and jackals which feed on dead animals. Decomposers cannot make food; in a sense, they are consumers. As they feed on dead plants and animals and waste materials, decomposers produce carbon dioxide and water as by-products. Thus, some of the matter of dead organisms and wastes is converted to carbon dioxide and water. These by-products are then recycled through the ecosystem. In general, decomposers recycle the minerals in the environment. Figure 33-6 summarizes the flow of matter and energy through an ecosystem.

33:5 Nitrogen Cycle

Nitrogen is an important element in all organisms. For example, it is an essential part of amino acids, proteins, and DNA. Nitrogen must be reused if an ecosystem is to survive. Nitrogen moves through ecosystems in what is called the **nitrogen cycle** (Figure 33-7). The nitrogen cycle includes three major pathways, each of which involves microorganisms.

In one pathway, decomposer bacteria in the soil attack proteins and other nitrogen compounds in dead animals and plants or waste products. Nitrogen in this form cannot be absorbed by plants. The complex organic compounds must be broken down. One group of bacteria convert the organic compounds to amino acids which are then metabolized, releasing ammonia (NH_3). Conversion of amino acids to ammonia is called **ammonification** (uh moh nuh fuh KAY shun). Ammonia reacts with water in the soil to make ammonium ions (NH_4^+). The ions are then changed by other bacteria to nitrite ions (NO_2^-) and then to nitrate ions (NO_3^-). This change is called **nitrification** (ni truh fuh KAY shun). During this process, the bacteria get energy for their needs.

During the nitrogen cycle, proteins of dead organisms and waste materials are converted to inorganic forms.

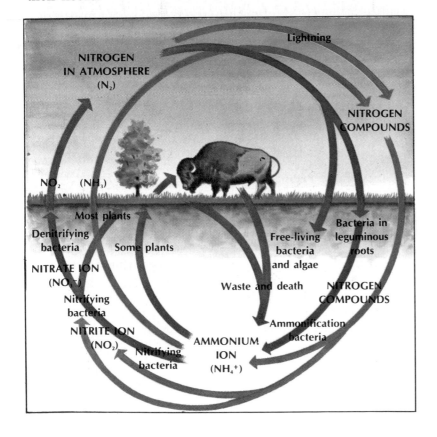

Lightning can produce nitrogen oxides from elementary nitrogen in the atmosphere. These oxides are carried into the soil by rain and converted to nitrates.

FIGURE 33-7. The nitrogen cycle is a complex pathway by which nitrogen moves through an ecosystem. It involves the interaction of organisms and nitrogen compounds.

FIGURE 33-8. Nitrogen-fixing bacteria inhabit root nodules, shown here as white knobs on roots of a clover plant. These bacteria convert atmospheric nitrogen to nitrate ions which the plant can absorb.

The gene for nitrogenase, the enzyme needed for fixing nitrogen, has been spliced into *E. coli* by recombinant DNA techniques. Production of nitrogenase by this method could reduce or eliminate the need for fertilizers.

FIGURE 33-9. An orchid is an epiphyte that is a commensal with the trees in which it lives.

Nitrate ions are the form of nitrogen most plants absorb from the soil. Plants use nitrate ions in making amino acids, proteins, and nucleotides (Section 9:2). These organic compounds become part of the food web. Thus, conversion of organic nitrogen compounds to nitrates is one way in which nitrogen is recycled.

Although the atmosphere contains about 78 percent nitrogen gas (by volume), most organisms cannot use nitrogen in that form (N_2). However, many forms of blue-green algae (Section 13:2) and several kinds of bacteria can use nitrogen gas. They can change nitrogen gas to a usable form, a process called **nitrogen fixation.** Nitrogen fixation is another pathway in the nitrogen cycle.

Some nitrogen-fixing bacteria live in the roots of a family of plants called legumes (peas, clover, and alfalfa). The bacteria enter the root through root hairs and travel to the cortex cells (Section 14:12) of the root. The cortex cells then become swollen areas called **nodules** (NAHJ ewlz). The bacteria can change nitrogen gas in the air to ammonia. Some ammonia enters the soil and is converted to nitrates. Most of the ammonia is converted by the bacteria to amino acids which enter the plant cells. The amino acids can be converted by plants to protein and other nitrogen compounds. In this relationship, the bacteria obtain materials needed for nitrogen fixation and their metabolism from the plant. Both organisms benefit.

A third pathway in the nitrogen cycle drains nitrogen from an ecosystem. By the process of **denitrification** (dee ni truh fuh KAY shun), some bacteria obtain energy by changing nitrates, nitrites, or ammonia, to nitrogen gas. Thus, some nitrogen which could be used by plants escapes to the atmosphere. Also, erosion can wash away soil containing nitrates. These events affect the nitrogen cycle, but the overall amount of nitrogen in the soil usually remains fairly stable.

33:6 Other Biotic Relationships

The most obvious biotic relationships involve eating or being eaten, but organisms also interact in other ways. Some biotic interactions are highly specialized.

Commensalism (kuh MEN suh lihz um) is a relationship in which one organism benefits from a host, without helping or harming the host. The benefiting organism is called a **commensal.** For example, in dense, tropical rain forests, the tree branches are so thick that the forest floor is dark. As a result, small plants cannot grow on the forest floor. Some small plants, such as orchids, live in the branches of trees and thus get enough light. Because of the high humidity in a rain forest, their roots can absorb water from the air. Plants like orchids which live in the tops of trees are called **epiphytes** (EP uh fites).

Relationships described in this section are broadly classified as symbiosis (living together). Previously, the term symbiosis was used to describe what is now called mutualism. Today, symbiosis refers to any such special relationship.

Tom Stack for Tom Stack and Associates

David M. Dennis

a

b

FIGURE 33-10. (a) A bromeliad is an epiphyte in rain forest trees. (b) Small tree frogs get moisture from plants, such as the bromeliad, that collect water.

certain mosquitoes, beetles, and crabs.

The bromeliad (broh MEE lee ad), a member of the pineapple family, is another epiphyte of rain forests. Not only is a bromeliad a commensal, it is also a small ecosystem. The leaves of a bromeliad overlap to form a hollow in which water collects. Many arthropods and even tree frogs live in the water. Some of these frogs live entirely in the treetops.

Another commensal is "Spanish moss," again, a member of the pineapple family. It is an epiphyte of oak trees in the southern United States.

Animals exhibit commensalism also. A remora (REM uh ruh) is a small fish which attaches itself to the belly of a larger animal such as a shark. The shark provides a "free ride" for the remora which feeds from the leftovers of the shark's meals.

FIGURE 33-11. (a) The red-billed ox picker exhibits commensalism with the warthog, eating lice and other insects from its coat. (b) The dramia crab "decorates" itself with sponges, aiding the crab in food getting.

a

b

Leonard Lee Rue III for Tom Stack and Associates

Ed Robinson for Tom Stack and Associates

Raymond A. Mendez/Animals Animals

Richard Brommer

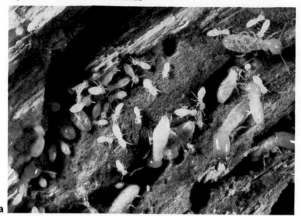

a

b

FIGURE 33-12. (a) Termites have protozoa within their intestines that enable them to eat wood. The relationship is mutualism. (b) Wasp larvae are parasites of the tomato horn worm.

In mutualism, two organisms depend on each other.

Mutualism (MYEW chuh lihz um) is an interaction in which two organisms depend on each other. In a lichen, the alga provides food for the fungus, and the fungus probably provides moisture and protection for the alga (Section 14:1). Neither organism could inhabit areas such as bare rock without the other. Nitrogen-fixing bacteria have a mutual relationship with legumes (Section 33:5). Termites are able to "eat" wood because their intestines contain certain protozoans which digest wood cellulose. In turn, termites supply the protozoan with materials for their metabolism.

Another example of mutualism is that of the yucca plant and yucca moth. Female moths transfer pollen from one yucca flower to another. These moths also deposit eggs in the developing seedpods of yucca plants. The eggs develop into larvae which feed on some of the seeds. The seeds not eaten can develop into yucca plants. Thus, the larvae have an adequate food supply, and pollination and reproduction of yucca plants are assured.

In parasitism, a parasite depends on the host which it usually harms.

Parasitism is another relationship between organisms. In **parasitism,** one organism, the parasite, is completely dependent at some point in its life cycle on a host which is usually harmed. Parasites cause many plant and animal diseases. Parasites may also be important in determining population size (Section 32:5).

Besides these specific relationships in ecosystems, many more general ones exist. Each ecological niche, an organism's place in nature, involves relationships among living and/or once living things. For example, some birds build nests in trees, some insect larvae live in rotten logs, and some seeds are dispersed by animals. Humans use parts of plants and animals for clothing, chemicals, and tools.

1. A community is a group of populations living in the same area. An ecosystem is the interaction of a community with its environment.
2. Materials and energy are interchanged between organisms and environment.

REVIEWING YOUR IDEAS

1. Distinguish between a community and an ecosystem.
2. In general, what things are interchanged between organisms and their environment?

3. Define biotic factors of the environment.
4. Distinguish among herbivore, carnivore, and omnivore.
5. What is transferred in a food chain? Distinguish between food chain and food web.
6. Distinguish among the three pyramids in ecosystems.
7. What organisms are necessary for the recycling of materials through an ecosystem?
8. How are epiphytes examples of commensals?

3. Biotic factors are the living elements of an ecosystem.
4. A herbivore feeds on plants. A carnivore is a meat eater. Omnivores feed upon both plants and animals.
5. Materials and potential energy are transferred in a food chain. A food chain is one possible way materials and energy are transferred. A food web is all the possible feeding relationships in an ecosystem.
6. The pyramids of energy, numbers, and biomass describe how each item decreases on higher levels of a food chain.
7. decomposers
8. Epiphytes live in the tops of trees where they can get light, but they neither harm nor help the trees.

ABIOTIC FACTORS OF ENVIRONMENT

In addition to the biotic factors of the environment, an ecosystem also is influenced by **abiotic** (ay bi AHT ihk) **factors.** Abiotic factors are the physical aspects of the surroundings. They can control the distribution and range of organisms and their reproduction, feeding, growth, and metabolism. An abiotic factor often can act as a limiting factor on a population (Chapter 32). Because populations live together in ecosystems, an entire ecosystem can be affected by abiotic factors. Study of abiotic factors and their importance is difficult because they interact to affect the makeup and functions of the ecosystem. The following physical factors are presented separately, but keep in mind that they work together.

Abiotic factors are the physical aspects of the environment. They interact to affect a community.

33:7 Medium

The substance in which an organism lives is called a **medium.** Most organisms live either in air (on land) or in water. These two media differ in many ways. Features of the medium determine the kinds of organisms that live in it.

FIGURE 33-13. Certain animals have special adaptations for movement through media. (a) Flying squirrels have skin folds that aid movement through air. (b) Salmon "jump" from the water when moving upstream to spawn.

Marty Stouffer/Animals Animals

Dale Johnson for Tom Stack and Associates

Frank Cezus

Steve Lissau

a

b

FIGURE 33-14. Water gives more resistance to movement than air does. (a) Swinging a bat in air requires less effort than (b) paddling a canoe through water.

Density differences of air and water are related to different modes of locomotion in each medium.

Organisms are supported by their medium. Water is over a thousand times more dense than air and provides more support than air. Because of this density, many aquatic animals can survive without a skeletal system. Most true land organisms have skeletal systems.

Water resists movement more than air does. Therefore, the medium affects *speed* of locomotion. Animals can move much faster through air or on the surface of the land than they can through water. The streamlined forms of many aquatic organisms are adaptations for locomotion in water.

Differences in density and resistance of air and water are also related to the *type* of locomotion in these media. The high resistance of water enables a jellyfish to move by jet propulsion and allows a fish to swim by "rowing" with its fins. Broad fins are an adaptation of some fish. Broad fins aid movement in the same way a paddle moves a canoe. These kinds of locomotion are not possible for most land animals because air does not provide enough resistance. Although birds and insects actually move through the medium (fly through air), most land animals either walk or run. Resistance necessary for this locomotion comes from the land surface rather than the medium. Have you ever tried to walk or run on ice?

FIGURE 33-15. An otter has a body that is streamlined and well-adapted for moving through water.

David M. Dennis

The medium also transports materials to and from some organisms. In water, animals such as sponges and clams are filter feeders (Section 25:7). They remove food from the medium as it passes through them. The medium is related in some ways to how other organisms get food, too. Food is trapped as it moves past a hydra in the water.

Water brings food to some animals.

Gas exchange also depends on the medium. Oxygen and carbon dioxide, for example, are dissolved in water and are part of the air.

33:8 Water

All living things need **water.** Water is important as a medium in which many organisms live. Water is also important to living things in other ways. It is a major part of protoplasm, a solvent in which many metabolic reactions occur, and is a reactant in some reactions. How is water important to humans?

All living things need water.

Water temperature changes much more slowly than air temperature. Thus, water tends to be a more stable environment (Section 33:11).

Water affects the distribution of land plants. All plants require water for photosynthesis, and plants such as mosses and ferns need water for reproduction. The amount of water on land is controlled by rainfall. The amount of rainfall, in combination with temperature, determines the type of plant which will be dominant in a given area. For example, forests are common in areas receiving 75 cm or more of rain per year. In regions where rainfall is from 25 to 75 cm per year, grasses are common. Water is scarce in desert regions. Thus, desert plants and animals are adapted to obtain and conserve water (Section 34:10).

Amount of rainfall, in combination with temperature, determines the dominant plant life of an area.

FIGURE 33-16. Water moves in a cycle. Water recycling depends on heat energy from the sun and metabolic activities of organisms.

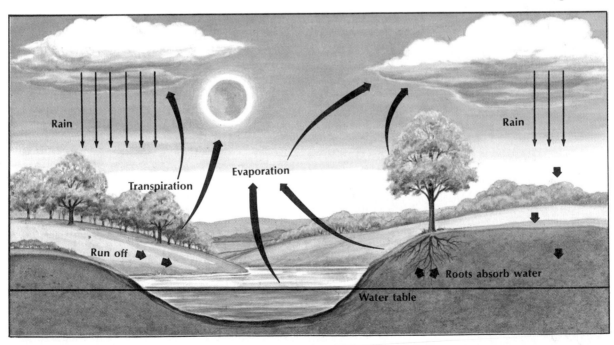

Rain

Rain

Transpiration

Evaporation

Run off

Roots absorb water

Water table

33:9 Soil

Soil is very important in several ways to land organisms. Most plants are anchored in soil. Soil is the substrate upon which many animals move and in which many organisms live. Decomposers in soil return materials to the ecosystem.

Living things help form soil. The beginning of soil formation is a mechanical process in which **weathering** (freezing, thawing, and erosion) breaks rocks into small particles which are the basis of soil. After small particles are formed, microorganisms and small plants begin to live there. The microorganisms' metabolism releases carbon dioxide which dissolves in water, forming a weak acid. The action of the acid and leaching continues the breakdown of the rock. **Leaching** is the dissolving of minerals out of rock or soil by water. Eventually, fine particles such as clay are formed.

After the breakdown of rock into soil begins, organic material is added as the first organisms die. More plants begin to live in the soil, and then animals. As the plants and animals die, they build up on the surface of the soil and decompose. The decayed remains of living things are called **humus** (HYOO muhs). Humus is an important part of soil because it contains organic material, and it enriches the soil. Thus, the remains of once living things provide the materials other organisms will use later. Humus also increases the soil's capacity for holding water and air necessary for plant growth. Humus is found in the upper, dark layers of soil called **topsoil.** Removal of topsoil by erosion (Section 35:10) can be a severe agricultural problem.

Soil fertility is determined by mineral content, organic content, and pH. Different plants are adapted for growth in different soils. Some plants can grow in acidic soils, while others grow best in neutral or basic soils. Lime, a basic material, often is added to acidic soils to make them neutral. Acid rain (Section 35:6) alters the pH of soil and may affect plant life. Acid rain is defined as rainwater with a pH of 5.6 or less.

Soil fertility is also determined by particle size. Few plants can grow well in loose, sandy soils. Most plants grow best in soil composed of small particles in which water and oxygen are plentiful.

Weathering and the action of simple organisms cause the breakdown of rock into smaller particles.

Soil formation is an excellent example of how organisms affect the physical aspects of their environment.

Humus enriches the soil and increases the soil's capacity to hold water.

FIGURE 33-17. Fertilizer is added to soil to restore minerals that have been lost. The three numbers indicated on fertilizer labels give the respective amounts of nitrogen, potassium, and phosphorus that the fertilizer contains.

Larry Hamill

10-6-4		
Guaranteed Analysis		
Total Nitrogen (N)...	10.00%	
10% Ammonical Nitrogen		
Available Phosphoric Acid (P_2O_5)...	6.00%	
Soluble Potash (K_2O)...	4.00%	
Primary plant nutrients derived from ammonium sulfate, ammoniated superphosphorus, muriate of potash.		

James N. Westwater

Hickson-Bender Photography

FIGURE 33-18. Light is essential for (a) photosynthesis by green plants. (b) Vision also requires light. Without light reflected from this biker, she would be impossible to see.

33:10 Light

Light, or radiant energy, is the source of energy for all ecosystems. By photosynthesis, light energy is changed to the chemical energy needed by every living thing.

Plant distribution is affected by the amount of light. Because light cannot penetrate deep into water, algae live near the surface of aquatic communities. In a forest, trees are exposed to the greatest amount of light. Tree leaf arrangements are adaptations for maximum light exposure. Other forest plants are adapted to grow in the dim light of the forest floor. Some of these other plants begin to grow before leaves appear on the trees. Epiphytes receive enough light by growing in tree branches.

Only about two percent of the light striking the earth is used for photosynthesis. Most of the light is absorbed by the atmosphere, land, and seas and is converted to heat or thermal energy. Thus, light energy raises the temperature of land and water and in this way, maintains the earth's temperature. Also, heat has many specific roles. For example, heat is needed for the transpiration of water from plants. Heat also causes the evaporation of water from oceans and rivers. Without heat, water could not be recycled.

Light is also important to organisms in other ways. Light is required for vision. Some animals see well in dim light, but no animals can see in the complete absence of light. Light also triggers migration of birds and the flowering of certain plants (Section 22:12). Light energy is needed to make vitamin D in humans (Table 25-2). Can you think of other examples?

33:11 Temperature and Distribution of Organisms

Temperature of the environment has an important role in the distribution of organisms. In general terms, temperature changes with altitude and latitude. That is, temperature

Light influences the distribution of plant life.

Light energy is transformed to heat necessary for many specific processes and also for life in general.

Light is necessary for vision and for triggering certain biological processes.

Temperature influences the type of communities in different areas.

FIGURE 33-19. Life forms vary with altitude and latitude. Community types parallel one another in altitudinal and latitudinal succession.

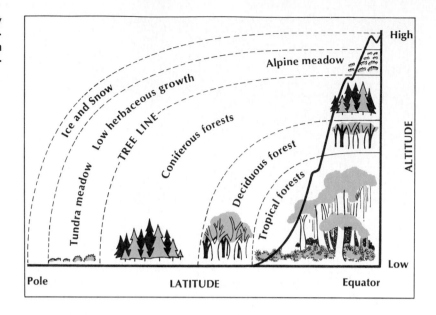

Tide flats are very unstable environments. The temperature varies greatly on both a daily and seasonal basis.

Temperature affects life on land more than it affects life in the water.

No active animal life is found above about 45°C and plants die above 56°C. Certain bacteria, however, can survive temperatures over 100°C.

By forming endospores, bacteria can withstand temperatures above the boiling point and below the freezing point of water.

decreases from the earth's surface upward and from the equator north and south to the poles. The differences in temperatures, along with factors such as wind and moisture, affect the distribution of life forms. As a result, there is a continuous progression of community types from the equator to the poles. This is called **latitudinal** (lat uh TEWD nul) **succession.** The same pattern occurs with changes in altitude. This change is called **altitudinal** (al tuh TEWD nul) **succession.** The two types of successions parallel one another (Figure 33-19).

Temperature varies with time as well as with space. Temperatures differ from day to night and from season to season. Temperature differences also exist between times of sunshine and times of cloudiness. Such changes affect land organisms more than water organisms because air temperatures change more rapidly and to a greater degree than water temperatures. Air temperature can change as much as 40 C° between day and night. In the same time period, the temperature of the surface (top ten meters) of the ocean changes no more than 4 C°. Below ten meters, there is little change in ocean temperature. Thus, in temperature, water is a more stable environment than land.

Temperature, especially on land, is an important ecological factor. Bacteria can live within the greatest temperature range. Some bacteria form endospores and can withstand temperatures above the boiling point and far below the freezing point of water (Section 13:3). For this reason, bacteria are found almost everywhere. Formation of spores or seeds is a feature of many plants. Some spores and seeds can survive temperatures that would kill a mature plant. In this way, the species survives extreme temperatures.

Warren Garst for Tom Stack and Associates

FIGURE 33-20. Many mammals, such as caribou, migrate in the winter. Caribou migrate from the valleys and plains up the slopes in winter where wind blows the snow cover off the sparse vegetation.

Temperature often starts biological processes. For example, peach trees bloom when it is warm. But, they are adapted to withstand chilling during winter so that the trees will not bloom without the chilling. Gypsy moth pupae will not develop into adults unless a freezing temperature has occurred. An adult, though, would die in freezing temperatures. These temperature requirements limit the distribution of the organisms. Peach trees and gypsy moths could not reproduce in the tropics.

Temperature is among the factors which can affect the movement of organisms from place to place. Many birds and some mammals migrate in the winter. Often this migration of animals, such as big-horn sheep, caribou, and many birds, aids in finding food. This lack of food is brought on by the temperature (weather) changes.

Temperature often is responsible for the beginning of biological processes.

Temperature changes can lead to a reduced food supply and the migration of animals.

33:12 Temperature and Metabolism

Metabolic rate in animals varies with external temperature. Up to about 45°C, metabolic rate increases two or three times for every ten degrees the temperature is raised. Approaching 50°C, the rate slows down. Then it falls off sharply to zero. At high temperatures, the enzymes needed for metabolism are destroyed. Therefore, most forms of life cannot survive in temperatures above 50°C (Figure 33-21).

Enzymes are denatured at high temperatures.

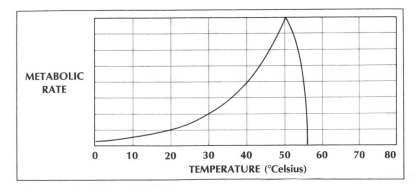

METABOLIC RATE

TEMPERATURE (°Celsius)

FIGURE 33-21. Metabolic rate is influenced by external temperature. Above about 50°C, the rate decreases rapidly because enzymes are destroyed. Most organisms cannot live at temperatures above 50°C.

FIGURE 33-22. (a) The snake, *Sonora simiannulata,* is a cold-blooded animal. Its internal temperature varies with its surroundings. (b) The pine grosbeak, *Pinicola enucleator,* is a warm-blooded animal, maintaining a fairly constant internal temperature.

David M. Dennis

Stephen J. Krasemann/DRK Photo

a

b

Ectotherms have many behavioral and physiological adaptations which enable them to survive temperature extremes.

Ectotherms (Section 16:12) have body temperatures close to that of the environment. These animals have behavioral and physiological adaptations which prevent severe changes in body temperature and metabolism. A desert lizard is active in the early morning when it is cool. However, it will spend the hottest part of the day where it is cooler, such as behind or under a rock. A frog may spend the winter buried in the mud at the bottom of a pond. The frog's metabolism and energy use are greatly reduced. This condition is called hibernation. A frog may again go through a dormant period during the summer. This period of summer dormancy is called **estivation** (es tuh VAY shun). It allows an organism to "escape" from the heat or from drought.

Body temperature of endotherms is maintained at a constant level favorable for metabolism.

Birds and mammals are endotherms (Section 16:13). Their body temperatures vary slightly and are controlled internally.

A human has a body temperature of about 37°C, in a polar bear it is about 38°C, and in an elephant it is about 36.2°C. Why are these temperatures so similar? They are points at which enzymes operate efficiently and metabolism occurs rapidly. Thus, enough energy is made available for the animals' complex activities. Endotherms also have physiological adaptations to

FIGURE 33-23. (a) Earthworms estivate and (b) a bat hibernates. During estivation and hibernation, body metabolism is slowed and less energy is expended.

a

b

Raymond A. Mendez/Animals Animals

David M. Dennis

survive severely cold weather. For example, many mammals, such as squirrels, bears, and bats, hibernate during the winter. During hibernation, body temperature decreases as the metabolic rate decreases. Body temperature in vertebrates is monitored and regulated by the hypothalamus (Section 30:9). The hypothalamus is sensitive to temperature, and it also receives temperature information from heat sensors located on the body.

Adjustments to external temperature involve both physiological and behavioral changes. For example, you may perspire when hot. As perspiration occurs, the skin is cooled. Also, some arteries in your skin get larger and heat escapes. You also tend to be less active, so less heat is generated by the muscles. When you are cold, you may become more active and even shiver. Arteries in the skin contract. These changes conserve heat.

See **Natural History,** October, 1981, for an entire issue devoted to adaptations to cold.

The hypothalamus regulates body temperature in vertebrates.

REVIEWING YOUR IDEAS

9. Define abiotic factors of the environment.
10. What are two media in which organisms live?
11. How is water necessary for life?
12. How is soil important to an ecosystem?
13. In general, how is light important to plants? How is it important to animals?
14. How do altitude and latitude affect temperature? What are several ways that temperature affects organisms?

9. Abiotic factors are the physical aspects of the environment.
10. air and water
11. Water is important as a medium for some organisms, is a major part of protoplasm, a solvent for many reactions, and is a reactant in many reactions.
12. Soil is the substrate upon which many animals move and in which many organisms live. Plants are anchored in soil and much decomposition occurs in soil.
13. Light is necessary for photosynthesis and limits the distribution of plants. It is important to animals for vision, in triggering migrations of birds, and in making vitamin D in humans.
14. Temperature decreases from the earth's surface upward and from the equator north and south to the poles. Temperature affects rate of metabolism and starts some biological processes. Migration is indirectly influenced by temperature.

CHAPTER REVIEW

SUMMARY

1. In an ecosystem, organisms interact with one another and with the physical factors of their environment.
2. Materials and potential energy are transferred through feeding levels within an ecosystem by food chains.
3. Because energy is lost along a food chain, less energy is available at each feeding level. Loss of energy results in a pyramid of energy.
4. Loss of energy also results in a pyramid of numbers and a pyramid of biomass.
5. Because energy cannot be recycled, a constant energy source, the sun, is needed to maintain an ecosystem.

6. Materials in an ecosystem are recycled. Carbon, hydrogen, and oxygen are recycled as a result of processes including respiration and photosynthesis and the activities of decomposers and scavengers.
7. Decomposer bacteria and nitrogen-fixing bacteria are important organisms in the nitrogen cycle.
8. Commensalism, mutualism, and parasitism are examples of special biotic relationships.
9. Adaptations of organisms are related to the medium in which they live.
10. Water is part of protoplasm, a solvent for cellular reactions, and a reactant in some cellular reactions. Amount of rainfall is important in the determination of dominant plant life in a given area.

All Chapter Review answers and additional chapter teaching suggestions are provided in the Teacher's Guide at the front of this text.

CHAPTER REVIEW

11. Type of soil influences the type of plant life and animal life in an ecosystem.
12. Light influences photosynthesis. It also is changed to heat which provides a suitable range of temperatures for life and which is necessary to "drive" the water cycle.
13. Variation in temperature influences the distribution of organisms. Temperature also triggers many biological processes.
14. Temperature affects metabolism. Animals have adaptations for survival in different temperature regions.

LANGUAGE OF BIOLOGY

abiotic factor
altitudinal succession
biotic factor
carnivore
commensalism
ecosystem
estivation
feeding level
first-order
  consumer
food chain
food web
herbivore
humus
latitudinal succession

medium
mutualism
nitrogen cycle
nitrogen fixation
nodule
omnivore
parasitism
pyramid of biomass
pyramid of energy
pyramid of numbers
scavenger
second-order
  consumer
third-order consumer
topsoil

CHECKING YOUR IDEAS

On a separate paper, complete each of the following statements with the missing term(s). Do not write in this book.

1. A first-order consumer is also called a(n) _____.
2. _____ are animals which feed upon other animals.
3. _____ is a relationship in which one organism benefits and the other is neither harmed nor helped.
4. Because of its diet, a human is an example of a(n) _____.

5. All possible feeding relationships in an ecosystem are known as a(n) _____.
6. Nitrogen fixation can be accomplished by blue-green algae and certain _____.
7. Rate of metabolism is related to an organism's _____.
8. _____ is the progression of community types from the equator to the poles.
9. In _____, two organisms live in close association and both benefit.
10. _____ is the rich, organic portion of topsoil.

EVALUATING YOUR IDEAS

1. Why is a constant supply of sunlight needed to maintain an ecosytem?
2. What are the general names for the links in a food chain?
3. Does each ecosystem have specific food chains? Explain.
4. What factors result in a pyramid of energy?
5. Why do large carnivores eat other large animals rather than small animals?
6. Why is there a pyramid of numbers?
7. Why is there a pyramid of biomass?
8. Why do plants need nitrogen? Explain the pathways by which nitrogen becomes available to plants in the nitrogen cycle. Include the activities and importance of nitrogen-fixing bacteria.
9. Distinguish between commensalism and mutualism. Give examples.
10. How does parasitism differ from commensalism and mutualism?
11. How does the medium affect (a) support, (b) locomotion, and (c) food getting?
12. How does availability of water determine the distribution of plants?
13. How is soil formed?
14. How does the nature of the soil help determine the structure of a community?
15. How does light affect the distribution of plants in a forest?

CHAPTER REVIEW

16. How is light energy converted to heat energy? How is heat energy important?

17. Distinguish between latitudinal succession and altitudinal succession.

18. In terms of temperature, which environment is more stable, water or land? Why?

19. How are spores and seeds an important adaptation to temperature?

20. How does temperature affect metabolism in animals?

21. Explain some ways in which ectotherms respond to changes in temperature.

22. In what ways is constant body temperature adaptive?

APPLYING YOUR IDEAS

1. Explain several ways that humans fit into food chains. Are humans usually preyed on by carnivores? Explain.

2. Describe a possible food chain in an aquatic community and a desert community.

3. Consider the sizes of predators and prey. Do you think there is a size relationship along food chains in ecosystems? Explain.

4. Allen's rule states that in general, mammals living in cold climates have shorter extremities (ears, tails, and so on) than the same mammals living in warmer climates. Can you explain why this phenomenon occurs?

5. Would you expect the root system of a cactus to grow deep into the soil or to grow sideways close to the surface of the soil? Explain.

6. In order for nitrogen fixation to occur, enzymes called nitrogenases are needed. Nitrogenase enzymes can be produced by recombinant DNA methods; how might they be used in a practical way?

7. Why is wood such a good source of energy?

8. Some people have suggested that if the human population size continues to increase, it may be necessary for all humans to become herbivores. Why would this change be necessary?

9. In what ways does a dog stay cool in hot weather?

10. How may clearing land for agriculture affect a natural ecosystem?

EXTENDING YOUR IDEAS

1. Assume that a small group of humans is leaving Earth to colonize another planet. You are on a committee to develop plans for a well-organized ecosystem in the new environment. Report on your plans.

2. A small pond or lake is a good place for studying biotic and abiotic factors of the environment. Obtain water samples from different areas and depths. Test your samples for temperature, turbidity (cloudiness), pH, and concentration of dissolved materials such as oxygen, carbon dioxide, nitrates, phosphates, iron, and copper. Correlate this information with a study of life forms in the areas which you studied.

3. Prepare a report on the place of humans in the ecosystem. Discuss their needs and how these needs are met. Also, discuss how humans have affected the ecosystem.

4. Phosphorus is an important mineral needed for life. Find out how phosphorus is recycled in an ecosystem.

SUGGESTED READINGS

Brill, Winston J., "Agricultural Microbiology." *Scientific American*, October, 1981.

Miller, Julie Ann, "Getting Warm." *Science News*, January 15, 1977.

Mosser, Jerry L., and Brock, Thomas D., "Taking the Heat." *Nat. Hist.*, Feb., 1979.

Ricklefs, Robert E., *The Economy of Nature.* Portland, OR, Chiron Press, 1976.

Schmidt-Nielson, Knut, "Counter-current Systems in Animals." *Sci. Am.*, May, 1981.

Street, Philip, *Animal Migration and Navigation.* New York, Chas. Scribner's Sons, 1976.

Additional student readings and suggested teacher readings are provided in the Teacher's Guide.

A community is a group of populations occupying the same area. During its development, a community undergoes an orderly series of changes called succession. This area is changing from a lake to a forest community. As the lake fills in with soil, different types of plants will grow in the area. What factors affect the life forms and changes of a community?

Introduction: Find some signs of "minisuccessions" near the school. These could be mosses or grasses growing in a crack in the sidewalk or a variety of life forms in standing water. Take advantage of these phenomena to make real the idea of succession. A variety of excellent teaching aids covering the world's biomes are available. See *Suggested Audio-Visuals* in the Teacher's Guide.

Chapter

34

ORIGIN AND DISTRIBUTION OF COMMUNITIES

Chapter 34 discusses primary and secondary succession and the character-istics of the major world biomes.

Many natural biological communities exist. They include lakes, forests, and open meadows. If you study any one of these communities, you can determine its common plants and animals. Also you can observe the effects of biotic and abiotic factors within it. In short, you can analyze the community as it exists today.

no Have the same plants and animals always been in the community? How did the plants and animals get there? Were the same biotic and abiotic factors important today also important in the past? Can a community change with time? Are there yes
no communities in other parts of the country and the world similar to the ones where you live? What factors might cause similarities? Keep these questions in mind as you study this chapter. └ climate, altitude, latitude, etc.

GOAL: You will gain an under-standing of ecological succession and the features and distribution of the world's major biomes.

Plants move into an area when their seeds or spores get there. Animals migrate in.

ECOLOGICAL SUCCESSION

Like any other biological level of organization, a community is a living system; it has a developmental history. The series of changes in a community during its development is called **ecological succession** (ee kuh LAHJ ih kul · suk SESH un). Succession may occur as a result of natural, orderly changes, or it may follow a disaster such as fire or disease. Each part of a community's history is well integrated and ordered. The "characters" and "stage" change with time, but the "plot" remains the same.

During its development, a com-munity undergoes a series of changes called ecological suc-cession.

34:1 Primary Succession

Succession that begins with bare rock is called **primary succession.** The first stage of primary succession involves "hardy" autotrophs which can grow under adverse conditions. This first stage of succession is called the **pioneering stage.**

Primary succession is ecological succession in an area that has not been previously occupied by a community.

655

FIGURE 34-1. The first stage in primary succession of a forest is lichens growing on bare rocks. As they die and form humus, larger plants such as mosses, grasses, ferns, and shrubs can grow.

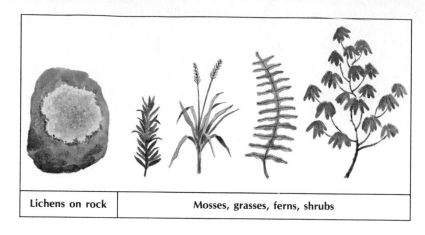

| Lichens on rock | Mosses, grasses, ferns, shrubs |

Succession is directional. Each stage is more mature than a previous one and usually has mostly different organisms.

Consider a natural forest community in New England. This forest might have begun long ago with lichens growing on bare rock. The lichens produce acids which may cause the rock to become corroded. Freezing and thawing of water in cracks in the rock then cause the rock to break into smaller fragments. As the lichens die, bacteria and other decomposers break them down. Small amounts of organic materials may collect in the cracks of the rock, thus, beginning soil formation (Section 33:9). Mosses may then root in the "primitive" soil. As the mosses die and become decomposed, they further enrich the soil. Later, more complex plants such as ferns, grasses, and shrubs appear. The decay of these plants further increases the humus content of the soil, making it thicker and richer.

"Hardy" organisms are the first to live in a new area.

While these changes in plant species are occurring, animal life is also changing. Animals such as nematodes and earthworms add to the richness of the soil, and insect life becomes abundant above the soil. The insects may help pollinate the plants and speed the population growth of the plants. Birds and small mammals may also enter the area.

Both plant and animal life changes during succession.

The kinds of plants and animals present at each stage of succession not only change the soil, but also change other abiotic and biotic factors. For instance, larger plants cast shadows that cause subtle differences in temperature, moisture, and light in some small parts of the community. These slight differences make areas that are known as **microenvironments.** Differences in organisms also influence food chains and energy flow (Section 33:1). All these changes result in the eventual replacement of the organisms of each stage. The organisms are replaced by different organisms in later stages.

Each stage of an ecological succession has a more complex set of organisms. Each stage of succession "prepares" for more complex stages.

In the New England community, pine trees gradually come to replace the grasses and shrubs. Seedlings of beech and maple trees grow in the shade of the pines. Gradually beeches and maples replace the pines by crowding them out.

Each stage of a succession essentially "leads to its own elimination" as a result of environmental modifications.

| Oaks and pines | Maples and beeches |

34:2 Climax Community

Beeches and maples are known as the **dominant species** in the New England forest. They are the final, stable stage in the development of the community called the **climax community.** The type of climax community in a given area depends on the interaction of all factors of the environment, both physical and biotic. The climax community in this example is a **beech-maple forest.** In the southeastern United States, the climax community might be an **oak-hickory forest.**

Because it is complex, a climax community tends to remain the same over a long period of time without further succession. But factors such as changes in climate, disease, a natural disaster, or human interference could be so severe that further succession might occur later.

34:3 Secondary Succession

New succession often begins as a result of natural destruction such as by fire or disease. It may also result from interference by humans. In either case, new succession begins when the dominant species of a plant community are removed. If the land is later left alone, **secondary succession** will occur.

During the early history of the United States, much of the forest land of New England was cleared and used for farming. As people moved westward, many of these farms were abandoned. Secondary succession then began in the abandoned fields. This type of succession is still occurring today in New England (and in other parts of the world). At first, hardy grasses and weeds appear in the fields. Later, shrubs grow and are then followed by junipers, poplars, and white pines. Eventually, beeches and maples begin to sprout in the shadow of the other trees so that what was once an open field becomes a beech-maple forest.

FIGURE 34-2. Succession leads to a climax community. Oaks and pines are replaced by beech and maple trees in a beech-maple climax community.

A climax community is stable and usually has a dominant plant species.

Chestnut trees were once dominant species in many North American forests, but they were destroyed by chestnut blight and replaced by other species.

Certain factors may alter a climax community and lead to further succession.

Secondary succession may occur in an area in which there has already been a community.

Roger K. Burnard

Roger K. Burnard

a

b

FIGURE 34-3. Secondary succession occurs when natural growth is disrupted. (a) After a forest fire, secondary succession occurs eventually resulting in formation of the forest again. (b) This abandoned farm shows early signs of secondary succession.

This sequence of development is different from that beginning with bare rock, but the climax community is the same. Some ecologists feel that a given geographic area will always produce the same climax community even though different origins and pathways are involved. Thus, all climax communities in New England would be beech-maple forests.

Other ecologists believe that each climax community is unique because its development depends on so many chance occurrences. Which view is correct is not known. A major problem in learning about the end product of succession is the vast amount of time needed for a climax community to develop.

34:4 From Lake to Forest

A lake is a body of water surrounded by land. It is a type of ecosystem in which green and blue-green algae are the main producers. Toward the shore, plants such as cattails also provide energy. Consumers consist of ciliates (SIHL ee ayts) and other protists, insect and other larvae, worms, crayfish, and fish. Study of a lake shows that it is a stable, well-organized ecosystem.

A lake is organized, but it is not a climax community. A lake is not a permanent ecosystem; it undergoes succession. The life span of a lake depends on its size and the conditions of the environment.

A lake is not a permanent ecosystem. It eventually undergoes succession.

Consider a lake surrounded by a beech-maple forest. As the lake ages, sediments collect at its bottom. The shallow portions around the shoreline become filled first. In this marshy soil, simple plants such as *Sphagnum* moss, insectivorous plants, and shrubs take root. Sediments continue to collect on the bottom of the lake. As land takes the place of more water, simple plants continue to grow. Meanwhile, the areas around the old shore

Succession of a lake occurs from the edges toward the middle.

Yes, pollution, for example, could alter succession.

undergo further succession. Shrubs are replaced by trees, and finally, beeches and maples become dominant. This pattern continues until no more water remains (Figure 34-3). A beech-maple forest, the climax community, gradually replaces the lake.

If you examine the area surrounding an old lake, you may see evidence of succession. Close to the lake are hardy, simple plants common to marshy areas. Areas farther from the lake support life of increasing complexity up to the climax community. Do human activities affect succession? Explain.

REVIEWING YOUR IDEAS

1. What is ecological succession?
2. What is the pioneering stage of ecological succession?
3. What is a climax community?
4. Distinguish between primary succession and secondary succession.
5. Is a lake a climax community? Explain.

Eventually a lake is replaced by the climax community of its area.

1. Ecological succession is the series of changes in a community during its development.
2. The pioneering stage is the first stage of a succession, characterized by hardy autotrophs.
3. A climax community is the final, stable stage of a succession.
4. Primary succession occurs in an area where no community has previously existed. Secondary succession follows removal of the dominant species from an already established community.
5. No, it undergoes further succession to become the climax community characteristic of its area.

PIONEER STAGE

CLIMAX COMMUNITY

Some ecologists refer to the natural succession of a lake as eutrophication. Others reserve that term for accelerated aging due to pollution.

FIGURE 34-4. A lake is not a permanent ecosystem. As time passes, the lake becomes filled and the surrounding climax community replaces it.

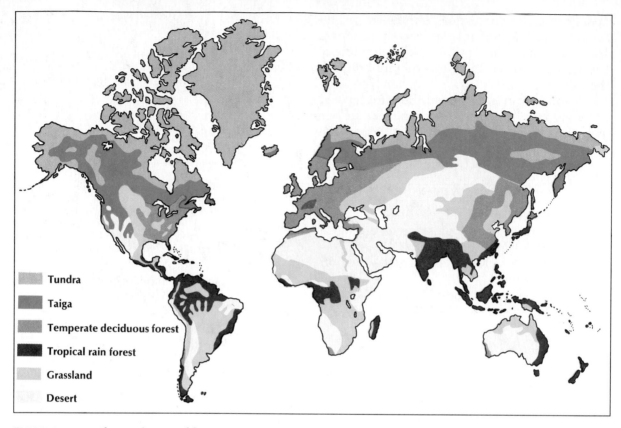

FIGURE 34-5. The major world biomes can be shown on a map. Notice how areas with similar climate have the same biomes.

Tundra

Taiga

Temperate deciduous forest

Tropical rain forest

Grassland

Desert

FIGURE 34-6. One major difference in the world's biomes is the average amount of annual rainfall. The rainfall directly affects the biome's life forms.

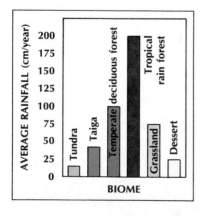

BIOMES

Several communities with the same major life forms make up a **biome** (BI ohm). Geography and climate determine the type of biome an area will be. These factors affect the producers which in turn affect the other life forms. Figure 34-5 shows the major world biomes. Distribution of these biomes shows a latitudinal succession. A similar altitudinal succession also occurs (Section 33:11). For example, mountaintops in lower latitudes have an alpine tundra.

34:5 Tundra

The **tundra** (TUN druh) biome is found at the northernmost latitudes. It has low average temperature and low annual precipitation. The precipitation of the tundra is mostly in the form of snow. Converted to rain, the annual precipitation would be about 12 cm per year. Because the growing season is short and rainfall is low, forests cannot develop. In the winter, water in the soil is frozen. Although a slight amount of thawing occurs in

Roger K. Burnard

Edwin Shay

a

b

summer, thawing extends down for only a few meters. Thus, there is always a layer of frozen ground called **permafrost** (PUR muh frawst) that prevents the rooting of large plants.

Producers of a tundra are lichens such as "reindeer moss," true mosses, and some low, stunted shrubs and bushes. Rodents such as mice, moles, and lemmings are common in the tundra. Other animal life includes snowshoe hares, polar bears, reindeer (caribou), and foxes. Some animals live in the tundra only in warmer weather. Mosquitoes and flies are common in the summer. Many birds migrate to the tundra in summer, though few birds stay all year.

The tundra is a very fragile biome which is being affected by humans. Disturbance of the vegetation which insulates the permafrost can cause widespread erosion. Footpaths used for one season may be visible decades later. Vehicles have left tracks that have eroded into gullies three meters deep. The search for oil in the area is also posing grave threats to the tundra, reducing grazing ranges, and disturbing the migratory patterns of animals such as caribou.

FIGURE 34-7. (a) The tundra contains (b) low shrubs and bushes. Harsh winters with strong winds, short summers, and lack of available water prevent growth of large plants.

Permafrost may extend downward for several hundred feet.

Lichens, mosses, and some shrubs are producers which can exist in the permafrost of the tundra.

FIGURE 34-8. Animals of the tundra are adapted for life in cold zones. (a) Musk oxen have thick fur which protects them. (b) Ptarmigans have feathers that cover their feet and protect against cold.

a

Stephen J. Krasemann/DRK Photo

b

Roger K. Burnard

FIGURE 34-9. The taiga, land characterized by coniferous forests, is the largest of the world's biomes.

Thomas Russell

34:6 Taiga

South of the tundra are the great coniferous (kuh NIHF rus) forests (Section 14:9) covering large portions of Canada, Alaska, and the U.S.S.R. This biome, called **taiga** (TI guh), is probably the largest of the world's biomes. The more southern areas of the taiga have a rainfall of about 35 to 40 cm per year. The taiga also has a lot of fog and a low evaporation rate which results in a very wet area. The soil is full of water and is acidic. There is no permafrost because the temperature is higher than in the tundra.

Trees can grow in taiga soil. Once spruce and firs begin to grow, they further change an area by creating microenvironments. Trees of the taiga provide shade, homes, and protection to many organisms. Trees also cause changes in the soil.

Animal life common in the taiga includes moose, caribou, weasels, mink, and ermine (UR mun). Crossbills are birds well adapted to the taiga. Because their upper and lower bills overlap like a pair of scissors, crossbills (Figure 34-10)are able to break apart cones and feed on the seeds.

Probably the largest of the earth's biomes is the taiga.

The taiga is slightly warmer than the tundra, has relatively little precipitation, and has no permafrost.

FIGURE 34-10. Taiga animals include (a) the moose, *Alces alces,* and (b) the crossbill, *Loxia curvirostra,* which are adapted to survive in coniferous forests.

a

Charlie Ott for Photo Researchers

b

Editorial Photocolor Archives

34:7 Temperate Deciduous Forest

Regions with a rainfall totaling about 100 cm per year make up the **temperate deciduous** (dih SIHJ uh wus) **forest** biome. A deciduous forest is one in which leaves regularly fall from the trees, and so at times, the trees are "bare." As the name suggests, these biomes are found in temperate regions where there are definite seasons. Most leaves fall in the autumn and new buds open in the spring.

Temperate deciduous forests are found in North America, South America, Europe, and Asia. Most of the region east of the Mississippi River is the temperate deciduous forest biome of the United States. This biome has several different climax communities. In the north, the beech-maple forest is common, while in the south, the climax community is usually the oak-hickory forest.

All forests have **vertical stratification** (strat uh fuh KAY shun), a series of **strata** (STRAYT uh), or layers, from top to bottom. The top layer is the **canopy** (branches) of the trees. The canopy shades the ground below and provides homes for animals such as insects, squirrels, and birds. Most of the food is produced in the canopy. Next is the **shrub** layer, under which is the **forest floor.** Light is scarce on the floor so only plants which can grow well in dim light are present. Insects, other arthropods, and snakes are common on the forest floor. A fallen, rotting log may contain a microcommunity of life. Beneath the ground, in the **soil,** is the lowest level. In this layer are many small arthropods, worms, and decomposers.

FIGURE 34-11. Temperate deciduous forests are found in regions that get about 100 cm of rain per year.

Forests have vertical stratification.

In summer, less than one percent of the sunlight may reach the forest floor.

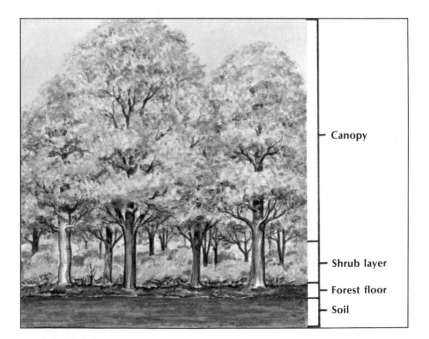

Canopy

Shrub layer

Forest floor

Soil

FIGURE 34-12. Forests show vertical stratification. Life forms in each layer vary.

a

b

FIGURE 34-13. Temperate deciduous forest areas appear much different in winter. (a) Spring brings the budding of trees and shrubs, and the area supports much animal life. (b) In winter, plant leaves are lost, and the area appears nearly lifeless.

Each level of the forest has its own set of environmental conditions. Each is a separate zone. Although an organism usually lives in only one level, the organization of the community depends on the interaction of all organisms.

A temperate deciduous forest changes with the seasons. The falling of leaves in the fall affects the community in many ways. Most important is that the food supply is reduced because food sources such as leaves, seeds, and fruits are less abundant. Also, without leaves, the effects of cold temperatures and wind are more severe. The net effect of these changes is a dormant period during the winter months. The forest floor is covered with dead leaves. Also, animal life is scarce as hibernation and long winter sleeps are common among the animals. In the spring, there is a rapid burst of growth as plants on the forest floor begin to bloom and leaves form on the trees.

During the winter, a temperate deciduous forest is dormant. The forest is full of life in the spring and summer months.

Some of the major animals of the temperate deciduous forest in the United States are Virginia deer, black bears, opossums, salamanders, and squirrels. Birds and insects are also abundant.

34:8 Tropical Rain Forest

Temperate rain forests also exist. In the northwestern United States, for example, rainfall exceeds evaporation in certain mountainous areas. Trees there are mainly conifers and epiphytes exist.

In the equatorial (ek wuh TOR ee ul) regions around the world is the **tropical rain forest** biome. These forests are found in Central and South America, central Asia, parts of Australia, and Africa. This biome is often called jungle, but a **jungle** is really a very dense growth resulting from secondary succession after a rain forest has been cleared. In a tropical rain forest, the temperature is almost constant at 25°C all year and rainfall is heavy. Rain falls almost every day for a total of more than 200 cm of rain per year. Heavy rainfall and high temperature produce a humid environment much like a florist's greenhouse and growth occurs constantly. The tropical rain forest has the most abundant growth of all the biomes.

A tropical rain forest is a year-round "hothouse" of luxuriant growth.

Ruth Dixon

FIGURE 34-14. Heavy rainfall and constantly warm temperatures contribute to the luxuriant growth of the tropical rain forest.

Most prominent of the tropical rain forest plants are large trees reaching 30 to 40 m in height. Unlike coniferous and deciduous forests, a tropical rain forest has no dominant species of trees. In fact, there may be hundreds of species in the same forest. The branches of the trees form a large canopy which is a major layer of the forest. The canopy is so thick that the forest floor may be dark, even at noon. Because the forest floor is dim, floor plant life is scarce. A few shrublike plants may survive, but often the soil is bare.

A tropical rain forest has no dominant species of trees.

Common in this biome are vinelike plants called **lianas** (lee AHN uz). Lianas are rooted in the ground, but their leaves are in the canopy where they receive sunlight. Also in the canopy are epiphytes such as the bromeliad. These plants trap and store water in the hollow areas where their leaves are joined. This water is used by the bromeliad (Section 33:6) and by the animals which live in the canopy.

Lianas and epiphytes are common in the canopy of a tropical rain forest.

a

b

Steve Martin for Tom Stack and Associates   *Tom McHugh for Photo Researchers*

FIGURE 34-15. (a) The slow loris is a tropical rain forest animal that is nocturnal and often sleeps hanging by its feet from a tree limb. (b) Lianas are vines which are rooted in the soil, but have their leaves in the canopy where they receive sunlight.

Although plants are more evident, animals abound. The forest is alive with many arthropods, such as beetles, and vertebrates, such as tree frogs. Most of the mammals in the rain forest live in the trees.

Tropical rain forests exist in several developing countries of the world. This biome supports a large amount of natural plant life. Thus, it seems that the land could be cleared and used for farming. However, the soil is not suitable for growing crops. Temperature and humidity cause rapid decay of dead organisms, and the products are quickly used by the existing plants. Therefore, little humus is formed, and water from the heavy rainfall leaches out minerals in the soil that does form. These processes make the soil infertile; most of the nutrients are in the organisms rather than the soil.

Even though the soil is not fertile, in recent years there has been great pressure to develop the land now occupied by the tropical rain forest. Roads are being cut, and many areas are still being cleared for agricultural purposes. Unlike forests in other biomes, the tropical rain forest is unable to recover through secondary succession once destroyed. Some scientists believe that all tropical rain forests will be destroyed by the year 2000 if current development of the land is not stopped.

The soil of tropical rain forests is not suitable for farming.

FIGURE 34-16. Careless farming of tropical rain forests has resulted in erosion of the land. Erosion of this former Colombian forest has caused the large gorges.

AID

Roger K. Burnard

Michael Collier

a

b

34:9 Grassland

Some areas in both temperate and tropical regions receive between 25 and 75 cm of unevenly distributed rainfall per year. Grasses are the major species of the climax community in these areas. Grasses will also grow where there is more than 75 cm of rain per year, but they are often crowded out in the shade of trees. Biomes in which grass is predominant have different names in different regions. These names include steppe, prairie, plain, pampa, and veldt. A savannah (suh VAN uh) is a biome in which grasses predominate but in which there also are scattered trees. However, in general, these biomes are called **grasslands.**

In the United States, grassland is found west of the Mississippi River to the foothills of the Rocky Mountains. Grasses are the natural climax species of this biome. The size of the grasses increases from west to east as average rainfall increases. At one time grasses close to two meters tall were common.

Animals of the grasslands at one time included grazing animals such as bison. Today, antelopes, jackrabbits, gophers, ground squirrels, and meadowlarks are common. Hunting of ground-nesting birds, such as the prairie chicken and ring-necked pheasant, is restricted to prevent extinction of them.

FIGURE 34-17. (a) An African savannah is a special type of grassland. **(b)** Although most of the U.S. grasslands are in the Great Plains, some are in other places, such as this area in California.

The grassland biome has a rainfall of between 25 and 75 cm per year.

FIGURE 34-18. (a) Giraffes and **(b)** zebras are among animals that live in the African savannah. Both live in herds of about a dozen, and mainly are killed by lions and humans.

a

Don C. Nieman

b

Don C. Nieman

Soil Conservation Service

FIGURE 34-19. This farm was abandoned because poor farming practices ruined the soil. Winds eroded the loose soil.

Grasslands are very important to humans because of their use in agriculture. To take advantage of the high fertility of grassland soils, humans have changed this biome. They have replaced the natural grasses with cereal grains such as wheat and corn.

Natural grasses have been replaced with cereal grains, and bison with cattle.

Humans have been careless with this biome. Much of the rich topsoil has been removed as a result of wind and water erosion of plowed soil. Constant plowing and lack of rain change the rich soil into loose dust. In the 1930's, winds picked up the soil and carried it for great distances. The south central part of the United States became known as the "dust bowl," and many farms had to be abandoned. The tragedy of the "dust bowl" was a major factor in starting conservation practices. How have humans benefited from the "dust bowl"?

Nutrients also are removed during harvesting of crops because with crop removal there is little organic material remaining available for decay and decomposition.

34:10 Desert

Where rainfall is less than 25 cm per year and evaporation is rapid, there is little plant and animal life. Such areas are desert biomes. **Deserts** are found in western United States, Africa, India, Asia, South America, and Australia. Depending on the amount of rainfall relative to the average temperature, deserts can be hot, cold, or temperate. The Mojave Desert of southern California is an example of a hot desert. The Northern Great Basin Desert in parts of Nevada, Utah, and California is a cold desert.

Deserts occur in areas receiving less than 25 cm of rain per year.

Deserts have little plant cover; bare ground is a common sight. The amount of water available to plants is small so little plant life can be supported. Plants that are present are widely spaced.

Desert plants are well spaced.

Not only is the amount of water small, there is no regular pattern of rainfall. Long periods of drought are not uncommon and may last for many years. Also, when it does rain, much of the water quickly runs off and is not usable by the plants.

Organisms in desert biomes have many adaptations to dryness and temperature extremes. In plants these include reduction of the surface area of leaves, storage of water in fleshy parts, and large root systems for absorbing water. The thorns of cacti are modified leaves which have little surface area and lose little water by evaporation. Some plants mature quickly and produce seeds in a few days when water is available. During droughts some parts of plants may die, but the remaining parts can produce new growth when water becomes available. Seeds of some desert plants can remain dormant for fifty years or more so that a species can survive even under the most adverse conditions. Other seeds have a chemical which prevents germination until the chemical is dissolved by water. Because a large amount of water is needed to dissolve the chemical, the plant starts to grow only when water is plentiful.

Seeds of desert plants have adaptations for surviving during long dry spells.

Animals, too, are adapted for desert life. Conservation of water is important in their survival. Desert animals can obtain water from their metabolism. Water produced as a by-product of the breakdown of foods can be used for other purposes. Also, animals such as a kangaroo rat excrete highly concentrated urine (Section 27:2) and thus conserve water.

Temperature extremes are common in deserts. Many desert animals are small burrowing rodents. By staying in their burrows, they avoid the heat of the day and the cold of the night. Some burrowing animals undergo a period of estivation (Section 33:11) which is like hibernation but occurs in hot weather. As in hibernation, metabolism is slowed down. In this way, an animal survives adverse conditions.

Estivation enables some desert animals to withstand temperature extremes.

Jumping animals live in deserts. The jackrabbit and kangaroo rat have a jumping locomotion. This allows them to move quickly from place to place. Large animals do not usually live in a desert. They would be unable to find enough food, and they are not adapted to drought and temperature extremes.

Also, some behavioral adaptations protect animals from temperature extremes. Many are active only at night. Others stay in shady places during the hottest part of the day (Section 33:11).

FIGURE 34-20. (a) The horned toad is a desert animal that estivates if the temperature gets too high. (b) Desert plants include peyote, the small bushy plants, and various other cacti.

David M. Dennis

Joey Jacques

R. G. Bachand

Richard Brommer

Joey Jacques

a b c

FIGURE 34-21. (a) The moray eel, (b) sea urchin, and (c) squirrel fish are ocean animals that live close to the surface where light penetrates.

34:11 Ocean

Other aquatic biomes are lakes, streams, rivers, and estuaries.

You are familiar with life on land. However, the earth is covered with more than twice as much water as land. Most of this water is in the **oceans**. The kinds and number of organisms living in the oceans far exceed those on land. How might this vast resource be best used?

Distribution of organisms in the oceans depends mostly on abiotic factors. Most important of these is light. Light intensity decreases with depth because light is both reflected and absorbed by the water. The penetration of light varies with the contents of the water and with latitude, but it generally does not reach a depth greater than 200 m. The oceans have an average depth of about 4000 m so the zone of water in which light is present is quite small. Producers, which affect the makeup of any ecosystem, only live where there is sufficient light for photosynthesis to occur. Thus, light is an important limiting factor of life in the ocean.

Limited penetration of light restricts photosynthesis to about the top two hundred meters of the oceans.

Temperature is also important to life in water. However, temperature does not vary as much in the ocean as on land (Section 33:11). Thus, the sea is a more stable environment than the land. In the mid North Atlantic Ocean, for example, water temperature varies only about 10 C° from top to bottom.

Ecologists classify marine organisms into three major groups. Organisms which float in the water are called **plankton** (PLANG tun). These include many types of unicellular algae, heterotrophic protists, and small multicellular animals. Copepods (KOH puh pahdz), microscopic crustaceans, are a major form of animal plankton. Jellyfish and their relatives and the larval forms of other animals are also plankton.

Plankton are organisms which float in water.

Plankton is further classified as phytoplankton (plants) and zooplankton (animals).

Animals which can move freely through the water under their own power are called **nekton** (NEK tun). Nektonic animals include fish, whales, arthropods, and squid.

Nekton are animals which move freely through water.

Animals which live attached to or crawl on the ocean floor are called **benthos** (BEN thahs). Included in this group are organisms such as barnacles, starfish, and clams. Benthic organisms are mostly found close to shore or in shallow water.

Benthos are bottom-dwelling animals.

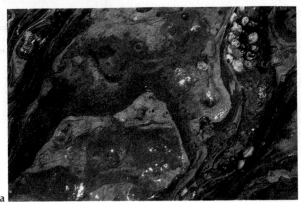

a

b

34:12 Ocean: Littoral and Neritic Zones

Conditions vary greatly from one part of the ocean to another. For this reason, the ocean is made up of many biomes which have certain features and life forms. For example, the area close to the shore is the **littoral** (LIHT uh rul) **zone.** The littoral zone is subject to the action of tides and is a transitional area between land and sea. Organisms of this biome, such as many types of algae, clams, crabs, and barnacles, are adapted to changing conditions. These organisms can survive exposure to both air and water and changes in temperature.

Along the continental shelf, the land begins to slope down and the ocean becomes deeper. This area is the **neritic** (nuh RIHT ihk) **zone.** Life in the neritic zone is different from life in the littoral zone. The environment is more stable because there is no direct exposure to air. Organisms in the neritic zone are strictly aquatic. Plankton and nekton abound in the surface waters. Also, there are many bottom dwellers.

34:13 Ocean: Abyssal Zone

The deepest part of the ocean is the **abyssal** (uh BIHS ul) **zone.** Here light is absent so no photosynthesis occurs. Some nektonic animals, mostly fish, exist here. These fish feed on other fish and on dead organisms settling from above. Some organisms of this zone have organs which give off light. A certain angler fish has a "lure" which emits light and attracts prey. Giving off a light in the abyssal zone may also be needed for reproduction.

Some animals live at great depths in the abyssal zone. Experiments have been done in which bait (food), lights, and movie cameras were lowered to a depth of 7000 m. It was found that within a few hours small fish, crustaceans, and even sharks were attracted to the bait, probably by its odor. The animals quickly ate most of the food and mollusks and echinoderms fed on the leftovers.

FIGURE 34-22. (a) The littoral zone is the ocean biome close to shore. A tide pool shows some of the life of the littoral zone. (b) A coral reef has organisms of the neritic zone.

Organisms inhabiting the littoral zone must be adapted to changing conditions.

Life in the neretic zone is more stable than life in the littoral zone.

In the abyssal zone, animals feed on other animals or dead organisms sinking from above.

Decomposition of ocean organisms occurs on the ocean bottom.

Materials produced by decomposition are constantly mixed and redistributed in the upper layers of the oceans as a result of temperature differences and wind.

6. geography and climate
7. tundra — arctic; lichens, mosses, and shrubs; taiga — Canada, Alaska, and USSR; conifers; temperate deciduous forest — North and South America, Europe, and Asia; deciduous trees; tropical rain forest — Central and South America, Asia, Australia, and Africa; lianas and epiphytes; grassland — North and South America, Europe, Africa, and Australia; grasses; desert — western U.S., Africa, India, Asia, South America, and Australia; cactus, etc.; oceans—throughout world; no dominant species.
8. rainfall
9. A jungle results from secondary succession following clearing of a rain forest.
10. Light can penetrate only the top. Thus, there are no producers in deeper waters and less energy to sustain life.

Teaching suggestion: Stress the uniqueness of these communities in that energy available to organisms comes originally from heat (geothermal) rather than light.

Decomposition of dead organic materials on the ocean floor is done by bacteria. The molecules are broken down into simpler forms such as carbon dioxide, nitrates, and phosphates. After decomposition, materials must be made available to producers. If materials continued to build up on the ocean bottom, a point would be reached where life could no longer continue because all the materials would be at the bottom of the ocean. An ecosystem can survive only if materials are recycled.

Return of materials to the surface of the oceans is affected mostly by water temperature and wind. In cold climates, surface water becomes colder than water below the surface. Because cold water is more dense than warm water, cold surface water sinks and warm bottom water rises. Also, the wind causes currents which move the surface water. Water below the surface rises to replace the water displaced by the wind. Although both of these processes return decomposed materials to the surface, water temperature differences account for almost all of the return.

REVIEWING YOUR IDEAS

6. What factors affect the type of biome an area will be?
7. Name the major world biomes. Where is each found? What is the dominant species of plant in each one?
8. What factor accounts for the different biomes east and west of the Mississippi River in the United States?
9. Distinguish between jungle and rain forest.
10. Why is there more life within a hundred meters of the ocean surface than on the ocean floor?

ADVANCES IN BIOLOGY

34:14 A Newly-Discovered Ocean Community

For the most part, the abyssal zone is a cold, barren, desertlike biome. Because light only penetrates about 100 m into ocean water, no photosynthesis can occur on the deep ocean floor. Without sunlight to provide an energy source, it was thought that very few life forms could survive. Recently, however, scientists studying the ocean floor have discovered communities of animals living almost 3 000 m below the ocean surface.

The first of these communities was found in 1977 off the Galapagos Islands (Section 10:8). Since then, similar communi-

Dr. Frederick Grassle,
Woods Hole Oceanographic Institution

ties have been discovered off the coasts of Mexico and Peru. These communities are located near places where the earth's solid crust forms cracks, or **rifts,** and splits into huge plates that move. At these cracks the huge plates move apart, and **magma,** molten material from deep within the earth, fills in the cracks and becomes the new ocean floor. Water seeps into these and other seafloor cracks and comes in contact with molten rock. The temperature of the water rises because of geothermal energy. **Geothermal energy** is energy due to the natural radioactivity of the earth. Because the water is under tremendous pressure, it gushes up through vents (openings that look like small volcanoes) in the new ocean floor. It is around these vents that the unusual communities exist.

An abundance of animal life never before seen has been found to inhabit these communities. Brown mussels and white clams which average 30 cm long live among mounds of cooling lava that look like pillows. Clusters of orange and white crabs, starfish, octopi, and strangely colored fish move around the vents. Strangest of all are clusters of giant tube worms, some of them as long as three meters, that live in colonies around the vents. Many other life forms collected from the sites differ so much from known animals that they have not yet been classified.

The warm water, ranging in temperature from 2°C to 350°C, helps the animals survive and grow and provides energy for the system. But because there are no plants, scientists did not know what organisms functioned as producers. By testing water samples, they found that the very hot water was reacting with minerals in rocks to produce hydrogen sulfide. Chemosynthetic bacteria (Section 13:3) metabolize the hydrogen sulfide and use its energy to make carbohydrates and function as producers in the community. The bacteria—the basis of the community's food chain—were found by the millions in the digestive tracts of mussels and clams. The shellfish, in turn, provide food for other members of the community.

Besides supplying the heat and food source for these abyssal communities, the hot water gushing from the vents may also be of economic importance. Important minerals, such as gold and silver, are also dissolved in the water with the hydrogen sulfide. When the hot water mixes with cold sea water, these minerals precipitate, or become solids again. Some scientists are trying to find inexpensive ways to collect these minerals.

It is thought that many of these communities must exist along the cracks in the earth's crust where seafloor spreading is occurring. As scientists continue to study these sections of the ocean floor, more information will be available about the interactions of these newly-discovered organisms with their geothermal environment.

FIGURE 34-23. Unusual life forms live at the vents. Shown here are tube worms and clams.

Ocean vent communities contain an abundance of newly discovered animal life.

FIGURE 34-24. Hot, sulfide-blackened water comes from a "chimney" at the East Pacific Rise near the Gulf of California. Water from the vents is as hot as 350°C and contains minerals that nourish the biological community.

Dudley Foster/
Woods Hole Oceanographic Institution

CHAPTER REVIEW

SUMMARY

1. The series of changes in the development of a community is ecological succession.

2. Each stage of primary succession from bare rock affects both biotic and abiotic factors and prepares the community for more complex stages which follow.

3. Eventually, primary succession results in a stable climax community with a dominant species.

4. Secondary succession occurs after a community has been affected in such a way that one of its dominant species is removed.

5. A lake is a community in the process of succession. It will eventually be replaced by the climax community of its area.

6. The type of biome in a given area is determined by geography and climate.

7. The tundra biome has permafrost and lacks large plants.

8. The taiga biome is a wet region composed of evergreen forests.

9. Temperate deciduous forests are found in areas of moderate rainfall. Most plant life is dormant during the winter.

10. Tropical rain forests develop in regions with heavy rainfall and constant warm temperature.

11. Grassland biomes receive less rain than forests. Much of the grasslands have been cleared for agriculture.

12. Deserts are biomes with sparse rainfall and they support little plant or animal life.

13. Oceans cover most of the earth. Many more kinds of organisms live in the oceans than on land.

14. The ocean is composed of three distinct zones: littoral, neritic, and abyssal.

15. Newly-discovered abyssal communities are powered by geothermal energy. In these communities, producers use energy of hydrogen sulfide to make carbohydrates.

LANGUAGE OF BIOLOGY

abyssal zone
benthos
biome
climax community
desert
dominant species
ecological succession
geothermal energy
grassland
littoral zone
nekton

neritic zone
ocean
plankton
primary succession
secondary succession
taiga
temperate deciduous
  forest
tropical rain forest
tundra
vertical stratification

CHECKING YOUR IDEAS

On a separate paper, indicate whether each of the following statements is true or false. Do not write in this book.

1. Conifers are dominant in the tundra.

2. A lake is a permanent climax community.

3. Abandonment of New England farms has led to secondary succession.

4. The first organisms to play a role in primary succession are small animals.

5. Each stage during an ecological succession modifies the environment and makes possible the next stage.

6. Plankton are free-swimming organisms.

7. The source of energy in newly-discovered abyssal zone communities is geothermal energy.

8. Wide spacing of plants is a characteristic of deserts.

9. No photosynthesis occurs in the abyssal zone.

10. Barnacles are examples of benthos.

EVALUATING YOUR IDEAS

1. Compare the events of primary succession in New England from bare rock and secondary succession on an abandoned farm.

2. How does a lake become a forest?

CHAPTER REVIEW

3. What is permafrost? How does permafrost affect the type of plant life in the tundra?

4. Describe the animal life in the tundra.

5. What is the climate of the taiga? How does the climate affect plant life there?

6. What are microenvironments? How do they affect a community?

7. What kinds of animals live in the taiga?

8. Describe the climate of a temperate deciduous forest.

9. What is vertical stratification? Describe vertical stratification of a temperate deciduous forest.

10. How does the climate of a tropical rain forest affect the plant life there?

11. Compare life in the canopy of a tropical rain forest to life on the forest floor.

12. Describe the climate of the grasslands.

13. How have the grasslands of the United States changed?

14. Why are the plants of a desert scattered rather than clumped together?

15. What kinds of animals live in a desert? How are they adapted for life there?

16. How does light affect the distribution of organisms in the oceans?

17. Distinguish the three kinds of ocean life.

18. Distinguish three major ocean zones.

19. How are materials of the ocean recycled?

20. Explain energy "flow" in newly-discovered abyssal communities.

APPLYING YOUR IDEAS

1. What might happen to a climax community if a parasite severely damaged the dominant species of plant?

2. How might life in the canopy layer of a temperate deciduous forest affect the shrub, floor, and soil levels?

3. What kinds of animal life would be affected if a forest were cleared? How?

4. Which type of life is most numerous in an ocean? Why?

5. Vertical stratification is common in forest biomes. Does vertical stratification also occur in oceans? Explain.

6. What kind of biome do you live in? How have human activities altered the characteristics of that biome?

7. Do you think that the newly-discovered abyssal biomes are permanent? Explain.

EXTENDING YOUR IDEAS

1. Examine an area near your home for evidence of secondary succession. Are there different kinds of plants in different areas? Make a model or drawing of the area.

2. Examine a natural area for microenvironments. Make a list of microenvironments and the special conditions in them. How do they affect the life of the community?

3. Find out about biomes called estuaries. What unique conditions exist there? How are organisms adapted for life in estuaries?

SUGGESTED READINGS

Cromie, William J., "Probing the Ocean's Metal 'Factories'." *Sciquest*, December, 1979.

del Moral, Roger, "Life Returns to Mount St. Helens." *Natural History*, May, 1981.

Fichter, George S., *The Future Sea*. New York, Sterling Publishing Co., 1978.

Godfrey, Michael A., "The Inevitable Forest." *National Wildlife*, August-September, 1977.

Horn, Henry S., "Forest Succession." *Scientific American*, May, 1975.

Lambert, Stan L., and Jones, James H., "Desert Shrews." *Natural History*, January, 1980.

MacDonald, Ken C., and Luyendyk, Bruce P., "The Crest of the East Pacific Rise." *Scientific American*, May, 1981.

Pringle, L., *The Gentle Desert: Exploring an Ecosystem*. New York, Macmillan, 1977.

Additional student readings and suggested teacher readings are provided in the Teacher's Guide.

Humans depend on and interact with the environment. Here, a photographer "shoots" a bull moose in Mt. McKinley National Park. How do you depend on the environment? How do you interact with the environment? What types of effects have humans had on the environment? What can you do to assure that a clean, healthy environment will be available to others in the future?

676

Introduction: You can begin this chapter by asking students in what ways humans have helped and hurt the environment. Not only will this probably produce a list of negative factors such as pollution, food and energy shortages, and over-population, but it may also lead to a spirited debate during which students can air their personal feelings about the environment. If you can get a word in, consider the following questions, too. How does economy affect our decisions involving environment? Would people in technological countries be willing to voluntarily return to a simpler way of life? Would it be better to educate people so they can make intelligent and farsighted decisions or to have governments legislate standards? Do people living today really think seriously about the quality of life their descendants may face? Is there recent evidence that the quality of the environment is improving? Does better technology necessarily mean progress?

HUMANS AND THE ENVIRONMENT

Chapter 35 explores the effect of humans on the biosphere.

Despite the fact that humans can avoid many of the forces of natural selection, they are part of the **biosphere,** the world of life. The biosphere is made up of ecosystems where organisms interact with their environment. The environment affects the lives of the organisms, and the organisms affect the total environment.

Humans depend on the environment, both directly and indirectly. They need food, fuel to run their machines, and other raw materials for modern-day life. Humans change their environment by clearing land, substituting one kind of life for another, and killing "pests." They also disrupt food chains and put waste materials into the air, water, and soil. The results of these actions are some of the most urgent problems of ecology. These changes which humans make in the environment are important to all organisms, including humans themselves.

GOAL: You will gain an understanding of the place of humans in the biosphere and how human influence on the environment can affect the destiny of humans and other organisms.

Humans have altered their natural surroundings in many ways.

Emphasize that the uniqueness of humans is the extent to which they draw from and alter their environment. All organisms do both, but only humans consciously alter the balance of nature.

PEST CONTROL AND POLLUTION

While agriculture and technological advances (Section 32:11) have been responsible for human successes and comforts, these advances have also produced unexpected and unwanted results. In growing crops and producing goods, many wastes have been released into the environment. Often these wastes cause **pollution** of air, water, and soil and decrease the quality of the environment. A major source of pollution has resulted from the effort to control organisms which compete with or cause disease in humans.

Introduction of wastes into the biosphere contributes to pollution.

677

David M. Dennis

Richard Brommer

a

b

FIGURE 35-1. Insect damage can ruin various crops. (a) Squash bugs harm squash plants and (b) Japanese beetles can ruin many kinds of fruit plants, such as this peach tree.

35:1 Pests and Pesticides

Many organisms are pests to humans. Termites destroy wood, moths destroy woolen products, and Japanese beetles attack fruit trees and other plants, to name a few. In addition to pests that may directly affect humans in and around the home, there are pests which cause severe damage to agricultural crops, livestock, and forests. Weeds cause nearly ten percent of crop losses each year by competing with and crowding out cultivated plants. Corn borers attack corn and bollworms (larvae of a moth) invade cotton. Fungi such as rusts (Section 19:7) damage wheat plants, and other fungi cause Dutch elm disease (Section 13:15). Nematode worms attack and destroy a variety of plant parts.

Some pests were accidentally brought to the United States.

Many pests, such as the Japanese beetle, gypsy moth, and Mediterranean fruit fly (medfly) were brought to the United States from other parts of the world either on purpose or accidentally. The gypsy moth was brought from Europe in 1868 for use in experiments. Japanese beetles first appeared in 1916, accidentally imported, probably in the form of larvae in soil around plants. The first invasion of medflies occurred in 1929 in fruit thought to be smuggled from Hawaii. With no natural predators, these insects flourished and became pests in the new environment.

Changes in natural ecosystems may increase the population density of pest organisms.

Humans have also contributed to pest problems by altering natural ecosystems and planting large areas with single food crops. These activities remove natural predators and create a high population density of hosts suitable for transmission of parasites (Section 32:5).

DDT is a chlorinated hydrocarbon. Other chemicals in this category are chlordane, dieldrin, and heptachlor.

DDT and other pesticides have been used to kill disease-causing and crop-destroying insects.

In trying to control pests, humans use chemicals called **pesticides,** poisons which kill the unwanted organisms. Insects are the most numerous pests. One of the most effective pesticides used to kill insects is a chemical known as DDT. DDT has been used to kill disease carriers such as *Anopheles* (uh NAHF uh leez) mosquitoes. These mosquitoes transmit the organism which causes malaria (Section 13:11).

USDA

FIGURE 35-2. These trees are being sprayed with pesticides to eliminate organisms which damage the crop.

DDT also has been used to kill insects around the home and those which destroy crops. Because DDT and other pesticides were effective and easily obtained, they became convenient weapons for farmers, orchard keepers, and homeowners.

35:2 Pesticides: Some Problems

Use of pesticides to eliminate pests and disease and to protect crops is extensive, and large areas are sprayed with pesticides. But DDT and other pesticides kill many organisms besides pests. In applying chemicals to large areas, entire ecosystems are affected.

Suppose that an insect pest is the natural prey of a larger, carnivorous insect. When DDT is used to kill the pest, both insect populations are affected. The predators, fewer in number than the pests (Section 32:4), may be completely destroyed by the pesticide. But some of the pests may survive, even after the effects of the pesticide wear off. In the absence of natural predators, the pest population would increase rapidly. The pest problem may get worse than it was before (Figure 35-3). Thus, in this case, pesticide use would have made conditions worse.

Pesticides have caused another unforeseen problem. When DDT was widely used in the 1940's, houseflies were easily killed. However, some flies were not affected because they were resistant (genetically) to DDT. These flies survived and passed their genes to later generations. Thus, as a result of natural selection, a resistant strain of houseflies resulted. In the same way, malarial mosquitoes have become resistant to DDT. It is estimated that a total of four hundred insect species and fifty species of fungi around the world are now resistant to currently used pesticides. Some organisms are resistant to only one type of poison, while others are resistant to several.

FIGURE 35-3. Dragonflies are natural predators of aphids. Spraying an area with DDT to kill aphids may kill all dragonflies. Some aphids may survive and, without the natural predator, the aphid population would grow.

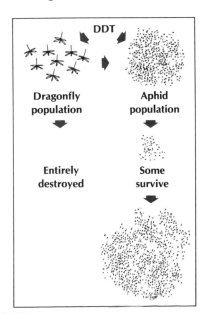

FIGURE 35-4. As a top level carnivore, the bald eagle can accumulate large concentrations of DDT. DDT and related pesticides are known to be involved in eggshell thinning in these and other birds.

Charlie Ott from National Audubon Society

35:3 Pesticides: Effects on Other Organisms

A biodegradable substance is one which can be broken down in organisms and thus be recycled through a community.

DDT is a synthetic product which cannot be metabolized, broken down, by animals. Chemicals structurally similar to DDT, such as DDD, DDE, and dieldrin, are also not broken down. A compound that is not chemically broken down into harmless, inactive compounds is called **nonbiodegradable** (nahn bi oh dih GRAYD uh bul).

DDT is a nonbiodegradable substance. It accumulates in the fatty tissues of animals. As it is passed upward along food chains, it becomes concentrated and, in larger amounts, can kill animals.

DDT, insoluble in water, is soluble in fats. Thus, DDT builds up in the fatty tissues of animals and is transferred along food chains from animal to animal. Because it is not broken down, the concentration of DDT increases as it passes higher up the food chain. This increased concentration of chemicals along a food chain is called **biological magnification.**

In small doses, DDT is not harmful to animals other than insects. But, as it builds up in other animals, DDT can be harmful, even lethal, to animals such as fish, birds, and mammals. As these animals die, the ecosystems of which they were a part are disrupted.

Birds often are affected by pesticides such as DDT. Top carnivores, such as the bald eagle and golden eagle, build up the most DDT. Studies show that these birds are rapidly decreasing in number. In fact, they are in danger of extinction. DDT does not kill the adult birds, but instead, affects the population's birthrate (Section 32:2). DDT causes eggshells to be very thin and so the eggs break easily. DDT may also interfere with breeding behavior. Ospreys, falcons, and pelicans are other birds affected

These pesticides, the organophosphates, inhibit cholinesterase. Even though biodegradable, they can affect a greater variety of harmless organisms than do the chlorinated hydrocarbons.

by DDT. The sizes of their populations also have been reduced by the use of pesticides.

Another group of pesticides, including parathion, malathion, and phosdrin, have different ecological actions. Unlike DDT and related substances, these pesticides tend to break down quickly. Thus, they do not spread through food chains and their effects are not magnified. However, these pesticides affect not only insects but also vertebrates, including humans, before they break down. When applied over a large area, they may kill many predators of pests, thus disturbing natural controls of pest populations. Malathion was widely used in California in 1981 to control a "foreign" pest, the medfly.

USDA

FIGURE 35-5. Because of damage done by medflies, samples of fruits shipped within, into, and out of the country are inspected for medfly larvae.

35:4 The Pesticide Dilemma

Use of pesticides such as DDT was widespread until their harmful ecological effects were fully realized. In 1972, DDT was banned for normal use in the United States. Since that time, the use of other dangerous pesticides also has been restricted.

But how does pesticide use affect the economy? In order to feed a growing world population, a high crop yield is needed. Without pesticides, pests would destroy a large portion of the crops and a lot of food would be lost.

Apart from the need for enough food for everyone, many shoppers in the United States expect a large selection of food in grocery stores. Consumers want to buy food which is pest free and which does not show signs of pest damage. For example, grocers must supply mold-free oranges and worm-free apples. Thus, pesticide use affects the economy in many ways.

Much pesticide research is still necessary to find ways to use pesticides with less harmful consequences. For example, new ways of applying pesticides besides aerial spraying must be found. The chemicals should be applied more directly to reduce the risk of harming other organisms. It is estimated that if pesticides could be applied directly to pests, 99 percent of the pesticides now used could be eliminated. Scientists are studying the use of pesticides in plastic capsules to reduce the risks to other organisms. The capsules would be placed in the soil where microorganisms would degrade the plastic. Thus, the pesticide would be in the soil and would not directly enter the air. Also, development of pesticides which quickly break down to form harmless products is being studied. Alternatives to control by pesticides are discussed in Section 35:14.

Because pesticides can be very beneficial, what should be done about the problems they cause? Many people defend pesticide use to avoid crop loss and damage. What do you think?

Teaching suggestion: Ask students if they would buy moldy or wormy fruit. Students will quickly see what the pesticide dilemma is.

Pesticide use can be beneficial at the same time it is harmful in other ways.

Pesticides should be applied to an ecosystem in such a way that organisms other than pests are not affected.

1. Humans depend on the environment for food, fuel, and raw materials.

2. Pesticides are poisons. They are used to combat organisms which are dangerous to or compete with humans.

3. A nonbiodegradable substance is one which does not break down into simpler, harmless compounds.

4. As it passes along food chains, DDT builds up in the fatty tissues of animals. Concentration of DDT increases as it passes up the food chain.

REVIEWING YOUR IDEAS

1. How do humans depend on their environment?
2. What are pesticides? Why are they used?
3. What is a nonbiodegradable substance?
4. Explain what happens to DDT as it is passed along food chains.

OTHER SOURCES OF POLLUTION

Pesticides and other chemicals are pollutants. A **pollutant** is any factor that damages or makes the environment unclean. Pollutants affect air, water, and soil and may endanger the health and lives of all forms of organisms.

35:5 Air Pollution

A major source of air pollution is the burning of fossil fuels.

Most air pollution is caused by the burning of fossil fuels. Burning of fuels is needed in industry, transportation, and homes. During this burning, substances which may damage organisms are released directly into the atmosphere.

One of the chief causes of air pollution is the burning of gasoline, mainly in automobiles. By-products of gasoline combustion include hydrocarbons (compounds of hydrogen and carbon), carbon monoxide, sulfur dioxide, nitrogen oxides, and lead compounds. Some hydrocarbons, also produced by oil refineries, are known to cause cancer. Carbon monoxide deprives animals of oxygen because it combines readily with hemoglobin (Section 26:9).

Nitrogen oxides are produced at high temperatures from the reaction between nitrogen and oxygen in the air. The nitrogen oxide, in turn, can combine in sunlight with hydrocarbons to form a compound called PAN, a chief ingredient in the kind of

FIGURE 35-6. (a) The U.S. Environmental Protection Agency developed the Pollutant Standards Index (PSI) to convey air pollution information and associated health effects to the public in a simple, uniform way. (b) Often, people think of air pollution as something that is outside. Air pollution inside cars and houses from smoking and poor ventilation can pose major health hazards.

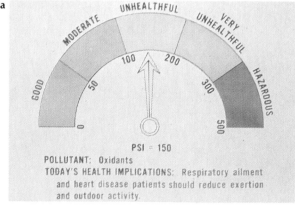

a

PSI = 150
POLLUTANT: Oxidants
TODAY'S HEALTH IMPLICATIONS: Respiratory ailment and heart disease patients should reduce exertion and outdoor activity.

EPA

b

Lightforce

smog which often surrounds large cities. A major effect of this type of smog is damage to the lungs. Damage of this kind can be extremely dangerous to people who suffer from other respiratory illnesses.

Nitrogen dioxide, a brownish-colored gas, is a compound which can kill lung cells and, in high amounts, cause a buildup of fluids in the lungs. How would fluid buildup affect respiration?

Some automobile engines require a form of gasoline containing lead compounds. As this gasoline is burned, lead compounds are released into the air along with other pollutants. Lead is a poison which can interfere with cellular metabolism by combining with proteins and interfering with enzymes. Because of lead's harmful effects, gasoline-using cars made in the United States since 1975 are built to run on unleaded gasoline. U.S. cars manufactured before 1975 and some imported cars still use gasoline containing lead.

Another air pollutant is sulfur dioxide, a compound produced by burning sulfur-containing fuel oil and coal. Sulfur dioxide is a gas which can damage the lining of the respiratory tract and lungs. The ciliated cells of the air passages are weakened, and the respiratory tract becomes more easily damaged by pollutants such as dust and other chemicals.

Sometimes the air over a highly industrialized area becomes trapped because of atmospheric conditions. Pollutants then become even more concentrated. Such a situation is called an **inversion** (ihn vur zhun). In 1952, an inversion occurred in London, England. A smog containing sulfur dioxide and other pollutants was trapped for four days and resulted in the death of more than 4000 people.

Burning of fossil fuels may have a long-range effect on average global temperatures. The amount of CO_2 in the atmosphere has increased greatly with the burning of fossil fuels in industry and transportation. Increased CO_2 in the atmosphere may cause some of the heat leaving the earth to be radiated back to the surface. Thus, some people feel that an increase in CO_2 in the environment may have an overall warming effect. One severe consequence of a prolonged warming effect would be melting of polar ice caps. The changing of ice to water would increase the depth of oceans, possibly submerging coastal regions. Other scientists feel that the increasing number of all particles in the air from pollution may have an opposite effect. They suggest that more sunlight will be reflected back into space before it reaches the earth's surface. This reflection could lead to a decline in temperatures on Earth. How might a decrease in temperature affect life on Earth?

Products of fuel combustion are not the only source of air pollution. Other dangerous chemicals include asbestos fibers, mercury, and a variety of organic compounds released during

FIGURE 35-7. Meters attached to exhaust pipes are used to test the emissions of cars. In many areas, persons with cars that have high exhaust emissions of hydrocarbons and carbon monoxide are not permitted to drive the vehicles until the emission problem is corrected.

An inversion is a state in which the air temperature increases with increasing altitude. This holds surface air (and its pollutants) down.

In an inversion, a layer of air is trapped close to the ground. Because of atmospheric conditions, the concentration of pollutants continues to increase. Serious health problems may result.

This warming is called the "greenhouse effect."

Pollution leads to a greater number of particles in the air. An increase in these particles may affect temperatures world-wide.

Another form of air pollution is that caused by open burning. For example, in San Joaquin Valley of California the air in the autumn is sometimes full of smoke from burning rice fields to kill insect pests.

industrial processes. One of the major difficulties in analyzing and dealing with air pollution is the fact that pollutants often interact with one another to form even more dangerous compounds. Thus, the effect of a pollutant often is difficult to learn. It can be concluded, though, that air pollution is a threat to health and requires a great deal of further study.

35:6 Acid Rain

Rain is normally slightly acidic, having a pH of 5.6 (Section 3:8). The acidity results from the dissolving of carbon dioxide in water forming weak carbonic acid.

Sulfur dioxide and nitrogen dioxide combine with water and/or oxygen in the air to form acids that lower the pH of rain.

Release of sulfur dioxide and nitrogen oxides into the atmosphere further lowers the pH of rain. These pollutants react with water and/or oxygen in the air to produce sulfuric and nitric acids. So much sulfur dioxide and nitrogen oxide are released into the atmosphere in urban areas that the pH of rain in some places may now be as low as 3! Rain with a low pH is known as **acid rain.**

In the United States, acid rain is most damaging in the northeast where the average pH is between 4.0 and 4.5. Rain that is only slightly more acidic than normal may increase the yield of some crops. However, as acidity continues to increase (as pH lowers), plant tissues are damaged or destroyed and photosynthesis and nitrogen fixation in legumes (Section 33:5) are affected. Changing the pH of soil also affects the types of plants that may grow (Section 33:5).

Acid rain may damage plant tissues and interfere with photosynthesis and nitrogen fixation.

Acid rain severely affects lake ecosystems. A pH lower than normal may cause nutrients to be removed from the water. A low pH may also lead to increased solubility of dangerous metals like mercury (Section 35:8). Greater acidity is lethal to a variety of organisms—plankton, eggs of fish and salamanders, frogs, and

FIGURE 35-8. (a) Salmon develop normally in neutral water and (b) abnormally in the presence of acid rain. (c) Radishes grow much larger at a neutral pH than (d) when grown at a low pH.

a

Hickson-Bender Photography

b

Hickson-Bender Photography

c
ph = 7.0

Brookhaven National Laboratory

d
pH = 2.6

Brookhaven National Laboratory

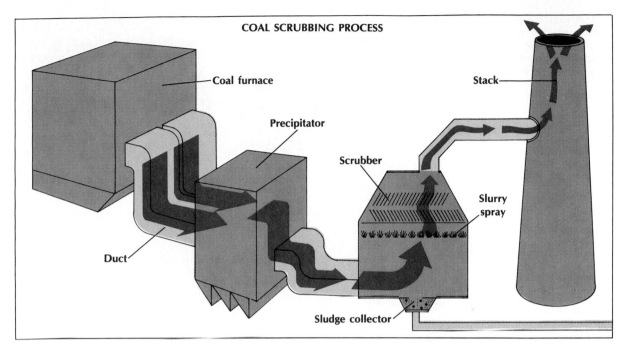

COAL SCRUBBING PROCESS

Coal furnace

Precipitator

Scrubber

Stack

Slurry spray

Duct

Sludge collector

adult fish. Because many bacteria also die, the rate of decomposition decreases and organic material accumulates at the bottom of the lake.

Acid rain is yet another problem which results from burning fossil fuels and is another reason why some people have suggested turning to other energy sources. Coal, also a fossil fuel, does not solve the problem because it contains sulfur, and when burned, releases sulfur dioxide. One answer may be the development of scrubbers and other devices which remove pollutants from gases escaping to the atmosphere. Alternate energy sources, such as nuclear (Section 35:11), solar, tidal, and wind power, do not release substances into the atmosphere which cause acid rain.

FIGURE 35-9. When burned, high sulfur coal releases sulfur, which can be removed from the emitted gases by a coal scrubbing process.

Some sources of energy do not release substances which cause acid rain and other problems of air pollution.

35:7 Water Pollution

Chemicals pollute water as well as air. Many industrial by-products are poured in large amounts into streams and rivers. Mercury is an example of an extremely dangerous by-product. The mercury settles to the bottom in a safe, insoluble form. But, bacteria in the bottom mud may change insoluble mercury to a soluble, poisonous form. This form of mercury enters the food chain where, like DDT, it becomes more concentrated along each link. People who eat mercury-poisoned fish may become ill and even die. Fishing has been prohibited in many areas because of high mercury levels. Swordfish, a large carnivore, was for a long time declared unsafe for human consumption in the United States because of its high mercury content.

Aquatic ecosystems are affected by poisons such as mercury produced by some industries.

The major source of mercury is the plastics industry. Mercury which settles to the bottom is metallic. It is converted to organic form, methylmercury, by bacteria.

FIGURE 35-10. An algal bloom is shown covering the surface of the water of this pond. Such an algae population explosion can lead to water stagnation.

Grant Heilman

PCBs are nonbiodegradable chemicals that harm aquatic organisms.

PCBs (polychlorinated biphenyls) are chemicals used in the manufacture of lubricants, adhesives, protective coatings, and electronic equipment. PCBs enter rivers and lakes from factories. Like some pesticides, PCBs are nonbiodegradable and accumulate in food chains. Because no method is available for removing PCBs from water, it is important that industries take steps to decrease the amount of PCBs which enter the water.

Water pollutants may play a role in the aging and death, or **eutrophication,** of a lake. In such a situation, the oxygen level of the lake becomes very low, and the ecological balance is destroyed. The following is an example of how eutrophication occurs.

Phosphates and nitrates can cause an algal bloom which may eventually cause a body of water to become stagnant.

Phosphates from home detergents may enter a lake from sewage treatment plants. Phosphates and nitrates from fertilizers enter from soil runoff. These phosphates and nitrates are important nutrients for algae. Thus, with large amounts of these chemicals and with warm weather, the algal populations thrive and grow rapidly in what is called an **algal bloom.** The algal population may become so large that the algae use up all available nutrients and begin to die. The dead algae settle to the bottom where they are decomposed. Huge amounts of oxygen are used up as decomposition occurs. As a result, less oxygen is available for other aquatic organisms and so many die. Death of a large number of organisms causes a disrupted food web. Continued decomposition of dead organisms uses more oxygen. Consumers, such as insect larvae, crustaceans, and fish, may die and other organisms, such as bacteria and mosquitoes, may thrive. The entire lake may become stagnant as the ecological balance is destroyed.

Pollution accelerates eutrophication and speeds the succession from a lake to dry land (Section 34:4). At one time Lake Erie was near destruction, but conservation efforts are saving it.

Water also can be polluted by heat! Addition of hot water to a natural body of water is called **thermal pollution.** Water from a nearby natural ecosystem is often used as a cooling agent in industries such as nuclear power plants. The temperature of the water increases and then the water is piped back to the lake, stream, or bay. One effect of thermal pollution is the lowering of oxygen content of water (Section 32:9). Animal life in the water may not be able to survive if enough oxygen is not present. Thermal pollution may also interfere with the spawning (mating) habits of fish and may kill organisms that cannot adapt to the warmer waters. Organisms better adapted to the warm water may increase, thus changing the balance of the ecosystem.

Thermal pollution lowers the oxygen content of water, interferes with spawning of fish, and may kill some organisms.

PEOPLE IN BIOLOGY

When toxic wastes, pollutants which are harmful to humans and other life forms, began to destroy her beautiful Japanese fishing village, Michiko Ishimure became a determined ecologist. For over twenty-five years she had watched the "cat's dance disease," which made cats go mad and drown themselves, spread throughout the village. Humans then became affected, becoming crippled and disfigured, and finally dying. University studies showed that the people were suffering from a nervous disorder which resulted from eating fish contaminated by mercury wastes discharged into the bay by a large chemical plant.

Ishimure attacked the toxic waste problem by writing books about the people who suffered from the poisoning. Her first book, *Kukai Jodo (Sea of Suffering),* made her an outcast in her village because the people were so dependent on the chemical plant for jobs. After her second book, *Rumin no Miyako (City of Drifters),* was published, the Japanese government began to take an interest in the toxic waste problem. With her books, Michiko Ishimure has led the fight in Japan to control the types of wastes which can be dumped by industry. Because of her efforts, and the efforts of many like her, governments have passed guidelines to control toxic wastes.

(1927 -   )

Michiko Ishimure

Doug Martin

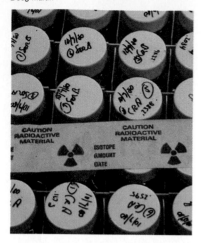

FIGURE 35-11. Radioactive substances are labeled with a standard symbol as a caution. These samples, made radioactive for biological study, are disposed of in a special way, so that radioactive contamination of other substances will not result.

Noise pollution can have a bad effect on hearing and behavior.

Industries are being encouraged to devise methods for reducing production of waste by-products.

35:8 Other Forms of Pollution

Radioactive isotopes (Section 10:1) which result from the testing of atomic devices and industry may pollute the air, water, and soil. These isotopes, examples of hazardous wastes, are subject to biological magnification and may increase the incidence of mutations (Section 9:9). Radioactive isotopes may also build up in cow's milk. If the level of these isotopes becomes too high, the milk is dangerous for humans (and calves) to drink. Young children are affected by the contaminated milk. Certain radioactive isotopes build up in their bones. Radioactive iodine may become concentrated in the thyroid gland (Section 29:2). Like some pesticides, radioactive isotopes are most harmful to top carnivores in a food chain. Presently, radioactive isotopes in the environment do not seem to pose a major threat. However, accumulation of more isotopes in the future may result in serious problems. Careful planning for the containment, transport, and safe storage of radioactive wastes is essential for future safety.

Humans harm their environment in other ways besides chemical pollution. They constantly dispose of trash and garbage, often as litter. As a result of poor farming methods, sediments build up in water and kill fish. Offshore oil spills and oil from routine cleaning of tankers destroy beaches and kill many birds and fish.

Noise pollution is increasing in urban areas. Increase in noise level can cause hearing loss. People who work in places with high noise levels are often required to wear protective ear coverings. Scientists also are concerned that excess noise can affect behavior unfavorably. How do you react to noise?

What are the answers to pollution problems? It seems unlikely that people will be willing to give up the comforts of life made possible by that technology. Are there alternatives? The government has formed guidelines for industry which will reduce the output of pollutants. Many industries have spent a lot of money to change their production processes to reduce waste emissions. Improved methods of sewage treatment have helped prevent water pollution. Also, methods have been found for recycling (reusing) wastes such as metal, glass, and paper.

REVIEWING YOUR IDEAS

5. What is a pollutant?
6. What is the major cause of air pollution?
7. How is acid rain formed?
8. What is eutrophication? Does this process occur naturally?
9. How may streams and rivers become polluted?
10. Name two kinds of pollution other than air and water.

5. A pollutant is any factor that damages the environment or makes it unclean.
6. burning of fossil fuels
7. Acid rain forms as nitrogen dioxide and sulfur dioxide combine with water and/or oxygen to form nitric and sulfuric acid.
8. Eutrophication is the aging of a lake. It occurs naturally but is accelerated by pollution.

9. Water can be polluted as a result of industrial by-products dumped into aquatic ecosystems and by heat.

10. hazardous wastes, noise. Students may give other answers.

CONSERVATION OF RESOURCES

Every organism takes from its environment the materials and energy needed for life. Humans depend on the entire biosphere for their needs. All the things taken from the environment are called **resources.** In a broad sense, resources are either renewable or nonrenewable. **Renewable resources** can be replaced; **nonrenewable resources** cannot. Humans must realize how their use of these resources affects other organisms and their own future.

Resources can be classified as renewable or nonrenewable.

35:9 Food

One of the most important of all resources is food. **Food** provides the energy needed by living systems. Because crops can be replanted and livestock can be bred, food is a renewable resource. But, the world population may become greater than the food supply. If this situation occurs, it may not be possible to renew the food supply fast enough. Current world population growth is causing a global food crisis.

See *Scientific American*, September, 1976, for an entire issue devoted to food and agriculture.

Food is a renewable resource as long as the population is not greater than the food supply.

Food shortages are most critical in developing countries where the combination of dense populations, primitive farming methods, and lack of money results in poor food supplies. Fuel for harvesting crops is hard to get and is expensive, so food production is decreased even more.

In the 1960's, plant breeders began concentrated efforts at development of new strains of plants such as rice and wheat. By selective breeding, plants are produced which have large heads of grain. Also, these plants respond well to fertilizers. These new strains have produced enough food to feed many more people than could be fed with "wild" varieties of rice and wheat. A problem with selective breeding of this type is that it reduces variation in the plant population. Geneticists are working to cross cultivate plants such as domestic wheat with its wild (natural) relatives. This process may result in new gene combinations which yield larger and more nutritious crops. Some new gene combinations, though, may result in undesirable or unexpected traits. For example, the offspring may be less resistant to certain diseases, or they may not develop as quickly as the original plants.

With food shortages, protein deficiency becomes a major problem. Protein is very important for growth and mental development. Geneticists have developed a strain of corn rich in protein. This corn has more protein than either beef or milk. However, there are some poor traits which must be bred out of this strain. The kernels are soft and the plants are not very

FIGURE 35-12. Millions of people around the world are malnourished. Food shortages in many areas cause survival problems, especially for children who often suffer from protein deficiency.

Edward Lettau for Photo Researchers

USDA

FIGURE 35-13. (a) The photosynthetic rate of a bean leaf is measured in this chamber. Photosynthetic rates are studied in an effort to breed and manage plants so that total seasonal photosynthesis increases and crop production improves. (b) Information obtained from satellites can be coupled with ground-based information to estimate crop yields. This statistician is mathematically combining Landsat satellite images with computer generated maps.

Certain plants are being used to add to the supply of protein.

A protein concentrate made from fish may be a way of solving protein shortage problems.

Removal of materials from farmlands results in soil depletion.

resistant to pests. Also, farmers must be convinced of the value of planting this strain.

Solving protein shortage problems may be helped by methods other than improved breeding. Many types of plant seeds are good sources of protein. Most widely used are soybean plants. Soybeans are legumes (Section 33:5) which resist drought and thrive in a variety of soils. In Asian countries, soybeans (the seeds of the plant) are used as food in fresh or dried form or are ground to make meal. By means of a special process, oil can be extracted from soybeans. Impurities in the remaining material are then removed, leaving concentrated protein. This protein can be used as a meat substitute. A method has been developed to give soy protein the texture of meats, fish, and shellfish. The protein can then be dried and sliced. When water is added to the dry protein, it can be used in dishes like stews or casseroles.

In the future, the sea may become an important source of protein. Much protein exists as part of fish which are not usually eaten by humans because they are too small or too oily. However, a protein concentrate could be made from these fish. The concentrate would have a high nutritive value and could be used as a meat substitute. Work is underway to produce fish protein concentrate by the use of enzymes or microorganisms.

35:10 Soil

Food production on land depends on the **soil.** The growing of crops removes nutrients from the soil. Normally the nutrients of plants would be returned to the soil by decay of the plants or animals that eat the plants. However, when humans use crops as food, they remove organic material so some nutrients are not returned to the soil. As a result, soil fertility is reduced. This process is called **soil depletion** (dih PLEE shun). Fertilizers are used in an effort to replace the nutrients which are removed.

James N. Westwater

David M. Dennis

Often farmers alternate crops, a process called **crop rotation.** In crop rotation, a soil-enriching plant such as a legume is alternated with a soil-depleting crop such as corn or wheat. The legumes contain nitrogen-fixing bacteria which return nitrogen to the soil (Section 33:5). Crop rotation is also often effective in reducing the number of insect pests.

Soil resources can be lost as a result of **erosion** (ih ROH zhun). Erosion is a natural process in which topsoil is removed by the action of water and wind. Under the cover of plants, soil is held in place. Plant cover limits the amount of erosion which occurs. However, careless farming methods increase the erosion rate (Section 34:9). Harvesting and plowing expose the topsoil by removing the plant cover. Under these conditions, water and wind carry topsoil away more easily (Figure 35-14).

Soil is a renewable resource because it is constantly being formed, but soil formation takes thousands of years. Thus, increased erosion due to human activity can cause soil to be nonrenewable.

Erosion can be reduced in several ways. **Contour plowing,** plowing along the contour of the land, reduces water runoff. **Terracing,** the creation of banks of land on a slope, also prevents runoff. The terraces slow the flow of water which slows the erosion rate. Wind erosion can be lessened by planting trees to break the wind. Also, plowing at right angles to the wind reduces erosion. Soil is not so easily removed because it piles up in low places between rows.

FIGURE 35-14. (a) Both water and wind can erode soil. (b) Careful plowing, such as the contour plowing shown, can prevent or minimize erosion damage.

Natural plant cover tends to minimize the effects of erosion. However, careless farming methods increase the rate of erosion.

Soil erosion can be prevented by contour plowing, terracing, proper planting of trees, and by plowing at right angles to the wind.

35:11 Fuels

Humans today rely on fossil fuels such as coal, oil, and natural gas, but supplies are rapidly dwindling. The supply of petroleum products required millions of years to form, but humans have almost totally used up the supply in a few hundred

FIGURE 35-15. Humans depend on fossil fuels. (a) An offshore drill rig is used to get oil that is in deposits under the ocean waters. (b) The Alaskan pipeline moves oil from northern Alaska to ports in southern Alaska for transport to places where the oil is refined.

Aerial Photo by Collier/Condit

Mobil Oil Corporation

a   b

Humans have used nearly all of the available fossil fuel resources.

years. New sources of oil and natural gas are constantly being sought. Offshore drilling may provide new supplies of these energy sources. Shale is another good source of oil. However, even if new supplies are found, the demand cannot be met for long as these supplies will soon run out, too.

As supplies of fossil fuels run low, scientists are developing alternative sources of energy. These alternative sources include nuclear, solar, geothermal, tidal, and hydrogen power.

Nuclear energy is generated in the United States and other countries by nuclear reactors. In one type of nuclear reactor, radioactive isotopes of uranium are split apart in a process called **nuclear fission.** During nuclear fission, energy is released. In a nuclear power plant, the energy is used to generate electricity. Only a small part of the electricity generated in the United States comes from nuclear power plants. Use of nuclear reactors conserves fossil fuels, but the radioactive isotopes of uranium used to produce nuclear energy are nonrenewable resources. Radioactive wastes produced by nuclear reactors pose difficult disposal problems, and the water used for cooling the reactors may cause thermal pollution in rivers and lakes. In a properly functioning reactor, radiation does not escape as fission occurs. However, in the event of a large accident, some radiation could escape and affect the environment.

Use of solar (sun) energy is slowly increasing. Currently, solar energy is used mainly for heating and cooling buildings. Solar panels are installed on houses or other buildings to collect heat. Other uses are also being found for solar energy. Solar cells are being used to light up calculators and watches, fuel a plant to

FIGURE 35-16. Fission reactions release energy in a nuclear fission reactor. Shown here is the reactor in which the reactions occur.

DOE

make fresh water out of salt water in Saudi Arabia, power satellites, and run field telephones for the military. Solar cells have even been used to power a specially made plane in England. As the cost of solar cells decreases, more uses for solar cells will be found.

What may the future hold? Hydrogen may be an energy source for the future. Hydrogen is readily available from water and, when burned, does not release pollutants. However, the process now being used to obtain hydrogen from water is very expensive. Therefore, hydrogen is not being used commonly as an energy source. It however, already has been used as a rocket fuel. Hydrogen also may be used as a nuclear fuel. Isotopes of heavy hydrogen (Section 3:2) may be used in a process called **nuclear fusion.** Nuclear fusion is a reaction in which small atoms collide to form larger atoms. As these collisions occur, a great deal of energy is released. Fusion is the reaction which fuels the sun. In order to "mimic" this reaction on Earth, large amounts of energy and extremely high temperatures are needed. Research is continuing to find an efficient way to control fusion and harness the energy it releases. Unless more energy is released from fusion than is used in the process, hydrogen fusion will not be an economical energy alternative.

Still other sources of energy are being investigated for future use. Possible sources of untapped energy include wind, geothermal energy (Section 34:14), and tidal power. These energy sources have two advantages—they are renewable and produce little or no pollution.

35:12 Wildlife and Forests

Humans have often interfered with natural food chains and caused the extinction of many species of plants and animals. The dodo bird and passenger pigeon have become extinct because of human interference. Also, the hunting of animals, such as bison and tigers, has nearly wiped out these animals.

People should understand the value of wildlife conservation. They should realize the long-range effects of extinction. It not only interferes with the natural balance of ecosystems but also removes forever a part of the world of life.

Once an organism is gone, it is gone forever. Thus, to prevent extinction, humans must conserve wildlife. To do so, preserves have been set aside to protect many species, and strict hunting and fishing limits have been imposed. Hunting is helpful in controlling the population size of some animals, but an overkill can reduce the size to a point very close to extinction. Plant species are also protected in certain areas by laws.

Michael DiSpezio

FIGURE 35-17. Solar collectors on this building help with heating by using energy from the sun. Water moving through the panels picks up heat and can be used as hot water or for heating the building.

FIGURE 35-18. The California condor is a bird that is nearly extinct. It is listed on the U.S. EPA endangered species list.

James L. Hawn for Tom Stack and Associates

Large forest areas have been used carelessly.

Humans have not only killed many animals, they have also wasted large areas of forests. At one time, forests covered most of the eastern and western United States. These forests were cleared for farmland and much of the timber was burned or used for other purposes. By the early 1900's, it was evident that too much of this natural resource had been removed.

Since that time, humans have begun to conserve forests and other plants and increase their value. Trees are planted every few years so that some will be ready for cutting at regular intervals. In this way, there is a continuous production of trees, and a sufficient supply of valuable, healthy trees is available each year. Forests are also conserved by not cutting an entire forest at once. Instead, blocks of trees are left to reseed the cut areas.

Humans can conserve forests by planting trees every few years, by not cutting an entire forest at once, and by selective cutting and improvement cutting.

Other forest conservation practices include **selective cutting** and **improvement cutting.** In selective cutting, mature trees are cut while young trees are left to mature. In improvement cutting, old, crooked, or diseased trees are removed. Thus, healthy trees can grow into large, valuable trees.

35:13 Cause for Optimism

Pollution of the environment, wasting of resources, and an expanding population are important problems facing humans. Humans must care about the environment now and in the future and do everything possible to solve these problems. If people ignore these problems, other problems connected with the human's place in nature will be compounded.

FIGURE 35-19. One cause for optimism is (a) formerly polluted areas that (b) are now being cleaned up. Lake Erie areas are shown.

John Youger

James N. Westwater

Fortunately, many people realize the results of pollution, poor conservation methods, and overpopulation. Scientists and nonscientists alike are aware of and concerned about these problems. Humans should continue to use their reason and intelligence to ensure their survival and that of all that is living.

REVIEWING YOUR IDEAS

11. What are resources? How are resources classified?
12. How can food become a nonrenewable resource?
13. What is soil depletion? How does soil depletion occur?
14. What is erosion? Explain what humans can do to prevent erosion.
15. How are fuels used today? Are fuels a renewable resource? Explain.
16. Distinguish between nuclear fusion and nuclear fission.
17. What has caused the extinction or near extinction of many animals?
18. Why has much of the original forest land of the United States been cleared?

11. Resources are things taken from the environment. They are either renewable or nonrenewable.
12. Food could become a nonrenewable resource if population size grows larger than the food supply.
13. Soil depletion is the removal of nutrients from soil. It occurs as humans use plant crops as food, removing organic nutrients which would otherwise be returned to the soil.
14. Erosion is a process in which topsoil is removed by the action of water and wind. Erosion of soil can be combated by contour plowing, terracing, planting trees to break the wind, and by plowing at right angles to the wind.
15. Fuels are used as source of heat and to power vehicles and machinery. They are not renewable because they are being used at a rate which exceeds the time needed to replace them.
16. Nuclear fission is a process in which radioactive isotopes are split apart. Nuclear fusion is the forceful combining of small atoms to make larger atoms. Both processes release energy.
17. Human activities such as hunting and disruption of natural ecosystems have caused extinction of many animals.
18. Much original forest land was cleared for agriculture or for timber used as fuel or in construction.

ADVANCES IN BIOLOGY

35:14 Alternative Solutions in Pest Control

Although the use of pesticides continues, it is not the only answer to pest control. Biological control methods are also being developed. **Biological control** is the use of organisms to check pest populations. Such methods retain a more natural, balanced ecosystem and avoid the disadvantages of chemicals.

One biological method used to control pests is to preserve their natural enemies—insects, spiders, frogs, and birds. Predators of pests may also be introduced into a new area. This method was first used in 1888 when an Australian ladybird beetle was introduced in California to reduce the numbers of a small insect that was destroying citrus crops. The beetle saved the citrus industry.

Wasps (Figure 35-20) are especially useful in controlling other insects as they act either as predators or parasites. Two species of parasitic wasps imported from India may prove useful in controlling gypsy moths. It is the gypsy moth caterpillar which causes damage. In 1981, they destroyed the leaves of thirteen million acres of U. S. trees. The wasps lay their eggs in the caterpillars. Within two to three weeks, the wasp larvae destroy the host caterpillars. Field tests are planned to determine how

FIGURE 35-20. This wasp is laying eggs in a gypsy moth pupa. When the eggs hatch, the wasp larvae will feed on and kill the pupa. Introduction of the parasitic wasps into the area thus can control the moths.

USDA

FIGURE 35-21. Japanese beetles can be controlled by use of sex attractants. The attractants in the dark patch on the trap lure the beetles which then fall into the trap.

Hormones are used to alter the developmental pattern of some insects.

Pheromones can be used as "bait" in traps or to interfere with the finding of mates.

effective the wasps may be. Currently, several species of insects have been approved for use in pest control in the United States. What precautions should be taken before introducing a "foreign" insect into an ecosystem?

Use of bacteria, viruses, fungi, and protozoa as agents of control is being studied and several products have been developed. Bacteria which control the larvae of Japanese beetles and a variety of other insects are already in use. Spores of the bacteria are applied over an area like an insecticide but affect only certain insects. The spores, once ingested by the insects, develop and become toxic, causing the insects to die. Spores of bacteria have been applied to crops, including lettuce and cabbage. Viruses are available for use against the cotton bollworm and gypsy moth. A problem with using microorganisms is that they often work slowly, and insects may cause a great deal of damage before dying. However, microorganisms usually attack only one pest species, leaving other organisms intact.

Another form of pest control is the sterilizing of male insects by radiation. This method in which insects contribute to their own destruction is called **autocidal control.** Insects are raised in a laboratory and sterilized at maturity. Then, these males are released into the ecosystem being treated for pests. Some sterile males will mate with females. When mating of this kind occurs, the eggs are not fertilized, and the size of the insect population is reduced. Scientists think that if there are ten times more sterile males than fertile ones in a population, many insect species could be eliminated within four generations. In California, use of sterile males was combined with malathion to control the spread of medflies. Other species of fruit flies have also been successfully controlled by sterilization procedures.

Hormonal control of insect pest development is also in use. These hormones affect the insect's rate of metamorphosis (Section 29:9). Some hormones may speed up the time needed to reach maturity and are effective in cases where an insect causes damage as a larva. Other hormones retard development and are effective in cases where the insect causes damage as an adult or where reproduction must be controlled. Hormones such as these are being used to control the development of fleas and mosquitoes.

Pheromones (Section 31:11) are also being used to control some insects. Pheromones can be placed in traps to attract insects. Pheromones also may be spread over a large area, "confusing" insects in search of mates. Both uses of pheromones lead to a reduction in the size of the insect population. The cotton bollweevil (a beetle) as well as the bark beetle which carries the fungus causing Dutch elm disease are being controlled with pheromones.

Cultural control is another means of dealing with pests. **Cultural control** involves the breeding, planting, and harvesting of crops by methods which reduce pest damage. Crop rotation is an example of a cultural control method. By alternating crops, pests are less likely to attack since the same crop is not present every year. The time when crops are planted or harvested is also important. With proper timing of these events, crops may escape the effects of potential pests.

Genetics is an important aspect of cultural control. Breeding of pest resistant crops is one way to combat damage and crop loss. Recombinant DNA techniques may be used in the future to produce pest-resistant plants. Such techniques, once developed, would change crops much more quickly than breeding, which often takes up to ten years.

Genetics can be used in the production of pest resistant crops.

The problems of pest control are complex, and solutions must be carefully thought out. As more is learned about the relationships among organisms, it becomes clear that a pest problem can rarely be solved using only one approach. Many people feel that integrated pest management may be the most effective plan of attack. **Integrated pest management** is a system in which a combination of techniques is used to control pests. This system involves the use of chemical pesticides along with biological and cultural controls. In every case, the goal of a program of pest control should be to preserve the natural balance of an ecosystem.

Integrated pest management may be the most sensible approach to pest control.

CHAPTER REVIEW

SUMMARY

1. Modern technology has accelerated pollution of the environment.
2. Pesticides are used to kill a variety of organisms that compete with or are harmful to humans.
3. Many pesticides are nonbiodegradable and accumulate in the tissues of animals. Other pesticides are degradable but may be toxic to organisms for which they are not intended.
4. Many insect species have become immune to pesticides.
5. Air pollution is caused mainly by the burning of fossil fuels.
6. Release of nitrogen oxides and sulfur dioxide has contributed to formation of acid rain which damages or kills a variety of organisms.
7. Radioactive isotopes are pollutants which may cause mutations. Careful planning is needed for control of nuclear materials.
8. Water pollution can lead to poisoning and death of organisms and to the destruction of entire ecosystems.
9. Littering, oil spills, and noise are other forms of pollution.
10. In many areas of the world, food is a resource which cannot be produced quickly enough to meet the increase in population size.

All Chapter Review answers and additional chapter teaching suggestions are provided in the Teacher's Guide at the front of this text.

CHAPTER REVIEW

11. Soil quality can be improved by farming methods which decrease erosion.

12. Fossil fuels are rapidly being used up as energy demands increase. New sources of energy must be developed.

13. Wildlife can be conserved through human concern in establishing protected areas and following hunting/fishing limits. Proper forestry techniques must also be continued.

14. An awareness of ecological problems and dedication by some to solving these problems are reasons for optimism about the future.

15. Pest control involves the use not only of pesticides but also of biological and cultural control methods. Integrated pest management may be the most effective means of controlling pests.

LANGUAGE OF BIOLOGY

acid rain
algal bloom
autocidal control
biological control
biological magnification
biosphere
crop rotation
cultural control
erosion
eutrophication
integrated pest
   management
inversion

nonbiodegradable
nonrenewable
   resource
nuclear fission
nuclear fusion
pesticide
pollutant
pollution
renewable resource
resources
soil depletion
thermal pollution

CHECKING YOUR IDEAS

On a separate paper, complete each of the following statements with the missing term(s). Do not write in this book.

1. A(n) _____ is any factor which makes the environment unclean.

2. _____ is the aging and death of a lake.

3. Substances such as DDT which are not broken down are said to be _____.

4. Fossil fuels are an example of a(n) _____ resource.

5. Large amounts of phosphates and nitrates may result in a population explosion of algae called a(n) _____.

6. _____ may be used to lure insect pests to traps or to prevent insects from finding mates.

7. _____ is the increased concentration of chemicals along a food chain.

8. _____ is a natural process that results in removal of topsoil.

9. _____ is a dangerous element present in some gasoline.

10. Alternation of crops to increase soil fertility is called _____.

EVALUATING YOUR IDEAS

1. Name some specific organisms which are pests to humans. What organisms do the pests affect?

2. How have humans contributed to pest problems?

3. What can happen if insects which prey on insect pests are also killed when exposed to a pesticide?

4. Why are some pesticides no longer effective against certain insects?

5. What are the effects of DDT on large birds?

6. How are pesticides such as malathion harmful to an ecosystem?

7. How do the pollutants given off by burning fuels affect organisms?

8. Describe the sequence of events leading to an algal bloom and eutrophication.

9. How may radioactive isotopes act as pollutants?

10. List several ways in which better crops have been produced to meet the food shortage.

CHAPTER REVIEW

11. What is crop rotation? How does crop rotation prevent soil depletion?

12. How can erosion be prevented?

13. Why are fossil fuels considered to be nonrenewable? What are some possible new energy sources?

14. Discuss the pros and cons of generating electricity by nuclear power.

15. How is solar energy being used today?

16. How can wildlife be conserved?

17. How are forests conserved? How would recycling help conserve forests?

18. What are the advantages of using microorganisms to control pests? What are the disadvantages?

19. Explain how hormones and pheromones may be used to control pests.

APPLYING YOUR IDEAS

1. Explain how insects have become resistant to DDT and other pesticides.

2. The amount of oxygen dissolved in water increases with lower temperatures. How might hot water produced by a factory affect life in a body of water?

3. Why must offshore drilling procedures be well controlled?

4. In what ways would an energy shortage affect a technological society?

5. Which areas of the United States are most heavily polluted? Are other areas safe from pollution? Explain.

EXTENDING YOUR IDEAS

1. How can you as an individual help in the fight against pollution? Do you have an obligation to keep the environment free of pollution? How can you inform others about the need for a healthy environment?

2. Use mounds of soil to illustrate the principles of contour plowing and terracing. Use other mounds as controls. Add the same amount of water to each mound and note the differences in the water that runs off.

3. Increased use of electricity means more pollution by electric plants that operate on fossil fuels. Increased electrical usage could also lead to the use of more nuclear power plants which cause thermal pollution and pose the threat of nuclear contamination. Which would you prefer, less electricity or more electricity and these possible consequences? Explain.

4. Investigate the processes for recycling wastes such as glass, aluminum cans, and paper and uses for recycled materials.

5. Study your home and school for ways to conserve energy and start an energy conservation program based on your findings.

SUGGESTED READINGS

Angier, Natalie, "Menace of the Medfly." *Discover*, September, 1981.

Drummond, A. H., Jr., "Carbon Monoxide: the Hidden Threat." *Sciquest*, March, 1980.

Gibbons, Don L., "Acidic Confusion Reigns." *Sciquest*, January, 1982.

Graves, C. K., "Rain of Troubles." *Science 80*, July-August, 1980.

"Infestation." *Sciquest*, November, 1981.

Lehmann, Phyllis, "Debugging with Bugs." *Sciquest*, September, 1980.

Likens, Gene E., Wright, Richard F., Galloway, James N., and Butler, Thomas J., "Acid Rain." *Scientific American*, October, 1979.

Pimentel, David and Pimentel, Marcia, "The Risks of Pesticides." *Nat. Hist.*, Mar., 1979.

Robinson, Paul R., "A Gas for When the Oil Is Gone." *Sciquest*, February, 1981.

Weintraub, Pamela, "A New Kind of Sea Power." *Discover*, April, 1981.

Yall, Irving, "A Petroleum-Eating Bacterium." *Natural History*, July-August, 1979.

Zimmerman, David R., "The Bald Eagle Bicentennial Blues." *Nat. Hist.*, Jan., 1976.

Additional student readings and suggested teacher readings are provided in the Teacher's Guide.

APPENDIX A
A Classification Of Living Systems

The following is a classification showing five kingdoms. Major phyla of these kingdoms are included. Several minor phyla have been omitted. Classification includes the classes for several phyla and important orders of insects and mammals. For more complete descriptions of most groups, refer to Chapter 13 (Monerans, Protists, and Fungi), Chapter 14 (Plants), and Chapters 15 and 16 (Animals).

KINGDOM MONERA
(All are prokaryotes.)

Phylum Schizomycophyta: Bacteria. Very small cells; usually unicellular; some chains or clusters; mostly heterotrophic.

Phylum Cyanophyta: Blue-green algae. Usually unicellular; some chains or filaments; chlorophyll throughout cells (chloroplasts absent).

KINGDOM FUNGI
(All are eukaryotes.)

Phylum Zygomycota: Sporangium fungi. Multicellular; heterotrophic; spores produced in sporangia.

Phylum Basidiomycota: Club fungi. Multicellular; heterotrophic; spores produced in basidia.

Phylum Ascomycota: Sac fungi. Mostly multicellular; heterotrophic; spores produced in asci.

KINGDOM PROTISTA
(All are eukaryotes.)

Phylum Euglenophyta: Euglenoids. Unicellular algae; mostly autotrophic; usually one flagellum for locomotion; mainly freshwater forms; some animal parasites.

Phylum Chrysophyta: Golden algae. Yellow-brown color; mostly unicellular; marine.

Phylum Pyrrophyta: Dinoflagellates. Unicellular; two flagella for locomotion; marine and freshwater forms.

Phylum Sarcodina: Sarcodines. Unicellular; pseudopods (false feet) for locomotion and obtaining food; heterotrophic.

Phylum Ciliophora: Ciliates. Unicellular; many cilia for both locomotion and obtaining food; heterotrophic.

Phylum Mastigophora: Flagellates. Unicellular; have flagella; heterotrophic.

Phylum Sporozoa: Sporozoans. Unicellular; reproduce by spores; no locomotion adaptations; parasitic.

Phylum Myxomycota: Slime molds. Mostly colonial; some cells amoebalike; spores; multinucleate.

KINGDOM PLANTAE

(All are eukaryotes.)

Phylum Chlorophyta: Green algae. Many unicellular; some filaments or colonies.

Phylum Phaeophyta: Brown algae. Multicellular; mostly sessile; mostly marine.

Phylum Rhodophyta: Red algae. Multicellular; filamentous and branchlike forms; often deep in ocean.

Phylum Bryophyta: Mosses and liverworts. Very small; multicellular; no vascular system; in moist environments; gametophyte generation predominant.

Phylum Tracheophyta: Plants with vascular tissue.

Subphylum Psilopsida: Psilopsids. Very rare; vascular tissue in stem only.

Subphylum Lycopsida: Club mosses. Vascular tissue throughout plant; cones.

Subphylum Sphenopsida: Horsetails. Vascular tissue throughout; branches and leaves in a whorled pattern; cones.

Subphylum Pteropsida: Most complex tracheophytes.

Class Filicineae: Ferns. Sporophyte generation predominant; rhizomes; sori.

Class Gymnospermae: Conifers. Seeds in cones; needlelike leaves; sporophyte generation predominant.

Class Angiospermae: Flowering plants. Flowers; seeds within fruits; flat leaves; sporophyte generation predominant.

Subclass Monocotyledonae: Monocots. Seeds with one cotyledon.

Subclass Dicotyledonae: Dicots. Seeds with two cotyledons.

KINGDOM ANIMALIA

(All are eukaryotes.)

Phylum Porifera: Sponges. Two cell layers; no symmetry; no locomotion; no nervous system; skeleton of mineral content; all aquatic.

Phylum Coelenterata: Coelenterates. Two cell layers; radial symmetry; nerve net; single body opening for mouth and anus; tentacles and stinging cells; all aquatic.

Phylum Ctenophora: Comb jellies. Two cell layers; radial symmetry; rows of cilia along body for swimming; single body opening; marine.

Phylum Platyhelminthes: Flatworms. Three cell layers; bilateral symmetry; flattened body; single body opening; many parasitic.

Phylum Nemertina: Proboscis worms. Three cell layers; bilateral symmetry; flattened body; cilia; two body openings; circulatory system lacking a heart; proboscis for food getting and defense; mostly marine.

Phylum Nematoda: Roundworms. Three cell layers; bilateral symmetry; round shape (cylindrical); two body openings; mostly parasitic.

Phylum Rotifera: Rotifers. Three cell layers; bilateral symmetry; microscopic but multicellular; ring of cilia around mouth for drawing in food; freshwater and marine.

Phylum Acanthocephala: Spiny-headed worms. Three cell layers; bilateral symmetry; no digestive system; young are parasites in arthropods; adults are parasites in vertebrates.

Phylum Bryozoa: Moss animals. Three cell layers; bilateral symmetry; colonial; tentacles surrounding mouth; protective secretion around colony; primitive nervous system; freshwater and marine.

Phylum Brachiopoda: Lamp shells. Three cell layers; bilateral symmetry; body in two shells like clam; two "arms" with tentacles; supported by stalk; many fossil forms; marine.

Phylum Annelida: Segmented worms. Three cell layers; bilateral symmetry; segmented body; two body openings; ventral nervous system; primitive dorsal circulatory system; many aquatic.

Phylum Mollusca: Mollusks. Three cell layers; bilateral symmetry; often with shells; complex digestive, respiratory, circulatory, and excretory systems; mostly aquatic.

Phylum Arthropoda: Arthropods. Three cell layers; bilateral symmetry; jointed appendages; tough exoskeleton; segmented; body in sections; all systems specialized.

Class Chilopoda: Centipedes. One pair of legs per segment.

Class Diplopoda: Millipedes. Two pairs of legs per segment.

Class Crustacea: Crustaceans. Five or more pairs of legs; two body sections; mandibles; mainly aquatic.

Class Insecta: Insects. Three pairs of legs; three body sections; mandibles; usually winged.

Order Coleoptera: Beetles. Membranous hind wings folded under hard front wings; chewing mouthparts.

Order Diptera: Flies and mosquitoes. One pair of wings; piercing and sucking mouthparts.

Order Hemiptera: True bugs. Wings thin out from base to tip; sucking mouthparts.

Order Homoptera: Cicadas, leafhoppers, and plant lice. Wingless or wings lifted above body; sucking mouthparts.

Order Hymenoptera: Ants, bees, and wasps. Front wings longer than hind wings (or wingless); chewing or sucking mouthparts; some with stingers.

Order Isoptera: Termites. Two pairs of wings of similar size, chewing mouthparts.

Order Lepidoptera: Butterflies and moths. Two pairs of scaly wings; sucking mouthparts.

Order Odonata: Damselflies and dragonflies. Two pairs of long wings; chewing mouthparts.

Order Orthoptera: Grasshoppers. Membranous hind wings folded under long, tough front wings; chewing mouthparts.

Class Arachnida: Arachnids. Four pairs of legs; two body sections; chelicerae.

Phylum Echinodermata: Echinoderms. Three cell layers; radial symmetry in adult; spiny body often with rays; all marine.

Phylum Hemichordata: Acorn worms. Burrow in mud; marine; feed on microorganisms in sand.

Phylum Chordata: Chordates. Three cell layers; bilateral symmetry; dorsal nervous system; ventral circulatory system; presence of gill slits and notochord during some stages of life; paired appendages.

Subphylum Cephalochordata: Lancelets. Fishlike; filter feeders; marine.

Subphylum Urochordata: Sea squirts. Sessile; chordate characteristics prominent only in larvae; marine; filter feeders.

Subphylum Vertebrata: Vertebrates. Backbone and general internal skeleton.

Superclass Pisces: Fish. Gills; skeleton of cartilage and/or bone.

Class Agnatha: Jawless fish. Lack paired fins; cartilaginous skeleton; notochord throughout life.

Class Chondrichthyes: Cartilaginous fish. Paired fins; cartilaginous skeleton; prominent gill openings; mostly marine.

Class Osteichthyes: Bony fish. Scaled; hard covering over gills; paired fins; marine and freshwater forms.

Superclass Tetrapoda: Vertebrates with two pairs of limbs.

Class Amphibia: Amphibians. Lungs in most adult forms; aquatic and terrestrial forms; external fertilization, development in water; moist, smooth skin.

Class Reptilia: Reptiles. Dry skin; lungs; internal fertilization; shelled egg; most live on land.

Class Aves: Birds. Feathers; endotherms; usually winged; lungs; internal fertilization; shelled egg.

Class Mammalia: Mammals. Endotherms; hair or fur; internal fertilization; usually internal development; mammary glands; lungs; mostly terrestrial.

Order Monotremata: Monotremes (duckbill platypus and spiny anteaters). Most primitive mammals; lay eggs; primitive mammary glands.

Order Marsupialia: Marsupials such as kangaroos, koalas, opossums, wallabies. Young develop in pouch of female; variety of body forms.

Order Insectivora: Moles, shrews, etc. Small burrowing forms; eat insects and other small animals.

Order Chiroptera: Bats. Forelimbs adapted for flight; active at night.

Order Rodentia: Rodents such as beaver, gopher, mouse, squirrel. Chisel-like teeth for gnawing; little body specialization but forelimbs adapted for variety of niches.

Order Lagomorpha: Hares, rabbits, pikas. Tooth structure similar to that of rodents but more incisors; use side to side mouth movements to eat plants; long ears.

Order Edentata: Armadillo, sloth, great anteater, etc. Most lack teeth but some have molars; eat small animals.

Order Cetacea: Dolphins, porpoises, whales. Streamlined body; hair vestigial or absent in adults; forelimbs modified as flippers; hind limbs absent; marine.

Order Sirenia: Manatees, dugongs, sea cows. Streamlined body; sparse amount of hair; forelimbs modified as flippers; hind limbs absent; flipperlike tail; freshwater.

Order Proboscidea: Elephants. Front teeth missing except for incisors (tusks); trunk; herbivorous.

Order Carnivora: Cat, dog, raccoon, seal, etc. Powerful jaws; large canine teeth for eating flesh; sharp claws.

Order Ungulata: Cow, giraffe, horse, rhinoceros, etc. Teeth adapted for grinding plants; feet modified as hoofs.

Order Primates: Primates such as lemurs, monkeys, orangutans, humans. Prehensile hands; large brain, erect or semi-erect posture; nails.

APPENDIX B

Material presented in Appendix B is intended for use with honors or advanced classes.

Respiration and Photosynthesis

Cellular Respiration

How is the energy of glucose changed to that of ATP in aerobic cell respiration? Aerobic respiration can be written generally as:

$$2ATP + 38ADP + 38 \; \text{—} \textcircled{P} + C_6H_{12}O_6 + 6O_2$$
$$\rightarrow 6CO_2 + 6H_2O + 38ATP + 2ADP + 2 \; \text{—} \textcircled{P}$$

Attempt to relate the details of aerobic respiration, which occurs in four major stages (Figure B-1), to the general purpose of ATP production. Also, compare the specific details to the general equation.

B:1 Glycolysis splitting of sugar

The first stage, **glycolysis** (gli KAHL uh sus), occurs in the cytoplasm. Glycolysis of one molecule of glucose, a six-carbon molecule (6C), produces two molecules of pyruvic (pi REW vihk) acid (3C) and *releases energy from glucose.* The reactions are regulated by specific enzymes. For each glucose molecule, two molecules of ATP are used, but enough energy is released to form 4 ATP, thus netting 2 ATP. The number of carbon atoms is not changed, but four hydrogen atoms are removed and join with a coenzyme, NAD*, to form 2 NADH$_2$. The fate and importance of the hydrogen atoms is discussed later. Glycolysis is an anaerobic process; it occurs in the absence of oxygen. It is the first stage of aerobic respiration because the reactions of glycolysis must occur before the aerobic reactions in later stages can occur.

B:2 Forming Acetyl-co-A pyruvic acid oxidation

Each pyruvic acid (3 C) produced in glycolysis is converted to acetic acid (2 C). The carbons removed in this step combine with oxygen and are given off as CO_2 (part of the CO_2 shown in the general equation for respiration). The acetic acid then combines with a compound called coenzyme A (co-A) to form acetyl-co-A. One glucose molecule entering glycolysis results in two molecules of acetyl-co-A. This releases four more hydrogen atoms which combine with NAD to form 2 NADH$_2$. The major importance of this stage is the release of four more hydrogen atoms (oxidation).

*nicotine adenine dinucleotide

oxaloacetic acid
B:3 Krebs Cycle citric acid cycle

The **Krebs cycle** occurs in the fluid of the mitochondria. Each acetyl-co-A formed combines with a 4 C molecule to form citric acid (6C). Each glucose molecule entering glycolysis produces 2 citric acid molecules in the Krebs cycle. In a series of steps, each citric acid is broken down to a 5 C molecule and finally to the original 4 C molecule, giving off two carbons in CO_2 (this CO_2 plus that from forming acetyl-co-A accounts for all the CO_2 in the general equation). For each acetyl-co-A that enters the Krebs cycle, 3 H$_2$O are used and 8 H are released. Because two acetyl-co-A enter for each glucose molecule being broken down, 6 H$_2$O are used and 16 H are produced in the Krebs cycle. Twelve combine with 6 NAD to form 6 NADH$_2$, and 4 H combine with FAD**, another coenzyme, to form 2 FADH$_2$. The Krebs cycle also produces 2 ATP molecules for each glucose molecule entering glycolysis.

oxidative
B:4 Electron Transport Chain phosphorylation

The 24 hydrogens produced in the previous stages are used in the **electron transport chain** (a series of special molecules which act as coenzymes) on the cristae. The 10 NADH$_2$ and 2 FADH$_2$ transfer 12 pairs of electrons to this chain, also called the **respiratory chain.** Some of the electron pairs enter at a lower energy level than others. All these electrons, which have high potential energy, are passed from one

**flavin adenine dinucleotide

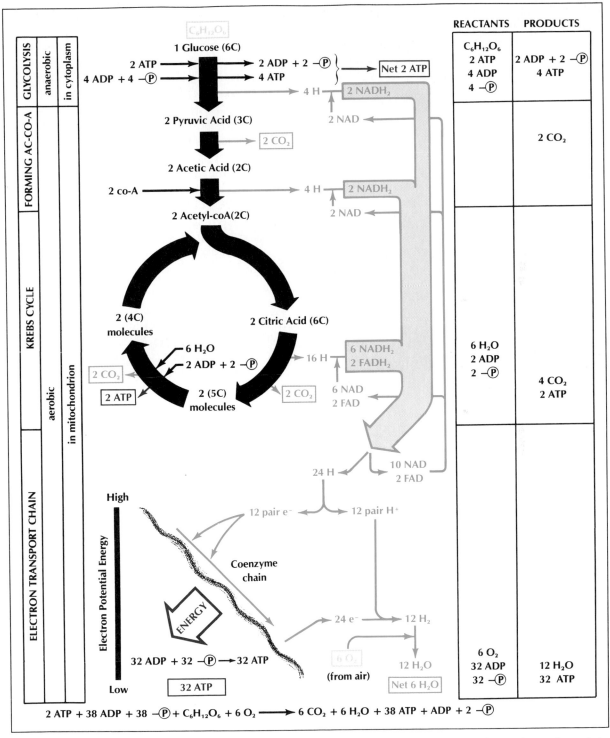

FIGURE B-1. In aerobic respiration, glucose is broken down yielding energy as ATP via the Krebs cycle and the electron transport chain.

⌐The respiratory chain contains molecules called cytochromes.
└molecule to another releasing enough energy to convert 32 ADP + 32 —Ⓟ to 32 ATP. The electrons then combine with hydrogen ions and oxygen to form water. Six H_2O were used in the Krebs cycle; thus, electron transport nets 6 H_2O (shown in the general equation). The oxygen used to form the water comes from the air (or it may come from that dissolved in water) and is necessary as the final electron acceptor in the electron transport chain. Because oxygen is needed, this respiration is aerobic. Aerobic respiration of one molecule of glucose produces 6 CO_2, 6 H_2O, and 36 ATP. Much of the potential energy of glucose is transferred to ATP; the rest is lost as heat.

B:5 Other Energy Sources

Glucose is the molecule most often broken down during respiration. Other energy-rich molecules, such as fats and proteins, can be broken down for energy. Fatty acids and amino acids can be changed to molecules which enter the Krebs cycle. This sends hydrogens to the respiratory chain releasing energy for ATP formation (Figure B-2).

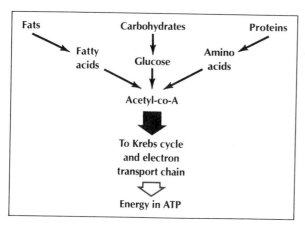

FIGURE B-2. Fatty acids and amino acids can also be converted to acetyl-co-A and used as energy sources.

B:6 Anaerobic Respiration

Anaerobic respiration is respiration without oxygen. Some organisms, such as some bacteria, cannot live in the presence of oxygen, and thus, respire anaerobically. Most other cells, including yeast, some bacteria, and most plant and animal cells, respire anaerobically when deprived of oxygen.

Anaerobic respiration in cells such as yeast produces alcohol and thus is called **alcoholic fermentation.** The first part of alcoholic fermentation is glycolysis which releases 4 H (that form 2 $NADH_2$) and 2 ATP molecules per glucose molecule broken down. Recall that glycolysis is anaerobic. The second part is the conversion of pyruvic acid to ethyl alcohol and carbon dioxide. Muscle cells undergo **lactic acid fermentation** which involves changing pyruvic acid to lactic acid. This conversion of pyruvic acid to ethyl alcohol or lactic acid also is anaerobic (Figure B-3). In anaerobic respiration the electrons carried in the 2 $NADH_2$ are accepted by the pyruvic acid.

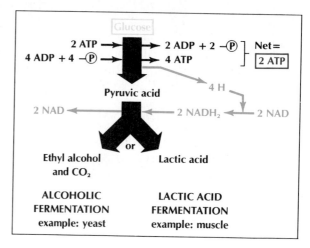

FIGURE B-3. Anaerobic respiration results in the production of ethyl alcohol or lactic acid.

Anaerobic respiration nets 2 ATP for each glucose molecule being broken down. Thus, it releases much less glucose energy in ATP than does aerobic respiration. This is because more of the original energy of glucose remains "locked" in the molecule of ethyl alcohol or lactic acid. The CO_2 product of aerobic respiration is smaller and simpler than ethyl alcohol or lactic acid of anaerobic respiration. Therefore, more energy is released in its formation. Also, more energy is released when oxygen is the final electron acceptor rather than the pyruvic acid of anaerobic respiration.

Anaerobic respiration is completed before most hydrogen atoms are removed. The four hydrogen atoms which are removed during glycolysis are transferred to pyruvic acid and become part of the end products.

Photosynthesis

A simple equation for photosynthesis shows the reactants and products. It also shows that enzymes, chlorophyll, and light energy are needed.

$$6CO_2 + 6H_2O \xrightarrow[\text{light energy}]{\text{enzymes, chlorophyll}} C_6H_{12}O_6 + 6O_2$$

It does not show the many, complicated reaction steps which were worked out by the efforts of many scientists over many years.

Photosynthesis involves the addition of hydrogen to carbon and is, therefore, a reduction reaction. It is also endergonic. Point out how these reactions are the opposite of aerobic respiration.

B:7 Source of Oxygen

It was known before 1900 that CO_2 and H_2O are reactants, that chlorophyll and light are needed, and that oxygen is given off when glucose is made. This can be represented by a simple, unbalanced equation.

$$CO_2 + H_2O \rightarrow [CH_2O] + O_2$$

Little else was known about photosynthesis chemistry.

From where does the O_2 given off come? Early researchers thought it came from CO_2 and that carbon joined water to form $[CH_2O]$. This idea was tested using an isotope (Section 3:2) of O_2 with ten neutrons (Figure B-4). Because oxygen (^{16}O) and the heavy oxygen isotope (^{18}O) differ in mass, it is possible to distinguish between them. An experiment was done in which plants were given $C^{18}O_2$ and $H_2^{16}O$ and the products of photosynthesis were analyzed. The heavy oxygen appeared in the glucose produced. Thus, the O_2 given off is not from the carbon dioxide.

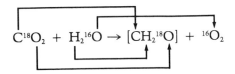

$$C^{18}O_2 + H_2^{16}O \rightarrow [CH_2^{18}O] + {}^{16}O_2$$

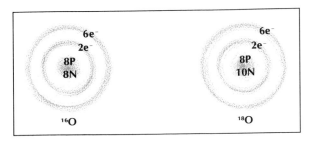

FIGURE B-4. Oxygen isotopes differ in mass because they differ in the number of neutrons.

Thus, what seemed to be a simple, logical explanation was wrong, and ideas about photosynthesis had to be changed.

B:8 The Light Reactions

How does light interact with chlorophyll, and how is radiant energy changed to chemical energy? The reactions of photosynthesis which require light are called the **light reactions.** They occur in the chloroplast grana. The reactions in the grana have been divided into two groups which are referred to as **photosystem I** and **photosystem II.** Each photosystem has a **pigment system** which is a group of chlorophyll and carotene molecules. The pigment molecules of pigment system I absorb light energy and transfer energy to a special kind of chlorophyll molecule in the pigment system. Light moves electrons of the chlorophyll to levels farther from the atoms' nuclei—to a higher energy level. These unstable, energy-rich atoms or molecules are then said to be in an **excited state.** The electrons are called **excited electrons.** In one series of reactions, excited electrons from pigment system I (in photosystem I) are passed down a chain of coenzymes (like the electron transport chain in a mitochondrion). The electrons return to the pigment system in the **ground state,** a low energy level (red path, Figure B-5). The energy of the electrons is used in forming ATP which will be used in the actual making of glucose.

Some electrons removed from the pigment system combine with hydrogen ions (H^+) to form hydrogen atoms. These atoms combine with NADP* forming $NADPH_2$. (Some hydrogen of $NADPH_2$ finally ends up in glucose.) The

*nicotinamide adenine dinudeotide phosphate

cyclic photophosphorylation

hydrogen ions used here are formed by the breakdown of water which in addition yields oxygen (shown in the general equation for photosynthesis).

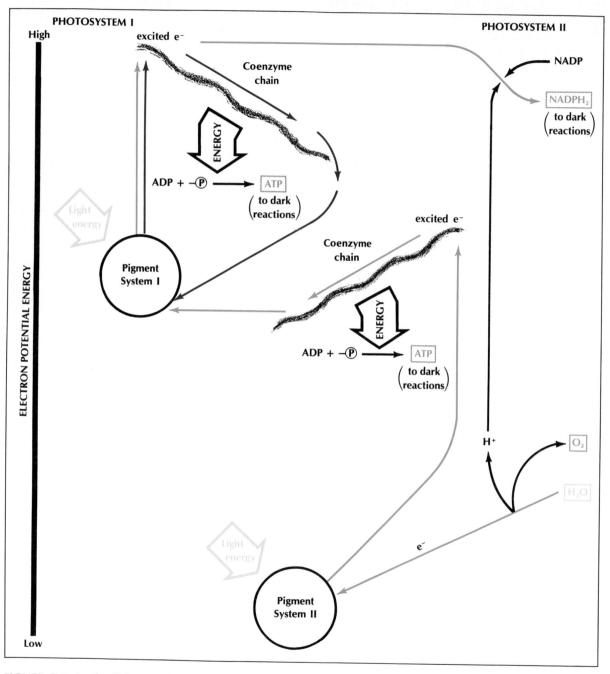

FIGURE B-5. In the light reactions of photosynthesis, light energy excites electrons. In the returning of these electrons to their ground state, energy is given off as ATP. This energy is used in the dark reactions.

Emphasize that the light reactions provide the energy and
hydrogen necessary for reduction of CO_2 in the dark reactions.

Light absorbed by pigment system II causes other electrons to become excited. These unstable electrons give off energy which forms ATP as they pass down a series of coenzymes. They eventually return to pigment system I at the ground state replacing those electrons removed earlier. Electrons produced from breaking down water replace those lost from pigment system II (blue path, Figure B-5).

Some of the details of the light reactions are still not worked out. Several hypotheses exist for how some reactions occur. Also, there are some known alternate pathways for electron flow. For these reasons, the reactants and products in Figure B-5 are not balanced. Note that the *light reactions produce chemically-bound energy* (in ATP) *and NADPH₂ for use in the dark reactions.* noncyclic photophosphorylation

B:9 The Dark Reactions

Actual synthesis of glucose occurs in a second series of reactions called the **dark reactions.** The dark reactions also occur in the chloroplast. They are so named because they can occur in the absence of light. After the light reactions, hydrogen (from water) in the form of $NADPH_2$, carbon dioxide (from air or water), and energy (from light) in the form of ATP are present. In a series of reactions called the **Calvin cycle,** each carbon dioxide molecule reacts with RDP* (5 C) to form two 3 C molecules (**carbon fixation**). RDP is then reformed to join with more incoming CO_2. Through reactions much like the reverse of glycolysis, glucose is then formed (Figure B-6). Analyze Figures B-5 and B-6 together and trace the reactants and products in the general reaction for photosynthesis.

*ribulose diphosphate

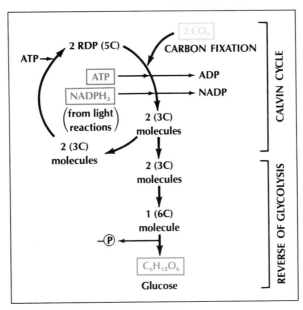

FIGURE B-6. In the dark reactions of photosynthesis, CO_2 is converted to glucose. ATP and $NADPH_2$, both produced in light reactions, are used.

APPENDIX C
Biology-Related Careers

Careers in biology-related fields are many and varied. Some jobs in these fields may require only on-the-job training. Others may require up to eight years of formal college training plus on-the-job training. Below is a list of a few of the biology-related careers with brief descriptions and training requirements. The training requirements may vary from place to place. You will want to check with local companies, schools, and professional groups for details.

Training and education are indicated below using the following abbreviations: On-the-job training—JOB, High school diploma—HS, Vocational or technical school training—VT, Junior college (2 yr)—JC, Bachelor of Science degree—BS, Master of Science degree—MS, Internship—IN.

LIFE SCIENCE. Life sciences often are divided into three broad categories—agriculture, biology, and medicine. Life scientists may do research to determine facts. They also may solve practical problems or teach. Improved plants, new drugs, and better food are some of the results of the work of life scientists.

Animal laboratory assistant (JOB, HS)—cares for lab animals

Biochemist (BS, MS)—studies substances such as foods and drugs and their changes in living systems

Biomedical engineer (BS)—applies engineering technology to medical and health problems

FIGURE C-1. An animal husbandry specialist does research on the breeding, feeding, and diseases of domestic farm animals.

USDA

Farmer (JOB, VT, BS)—cultivates land, raises crops and/or livestock

Horticulturist (BS)—breeds plants, raises flowers, fruits, vegetables, and decorative plants

Microbiologist (BS, MS)—studies microscopic organisms

Science teacher (BS, MS)—instructs students about general or specific areas of science

Soil scientist (BS)—studies biological, physical, and chemical properties of soil

ENVIRONMENTAL CONSERVATION. Persons in conservation and environmental occupations help us live within our physical environment. Some help protect, develop, and manage our forests, rangelands, wildlife, soil, and water. Others study our surroundings to improve the quality of life. All play an important role in solving environmental pollution problems.

Forester (BS)—manages, protects and develops forests

Forestry technician (VT)—aids forester; prevents and controls fires; supervises woodcutting

Geologist (MS)—studies composition, structure, and history of earth's crust

Geophysicist (BS)—studies chemical and physical traits of earth and other planets

Meteorologist (BS)—studies atmosphere and its effects; forecasts weather

HEALTH CARE. The availability of health service is important to people who are sick or injured. These services depend on people employed in health occupations. Certain careers in some professional health fields—medicine, dentistry, pharmacy—require not only several years of preprofessional college training but also professional school education and a passing score on a state board examination. However, other careers in these fields require less specialized training.

Dentistry

Dental assistant (JOB, VT)—prepares patients; helps dentist

Dental hygienist (VT or BS)—cleans teeth, gives oral hygiene instruction

Dental laboratory technician (JOB)—prepares dentures, inlays, and dental appliances

Dentist (Doctor of Dental Surgery degree-6 yr.)—examines and treats people with tooth-related problems

Medical secretary (VT, SC)—office work for doctors, insurance companies, and others

Medical Practitioners

Chiropractor (Doctor of Chiropractics degree-4 yr.)—treats human patients by manual manipulation of body parts; cannot prescribe medication

Optometrist (Doctor of Optometry degree-6 yr.)—examines eyes for vision problems and disease

Osteopathic physician (Doctor of Osteopathy degree-7 yr., IN)—diagnoses and treats human diseases, especially by manipulation of skeletal and muscular systems; can use all accepted methods of medical care

Physician (Doctor of Medicine degree-7 yr., IN)—examines, diagnoses, and treats human disease and injury; often specialized

Podiatrist (Doctor of Podiatric Medicine degree-6 yr.)—treats foot injury and disease

Veterinarian (Doctor of Veterinary Medicine-6 yr)—diagnoses and treats animal disease and injury

Doug Martin

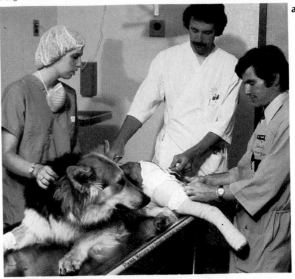

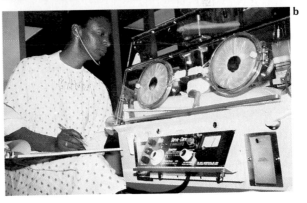

FIGURE C-2. Biology-related careers include the care of both animals and humans. (a) A veterinarian checks the leg of an injured dog. (b) A nurse carefully monitors the life functions of a prematurely born infant.

Nursing

Licensed practical nurse, LPN (HS, 1 yr training)—provides nursing care to sick or injured patients

Nursing assistant (JOB)—serves meals; provides for patient comfort; frees registered nurse and licensed practical nurse for more critical work

Registered nurse, RN (Nursing school-2 to 5 yr.)—gives medication ordered by physician; observes patient symptoms and progress; supervises nursing assistants; teaches

Dietician (BS)—plans nutritious meals; supervises food service workers

Food technologist (BS)—investigates nature of food and applies this to processing, packaging, and storage of foods

Immunologist (MS)—studies how the body fights disease

Medical assistant (paramedic) (JOB, VT)—helps physician examine and treat patients; does clerical work

Medical lab worker: Assistant (JOB), Technician (College-2yr.), Technologist (College-4 yr.)—works in laboratory performing various medical tests; responsibility and test complexity depend on training and experience

Pharmacist (Pharmacy degree-5 yr., IN)—dispenses drugs and medicines prescribed by medical practitioners

Physical therapist (Physical therapy degree-4 yr.)—provides training and helps rehabilitate persons with muscle, bone, and nerve disease or injury

Physical therapy aide (JOB, JC)—assists physical therapist

Additional Information

The following is a list of addresses for a few sources of additional information. Further information about biology-related careers and a more complete listing of additional sources can be found in the *Occupational Outlook Handbook* and *Keys to Careers in Science and Technology*. Check also with your school guidance counselors for any information they may be able to provide.

American Dental Association
Council on Dental Education
211 East Chicago Avenue
Chicago, IL 60611

American Institute of Biological Sciences
3900 Wisconsin Avenue, NW
Washington, DC 20016

American Medical Association
Council on Medical Education
535 North Dearborn Street
Chicago, IL 60610

ANA Committee on Nursing Careers
American Nurses' Association
2420 Pershing Road
Kansas City, MO 64108

Keys to Careers in Science and Technology
National Science Teachers Association
1742 Connecticut Avenue, NW
Washington, DC 20009

Occupational Outlook Handbook
U.S. Department of Labor
Bureau of Labor Statistics
Washington, DC 20212

Opportunities in Biological Science Careers
Vocational Guidance Manuals
Division of Data Courier, Inc.
Louisville, KY 40200

U.S. Civil Service Commission
Washington, DC 20415

U.S. Department of Agriculture
Forest Service
Washington, DC 20250

U.S. Department of Agriculture
Soil Conservation Service
Washington, DC 20250

APPENDIX D
Chemical Symbols and Formulas

TABLE D-1. THE ELEMENTS AND THEIR SYMBOLS

Element	Symbol	Element	Symbol	Element	Symbol	Element	Symbol
Actinium	Ac	Europium	Eu	Molybdenum	Mo	Scandium	Sc
Aluminum	Al	Fermium	Fm	Neodymium	Nd	Selenium	Se
Americium	Am	Fluorine	F	Neon	Ne	Silicon	Si
Antimony	Sb	Francium	Fr	Neptunium	Np	Silver	Ag
Argon	Ar	Gadolinium	Gd	Nickel	Ni	Sodium	Na
Arsenic	As	Gallium	Ga	Niobium	Nb	Strontium	Sr
Astatine	At	Germanium	Ge	Nitrogen	N	Sulfur	S
Barium	Ba	Gold	Au	Nobelium	No	Tantalum	Ta
Berkelium	Bk	Hafnium	Hf	Osmium	Os	Technetium	Tc
Beryllium	Be	Helium	He	Oxygen	O	Tellurium	Te
Bismuth	Bi	Holmium	Ho	Palladium	Pd	Terbium	Tb
Boron	B	Hydrogen	H	Phosphorus	P	Thallium	Tl
Bromine	Br	Indium	In	Platinum	Pt	Thorium	Th
Cadmium	Cd	Iodine	I	Plutonium	Pu	Thulium	Tm
Calcium	Ca	Iridium	Ir	Polonium	Po	Tin	Sn
Californium	Cf	Iron	Fe	Potassium	K	Titanium	Ti
Carbon	C	Krypton	Kr	Praseodymium	Pr	Tungsten	W
Cerium	Ce	Lanthanum	La	Promethium	Pm	Uranium	U
Cesium	Cs	Lawrencium	Lr	Protactinium	Pa	Vanadium	V
Chlorine	Cl	Lead	Pb	Radium	Ra	Xenon	Xe
Chromium	Cr	Lithium	Li	Radon	Rn	Ytterbium	Yb
Cobalt	Co	Lutetium	Lu	Rhenium	Re	Yttrium	Y
Copper	Cu	Magnesium	Mg	Rhodium	Rh	Zinc	Zn
Curium	Cm	Manganese	Mn	Rubidium	Rb	Zirconium	Zr
Dysprosium	Dy	Mendelevium	Md	Ruthenium	Ru	Element 104	(Rf)
Einsteinium	Es	Mercury	Hg	Samarium	Sm	Element 105	(Ha)
Erbium	Er						

TABLE D-2. SOME COMMON COMPOUNDS

Name	Formula	Name	Formula	Name	Formula
ammonia	NH_3	fructose	$C_6H_{12}O_6$	rust	Fe_2O_3
calcium carbonate	$CaCO_3$	glucose	$C_6H_{12}O_6$	sodium hydroxide	$NaOH$
carbon dioxide	CO_2	glycerol	$C_3H_8O_3$	sucrose	$C_{12}H_{22}O_{11}$
chlorophyll-a	$C_{55}H_{72}O_5N_4Mg$	glycine	$C_2H_5O_2N$	table salt	$NaCl$
ethyl alcohol	C_2H_5OH	lactic acid	$CH_3CHOHCOOH$	water	H_2O

APPENDIX E
SI Measurement

The SI system is a convenient, widely used system of measurement which has the advantage of units based on ten and multiples and fractions of ten. Table E-1 that follows is an extended version of Table 2-1. Information about converting from one SI unit to another follows the table.

TABLE E-1. SI PREFIXES				
Prefix	Symbol	Meaning	Multiplier (Numerical)	Multiplier (Exponential)
			Greater than 1	
tera	T	trillion	1 000 000 000 000	10^{12}
giga	G	billion	1 000 000 000	10^9
mega	M	million	1 000 000	10^6
kilo	k	thousand	1 000	10^3
hecto	h	hundred	100	10^2
deka	da	ten	10	10^1
			Less than 1	
deci	d	tenth	0.1	10^{-1}
centi	c	hundredth	0.01	10^{-2}
milli	m	thousandth	0.001	10^{-3}
micro	μ	millionth	0.000 001	10^{-6}
nano	n	billionth	0.000 000 001	10^{-9}
pico	p	trillionth	0.000 000 000 001	10^{-12}
femto	f	quadrillionth	0.000 000 000 000 001	10^{-15}
atto	a	quintillionth	0.000 000 000 000 000 001	10^{-18}

The basic units for length, volume, and mass are the meter, liter, and kilogram respectively. The basic unit of time is the second. Larger and smaller units of measurement in SI are obtained by multiplying or dividing the base unit by some multiple of ten. Multiply to change from larger units to smaller units. Divide to change from smaller units to larger units. For example, to change 10 kg to g, multiply 10 kg × 1000 (for kilo-) = 10 000 g. To change 10 g to kg, divide 10 g ÷ 1000 (for kilo-) = 0.01 kg.

GLOSSARY

abdomen: posterior body region of an arthropod; region in vertebrates housing many internal organs

abiotic (ay bi AHT ihk) **factors:** physical (nonliving) aspects which interact with the organisms of an ecosystem

abscission (ab SIHZH un): the falling of leaves from trees

abscission layer: group of cells which forms between the stem and the petiole of a leaf

absorption spectra (ub SORP shun • SPEC truh): spectra which have some wavelengths of light either reduced or absent

abyssal (uh BIHS ul) **zone:** deepest part of the ocean where light is absent

acceleration center: area in the medulla oblongata from which the accelerator nerves originate

accelerator nerves: nerves which increase the heartbeat by stimulating the S-A node

acetylcholine (uh seet ul KOH leen): neurotransmitter which is produced by the vagus nerves and inhibits the rate of contraction of heart muscle in humans

acid: substance which in solution has a greater concentration of hydrogen ions than hydroxide ions

acid rain: rain with a low pH

acquired characteristic: change in an organism caused by use or disuse of certain body parts

actin (AK tun): protein which makes up part of the filaments in striated muscle

action potential: reversal of polarity and flow of ions in a neuron caused by a stimulus

activation energy: energy necessary to start some chemical reactions

active immunity (ihm YEW nut ee): immunity or disease resistance resulting from production of antibodies by the host

active site: particular portion of an enzyme molecule which fits a substrate

active transport: energy-requiring process in which a membrane has an active role in the passage of materials across it

adaptation: inherited characteristic which promotes survival and reproduction in a natural environment

adaptive advantage: possessing a trait which makes a species better suited to its environment and makes its chances of reproducing better

adaptive radiation: the evolution of many new species from a common ancestor in a new environment

adenine (AD un een): one of the bases in nucleic acids

adenosine diphosphate (uh DEN uh seen • di FAHS fayt) **(ADP):** complex molecule containing adenine, ribose, and two phosphates

adenosine triphosphate (uh DEN uh seen • tri FAHS fayt) **(ATP):** complex molecule containing adenine, ribose, and three phosphates; used as an energy source in all organisms

adhesion (ad HEE zhun): attraction between unlike molecules

adrenal (uh DREEN ul) **cortex:** outer portion of the adrenal gland

adrenal gland: endocrine gland on top of each kidney

adrenal medulla (muh DUL uh): inner portion of the adrenal gland

adrenaline (uh DREN ul un): hormone secreted by the adrenal medulla; helps the body respond to emergencies; also called epinephrine

adrenocorticotrophic hormone (ACTH): hormone secreted by the anterior pituitary; stimulates the adrenal cortex to secrete its hormones

adventitious (ad ven TIHSH us) **roots:** roots which grow from the stems of plants allowing them to be vegetatively propagated

aerobe: organism which uses oxygen in respiration

aerobic (er ROH bihk) **respiration:** respiration which occurs in the presence of oxygen

African sleeping sickness: disease caused by a parasitic flagellate

afterbirth: part of the placenta that is expelled from the body after the birth of a baby

agar: substance made from brown algae used to make culture media gel

agglutination: process in which red blood cells clump together

agglutinin (uh GLEWT uh nun): antibody in blood that causes it to clump

air sac: respiratory structure in birds which fill with air as the lungs fill

alcoholic fermentation: type of anaerobic respiration used by plant cells and microbes

aldosterone (al DAWS tuh rohn): hormone secreted by the adrenal cortex; controls salt level in the blood

algae: unicellular or multicellular photosynthetic protists

algal bloom: rapid growth of algae

alimentary (al uh MEN tree) **canal:** long, hollow tube in animals through which food passes during digestion

allantois (uh LANT uh wus): sac which collects metabolic waste products in the shelled egg; also functions with the chorion in gas exchange

allele (uh LEEL): dominant or recessive form which a gene may take

all or none response: a muscle fiber contracts fully or does not contract at all; a neuron either carries an impulse or does not carry it at all

alternation of generations: life cycle in plants and plant-like protists, diploid and monoploid generations follow each other

altitudinal (al tuh TEWD nul) **succession:** continuous succession of community types from low to high altitudes

alveoli (al VEE uh li): small, moist sacs in the lungs; sites of gas exchange

amino (uh MEE noh) **acids:** compounds which are the building blocks of proteins

amino group: part of all amino acids which has the structural formula ($-NH_3$)

ammonia (NH_3): nitrogenous waste excreted by planaria

ammonification (uh moh nuh fuh KAY shun): stage of the nitrogen cycle during which bacteria metabolize amino acids and produce ammonia

amniocentesis (am nee oh sen TEE sus): technique in which some of the amniotic fluid surrounding an embryo is removed for analysis

amnion (AM nee ahn): fluid-filled sac surrounding the embryo; protects the embryo and keeps it moist

amoebocyte (uh MEE buh site): type of cell in sponges that moves in amoeboid fashion

amoeboid (uh MEE boyd) **motion:** movement by pseudopodia; motion of amoebae and amoebalike cells

amphetamines: stimulant drugs used for appetite control

amphibians: vertebrates which live both on land and in water; class Amphibia

amplexus: clasping of the female frog by the male that results in gametes being released at the same time

ampulla: bulb-shaped structure in the water-vascular system of starfish

anaerobe: organism which does not use oxygen in respiration

anaerobic (an uh ROH bihk) **respiration:** respiration in the absence of oxygen

anal pore: structure in ciliates which allows egestion of undigested materials

anaphase (AN uh fayz): phase of mitosis during which one strand of each chromosome is pulled to each pole of the cell; phase in meiosis I in which homologous chromosomes are separated and pulled to each pole of the cell

anatomy: study of the structures of organisms

androgens (AN druh junz): male sex hormones

anemia (uh NEE mee uh): disease in which the blood is low in red blood cells, hemoglobin, or total volume

angiosperms (AN jee uh spurmz): flowering plants

animal: multicellular, heterotrophic organism, usually mobile

animal pole: top half of a frog egg composed of cytoplasm and a dark pigment

annelids: segmented worms; phylum Annelida

annual rings: circular lines in a woody stem which represent growth during a year

antennae: sensory organs of arthropods

anterior (an TIHR ee ur): front part of an animal

anterior pituitary: one of the lobes of the pituitary gland; many of its hormones control other endocrine glands

anther (AN thur): male sporangium at the tip of stamens

antheridium (an thuh RIHD ee um): male sex organ in bryophytes and ferns

anti-A agglutinin: antibody contained in the plasma of blood type B

anti-B agglutinin: antibody contained in the plasma of blood type A

antibiotic: drug which cures certain bacterial diseases

antibody (ANT ih bohd ee): chemical formed in response to a virus or other foreign microorganism in the blood or tissues

anticodon: set of three bases at one end of tRNA; fits only with certain codon of mRNA

antigen (ANT ih jun): specific protein on the surfaces of red blood cells; any foreign protein which causes antibody formation

antiserum: solution of antibodies and blood serum used to fight disease

anus (AY nus): opening through which undigested materials are expelled

aorta (ay ORT uh): large artery leading from the heart

aortic (ay ORT ihk) **arches:** five pairs of enlarged tubes, "hearts," in annelids

apical (AY pih kul) **dominance:** retardation of growth of lateral buds in the presence of the apical bud

apical meristem: plant growth tissue located at the tip of roots and stems

appendage (uh PEN dihj): limb or other projection attached to the main trunk of an animal

appendix: small organ attached to the large intestine; vestigial in humans

applied science: using scientific knowledge to solve real problems

aquatic (uh KWAHT ihk): having to do with water

arachnids (uh RAK nudz): class of arthropods; spiders, ticks, mites, and scorpions

arboreal: tree dwelling

archegonium (ar kih GOH nee um): female sex organ in bryophytes and ferns

archenteron (ar KENT uh rahn): internal cavity in the developing embryo; develops into the alimentary canal

artery: blood vessel which carries blood away from the heart to the body

arthropods: animals having an exoskeleton and jointed appendages; phylum Arthropoda

artificial selection: procedure in which humans choose organisms to breed that have desirable features

ascending colon: portion of the large intestine into which undigested materials from the small intestine pass

ascus: saclike structure in which spores are produced by meiosis in certain fungi

asexual (ay SEK shul) **reproduction:** reproduction in which a single parent produces one or more offspring by mitosis

association neuron: neuron which connects sensory neurons and motor neurons in the brain and spinal cord

asthma: respiratory condition in which the muscles of the bronchial system contract, reducing the diameter of the air passages

atherosclerosis (ath uh roh skluh ROH sus): condition in which the arteries become lined with fatty deposits

atom: smallest particle of an element; basic building block of all matter

ATP-ADP cycle: series of reactions by which ATP is converted to ADP and ADP is converted back to ATP

atrioventricular (ay tree oh ven TRIHK yuh lur) **node (A-V node):** small bundle of tissue between atria and ventricles which receives the current from the S-A node

atrium (AY tree uhm): heart chamber which receives blood in vertebrates; also called auricle

Australopithecus (aw stray loh PIHTH uh kus): genus of prehumans that lived around 2 million years ago in southern Africa

autoclave (AWT oh klayv): kind of equipment used in labs and hospitals to kill bacteria

autonomic nervous system: system which controls involuntary responses

autosome (AWT uh sohm): body chromosome, as distinguished from sex chromosome

autotroph (AWT uh trohf): organism which can produce its own food

auxin (AWK sun): plant hormone

Aves: class of vertebrates characterized by feathers and lightweight bones for flight

axon (AK sahn): long part of a neuron leading away from the cell body; transmits impulses away from the cell body

bacilli (buh SIHL i): rod shaped bacteria

bacteria: very small, prokaryotic, unicellular, heterotrophic organisms (lack nuclei and some organelles)

bacterial transformation: form of genetic recombination which occurs when one bacterium breaks open and part of its DNA enters another bacterium

bacteriophage (bak TIHR ee uh fayj): virus which reproduces in bacteria; also called phage

balance: scientific instrument used for measuring mass; process of making the number of atoms of each element agree on both sides of a chemical equation

balanced equation: chemical equation in which the number of atoms of each element agree on both sides

ball and socket joint: type of joint that can rotate as well as move side to side and back and forth

barbiturates: most powerful and most often abused depressants

bark: outermost layers of a woody stem

basal body: structure that attaches cilia and flagella to the inside of a cell

base: substance which in solution has a greater concentration of hydroxide ions than hydrogen ions; an alkaline solution; compound containing nitrogen which makes up part of a nucleic acid

basic irritability: cytoplasmic response to stimuli

basidia (buh SIHD ee uh): club-shaped, spore-producing structures in certain fungi

B-cell: lymphocyte which does not pass through the thymus gland; divides to form a clone and produces antibodies

beech-maple forest: climax community in northeastern United States

behavior: responses made by an organism to the stimuli of its environment

behavioral (bih HAY vyuh rul) **adaptation:** adaptation involving reactions to the environment

benthos (BEN thas): animals which live attached to or crawl on the ocean floor

beriberi: deficiency disease caused by lack of vitamin B_1

beta cell: type of islet of Langerhans cell that produces insulin

bicuspid (bi KUS pud) **valve:** valve which prevents blood from being forced back into the left atrium when the left ventricle contracts

bilateral (bi LAT uh rul) **symmetry:** body pattern in which only one longitudinal cut will produce two sides that are mirror images

bile: greenish liquid produced by the liver and stored in the gall bladder; emulsifies fat in the small intestine

bile salts: substances contained in the gall bladder that break up fat globules in the intestine

binomial nomenclature (bi NOH mee ul • NOH mun klay chur): two-term naming system used in classifying organisms

biogenesis (bi oh JEN uh sus): theory which states that at the present time and under present conditions on earth, all living things are produced from other living things

biological clock: mechanism which controls certain time-related activities of animals

biological control: using natural, biological methods of controlling pest populations

biological magnification: increased concentration of chemicals along a food chain

biologist: one who studies biology

biology: study of life

biomass (BI oh mas): total mass of a group of organisms per unit of area

biome (BI ohm): communities characterized by the same major life forms, such as tundra

biosphere (BY uh sfir): total world of life

biotic (bi AHT ihk) **factors:** relationships among living organisms in an ecosystem

biotic potential: tendency of all organisms to reproduce in large numbers; reproductive potential

bipedal (bi PED ul) **locomotion:** locomotion on two feet

birth: expulsion of the baby from the uterus

birthrate: number of organisms born in a given time period

bivalves (BI valvz): mollusks which have two shells; includes clams, oysters, and mussels

blade: expanded part of a leaf

blastocoel (BLAS tuh seel): fluid-filled cavity inside the blastula

blastocyst: ball of cells formed as a zygote begins to divide

blastopore (BLAS tuh por): opening formed by the dorsal lip cutting into the blastula

blastula (BLAS chuh luh): hollow ball of cells in the early development of an embryo

blood: liquid which serves as an exchange medium between the internal parts of an organism and its external environment

blood clot: network of fibers and other blood parts which covers a wound and prevents the loss of excess blood

blood pressure: pressure exerted by the blood on the walls of the blood vessels

body stalk: structure which connects the trophoblast and the embryo to the uterine wall

bone: living tissue which makes up the endoskeleton of most vertebrates

bone marrow: tissue in the hollow part of bones

bony layer: layer of bone which contains minerals

botulism (BACH uh lihz um): a sometimes fatal disease resulting from bacterial wastes in improperly canned food

Bowman's capsule: cup-shaped part of a nephron

brain: major coordinating center in vertebrates; nerve center in invertebrates similar in position and function to the vertebrate brain

breathing: movement of air into and out of the lungs of complex animals

breathing center: area in the medulla oblongata which controls the breathing rate

bromeliad: epiphyte that lives in the canopy of the tropical rain forest

bronchi (BRAHN ki): two large tubes branching from the trachea in the lungs

bronchial tubes: small branches of the bronchi

bronchioles (BRAHN kee ohlz): tiny branches of the bronchial tubes

bryophytes (BRI uh fites): most primitive of true land plants; mosses and liverworts

bud: protected, dormant meristem which may develop into new stems, flowers, or leaves

bud scale: modified leaf which protects a bud

bud scale scar: place where bud scales surrounded a bud

budding: type of vegetative propagation in which an outgrowth forms on the parent organism and later separates giving rise to a new organism

bulb: short underground stem surrounded by many scales (modified leaves)

Calvin cycle: cyclic pattern of reactions in the dark reaction of photosynthesis

cambium: tissue which produces additional xylem and phloem cells as a plant grows in diameter

camouflage (KAM uh flahj): any means of blending with the environment

cancer: disease characterized by lack of control of cell division

canopy: top layer of a forest where most of the food is produced

cap: top, umbrellalike portion of a mushroom; guanine at the end of mRNA

capillaries: smallest branches of blood vessels where materials of the blood and cells are exchanged; connect arteries and veins

carbohydrates: organic compounds composed of carbon, hydrogen, and oxygen; used for energy sources in organisms

Carbon-14: a radioactive isotope with a half-life of 5730 years

carbon compound: chemical compound containing carbon

carboxyl (kar BAHK sul) **group:** part common to all fatty acids that has a structural formula of (-COOH)

carboxyhemoglobin: molecule formed when carbon dioxide combines with hemoglobin in blood

cardiac (KARD ee ak) **muscle:** muscle of which the heart is composed

carnivore (KAR nuh vor): consumer which feeds on other consumers; meat eater

carotenes (KER uh teenz): yellow or orange pigments present in most autotrophs

carrier molecule: protein that combines with certain particles and helps them pass across the cell membrane

carrying capacity: number of individuals of a population which a particular environment can support

cartilage (KART ul ihj): tough, flexible, connective tissue which does not contain minerals

cell: smallest living unit of which all organisms are composed

cell body: portion of a neuron most resembling other cells; contains a nucleus and cytoplasm

cell fractionation: separation of cell parts

cell membrane: structure that separates the components of a cell from its environment

cell plate: structure completed in plants to separate the daughter cells formed in mitosis

cell theory: concept which applies to all living things; the cell is the basic unit of structure and function and all cells are produced from other cells

cell wall: structure which surrounds the plasma membrane of plant cells; composed of cellulose or other carbohydrates

cellular respiration: process by which the energy of glucose is converted to the energy of ATP in a cell

cellulose: polysaccharide of plants

Celsius (SEL see us): scale for measuring temperature which has 0° as the freezing point and 100° as the boiling point of water

cenozoic: era of the geologic timetable which lasted from 75 000 000 years ago to the present

centimeter: measurement of length in the SI system equal to 1/100 of a meter

centipede: member of class of arthropods characterized by one pair of legs per segment; class Chilopoda

central disc: center part of a starfish from which arms stick out

central nervous system: control center for the entire nervous system

centrifuge: instrument that spins materials at high speed

centrioles (SEN tree olz): pair of organelles which play an important role in division of animal cells

centromere (SEN truh mihr): round body made of chromatin which holds the two strands of a chromosome together

cephalothorax (sef uh luh THOR aks): one of the two body sections of crustaceans; the result of fusion of the head and thorax

cerebellum (ser uh BEL um): convoluted region of the hindbrain lying at the back of the head below the cerebrum

cerebral cortex: convoluted surface of the cerebrum

cerebrospinal fluid: fluid in brain and spinal cord; protects brain from shock

cerebrum (suh REE brum): forebrain of humans

cervix (SUR vihks): small opening between the vagina and uterus

chelicerae (kih LIHS uh ree): fanglike or pincerlike mouthparts in arachnids

chemical bond: force which holds atoms together

chemical change: process by which atoms or molecules are rearranged; also called chemical reaction

chemical energy: energy within molecules

chemical equation: statement using formulas to describe a chemical reaction

chemical formula: combinations of symbols which represent the number and kind of each atom in a compound

chemical property: property of a substance which depends on how the substance reacts with other substances

chemical reaction: chemical change; rearranging of the atoms or molecules of substances to form completely new substances with new properties

chemical symbol: shorthand method of representing an element

chemosynthesis (kee moh SIHN thus sus): process in which inorganic materials such as iron, sulpher, and nitrogen compounds are used to make carbohydrates

chemotherapy: use of chemicals to treat disease

chiliped (KEE luh ped): legs modified as claws found on some crustaceans used for trapping food and for defense

chitin (KITE un): carbohydrate material forming the walls of most fungi; carbohydrate material forming one of the main components of an arthropod's exoskeleton

chlorophyll: green pigment which is essential for the conversion of light energy to chemical energy in autotrophic organisms

chloroplast (KLOR uh plast): cellular organelle in autotrophs which contains chlorophyll

cholinesterase (koh luh NES tuh rays): enzyme that breaks down acetylcholine into two smaller molecules

chordates (KOR dates): members of phylum Chordata, includes vertebrates

chorion (KOR ee ahn): thin membrane inside the shell of a land egg which functions in gas exchange; a membrane in mammals contributing to the formation of the placenta

chromatid (KROH muh tid): individual strand in a double-stranded chromosome

chromatin (KROH mut un): mass of material inside the nuclear membrane which appears as chromosomes during cell division

chromatophore (kroh MAT uh for): cell containing one or more pigments

chromosome (KROH muh sohm): distinct body in the nucleus which appears during cell division; contains genes

chromosome theory of heredity: genes are located on chromosomes

chunk feeder: animal which eats pieces of food material

chyme (KYM): liquid acid form of food after digestion in the stomach

cilia (SIHL ee uh): tiny, hairlike projections; used for locomotion in some one-celled organisms; also present on some cells of multicellular organisms

ciliary (SIHL ee er ee) **motion:** locomotion achieved by movement of cilia

ciliates (SIHL ee ayts): protozoa which have cilia

circulatory (SUR kyuh luh tor ee) **system:** system made up of the blood and the structures through which it passes

cirri: large bundles of cilia found in some protists

class: division of classification system which represents a subdivision of a phylum

cleavage (KLEE vihj): series of many cell divisions in the developing embryo

climax community: final stage in the evolution of a community

cloaca (kloh AY kuh): a common chamber that receives the digestive and excretory wastes as well as products of the reproductive system

clone: strain of genetically identical cells

closed circulatory system: system in which blood is always in the blood vessels

cocci (KAHK si): round- or sphere-shaped bacteria

cochlea: fluid-filled canal in the inner ear

codon (KOH dohn): sequence of three bases representing a certain amino acid

coelenterates: simple animals characterized by tentacles with stinging cells, two cell layers, and a single body opening; phylum Coelenterata

coelom (SEE lum): body cavity which houses the major organs in annelids and more complex animals

coenzyme: molecules with which enzymes temporarily join during a reaction

cohesion (koh HEE zhun): clinging together of the same kind of molecules

coleoptile (koh lee AHP tul): leafy tip of a seedling

collar cells: flagellated endoderm cells which line the body cavity of sponges; function in trapping food

colon (KOH lun): large intestine

colorblindness: generic, sex-linked trait that makes a human unable to distinguish red or green

commensalism (kuh MEN suh lihz um): relationship in which one organism (commensal) benefits from another organism (host) without affecting it

common bile duct: canal formed by the merging of the bile duct and the pancreatic duct; empties into the duodenum

communication: use of symbols to represent ideas

community: naturally occurring group of organisms living in a certain area

companion cells: cells with nuclei that lie next to seive tubes in a stem

comparative anatomy: studies of similar structures among organisms

comparative biochemistry: studies of chemical similarities among organisms

comparative embryology: studies of similar development among different organisms

competitive exclusion principle: two populations cannot occupy the same ecological niche

complement: set of enzymes in the bloodstream which attacks foreign cells

complete metamorphosis: four-stage process of development in insects

compound: substance composed of different kinds of atoms

compound leaf: leaf blade subdivided into leaflets

concept: idea

concussion: brain injury which may result from a severe fall or blow to the head

conditioned response: involuntary response to a stimulus that does not normally cause the response; voluntary response to get a desired effect; depends on type of conditioning

conditioning: type of learning in animals

conductor: structure that transmits nerve impulses

conidium (kuh NIHD ee um): spore formed by mitosis at the tip of a conidiophore

conidiophore (kuh NIHD ee uh for): hyphae found in some molds on which conidia are produced

cone: seed-bearing or pollen-bearing structure of gymnosperms

conifers (KAHN uh furs): pines and their relatives; cone-bearing gymnosperms

conjugation: fusion of nuclear material of two cells

consumer: living things which obtains food from other organisms

continuous variation: existence of varying degrees of a characteristic; controlled by more than one pair of genes

contour plowing: conservation practice in which land is plowed along its natural contours, reducing erosion from water runoff

contractile (kun TRAK tul) **vacuole:** organelle which pumps excess water from a protozoan

control group: group which is identical to the experimental group except for the variable being tested

controlled experiment: experiment in which all factors are identical except the one being tested

convergence (kun VUR junts): evolutionary process in which distantly related species produce descendants which resemble each other

convolutions (kahn vuh LEW shunz): folds in the cerebral cortex

cork: cells which make up the outer bark of trees and woody shrubs

corpus luteum (KOR pus • LEWT ee um): yellow tissue that forms from the ruptured follicle

corpus luteum stage: stage in the menstrual cycle during which the corpus luteum produces progesterone to maintain the uterus for pregnancy.

cortex: food storage area in roots and stems; outer part of kidney; outer part of adrenal gland; outer part of cerebrum

cortisol: hormone which causes fats and proteins to be converted to glucose; secreted by the adrenal cortex

cortisone: hormone secreted by the adrenal cortex, often administered in synthetic form to counteract pain and swelling

cotyledon (kaht ul EED un): seed leaf, stores food for the embryo

courtship patterns: signals used by animals to identify members of their own species ready for mating

courtship behavior: complex behavior of animals

covalent (koh VAY lunt) **bonds:** sharing of electrons between atoms

cranial nerves: nerves from the brain which carry impulses of the sensory-somatic system

creatine phosphate (CP): compound that can quickly be converted to ATP for energy for muscle movement

cretin: malformed, mentally retarded dwarf suffering from cretinism

cretinism (KREET uhn ihz um): disease caused by a great deficiency of thyroxine in early childhood; victim is called a cretin

cristae (KRIS tee): folds on the inner layer of mitochondria

Cro-Magnon: type of modern human that lived 20 000 to 50 000 years ago

crop: food storage organ in the alimentary canal of an earthworm

crop rotation: conservation practice in which different crops are planted in a field from year to year

cross-over: an exchange of segments of chromosomes between two homologous chromatids

crossing-over: exchange of segments of chromosomal material between two strands of a tetrad; occurs during prophase of meiosis I

cross-pollination: pollination between flowers of separate plants

crustaceans (krus TAY shee uns): class of arthropods which includes lobsters, crayfish, shrimp, and crabs

cryptic coloration: type of camouflage in which the color of an organism blends with the environment

cultural control: the breeding, planting, and harvesting of crops by methods which reduce pest damage

cultural evolution: changes in culture which have reduced natural selection for humans

culture: knowledge, customs, and laws into which each person is born

curare: muscle relaxant that combines with receptors for acetylcholine on muscle cells

cutin: waxy material covering the epidermis of a leaf that helps prevent water loss

cyclic AMP: "second messenger" formed by adrenaline

cytochrome (SITE uh krohmz): chemicals contained in mitochondria that function in aerobic respiration

cytoplasm (SITE uh plaz um): protoplasm outside the nucleus of the cell

cytosine (SITE uh seen): one of the bases in the nucleic acids

dark reaction: phase of photosynthesis in which the actual synthesis of glucose occurs

Darwinism: theory of evolution first proposed by Charles Darwin stating that the organisms best adapted to an environment are the ones that survive and reproduce

data: scientific facts

daughter cells: two cells formed as the result of mitosis of a single cell

day-neutral plant: plant whose flowering does not depend on the length of daylight or darkness

DDT: pesticide which kills insects by attacking the nervous system; nonbiodegradable, passed along food chains

death rate: number of organisms that die in a given period of time

deciduous (dih SIHJ uh wus) **forest:** forest in which leaves are periodically shed from the trees

decomposer: organism such as bacteria or fungi which causes decay

degenerative (dih JEN uh ruh tihv) **evolution:** process in which organisms lose some of their features as they evolve from a more complex form into a simpler one

dehydration synthesis: chemical reaction in which a large molecule is formed from smaller molecules by removing water

dehydrogenase: an enzyme that removes hydrogen

dendrite (DEN dritc): highly branched structure at one end of a neuron

denitrification (dee ni truh fuh KAY shun): process by which nitrogen is released from the soil by the action of denitrifying bacteria

density: the amount of matter that something contains in a certain volume

deoxyribonucleic (dee AHK sih ri boh noo klay ihk) **acid (DNA):** nucleic acid that contains the "genetic message"

deoxyribose: a sugar which joins with a nitrogen base and a phosphate group to form a nucleotide

depressant: one of a major group of drugs which reduce the reactions of the central nervous system

descending colon: section of the large intestine which leads to the rectum

desert: biome of arid regions where rainfall is less than 25 cm per year; sparse, widely-spaced vegetation

desmids: form of green algae

development: series of changes a living thing undergoes in attaining its final form

diabetes insipidus (ihn SIHP ud us): disease caused by secretion of too little vasopressin, characterized by frequent urination and constant thirst

diabetes mellitus (MEL ut us): disease in which a sufficient quantity of the hormone insulin is not produced; characterized by frequent urination and constant thirst as a result of a high blood sugar level, also called sugar diabetes

diaphragm: large, muscular sheet which separates the chest from the abdomen, important in breathing

diastole (di AS tuh lee): short period of "rest" after the heart contracts

diatomaceous earth: huge deposit of cell walls of dead diatoms

diatoms (DI uh tahmz): unicellular golden algae

dicot (DI kaht): plants whose seeds contain two cotyledons

differentiation (dihf uh ren chee AY shun): series of changes which result in the formation of specialized body cells and parts

diffusion (dihf YEW zhun): random movement of particles resulting in their movement from a region of greater concentration to one of lesser concentration

digestion: process of breaking large molecules into smaller ones by chemical and physical means

dinoflagellates: unicellular algae with two flagella for locomotion

dipeptide: two amino acids joined together by a peptide bond

diploid (DIHP loyd) **number:** a chromosome number equal to twice that found in the gametes

disaccharide: double sugar formed by the combination of two monosaccharides

dissociation: process in which the ions of ionic compounds separate in solution

divergence (di VUR junts): evolution of a species into two or more species with different characteristics

division of labor: organization of parts or organisms for specific jobs

dominant (DAHM un nunt) **species:** characteristic species of a community

dominant trait: genetic trait which dominates or prevents the expression of the recessive trait

dormancy (DOR mun see): period of inactivity of a seed or spore before germination; period of little or no activity in some types of animals

dorsal (DOR sul): toward the back

dorsal aorta: aorta that carries blood from the gills to all parts of a fish

dorsal blood vessel: major blood vessel on the back side of an annelid worm

dorsal lip: edge of blastopore dorsal to the embryo

Down's syndrome: abnormality caused by nondisjunction, characterized by eye shape that looks like that of people of the Mongoloid race, mental retardation, short arms and legs, and internal malformations; Mongolism

drone: male bee which developed from an unfertilized egg

duet rule: atoms with only one energy level acquire two electrons in forming molecules

duodenum (dew uh DEE num): portion of the small intestine closest to the stomach

dynamic equilibrium (di NAM ihk • ee kwul LIHB ree um): state in which the number of particles entering and leaving a cell is equal

ecdyson (EK duh sahn): hormone which causes molting

echinoderms: marine animals characterized by spiny skin and radial symmetry; phylum Echinodermata

ecological niche: the specific role an organism plays in a community

ecological succession (ee kuh LAHJ ih kul • suk SESH un): series of changes in a community during its evolution

ecology: study of the relationships between organisms and their environment

ecosystem (EE koh sihs tum): interaction of a community with its physical environment; an ecological system

ectoderm (EK tuh durm): outer layer of cells in an embryo or mature animal

ectotherm (EK tuh thurm): cold-blooded animal; animal whose body temperature is not internally regulated but rather approximates that of the environment

effector (ih FEK tur): organ which carries out the appropriate response to a stimulus

egestion: the elimination of undigested food

egg: female reproductive cell, also called an ovum

electron: negatively-charged particle of an atom

electron cloud: description of probable electron location around the nucleus of an atom

electron microscope: microscope which uses a beam of electrons instead of light

element: substance composed of only one type of atom

elephantiasis: a disease caused by *Filaria* roundworms

elongation region: cells of the meristem which grow only in length adding to the length of a young stem or root

embryo: developing plant or animal after fertilization

embryology (em bree AHL uh jee): study of development

embryonic induction (em bree AHN ihk • ihn DUK shun): hypothesis that a particular section of an embryo influences, or induces, the development of an adjacent region

emigration: movement of animals out of an area

emphysema: respiratory disease linked to smoking in which the bronchioles become inflamed

end brush: filaments forming the end of an axon

endergonic (en dur GAHN ihk) **reaction:** chemical reaction which requires energy

endocrine (EN duh krun) **gland:** ductless gland, pours hormones directly into blood

endocrinology (en duh krih NAHL uh jee): study of endocrine glands and hormonal control

endocytosis (en duh si TOH sus): process in which a cell uses energy to surround and take in large substances

endoderm (EN duh durm): inner layer of cells in an embryo or mature animal

endoplasmic reticulum (en duh PLAZ mihk • rih TIHK yuh lum): network of tubelike structures in most cells; may be a transport system for cellular materials

endoscope: device which allows a fetus to be viewed while it is still in the mother

endoskeleton (en doh SKEL ut un): internal skeleton

endosperm (EN duh spurm): mass of tissue in a seed, the food source for the germinating plant

endosperm nucleus: $3n$ structure formed when the sperm nucleus joins with the polar nuclei in a flower

endospore: type of spore formed from a bacterial cell during unfavorable conditions

endotherm (EN duh thurm): warm-blooded animal, a fairly constant body temperature regulated internally

endotoxin: poisonous chemical released when bacteria die and break open

energy: ability to do work and cause changes

energy level: distance at which an electron travels around the nucleus of an atom

enkephalin: neuropeptide that reduces pain

environment: all factors that act upon an organism

environmental resistance: total of the environmental factors which check the biotic potential of a population

enzyme (EN zime): protein which activates a chemical reaction in a cell

enzyme induction: process in which a substance entering a cell causes the cell to start producing a certain enzyme

epicotyl (EP ih kaht ul): embryonic seed structure, first true leaves of the plant

epidermis (ep uh DUR mus): outermost layer of cells of an organism

epiglottis (ep uh GLAHT us): structure which covers the opening to the trachea when a person swallows food

epinephrin: main hormone of the adrenal medulla which prepares the body to cope with stress

epiphyte (EP uh fite): plant which lives as a commensal in the canopy of trees

era: division of time used by geologists to divide the earth's history

erosion (ih ROH zhun): naturally-occurring process in which topsoil is removed by the action of water and wind

erythrocyte (ih RIHTH ruh site): red blood cell, produced in bone marrow; important in transport of oxygen and carbon dioxide

esophagus (ih SAHF uh gus): tube which passes food from the mouth or throat to other digestive organs in a variety of animals

essential nutrient: material needed by cells for life

estivation (es tuh VAY shun): period of inactivity and low metabolism similar to hibernation but occurring in hot weather

estrogen (ES truh jun): female sex hormone

estrous (ES trus) **cycle:** entire series of chemical and physical changes leading up to the production of mature eggs

eukaryote (yew KER ee oht): organism with cells that have true nuclei

Eustachian tube: a canal which connects the middle ear to the nasal passages and throat

eutrophication: aging and death of a lake, the result of upsetting the ecological balance

evolution: process of change with time during successive generations among living things

excretion: release and removal of harmful metabolic by-products

excretory canal: structure in a planarian which collects excess water from tissues

excretory duct: branch of excretory canal which opens as a pore on the surface of a planarian; excess water leaves through the pore

excurrent pore: opening in a sponge through which water leaves

exergonic (ek sur GAHN ihk) **reaction:** chemical reaction which releases energy

exocytosis (ek soh si TOH sus): process in which materials are expelled from a cell through the action of membranes fusing

exon: sections of DNA that contain the information that codes for the protein product of the gene

exoskeleton (ek soh SKEL ut un): external skeleton

exotoxin: poisonous chemical released by living bacteria

experimental group: part of an experiment in which the variable factor is tested

experimentation: scientific testing of a hypothesis

expiration: process in which air is expelled from the lungs

extensor (ihk STEN sur): muscle which, when contracted, causes a joint to straighten

external fertilization: fertilization in animals in which the egg is fertilized outside the female's body

external respiration: exchange of gases between the circulating fluid and the external environment

extinct: no longer existing form of life

extracellular (ek struh SEL yuh lur) **digestion:** digestion which occurs outside cells

extract: solution of a chemical obtained from cells

eyespots: two light-sensitive organs at the anterior end of planarians

facillitated diffusion: process in which carrier molecules help other molecules to move across cell membranes

fact: observed phenomenon agreed upon by a number of people; something about which there is no doubt

FAD: flavin adenine dinucleotide; a coenzyme that transports hydrogens and thus electrons in respiration

Fallopian (fuh LOH pee un) **tube:** another name for oviduct

family: subdivision of an order in the complete classification of an organism

fatty acid: complex molecule containing a carboxyl group; part of a fat molecule

feces (FEE seez): solid waste material, egested through the anus

feedback mechanism: system in which control over the glands depends on information received from them

feeding level: level of energy transfer in an ecosystem

fermentation: anaerobic respiration

ferns: vascular plants that have roots, stems, leaves, and rhizomes and reproduce by spores

fertility factor: genetic information located on plasmid in certain bacteria that are designated F⁺ (Other bacteria without this factor are F⁻.)

fertilization: fusion of sperm and egg

fetoscopy (fee TAHS kuh pee): medical test which allows direct observation of the fetus and surrounding tissues

fetus (FEET us): an embryo that is at least eight weeks old

fiber: a skeletal muscle cell

fibril: unit which makes up fibers of striated muscle

fibrin (FI brun): long strands of protein which form a blood clot

fibrous (FI brus) **root system:** system of many secondary roots and root hairs

filament: stalklike portion of a stamen; unit which makes up fibrils in striated muscle

filter feeder: animal which takes food from water as it flows through the animal

first filial (FIHL ee ul) **generation:** first offspring produced from a parental cross

first-order consumer: consumer which feeds directly on a producer; herbivore

first polar body: one of the two cells produced from the primary oocyte during meiosis I; very small cell

fission (FIHSH un): asexual reproduction in which one organism divides into two small organisms of equal size

flagella (fluh JEL uh): long, whiplike projections of a cell used for locomotion

flagellar motion: locomotion achieved by movement of flagella

flagellate: protozoan which moves by means of flagella

flame cell: cell with flagella which moves water into and along the excretory canal in a planarian

flatworms: bilaterally symmetrical, aquatic, semi-aquatic, or parasitic organisms; members of phylum Platyhelminthes

flexor (FLEK sor): muscle which causes the bending of a joint

florigen: hormone that promotes flowering

flourescence: energy given off as light

flower: reproductive organ in angiosperms

flower scar: place on the stem where a flower was once attached

follicle (FAHL ih kul): cell nest within an ovary; site of egg development

follicle stage: stage in the menstrual cycle during which an egg matures and the preparation of the uterus for a possible pregnancy begins

follicle-stimulating hormone (**FSH**): hormone which stimulates the ripening of eggs within the follicle of the ovary; hormone that stimulates sperm production in males

food: substance which provides energy required by living systems

food chain: passage of energy and materials through a community

food vacuole: structure within some protozoa that collects and digests food

food web: all the possible feeding relationships in an ecosystem

foot: muscular organ in mollusks used for locomotion

forebrain: one of the three general areas of the vertebrate brain

forest floor: bottom-most strata of a forest

fossil: any evidence or part of a once-living thing

fossil fuels: fuels made from the remains of once-living organisms

fragmentation: form of vegetation propagation in which a part of an organism breaks off and grows

fraternal (fruh TURN ul) **twins:** twins which develop when two different eggs are fertilized

frond (FRAHND): fern leaf, highly branched, often with a lacy appearance

fruit: enlarged ovary of a plant that aids in seed dispersal

fruit scar: place on a stem where a fruit was once attached

fungi: plantlike, heterotrophic protists; members of phylum Mycophyta

fungi: heterotrophic, plantlike organisms which reproduce by forming spores and by other means

fusion: uniting of two sets of DNA; sexual reproduction

galactose: a simple sugar found in milk

galactosemia: a genetic disease in which galactose cannot be converted to glucose and instead builds up and causes nerve damage

gall bladder: organ beneath the liver in which bile is stored

Galapagos (guh LAHP uh gus) **Islands:** islands located about 1000 km west of South America at the equator

gametes (GAM eets): sex cells; sperms and eggs

gametophyte (guh MEET uh fite) **generation:** the monoploid part of the life cycle of a plant or plantlike protist

ganglia (GANG glee uh): knotlike bundle of nerve tissue

gas exchange: movement of oxygen and carbon dioxide between organisms and their environment

gasohol (GAS uh hahl): alcohol mixed with gasoline and used for fuel

gastric glands: glands in the stomach that secrete gastric juice

gastric juice: fluid secreted into the stomach by gastric glands that contains enzymes necessary for digestion

gastrin (GAS trun): hormone which stimulates the secretion of gastric juice

gastrovascular (gas troh VAS kyuh lur) **cavity:** internal area of coelenterates

gastrula: stage of the developing embryo following the blastula stage

gastrulation (gas truh LAY shun): movement of cells from the outside surface of the blastula through the blastopore into the interior of the blastula; process in which cell layers are formed

Geiger counter: instrument that detects radioactive particles being given off

gel: somewhat solidified state such as is characteristic of the cytoplasm at times

gemmule (JEM yewlz): reproductive cell of a sponge enclosed by a tough, outer covering that is highly resistant to dryness and cold

gene: unit responsible for transmitting hereditary traits; segment of a DNA molecule

gene linkage: presence of genes for different traits on the same chromosome

gene pool: all the genes of a population; sum of genetic information which will be passed to each new generation

generative nucleus: nucleus of a pollen grain, produces two monoploid sperm nuclei

genetic continuity: reproduction of offspring having the same set of features as the parent

genetic counseling: type of counseling in which parents can be advised of their chances of having offspring with a hereditary disease

genetic engineering: altering an organism's genetic makeup

genetic map: diagram indicating locations of genes on a chromosome

genetic recombination: rearranging of genetic instructions

genetics (juh NET ihks): science of heredity

genotype (JEE nuh tipe): particular combination of alleles of an organism

genus (JEE nus): classification division between family and species; first name in the scientific name of an organism

geographic isolation: division or separation of populations by geographical features

geothermal energy: energy created by the natural heat of the earth

geotropism (jee oh TROH pihz um): plant growth response to gravity

germ theory of disease: theory proposed by Louis Pasteur that stated that bacteria can cause disease

germinate (JUR muh nayt): begin development

gestation (jeh STAY shun) **period:** length of pregnancy

gibberellin (jihb uh REL un): chemical regulator affecting plant growth

gill: respiratory organ in fish and other aquatic animals; spokelike structure in the cap of a mushroom where spores are produced

gill chamber: area in which gills are located in fish

gill filaments: double rows of thin-walled tissue in gills through which capillaries pass

gizzard: digestive organ in which food is ground up in earthworms and birds

gliding joint: joint in which bones move easily over one another in a back and forth motion

glomerulus (gluh MER uh lus): mass of capillaries in the center of each Bowman's capsule of a kidney

glucose: simple sugar produced by photosynthesis

glycerol: complex molecule that is part of fats

glycogen (GLI kuh jun): starchlike carbohydrate in animals

glycolysis: series of energy-releasing reactions in a cell in the absence of oxygen; stage one of aerobic respiration though it does not require oxygen; process of anaerobic respiration

goiter: disease characterized by enlargement of the thyroid gland, often caused by lack of iodine in the diet

Golgi (GAWL jee) **body:** cell organelle which appears as stacks of flattened discs, thought to be involved with production of large carbohydrates and the storage and secretion of cellular substances

gonads (GOH nadz): sex organs; ovaries and testes

grana (GRAY nuh): platelike structures which contain chlorophyll in a chloroplast

grassland: biome of plains regions, characterized by grasses

gray matter: neuron cell bodies which make up the cerebral cortex and the interior of the spinal cord

growth: increase in the amount of living material in an organism; increase in the number of individuals in a population

guanine (GWAHN een): one of the bases in nucleic acids

guard cells: cells which surround and control the size of the stomata in leaves of complex plants

gymnosperms (JIM nuh spurmz): class of seed plants; plants in which seeds develop unprotected on the scales of cones; phylum Gymnospermae

half-life: time necessary for one half of a radioactive material to decay

Haversian (huh VUR zhun) **canals:** channels running throughout the bony layer that contain blood vessels and nerves which supply osteocytes

hazardous wastes: wastes dangerous to humans and other life forms

head-foot mollusk: mollusk which has tentacles originating in the head region such as squid and octopus

heart: muscular pump which circulates blood throughout an animal

hemocoel (HEE muh seel): body cavity, spaces through which blood passes in an open circulatory system

hemoglobin (HEE muh gloh bun): complex protein in red blood cells containing iron which combines with oxygen, important in oxygen transport

hemophilia (hee muh FIHL ee uh): sex-linked hereditary disease in which the blood fails to clot properly

hepatic (hih PAT ihk) **portal vein:** vein which carries blood from the intestine to the liver

herbaceous (hur BAY shus) **stem:** soft, green stem of plants which live for only one growing season

herbivore (HUR buh vor): consumer which eats producers (plants); plant eater

heredity (huh RED ut ee): transmission of characteristics from one generation to the next

hermaphrodite (hur MAF ruh dite): organism which has both ovaries and testes

heterocyst (HET uh roh sihst): special cell in a filament of blue-green algae that has thick walls, no DNA, and appears empty

heterotroph (HET uh ruh trohf): organism which cannot make its own food and so depends on other living or dead things for food

heterozygous (het uh roh ZI gus): having two different alleles for a given character at the corresponding sites on homologous chromosomes

hibernation: state in which metabolism is reduced and energy expenditure is minimized; occurs in some animals during the winter months

high energy bond: bond which when broken provides a large amount of chemical energy

high energy phosphate: phosphate group containing high energy bonds

hindbrain: one of the three general areas of the vertebrate brain

hinge joint: joint which moves in one direction and does not rotate

histones: very basic proteins that play an important role in chromosome structure

holdfast: special anchoring cell found in some algae

homeostasis (hoh mee oh STAY sus): maintaining of a constant internal environment

hominid: early human

Homo erectus: prehuman that lived about 1.5 million years ago; may have led to the extinction of *Australopithecus*

Homo habilis: prehuman that lived 2 to 3 million years ago; thought to be a toolmaker

Homo sapiens (HOH moh • SAY pee unz): scientific name for modern humans

homogeneous (hoh muh JEE nee us): the same throughout

homologous (huh MAHL uh gus): those parts in various animals having the same shape, structure, and origin

homologs (HOH muh lawgs): the two chromosomes of a pair with the same kinds of genetic messages

homozygous (hoh muh ZI gus): having two identical alleles for a given character at the corresponding sites on homologous chromosomes

hormone: a chemical regulator that is produced in one part of the organism and affects other parts; complex molecules that direct chemical control within the body

host: organism from which another organism benefits

humus: rich layer of soil containing decayed remains of organisms

hybridoma (hi brih DOH muh): cell used to make cancer cells in the laboratory

hydrocarbons: compounds of hydrogen and carbon produced when fossil fuels are burned

hydrogenase (hi DRAHJ uh nays): an enzyme that removes hydrogen

hydrolysis (hi DRAHL uh sus): chemical reaction in which large molecules are broken into small molecules by the addition of water

hyphae (HI fee): filamentous strands filled with cytoplasm and many nuclei that compose the bodies of most true fungi

hypocotyl (HI puh kaut ul): embryonic seed structure, develops into part of the root and stem; embryonic part between the epicotyl and radicle

hypothalamus (hi poh THAL uh mus): region of the brain which controls many of the body's internal activities; brain region involved in many feedback mechanisms of internal control

hypothesis: idea or statement which explains the relationship among observed facts

identical twins: twins which have the same genotypes, resulting from the splitting of a zygote into two separate parts

ileum (IHL ee um): bulk of the small intestine in which most chemical digestion takes place; last portion of small intestine between jejunum and colon

immune system: cells and tissues which identify and defend the body against foreign chemicals and organisms

immunity: resistance to disease

immunology: study of how the body protects itself from invading organisms and chemicals

imperfect flower: flower which contains only the male or female organs

implantation: attachment to and embedding of the embryo in the uterine wall

imprinting: simple, rapid, irreversible form of learning by which an animal forms a social attachment to an object or organism shortly after hatching or birth

improvement cutting: removing old, crooked, or diseased trees while leaving the healthy trees

impulse: series of action potentials

incomplete dominance: condition in which the heterozygous genotype for certain alleles gives rise to a phenotype intermediate between the dominant and recessive traits

incomplete metamorphosis: three stage process of development in insects

incurrent pore: opening or perforation through which water enters a sponge

indoleacetic (IHN dohl uh seet ihk) **acid (IAA):** auxin necessary for the lengthening of plant cells

inducer: substance which causes enzyme induction

industrial melanism (MEL uh nihz um): phenomenon in which a color change in a population of peppered moths in England evolved during a period of industrialization

infectious disease: disease caused by a pathogen

infusion: nutrient-rich solution in which microorganisms can live

ingestion: taking in of bits of food not yet digested

inheritance of acquired characteristics: invalid hypothesis which states that characteristics which each individual acquires during its lifetime are passed on to the offspring of that individual

inhibition (ihn uh BIHSH un) **center:** area of the medulla oblongata from which the vagus nerves originate

innate (ihn AYT) **behavior:** behavior that is genetically passed from parent to offspring; behavior which does not change

inner bark: layer of a woody stem made up of cortex and phloem tissue

inner cell mass: one of the two regions of cells that form as the cells of a blastocyst divide

insectivorous plant: plant which feeds on insects

insects: largest class of arthropods; arthropods with three pairs of legs, three body sections, and usually wings

insight: ability to plan a response to a new situation

inspiration: process in which air is taken into lungs

instinct: innate behavior that involves complicated responses to a stimulus or stimuli

insulin: hormone which regulates the level of sugar in the blood; hormone secreted by beta cells of the islets of Langerhans

insulin pump: device which supplies the body with a constant flow of insulin

integrated pest management: system in which a combination of techniques is used to control pests

integument (ihn TEG yeh ment): outer covering of a seed; skin

interferon (ihnt ur FIHR ahn): protein produced by some cells after exposure to viruses which inhibits further virus growth

internal fertilization: process in animals in which sperms are deposited inside the female reproductive organs where fertilization occurs

internal respiration: exchange of gases within the body of an organism

International System of Measurement: special language of measurements and their symbols used by scientists and by other people in most countries throughout the world

interphase (IHNT ur fayz): period between mitoses during which chromosomes are replicated; period before meiotic division

interpretation: the logical conclusion drawn from observations made in the laboratory

interspecific (ihn tur spih SIHF ihk) **competition:** competition between populations of different species

intestine: alimentary canal organ where some or most food is chemically digested

intracellular (ihn truh SEL yuh lur) **digestion:** digestion which occurs within individual cells

intraspecific (ihn truh spih SIHF ihk) **competition:** competition between members of the same species

intron: DNA sequence that does not code for a protein

invertebrates: animals without backbones

involuntary muscles: muscles which an organism cannot consciously control

ion: charged atom or group of atoms

ionic bond: attraction between ions of opposite charge

ionic compound: combination of different ions

islets (I lutz) **of Langerhans** (LAHNG ur hahnz): endocrine cells within the pancreas which secrete insulin and glucagon

isomers (I suh murz): compounds which have the same chemical formula but different structural formulas

isotopes (I suh tophs): two or more atoms of the same element differing only in the number of neutrons

Java people: variety of *Homo erectus* that lived about 500 000 years ago

jejunum (jih JEW num): short section of the small intestine between the duodenum and the ileum

joint: where body segments of arthropods meet; where bones of vertebrates meet

jungle: dense forest community resulting from secondary succession of a rain forest

juvenile hormone: hormone involved in the final transition of an insect pupa to the adult form

karyotype (KER ee uh tipe): characteristics of all chromosomes in a cell including size and number

kelp: seaweed

kidneys: excretory organs in vertebrates

kilogram: an SI unit of measure for mass, equal to 1000 grams

kinetic energy: energy of motion or energy at work

kingdom: broadest division in the classification of living organisms; the three kingdoms are animals, plants, and protists

Klinefelter Syndrome: genetic problem of males with an XXY chromosome pattern

Koch's postulates: the methods by which Koch determined that a bacterium causes a specific disease

Krebs cycle: stage three in aerobic respiration; stage in which 16 hydrogen atoms and 2 ATP molecules are released per glucose molecule entering glycolysis

labor: series of contractions of the uterine muscles prior to giving birth

lactase: enzyme that breaks down lactose

lacteal (LAK tee ul): lymph vessel in villi which absorbs fatty acids and glycerol

ladder-type nervous system: nervous system in planarians and other flatworms; system composed of two ganglia and two major nerve cords connected at regular intervals by nerves

Lamarckism: theory of evolution proposed by Jean Baptiste de Lamarck; ideas which explained evolution of adaptations through laws of use and disuse and inheritance of acquired characteristics

language: form of communication in which symbols are used to represent ideas

large intestine: organ in humans which absorbs water from the undigestible materials, also called the colon

larva: developing organism leading an independent existence

lateral aspects: side edges of a bilaterally symmetrical organism

lateral bud: bud along the sides of branches that gives rise to new branches

latitudinal (lat uh TEWD nul) **succession:** continuous succession of community types from the equator to the poles

law of conservation of energy: energy can neither be created nor destroyed, but can be transformed into other kinds of energy

law of conservation of mass: during a chemical reaction, mass can neither be created nor destroyed

law of dominance (DAHM uh nuhns): the dominant form of a trait dominates or prevents the expression of the recessive form

law of independent assortment: different chromosomes separate independently during gamete formation

law of segregation (seg rih GAY shuhn): during gamete formation the pair of alleles responsible for each trait separate so each gamete contains only one allele for each trait

law of use and disuse: assumption that an animal could strengthen or develop part of its body by using it and that if a certain body part were not used, it would disappear; one of the two laws of Lamarckism

leaching: dissolving of minerals out of rock and soil by water

leaf: major photosynthetic organ of complex plants

learned behavior: behavior that can be changed

lenticel (LENT uh sel): tiny pore on a stem; site of gas exchange between the stem and atmosphere

left ventricular assist device (LVAD): device which takes over for the heart until a donor heart becomes available for a transplant

lethal (LEE thuhl): causing death

lethal gene: an allele that causes death

leukemia: cancer of blood-forming tissue

leukocyte (LEW kuh site): white blood cells produced in bone marrow, the spleen, and lymph nodes; protects the body against infection

levels of organization: different groups of biological parts (cells, tissues, and so on) organized to perform particular functions

liana (lee AHN uh): vinelike plant common in rain forests; rooted in the ground but with leaves in the canopy

lichen (LI kun): mutualistic combination of a fungus and an alga; often lives on rock or in other barren places

ligament (LIHG uh munt): connective tissue which connects bones together

light: radiant energy

light reaction: series of photosynthetic reactions which depend on light; portion of photosynthesis in which light energy is converted to chemical energy

linear density gradient: gradient in which density increases from one end of the tube to the other, but not in distinct steps

linkage: genes occurring on the same chromosome

limiting factor: aspect of the environment which prevents an increase in population size at any given time

lipids: class of organic compounds which includes fats, waxes, and oils; composed of carbon, hydrogen, and oxygen

littoral (LIHT uh rul) **zone:** area of the ocean close to shore and subject to the action of tides

liver: digestive organ; produces bile, destroys old red blood cells, stores glycogen; important in many processes of metabolism

lock and key hypothesis: each enzyme is specific for a given substrate because its shape matches that of the substrate

locomotion: movement of the total organism

long-day plant: plants whose flowering is dependent on long periods of light exposure

low energy phosphate: a phosphate group containing low energy bonds

luminescent: glows in the dark

lungs: moist internal organs for gas exchange in most amphibians and all reptiles, birds, and mammals

luteinizing (LEW teen i zing) **hormone (LH):** hormone which causes the follicle to rupture and the ruptured follicle to change to the corpus luteum; causes production of testosterone in males

lymph: fluid which escapes from the capillaries into the intercellular spaces and exchanges many materials with the cells

lymph nodes: structures scattered throughout the body, remove harmful substances from lymph

lymph vessel: vessel which channels lymph throughout the body

lymphatic (lihm FAT ihk) **system:** network of lymph vessels and lymph nodes

lymphocyte (LIMH fuh site): white blood cell involved in the formation of antibodies which destroy foreign protein

lysis (LI sus): destruction of bacteria or other cells by breaking of the membrane

lysogenic (li suh JEN ihk) **cycle:** viral life cycle in which the DNA of a phage becomes part of the bacterial host's DNA and is replicated when the bacterium reproduces

lysosome (LI suh sohm): organelle containing chemicals which hydrolyze large molecules brought into the cell

lytic cycle: viral life cycle in which viral DNA takes over a bacterial cell, uses the bacterium's materials to reproduce, and destroys the bacterial cell

macronucleus: large structure in ciliates that controls the basic activities of a cell

macrophage (MAK ruh faj): kind of white blood cell involved in immunity

magma: molten material from deep within the earth

magnification: the amount an object is made bigger through the use of instruments such as microscopes

malaria: protozoan disease transmitted by mosquitoes which causes bursting of red blood cells

malnutrition: inadequate supply of one or more essential nutrients in a person's diet

Malpighian (mal PIHG ee un) **tubules:** cluster of stringlike structures attached to the intestine of a grasshopper that absorb nitrogenous wastes

maltase: enzyme that breaks down maltose

mammals: complex vertebrates which have hair or fur and mammary glands, and bear their young alive; class Mammalia

mandible: mouthpart adapted for biting and chewing

mantle: folded tissue in mollusks covering the internal organs

marrow: tissue in the hollows of some bones; produces blood cells or stores excess fat

marsupials (mar SEW pee ulz): group of pouched mammals in which partial development of embryos occurs internally

masked message: RNA sequence coated with protein and stored in the cytoplasm of a cell

mass: amount of material in an object

matter: anything which has mass and occupies space

maturation region: area of meristem where cells are large and develop into different types of specialized tissue

medium: substance in which an organism lives

medulla (mih DEW luh): inside part of a kidney; inside section of an adrenal gland

medulla oblongata (mih DEW luh • ahb long GAHT uh): portion of the hindbrain; controls involuntary responses of internal organs

medusa: jellyfish form of many coelenterates

megaspore (MEG uh spor): cell which divides in a female plant to form eight monoploid nuclei to form the female gametophyte generation

meiosis (mi OH sus): process of division whereby each sperm and egg receives the monoploid number of chromosomes

melanin (MEL uh nun): a dark pigment

membrane potential: condition in which the outside of the membrane is more positively charged than the inside; also called resting potential

meninges (muh NIHN jeez): membranes which protect and nourish the spinal cord and brain

menopause: period when the menstrual cycle of human females ends, usually occurs in the 40's

menstrual (MEN strul) **cycle:** monthly series of hormonal changes leading to egg maturation and uterine preparation for a possible pregnancy

menstruation (men STRAY shun): stage of the menstrual cycle usually lasting from three to five days during which blood, some uterine tissue, and the unfertilized egg are expelled from the vagina

meristem (MER uh stem): special regions of plant tissue where cell division occurs

mesozoic: era of the geologic timetable which lasted from 205 555 555 to 75 000 000 years ago

mesoderm (MEZ uh durm): layer of cells between the ectoderm and the endoderm

mesoglea (mez uh GLEE uh): jellylike layer between the two cell layers of coelenterates

messenger RNA: RNA which carries the genetic code of DNA; necessary for protein synthesis

metabolism (muh TAB uh lihz um): total of the chemical reactions which build up and tear down complex molecules within a cell

metamorphosis (met uh MOR fuh sus): series of changes in form during development of an immature form to an adult

metaphase (MET uh fayz): phase of mitosis in which chromosomes move to the "equator" of the cell and become attached to spindle fibers by their centromeres

meter: SI unit of linear measure

methyl group: a carbon atom bonded to three hydrogen atoms

methylation: adding of methyl groups to inactive genes to make them active

microbe: microscopic living thing

microenvironment: small area in an ecosystem which differs from the rest of the area

microfilament: structure that makes up the fibrils of skeletal muscle

micron: unit of length equal to 0.001 mm

micronucleus: small structure in celiates involved in reproduction

microorganism: living thing too small to be seen with the unaided eye; microbe

micropyle (MI kruh pile): opening in the ovule of a flowering plant through which sperm nuclei enter

microscope: a scientific instrument used to magnify small objects so that they can be easily seen

microscopic (mi kruh SKAHP ihk): too small to be seen with the naked eye

microspores: monoploid cells produced in the anthers of flowers

microtubule: long, thin structure that provides support and shape to a cell

midbrain: one of the three general areas of the vertebrate brain

migration: seasonal movement of animals

millimeter: linear measurement in SI that equals 1/1000 of a meter

millipede: member of class of arthropods characterized by two pairs of legs per segment; class Diplopoda

mimicry (MIHM ih kree): protective adaptation in which one organism (the mimic) resembles another organism (the model)

mineral: essential nutrient needed for maintenance of an organism

mitochondria (mite uh KAHN dree uh): organelles scattered throughout the cytoplasm; involved in energy release of respiration

mitosis (mi TOH sus): process of nuclear replication in a cell

mixed nerves: spinal nerves which contain both sensory and motor neurons

model: organism a mimic is similar to; image of an idea or object that helps simplify understanding the idea or object

molecule: a combination of two or more atoms joined by a covalent bond

mollusks (MAHL usks): soft-bodied, mostly marine animals, usually enclosed within a hard outer shell of calcium carbonate; phylum Mollusca

molting: process of shedding the exoskeleton in arthropods; process in some birds and reptiles in which the outer skin or feathers are shed and replaced by new growth

moneran: an organism in the Kingdom Monera

monoclonal antibody: antibody produced by one type of clone of cancer cells

monocotyledonous plants (**monocots**): plants whose seeds contain one cotyledon

monoploid (MAHN uh ployd) **number:** number of chromosome pairs in each cell; number of chromosomes in the gametes

monosaccharide (mahn uh SAK uh ride): single sugar; basic building block for complex carbohydrates

monotreme: group of primitive egglaying mammals; includes platypus and spiny anteater

morphogenesis (mor fuh JEN uh sus): series of embryonic changes in which migration of cells results in a change of form

morphological (mor fuh LAHJ ih kul) **adaptation:** adaptation which involves the structures of organisms

mosaic: mottled

motivation (moht uh VAY shun): drive necessary for the learning process of most animals

motor neuron: neuron which transmits outgoing impulses from the brain or spinal cord to the effectors

mouthbreeder: an animal which picks up and holds their fertilized eggs in its mouth until the eggs hatch

mucin (MYEWS un): substance in saliva which moistens food so it can be swallowed easily; mucus

multicellular: composed of many cells

multiple alleles: three or more alternate genes which can be at one site at different times giving different phenotypes, such as A, B, O genes for blood types

multiple genes: crosses in which many genes may affect a single trait

multiple sclerosis: disease which leads to the slow destruction of the nervous system

murein (MYOOR ee un): material that composes the cell wall of prokaryotes

muscle: specialized tissue which contracts

muscle tone: condition in which muscles are always slightly contracted

mutagen (MYEWT uh jun): agent which causes mutations by altering the structure of DNA molecules

mutation (MYEWT ay shun): change in the genetic code of an organism

mutualism (MYEW chuh lihz um): relationship in which two organisms live in a mutually beneficial and usually necessary association

mycelium (mi SEE lee um): mass of hyphae

myelin (MI uh lun) **sheath:** fatty outer layer which encloses the axon of many neurons

myosin (MI uh sun): protein which makes up part of the filaments in striated muscle

NAD: nicotinamide adenine dinucleotide, coenzyme which transports hydrogens and thus electrons in respiration

NADP: nicotinamide adenine dinucleotide phosphate, coenzyme which transports hydrogens and thus electrons during light reactions of photosynthesis

nanometer: SI unit of measurement used for very small things such as cell parts

natural birth control: method of birth control in which the chance of fertilization is reduced by abstaining from sexual intercourse near the time of ovulation

natural selection: process by which the better adapted organisms survive and reproduce

navel: point at which the umbilical cord was attached to the body of the baby during its development in the uterus

Neanderthals (nee AN dur thawl): humans that lived 35 000 to 100 000 years ago; classified as *Homo sapiens*

nekton (NEK tun): ocean animals which can move freely through the water under their own power

nematocyst (nih MAT uh sihst): stinging cell of coelenterates such as hydra; used in trapping food

nematodes: roundworms; phylum Nematoda

neoteny (nee AWT un ee): retaining immature traits in the adult form

nephridia (nih FRIHD ee uh): pairs of excretory units in almost every segment of an earthworm

nephridiopore (nih FRIHD ee up por): small opening of each bladder to the outside of an earthworm; releases wastes

nephron (NEF rahn): tiny excretory unit in the human kidney

nephrostome (NEF ruh stohm): funnel-shaped part of nephridia

neritic (nuh RIHT ihk) **zone:** area of ocean along the continental shelf beyond the littoral zone

nerve: bundle of neuron fibers

nerve impulse: series of action potentials sweeping down an axon

nerve net: diffuse nerve system within the mesoglea of coelenterates

nervous system: system which controls rapid responses to stimuli

neural (NOOR ul) **folds:** raised cells of the neural plate in the developing embryo

neural plate: rapidly dividing ectoderm cells which form a flat section along the dorsal side of an embryo

neural tube: hollow groove formed by the fusion of the neural folds; becomes the brain and spinal cord of the organism

neurofibril (noor oh FIBE rul): structure which transmits impulses in some protists

neuron (NOO rahn): specialized cell of the nervous system which conducts impulses; nerve cell

neuropeptide: small protein that functions in the nervous system

neurotransmitter: hormonelike chemical stored and released from tiny cavities at the ends of presynaptic fibers; secreted across synapses

neutral solution: solution which is neither acidic nor basic

neutron: neutral particle in the nucleus of an atom

nicotine: stimulant found in cigarette smoke

night blindness: disease caused by lack of vitamin A

nitrification (ni truh fuh KAY shun): process in which bacteria oxidize ammonium ions into nitrite ions and then to nitrate ions

nitrogen base: a compound that makes up part of a nucleic acid

nitrogen cycle: the movement of nitrogen through an ecosystem

nitrogen fixation: process in plants in which nitrogen gas is changed to a usable form

nitrogen-fixing bacteria: bacteria which convert atmospheric nitrogen to nitrate ions

nitrogenous (ni TRAHJ uh nus) **waste:** animal waste product, contains nitrogen

node: place on a stem where leaves develop

nodes of Ranvier: points where the myelin sheath does not cover the axon

nodule (NAHJ ewlz): swollen area on a root; contains nitrogen-fixing bacteria

nonbiodegradable (nahn bi oh dih GRAYD uh bul) **substance:** material which cannot be converted chemically to inactive compounds

nondisjunction (nahn dihs JUNK shun): failure of homolog to segregate during meiosis

nonrenewable resource: resource which once used cannot be replaced

nonsymbiotic theory: theory that explains the origin of eukaryotes through direct evolution of prokaryotes

nonvascular plants: plants that do not have vascular (conductive) tissue for transport of food, water, and minerals

noradrenaline (nor uh DREN ul un): neurochemical which excites heart muscle and inhibits alimentary canal muscles in humans

notochord (NOHT uh kord): stiff rod of cartilage along the dorsal side of chordates at some stage of their life cycle; becomes the vertebral column in most adult chordates

nuclear fission: process in which radioactive isotopes of uranium are split

nuclear fusion: reaction in which small atoms collide to form larger atoms, releasing energy

nuclear membrane: membrane which surrounds the nucleus

nucleic (noo KLAY ihk) **acids:** large, complex molecules, control heredity (DNA and RNA)

nucleoli (new KLEE uh li): small bodies within the nuclei of most eukaryotic cells; site of synthesis of RNA or ribosomes

nucleoplasm (NEW klee uh plaz um): protoplasm inside the nucleus

nucleoprotein (new klee oh PROH teen): combination of nucleic acid and protein; makes up chromosomes of eukaryotes

nucleotide (NEW klee uh tide): subunit of nucleic acids, composed of a sugar, a phosphate group, and a nitrogen base

nucleus: central, round body that is the control center of a cell

nutrient (NEW tree unt): in general, materials required by cells

nutrient broth: substance used for growing bacteria

nutrition: the study of foods and how they are used by the body

nymph (NIHMF): second stage in the process of incomplete metamorphosis

oak-hickory forest: climax community in the southeastern United States

observation: a noticed and recorded event

ocean: aquatic community covering over two thirds of the Earth's surface

octet rule: rule which states that atoms combine so that outer energy levels acquire eight electrons

omnivore (AHM nih vore): consumer which feeds on both producers and other consumers; consumer that eats plants and animals

ootid: cell produced in meiosis II that develops into a mature ovum

open circulatory system: system in which blood is not always in the blood vessels

operator gene: region of DNA with which a repressor combines inhibiting enzyme formation

operculum (oh PUR kyuh lum): hard covering of the gill chamber of fish

oral groove: opening in *Paramecium* through which food is ingested

order: subdivision of a class in the complete classification of an organism

organ: group of specialized tissues performing a specific function

organelle (or guh NEL): specialized cell part

organic chemistry: the study of chemistry of carbon compounds

organic compounds: molecules which contain the element carbon

organism: living thing

organization: the orderly functioning of a living system

organizer: tissue which induces other tissues of an embryo to differentiate

organ of Corti: special hair cells in the cochlea of the ear

osculum (AHS kyuh lum): large opening in the body of sponges; also called excurrent pore

osmosis (ahs MOH sus): diffusion of water across a semipermeable membrane

osmotic (ahs MAHT ihk) **balance:** equilibrium of water concentration inside and outside a cell

ossification (ahs uh fuh KAY shun): hardening of cartilage tissue into bone by the addition of minerals

osteocyte (AHS tee uh site): living bone cell

ostia (AHS tee uh): tiny openings through which blood passes into the heart of a grasshopper

outer bark: outermost part of a woody stem made up of cork

oval window: membrane in the middle ear

ovary (OHV ree): swollen lower region of the pistil in flowering plants; female gonad in animals; where eggs are produced

oviduct (OH vuh dukt): tube close to each ovary in the mammalian female; conveys egg from ovary to uterus; also called Fallopian tube

ovipositor: posterior abdominal segments of female grasshoppers used to tunnel into the soil

ovisac: structure in female frogs that stores eggs

ovulation (ahv yuh LAY shun): short stage in the menstrual cycle in which the follicle bursts and the mature egg is released

ovule (OHV yewl): female sporangium within the ovary of a flowering plant

ovum: egg

oxidation reaction: exergonic reaction in which oxygen is added to a substance, hydrogen is removed, or electrons are removed from a substance

oxygen debt: the amount of oxygen needed to remove the lactic acid from muscle cells and restore the supplies of stored energy

oxyhemoglobin (ahk sih HEE muh gloh bun): compound containing oxygen and hemoglobin; form in which oxygen is transported by red blood cells

oxytocin (ahk sih TOHS un): hormone secreted by the posterior pituitary; stimulates contraction of uterine muscles during labor

pacemaker: small bundle of tissue in the right atrium where the impulse for the heartbeat originates; also known as the sinoatrial node

paleozoic: era of the geologic timetable which lasted from 500 000 000 to 205 000 000 years ago

palisade cells: long cells arranged vertically under the epidermis of a leaf; site of photosynthesis

palmate (PAL mayt): venation pattern in which large veins originate and spread out from the point where the petiole is attached to the blade

palmately compound: leaf pattern in which leaflets are all attached to the petiole at a central point

PAN: compound of nitrogen oxides and hydrocarbons which pollutes the air, damaging lungs and irritating eyes

pancreas (PAN kree us): organ which secretes enzymes for intestinal digestion and the hormones insulin and glucagon

pancreatic amylase: enzyme which changes starch to maltose

pancreatic duct: duct which transports digestive enzymes from the pancreas to the duodenum

parapods: paired, bristled paddles that extend from the segments of some annelids, function in locomotion and respiration

parasite: organism that lives in or on a host and gets nourishment from the host

parasitism (PER uh suh tihz um): relationship in which one organism (parasite) is completely dependent on a host organism; the host is usually harmed

parasympathetic (per uh sihm puh THET ihk) **system:** division of the autonomic nervous system; counteracts the results of the sympathetic system's actions returning the body to normal after an emergency

parental cross: mating of two organisms to produce offspring; usually refers to first mating in a series

parthenogenesis: process in which male bees are hatched from unfertilized eggs

passive immunity: immunity to a disease brought about by the injection of an antiserum

passive transport: exchange of materials across the cell membrane in which the cell does not expend energy

pasteurization: heating and then rapidly cooling a substance to kill bacteria

pathogen (PATH uh jun): disease-causing organism

pathogenic: causing disease

pecking order: levels of authority in chickens and other animals; also called social hierarchy

pedipalp: a pair of appendages on spiders which hold and tear apart food

Peking people: variety of *Homo erectus* similar to Java people

pellicle (PEL ih kul): stiff covering on Ciliates

pelvis: central, hollow cavity of the kidney

penicillin: chemical produced by the mold, *Penicillium*; kills certain disease-causing bacteria

penis: male reproductive organ in animals which have internal fertilization

pepsin: enzyme which hydrolyzes proteins into polypeptides

pepsinogen (pep SIHN uh jun): protein present in gastric juice

peptidase: enzyme that converts small polypeptides to amino acids

peptide: two or more amino acids joined together

peptide bond: bond which holds amino acids together

perfect flower: flower which contains both male and female organs

pericycle: layer of root cells which gives rise to branch roots

period: subdivision of an era in the geologic timetable

periostium (per ee AHS tee um): outer layer of bones, encloses long bones such as arm and leg bones

peripheral (puh RIHF rul) **nervous system:** system which sends information from the receptors to the brain and spinal cord and transmits impulses from them to the effectors

peristalsis (per uh STAHL sus): series of alternating muscular contractions and relaxations, moves food along the digestive tract

peritoneum (per ut un EE um): thin sheet of tissue lining the coelum of segmented worms

permafrost (PUR muh frawst): layer of frozen ground in the tundra that never thaws

pesticide: chemical such as DDT that kills pests

petiole (PET ee ohl): slender stalk of a leaf, attaches leaf to the stem

petrochemical (peh troh KEM ih kul): extracts from fossil fuels

pH scale: scale of numbers representing the concentration of hydrogen ions and hydroxide ions in a solution

phage: a virus which attacks a bacterium

phagocyte: amoebalike white blood cell which engulfs and destroys invading microorganisms

phagocytosis (fag uh si TOH sus): engulfing of a solid particle by a cell

pharynx (FER ingks): tube through which food passes after it leaves the mouth in planarians and earthworms; in vertebrates, passageway for gases and food; throat

phenylketonuria (PKU): genetic disease in which a missing enzyme leads to severe mental retardation

phenotype (FEE nuh tipe): physical or visible characteristic which a genotype determines

pheromone (FER uh mohn): substance secreted by an organism into the environment which affects the physiology or behavior of other members of the same species

phloem (FLOH em) **cells:** cells which transfer food materials synthesized by the leaf to other parts of the plant

photoperiodism: response of flowering plants to light and dark conditions

photosynthesis: process by which light energy is absorbed and then converted to the chemical energy of glucose

phototropism (foh toh TROH pihz um): plant response to light

phycocyanin: a blue pigment found in blue-green algae

phylum: major classification division of a kingdom

physical change: any change in the physical properties of a substance

physical property: characteristic which describes a piece of matter

physiological adaptations: adaptations involved with the physical and chemical needs of organisms

physiology (fihz ee AHL uh jee): study of the functions of parts of living things

phytochrome (FITE uh krohm): pigment in leaves thought to be involved in flowering of flowering plants

pinnate (PIHN ayt): venation pattern in which veins branch from a central vein

pinnately compound: leaf pattern in which leaflets branch out along different parts of the petiole

pinocytosis (pi noh si TOH sis): a type of endocytosis in which liquids and small particles are taken into a cell

pioneering stage: first stage in ecological succession; usually involves hardy autotrophs

pistil (PIHS tul): long, vase-shaped female organ of a flower

pith: central part of stems

pith ray: cells which transport materials horizontally between pith, wood, and bark

pituitary (puh TEW uh ter ee) **gland:** tiny, endocrine gland at the base of the brain; secretes hormones which control other endocrine glands; also called the hypophysis

pivot joint: joint which moves in one direction as well as rotating

placenta (pluh SENT uh): mass of small blood vessels and associated tissues across which materials are exchanged between embryo and mother

placentals (pluh SENT ulz): group of mammals in which the entire development of the embryo occurs internally with material exchange occurring through the placenta

plankton (PLANG tun): marine organisms which float in the water

plant: autotrophic, complex, multicellular organism with chlorophyll in chloroplasts

plasma cells: clone of cells formed from a B-cell

plasma membrane: boundary which separates a cell from its environment; also called cell membrane

plasmid: circular segment of DNA in bacteria

plasmodium (plaz MOHD ee um): slimy mass of material in some species of slime molds, contains many nuclei but no cell walls

plasmolysis (plaz MAHL uh sus): loss of water from cells due to osmosis

plastids (PLAS tudz): organelles in plant cells, chloroplasts are the most common kind

platelet (PLAYT lut): blood cell fragments lacking nuclei; involved in blood clotting

pneumonia: respiratory disease that may be caused by bacteria, viruses, or fungi

point of insertion: site where a muscle attaches to a bone that moves

point of origin: site where a muscle attaches to a bone that does not move

polar nuclei: two monoploid nuclei within the ovule of a flowering plant that fuse with one of the sperm nuclei to form the endosperm nucleus

polarity: ionic charge

polarized: having an unequal distribution of ions (charge)

pollen: extension of the pollen grain through which sperm nuclei travel to the ovule

pollen grain: structure which contains the male sex cells of a flowering plant

pollen sac: male sporangium contained in flower anthers

pollen tube: structure formed by the tube nucleus that "digs" through the style to the ovary of a flower

pollination: process by which pollen reaches the female gametes

pollutant: any substance that makes water, soil, or air unclean

pollution: introduction of materials into the environment which decreases the purity, or cleanliness, of the environment

polyp (PAHL up): one of the body forms of coelenterates; sessile, cylindrical body

polypeptide: molecule formed by the union of many amino acids

polysaccharide: compound composed of many monosaccharides

population: group of organisms which naturally interbreed

population density: number of individuals per given area

population genetics: study of gene pools and their evolution

population growth: change in size of population with time

population growth rate curve: a graph of the rate of increase in the size of a population with time

population size: number of individuals in a population

posterior (pah STIHR ee ur): hind end of an organism

posterior pituitary: lobe of the pituitary gland; secretes oxytocin and vasopressin; does not directly influence other endocrine glands

post-transcriptional event: events that occur after transcription of DNA that can determine if the product of the gene is made

postsynaptic (pohst suh NAP tihk) **fiber:** fiber which receives an impulse after it crosses the synapse

potential energy: energy due to position; stored energy

precambrian: era of the geologic timetable which lasted from 5 000 000 000 to 500 000 000 years ago

precipitate: become solid

predation (prih DAY shun): feeding of one organism on another

predator (PRED ut ur): animal that preys on another organism

prehensile (pree HEN sul): able to grasp, like the human hand

pressure-flow hypothesis: explanation of food transport in plants in which pressure differences in sieve cells from leaves to roots account for the downward movement of food

presynaptic (pree suh NAP tihk) **fiber:** fiber which carries an impulse toward a synapse

primary oocyte: cell which divides in meiosis I to produce the secondary oocyte and first polar body

primary spermatocyte: cell which divides in meiosis I to produce two secondary spermatocytes

primary succession: ecological succession that begins with bare rock; the first succession in an ecosystem

primate: order of mammals which includes lemurs, monkeys, great apes, and humans

proboscis (pruh BAHS us): modified mouthparts of insects, used for obtaining food

producer: living thing which can make its own food

product: substance which results from a chemical reaction

progesterone (proh JES tuh rohn): hormone secreted by the corpus luteum; maintains the uterus in its prepared condition for pregnancy

prokaryote (proh KER ee oht): organism that does not have distinct nuclei; blue-green algae and bacteria

prolactin: hormone secreted by the anterior pituitary that stimulates milk production

prophase (PROH fayz): first stage in mitosis during which the nucleolus and the nuclear membrane disappear and chromosomes become clearly visible as separate bodies; stage in meiosis I when homologous chromosomes pair; stage in meiosis II

prostaglandin: special group of hormones made from fatty acids

protease (PROHT ee ays): enzyme which breaks down proteins

protein: large, complex molecule; contains carbon, hydrogen, oxygen, and nitrogen; building block of living material

prothallium (pro THAL ee um): small, heartshaped gametophyte of the fern

prothrombin: chemical needed for the clotting of blood

protist: simple, eukaryotic organism; includes simple algae, protozoa, and slime molds; Kingdom Protista

proton: positively charged particle in the nucleus of an atom

protonema (proht uh NEE muh): small, monoploid moss structure which grows into a mature gametophyte

protoplasm (PROHT uh plaz um): all the living substance of a cell

protoplasmic streaming: flow of protoplasm in a cell which distributes cellular material and, in some cases, aids locomotion

protozoan: unicellular, animallike protist

provirus: a virus which has become part of its host's DNA

pseudopodia (sewd uh POHD ee uh): structures of locomotion and foodgetting, false feet in amoeba

psychology: study of behavior

puberty (PYEW burt ee): onset of the development of secondary sexual characteristics

pulmonary (PUL muh ner ee) **artery:** artery in birds and mammals which takes deoxygenated blood from the right atrium to the lungs

pulmonary veins: veins in amphibians, reptiles, birds, and mammals which take oxygenated blood from the lungs to the left atrium

Punnett (PUN ut) **square:** chart used to determine the possible genotypes of the offspring of a cross

punishment: negative reinforcement

pupa (PYEW puh) **:** stage of an insect life cycle in which the tissues of the organism are completely reorganized during complete metamorphosis

pyloric sphincter: structure that regulates the flow of chyme from the stomach into the small intestine

pyramid of biomass: relationship showing the decrease of biomass with each higher feeding level

pyramid of energy: relationship showing the loss of energy as it is transferred along a food chain

pyramid of numbers: relationship showing the decrease in the number of organisms with each higher feeding level

pyrenoid (pi REE noyd) **:** structure on a chloroplast that stores excess food

queen bee: central figure in a beehive; mates only once and produces thousands of offspring

radial symmetry (SIH muh tree) **:** body plan in which a cut lengthwise through the middle in any direction produces two identical halves

radicle (RAD ih kul) **:** embryonic seed structure, becomes the primary root

radiant energy: energy given off as lightwaves

radioactive elements: isotopes with unstable nuclei which disintegrate, releasing nuclear energy

radiocarbon dating: method of dating fossils that uses the half-life of radioactive materials

radula (RAJ uh luh) **:** structure with toothlike projections used by univalves and other mollusks to obtain food

reactant: substance which enters into a chemical reaction

receptacle: branch of a thallus of brown algae which contains sex organs

receptor (rih SEP tur) **:** structure which detects stimuli; protein which "recognizes" and combines with certain other molecules (antigens, hormones)

recessive (rih SES ihv) **trait:** form of a trait which is dominated by another form

recombinant DNA: DNA that results from the combination of DNA from two organisms; recombined DNA

recombination gametes: gametes which have different allele combinations than the parental cells

rectum (REK tum) **:** end of large intestine; storage area for solid wastes in mammals

red cell: blood cell that transports oxygen and some carbon dioxide

red tide: large population of dinoflagellates that present a danger to seafood and fish

reflex: innate behavior pattern resulting from the fixed pathways of the nervous system; simple response which involves no conscious control; also called reflex act

reflex arc: path of the impulse in a reflex

refractory (rih FRAK tree) **period:** interval of time in which the membrane potential of a neuron is being restored

regeneration (rih jen uh RAY shun) **:** regrowing of missing parts; a method of vegetative propagation

regulator gene: gene which controls the production of a genetic repressor

releasing factor: hormone secreted by the hypothalamus if thyroxine levels fall below normal

renal (REEN ul) **arteries:** blood vessels which bring blood containing wastes to the kidneys

renal veins: blood vessels which return purified blood from the kidneys to the general circulation

renewable resource: resource which can be replaced

replication: duplication

repressor: special protein synthesized by mRNA that binds to operator gene and inhibits its function

reproduction: process in which new organisms are produced

reproductive isolation: any barrier to interbreeding

reptiles: vertebrates characterized by dry, scaly skin, internal fertilization and development within shelled eggs; class Reptilia

resource: anything humans take from the environment

resolving power: ability to distinguish two objects as two separate things

respiration: exchange of oxygen and carbon dioxide between cells and the environment

respiratory system: system made up of special regions for gas exchange and methods of transporting gases

resting potential: another name for membrane potential

reverse transcription: process in RNA tumor viruses in which DNA is made from RNA

reward: positive reinforcement for a behavior

Rh factors: antigens in the blood; first discovered in the blood of Rhesus monkeys

Rh negative blood: blood which does not have the Rh factors

Rh positive blood: blood which has the Rh factors

rhizoid (RI zoyd): rootlike structure which anchors certain fungi to the food source and secretes enzymes into it; rootlike structure in bryophytes

rhizome (RI zohm): underground fern stem from which roots and leaves develop

ribonucleic (ri boh noo KLAY ihk) **acid (RNA):** large, complex molecule which works with DNA in carrying out the instructions of the genetic code

ribose: sugar contained in RNA

ribosomal RNA: type of RNA that makes up ribosomes

ribosome (RI buh sohm): organelle in cytoplasm which is the site of protein synthesis

rickets: disease caused by lack of vitamin D which results in the improper development of bone

rickettsia (rihk ET see uh): group of disease-causing organisms which are parasites

rift: crack in the Earth's crust

RNA processing: post transcriptional event which occurs in the nucleus of a cell

RNA tumor virus: virus known to cause tumors in animals

root cap: protective cells covering the tip of a growing root

root hair: outgrowth of a root epidermis cell

root pressure: pushing force caused by water in the xylem

round dance: bee behavior which means there is food within 100 m

rust: club fungi which causes disease in plants

saliva (suh LI vuh): liquid secretion of the salivary glands; moistens food and contains an enzyme which breaks starch into maltose

salivary (SAL uh ver ee) **glands:** three pairs of glands which secrete saliva

saprophyte (SAP ruh fite): organism which obtains its food from dead organisms or from waste products of living things

scanning EM: electron microscope which passes a beam of electrons through a live sample, forming an image which can be viewed on a screen

scavenger (SKAV un jur): animal which feeds on dead animals

science: a body of organized knowledge about nature; method of solving problems

scrotum (SKROHT um): external sac which encloses the testes of a mammal

second: basic unit of time in SI

second filial generation: generation of offspring produced from interbreeding offspring of the first filial generation

second messenger hypothesis: idea that hormones cause cells to produce a second compound which acts as a messenger and causes chemical changes in the cells

second-order consumer: consumer which eats a first-order consumer

second polar body: cell produced from the secondary oocyte during meiosis II that dies

secondary oocyte: cell which undergoes meiosis II to produce the ootid, and a second polar body

secondary spermatocytes: two cells produced by meiosis I which undergo meiosis II to produce the spermatids

secondary succession: series of ecological changes which occur when species of a climax community are removed

secretion: process by which an organism releases some material; the material released

seed: reproductive structure which contains an embryo plant and endosperm

seed coat: hardened outer covering of a seed

seed dispersal: the scattering of seeds

segmentation: division of a body plan into more or less similar parts

segmented: divided into units

segregate: separate

selective breeding: mating of animals or plants to produce offspring with desired features

selective cutting: cutting of mature trees while leaving the young trees to mature

self-pollination: pollination which occurs in a single flower or between flowers on the same plant

semen (SEE mun): combination of sperms and fluid

semilunar (sem ih LEW nur) **valve:** valve at the base of the pulmonary artery or aorta; prevents blood from flowing back into the ventricle after it contracts

semipermeable (sem ih PER mee uh bul) **membrane:** membrane which allows only certain materials to pass through it

sensory neuron: cell which transmits incoming impulses from receptors to a coordinating center such as the brain or spinal cord

sensory-somatic system: division of the peripheral nervous system; controls the exchange of information between receptors, the central nervous system, and the skeletal muscles

septum (SEP tum): in some vertebrates, wall dividing ventricle which keeps oxygenated and deoxygenated blood separated

sessile (SES ul): permanently attached

setae (SEE tee): bristles on each segment of segmented worms; aid in locomotion

sex chromosomes: chromosomes (X and Y) which determine sex

sex-linked characteristic: trait whose genes are carried on the X chromosomes

sexual reproduction: union of two sets of DNA; fusion process

sexually transmitted disease: a venereal disease such as syphilis and gonorrhea

shelled egg: embryo surrounded by a tough shell; protects embryo as it develops outside the mother; permits development away from water

short-day plant: plant whose flowering depends on short periods of light exposure

sickle-cell anemia: hereditary disease in which hemoglobin is abnormal and red blood cells are shaped like sickles

sieve tube: another name for a phloem cell because the end walls are perforated, resembling a sieve

simple formula: chemical formula showing the kinds and numbers of atoms per molecule

sinoatrial (si noh AY tree ul) **node (S-A node):** small bundle of tissue in the right atrium in which the impulse for the heartbeat originates; also called the pacemaker

sinus (SI nus): space in the body cavity through which blood passes in animals with an open circulatory system

sinus venosus (SI nus • vih NOH sus): saclike structure in fishes and frogs which collects blood as it returns to the heart

skeletal muscles: another name for striated muscles

skeletal system: specialized support system in most complex organisms

sliding filament hypothesis: theory which explains muscle contraction

slime capsule: outer protective covering which encloses some bacteria cells

slime mold: fungi-related protist; phylum Myxomycophyta

small intestine: digestive organ in humans in which most chemical digestion occurs

smooth ER: endoplasmic reticulum without ribosomes

smooth muscle: muscle which moves many of the internal parts of the body; also called nonstriated or involuntary muscle

smut: club fungi which causes disease in plants

social hierarchy (HI rar kee): levels of authority in animals

society: group of animals of the same species living together in an organized way

sodium-potassium pump: process occurring in a neuron where sodium ions are actively transported out of and potassium ions into a cell

soil depletion: reduction of soil fertility as a result of nutrients being removed by crops

sol (SAHL): liquified state which the cytoplasm may take

solute (SAHL yewt): portion of a solution in lesser quantity

solution: homogeneous material with variable composition

solvent (SAHL vunt): portion of a solution in greater quantity

sori (SOR i): circular structures on the underside of leaves in some species of ferns; contain sporangia

speciation: evolution of a new species

species: classification division after genus; group of organisms which normally interbreed in nature to produce fertile offspring; second name in scientific name

sperm: male reproductive cell

sperm duct: area in the male reproductive system where fluids are added to the sperm

sperm nuclei: two monoploid nuclei produced by mitosis from the generative nucleus in the pollen tube

sperm receptacle: special sac attached to the vagina of a grasshopper used for sperm storage

spermatids: four monoploid cells produced during meiosis II which mature into sperm cells

spicule (SPIHK yewl): minerallike structure which supports a sponge

spinal cord: major nerve cord running along the dorsal side of vertebrates

spinal nerves: thirty-one pairs of nerves that connect body parts with the spinal cord in humans

spindle: oval-shaped structure composed of fibers between opposite poles of the cell; structure to which chromosomes become attached in mitosis and meiosis

spinneret: structures in a spider's body which release threads of silk for making webs

spiracle (SPIHR ih kul): small opening through which air enters a terrestrial arthropod; external opening of a trachea

spirilla (spi RIHL uh): spiral-shaped bacteria

spleen: saclike abdominal organ which mainly stores blood, destroys dead blood cells, and produces lymphocytes

split gene: gene which contains exons and introns

sponges: sessile, mostly marine animals with two cell layers; phylum Porifera

spongy layer: layer of cells beneath the palisade cells in leaves; contains chlorophyll

spontaneous (spahn TAY nee us) **generation:** mistaken belief that organisms can be produced from non-living sources

sporangiophore (spuh RAN jee uh for) **hypha:** upright structure upon which sporangia are located; present in common bread mold

sporangium: case in which spores are produced and stored

spore: specialized reproductive cell which gives rise to a new organism

sporophyte (SPOR uh fite) **generation:** generation of a plant in which the cells are diploid and spores are produced

sporozoans (spor uh ZOH unz): phylum of protozoa that have no way of moving and reproduce by means of spores

spring wood: wood produced in the spring, consisting mainly of large xylem vessels

S-shaped curve: population growth curve

stamen (STAY mun): male reproductive organ of a flower

starch: large, complex molecule made up of hundreds of monosaccharides

stele (STEEL): central cylinder of the cortex of a root, xylem and phloem

stem: main stalk of vascular plants; supports the plant and transports materials

step density gradient: tube containing liquids in zones or steps of different density

sterile: free of life

steroids (STIHR oydz): group of organic compounds that includes cholesterol, sex hormones, hormones from the adrenal cortex, and vitamin D

stigma: structure on *Euglena* sensitive to light; sticky part of a female flower

stimulant: one of a major group of drugs which works by increasing the reactions of the central nervous system

stimulus: anything that causes activity or change in an organism

stipe: stalklike section of a mushroom

stolon (STOH lun): hypha which grows along the surface of the food supply

stomata (STOH mut uh): tiny pore in a leaf

stomach: large, hollow organ where protein digestion begins

strata: layers

striated (STRI ayt ud) **muscle:** muscle attached to bones; sometimes called skeletal muscle or voluntary muscle

stroma: liquid within a chloroplast which produces glucose

structural formula: formula which shows the arrangement of the atoms of a molecule

structural gene: gene which directs synthesis of a protein or polypeptide

style: stalklike portion of a pistil

suberin (SEW buh run): oily material which coats cork cells and protects against water loss

subspecies: division of species; capable of interbreeding with other subspecies of the same species; also called race

substrate (SUB strayt): molecule or molecules upon which a certain enzyme operates; surface upon which an organism lives or moves

successive osmosis: process in which water passes by osmosis from cell to cell and then into the xylem of roots

sucrase: enzyme that breaks down sucrose

summer wood: wood produced in the summer; made up of vessels that are smaller in diameter than those in spring wood

survival of the fittest: major point of Darwin's theory of evolution; the best-adapted organisms survive to reproduce

swimmeret: appendage on some crustaceans used for swimming

swarm cells: flagellated cells of slime molds which can fuse to form a zygote

symbiosis: a relationship in which two organisms live in close association and in general, both benefit from the relationship

symbiotic theory: theory that explains the origin of eukaryotes through symbiosis of prokaryotes

sympathetic (sihm puh THET ihk) **system:** division of the autonomic nervous system; initiates responses which prepare the body for emergencies

synapse (SIHN aps): gap between two neurons or between a neuron and effector

synapsis (suh NAP sus): process in which homologous chromosomes pair during prophase of meiosis I

synfuels (SIHN fyewlz): fuels made by artificial processes

synthesize (SIHN thuh size): build up

synthetic vaccine: vaccine made from pure antigens

system: group of organs working together to perform a specific function

systole (SIHS tuh lee): contraction of the heart chambers

taiga (TI guh): biome characterized by coniferous forests

tail: adenine molecules on the end of mRNA

taproot system: root system in which plants have one large, primary root

target organ: organ affected by a particular hormone

taxonomy: science of classifying things

Tay-Sachs disease: genetic disease in which the nervous system fails to develop properly

T-cell: lymphocyte which passes through the thymus gland

technology: applying scientific knowledge to real problems

telophase (TEL uh fayz): last phase of mitosis in which the events are opposite those of prophase; stage in meiosis I and meiosis II

temperate deciduous forest: biome characterized by an even distribution of rain totaling about one hundred centimeters per year; region in which leaves are periodically all shed from the trees

tendon (TEN dun): tough, elastic connective tissue which attaches muscle to bone

tentacles (TENT ih kulz): structures that surround the mouth of some animals, used in food getting

terminal bud: bud at the tip of a branch responsible for lengthening stems

terracing: conservation practice in which banks of land are created on slopes to prevent erosion from water runoff

territoriality (ter uh tor ee AL ut ee): adaptation in many animals to occupy and defend specific territories

testis (TES tus): male gonad

testosterone (teh STAHS tuh rohn): androgen which stimulates the formation of secondary sexual characteristics in males

tetanus: bacterial disease resulting in continuous muscle contraction

tetrad (TEH trad): pair of double-stranded chromosomes

thallus: the entire body of an alga

theory: fundamental hypothesis which has survived the test of time

third-order consumer: consumer which eats a second-order consumer

thoracic duct: major tube in the chest region for collecting lymph

thorax: chest region

threshold: level of intensity necessary to cause a nerve impulse

thromboplastin: chemical needed for the clotting of blood

thymine (THI meen): one of the bases in nucleic acids

thymus gland: gland beneath the breastbone; thought to control the production of certain antibodies in juveniles

thyroid (THI royd) **gland:** small endocrine gland on the trachea; secretes thyroxine

thyroid-stimulating hormone (**TSH**): hormone secreted by the anterior pituitary that stimulates thyroxine production

thyroxine (thi RAHK sun): hormone which controls the metabolic rate of the body cells; produced by the thyroid gland

tissue: similar groups of cells organized to perform certain functions

tissue fluid: fluid which passes out of the blood vessels and exchanges materials with tissue cells

T-maze: maze shaped like a T so an animal has a choice of one of two turns

topsoil: dark, upper layer of soil; most fertile layer

toxin (TAHK sun): poisonous chemical

trachea (TRAY kee uh): windpipe, tube leading from mouth to bronchi; tube in insects and spiders which opens to the outside, functions in gas exchange

tracheal (TRAY kee ul) **system:** system made up of spiracles, tracheae, and tracheoles; respiratory system in terrestrial arthropods

tracheid (TRAY kee ud): type of xylem cell

tracheole (TRAY kee ohl): tiny air sac which contains water; part of the tracheal system in terrestrial arthropods; site of gas exchange with cells

tracheophytes: plants characterized by vascular tissue; phylum Tracheophyta

tranquilizers: drugs which depress the central nervous system

transaminase (tranz AM uh nays): an enzyme that transfers an amino group

transcription (trans KRIHP shun): transferring the genetic code from DNA to RNA in protein synthesis

transduction (trans DUK shun): injection of portion of one bacterial chromosome into another bacterium by a bacteriophage

transfer RNA: RNA which brings amino acids to messenger RNA in protein synthesis

transformation: reproductive process which occurs when one bacterium breaks open and part of its DNA enters another bacterium

transformer: bacterium which converts nitrogen from organic to inorganic form

transforming principle: chemical involved in bacterial transformation; DNA

translation: operation and interaction of messenger RNA, transfer RNA, and amino acids to form a protein

translocation (trans loh KAY shun): transport of food in a v cular plant; occurs within phloem cells

transmission EM: electron microscope which passes a beam of electrons through a very thinly sliced sample

transpiration (trans puh RAY shun): process in which water constantly escapes from the leaves of plants through the stomata

transpiration-cohesion theory: theory that states that water is pulled up a stem because water loss through the leaf pulls on the water column in the xylem

transpiration pull: tension created by cohesion of water molecules to one another

transport system: system for exchange of materials between cells and the environment

transverse colon: section of the large intestine

trial and error: simple learning in which an organism repeatedly tries a task and learns by its mistakes

trichinosis: painful disease caused by the eating of pork containing *Trichinella* worms

trichocyst: structure in *Paramecium* used for protection

tricuspid (tri KUS pud) **valve:** valve between the right atrium and right ventricle; prevents blood from returning to the right atrium when the right ventricle contracts

trimming: removal of cap and tail of mRNA in the nucleus

triploid (TRIHP loyd): 3n structure

tropical rain forest: biome of equatorial regions, characterized by heavy rainfall, constant warm temperature, dense growth of many different species of trees

trophoblast: outer layer of cells which develops as the cells of the blastocyst divide

tropism (TROH pihz um): plant growth response caused by unequal stimulation on opposite sides of the plant

trypsins: protein-digesting enzymes secreted by pancreas

tube feet: hollow structures on the underside of a starfish; used in locomotion and food-getting

tube nucleus: one of the two monoploid nuclei formed in the anther of a flower

tuber: modified, swollen underground stem

tubule: tube which leads to the bladder in each nephridium of an earthworm; long, coiled tube leading from each Bowman's capsule in a kidney

Turner Syndrome: genetic problem resulting from nondisjunction of the sex chromosomes leaving the person with one X and no Y chromosome

tundra (TUN druh): biome characterized by low average temperature, permafrost, low average rainfall, lack of large plants

turgidity (tur JIHD ut ee): stiffness caused by the pressure of water in cells

tympanic membrane: eardrum

ultrasonography (ul truh suh NAUG ruh fee): technique used to determine the position and anatomy of a fetus

umbilical (um BIHL ih kul) **cord:** structure which contains blood vessels; transports blood between the embryo and the placenta

uncoating: the exit of RNA from the protein coat of a virus

unicellular: made up of only one cell

univalve (YEW nih valv): one-shelled mollusk

universal donor: person having type O blood

universal recipient: person having type AB blood

uracil (YOOR uh sihl): a base in RNA but not in DNA

urea (yoo REE uh): nitrogenous waste in amphibians and mammals; component of urine

ureter (YOOR ut ur): tube which transports urine from the kidney to the urinary bladder

urethra: canal from which urine is expelled from the body and in males transports sperms

uric acid: nitrogenous waste produced by insects and some other animals

urinary bladder: hollow organ which stores urine

urine: combination of urea, excess salts, and water

uterus (YEWT uh rus): thick-walled, muscular organ in female mammals; organ in which the embryo develops; also called the womb

vaccine: solution of weakened or killed microorganisms administered to prevent disease by producing immunity

vacuole (VAK yuh wohl): cellular organelle used for storage

vagina (vuh JI nuh): the organ in the female that receives sperm from the male

vagus (VAY gus) **nerves:** pair of nerves which originate in the medulla oblongata that decrease the heartbeat rate

valve: another name for *shell* in mollusks

variable factor: factor being tested in an experiment

vascular bundle: group of xylem and phloem tissue

vascular cambium: meristem which produces cells that later develop into xylem and phloem tissue

vascular plants: plants which have specialized tissue for the transport of food, water, and minerals

vascular tissue: tissue which transports food, water, and minerals throughout plants

vasopressin (vay zoh PRES un): hormone secreted by the posterior pituitary gland that controls water balance in the body

vegetal (VEJ ut ul) **pole:** ventral part of a frog egg; contains the yolk

vegetative propagation (VEJ uh tayt ihv • praph uh GAY shun): reproduction from a nonsexual, or vegetative, part of an organism

vein: conducting tissue of leaves (xylem and phloem); blood vessel which carries blood toward the heart from the body

venation (ve NAY shun): vein pattern in a leaf

ventral (VEN trul): belly side of an organism; toward the belly

ventral aorta: aorta that carries blood from the heart to the gills of a fish

ventral blood vessel: major blood vessel on the front side of an annelid worm

ventricle (VEN trih kul): chamber which pumps blood away from the heart; cavity or space within the brain

vertebrae (VUR tuh bray): bony structures which connect to form the spinal column in vertebrates

vertebrates (VURT uh brayts): animals with backbones

vertical stratification: layers of a forest from top to bottom

vesicle: sac which stores neurotransmitters

vessel: type of xylem cell

vestige (VES tihj): structure which is no longer functional

villi (VIHL i): structures on the intestinal lining which extend into the hollow of the intestine; increase the surface area for absorption of digested food

viroid: small segment of RNA known to cause disease in a variety of plants

virus: microscopic "organism" which depends on a specific host cell for its reproduction

visible spectrum: band of colors created when white light is separated into different wavelengths

vitamin: an organic substance necessary in small amounts for the proper metabolic functioning of an organism

volume: cubic capacity of an object

voluntary muscles: muscles that can be controlled

waggle dance: bee behavior which indicates distance (over 100 m) and direction to food source

warning coloration: display of various bright colors which announce rather than conceal the presence of an animal

water-vascular system: system which controls movement and food-getting in a starfish

wavelength: distance between consecutive crests of two waves

weight: measure of gravitational attraction between two objects

weathering: mechanical process of freezing, thawing, and erosion

white matter: axons with myelin sheaths in the interior of the human brain and exterior of the spinal cord

womb: uterus

woody stem: stem which contains woody tissue derived from xylem

worker bee: sterile female bee which performs most of the tasks necessary for maintaining a beehive

X chromosome: one of the chromosomes which determines sex; a sex chromosome

X-ray crystallography (krihs tuh LAHG ruh fee): scientific technique which uses X-rays to determine the structure of substances

xylem (ZI lum): vascular tissue in plants; carries water and minerals to the leaves

Y chromosome: one of the chromosomes which determines sex; a sex chromosome

yolk sac: structure in the shelled egg which contains yolk, the food source for the developing embryo

zero population growth: condition in which the birth rate equals the death rate

Zinjanthropus (zihn JAN thruh pus): prehuman that lived about 1.75 million years ago, now thought to be a member of the genus _Australopithecus_

Z-line: crossband to which actin is attached

zoospore: asexual reproductive cell produced from sporangium cells

zygospore: diploid zygote with tough outer shell

zygote (ZI goht): fertilized egg resulting from the union of a sperm and an egg

INDEX